Scandinavia

THE ROUGH GUIDE

There are more than one hundred Rough Guide titles
covering destinations from Amsterdam to Zimbabwe

Forthcoming titles include
Jamaica • New Zealand
South Africa • Southwest USA

Rough Guide Reference Series
Classical Music • The Internet • Jazz • Opera • Rock Music • World Music

Rough Guide Phrasebooks
Czech • French • German • Greek • Indonesian • Italian • Mandarin Chinese
Mexican Spanish • Polish • Portuguese • Spanish • Thai • Turkish
Vietnamese

Rough Guides on the Internet
http://www.roughguides.com/
http://www.hotwired.com/rough

ROUGH GUIDE CREDITS

Text editor: Kate Berens
Series editor: Mark Ellingham
Editorial: Martin Dunford, Jonathan Buckley,
   Jo Mead, Samantha Cook, Amanda Tomlin,
   Ann-Marie Shaw, Paul Gray, Vivienne Heller,
   Sarah Dallas, Chris Schüler, Helena Smith,
   Kirk Marlow, Julie Kelly (UK),
   Andrew Rosenberg (US)
Online Editors: Alan Spicer (UK),
   Andrew Rosenberg (US)

Production: Susanne Hillen, Andy Hilliard,
   Judy Pang, Link Hall, Nicola Williamson,
   Helen Ostick
Cartography: Melissa Flack, David Callier
Finance: John Fisher, Celia Crowley,
   Catherine Gillespie
Marketing & Publicity: Richard Trillo,
   Simon Carloss, Niki Smith (UK),
   Jean-Marie Kelly (US)
Administration: Tania Hummel, Mark Rogers

ACKNOWLEDGEMENTS

Thanks are due to: Andrew Hutter, Johnny Moore, Ruth Rigby, the many Norwegian tourist board offices, *Braathens SAFE*, *NSB Railways*, *Oslo Promotion A/S*, the Swedish Youth Hostel Association, Anne-Charlotte Carlsson at the Swedish Travel & Tourism Council in London, Jane Wilde, Juliet Shaffer, Per Henriksson in Stockholm, all the Swedish tourist offices, Adam Claus, Claus Feldthusen in Malmö, Tomas Larson in Gothenburg, Eric Lindfeldt in Jönköping, Jonas Ludvigsson in Lidköping, Brita Anhoff, Christer Jacobsson, Charlotta Lindell, Per Nilsen, Riitta Balza at the Finnish Tourist Board in London, Meta Mannerheim, Tommi Lattunen in Helsinki, Karmela Belinki and Jorma Kotinen in Helsinki, Artzi Pekka Heino in Oulu, Lasse Kekki in Turku.

Thanks also to Daniel Jacobs for additional Basics research; David Callier, Mick Bohoslawec, Andy & Mike at KPG for cartography; Gareth Nash for proofreading; Link Hall, Nicola Williamson and Sue Grimshaw for wading through the production; and to Jonathan Buckley and Chris Schüler for off-site assistance.

PUBLISHING INFORMATION

This fourth edition published June 1997 by Rough Guides Ltd, 1 Mercer St, London WC2H 9QJ. Previous editions published 1988, 1990, 1993.
Distributed by the Penguin Group:
Penguin Books Ltd, 27 Wrights Lane, London W8 5TZ
Penguin Books USA Inc., 375 Hudson Street, New York 10014, USA
Penguin Books Australia Ltd, 487 Maroondah Highway, PO Box 257, Ringwood, Victoria 3134, Australia
Penguin Books Canada Ltd, 10 Alcorn Avenue, Toronto, Ontario, Canada M4V 1E4
Penguin Books (NZ) Ltd, 182–190 Wairau Road, Auckland 10, New Zealand
Typeset in Linotron Univers and Century Old Style to an original design by Andrew Oliver.
Printed in England by Clays Ltd, St Ives PLC.
Illustration on p.1 by Tommy Yamaha; other illustrations by Edward Briant.

Scandinavia

THE ROUGH GUIDE

Written and researched by

Jules Brown and Mick Sinclair

With

**Peter Bejder, Kim Boye Holt, Phil Lee,
James Proctor and Neil Roland**

THE ROUGH GUIDES

THE ROUGH GUIDES

TRAVEL GUIDES • PHRASEBOOKS • MUSIC AND REFERENCE GUIDES

 We set out to do something different when the first Rough Guide was published in 1982. Mark Ellingham, just out of university, was travelling in Greece. He brought along the popular guides of the day, but found they were all lacking in some way. They were either strong on ruins and museums but went on for pages without mentioning a beach or taverna. Or they were so conscious of the need to save money that they lost sight of Greece's cultural and historical significance. Also, none of the books told him anything about Greece's contemporary life – its politics, its culture, its people, and how they lived.

So with no job in prospect, Mark decided to write his own guidebook, one which aimed to provide practical information that was second to none, detailing the best beaches and the hottest clubs and restaurants, while also giving hard-hitting accounts of every sight, both famous and obscure, and providing up-to-the-minute information on contemporary culture. It was a guide that encouraged independent travellers to find the best of Greece, and was a great success, getting shortlisted for the Thomas Cook travel guide award,

and encouraging Mark, along with three friends, to expand the series.

The Rough Guide list grew rapidly and the letters flooded in, indicating a much broader readership than had been anticipated, but one which uniformly appreciated the Rough Guide mix of practical detail and humour, irreverence and enthusiasm. Things haven't changed. The same four friends who began the series are still the caretakers of the Rough Guide mission today: to provide the most reliable, up-to-date and entertaining information to independent-minded travellers of all ages, on all budgets.

We now publish 100 titles and have offices in London and New York. The travel guides are written and researched by a dedicated team of more than 100 authors, based in Britain, Europe, the USA and Australia. We have also created a unique series of phrasebooks to accompany the travel series, along with an acclaimed series of music guides, and a best-selling pocket guide to the Internet and World Wide Web. We also publish comprehensive travel information on our two web sites:

http://www.hotwired.com/rough
and http://www.roughguides.com/

HELP US UPDATE

We've gone to a lot of effort to ensure that this fourth edition of *The Rough Guide to Scandinavia* is accurate and up-to-date. But things change and, if you feel there are places we've under-rated or over-praised, or know of good hotels we've missed or others that have closed – or deteriorated – then please write. If you can remember the address, the price, the time, the phone number, so much the better.

We'll credit all contributions, and send a copy of the next edition (or any other Rough Guide if you prefer) for the best letters. Please mark letters: "Rough Guide to Scandinavia Update" and send to:
Rough Guides, 1 Mercer St, London WC2H 9QJ, or
Rough Guides, 375 Hudson St, 9th floor,
New York NY 10014.

Or send e-mail to: mail@roughguides.co.uk
Online updates about this book can be found on Rough Guides' website at http://www.roughguides.com/

CONTENTS

Introduction xi

| PART ONE | BASICS | 1 |

Getting there from Britain 3 / Getting there from Ireland 11 / Getting there from North America 12 / Getting there from Australasia 18 / Red tape and visas 21 / Money and banks 22 / Post and phones 23 / Health 24 Insurance 25 / Information and maps 26 / Getting around 29 / Accommodation 30 / Police and crime 32 Sexual harassment & the women's movement 32 / Gay Scandinavia 33 / Disabled travellers 34 / Outdoor activities 35 / Work 36 / Books 37 / Directory 42

| PART TWO | DENMARK | 43 |

Introduction 45 / Getting there 45 / Costs, money and banks 47 / Post and phones 47 / The Media 47 / Getting around 48 / Accommodation 50 / Food and drink 51 / Directory 55 / History 56 / Danish language 67

● CHAPTER 1: ZEALAND 69—108

Copenhagen 69
Helsingør 95
Hillerød 98

Roskilde 99
Falster, Lolland & Møn 104
Bornholm 106

● CHAPTER 2: FUNEN 109—120

Odense 111
Kerteminde 116

Southern Funen 117
Langeland and Æro 119

● CHAPTER 3: JUTLAND 121—153

Esbjerg 123
Ribe 125
Århus 133

Viborg 142
Aalborg 146
Skagen 151

| PART THREE | NORWAY | 155 |

Introduction 157 / Getting there 158 / Costs, money and banks 158 / Post and phones 159 / The Media 159 / Getting around 160 / Accommodation 165 / Food and drink 167 / Directory 171 / History 173 / Norwegian language 182

● CHAPTER 4: OSLO & AROUND 185—221

Arrival and information 187
City transport 191
Accommodation 193
The city centre 196
Akershus castle and fortress 203
Bygdøy peninsula 205

Munch Museum 208
Vigeland Sculpture Park 209
The Nordmarka 211
Eating: cafés and restaurants 211
Entertainment and nightlife 215
Around Oslo: Fredrikstad 219

• CHAPTER 5: SOUTH AND CENTRAL NORWAY 222–243

Lillehammer 226
Jotunheim & Rondane national parks 227
Røros 230

Kongsberg 234
The South Coast 236
Kristiansand 239

• CHAPTER 6: BERGEN & THE WESTERN FJORDS 244–288

Bergen 245
Stavanger 261
The Hardangerfjord 267
Voss 269
Flåm & the Aurlandsfjord 271

The Sognefjord: Balestrand 273
Jostedalsbreen glacier 277
The Geraingerfjord 280
The Romsdalsfjord: Åndalsnes 282
Ålesund 284

• CHAPTER 7: CENTRAL NORTHERN NORWAY – TRONDHEIM TO THE LOFOTENS 289–322

Trondheim 291
Mo-i-Rana 300
The Arctic Circle 300

Bodø 302
Narvik 305
The Lofoten and Vesterålen islands 308

• CHAPTER 8: NORTH NORWAY 323–343

Tromsø 325
Alta 331
The Finnmarksvidda 332
Hammerfest 335

Nordkapp 337
Kirkenes 340
Svalbard: Spitzbergen 341

PART FOUR SWEDEN 345

Introduction 347 / Getting there 347 / Costs, money and banks 348 / Post and phones 349 / The Media 349 / Getting around 350 / Accommodation 352 / Food and drink 354 / Directory 358 / History 359 / Swedish language 369

• CHAPTER 9: STOCKHOLM & AROUND 371–416

Stockholm 372
Drottningholm 406
The Stockholm archipelago 407

Mariefred and Gripsholm 409
Uppsala 411

• CHAPTER 10: GOTHENBURG & AROUND 417–447

Gothenburg 418
The Bohuslän coast 437
The Göta Canal 442

Trollhättan 442
Vänersborg 443
Vastergötland 444

• CHAPTER 11: THE SOUTHWEST 448–490

Varberg 451
Falkenberg 453
Halmstad 454
Båstad and the Bjäre peninsula 455
Ängelholm 457
Helsingborg 458

Lund 463
Malmö 467
Ystad 477
Kristianstad 482
Karlskrona 487

• CHAPTER 12: THE SOUTHEAST 491–529

Kalmar 492
Öland 497
Växjö 501
The Glass Kingdom 503
Jönköping 504
Lake Vättern 505

Vadstena and Motala 507
Örebro 510
Linköping 512
Norrköping 514
Nyköping 517
Gotland 519

• CHAPTER 13: THE BOTHNIAN COAST – GÄVLE TO HAPARANDA 530–559

Gävle 532
Söderhamn and Hudiksvall 536
Sundsvall 538
Härnösand 542
The Höga Kusten 543

Umeå 546
Skellefteå 550
Luleå 552
Boden 556
Haparanda 557

• CHAPTER 14: CENTRAL AND NORTHERN SWEDEN 560–590

Dalarna 562
Östersund 570
Arvidsjaur and the Arctic Circle 578
Jokkmokk 579

Gällivare 581
Kiruna 585
The Torne Valley 588

PART FIVE FINLAND 591

Introduction 593 / Getting there 594 / Costs, money and banks 595 / Post and phones 595 / The Media 595 / Getting around 596 / Accommodation 598 / Food and drink 600 / Directory 604 / History 606 / Finnish language 618

• CHAPTER 15: HELSINKI AND THE SOUTH 621–661

Helsinki 622
Järvenpää and Ainola 647
Kotka 650

Turku 652
Rauma and Pori 658
The Åland Islands 660

• CHAPTER 16: THE LAKE REGION 662–688

Tampere 663
Jyväskylä 669
Lahti 670
Mikkeli 672

Lappeenranta 675
Savonlinna 677
Joensuu 682
Kuopio 684

• CHAPTER 17: OSTROBOTHNIA, KAINUU & LAPPLAND 689–711

Vaasa 691
Oulu 692
Kajaani 697

Rovaniemi 701
The Arctic Circle 703
The Arctic North 704

Index 712

LIST OF MAPS

Scandinavia map	xii	**SWEDEN**	345

DENMARK	43
Zealand	70
Copenhagen	72
Copenhagen: Indre By & Christianborg	77
Helsingor	95
Roskilde	99
Funen	110
Odense	112
Jutland	122
Esbjerg	124
Fredericia	130
Århus	134
Viborg	143
The Hald Area	144
Aalborg	147
NORWAY	155
Oslo & Around	186
Oslo	188
Central Oslo	198
South & Central Norway	223
Røros	231
Kristiansand	239
Bergen & the Western Fjords	246
Bergen	248
Stavanger	262
Sognefjord	273
Nordfjord	277
The Geraingerfjord & Romsdalsfjord	281
Ålesund	285
Central Northern Norway	290
Trondheim	292
Bødo	303
Narvik	305
Lofoten & Vesterålen Islands	310
North Norway	324
Tromsø	326

SWEDEN	345
Stockholm & Around	371
Stockholm	374
Tunnelbana & Pendeltåg	377
Gamla Stan & Norrmalm	383
Uppsala	412
Gothenburg & Around	417
Tram Routes	420
Gothenburg	424
Southwest	449
Helsingborg	459
Lund	464
Malmö	468
Ystad	478
Kristianstad	483
Karlskrona	487
The Southeast	491
Kalmar	493
Öland	496
Örebro	510
Gotland	520
Visby	522
The Bothnian Coast	531
Central Gavle	532
Sundsvall	539
Umeå	547
Luleå	553
Central & Northern Sweden	561
Östersund	571
Gällivare	581
Northern Lappland	584
Kiruna	586
FINLAND	591
Helsinki & The South	621
Helsinki	624
Turku	653
The Lake Region	662
Tampere	664
Jvväskvlä	669

Lahti	671	**Ostrobothnia, Kainuu & Lapland**	690
Mikkeli	673	Oulu	693
Savonlinna	677	Kajaani	697
Kuopio	685	Rovaniemi	702

MAP SYMBOLS

═══	Motorway	∴	Ruin
═══	Major road	◆	General point of interest
═══	Minor road	▲	Mountain peak
- - - -	Path	ⓘ	Tourist office
━━	Railway	⊠	Post office
▬▬▬	Wall	ⓒ	Telephone
— —	Ferry route	▣	Parking
───	Waterway	⬥	Swimming pool
┴┴┴┴	Canal	✡	Synagogue
▬ ▬ ▬	Chapter division boundary	★	Bus stop
▬▪▬▪▬	International boundary	▰	Building
▬ ▫ ▫ ▬	County boundary	➡	Church (town map)
✈	Airport	⁺₊⁺	Cemetery
◉	Hotel		Park
♕	Castle		National park
🏛	Stately home		Forest
⬛	Church		Sand/beach
♦	Museum		Glacier

READERS' LETTERS

The following people wrote in with useful comments and contributions to the last edition. Thanks to you all and please keep writing! Olav Aalberg; Marc Albers; Dawn Alderson; Dr J. K. Anand; Rikst Audenaert; Rebecca Ball; Maria Bergestig; M. J. Bilbie; Katja Bremer; Garry Brooks; Flavio Cali; Benjamin Chisholm; Claes & Rober; Jane Clough & Victoria Hayes; David A. Corfield; R. M. Cubitt; R. J. Davies; G. T. Drost; Christian Duckworth; Irene van Enckevort & Gerben Ruessink; Cherie Fellows; Keith Fender; Ruth Foley; Clinton Graves; Julie & Jonathan Green; Kirsten Guthrie; Julia Hacking; Robert Dale Hajek; 'Elz' Hilsen; Andrew Hutter; Dr J. Jacobs; Margaret P. Kerr; Enrique Lamont; Britt S. Lightbody; Jonas Ludvigsson; Martin Lunnon; Mikkel Impgaard Madsen; Diran Meghreblian; Erika Mitchell; Chris Munns; Jon Murnick; Laurie M. Naumann; Jackie Nightingale; Salvatore Piazzolla; Richard Peterson; Erna-Karin Polden, Gunnar Rønnestad & Inki Roald; Judith A. Pretty; Carl P. Salicath; Mark Seidenberg; Stephanie Strøm; Samantha Tasker; Gordon Taylor; Judy Upton; Natalie Viola; Dr Liqun Wang; Nicholas Watkinson; Frances & David Watling; Laurie Wedd; Alison Welch; Derek Wilde; Nigel Wilson; Ian & Betty Wood; Pam & Rog Wortley; P. Y. Yee & Y. M. Lee; Dr Robert J. Young.

INTRODUCTION

Scandinavia – Denmark, Norway, Sweden and Finland – conjures resonant images: wild, untamed lands, reindeer and the Midnight Sun; wealthy, healthy, blue-eyed blondes enjoying life in a benevolent welfare state. Yet it's a picture that's only partially accurate. Certainly, by western European standards Scandinavia is affluent, with a high standard of living and the near eradication of poverty. And for travellers it holds some of Europe's most unspoilt terrain. But it's by no means paradise: there's a social conformity that can be stifling, and the problems of other industrialized countries – drug addiction, racism, street violence – are beginning to make themselves felt. The larger part of the population clusters in the south, where there's all the culture, nightlife and action you'd expect. But no one capital fully reflects its society. With the exception of Denmark these are large, often physically inhospitable countries and rural traditions remain strong, not least in the great tracts of land above the Arctic Circle, where the Sami (Lapps) survive as they have done for thousands of years – by reindeer herding, hunting and fishing.

Historically, the Scandinavian countries have been closely entwined, though in spite of this they remain strikingly individual. For visitors, the efficient and well-organized tourist infrastructure lessens the shock of getting about in what are, after all, Europe's most expensive countries. **Denmark** is the geographical and social bridge between Europe and Scandinavia – easy to reach and the best known of the Scandinavian countries. The Danes are much the most gregarious of the Nordic peoples, something manifest in the region's most relaxed and appealing capital, Copenhagen, and the decidedly more permissive attitude to alcohol.

Norway features great mountains, a remote and bluff northern coast and the mighty western fjords: raw, often inaccessible landscapes which can demand long, hard travel. Even by Scandinavian standards the country is sparsely populated, and people live in small communities along a coastline which stretches from the lower reaches of the North Sea right up to the Russian border.

Sweden is the most "Scandinavian" country in the world's eyes: affluent and with a social system and consensus politics that are considered an enlightened model, though confidence in the country's institutions has been shaken of late with the collapse of the economy and the fragmentation of old alliances; crime and unemployment are rising, too. Travelling is simple enough, although Sweden has Scandinavia's least varied landscape – away from the southern cities and coastal regions an almost unbroken swathe of lakes, forests and hills, in which every Swede has a second, peaceful, weekend home.

Finland is perhaps the least known of the mainland Scandinavian countries. Ruled for hundreds of years by the Swedes and then the Russians, it became independent only this century and has grown into a vibrant, confident nation. Its vast coniferous forests and great lake systems have shaped for the Finns an empathy with their country and its nature which is hard to ignore. Also, though Finland is undeniably Scandinavian and looks to the west for its lifestyle, there are, historically and culturally, a number of similarities between Finland and eastern Europe.

Connections and costs

Travelling in Scandinavia is easy. Public transport is efficient and well co-ordinated, there are a minimum of border formalities between the countries, and there are excellent connections between all the main towns and cities: indeed, on one trip it's perfectly feasible to visit several, if not all, of the mainland countries. From western Europe it's

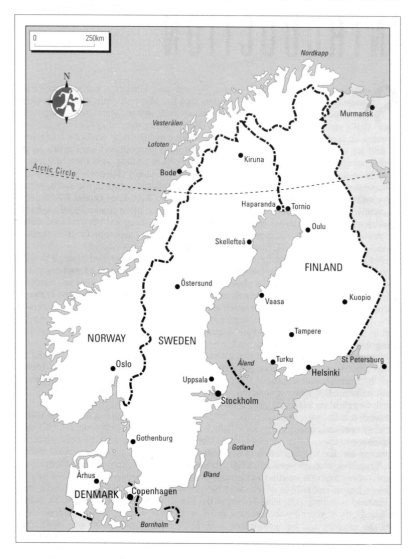

simplest to enter Denmark, from where you can continue northwards into Norway (by boat) or Sweden (by boat or train), the two countries separated by a long north–south border. From Sweden's east coast there are regular ferries across to Finland, as well as a land border between the two in the far north.

As for **costs**, the Scandinavian countries are expensive by north European standards – but not excessively so. Their reputation for high prices is largely based on the cost of consumables – from books to meals and beer – rather than more substantial items, particularly accommodation, where first-rate budget opportunities are ubiquitous.

When to go

Deciding **when to go** isn't easy, since, except for Denmark, Scandinavia experiences intense seasonal changes. The short summers (roughly mid-June to mid-August) can be as hot as in any southern European resort, with high temperatures regularly recorded in Denmark, southern Norway and Sweden, and the Baltic islands. Even the northern areas of each country are temperate, and the whole of the Norwegian west coast, for example, is warmed by the Gulf Stream. Rain, though, is regular, and in the far north of Norway especially, and to a lesser extent in Sweden and Finland, summer temperatures can plunge extremely low at night, so campers need decent equipment for extended spells of sleeping out. One bonus this far north, though not exactly a boon to sleep, is the almost constant daylight lent by the Midnight Sun.

The **summer** is celebrated everywhere with a host of outdoor events and festivities, and is the time when all the facilities for travellers (tourist offices, hotel and transport discounts, summer timetables) are functioning. However, it's also the most crowded time to visit, as the Scandinavians are all on holiday too: go either side of summer (late May/early June or September), when the weather is still reasonable, and you'll benefit from more peace and space. Autumn, especially, is a beautiful time to travel, with the trees and hillsides turning golden brown in a matter of days.

In **winter**, from November to around late May, only Denmark retains a semblance of western European weather, while the other countries suffer long, dark and extremely cold days. The cold may be severe but it is crisp and sharp, never damp, and if you're well wrapped up the cities at least needn't be off-limits – though, unless you're exceptionally hardy, the far north is best left to its own, gloomy devices. You'll find broad climatic details in each country's "Introduction"; for mean temperatures all year round, check the **temperature chart** below.

What to take

It's as well to give some thought as to **what to take** – and worth packing that bit more to stave off despair later. Expect occasional rain throughout the summer and take a waterproof jacket and a spare sweater. A small, foldaway umbrella is useful too. If camp-

	Jan	Feb	March	April	May	June	July	Aug	Sept	Oct	Nov	Dec
AVERAGE TEMPERATURE °F												
Denmark												
Copenhagen	32	32	35	44	53	60	64	63	57	49	42	36
Norway												
Oslo	23	25	30	41	52	59	63	61	52	43	34	28
Bergen	35	35	37	43	50	55	59	59	54	46	41	37
Tromsø	26	25	28	32	38	48	54	54	45	37	32	28
Sweden												
Stockholm	27	30	30	39	53	57	64	62	51	45	40	34
Östersund	18	26	22	33	50	52	59	54	44	39	30	27
Haparanda	14	21	15	30	48	56	61	55	44	36	25	22
Finland												
Helsinki	22	21	26	37	48	58	63	61	53	43	35	28
Tampere	17	17	23	35	47	56	61	59	50	40	32	25
Ivalo	8	8	16	27	39	49	56	52	42	31	21	14

Note that these are *average temperatures*. The Gulf Stream can produce some very temperate year-round weather and, in summer, southern Scandinavia can be blisteringly hot. In winter, on the other hand, temperatures of -40°F are not unknown in the far north.

ing, a warm sleeping bag is vital and good walking shoes essential (comfortable, too, in sprawling cities and the flat southern lands). Mosquitoes are a pest in summer, especially further north and in lake regions, and some form of barrier/treatment cream is necessary. For winter travel, take as many layers as you can pack. Gloves, a hat or scarf that covers your face, thick socks and thermal underwear are all required.

GETTING THERE FROM BRITAIN

The details below cover routes to Denmark, Norway, Sweden and Finland from Great Britain. See p.11 for details on getting to Scandinavia from Ireland. For connections within Scandinavia itself, see the "Getting There" sections for each individual country.

BY PLANE

Flying to Scandinavia isn't especially cheap. Low-cost charter flights do exist, but they're few and far between, and serve only limited destinations; *Strata* (see "Discount Agents" in the box overleaf) is a good source of tickets when they're available. Often the best starting point for the cheapest deals to Scandinavia are the classified sections in the Sunday newspapers (*The Sunday Times* especially) or, if you live in London, *Time Out* magazine or the *Evening Standard*. Failing that, go straight to a **discount flight agent** like *STA Travel* or *Campus Travel* (addresses in the box overleaf); they specialize in youth flights, and generally have good deals if you're under 26 or a student, as well as ordinary discounted tickets if you're not.

It's also worth contacting the major scheduled **airlines** – *British Airways*, *SAS* (the airline of Denmark, Norway and Sweden) or *Finnair* – since seasonal deals can mean that regular APEX or SuperAPEX tickets (*SAS* call their equivalent "Jackpot") cost no more than the fare quoted by an agent. These tickets do, however, carry restrictions, such as having to book seven (sometimes 14) days in advance and stay at least one Saturday night abroad, and you have no option to change your

flight. It's not usually worth shopping around the major airlines since their fares are pretty well matched. However, if you are under 25, ask about the availability of **youth fares**, which should save you a few pounds. The smaller airlines tend to offer cheaper seats, especially from regional airports: further details are given below, but bear in mind that small firms may come and go, so it's worth keeping an eye out for what's new on the market.

When no direct flights are available, airlines can usually offer you **connections** to Scandinavian airports via a Scandinavian partner (*British Midland* with *SAS*, or *British Airways* with *Sun Air* for example). You might also want to consider buying an **air pass**, usually sold only in conjunction with your ticket from Britain, which can be useful for getting across the vast expanses of Scandinavia. **SAS Air Passes**, which have to be bought in conjunction with a "Jackpot" ticket, allow you to buy up to six vouchers at £50 each, valid on flights within and between Denmark, Norway and Sweden and between Sweden and Finland. The **Nordic Air Pass**, offered by *Transwede*, *Finnair/Braathens* and *Maersk Air*, takes in countless routes in Finland with *Finnair*, in Norway with *Braathens* and in Denmark with *Maersk*, though it's less useful if you're planning much air travel in Sweden.

Finally, it is also worth considering a **package deal**, particularly if you're clear on where you want to go and intend to stay for no more than a week; city breaks, especially, can work out at very good value. Again, full details below.

TO DENMARK

Denmark is the closest Scandinavian country to Britain and the best served by the airlines. *SAS* run five daily flights **from London** Heathrow to **Copenhagen** (1hr 45min), while *British Airways* operate another four on most days, plus two out of Gatwick. On weekdays, there are also two or three flights a day to Copenhagen operated by *Air UK* from Stansted, *Maersk Air* from Gatwick, and *Debonair* out of Luton, all with slightly reduced services at weekends. A more exotic alternative is the Brazilian airline *Varig*, which flies from Heathrow three times a week. You can also fly direct from London to **Århus** with *SAS* (daily from Heathrow), and to Billund with *Maersk Air* (2–3 daily from Gatwick).

AIRLINE ADDRESSES AND ROUTES

Air UK, Stansted Airport, Essex CM24 1QT (☎0345/666 777); http://www.airuk.co.uk. *London Stansted to Copenhagen; Aberdeen to Stavanger and Bergen.*

Braathens SAFE, Newcastle International Airport, Woolsington, Newcastle-upon-Tyne NE13 8BZ (☎0191/214 0991 or ☎0800/526938). *London Gatwick and Newcastle to Oslo, Stavanger and Bergen.*

British Airways, 156 Regent St, London W1R 6LB, and branches nationwide (☎0345/222111); http://www.british-airways.com. *London Heathrow and Gatwick to Copenhagen, Oslo, Stavanger, Stockholm, Gothenburg and Helsinki.*

British Midland Airways, Donington Hall, Castle Donington, Derby DE74 2SB (☎0345/554554). *London Heathrow to Bergen; Edinburgh and Glasgow to Copenhagen.*

Business Air, Cargo Building, Mercury Way, Dundee DD2 1UH (☎0500/340146). *Aberdeen to Esbjerg.*

Debonair Airways, 146 Prospect Way, Luton, Bedfordshire LU2 9BA (☎0500/146200). *London Luton to Copenhagen.*

Finnair, 14 Clifford St, London W1X 1RD (☎0171/408 1222); http://www.finair.fi. *London and Manchester to Helsinki and Stockholm; London Gatwick to Turku.*

Maersk Air, Terminal House, 52 Grosvenor Gardens, London SW1W 0AU (☎0171/333 0066). *London Gatwick to Copenhagen, Billund and Kristiansand.*

Maersk Air Limited, 2245 Coventry Rd, Birmingham B26 3NG (☎0121/743 9090). *Birmingham to Copenhagen.*

Malmö Aviation, Première Three, Betts Way, Crawley, West Sussex RH10 2GB (☎01293/530839). *London City to Malmö.*

New Air, Room 20, Level 5, Terminal 1, Manchester Airport, Manchester M90 3FE (☎0161/489 2802). *Manchester and Birmingham to Billund; Newcastle to Copenhagen.*

SAS, 52–53 Conduit St, London W1R 0AY (☎0171/734 4020); Level 5, Terminal 1, Manchester Airport, Manchester M90 3FE (☎0161/499 1441); Aberdeen Airport, Aberdeen AB9 1WH (☎01224/770220); http://www.sas.se. *London Heathrow to Copenhagen, Århus, Oslo, Stavanger, Stockholm and Gothenburg; Manchester to Copenhagen, Oslo, Stockholm and Helsinki; Aberdeen to Stavanger.*

Varig, 61 Conduit St, London W1R 0HG (☎0171/287 1414). *London Heathrow to Copenhagen.*

DISCOUNT FLIGHT AGENTS

Alpha Flights, 173 Uxbridge Rd, London W7 3TH (☎0181/579 3508).

APA Travel, 138 Eversholt St, London NW1 1BL (☎0171/387 5337).

Benz Travel, 93 Regent St, London W1R 7TG (☎0171/437 2377).

Campus Travel, 52 Grosvenor Gardens, London SW1W 0AG (☎0171/730 3402); 541 Bristol Rd, Selly Oak, Birmingham B29 6AU (☎0121/414 1848); 61 Ditchling Rd, Brighton BN1 4SD (☎01273/570226); 39 Queen's Rd, Clifton, Bristol BS8 1QE (☎0117/929 2494); 5 Emmanuel St, Cambridge CB1 1NE (☎01223/324283); 53 Forrest Rd, Edinburgh EH1 2QP (☎0131/668 3308); 105–106 St Aldates, Oxford OX1 1BU (☎01865/484730). *Student/youth travel specialists, with branches also in YHA shops and on university campuses all over Britain.*

Council Travel, 28a Poland St, London W1V 3DB (☎0171/437 7767). *Flights and student discounts.*

North South Travel, Moulsham Mill Centre, Parkway, Chelmsford, Essex CM2 7PX (☎01245/492882). *Friendly, competitive travel agency, offering discounted fares world wide – profits are used to support projects in the developing world.*

STA Travel, 86 Old Brompton Rd, London SW7 3LH; 117 Euston Rd, London NW1 2SX; 38 Store St, London WC1 (☎0171/361 6161); 25 Queens Rd, Bristol BS8 1QE (☎0117/929 4399); 38 Sidney St, Cambridge CB2 3HX (☎01223/366966); 75 Deansgate, Manchester M3 2BW (☎0161/834 0668); 88 Vicar Lane, Leeds LS1 7JH (☎0113/244 9212); 36 George St, Oxford OX1 2OJ (☎01865/792800); and branches in Birmingham, Canterbury, Cardiff, Coventry, Durham, Glasgow, Loughborough, Nottingham, Warwick and Sheffield; http://www.futurenet.co.uk/STA/Guide/Europe/GetThere.html. *Worldwide specialists in low cost flights and tours for students and under-26s.*

contd.

Strata Travel, 9 Central Parade, Green St, Enfield, Middlesex EN3 7HG (☎0181/805 1555). *Cheap charter and scheduled flights to Scandinavia.*

Trailfinders, 42–50 Earls Court Rd, London W8 6FT (☎0171/937 5400); 194 Kensington High St, London, W8 7RG (☎0171/938 3939); 58 Deansgate, Manchester M3 2FF (☎0161/839 6969); 254–284 Sauchiehall St, Glasgow G2 3EH (☎0141/353 2224); 22–24 The Priory, Queensway, Birmingham B4 6BS (☎0121/236 1234); 48 Corn St,

Bristol BS1 1HQ (☎0117/929 9000). *One of the best informed and most efficient agents.*

Travel Bug, 597 Cheetham Hill Rd, Manchester M8 5EJ (☎0161/721 4000); 125a Gloucester Road, London SW7 4SF (☎0171/835 2000). *Large range of discounted tickets.*

Travel CUTS, 295a Regent St, London W1R 7YA (☎0171/255 1944); 33 Prince's Square, London W2 4NG (☎0171/792 3770). *British branch of Canada's main youth and student travel specialist.*

Several airlines fly to Denmark from **regional airports**. There are currently services from **Aberdeen** to Esbjerg (with *Business Air*), **Birmingham** to Copenhagen (*Maersk Air Ltd*) and Billund (*New Air*), **Edinburgh** and **Glasgow** to Copenhagen (*British Midland*), **Manchester** to Copenhagen (*SAS*) and Billund (*New Air*), and **Newcastle** to Copenhagen (*New Air*). All of these carriers operate at least one flight a day, though services may be reduced at weekends.

The lowest regular **fare** at present is *Debonair's* at £51 each way before tax; otherwise, you can expect to pay around £180 plus tax for a regular SuperAPEX or similar return ticket from Britain to Denmark bought directly from *SAS*, *British Midland* or *BA* (though watch out for occasional offers that bring fares down to as low as £100 return), £30–60 less with the smaller airlines, and a minimum of around £110 return for a ticket from a discount agent.

TO NORWAY

From **London** Heathrow to **Oslo**, there's a good choice of flights, with *SAS* operating three or four daily and *BA* another three. From Gatwick, *BA* has six Oslo flights a week, and the Norwegian airline *Braathens SAFE* flies there daily. *Braathens SAFE* also flies direct to the fjords, with a daily service from Gatwick to **Bergen** via Stavanger; from Heathrow, there's a daily *British Midland* flight to Bergen. **Stavanger** is also served by *SAS* (2 daily from Heathrow) and *BA* (6 a week from Gatwick). The other Norwegian destination reached directly from London is **Kristiansand**, with six *Maersk Air* flights a week from Gatwick.

If you're heading directly to the fjords, flights from regional airports are fast and regular. *Air UK* and *SAS* fly from **Aberdeen** to Stavanger at least once a day, with *Air UK* also flying to Bergen six

times a week. From **Newcastle** *Braathens SAFE* flies to Bergen (via Stavanger) and Oslo, more or less daily. *SAS* flies between **Manchester** and Oslo every day except Saturday.

Airlines charge a minimum of around £200 plus tax for a return to Oslo (SuperAPEX or youth fare). *British Midland* currently does the lowest fares to Bergen (£145 return before tax, well ahead of *Air UK's* £170–180 out of Aberdeen – though all these are liable to change, of course). Discount agents offer Oslo tickets for upwards of £155 return before tax.

TO SWEDEN

Flying to Sweden, the choice of routes is not as wide as you might expect, though routes from **London** to Stockholm and Gothenburg are well served. There are ample flights to **Stockholm**, with *SAS* (4–5 daily from Heathrow), *Finnair* (1 daily from Gatwick), and *British Airways* (4 daily from Heathrow, 1–2 daily from Gatwick). To **Gothenburg**, *SAS* and *BA* each operate two flights a day from Heathrow, with another *BA* service out of Gatwick. A recent and welcome addition to these is *Malmö Aviation's* daily flight (except Sat) from London City Airport to Malmö. Apart from London, only **Manchester** has direct flights to Sweden, with *Finnair* (daily), and *SAS* (daily except Sat) to Stockholm.

Barring special offers, which may be as low as £130 return, minimum fares tend to hover around the £200 mark. Discount agents may be able to offer small savings on these.

TO FINLAND

As you might expect, *Finnairs* offer the best choice of flights to Finland, with three a day from **London** Heathrow to **Helsinki**, and another from Gatwick. *BA* runs two a day from Heathrow and one daily except Saturday from Gatwick. *Finnair* also flies every day except Saturday from Gatwick to **Turku**, the only direct service to any Finnish airport outside the capital. From **Manchester**, you can fly to Helsinki on *Finnair* (daily) or *SAS* (daily except Saturday). No other British airports have direct flights to Finland, though you can get connecting services through *SAS*, *British Midland* and *BA*, among others.

You should be able to get a return ticket to Helsinki for around £200 if you are prepared to accept the restrictions of an APEX or SuperAPEX fare. Special offers may also mean that return tickets are available for as little as £130 at certain times of the year (usually Jan–March).

BY TRAIN

Taking a train can be a more relaxed way of getting to Scandinavia, though it doesn't work out a lot cheaper than flying, and is even more expensive if you're over 26. However, a number of deals valid for all the mainland countries make it possible to cut costs, especially if you're intending to do a lot of travelling around once there.

One of the most popular if you're under 26 is to purchase a **BIJ ticket**, which gives up to 50 percent discount on ordinary fares. Available through *Wasteels*, and sometimes *British Rail International*, these allow as many stopovers as you like and are valid for two months. Various routes are available, including several Scandinavian destinations. Tickets are available either direct from the operators (addresses below), or from youth and student travel agents.

If you have no clear itinerary, the **InterRail pass** might be a better bet. The pass gives you free travel in theory on all state railways in the countries it covers (though with supplements payable on the trains you'll most want to use, especially high-speed trains, and only a 50 percent discount in the country where you buy it), as well as discounts on many private railways, buses and ferries (including those from Newcastle and Harwich to Gothenburg and Esbjerg, as well as several in Scandinavia and between Scandinavia and Germany – some of the very short ones are free). Passes are valid in up to seven zones covering most of Europe, the British Isles, Turkey and Morocco, usually for a month (though 15-day passes are available). To qualify for one, you have to provide proof that you've been resident for at least six months in one of the countries it covers. Norway, Sweden and Finland are all in Zone B; Denmark is in Zone C, along with Germany, Switzerland and Austria. Depending on what route you want to take, you may have to buy a pass that covers Zone E (France, Belgium, the Netherlands and Luxembourg) too. A pass covering only one zone (valid only for 15 days) is £185, for two zones (and a month) £224, for three zones £249, for four or more £279. The passes are available from many train stations as well as youth and student travel agencies. If you are **over 26**, you can buy a pass covering some of the countries in the scheme, including Denmark, Norway, Sweden and Finland, as well as the Netherlands and Germany, but not France or Belgium; current prices are £279 for a month, £215 for 15 days.

Eurail passes are available in Britain from *SNCF* (see box opposite) for non-residents of Europe, North Africa or the British Isles, and cover Denmark, Norway, Sweden and Finland, and all the countries you'll need to pass through on your way from Britain, but not the UK itself. They are valid on more express trains than the *InterRail*. The *Eurail Youthpass* (for under-26s) costs £327 for 15 days, £468 for 1 month, or £625 for 2 months; if you are over 26, you'll have to buy a first-class version (£409/657/899). You stand more chance of getting your money's worth from a *Eurail Flexipass*, good for ten or fifteen days in a two-month period. For under-26s these cost £343 and £461 respectively, £483 and £636 for first-class or over-26s.

If you're flying to Scandinavia and only planning to travel by train once you get there, you're probably better off buying a **Scanrail** pass, which covers all the Scandinavian countries and comes in a variety of versions; for further details, see p.29. There are also certain individual country passes available; for more details on these, see the country's "Getting Around" section. A final alternative for travelling in Scandinavia is *British Rail*'s **Freedom Pass**, which offers unlimited train travel (including supplements on high speed trains) within any one of 25 European countries including Sweden, Denmark, Finland and Norway. For each country you have to buy a separate pass, which comes in under-26 and standard-class versions: 3 days' travel within a month costs £69/£99, 5 days £99/ £129 and 10 days £129/£179. Exactly the same deal can also be purchased from *Eurotrain*, under the name **EuroDomino**.

If you're 60 or over, the **Rail Europ Senior Card** gives up to 30 percent discounts on any journeys which cross international frontiers (but not on journeys within countries) in most of Western Europe, including Scandinavia. To obtain it, you must first have a Senior Citizen Rail Card (£16 from any train station) and pay an extra £5 at any British Rail Travel Centre or travel agent specializing in European rail travel.

Anyone thinking of travelling extensively by train would be wise to pick up a copy of the latest monthly *Thomas Cook European Rail Timetable* (the red volume), which contains schedules of all major train and ferry routes throughout Europe.

TO DENMARK

To Denmark, there's a choice of **four routes** from London. The longest and cheapest, via the **Harwich–Esbjerg** ferry, runs three times a week (except Jan) and takes around 28 hours to reach Copenhagen, with cabin reservations obligatory and best booked well in advance. Fares on this route are currently £161 one-way and £314 return to Copenhagen, £157 and £307 as far as Århus. Under-26 fares are available to Copenhagen for £142/£243.

The fastest and priciest route, on the other hand, is via the Channel Tunnel on **Eurostar**, leaving Waterloo daily at around midday for Brussels Midi/Zuid, where you connect with the Nord Express for Copenhagen, arriving 8.30am next morning (couchettes are available). Make sure you are in the correct part of the train, as not all of it goes the whole way. Fares on this route start at £202 one-way and £245 return, or £159/235 if you are under 26.

The Nord Express can also be picked up at **Ostend**, reached by taking the train from Victoria to connect with Ramsgate–Ostend ferry. Going this way at present costs £161 one-way and £314 return, £128/£256 if you are under 26. Further savings can be made by taking the early-evening boat train from Liverpool Street for the night ferry from Harwich to the **Hook of Holland**, where you can take a train to Copenhagen by changing at Amersfoort, Osnabrück and Hamburg (£142/143, £113/213 under-26). Certain outlets may be unwilling to sell you a ticket via this route, but *Wasteels* will do so. If coming from the north of England or from Scotland, you can travel overnight with *North Sea Ferries* from Hull to **Rotterdam**, where you can catch the train to Copenhagen

via Amersfoort, Osnabrück and Hamburg. *Wasteels* also sell Mini-Tours: one from London, through Denmark to Copenhagen, and returning through Hamburg and Amsterdam, costs around £188.

Timings and connections are subject to change, so it's vital to check the details with an agent or ticket office before buying a ticket.

TO NORWAY, SWEDEN AND FINLAND

Getting to Norway, Sweden or Finland by train from Britain involves first travelling to Copenhagen, as described above, and then taking an onward service. Unfortunately connections aren't necessarily convenient. From Copenhagen to **Stockholm**, there is a morning and an evening service (total journey time 31hr), the former connecting for the *Silja* ferry to **Helsinki** (journey time over 46hr). Only the Hook of Holland route from London to Copenhagen allows connections to **Oslo**, of which there are also two daily. Total journey time is just over 35 hours.

Current **fares** from London to **Stockholm** are £204 one-way, £401 return (£167/333 under-26) via Ostend, £186/330 (£152/290) via the Hook of Holland, £168/291 (£119/215) via Esbjerg, and from £240.50/311 (£197.50/301 under-26 if bought in London) via the Channel Tunnel. To **Oslo**, the fare is £204/367 (£168/322) via the Hook of Holland. To **Finland** the fare ranges from £365 to £481 return.

TRAIN TICKET OFFICES

British Rail International Travel Centre, by platform 2, Victoria Station, London SW1V 1JY (☎0171/834 2345). *Through tickets via Channel Tunnel or ferry connections.*

Eurostar, Eurostar House, Waterloo Station, London SE1 8SE (☎0345/303030). *Channel Tunnel services; no through tickets to Scandinavia.*

SNCF French Railways, 179 Piccadilly, London W1V 0BA (☎0990/300003). *Eurail passes for non-European residents.*

Wasteels, by platform 2, Victoria Station, London SW1V 1JY (☎0171/834 7066). *Youth ticket specialists.*

COACH COMPANIES

Eurolines, 52 Grosvenor Gardens, London SW1W 0AU (☎0990/808080).

BY COACH

A coach journey to Scandinavia can be an endurance test. It is often the cheapest option, but not always, and rarely by much, and the saving over an air fare is offset by the time spent on the journey. Only if time is no object and price all-important, or if you specifically do not want to fly, is it really worth taking the bus.

Eurolines run two direct services a week from London to **Copenhagen** (20hr 30min), plus one weekly involving a change of bus at Amsterdam (total journey time 24hr); all continue to **Gothenburg** (25hr 20min–29hr), where they connect for **Oslo** (30hr 50min–36hr 50min from London), and to **Stockholm** (30hr 10min–34hr 10min), where the weekly service via Amsterdam connects for **Turku** (45hr 30min), **Helsinki** (48hr 30min), **Vaasa** (51hr 20min) and **Oulu** (56hr 20min). The two direct weekly buses from London to Gothenburg connect there for **Vanesborg** (27hr 55min), **Karlstad** (30hr 25min) and **Kristinehamn** (30hr 20min). Two direct weekly buses from London also run to **Hirtshals** (22hr 25min) via **Århus** (19hr 50min) and **Ålborg** (21hr 15min), supplemented by later departures the same days connecting at Amsterdam and taking some four to five hours longer.

Fares to all Danish destinations are £67 one-way, £94 return, with a £5 reduction if you are under 26 or over 60. All Norwegian destinations currently cost £115 one-way, £183 return (£108/£176 under-26 or over-60); Stockholm fares go for £107/£154 (£98/147); and to Helsinki you'll be paying £138/216 (£127/205).

Independent operators occasionally offer competition, but at time of writing there are none in the field. Nor are there any through services from anywhere in Britain outside London, so you will either have to go there first, or take a ferry to the Netherlands or Germany and a bus from there.

BY CAR: THE FERRIES

Ferry connections out of Harwich and Newcastle link Britain with Denmark, western Sweden and southern Norway. Fares aren't cheap, but discounts and special deals can cut costs greatly. *Scandinavian Seaways*, for example, offer "Seapex" midweek return fares, which have to be booked at least 21 days before departure (and are not valid on Friday or Saturday sailings). There are also 25 percent discounts on all fares for senior citizens and students. Unless otherwise stated, we've quoted the cheapest possible fares for a one-way passage. Not surprisingly, all fares are usually at their lowest between January and March.

Apart from the direct routes to Scandinavia, it is possible to get a ferry over to **Holland** or **Germany**, even Belgium or France, and drive or hitch from there. Obviously, these crossings are shorter and less costly, but they mean a longer drive for you when you get to the Continent. *Scandinavian Seaways* crossings from Harwich to Hamburg and *Stena Line*'s from Harwich to the Hook of Holland are really the only crossings that make sense, though you might just want to sail from Hull to Rotterdam with *North Sea Ferries* (handy for train connections – see p.7) or Ramsgate to Ostend with *Sally Line*.

Hitching is generally possible in Belgium, the Netherlands and, especially, Germany, but notoriously bad in Scandinavia itself. On the Puttgarten–Rødby ferry, it is best to ask around drivers boarding their cars as the ferry arrives at port.

BRITAIN TO SCANDINAVIA DIRECT

From the UK **to Denmark**, *Scandinavian Seaways* sail from **Harwich to Esbjerg** three or four times a week, a trip of nearly 20 hours. Fares in low season start at £67 one-way/£82 return per passenger plus £42/69 for a car (£270/370 for a car and four passengers), rising to £123/186 plus £64/119 (£580/680) in high season; many of the cheaper fares require 21-day advance booking.

Most of the year, the only services from Britain to **Norway** are the two or three sailings a week with *Color Line* from **Newcastle to Stavanger** (21hr) and **Bergen** (25hr), sometimes calling at Haugesund too. Minimum fares in winter are £30 each way per person, plus £40 for a car, rising to £93 plus £60 on Friday sailings in summer. Motorbikes are carried for £20 year-round, while bicycles go free. Students, senior citizens and registered disabled people get a 50 percent discount. In July and August, *P&O Scottish Ferries* run a weekly service to **Bergen** from **Aberdeen** (28hr 30hr), and **Lerwick** in Shetland (12hr 30hr). Fares start at £92 per passenger plus £80 per car (motorbikes £40, bicycles £10) from Aberdeen, £57 plus £50

(£20/£5) from Lerwick, with 20–25 percent discounts for students and senior citizens. Stopovers in Lerwick, and round trips using the routes Aberdeen–Lerwick–Bergen/Stavanger–Newcastle (or vice versa) are also available in conjunction with *Color Line*.

To Sweden, *Scandinavian Seaways* operate two routes: from **Harwich to Gothenburg** twice weekly, a 24-hour trip, and – in July and August only – **Newcastle to Gothenburg** once weekly, a 23-hour journey. Prices on both routes start at £102 per person each way, with an add-on fare of £42 for a car. A return fare of £400 is available for a car with up to five passengers.

There are no direct passenger ferries from Britain to **Finland**.

CROSSINGS FROM OTHER COUNTRIES

If you're driving or hitching, bear in mind also that there are ferry links to Scandinavia from other European countries. The main routes are given below, and note that there are also minor connections to the Danish islands. More details from ferry companies and travel agents, and in the relevant "Travel Details" sections of the guide.

From **Germany**, the most useful route is the hour-long crossing from Puttgarten to Rødby, on the way to Copenhagen. Ferries run half-hourly round the clock all year. Other routes include Rostock to Gedser (9–11 daily; 2hr), Kiel to Oslo (1 daily; 19hr 30min), Kiel to Gothenburg (1 daily; 14hr), Rostock to Trelleborg (boat: 4–5 daily; 5hr 30min–7hr; catamaran: 2–3 daily; 2hr 45min) and Sassnitz to Trelleborg (4–5 daily; 3hr 30min). From Travemünde, you can get ferries to Rødby (1 daily; 2hr 30min), Malmö (2 daily; 9hr) and Trelleborg (2–6 daily; 7–8hr), and there are services from

Travemünde and Lubeck to Helsinki (1–3 weekly each; 22hr and 36hr respectively).

From **Poland**, ferries run from Swinoujscie to Copenhagen (5 weekly; 9hr 15min), Malmö (1–2 daily; 9hr) and Ystad (1 daily; 6hr 45min), Gdansk to Oxelosund (3–6 weekly; 18hr 30min), and Gdynia to Karlskrona (6 weekly; 10hr 30min). They also run from Tallinn, the capital of **Estonia**, to Helsinki (boat: 6 daily; 3hr 30min–6hr 45min; hydrofoil: 4–6 daily; 1hr 30min; catamaran: 2–3 daily; 1hr 45min) and Stockholm (1 daily; 15hr).

PACKAGE TOURS

Don't be put off by the idea of an **inclusive package**. In such an expensive part of Europe, it can be the cheapest way to do things, and may also be the only way to reach remote parts of the region at inhospitable times of year. If you just want to see one city and its environs, then **city breaks** invariably work out cheaper than arranging the same trip independently. Prices include return travel, usually by plane, and accommodation (with breakfast), most operators offering a range from hostel to luxury-class hotel. As a broad guide, two-night hotel stays in Copenhagen or Stockholm start at around £250 per person out of season; in Oslo, prices start at around £280, while two nights in Helsinki will cost from £260. If you stay for a week in any of these places, rates per night fall considerably.

There are also an increasing number of operators offering special interest holidays to Scandinavia, from camping tours to Arctic cruises (see box overleaf). Prices for these are a good bit higher, but are generally excellent value for money.

FERRY OPERATORS

Color Line, International Ferry Terminal, Royal Quays, North Shields, Tyne and Wear NE29 6EE (☎0191/296 1313). *Newcastle to Stavanger, Haugesund and Bergen; Kiel to Oslo.*

North Sea Ferries, King George Dock, Hedon Rd, Kingston-upon-Hull HU9 5QA (☎01482/377177). *Hull to Rotterdam.*

P&O Scottish Ferries, PO Box 5, Jamieson's Quay, Aberdeen AB11 5NP (☎01224/574411). *Aberdeen and Lerwick to Bergen.*

Sally Line, 81 Piccadilly, London W1V 9HF (☎0171/409 2240). *Ramsgate to Ostend.*

Scandinavian Seaways, Scandinavia House, Parkeston Quay, Harwich, Essex CO12 4QG (☎0990/333000); 15 Hanover St, London W1R 9HG (☎0171/409 6060); Tyne Commission Quay, North Shields, NE29 6EA (☎0191/296 0101). *Harwich to Esbjerg; Harwich and Newcastle to Gothenburg.*

Stena Line, Charter House, Park St, Ashford, Kent TN24 8EX (☎0990/707070). *Harwich to the Hook of Holland.*

SPECIALIST OPERATORS

Aeroscope, Scope House, Morerton-in-Marsh, Gloucestershire GL56 0BQ (☎01608/650103). *One- and two-centre city breaks.*

Alfred Gregory Photographic Holidays, Woodcock Travel, 25–31 Wicker, Sheffield S3 8HW (☎0114/272 9619). *Annual Lapland dog-sledge trip for photographers.*

Anglers World Holidays, 46 Knifesmith Gate, Chesterfield, Derbyshire S40 1QR (☎01246/221717). *Angling holidays in Denmark and Sweden; cottage and hotel stays.*

Arctic Experience/Discover the World, 29 Nork Way, Banstead, Surrey SM7 1PB (☎01737/218800); http://www.arctic-discover.co.uk. *Specialist adventure tours including whale watching in Norway and dog-sledging in Lapland.*

Ashley Tours, "Cleve", Well Lane, Little Witley, Worcester WR6 6LN (☎01886/888335). *Annual tours to the Gothenburg jazz festival.*

Branta, 7 Wingfield St, London SE15 4LN (☎0171/635 5812). *Birdwatching tours.*

City Breaks, 2 Blair Court, North Ave, Clydebank Business Park, Clydebank G81 2LA (☎0141/951 8411). *One- and two-centre city breaks in Copenhagen, Stockholm, Oslo and Helsinki.*

Crystal Holidays, Crystal House, Arlington Rd, Surbiton, Surrey KT6 6BW (☎0181/399 5144); http://www.crystalholidays.co.uk. *One- and two-centre city breaks, lakes, mountains and skiing.*

DA Study Tours, Williamson House, Low Causeway, Culross, Fife KY12 8HL (☎01383/882200). *Coach tours for culture vultures.*

Finman Travel International, 87–89 Church St, Leigh, Greater Manchester WN7 1AZ (☎01942/262662). *Tailor-made holidays in Finland and Sweden, Helsinki city breaks, winter cruises and survival training in Lappland.*

Flying Ghillies, PO Box 1, Morpeth, Northumberland NE61 6YX (☎01670/789603). *Salmon-fishing holiday specialists, with sidelines in Norwegian walking and outdoor holidays.*

Insight, 26–28 Paradise Rd, Richmond, Surrey TW9 1SE (☎0990/143433). *Coach tours and tailor-made holidays.*

Inntravel, Hovingham, York YO6 4JZ (☎01653/628741). *Outdoor holidays in Norway including skiing, walking, fjord cruises, and whale and reindeer watching.*

King's Angling Holidays, 27 Minster Way, Hornchurch, Essex RM11 3TH (☎01708/453043). *Angling in Denmark and Sweden.*

Norvista, 227 Regent St, London W1R 8PD (☎0171/409 7334). *Finland specialists with a variety of tours and holidays, and some in Sweden too.*

Scandinavian Seaways, Scandinavia House, Parkeston Quay, Harwich, Essex CO12 4QG (☎0990/333111). *Breaks in Denmark and Sweden, including two nights on board ship and two or three nights abroad – good deals out of season.*

Scandinavian Travel Service, 2 Berghem Mews, Blythe Rd, London W14 0HN (☎0171/559 6666). *City breaks, tours, cruises and Scanrail passes.*

ScanMeridian, 28b High St, Hampstead, London NW3 1QA (☎0171/431 5322). *Scandinavia specialists offering city breaks, fly-drive, cottage holidays, cruises and tailor-made holidays.*

Scantours, 21–24 Cockspur St, London SW1Y 5BN (☎0171/839 2927). *Scandinavia specialists with a wide range of packages and tailor-made holidays.*

Ski Scandinavia, Whetstone Lodge, The Dicken, Whetstone, Leicestershire LE8 6LE (☎01162/752750). *Year-round skiing in Norway and Sweden.*

Specialised Tours, Suite 1, Copthorne Business Centre, Church Rd, Crawley, West Sussex RH10 3RA (☎01342/712785). *City breaks, motoring, cycling and tailor-made holidays, even the odd spot of whale watching.*

Taber Holidays, 126 Sunbridge Rd, Bradford, West Yorkshire, BD1 2SX (☎01274/735611). *Their "Norway Only" brochure has dozens of options, including self-catering holidays, fjord cruises, motoring tours and guided coach tours.*

Tracks, Evegate Park Barn, Smeeth, Ashford, Kent TN25 6SX (☎01303/814949). *Coach camping tours for 18- to 38-year-olds, including a 31-day "Midnight Sun Tour" of Scandinavia, and a 48-day "Hussar Tour" taking in some of Eastern Europe too.*

GETTING THERE FROM IRELAND

The only direct **flights from Dublin** to Scandinavia are to **Copenhagen** (daily with *SAS*, daily except Saturday with *Aer Lingus*; 2hr). For most other destinations, your best bet is either an onward connection with one of these airlines, or else a connection via London or Manchester with either *British Airways*, or a combination of *Aer Lingus* or *British Midland* and *SAS* and *Finnair*, or else with *Air France* via Paris, which is often the cheapest route. Official **fares** to Copenhagen start at around IR£240 plus tax for a "Jackpot" or APEX return ticket,

AIRLINES

Aer Lingus, 40 O'Connell St, Dublin 1 (☎01/844 4777); 46 Castle St, Belfast BT1 1HB (☎01232/314844); 2 Academy St, Cork (021/327155); 136 O'Connell Street, Limerick (☎061/474239).

British Airways, in the Republic c/o *Aer Lingus* (address above; reservations ☎1800/626747); in

Northern Ireland at 1 Fountain Centre, Fountain St, Belfast BT1 6HR (reservations ☎0345/222111).

British Midland, Nutley, Merrion Rd, Dublin 4 (☎01/283 8833); Suite 2, The Fountain Centre, College St, Belfast 1 (☎0345/554554).

SAS, Terminal Building, Dublin Airport (☎01/844 5440).

DISCOUNT AGENTS

Discount Travel, 4 South Great Georges St, Dublin 2 (☎01/679 5888).

Flight Finders International, 13 Baggot St Lower, Dublin 2 (☎01/676 8326).

Joe Walsh Tours, 8–11 Baggot St, Dublin (☎01/676 3053). *General budget fares agent.*

Student & Group Travel, 71 Dame St, Dublin 2 (☎01/677 7834). *Student specialists.*

Trailfinders, 4–5 Dawson St, Dublin (phone number not available at time of writing).

Travel Shop, 35 Belmont Rd, Belfast 4 (☎01232/471717).

USIT, O'Connell Bridge, 19–21 Aston Quay, Dublin 2 (☎01/679 8833); Fountain Centre, Belfast BT1 6ET (☎01232/324073); 10–11 Market Parade, Patrick St, Cork (☎021/270900); 33 Ferryquay St, Derry (☎01504/371888); Victoria Place, Eyre Square, Galway (☎091/565177); Central Buildings, O'Connell St, Limerick (☎061/415064); 36–37 Georges St, Waterford (☎051/72601). *Ireland's main student and youth travel specialists.*

FERRY COMPANIES

Irish Ferries, 2–4 Merrion Row, Dublin 2 (☎01/661 0511); 16 Westmoreland St, Dublin 2 (☎01/661 0715, 24hr); St Patrick's Buildings, Cork (☎021/504333). *Irish agents for Scandinavian Seaways.*

P&O European Ferries, The Terminal Building, Larne Harbour, Co. Antrim BT40 1AQ (☎0990/980777).

TOUR OPERATORS

Falcon Travel, 19 Lower Camden St, Dublin 2 (☎01/478 1843). *City breaks and cruises.*

Crystal Holidays, 38 Dawson St, Dublin 2 (☎01/670 8444). *One- and two-centre city breaks, lakes, mountains and skiing.*

Express Travel Service, 18a Upper Merrion St, Dublin 2 (☎01/676 4806).

Thomas Cook, 11 Donegall Place, Belfast (☎01232/240833); 118 Grafton St, Dublin (☎01/677 1721). *Package holiday and flight agent, with occasional discount offers.*

although special offers below IR£200 are sometimes available, and a discount agent such as *USIT* (see box below) may have youth, student or discounted tickets for even less. Scheduled fares to **Stockholm**, **Oslo** or **Helsinki** tend to start at around IR£280 return, although again you may be able to get cheaper tickets through a discount agent.

From Belfast, there are no direct flights to Scandinavia, and your best bet is probably flying via London with *British Airways*, *British Midland* or *SAS*. **Prices** to Copenhagen, Stockholm or Oslo usually start at about £300 for an APEX return, £350 to Helsinki, but special offers can take these as low as £175 return to Copenhagen, and just over £200 to other Scandinavian capitals. Failing that, you should be able to get a reasonable deal through a discount agent, either in Northern Ireland or in Great Britain.

If you are planning to travel from Ireland **by train**, your best bet by far would be an *Inter Rail* pass, details of which are given in the train section of "Getting There from Britain" (p.6). Getting to Scandinavia by bus would involve going to London and picking up a connection there. For motorists, combined ferry fares covering Irish Sea and North Sea crossings are generally available through *Irish Ferries* from the Republic or *P&O* from the North (see box p.11 for addresses).

Not many operators run **package tours** to Scandinavia from Ireland, but a package tour may well be the cheapest way to travel and sometimes the only way to reach remote parts of the region at inhospitable times of year. Booking a city break may well work out cheaper than arranging the same trip independently. British operators are listed on p.10, those based in Ireland are given above.

GETTING THERE FROM NORTH AMERICA

The four countries of Scandinavia are well served by numerous American and European airlines, though only SAS, American and Finnair provide direct flights. If you are visiting more than one country, an air pass might be your best bet.

SHOPPING FOR TICKETS

Barring special offers, the cheapest of the airlines' published fares is usually an **Apex** (Advance Purchase Excursion) ticket, although this will carry certain restrictions: you have to book – and pay – at least 21 days before depar-

ture, spend at least seven days abroad (maximum stay three months), and you tend to get penalized if you change your schedule. On transatlantic routes, there are also winter **Super Apex** tickets, sometimes known as "Eurosavers" – slightly cheaper than an ordinary Apex, but limiting your stay to between 7 and 21 days. Some airlines also issue **Special Apex** tickets to people younger than 24, often extending the maximum stay to a year. Many airlines offer youth or student fares to under-26s; a passport or drivers licence are sufficient proof of age, though these tickets are subject to availability and can have eccentric booking conditions. It's worth remembering that most cheap return fares involve spending at least one Saturday night away and that many will only give a percentage refund if you need to cancel or alter your journey, so make sure you check the restrictions carefully before buying a ticket.

You can normally cut costs further by going through a **specialist flight agent** – either a **consolidator**, who buys up blocks of tickets from the airlines and sells them at a discount, or a **discount agent**, who in addition to dealing with discounted flights may also offer special student and youth fares and a range of other travel-related services such as travel insurance, rail passes, car rental, tours and the like. Bear in mind, though, that penalties for changing your plans can be stiff. Remember too that these companies make their money by dealing in bulk – don't expect them to answer lots of questions. Some agents specialize in **charter** flights, which may be cheaper than anything available on a scheduled flight, but again departure dates are fixed and withdrawal penalties are high (check the refund policy). If you travel a lot, **discount travel clubs** are another option – the annu-

---

DISCOUNT TRAVEL COMPANIES IN NORTH AMERICA

Air Brokers International, 323 Geary St, Suite 411, San Francisco, CA 94102 (☎1-800/883-3273 or 415/397-1383; fax 415/397-4767). *Consolidator.*

Air Courier Association, 191 University Blvd, Suite 300, Denver, CO 80206 (☎303/278-8810). *Courier flight broker.*

Airhitch, 2641Broadway, New York, NY 10025 (☎1-800/326-2009 or 212/864-2000). *Standby seat broker. For a set price, they guarantee to get you on a flight as close to your preferred destination as possible, within a week.*

Airtech, 584 Broadway, Suite 1007, New York, NY 10012 (☎1-800/575-TECH or 212/219-7000). *Standby seat broker; also deals in consolidator fares and courier flights.*

Cheap Tickets, Inc. Offices nationwide (☎1-800/377-1000 or 212/570-1179). *Consolidator.*

Council Travel, 205 E 42nd St, New York, NY 10017 (☎1-800/226-8624), and branches in many other US cities. *Student/budget travel agency. A sister company,* **Council Charter** (☎1-800/800-8222), *specializes in charter flights.*

Educational Travel Center, 438 N Frances St, Madison, WI 53703 (☎1-800/747-5551 or 608/256-5551). *Student/youth and consolidator fares.*

High Adventure Travel, 353 Sacramento St, Suite 600, San Francisco, CA 94111 (☎1-800/428-8735 or 415/912-5600; fax 415/912-5606; Website http://www.highadv.com; E-mail airtracks@highadv.com

International Student Exchange Flights, 5010 E Shea Blvd, Suite 104A, Scottsdale, AZ 85254 (☎602/951-1177). *Student/youth fares, student IDs.*

Interworld Travel, 800 Douglass Rd, Miami, FL 33134 (☎1-800/468-3796). *Consolidator specializing in Scandinavia.*

Last Minute Travel Services. Offices nationwide (☎1-800/LAST-MIN). *Specializes in standby flights.*

Nouvelles Frontières/New Frontiers, 12 E 33rd St, New York, NY 10016, and other branches in Los Angeles and San Francisco (☎1800/366-6387); in Canada: 1001 Sherbrook E, Suite 720, Montréal, H2L 1L3 (☎514/526-8444). *French discount travel firm.*

Now Voyager, 74 Varick St, Suite 307, New York, NY 10013 (☎212/431-1616). *Courier flight broker and consolidator.*

Skylink, 265 Madison Ave, 5th Floor, New York, NY 10016 (☎1-800/AIR-ONLY or 212/573-8980), with branches in Chicago, Los Angeles, Montréal, Toronto and Washington, DC. *Consolidator.*

STA Travel, 10 Downing St, New York, NY 10014 (☎1-800/777-0112 or 212/627-3111), and other branches in Los Angeles, San Francisco and Boston. *Worldwide discount travel firm specializing in student/youth fares.*

TFI Tours International, 34 W 32nd St, New York, NY 10001 (☎1-800/745-8000 or 212/736-1140), and other offices in Las Vegas and Miami. *Consolidator.*

Travac Tours, 989 6th Ave, New York NY 10018 (☎1-800/872-8800 or 212/563-3303). *Consolidator and charter broker. If you have a fax machine you can have a list of fares faxed to you by calling toll-free 888/872-8327.*

Travel Avenue, 10 S Riverside, Suite 1404, Chicago, IL 60606 (☎1-800/333-3335 or 312/876-6866). *Full-service travel agent that offers discounts in the form of rebates.*

Travel CUTS (Canada), 187 College St, Toronto, ON M5T 1P7 (☎416/979-2406), and other branches nationwide. *Canadian student travel organization specializing in student fares, IDs and other travel services.*

Travelers Advantage, 311 W Superior St, Chicago, IL 60610 (☎1-800/255-0200). *Travel club; annual membership fee.*

UniTravel, 1177 N Warson Rd, St Louis, MO 63132 (☎1-800/325-2222 or 314/569-2501). *Consolidator.*

Worldtek Travel, 111 Water St, New Haven, CT 06511 (☎1-800/243-1723 or 203/772-0470). *Discount travel agency.*

Worldwide Discount Travel Club, 1674 Meridian Ave, Miami Beach, FL 33139 (☎305/534-2082). *Travel club; annual membership fee.*

AIRLINES IN THE USA AND CANADA

Air Canada

BC ☎1-800/663-3721; Alberta, Saskatchewan and Manitoba ☎1-800/542-8940; eastern Canada ☎1-800/268-7240; US ☎1-800/776-3000.

Daily fom Toronto to Frankfurt and Zurich (daily), and Paris (5 a week), to connect with SAS and Air France flights to all major Scandinavian cities. West Coast Canadians can connect in Toronto, or fly from Vancouver via London or Frankfurt.

Air France

US ☎1-800/237-2747; Canada ☎1-800/667-2747.

Daily flights from many major cities in the US and Canada to Paris, with connecting flights to all major Scandinavian cities.

American Airlines

☎1-800/433-7300.

Direct flights to Stockholm daily from Chicago and Miami. Connections with all major cities in North America.

British Airways

US ☎1-800/247-9297; Canada ☎1-800/668-1059.

Daily flights from 22 North American cities to London; connecting flights on to all major Scandinavian cities.

Continental Airlines

☎1-800/231-0856.

New York (Newark) to many major European cities with connecting flights to Scandinavia on another carrier. Also connects most major North American cities with direct SAS flights from Newark to Copenhagen, Stockholm and Oslo.

Delta Airlines

☎1-800/241-4141.

Daily flights from many major North American cities via Atlanta and New York (JFK) to Brussels; connecting flights to Scandinavia on Sabena Airlines.

Finnair

US ☎1-800/950-5000; Canada ☎1-800/461-8651.

Direct flights to Helsinki from New York (year-round, 6–7 a week), San Francisco (mid-May to Aug, 3 a week), Miami (Sun in winter) and Toronto (mid-May to Aug, 2 a week). In winter flights from San Francisco and Toronto connect through New York. Also connections on from Helsinki, plus a stopover fare allowing up to three nights in Helsinki en route to other destinations. Check out also Finnair's Nordic Air Pass.

Icelandair

☎1-800/223-5500.

Flights to Reykjavik (Iceland) from New York (daily), Baltimore (6 a week), Boston (4 a week), Orlando (3 a week) and Halifax, Nova Scotia (2 a week); onward flights from Reykjavik to all major

al membership fee may be worth it for benefits such as cut-price air tickets and car rental.

Don't automatically assume that tickets purchased through a travel specialist will be cheapest – once you get a quote, check with the airlines and you may turn up an even better deal. Be advised also that the pool of travel companies is swimming with sharks – exercise caution and never deal with a company that demands cash up front or refuses to accept payment by credit card.

Students might be able to find cheaper flights through the major student travel agencies, such as *STA Travel, Nouvelles Frontières* or, for Canadian students, *Travel Cuts* (see box on p.13 for addresses and phone numbers).

A further possibility is to see if you can arrange a **courier flight**, although the hit-or-miss nature of these makes them most suitable for the single traveller who travels light and has a very flexible schedule. In return for shepherding a parcel through customs and possibly giving up your baggage allowance, you can expect to get a major discounted ticket. For information about courier flights you could contact *Halbart Express* (☎718/656-5000) or *Now Voyager* (☎212/431-1616). For more options, consult *A Simple Guide to Courier Travel* (Pacific Data Sales Publishing).

If you are travelling to Scandinavia as part of a longer trip, you might want to consider buying a **Round-the-World** (RTW) ticket. Since Scandinavia is not one of the more obvious destinations for round-the-world travellers, you would probably have to have a custom-designed RTW ticket (more expensive than an "off-the-shelf" RTW ticket) assembled for you by a travel agent, which can be quite expensive.

Scandinavian cities. Frequency of flights varies according to season. Can book connections with all major North American cities. Also flights with a stopover in Reykjavik.

KLM

☎1-800/374-7747.

Flights to Amsterdam from 10 US gateways (Atlanta, Boston, Chicago, Detroit, Houston, Los Angeles, Memphis, Minneapolis/St Paul, New York and San Francisco) and 6 Canadian cities (Calgary, Halifax, Montréal, Ottowa, Toronto and Vancouver), with connections to most major Scandinavian cities.

Lufthansa

☎1-800/645-3880.

Flights to Scandinavia from major cities in the United States (and from Toronto and Vancouver in Canada) via Frankfurt.

Sabena

☎1-800/955-2000.

Flights from all major US cities via Brussels.

Scandinavian Airlines (SAS)

☎1-800/221-2350.

Direct flights to Copenhagen from New York Newark (daily), Chicago (Wed–Sun) and Seattle (daily except Wed). Also direct flights daily from New York (Newark) to Stockholm and Oslo, with onward connections. Connections with most major cities in North America via United Airlines. Note that

SAS also offers the Visit Scandinavia Air Pass.

Swissair

☎1-800/221-4750.

Flights to Zurich from Atlanta, Boston, Chicago, Los Angeles, New York, Toronto and Montréal, with connections to Scandinavia on either Swissair or SAS.

TWA

☎1-800/892-4141.

Flights to Frankfurt or Paris via all major cities in North America. Connects with Lufthansa or SAS flights to Scandinavia.

United Airlines

☎1-800/538-2929.

Connects most major North American cities with direct SAS flights from New York (Newark) to Copenhagen, Stockholm and Oslo.

US Air

☎1-800/622-1015.

Flights from Philadelphia or Boston hubs to many major European cities, with connecting flights to Scandinavia on other carriers.

Virgin Atlantic Airways

☎1-800/862-8621.

Daily flights from a number of North American cities to London, with connections to major Scandinavian cities on another carrier.

The newest option for seaching for lowest price air fares is the World Wide Web. There are a number of new **Web sites** where you can look up fares and even book tickets. You can search in the travel sections of your Web Browser, or try one of the following: Travelocity at http://www.travelocity.com, Travel Information Service at http://www9.ibm.tiss.com, or FLIFO Cyber Travel Agent at http://www.flifo.com

FLIGHTS FROM THE USA AND CANADA

The majority of flights to Scandinavia from North America involve **changing planes** in London, Reykjavik, Brussels, Amsterdam, Paris, Frankfurt or Zurich. And if you don't live in one of the gateway cities in North America you might have to change planes more than once. **Direct flights**, of

which there are a few, might be more desirable but it is worth shopping around to get the cheapest fares for the dates you want to travel, as prices can vary widely, especially in the low season. Following is a guide to the fares you can expect to pay and information on direct flights; for airline contact numbers and details on specific routings, see the box above.

Fares to the four countries are fairly comparable, with those to Denmark being the cheapest and those to Finland the most expensive, though the difference is minimal. The cost of flying to either Copenhagen, Oslo, Stockholm or Helsinki on a round-trip midweek Apex economy class ticket (excluding taxes and airport fees) from **New York** (journey time can range from 7hr 30min to at least 10hr on an indirect flight) is around US$900–1100 during the high season, US$600–850 during the shoulder seasons and anywhere between US$400 and $600 in the low season. You can fly direct to **Helsinki** from New York on *Finnair* and to **Copenhagen**, **Stockholm** and **Oslo** on *SAS*.

The fare from **Chicago** to Stockholm (journey time on a direct flight is 8hr 30min; at least 11hr on an indirect flight) is likely to be US$900–1100 during the high season, US$650–850 during the shoulder seasons and US$550–650 in the low season. *American Airlines* flies direct from Chicago to **Stockholm** while *SAS* flies direct to **Copenhagen**.

From the **West Coast** (journey time can be at least 12hr on an indirect flight) fares are a little higher: US$1200–1300 during the high season, US$1000–1050 during the shoulder seasons and US$550–$750 in the low season. *SAS* flies direct from **Seattle** to **Copenhagen** and *Finnair* flies direct from **San Francisco** to **Helsinki** in the summer months.

From **Canada** there are very few direct flights and flying time can vary between 9hr and 12hr 30min from Toronto, and 13–18hr from Vancouver, depending on connections. From **Toronto** high-season fares are around CDN$1000–1300, in the low season CDN$750–960n, with shoulder season fares somewhere in between. Flying from **Vancouver**, fares range from CDN$1300 to $1700 during the high season and CDN$1150–1300 in the low season (as a rule of thumb, fares from Vancouver are around $400 more than the Toronto fare). *Finnair* flies from Toronto to **Helsinki** twice a week in the summer (via New York in the winter). You might also want to look into cheap flights to New York or Chicago, and connecting flights from there using another carrier.

If you're considering getting around Scandinavia by air, check out the **Visit Scandinavia Air Pass** offered by *SAS*. A book of discount coupons for air travel within Norway, Sweden and Denmark (not Finland), it must be pur-

chased in the US or Canada along with an intercontinental ticket. The coupons are valid for three months from arrival and cost between $80 and $420, depending on the number purchased. *Finnair* offers the similar **Nordic Air Pass**. For airline contact numbers, see the box on pp. 14–15.

TRAVELLING VIA EUROPE

If fares seem high you might want to consider flying to **London**, one of the cheapest European cities to get to, and taking a flight or a train and ferry onward to Scandinavia (see "Getting There from Britain", p.3). If you are visiting Scandinavia as part of a wider tour of Europe, it may be worth buying a **Eurail pass** (which you'll need to purchase before you leave home), which can get you by train to Scandinavia from anywhere in Europe. Allowing unlimited first-class train travel in seventeen European countries, the basic *Eurail* pass costs $522 for 15 days, $678 for 21 days, $838 for 1 month, $1148 for 2 months and $1468 for 3 months. The **Eurail Flexipass** is cheaper if you are not planning to travel every day of your stay: $616 for 10 days of travel within 2 months and $812 for 15 days in 2 months. **Under-26s** are eligible for the even better value **Eurail Youthpass**, which costs $418 for 15 days, $598 for 1 month or $798 for 2 months, while the **Under-26 Flexipass** costs $438 for 10 days of travel within 2 months and $588 for 15 days in 2 months. Note, however, that the youth passes only cover second-class travel. A final option, if there are two of you (three in summer), is the **Eurail Saverpass**, which can knock about 15 percent off the cost of the standard Eurail offerings.

If you're planning to travel by train only once in Scandinavia, then you're better off with a Scandinavia-wide **Scanrail** pass (see p.29), or a single-country train pass (see the relevant country's "Getting Around" section).

RAIL CONTACTS IN NORTH AMERICA

Borton Overseas (☎1-800/843-0602). *Sells all Eurail and Scanrail passes.*

CIT Tours (☎1-800/223-7987). *Eurail passes only.*

DER Tours/Derrail (☎1-800/782-2424; ☎1-800/205-5800 in Canada). *Eurail and Scanrail passes.*

Rail Europe (☎1-800/4-EURAIL in USA; ☎1-800/361-RAIL in Canada). *Official Eurail Pass agent in North America; also sells the Scanrail pass.*

ScanTours (☎1-800/223-7226). *Eurail and Scanrail passes.*

NORTH AMERICAN TOUR OPERATORS

American Express Vacations (☎1-800/446-6234). *Flight-plus-hotel packages to major Scandinavian cities.*

Backroads (☎1-800-462-2848) Website http://www.backroads.com. *Offers a 7-day bicycling holiday in the Vesteralen and Lofoten Islands of Norway and an 8-day hiking tour of the mountains, glaciers and fjords of Norway.*

Bennett Tours (☎1-800-221-2420) Website http://www.bennett-tours.com. *Scandinavia specialists. Cheap weekend breaks or fully escorted bus tours throughout Scandinavia.*

Bergen Line (☎1-800/323-7436). In Canada call Finncharter (☎1-800/461-8651 or 416/222-0740). *Cruises around the Swedish archipelago, the Norwegian fjords and the Baltic Sea.*

Borton Overseas (☎1-800/843-0602). *Company specializing in adventure vacations (hiking, rafting, birdwatching, dog-sledging, cross-country skiing etc) and farm and cabin stays in Scandinavia.*

Brekke Tours (☎1-800/437-5302). *Escorted tours and cultural tours of Scandinavia. Call for a brochure.*

Contiki Tours (☎1-800/CONTIKI). *Tours of Scandinavia and Russia for 18- to 35-year-olds.*

Euro-Bike (☎1-800/321-6060). *Summer bicycling tours of Sweden and Denmark.*

EuroCruises (☎1-800/688-3876). *Cruises of the Baltic Sea, the fjords of Norway and the canals of Sweden.*

Euroseven (☎1-800/890-3876). *Independent hotel-plus-flight packages from New York, Baltimore or Boston to Scandinavia.*

Loma Travel (☎1-800/294-3261). *Canadian tour operator based in Vancouver and advertised as "The Scandinavian Connection"; cheap flights, tours and cruises.*

Nordique Tours (☎1-800/995-7997). *Specializes in package tours of the Norwegian fjords.*

Passage Tours (☎1-800-548-5960). *Scandinavian specialist offering escorted and unescorted tours and cheap weekend breaks.*

Pedersen World Tours (☎1-800/933-6627; in Canada 1-800/973-3377). *Canadian tour operator specializing in Swedish tours.*

SAS (☎1-800/221-2350 ext 4). *Scandinavian airline which also offers tours.*

Scanam World Tours (☎1-800/545-2204 or 201/835-7070). *Specializes in Scandinavian tours and cruises for groups and individuals. Also cheap weekend breaks.*

Scand-America Tours (☎1-800/886-8428; 813/447-8687). *Offers a wide variety of packages – everything from dog-sledging to garden tours – throughout Scandinavia.*

Scanditours (☎1-800-432-4176). *Canadian Scandinavian specialist with offices in Toronto and Vancouver.*

Scandinavian Special Interest Network (☎201/729-8961; Website http://www.sitravel.com. *Hundreds of different special-interest tours in Scandinavia.*

Scantours (☎1-800/223-7226). *Major Scandinavian holiday specialists offering vacation packages and customized itineraries, including cruises and city sightseeing tours.*

Ski-See Norway (☎1-800/447-5473). *As the name suggests, this company books alpine and cross-country skiing holidays in Norway.*

Vantage Deluxe World Travel (☎1-800/322-6677). *Deluxe group tours and cruises in Scandinavia.*

The companies listed in the box opposite specialize in the passes indicated, though the more common European passes can be purchased through most travel agents.

PACKAGES AND ORGANIZED TOURS

There are a number of companies operating **organized tours** of Scandinavia, ranging from deluxe cruises to bicycling holidays. Group tours can be very expensive, and occasionally do not include the air fare, so check what you are getting for the price. If your visit is centred on cities you could simply book a hotel-plus-flight package (which can work out cheaper than booking the two separately). *Bennett Tours, Euroseven, Scanam* and *Passage Tours* offer very reasonable weekend deals in the low season (see box above). Tour reservations can often be made through your local travel agent.

GETTING THERE FROM AUSTRALASIA

There are no direct flights from Australia or New Zealand to Scandinavia; instead you have to fly to either a European or Asian gateway city where you can get a connecting flight or alternative transport. Fares are pretty steep, so if you're on a tight budget it's worth flying to London (see "Getting There from Britain"), Amsterdam or Frankfurt first and picking up a cheap flight. If you intend to take in a number of other European countries on your trip, it might well be worth buying a Eurail pass before you go.

Fares from major **Eastern Australian** cities are common rated, with flights from Perth and Darwin A$100–200 less via Asia or A$200–400 more via Canada and the US. Fares from Christchurch and Wellington are between NZ$150–300 more than from Auckland. Prices also vary significantly with the **season**. For most major airlines, low season runs from mid-January to the end of February and during October and November; high season runs from mid-May to the end of August and from December to mid-January; the rest of the year is counted as shoulder season. Tickets purchased direct from the **airlines** tend to be expensive, with published fares ranging from A$2399/NZ$2699 in low season, to A$2599–2799/NZ$2899–3150 in shoulder season, up to high-season fares of A$2999/NZ$3399.

DISCOUNT AGENTS

Accent on Travel, 545 Queen St, Brisbane (☎07/3832 1777).

Anywhere Travel, 345 Anzac Parade, Kingsford, Sydney (☎02/9663 0411).

Brisbane Discount Travel, 260 Queen St, Brisbane (☎07/3229 9211).

Budget Travel, 16 Fort St, Auckland; other branches around the city (☎09/366 0061; toll-free 0800/808 040).

Destinations Unlimited, 3 Milford Rd, Milford, Auckland (☎09/373 4033).

Flight Centres Australia: Circular Quay, Sydney (☎02/9241 2422); Bourke St, Melbourne (☎03/9650 2899); plus other branches nation wide. New Zealand: National Bank Towers, 205–225 Queen St, Auckland (☎09/209 6171); Shop 1M, National Mutual Arcade, 152 Hereford St, Christchurch (☎03/379 7145); 50–52 Willis St, Wellington (☎04/472 8101); other branches nation wide.

Harvey World Travel, 631 Princes Highway, Kogarah, Sydney (☎02/9567 6099); branches nation wide.

Northern Gateway, 22 Cavenagh St, Darwin (☎08/8941 1394).

Passport Travel, Kings Cross Plaza, Suite 11a, 4010 St Kilda Rd, Melbourne (☎03/9824 7183).

STA Travel, Australia: 855 George St, Ultimo, Sydney (☎02/9212 1255; toll-free 1800/637 444); 256 Flinders St, Melbourne (☎03/9654 7266); other offices in Townsville, state capitals and major universities. New Zealand: Travellers' Centre, 10 High St, Auckland (☎09/309 0458); 233 Cuba St, Wellington (☎04/385 0561); 90 Cashel St, Christchurch (☎03/379 9098); other offices in Dunedin, Palmerston North, Hamilton and major universities.

Thomas Cook, Australia: 321 Kent St, Sydney (☎02/9248 6100); 330 Collins St, Melbourne (☎03/9602 3811); branches in other state capitals. New Zealand: Shop 250a St Luke's Square, Auckland (☎09/849 2071).

Topdeck Travel, 65 Glenfell St, Adelaide (☎08/8232 7222).

Tymtro Travel, 428 George St, Sydney (☎02/9223 2211).

UTAG Travel, 122 Walker St, North Sydney (☎02/9956 8399); branches throughout Australia.

AIRLINES

Air New Zealand, 5 Elizabeth St, Sydney (☎02/9223 4666); 17th floor, Quay Tower, Customs St, Auckland (☎09/366 2803).

Several flights weekly to London via Auckland and LA; daily flights to Bangkok (to connect with SAS) from major cities.

Britannia Airways, Aus-Extras Level 6, 210 George St, Sydney (☎02/9251 1299). No NZ office.

Several charter flights to London and Amsterdam per month (Nov–March) from major Australian cities and Auckland via Singapore and Abu Dhabi.

British Airways, Level 26, 201 Kent St, Sydney (☎02/9258 3300); 154 Queen St, Auckland (☎09/356 8690).

Daily flights to London from major Australian cities via Asia and from New Zealand cities via Los Angeles.

Canadian Airlines, 30 Clarence St, Sydney (☎02/9299 7843); Floor 15, Jetset Centre, 44 Emily Place, Auckland (☎09/309 0735).

Twice weekly to Vancouver and Toronto from Sydney, Melbourne and Auckland, connecting with SAS.

Finnair, 20 Bay St, Double Bay, NSW (☎02/9326 2999). No NZ office.

In conjunction with Qantas/Thai 4 flights weekly from Sydney via Bangkok/Tokyo to Helsinki; with Singapore Airlines twice weekly from Auckland via Singapore to Helsinki and then on to other major Scandinavian cities.

Garuda, 55 Hunter St, Sydney (☎02/9334 9944); 120 Albert St, Auckland (☎09/366 1855).

Several flights weekly via Jakarta or Denpasar to Gatwick and Amsterdam from major Australian cities and from Auckland twice weekly.

Lufthansa/Lauda-air, 143 Macquarie St, Sydney (☎02/9367 3888); Lufthansa House, 36 Kitchener St, Auckland (☎09/303 1529).

Three flights weekly to Frankfurt and Vienna from major Australian cities and Auckland via Sydney and Singapore.

Malaysia Airlines, 16 Spring St, Sydney (local call rate ☎13 2627); Floor 12, Swanson Centre, 12–26 Swanson St, Auckland (☎09/373 2741).

Several flights weekly to London, Amsterdam, Paris and Zurich from major Australian and New Zealand cities via Kuala Lumpur.

Philippine Airlines, 49 York St, Sydney (☎02/9262 3333). No NZ office.

Twice weekly to London and Frankfurt from Brisbane, Sydney and Melbourne via Manila.

Qantas, Chifley Square, cnr Hunter and Phillip streets, Sydney (☎02/9957 0111); Qantas House, 154 Queen St, Auckland (☎09/357 8900).

Daily to London, Singapore and Bangkok from major cities in Australia and New Zealand, connecting with SAS and Finnair to destinations in Scandinavia.

SAS Scandinavian Airlines, 350 Kent St, Sydney (☎02/9299 6688); 52 Quay St, Auckland (☎09/309 7750).

SAS-Qantas/Air New Zealand have several flights weekly to Oslo, Stockholm, Helsinki and other destinations in Scandinavia from major cities in Australia and New Zealand via Copenhagen.

Singapore Airlines, 17–19 Bridge St, Sydney (local call rate ☎13 1011); Lower Ground Floor, West Plaza Building, cnr Customs and Albert streets, Auckland (☎09/379 3209).

Several flights weekly to London via Singapore from major Australian cities and twice weekly from Auckland, connecting with Finnair to Helsinki.

Thai Airlines, 75–77 Pitt St, Sydney (☎02/9844 0999; toll-free 1800/422 020); Kensington Swan Building, 22 Fanshawe St, Auckland (☎09/377 3886).

Several times weekly to Stockholm and Copenhagen via Paris and Bangkok from major Australia cities and Auckland. Connections with Finnair.

Travel agents offer better deals on fares and have the latest information on limited special deals such as free stopovers en route and fly-drive-accommodation packages. *Flight Centres* and *STA* (see box opposite for addresses) generally offer the best discounts, especially for students and those under 26.

To Sweden, **Norway**, **Denmark** and **Finland**, airlines flying out of Australia and New Zealand often use *SAS* and *Finnair* for connecting services, with daily flights to major towns and cities in the region. To get to Copenhagen, Helsinki or Stockholm you can expect to pay around A$2100/2400/2700 or NZ$2250/2600/2900.

For flights to other **European cities**, the lowest fares are with *Britannia* to London, during its limited charter season from November to March, when you can expect to pay A$1200/1450/1800 or NZ$1420/1840/2130. Among the scheduled flights, count on paying A$1499/NZ$1899–A$1999/NZ$2450 on *Philippine Airlines* and *Garuda*; A$1800/NZ$2100–A$2350/NZ$2700 on *Malaysia Airlines*, *Thai Airways* and *Lufthansa/Lauda-air*, and A$23999/NZ$2699–A$2999/NZ$3399 on *British Airways*, *Qantas*, *Singapore Airlines*, *Air New Zealand* and *Canadian Airways* depending on the season. See the box above for a full rundown of airlines and routes.

Air passes that allow for discounted flights within Europe and Scandinavia, such as the *SAS* "Visit Scandinavia Pass" and *BA-Qantas* "Air Pass" are only available in conjunction with a flight to Scandinavia, and must be bought at the same time. Expect to pay between A/NZ$120 and A/NZ$180 per coupon.

For extended trips, **Round The World** tickets, valid up to a year, can be good value. Tickets that take in Scandinavia include the combined *SAS-Thai-United* fare (A$2999/NZ$3299) with six stopovers, open-jaw travel and backtracking permitted, and the *Qantas-BA* "Global Explorer" (A$2499/3099; NZ$2399/2999), which doesn't allow backtracking.

Travellers who want to take a **package holiday** to Scandinavia will find there are very few to choose from. Your best bet is *Bentours* (see box below for details), who will put together a package for you, and are about the only agents willing to deal with skiing holidays. Alternatively you could wait until you get to Europe, where there's a greater choice of holidays and prices (see "Getting there from Britain") – none of the prices given in the box below include the plane fare.

If you're planning to travel a lot **by train**, or use trains to get to Scandinavia from another European country, it's worth considering a train pass. **Eurail passes**, which come in numerous versions (see pp.6–7 for a rundown) are available from most travel agents, or from *CIT*, 123 Clarence St, Sydney (☎02/9267 1255; offices in Melbourne, Brisbane, Adelaide and Perth), or *Thomas Cook World Rail* (Australia ☎1800/422 747; New Zealand ☎09/263 7260). There's also a specific pass for Scandinavia, the **Scanrail** pass, which is sold by *Bentours* – further details on p.29.

SPECIALIST TOUR OPERATORS

Bentours, level 11, 2 Bridge St, Sydney (☎02/9241 1353). *Ferry, rail, bus and hotel passes and a host of scenic tours throughout Scandinavia such as fjord-hopping, cycling in Denmark and a 4-day ferry journey down the Göta Canal between Stockholm and Gothenburg; from A$1190/NZ$1300 including meals.*

Explore Holidays, 1st Floor, Oasis Centre, cnr Pennent Hills and Marsden Rds, Carlingford, Sydney (☎02/9872 6222). *Stockholm mini-stays from A$490/NZ$517, and 21 day-adventure tour through central and northern Sweden and coastal Norway from A$1660/NZ$1700.*

European Travel Office, 122 Rosslyn St, West Melbourne (☎03/9329 8844); Level 20, 133 Castlereagh St, Sydney (☎02/9267 7727); 407 Great South Rd, Penrose, Auckland (☎09/525 3074). *Oslo, Stockholm and Copenhagen hotel accommodation from A$79 twin share; sightseeing tours by coach or boat.*

Wiltrans/Maupintour, Level 10, 189 Kent St, Sydney (☎02/255 0899). *Luxury all-inclusive 14- to 21-day tours of Scandinavia travelling by boat and train and overnighting in spendid hotels and lodges from $2869.*

YHA Travel Centres

Sydney: 422 Kent St (☎02/9261 1111).
Melbourne: 205 King St (☎03/9670 9611).
Adelaide: 38 Stuart St (☎08/8231 5583).
Brisbane: 154 Roma St (☎07/3236 1680).
Perth: 236 William St, Northbridge (☎08/9227 5122).
Darwin: 69a Mitchell St (☎08/8981 2560).
Hobart: 28 Criterion St (☎03/6234 9617).
Auckland: 36 Customs House (☎09/379 4224).
Budget accommodation throughout Scandinavia for YHA members.

RED TAPE AND VISAS

European Union, US, Canadian, Australian and New Zealand citizens need only a valid passport to enter Denmark, Norway, Sweden or Finland for up to three months. All other nationals should consult the relevant embassy about visa requirements. For longer stays, EU nationals can apply for a residence permit while in the country, which, if it's granted, may be valid for up to five years. Non-EU nationals can only apply for a one-year residence permit before leaving home, and must be able to prove they can support themselves without working.

In spite of the lack of restrictions, **checks** are frequently made on travellers at the major ports of entry. If you are young and have a rucksack, be prepared to prove that you have enough money to support yourself during your stay. You may also be asked how long you intend to stay and why. Be polite. It's the only check that will be made, since once you get into Scandinavia there are few passport controls between the individual countries.

SCANDINAVIAN EMBASSIES AND CONSULATES

AUSTRALIA: **Denmark** 15 Hunter St, Yarralumla, Canberra, ACT 2600 (☎06/273 2195); **Norway** 17 Hunter St, Yarralumla, Canberra ACT 2600 (☎06/273 3444); **Sweden** 5 Turrana St, Yarralumla, Canberra ACT 2600 (☎06/273 3033); **Finland** 10 Darwin Ave, Yarralumla, Canberra ACT 2600 (☎06/273 3800).

CANADA: **Denmark** 47 Clarence St, Suite 450, Ottawa, Ontario, K1N 9K1 (☎613/562-1811); **Norway** Royal Bank Center, 90 Sparks St, Suite 532 CDN, Ottawa, Ontario, K1P 5B4 (☎613/238-6570); **Sweden** 377 Dalhousie Street, Ottawa, Ontario K1N 9N8 (☎613/241-8553); **Finland** 55 Metcalfe St, Suite 850, Ottawa, Ontario, K1P 6L5 (☎613/236-2389).

IRELAND: **Denmark** 121–122 St Stephen's Green, Dublin 2 (☎0353/4756 404); **Norway** 34 Molesworth St, Dublin 2 (☎01/662 1800); **Sweden** Sun Alliance House, 13–17 Dawson St, Dublin 2 (☎01/715 822); **Finland** Russell House, Stokes Place, St Stephen's Green, Dublin 2 (☎01/781 344 or 348).

NEW ZEALAND: **Denmark** CG, 18th Floor, Marrac House, 105–109 The Terrace, PO Box 10035, Wellington 1 (☎04/720 020); **Norway** PO Box 25-319, St Heliers, Auckland (☎9/377 1944); **Sweden** Greenock House, 8th Floor, 39 The Terrace, Wellington 1 (☎04/720 909); **Finland** (see Australia).

UK: **Denmark** 55 Sloane St, London SW1 (☎0171/235 1255); **Norway** 25 Belgrave Square, London SW1 (☎0171/235 7151); 86 George St, Edinburgh (☎0131/226 5701); **Sweden** 11 Montague Place, London W1 (☎0171/724 2101); **Finland** 38 Chesham Place, London SW1 (☎0171/235 9531).

USA: **Denmark** 3200 Whitehaven St NW, Washington DC 20008 (☎202/234-4300); **Norway** 2720 34th St NW, Washington DC 20008 (☎202/333-6000); **Sweden** 1501 M St NW, Washington, DC 20005 (☎202/467-2600); **Finland** 3301 Massachusetts Ave NW, Washington, DC 20008 (☎202/298-5800).

MONEY AND BANKS

Of Scandinavia's currencies, Denmark and Norway use *kroner,* **Sweden** *kronor –* **abbreviated respectively as DKr, NKr and SKr, or as DKK, NOK and SEK.**

In this guide, we've abbreviated each as "kr", except where it's not clear to which country's money we're referring. Though they share a broadly similar exchange rate (currently 8–10kr to £1, 5–7kr to US$1), the currencies are not interchangeable. Finland uses the *markka,* abbreviated as Fmk or just mk, and the rate right now is around 7.10mk to £1, 10.65mk to US$1.

TRAVELLERS CHEQUES AND CREDIT CARDS

It's easiest and safest to carry money as **travellers cheques**, available for a small commission (usually 1 percent of the amount ordered) from any bank and some building societies, whether or not you have an account. In Britain, banks also issue current account holders with a **Eurocheque card** and cheque book, with which you can get cash from most banks in Scandinavia; you'll pay a few pounds service charge a year but usually no commission on transactions.

The major **credit and charge cards** – *Visa, Mastercard, American Express* and *Diners Club –* are accepted almost everywhere in return for goods or cash, while *Visa* card holders (and holders of some other bank cards) can use them to withdraw local currency from cashpoint machines (ATMs). Before leaving, check with your bank to see if this facility extends to you and, if so, what the charges are.

EXCHANGING MONEY

Exchanging money is easy but usually expensive. Banks have standard exchange rates, but commissions can vary enormously and it's always worth shopping around. Some places charge per transaction, others per cheque, so it's common sense to carry large denomination cheques, or to try to change several people's money at once.

Banking hours vary from country to country – check each country under "Costs, Money and Banks". Outside those times, and especially in the more remote areas, you'll often find that you can change money at hostels, hotels, campsites, tourist offices, airports and ferry terminals – though usually at worse rates than at the bank.

POST AND PHONES

Post office opening hours and more specific information on using the mail and tele- phones is given under each individual country's section on "Post and Phones".

You can have letters sent **poste restante** (general delivery) to any post office in Scandinavia by addressing them "Poste Restante" followed by the name of the town and country. When picking mail up you'll need to take your passport, and make sure they check under middle names and initials, as letters often get misfiled.

Phone boxes are plentiful and almost invariably work; English instructions are normally posted up inside. To make a collect call, dial the operator, who will speak English.

To make a **direct call** to Britain or North America, dial the international access and country code, wait for the tone, then dial the area code, omitting the first 0 if there is one, and subscriber number. For further phone information, see each individual country's section on "Communications".

INTERNATIONAL DIALLING CODES

To Scandinavia:

Dial your country's international access code, then

Denmark ☎45	**Sweden** ☎46
Norway ☎47	**Finland** ☎358

From Denmark to:
Britain ☎0044
USA & Canada ☎001
Australia ☎0061
New Zealand ☎0064
Ireland ☎00353

From Sweden to:
Britain ☎009-44
USA & Canada ☎009-1
Australia ☎009-61
New Zealand ☎009-64
Ireland ☎009-353

From Norway to:
Britain ☎095-44
USA & Canada ☎095-1
Australia ☎095-61
New Zealand ☎095-64
Ireland ☎095-353

From Finland to:
Britain ☎990-44
USA & Canada ☎990-1
Australia ☎990-61
New Zealand ☎990-64
Ireland ☎990-353

HEALTH

Health care in Scandinavia is excellent and widely available. Language is rarely a problem and the nearest tourist office will be able to recommend local doctors and hospitals.

EU nationals can take advantage of health services in **Denmark**, **Sweden** and **Finland** under the same terms as residents of the country. For this you'll need form E111, which you can get over the counter at the post office or by applying on form SA30 by post, one month in advance, to any DSS office in Britain. Norway also has a **reciprocal health agreement** with Britain, which is detailed below.

North American visitors will find that medical treatment is far less expensive than they're accustomed to in the United States, but even so it's essential to take out travel insurance. In the case of an emergency, you should go to a hospital, since this will prove less expensive than a doctor's visit. Prescription drugs are also cheap, but pharmacies will only fill prescriptions written by EU doctors.

HEALTH PROBLEMS

In **Denmark**, tourist offices and health offices (*kommunes social og sundhedforvaltning*) have lists of doctors. If the doctor decides you need hospital treatment, it'll be arranged for free but always take your E111 with you. For doctors' consultations and prescriptions (available from an *Apotek*) you will have to pay the full cost on the spot, but keep a receipt and take this together with your E111 and passport to the local health office for a refund – a sometimes long and frustrating process. Health care here is free for American visitors, provided it doesn't look like you have come to Denmark with the intention of having a serious illness treated for free.

In **Norway**, hotels and tourist offices have lists of local doctors and dentists, and there'll usually be an emergency department you can go to outside surgery hours. You'll pay 100kr for an appointment but EU citizens will be reimbursed for part of the cost of any treatment; ambulance travel and hospital stays are free. Get a receipt (*Legeregning*) at the time of payment, and take it and your passport to the social insurance office (*Trygdekasse*) of the district where treatment was obtained. For prescription drugs, go to a pharmacy (*Apotek*); late-opening ones in the main cities are detailed in the guide.

In **Sweden** there is no local doctor system: go to the nearest hospital with your passport and they'll treat you for a fee of around 140kr. If you need medicine you'll get a prescription to take to a pharmacy (*Apotek*), for which the maximum charge is normally around 100kr. Hospital stays cost 80kr per day; the emergency department is the *Akutmottagning*.

In **Finland**, treatment at a doctor's surgery (*Terveyskeskus*), found in all towns and villages, is free, but medicines have to be paid for at a pharmacy (*Apteekki*) – although, provided you have your passport, you won't be charged more than Finns. Hospitals levy charges whether you stay in a bed or are treated as an outpatient.

INSURANCE

Most people will find it essential to take out some kind of comprehensive travel insurance. Bank and credit cards often have certain levels of medical or other insurance included, especially if you use them to pay for your trip. This can be quite comprehensive, anticipating anything from lost or stolen luggage and missed connections. Similarly, if you have a good "all risks" home insurance policy it may well cover your possessions against loss or theft even when overseas, and many private medical schemes also cover you when abroad – make sure you know the procedure and the helpline number.

If you plan to participate in **winter sports**, or do some **hiking**, you'll probably have to pay an extra premium; check carefully that any insurance policy you are considering will cover you in case of an accident. Note also that very few insurers will arrange on-the-spot payments in the event of a major expense or loss; you will usually be reimbursed only after going home. In all cases of loss or **theft** of goods, you will have to contact the local **police** to have a **report** made out so that your insurer can process the claim; for medical claims, you'll need to provide supporting bills. Keep photocopies of everything you send to the insurer and note any time period within which you must lodge any claims.

BRITISH AND IRISH COVER

In Britain and **Ireland**, travel insurance schemes (from around £23 a month) are sold by

---

TRAVEL INSURANCE SUPPLIERS

AUSTRALIA AND NEW ZEALAND

AFTA, 181 Miller St, North Sydney (☎02/9956 4800).

Cover More, Level 9, 32 Walker St, North Sydney (☎02/9968 1333; toll-free 1800/251 881).

Ready Plan, 141–147 Walker St, Dandenong, Victoria (toll-free ☎1800/337 462); 10th Floor, 63 Albert St, Auckland (☎09/379 3399).

UTAG, 347 Kent St, Sydney (☎02/9819 6855; toll-free 1800/809 462).

BRITAIN AND IRELAND

Campus Travel, ☎0171/730 8111.
Columbus Travel Insurance, ☎0171/375 0011.
Endsleigh Insurance, ☎0171/436 4451.
Frizzell Insurance, ☎01202/292333.

STA, ☎0171/361 6262.
USIT, Belfast ☎01232/324073; Dublin ☎01/679 8833.

USA AND CANADA

Access America (☎1-800/284-8300).
Carefree Travel Insurance (☎1-800/323-3149).
Desjardins Travel Insurance – Canada only (☎1-800/463-7830).
International Student Insurance Service (ISIS) – sold by *STA Travel* (☎1-800/777-0112).

Travel Assistance International (☎1-800/821-2828).
Travel Guard (☎1-800/826-1300).
Travel Insurance Services (☎1-800/937-1387).

many **travel agents**, **banks** and by **specialist insurance companies**. Policies issued by *Campus Travel* or *STA*, *Endsleigh Insurance*, *Frizzell Insurance*, *USIT* or *Columbus Travel Insurance* are all good value. *Columbus* also does an annual multi-trip policy which offers twelve months' cover for £125.

US AND CANADIAN COVER

Before buying an insurance policy, check that you're not already covered. **Private health plans** typically provide some overseas medical coverage, although they are unlikely to pick up the full tab in the event of a mishap. Holders of official **student/teacher/youth cards** are entitled to accident coverage and hospital in-patient benefits – the annual membership is far less than the cost of comparable insurance. **Students** may also find that their student health coverage extends during the vacations and for one term beyond the date of last enrollment. Homeowners' or renters' insurance often covers theft or loss of documents, money and valuables while overseas. After exhausting the possibilities above, you might want to contact a specialist **travel insurance** company; your travel agent can usually recommend one, or see the box above.

The best **premiums** are usually to be had through student/youth travel agencies – *ISIS* policies, for example, cost US$48–69 for 15 days (depending on level of coverage), US$80–105 for 1 month, US$149–207 for 2 months, US$510–700 for 1 year. If you're planning to do any "dangerous sports" (skiing, mountaineering etc.), be sure to ask whether these activities are covered: some companies levy a surcharge.

Most North American travel policies apply only to items lost, stolen or damaged while in the custody of an identifiable, responsible third party – hotel porter, airline, luggage consignment, etc. Even in these cases you will have to contact the local police within a certain time limit to have a complete report made out so that your insurer can process the claim.

AUSTRALIAN AND NEW ZEALAND COVER

Travel insurance is available from travel agents or direct from insurance companies (see box above). Policies are broadly comparable in premuim and coverage: a typical one will cost A$190/NZ$220 for 1 month, A$270/NZ$320 for 2 months and A$330/NZ$400 for 3 months.

INFORMATION AND MAPS

Before you leave, it's worth contacting the national tourist boards for free maps and brochures – though don't go mad: much of it can easily be obtained later in Scandinavia.

The train/ferry/bus **timetables** for the most popular tourist routes are worth taking, as are the **accommodation** listings booklets. Addresses of the national tourist boards are given below.

TOURIST OFFICES

Once in Scandinavia, every town and some villages have a **tourist office**, where you can pick up free town plans and information, brochures and other bumph. Many book private rooms (sometimes youth hostel beds), rent bikes, sell local discount cards and change money too. During summer, they're open daily until late evening; out of high season, shop hours are more usual, and in winter they're sometimes closed at weekends. You'll find full details of individual offices throughout the text.

NATIONAL TOURIST BOARD OFFICES

AUSTRALIA: No tourist board office, but the embassy handles tourist information (see p.21).

BRITAIN: **Denmark** 55 Sloane St, London SW1 (☎0171/259 5958); **Norway** Charles House, 5–11 Lower Regent St, London SW1 (☎0171/839 2650); **Sweden** 11 Montagu Place, London W1 (☎0171/724 5868); **Finland** 30–35 Pall Mall, London SW1 (☎0171/839 4048).

CANADA: Contact the tourist board in the USA.

IRELAND: No tourist board office, but the embassy handles tourist information (see p.21).

NEW ZEALAND: Again, the embassy supplies tourist information.

USA: **Scandinavian Tourist Board**, 655 Third Ave, New York, NY 10017 (☎212/949-2333); **Sweden** PO Box 4649, Grand Central Station, New York, NY 10163 (☎212/949-2333).

MAPS

The **maps and plans** we've printed should be fine for reference, but drivers, cyclists and hikers may require something more detailed. Tourist offices often give out reasonable road maps and town plans but anything better you'll have to buy. There's a list of specialist map shops in the box below.

For **Scandinavia** as a whole, *Kümmerley & Frey* produces a road map on a scale of 1:1,000,000; *Rand McNally* produces a good road atlas of Scandinavia. For really detailed plans of the **capital cities**, the fold-out *Falk* maps are excellent and easy to use.

As for the individual countries, maps of **Denmark** are produced by *Kümmerley & Frey* (1:300,000), *Ravenstein* (1:500,000), and *Baedekers* (1:400,000); **Finland** is covered by *Kümmerley & Frey* (1:1,000,000). For **Norway**, you're best off with the *Kümmerley & Frey* (1:1,000,000), or the *Roger Lascelles* 1:800,000 map, which also has a place name index. For **Sweden** as a whole, the best maps are produced by *Terrac* and *Hallwag*.

If you're staying in one area for a long time, or are **hiking** or **walking**, you'll need something more detailed still – a minimum scale of 1:400,000, much larger (1:50,000) if you're doing any serious trekking. For Norway, the 1:400,000 *Kummerley & Frey* regional maps are very good; for Sweden there is the 1:300,000 *Esselte Kartor* series and the 1:400,000 *Kartförlaget* series; the provinces of Denmark are covered by the 1:200,000 *Kort og Matrykelstyren* series; and *Kümmerley & Frey* produces a number of regional Finnish maps at a scale of 1:400,000. Also, the larger tourist offices sometimes have decent hiking maps of the surrounding area. In Norway, the government agency *Statens Kartverk* produces a high-quality series of 1:50,000 maps covering the entire country; these are widely available from tourist offices and bookshops, and also from the national hiking organization, *DNT*, Stortingsgate 28, Oslo. Sweden's hiking organization, *STF*, can be contacted at Box 25, S-101 20 Stockholm. In Finland, the best source of hiking maps is *Aleksi*, Unioninkatu 32, Helsinki.

MAP OUTLETS

AUSTRALIA AND NEW ZEALAND

The Map Shop, 16a Peel St, Melbourne, VIC 3000 (☎08/8231 2033).

Bowyangs, 372 Little Burke St, Adelaide, SA 5000 (☎03/9670 4383).

Perth Map Centre, 891 Hay St, Perth, WA 6000 (☎08/9322 5733).

Specialty Maps, 58 Albert St, Auckland (☎09/307 2217).

Travel Bookshop, 20 Bridge St, Sydney, NSW 2000 (☎02/9241 3554).

BRITAIN

Daunt Books, 83 Marylebone High St, London, W1 (☎0171/224 2295).

John Smith and Sons, 57–61 St Vincent St, Glasgow G2 5TB (☎0141/221 7472).

National Map Centre, 22–24 Caxton St, London, SW1 (☎0171/222 4945).

Stanfords*, 12–14 Long Acre, London, WC2 (☎0171/836 1321); 52 Grosvenor Gdns, London SW1W 0AG; 156 Regent St, London W1R 5TA.

The Travel Bookshop, 13–15 Blenheim Crescent, London W11 2EE (☎0171/229 5260).

*Note maps by **mail or phone order** are available from *Stanfords* (☎0171/836 1321).

CANADA

Open Air Books and Maps, 25 Toronto St, Toronto, ON M5R 2C1 (☎416/363-0719).

Ulysses Travel Bookshop, 4176 St-Denis, Montréal (☎514/289-0993).

World Wide Books and Maps, 1247 Granville St, Vancouver, BC V6Z 1E4 (☎604/687-3320).

IRELAND

Easons Bookshop, 40 O'Connell St, Dublin 1 (☎01/873 3811).

Fred Hanna's Bookshop, 27–29 Nassau St, Dublin 2 (☎01/677 1255).

Hodges Figgis Bookshop, 56–58 Dawson St, Dublin 2 (☎01/677 4754).

Waterstone's, Queens Bldg, 8 Royal Ave, Belfast BT1 1DA (☎01232/247355).

USA

The Complete Traveler Bookstore, 199 Madison Ave, New York, NY 10016 (☎212/685-9007); 3207 Fillmore St, San Francisco, CA 92123 (☎415/923-1511).

Forsyth Travel Library, 9154 W 57th St, Shawnee Mission, KS 66201 (☎1-800/367-7984).

Map Link Inc, 25 E Mason St, Santa Barbara, CA 93101 (☎805/965-4402).

Phileas Fogg's Books & Maps, #87 Stanford Shopping Center, Palo Alto, CA 94304 (☎1-800/233-FOGG in California; ☎1-800/533-FOGG elsewhere in US).

Rand McNally*, 444 N Michigan Ave, Chicago, IL 60611 (☎312/321-1751); 150 E 52nd St, New York, NY 10022 (☎212/758-7488); 595 Market St, San Francisco, CA 94105 (☎415/777-3131); 1201 Connecticut Ave NW, Washington, DC 20003 (☎202/223-6751).

Sierra Club Bookstore, 730 Polk St, San Francisco, CA 94109 (☎415/923-5500).

Travel Books & Language Center, 4931 Cordell Ave, Bethesda, MD 20814 (☎1-800/220-2665).

Traveler's Bookstore, 22 W 52nd St, New York, NY 10019 (☎212/664-0995).

*Note: *Rand McNally* now has 24 stores across the USA; call ☎1-800/333-0136 (ext 2111) for the other location of your nearest store, or for maps by mail order.

GETTING AROUND

Public transport systems are good throughout Scandinavia. Denmark, Norway, Sweden and Finland have a fairly comprehensive rail network which runs as far north as it dares before plentiful buses take over. Fjords and inordinate amounts of water – lakes, rivers and open sea – make ferries a major form of transport too.

For further information see each country's individual "Getting Around" section, and the "Travel Details" at the end of every chapter.

RAIL PASSES

Nowhere does travel come cheap, but a number of **passes** can ease the burden. If you're travelling by train there is, of course, the *InterRail* or *Eurail* pass (see the "Getting There" sections). But if you don't qualify for one of these, or you're planning train travel only in Scandinavia, it's well worth considering a **Scanrail** pass, which covers all four countries and is available to anyone.

The pass comes in two forms, the *Scanrail* and *Scanrail Flexi*. The regular *Scanrail* allows a full month's unlimited travel, which costs £254/US$404/A$595; 12–25 year olds get around 25 percent discount. There's a 21-day version that costs proportionally less. *Scanrail Flexi* is available for travel on any 5 days in a 15-day period (adult £130/US$278/A$236; youth £98/US$132/A$177) or any ten days in a month (adult £176/US$278/A$392; youth £132/US$209

/A$294). The pass also gives 50 percent discount on a number of ferry routes. You need to buy it before leaving home: see the "Getting There" sections for addresses of train ticket and specialist agents.

Train passes specific to one country are covered in the relevant country's "Getting Around" section.

FLIGHTS

Internal Scandinavian **flights**, surprisingly, can also work out to be a good bargain. During the summer – usually July and the early part of August – *SAS* generally has cheap set-price tickets (one-way and return) to anywhere in mainland Scandinavia except Finland; plus other discounts for families and young people. These flights can also save a great deal of time, particularly if you're heading for the far northern reaches. Contact *SAS* offices in Danish, Norwegian and Swedish cities for the latest deals – they're detailed under "Listings" in the accounts of the capital cities. Also, check out the **air passes** on offer before leaving home; these have to be bought in conjunction with a ticket to Scandinavia and are detailed in the "Getting There" sections.

CAR RENTAL

Car rental is pricey, although some tourist offices do arrange summer deals which can bring the cost down a little. On the whole, expect to pay at least £350/$480 a week for a small car plus fuel; see each country's "Getting Around" section for specific prices and details of rules of the road and documentation.

You may well find the it cheaper, especially if you are travelling from North America, to arrange things before you go; airlines sometimes have special deals with car rental companies if you book your flight and car through them. Alternatively if you don't want to be tied down, try an agency such as *Holiday Autos*, who will arrange advance booking through a local agent and can usually undercut the big companies considerably (see the box below for details of car rental firms).

CAR RENTAL FIRMS

AUSTRALIA

Avis ☎1800/225 53.
Buget ☎13 2848.

Hertz ☎13 1918.

BRITAIN

Avis ☎0181/848 8733.
Europcar/InterRent ☎01345/222525.
Eurodollar 01895/233300.

Budget ☎0800/181181.
Hertz ☎0990/996699.
Holiday Autos ☎0990/300400.

IRELAND

Avis ☎01232/240404.
Budget Rent-A-Car ☎01232/230700.
Europcar ☎01232/450904 or 01232/423444.

Hertz ☎01/660 2255.
Holiday Autos ☎01/454 9090.

NEW ZEALAND

Avis ☎09/525 1982.
Budget ☎09/275 2222.

Hertz ☎09/309 0989.

NORTH AMERICA

Auto Europe ☎1-800/223-5555.
Avis international ☎1-800/331-1084.
Budget ☎1-800/527-0700.
Dollar ☎1-800/421-6868.

Europe by Car ☎1-800/223-1516.
Hertz international ☎1-800/654-3001; in Canada
  ☎1-800/263-0600.
Holiday Autos ☎1-800/422-7737.

For addresses of car rental firms in Scandinavia, see the "Listings" sections of major cities.

ACCOMMODATION

Accommodation is going to be your major daily expense in Scandinavia. If you plan ahead, however, there are a number of ways you can avoid paying over the (already high) odds. Using youth hostels, camping cabins and campsites are the obvious options, and not just for tourists – they're popular with Scandinavians, too. There's also a series of hotel cheques and discount passes available, for use in hotel chains all over mainland Scandinavia.

HOTELS

Scandinavian **hotels** aren't as expensive as you might think; certainly not if you compare them with equivalent accommodation in London, say, or New York. Lots of Scandinavian hotels, usually dependent on business travellers, drop their prices drastically during the summer holiday period and at weekends year-round, so it's always worth enquiring in the tourist office

YOUTH HOSTEL ASSOCIATIONS

AUSTRALIA
Australian Youth Hostel Association, Level 3, 10 Mallet St, Camperdown, Sydney (☎02/9565 1325). *Annual membership costs A$42.*

CANADA
Hostelling International/Canadian Hostelling Association, Room 400, 205 Catherine St, Ottawa, ON K2P 1C3 (☎613/237-7884 or ☎1-800/663-5777). *Annual membership adults CAN$26.75, children under 18 free when accompanied by parents; two-year membership costs CAN$35.*

ENGLAND AND WALES
Youth Hostel Association (YHA), Trevelyan House, 8 St Stephen's Hill, St Alban's, Herts AL1 2DY (☎01727/855215). London information office: 14 Southampton St, London WC2 7HY (☎0171/836 1036). *Annual membership costs £9.30.*

IRELAND
Youth Hostel Association of Northern Ireland, 22 Donegall Rd, Belfast BT12 5JN

(☎01232/324 733); **An Oige**, 61 Mountjoy St, Dublin 7 (☎01/830 4555). *The price in Northern Ireland is the same as in England and Wales; in the Republic annual membership costs £7.50.*

NEW ZEALAND
Youth Hostel Association of New Zealand PO Box 436, Christchurch (☎03/379 9970). *Annual membership costs NZ$45.*

SCOTLAND
Scottish Youth Hostel Association, 7 Glebe Crescent, Stirling, FK8 2JA (☎01786/451181). *Annual membership £6.*

USA
Hostelling International-American Youth Hostels (HI-AYH), 733 15th St NW, Suite 840, PO Box 37613, Washington, DC 20005 (☎202/783-6161). *Annual membership adults US$25, youths (under 18) US $10, seniors (55 or over) US$15, families US$35.*

---

about the availability of special local deals. Also, the capitals and other major cities feature cheap "packages", usually involving a night's hotel accommodation and a free city discount card. More details, and a guide to prices, are given under each country's "Accommodation" section, as well as under the specific town and city accounts.

In addition, some Scandinavia-wide hotel chains operate a discount or **hotel cheque system** which you can organize before you leave. Either you purchase cheques in advance, redeemable against a night's accommodation in any hotel belonging to the particular chain or you buy a **hotel pass** which entitles you to a hefty discount on normal room rates. There are a bewildering number of schemes available, but most only operate from June to September and they all offer basically the same deal: consult your travel agent, or one of the national tourist boards.

YOUTH HOSTELS

Joining the **Hostelling International** association gives you access to what is sometimes the only budget accommodation available in

Scandinavia. Non-members can use most of the hostels but will pay slightly more – a sizeable sum over a couple of weeks considering the low cost of annual membership. Another thing you'll need is a **sheet sleeping bag**, the only kind allowed in *HI* hostels, either rentable at the hostels or on sale at camping shops; alternatively, you can simply stitch a couple of old sheets together and take a pillowcase. If you're planning to cook for yourself using youth hostel kitchens, bear in mind that many don't provide pots, pans and utensils – take at least the basic equipment with you.

Addresses for joining your own national youth hostel association are given in the box below; under each country's "Accommodation" section you'll find the addresses of Scandinavian national organizations, where you can also join. It would be impossible to list all the hundreds of youth hostels in this guide – instead consult *Hostelling International: Europe and the Mediterranean*, which lists every hostel in Scandinavia.

CAMPING

Camping is hugely popular in all Scandinavian countries and covered in more detail in each country's "Accommodation" section. But a number of points common to all the countries are worth noting. In order to use certain sites you may need a camping carnet, which you can buy at the first site you visit; camping rough is, with certain exceptions, legal in Norway and Sweden; and most campsites have furnished **cabins**, though if you intend to use these take a sleeping bag as bedding is not usually provided.

POLICE AND CRIME

Scandinavia is one of the least troublesome corners of Europe. You will find that most public places are well lit and secure, most people genuinely friendly and helpful, and street crime and street hassle have a relatively low profile.

PETTY CRIME AND MINOR OFFENCES

It would be foolish, however, to assume that problems don't exist. The capital cities have their share of **petty crime**, fuelled – as elsewhere – by a growing number of drug addicts and alcoholics after easy money. But keep tabs on your cash and passport (and don't leave anything visible in your car when you leave it) and you should have little reason to visit the **police**. If you do, you'll find

them courteous, concerned, and, most importantly, usually able to speak English. If you have something stolen, make sure you get a **police report** – essential if you are to make a claim against your insurance.

As for **offences** *you* might commit, **nude sunbathing** is universally accepted in all the major resorts (elsewhere there'll be no one around to care); and **camping rough** is a tradition enshrined in law in Norway and Sweden, and tolerated in Finland, though in Denmark it's more difficult. However, you are not allowed to drink alcohol in public places, and being **drunk** on the streets can get you arrested – **drinking and driving** is treated especially rigorously. **Drugs** offences, too, meet with the same harsh attitude that prevails throughout the rest of Europe.

SEXUAL HARASSMENT & THE WOMEN'S MOVEMENT

In general, the social and economic position of women in Scandinavia is more advanced than in almost all other European countries – something which becomes obvious after a short time there. Many women are in traditionally male occupations, and sexual harassment is less of a problem than elsewhere in Europe.

You can walk almost everywhere in comparative comfort and safety, and although in the capital cities you can expect to receive unwelcome attention occasionally, it's very rarely with any kind of violent intent. Needless to say, travelling alone on the underground systems in Copenhagen, Oslo, Stockholm and Helsinki late at night is unwise. If you do have any problems, the fact that almost everyone understands English

makes it easy to get across an unambiguous response.

WOMEN'S ORGANIZATIONS

Denmark's women's movement is in a state of flux: the once prominent *Rødstrømper* (Red Stockings) – the Radical Feminists – are now less active. But there are lots of feminist groups around the country, and in Copenhagen a couple of active women's centres: *Dannerhuset*, Nansensgade 1 (☎33/141676), and *Kvindehuset*, Gothersgade 37 (☎33/142804).

Norway's women's movement is highly developed, assisted by progressive government and a 1986–89 Labour administration led by a woman, Dr Gro Harlem Brundtland, which endeavoured to even out parliamentary representation by promoting women into the cabinet. Contacts in Oslo can be made through the *Norsk Kvinnesaksforening* (☎22 60 42 27).

In **Sweden**, the women's movement is also strongly developed, riding on the back of the social welfare reforms introduced by the Social Democratic governments of the last forty years. You'll find women's centres in most major towns, contacts in Stockholm including *Grupp 8* at Snickarbacken 10, an active socialist-feminist group.

Women in **Finland** were the first to achieve suffrage, but in spite of that its women's movement is lagging behind the rest of Scandinavia, and there have been fewer reforms to benefit the lot of women over the years. The major feminist organization, *Unioni*, first established in 1892 in Helsinki, is the best place for up-to-date information (Bulevardi 11A; ☎09/64 31 58; closed mid-June to July).

GAY SCANDINAVIA

Scandinavia comprises some of the most liberated and tolerant countries in Europe. Gays are rarely discriminated against in law, and the age of consent is almost uniformly the same as for heterosexuals – usually fifteen or sixteen. However, in all four mainland countries you'll not find much of a scene outside the capitals.

ATTITUDES AND THE LAW

Denmark used to have a reputation for being the gay pornography capital of the world, and although this is no longer so, there is a very good gay scene in Copenhagen. As far as the law goes, in 1989 the Danish parliament voted to make a form of homosexual marriage legal, and it has continued to investigate other ways of eliminating discrimination against gays. For more information, contact the *Landsforeningen for bøsser og lebiske*, in Copenhagen at Teglgårdsstræde 13 (☎33/13 19 48), in Århus at Jægergårdsgade 42–44 (☎86/13 19 48).

Norway was one of the first countries in the world – in 1981 – to pass a law making discrimination against homosexuals illegal. Norwegian society is reasonably tolerant of homosexuality. There is a strong and effective gay and lesbian organization, with a national HQ in Oslo (*L.L.H.*, PO Box 68, 38 St Olavsplass; ☎22 36 19 48; fax 22 11 47 45) and branches throughout the country.

In **Sweden** gay marriage is now legal. However, there are very few gay bars, and gay saunas and video shops with cubicles have been outlawed since mid-1987. The national organization, the *RFSL*, can be contacted at Sveavägen 57–59, PO Box 350, 10126 Stockholm (☎08/736 02 13; fax 30 47 30).

From a legal point of view, there is some discrimination against gays in **Finland**. The country's penal code forbids the public encouragement of homosexuality, and, unlike the other Scandinavian countries, the homosexual age of consent is 18. However, nobody has ever been convicted for breaking the anti-gay laws. *SETA* (Organization for Sexual Equality in Finland), at Mäkelänkatu 36 A5, Helsinki, can provide further information – on Helsinki and elsewhere – and publishes a bi-monthly nationwide magazine; during the summer they also print useful pages of information in English for foreign visitors to Helsinki.

DISABLED TRAVELLERS

Scandinavia is, in many ways, a model of awareness for the disabled traveller: wheelchair access, other facilities and help are generally available at hotels, hostels, museums and public places. Getting there, too, is getting easier: *Scandinavian Seaways* ferries have specially adapted cabins, and *Silja Line* offers discounts for disabled passengers.

PLANNING A HOLIDAY

There are **organized tours and holidays** specifically for people with disabilities – the contacts in the box below will be able to put you in touch with any specialists for trips to Scandinavia. If you want to be more independent, it's important to become an authority on where you must be self-reliant and where you may expect help, especially regarding transportation and accommodation. It's also vital to be honest with travel agencies, insurance companies and travel companions. It's worth thinking about your limitations and making sure others know them, too. If you don't use a wheelchair all the time but your walking capabilities are limited, remember that you are likely to need to cover greater distances while travelling (sometimes

TRAVEL AGENCIES AND ORGANIZATIONS

AUSTRALIA AND NEW ZEALAND

ACROD (Australian Council for Rehabilitation of the Disabled), PO Box 60, Curtin ACT 2605 (☎06/682 4333); 55 Charles St, Ryde (☎02/9809 4488).

Disabled Persons Assembly, PO Box 10, 138 The Terrace, Wellington (☎04/472 2626).

BRITAIN AND IRELAND

Disability Action Group, 2 Annadale Ave, Belfast BT7 3JH (☎01232/91011).

Holiday Care Service, 2nd floor, Imperial Building, Victoria Rd, Horley RH6 9HW (☎001293/774535).

Irish Wheelchair Association, Blackheath Drive, Clontarf, Dublin 3 (☎01/833 8241). *A national voluntary organization working with people with disabilities with related services for holidaymakers.*

Holiday Scandinavia Ltd, 28 Hillcrest Rd, Orpington BR6 9AW (☎01689/824958).

RADAR, 12 City Forum, 250 City Rd, London EC1V 8AS (☎0171/250 3222; Minicom ☎0171/250 4119). *A good source of advice on holidays and travel abroad.*

Tripscope, The Courtyard, Evelyn Rd, London W4 5JL (☎0181/994 9294).

US AND CANADA

Directions Unlimited, 720 N Bedford Rd, Bedford Hills, NY 10507 (☎1-800/533-5343). *Tour operator specializing in custom tours for people with disabilities.*

Mobility International USA, PO Box 10767, Eugene, OR 97440 (Voice and TDD: ☎503/343-1284). *Information and referral services, access guides, tours and exchange programs. Annual membership $20 (includes quarterly newsletter).*

Society for the Advancement of Travel for the Handicapped (SATH), 347 5th Ave, New York, NY 10016 (☎212/447-7284). *Non-profit*

travel-industry referral service that passes queries on to its members as appropriate; allow plenty of time for a response.

Twin Peaks Press, Box 129, Vancouver, WA 98666; ☎206/694-2462 or 1-800/637-2256). *Publisher of the Directory of Travel Agencies for the Disabled (US$19.95), listing more than 370 agencies world wide; Travel for the Disabled (US$19.95); the Directory of Accessible Van Rentals (US$9.95) and Wheelchair Vagabond (US$14.95), loaded with personal tips.*

over rougher terrain and in hotter/colder temperatures than you are used to. If you use a wheelchair, it is always wise to have it serviced before you go and carry a repair kit.

People with a pre-existing medical condition are sometimes excluded from travel **insurance policies**, so read the small print carefully. To make your journey simpler, ask your travel agent to notify airlines or bus companies, who can cope better if they are expecting you, with, for example, a wheelchair provided at airports and staff primed to help. A **medical certificate** of your fitness to travel, provided by your doctor, is also extremely useful; some airlines or insurance companies may insist on it. Make sure that you have extra supplies of drugs – carried with you if you fly – and a prescription including the generic name in case of emergency. Carry spares of any clothing or equipment that might be hard to find; if there's an association representing people with your disability, contact them early in the planning process.

FACILITIES IN SCANDINAVIA

In **Denmark**, facilities are generally outstanding. The Danish Tourist Board (see p.27 for addresses) publishes a comprehensive 100-page brochure called *Access in Denmark – a Travel Guide for the Disabled*, which covers everything from airports to zoos.

The **Norwegian** Tourist Board uses the wheelchair symbol throughout its publications to denote accessibility. Transport is not too much of a problem: *Norwegian State Railways* have special carriages on most main routes with wheelchair space, hydraulic lifts and a disabled toilet; new ships on the *Hurtigrute* Coastal Express route have lifts and cabins for disabled people; and new fjord ferries also have lifts from the car deck to the lounge and toilets. According to Norwegian law, all new public buildings must be accessible to disabled people. For further information, contact the *Norwegian Association of the Disabled*, PO Box 9217, Gronland, N-0134 Oslo (☎22 17 02 55; fax 22 17 61 77).

In **Sweden**, many hotels are provided with specially adapted rooms, and camping-cabin holidays are not beyond wheelchair users either, as some chalet-villages have cabins with wheelchair access. The Stockholm T-bana system has elevators at most stations, and there are specially converted minivans and taxis for hire. A useful holiday guide with more information is available from Swedish tourist offices. Or contact the *Swedish Federation of Disabled Persons (DHR)*, Katrinebergsvägen 6, S-117 43 Stockholm (☎08/18 91 00; fax 645 6541).

Finland is as welcoming to the disabled traveller as the other Scandinavian countries. The Finnish Tourist Board issues a free leaflet, *Tourist Services for the Disabled*, giving a brief overview of facilities; and further information can be obtained from Mr Jens Gellin, *Rullaten ry*, Vartiokyläntie 9, 00950 Helsinki (☎09/322069).

OUTDOOR ACTIVITIES

Scandinavia is a wonderful place if you love the great outdoors, with great hiking, fishing and, of course, skiing opportunities. Best of all you won't find the countryside overcrowded – there's plenty of space to get away from it all, especially in the north. As you might expect, any kind of hunting is forbidden without a permit, and fishing usually requires a special licence, available from local tourist offices.

HIKING

Scandinavia offers the ultimate in hiking experiences – a landscape of rugged mountains, icy glaciers and deep green fjords, much of the time miles away from the nearest road. Many of the best hiking areas have been set aside as **national parks**, with information centres, lodges and huts dotted along well-marked trails. Huts are usually run by national or local hiking organizations, and you will have to become a member to be able to use them. See "Maps and Information" for addresses and map suppliers, and note also that **tourist offices** in the hiking areas supply maps and leaflets describing local routes. Where hiking routes are covered in the guide we've listed the best source of local information. It's essential to plan your route thoroughly before setting out, taking into account weather conditions, and not to overestimate what you can manage in the time. In many areas solo hiking is strongly advised against.

As far as **equipment** goes, for day walking you'll need warm clothing and gloves, waterproofs, and sun and mosquito protection; on all but the easiest and shortest hikes, a compass is a good idea – as long as you know how to use it. For long-distance treks you'll also need a sleeping bag, medical kit and a torch, plus a pair of sturdy, comfortable boots.

Especially if you're planning to camp, you should be aware of some specific **ground rules**. The landscape is there for everyone's use and camping rough is legal much of the time – but the Scandinavians are concerned to protect the environment both from the damage caused by excessive tourism and the potential disasters that can result from ignorance or thoughtlessness.

Don't **light fires** anywhere other than at designated spots – and even these shouldn't be used in times of drought. **Tents** may only be placed on marked sites or, on some hikes, in other designated areas. When camping, do not **break tree branches** or leave rubbish; and try not to disturb nesting **birds**, especially in the spring.

In the northern reaches of Scandinavia, be wary of frightening **reindeer herds**, since if they scatter it can mean several extra days work for the herder; also, avoid tramping over moss-covered stretches of moorland – the reindeer's staple diet. **Picking flowers, berries and mushrooms** is also usually prohibited in the north. If you are going to pick and eat anything, however, it's a wise idea, post-Chernobyl, to check on the latest advice from the authorities – tourist offices should know the score.

WINTER SPORTS

Aside from the cities, which maintain their usual roster of activities and attractions, though sometimes with reduced opening hours, the big incentive for coming to Scandinavia in winter is the range of participant **winter sports** available – from ice fishing to dog-sledging. Although you're not likely to come on a skiing package to Scandinavia (it's nearly always cheaper to go to other European resorts), it's easy to arrange a few days **cross-country skiing** wherever you end up: even in Oslo and Stockholm there are ski runs within the city boundaries, and plenty of places to rent equipment.

WORK

Norway, Sweden and Finland in particular are extremely suspicious of potential foreign workers, and you may have to prove

on entry that you are not there to seek work (by showing return tickets and sufficient cash, for instance). The chances of finding casual work are, anyhow, slim to say the least.

THE PAPERWORK

If you're serious about **working**, though, and an EU citizen, **Denmark** and **Sweden** are the best options, though for other than relatively low-paid bar/restaurant/hotel work you really need to speak the language. You can stay for up to three months while you look for work, and, if you find it, a residence permit should be granted. Fast-food restaurants and larger hotels have a fairly high turnover of foreign staff, and private employment agencies can sometimes place unskilled foreign workers. Non-EU citizens are not allowed to look for work after arriving and need to set up employment before leaving home.

OTHER OPTIONS

The best-paid opportunity to live and work in Scandinavia for a short period is by **working on a farm**. You live with a farming family, work incredibly hard and receive board and lodging and pocket money in return. Vacancies are usually for the spring and summer although some jobs stay open for a full year. Serious vacancies (ie for young farmers and/or people with experience) are dealt with by the *International Farm Experience Programme*, YFC Centre, National Agricultural Centre, Kenilworth, Warwickshire CV8 2LG. For summer farm work (no experience necessary), 18- to 30-year-olds should contact the *Norwegian Youth Council* (*Landsradet for Norske Ungdomsorganisasjoner*), Working Guest Programme, Rolf Hofmosgate 18, Oslo 6, Norway (apply by April 15).

If you would like to do **voluntary work** in mainland Scandinavia, send an sae to *International Voluntary Service*, Ceresole House, 53 Regent Rd, Leicester LE1 6YL. They organize international work camps two to three weeks long, with food and accommodation provided. You must be at least 18 and pay your own travel expenses. In the USA, *The Council on International Educational Exchange* produces a booklet called *Volunteer*, which lists over 170 organisations that deal with short- and long-term volunteer work overseas, including Scandinavia.

INFORMATION

For more information about working in Scandinavia – paid or voluntary – consult the series of books published in Britain by *Vacation Work*, which all have sections on the Scandinavian countries: *The International Directory of Voluntary Work, Summer Jobs Abroad* and *Work Your Way Around the World*.

BOOKS

Books on Scandinavia in English are remarkably scant: surprisingly few travellers have written well (or indeed at all) about the region over the years, and historical or political works tend to concentrate almost exclusively on the Vikings.

However, Scandinavian literature is appearing more and more in translation – notably the Icelandic Sagas and selected modern novelists – and it's always worth looking out for a turn-of-the-century Baedeker's *Norway and Sweden*, if only for the phrasebook, from which you can learn the Swedish and Norwegian for "Do you want to cheat me?", "When does the washerwoman

come?" and "We must tie ourselves together with rope to cross this glacier."

Of the publishers, *Peter Owen* and *Forest Books* regularly produce fine new translations of modern Scandinavian novels. *Norvik Press*, too, is a good source of new translations of old and new Scandinavian writing; for their catalogue write to them at EUR/University of East Anglia, Norwich NR4 7TJ. Titles go in and out of print regularly; if your library doesn't have copies, your local bookshop may be able to order them for you.

SCANDINAVIA

TRAVEL AND GENERAL

Jeremy Cherfas *The Hunting of Whale*. Subtitled "A tragedy that must end", this is a convincing condemnation of whaling and all those – like Norway – involved in it.

Tom Cunliffe *Topsail and Battleaxe*. The intertwined stories of the tenth-century Vikings who sailed from Norway, past the Faroes and Iceland to North America, and the author's parallel trip in

1983 – made in a 75-year-old pilot cutter. Enthusiastically written, with good photos.

John McCormick *Acid Earth*. Good for the background on the burning issue of acid rain, of which the Scandinavian countries are net recipients – especially from Britain.

Christoph Ransmayr *The Terrors of Ice and Darkness*. Clever mingling of fact and fiction as the book's main character follows the route of the 1873 Austro-Hungarian expedition to the Arctic. A story of obsession and, ultimately, madness.

Mary Wollstonecraft *A Short Residence in Sweden, Norway and Denmark*. A searching account of Wollstonecraft's three-month solo journey through southern Scandinavia in 1795.

HISTORY, MYTHOLOGY AND ART

Johannes Brøndsted *The Vikings*. Classic and immensely readable account of the Viking period, with valuable sections, too, on social and cultural life, art, religious beliefs and customs.

H.R. Ellis Davidson *The Gods and Myths of Northern Europe*. A handy Saga companion, this is a Who's Who of Norse mythology, including some useful reviews of the more obscure gods. Displaces the classical deities and their world as the most relevant mythological framework for northern and western European culture.

P.V. Glob *The Bog People*. A fascinating study of the various Iron Age bodies discovered preserved in full in northwestern European peat-bogs, most of which have been found in Denmark. Excellent, if ghoulish, photographs.

Gwyn Jones *A History of the Vikings*. Probably the best book on the subject: a superb, thoughtful and thoroughly researched account of the Viking period.

F. Donald Logan *The Vikings in History*. Scholarly – and radical – re-examination of the Vikings' impact on medieval Europe, indispensable for the Viking fan.

Geoffrey Parker *The Thirty Years' War*. One of the more recent accounts of this turbulent period, acknowledged as authoritative but a dry read.

Else Roesdahl *The Vikings*. A lucid and recent account of the 300-year reign of Scandinavia's most famous (and most misunderstood) cultural ambassadors, and the traces that they've left throughout northern Europe.

DENMARK

HISTORY AND PHILOSOPHY

Inga Dahlsgård *Women in Denmark, Yesterday and Today*. A refreshing presentation of Danish history from the point of view of its women.

W. Glyn Jones *Denmark: A Modern History*. A valuable account of the present century (up until 1984), with a commendable outline of pre-twentieth-century Danish history. Strong on politics, useful on social history and the arts, but disappointingly brief on recent grass roots movements.

Søren Kierkegaard *Either/Or*. A new translation of Kierkegaard's most important work, packed with wry and wise musings on love, life and death in nineteenth-century Danish society; includes the (in)famous Seducer's Diary.

Roger Poole and Henrik Stangerup (eds) *A Kierkegaard Reader*. By far the best and most accessible introduction to this notoriously "difficult" nineteenth-century Danish philosopher and writer, with a sparkling introductory essay.

LITERATURE AND BIOGRAPHY

Hans Christian Andersen (ed. Naomi Lewis) *The Fairy Tales of Hans Christian Andersen*. Still the most internationally prominent figure of Danish literature, Andersen's fairy-tales are so widely translated and read that the full clout of their allegorical content is often overlooked: interestingly, his first collection of such tales (published in 1835) has condemned for its "violence and questionable morals". *A Visit to Germany, Italy and Malta, 1840–1841* is the most enduring of his travel works. And his autobiography, *The Fairy Tale of My Life*, is a fine riposte to the numerous sycophantic biographies which have appeared since.

Steen Steensen Blicher *Diary of a Parish Clerk; Twelve Stories*. Blicher was a keen observer of Jutish life, writing stark, realistic tales in local dialect and gathering a seminal collection of Jutish folk tales – published as *E Bindstouw* in 1842.

Karen Blixen (Isak Dinesen) *Out of Africa; Letters from Africa; Seven Gothic Tales*. *Out of Africa*, the account of Blixen's attempts to run a coffee farm in Kenya after divorce from her husband, is a lyrical and moving tale. But it's in *Seven Gothic Tales* that Blixen's fiction was at its zenith: a flawlessly executed, weird, emotive work, full of twists in plot and strange, ambiguous characterization.

Tove Ditlevsen *Early Spring*. An autobiographical novel of growing up in the working-class Vesterbro district of Copenhagen during the 1930s. As an evocation of childhood and early adulthood, it's totally captivating.

Martin A. Hansen *The Liar*. An engaging novel, showing why Hansen was one of Denmark's most perceptive – and popular – authors during the postwar period. Set in the 1950s, the story examines the inner thoughts of a lonely schoolteacher living on a small Danish island.

Peter Høeg *Miss Smilla's Feeling for Snow*. A worldwide bestseller, published in the USA as *Miss Smilla's Sense of Snow*, this is a compelling thriller dealing with Danish colonialism in Greenland and the issue of cultural identity.

Judith Thurman *Isak Dinesen: The Life of Karen Blixen*. The most penetrative biography of Blixen, with elucidating details of the farm period not found in the two "Africa" books.

Dea Trier Mørch *Winter's Child*. A wonderfully lucid sketch of modern Denmark as seen through the eyes of several women in the maternity ward of a Copenhagen hospital. See also *Evening Star*, which deals with the effect of old age and death on a Danish family.

NORWAY

HISTORY AND SOCIOLOGY

Oddvar K. Hoidal *Quisling: A Study in Treason*. A long and comprehensive biography of the world's most famous traitor, Vidkun Quisling, the man presented in all his unpleasant fullness.

Gwyn Jones *The Norse Atlantic Saga*. An excellent companion account of the (mainly Norwegian) discovery and settlement of Iceland, Greenland and North America, interspersed with extracts from the Sagas.

Francois Kersaudy *Norway 1940*. A short history of the Norwegian resistance – in 1940 – to the Nazi invasion of their country. A well-informed account, including coverage of the role of the British forces who helped the Norwegians in their fight.

Magnús Magnússon and Hermann Palsson (trans.) *The Vinland Sagas: The Norse Discovery of America*. This tells, in contemporary reportage, of the Viking Norwegians' "discovery" of North America in the tenth century.

LITERATURE AND ART

Knut Faldbakken *The Sleeping Prince*. Shades of *The Lonely Passion of Miss Judith Hearne* in this story of the fantasy created in the mind of a middle-aged spinster as she awaits her sleeping prince – an absorbing and spirited novel by one of Norway's finest writers. Other novels in print include *Insect Summer* and the less accessible *Adam's Diary*.

Jostein Gaarder *Sophie's World*. A cross between a children's story and a philosophical ramble, which makes for an excellent, thoroughly enjoyable read.

Janet Garton and Henning Sehmsdorf *New Norwegian Plays*. Four plays written between 1979 and 1983, including work by the feminist writer Bjørg Vik (see below) and a Brechtian analysis of Europe in the nuclear age by Edvard Hoem.

Knut Hamsun *Hunger; The Wanderer; Mysteries; The Women at the Pump; Wayfarers; Growth of the Soil; Pan*. Hamsun's novels are enjoying a resurgence of interest after a backlash initiated by his pro-Nazi sympathies during the last war. They're thoughtful, lyrical works on the whole, deliberately simple in style but with an underlying, sometimes sinister, ambivalence.

Henrik Ibsen *Ibsen Plays, Vols. 1–6*. The key international figure of Norwegian literature, Ibsen was a social dramatist, keen through his characters to portray contemporary society in all its forms and hypocrisies. Comparatively few of his plays are ever performed in Britain, though some – *A Doll's House* and *Hedda Gabler*, for example – are household names. All the major plays are contained in the six-volume set.

Jonas Lie *The Seer*. The celebrated nineteenth-century Norwegian writer – who spent over thirty years living abroad – is represented here by his first great success, the novella *The Seer*, and eight other short stories.

Øystein Lønn *Tom Reber's Last Retreat*. A recent novel by one of Norway's best-known contemporary writers. It examines a businessman's past and his increasingly complicated present in typically tense style.

Sigbjørn Obstfelder *A Priest's Diary*. The last, uncompleted work of a highly regarded Norwegian poet who died of consumption in 1900 aged 33. A moody, intense piece, it forms only a segment of an ambitious work that Obstfelder intended to be his life's major undertaking.

Cora Sandel *Alberta and Jacob; Alberta and Freedom; Alberta Alone.* The celebrated *Alberta* trilogy follows the struggle of a young woman to prove herself in a hostile environment. With its depth of insight and contemporary detail, it ranks as a key work of twentieth-century Norwegian literature. Also available are *Krane's Café*, *The Leech* and *The Silken Thread*.

Amalie Skram *Betrayed.* A psychological study of nineteenth-century sexual mores, concerning the marriage of a shy young bride to an older sea captain.

Bjørg Vik *Aquarium of Women.* A collection of nine connected short stories by one of Norway's best-known feminist writers. Recommended.

CRITICISM AND BIOGRAPHY

J.P. Hodin *Edvard Munch.* The best available general introduction to Munch's life and work, with much interesting historical detail.

Michael Meyer *Ibsen on File.* The best brief introduction to Ibsen's work for the general reader. For more depth, Meyer's biography, *Ibsen*, is invaluable, and a marvellous read to boot.

SWEDEN

HISTORY AND POLITICS

Eric Elstob *Sweden: A Traveller's History.* An introduction to Swedish history from the year dot, with useful chapters on art, architecture and cultural life.

Alan Palmer *Bernadotte.* First English biography for over fifty years of Napoleon's marshal, later Sweden's King Karl Johan XIV. Lively but comprehensive – for enthusiasts only.

Michael Roberts *The Early Vasas; A History of Sweden 1523–1611.* This logical and general account of the period is complemented by his more recent *Gustavus Adolphus and the Rise of Sweden* which, more briefly and enthusiastically, covers from 1612 to the king's death in 1632.

LITERATURE

Sigrid Cambüchen *Byron.* A highly regarded Swedish literary critic, Cambüchen has taken as her starting point the exhumation of the poet Byron's body by devotees in the 1930s – developing this into a brilliantly realized biography.

Stig Dagerman *The Games of Night.* Intense short stories, including an autobiographical piece, by a prolific young writer who had written four novels, four plays, short stories and travel sketches by the time he was 26. He committed suicide in 1954 at the age of 31. This is some of the best of his work.

Robert Fulton (trans.) *Preparations for Flight.* Eight Swedish short stories from the last 25 years, including two rare prose outings from the poet Niklas Rådström.

P.C. Jersild *A Living Soul.* A social satire based around the "experiences" of an artificially produced, bodiless human brain floating in liquid. Entertaining, provocative reading from one of Sweden's best novelists.

Sara Lidman *Naboth's Stone.* A novel set in 1880s Västerbotten, in Sweden's far north, charting the lives of settlers and farmers as the industrial age – and the railway – approaches.

Agneta Pleijel *The Dog Star.* By one of Sweden's leading writers, *The Dog Star* is the powerful tale of a young girl's approach to puberty. One of Pleijel's finest novels, full of fantasy and emotion.

Clive Sinclair *Augustus Rex.* August Strindberg dies in 1912 – and is then brought back to life by the Devil in 1960s Stockholm. Bawdy, imaginative and very funny treatment of Strindberg's well-documented neuroses.

Bent Söderberg *The Mysterious Barricades.* Leading Swedish novelist writes of the Mediterranean during the wars – a part of the world he's lived in for over thirty years.

Hjalmar Söderberg *Short Stories.* Twenty-six short stories from the stylish pen of Söderberg (1869–1941). Brief, ironic and eminently ripe for dipping into.

August Strindberg *Strindberg Plays: One* (including *The Father*, *Miss Julie* and *The Ghost Sonata*); *Strindberg Plays: Two* (*The Dance of Death*, *A Dream Play* and *The Stranger*). *Motherly Love/Pariah/The First Warning*). *By the Open Sea.* Strindberg is now seen as a pioneer in both his subject matter and style. His early plays were realistic in a manner not then expected of drama, and confronted themes that weren't considered suitable viewing at all, examining with deep psychological analysis the roles of the sexes both in and out of marriage. A fantastically prolific writer, only a fraction of his sixty plays, twelve historical dramas, five novels, short stories, numerous autobiographical volumes and poetry has ever been translated into English.

CRITICISM AND BIOGRAPHY

Peter Cowie *Ingmar Bergman*. New edition of an already fine critical biography of the director; a well-written, sympathetic account of Bergman's life and career.

Michael Meyer *Strindberg on File*. A useful brief account of Strindberg's life and work, though for a more stirring biography the same author's *Strindberg* is the best and most approachable source.

ART AND ARCHITECTURE

Henrik O. Andersson and Frederic Bedoure *Svensk Arkitektur*. Seminal book on Swedish architectural history from 1640 to 1970, with text in English and Swedish. Colour plates illustrate the works of each architect. One to borrow from the library.

Roger Tanner (trans.) *A History of Swedish Art*. Covers architecture, design, painting and scuplture, ranging from prehistoric rock carvings up to postmodernist works. Well illustrated.

Barbro Klein and Mats Widbom (eds) *Swedish Folk Art – All Tradition Is Change*. Lavishly produced volume on the folk art movement, illustrating the influences of local culture on art and design. Includes a section on the *Ikea* home furnishing phenomenon.

FINLAND

HISTORY

D.G. Kirby *Finland in the Twentieth Century – A History and Interpretation*. By far the best insight into contemporary Finland and the reshaping of the nation after independence. Recommended.

Fred Singleton *A Short History of Finland*. A very readable and informative account of Finland's past, lacking the detail of most academic accounts but an excellent starting point for general readers.

LITERATURE

Tove Jansson The *Moomin* books. Enduring children's tales, and with evocative descriptions of a Finnish nature.

Matti Joensuu *Harjunpää and the Stone Murders*. The only one of the Harjunpää series, involving the Helsinki detective, Timo Harjunpää, to have been translated into English. It's set in contemporary Helsinki during a bout of teenage gang warfare.

Christer Kihlman *The Rise and Fall of Gerdt Bladh*. Supremely evocative study of personal anguish set against a background of Finland's ascent from rural backwater to modern, prosperous nation.

Väinö Linna *The Unknown Soldier*. Using his experiences fighting in the Winter War, Linna triggered immense controversy with this book, depicting for the first time Finnish soldiers not as "heroes in white" but as men who drank and womanized.

Elias Lönnrot *Kalevala*. A collection of previously oral folk tales gathered over twenty years by Lönnrot, a rural doctor, and *the* classic tome of Finnish literature. Set in an unspecified point in the past, the plot centres on a state of war between the mythical region of Kalevala (probably northern Karelia) and Pohjola (possibly Lappland) over possession of a talisman called the *Sampo*. The story is regarded as quintessentially Finnish, but it's not an easy read, due mainly to its length (some 22,750 lines), and the non-linear course of the plot. Its influence on Finnish literature is huge, and it was a linchpin of the Finnish nationalist and language movements.

Oscar Parland *The Year of the Bull*. A steadily absorbing look at the civil-war-torn Finland of 1918 through the eyes of a young boy.

Kirsti Simonsuuri (ed.) *Enchanting Beasts*. A slender but captivating tome, and one of the few English translations of the best of Finland's modern female poets.

DIRECTORY

ADDRESSES In Scandinavia addresses are always written with the number after the street name. In multi-floored buildings the ground floor is always counted as the first floor, the first the second, etc.

ALCOHOL With the exception of Denmark, this is very expensive throughout Scandinavia. For spirits especially, you'll find it cheaper to exceed your duty-free limit and pay the duty than buying when you get there.

ALPHABET The letters Å, Æ, Ø, Ä and Ö come at the end of the relevant alphabets, after Z.

ARCTIC CIRCLE This, an imaginary line drawn at 66° 33' latitude, stretches across three mainland Scandinavian countries – Norway, Sweden and Finland – and denotes the limit beyond which there is at least one day in the year on which the sun never sets, and one on which it never rises.

BOOKS You'll find English-language books in almost every bookshop, though at about twice the price you'd pay at home.

BRING An alarm clock is useful for early-morning buses and ferries, mosquito repellent and antiseptic cream handy (vital in the far north), and a raincoat or foldaway umbrella more or less essential.

CAMPING *Camping Gaz* is only available from selected outlets in Scandinavia – details from national tourist boards – so take your own can. For hiking campers, a plastic survival bag keeps you and your pack dry. And take a torch.

GLACIERS These slow-moving masses of ice are in constant, if imperceptible, motion, and are therefore potentially dangerous. Never climb a glacier without a guide, never walk under one and always heed the instructions at the site. Guided crossings can be terrific; local tourist offices and hiking organizations have details – see the relevant accounts in the guide.

LUGGAGE There are lockers in most train stations, ferry terminals and long-distance bus stations.

MUSEUMS AND GALLERIES As often as not there's a charge to get in, though other than for the really major collections it's rarely very much; *ISIC* cards are valid for reductions at most. Opening times vary greatly: in winter they are always reduced; the likely closing day is Monday.

NEWSPAPERS You'll find British newspapers on sale in every capital city – often on the day of issue – as well as in many other large towns. Your only other choices are likely to be the *International Herald Tribune* or *USA Today*.

NORTHERN LIGHTS (*Aurora Borealis*) A shifting coloured glow visible during winter in the northern parts of Scandinavia, usually above the Arctic Circle, and caused by the solar wind bringing electronically charged particles into contact with the Earth's atmosphere. You'll need to be in luck to see a really good display.

TIME Denmark, Sweden and Norway are one hour ahead of **the UK**; Finland is two hours ahead. Denmark, Sweden and Norway are six to nine hours ahead of the **continental US**, and Finland is seven to ten hours ahead.

WORLD SERVICE You can keep in touch with British and world events by listening to the BBC World Service, which is broadcast to all of mainland Scandinavia. Frequencies vary according to area and usually change every few months. For the latest details write for the free *Programme Guide* to BBC External Services Publicity, Bush House, PO Box 76, Strand, London WC2.

PART TWO

DENMARK

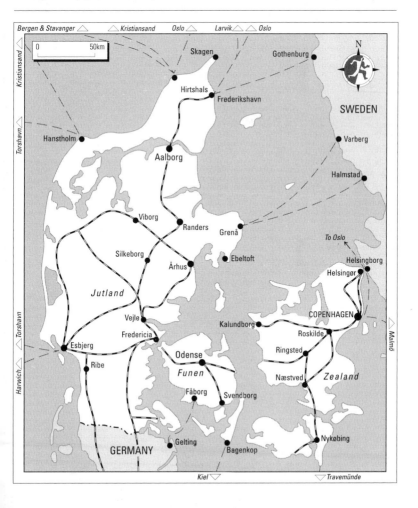

Introduction

Delicately balanced between Scandinavia proper and mainland Europe, **Denmark** is a difficult country to pin down. In many ways it shares the characteristics of both regions: it's an EU member, and has prices and drinking laws that are broadly in line with the rest of Europe. But Danish social policies and style of government are distinctly Scandinavian: social benefits and the standard of living are high, and its politics are very much that of the consensus.

It may seem hard to believe, but it wasn't so long ago that tiny Denmark ruled a good chunk of northern Europe. Since imperialist times, however, the country's energies have been turned inwards, towards the development of a well-organized but rarely over-bureaucratic society that does much to foster a pride in Danish arts and culture and uphold the freedoms of the individual. Indeed, once here, it becomes easy to share the Danes' puzzlement over why other small, ex-empire owning nations haven't followed their example.

■ Where to go

While Denmark is the easiest Scandinavian country in which to travel – both in terms of cost and distance – the landscape itself is the region's least dramatic: very green, flat and rural, largely farmland interrupted by innumerable fairy-tale half-timbered villages. There are surprisingly few urban settlements. Apart from a scattering of small islands, three main land masses make up the country – the islands of Zealand and Funen and the peninsula of Jutland, which extends northwards from Germany.

The vast majority of visitors make for **Zealand** (*Sjælland*) and, more specifically, **Copenhagen**, the country's one truly large city and an atmospheric and exciting focal point. The compact capital really has everything: a beautiful old centre, a good array of museums – both national collections and smaller oddball establishments – and a boisterous nightlife. But Copenhagen has little in common with the rest of Zealand, which is largely quiet and rural – much like the rest of the country. Zealand's smaller neighbour, **Funen** (*Fyn*), has only one positive urban draw in **Odense**, and is otherwise sedate, renowned for the cuteness of its villages, the sandy beaches of its southern coast – a major holiday destination – and numerous explorable small islands.

Only **Jutland** (*Jylland*) is far enough away from Copenhagen to enjoy a truly individual flavour, as well as Denmark's most varied scenery, ranging from soft green hills to desolate heathlands. In **Århus**, Jutland also has the most lively and enjoyable city outside the capital.

■ When to go

Copenhagen attracts visitors all year round, but the intake peaks during July and August – which means May, early June and September are probably the most pleasant times to be there, although there's plenty happening in the city throughout the year. Anywhere else is enjoyably crowd-free all year round except for July, the Danish vacation month, when the population heads en masse for the countryside and the coastal strips – though, even then, only the most popular areas are uncomfortably crowded. Many outdoor events – from big rock festivals to local folk dance displays – take place between mid-June and mid-August, when all tourist facilities and transport services (including the more minor ferry links) are operating in full. In more isolated areas things begin to slacken off in September.

Denmark has the least extreme **climate** of the Scandinavian countries, but due to the proximity of the sea the weather can fluctuate rapidly. A wet day will as likely be followed by a sunny one and vice versa, and stiff breezes are common, especially along Jutland's west coast, where they can be particularly strong. **Summer** is on the whole sunny and clear: throughout July the temperature averages 20°C (68°F), often reaching 26°C (78°F). **Winter** conditions are cold but not severe: there's usually a snow covering from December to early February, and the temperature can at times drop as low as -15°C (5°F), but generally it hovers around or just below freezing point.

Getting There

One look at a map will show you there'll be few problems getting to Denmark from the other Scandinavian countries. Links by rail, sea and air are quick and frequent all year round, and, generally speaking, the journey to Denmark can be a rewarding part of your trip rather than a chore. See *Basics* for details of getting to Scandinavia from Britain and Ireland, the USA and Canada, and Australia and New Zealand.

■ By train

Copenhagen is a major junction for **trains** between Europe and the rest of Scandinavia. There are usually several daily services to Copenhagen from the major Scandinavian cities – Stockholm, Gothenburg, Oslo, Bergen, Turku and Helsinki – and less frequent links (usually one a day in summer) with remoter spots in the far north, such as Narvik (in Norway) and Kiruna (in Sweden). *InterRail/Eurail*, *BIJ* and *Nordturist* cards are valid on all the international routes into Denmark (see *Basics*).

■ By bus

There are several direct **bus** links between the major Danish cities and the rest of Scandinavia, using the ferry routes outlined below. To Copenhagen from Sweden there are usually two buses a day from Halmstad, and nine a day from Malmö and Lund, using the Limhamn–Dragør ferry. For long-distance enthusiasts, there's also a bus from Helsinki twice a week in summer, travelling via Stockholm to Copenhagen.

■ By ferry

Precise details of the numerous **ferries** into Zealand and Jutland from Norway and Sweden are best checked in the ferry companies' latest brochures or at any Scandinavian tourist office, since timetables and prices fluctuate constantly. There are sometimes reductions for holders of railcards (see *Basics*), and fares are usually a lot cheaper outside the peak period from the end of June to early August – though bear in mind that services are likely to be less frequent out of season, and possibly nonexistent in winter. Even if you're heading for Copenhagen, don't disregard the possibility of a quicker, and cheaper, crossing into north Jutland – an interesting part of Denmark, and with easy rail links to the capital; or, from Sweden, reaching Denmark by way of the very explorable island of Bornholm.

From Sweden

The quickest route **from Sweden** to Denmark is the twenty-minute *Scanlines* crossing from Helsingør to Helsingør (32Skr return), which runs round the clock; you can walk or cycle straight on board. Stockholm–Copenhagen trains also use this ferry, completing the trip to Copenhagen fifty minutes later. Two other opera-

tors make the same crossing – see the "Helsingør" section (p.96) for details.

Another inexpensive link is the ferry service from Limhamn to Dragør (30Skr, car from 395Skr), which takes just under an hour and leaves you a half-hour's bus ride (bus #30 and #33) from central Copenhagen. The most direct link to Copenhagen (Havnegade; buses #27 and #26E), however, is the 45-minute catamaran journey from Malmö with *Flygbåtarna*, though this is comparatively expensive at 97Skr one-way and doesn't run when the sea is frozen – quite likely between mid-November and mid-March. A cheaper option is the catamaran operated by *Pilen* (20Skr one-way).

With time to spare, you could reach Denmark proper by way of Bornholm, a sizeable Danish island that's actually nearer to Sweden. There's a daily ferry from Ystad to Rønne, and in summer several daily catamaran crossings from Simrishamn to Allinge. From Rønne, you can take the twice-daily (once in winter) ferry to Copenhagen.

Stena sails several times a day in summer from Gothenburg to Frederikshavn in Jutland (60Skr one-way, cars from 395Skr), and there's also the hydofoil *SeaCat*, which takes two hours and costs 70Skr return (cars 490Skr). *Lion Ferry* sail daily from Halmstad and Varberg to Grenå (for Århus), for a basic fare of 80Dkr one-way (cars 395Skr). See "Travel Details" at the end of the *Jutland* chapter for the full picture.

From Norway

The only direct connection **from Norway** to Copenhagen is the daily *DFDS* overnight crossing from Oslo (from 470Nkr), though you'll save a lot of money by taking one of the numerous routes to either Frederikshavn or Hirtshals in Jutland. From Oslo to Frederikshavn there are four to seven crossings a week with *Stena* (from around 200Nkr one-way), and a similar number with the slightly cheaper *Color Line*, which also sails to Hirtshals (from 150Nkr). There are also comprehensive connections from Larvik and Moss to Frederikshavn (with *Stena* and *Larvik Lines*), and from Kristiansand to Hirtshals with *Color Line* (all from 170–180Nkr) – any of which should save money over the fare from Oslo. Again, for fuller facts, see "Travel Details".

■ By plane

SAS operates nine **flights** daily into Copenhagen from Oslo and Stockholm, five daily from Helsinki;

Finnair flies three or four times daily to Copenhagen from Helsinki. Contact a tourist office or travel agent to find out about special reduced fare deals between the Scandinavian capitals – there are usually several each summer. Copenhagen is very much the Danish hub of the *SAS* network (Århus is a poor second) and international arrivals often dovetail with domestic flights to other Danish cities, which cost little extra on top of the international fare.

A smaller Scandinavian airline, *North Flying*, has daily flights from Bergen and Stavanger to Aalborg and Århus; one-way fares are upwards of 1500Nkr but under-26s can enjoy substantial discounts – sometimes paying as little as 500Nkr.

Costs, Money and Banks

Costs for virtually everything – eating, sleeping, travelling and entertainment – are far lower in Denmark than in any other Scandinavian country.

If you come for just a few days, stay in youth hostels or on campsites and don't eat out, it's possible to survive on £15/$22 a day. Otherwise, moving around the country, combining campsites or hostels with cheap hotel accommodation, visiting museums, eating a full meal each day plus a few snacks and going for a drink in the evening, you can expect to spend a minimum of £25–30/$38–45 per day.

Danish currency is the *krone* (plural *kroner*), made up of 100 *øre*, and it comes in notes worth 1000kr, 500kr, 100kr, 50kr and 20kr, and coins worth 20kr, 10kr, 5kr, 1kr, 50øre and 25øre.

Banks are the best places to change travellers cheques and foreign cash; there's a uniform commission of 20kr per transaction – so change as much as is feasible in one go. Banking hours are Mon–Wed & Fri 9.30am–4pm, Thurs 9.30am–6pm. Most international airports and ferry ports have late-opening exchange facilities. Alternatively, the red *Kontanten* high-street **cash machines** give cash advances on *Visa* and *Eurocheque* cards and, depending on your banking arrangements, these can work out cheaper than changing cash or travellers cheques.

Post and phones

As a geographically close-knit country, it's no surprise that communications in Denmark are safe and speedy. Whether you're sending a postcard home or phoning a ferry office at the other end of the country, you'll have few difficulties.

Like most other public bodies in the country, the Danish **post office** runs an exceedingly tight ship. Anything you post is almost certain to arrive within two days. You can buy **stamps** from most newsagents, and from post offices, most of which are open Mon–Fri 9am–6pm, Sat 9am–1pm, with reduced hours in smaller communities. If you're more worried about receiving mail than sending it, **poste restante** is available at any post office, and many hotels, youth hostels and campsites will hold mail ahead of your arrival.

The old-style Danish **public telephones** frustratingly keep one of your coins even if the number is engaged, which obviously means you should only insert the minimum amount to start with – two 1kr coins. The newer phones give refunds and change – don't insert any money until the call is answered. **Card phones** are becoming more common in the bigger cities; you can buy phone cards (*telekort*) in 20kr, 50kr and 100kr denominations from post offices, general kiosks, and the kiosks run by Danish State Railways (*DSB*) – look for the parrot logo. Most hotel rooms have a phone but it's much cheaper to make calls from the public phone at reception. Youth hostels and campsites generally have public phones; if not, the warden will probably let you use the house one for a pay-phone fee.

One thing to remember when dialling Danish numbers is *always*, even if you're already within the area concerned, to use the **area code** – a two-figure number which precedes the six-figure subscriber number. Calling from abroad, the **international code** for Denmark is ☎45; codes for international calls from Denmark are given in *Basics*. To make a **collect international call**, dial ☎141 for the operator and ask to be connected to the operator in your own country, who will put through the collect call – full instructions for this "Country Direct" system are displayed in phone booths. Be warned that **directory enquiries** (international ☎113, domestic ☎118) is expensive, with a minimum charge of 20kr per call.

The Media

For a country of its size, Denmark has an impressive number of newspapers and freesheets. By the lowest-common-denominator standards of the modern global media, the **Danish press**, with its predominantly serious and in-depth coverage of worthy issues, can't help but seem a little anachronistic. The main newspapers, each costing 7–10kr, are *Politiken*, a reasonably impartial newssheet with strong arts features; *Berlingske Tidende*, conservative/centrist; *Aktuelt*, a trade union paper; *Kristeligt Dagblad*, a Christian paper; *Jyllands-Posten*, a well-respected right-wing paper; and *Information*, left-wing and intellectual. The weekly *Weekendavisen*, published on Fridays, has excellent background features. The best sports coverage can be found in the two tabloids – *B.T.*, which has a conservative bias, and *Ekstra Bladet*, akin to Britain's *Daily Mirror*.

You'll find excellent **entertainment listings** in both *Jyllands-Posten* and *Politiken*, and every Thursday *Information* has a section devoted to listings too. The free Danish **rock music** paper, the monthly *Gaffa*, lists most of the bigger rock shows, and innumerable similar regional papers do the same for their areas – find them in cafés, record shops and the like. You can keep in touch with global current affairs with the **overseas newspapers**, sold in all the main towns: most UK weekday titles cost 15kr and are available the day after publication at train stations and the bigger newsagents, which are also likely to stock recent issues of *USA Today*. There's also a very short "News In English" on the Danish radio station DR – 90.8Mhz.

Danish television on first acquaintance seems as outmoded as the national press. There are three national channels: the non-commercial Channel 1 and DR 2, and the commercial Channel 2 – though, apart from the advertising, you'll probably struggle to spot the difference between them. The fourth station, Channel 3, a cable channel, is shared with Sweden and Norway. None of these start up until mid-afternoon, and all close down before midnight; the evening news programmes begin at 7pm and 7.30pm. If you're staying in a hotel, or a youth hostel with a TV room, you may also have the option of German and Swedish channels – plus a handful of cable and satellite stations.

Getting Around

Despite being largely made up of islands, Denmark is a swift and easy country in which to travel. All types of public transport – trains, buses and the essential ferries – are punctual and efficient, and where you need to switch from one type to another, you'll find the timetables impres-

sively well integrated. And with Denmark being such a small country, you can get from one end to the other in half a day; even if, as is more likely, you're planning to see it all at leisure, you'll rarely need to do more than an hour's daily travelling. Besides being small, Denmark is also very flat, with scores of villages linked by country roads – ideal for effortless, problem-free cycling.

■ Trains

Trains are easily the best way to get about. *Danske Statsbaner* (*DSB*) – Danish State Railways – run an exhaustive and highly reliable network. *InterRail*, *Eurail*, *BIJ* and *Nordturist* passes are valid on all routes except the few private lines that operate in some rural areas. There are just a few out-of-the-way regions that trains fail to penetrate, though these can be easily crossed by buses, which often run in conjunction with local train connections. Some of these buses are operated privately, some by *DSB*, in which case train passes are valid (for more on buses, see below).

Trains range from **inter-city expresses (ICs)**, which have six-seat compartments and a buffet car, to smaller **local** trains (**regionaltog**), with open-plan carriages. Departure times are listed on notices both on station concourses and on the platforms (departures in yellow, arrivals in white), and announced over the loudspeaker. On the train, each station is usually called a few minutes before you arrive. Watch out for *stillekupé* – special quiet compartments, for which you pay extra (unless you have a first-class ticket) on top of the normal fare.

Tickets should be bought in advance from the station – you also need an advance seat reservation for an IC (see below) – although you can buy tickets for *regionaltog* on board. One-way tickets allow you to break your journey once, but travel must be completed on a single day. All trains have an inspector who checks tickets: he or she is almost certain to speak English and is normally willing to answer your questions about routes and times. **Fares** are calculated on a zonal system: Copenhagen–Odense, for example, costs 146kr one-way, Copenhagen–Århus (probably the longest single trip you'll make) 237kr, including seat reservation. Buying a return ticket offers no savings over two one-ways, but avoiding travel on a Sunday, Monday or Friday can save 30–40kr over a long trip; it's the off-peak fares we've listed above. If you don't have a rail pass but are a student, there are various **discounts** of up to 50 percent available through *DIS*, the Danish student travel organization. Those **over 65** qualify for 30–50 percent discounts on certain routes, and people travelling in a group of three or more are also entitled to discounts of up to 50 percent – get details from any Danish tourist office.

Seat reservations, costing 30kr from the station ticket office, can be a good idea (especially if you've luggage to hump) on busy routes – typically those to and from ferry terminals, and in and out of major cities at holiday times; ask at a tourist office or station for advice. Reservations are compulsory on crossings of the Store Bælt, the sea dividing Zealand from Funen and Jutland. If you're taking a *regionaltog* on this route, you can buy one from the inspector on board; in the unlikely event of there being no spare seats, you'll be turfed off at the ferry port and will have to wait for the next train.

As for **timings**, *DSB*'s *Køreplan* (30kr from any newsagent) details all *DSB* train, bus and ferry services inside (and long-distance routes outside) the country, including the local Copenhagen S-train system and all private services, and is a sound investment if you're planning a lot of travelling within the country. If you're not, smaller **timetables** detailing specific routes can be picked up for free at tourist offices and station ticket offices.

■ Buses

There are only a handful of **long-distance bus** services in Denmark: Århus–Copenhagen (150kr), Århus–Ålborg (98kr), Ålborg–Copenhagen (180kr) and Frederikshavn–Esbjerg (190kr). These fares represent quite a saving over full train fares, but, while just as efficient, long-distance buses are much less comfortable than trains. Where buses really come into their own, however, is in the few areas where trains are scarce or the connections complicated. Much of Funen and northeast Jutland are barely touched by trains, for example, and if you're travelling from Esbjerg to Frederikshavn or Aalborg you save several hours – and a lot of timetable reading – by taking the bus. Companies worth checking out are *Abildskous Rutebiler* (☎86/784888), *Fjerritslev-København* (☎98/116600) and, around Jutland, *X-busser* (☎98/900900). Buses are also often the best way of getting to smaller outlying towns and your best source of information is the local tourist office or bus station.

■ Ferries

Ferries connect all the Danish islands, and vary in size from the train-carrying *DSB* ferries linking Zealand, Funen and Jutland, to raft-like affairs serving tiny, isolated settlements a few minutes off the (so-called) mainland. Where applicable, train and bus fares include the cost of ferry crossings (although you can also pay at the terminal and walk on), while the smaller ferries commonly charge 10–40kr for foot passengers. Get the full picture from the nearest tourist office, and check "Travel Details" at the end of each chapter for frequencies and journey times.

■ Planes

Domestic flights, operated by *SAS*, are hardly essential in a country of Denmark's size, but can be handy if you're in a rush: from Copenhagen it's less than an hour's flying time to anywhere in the nation. There are three kinds of fare: "red departures" are returns valid on weekdays; "green departures" are weekend returns and slightly pricier; and "blue departures" are valid for travel any time and therefore the most expensive, with returns costing twice as much as a one-way. To give an idea of the differences, a blue one-way ticket costs the same as a red return. If you're **under 26** or **over 60**, regular air fares can be cut with the 300kr **standby ticket**; get details from an *SAS* desk or tourist office. Remember, too, that taking a domestic flight when you arrive in Denmark from abroad will rarely cost more than the international fare.

■ Cycling

Cycling is the best way to appreciate Denmark's pastoral, and mostly flat, landscape, as well as being a good method of getting about in the towns. Traffic is sparse on most country roads and all large towns have cycle tracks – though watch out for sometimes less-than-careful drivers on main roads. Bikes can be **rented** at nearly all youth hostels and tourist offices, at most bike shops, and some train stations, for around 40–50kr per day or 200kr per week, plus there's often a 200kr deposit. For long-distance cycling, **plan your route** taking into account the frequent westerly winds – pedalling is easier facing east than west.

If the wind gets too strong, or your legs get too tired, you can take your bike on all types of public transport except city buses. Unless you're travelling more than 100km, however, you can't use *IC*s and will have to take the slower local trains – and pay 12–30kr for your machine. The brochure called *Cykler i tog* lists rates and rules in full and is free from train stations. For a similar fee, long-distance buses have limited cycle space, while ferries let bikes on free or for a few kroner. Domestic flights charge around 100kr for airlifting your bike.

■ Driving and hitching

Given the excellent public transport system, the size of the country, and the comparatively high price of petrol, **driving** isn't really economical unless you're in a group. **Car rental** is expensive too, though it's worth checking the cut-price deals offered by some ferry lines. You'll need an international driving licence and must be aged at least 20 to take to the roads, although many firms won't rent vehicles to anyone under 25. Danes drive on the right, and there's a speed limit in towns of 50kph, 80kph in open country and 110kph on motorways. As in Sweden and Finland, headlights need to be used at all times. There are random breath tests for suspected drunken drivers, and the penalties are severe. When parked in a town, not on a meter, a parking-time disc must be displayed; get one from a tourist office, police station or bank. As for **hitching**, this is illegal on motorways but otherwise it's a fairly easy and reasonably safe way to get around.

■ City transport

Transport in towns is by bus, or in Copenhagen by bus and S-Train. Single fares are 10–13kr, and tickets are usually valid for any number of journeys within an hour. If you're in one town for a while and using the buses a lot, either get a *klippekort* – a coupon usually equivalent to ten single tickets but slightly cheaper – or a discounted pass from the tourist office, which covers transport over a wider area, usually for 24 hours. Generally, unless several people are sharing, **taxis** are a raw deal. Expect to pay around 18kr plus 7–10kr per kilometre, inclusive of tip.

Accommodation

While much less costly in Denmark than in other Nordic countries, accommodation is still going to be your major daily expense and you should plan

---

HOTEL PRICES

The Danish hotels listed throughout the guide have been divided into the following price bands, based on their rates for a double room, with bathroom usually included, in summer.

① Up to 300kr ③ 450–600kr
② 300–450kr ④ over 600kr

---

it carefully. Hotels, however, are by no means off limits if you seek out the better offers, and both youth hostels and campsites are plentiful – and of a uniformly high standard.

■ Hotels and private rooms

Coming to Denmark on a standard package trip (see *Basics*) is one way to stay in a **hotel** without spending a fortune. Another way is simply to be selective. Most Danish hotels charge around 600kr for a double room (singles from around 380kr) with a bathroom, TV and phone, but going without the luxuries can result in big savings. In most large towns you'll find several hotels offering rooms without bathrooms for as little as 300kr for a double (200kr for a single), and some **inns** (or *Kro*) in country areas match this price for rooms with full facilities. Other advantages of staying in a hotel or inn are the lack of a curfew (common in hostels in big cities) and the inclusion of an all-you-can-eat breakfast – so large you won't need to buy lunch.

Only in peak season will you need to make **reservations** in advance, although obviously for the cheaper places you should book as early as you can. Danish tourist offices overseas (see p.27) will give you a free list of hotels (and approximate prices) throughout the country, though much more accurate and extensive information can, not surprisingly, be found at local tourist offices. We detail the most attractive deals and prices in the guide but often the best way to locate what's currently on offer is simply to phone the local tourist office and ask – then call the hotel directly. Tourist offices get no commission so they're unbiased. Local tourist offices will also have details of **private rooms** in someone's home, vaguely akin to British-style bed and breakfast (often without the breakfast). These vary greatly but reckon on paying 200–300kr a double. An increasingly popular option is to stay on a **farm** (*Bondegårdsferie*) – get information from *Ferie på Landet*, Sandegade 26, 8700 Horsens (☎70/104190).

■ **Youth hostels**

Youth hostels (*vandrerhjem*) are the cheapest option under a roof. Every town has one, they're much less pricey than hotels, and they have a high degree of comfort thanks to a campaign by the Danish hostelling association (*Danmarks Vandrerhjem*) to raise their profile and attract families. Most hostels offer a choice between private rooms, often with toilets and showers, and dormitory accommodation, and nearly all have cooking facilities. **Rates** range from 160kr per person in a private room to 36–79kr for a dormitory bed. It's rare for hostels other than those in major towns or ferry ports to be full, but during the summer it's still wise to phone ahead to make a reservation, and to check on the hostel's location – some are several kilometres outside the town centre.

As with all Scandinavian hostels, sleeping bags are not allowed, so you need to bring either a sheet sleeping bag or rent hostel linen – which can become expensive over a long stay. It's a good idea, too, to get an **HI card**, since without one you'll be lumbered with the cost of either an overnight card (25kr) or a year-long Danish membership card (50kr). If you're intent on doing a lot of hostelling, it's worth contacting *Danmarks Vandrerhjem*, Vesterbrogade 39, DK-1620, Copenhagen V (☎31/313612), for their guide to Danish hostels (*Vandrerhjem i Danmark*, free, but there's a charge for postage) – published in several languages, including English.

Sometimes cheaper still, and occasionally free, are **Sleep-Ins**, run by local authorities and usually open for a two-week period during July or August. Copenhagen has a well-established one which operates all summer, offering a bed, shower and breakfast for around 100kr, and most other towns have downmarket versions, often no more than a mattress on the floor. You need your own sleeping bag, sometimes only one night's stay is permitted and there may be an age restriction (typically 16- to 24-year-olds only, although this may not be strictly enforced). Sleep-ins come and go, so check the current situation at a local tourist office, or with *Use-It* in Copenhagen (see p.71).

■ **Camping**

If you don't already have an International Camping Card from a camping organization in your own country, you'll need a **Visitor's Pass** to camp in Denmark, which costs 24kr per person (48kr for a family) from any campsite and is valid on all official sites until the end of the year. **Camping rough** without the landowner's permission is illegal, but possible if you stay out of sight; a dim view is taken of camping on beaches and an on-the-spot fine may well be imposed. In a few rural spots, the local tourist office will be able to inform you about a corner of a nearby field that is designated for rough camping.

In any case, **campsites** (*campingplads*) can be found virtually everywhere. All sites are open in June, July and August, many are open from April right through to September, and a few operate all year round. There's a rigid grading system: one-star sites have drinking water and toilets, two-star sites have, in addition, kitchen, showers, laundry and a food shop within a kilometre, while three-star sites, by far the majority, have all the above plus a TV room, on-site shop, cafeteria, etc. Prices vary only slightly, three-star sites charging 32–42kr per person, the others a few kroner less. Many sites also have **cabin accommodation**, usually with cooking facilities, which at 50–70kr a night represents massive savings for several people sharing, although on busy sites cabins are often booked up throughout the summer. Any Danish tourist office will give you a free leaflet listing all the sites and the basic camping rules, or there's an official guide, *Camping Danmark*, available from kiosks, bookshops and tourist offices (70kr). For further information, contact *Dansk Camping Union*, Gl. Kongevej 74D, DK-1850 Frederiksberg C (☎31/210600).

Food and Drink

Although good food can cost a lot, there are plenty of ways to eat affordably and healthily in Denmark, and with plenty of variety too. Much the same applies to drink: the only Scandinavian country free of social drinking taboos, Denmark is an imbiber's delight – both for its huge choice of tipples, and for the number of places where they can be sampled.

■ **Food**

Traditional Danish **food** is centred on meat and fish: beef, veal, chicken and pork are frequent

GLOSSARY OF DANISH FOOD AND DRINK TERMS

Basics

Brød	Bread	*Pølser*	Frankfurter/	*Sukker*	Sugar
Bøfsandwich	Hamburger		sausages	*Sødmælk*	Full cream milk
Chokolade	Chocolate	*Nogle småkager*	Biscuits	*Te*	Tea
(Varm)	(Hot)	*Ostebord*	Cheese board	*Wienerbrød*	Pastry
Det kolde bord	Help-yourself	*Sildebord*	A selection of		
	cold buffet		spiced and	**Egg (*æg*) dishes**	
Is	Ice Cream		pickled herring	*Kogt æg*	Boiled egg
Kaffe (med	Coffee (with	*Skummetmælk*	Skimmed milk	*Omelet*	Omelette
fløde)	cream)	*Smør*	Butter	*Røræg*	Scrambled
Letmælk	Low-fat milk	*Smørrebrød*	Open		eggs
Mælk	Milk		sandwiches	*Spejlæg*	Fried eggs

Fish (*Fisk*)

Forel	Trout	*Krebs*	Crayfish	*Sardiner*	Sardines
Gedde	Pike	*Laks*	Salmon	*Sild*	Herring
Helleflynder	Halibut	*Makrel*	Mackerel	*Store rejer*	Prawns
Hummer	Lobster	*Rejer*	Shrimp	*Søtunge*	Sole
Karpe	Carp	*Rogn*	Roe	*Stør*	Sturgeon
Klipfisk	Salt cod	*Rødspætte*	Plaice	*Torsk*	Cod
Krabbe	Crab	*Røget Sild*	Kipper	*Ål*	Eel

Meat (*Kød*)

And(ung)	Duck(ling)	*Hare*	Hare	*Lever*	Liver
Bøf	Beef	*Kalkun*	Turkey	*Pølser*	Sausages
Dyresteg	Venison	*Kanin*	Rabbit	*Rensdyr*	Reindeer
Fasan	Pheasant	*Kylling*	Chicken	*Skinke*	Ham
Gås	Goose	*Lam*	Lamb	*Svinekød*	Pork

Vegetables (*Grøntsager*)

Artiskokker	Artichokes	*Kartofler*	Potatoes	*Ris*	Rice
Asparges	Asparagus	*Linser*	Lentils	*Rosenkål*	Sprouts
Blomkål	Cauliflower	*Løg*	Onions	*Rødbeder*	Beetroot
Champignons	Mushrooms	*Majs*	Sweetcorn	*Rødkål*	Red cabbage
Grønne bønner	Runner beans	*Majskolbe*	Corn on the cob	*Salat*	Lettuce, salad
Gulerødder	Carrots	*Nudler*	Noodles	*Salatgurk*	Cucumber
Hvide bønner	Kidney beans	*Peberfrugt*	Peppers	*Selleri*	Celery
Hvidløg	Garlic	*Persille*	Parsley	*Spinat*	Spinach
Julesalat	Chicory	*Porrer*	Leeks	*Turnips*	Turnips

Fruit (*Frugt*)

Abrikoser	Apricots	*Ferskner*	Peaches	*Rabarber*	Rhubarb
Ananas	Pineapple	*Grapefrugt*	Grapefruit	*Rosiner*	Raisins
Appelsiner	Orange	*Hindbær*	Raspberries	*Solbær*	Blackcurrants
Bananer	Bananas	*Jordbær*	Strawberries	*Stikkelsbær*	Gooseberries
Blommer	Plums	*Kirsebær*	Cherries	*Svesker*	Prunes
Blåbær	Blueberries	*Mandariner*	Tangerines	*Vindruer*	Grapes
Brombær	Blackberries	*Melon*	Melon	*Æbler*	Apples
Citron	Lemon	*Pærer*	Pears		

Danish Specialities

Boller i karry	Meatballs in curry sauce served with rice	*Røget sild*	Smoked herring on rye bread garnished with a raw egg yolk, radishes and chives
Flæskesteg	A hunk of pork with red cabbage, potatoes and brown sauce	*Skidne æg*	Poached or hard-boiled eggs in a cream sauce, spiced with fish
Frikadeller	Pork rissoles		mustard and served with rye
Hakkebøf	Minced beef rolled into balls and fried with onions		bread, decorated with sliced bacon and chives
Skipper labskovs	Danish stew: small squares of beef boiled with potatoes, peppercorns and bay leaves	*Ålesuppe*	Sweet and sour eel soup
		Stegt ål med stuvede kartofler	Fried eel with diced potatoes and white sauce
Kalvebryst i frikasseé	Veal boiled with vegetables and served in a white sauce with peas and carrots	*Æbleflæsk*	Smoked bacon with onions and sautéed apple rings
Grillstegt kylling	Grilled chicken with salad	*Æggekage*	Scrambled eggs with onions, chives, potatoes and bacon pieces
Medisterpølse	A spiced pork sausage, usually served with boiled potatoes or stewed vegetables	*Kogt torsk*	Poached cod in mustard sauce with boiled potatoes
Sild i karry	Herring in curry sauce		

Drink (*Drikke*)

Appelsinvand	Orangeade	*Vin*	Wine	*Øl*	Beer
Citronvand	Lemonade	*Husets vin*	House wine	*Eksport-Øl*	Export beer (very strong lager)
Kærnemælk	Buttermilk	*Rødvin*	Red wine		
Mineralvand	Soda water	*Hvidvin*	White wine	*Fadøl*	Draught beer
Tomatjuice	Tomato juice	*Æblemost*	Apple juice	*Guldøl*	Strong beer

menu items – though rarely bacon, which is mainly exported – along with various forms of salmon, herring, eel, plaice and cod. Combinations of these are served with potatoes and another, usually boiled, vegetable. Ordinary restaurant meals can be expensive, especially in the evening, and are often no-go areas for vegetarians – but there are other ways to eat Danish food that won't ruin your budget or your diet.

Breakfast

Breakfast (*morgenmad*) can be the tastiest and is certainly the healthiest (and most meat-free) Danish meal. Almost all hotels offer a sumptuous breakfast as a matter of course, and if you're staying in a rural youth hostel you can often attack a help-yourself table laden with cereals, bread, cheese, fruit juice, milk and tea for around 38kr – though city hostels' breakfasts tend to be less exciting. Breakfast elsewhere will be far less substantial: many cafés offer a very basic one for around 20kr, but you're well advised to hold out until lunchtime.

Lunch and snacks

You can track down an excellent-value **lunch** (*frokost*) simply by walking around and reading the signs chalked up outside any café, restaurant or *bodega* (a kind of bar that also sells basic food). On these notices, put out between 11.30am and 2.30pm, you'll often see the word *tilbud*, which refers to the "special" priced dish, or *dagens ret*, meaning "dish of the day" – a plate of chilli con carne or lasagne for around 45kr, or a two-course set lunch for about 60kr. Some restaurants carry a fixed-price (75–90kr) three-course lunch where you can pick from a selection of dishes. A variation on this idea is a choice of *smørrebrød*, or open sandwiches: slices of rye bread heaped with meat (commonly either ham, beef or liver pâté), fish (salmon, eel, caviar, cod roe, shrimp or herring) or cheese, and generously piled with assorted trimmings (mushrooms, cucumber, pickles or slices of lemon). A selection of three or four of these costs about 75kr.

Elsewhere, the American **burger** franchises are as commonplace and as popular as you'd expect, as are **pizzerias**, which are dependable and affordable at any time of day, many offering special deals such as all-you-can-eat-salad with a basic pizza for 45kr, or a more exotic dish or pizza topping for 45–70kr. You can also get a very ordinary self-service meat, fish or omelette lunch in a **supermarket cafeteria** for 40–75kr.

Most Danes buy **snacks** from the very popular fast-food stands (*pølsevogn*) found on all main streets and at train stations. These serve various types of **hot sausage** (*pølser*) for 12–20kr: the long thin *wiener*, the fatter *frankfurter*, or the *franske*, a sausage inside a cylindrical piece of bread. Alternatives include a **toasted ham and cheese sandwich** (*parisertoast*) for 15kr – vegetarians can ask for the ham to be left out – and **chips** (*pommes frites*), which come in big (*store*) and small (*lille*) forms. All of the above come with various types of ketchup and mustard to order.

If you just want a cup of **coffee** (always fresh) or **tea** (usually a fairly exotic teabag brew), drop into the nearest café, where either will cost 10–14kr. You help it down with a **Danish pastry** (*wienerbrød*), tastier and much less sweet than the imitations sold under the name abroad.

Dinner

Dinner (*aftensmad*) in Denmark presents as much choice as does lunch, but the cost is likely to be much higher. Pizzerias and similar places (see above) keep their prices unchanged from lunchtime, and many youth hostels serve simple but filling evening meals for up to 60kr, though you have to order it in advance – as with breakfast, the best tend to be in rural areas. The most cost-effective dinners (80–100kr), however, are usually found in **ethnic restaurants** (most commonly Chinese and Middle Eastern, with a smaller number of Indian, Indonesian and Thai), which, besides à la carte dishes, often have a help-yourself table – ideal for gluttonous overindulgence – and you usually get soup and a dessert thrown in as well. Often the same **Danish restaurants** that are promising for lunch turn into expense-account affairs at night, offering an atmospheric, candle-lit setting for the slow devouring of immaculately prepared meat or fish, where you'll be hard pushed to spend less than 200kr each.

Shops and markets

An especially tight budget may well leave you dependent on **shopping** for food. *Brugsen, Føtex*

and *Irma* are the most commonly found **supermarkets** (usually open Mon–Fri 9am–5.30pm, later on Thurs & Fri, Sat 9am–5pm), and there's little difference in price, although you'll also come across *Netto*, which can be slightly cheaper but is mostly filled with freezer food. Smaller supermarkets may be open shorter hours, especially on Saturday, when they close at 1 or 2pm except on the first Saturday of the month.

Late-night shopping is generally impossible, although in bigger towns, the *DSB* supermarket at the train station is likely to be open until midnight.

The best spots for fresh fruit and veg are the Saturday and (sometimes) Wednesday **markets** held in most towns, and you can buy *smørrebrød* (see above) for 15–40kr a piece from the special *smørrebrød* shops, at least one of which will be open until 10pm.

■ Drink

If you've arrived from near-teetotal Norway or Sweden, you're in for a shock. Not only is alcoholic **drink** entirely accepted in Denmark, it's unusual *not* to see people strolling along the pedestrianized streets swigging from a bottle of beer. Although extreme drunkenness is frowned upon, alcohol is widely consumed throughout the day by most types of people.

Although you can buy booze more cheaply from supermarkets, the most sociable **places to drink** are pubs and cafés, where the emphasis is on beer – although you can also get spirits and wine (or tea and coffee). There are also bars and *bodegas* (see "Food"), in which, as a very general rule, the mood tends to favour wines and spirits, and the customers are a bit older than café patrons.

The cheapest type of beer is **draught beer** (*fadøl*), half a litre of which costs 15–20kr. Draught is a touch weaker than **bottled beer**, which costs 17–18kr for a third of a litre, and a great deal less potent than the **export beers** (*guldøl* or *eksport-Øl*) costing 25–30kr per bottle. All Danish beer is actually lager, the most common brands being *Carlsberg* and *Tuborg*, and although a number of towns have their own locally brewed rivals, you'll need a finely tuned palate to spot much difference between them. One you will notice the taste of is *Lys Pilsner*, a very low-alcohol lager.

Most international **wines and spirits** are widely available, a shot of the hard stuff costing 18–20kr in a bar, a glass of wine upwards of 15kr.

While in the country you should investigate the many varieties of the schnapps-like **Akvavit**, which Danes consume as eagerly as beer, especially with meals; more than two or three turn most non-Danes pale. A tasty relative is the gloriously hot and strong *Gammel Dansk Bitter Dram* – Akvavit-based but made with bitters – only ever drunk with food at breakfast time.

Directory

EMERGENCIES ☎112. Ask for fire, police or ambulance.

FESTIVALS A wide range of music festivals – rock, folk, jazz and various combinations – takes place all over Denmark throughout the summer. Some feature leading names and require tickets, but many are cheap or free. Get the details from the free music monthly, *Gaffa*, or one of the many regional freesheets from places like record shops or cafés. The tourist office also produces a free festival calendar in Danish and English.

FISHING Well stocked with bream, dace, roach, pike, trout, zander and much more, Denmark's lakes and rivers are a fishing enthusiast's dream. The only problem is bringing enough bait (more expensive than you might expect) to cope with the inevitably large catch. The time to come is in early or late summer, and the prime areas are in central Jutland, around Randers and Viborg, and slightly further north around Silkeborg and Skanderborg. For specialist angling trips, see the "Getting There" sections in *Basics*.

FOOTBALL The success of Denmark's national football team in the European Championship of 1992 stimulated interest in the country's domestic soccer scene. Teams especially worth watching are Brøndby (Copenhagen), AaB (Ålborg), AGF (Århus) and OB (Odense). The season divides into two

halves, from April to early June (*Forår*) and from August to October (*Efterår*), with most matches played on Sunday afternoon; admission is 40–60kr and the local newspapers (look under *Fodbold*) and tourist office will have details.

MARKETS Virtually every town has a market, usually on Wednesday and Saturday mornings.

NUDE BATHING Trying for an all-over tan is accepted practice in Denmark, although you'll be arrested if you try it anywhere except at the designated beaches – which exist in most popular bathing areas. Details from the local tourist office.

PUBLIC HOLIDAYS All shops and banks are closed on the following days, and public transport and many museums run to Sunday schedules: January 1, the afternoons of May 1 and June 5 (Constitution Day), December 24 (afternoon only), December 25, December 26, Maundy Thursday, Good Friday, Easter Monday, Prayer Day (fourth Friday after Easter), Ascension Day (around mid-May) and Whit Monday.

SAILING Experienced sailors can rent sailing and motorboats on many parts of the Danish coast; Kerteminde and Svenborg, on Funen's northeast and south coast respectively, are particularly well-established sailing centres. The Danish Tourist Board can supply full details. Danish marine charts can be bought at *Søkortafdelingen*, Esplanaden 19, DK-1263 Copenhagen K.

SALES TAX A tax of 25 percent is added to almost everything you'll buy – but it's always included in the marked price.

SHOPS Shop hours are Mon–Thurs 9am–5.30pm, Fri 9am–7 or 8pm, Sat 9am–1 or 2pm, Sun closed. On the first Saturday of the month shops stay open until 5pm.

TIPS Unless you're in the habit of having porters carry your luggage, you'll never be expected to tip – restaurant bills include a 15 percent service charge.

History

Spending much time at all in Denmark soon makes you realize that its history is entirely disproportionate to its size. Nowadays a small – and often overlooked – nation, Denmark has nonetheless played an important role in key periods of European history, firstly as home-base of the Vikings, and later as a medieval superpower. Markers to the past, from prehistory to the wartime resistance movement, are never hard to find. Equally easy to spot are the benefits stemming from one of the earliest welfare state systems and some of western Europe's most liberal social policies.

■ Early settlements

Traces of human habitation, such as deer bones prised open for marrow, have been found in central Jutland and dated at 50,000 BC, but it is unlikely that any settlements of this time were permanent, as much of the land was still covered by ice. From 14,000 BC tribes from more southerly parts of Europe arrived during the summer to hunt reindeer for meat and antlers, which provided raw material for axes and other tools. The melting ice caused the shape of the land to change and the warmer climate enabled vast forests to grow in Jutland. From about 4000 BC, settlers with agricultural knowledge arrived: they lived in villages, grew wheat and barley and kept animals, and buried their dead in **dolmens** or megalithic graves.

The earliest metal and bronze finds are from 1800 BC, the result of trade with southern Europe. The richness of some pieces indicates an awareness of the cultures of Crete and Mycenae. By this time the country was widely cultivated and densely populated. Battles for control over individual areas saw the emergence of a ruling warrior class, and, around 500 AD, a tribe from Sweden calling themselves **Danes** migrated southwards and wrested control of what became known as **Danmark**.

■ The Viking era

Around 800 AD, under **King Godfred**, the Danish boundaries were marked out. However, following Charlemagne's conquest of the Saxons in Germany, the Franks began to threaten the Danes' territory and they had to prepare an opposing force. They built fast seaworthy vessels and defeated Charlemagne easily. Then, with the Norwegians, they attacked Spanish ports and eventually invaded Britain. By 1033, the Danes controlled the whole of England and Normandy and dominated trade in the Baltic.

In Denmark itself, which then included much of what is now southern Sweden, the majority of people were farmers: the less wealthy paid taxes to the king and those who owned large tracts of land provided the monarch with military forces. In time, a **noble class** emerged, expecting and receiving privileges from the king in return for their support. Law-making was the responsibility of the *ting*, a type of council consisting of district noblemen. Above the district *ting* there was a provincial *ting*, charged with the election of the king. The successful candidate could be any member of the royal family, which led to a high level of feuding and bloodshed.

In 960, with the baptism of King **Harald ("Bluetooth")**, Denmark became officially Christian – principally, it's thought, to stave off imminent invasion by the German emperor. Nonetheless, Harald gave permission to a Frankish monk, **Ansgar**, to build the **first Danish church**, and Ansgar went on to take control of missionary activity throughout Scandinavia. Harald was succeeded by his son **Sweyn I ("Forkbeard")**. Sweyn was a pagan but he tolerated Christianity, even though he suspected the missionaries of bringing a German influence to bear in Danish affairs. In 990 he joined with the Norwegians in attacking Britain, where Alfred had been succeeded by the well-named Ethelred "the Unready". Sweyn's son, **Knud I ("the Great")** – King Canute of England – married Ethelred's widow, took the British throne and soon controlled a sizeable empire around the North Sea – the zenith of Viking power.

■ The rise of the Church

During the eleventh and twelfth centuries, Denmark was weakened by violent internal struggles, not only between different would-be rulers but also among the Church, nobility and monarchy. Following the death of **Sweyn II** in 1074, two of his four sons, Knud and Harald, fought for the throne – Harald, supported by the peasantry and the Church, emerging victorious. A mild and introspective individual, Harald was nonetheless a competent monarch, and introduced the first real Danish currency. He was constantly derided by Knud and his allies, however, and after his death in 1080 his brother became **Knud II**. He made generous donations to the Church, but his introduction of higher taxes and the absorption of all unclaimed land into the realm enraged the nobility. The farmers of North Jutland revolted in 1086, forcing Knud to flee to Odense, where he was slain on the high altar of Skt Alban's Kirke. The ten-year period of poor harvests that ensued was taken by many to be divine wrath, and there were reports of miracles occurring in Knud's tomb, leading to the murdered king's canonization in 1101.

The battles for power continued, and eventually, in 1131, a **civil war** broke out that was to simmer for two decades, various claimants to the throne and their offspring slugging it out with the support of either the Church or nobility. During this time the power of the clergy escalated dramatically by way of **Bishop Eskil**, who enjoyed a persuasive influence on the eventual successor, Erik III. Following Erik's death in 1143, the disputes went on, leading to the division of the kingdom between two potential rulers, Sweyn and Knud. Sweyn's repeated acts of tyranny resulted in the death of Knud in Roskilde, but Knud's wounded aide, Valdemar, managed to escape and raise the Jutlanders in revolt at the battle of Grathe Heath, south of Viborg.

■ The Valdemar era

Valdemar I ("the Great") assumed the throne in 1157, strengthening the crown by ending the elective function of the *ting*, and shifting the power to choose the monarch to the Church. Technically the *ting* still influenced the choice of king, but in practice hereditary succession became the rule.

After Bishop Eskil's retirement, **Absalon** became Archbishop of Denmark, erecting a fortress at the fishing village of **Havn** (later to become København — Copenhagen). Besides being a zealous churchman, Absalon possessed a sharp military mind and came to dominate the monarch and his successor, Knud IV. Through him Denmark saw some of its best years, expanding to the south and east, and taking advantage of internal strife within Germany. In time, after Absalon's death and the succession of **Valdemar II**, Denmark controlled all trade along the south coast of the Baltic and in the North Sea east of the Ejder. Valdemar was also responsible for subjugating Norway, and in 1219 he set out to conquer Estonia and take charge of Russian trade routes through the Gulf of Finland. According to

Danish legend, the national flag, the *Dannebrog*, fell down from heaven during a battle in Estonia in 1219.

However, in 1223 Valdemar was kidnapped by Count Henry of Schwerin (a Danish vassal) and forced to give up many Danish possessions. There was also a redrawing of the southern boundary of Jutland, which caused the Danish population of the region to be joined by a large number of Saxons from Holstein.

Within Denmark, the years of expansion had brought great prosperity. The laws of the *ting* were written as the **Jutlandic Code**, which unified the laws all over the country, in so doing marking a shift towards law-making being carried out by the king rather than by the *ting*. The increasingly affluent nobles demanded greater rights if they were to be counted on to support the new king. The Church was envious of the growing power of the nobles and much bickering ensued in the following years, resulting in the eventual installation of Valdemar II's son, Christoffer I, as monarch.

Christoffer died suddenly in Ribe when his only son Erik was two years old; Queen Margrethe took the role of regent until **Erik V** came of age. Erik's overbearing manner and penchant for German bodyguards annoyed the nobles, and they forced him to a meeting at Nyborg in 1282 where his powers were limited by a *håndfæstning*, or charter, that included an undertaking for annual consultation with a *Danehof*, or forum of nobles. In 1319 **Christoffer II** became king, after agreeing to an even sterner charter, which allowed for daily consultations with a *Råd* — a council of nobles. In 1326, in lieu of a debt which Christoffer had no hope of repaying, Count **Gerd of Holstein** occupied a large portion of Jutland. Christoffer fled to Mecklenburg and Gerd installed the twelve-year-old Valdemar, Duke of Schleswig, as a puppet king.

As they proceeded to divide the country among themselves, the Danish nobles became increasingly unpopular with both the Church and the peasantry. Christoffer attempted to take advantage of the internal discord to regain the crown in 1329 but he was defeated in battle by Gerd. Under the peace terms Gerd was given Jutland and Funen, while his cousin, Count Johan of Plön, was granted Zealand, Skåne and Lolland-Falster. In 1332 Skåne, the richest Danish province, inflicted a final insult on Christoffer when its inhabitants revolted against Johan and transferred their allegiance to the Swedish king, Magnus.

Gerd was murdered in 1340. The years of turmoil had taken their toll on all sections of Danish society: from Christoffer's death in 1332, the country had been without a monarch and it was felt that a re-establishment of the crown was essential to restoring stability. The throne was given to **Valdemar IV**. The monarchy was strengthened by the taking back of former crown lands that had been given to nobles, and within twenty years Denmark had regained its former territory, with German forces driven back across the Ejder. The only loss was Estonia, a Danish possession since 1219, which was sold to the Order of Teutonic Knights.

In 1361, the buoyant king attacked and conquered Gotland, much to the annoyance of the Hanseatic League, who were using it as a Baltic trading base. A number of anti-Danish alliances sprang up and the country was slowly plundered until peace was agreed in 1370 under the **Treaty of Stralsund**. This guaranteed trade for the Hanseatic partners by granting them control of castles along the west coast of Skåne for fifteen years. It also laid down that the election of the Danish monarch had to be approved by the Hanseatic League – the peak of their power.

■ The Kalmar Union

Valdemar's daughter Margrethe forced the election of her five-year-old son, Olav, as king in 1380, installing herself as regent. After his untimely death after only a seven-year reign, Margrethe became Queen of Denmark and Norway, and later of Sweden as well – the first ruler of a united Scandinavia. In 1397, a formal document, the **Kalmar Union**, set out the rules of the union of the countries, which allowed for a Scandinavian federation under the same monarch and foreign policy, within which each country had its own internal legislation. It became evident that Denmark was to be the dominant partner within the union when Margrethe placed Danish nobles in civic positions in Norway and Sweden but failed to reciprocate with Swedes and Norwegians in Denmark.

Erik VII ("of Pomerania") became king in 1396, and was determined to remove the Counts of Holstein who had taken possession of Schleswig. In 1413 he persuaded a meeting of the *Danehof* to declare the whole of Schleswig to be crown property, and three years later war broke out with the German-influenced nobility of the region. Initially the Hanseatic League supported

the king, unhappy with the Holstein privateers who were interfering with their trade. But Erik also introduced important economic reforms within Denmark, ensuring that foreign goods reached Danish people through Danish merchants instead of coming directly from Hanseatic traders. This led to a war with the League, after which, in 1429, Erik imposed the **Sound toll** (*Øresundstolden*) on shipping passing through the narrow strip of sea off the coast of Helsingør.

The conflicts with the Holsteiners and the Hanseatic League had, however, badly drained financial resources. Denmark still relied on hired armies to do its fighting, and the burden of taxation had caused widespread dissatisfaction, particularly in Sweden. With the Holstein forces gaining ground in Jutland, Erik fled to Gotland and in 1439 Swedish and Danish nobles elected in his place **Christoffer III**, who acquiesced to the nobles' demands and ensured peace with the Hanseatic League by granting them exemption from the Sound toll.

His sudden death in 1448 left – after internal struggle – **Christian I** to take the Danish throne. Following the death of his uncle and ally, the Count of Holstein, he united Schleswig and Holstein at Ribe in 1460 and became Count of Holstein and Duke of Schleswig. In Denmark itself he also instigated the *stændermøde*: a council of merchants, clergy, freehold peasants and nobility in place of the exclusively noble *Danehof*, thereby maintaining his pledge to work in close liaison with the nobles, and forging a powerful position for the crown – a policy that was continued by his successor, Hans.

Hans died in 1513 and **Christian II** came to the throne, seeking to re-establish the power of the Kalmar Union and reduce the trading dominance of the Hanseatic League. He invaded Sweden in 1520 under the guise of protecting the Church, but soon crowned himself King of Sweden at a ceremony attended by the cream of the Swedish nobility, clergy and the merchant class – an amnesty being granted to those who had been opposed to him. It was, however, a trick. Once inside the castle, 82 of the "guests" were arrested on charges of heresy, sentenced to death, and executed – an event that became known as the **Stockholm Bloodbath**. This was supposed to subdue Swedish hostility to the Danish monarch but in fact had the opposite effect. Gustavus Vasa, previously one of six Swedish hostages held by Christian in Denmark, became the leader of a revolt that ended Christian's reign in Sweden and finished the Kalmar Union.

Internally, too, Christian faced a revolt, to which he responded with more brutality. At the end of 1522, a group of Jutish nobles banded together with the intention of overthrowing him, joining up with Duke Frederik of Holstein-Gottorp (heir to half of Schleswig-Holstein), who also regarded the Danish king with disfavour. The following January, the nobles renounced their royal oaths and, with the support of forces from Holstein, gained control of all of Jutland and Funen. As they prepared to invade Zealand, Christian fled to Holland, hoping to assemble an army and return. In his absence, Frederik of Holstein-Gottorp became **Frederik I**.

■ The Reformation

At the time of Frederik's acquisition of the crown there was a growing unease with the role of the Church in Denmark, especially with the power – and wealth – of the bishops. Frederik was a Catholic but refused to take sides in religious disputes and did nothing to prevent the destruction of churches, well aware of the groundswell of peasant support for Lutheranism. Frederik I died in 1533 and the fate of the Reformation hinged on which of his two sons would succeed him. The elder and more obvious choice was Christian, but his open support for Lutheranism set the bishops and nobles against him. The younger son, Hans, was just 12 years old but favoured by the Church and the nobility. The civil war that ensued became known as the **Counts' War**, and ended in 1536 with **Christian II** on the throne and the establishment of the new Danish Lutheran Church, with a constitution placing the king at its head.

■ Danish–Swedish conflicts

New trading routes across the Atlantic had reduced the power of the Hanseatic League, and the young and ambitious successor to Christian, **Frederik II**, saw this as a chance for expansion. Sweden, however, was also seeking to expand, with the result that the **Seven Years' War** was fought between the two countries from 1563 to 1570. The conflict caused widespread devastation and plunged the Danish economy into crisis – though this was short-lived: price rises in the south of Europe enabled Danish wealth to grow, and the increasing affluence of the time was marked by the building of the elaborate castle of Kronborg in Helsingør.

By the time **Christian IV** came to the throne in 1596, Denmark was a solvent and powerful nation. His reign was to be characterized by bold new town layouts and great architectural works. Copenhagen became acknowledged as a major European capital, gaining both a large increase in population and much of today's skyline, including Rosenborg, Børsen and Rundetårnet. To stem the rise of Swedish power after the Seven Years' War, Christian IV took Denmark into the abortive **Thirty Years' War** in 1625, in which Danish defeat was total, and the king was widely condemned for his lack of foresight. The war led to increased taxes, inflation became rampant, and a number of merchants displayed their anger by petitioning the king over tax exemptions and other privileges enjoyed by nobles.

In 1657 Sweden occupied Jutland, and soon after marched across the frozen sea to Funen with the intention of continuing to Zealand. Hostilities ceased with the signing of the **Treaty of Roskilde**, under which Denmark finally lost all Swedish provinces. Sweden, however, was still suspicious of possible Danish involvement in Germany, and broke the terms of the treaty, commencing an advance through Zealand towards Copenhagen. The Dutch, to whom the Swedes had been allied, regarded this as a precursor to total Swedish control of commercial traffic through the Sound and sent a fleet to protect Copenhagen. This, plus a number of local uprisings within Denmark and attacks by Polish and Brandenburg forces on Sweden, halted the Swedes' advance and forced them to seek peace. The **Treaty of Copenhagen**, signed in 1660, acknowledged Swedish defeat but allowed the country to retain the Sound provinces acquired under the Treaty of Roskilde, so preventing either country from monopolizing Sound trade.

■ Absolute monarchy

In Denmark, the financial power of the nobles was fading as towns became established and the new merchant class grew. The advent of firearms caused the king to become less dependent on the foot-soldiers provided by the nobles, and there was a general unease about the privileges – such as exemption from taxes – that the nobles continued to enjoy. Equally, few monarchs were content with their powers being limited by *håndfæstning*.

During the Swedish siege of Copenhagen, the king had promised special concessions to the city and its people, in the hope of encouraging them to withstand the assault. Among these was the right to determine their own rate of tax. A meeting of the city's burghers decided that everyone, including the nobility, should pay taxes. The nobles had little option but to submit. Sensing their power, the citizens went on to suggest that the crown become hereditary and end the *håndfæstning* system. Frederik III accepted and, with a full-scale ceremony in Copenhagen, was declared hereditary monarch. The task of writing a new constitution was left to the king and its publication, in 1665, revealed that he had made himself absolute monarch, bound only to uphold the Lutheran faith and ensure the unity of the kingdom. The king proceeded to rule, aided by a Privy Council in which seats were drawn mainly from the top posts within the civil service. The noble influence on royal decision-making had been drastically cut.

Christian V, king from 1670, instigated a broad system of royal honours, creating a new class of landowners who enjoyed exemptions from tax, and whose lack of concern for their tenants led Danish peasants into virtual serfdom. In 1699 **Frederik IV** set about creating a Danish militia to make the country less dependent on foreign mercenaries. With Sweden changing its allegiance towards Britain and Holland, Denmark re-established its relations with the French, which culminated in the **Great Northern War** from 1709 to 1720. This resulted in the emergence of Russia as a dominant force in the region, while Denmark emerged with a strong position in Schleswig, and Sweden's exemption from the Sound Toll was ended.

The two decades of peace that followed saw the arrival of **Pietism**, a form of Lutheranism which strove to renew the devotional ideal. Frederik embraced the doctrine towards the end of his life, and it was adopted in full by his son, **Christian VI**, who took the throne in 1730. He prohibited entertainment on Sunday, closed down the Royal Theatre, and made court life a sombre affair: attendance at church on Sundays became compulsory and confirmation obligatory.

■ **The Enlightenment**

Despite the beliefs of the monarch, Pietism was never widely popular, and by the 1740s its influence had waned considerably. The reign of **Frederik V**, from 1746, saw a great cultural awakening: grand buildings such as Amalienborg and Frederikskirke were erected in Copenhagen (though the latter's completion was delayed for twenty years), and there was a new flourishing of the arts. The king, perhaps as a reaction to the puritanism of his father, devoted himself to a life of pleasure and allowed control of the nation effectively to pass to the civil service. **Neutrality** was maintained through several international conflicts and the economy benefited as a consequence.

In 1766 Frederik's heir, **Christian VII**, who had scarcely more credibility as a ruler, took the crown. His mental state was unstable, his moods ranging from deep lethargy to rage and drunkenness. By 1771 he had become incapable of carrying out even the minimum of official duties. The king's council, filled by a fresh generation of ambitious young men, insisted that the king effect his own will – under guidance from them – and disregard the suggestions of his older advisers.

Decision-making became dominated by a German court physician, **Johann Freidrich Struensee**, who had accompanied the king on a tour of England and had gained much of the credit for the good behaviour of the unpredictable monarch. Struensee combined personal arrogance with a sympathy for many of the ideas then fashionable elsewhere in Europe; he spoke no Danish (German was the court language) and had no concern for Danish traditions. Through him a number of sweeping **reforms** were executed: the Privy Council was abolished, the Treasury became the supreme administrative organ, the death penalty was abolished, the moral code lost many of its legal sanctions, and the press was freed from censorship.

There was opposition from several quarters. Merchants complained about the freeing of trade, and the burghers of Copenhagen were unhappy about their city losing its autonomy. In addition, there were well-founded rumours about the relationship between Struensee and the queen. Since nothing was known outside the court of the king's mental state, it was assumed that the monarch was being held prisoner. Struensee was forced to reintroduce censorship of the press as their editorials began to mount attacks on him. The Royal Guards mutinied when their disbandment was ordered, while at the same time a coup was being plotted by Frederik V's second wife, Juliane Marie of Brunswick, and her son, Frederik. After a masked ball at the palace in 1772, Struensee was arrested and tried, and soon afterwards beheaded. The dazed king was paraded before his cheering subjects.

The court came under the control – in ascending order of influence – of Frederik, Juliane, and a minister, **Ove Høegh-Guldberg**. All those who had been appointed to office by Struensee were dismissed, and while Høegh-Guldberg eventually incurred the wrath of officials by operating in much the same arrogant fashion as Struensee had, he recognized – and exploited – the anti-German feelings that had been growing for some time. Danish became the language of command in the army and later the court language, and in 1776 it was declared that no foreigner should be given a position in royal office.

In the wider sphere, the country prospered through dealings in the Far East, and Copenhagen consolidated its role as the new centre of Baltic trade. The outbreak of the American War of Independence provided neutral Denmark with fresh commercial opportunities. In 1780 Denmark joined the **League of Armed Neutrality** with Russia, Prussia and Sweden, which had the effect of maintaining trading links across the Atlantic until the end of the war.

Faced with the subsequent conflict between Britain and revolutionary France, Denmark joined the second armed neutrality league with Russia and Sweden, until a British naval venture into the Baltic during 1801 obliged withdrawal. British fears that Denmark would join Napoleon's continental blockade resulted in a British attack led by Admiral Nelson, which destroyed the Danish fleet in Copenhagen. The pact between France and Russia left Denmark in a difficult situation. To oppose this alliance would leave them exposed to a French invasion of Jutland. To oppose the British and join with the French would adversely affect trade. As the Danes tried to stall for time, the British lost patience, occupying Zealand and commencing a three-day bombardment of Copenhagen. On their inevitable surrender, the Danes were left with little option but to join with Napoleon, although it was becoming clear that his was to be the losing side. Sweden had aligned with the British and was demanding the ceding of Norway if Denmark were to be defeated – which, under the **Treaty of Kiel**, is what happened.

■ The Age of Liberalism

The Napoleonic Wars destroyed Denmark's international prestige and left the country bankrupt, and the period up until 1830 was spent in recovery. But the king remained popular, believed to have the welfare of his subjects at heart.

Meanwhile, in the arts, a **national romantic movement** was gaining pace. The sculptor Thorvaldsen and the writer/philosopher Kierkegaard are perhaps the best-known figures to emerge from the era, but the most influential domestically was a theologian called **N.F.S. Grundtvig**, who, in 1810, developed a new form of Christianity – one that was free of dogma and drew on the virtues espoused by the heroes of Norse mythology. In 1825 he left the intellectual circles of Copenhagen and travelled the rural areas to guide a religious revival, eventually modifying his earlier ideas in favour of a new faith in the wisdom of "the people" – something that was to colour the future liberal movement.

On the political front, there was trouble brewing in Danish-speaking **Schleswig** and German-speaking **Holstein**. The Treaty of Kiel had compelled the king to relinquish Holstein to the Confederation of German States – although, confusingly, he remained duke of the province. He promised the setting up of a consultative assembly for the region, while within Holstein a campaign sought to pressure the king into granting the duchy its own constitution. The campaign was stamped on hard, but the problems of the region still weren't resolved. Further demands called for a complete separation from Denmark, with the duchies being brought together as a single independent state. The establishment of consultative assemblies in both Holstein and Schleswig eventually came about in 1831, though they lacked any real political muscle.

Although absolutism had been far more benevolent towards the ordinary people in Denmark than to their counterparts elsewhere in Europe, interest was growing in the liberalism that was sweeping through the continent. In Copenhagen a group of scholars proffered the idea that Schleswig be brought closer into Danish affairs, and in pursuit of this they formed the Liberal Party and brought pressure to bear for a new liberal constitution. As the government wavered in its response, the liberal movement grew and its first newspaper, *Fædrelandet*, appeared in 1834.

In 1837 the crown agreed to the introduction of elected town councils and, four years later, to elected bodies in parishes and counties. Although the franchise was restricted, many small farmers gained political awareness through their participation in the local councils.

Frederik IV died in 1839 and was replaced by **Christian VIII**. As Crown Prince of Norway, Christian had approved a liberal constitution in that country but surprised Danish liberals by not agreeing to a similar constitution at home. In 1848 he was succeeded by his son **Frederik VII.** Meanwhile, the liberals had organized themselves into the **National Liberal Party**, and the king signed a **new constitution** that made Denmark the most democratic country in Europe, guaranteeing freedom of speech, freedom of religious worship, and many civil liberties. Legislation was to be put in the hands of a *Rigsdag* elected by popular vote and consisting of two chambers – the lower *folketing* and upper *landsting*. The king gave up the powers of an absolute monarch, but his signature was still required before bills approved by the *Rigsdag* could become law. And he could select his own ministers.

Within Schleswig-Holstein, however, there was little faith that the equality granted to them in the constitution would be upheld. A delegation from the duchies went to Copenhagen to call for Schleswig to be combined with Holstein within the German Confederation. A Danish compromise suggested a free constitution for Holstein with Schleswig remaining as part of Denmark, albeit with its own legislature and autonomy in its internal administration. The Schleswig-Holsteiners rejected this and formed a provisional government in Kiel.

The inevitable war that followed was to last for three years and, once Prussia's support was withdrawn, it ended in defeat for the duchies. The Danish prime minister, C.C. Hall, drew up a fresh constitution that included Schleswig as part of Denmark but totally excluded Holstein. Despite widespread misgivings within the *Rigsdag*, the constitution was narrowly voted through. Frederik died before he could give the royal assent and it fell to **Christian IX** to put his name to the document that would almost certainly trigger another war.

It did, and under the peace terms Denmark ceded both Schleswig and Holstein to Germany, leaving the country smaller than it had been for centuries. The blame was laid firmly on the National Liberals, and the new government, appointed by the king and drawn from the affluent landowners, saw its initial task as replacing the constitution, drawn up to deal with the Schleswig-Holstein crisis, with one far less liberal in content. The election of 1866 resulted in a narrow majority in the *Rigsdag* favouring a new constitution. When this came to be implemented, it retained the procedure for election to the *folketing*, but made the *landsting* franchise dependent on land and money and allowed 12 of the 64 members to be selected by the king.

The landowners worked in limited co-operation with the National Liberals and the Centre Party (a less conservative version of the National Liberals). In opposition, a number of interests, encompassing everything from leftist radicals to followers of Grundtvig, were shortly combined into the **United Left**, which put forward the first political manifesto seen in Denmark. It called for equal taxation, universal suffrage in local elections, more freedom for the farmers, and contained a vague demand for closer links with the other Scandinavian countries. The United Left became the majority within the *folketing* in 1872.

The ideas of **revolutionary socialism** had begun percolating through the country around 1871 via a series of pamphlets edited by Louis Pio, who attempted to organize a Danish *Internationale*. In April 1872, Pio led 1200 bricklayers into a strike, announcing a mass meeting on May 5. The government banned the meeting and had Pio arrested: he was sentenced to five years in prison and the Danish *Internationale* was banned. The workers began forming trade unions and workers' associations.

The intellectual left also became active. A series of lectures delivered by Georg Brandes in Copenhagen cited Danish culture, in particular its literature, as dull and lifeless compared to that of other countries. He called for fresh works that questioned and examined society, instigating a bout of literary attacks on institutions such as marriage, chastity and the family. As a backlash, conservative groups in the government formed themselves into the **United Right** under Prime Minister **J.B.S. Estrup**.

The left did their best to obstruct the government but, as time went on, they lost seats while the strength of the right grew. In 1889, the left issued a manifesto calling for reductions in military expenditure, a declaration of neutrality, the provision of old age pensions, sick pay, a limit to working hours, and votes for women. The elections of 1890 improved the left's position in the *folketing*, and also saw the election of two **Social Democrats**. With this, the left moved further towards moderation and compromise with the right. The trade unions, whose membership escalated in proportion to the numbers employed in the new industries, grew in stature, and were united as the Association of Trade Unions in 1898. The Social Democratic Party grew stronger with the support of the industrial workers, although it had no direct connection with the trade unions.

■ Parliamentary democracy and World War I

By the end of the century the power of the right was in severe decline. The elections of 1901, under the new conditions of a secret ballot, saw them reduced to the smallest group within the *folketing* and heralded the beginning of **parliamentary democracy**.

The government of 1901 was the first real democratic government, assembled with the intention of balancing differing political tendencies – and it brought in a number of reforms. Income tax was introduced on a sliding scale, and free schooling beyond the primary level began. As years went by, Social Democrat support increased, and the left, such as they were, became increasingly conservative; indeed they were barely left-wing at all and are better referred to under their Danish name, *Venstre*. In 1905 a breakaway group formed the **Radical Left**, *Det Radikale Venstre* (politically similar to the English Liberals), calling for the reduction of the armed forces to the status of coastal and border guards, greater social equality, and votes for women.

An alliance between the Radicals and Social Democrats enabled the two parties to gain a large majority in the *folketing* in the election of 1913, and a year later conservative control of the *landsting* was ended. Social advances were made, but further domestic progress was halted by international events as Europe prepared for war.

Denmark had enjoyed good trading relations with both Germany and Britain in the year preceding **World War I** and was keen not to be seen to favour either side in the hostilities. On the announcement of the German mobilization, the now Radical-led cabinet, with the support of all the other parties, issued a **statement of neutrality** and was able to remain clear of direct involvement in the conflict.

At the conclusion of the war, attention was turned again towards Schleswig-Holstein, and under the **Treaty of Versailles** it was decided that Schleswig should be divided into two zones

for a referendum. In the northern zone a return to unification with Denmark was favoured by a large percentage, while the southern zone elected to remain part of Germany. A new German–Danish border was drawn up just north of Flensburg.

High rates of unemployment and the success of the Russian Bolsheviks led to a series of strikes and demonstrations, the unrest coming to a head with the **Easter crisis** of 1920. During March of that year, a change in the electoral system towards greater proportional representation was agreed in the *folketing* but the prime minister, **CTh Zahle**, whose Radicals stood to lose support through the change, refused to implement it. The king, Christian X, responded by dismissing him and asking **Otto Liebe** to form a caretaker government to oversee the changes. The royal intervention, while technically legal, incensed the Social Democrats and the trade unions, who were already facing a national lockout by employers in response to demands for improved pay rates. The unions, perceiving the threat of a right-wing coup, began organizing a general strike to begin after the Easter holiday. There was a large republican demonstration outside Amalienborg.

On Easter Saturday, urgent negotiations beween the king and the existing government concluded with an agreement that a mutually acceptable caretaker government would oversee the electoral change and a fresh election would immediately follow. Employers, fearful of the power the workers had shown, met many of the demands for higher wages.

The next government was dominated by the *Venstre*. They fortified existing social policies, and increased state contributions to union unemployment funds. But a general economic depression continued, and there was widespread industrial unrest as the *krone* declined in value and living standards fell. A **general strike** lasted for a month and a workers' demonstration in Randers was subdued by the army.

Venstre and the Social Democrats jostled for position over the next decade, though under the new electoral system no one party could achieve enough power to undertake major reform. The economy did improve, however, and state influence spread further through Danish society than ever before. Enlightened reforms were put on the agenda, too, making a deliberately clean break with the moral standpoints of the past – notably on abortion and illegitimacy. Major public works were funded, such as the bridge between Funen and Jutland over the Lille Bælt, and the *Stormstrømsbro*, linking Zealand to Falster.

■ The Nazi occupation

While Denmark had little military significance for the Nazis, the sea off Norway was being used to transport iron ore from Sweden to Britain, and the fjords offered good shelter for a fleet engaged in a naval war in the Atlantic. To get to Norway, the Nazis planned an invasion of Denmark. At 4am on April 9, 1940, the German ambassador in Copenhagen informed Prime Minister Stauning that German troops were preparing to cross the Danish border and issued the ultimatum that unless Denmark agreed that the country could be used as a German military base – keeping control of its own affairs – Copenhagen would be bombed. To reject the demand was considered a postponement of the inevitable, and to save Danish bloodshed the government acquiesced at 6am. "They took us by telephone," said a Danish minister.

A national coalition government was formed which behaved according to protocol but gave no unnecessary concessions to the Germans. Censorship of the press and a ban on demonstrations were imposed, ostensibly intended to prevent the Nazis spreading propaganda. But these measures, like the swiftness of the initial agreement, were viewed by some Danes as capitulation and were to be a thorn in the side of the Social Democrats for years to come.

The government was reshuffled to include non-parliamentary experts, one of whom, **Erik Scavenius**, a former foreign minister, conceived an ill-fated plan to gain the confidence of the Germans. He issued a statement outlining the government's friendly attitude to the occupying power, and even praised the German military victory – which upset the Danish public and astonished the Germans, who asked whether Denmark would like to enter into commercial agreement immediately rather than wait until the end of the war. Scavenius was powerless to do anything other than agree, and a deal was signed within days. Under its terms, the krone was to be phased out and German currency made legal tender.

Public reaction was naturally hostile, and Scavenius was, not surprisingly, regarded as a traitor. Groups of Danes began a systematic display of antipathy to the Germans. Children wore red, white and blue "RAF caps", Danish customers walked out of cafés when Germans entered, and the ban on demonstrations was flouted by groups who gathered to sing patriotic songs. On September 1, 1940, an estimated 739,000 Danes around the country gathered to sing the same song simultaneously. The king demonstrated his continued presence by riding on horseback each morning through Copenhagen.

Meanwhile, the Danish government continued its balancing act, knowing that failure to cooperate at least to some degree would lead to a complete Nazi takeover. It was with this in mind that Denmark signed the Anti-Comintern Pact making communism illegal, but insisted on the insertion of a clause that allowed only Danish police to arrest Danish communists.

Vilhelm Buhl, who was appointed prime minister on May 3, 1942, had been an outspoken opponent of the signing of the Anti-Comintern Pact and it was thought he might end the apparent appeasement. Instead, the tension between occupiers and occupied was to climax with Hitler's anger at the curt note received from Christian X in response to the Führer's birthday telegram. Although it was the king's standard reply, Hitler took the mere "thank you" as an insult and immediately replaced his functionaries in Denmark with hardliners who demanded a new pro-German government.

Scavenius took control, and, in 1943, with the idea of showing that free elections could take place under German occupation, elections were called. The government asked the public to demonstrate faith in national unity by voting for any one of the four parties in the coalition, and received overwhelming support in the largest ever turnout for a Danish election.

Awareness that German defeat was becoming inevitable stimulated a wave of strikes throughout the country. Berlin declared a state of emergency in Denmark, and demanded that the Danish government comply – which it refused to do. Germany took over administration of the country, interning many politicians. The king was asked to appoint a cabinet from outside the *folketing*, and Germans were free for the first time to round up Danish Jews. Resistance was organized under the leadership of the **Danish Freedom Council**. Sabotage was carefully coordinated, and an underground army, soon comprising over 43,000, prepared to assist in the Allied invasion. In June 1944, rising anti-Nazi violence led to a curfew being imposed in Copenhagen and assemblies of more than five people being banned, to which workers responded with a spontaneous general strike. German plans to starve the city had to be abandoned after five days.

■ The postwar period

After the German surrender in May 1945, a **liberation government** was created, composed equally of prewar politicians and members of the Danish Freedom Council, with Vilhelm Buhl as prime minister. Its internal differences earned the administration the nickname "the debating club".

While the country had been spared the devastation seen elsewhere in Europe, it still found itself with massive economic problems and it soon became apparent that the liberation government could not function. In the ensuing election there was a swing to the Communists, and a minority *Venstre* government was formed. The immediate concern was to strengthen the economy, although the resurfacing of the southern Schleswig issue began to dominate the *Rigsdag*.

Domestic issues soon came to be overshadowed by the **international situation** as the Cold War began. Denmark had unreservedly joined the United Nations in 1945, and had joined the IMF and World Bank to gain financial help in restoring its economy. In 1947 Marshall Plan aid brought further assistance. As world power became polarized between East and West, the Danish government at first tried to remain impartial, but in 1947 agreed to join NATO – a total break with the established concept of Danish neutrality (though, to this day, the Danes remain opposed to nuclear weapons).

The years after the war were marked by much political manoeuvring among the Radicals, Social Democrats and Conservatives, resulting in many hastily called elections and a number of ineffectual compromise coalitions distinguished mainly by the level of their infighting. Working-class support for the Social Democrats steadily eroded, and support for the Communists was largely transferred to the new, more revisionist, Socialist People's Party.

Social reforms, however, continued apace, not least in the 1960s with the abandoning of all forms of censorship and the institution of free abortion on demand. Such measures are typical of more recent social policy, though Denmark's odd position between Scandinavia and the rest of mainland Europe still persists. A referendum held

in 1972 to determine whether Denmark should join the EC resulted in a substantial majority in favour, making Denmark the first Scandinavian country in the community – Sweden joined the EU in 1995 – though public enthusiasm remained lukewarm.

■ The 1970s and 1980s

Perhaps the biggest change in the 1970s was the foundation – and subsequent influence – of the new **Progress Party** (*Fremskridtspartiet*), headed by Mogens Glistrup, who came to national attention on TV, claiming to have an income of over a million kroner but to be paying no income tax at all through manipulation of the tax laws. The Progress Party stood on a ticket of drastic tax cuts and Glistrup went on to compare tax avoidance with the sabotaging of Nazi railway lines during the war. He also announced that if elected he would replace the Danish defence force with an answering machine saying "we surrender" in Russian. Eventually he was imprisoned after an investigation by the Danish tax office; released in 1985, he set himself up as a tax consultant.

What the success of the Progress Party pointed to was dissatisfaction with both the economy and the established parties' strategies for dealing with its problems. In September 1982, after yet more *Venstre*/Social Democrat/Socialist coalitions, **Poul Schlüter** became the country's first Conservative prime minister of the twentieth century, leading the widest-ranging coalition yet seen – the Conservatives joined by the *Venstre*, Centre Democrats and Christian People's Party.

In keeping with the prevailing political climate in the rest of Europe, the prescription for Denmark's economic malaise was seen to be spending cuts, not sparing the social services, and an extension of taxation into previously untapped areas such as pension funds. A 4 percent ceiling was set on wage increases. The government failed to win a sufficient majority in the *folketing* and an early election was called for January 1984. The goverment was returned, and felt the public had given it a mandate to continue its policies, which it did until the call for a snap election in 1987.

The result was a significant swing to the left. The centre-right coalition lost seven seats and the Social Democrats, despite losing two seats, became by far the largest party in the *folketing*. The People's Socialists fared extremely well, finishing with 27 MPs. Schlüter resigned as prime minister but was then asked to form a new government after being nominated to do so by six of the nine party leaders within the *folketing*. His failure to consult non-government parties in seeking a majority was regarded as highly irregular but not unconstitutional. He made an informal agreement with the Progress Party in order to gain a single-seat working majority in the *folketing*. Three of the four seats lost by the Conservatives had gone to the Progress Party, who espoused tax cuts and immigration curbs. Their former leader, Mogens Glistrup, was returned to the *folketing* and announced his intention to be prime minister in "five to ten years".

A further election, in May 1988, largely served to affirm the new Schlüter-led government, if only, perhaps, because of the apparent lack of any workable alternative.

■ The current political scene

In January 1993 Schlüter's government was forced to resign over a political scandal, when it was revealed that asylum had been denied to Sri Lankan Tamil refugees in the late 1980s and early 1990s, in contravention of Danish law. The Social Democrats, led by **Poul Nyrup Rasmussen**, took power and formed a four-party coalition. For the first time in ten years Denmark was ruled by a majority government. Since the 1994 election Nyrup Rasmussen has presided over a centre-left majority coalition, which has been criticized for its weak policies on tax reform, the welfare state and the thorny issue of **European union**.

Though traditionally a reluctant member of the EC, Denmark was carried into the European **Exchange Rate Mechanism** (or ERM, widely viewed as the first step towards a single European currency) by Schlüter at the start of the 1990s, a move that transformed the Danish economy into one of the strongest in Europe and made its inflation rate the lowest of any EC member. The price for this, however was soaring unemployment and further cuts in public spending.

The outcome of the **referendum on the Maastricht treaty** (the blueprint for European political and monetary union) in June 1992, however, provided an unexpected upset to the Schlüter apple cart. Despite calls for a "Yes" vote not only from the government but also from the opposition Social Democrats, over 50 percent of Danes rejected the treaty – severely embarrassing the prime minister and sending shivers down the spine of every western European government.

The Danish **anti-Maastricht camp** was a curious alliance of the reformed Marxists of the People's Socialists, the right-wingers of the Progress Party, and assorted environmentalists and peace campaigners – an indication of how fears of a European Superstate and a loss of national sovereignty were spread across a broad cross-section of the population. The government and other pro-Europe parties didn't give up, however, but set to work on a revised version of the Maastricht Treaty, with the emphasis on protecting national interests – it included a pledge allowing the Danish people to reject citizenship of a United Europe. A **second referendum** in May 1993 was a triumph for the government, with almost 57 percent of the Danish population voting in favour of the new Treaty. Anti-European feelings, already intense, reached boiling point, and the night after the referendum young left-wingers and anarchists came together in central Copenhagen to declare the area a "EU-free zone". The police moved in to break up the demonstration, battles with the demonstrators ensued, and for the first time ever the Danish police opened fire against a crowd of civilians. Fortunately nobody died, but the incident sparked off a major investigation into the actions of the police, which is still ongoing. While Denmark has successfully avoided the risk of economic isolation in an increasingly integrated European community, doubts among the Danish people remain, along with a continuing dissatisfaction at the way the yes vote was achieved.

A BRIEF GUIDE TO DANISH

Danish in some ways is similar to German, but there are significant differences in pronunciation, Danes tending to swallow the ending of many words and leave certain letters silent. English is widely understood, as is German; young people especially often speak both fluently. And if you can speak Swedish or Norwegian then you should have little problem making yourself understood – all three languages share the same root. A handy phrasebook to take is *Traveller's Scandinavia* (Pan) – which, as well as Danish, covers Norwegian and Swedish.

PRONUNCIATION

In **pronunciation**, unfamiliar **vowels** include:

æ when long between a**i**r and t**ai**lor. When short like g**e**t. When next to "r" sounds more like h**a**t.

å when long like s**a**w, when short like **o**n.

ø like f**u**r but with the lips rounded.

e, when long, is similar to pl**a**te, when short somewhere between pl**a**te and h**i**t; when unstressed it's as in **a**bove.

Consonants are pronounced as in English, except:

d at the end of a word after a vowel, or between a vowel and an unstressed "e" or "i", like **th**is. Sometimes silent at the end of a word.

g at the beginning of a word or syllable as in **g**o. At the end of a word or long vowel, or before an unstressed e, usually like **y**et but sometimes like the Scottish lo**ch**. Sometimes mute after an a, e, or o.

hv like **v**iew

hj like **y**et

k as English except between vowels, when it's as in **g**o.

p as English except between vowels, when it's as in **b**it.

r pronounced as in French from the back of the throat but often silent.

sj as in **sh**eet

t as English except between vowels, when it's as in **d**o. Often mute when at the end of a word.

y between b**ee** and p**oo**l

BASICS

Do you speak English?	*Taler De engelsk?*	Goodnight	*Godnat*
Yes	*Ja*	Goodbye	*Farvel*
No	*Nej*	Yesterday	*I går*
I don't understand	*Jeg forstår det ikke*	Today	*I dag*
I understand	*Jeg forstår*	Tomorrow	*I morgen*
Please	*Værså venlig*	Day after	*I overmorgen*
Thank you	*Tak*	tomorrow	
Excuse me	*Undskyld*	In the morning	*Om morgenen*
Good morning	*Godmorgen*	In the afternoon	*Om eftermiddagen*
Good afternoon	*Goddag*	In the evening	*Om aftenen*

SOME SIGNS

Entrance	*Indgang*	Arrival	*Ankomst*
Exit	*Udgang*	Departure	*Afgang*
Push/pull	*Skub/træk*	Police	*Politi*
Danger	*Fare*	No Smoking	*Rygning forbudt/Ikke rygere*
Gentlemen	*Herrer*	No Entry	*Ingen adgang*
Ladies	*Damer*	No Camping	*Campering forbudt*
Open	*Åben*	No Trespassing	*Adgang forbudt for*
Closed	*Lukket*		*uvedkommende*

continued overleaf...

A BRIEF GUIDE TO DANISH contd.

QUESTIONS AND DIRECTIONS

Where is?	*Hvor er?*	Near/far	*Er det nær/fjern*
When?	*Hvornår?*	Left/right	*Venstre/højre*
What?	*Hvad?*	Straight ahead	*Ligeud*
Why?	*Hvorfor?*	I'd like. . .	*Jeg vil gerne ha. . .*
Who?	*Hvem?*	Where is the youth	*Hvor er vandrerhjemmet?*
How much?	*Hvor meget?*	hostel?	
How much does it	*Hvad koster det?*	Can we camp here?	*Må vi campere her?*
cost?		It's too expensive	*Det er for dyrt*
Here	*Her*	Where are the toilets?	*Hvor er toiletterne ?*
There	*Der*	How far is it to. . .?	*Hvor langt er der til. . .?*
Good/bad	*God/dårlig*	Where can I get a	*Hvor kan jeg tage/*
Cheap/expensive	*Billig/dyr*	train/bus/ferry to. . .?	*bussen/færgen til. . .?*
Hot/cold	*Varm/kold*	At what time does. . .?	*Hvornår går. . .?*
Better/bigger/cheaper	*Bedre/større/billigere*	Ticket	*Billet*

NUMBERS

0	*Nul*	9	*Ni*	18	*Atten*	80	*Firs*
1	*En*	10	*Ti*	19	*Nitten*	90	*Halvfems*
2	*To*	11	*Elleve*	20	*Tyve*	100	*Hundrede*
3	*Tre*	12	*Tolv*	21	*Enogtyve*	101	*Hundrede og et*
4	*Fire*	13	*Tretten*	30	*Tredive*	151	*Hundrede og*
5	*Fem*	14	*Fjorten*	40	*Fyrre*		*enoghalvtreds*
6	*Seks*	15	*Femten*	50	*Halvtreds*	200	*To hundrede*
7	*Syv*	16	*Seksten*	60	*Tres*	1000	*Tusind*
8	*Otte*	17	*Sytten*	70	*Halvfjerds*		

DAYS AND MONTHS

Monday	*mandag*	January	*januar*	July	*juli*
Tuesday	*tirsdag*	February	*februar*	August	*august*
Wednesday	*onsdag*	March	*marts*	September	*september*
Thursday	*torsdag*	April	*april*	October	*oktober*
Friday	*fredag*	May	*maj*	November	*november*
Saturday	*lørdag*	June	*juni*	December	*december*
Sunday	*søndag*				

(Days and months are never capitalised)

GLOSSARY OF DANISH TERMS AND WORDS

Banegård	Railway station	*Herregård*	Manor house	*Rutebilstation*	Bus station
Bakke	Hill or ridge	*Jernebane*	Railway	*Rådhus*	Town hall
Domkirke	Cathedral	*Kirke*	Church	*Skov*	Wood or forest
Gammel or	Old	*Klint*	Cliff	*Stue*	Room
Gamle		*Kloster*	Monastery	*Sø*	Lake
Hav	Sea	*Kro*	Inn	*Torvet*	Market square
Havn	Harbour	*Plads*	Square	*Tårn*	Tower
				Vand	Water

CHAPTER ONE

ZEALAND

A s home to Copenhagen, **Zealand** (*Sjælland*) is Denmark's most important – and most visited – region. Tucked away on the east coast of the biggest Danish island, the nation's capital, though not an especially large city, dominates much of Zealand, and the nearby towns, while far from being drab suburbia, tend inevitably to be dormitory territory. Only much further away, towards the west and south, does the pace become more provincial.

It would be perverse to come to Zealand and not visit **Copenhagen** – easily the most extrovert and cosmopolitan place in the country, and as lively by night as it is by day. But once there you should make at least a brief journey out of the city to see how different the rest of Denmark can be. Woods and expansive parklands appear almost as soon as you leave the city – and even if you don't like what you find, the swiftness of the metropolitan transport network, which covers almost half the island, means that you can be back in the capital in easy time for an evening drink.

North of Copenhagen, the coastal road passes the outstanding modern art museum of **Louisiana** and the absorbing Karen Blixen museum at **Rungsted**, before reaching **Helsingør**. The only place where you can cross by train into Sweden, this is also the site of the renowned **Kronborg Slot** – an impressive fortification, though quite unfairly stealing the spotlight from **Frederiksborg Slot**, the castle at nearby **Hillerød**. West of Copenhagen and on the main route to Funen is **Roskilde**, a former capital with an extravagant cathedral that's still the last resting place for Danish monarchs, and with a gorgeous location on the Roskilde fjord – from where five Viking boats were salvaged that are now restored and displayed in a specially built museum. South of Copenhagen, at the end of the urban S-train system, is **Køge**, which – beyond the industrial sites that flank it – has a well-preserved medieval centre and long, sandy beaches lining its bay.

Further out from the sway of Copenhagen, Zealand's towns are appreciably smaller, more scattered, and far less full of either commuters or day-trippers. **Ringsted**, plumb in the heart of the island, is another one-time capital, a fact marked by the twelfth- and thirteenth-century royal tombs in its church. Further south, **Næstved**, surrounded by lush countryside, gives access to three smaller islands just off the coast: **Lolland**, **Falster** and **Møn**. Each of these is busy during the summer but outside high season you'll find them green and peaceful, with Lolland forming a leisurely backdoor route, via Langeland, to Funen.

Not part of Zealand, but conveniently reached by ferry from Copenhagen, is the island of **Bornholm**. A huge slab of granite in the Baltic, it houses a few small fishing communities, and has some fine beaches and an unusual history, making a stimulating detour if you're heading for Sweden – it's nearer Sweden than Denmark, with regular ferry connections.

COPENHAGEN

COPENHAGEN, as any Dane will tell you, is no introduction to Denmark; indeed, a greater contrast with the sleepy provincialism of the rest of the country would be hard to find. Despite that, the city completely dominates Denmark: it is the seat of all the

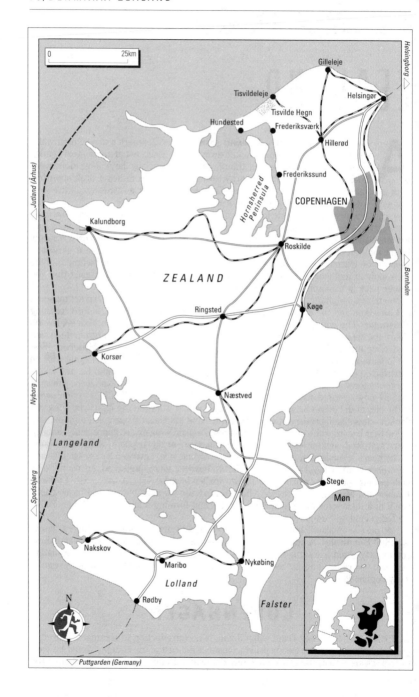

nation's institutions – politics, finance, the arts – and provides the driving force for the country's social reforms. Copenhagen is also easily Scandinavia's most affordable capital, and one of Europe's most user-friendly cities: small and welcoming, a place where people rather than cars set the pace, as evidenced by the multitude of outside-café tables and a small centre largely given over to pedestrians. In summer especially there's a varied range of lively street entertainment, while at night there are plenty of cosy bars and an intimate club and live music network that can hardly be bettered. This is not to mention the city's beckoning history collections and galleries of Danish and international art, as well as a worthy batch of smaller museums. If you're intent on heading north into Scandinavia's less populated (and pricier) reaches, you'd certainly be wise to spend a few days living it up in Copenhagen first.

There was no more than a tiny fishing settlement here until the twelfth century, when Bishop Absalon oversaw the building of a castle on the site of the present Christiansborg. The settlement's prosperity grew after Erik of Pomerania granted it special privileges and imposed the Sound Toll on vessels passing through the Øresund, then under Danish control – which gave the expanding city tidy profits and enabled a self-confident trading centre to flourish. Following the demise of the Hanseatic ports, the city became the Baltic's principal harbour, earning the name København ("merchant's port"), and in 1443 it was made the Danish capital. A century later, Christian IV began the building programme that was the basis of the modern city: up went Rosenborg Slot, Børsen, Rundetårnet, and the districts of Nyboder and Christianshavn; and in 1669 Frederik III graced the city with its first royal palace, Amalienborg, for his queen, Sophie Amalie.

Like much of the Copenhagen of that time, these structures still exist, and the taller of them remain the major peaks on what is a refreshingly low skyline. It's an easy city to get around: you're unlikely to need to venture far from the central section, still largely hemmed in by the medieval ramparts (now a series of parks), which is where most of the activity and sights are contained.

Arrival, information and city transport

However you get to Copenhagen you'll be within easy reach of the centre. Trains pull into the **Central Station** (*Hovedbanegården*), near Vesterbrogade. Downstairs, the *InterRail Centre* (July to mid-Sept daily 7am–1am), restricted to *InterRail* or *Eurail* pass holders, is a useful refuge for long-distance travellers, with large left-luggage lockers, showers (20kr), cooking facilities, a rest area and a message board. **Long-distance buses** from other parts of Denmark stop only a short bus or S-train ride from the centre: buses from Århus stop at Valby; buses from Aalborg at Ryparken Station on S-train line H; and those from Hanstholm and Fjerritsslev on Hans Knudsens Plads. **Ferries** from Norway and Sweden dock close to Nyhavn, a few minutes' walk from the inner city. From **Kastrup Airport**, 8km from the city, *SAS* coaches run every twenty minutes to Central Station (20min; 35kr), or there's a slower but cheaper city bus (#32) to Rådhuspladsen.

Information

Once here, your first stop should be **Use-It**, centrally placed at the back of the *Huset* complex at Rådhusstræde 13 (mid-June to mid-Sept daily 9am–7pm; rest of the year Mon–Fri 10am–4pm; ☎33/156518). They provide a full rundown on budget accommodation, eating, drinking and entertainment, a free city map, will hold mail and store luggage, and in summer issue *Playtime*, a small but vital free newspaper. There's also a regular **tourist office** at Bernstorffsgade 1 (May Mon–Fri 9am–5pm, Sat 9am–2pm,

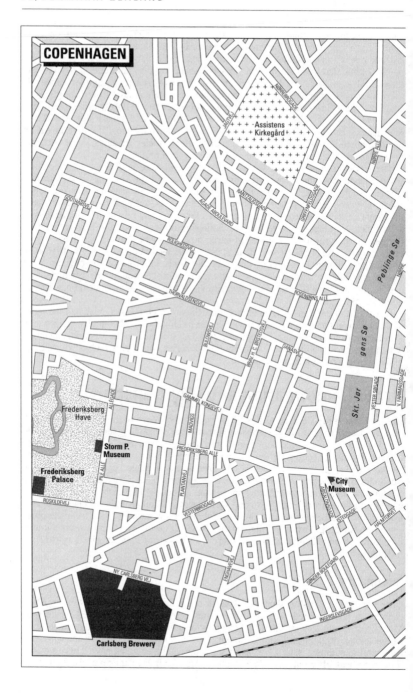

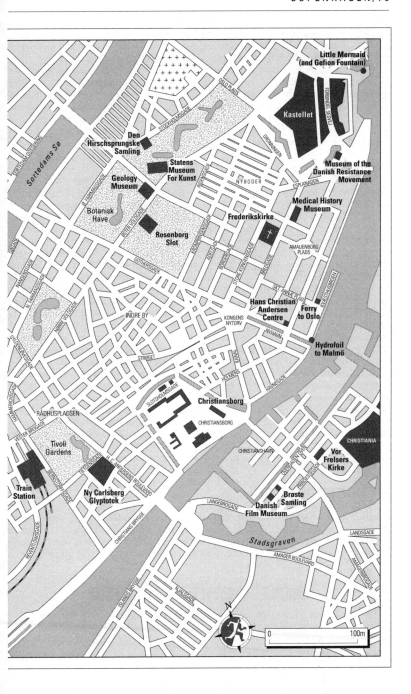

Little Mermaid
(and Gefion Fountain)

Kastellet

Den
Hirschsprungske
Samling

Statens
Museum
For Kunst

Geology
Museum

Museum of the
Danish Resistance
Movement

NYBODER

ESPLANADEN

Botanisk
Have

Medical History
Museum

Frederikskirke

AMALIENBORG
PLADS

Rosenborg
Slot

GOTHERSGADE

INDRE BY

Hans Christian
Andersen
Centre

Ferry
to Oslo

KONGENS
NYTORV

NYHAVN

Hydrofoil
to Malmö

STRØGET

SLOTSHOLMSGADE

Christiansborg

RÅDHUSPLADSEN

CHRISTIANSBORG

Tivoli
Gardens

CHRISTIANIA

CHRISTIANSHAVN

Vor
Frelsers
Kirke

Train
Station

Ny Carlsberg
Glyptotek

H. C. ANDERSENS BOULEVARD

LANGEBROGADE

Brøste
Samling

Danish
Film Museum

Stadsgraven

LANDSGADE

AMAGER BOULEVARD

CHRISTIANS BRYGGE

ISLANDS BRYGGE

N

0   100m

Sun 9am–1pm; June to mid-Sept daily 9am–6pm; mid-Sept to April Mon–Fri 9am–5pm, Sat 9am–noon; ☎33/111325), which provides countrywide information and distributes the free *Copenhagen This Week*, an up-to-date news and listings magazine.

If you plan on visiting many museums, either in Copenhagen or in nearby towns like Helsingør, Roskilde and Køge, consider purchasing a **Copenhagen Card** – valid for transport on the entire metropolitan system (which includes the towns mentioned above) and giving entry to virtually every museum in the area. Obviously its worth will depend on your itinerary, but the three-day card (295kr) can certainly save money if well used. It's available from the tourist office, travel agents, hotels and most train stations in the metropolitan region.

City transport

The best way to see most of Copenhagen is simply to **walk**: the inner city is compact and much of the central area pedestrianized. There is, however, an integrated zonal network of **buses** and electric **S-trains** (*S-tog*) covering Copenhagen and the surrounding areas, which run about every ten to fifteen minutes between 5am and 12.30am, after which a **night bus** (*Natbusserne*) system comes into operation – less frequent but still running once or twice an hour. You can use *InterRail* or *Eurail* cards on the S-trains, but otherwise the best option is a blue *Rabatkort* (80kr), a **ticket** with ten stamps that you cancel individually according to the length of your journey: one stamp gives unlimited transfers within one hour in one zone (ie around the centre), two stamps are good for ninety minutes and three stamps allow two hours – two or more people can use a *Rabatkort* simultaneously. For a short single journey of less than an hour, use a *Grundbillet* (12kr), which is valid for unlimited transfers within two zones in that time. Tickets can be bought on board buses or at train stations and should be stamped when boarding the bus or in the machines on station platforms. Except on buses, it's rare to be asked to show your ticket, but if you don't have one you face an instant fine of 250kr. **Route maps** cost 10kr from stations, but most free maps of the city include bus lines and a diagram of the S-train network.

Bikes can also be a good way to get around the city, and are handy for exploring the immediate countryside. The best place to rent one is *Københavns Cyklebørs*, Gothersgade 157 (☎33/140717), which charges 40–50kr a day plus a deposit of 100kr, or try any of the outlets mentioned on p.92. The basic **taxi** fare is 18kr plus 8kr per kilometre (rates increase after 6pm and at weekends) – only worth while if several people are sharing; phone *Taxa* (☎31/353535) if you need a cab, hail one in the street if it's showing the "Fri" sign, or try the rank outside Central Station.

Accommodation

Whether it's a hostel bed or a luxury hotel suite, **accommodation** of all kinds is easy to come by in Copenhagen, and almost all of it is centrally located. If you're going to be arriving late or during July and August – the busiest time of year – it is wise, especially if you're looking for a cheap place, to book in advance, if only for the first night.

ACCOMMODATION PRICE CODES

The Danish hotels listed throughout the guide have been graded according to the following price bands, based on the rate for a double room in summer, with a private bathroom usually included.

① Up to 300kr   ② 300–450kr   ③ 450–600kr   ④ over 600kr

Hotels

You won't find a grotty **hotel** in Copenhagen, but the cheaper ones often forgo the pleasures of private bathroom, phone and TV – although prices almost always include breakfast. Most of the least expensive hotels are just outside the inner centre, around Istedgade – a slightly seedy (though rarely dangerous) area on the far side of the train station. This area is also home to a number of mid-range hotels, and there's a further choice of mid-priced hotels around Nyhavn, on the other side of Indre By.

Absalon, Helgolandsgade 15 (☎31/242211). Clean and modern, with soundproofing that makes it extremely quiet and relaxing. ③

Admiral, Toldbodgade 24–28 (☎33/118282). A 200-year-old-granary beside the harbour, converted into comfortable wood-beamed rooms. ④

Ansgar, Colbjørnsensgade 29 (☎31/212196). Compact and tidy, this place actually lowers its prices in high season. No alcohol served. ③

Ibsens, Vendersgade 23 (☎33/131913). Relaxed and friendly place, popular with businessmen from Jutland. ③

Jørgensens, Rømersgade 11 (☎33/139743 or 138186). North of Istedgade, just across the Peblinge Sø from the inner centre. Though not an exclusively gay hotel, it's become popular with gay travellers; hostel-type accommodation is also on offer in the summer months (see below). ②

Mayfair, Helgolandsgade 3 (☎31/314801). Old-Danish style elegance coupled with every modern convenience. ④

Missionshotellet Nebo, Istedgade 6 (☎31/211217). Small and friendly, and one of the best deals in the price bracket in this part of the city, though they don't serve alcohol. ③

Sophie Amalie, Skt Annæ Plads 21 (☎33/133400). Large luxurious rooms, right by the harbour. ④

Triton, Helgolandsgade 7–11 (☎31/313266). A showpiece of contemporary Danish design, and well-suited to a cosy stay. ④

Turisthotellet, Riverdilsgade 5 (☎31/229839). Close to the train station; simple, friendly and good value. ②

Weber, Vesterbrogade 11b (☎31/311432). Plush, cosy, and full of charm. ④

Hostels, pensions and student accommodation

For those on a tighter budget, Copenhagen has a great selection of **hostel accommodation,** where a dormitory bed costs 80–100kr (less in the official *HI* hostels). Space is only likely to be a problem in the peak summer months, and during this time you should call ahead or turn up as early as possible to be sure of a place. For the most up-to-date information ask at *Use-It*, and check the accommodation reviews in *Playtime*.

If you're staying for more than couple of weeks, **pensions** can save a lot of money over hotels, as can **subletting a room** in a student hall or shared flat, or renting a **private room** in someone's home (from 100kr per person) – ask at *Use-It*. You can also arrange private rooms through the tourist office (Mon–Sat; ask for *Værelsesanvisningen*) for a fee of 15kr per person.

Official youth hostels

Bellahøj, Herbergvejen 8, in the Brønshøj district (☎31/289715). More homely than its rivals, situated in a residential part of the city. Simple to reach, too: about 15min from the city centre on bus #2 (night bus #902) to Herbergvejen. Buses #8, #63 and #68 also stop close by. Jan–Nov; reception closed 10am–noon; no curfew.

Copenhagen, Vejlandsallé 200 (☎32/522908). Hostel with frugal two- and four-bedded rooms. Tends to be crowded and noisy, and while there's a laundry there's no kitchen. Bus #46 (daytime only), or S-train line C to Valby or Sjælør (line A or E), then a #37 bus towards Holmens Bro – all of which takes about half an hour. No curfew.

Lyngby, Rådvad 1 (☎42/803074). Its distance from the city and early lock-up (11pm) make this a poor base for exploring Copenhagen. S-train to Lyngby (line A), then bus #187 to Rådvad. Mid-May to Oct.

Other hostels

Inter Point, Valdemarsgade 15 (☎31/311574). Run by the Danish *YMCA/YWCA*, dormitory beds cost 70kr and breakfast is 30kr. About ten minutes' walk from Central Station, or take bus #6 or #16. July to mid-Aug; curfew 12.30am.

Jørgensens, Rømersgade 11 (☎33/139743). A basic regular hotel that in summer offers six-bed dormitory accommodation for 100kr per person, including breakfast. Those without a sleeping bag can rent blankets for 30kr.

Sleep-In, Blegdamsvej 132 (☎35/265059). A vast hall divided into four-bed compartments. Nice, if busy, atmosphere, with a young and friendly staff and sporadic free gigs by local bands. Beds 70kr (breakfast 30kr) and if you don't have a sleeping bag you can rent blankets for 20kr (plus 40kr deposit). Bus #1 from Rådhuspladsen. Mid-June to Aug; closed daily noon–4pm; no curfew.

Vesterbro Ungdomsgård/City Public Hostel, Absalonsgade 8 (☎31/312070). Handily placed, ten minutes' walk from the train station between Vesterbrogade and Istedgade. There's a noisy sixty-bed dormitory on the lower floor, but less crowded conditions (4–20 beds) on other levels. Also has kitchen. Reports vary, but the atmosphere is easy-going and there's no curfew. 120kr per person, including breakfast; bed linen 30kr. Buses #6, #8 and #10 stop close by. May–Aug.

Campsites

Of Copenhagen's five **campsites**, only one is close to the city centre, although the others are fairly easily reached by public transport. There's little difference in price among them.

Absalon, Korsdalsvej 132, Rødovre (☎36/410600). About 9km to the southwest of the city and open all year. Take S-train line B to Brøndbyøster.

Bellahøj, on Hvidkildevej, near the Bellahøj youth hostel (☎31/101150). Central but grim, with long queues for the showers and cooking facilities. Buses #2, #8, #63 and #68. June–Aug.

Charlottenlund Strandpark, Strandvejen 144B, Charlottenlund (☎39/623688). Beautifully situated at Charlottenlund Beach, reached on the #6 bus route. May–Sept.

Nærum on Ravnebakken (☎42/801957). Quite a way from the centre but very pleasant: take a train to Jægersborg, then private train (*InterRail* and *Eurail* not valid) to Nærum. Cabins also available. Mid-April to mid-Sept.

Strandmøllen, Strandmøllevej 2 (☎45/505510). Around 14km north of the city, a twenty-minute ride away on S-train line C (to Klampenborg), then bus #188 towards Helsingør. Mid-May to Aug.

The City

Seeing Copenhagen is supremely easy. Most of what you're likely to want to see can be found in the city's relatively small – and effortlessly walkable – centre, between the long scythe of the harbour and a semicircular series of lakes. Within this area the divisions are well defined. **Indre By** forms the city's inner core, an intricate maze of streets, squares and alleys whose pleasure is as much in joining their daily bustle as viewing specific sights. The area **north of Gothersgade** is quite different, boldly proportioned grid-pattern streets and avenues built to accommodate the Danish nobility in the seventeenth century, reaching a pinnacle of affluence with the palaces of Amalienborg and Rosenborg. The far end of this stretch is guarded, now as three hundred years ago, by the Kastellet, which lies within the fetching open spaces of the Churchill Park. Separated by moat from Indre By, **Christiansborg** is the administrative base for the whole country, housing the national parliament and government offices as well as a number of museums and the ruins of Bishop Absalon's original castle. **Christianshavn**, across Inder Havnen – the inner harbour – provides further contrast, a tightly proportioned and traditionally working-class quarter, with a pretty waterfront lined by Dutch-style dwellings. A few blocks away lies **Christiania**, colonized by the young and homeless in the early 1970s, whose "alternative society" is an enduring con-

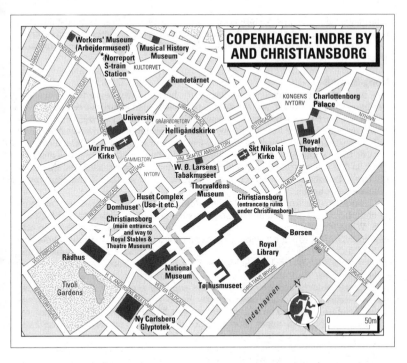

troversy in Danish life – and merits at least a look. **Vesterbrogade** is the prime route out of the city centre to the southern suburbs, but its course begins with the carefree delights of the Tivoli Gardens and leads on to the slightly less wholesome goings-on around Istedgade, before reaching the city fringes at Frederiksberg Have.

Indre By

While not actually part of **Indre By**, the main route into the inner city leads off from the buzzing open space of Rådhuspladsen. Here, the **Rådhus** (Mon–Fri 10am–3pm; free) has a spacious and elegant main hall that retains many of its original turn-of-the-century features, not least the highly polished sculptured bannisters heading up from the ground floor. There's a lift up to the belltower (at 10am, noon & 2pm; 10kr) for a not madly impressive view over the city, but more interesting is the **Jens Olsen's World Clock** (Mon–Fri 10am–4pm, Sat 10am–1pm; 10kr), in a side room close to the entrance. What looks like a mass of inscrutable dials is an astronomical timepiece which took 27 years to perfect and contains a 570,000-year calendar plotting moon and sun eclipses, solar time, local time and various planetary orbits – all with incredible accuracy. At no. 57 on Rådhuspladsen, and with an appeal of an entirely different kind, **Ripley's Believe It Or Not!** (mid-June to mid-Sept daily 10am–11pm; rest of the year Mon–Sat 10am–4.30pm; 50kr) is one of a growing international band of tourist-aimed assemblages of oddities. A model of the world's tallest man and a bicycle made from matchsticks are just two of hundreds of exhibits derived from the cartoons of American Robert L. Ripley.

Indre By proper begins with **Strøget** (literally "level measure"), a series of streets – namely Vesterbrogade, Frederiksbergade, Nygade, Vimmelskaftet Amager Torv and

Østergade – lined by pricey stores and graceless fast-food dives. Its appeal lies in the walkers, cyclists, roller-skaters and, even during the freezing winters, street entertainers who parade along it. You'll find most of Indre By's charm and historic sights in the streets northwest of Strøget.

Along Strøget

Very much the public face of Copenhagen, it's hard to imagine anything unpleasant ever happening on Strøget, and the strip is perfectly suited to stress-free ambling. The most active part is usually around Gammeltorv and Nytorv, two squares ("old" and "new") on either side of Strøget, where there's a morning fruit and vegetable market, stalls selling handmade jewellery and bric-à-brac – and frequent political rallies. It was between these squares that the fifteenth-century Rådhus stood before it was destroyed by fire in 1795. A new Rådhus was erected on Nytorv a century later, and this is now the city's **Domhuset**, or Law Courts, marked by a suitably forbidding row of Neoclassical columns.

A few minutes' further on is the **Helligåndskirken** (daily 11am–4pm), one of the oldest churches in the city, founded in the fourteenth century though largely rebuilt from 1728. While it's still in use as a place of worship, there are often art shows and other exhibitions inside, which provide a good excuse for a peek at the church's vaulted ceiling and its slender granite columns. Of equally low-key appeal is the tobacco shop directly across Strøget, which holds the **W.Ø. Larsens Tobaksmuseet** (Mon–Fri 9.30am–5pm, Sat 9am–1pm; free) and its briefly diverting clutter of vintage pipes, ornate cigar holders and every conceivable smoking accessory, plus paintings and drawings satirizing the deadly habit's rituals. Just beyond, a path leads east off Strøget, through Højbro Plads and on to the grandiose **Skt Nikolai Kirke**, where religion really takes a back pew. The upper floors of the church are used primarily as an exhibition space for contemporary artists, while at ground level there's a daytime café.

The final section of Strøget is **Østergade**, where you'll find another international tourist pull – the **Guinness World of Records Museum** (daily 10am–8pm; 48kr). It's much as you'd expect, with family-oriented exhibits on the world's tallest, fastest and smallest. Beyond, Østergade flows past the swish and chic *Hotel D'Angleterre* into the biggest of the city squares, **Kongens Nytorv**. Built on what was the edge of the city in medieval times, the square has an equestrian statue of its creator, Christian V, in its centre and a couple of grandly ageing structures around two of its shallow angles. One of these, the *Kongelige Teater* or **Royal Theatre**, dates from 1874, but the other, **Charlottenborg**, next door, was finished in 1683, at the same time as the square itself, for a son of Frederik III. It was later sold to Queen Charlotte Amalie but since 1754 has been the home of the Royal Academy of Art, which uses some of the spacious rooms for very eclectic art exhibitions. Drop in if the building's open, just to glimpse the elegant interior.

Northwest of Strøget

Don't think that by walking the length of Strøget, you've exhausted Indre By. There's much more to see among the tangle of buildings and streets **northwest of Strøget** (to the left as you walk from Rådhuspladsen). Crossing Gammeltorv and following Nørregade leads to the old university area, sometimes called the **Latin Quarter**, parts of which retain an academic function, which accounts for the book-carrying students milling around. The old university building is overlooked by **Vor Frue Kirke** (May–Aug Mon–Sat 9am–5pm, Sun noon–4.30pm; Sept–April Sun only), the cathedral of Copenhagen. Built on the site of a twelfth-century church, this dates only from 1829, rising from the devastation caused by the British bombardment in 1807. The weighty figure of Christ behind the altar and the solemn statues of the apostles, some crafted by Bertel Thorvaldsen (for more on whom, see p.82), others by his pupils, merit a quick call. From the cathedral, dodge across Skindergade into Gråbrødretorv, a cobbled square often crowded with buskers and best enjoyed from a table at one of the terrace cafés, on the way to the **Rundetårnet** (April, May, Sept & Oct Mon–Sat 10am–5pm, Sun noon–4pm; June–Aug Mon–Sat 10am–8pm, Sun noon–8pm; Nov–March Mon–Sat 11am–4pm, Sun noon–4pm, Tues & Wed also 7–10pm; 12kr). With a gradually ascending spiral ramp winding up to its summit, the round tower was built by Christian IV as an observatory, and perhaps also to provide a vantage point for his subjects to admire his additions to the city. Today the best views are of the more immediate hive of medieval streets and the pedestrian processions filling them. Legend has it that Tsar Peter the Great sped to the top on horseback in 1715, pursued by the Tsarina in a six-horse carriage – a smoother technique than descending the cobbles on a skateboard, a short-lived fad in more recent times.

After leaving the Rundetårnet, you could easily spend half an hour browsing the bookshops of Købmagergade, or visit the **Museum Erotica** (May–Aug daily 10am–11pm; Sept–April daily 10am–6pm), which lurks along here at no. 24: for the most part an exhibition on erotic art through the ages, it also boasts an up-to-date porn cinema. If your tastes are more culturally inclined, you might prefer the **Musical History Museum**, just off Kultorvet at Åbenrå 30 (Tues & Wed 10am–1pm, Fri–Sun 1–4pm; free), a deceptively large place holding an impressive quantity of musical instruments and sound-making devices, spanning the globe and the last thousand years. Naturally the bulk come from Denmark and there are some subtle comments on the social fabric of the nation to be gleaned from the yellowing photos of country dances and other get-togethers, hung alongside the instruments. Many musical recordings can be listened to through headphones, and guided tours take place every Wednesday at 11am.

Less musical sounds are provided by the cars hurtling along Nørre Voldgade, at the top of Kultorvet, which marks the edge of the pedestrianized streets of the old city. There are two reasons to queue up at the traffic lights and cross over: the first is the fruit and vegetable **market** – and Saturday flea market – on Israel Plads; the second is the **Workers' Museum** at Rømersgade 22 (*Arbejdermuseet*; Tues–Fri 10am–3pm, Sat & Sun 11am–4pm; 25kr), an engrossing and thoughtful guide to working-class life in Copenhagen from the 1930s to the 1950s, using reconstructions and authentic period materials. Entering the museum, you can walk down a reconstructed Copenhagen street complete with passing tram and a shop window hawking the consumer durables of the day, and continue, via a backyard where washing hangs drying, through a printing works subsidized by the Marshall Plan, and into a coffee shop, which sells an old-fashioned coffee and chicory blend by the cup. Elsewhere, mock-up house interiors contain family photos, newspapers and TVs showing newsreels of the time. The fixed exhibits are backed up by some outstanding temporary exhibitions from labour movements around the world.

North of Gothersgade

There's a profound change of mood once you cross **Gothersgade**, the road marking the northern perimeter of Indre By. The congenial alleyways and early medieval markers of the old city give way to long, broad streets and a number of proud, aristocratic structures. There is a whole group of these in the **harbour area** near Nyhavn just to the east, the obvious route if you're walking from Indre By, although perhaps the most impressive building of all is Rosenborg Slot, a short way to the west away from the harbour and close to several major museums.

From Nyhavn to Esplanaden

Running from Kongens Nytorv at the top of Strøget, a slender canal divides the two sides of **Nyhavn**, a wide but quite short street, until recently frequented by sailors – who earned the area a racy reputation – but now in the advanced stages of gentrification. One or two of the old tattoo shops remain, but they're mostly here to artificially flavour the atmosphere and are outnumbered by small but expensive restaurants and a growing band of refined antique shops. The canalside is quite picturesque, however, with yachts moored on the water and preserved eighteenth-century houses lining the street, three of which (nos. 18, 20 and 67) were lived in at various times by Hans Christian Andersen. At no. 69, the **Hans Christian Andersen Centre** (daily April–Sept 10am–9pm; Oct–March noon–5pm; 35kr) manages to fill five floors with a motley collection of sculptures and watercolours inspired by Andersen's stories; only the writer's re-created study and a few souvenirs of his travels relate directly to his life. To find the definitive Andersen collection you'll need to travel to his birthplace, Odense (see p.111). The far end of Nyhavn is also the departure point for the catamaran to Malmö, boats to Rønne and, a block away at the end of Skt Annæ Plads, ferries for Oslo.

From Skt Annæ Plads, Amaliegade leads under a colonnade into the cobbled **Amalienborg Plads**, with a statue of Frederik V in its centre that reputedly cost more than the construction of all four identical Rococo palaces that flank it. Dating from the mid-eighteenth century, the quartet of imposing buildings provides a sudden burst of welcome symmetry into the city's generally haphazard layout. Two of them now serve as royal residences and there's a changing of the guard each day at noon when the monarch is at home – generally attended by gangs of camera-toting tourists.

Between the square and the harbour are the lavish gardens of **Amaliehaven**, while in the opposite direction, on Bregade, looms the great marble dome of **Frederikskirken**, also known as the "Marmorkirken" (Mon–Sat 11am–2pm; free guided tours Sat 11am). Modelled on – and intended to rival – St Peter's in Rome, the church was begun in 1749, but because of its enormous cost lay unfinished until a century and a half later, when its most prominent feature (one of Europe's largest domes) was completed with Danish rather than the more expensive Norwegian marble. If you can coincide with the guided tour, the reward is the chance to climb first to the whispering gallery and then out onto the rim of the dome itself. From here there's a stunning, and usually blustery, view over the sharp geometry of Amalienborg and across the sea to the factories of Malmö in Sweden.

Further along Bredgade, at no. 22, the former Danish Surgical Academy now holds the **Medical History Museum** (guided tours only; in English on Wed, Thurs, Fri & Sun at 2pm; free) – not a place to visit if you've spent the morning on a brewery binge. The enthusiastically presented hour-long tour features aborted foetuses, strait-jackets, methods of syphilis treatment, amputated feet, eyeballs and a dissected head.

The Kastellet and around

A little way beyond the museum, Bredgade concludes at Esplanaden, facing the green space of the Churchill Park. To the right, the German armoured car that was commandeered by Danes and used to bring news of the Nazi surrender marks the entrance to the **Museum of the Danish Resistance Movement** (*Frihedsmuseet*; May to mid-Sept Tues–Sat 10am–4pm, Sun 10am–5pm; mid-Sept to April Tues–Sat 11am–3pm, Sun 11am–4pm; free). Initially, the Danes put up little resistance to the German invasion, but later the Nazis were given a systematically wretched time. The museum records the growth of the organized response and has a special section on the youths from Aalborg who formed themselves into the "Churchill Club". Feeling the adults weren't doing enough, this gang of fifteen-year-olds set about destroying German telegraph cables, blowing up cars and trains and stealing weapons. There's also a small, but inevitably moving, collection of artworks and handicrafts made by concentration camp inmates.

The road behind the museum crosses into the grounds of the **Kastellet** (daily 6am–10pm; free), a fortress built by Christian IV and expanded by his successors through the seventeenth century, after the loss of Danish possessions in Skåne had put the city within range of Swedish cannonballs. It's now occupied by the Danish army and closed to the public. The tall arches and gateways, however, are an enjoyable setting for a stroll, as are the grassy slopes beside the moat. In a corner of the park, perched on some rocks just off the harbour bank, the **Little Mermaid** (*Den Lille Havfrue*) exerts an inexplicable magnetism on tourists. Since its unveiling in 1913, this bronze statue of a Hans Christian Andersen character, sculpted by Edvard Erichsen and paid for by the boss of the Carlsberg brewery, has become the best-known emblem of the city – a fact which has led to it being the victim of several subversive pranks: the original head disappeared in 1964, a cow's head was forced over the replacement in 1986, and more recently one of its arms was stolen. But it's worth enduring the crowds gawping at the mermaid for the spectacular **Gefion Fountain**, a hundred metres away. The fountain's sculpted figure is by Anders Bundgaard and shows the goddess Gefion with her four sons, whom she's turned into oxen having been promised, in return, as much land as she can plough in a single night. The legend goes that she ploughed a chunk of Sweden, then picked up the piece of land (creating Lake Vänern) and tossed it into the sea – where it became Zealand.

West from the harbour: Rosenborg Slot and the museums

Still north of Gothersgade, but away from the harbour across Store Kongensgade, lies **Nyboder**, a curious area of short, straight and narrow streets lined with rows of compact yellow dwellings. Although some of these are recently erected apartment blocks, the original houses, on which the newer constructions are modelled, were built by Christian IV to encourage his sailors to live in the city. The area had at one time declined into a slum, but a recent vigorous revamping has made it an increasingly sought-after district. The oldest (and prettiest) houses can be found along Skt Pauls Gade.

Across Sølvgade from Nyboder is the main entrance to **Rosenborg Slot** (May & mid-Sept to Oct daily 11am–3pm; June–Aug daily 10am–4pm; rest of the year Tues–Sun 11am–3pm; 50kr), a Dutch Renaissance palace and one of the most elegant buildings bequeathed by Christian IV to the city. Though intended as a country residence, Rosenborg served as the main domicile of Christian IV (he died here in 1648) and, until the end of the nineteenth century, the monarchs who succeeded him. It became a museum as early as 1830 and in the main building you can still see the rooms and furnishings used by the regal occupants. The highlights, though, are in the downstairs treasury (separate entrance; same hours), which displays the rich accessories worn by Christian IV (and his horse), the crown of absolute monarchs and the present crown jewels. Outside, the splendidly neat squares of Rosenborg Have can be reached by leaving the palace itself and using the park's main entrance on the corner of Østervoldgade and Sølvgade. On the west side of the Slot is Kongens Have, the city's oldest public park and a popular place for picnics, and, close by, the **Botanical Garden** (*Botanish Have*; daily April–Sept 8.30am–6pm; Oct–March 8.30am–4pm; free).

Opposite the castle, marked by a few runic stones, is the **Geology Museum** (Tues–Sun 1–4pm; free), which has a great meteorite section but is otherwise quite missable unless you're a mineral freak (although the microscopic fragment of moon rock brought back by an Apollo mission and presented by Richard Nixon to the Danish people in the name of "world peace" is one of Copenhagen's greater ironies). Only slightly more worth while is the neighbouring royal art museum, the **Statens Museum for Kunst** (Tues–Sun 10am–4.30pm; 20kr), a mammoth collection that's too large to take in on a short visit and too dull to warrant a longer one. While all the big cheeses have their patch – there are some minor Picassos and more major works by Matisse and Braque, Modigliani, Dürer and El Greco – it's the works of Emil Nolde, with his gross pieces showing bloated ravens, hunched figures and manic children, that best capture the mood of the place.

Art fans will find greater things across the park behind the museum, in the **Den Hirschsprungske Samling** (Wed–Sat 1–4pm, Sun 11am–4pm; 20kr) on Stockholmsgade. Heinrich Hirschsprung was a late nineteenth-century tobacco baron who sunk some of the industry's profits into patronage of emergent Danish artists, including the Skagen artists (see p.151) and a batch of others later to become significant. It was Hirschsprung's wish that on his death the collection – which also features Eckersburg, Købke and lesser names from the Danish mid-nineteenth-century Golden Age – would be given to the nation, but the government of the day vetoed the plan, and Hirschsprung set up his own gallery. Despite a lack of masterpieces, you can easily spend an hour on this fine collection.

Christiansborg

Christiansborg sits on the island of Slotsholmen, tenuously connected to Indre By by several short bridges: a mundane part of the city, but administratively – and historically – an important one. It was here, in the twelfth century, that Bishop Absalon built the castle that instigated the city, and the drab royal palace that occupies the site, completed in 1916, is nowadays primarily given over to government offices and the state parliament or **Folketinget** (guided tours July & Aug daily on the hour 10am–4pm; rest of the year Sun only; free). Close to the bus stop on Christiansborg Slotsplads is the entrance to the **Ruins under Christiansborg** (May–Sept daily 9.30am–3.30pm; Oct–April closed Mon & Sat; 15kr), where a staircase leads down to the remains of Absalon's original building. The first fortress suffered repeated mutilations by the Hanseatic League, and Erik of Pomerania had a replacement erected in 1390, into which he moved the royal court. This in turn was pulled down by Christian IV and another castle built between 1731 and 1745. The stone and brick walls that comprise the ruins, and the articles from the castles stored in an adjoining room, are surprisingly absorbing, the mood enhanced by the semi-darkness and lack of external noise.

In and around Christiansborg's courtyard there are a number of other, less captivating museums, to which the information office close to the ruins' entrance can provide directions – the confusing array of buildings makes it easy to get lost. That said, you could probably sniff your way to the **Royal Stables** (May–Oct Fri–Sun 2–4pm; Nov–April Sat & Sun 2–4pm; 10kr), though, unsurprisingly, this is among the country's least essential collections. Nearby, the **Theatre Museum** (Wed 2–4pm, Sun noon–4pm; 20kr) is more interesting, housed in what was the eighteenth-century Court Theatre and displaying original costumes, set-models and the old dressing rooms and boxes. Exiting the courtyard and walking through Tøjhusgade takes you past the **Armoury Museum** (*Tøjhusmuseet*; mid-June to mid-Sept Tues–Sun 10am–4pm; rest of the year Tues–Fri 1–3pm, Sat & Sun noon–4pm; 20kr), where you can view weaponry from Christian IV's arsenal and a host of crests and coats of arms. A few strides further on, a small gateway leads into the gorgeous tree-lined grounds of the **Royal Library** – an excellent venue for a picnic. The library itself (closed for restoration until mid-1998, but previously open Mon–Fri 9am–6pm, Sat 9am–6pm) contains original manuscripts by Hans Christian Andersen, Karen Blixen and Søren Kierkegaard (of whom there's a statue in the gardens), though you can only get to see them if you can convince those at reception that you're a bona fide scholar (a student card should suffice). Adjacent to Christiansborg Slotsplads is the low, long form of the seventeenth-century **Børsen**, or Stock Exchange – with its spire of four entwined dragons' tails, one of the most distinctive buildings in the city.

The Thorvaldsens and national museums

On the far side of Slotsholmen, the **Thorvaldsens Museum** (Tues–Sun 10am–5pm; free) is the home of an enormous collection of work and memorabilia (and the body) of Denmark's most famous sculptor. Bertel Thorvaldsen lived from 1770 to 1844 and despite negligible schooling drew his way into the Danish Academy of Fine Arts, from there moving on to Rome where he perfected the heroic, classical figures for which he became famous. Nowadays he's not widely known outside Denmark, although in his day he enjoyed international renown and won commissions from all over Europe.

Other than a selection of early works in the basement, the labels of the great, hulking statues read like a roll-call of the famous and infamous: Vulcan, Adonis, John Russell, Gutenberg, Pius VII and Maximilian; and the Christ Hall contains the huge casts of the Christ and Apostles statues which can be seen in Vor Frue Kirke (see p.78). A prolific and gifted sculptor, Thorvaldsen was something of a wit too. Asked by the Swedish artist J.T. Sergel how he managed to make such beautiful figures, he held up the scraper with which he was working and replied, "With this."

There's another major collection a short walk away over the Slotsholmen moat to the west: the **National Museum** (Tues–Sun 10am–5pm; 30kr), which has an ethnographic section in a separate wing at Ny Vestergade 10, but is really strongest (as you'd expect) on Danish history; if you've any interest at all in the subject you could spend a good couple of hours here. Much of the early stuff, ranging from prehistory to the Viking days, comes from Jutland – jewellery, bones and even bodies, all of it remarkably well preserved and much only discovered after wartime fuel shortages led to large-scale digging of the Danish peat bogs. Informative explanatory texts help clarify the Viking section, whose best exhibits – apart from the infamous horned helmets – are the sacrificial gifts, among them the Sun Chariot, a model horse carrying a sun disc with adornments of gold and bronze. Further floors store a massive collection of almost anything and everything that featured in Christian-era Denmark up to the nineteenth century – finely engraved wooden altarpieces, furniture, clothing and more – as well as a good section on peasant life.

Christianshavn

From Christiansborg, a bridge crosses the Inder Havnen to the island of Amager and into **Christianshavn**, built by Christian IV as an autonomous new town in the early sixteenth century to provide housing for workers in the shipbuilding industry. It was given features more common to Dutch port towns of the time, even down to a small canal (Wilders Kanal), and in parts the area is more redolent of Amsterdam than Copenhagen. Although its present inhabitants are fairly well-off, Christianshavn still has the mood of a working-class quarter, with a grouping of second-hand shops along the main street through the district, Torvegade, and some immaculately preserved houses along Overgaden oven Vandet on the canalside.

Besides the houses, take a walk down here for the *Filmhuset*, on the corner of Store Søndervoldstræde, a small building but one that is the base of the national film industry and holds the **Danish Film Museum** (Mon, Tues, Thurs & Fri noon–4pm, Sept–May until 9pm Tues; free). Here the dust is kept off the cameras, props and other remnants of an early film industry that before Hollywood and the advent of the talkies was among the world's most successful and advanced.

Poking skywards through the trees on the other side of Torvegade is the blue and gold spire of **Vor Frelsers Kirke** (June–Aug Mon–Sat 9am–4.30pm, Sun noon–4.30pm; mid-March to May, Sept & Oct Mon–Sat 9am–3.30pm, Sun noon–3.30pm; Nov to mid-March Mon–Sat 10am–1.30pm, Sun noon–1.30pm; spire 10kr), on the corner of Prinsessegade and Skt Annægade. The spire, with its helter-skelter-like outside staircase, was added to the otherwise plain church in the mid-eighteenth century, instantly becoming one of the more recognizable features on the city's horizon. Climbing the spire is fun, but not entirely without risk (though the rumour that the builder fell off it and died, while plausible, is untrue). To get to the spire, go through the church and up to a trap door which opens onto the platform where the external steps begin: there are four hundred of them, slanted and slippery (especially after rain) and gradually becoming smaller. The reward for reaching the top is a great view of Copenhagen and beyond.

Christiania

A few streets east of Vor Frelsers Kirke, **Christiania** occupies an area that was for centuries used as a barracks, before the soldiers moved out and it was colonized by young and homeless people. It was declared a "free city" on September 24, 1971, with a view to its operating autonomously from Copenhagen proper, and its continued existence has fuelled one of the longest-running debates in Danish (and Scandinavian) society. One by-product of its idealism and the freedoms assumed by its residents (and, despite recent lapses, generally tolerated by successive governments and the police) was to make Christiana a refuge for petty criminals and shady individuals from all over the city. But the problems have inevitably been overplayed by Christiania's critics, and a surprising number of Danes – of all ages and from all walks of life – do support the place, not least because Christiania has performed usefully, and altruistically, when established bodies have been found wanting. An example has been in the weaning of heroin addicts off their habits. Once, a 24-hour cordon was thrown around the area to prevent dealers reaching the addicts inside: reputedly the screams – of deprived junkies and suppliers being "dealt with" – could be heard all night. And Christiania residents have stepped in to provide free shelter and food for the homeless at Christmas when the city administration declined to do so.

The population is around one thousand, swelled in summer by the curious and the sympathetic – although the residents ask people not to camp here, and tourists not to point cameras at the weirder-looking inhabitants. The craft shops and restaurants are – partly because of their refusal to pay any kind of tax – fairly cheap, and nearly all are good, and there are a couple of innovative music and performance art venues. These, and the many imaginative dwellings, including some built on stilts in a small lake, make a visit worth while. Additionally, there are a number of alternative political and arts groups based in Christiania; for information on these – and on the free city generally – call in to *Galopperiet* (daily noon–5pm), to the left of the main entrance on the corner of Bådsmandsstræde and Prinsessegade. Two-hour guided tours of Christiania operate in summer (20kr per person; information and reservations on ☎31/579670).

Along Vesterbrogade

Hectic **Vesterbrogade** begins on the far side of Rådhuspladsen from Strøget, and its first attraction is Copenhagen's most famous after the Little Mermaid – the **Tivoli Gardens** (May to mid-Sept daily 11am–midnight; 44kr). This park of many bland amusements, which first flung open its gates in 1843, was modelled on the Vauxhall Gardens in London, and in turn became the model for the Festival Gardens in London's Battersea Park. The name is now synonymous with Copenhagen at its most innocently pleasurable, and the opening of the gardens each year on May 1 is taken to mark the beginning of summer. There are fairground rides, fireworks (Wed, Fri & Sat nights) and fountains, and nightly entertainment in the central arena, encompassing everything from acrobats and jugglers to the mid-Atlantic tones of various fixed-grin crooners. Naturally, it's overrated and overpriced, but an evening spent wandering among the revellers of all ages indulging in the mass consumption of ice cream is an experience worth having – once, at any rate. Close to the gardens' Vesterbrogade entrance is the predictable **Holography Museum** (daily mid-April to mid-Sept 10am–midnight; rest of the year 10am–6pm; 32kr) – once you've seen through one hologram you've seen through them all – and the abysmal **Louis**

Tussaud's Wax Museum (daily May to mid-Sept 10am–11pm; mid-Sept to April 10am–7pm; 48kr).

Behind the Tivoli, across Tietgensgade towards the harbour, is the dazzling **Ny Carlsberg Glyptotek** (May–Aug Tues–Sun 10am–4pm; Sept–April Tues–Sat noon–3pm, Sun 10am–4pm; 15kr, free to art students and *ISIC* or *FIYTO* cardholders), opened in 1897 by brewer Carl Jacobsen as a venue for ordinary people to see classical art exhibited in classical style. Its centrepiece is the conservatory: "Being Danes", said Jacobsen, "we know more about flowers than art, and during the winter this greenery will make people pay a visit; and then, looking at the palms, they might find a moment for the statues." It's an idea that succeeded, and even now the gallery is well-used – and not just by art lovers: there's a programme of electronic music daily at 1pm, as well as a seasonal roster of other free events; pick up a schedule at the entrance.

As for the contents, this is by far Copenhagen's finest gallery, with a stirring array of Greek, Roman and Egyptian art and artefacts, as well as what is reckoned to be the biggest (and best) collection of Etruscan art outside Italy. There are, too, excellent examples of nineteenth-century European art, including a complete collection of Degas casts made from the fragile working sculptures he left on his death, Manet's *Absinthe Drinker*, and two small cases containing tiny caricatured heads by Honore Daumier. Easily missed, but actually the most startling room in the place, is an antechamber with just a few pieces – early works by Man Ray, some Chagall sketches and a Picasso pottery plate.

Beyond the Tivoli Gardens

The streets between Vesterbrogade and **Istedgade**, just west of the train station, used to be Copenhagen's token red-light area, and the only part of the city where you may have felt unsafe. Over recent years, the low rents have attracted students and a large number of immigrant families: walk along Istedgade and you're likely to see dreadlocked rastas, and Turks sipping tea from tulip glasses, and to stumble across a number of diverse (but uniformly well-priced) ethnic eateries.

At Vesterbrogade 59 is the **City Museum** (*Københavns Bymuseum*; Tues–Sun May–Sept 10am–4pm; Oct–April 1–4pm; free), which has reconstructed ramshackle house exteriors and tradesmen's signs from early Copenhagen. Looking at these, the impact of Christian IV becomes resoundingly apparent. There's a large room recording the form and cohesion that this monarch and amateur architect gave the city, even including a few of his own drawings. The rest of the city's history is told by paintings – far too many paintings, in fact – and you should head straight upstairs for the room devoted to **Søren Kierkegaard**, filled by bits and bobs that form an intriguing footnote

---

SØREN KIERKEGAARD

Kierkegaard is inextricably linked with Copenhagen, yet his championing of individual will over social conventions, and his rejection of materialism, did little to endear him to his fellow Danes. Born in 1813, Kierkegaard believed himself set on an "evil destiny" – partly the fault of his father, who is best remembered for having cursed God on a Jutland heath. Kierkegaard's first book, *Either/Or*, published in 1843, was inspired by his love affair with one Regine Olsen; she failed to understand it, however, and married someone else. Few other people understood *Either/Or*, and Kierkegaard, though devasted by the broken romance, came to revel in the enigma he had created, becoming a "walking mystery in the streets of Copenhagen" (he lived in a house on Nytorv). He was a prolific author, sometimes publishing two books on the same day and often writing under pseudonyms. His greatest philosophical works were written by 1846 and are generally claimed to have laid the foundations of existentialism.

to the life of the nineteenth-century Danish writer and philosopher, and much the most interesting part of the museum (see box below).

A few minutes to the north of Vesterbrogade, at Gammel Kongevej 10, on the corner with Vester Søgade, is the **Tycho Brahe Planetarium** (Tues–Sun 10.30am–9pm, May–Sept also Mon; shows 70kr), the biggest in Scandinavia, named after the world-famous Danish astronomer who invented instruments to accurately plot the sun, planets and stars for the first time.

West to the Carlsberg Brewery and Frederiksberg Have

Way out west along Vesterbrogade (save your legs by taking bus #6 or #18), down Enghavevej and along Ny Carlsbergvej, you'll find the **Carlsberg Brewery**; the tours (Mon–Fri 11am & 2pm; free; reservations ☎33/271313), beginning from the hut to the left, are well worth joining, if only for the free booze provided at the end. If you're in the vicinity, pass by anytime to admire the **Elephant Gate** – four elephants carved in granite supporting the building that spans the road.

Vesterbrogade finishes up opposite the **Frederiksberg Have**, which contains the Frederiksberg Palace, now used as a military academy and closed to the public. Throughout the eighteenth century, the city's top nobs came here to mess about in boats along the network of canals that dissect the copious lime-tree groves, and its pleasant surrounds are now a popular weekend picnic spot for locals, and refreshingly free of tourists. While here, you might call in at the entertaining **Storm P. Museum** (May–Aug Tues–Sun 10am–4pm; Sept–April Wed, Sat & Sun 10am–4pm; 20kr), by the gate facing Frederiksberg Allé, packed with the satirical cartoons that made "Storm P." (Robert Storm Petersen) one of the most popular bylines in Danish newspapers from the 1920s. Even if you don't understand the Danish captions, you'll leave the museum with an insight into the national sense of humour.

Beyond the Frederiksberg Palace, at Roskildevej 32 (buses #27 and #28), is Copenhagen's **Zoo**, which has a special children's section as well as the usual array of caged lions, elephants and monkeys (daily June–Aug 9am–6pm; rest of the year 9am–4pm; 55kr, children 27kr).

Out from the centre

Unlike many other major European cities, Copenhagen has only a few miles of drab housing estates on its periphery before the countryside begins. A number of things are worth venturing out from the centre to see, although none of them need keep you away from the main action for long.

Just outside the inner city, only a few minutes on foot from Indre By, is **Assistens Kirkegård**, a cemetery built to cope with the dead from the 1711–12 plague. More interestingly, it contains the graves of Hans Christian Andersen and Søren Kierkegaard – both well signposted, although not from the same entrance. If you get lost, look at the handy catalogue by the gate on Kapelvej. The cemetery is off Nørrebrogade in the district of Nørrebro: walk from the Nørreport station along Frederiksborggade and over the lake. Alternatively buses #5, #7, #16 and #18 run along the graveyard's edge.

Slightly further out is **Grundtvigs Kirke** (mid-May to mid-Sept Mon–Sat 9am–4.45pm, Sun noon–4pm; rest of the year Mon–Sat 9am–4pm, Sun noon–1pm), an astonishing yellow-brick creation whose gabled front resembles a massive church organ which rises upwards and completely dwarfs the row of terraced houses that share the street. The church, named after and dedicated to the founder of the Danish folk high schools, was designed by Jensens Klint and his son in 1913, but was not finished until 1926. To reach it from the city centre takes about twenty minutes on buses #10, #16, #19 or #21. Get off in the small square of Bispetorv soon after passing the Bispebjerg Hospital; the church itself is in På Bjerget.

South

If the weather's good, take a trip south to the Amager **beaches**, about half an hour away by bus #12 along Øresundsvej (ask for Helgoland). On the other side of the airport from the beaches (take bus #30 or #33) lies the village of **DRAGØR**, an atmospheric cobbled fishing village from where **ferries** depart for Limhamn in Sweden. There are a couple of good local history collections in the **Dragør Museum** by the harbour (May–Sept Tues–Fri 2–5pm, Sat & Sun noon–6pm; 15kr), and the **Amager Museum** (June–Aug Wed–Sun 11am–3pm; rest of the year Wed & Sun 11am–3pm; 15kr), a few minutes' walk away. Beware that at present Amager and its immediate area resembles a gigantic building site thanks to the construction of the Copenhagen–Malmö road and rail link – work is projected to finish by the year 2000, but this date seems somewhat optimistic.

Further out, on the road to Køge, the southern suburb of **Ishøj** is home to many ethnic communities, mainly from the Middle East, and an excellent museum of modern art, **Arken** (April–Sept daily 10am–6pm, Wed until 10pm; Oct–Dec daily 10am–5pm, Wed until 10pm; 40kr). From central Copenhangen take the S-train to Ishøj station and then bus #128 – a 45-minute journey altogether.

North

If you're tired of history, culture and the arts, you might fancy a guided tour around the **Tuborg Brewery**, the headquarters of other major Danish brewer (Mon–Fri 10am, 12.30pm & 2.30pm; free), which ends with a free drinking session. Take bus #6 or #21 north to Hellerup; the brewery is at Strandvejen 54. Next door to the brewery, in a former bottling hall, the **Eksperimentarium** (Mon–Fri 9am–6pm, Tues & Thurs until 9m, Sat & Sun 11am–6pm; 69kr, children 49kr) is a workshop/museum intended to raise scientific awareness through some interesting and entertaining hands-on exhibits, such as a disco which beats to your bio-rhythms.

Just outside the city limits, reached by bus #6, **CHARLOTTENLUND** has a lovely beach, good for sunbathing – as long as you can ignore the chimneys in the background. Its main attraction these days is the **Danmarks Akvarium** (daily 10am–4pm; 45kr), with its impressive collection of tropical fish, sharks, crocodiles and turtles. Nearby **Charlottenlund Fort** (free entry) has a few abandoned cannons and is only worth bothering with for the great views over the city and out to sea. You're better off making for **Charlottenlund Slotshave**, a former manor house with a gorgeous park perfect for strolling and picnicking.

If you're in the mood for an amusement park but can't face (or afford) Tivoli, venture out to **Bakken** (late March to late Aug daily 2pm–midnight; free), close to the Klampenborg stop at the end of line C on the S-train network. Set in a corner of Kongens Dyrehave (the Royal Deer Park), it's a lot more fun than its city counterpart, and besides the usual swings and roller-coasters, offers easy walks through woods of sturdy oaks and beeches. Strolling back towards Klampenborg along Christiansholmsvej, a left turn at the restaurant *Peter Lieps Hus* gives superb views over the Øresund.

Finally, half an hour's bus journey (#184) to the north is the village of **LYNGBY**, and its **Open-Air Museum** (*Frilandsmuseet*; April–Nov Tues–Sun 10am–5pm; 30kr), set inside a large park and comprising restored seventeenth- to mid-nineteenth-century buildings, drawn from all over Denmark and its former territories. A walk through the park leads to the **Sorgenfri Palace**, one-time home of Frederik V and closed to the public. Take S-train line A or Cc to Sorgenfri.

Eating

Whether you want a quick coffee and croissant, or to sit down to a five-course gourmet dinner, you'll find more choice – and lower prices – in Copenhagen than in any other

Scandinavian capital. Many of the city's innumerable **cafés** offer good-value, highly filling lunches, and there are plenty of **pizzerias**, again many with daily specials and all-you-can-eat salad deals. Most **restaurants** are open for lunch and dinner: prices tend to be higher in the evenings, but there are generally good-value deals at lunchtime, so those on a budget needn't deprive themselves of a blow-out.

If you're stocking up for a **picnic** – or a trip to Sweden or Norway – take advantage of the numerous *smørrebrød* outlets; *Smørrebrødskunsten*, on the corner of Magstræde at Rådhusstræde, and *Københavns Smørrebrød*, Vesterbrogade 6c, are two of the most central. For more general food shopping, use one of the **supermarkets**. *Brugsen* at Axeltorv 2, and *Irma* at Vesterbrogade 1 and Borgergade 28, are cheaper than their counterparts along Strøget.

Cafés and pizzerias

Alexanders Pizza House, Lille Kannikestræde 5. Brilliant-value all-you-can-eat deals.

Bar Bar Bar, Vesterbrogade 53. A stylish and relaxed place for a coffee, drink or light snack.

Café au lait, Nørre Voldgade 27. Opposite the Nørreport S-train station, a pleasantly unflustered place for a coffee or snack. Branches at Gothersgade 11, Vesterbrogade 16 and Vornedamsvej 16.

Caféen i Nikolaj, Nikolaj Plads 22. Nibble a light lunch or pastry and then tour the rest of this former church, which now houses an art gallery. Closed Sun.

Floras Kaffebar, Blågårdsgade 27. Daily specials at 45kr, plus soups and cakes, served in an easygoing atmosphere. Come back at night for cheaper-than-average beer.

Klaptræet, Kultorvet 13. Very cheap breakfasts and good-value eating throughout the day.

Rust, Guldbergsgade 8. A bar and rock venue that also houses a good-value restaurant; 100kr buys a couple of satisfying courses.

Shawarwa, Strøget, close to Rådhuspladsen. Excellent Middle-Eastern snacks: shawarwas, pitta bread with falafels and kebabs, starting at 22kr.

Café Sonja, Saxogade 86. Pasta and salad main courses for under 50kr.

Vagabondo's Cantina, Vesterbrogade 70. The most central of several branches of this dependable pizza chain, where pizza and pasta dishes start at 50kr.

Restaurants

Many of the city's **Danish restaurants** knock out affordable (around 80kr) and very high-quality lunches, either from a set menu or from an open table – dinner will always be more expensive. However, huge **dinners** can be enjoyed more cheaply in one of Copenhagen's growing band of **ethnic restaurants**, many of which have adopted the Scandinavian open table idea, offering all-you-can-eat meals from around 60kr. These are usually the best bet for finding **vegetarian** food, too, but don't plan a night's dancing after wading through one.

Danish restaurants

DSB Bistro, Banegårdspladsen 7. Believe it or not, it's here at the train station restaurant that you'll get a broad, comparatively low-cost, introduction to Danish food. Allow a couple of hours to explore the massive cold buffet served from 11.30am to 9.30pm for 139kr; far cheaper are the daily specials.

Els, Store Strandstræde 3. Very plush, with a game-orientated menu and walls lined with elegant mid-nineteenth-century Danish art. A full meal will set you back around 300kr.

Nyhavns Færgekro, Nyhavn 5. Unpretentious and thoroughly tasty traditional food, either from the lunchtime fish-laden open table (80kr), or the à la carte restaurant upstairs.

Peder Oxe, Gråbrødretorv 11. Especially worth while at lunchtime, when prices are lower. Also has a lively wine cellar.

Café Rosenkælderen, Rosengården 5. Central and cheap, with stacks of daily specials and lunch and dinner plates starting at around 50kr.

Spisehuset, Rådhusstræde 13. In the *Huset* building, with a varied but always wholesome and fairly cheap menu, including 70kr daily specials.

Spiseloppen, Bådsmandsstræde 43, Christiania. Superb food that won't break the bank.

Skt Gertruds Kloster, Hauser Plads 32. In the vaults of a medieval cloister and smoulderingly romantic – though you'll spend a fortune.

Foreign restaurants

A/S Bananrepublikken, Nørrebrogade 13. Serving ethnic foods with a modern Danish edge, from around 100kr, including the best tapas in Denmark. See also "Nightlife".

Bali, Lille Kongensgade 4. Tread carefully around the bamboo plants and you'll find a fine Indonesian restaurant; the house special is *rijsttafel*, costing 128kr.

Govindas, Nørre Farimagsgade 82. Work up an appetite on the twenty-minute walk from Indre By then satiate at this Krishna-run restaurant which produces seven-course lacto-vegetarian meals for 35kr (45kr after 3pm). Closed Sun.

Kashmir, Nørrebrogade 35. Indian food and a 79kr lunchtime buffet offering the best value for miles.

Koh I Nor, Vesterbrogade 33. A mix of Indian, Pakistani and Halal, with vegetarian dishes available; the set dinner costs 89kr.

Café Latino, Gothersgade 113. A tiny and likeable restaurant serving Latin American dishes from 50kr.

Merhaba, Abel Cathrinesgade 7. Good Turkish food with prices starting at 50kr. There's sometimes a three-course set meal on offer for 59kr.

Mexicali, Åboulevarden 12, Nørrebro. Decent Mexican food from around 80kr.

Pasta Basta, Valhendorfsgade 22. An array of fish and meat pasta dishes, plus nine cold pasta bowls from which you can help yourself for 69kr. Open until 5am, this is a favourite final stop for late-night groovers.

The Pyramids, Gothersgade 15. Gloriously over-the-top Egyptian restaurant – belly dancers provide entertainment while you eat.

Rama, Bredgade 29. Top-class Thai food with a choice of set menus for 110kr.

Riz-Raz, Kompagnistræde 20. Middle-Eastern vegetarian buffet for 49kr at lunchtime, 69kr in the evenings.

Shezan, Viktoriagade 22. Excellent Pakistani dishes – if it's too busy, try *Indus*, across the street.

Zorba, Gråbrødrestræde 23. A dependable Egyptian diner, worth a call for its open table: 98kr for dinner, 54kr at lunchtime.

LATE-NIGHT FOOD

For **late-night eating**, as well as *Pasta Basta*, listed above, and the late-opening cafés mentioned under "Nightlife", you might want to join the thespians munching fresh bread and rolls in *Herluf Trolle*, on Herluf Trolles Gade, just behind the Royal Theatre.

Drinking and nightlife

An almost unchartable network of **cafés and bars** covers Copenhagen. You can get a drink – and usually a snack too – in any of them, although some are especially noted for their congeniality and youthful ambience, and it's these we've listed below. Almost all the better cafés and bars are in – or close to – the districts of Indre By and Nørrebro just beyond, and it's no hardship to sample several on the same night, though bear in mind that Fridays and Saturdays are very busy, and you'll probably need to queue before getting in anywhere.

Another area the city excels in is **live music**. Major international names visit regularly but it's with small-scale shows that Copenhagen really excels. Minor gigs early in the week in cafés and bars will often be free, making it a cheap and simple business to take in several places until you find something to your liking – though later in the week smaller venues may have a modest cover charge. There are also a number of medium-sized halls that host the best of Danish and overseas rock, jazz, hip-hop and funk. Things normally kick off around 10pm and, if not free, admission is 25–75kr. Throughout the summer, there are many **free concerts** in the city parks, some featuring the leading Danish bands. You can find out who's playing where by reading the latest copy of *Gaffa*, free from music and record shops; or *Huset*, a monthly magazine available from the *Huset* building at Rådhusstræde 13, which lists what's on at its own three music venues.

With the plethora of late-opening cafés and bars, you'll never have to choose between going to a **club** and going to bed. If you do get a craving for a dancefloor fling, however, you'll find the discos much like those in any major city – but more preoccupied with providing entertainment than defining the cutting edge of fashion. You'll be dancing alone if you turn up much before midnight, although after that time, especially on Fridays and Saturdays, they fill rapidly – and stay open until 5am. There are dress codes but these are fairly easy-going – anything casual and clean will usually suffice. Another plus is that drink prices are seldom hiked up and admission is fairly cheap at 25–45kr.

For full **listings** of events and all kinds of entertainment, check out the free monthly tourist magazines, *Copenhagen This Week* and *Cope City Guide*, and keep an eye out for notices in *Use-It* and city cafés.

Bars and cafés

Barcelona, Fælledvej 21. Chic, and very much the place to be seen, though you pay over the odds for the privilege.

Café Dan Turell, Store Regnegade 3. Something of an institution with the artier student crowd (it takes its name from a famous Danish writer) and a fine place for a sociable tipple. Spot it by the rows of bicycles parked outside.

Hard Rock Café, Vesterbrogade 3. As seen on a million T-shirts worldwide; it's as popular as you'd expect. Occasional live music.

Krasnapolsky, Vestergade 10. The Danish avant-garde art hanging on the wall reflects the trend-setting reputation of this ultra-modern watering hole. Come here at least once.

Peder Hvitfeldt, P. Hvitfeldtsstræde 15. Spit-and-sawdust-type place and immensely popular with a youthful crowd. Come early if you want to sit down.

Café Rust, Guldbergsgade 8. A late-night rock'n'roll bar, lively and popular.

Sabines Cafeteria, Teglgårdsstræde 4. Where the young and good-looking begin their evening's drinking.

Café Sommersko, Kronprinsensgade 6. Sizeable, but crowded most nights, with free live music on Sunday afternoons to soothe away hangovers.

Universitetscaféen, Fiolstræde 2. A prime central location and long hours (open until 5am) make this a good spot to hit, early or late, for a leisurely beer.

Live music

A/S Bananrepublikken, Nørrebrogade 13. One of the best places to hear world music; also has a good range of ethnic foods (see p.89).

Copenhagen Jazz House, Niels Hemmingsensgade 10. The country's premier jazz venue, featuring international big names and Denmark's finest. Can be pricey but students get substantial discounts. Closed Sun & Mon.

Femøren, Amager. Huge open-air rock concerts from June to August. Bus #12 or #13.

La Fontaine, Kompagnistræde 11. Jazz club open from 9pm right through to 5am.

Loppen, in Christiania. On the edge of the "free city" and a sympathetic setting for both established and experimental Danish rock, jazz and performance artists, and quite a few British and American ones too.

Musikcaféen, Rådhusstræde 13 (☎33/320066). The mainstream rock part of *Huset*, a sizeable hall but small enough to have plenty of atmosphere on good nights – of which there are several most weeks.

Musikloppen, Christiania. Rock'n'roll or Danish pop plays here mainly at weekends.

Café Pavillon, Fælledparken. In summer, this open-air venue serves a barbecue Thurs–Sat nights and follows it up with a diverse selection of Danish rock bands.

Pumpehuset, Studiestræde (☎33/320066). Not part of *Huset* but run by the same people, and offering a broad sweep of middle-strata rock, hip-hop and funk groups from Denmark and around the world about three times a month.

Café Rust, Guldbergsgade 8, Nørrebro. Bands play at weekends and often on Thursdays too.

Sofies Kælder, Sofiegade, Christianshavn. Hosts rock bands in the evenings, with a jazz concert every Saturday afternoon (3–6pm).

Clubs

Annabell's, Lille Kongensgade 16. Comparatively upmarket but worth a fling on Fridays and Saturdays when there's a younger, brasher crowd.

Bar Bue, Rådhusstræde 13. Mixtures of punk, funk and hip-hop burst out in this compact and sweaty room (see also "Live music"), usually Fri & Sat only.

Daddy's, Axeltorv 5. A bit staid, with an older clientele, but fine if you're looking to tango until dawn.

U-matic, Vestergade 10, in the basement of *Krasnapolsky* (see "Bars and cafés"). With the trendiest sounds and the weirdest-dressed people, this is the nearest thing to a poseurs' paradise that the city has – though sociable enough to make anyone feel part of the scene. Closed Sun & Mon.

Woodstock, Vestergade 12 (☎33/112071). Pulls a large, fun-loving crowd eager to dance to anything with a beat – though the music is predominantly 1960s.

Gay and lesbian Copenhagen

Copenhagen has a lively **gay** scene, which includes a good sprinkling of gay bars and clubs, a bookshop and a sauna, and a couple of gay-friendly hotels. For **contacts and information**, ignore the misleadingly named "Copenhagen Gay Centre" (no more than a glorified sex emporium) and contact the **National Organization for Gay Men and Women** (*Landsforeningen for bøsser og lesbiske*), based at Teglgårdsstræde 13 (☎33/131948). They provide information and advice, along with a bookshop, travel agency and café (Tues & Sun 1pm–3am, Wed & Thurs 1pm–4am, Fri 1pm–5am, Sat 1pm–6am), as well as the *Pan Club* disco (see below). There's also a **gay switchboard** (☎33/130112) and further information can be gleaned from *Pan* magazine, which does not have listings but does have ads announcing the latest happenings – in Danish but easily understood. The **Gay Liberation Movement** (*BBF*) meets each Monday at 8pm in the Bøssehuset on Karlsvognen in Christiania.

For **accommodation**, two hotels cater to gay visitors although neither is exclusively gay: *Jørgensen's*, Rømersgade 11 (☎33/139743; ②), is detailed on p.75; *Hotel Windsor*, Frederiksborggade 30 (☎33/110830; ②), has one wing reserved for gay men. Both hotels are near Israel Plads, about a fifteen-minute walk from the city centre and a few minutes from the Nørreport S-train station. Both dispense handy maps showing the main gay spots in the city.

Bars and clubs

Amigo Bar, Schønbergsgade 4. Serves snacks and is frequented by gay men of all ages.

Café Babuska, Turesensgade 6. Lesbian-only café.

Can Can, Mikkel Bryggersgade 11. One of the favourite spots for late drinking.

Centralhjornet, Kattesundet 18. An ordinary and somewhat dreary bar.

Club Amigo, Studiestræde 31A. Enormous club with bar, cinemas, sauna and solarium, pool room, video room and much more. Gay men only.

Cosy Bar, Studiestræde 24. Gets busy late, mainly with clones and motorbike boys.

Masken Bar, Studiestræde 33. Relatively staid bar popular with an older clientele.

Men's Bar, Teglgårdsstræde 3. The most macho bar, popular with leather and motorbike types. Daily 4pm–2am.

Pan Club, Teglgårdsstræde 13. Part of the biggest and most popular gay centre in the country (see above). The disco is also big – and very enjoyable. Mon–Wed & Sun 10pm–3am, Fri & Sat 10pm–5am.

Sebastian, Hyskenstræde 10. The newest, brightest and most popular of the late-night café-restaurants.

Listings

AIDS hotline ☎33/911119 daily 9am–11pm.

Babysitters *Minerva-Studenternes Baby Sitters*, Smallegade 52A (☎31/229696). Bookings taken Mon–Thurs 6.30–9am & 3–6pm, Fri 3–6pm, Sat 3–5pm.

Banks and exchange Central branches include *Det Danske Bank*, Amagertorv 12 (Mon–Fri 9.30am–4pm, Thurs until 6pm). There's also an *American Express* office at Amagertorv 18, and a *Bank of Tivoli* at Vesterbrogade 3 (May to mid-Sept 10am–11pm). For changing money outside bank hours – at bank rates – there are bureaux at Central Station (daily 7am–9pm), the airport arrival hall (6.30am–10pm) and departure hall (6.30am–8.30pm), and the Tivoli office (noon–11pm) in Tivoli season.

Bike rental *Cykeltanken*, Godthåbsvej 247 (☎31/871423), and *DSB Cykelcenter*, on Reventlowsgade, near Central Station. From April to Oct also at the train stations at Klampenborg and Lyngby.

Boat tours Leave frequently from Gammel Strand and sail around the canals and harbour. Prices 40–120kr per person; just turn up.

Bookstores Most of the city's bookstores are in the area around Fiolstræde and Købmagergade. *The Book Trader*, Skindergade 23, has a varied selection of old and new books in English; *Kupeen DIS Rejser*, Skindergade 28, has guidebooks and maps for budget travellers. Chief places for new books are *G.E.C.Gad*, Vimmelskaftet 32; *Arnold Busck*, Købmagergade 49 (with a discount branch at Østergade 16); and *Boghallen i Politikens Hus*, Rådhuspladsen 37.

Car rental *Avis*, Kampmannsgade 1 (☎33/152299); *Hertz*, Ved Vesterport (☎33/127700); *Europcar*, Gyldenløvesgade 17 (☎33/116200).

Dental emergencies *Tandlægevagten*, Oslo Plads 14, open nightly for emergencies only 8–9.30pm, Sat & Sun also 10am–noon. Turn up and be prepared to pay at least 150kr on the spot.

Doctors and hospitals Call ☎33/936300 Mon–Fri 8am–4pm and you'll be given the name of a doctor in your area. There's a night fee of around 300kr to be paid in cash. For non-urgent treatment, get a list of doctors from the tourist office, *Use-It*, or a local health department (*Kommunens social og sundhedsforvaltning*). The local emergency department is at *Rigshospitalet*, Blegdamsvej 9 (☎35/453545); free treatment for EU and Scandinavian nationals, though others are unlikely to have to pay.

Embassies *Australia*, Kristianiasgade 21 (☎35/262244); *Canada*, Kristen Bernikows Gade 1 (☎33/122299); *Ireland*, Østbanegade 21 (☎31/423233); *New Zealand* (use UK); *UK*, Kastelsvej 40 (☎35/264600); *USA*, Dag Hammerskjölds Allé 24 (☎31/423144).

Emergencies ☎112 for fire, police or ambulance.

Films New releases, often in English with Danish subtitles, are shown all over the city; more esoteric fare is screened at *Græshoppen* in *Huset*, the *Delta Bio*, Kompagnistræde 19, or the *Park Bio*, on Østergade. Full listings are printed in all newspapers. For kids, there's a special cinema, *Tivoli Bio for Børn*, by the main entrance to Tivoli Gardens.

Flea markets There's a good, rummageable flea market at Israel Plads on Saturday mornings May–Sept, and a Salvation Army market, selling bric-à-brac and old clothes, at Hørhusvej

(Tues–Thurs 1–5pm, Fri 1–6pm, Sat 9am–1pm); take bus #30, #3 or #4 to Brydes Allé. Try also the Saturday morning market held in summer behind Frederiksberg Rådhus – take bus #1 or #12.

Football The city has four first division football teams, by far the most successful of which is Brøndby. Take S-train line A to Brøndbyøster and follow the crowds. Big matches, and other league games, are played closer to the centre in Idrætsparken: take bus #6, #7 or #14. Fixture details from *Use-It*, tourist magazines, newspapers and other listings sources.

Health food shops *Urtekræmmeren*, Lars Bjørnsstræde 20; *Sæbehuset*, Studiestræde 18; *City Helse*, Linnégade 14.

Hitching First check the car-share notices on *Use-It* noticeboards. If they don't deliver anything, use the following routes. Heading south to Germany, take S-train line A to Ellebjerg, which leaves you by the ring road, near the start of motorway E20. North to Helsingør and Sweden, take S-train line B or F to Ryparken (or bus #6, #24 or #84 to Hans Knudsen Plads) and hitch along Lyngbyvej (for the E4). West for Funen and Jutland, take S-train line Bb to Tåstrup, then walk along Køgevej and hitch from Roskildevej (A1).

Late shops The supermarket at Central Station is open daily until midnight.

Laundry Central places to do washing include *Vascomat*, Borgergade 2, *Møntvask*, Istedgade 29, and *Møntvask*, Nansengade 39; an average load costs about 40kr.

Left luggage Office (*DSB Garderobe*) on Central Station concourse stores luggage for 20kr per day per pack. There are also lockers in the *InterRail Centre* and at *Use-It*.

Library *Hovedbiblioteket*, Kultorvet 2 (Mon–Fri 10am–7pm, Sat 10am–2pm). *Huset* has a very well-stocked reading room, with international magazines and newspapers.

Lost property The general lost property office is at Carl Jacobsvej 20, Valby (☎31/161406). Otherwise, for things lost on a bus, contact the *HT* office on Vester Voldgade (☎33/147448); lost on a train, the *DSB* office at Central Station (call in person only); lost on a plane (Mon–Fri 8am–noon & 1–4pm; ☎31/503211).

Media *Playtime* and its updates throughout the summer are essential reading, free from *Use-It* and many cafés. The alternative radio station, *Radio Sokkelund*, broadcasts on 101.7MHz: all programmes are in Danish but contain up-to-the-minute news of events in the city. News in English is broadcast daily at 8.30am on *Danmarks Radio 3* (93.8FM). Overseas newspapers are on sale from the stall in Rådhuspladsen and some newsagents along Strøget.

Parking Usually pay and display, with different rates depending on zone colour: in descending level of expense, red, yellow, green, blue, white.

Pharmacies *Steno Apotek*, Vesterbrogade 6, and *Sønderbro Apotek*, Amagerbrogade 158, are open 24 hours.

Post office Main office at Tietgensgade 35 (Mon–Fri 9am–6pm, Sat 9am–1pm). Also at Central Station (Mon–Fri 8am–10pm, Sat 9am–4pm, Sun 10am–5pm). Poste restante at *Use-It* or any named post office.

Saunas Public saunas at Borgergade 12, Sjællandsgade 12 and Sofiegade 15. Generally open Mon–Fri 8am–6.30pm, Sat 8am–2pm; 30kr per person.

Student travel *KILROY Travels*, Skindergade 28 (☎33/110044), can give advice on travelling around Denmark, the rest of Scandinavia and Europe.

Women's movement The main women's centre is *Dannerhuset* (☎33/141676) at Nansensgade 1, a renovated old building. There's a café (Mon–Wed 5–8pm), a bookshop (Mon–Fri 5–10.30pm), and a range of facilities including a film club, counselling and self-defence courses – though these shut down during summer. *Kvindehuset*, Gothersgade 37 (☎33/142804), is another, rather less organized, centre with a cheap café (Mon–Fri noon–6pm) and bookshop.

AROUND ZEALAND

It's easy to see more of Zealand by making day trips out from the capital, although, depending on where you're heading next, it's often a better idea to pack your bags and leave the city altogether. Transport links are excellent throughout the region, making much of northern and central Zealand commuter territory for the capital; but that's hardly something you'd notice as you pass through dozens of tiny villages and large forests on the way to historic centres such as **Helsingør**, **Køge** and – an essential call if you're interested in Denmark's past – **Roskilde**. Except for the memorable vistas of the **northern coast**, and the explorable smaller **islands** off southern Zealand and **Bornholm** to the east, however, you'll find the soft green terrain varies little; and, unless you're a true nature lover, you'll soon want to push on (which is easily done) to the bigger cities in Funen and Jutland.

North Zealand: Helsingør and the coast

The **coast** north of Copenhagen, as far as Helsingør, rejoices under the tag of the "Danish Riviera", a handy label to describe its line of tiny one-time fishing hamlets now inhabited almost exclusively by the extremely rich. It's best seen on the hour-long bus journey (#188) from Klampenborg, last stop on line C of the S-train system – the views of beckoning beaches are lovely. There's also a frequent train service between Copenhagen and Helsingør that's slightly quicker than the bus, but you won't see much unless you break the journey, since the views from the train are obscured by trees.

The Karen Blixen Museum, Humlebæk and Louisiana

There are two good reasons to stop before Helsingør. A fifteen-minute walk from Rungsted Kyst train station, the **Karen Blixen Museum** (May–Sept daily 10am–5pm; Oct–April Wed–Fri 1–4pm, Sat & Sun 11am–4pm; 30kr) is sited in the family home of the writer who, while long a household name in Denmark for her short stories (often written under the pen-name of Isak Dinesen) and outspoken opinions, enjoyed a resurgence of international popularity during the mid-1980s when *Out of Africa* – a Hollywood film based on Blixen's 1937 biographical account of running a coffee plantation in Kenya – was released. After returning from Africa, Blixen lived here until her death in 1962, and much of the house is maintained as it was during her final years. Texts describing Blixen's eventful life (among other things, her father committed suicide and she married the twin brother of the man she loved) line the walls and the exhibits include a collection of first editions and the tiny typewriter she used in Africa. Even if you've never read a word of Blixen, it's hard not to be impressed by her spirit and strength, which shines through the museum. After seeing the house, make for the well-tended flower garden, where Blixen's simple grave lies beneath a protective beech tree.

In **HUMLEBÆK**, the next community of any size, you'll find **Louisiana** (daily 10am–5pm, Wed until 10pm; 48kr), a modern art museum on the northern edge of the village at Gammel Strandvej 13, a short walk from the train station. Even if you go nowhere else outside Copenhagen, it would be a shame to miss this: the setting alone is worth the journey, harmoniously combining art, architecture and the natural landscape. The entrance is in a nineteenth-century villa, off which two carefully – and subtly – designed modern corridors contain the indoor collection, their windows allowing views of the outside sculpture park and the Øresund.

It seems churlish to mention individual items, but the museum's American section, in the south corridor, sticks in the mind. It includes some devastating pieces by Edward Kienholz, Malcolm Morley's scintillatingly gross *Pacific Telephone Los Angeles Yellow Pages*, in which the telephone directory cover expands to monstrous proportions and coffee stains rib the city skyline like a weird metallic grid, and (in the reading room) Jim Dines' powerful series, *The Desire*. You'll also find some of Giacometti's strange, gangly figures haunting a room of their own off the north corridor, and an equally affecting handful of sculptures by Max Ernst, squatting outside the windows and leering inwards. Except for some collages by Arthur Køpcke, and paintings by various Danish luminaries of the CoBrA group, homegrown artists have a rather low profile, although their work is often featured in temporary exhibitions.

Helsingør

First impressions of **HELSINGØR** are none too enticing. The **bus** stops outside the noisy **train station**, outside which Havnepladsen is usually full of transit passengers loitering around fast-food stalls before making for the **ferry terminal**, 100m distant. But away from the hustle, Helsingør is really a quiet and likeable town. Its position on the four-kilometre strip of water linking the North Sea and the Baltic brought the town prosperity when, in 1429, the Sound Toll was imposed on passing vessels – an upturn only matched in magnitude by the severe decline following the abolition of the toll in the nineteenth century. Shipbuilding brought back some of the town's self-assurance, but today it's once again the whisker of water between Denmark and Sweden, and the ferries across it to Helsingborg, which account for most of Helsingør's through-traffic.

The Town

The town's other great draw, on a sandy curl of land extending seawards, is **Kronborg Slot** (April & mid-Sept to Oct Tues–Sun 11am–4pm; mid-July to mid-Aug daily 9.30am–5pm; May to mid-July & mid-Aug to mid-Sept daily 10.30am–5pm; Nov & March Tues–Sun 11am–3pm; 30kr, 45kr joint ticket with Maritime Museum), principally because of its literary association as Elsinore Castle, whose ramparts Shakespeare's Prince Hamlet supposedly strode. Actually, the playwright never visited Helsingør, and his hero was based on Amleth (aka Amled), a tenth-century character shrouded in the fogs of Danish mythology and certainly predating the castle. Nevertheless, there are still hundreds of requests each year for the whereabouts of "Hamlet's bedroom" and a thriving Hamlet souvenir business. During the winter, guided tours leave from the entrance every half-hour; summer numbers make these impossible and, instead, a well-informed attendant hovers in every room ready to answer questions.

During the sixteenth century, Frederik II instigated construction of the present castle on the site of Erik of Pomerania's fortress, commissioning the Dutch architects Van Opbergen and Van Paaschen, who took their ideas from the buildings of Antwerp.

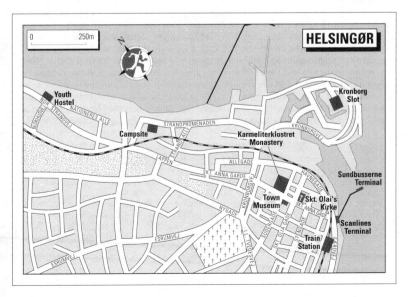

Various bits have been destroyed and rebuilt since, but it remains a grand affair, enhanced immeasurably by its setting and with an interior, particularly the royal chapel, that is spectacularly ornate – though appreciation is hampered by the steady flow of tourists. Crowds are less of a problem in the labyrinthine cellars, which can be seen on a half-hourly guided tour (departing from the cellar entrance). The guide delivers the details then lets visitors wind their way around the cold, damp corridors, dimly lit by oil lamps. The body of Holger Danske, a mythical hero from the legends of Charlemagne, is said to lie beneath the castle, ready to wake again when Denmark needs him; however, the tacky Viking-style statue representing the legend detracts somewhat from the cellars' authentic decay. The castle also houses the national **Maritime Museum**, an uninteresting collection of model ships and nautical knick-knacks.

Away from Kronborg and the harbour area, Helsingør has a well-preserved **medieval quarter** worth taking a walk through. **Stengade** is the main pedestrianized street, linked by a number of narrow alleyways to **Axeltorv**, the town's small market square and usually a good spot to linger over a beer – alternatively, stroll into nearby Brostræde, a street that's famous for the immense ice creams made with traditional ingredients sold here. Near the corner of Stengade and Skt Annagade, the spired **Skt Olai's Kirke** is connected to the Karmeliter Klosteret, which was built by monks as a hospital, became the local poorhouse in 1630, and now contains the **Town Museum** (daily noon–4pm; 10kr). While a hospital, the place prided itself on brain operations, and the unnerving tools of this profession are still *in situ*, together with diagrams of the corrective insertions made into patients' heads. These, combined with various dark remnants from the poorhouse times, evoke a sadness not entirely alleviated by the more upbeat memories from the town's prosperous days. If after this you feel the need to lighten your mood, seek out the oddball **Journeymen's Club** (*Naverhulen*) in a nearby courtyard, cluttered with souvenirs of world travel, such as crab puppets and armadillo lampshades. Act interested and you might get a free guided tour.

Practicalities

You can pick up a free map and information on Helsingør from the **tourist office** at Havnepladsen 3 (June, July & Aug Mon–Sat 9am–7pm, Sun 9am–noon; Sept–May Mon–Fri 9am–5pm, Sat 9am–1pm; ☎49/211333), across Strandgade from the train station, or from the tourist counter in the station itself. Due to the tourist trade, however, the closest thing to a cheap **hotel** in the town is *Skandia*, Bramstræde 1 (☎49/210902; ③), which is decent and clean. If you can afford it, treat yourself to the "Hamlet" or "Ophelia" suites offered at the *Hamlet*, Bramstræde 5 (☎49/210591; ④). There is also a **youth hostel** (☎49/211640; Feb–Nov), literally on the beach, a twenty-minute walk to the north along the coastal road (Ndr. Strandvej); or take bus #340 from the station and get off just after the sports stadium. The **campsite**, at Campingvej 1 (☎49/215856), is

---

FERRIES TO SWEDEN

Three **ferry lines** cross from Helsingør to Helsingborg in Sweden, though only two take foot passengers. The main one, and probably the best option, is the *Scanlines* boat leaving from the main terminal by the train station (see above) and costing 28kr return. The *Sundbusserne* crossing, by small craft which are often heavily buffeted by the choppy waters, also costs 28kr return. The third line, *Sundbroen*, takes cars only. It's perfectly feasible, and on a sunny day very enjoyable, to rent a **bike** from the courtyard behind the tourist office (40kr a day) and cross to Helsingborg for a day's cycling along the Swedish coast. But take food and drink with you – both are much more expensive in Sweden than in Denmark.

closer to town and also by a beach, between the main road Lappen (which begins where Skt Annagade ends) and the sea.

The usual pizza and fast-food outlets are two-a-penny around Stengade, but for healthier **eating**, *Kloster Caféen*, Skt Annagade 35, is the prime lunchtime spot for its set menu and sizeable sandwiches. A little more expensively, there's fine Danish food in the atmospheric *Hos Anker*, Bramstræde 1, or *Færgegården*, Stengade 81b. Given the proximity of the capital, nightlife of note is a rare commodity in Helsingør, but for an evening **drink**, stroll the streets on either side of Stengade, where there are several decent *bodegas* (bars). Rowdier boozing goes on at the top end of Axeltorv, the bar here popular with Swedes taking advantage of Denmark's more liberal licensing laws.

Onwards from Helsingør: the North Zealand coast

Some of the best beaches in Zealand and several picture-postcard fishing villages are within easy reach of Helsingør, either by bike, local buses or a network of private trains (Copenhagen Card valid, *InterRail* and *Eurail* not). No one place has the power to hold you for long but the region is hard to beat for a few days of idle relaxation after exhausting yourself in Copenhagen. From the western extremity at Hundested there used to be a ferry to Grenå in Jutland, but at the time of writing services had been suspended; check with the tourist office to find out whether it's running again.

Hellebæk and Hornbæk
A string of fine sands can be found simply by following Ndr. Strandvej from Helsingør towards the sleepy village of **HELLEBÆK**, some 5km north. At Hellebæk itself, part of the beach is a well-known, if unofficial, venue for nude bathing.

Trains from Helsingør stop at Hellebæk and then continue for 7km to the moderately larger **HORNBÆK**, blessed with excellent beaches and fabulous views over the sea towards Kullen, the rocky promontory jutting out from the Swedish coast. Though fast becoming a playground for yacht-owners and their cronies, Hornbæk is a lovely spot to stay over. In a library just off the main street, the **tourist office** (Mon, Tues & Thurs 2–7pm, Wed & Fri 10am–4pm, Sat 10am–1/3pm; ☎49/704747) can find private rooms and summer cottages, or try the inexpensive pension *Ewaldsgården*, Johannes Ewalds Vej 5 (☎49/700082; ②), close by the train station. Just a few minutes' walk away is Hornbæk's exceptionally inexpensive **campsite** (mid-April to mid-Sept; ☎49/700223).

Gilleleje and Tisvildeleje
From Hornbæk, trains continue along the coast to **GILLELEJE**, twenty minutes further on, another pretty fishing village that does a roaring tourist trade and one with as much appeal as Hornbæk as a short-term stopover. Unfortunately, **accommodation** tends to be booked far in advance and the only hotel in town is the Swiss-chalet-style *Strand*, Vesterbrogade 4B (☎48/300512; ③). The budget option is the all-year campsite, just outside the village at Bregnerødvej 21 (☎49/719755). An alternative is to head west to the youth hostel in Tisvildeleje (see below).

While in Gilleleje, negotiate at least some of the **footpath** that runs along the top of the dunes, where, in 1835, **Søren Kirkegaard** took lengthy contemplative walks, later recalling: "I often stood there and reflected over my past life. The force of the sea and the struggle of the elements made me realize how unimportant I was." Ironically, so important would Kirkegaard become that a monument to him now stands on the path, bearing his maxim: "Truth in life is to live for an idea."

From Gilleleje, bus #343 largely follows the coast to **TISVILDELEJE** (a thirty-minute journey), where there are yet more beaches and Tisvilde Hegn (locally called simply "Hegn"), a forest of wind-tormented trees planted here during the eighteenth century to prevent sand drifts. The **youth hostel** (☎42/309850) forms part of a new holiday complex, *Sankt Helene Centeret*, at Bygmarken 30.

Inland from the coast

It's hard to continue along the coast without first detouring inland, and frankly the effort is barely worthwhile. Trains from both Tisvildeleje and Gilleleje run to Hillerød, in the heart of north Zealand, which – thanks to its magnificent castle – is the place to make for. On the way, though, you might spend a few hours at another royal residence, **Fredensborg Slot** (July only noon–5pm; guided tours 10kr), built by Frederik IV to commemorate the 1720 Peace Treaty with Sweden. Even if the castle is closed, its grand, statue-lined gardens (open all year; free), stretching down to an expansive lake, have distinct appeal.

Hillerød: Frederiksborg Slot

HILLERØD, half an hour by train from Helsingør, and a similar distance from Copenhagen (last stop on line E of the S-train network), has a castle which pushes the more famous Kronborg well into second place: **Frederiksborg Slot** (daily May–Sept 10am–5pm; April & Oct 10am–4pm; Nov–March 11am–3pm; 30kr), which lies decorously across three small islands within an artificial lake. Buses #701 and #703 run from the train station to the castle, but it only takes about twenty minutes to walk there, following the signs (*Slottet*) through the town centre.

The castle was the home of Frederik II and birthplace of his son Christian IV. At the turn of the seventeenth century, under the auspices of Christian, rebuilding began in an unorthodox Dutch Renaissance style. It's the unusual aspects of the monarch's design – prolific use of towers and spires, pointed Gothic arches and flowery window ornamentation – that still stand out, despite the changes wrought by fire and restoration.

You can see the exterior of the castle for free simply by walking through the main gates, across the seventeenth-century S-shaped bridge, and into the central courtyard. Since 1882, the **interior** has functioned as a **museum of Danish history**, largely funded by the Carlsberg brewery magnate Carl Jacobsen in an attempt to create a Danish Versailles, and to heighten the nation's sense of history and cultural development. It's a good idea to buy (25kr), or at least try to borrow, the illustrated guide to the museum, since without it the contents of the sixty-odd rooms are barely comprehensible. Many of the rooms are surprisingly free of furniture and household objects, and attention is drawn to the ranks of portraits along the walls – a motley crew of nobility, statesmen and royalty, who between them ruled and misruled Denmark for centuries. A succession of flat-faced kings and thin consorts gives way in the later rooms to politicians, scientists and writers.

Two rooms deserve special mention. The **chapel**, where monarchs were crowned between 1671 and 1840, is exquisite, its vaults, pillars and arches gilded and embellished, and the contrasting black marble of the gallery riddled with gold lettering. The shields, in tiered rows around the chapel, are those of the knights of the Order of the Elephant, who sat with the king in the late seventeenth century. The **Great Hall**, above the chapel, is a reconstruction, but this doesn't detract from its beauty. It's bare but for the staggering wall and ceiling decorations: tapestries, wall reliefs, portraits and a glistening black marble fireplace. In Christian IV's day the hall was a ballroom, and the polished floor still calls up some fancy footwork as you slide up and down its length.

Away from the often crowded interior, the **gardens**, on the far side of the lake, have some photogenic views of the castle from their stepped terraces and are a good spot for a rest. The quickest way to them is through the narrow Mint Gate to the left of the main castle building, which adjoins a roofed-in bridge leading to the King's Wing. In summer you can also cross the lake on the hourly *M/F Frederiksborg* ferry (May–Sept daily).

Though Frederiksborg is the main reason to come to Hillerød, while here you could also visit the **Money Historical Museum** (open during banking hours; free) at Slotsgade 16–18. During the reigns of Frederik II and Christian IV all Danish coins were minted in Hillerød. Besides samples of these, the place displays currencies from all over the world.

Few of Hillerød's **hotels** can match the prices you might find in Copenhagen, but if you do want to stay, try the *Hillerød*, Milnersvej 41 (☎48/240800; ③). The only budget option is the campsite (Easter to mid-Sept; ☎42/264854) at Blytækkervej 18. The **tourist office** at Slotsgade 52 (June–Aug Mon–Fri 9am–6pm, Sat 10am–5pm; Sept–May Mon–Fri 9am–4pm, Sat 10am–1pm; ☎42/262852) can arrange private rooms.

West from Copenhagen: Roskilde and beyond

There's very little between Copenhagen and the West Zealand coast in the way of things to see and explore, except for the ancient former Danish capital of **ROSKILDE**, less than half an hour by train from the big city. There's been a community here since

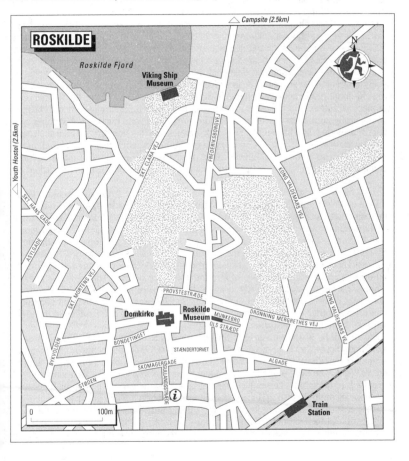

prehistoric times and later the Roskilde fjord provided a route to the open sea that was utilized by the Vikings. But it was the arrival of Bishop Absalon in the twelfth century that made the place the base of the Danish church – and, as a consequence, the national capital. Importance waned after the Reformation and Roskilde came to function mainly as a market for the neighbouring rural communities – much as it does today, as well as being dormitory territory for Copenhagen commuters. In high season especially, it can be crammed with day-trippers seeking the dual blasts from the past supplied by its royal tombs and Viking boats; and the town sees a massive influx every July, when it hosts the **Roskilde Festival** – northern Europe's biggest open-air rock event. Yet at any other time, or for more than a swift visit, the ancient centre is one of Denmark's most appealing towns, and the surrounding countryside quiet and unspoilt.

The Town

The major pointer to the town's former status is the fabulous **Roskilde Domkirke** (April & Sept Mon–Fri 9am–4.45pm, Sat 11.30am–4.45pm, Sun 12.30–4.45pm; May–Aug Mon–Sat 9am–4.45pm, Sun 12.30–4.45pm; Oct–March Mon–Sat 10am–3.45pm, Sun 12.30–3.45pm; 6kr), founded by Bishop Absalon in 1170 on the site of a tenth-century church erected by Harald Bluetooth, and finished during the fourteenth century – although portions have been added right up to the present century. The result is a mishmash of architectural styles, though one that hangs together with surprising neatness; every square inch seems adorned by some curious mark or etching. But it's the claustrophobic collection of coffins containing the regal remains of twenty kings and seventeen queens in four large **royal chapels** that really catch the eye. The most richly endowed chapel is that of Christian IV, a previously austere resting place jazzed-up – in typical early nineteenth-century Romantic style – with bronze statues, wall-length frescoes and vast paintings of scenes from his reign. A striking contrast is provided by the simple red-brick chapel just outside the cathedral, where Frederik IX was laid to rest in 1972. Try to get to the cathedral just before the hour to see and hear the animated medieval clock above the main entrance: a model of Saint Jørgen gallops forward on his horse to wallop the dragon and the hour is marked by the creature's squeal of death.

From one end of the cathedral, a roofed passageway, the **Arch of Absalon**, feeds into the yellow **Bishop's Palace**. The incumbent bishop nowadays confines himself to one wing, making way for three showplaces for (predominantly) Danish art. The main building houses the **Museum for Contemporary Art** (*Museet for Samtidskunst*; Mon–Fri 11am–5pm, Sat & Sun noon–4pm; free) and its diverse temporary exhibitions reflecting current trends. The theme continues in the west wing, where **Palæhøjen** (Tues–Fri & Sun noon–4pm, Sat 10am–2pm; free), run by the local arts society, extends outdoors, turning up a collection of striking sculpture beneath the fruit trees of the bishop's garden. The art rightly draws you away from the **Palace Collections** (May–Sept daily 11am–4pm; Oct–April Sat & Sun 1–3pm; 5kr), made up of paintings, furniture and other artefacts belonging to the wealthiest Roskilde families of the eighteenth and nineteenth centuries.

The **Roskilde Museum**, close to the cathedral at Skt Ols Gade 18 (June–Aug daily 11am–5pm; Sept–May Mon–Fri & Sun 2–5pm; 10kr) is a little more enticing, with strong sections on medieval pottery and toys. Look out for the strange photos that satirist Gustav Wied, who lived in Roskilde for many years and whose rooms are reconstructed here, took of his family. The museum extends to Ringstedgade 6, a shop in 1910-style, where locals dutifully turn up to buy traditional salted-herring and sugar loaves.

More absorbing, and better known, is the **Viking Ship Museum** (*Vikingeshibshallen*; daily April–Oct 9am–5pm; Nov–March 10am–4pm; 30kr) in Strandengen, on the banks of the fjord ten minutes' walk north of the centre. Here, five excellent specimens of

Viking shipbuilding are given the space they deserve: there's a deep-sea trader, a merchant ship, a warship, a ferry and a longship, each one retrieved from the fjord where they had been sunk to block invading forces. Together, they give an impressive indication of the Vikings' nautical versatility, and their skills in boat-building.

Practicalities

Evening entertainment in Roskilde amounts to visiting the sprinkling of bars around the town centre, taking in the occasional free event in the town park, or a pleasant walk along the banks of the fjord. Serious revellers make for Copenhagen, but if you're heading towards Funen or further south in Zealand it's not really worth returning there just for a night. If you do decide to stay, the only central **accommodation** is the pricey *Prindsen*, Algade 13 (☎46/358010; ④). There's a campsite (mid-April to mid-Sept; ☎46/757996) on the wooded edge of the fjord – an appealing setting that means it gets very crowded at peak times; it's linked to the town centre by bus #602. The youth hostel is further out, set amid countryside about 3km from the centre of Roskilde at Hørhusene 61 (☎46/352184). It's open all year and buses #601 and #604 from the train station pass close by; get off after the hospital and take a less-than-obvious route along a footpath through a field. For more information, or to arrange a private room, call in at Roskilde's **tourist office** (summer Mon–Fri 9am–7pm, Sat 9am–5pm, Sun 10am–2pm; shorter hours rest of the year; ☎46/352700) at Gullandstræde 15.

Eating isn't a problem in Roskilde, with plenty of mainstream restaurants lining Skomagergade. Other options include *Mulle & Ruoi*, off Djalma Lunds Gaard, with good snacks and espresso coffee; and, next door to *Hotel Prindsen* (see above), *Café Sachmo*, which provides decent salads and sandwiches – and backgammon tables.

THE ROSKILDE FESTIVAL

Neither the hostel nor campsite are worth bothering with if you're going to the **Roskilde Festival**, which has grown from humble beginnings to attract around 80,000 people annually to its weekend of live rock. The festival takes place over the last weekend in June and there's a special free camping ground beside the festival site, to which shuttle buses run from the train station every ten minutes. Tens of thousands of tickets are sold in advance – contact the tourist office for more information.

Lejre Historical-Archeological Centre

Iron Age Denmark is alive and well and re-enacted at the **Lejre Historical-Archeological Centre**, 12km west of Roskilde, by the volunteer families who spend the summer living in a reconstructed Iron Age settlement, farming and carrying out domestic chores using implements – and wearing clothes – copied from those of the period. Modern-day visitors are welcome (May–Sept daily 10am–4pm; 50kr), and can try their hand at grinding corn, paddling a dugout canoe and cooking rough pancakes. The scientific purpose is to gain understanding of family life in Denmark 2500 years ago, but the centre can be a lot of fun to visit as a day trip. Local trains from Roskilde stop at the village of Lejre; from the station, bus #233 covers the 4km to the historical centre's entrance.

Beyond Roskilde: West Zealand

Beyond Roskilde, West Zealand is flat and bland. You might, however, be journeying through to **Kalundborg** to pick up ferries to Århus in Jutland or to the island of Samsø;

and you can also take ferries from **Korsør**, the other main town of the western coast, to the island of Langeland, or to Nyborg on Funen. Apart from these, the only real interest lies in the **Hornsherred Peninsula**, which divides the Roskilde fjord and Isefjord. There are long, quiet beaches along the peninsula's western coast, though the lack of a railway and a skeletal local bus service means it's a place best toured by bike. Make for the medieval frescoes in the eleventh-century churches at **Skibby** or **Dråby**, or keep on northward for **Jægerspris** and its **castle** (May–Sept daily 10am–noon & 1–5pm; 20kr), built during the fifteenth century as a royal hunting seat and last used by the eccentric Frederik VII, who lived here during the mid-1800s with his third wife. She inherited the castle after the king's death and turned it into an institution for "poor and unfortunate girls".

South from Copenhagen: Køge and around

Not too long ago, **KØGE** was best known for the pollution caused by the rubber factory and chemical works on its outskirts. Despite the town's fine sandy beaches, few ventured here to sample the waters of Køge Bay. In recent years, though, the place has been considerably cleaned up, an achievement acknowledged by the extension of line E of the Copenhagen S-train network to the town, which put its evocatively preserved medieval centre and the bay's beaches within easy reach of the capital. It's also a good base for touring around the Stevns Peninsula, which bulges into the sea just south of the town.

The town and beaches

Saturday is the best day to visit Køge: a variety of free entertainment sweeps through the main streets until early afternoon and there are lively goings-on in the harbourside bars. Walk from the **train station** along Jernbanegade and turn left into Nørregade for Torvet, which is the hub of the action. On a corner of the square is the **tourist office** (Mon–Sat 9am–5pm; ☎53/655800), while nearby, at Nørregade 4, the **Køge Museum** (June–Aug daily 10am–5pm; Sept–May Mon–Fri 2–5pm, Sat & Sun 1–5pm; 15kr) contains remnants from Køge's bloody past, not least the local executioner's sword. If the tales are to be believed, the beheading tool was wielded frequently on Torvet, a place which, perhaps not surprisingly, has also been the scene of several incidences of witchcraft and haunting. On the site of what is today a clothes shop, the Devil is said to have appeared in the forms of a clergyman, a frog, a dog and a pig, to have thrown a boy from his bed out into the yard, and caused hands to swell – among other unwholesome ailments.

Once its market stalls are cleared away, a suitably spooky stillness falls over Torvet and the narrow cobbled streets that run off it. One of these streets, Kirkestræde, is lined with sixteenth-century half-timbered houses and leads to **Skt Nikolai Kirke** (mid-June to July daily 10am–4pm; Aug to mid-June Mon–Fri & Sun 10am–noon), where, in the heyday of sea piracy, plunderers captured in Køge Bay were hung from the tower. Along the nave, some of the carved angel faces on the pew ends lack noses, the wooden snouts having been sliced off by drunken Swedish soldiers during the mid-seventeenth century, while the font, an unattractive black marble and pine item, replaces an earlier one defiled by a woman who performed "an unspeakable act" in it. On a more aesthetic level, Brogade, one of the narrow passageways off Nørregade, contains the **Køge Gallery and Collection** (daily 11am–5pm; free). Besides hosting temporary exhibitions by new artists, the gallery keeps examples of works-in-progress bequeathed by established Danish artists.

The town's **beaches**, which draw many jaded Copenhageners on weekends, stretch along the bay to the north and south of the town. To take full advantage of the sands, stay at one of the two **campsites** beside the southerly beach: *Køge Sydstrand*

(April–Sept; ☎53/650769) is virtually on the beach, and *Vallø* (open all year; ☎53/652851), which also has cabins, is across Strandvejen, close to a pine wood. Further away, 2km from the town centre along Ølbyvej, is Køge's **youth hostel** (mid-May to Aug; ☎53/651474). Take bus #245 from the train station and get off when the bus turns into Agerskovvej. Staying in the town centre isn't expensive; head for the small and comfortable *Centralhotellet* (☎53/650696; ②), next door to the tourist office.

Around Køge: Stevns Peninsula

Stevns Peninsula, easily reached from Køge, is a fairly neglected part of Zealand, mainly because the coastline here is more rugged and less suited to sunbathing than immediately around Køge or in North Zealand. The town of **STORE HEDDINGE**, where you'll find a curious octagonal limestone church, is the obvious starting point for explorations; you can get there by private train (*InterRail* and *Eurail* passes not valid) from Køge in half an hour. In Store Heddinge you'll find a **youth hostel** at Ved Munkevænget 1 (mid-March to Sept; ☎53/702022). While there are several campsites on the beaches to the south, the nearest to Køge is *Nordstevns*, Strandvejen 29 (☎53/677003), in the woodlands around **Strøby**, accessible by frequent bus #209.

Central Zealand: Ringsted

Though now little more than a small farming town, **RINGSTED**'s central location made it one of the most important settlements in Zealand from the end of the Viking era until the Reformation. It was the burial place of medieval Danish monarchs as well as being site of a regional *ting*, the open-air court where prominent merchants and nobles determined the administrative decisions for the province.

The three *ting* stones around which the nobles gathered remain in Ringsted's market square, but they're often concealed by the market itself or the backsides of weary shoppers. It's the sturdy **Skt Bendt's Kirke** (May to mid-Sept Mon–Fri 10am–noon & 1–5pm; mid-Sept to April Mon–Fri 10am–noon) that dominates the square, as it has done for over eight hundred years. Erected in 1170 under the direction of Valdemar I, the church was the final resting place for all Danish monarchs until 1341. Four thousand people are said to have been present for the church's consecration, and although these days it receives a mere trickle of visitors compared to those flocking to the more ornate and recent royal tombs at Roskilde, it represents a substantial chunk of Danish history. Many of the most affluent Zealanders also had themselves buried here, presumably so that their souls could spend eternity mingling with those of the royals. During the seventeenth century a number of the coffins were opened and the finds are collected in the Museum Chapel within the church. Besides the lead slab found inside Valdemar I's coffin, there are plaster casts of the skulls of Queen Bengård and Queen Sofia, a collection of coins found in the church and, unfortunately, only a replica of the Dagmar Cross, discovered when Queen Dagmar's tomb was opened in 1697 – the original is in the National Museum in Copenhagen.

Once you've seen the church you've more or less exhausted Ringsted. The town's only other attraction is the **Agricultural Museum** (Mon–Thurs 11am–4pm, Fri 11am–3pm, Sun 1–4pm; 20kr), off Skt Bendtsgade to the rear of the church, an unexpectedly interesting documentation of the local farming community – but seeing it won't take up more than half an hour.

For accommodation, the **youth hostel** (☎53/611526) is handily situated across the road from the church – with no campsites nearby, this is the only budget option. Ringsted does have some pricey hotels, however, and the **tourist office** (summer Mon–Fri 10am–5pm, Sat 10am–noon; winter Mon–Fri 9am–noon; ☎53/613400), a few doors along, between the hostel and Torvet, can advise on these, as well as arranging private rooms (from 100kr per person).

Southern Zealand and the islands

Southern Zealand is seriously rural, almost solely made up of rich, rolling farmland and villages. South from Ringsted, most routes lead to **NÆSTVED**, by far the largest town in the area. Aside from a smartly restored medieval centre and a couple of minor museums, however, Næstved has little in its favour except proximity to unspoilt countryside and the River Suså, which makes it a good base for novice **canoe trips**. The river's lack of rapids and negligible current enable simple manoeuvring in either direction, and although busy at weekends it's free of crowds at other times. Canoes can be rented at *Suså Kanoudlejning*, Vestbyholmallé 6, in nearby Glumsø (☎53/646144), for around 280kr a day. Off the river, time in the town is best spent strolling amid the half-timbered buildings and dropping into the **Næstved Museum** at Ringstedgade 4 (Tues–Sun 9am–4pm; 20kr) for its jumble of (mainly religious) oddments and a fairly ordinary selection of historical arts and crafts from the town.

The local **tourist office** (May–Oct Mon–Fri 10am–5pm, Sat 9am–noon; Nov–April Mon–Fri 10am–5pm; ☎53/721122) in Det Gule Pakkus, Havnen 1, can fill you in on practical details, and offer suggestions for staying over in Næstved, or try for a room at the *Vinhuset* (☎53/720807; ③), centrally located on the church square, Skt Peders Kirkeplads. The only really cheap spot is the **youth hostel** at Frehasevej 8 (mid-May to mid-Sept; ☎53/722091); from the train station (which is about 1km from the centre on Jernbanegade), turn left into Imagesvej and left again along Præstøvej. There's also a **campsite** (☎53/722091) beside the hostel.

If you have the opportunity, take a trip to the island of **Gavnø**, a few miles south of Næstved, to see its eponymous eighteenth-century Rococo palace (May–Aug daily 10am–5pm; 15kr), an imposing structure enhanced by a delightful leafy setting. Parts of the building are still occupied by the descendants of the original owners, but it has a small viewable collection of books and paintings. Bus #85 runs about four times a day during the summer between Næstved town centre and the palace.

Falster, Lolland and Møn

Off the south coast of Zealand lie three sizeable islands – **Falster**, **Lolland** and **Møn**. All three are connected to the mainland by road, and Falster and Lolland have rail links, too, making them relatively easy to reach, but once there you'll need your own transport – bikes can be rented from virtually all tourist offices and campsites – to do any serious exploration outside the larger communities, since local buses are rare.

Falster
Falster is much the least interesting of the trio. There are some nice woods on the eastern side and some good, but very crowded, beaches along its western coast, particularly around the major resort of **MARIELYST**. There's not much to do in Marielyst except enjoy the beach, but it's got plenty of bars, cafés and accommodation. The most affordable **hotel** is the *Marielyst Strand*, near the beach (☎54/136888; ③), or you could ask at the tourist office (☎54/136298) for their list of private rooms. There are two **campsites**, *Smedegårdens* (☎54/136617) and *Marielyst Camping* (☎54/135307), both close to the beach.

The island's main town, **NYKØBING** – usually written Nykøbing F – has a major sugar industry and a quaint medieval centre, and is of practical use for its tourist office at Østerågade 2 (☎54/851301), which handles enquiries for all three islands. There's also the island's only **youth hostel** at Østre Allé 112 (☎54/854545), about 2km from the Nykøbing train station, with an adjoining campsite (☎54/854545), both open from May to mid-September. If you're here with children, don't miss the **Folkepark Zoo** (daily 9am–4pm; free), which offers the chance to come face to face with a llama, and some native Danish creatures.

If you're ultimately making for the port of **Gedser**, to the south of Falster, for ferries to Warnemünde in Germany, don't bother getting off the train before the ferry dock. Gedser itself doesn't have much to offer except for a decent beach to the east of town.

Lolland

Larger and less crowded than Falster, Lolland is otherwise much the same: wooded, with excellent beaches and lots of quiet, explorable corners. A private railway (*Inter/Eurail* passes not valid) runs to the island from Nykøbing in less than an hour, taking in Sakskøbing, Maribo and finally Nakskov, at the western extremity of the island, near to where ferries cross to Langeland; there's also a *DSB* train from Nykøbing and Saksøbing to Rødby on the south coast. Each town has a tourist office, youth hostel and campsite, but **MARIBO**, delectably positioned on the Søndersø lake, is the most scenic setting for a short stay, with a youth hostel at Skelstrupsvej 19 (March to mid-Dec; ☎53/883314), a campsite at Bangshavevej 25 (Easter to early Sept; ☎53/880071), and a good-value hotel, *Ebsens*, near the train station at Vestergade 32 (☎53/881044; ②).

After the beaches, the island's top attraction is probably **Aalholm Slot** in the southeast, a twelfth-century castle whose sumptuously furnished rooms and rather less attractive torture chamber are open to the public; next door to the castle is an **Automobile Museum** containing two hundred antique cars (both July & Aug daily 11am–5pm; Sept–June Sat & Sun 11am–5pm; joint ticket 90kr, children 35kr). Though Lolland is not the likeliest of places to spot big game, you can see antelopes, zebra, giraffes and more at the drive-through **Knuthenborg Safari Park**, 7km north of Maribo (May–Sept 9am–6pm; 70kr).

Møn

Møn is the most difficult of the three islands to get to from Zealand, since it's not connected by rail, though it's well worth the effort of getting there: take bus #64 from Vordingborg (accessible on the Nykøbing F–Copenhagen rail line). The island is known for its white chalk cliffs – the only cliffs in Denmark – but what really sets Møn apart are its **Neolithic burial places**, which litter the island by the score, and its unique whitewashed churches, many of which feature fourteenth-century frescoes depicting rural life – the work, apparently, of one peasant painter. The main town, **STEGE**, is, at least for those without their own transport, the most feasible base, since it's the hub of the island's (minimal) bus service and has a campsite (May–Aug; ☎55/815325), on Falckvej. Of the five campsites on the island, *Camping Møns Klint*, Klintevej 544 (☎ 55/812025) in **Borre**, to the east, is the best, while *Ulvshale Camping* (☎55/815325) is right on the beach at the island's northenmost point. If you'd rather sleep in a bed, check out current options with the helpful Stege **tourist office**, by the bus station at Storegade 2 (mid-June to Aug Mon–Sat 9am–6pm, Sun 10am–noon; rest of the year Mon–Fri 9am–5pm, Sat 9am–noon; ☎55/814411).

The best of the Neolithic barrows is **Kong Asker's Høj**, about 20km from Stege near **Sprove**, while the foremost frescoes can be admired at **ELMELUNDE** (bus #51 from Stege) and at **FANEFJORD** (take the Vordingborg bus from Stege and get out at Store Damme, then walk), which also has a Neolithic barrow in the churchyard. As for the cliffs (*Møn Klint*), they're at the eastern end of the island and stretch for about 8km. Bus #51 runs between the cliffs and Stege four or five times a day depending on the season. Fifteen minutes' walk from the cliffs, at Langebjergvej 1, is a **youth hostel** (closed Dec; ☎55/812030).

Bornholm

Although much nearer to Sweden, **Bornholm** has been a Danish possession since 1522. Once an important Baltic trading post, its population now lives by fishing, farming and, increasingly, tourism. The coastline is blessed with great beaches in the south, with some invitingly rugged cliffs and hilly landscapes on the northern side, while the island's centre is marked by some very walkable woods. It's no wonder that holiday-making Scandinavian and German families fill Bornholm each summer. Despite the crowds, Bornholm is an intriguing and unusual place to visit, easily reached by ferry from Copenhagen, and quite feasible as a stopover if you're going from Denmark to Sweden or Germany on one of several ferry crossings (see "Travel Details").

To get the most out of Bornholm, you really need to travel around the whole coast – not difficult, since the island is only about 30km across from east to west – and spend three or four days doing it. **Getting around** is easy and best done by **bike**: the island is criss-crossed by some two hundred bike trails, and bikes can be rented in Rønne at *Bornholms Cykeludlejning*, Nordre Kystvej 5 (☎56/951395), and from most of the island's tourist offices. If this seems too energetic, you can travel by **bus** (all buses are equipped to carry bikes; information on ☎56/952121). **Accommodation** is straightforward, too: there's a youth hostel in each of the main settlements and campsites are sprinkled fairly liberally around the coast. The peak weeks of the summer are very busy, and you should phone ahead to check space. But at any other time of year there'll be little difficulty. The nightlife on the island can also be surprisingly lively, although often limited to one spot in each town – invariably the café in the main square.

Ferries from Copenhagen arrive seven hours later in **RØNNE**, the main town on the island, where a **tourist office** (late June to Aug Mon & Fri–Sun 8am–9pm, Tues–Thurs 8am–5pm; Sept to late June daily 9am–5pm; ☎56/950810) can fill you in on accommodation and transport details, and give you a copy of *Bornholm Denne Uge*, the free weekly listings magazine. If you've arrived on the 6.30am boat, you can celebrate your arrival with breakfast at *Det Røde Pakhus*, Snellemark 30, or with freshly baked bread from the bakery opposite. Otherwise, though, it's best to move on immediately: Rønne lacks the character of many of the other island settlements. If you do need to **stay over**, there are plenty of options: a youth hostel at Sønder Allé 22 (April–Oct; ☎56/951340); a campsite at Strandvejen 4 (mid-May to Aug; ☎56/952320); private rooms start from around 125kr per person – contact the tourist office, or the *Sverres* hotel at Skt Mortensgade 42B (☎56/950303; ③).

If you're eager to get to the beach, make for **DUEODDE**, where there's nothing but sands, a youth hostel at Skrokkegårdsvej 17 (May–Sept; ☎56/988119), and a string of campsites. In summer Dueodde lighthouse is open to the public (5kr), offering superb views. At the other corner of the eastern coast, **SVANEKE** is a quiet place favoured by Danish retirees, but has more spectacular scenery and the beaches are, once again, superb. In the mid-1970s Svaneke won a Council of Europe prize for town preservation and these days upmarket hotels and restaurants occupy some of the renovated old buildings. If you want **to stay**, first choice is the excellent *Siemsens Gaard*, Havnebryggen 9 (☎ 56/496149; ③), whose front rooms give great views. Otherwise, there's a youth hostel at Reberbanevej 5 (mid-April to Oct; ☎56/496242), and two campsites. The **tourist office** at Staregade 24 (☎56/496350) should be able to help with any queries.

Halfway along the north coast, **GUDHJEM** is pretty too, its tiny streets winding their way around the foot of a hill. Buses run the 5km or so north to the **Bornholms Kunstmuseum** (daily 10am–5pm), a gallery displaying works from the Bornholm School that thrived here in the first half of this century. Gudhjem is also a good jumping-off point for the six-kilometre trip inland to **ØSTERLARS**, site of the largest and most impressive of the island's fortified round churches, which date from the twelfth and thirteenth centuries. A similar distance further inland, right in the centre of the island, is Bornholm's largest forest, **Almindingen**; there's a lookout tower for some fabulous views. **SANDVIG**, on the island's northwest corner, is the start of another worthwhile walk, along **Hammeren**, the massive granite headland that juts out towards Sweden. Just south of Sandvig are the remains of the thirteenth-century **Hammershus**, not much in themselves but worth a visit for the views from the tall crag which the castle occupied.

If Bornholm suddenly seems too big, and the weather's good, take one of the daily ferries (from Svaneke, Gudhjem or Sandvig; check with any tourist office for the latest details) to the tiny island of **Christiansø**, some 25km away – a speck in the Baltic that served as a naval base during the seventeenth century, and later as a prison, though these days the minuscule population prides itself on its spiced herring. From Christiansø there's a footbridge over to the island of **Frederiksø**, a breeding ground for eider duck. If you want to savour the peace of these little islands, you can stay at an inn, the *Gæstgiveriet* (☎56/462015; ②), on Christiansø.

As for **leaving Bornholm**, if you're not going back to Denmark, ferries to Sweden depart from Rønne for Ystad, and from Allinge, near Sandvig, there's a summer-only catamaran link to Simrishamn. There are also crossings from Rønne to Travemünde and Sassnitz in Germany.

travel details

Trains

Copenhagen to: Århus (6 daily; 5hr); Esbjerg (20 daily; 4hr 30min); Helsingør (30 daily; 50min); Næstved (20 daily; 1hr 30min); Nykøbing (20 daily; 2hr); Odense (25 daily; 3hr); Ringsted (20 daily; 55min); Roskilde (25 daily; 26min).

Helsingør to: Gilleleje (17 daily; 41min); Hellebæk (17 daily; 12min); Hillerød (23 daily; 30min); Hornbæk (17 daily; 24min).

Køge to: Fakse (16 daily; 38min); Store Heddinge (19 daily; 31min).

Nykøbing F to: Nakskov (21 daily; 49min); Rødby (20 daily; 29min); Sakskøbing (21 daily; 16min).

Roskilde to: Kalundborg (5 daily, connects with ferry to Jutland; 1hr 15min); Korsør (25 daily, connects with ferry to Funen; 54min).

Buses

Copenhagen to: Aalborg (2 daily; 6hr); Århus (2 daily; 4hr); Helsingør (30 daily; 1hr); Hanstholm (1 daily; 6hr 45min).

Ferries

Allinge to: Christiansø (May–Oct Mon–Sat 1 daily; 1hr 10min).

Copenhagen to: Rønne (1 daily in summer, 2 daily in peak season; 7hr).

Gudhjem to: Christiansø (May–Sept 1 daily; July & Aug 3 daily; 1hr).

Kalundborg to: Århus (15 daily; 1hr 20min–3hr).

Korsør to Lohals (5 daily; 1hr 30min); Nyborg (15–25 daily; 70min).

Sjællands Odde to: Ebeltoft (12–15 daily; 45min–1hr 40min).

Svaneke to: Christiansø (Mon–Fri 1 daily; 1hr 30min).

Tårs (Langeland) to: Spodsbjerg (16–18 daily; 45min).

International Trains

Copenhagen to: Bergen (2 daily; 19hr); Gothenburg (4 daily; 4hr 30min); Helsinki (3 daily; 25hr); Kiruna (1 daily; 29hr); Narvik (1 daily; 29hr); Oslo (3 daily; 9hr 30min); Stockholm (4 daily; 10hr); Turku (2 daily; 21hr).

International Ferries

Copenhagen to: Malmö (catamaran: 18 daily; 45min; boat: 5 daily; 1hr 30min); Oslo (1 daily; 16hr); Swinoujscie (5 weekly; 10hr).

Dragør to: Limhamn (20 daily; 55min).

Gedser to: Warnemünde, Germany (6 daily in summer; rest of year 3 daily; 2hr).

CHAPTER TWO

FUNEN

K nown as "the Garden of Denmark", partly for the lawn-like neatness of its fields and partly for the immense amount of fruit and vegetables that come from them, **Funen** (*Fyn*) is the smaller of the two main Danish islands – and it's true you wouldn't be missing a lot by passing quickly through on your way between Zealand and Jutland. The pastoral outlook of the place and the coastline draw many, but its attractions are mainly worthy but low-profile cultural aspects such as the various collections of the Funen painters and the birthplaces of writer Hans Christian Andersen and composer Carl Nielsen, who eulogized the distinctive sing-song Funen accent and claimed it inspired his music. If you are keen, the island's best seen by cycling; otherwise, you'll be getting around on buses more often than trains, which are relatively scarce here.

Arriving from Zealand brings you through **Nyborg**, a town with a heavily restored twelfth-century castle, though there's really little reason to linger long on the **east coast**, and it's preferable to stick to the cross-country railway that continues to **Odense**. This is Denmark's third largest city and the obvious base if you're intent on picking through the small surrounding communities by day but want something other than rural quiet to fill the evenings. Close by, the former fishing town of **Kerteminde** retains some faded charm, and is within easy reach of the **Ladby Boat**, an important Viking relic, and the isolated **Hindsholm peninsula**. To the **south**, Funen's coastal life centres on **Svendborg** – connected by train with Odense, the island's only other rail line – which has good beaches and a fragmented archipelago of **islands**: vacation territory for the most part, and all served by ferries. The **west** of Funen has the thickest gathering of manor houses in the country, although few of them are open to the public, and you'd do well to hurry through, either to the offshore islands or on to Jutland.

East Funen

Crossing from Zealand to Funen over the **Store Bælt** ("Great Belt") involves using the frequent ferries (which accommodate cross-country trains) between Korsør and **Nyborg**, the easternmost Funen town and one that few people see more of than the web of railway lines feeding out from its ferry terminal.

Unless you're in a rush to reach Odense, however, allocate a few hours to Nyborg's strollable old streets and the town's thirteenth-century castle, which spent two hundred years as the seat of Danish political power. Other than countless lookalike villages, there's little else in East Funen worthy of attention, although the Storebælt Exhibition Centre, within a short bus ride of Nyborg, offers an uncritical appraisal of the biggest engineering project ever seen in Denmark: the construction of a fixed road and rail link between Funen and Zealand.

Nyborg

Leaving the ferry terminal, you'll soon find that **NYBORG** is small and easily navigated and will have no trouble making your way to **Nyborg Slot**, completed around 1200

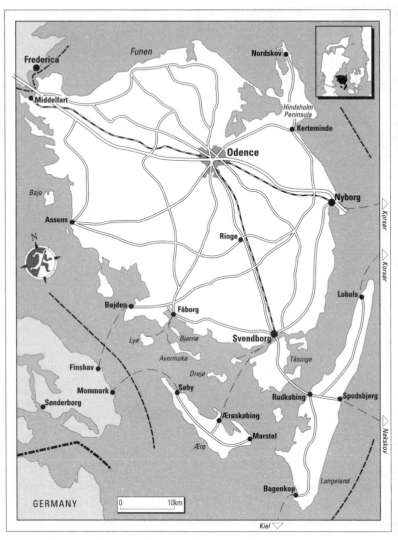

and instigated by Valdemar the Great as part of a chain of coastal fortresses to guard against Wend piracy. For over two hundred years, the *Danehof* – a summertime national assembly involving king, clergy and nobility – met here (in 1282 drawing up the first Danish constitution), which effectively made Nyborg the Danish capital until 1443, when power moved to Copenhagen. The castle bears little evidence of the years of power-broking, however. Many of the surrounding fortifications have been adapted as ordinary homes and all that remains on view is the narrow building holding the living quarters, its distinctive harlequin brickwork a result of 1920s restoration. Inside, the **museum** (daily June–Aug 10am–5pm; April, May, Sept & Oct 10am–3pm; 25kr) leads through low-beamed rooms and emerges into an expansive attic, in themselves much more evocative of the past than the odd table, chest, or suit of armour used to decorate them.

With the nightlife of Odense just 25km away to the west, there's little temptation to spend a night in Nyborg. If you decide to do so, though, *Missionshotellet*, on Østervoldgade (☎65/301188; ②), is a fair-priced hotel choice; and the **youth hostel** is centrally placed at Havnegade 28 (☎65/312704). Bus route #2 (which runs to the Storebælt Exhibition Centre, see below) is the link to the cabin-equipped beachside **campsite** (☎65/310256) at Hjejlegade 99. For further information, drop in to the **tourist office** at Torvet 9 (mid-June to Aug Mon–Sat 9am–5pm; Sept to mid-June Mon–Fri 9am–5pm, Sat 9am–noon; ☎65/310280).

The Storebælt Exhibition Centre

There's been a regular ferry between Nyborg and Korsør for more than two centuries and archeological research on the mid-channel island of Sprogø suggests that Danes have been boating back and forth for many thousands of years. The latest twist in the saga of Funen–Zealand travel is a multimillion-kroner combined bridge and tunnel to carry road and rail traffic across the eighteen-kilometre-wide Store Bælt, a task expected to be completed in 1998.

At Knudshoved, about 5km from Nyborg (bus #2) at Funen's eastern extremity, the **Storebælt Exhibition Centre** (May–Sept daily 10am–8pm; Oct–April Tues–Sun 10am–5pm; 35kr) will explain more than you need to know about the engineering expertise that has made the project – part of which involves constructing the world's longest suspension bridge – possible, and somewhat less about the British-built drilling machines that have put the project way behind schedule. The hour-long gap between Nyborg buses should give you plenty of time to get your fill of the centre's robotic models, videos and interactive computer simulations.

Odense

Funen's sole industrial centre and one of the oldest settlements in the country, **ODENSE** – named after Odin, chief of the pagan gods – gained prominence in the early nineteenth century when the opening of the Odense canal linked the city to the sea and made it the major transit point for the produce of the island's farms. Nowadays it's a pleasant provincial town, with a large manufacturing sector hugging the canal bank on the northern side of the city, well out of sight of the compact old centre – which houses some fine museums and a surprisingly vigorous nightlife. Odense is also known, throughout Denmark at least, as the birthplace of Hans Christian Andersen, and although it's all done quite discreetly, the fact is as celebrated as you might expect: souvenir shops and new hotels cater for travellers lured by the prospect of a romantic Andersen experience – something they (almost inevitably) won't find.

Arrival, information and accommodation

Long-distance **buses** terminate at the **train station**, a ten-minute walk from the city centre, where you'll find the **tourist office** (mid-June to Aug Mon–Sat 9am–7pm, Sun 11am–7pm; Sept to mid-June Mon–Fri 9am–5pm, Sat 9am–noon; ☎66/127520) on the ground floor of the nineteenth-century Rådhus. On Odense's **public transport** system you pay at the end of the trip: if you have to use more than one bus, ask the driver for a "change ticket" (*omstigning*). Better value if you're planning to see Odense's museums is the two-day **Adventure Pass** (*Odense Eventyrpas*), which for 90kr gets you into

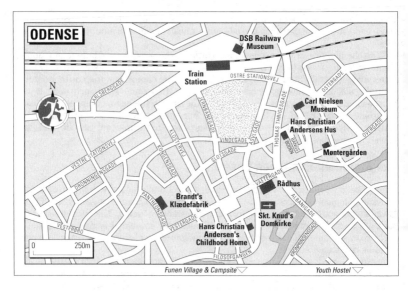

Funen Village & Campsite ▽   Youth Hostel ▽

all of them except the train museum (though there's a discount) and allows unlimited travel on local buses, along with reductions on the *Odense Åfart* boat and the zoo (see below); buy it from any tourist office, most train stations, youth hostels, campsites and hotels on Funen. If you can't face the buses, you can **rent a bike** at *City Cykler*, Vesterbro 27, among other outlets.

Accommodation

Hans Christian Andersen may well be responsible for Odense's plethora of pricey **hotels**; there are several affordable alternatives, though. Cheapest are the *Ansgarhus Motel*, Kirkegård Allé 17–19 (☎66/128800; ②), and the friendly *Det Lille Hotel*, Dronningensgade 5 (☎66/122821; ②); also worth trying are *Turisthotellet*, Gerthasminde 64 (☎66/112692; ③), and *Hotel Domir*, Hans Tausens Gade 19 (☎66/121427; ③); note that breakfast costs extra at all of them. Odense also has a **youth hostel** at Kragsbjergvej 121 (mid-Jan to Nov; ☎66/130425) – take a bus #6 going south to Holluf Pile/Fraugade or Hjallese and get out along Munkebjergvej at the junction with Vissenbjergvej.

The only **campsite** actually in Odense is at Odensevej 102 (late April to mid-Sept; ☎66/114702), near the Funen Village: take buses #41, #91 or #92 from the Rådhus or train station. The next closest site, which also has a few cabins, is *Blommenslyst*, about 10km from Odense at Middelfartvej 494 (May to mid-Sept; ☎66/967641); hourly buses #830 or #832 from the train station take twenty minutes.

ACCOMMODATION PRICE CODES

The Danish hotels listed throughout the guide have been graded according to the following price bands, based on the rate for a double room in summer, with a private bathroom usually included.

   ① Up to 300kr   ② 300–450kr   ③ 450–600kr   ④ over 600kr

The Town

Save for two outlying museums a bus ride away, Odense is easily explored on foot. There's a lot to be said for simply wandering around the compact centre with no particular destination in mind, but you shouldn't pass up the chance to visit the Hans Christian Andersen museums – very much what the town is known for – or fail to take in at least one of several absorbing art collections. Two other museums provide more offbeat fare: one celebrates composer Carl Nielsen – after Andersen, Odense's most famous son – and the other eulogizes Danish railways.

The Hans Christian Andersen museums and the cathedral

Odense's showpiece museum is the **Hans Christian Andersens Hus** at Hans Jensen Stræde 37–45 (daily June–Aug 9am–6pm; April, May & Sept 10am–5pm; Oct–March 10am–3pm; 20kr), in the house where the writer spent his early childhood and which he described in *The Fairy Tale of My Life*. Oddly enough, Andersen was only really accepted in his own country towards the end of his life; his real admirers were abroad, which was perhaps why he travelled widely and often, and left Odense at the first opportunity. The son of a hard-up cobbler, Hans Christian Andersen's first home was a single room that doubled as a workshop in what was then one of Odense's slum quarters. It was a rough upbringing: Hans' ill-tempered mother was fifteen years older than his father, whom she married when seven months pregnant with Hans (she also had an illegitimate daughter by another man); his grandfather was insane; and descriptions of his grandmother, often given charge of the young Hans, range from "mildly eccentric" to "a pathological liar". Andersen wrote novels and a few (best-forgotten) plays, but since his death it's his fairy tales that have gained most renown, partly autobiographical tales (not least *The Ugly Duckling*) that were influenced by *The Arabian Nights*, German folk stories, and the traditional Danish folk tales passed on by the inmates of the Odense workhouse where his grandmother looked after the garden.

Few of the less-than-fairy-tale aspects of Andersen's life are touched upon in the museum, which was founded on the centenary of Andersen's birth, when Odense began to cash in on its famous ex-citizen. There's a nagging falseness about some aspects of the collection, but since Andersen was a first-rate hoarder it is stuffed with intriguing items: bits of school reports, his certificate from Copenhagen University, early notes and manuscripts of his books, chunks of furniture, his umbrella, and paraphernalia from his travels, including the piece of rope he carried to facilitate escape from hotel rooms in the event of fire. A separate gallery has a library of his works in seventy languages and headphones for listening to some of Andersen's best-known tales read by the likes of Laurence Olivier and Michael Redgrave. Nearby, a sloppy slide-show purports to tell the life story of Andersen, to the accompaniment of a warped pianola soundtrack.

The area around the museum, all half-timbered houses and spotlessly clean, car-free cobbled streets, lacks character; indeed, if Andersen was around he'd hardly recognize the neighbourhood, which is now one of Odense's most expensive. For far more realistic local history, head to the **Møntergården** (daily 10am–4pm; 15kr), a few streets away at Overgade 48–50, where there's an engrossing assemblage of artefacts dating from the city's earliest settlements to the Nazi occupation, plus an immense coin collection – from as long ago and as far afield as England under Danelaw and Danish rule in Estonia – which might engage you for twice as long as the Andersen museum.

There's more, but not much more, about Andersen at Munkemøllestræde 3–5, between Skt Knud Plads and Klosterbakken, in the tiny **Hans Christian Andersen's Childhood Home** (daily April–Sept 10am–5pm; Oct–March noon–3pm; 5kr), where Andersen lived from 1807 to 1819. More interesting, though, is the nearby **Skt Knud's**

Domkirke (April, early May & late Sept Mon–Sat 10am–4pm; mid-May to mid-Sept Mon–Sat 10am–5pm, June–Aug also Sun 11.30am–3.30pm; Oct–March Mon–Fri 10am–4pm), whose crypt holds one of the most unusual and ancient finds Denmark has to offer: the **skeleton of Knud II**. Knud was slain in 1086 by Jutish farmers, angry at the taxes he'd imposed on them, in the original Skt Albani Kirke – the barest remains of which were found several years ago in the city park. The king was laid to rest here in 1101, and the miraculous events of proceeding years (see "History", p.56 for more) resulted in his canonization as Knud the Holy. Close to Knud's is another coffin, thought to hold the remains of his brother, Benedict (though some claim them to be Saint Alban, whose body was brought to Denmark by Knud); displayed alongside is the fading, but impressive, Byzantium-style silk tapestry sent as a shroud by Knud's widow, Edele. The cathedral itself is noteworthy, too. Mostly late thirteenth-century, it's the only example of pure Gothic church architecture in the country, set off by a finely detailed sixteenth-century wooden altarpiece that's rightly regarded as one of the greatest works of the Lübeck mastercraftsman, Claus Berg.

Odense's art museums

While it doesn't specialize in the paintings of the best-known Funen artists (for which see p.116 and p.118), it's in the **Art Museum of Funen**, at Jernbanegade 13 (*Fyns Kunstmuseum*; daily 10am–4pm, Wed also 7–10pm; 15kr, free on Wed evenings and winter Sun), a few minutes' walk from the cathedral, that you can get an idea of the region's importance to Danish art during the late nineteenth century, when a number of Funen-based painters forsook portraiture of the rich in favour of impressionistic landscapes, nature studies, and recording the lives of the peasantry. The collection also contains some stirring works by many Nordic greats, among them Vilhelm Hammershøi, P.S. Krøyer, and Michael and Anne Ancher, but most striking of all is H.A. Benedekilke's enormously emotive *The Cry*. The modern era isn't forgotten, with selections from Asger Jorn, Richard Mortensen and Egill Jacobsen, among many others, drawn from the museums' large stock and shown in rotation.

For more modern art, walk along Vestergade to **Brandt's Klædefabrik**, a large former textile factory now given over to a number of cultural endeavours: three museums, an art school, a music library and a cinema, along with cafés and restaurants. The **Art Exhibition Hall** here (Tues–Sun 10am–5pm; 25kr) is an increasingly prestigious spot for high-flying new talent in art and design to show off; close by are the varied displays of the **Museum of Photographic Art** (same hours; 20kr), taken from the cream of modern (and some not so modern) art photography and almost always worth a view. There's also the more down-to-earth **Danish Graphic Museum** (Mon–Fri 10am–4pm, Sat & Sun 11am–5pm; 20kr), with its bulky machines and devices chronicling the development of printing, book-binding and illustrating from the Middle Ages to the present day. You can buy a combined ticket for all three museums for 40kr.

The Carl Nielsen and railway museums

Odense's newest museum, and one that might be considered long overdue given the importance of the man it celebrates, is the **Carl Nielsen Museum**, inside the concert hall at Carls Bergs Gade 11 (daily 10am–4pm; 15kr). Though remembered in Denmark mostly for his popular songs, it was Nielsen's opera scores, choral pieces and symphonies that established him as a major international composer around the turn of the century. Born in a village just outside Odense, Nielsen displayed prodigious musical gifts from an early age and joined the Odense military band as a cornet player when just 14 (wearing a specially shortened uniform). From there he went to study at the Copenhagen conservatoire and then on to gain worldwide acclaim, the musical cognoscenti in his own country regarding him as having salvaged Danish music from a period of decline. Despite his travels, and long period of residence in Copenhagen, Nielsen continually praised the inspirational qualities of Funen's nature and the island's tuneful dialect, even writing a somewhat sentimental essay romanticizing the landscape in which "even trees dream and talk in their sleep with a Funen lilt". If you've never heard of Nielsen, be assured that his music is nowhere near as half-baked as his prose: in the museum you can listen to some of his work on headphones, including excerpts from his major pieces and the polka he wrote when still a child. The actual exhibits, detailing Nielsen's life and achievements, are enlivened by the accomplished sculptures of his wife, Anne Marie, many of them early studies for her equestrian statue of Christian IX that now stands outside the Royal Stables in Copenhagen.

The final museum in central Odense is hardly essential viewing but anyone impressed with the comfort and efficiency of modern Danish trains may regard a visit to it as a pilgrimage. The **DSB Railway Museum** (*Jernbanemuseet*; May–Sept daily 10am–4pm; Oct–April Mon–Sat 10am–3pm; 15kr, free to *InterRail*, *Eurail* and *Nordturist* pass holders, half-price with an Adventure Pass), immediately behind the station, houses some of *DSB*'s most treasured artefacts, which include royal and double-decker carriages and the reconstruction of an entire early 1900s station, as well as a feast of otherwise forgotten facts pertaining to the rise and rise of Danish railways.

Funen Village and Funen Prehistoric Museum

South of Odense's centre, the **Funen Village** (April, May, Sept & Oct daily 9am–4pm; June–Aug daily 9am–6.30pm; Nov–March Sun 10am–4pm; 20kr) is an open-air museum, a reconstructed nineteenth-century country village lent an air of authenticity by its wandering geese, and the gardens planted and maintained in the style of the time. From the farmhouse to the poorhouse, all the buildings are originals from other parts of Funen, with their exteriors painstakingly reassembled and interiors carefully refurnished. In summer, the old trades are revived in the former workshops and crafthouses, and there are free shows at the open-air theatre. Though often crowded, the village is well worth a call, and you should look out for the village-brewed beer – it tastes rather disgusting but is handed out free on special occasions. Buses #21 and #22 run to the village from the city centre (get out at the *Den Fynske Landsby* sign), or do what the locals do and rent a boat to float here along the river through Hunderup Skov. Between May and August you can also get here on the *Odense Åfart* boat from Munkemose to the Village, stopping off at Odense zoo on the way (5 daily 9am–5pm; 45kr, children 22kr; information ☎65/957996).

Also easily reached from the town centre, on bus #81, is the **Funen Prehistoric Museum** (Tues–Sun noon–5pm; 10kr), one of many prehistoric collections in Denmark, but one that at least makes an effort to be different, with an unusually accessible style of presentation. There is, for example, a simulated Bronze Age TV news broadcast, alongside displays describing how ancient symbols are used in modern times. The museum occupies several buildings in the grounds of a sixteenth-century manor house, whose very walkable landscaped gardens (open dawn to dusk) are decorated by sculptures from the Danish Academy of Fine Arts.

Eating, drinking and nightlife

Most of Odense's **restaurants and snack bars** are squeezed into the central part of town, which means there's a lot of competition and potentially some very good bargains during the day. If the weather is right for outdoor eating, pick up a sandwich from *Raadhusbageriet*, Vestergade 17. *Café Biografen* at Brandt's Klædefabrik serves cheap sandwiches, and in the same building there's also *Brandt's Café and Restaurant*, with staple dishes like lasagne and chilli from around 50kr. Decent, reasonably priced can also be had at *Eventyr*, Overgade 18, and at *Restaurant Tinsoldaten*, just around the corner on Frue Kirkestræde (which is also the place to be at 6am for breakfast after a night's clubbing).

In the evening, relatively inexpensive Danish menus are a feature of *Målet*, Jernbanegade 17. Reliable pizzas and pasta can be found at *Pizza Ristorante Italino*, Vesterbro 9, and *Mamma's*, Klaregade 4. Mexican dishes make up the menu at *Birdy's Café*, Nørregade 21, while carnivores should head for Odense's branch of the steak restaurant chain, *Jensens Bøfhus*, at Kongensgade 10.

Nightlife and live music

Lately, Odense has gained a plethora of late-opening cafés that have usurped the role of nightclubs as **evening** hang-outs. Easily the most fashionable, and decorated with a dazzling display of movie posters, is *Café Biografen* (see above). From there you could move on to *Boogie Dance Café*, downstairs from *Birdy's Café* at Nørregade 21, which is one of the few spots with any life early in the week. For unpretentious drinking, *On-Off*, Ny Vestergade 18, is the place for knocking back the Carlsberg. Should you be in the mood for a gamble, you can try your luck at the **casino** in the *SAS Hotel* on Claus Bergs Gade (☎66/147800, open from 7pm right through to 7am (60kr). For details on Odense's **gay and lesbian** scene, contact the *Lambda* organization (☎66/177692).

Odense also has a **live music** scene worth investigating. Read the free local magazine *Jam* (from most cafés, music shops, and the tourist office) for listings. The magazine originates at *Rytmeposten*, Østre Stationsvej 27a, a converted post office where you'll often find heavy rock bands performing. Another busy spot is the radical politics/arts centre *Badstuen*, Østre Stationsvej 26. Other likely venues are *Café Oscar*, Vestergade 75; *Musikhuset*, Vestergade 68; and, for jazz and blues, *Musik Kælderen*, Dronningensgade 2B, and *Kabyssen*, Vindegade 65.

Kerteminde and around

A half-hour bus ride (#890) northeast from Odense, past the huge cranes and construction platforms at Munkebo – until recently a tiny fishing hamlet but now the home of Denmark's biggest shipyard – lies **KERTEMINDE**, itself having firm links with the sea: originally in fishing and now, increasingly, in tourism. The town is a sailing and holiday centre and can get oppressively busy during the peak weeks of the summer. At any other time of year, though, it makes for a well-spent day, split between the town itself and the Viking-era Ladby Boat, just outside.

The heart of the town, around the fifteenth-century Skt Laurentius Kirke and along Langegade and Strandgade, is a neatly and prettily preserved nucleus of shops and houses. On Strandgade itself, the **town museum** (*Farvergården*; daily 10am–4pm; 20kr) has five reconstructed craft workshops and a collection of fishing equipment gathered locally. On a grander note, Kerteminde was home to the "birdman of Funen", the painter Johannes Larsen, and a fairly lengthy stroll around the marina and on along Møllebakken brings you to his one-time house, now the **Johannes Larsen Museum** (June–Oct Tues–Sun 10am–4pm; 30kr). During the late nineteenth century, Larsen produced etchings of rural locales and ornithology, going against the grain of prevailing art world trends in much the same way as the Skagen artists (see p.151). The house is kept as it was when Larsen lived there, with his furnishings and knick-knacks, many of his canvases and, in the dining room, his astonishing wall paintings. To the chagrin of the pious locals, the house in its day became a haunt of the country's more bacchanalian artists and writers. In the garden is a sculpted female figure by Kai Nielsen, a frequent visitor to the house. A story goes that during one particularly drunken party the piece was dropped and the legs broke off. Someone called the local *falck*, but despite much inebriated pleading, the (sober) officer who rushed to the scene refused to take the sculpture to hospital.

Practicalities

The **tourist office**, opposite the Skt Laurentius Kirke, across a small alleyway (May–Sept Mon–Fri 9am–5pm, Sat 9am–1pm; Oct–April Mon–Fri 9am–1pm; ☎65/321121), can give you details on Kerteminde's winter hotel accommodation bargains. If you want to stay over at any other time, the only low-cost option is the **youth hostel** (Nov–mid-Jan; ☎65/323929) at Skovvej 46, a twenty-minute walk from the centre (cross the Kerteminde fjord by the road bridge, take the first left and then turn almost immediately right to reach it). There's also a **campsite**, not far from the Larsen museum (late April to Aug; ☎65/321971) at Hindsholmvej 80, on the main road running along the seafront – a thirty-minute walk from the centre.

Around Kerteminde: the Ladby Boat and Hindsholm Peninsula

About 4km from Kerteminde, along the banks of the fjord at Vikingvej 123, is the **Ladby Boat** (*Ladbyskibet*; May–Oct Tues–Sun 10am–6pm; Nov–April Tues–Sun 10am–3pm; 20kr), a vessel dredged up from the fjord that was found to be the burial ship of a Viking chieftain. The 22-metre craft, along with the remains of the weapons, hunting dogs and horses that accompanied the deceased on his journey to Valhalla, is kept in a tiny purpose-built museum. It's an interesting find, but you'll need only half an hour for a close inspection. Bus #482 runs to the museum several times a day Monday to Friday, and in summer you can also get a motor boat, but it's a pleasant alternative to rent a bicycle in town and pedal there.

Cycling is the best way to explore the **Hindsholm Peninsula**, north of Kerteminde, since it's quite small; if this seems too energetic, the tourist office should have the latest bus schedules. There's not actually much to see, save perhaps the ancient **underground burial chamber** (*Mårhøj Jættestue*) near Martofte, which is open to the public (though the bodies, of course, are long gone), but – outside of high season – the area is an unparalleled spot to pitch a tent and revel in the quiet seclusion. Further into the peninsula are two **campsites**: *Bøgebjerg Strand* (mid-April to Sept; ☎65/341052), on the shore opposite the island of Romsø; and, on the northernmost tip just past Nordskov at Fynshovedvej 748, *Fyns Hoved* (May to mid-Sept; ☎65/341014).

Southern Funen and the islands

Southern Funen is noted above all for its many miles of sandy beaches, which are filled by a near shoulder-to-shoulder tourist crush during the peak season. In July and August, the islands of the southern archipelago are more enticing: connected by an efficient network of ferries, they range from larger chunks of land such as Tåsinge, Langeland and Ærø – the second two certainly worth a few nights' stay – to minute and sparsely populated places like Lyø, Avernakø, Drejø or Skarø, which are a pleasure to explore, if only for a few hours. From Odense, the simplest plan is to take the train to Svendborg, very much the hub of south coast activity, although you might well find the smaller Fåborg, an hour's bus ride (#960 or #962) from Odense, a better base.

Svendborg

A principal hang-out of the Danish yachting fraternity, with marinas clogging the coastline from here to Fåborg, 24km west, **SVENDBORG** is unexciting in itself though a pleasant enough place to plot your travels around the archipelago (or to spend a day on the *Helge* steamer; see the box below) and to spend an hour or two meandering the narrow backstreets, spattered with beautiful bronzes by one of Denmark's best-known sculptors, locally born Kai Nielsen.

A couple of historical collections might occupy a bit more time. The **county museum**, Grubbemøllevej 13 (*Viebæltegård*; May to mid-June daily 10am–4pm; mid-June to Oct daily 10am–5pm; Nov–April Mon–Fri afternoons only; 20kr), has the usual regional collections as well as well-preserved finds from a Franciscan monastery. More entertaining is the **L. Lange & Co Stove Museum**, Vestergade 45 (mid-May to mid-Aug daily 10am–5pm; 15kr), an eccentric horde of cookers and burners produced by a Svendborg-based firm from 1850 to 1984. Lastly, there's the **Toy Museum** (*Legetøjsmuseet*; daily 10am–4pm; 30kr), Skt Nicolajgade 18, with a collection that should appeal to kids and adults alike.

The Lange company's former foundry, next door to the Lange museum, is now the town's **youth hostel** (☎62/216699), and on Brogade you'll find the reasonably priced *Hotel Ærø* (☎62/210760; ②). The **tourist office** on Centrumpladsen (mid-June to mid-Aug Mon–Fri 9am–7pm, Sat 9am–5pm; rest of the year Mon–Fri 9am–5pm, Sat 9am–noon; ☎62/210980) can provide details of other accommodation, including 125kr-a-night private rooms and the numerous local **campsites**, as well as the latest local ferry timetables.

THE HELGE STEAMER

Between June and August, the *Helge* steamer (built in 1928) leaves Svendborg three to five times daily for the island of **Tåsinge**, calling at Vindeby, Svendborg's extension just across the Svendborg Sund, the thatched village of Troense – criss-crossed by quiet streets where the houses are strapped with preservation orders – and the seventeenth-century Valdemar's Slot. The return sailing time is two hours but tickets (60kr from the harbour) can be used to get on and off all day.

The *Helge*'s last stop is the best: **Valdemar's Slot**, an imposing pile with Baroque interiors instigated by Christian IV and continued by his son, Valdemar, who died before taking up residence. Filled with three centuries of furniture, paintings and tapestries, the castle serves as a **museum** (May–Sept daily 10am–5pm; 45kr). Outside the castle, while waiting for the *Helge* to carry you back to Svendborg, have tea at the reasonably priced *Tea Pavillon*, from where there are great views out to the long, narrow island of Langeland.

Should you want to stay over on Tåsinge, there are four **campsites** on the island, plus a couple of **hotels** – *Det Lille Hotel* (☎62/225341; ②) and Hotel Troense (☎62/225412; ③) – both in Troense.

Fåborg

FÅBORG is an alternative base for the south coast, a likeably small and sedate place, rarely as overwhelmed by holiday-makers as Svendborg and with equally good connections to the archipelago (ferries sail to Søby on Ærø, to Lyø and Avernakø, and to Gelting in Germany). If you've an interest in Danish art, the town's other big attraction is the **Fåborg Museum** (June–Aug daily 10am–5pm; April, Sept & Oct daily 10am–4pm; Nov–March Sat & Sun 11am–3pm; 25kr) at Grønnegade 75. The museum opened in 1910 and quickly became the major showcase for the Funen Artists, particularly the work of Fritz Syborg and Peter Hansen, both of whom studied under the influential Kristian Zhartmann in Copenhagen and typically filled their canvases with richly coloured depictions of Funen landscapes. Apart from the chance to admire the skills of the painters, it's interesting to view the works and see how little the Funen countryside has changed since their completion.

Almost next door to the museum at Grønnegade 72–73, just 200m from the harbour, is the country's quaintest **youth hostel** (April–Oct; ☎62/611203); and there's a **campsite** with cabins at Odensevej 54 (mid-May to Aug; ☎62/610399). You can check local travel details at the **tourist office** at Havnegade 2 (Mon–Fri 9am–5pm, Sat 10am–6pm; ☎62/610707).

Around Fåborg: Egeskov Castle and the smaller islands

In Kværndrup, just ten minutes from Fåborg by bus, **Egeskov Slot** ("Oak-forest castle") is a Renaissance castle, and you're allowed inside, though it's more impressive from outside (daily 10am–5pm; 100kr). The same ticket also gives admission to the nearby **Egeskov Veteranmuseum** (daily 10am–4pm), which displays around three hundred antique cars.

If you're looking for some quiet, it's easy enough to visit one of the three small islands of **Bjørnø**, **Lyø**, and **Avernakø**. All are connected with Fåborg by small, daily ferries (at least 5 daily; journey time 10–20min; information on ☎30/668050 or ☎62/612307). There's not much to do on the islands apart from walking in the beautiful countryside or chatting with locals. If you want to stay overnight, contact the tourist office (☎62/610707) in Fåborg, who can arrange stays with local families for around 125kr per person.

Langeland and Ærø

You don't need to catch a ferry to reach the largest of the southern islands, **Langeland**, which lies off the southeast coast of Funen, connected by road bridge. A long, thin, fertile island, Langeland is peaceful and has fine sea views. Frequent buses make the half-hour journey from Svendborg to **RUDKØBING**, the island's main town, from where there are ferry links on to Æro; there's also a ferry to Lolland (see p.105), leaving from Spodsbjerg, about 6km to the east. Rudkøbing in itself doesn't have a lot to offer except for a pleasant fishing harbour and the historical collection in the **Langelands Museum** (daily 10am–2pm; 15kr), and unless you want to stay on the island, you're best off moving on. The town's **tourist office**, at Torvet 5 (☎62/513505), can give advice on **accommodation**; or head for the **youth hostel** at Bagvejen 8 (☎62/511830), or one of the two **campsites**, at Spodsbjergvej no. 277 (☎62/501092) and no. 182 (☎62/501006). North of Rudkøbing, the island consists mostly of farmland and the occasional village, with just one target to head for: the fairy-tale thirteenth-century **Tranekær Slot**, surrounded by a beautiful park dotted with sculptures made from natural materials. There's a **museum** (May–Sept daily 10am–5pm; 15kr) covering the history of the village and its castle in the old water-mill opposite. To find the island's best **beaches** – **Ristinge** is the most popular – head for the southern coast, where there are also a couple of **bird sanctuaries**, Gulstav Mose and Tryggelev Nor. Local buses serve all the main sites on the island.

For a more varied few days, take the ferry west to the island of **Ærø**, where there are ancient burial sites, abundant stretches of sandy beach, and a peach of a medieval merchants' town in **ÆRØSKØBING**. The town's narrow streets, lined with tidy houses, are made for wandering – look out for the oldest building, dating from 1645, at Søndergade 36. If it's raining, you could drop into the **Bottle Ship Collection** and **Memorial Rooms** (both May–Sept daily 9am–5pm; Oct–April 10am–4pm; 15kr) at Smedegade 22, for an eye-straining collection of ships in bottles in the former, and a riot of wood carvings, furnishings and timepieces from bygone days in the latter. Ærøskøbing's **tourist office** (June–Aug Mon–Fri 9am–5pm, Sat 9am–1pm, Sun 9am–noon; Sept–May Mon–Fri 9am–4pm; ☎62/521300), on Torvet, can give information on the island's burial places and numerous secluded spots. As for **accommodation**, there's a youth hostel at Smedevejen 13 (☎62/521044; April–Sept) and a cabin-equipped campsite at Sygehusvej 40b (☎62/521854; mid-May to mid-Sept), appealingly sited next to the beach. There's a local bus service, but the best way to **get around** the island is by **bike**, though you'll need to pedal hard to get up some of the hills; the tourist office supplies free bike maps to help plan your route, and bikes can be rented for 40kr a day at *Pilebækkens Cykelservice* (☎62/521110).

If you're looking to escape the tourists, then **MARSTAL**, at the east end of the island and reached by bus from Ærøskøbing, is a good alternative base. Once there, don't miss the superb **Marstal Søfartsmuseum** (daily 10am–5pm; 25kr), a collection of maritime paintings and ship models from Marstal's nineteenth-century golden age, when it was one of the busiest harbours in Denmark. There are a few options for staying over: the **youth hostel** (☎62/531064) is conveniently close to the town centre and the harbour, while the **campsite**, *Marstal Camping* (☎62/533600), is almost on the beach; the nicest hotel is the *Marstal* (☎62/531352; b) at Dronningestræde 1A. For more information, contact the **tourist office** (☎ 62/531960) on Havnegade, near the youth hostel. **Bikes** can be rented at *Nørremark Cykelforretning*, Møllevejen 77(☎62/531477).

travel details

Trains
Odense to: Århus (30 daily; 2hr); Copenhagen (32 daily; 3hr); Esbjerg (30 daily; 2hr); Nyborg (32 daily, linking with the *DSB* ferry to Korsør; 19min); Svendborg (20 daily; 1hr).

Buses
Kerteminde to: Nyborg (17 daily; 33min).

Odense to: Assens (14 daily; 1hr); Fåborg (30 daily; 55min–1hr 18min); Kerteminde (42 daily; 30min); Nyborg (14 daily; 1hr 5min); Svendborg (18 daily; 1hr 24min).

Rudkøbing to: Lohals (23 daily; 44min); Spodsbjerg (5 daily; 15min).

Svendborg to: Fåborg (29 daily; 43min); Rudkøbing (27 daily; 30min).

Ferries
Bøjden to: Fynshav (7 daily; 50min).

Nyborg to: Korsør (21 daily; 70min).

Søby to: Mommark (2–4 daily in summer; 1hr).

South Coast Ferries
There's a mass of connections around the **south coast archipelago** and it's best to check the fine details locally. Some sailings continue year-round, others only operate during the summer. Fares are 30–45kr per person. Frequencies given below are for weekdays; sailings are often reduced on weekends and public holidays.

Assens to: Bågø (4–6 daily; 30min).

Fåborg to: Lyø (6 daily via Avernakø; 1hr); Søby (6 daily; 1hr).

Lohals to: Korsør (5 daily; 1hr 30min).

Marstal to: Rudkøbing (5 daily; 1hr).

Spodsbjerg to: Tårs (16–20 daily; 45min).

Svendborg to: Ærøskøbing (5 daily; 1hr 15min); Drejø (4 daily via Skarø; 1hr 30min).

International Trains
Odense to: Hamburg (6 daily; 4hr 40min).

International Ferries
Bagenkop to: Kiel (3 daily; 2hr 30min).

Fåborg to: Gelting (2–3 daily; 2hr).

CHAPTER THREE

JUTLAND

Long ago, the people of **Jutland** (*Jylland*), the Jutes, were a quite separate tribe from the more warlike Danes who occupied the eastern islands. In pagan times, the peninsula had its own rulers and much power, and it was here that the legendary ninth-century monarch Harald Bluetooth began the process that turned the two tribes into a unified Christian nation. By the dawn of the Viking era, however, the battling Danes had spread west, absorbing the Jutes, and real power in Denmark gradually shifted towards Zealand.

This is where it has largely stayed, making unhurried lifestyles and rural calm (except for a couple of very likeable cities) the overriding impression of Jutland for most visitors. Yet there's much to enjoy in the unspoilt towns and villages, and Jutland's comparative large size and distance from Copenhagen – and the fact that most locals still like to consider themselves a cut above the Danes to the east – make it perhaps the most distinct and interesting area in the country.

There are also more regional variations in Jutland than you'll find elsewhere in Denmark. In the south, **Schleswig** is a territory long battled over by Denmark and Germany, though beyond the immaculately restored town of **Ribe**, it holds little of abiding interest. **Esbjerg**, further north, is fairly dull too, but as a major ferry port you might well arrive or leave from here, and it gives easy access to the hills, meadows and woodlands of eastern Jutland, and to some of the peninsula's better-known sights – from the old military stronghold of **Fredericia** to the ancient runic stones at **Jelling** and the modern bricks of **Legoland**.

Århus, halfway up the eastern coast, is Jutland's main urban centre and Denmark's second city, and here, besides a wealth of history and cultural pursuits, you'll encounter the region's best nightlife. It's handy, too, for the optimistically titled "Lake District", a small but appealing area of inland water between **Skanderborg** and **Silkeborg**. Further inland, the retreat of the ice-sheets during the last Ice Age has bequeathed a sharp clash of terrain: stark heather-clad moors break suddenly into dense forests with swooping gorges and wide rivers – contrasts epitomized by the wild memorial park at **Kongenshus** and the grassy vistas of the **Hald Ege**. Ancient **Viborg** is a better base for seeing all this than dour **Randers**, and from here you can head north, either to the blustery beaches of **Limfjordslandet**, or to vibrant **Aalborg**, which sits on the Limfjorden's southern bank.

Across the Limfjorden is Jutland at its most dramatic: a sandy semi-wilderness that reaches a crescendo of storm-lashed savagery around **Skagen**, at the very tip of the peninsula. **Frederikshavn**, on the way, is the port for boats to Norway and Sweden, and is usually full of those countries' nationals stocking up with what is for them cheap liquor.

South Jutland

Best known as an entry and exit point (to the UK by sea, to Germany overland), more people pass through **south Jutland** than probably any other part of the country. Few of them stop here longer than they have to, however, with most heading straight for the bright lights of Copenhagen or the holiday areas of the northwest coast. This might seem strange

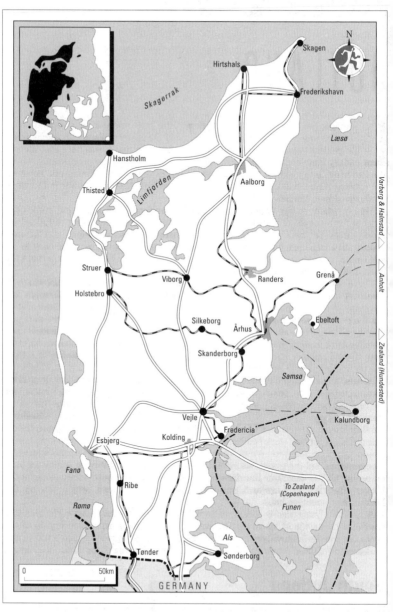

for an area that, as Schleswig, was at the heart of some prolonged and bitter international bickering, but the reasons become clearer once you've passed through. South Jutland's landscape and run-of-the-mill villages, while pleasant enough, are not exactly diverting.

Esbjerg

The area's only city (though not technically part of Schleswig) is **ESBJERG**, home to the world's biggest fish-oil factory, the stench from which matches the gloomy tenor of what must rank as Denmark's least appealing place. If this is your first view of the country, bear in mind it's an entirely untypical one. Esbjerg is a baby by Danish standards, purpose-built as a deep-water harbour during the nineteenth century with none of the older remnants that are a feature of most communities. That said, there are a few places worth a visit, and since the *Scandinavian Seaways* ferries from the UK berth here, you may well have the time to see them.

Arrival, information and accommodation

The Esbjerg **tourist office**, at Skolegade 33 (mid-June to Aug Mon–Fri 9am–6pm, Sat 9am–5pm; Sept to mid-June Mon–Fri 9am–5pm, Sat 9am–noon; ☎75/125599), on a corner of the main square, can give you all the practical information you might need, as well as a leaflet describing a short, self-guided walking tour of the city's turn-of-the-century buildings. The **passenger harbour** is a ten-minute well-signposted walk from the city centre, and trains to and from Copenhagen connect directly with the ferries at the harbour station. Otherwise, there are frequent departures to all Danish cities from the main **train station** at the end of Skolegade.

If you're staying, the tourist office can help in finding bed and breakfast-type **accommodation**; otherwise you'll find the cheapest hotel is the *Park* at Torvegade 31 (☎75/120868; ②), while the central *Ansgar*, Skolesgade 36 (☎75/128244; ③), is a little more upmarket. For those who can afford it, the top hotel in town is the *Britannia* on Torvet (☎75/130111; ④). The youth hostel is at Gammel Vardevej 80 (☎75/124258; closed late Dec & Jan), 25 minutes' walk away, or take a bus (#1, #4, #9, #11, #12 or #31) from Skolegade. There's a well-equipped **campsite** with cabins at Gudenåvej 20 (mid-May to mid-Sept; ☎75/158822), reached by bus #2.

The Town

The best way to get a sense of the city's newness is by dropping into the **Esbjerg Museum** (Tues–Sun 10am–4pm; 20kr) at Nørregade 25, where the meatiest of the few displays recalls the so-called "American period" of the 1890s, when Esbjerg's rapid growth matched that of the US gold-rush towns; here the massive population influx was caused by herring fishing. Also within easy reach of the centre is the **Museum of Art** (*Esbjerg Kunstmuseum*; Tues–Sun 10am–5pm; 20kr) at Havnegade 20, although its modern Danish artworks are fairly limp affairs; better to call in for the temporary shows, which often give insights into current trends. If your tastes are more technical, miss out the art in favour of the **Museum of Printing** (*Bogtrykmuseet*; Tues–Sun 10am–4pm; 15kr), at Borgergade 6, just off the pedestrianized strip of Kongensgade, which has an entertaining assortment of hand-, foot- and steam-operated presses as well as more recent, still functioning, printing machines (demonstrations on Tues).

With more time to spare, take a bus (#21, #23 or #30 from Skolegade) to the large **Fisheries and Maritime Museum and Sealarium** on Tarphagevej (daily June–Aug

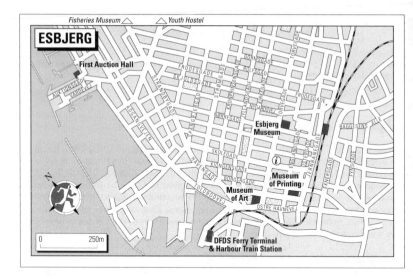

10am–6pm; Sept–May 10am–4pm; 35kr), where you can cast an eye over the vestiges of the early Esbjerg fishing fleet, see a representative of every type of fish found in Danish waters, and clamber around inside a dark and spooky wartime bunker built by the Germans. The Sealarium is part of a seal research centre, which often rescues seal pups marooned on sandbanks: you can see them swimming and, at 11am and 2.30pm, being fed. Just a few minutes' walk from the museum – follow the main road up the hill – is another of Esbjerg's more notable features, the **Sædden Kirke** (Mon–Fri 9am–1pm, Sat 9am–noon), whose completely red-brick interior is almost hypnotic, especially when the hundreds of hanging lightbulbs are lit – a modern reworking of traditional church architecture, made even more unusual by its location inside a shopping centre.

With an hour to kill before your boat leaves, nip around the harbour to the **Lightship Museum** (mid-May to mid-Oct daily 10am–4.30pm; 10kr), which gives a vivid impression of the North Sea lightshipmen's lot.

Eating, drinking and nightlife

Esbjerg's **eating** options are fairly limited if you're on a tight budget, although you can get a decent two-course lunch for around 50kr at the *Park Hotel*, on Torvegade, around the corner from the tourist office. Elsewhere, medium-priced ethnic eateries are plentiful: pick of the bunch is *La Bamba*, Danmarksgade 8, with a 99kr buffet. For traditional Danish food — and service – try *Sands*, Skolegade 60 (closed Sun), whose owner, incidentally, was decorated for sheltering Jews during the German occupation of Denmark in World War II. More expensively, for around 120kr each, you can sample Esbjerg-style nouvelle cuisine (basically well-prepared fresh fish with everything) at *Pakhuset*, Dokvej 3, in the dock area. A good place for lunch or an early-evening beer or coffee is the popular *Café Christian IX*, overlooking Torvet and named after the monarch commemorated by the square's equestrian statue – they sometimes have live music at weekends. Also good value at lunchtime is the steak restaurant *Jensens Bøfhouse*, on Kongensgade.

What little **nightlife** Esbjerg has is also based around Torvet, chiefly at *La Bonne*, a combined bar, restaurant and disco, and *5 Eifel*, a jazz pub. *Café Biografen*, Finsensgade

1, perks up with live music late in the week. If you've just arrived from Britain and want to make the transition to Danish culture (and prices) slowly, sup a beer or two at *The English Pub*, Kongensgade 10, or the *Andy Capp Pub*, Skolegade 17, which shares premises with the *John Wayne Saloon*.

Around Esbjerg: Fanø

From Esbjerg it's a straightforward fifteen-minute ferry trip to **Fanø**, a long, flat island with superb beaches that draw German holiday-makers here in droves during the summer. *DSB* ferries (information on ☎75/134500 or ☎75/120000) run frequently between Esbjerg and the island's main village, **Nordby**, where the **tourist office** at the harbour (early June to early Sept Mon–Fri 8.30am–6pm, Sat 9am–5pm, Sun 9am–7pm; rest of the year Mon–Fri 8.30am–5.30pm, Sat 9am–1pm; ☎75/162600) can provide information on accommodation and the few sights (a couple of fairly ordinary local museums and a windmill). There are eight campsites, of which the best is *Feldberg Familie Camping* (☎75/163680), almost on the beach.

Ribe

Just under an hour by train south from Esbjerg lies the exquisitely preserved town of **RIBE**. In 856 Ansgar built one of the first Danish churches here as a base for his missionaries arriving from Germany; a hundred years later the town was a major stopover point for pilgrims making their way south to Rome. Proximity to the sea allowed Ribe to evolve into a significant trading port, but continued expansion was thwarted by the dual blows of the Reformation and the sanding-up of the harbour. Since then, not much appears to have changed. The surrounding marshlands, which have prevented the development of any large-scale industry, and a long-standing house-preservation programme have enabled Ribe to keep the appearance and size of medieval times, and its old town is a delight to wander in.

The Town

From Ribe's train station, Dagmarsgade cuts an uncharacteristically straight path to Torvet and the **Domkirke** (June–Aug Mon–Sat 10am–6pm, Sun noon–6pm; May & Sept Mon–Sat 10am–5pm, Sun noon–5pm; Oct–April Mon–Sat 11am–3pm, Sun 1–3pm; 5kr), which towers above the town and dominates the wetlands for miles around. A sequel to Ansgar's original church, the cathedral was begun around 1150 using tufa – a suitably light material for the marshy base – brought, along with some of the Rhineland's architectural styles, by river from southern Germany.

Originally raised on a slight hill, the cathedral is now some 2–3m below the immediate streets, their level having risen due to the many centuries' worth of debris accumulated beneath them. The **interior** is not as spectacular as the cathedral's size and long history might suggest, having been stripped of much of its decoration by Hans Tausen, bishop of Ribe for twenty years from 1541 (arriving thirteen years after his revolutionary preachings in Viborg; see p.142). The thirteenth-century "Cat's Head Door" on the south side, a good example of the imported Romanesque design, is one of the few early decorative remains. More recent additions that catch the eye are the butcher's-slab altar and the frescoes and mosaics by Carl-Henning Pedersen, added in the mid-1980s. After looking around, climb the 248 steps to peer out from the top of the red-brick **Citizens' Tower**, so named since it doesn't belong to the church but to the people whose taxes pay for its upkeep. In an act worthy of *The Omen*, the tower's predecessor toppled into the nave on Christmas morning, 1283.

Heading away from the cathedral along Overdammen, you cross three streams, channelled around 1250 to provide water power for a mill. The houses on the right are

---

THE NIGHTWATCHMAN OF RIBE

At 10pm every evening between May and mid-September – and also at 8pm from June to August – the **Nightwatchman of Ribe** emerges from the bar of the *Weis' Stue* inn, Torvet 2, and makes his rounds. Before the advent of gas lighting, a nightwatchman would patrol every town in Denmark, looking through windows for unattended candles that might cause fires. The last real nightwatchman in Ribe made his final tour around the turn of the century, but thanks to the early development of tourism in the town, within thirty years the custom had been reintroduced.

Dressed in a replica of the original uniform and carrying an original morning-star pike and lantern (the sharp tip doubling as a weapon), the watchman walks the narrow alleys of Ribe singing songs written by Hans Adolf Brorson, bishop of Ribe in the mid-eighteenth century (whose statue you may have noticed outside the cathedral), and talking about the town's history while stopping at points of interest. One song tells people to go to bed and not light fires – sensible advice, even after 1554 when thatched roofs were officially banned. It's obviously laid on for the tourists, but the tour is free and can be fun.

---

the best of Ribe's many half-timbered structures and one of them, **Quedens Gaard**, at the corner of Sortebrødregade, operates as a museum (June–Aug Tues–Sun 10am–5pm; May, Sept & Oct Tues–Sun 11am–3pm; Nov–April Tues–Sun 11am–1pm; 10kr), with sixteenth-century interiors and exhibitions on medieval Ribe. Turn left off Overdammen and walk along the riverside Skibbroen and you'll spot the **Flood Column** (*Stormflodssøjlen*), a stout wooden pole showing the levels of the numerous floods that plagued the town before dykes were successfully built a century ago.

Continuing along Overdammen, Skt Nicolaj Gade cuts right to **Ribe Art Gallery** (mid-June to mid-Sept Tues–Sun 11am–4pm; rest of the year Tues–Sun 1–4pm; 20kr), housing a reasonable display of works by Danish artists in a chronological progression that takes you from noble portraiture through pre-Raphaelite concerns to natural reportage. On the ground floor the highlight is *The Christening*, by Skagen painter Michael Ancher (see p.151). A handful of accomplished bronze sculptures are supplemented by larger pieces on the back lawn, from where paths and footbridges lead back across the river to the town centre.

Ribe has recently gained a couple of museums celebrating the town's Viking era. The **Ribes Vikinger** (daily 10am–4pm; closed Mon in winter; 30kr), opposite the train station, displays remains that have been excavated locally, along with a full-size reconstructed Viking ship. If you've not had your fill, head for the **Ribe Vikingecenter** (mid-June to mid-Aug daily except Fri 11am–4pm; 30kr), 3km south of the centre on Lystrupvej, which attempts to re-create the Viking lifestyle, with appropriately costumed attendants demonstrating traditional Viking crafts such as pottery and cooking over open fires.

That's more or less all there is to Ribe, save for the paltry remains of **Ribehus Slotsbanke**, a twenty-minute walk away on the northern side of the town. The twelfth-century castle that stood here was a popular haunt with Danish royalty for a couple of centuries but was already fairly dilapidated when it was demolished by Swedish bombardment in the mid-seventeenth century. The **statue** of Queen Dagmar, a recent addition to the site and standing in bewitching isolation, makes the trek worthwhile.

Practicalities

Besides the usual services, the **tourist office** (June Mon–Fri 9am–5.30pm; July & Aug Mon–Fri 9am–5.30pm, Sat 10am–1/4pm, sometimes Sun 10am–2pm; Sept–May Mon–Fri 9am–5pm; ☎75/421500), across the road to the rear of the cathedral, offers the free *Denmark's Oldest Town* leaflet, a useful aid to self-guided exploration.

If you intend to stick around for the nightwatchman's tour, you'll need to **stay overnight**. Taking a room at the seventeenth-century *Weis' Stue*, Torvet 2 (☎75/420700; ②), is an atmospheric way to imbibe more of the town's historic atmosphere, or, if you can afford it, try the beautifully restored *Dagmar*, opposite the Domkirke (☎75/420033; ④), which dates from 1581 and claims to be the oldest hotel in Denmark. Most intriguing of the lot is *Den Gamle Arrest*, Torvet 11 (☎75/423700; ③–④), built as a girls' boarding school and serving until 1989 as the town's jail – the rooms are in the former cells, which these days lock from the inside. The youth hostel at Skt Pedersgade 16 (May to mid-Sept; ☎75/420620) is a simple walk over the river from the town centre. The nearest **campsite** (☎75/410777), 2km distant along Farupvej (use bus #771), is equipped with cabins and stays open all year. The tourist office publishes a list of private rooms.

Following the crowds is as good a way as any of finding somewhere to **eat** close to the cathedral; one reputable spot is *Vægterkælderen*, in the basement beneath *Hotel Dagmar*, serving two- (59kr) and three-course (74kr) lunches, and two-course dinners for 125kr. Also on Torvet, the *Weis' Stue* does reasonably priced fish lunches. *Café Nicolaj*, beside the art gallery, is open late for coffee and drinks and serves 50kr meals from noon to 2pm and from 6 to 8pm. At night, *Vægterkælderen* (see above) has a lively **bar**, though the beer is cheaper at *Pepper's* and *Stenbohus*, facing each other just up the street.

Rømø and Tønder

From Skærbæk, a few kilometres south of Ribe by bus, you can take a bus (#29) across 12km of tidal flats to the island of **Rømø**. The actions of sea and wind have given the island a wild and unkempt appearance, as well as causing a wide beach to form along the eastern side and allowing wildlife to flourish all over. There's a good chance of seeing seals basking during the spring, while at the end of the summer many migratory wading birds can be found, dodging the island's plentiful sheep.

Rømø's **tourist office** (summer Mon–Fri 9am–5pm, Sat & Sun 9am–4pm; shorter hours the rest of the year; ☎74/755130), just south of the causeway in the main village of **HAVNEBY**, can provide details on the island's bus service, which operates special routes in summer. There are several spots on Rømø to **stay** overnight: ask at the tourist office for details of private rooms or summer cottages for rent. The best hotel on the island is the *Kommandørgården* (☎74/755122; ③) in Østerby, a kilometre or so north of Havneby. There's a **youth hostel** in Havneby itself at Lyngvejen 7 (mid-March to Oct; ☎74/755188), and just to the north of the town at Havnebyvej 201, on the #29 bus route, is a **campsite** (☎74/755122) with cabins.

Besides enjoying the sands, and the fact that Rømø is a noted **nude bathing** spot, it's possible to **cross the border** to Germany without returning to the Danish mainland by using the ferry that sails from Havneby to List, on the German island of Sylt (information on ☎74/755303).

Tønder

On the mainland, the chief town on the Danish side, close to the border, is **TØNDER**. Founded in the thirteenth century, the town's cobbled streets still contain many ancient gabled buildings and it makes an attractive low-key base for a day or two, especially if you're here around the end of August, when the annual **jazz and folk festival** features many free street events – contact the *Tønder Festival* organization (☎74/724610) for more details. Otherwise, the main sights in town are the **Tønder Museum**, in the gatehouse of the sixteenth-century castle, and the adjoining **South Jutland Art Museum** (closed Mon), with its changing exhibitions of twentieth-century Danish works. Danish Prince Joachim and Princess Alexandra live 4km to the west of Tønder in **Schackenborg**

Castle, in the village of Møgeltønder (bus #66) – there's no entry to the public, but the castle park is good for an hour's strolling and the possibility of a peek at the royals.

First call for local information should be the **tourist office** on Torvet (summer Mon–Fri 9am–5.30pm, Sat 9.30am–3pm; rest of the year Mon–Fri 9am–4pm, Sat 9am–noon; ☎74/721220). Tønder has the charm to make you want to **stay** at least a night before moving on, and to this end there's a **youth hostel** at Sønderport 4 (☎74/723500; closed Christmas & Jan), 1km from the train station, a **campsite** at Holmevej 2a (April–Sept; ☎74/721849), and the functional *Hotel Tønderhus* at Jomfrustien 1, opposite the museum (☎74/722222; ③).

Kolding

Handily placed on the main road and rail axes north of Tønder, **KOLDING** doesn't attract a lot of attention, except from the shoppers who stroll through its excessively pedestrianized centre. If you do find yourself here for longer than you want to be, then head a short way north from the centre to the Slotsø lake, where the imaginatively renovated **Koldinghus** (May–Sept daily 10am–5pm; 35kr) is a harmonious mix of ruined and modern structures housing sparsely furnished period rooms. Another worthwhile call in this direction, 3km beyond the lake (bus #4 from the train station), is the **Trapholt Art Museum** (May–Sept daily 10am–5pm; Oct–April Mon–Fri noon–4pm, Sat & Sun 10am–noon; 26kr), its angular glass walls and shrill white interiors flooding the (mostly) modern art with natural light.

The **tourist office** is at Akseltorv 8 (Mon–Fri 9am–5pm, Sat 9am–noon; closed Sat in winter; ☎75/532100). Predictably, the cheapest **accommodation** option is the youth hostel, Ørnsborgvej 10 (☎75/509140), though the *Saxildhus* at Banegårdspladsen, opposite the train station, isn't bad value (☎75/521200; ②–③). The closest **campsite** is at Vonsildvej 19 (☎75/534725), 3km from the town centre by bus #3. Further away are several beachfront **campsites** – contact the tourist office for full details. For a quiet, inexpensive place to **eat**, look no further than *Café Paraplyen* on Akseltorv, open until 10pm. Or try the excellent-value pizza buffet and salad bar at the *Den Italienske*, also on Akseltorv.

Sønderborg

Despite lush green landscapes that gently subside into a peaceful coastline, the eastern section of southern Jutland holds comparatively few spots of interest and is best seen as part of a southerly route to Funen or Ærø (covered in the previous chapter). A lively provincial town in an area claustrophobically laden with campsites, **SØNDERBORG** straddles the once strategically important **Alssund**, a deep and slender channel dividing the island of Als from the Jutland mainland. The campsites are evidence of the appeal of the region's sandy coastline, while the line of preserved and enhanced earthworks on the mainland side are testament to the town's crucial place in Danish history. Beside them, the **Battlefield Centre** (*Historiecenter Dybbøl Banke*; June–Aug daily 10am–6pm; Sept–May 10am–5pm; 30kr) has multimedia displays that trace the details of the battle that took place here on April 18, 1864, when the Danes were defeated at the hands of the Prussians and medieval Sønderborg was all but destroyed. From then, northern Schleswig (in which Sønderborg stands) became part of Germany until the plebiscite of 1918 returned it to Denmark.

The bulk of the town lies across the Alssund, where your attention should focus on **Sønderborg Slot**, which may not be the grandest but is certainly one of Denmark's oldest castles, thought to have been started by Valdemar I in 1170 as a defence against the Wends. Inside the castle, the **Museum of South Jutland** (daily May–Sept 10am–5pm; Oct–April 10am–4pm; 20kr) comprises room after room of military mementoes. One of the more interesting sections tells of the four-day Als Republic of 1918, born as the German Reich's dissenting northern ports – Sønderborg, Bremen, Hamburg, Kiel – rebelled against the Kaiser, and, on the heels of the Russian Revolution, a red banner was raised over the town's barracks.

Practicalities

Trains go no further than the mainland section of the town, though long-distance **buses** continue across the graceful modern road bridge to Als and the bus station on Jernbanegade. Just downhill from the bus station, you'll find the **tourist office**, on Rådhustorvet (mid-June to Aug Mon–Sat 9am–5pm; Sept to mid-June Mon–Fri 9am–4pm, Thurs until 5pm, Sat 9am–noon; ☎74/423555). Of the central **hotels**, the *Arnkilhus*, Arnkilgade 13 (☎74/422336; ②), is unbeaten for price, though the grandest place in town is undoubtedly the *Scandic*, Rosengade 2 (☎74/421900; ④). The shiny modern **youth hostel** (Feb–Nov; ☎74/423112) is a twenty-minute walk along Perlegade and Alsgade, and a little less centrally placed than the waterfront **campsite** (☎74/424189).

Perlegade, close to the tourist office, is the town's main shopping street, bisected by the Rådhus into Store Rådhusgade and Lille Rådhusgade, an area that takes on a Mediterranean air on warm evenings as smartly dressed Danes mill from bar to bar. On the former, *Café Druen* has filling, low-cost snacks; further on, there are 50kr pizzas to be had at *Casa Letizia*, while nearby on Bagergade *Tortilla Flat* offers Mexican main courses for 80kr. There's a branch of the ubiquitous steakhouse chain, *Jensens Bøfhus* at Løkken 24.

Fredericia, Vejle and around

There's little that's unique about **east Jutland**, although its thick forests are a welcome change if you're coming directly from the windswept western side of the peninsula. As the main route between Funen and the big Jutland cities, it's a busy region with good transport links, but the area has only two sizeable towns: **Fredericia** is the more unusual, **Vejle** the more appealing – though neither justifies a lengthy stay.

Fredericia

FREDERICIA – junction of all the rail routes in east Jutland and those connecting the peninsula with Funen – has one of the oddest histories (and layouts) in Denmark. It was founded in 1650 by Frederik III, who envisaged a strategically placed reserve capital and a base from which to defend Jutland. Three nearby villages were demolished and their inhabitants forced to assist in the building of the new town – afterwards they had no option but to live in it. Military criteria resulted in wide streets that followed a strict grid system and low buildings enclosed by high earthen ramparts, making the town invisible to approaching armies. The railway age made Fredericia a transport centre and its harbour expanded as a consequence. But it still retains a soldiering air, full of memorials to heroes and victories, and is the venue of the only military tattoo in Denmark – an event that failed elsewhere due to lack of interest.

The half-hour walk from the **train station** along Vesterbrogade into the town centre takes you through Danmarks Port and the most impressive section of the old ramparts. They stretch for 4km and rise 15m above the streets, and walking along the top gives a good view of the layout of the town. But it's the **Landsoldaten** statue, opposite Princes Port, that best exemplifies the local spirit. The bronze figure holds a rifle in its left hand, a sprig of leaves in the right, and its left foot rests on a captured cannon. The inscription on the statue reads "6 Juli 1849", the day the town's battalion made a momentous sortie against German troops in the first Schleswig war – an anniversary celebrated as

Fredericia Day. The downside of the battle was the five hundred Danes who were killed and lie in a mass grave in the grounds of **Trinitatis Kirke** in Kongensgade.

Predictably, three hundred years of armed conflict form the core of the displays in the **Fredericia Museum** at Jernbanegade 10 (mid-June to mid-Aug daily 10am–5pm; rest of the year Tues–Sat noon–4pm, Sun 10am–4pm; 15kr). There are also typical local house interiors from the seventeenth and eighteenth centuries, and a dreary selection of archeological finds only offset by the glittering cache of silverware in the crafts section.

Practicalities

Unless you want to laze on Fredericia's fine **beaches**, which begin at the eastern end of the ramparts, there's little reason to hang around for very long. If you do want to stay, however, the cheapest **hotel** is the *Sømandshjemmet* on Gothersgade (☎75/920199; ②–③), near the harbour. There's a **youth hostel** at Skovløbervænget 9 (mid-Feb to Nov; ☎75/921287), which is slightly awkward to reach, 2km from the train station and further still from the town centre (bus #3 covers the town route, but only once an hour). Alternatively, use the **campsite** (April–Oct; ☎75/957183) on the Vejle fjord, adjacent to a public beach and very crowded during fine weather and at holiday times. You can arrange private rooms with the centrally placed **tourist office** (☎75/921377) on Danmarksgade.

Vejle

A twenty-minute train ride north of Fredericia, **VEJLE**, a compact harbour town on the mouth of the Vejle fjord, is home to the *Tulip* factory, from where 400 million sausages a year begin their journey to British breakfast tables. It's also the best base for exploring the contrasting pleasures of the Viking burial mounds at Jelling and – rather more famously – the Legoland complex at Billund, both within easy reach by bus or train.

Chief attraction in Vejle itself is **Skt Nicolai Kirke** (Mon–Fri 9am–5pm, Sat 9am–noon, Sun 9am–11.30am) in Kirke Torvet, in which a glass-topped coffin holds the peat-preserved body of a woman found in the Haraldskær bog in 1835. Originally the body was thought to be the corpse of a Viking queen, Gunhilde of Norway, but the claim was disputed and carbon tests carried out in 1977 dated the body at around 490 BC – too old to be a Viking but nonetheless still the best preserved "bog body" in the country. Unfortunately, it is hidden away behind bars in the north transept, which gives a view mainly of the feet. The Tollund Man, displayed in Silkeborg (see p.133), is a better displayed example of a preserved Iron Age corpse. Another macabre feature of the church, though you can't see it, are the 23 skulls hidden in sealed holes in the northern transept. Legend has it that the skulls belong to 23 thieves who were executed in 1630.

The **Museum of Art** and **Vejle Museum** (both Tues–Sun 11am–4pm; free) are conveniently placed next to each other at Flegborg 16 and 18, but they're time-killers rather than collections of importance. The art museum specializes in graphics and drawings, has a collection of twentieth-century painting and sculpture and often stages innovative temporary exhibitions from around the world; the Vejle Museum has a small collection of local historical and archeological finds. Also run by the museum, and perhaps a better destination on a sunny day, is Vejle **Vindmølle**, a disused windmill still with its full complement of ropes, shafts and pinions, and displaying a through-the-ages account of milling, from Neolithic blocks to modern roller mills. From the windmill, reached by climbing Kid Desvej (which leads off Søndergade), there are stupendous views across Vejle and its fjord.

Practicalities

Tucked into a small courtyard off the pedestrianized Søndergade, the Vejle **tourist office** (mid-June to Aug Mon–Sat 9am–5.30pm; Sept to mid-June Mon–Thurs 9am–5pm; ☎75/821955) has a list of accommodation in 250kr private rooms, but charges a steep 40kr booking fee. Otherwise, try for a room at the *Park* (☎75/822466; ②–③) at O. Lehmannsgade 5, or the *Munkebjerg,* Munkebjergvej 15 (☎75/723500; ④). Any of these options is more convenient than staying at the **youth hostel** on Gammel Landevej (☎75/825188), which is a bus journey away (#1, or on weekdays #9), or the **campsite** at Helligkildevej 5 (☎75/823335), a few kilometres east.

Central Vejle has plenty of inexpensive places to **eat**. In the same courtyard as the tourist office, *Den Smitske* serves substantial salads and *smørrebrød* through the afternoon and drinks until midnight. Around the corner on Søndergade, the glass-walled *Madværkstedet* has simple food for around 50kr. For a fuller evening meal, make for *Café Biografen*, Klostergade 1, also good simply for a drink.

Around Vejle: Jelling and Legoland

About 12km from Vejle, just a twenty-minute train ride away, the village of **JELLING** is known to have been the site of pagan festivals and celebrations, and it has two **burial mounds** thought to have contained King Gorm, Jutland's tenth-century ruler, and his queen, Thyra. The graves were found early this century and, although only one coffin was actually recovered, there is evidence to suggest that the body of Gorm was removed by his son, Harald Bluetooth, and placed in the adjacent church – which Bluetooth himself built around 960 after his conversion to Christianity. Excavations carried out on the site of the church revealed a skeleton and items similar to ones discovered in the empty mound, backing up the theory that Harald exhumed his pagan father to give him a Christian burial. In the grounds of the present church are two big **runic stones**, one erected by Gorm to the memory of Thyra, the other raised by Harald

Bluetooth in honour of Gorm. The texts, hewn into the granite, record the era when Denmark began the transition to Christianity.

Train services from Vejle to Struer or Herning stop at Jelling: both run about once an hour on weekdays and less frequently at weekends. If you can stomach such things, a **vintage train** operates between Vejle and Jelling every Sunday in July and on the first Sunday in August. By **bike**, the most direct route from Vejle is the A18, although a more scenic choice is through the hamlet of Uhre and along the shores of Fårup Sø. For overnight stays, the *Jelling Kro*, Gormsgade 16 (☎75/871006; ②), is pleasant and serves filling meals, or head for Jelling's **campsite** (☎75/871653; mid-April to mid-Sept) with cabins, about 1km west of the church, on Mølvangsvej.

Legoland Park
Twenty kilometres west of Vejle – linked by train or bus #211 – the village of **Billund** has been transformed into a major tourist centre, complete with international airport and rows of pricey hotels. It's all thanks to **Legoland Park** (May to mid-Sept daily 10am–8pm, July until 9pm; all-inclusive ticket 100kr, children 90kr), a theme park that celebrates the tiny plastic bricks that have filled many a child's Christmas stocking since they were developed by the Lego company in 1949 – seventeen years after a Danish carpenter, Ole Kirk Christiansen, had started making wooden toys collectively named "Lego", derived from the Danish phrase "Leg Godt", or "play well".

A cornucopia of elaborate model buildings, animals, planes and many other weird and wonderful things (such as Titania's Palace – home for the queen of the fairies) assembled from the toy bricks, the park is chiefly of appeal to kids, but anybody whose efforts at Lego construction have resulted in tears of frustration over missing corner bricks or a lack of right-sized windows might like to discover what can be achieved when someone has 45 million Lego bricks to play with.

North of Vejle: Horsens

Travelling north from Vejle, there's every chance that you'll pass through **HORSENS**, a likeable though hardly exciting town which claims to have the widest main street (Søndergade) in Denmark. Less trivially perhaps, Horsens was the birthplace in 1681 of **Vitus Bering**. It was he, in the employ of the Russian navy and on a mission from Peter the Great to find an Asian–American land bridge, who discovered what became the Bering Strait, between Alaska and Siberia. A memorial to Bering stands in the park which, like the strait, bears his name.

In another park, Caroline Amalielunden, just north of Sundvej, are the **Horsens Museum** (July & Aug daily 10am–4pm; Sept–June Tues–Sun 11am–5pm; 10kr), which carries a run-of-the-mill collection of local knick-knacks, and the more enticing **Art Museum** (Tues–Sun 11am–4pm; free), displaying some Danish Golden Age masters and an honourable collection of works by local artists.

The Lake District

The grandly titled Danish lake region sits within the triangle formed by Vejle, Århus and Viborg, and comprises green, rolling woodlands, several small lakes, and innumerable campsites. If you've seen only Denmark's larger towns, this is a region well suited to a couple of days' rural exploration. The north–south rail route passes through **Skanderborg**, which boasts some attractive eighteenth-century houses, many of them built with bricks from the town's medieval castle (of which only the church remains), but it's the lake region's other main town, **Silkeborg**, which is the area's liveliest centre, handsomely spread across several tongues of water.

Silkeborg

SILKEBORG has little history of its own – it was still a small village in 1845, when the local river was harnessed to power a paper mill that brought a measure of growth and prosperity – but the well-preserved body of an Iron Age woman, discovered ten miles west of Silkeborg in 1928, adds greatly to the appeal of the town's **Culture Museum**, on Hovedgården (mid-April to mid-Oct daily noon–5pm; rest of the year Wed, Sat & Sun noon–4pm; 20kr). As preserved bodies go, however, the so-called Elling Girl has been overshadowed since 1952 by the discovery of the Tollund Man, a corpse of similar vintage also on display at the museum. Gory as it may sound, the man's head is in particularly good condition, with stubble still visible on the chin.

An equally worthwhile call is to the excellent collection of abstract works by Asger Jorn and others inside the **Museum of Art**, Gudenå 7 (April–Oct Tues–Sun 10am–5pm; Nov–March Tues–Fri noon–4pm, Sat & Sun 10am–4pm; 30kr). It was to Silkeborg that Jorn, Denmark's leading modern painter and founder member of the influential CoBrA group, came to recuperate from tuberculosis. From the 1950s until his death in 1973, Jorn donated an enormous amount of his own work, and that of other artists, to the town, which displays them proudly in this purpose-built museum.

For a less cultural few hours, visit the town's aquarium, **Aqua** (summer daily 10am–6pm; rest of the year Tues–Sun 10am–4pm; 40kr, children 20kr), at Vejsøvej 55, on the southern edge of town. In keeping with the location, the exhibits here are all freshwater beasts – apart from the fish, there are numerous water birds and mammals, including some cute otters.

Practicalities

The helpful staff at the **tourist office**, Godthåbsvej 4 (mid-June to Aug Mon–Sat 9am–5pm; Sept to mid-June Mon–Fri 9am–4pm, Sat 9am–noon; ☎86/821911), have the usual practical details and a lengthy list of affordable accommodation in what's a surprisingly expensive town: the old and atmospheric *Dania*, on Torvet (☎86/820111; ④), is the least costly central hotel. There are many cheaper *kroer* in the outlying countryside, such as *Linå Kro* (☎86/841443; ②), 8km distant on the road to Århus (bus #113). Truly budget accommodation is limited to the **youth hostel**, Åhavevej 55 (☎86/823642), and several **campsites**: *Indelukkets* (☎86/822201), to the south, and *Silkeborg Sø* (☎86/822824), on the Århus road, are the closest. The tourist office can also help to organize a **canoe trip**, advising on distances and booking you in at campsites along the way. For going it alone, many of the campsites rent out canoes, or try *Slusekioskens Kanoudlejning* (☎86/800893) at the harbour.

Århus

Geographically at the heart of the country and often regarded as Denmark's cultural capital, **ÅRHUS** typifies all that's good about Danish cities: it's small enough to get to know in a few hours, yet big and lively enough to have plenty to fill both days and nights; indeed, you can even socialize around the clock if you want to. More unusually, it's also something of an architectural showcase, with several notable buildings spanning a century of top Danish and international design. A number of these buildings form the city's university campus, whose many students – during the 1960s the most radical in the country – contribute to a nightlife that's on a par with that of Copenhagen; it's no fluke, either, that the city is at the centre of the Danish rock music scene.

Despite Viking-era origins, the city's present-day prosperity is due to its long sheltered bay, on which the first harbour was constructed during the fifteenth century, and the more recent advent of railways, which made Århus a nationally important trade and

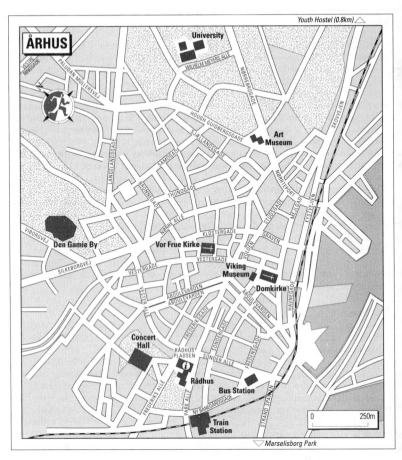

transport centre. Easily reached by train from all the country's bigger towns, and at one end of the only direct ferry link between Jutland and Zealand, Århus also receives non-stop international flights. There's certainly no better place for a first taste of Denmark.

Arrival, information and city transport

Whichever form of public transport brings you to Århus, you'll be deposited within easy reach of the hotels and main points of interest. **Trains and buses** stop on the southern edge of the city centre, from where it's a straightforward walk to the **tourist office** on the ground floor of the Rådhus (mid-June to mid-Aug daily 9am–8pm; mid-Aug to mid-Sept daily 9am–7pm; mid-Sept to mid-June Mon–Fri 9.30am–4.30pm, Sat 10am–1pm; ☎86/121600); **ferries** from Zealand dock just west of the centre, a short distance from the heart of Old Århus. **Airport buses** from Tirstrup arrive at (and leave from) the train station; the one-way fare for the fifty-minute journey is 50kr.

Getting around is best done on foot: the city centre is compact and you'll seldom need to use the **buses** at all unless you're venturing out to the beaches or woods on the city's outskirts. If you do, note that the transport system divides into four zones: one and two cover the whole central area, three and four reach into the countryside. The basic ticket is the so-called **"cash ticket"**, which costs 13kr from the machine at the rear of the bus and is valid for any number of journeys during the time stamped on it (usually about two hours from the time of purchase). If you're around for several days and doing a lot of bus hopping (or using local trains, on which these tickets are valid), it's best to buy either an **Århus Pass**, which costs 110kr for 48 hours and includes entry to numerous museums, including Den Gamle By, or a **multi-ride ticket**, which can be used ten times and costs 80kr for rides within the immediate city area; it can also be used by more than one person at once. These tickets can be bought at newsstands, campsites and shops displaying the *Århus Sporveje* sign. The driver won't check your ticket but a roving inspector might, and there's an instant fine of 150kr for travelling without one. The **bus information office** is at Banegårdspladsen 20 (Mon–Fri 8am–6pm, Sat 9am–noon; ☎89/465600).

Cycling is another viable way to get around, particularly if you're heading out along the coast to Moesgård. There are the usual number of outlets around the city, the most central being *Asmussen Cykler*, opposite the bus station at Fredensgade 54, which rents out single-speed roadsters for 50kr a day.

Accommodation

One of the best-priced and best-located **hotels** in the city is the *Missionshotellet Ansgar*, Banegårdsplads 14 (☎86/124122; ②–③). If you want something slightly more luxurious, there are plenty of mid-range hotels, such as *Hotel Windsor*, close to the harbour on Skolebakken (☎86/122300; ③), or the much more central *Ritz* on Banegårdspladsen (☎86/134444; ③–④); the tourist office has a long list of other options.

Århus' **youth hostel** is at Marienlundsvej 10 (☎86/167298, closed mid-Dec to mid-Jan), beautifully located 4km outside town in the middle of Risskov wood, close to a popular beach, and served by buses #1 and #9. If you're planning to spend most of your time in the centre, then the **Sleep-In** at Havnegade 20 (☎86/192055; ①) is a much better option: bunks cost 75kr and private rooms 180kr, or 240kr with a private bathroom; guests without their own sleeping bags can rent sheets and blankets (30kr). Other facilities include a café with a good noticeboard and bike rental for 50kr per day.

Of a number of **campsites** in the Århus area, two are handier than the others for commuting to the city: *Blommehaven* (mid-April to mid-Sept; ☎86/270207), overlooking the bay about 7km from the city centre, reached with bus #19 or less directly with bus #6; and the less convenient *Århus Nord* (☎86/231133), 8km north of the city and accessible by bus #117 or #118 from the bus station. Both campsites have cabins: the cheapest sleep two or three people and cost 330–500kr, depending on the season.

The City

For reasons of simple chronology, Århus divides into two clearly defined parts: even combined, these fill a small and easily walkable area. The old section, close to the cathedral, is a tight cluster of medieval streets with several viewable churches and a couple of museums, as well as the bulk of the city's nightlife. The more recent sections of Århus form a collar around the old centre, inevitably with less character, but nonetheless holding plenty that's worth seeing, not least the city's major architectural works.

Old Århus

Søndergade is Århus's main street, a pedestrianized strip lined with shops and overpriced snack bars that leads down into Bispetorvet and the old centre, whose streets form a web around the **Domkirke** (May–Sept Mon–Sat 9.30am–4pm; Oct–April

Mon–Sat 10am–3pm). Take the trouble to push open the cathedral's sturdy doors, not just to marvel at the soccer-pitch length – this is easily the longest church in Denmark – but for a couple of features that spruce up the plain Gothic interior, which is mostly a fifteenth-century rebuilding after the original twelfth-century structure was destroyed by fire. At the eastern end is one of few pre-Reformation survivors, a grand triptych altarpiece by the noted Bernt Notke. Look also at the painted – as opposed to stained – glass window behind the altar, the work of the Norwegian Emmanuel Vigeland (brother of Gustav), most effective when the sunlight is directly on it.

From the time of the first settlement here, in the tenth century, the area around the cathedral has been the core of Århus life. A number of Viking remains have been excavated on Clements Torv, across the road from the cathedral, and some of them are now displayed in the bank here as the **Viking Museum** (Mon–Fri 9.30am–4pm, Thurs until 6pm; free; enter the bank and turn left), including sections of the original ramparts and Viking tools, alongside informative accounts of early Århus. Also within a few strides of the cathedral, in a former police station at Domkirkeplads 5, the **Women's Museum** (*Kvindemuseet*; daily June to mid-Sept 10am–5pm; mid-Sept to May 10am–4pm; 15kr) is one of Denmark's most innovative museums, staging temporary exhibitions on aspects of women's lives and lifestyles past and present. After seeing the museums, venture into the small, very strollable streets close by, lined by innumerable preserved buildings, many of them housing antique shops, record shops or chic boutiques, and all good for a browse. The area is also home to some of the city's most enjoyable cafés, and is popular drinking territory after dark (see "Nightlife", below).

West along Vestergade from the Domkirke, the thirteenth-century **Vor Frue Kirke** (May–Aug Mon–Fri 10am–4pm, Sat 10am–2pm; Sept–April Mon–Fri 10am–2pm, Sat 10am–noon) is actually the site of three churches, most notable of which is the eleventh-century **crypt church** (go in through the main church entrance and walk straight ahead), which was discovered, buried beneath several centuries' worth of rubbish, during restoration work on the main church in the 1950s. There's not exactly a lot to see, but the tiny, rough-stone church – resembling a hollowed-out cave – is strong on atmosphere, especially during the candle-lit Sunday services. Except for Claus Berg's detailed altarpiece, there's not much to warrant a look in the main church. However, you should make your way through the cloister (to the left of the entrance) that remains from the pre-Reformation monastery – now an old folks' home – to see the medieval frescoes inside the third church, which depict local working people rather than the more commonly found biblical scenes.

Modern Århus

They may lack the intimacy of the old town's winding alleyways, but along the broad and busy streets of modern Århus you'll discover some notable examples of recent Danish architecture, a comprehensive re-creation of an old Danish town, and a quality collection of the nation's art.

If you've visited the tourist office, you've already been inside the least interesting section of one of the modern city's major sights: the functional-style **Rådhus**, completed in 1941 and as capable of inciting high passions – for and against – today as it was when it opened. From the outside, it's easy to see why opinions should be so polarized: the coating of Norwegian marble lends a sickly pallor to the building and the main block has the shape of a bloated Nissen hut. But on the inside (enter from Rådhus Pladsen), the finer points of architects Arne Jacobsen and Erik Møller's vision make themselves plain, amid the harmonious open-plan corridors and the extravagantly used glass. You're free to walk in and look for yourself, but consider taking a **guided tour** (10kr) – they're conducted in English at 11am on summer weekdays, and reveal a mass of fascinating details. Above the entrance hangs Hagedorn Olsen's huge mural, *A Human Society*, symbolically depicting the city emerging from the last war to face the future with optimism. In the council chamber, the lamps appear to hang suspended in mid-air (in fact they're held by almost invisible threads), and the shape of the council leader's chair is a distinctive curvy form mirrored in numerous smaller features throughout the building, notably the ashtrays in the lifts – though many of these have been pilfered by tourists. Perhaps most interesting of all, however, if only for the background story, are the walls of the small civic room, covered by the intricate floral designs of the artist Albert Naur: the work took place under the Nazi occupation and in it Naur concealed various Allied insignia. Finally, a lift (open to the public at 11am, noon, 2pm & 4pm during the summer; 5kr) climbs to the bell tower for a view over the city and across the bay.

A more recent example of Århus's municipal architecture is the glass-fronted **Concert Hall** (*Musikhuset*), a short walk behind the Rådhus, which has been the main venue for opera and classical music in the city since it opened in 1982. It's worth dropping into, if only for the small café where you might be entertained for free by a string quartet or a lone fiddler. A monthly list of upcoming concerts and events is available from the box office or the tourist office.

It's just a few minutes' walk from the Concert Hall to Viborgvej and the city's best-known attraction, **Den Gamle By** (daily June–Aug 9am–6pm; May & Sept 10am–5pm; shorter hours during the rest of the year; 40kr depending on season). An open-air museum of traditional Danish life, it consists of sixty-odd half-timbered houses from all over the country, dismantled and moved here piece by piece since the museum's inception in 1909. With many of the craftsmen's buildings used for their original purpose, the overall aim of the place is to give an impression of an old Danish market town. This is done very effectively, although sunny summer days bring big crowds here, and the period flavour is strongest outside of high season, when the visitors are fewer.

If you're at all interested in Danish art, you may as well miss out Den Gamle By in favour of the **Art Museum** (Tues–Sun 10am–5pm; 30kr) in the Vennelystparken, on the eastern edge of the centre. There's enough in the museum to give a good overview of the main national trends, from the late eighteenth-century formal portraits and landscapes by Jens Juel, and the finely etched scenes of domestic tension by Jørgen Sonne, through to the more internationally renowned names, particularly Vilhelm Hammershoi, represented here by some of his moody interiors. There's lots of viewable modern stuff, too. Besides the radiant canvases of Asger Jorn and Richard Mortensen, don't miss Bjørn Nørgård's sculpted version of Christian IV's tomb: the original, in Roskilde Cathedral, is stacked with riches; this one features a coffee cup, an egg and a ballpoint pen.

Though it's so plain you'd barely notice it, the Art Museum building is often on the itinerary of architects visiting the city. It's reckoned to be a prime example of the modern Danish style: red bricks and white-framed rectangular windows, with no decoration at all. There's much more of this look on the **university campus**, a short way up Høegh Guldbergs Gade, sprawling across the hillside and overlooking the rest of the city (from the centre take bus #1, #2, #3, #11, #13, #56 or #58). Most of the university buildings were designed by C.F. Møller and completed just after the last war. While on campus, there are two museums that might appeal: the **Natural History Museum** (daily 10am–4pm; 25kr) has a large collection of stuffed birds and animals alongside some exhibits on Danish ecology, while the **Steno Museum** (daily 10am–4pm; 30kr) focuses on medical matters and includes a small planetarium too.

Out from the centre

On Sundays Århus resembles a ghost town, with most locals spending the day in the parks, woodlands or beaches on the city's outskirts. If you are around on a Sunday – or, for that matter, any sunny day in the week – you could do much worse than join them. The closest beaches (and woods) are just north of the city at **Risskov**, near the youth hostel, easily reached with buses #1, #6 or #9.

For a more varied day, head **south** through the thick Marselisborg Skov and on to the prehistoric museum at Moesgård. Bus #6 runs directly to the museum, while bus #19 takes a more scenic route along the edge of Århus Bay, leaving you with a two-kilometre walk to the museum. If you don't fancy the buses, be advised that this is ideal territory for cycling, or gentle hiking.

Marselisborg Skov and Dyrehaven

The **Marselisborg Skov** is a large park that contains the city's football and horse-trotting stadiums and sees a regular procession of people exercising their dogs. It also holds the diminutive **Marselisborg Slot**, summer home of the Danish royals, the landscaped grounds of which can be visited when they're not around (open dawn to dusk). Further south, across Carl Nielsen Vej, the park turns into a dense forest, criss-crossed with footpaths but still easy to get lost in.

A simpler route to navigate, and one with better views, is along Strandvejen, which runs between the eastern side of the forest and the shore. Unbroken footpaths run along this part of the coast and give many opportunities to scamper down to rarely crowded (though often pebbly) beaches. Also on this route, near the junction of Ørneredevej and Thorsmøllevej, is the **Dyrehaven**, or Deer Park – as the name suggests, a protected section of the wood that's home to many deer. The animals can be seen (if you're lucky – they're not the most gregarious of creatures) from the marked paths running through the park from the gate on the main road. A short way from the Dyrehaven entrance is the *Blommehaven* campsite (see "Accommodation"), and, several kilometres further on, part of the prehistoric trackway belonging to the Moesgård prehistoric museum.

Moesgård Prehistoric Museum

Occupying the buildings and grounds of an old manor house, **Moesgård Prehistoric Museum** (April–Oct daily 10am–5pm; Nov–March Tues–Sun 10am–4pm; 30kr, students 10kr) records Danish civilizations from the Stone Age onwards with copious finds and easy-to-follow illustrations. However, it's the Iron Age which is most comprehensively covered and holds the most dramatic single exhibit – the **Grauballe Man**, a skeleton dated at 80 BC discovered to the west of Århus. Found in a peat bog, which kept it in amazingly good condition, it was even possible to discover what the deceased had eaten for breakfast (burnt porridge made from rye and barley) on the day of his death. Only a roomful of imposing runic stones, further on, captures the imagination as powerfully as does the peat body, and you'll fully exhaust the museum in an hour.

The rest of your time should be spent following the "**prehistoric tramway**", which runs from the grounds of the museum (from the far corner of the courtyard) to the sea and back again. A detailed trail guide is available in English (10kr). The three kilometre path leads through fields and woods, past a scattering of reassembled prehistoric dwellings, monuments and burial places. On a fine day, the walk itself is as enjoyable as the actual sights, and you could easily linger for a picnic when you reach the coast, or stop for a coffee and a snack at the small but popular *Skovmøllen* restaurant in the woods. If you don't have the energy for any more walking, you can take a #19 bus back to the city from here; the stop is a hundred metres to the north of the trail's end.

Eating

You'll find the best **lunch** bargains simply by cruising the cafés and restaurants of the old city and reading the notices chalked up outside them. *Mackie's Pizza*, on Skt Clemens Stræde, has lunchtime specials for around 50kr; turning the corner into Skolegade turns up a number of unpretentious eateries (so unpretentious, in fact, that they often look closed when they're open). *Pinds Café*, no. 11, is a case in point, and does excellent *smørrebrød* and set lunches for 60kr. *Gyngen*, at Mejlgade 53, does filling and healthy dishes at reasonable prices, while *Kokken*, the restaurant section of *Huset*, Vester Allé 15 (see also "Nightlife"), has a selection of mouth-watering vegetarian snacks at 25kr.

Dinner is going to be much more pricey unless you stick to the pizzerias – *Italia* at Åboulevarden 9 is a good one – or the ethnic restaurants, such as the Persian *Det Grønne Hjørne*, Frederiksgade 60, which does an oriental buffet with a good salad bar for 69kr (49kr at lunchtime), or the slightly cheaper Tunisian cuisine at *Kif Kif Gallorant*, Mejlgade 41. For Mexican food, *Rio Grande* in Vestergade and *Alimento*, Åboulevarden 46, are the top choices. If you want to splash out a bit, head for the harbour, Marselisborg Havn, where there are a number of fish restaurants – best is the pricey *Seafood* – plus a pizzeria and a creperie.

If finances are tight, or you just want to stock up for a **picnic**, use the *Special Smørrebrød* outlet at Sønder Allé 2. *Hjørnet,* Mejlgade 24, sells delicious picnic ingredients – it's next door to a smokers-only bar. For more general food shopping, there's a branch of *Brugsen* on Søndergade, and a **late-opening supermarket** (8am–midnight) at the train station.

Nightlife

Århus is the only place in Denmark with a **nightlife** to match that of Copenhagen. There's a diverse assortment of ways to be entertained, enlightened, or just inebriated, almost every night of the week. And while things sparkle socially all year round, if you visit during the **Århus Festival**, an orgy of arts events held annually over the first week in September (check what's on with the tourist office), you'll find even more to occupy your time.

Cafés
The city has a wonderful endowment of **cafés**, many situated in the medieval streets close to the cathedral, an area that sprang to life a few years ago following a clean-up and restoration campaign. There's little to choose between the cafés themselves: each pulls a lively cosmopolitan crowd, roughly in the 23–35 age bracket, and gets crowded on Fridays and Saturdays, less so earlier in the week. The best technique is really to wander around and try a few. A likely starter is the movie-themed *Casablanca*, at Rosensgade 12, from where you could continue to either *Carlton*, Rosensgade 23, *Café Jorden*, Badstuegade 5, *Drudenfuss*, Graven 30, *Englen*, Studsgade 3, or *Kindrødt*, Studsgade 8. Slightly more upmarket is the classical music-oriented *Café Mozart*, just outside the old centre at Vesterport 10. Or try the newly opened and popular *Café Viggo* on Åboulevarden. All of the above close at midnight or 2am depending on the day of the week and, if they're not heading for a club, revellers with stamina aim for one of the city's **late-night cafés**, such as *Café Paradis*, at Paradisgade 9.

Live music
There's plenty of **live music** in Århus. You can get basic details of all events from the tourist office, but a better source for rock music news is the *Århus Billet Bureau*, at Studsgade 44, where you can pick up a variety of free local magazines and flyers advertising forthcoming gigs.

The cream of Danish and international independent **rock** acts can be found at either *Huset*, Vester Allé 15 (☎86/122677) – which has a restaurant and cinema almost next door, called *Ridehuset* – or *58*, Vestergade 58 (☎86/130217). Gigs take place at both three or four nights a week; admission runs from 20kr to 100kr, with doors opening at 10pm and the main band on at midnight. More run-of-the-mill Danish bar bands turn up at *Fatter Eskild*, Skolegade 25 (☎86/194411), and *Gyngen*, Fronthuset, Mejlgade 53 (☎86/192255). Only the latter ever charges for entry. The small *Æsken*, at Anholtsgade 4 (☎86/138561), features anything from country to rock'n'roll on Thursday to Sunday nights.

The leading **jazz** venue is the smoky, atmospheric pub, *Bent J*, at Nørre Allé 66 (☎86/120492). There are free jam sessions here several nights a week; for a name band expect to pay 50–90kr. On Wednesday nights **Latin** fans congregate at Club Havana in the *Musikcafeen*, Mejlgade 53, where there are free salsa lessons for the first hour. For **classical music and opera**, check out the regular performances at the concert hall (☎89/318210).

Clubs and discos

Both *Huset* and *58* (see above) host rock and new wave **discos** on nights without live bands, although the city's coolest club right now is *Blitz*, at Klostergade 34 (☎86/191099). More mainstream discos are plentiful, the best of which are *Alexis*, Frederiksgade 72 (☎86/127755), *Don Quijote*, Mejlgade 14 (☎86/130254) or *Cocoon*, Store Torv 4 (☎86/139577) – which has the advantage of freshly made pizza, available from midnight, and is liveliest early in the week. If you fancy a night of 1950s and 60s nostalgia, the place to go is *Locomotion*, at M.P. Bruuns Gade 15 (☎86/124333). Early in the week, **admission** to any disco is likely to be free; on Thursday, Friday or Saturday, you'll pay 20–40kr.

Gay and lesbian nightlife

Although Århus doesn't have the wide network of **gay** clubs you'll find in the Danish capital, there is the long-established *Pan Klubben*, at Jægergårdsgade 42, a gay social centre with a café and disco, which has lesbian-only nights on Thursdays, and is mixed on Wednesday, Friday and Saturday. For details of events that may be of special interest to **women**, drop into *Kvindehuset*, at Domkirkepladsen 5.

Listings

Airport Tirstrup (☎86/363611), 44km northeast of the city. Airport buses, linking with all flights, leave from outside the train station; the fare is 50kr and the journey takes fifty minutes.

Airlines *SAS/DanAir* domestic ☎70/103000; international ☎70/102000.

Bike rental See "Arrival, information and getting around".

Bookshops The *Secondhand English Bookstore*, Frederiks Allé 53, fully lives up to its name, open Mon–Fri 11.30am–6pm, Sat 10.30am–1pm.

Car rental *Avis*, Jens Baggesens Vej 88 (☎86/161099); *Europcar*, Fredensgade 17 (☎86/132133).

Doctor Between 4pm and 9am, call ☎86/201022.

Hospitals Emergency at Århus Kommunehospital, on Nørrebrogade.

Late shopping The *DSB* supermarket at the train station is open daily 8am–midnight.

Market There's a fruit, veg and flower market every Wed and Sat on Bispetorv, beside the cathedral, though the one on Ingerslevs Boulevard on Sat mornings is livelier.

Pharmacy *Løve Apoteket*, at Store Torv 5 (☎86/120022), is open 24 hours.

Police Århus Politisation, Ridderstræde 1 (☎86/133000).

Post office On Banegårdspladsen, by the train station, open Mon–Fri 9am–5.30pm, Sat 9am–noon.

Transport information Local buses and trains ☎86/126703 or 181733. Long-distance trains and *DSB* ferries ☎86/181778. Århus–Copenhagen coach reservations ☎86/784888. Hydrofoil to Zealand, *Cat-Link* ☎86/131700 (car information ☎33/151515).

Travel agents *KILROY travels*, Fredensgade 40 (☎86/201144), specializes in cheap fares for students and under-26s.

Central Jutland: Randers, Viborg and around

From rugged windswept heathlands to lush valleys and thick belts of forest, **central Jutland** boasts some of the most varied landscapes in Denmark, which, together with the area's historical remnants, are sufficient ingredients for a couple of days' pleasurable rambling. The region is easily accessed by train, although, if coming from Århus, you'll need to change at Langå to get straight into the best of it – the patch around Viborg. Failing that, stay on the train and base yourself instead in the countryside close to Randers, seeing the rest by bike or local buses.

Randers

A trading and manufacturing base since the thirteenth century, **RANDERS** is not a promising introduction to central Jutland. Its growth has continued apace over the years, leaving a tiny medieval centre miserably coralled by a bleak new industrial one. The town's main historical sight is the house at Storegade 13, said to be the place where Danish nobleman Niels Ebbesen killed the German Count Gerd of Holstein, in 1340, and a shutter on the upper storey is always left open to allow the Count's ghost to escape, lest the malevolent spirit should cause the house to burn down. But Randers' biggest tourist attraction these days – one of the most popular in Jutland – is the **Randers Regnskov** (Randers Rainforest; daily May–Sept 10am–6pm; Oct–April 10am–4pm; 50kr, children 35kr), a re-creation of a tropical rain forest alongside the River Gudenåen. Visitors wander through the dense, damp foliage, enclosed within two giant domes, watching out for the birds and animals. The best part is undoubtedly the dark and spooky "night zoo", located in a dripping stone cave.

Practicalities

The **bus station** is right in the centre at Dytmærsken 12, while the **train station** is ten minutes' walk out of town at Jernbanegade 29. First stop should be the **tourist office**, near Randers Regnskov at Tørvebryggen 12 (mid-June to Aug Mon–Fri 9am–6pm, Sat 9am–3pm; reduced hours rest of the year; ☎86/424477), which hands out a list of private rooms to rent from 100kr per person – beware that some of them are a long way outside town. One of the best value **hotels** is the *Kronjylland* (☎86/414333; ②–③), on Vestergade, close to the train station. More upmarket are the *Randers*, Torvegade 11 (☎86/423422; ④), and the *Scandic Hotel Kongens Ege* (☎86/430300; ④), on Gl. Hadsundvej, whose rooms give superb views over the city. Randers' **youth hostel**, with dorms and private rooms, is only five minutes from the centre at Gethersvej 1 (☎86/425044; closed Jan). The nearest **campsite**, with cabins and a swimming pool, is at Fladbro, 6km west of the town (☎86/429361): take bus #10 to the *Fladbro Kro*, from where it's a ten-minute walk through the woods.

Randers has plenty of relatively cheap **restaurants**: try the Greek dishes at *Hellas*, Vester Kirkestræde 3, or the filling lunchtime deals at *Maren Knudsen, Øl & Vinkælder*, on Støregade. As for **nightlife**, Storegade holds a good selection of bars where you can sample the local beer (*Thor*), such as the popular *Tante Olga*, which has live rock bands at weekends. *Café von Hatten*, onVon Hatten Stræde, has a more peaceful atmosphere. In early August the town celebrates **Randers Ugen**, a week packed with all sorts of cultural events; the rest of the year, major rock concerts and theatre performances are regularly put on at *Værket*, a converted power station on Mariagervej – ask at the tourist office to find out what's on.

The best way to see the countryside around Randers is by **bike**. *Schmidt Cykler*, Vestergade 35 (☎86/412903), rents them for 50kr per day.

East of Randers: Djursland and Mols

East of Randers stretches the peninsula known jointly as **Djursland** (the north side) and **Mols** (the south), which, with its hilly, wooded landscape, edged with some fine beaches, attracts an increasing number of tourists every year. **EBELTOFT** is the most popular destination, most easily reached by regular bus from Århus. A thriving market centre in medieval times, it was sacked by the invading Swedes in 1659 and has only recently emerged from economic decline, thanks to tourism: in summer you should aim to get there early, before the cobbled streets are overrun by the hordes shopping for souvenirs. The main sight in town is the **Fregatten Jylland**, a wooden frigate dating from the nineteenth century (June–Aug daily 9am–7pm; rest of the year daily 10am–5pm; 40kr, children 20kr). Should you fancy staying in town, the best-value **hotel** is the small *Ebeltoft* on Adelgade (☎86/341090; ②), or there's the **youth hostel** at Søndergade 43 (☎86/341400). Along the bay there are several **campsites**, best of them the cabin-equipped *Vibæk Camping* (☎86/341214), right on the beach a little way north of town.

Located at Jutland's easternmost point, **GRENÅ** grew up around its harbour in the nineteenth century, and it's still an important port, with frequent ferry services to Sweden (Varberg and Halmstad). Though the town centre is pleasant enough, the main draw apart from the transport links are the beaches south of town. If you need to **stay** overnight, try for a room at the *Grenaa Strand*, close to the harbour (☎86/326814; ③); alternatively, there's a **youth hostel** at Ydesvej 4 (☎86/326622; closed Dec & Jan), while the best of the local **campsites** is *Polderrev Camping*, south of the harbour (☎86/321718). Grenå is reachable by train from Århus (2hr), though buses from Randers (#214) run roughly hourly through the day from the bus station, the journey taking about ninety minutes.

If it's really the beaches you're after, better to head 10km north of Grenå by local bus to **GJERRILD**, where you'll find one of the best in the country: Nordstranden, far preferable to the pebbly Stranden in the opposite direction. Just a kilometre outside the village is **Sostrup Castle**, home to fifteen Cistercian nuns, who have converted part of the castle into a hotel, café and restaurant (☎86/384111; ②). Other **accommodation** alternatives are Gjerrild's **youth hostel** (☎86/321200) and an excellent **campsite** (April–Oct; ☎86/384200) 500m from the sands at Nordstranden.

Viborg

For many years **VIBORG** was one of the most important communities in the country, at the junction of all the major roads across Jutland. From Knud in 1027 to Christian V in 1655, every Danish king was crowned here; Hans Tausen's Lutheran preachings began in Viborg in 1528, eight years before Denmark's official conversion from Catholicism; and until the early nineteenth century the town was the seat of a provincial assembly. As the national administrative axis shifted towards Zealand, however, so Viborg's importance waned, and although it's still home to the high court of West Denmark, it's now primarily a market town for the local farming community.

Viborg's centre is concentrated in a small area and most parts of the old town are within a few minutes' walk of each other. The twin towers of the **Domkirke** (April, May & Sept Mon–Fri 9am–5pm, Sat 9.30am–12.30pm; June–Aug Mon–Sat 9am–5pm; Oct–April Mon–Fri 8am–4pm, Sat 9.30am–12.30pm) are the most visible feature; indeed the cathedral – instigated by Bishop Eskil in 1130 – is the most compelling reminder of the town's former glories. It was destroyed by fire in 1726 and rebuilt in Baroque style by one Claus Stallknecht, though so badly that it had to be closed for two

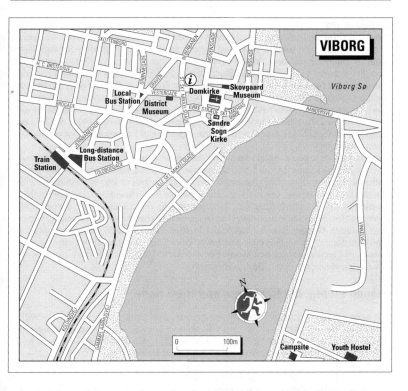

years and the work begun again. The interior is now dominated by the brilliant frescoes of Joakim Skovgaard, an artist commemorated by the **Skovgaard Museum** (daily May–Sept 10am–5pm; Oct–April 1.30–5pm; free), inside the former Rådhus across Gammel Torv – a neat building with which Claus Stallknecht made amends for his botching of the cathedral. There's a good selection of Skovgaard's paintings in the museum – although they can't fail to be a little anti-climactic after viewing the works in the cathedral – along with those by other members of his family.

Two minutes' walk away on Kirke Stræde, the late Romanesque **Søndre Sogn Kirke** (Mon–Fri 9am–1pm, Thurs also 3–5.30pm, Sat 9am–noon; sometimes locked at these hours, key available from the building to the right) is all that remains of the cloisters of the Dominican Black Friars, one of four monastic orders in Viborg that were ended by the Reformation. Inside the church, the sixteenth-century Belgian altarpiece is the star turn, with 89 gilded oak figures in high relief around the central Crucifixion scene. If you express sufficient interest, you may be permitted to scramble down into the crypt, which, though now a dusty shell, was once unhygienically used for burials and food storage.

For a broader perspective of Viborg's past, keep an hour spare for exploring the **District Museum** (*Stiftsmuseum*; June–Aug daily 11am–5pm; Sept–May Tues–Fri 2–5pm, Sat & Sun 11am–5pm; free), on the northern side of Hjultorvet between Vestergade and Skt Mathias Gade. The museum's three well-stocked floors hold everything from prehistoric and archeological artefacts to clothes, furniture and household appliances, which help record the social and cultural changes in Viborg over more recent decades.

Practicalities

Trains and buses both arrive on Viborg's western side, roughly 1km from the centre, where you'll find the **tourist office** on Nytorv (mid-June to Aug Mon–Sat 9am–5pm; April to mid-June & Sept Mon–Fri 9am–5pm, Sat 9.30am–12.30pm; Oct–March Mon–Fri 8am–4pm, Sat 9.30am–12.30pm; ☎86/611666). All Viborg's **hotels** are fairly pricey, though reduced rates can sometimes be negotiated at *Palads Hotel*, Skt Mathias Gade 5 (☎86/623700; ③); if money's no object and a lake view appeals, try *Golf Hotel Viborg*, Randersvej 2 (☎86/610222; ④). Close to the same lake, but on the opposite side to the town (a 2km walk or local bus #707), are the **youth hostel** (☎86/671781) and **campsite** (☎86/671311). Contact the tourist office about the possibility of arranging a private room.

During the day, you could do far worse than pick up some *smørrebrød* (the best outlet is at Jernbanegade 14) and **eat** alfresco in one of the numerous parks or on the banks of the lake. Plenty of reasonably priced eating places can be found along Skt Mathias Gade, however; one is the popular *Messing Jens* (closed Sun), with 89kr three-course dinners. A little further out, *Medborgerhuset*, Vesterbrogade 13, serves a 40kr *dagens ret* from noon to 8pm on weekdays, as well as cheap coffee and cakes. The cellar restaurant, *Brygger Bauers Grotter*, Skt Mathias Gade 61, is by far the top spot for a candle-lit dinner, although you'll find lower prices and more activity at the Mexican restaurant *Tortilla Flat* (closed Mon). For a drink and a game of darts in the company of Viborg's youth, try *Sam's Bar* on Hjultorvet.

Around Viborg: the Hald Area and Hjerl Hede

The area around Viborg is excellent for cycling, with plenty of pleasant spots within easy reach; there's also a decent local bus service. Leaving Viborg and heading south on Koldingvej (an alternative minor route to the A13), you come to **Hald Ege**, a beautiful area of soft hills and meadows on the shores of Hald Sø. For all its peace, though, the district's history is a violent one. This is where Neils Bugge led a rebellion of Jutland squires against the king in 1351, and where the Catholic bishop, Jorgen Friis, was besieged by Viborgers at the time of the Reformation. Much of the action took place around the manor houses, or *Halds*, that stood here, the sites and ruins of which can be reached by following a **footpath** marked by yellow arrows. The path starts close to **Hald Laden**, a restored barn by the side of the road, where an exhibition (June–Aug daily noon–6pm; Sept–May Sat & Sun noon–6pm; free) details the history and geology of the area, and the battle against the pollution that is killing Hald Sø. About 10km from Viborg lies the hilly lakeside area of Dollerup Bakker, where from June to August rowing boats are available for rent.

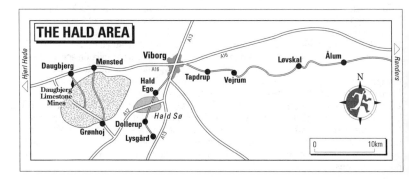

Lysgård and Mønsted

Just to the south of Dollerup Bakker, a road leads from the village of Dollerup to **LYSGÅRD** and **E. Bindstouw** (mid-April to mid-Sept Tues–Sun 9am–5pm; 10kr), the old school house where **Steen Steensen Blicher** recorded his famous nineteenth-century short stories. Blicher would sit here in the evenings while the local poor wove socks beside the stove and told folk tales, which Blicher noted down for posterity. The small building is still in its original location and contains the fixtures and fittings of Blicher's time, including his writing board, stove, and even a few socks.

About 9km west of Viborg, beside the A16 between **MØNSTED** and Raunstrup, the **Jutland Stone** marks the precise geographical centre of Jutland. There's not much to see, just a big inscribed rock and lots of cigarette ends. A few kilometres further, and markedly more interesting, are the **Mønsted Limestone Mines** (mid-June to mid-Aug daily 9am–6pm; late March to mid-June & mid-Aug to late Oct daily 10am–4pm; 30kr), which wind 35km into the earth and have a constant temperature, regardless of external weather. Wandering around in their cool, damp innards can be magically atmospheric, although a century ago conditions for the mine workers here were so horrific that when Frederik IV visited the place he was sufficiently appalled to bring about reforms – which led to the mines becoming known as "Frederik's Quarries" or, more venomously, "The King's Graves".

Daugbjerg and Kongenshus Mindepark

There's another set of **limestone mines** (times and price as at Mønsted) near **DAUGBJERG**, unlit and narrower than the Mønsted mines, with a guide who accompanies visitors with an oil lamp. The entrance to the mines was found by chance fifty years ago and no one has yet charted the full extent of the passages; it's said that work began here at the time of Gorm, the tenth-century King of Jutland, and that the tunnels were used as hideouts by bandits.

A few kilometres south of Daugbjerg is **Kongenshus Mindepark** (mid-April to mid-Oct daily 10am–6pm; 10kr for cars, pedestrians free) – 3000 acres of protected moorland on which there have been attempts at agriculture since the mid-eighteenth century, when an officer from Mecklenburg began keeping sheep here. For his troubles, the would-be shepherd received a grant from the king, Frederik V, and built the house that gives the park its name: *Kongenshus* (the King's House). A few years later, a thousand or so German migrants (the so-called "potato Germans") also tried to cultivate the place but to little avail. In the centre of the park is a memorial to the early pioneers; standing here, as the wind howls in your ears and you look around the stark and inhospitable heath, you can only marvel at their determination.

If you're not put off, there are several **campsites** around Kongenshus: *Hessellund-Sø* (April–Sept; ☎97/101604), to the south near Karup, and *Haderup* (April–Sept; ☎97/452188), off Jens Jensenvej to the west, are just two.

Hjerl Hede

Just to the west of Viborg is one of the most successful of Denmark's heritage tourism projects, the **Hjerl Hedes Frilandsmuseum** (April–Oct daily 9am–5pm; 50kr, children 20kr). This open-air museum attempts to re-create the development of a local village from the years 1500 to 1900, with examples of a forge, an inn, a school, mills, a vicarage, a dairy, a grocer's shop and farms, all relocated here from their original sites all over Jutland. By far the best time to come is in summer (mid-June to mid-Aug), when the place is brought to life by a hundred or so men, women and children dressed in traditional costumes, who provide demonstrations of the old crafts and farming methods. To get there, take the train to Vinderup (5–10 a day; journey time 30min), from where it's a three-kilometre walk to the museum.

Northwest Jutland: Limfjordslandet and around

Limfjordslandet is the land around the western portion of the **Limfjorden**, the body of water that splits northern Jutland from the rest of the peninsula. In the northwestern half, both the North Sea coast and the coast of the Limfjorden itself – which here resembles a large inland lake – attract legions of holidaying northern Europeans during the summer months, at which time it's a smart move to arrange accommodation in advance. At other times this is a rarely visited quarter of the country. There are fine beaches and plenty of opportunities to mess about in boats – and to catch them to Norway and beyond – and a number of small, neat old towns with a smattering of mildly diverting museums. But the weather here is unpredictable, with sharp winds prone to bluster in off the North Sea, and getting around is difficult: trains only reach to the fringes, so you'll need to rely on buses. In other words, don't bother to come here unless you're a hardy and determined traveller.

For a quick taste of the area, take the train from Viborg and change at Struer for the short journey south to **HOLSTEBRO**, the largest town in the region, and one with an easy-going atmosphere and a small, walkable centre. There's a commendable **Art Museum** (mid-June to mid-Aug Tues–Sun 11am–5pm; rest of the year Tues–Fri noon–4pm, Sat & Sun 11am–5pm; 20kr) here with a strong contemporary Danish collection and quality international pieces, including works by Matisse and Picasso. In the town park, the **Holstebro Museum** has a fair local history collection. The **tourist office** at Brostræde 2 (☎97/425700) can supply information for travelling deeper into Limfjordslandet. For staying overnight, there's a **youth hostel** at Søvej 2 (mid-March to mid-Nov; ☎97/420693), 2.5km from the centre, off Ringevejen, and a **campsite** equipped with cabins at Birkevej 25 (April to mid-Oct; ☎97/422068).

Also reachable from Struer, **Thisted**, at the end of the local rail line, has access to good beaches and a youth hostel and campsite, but little else of interest beyond its link (by bus #40) to **Hanstholm**, from where ferries leave for Kristiansund and Egersund in Norway.

Northeast Jutland

Much easier to get to and travel around than Limfjordslandet, **northeast Jutland** is nonetheless another portion of Denmark often missed by foreigners. It's a shame, as the region has a highly convivial major city in **Aalborg**, as well as ferries to Sweden and Norway. What's more, once you cross the Limfjorden, it boasts a landscape wilder than anywhere else on the peninsula: lush green pastures giving way to strangely compelling views of bleak moorland and windswept dunes.

Aalborg

The main city of north Jutland and the fourth largest in Denmark, **AALBORG**, hugging the south bank of the Limfjorden, is the obvious place to spend a night or two before venturing into the wilder countryside further on. It's the main transport terminus for

Some years ago, it was officially decreed that the Danish double "A" would be written as Å. The mayor of Aalborg, and many locals, resisted this change and eventually forced a return to the previous spelling of their city's name – though you may still see some maps and a few road signs using the "Å" form.

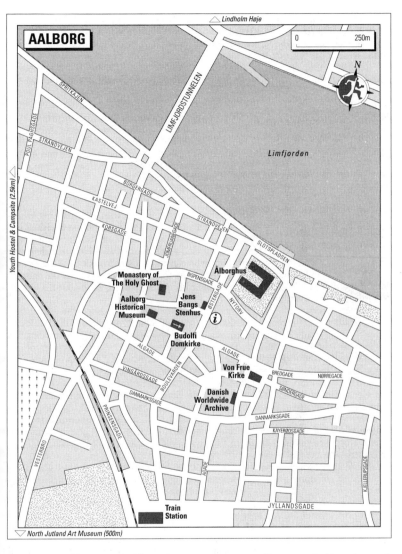

the region, and boasts a notable modern art museum, a well-preserved old section, and the brightest (indeed only) nightlife for miles around.

Information and accommodation

The **tourist office** is centrally placed at Østerå 8 (mid-June to mid-Aug Mon–Fri 9am–8pm, Sat 9am–2pm, Sun 10am–1pm; rest of the year Mon–Fri 9am–4.30pm, Sat 9am–noon; ☎98/126022) and has information on the town, though if you want to **stay** in Aalborg, be aware that bargain-priced hotels are hard to find. The three cheapest are the *Aalborg Sømandshjem*, Østerbro 27 (☎98/121900; ②), the *Prinsens*, Prinsensgade 14 (☎98/133733; ②–③), and *Missionshotellet Krogen*, Skibstedvej 4 (☎98/121705; ②). If these are too costly, make for the large **youth hostel** (March to mid-Dec; ☎98/116044) to the west of the town on the Limfjorden bank beside the marina – take bus #8 from the centre to the end of its route. The same bus takes you to the **campsite**, *Strandparken* (mid-May to Sept; ☎98/127629), about 300m from the youth hostel.

The Town

Since its beginnings, Aalborg has been known as a trading centre, and the profits from the seventeenth-century herring boom made it the biggest and wealthiest Danish town outside Copenhagen. Much of what remains of **old Aalborg** – chiefly the area within Østerågade (commonly abbreviated to Østerå), Bispensgade, Gravensgade and Algade – dates from that era, standing in stark contrast to the new roads that slice through it to accommodate the traffic using the Limfjorden bridge.

OLD AALBORG

The tourist office is as good a place as any to start exploring, with one of the major seventeenth-century structures standing directly opposite. The **Jens Bangs Stenhus** is a grandiose five storeys in Dutch Renaissance style, and, incredibly, has functioned as a pharmacy since it was built. Jens Bang himself was Aalborg's wealthiest merchant but was not popular with the governing elite, who conspired to keep him off the local council. The host of goblin-like figures carved on the walls allegedly represent the councillors of the time, while another figure, said to be Bang himself, pokes out his tongue towards the former Rådhus, next door.

The commercial roots of the city are further evidenced by portaits of the town's merchants (rather than the more customary portraits of nobles) inside **Budolfi Domkirke** (Mon–Fri 9am–3pm, Sat 9am–noon), easily located by its bulbous spire, just a few steps behind the Jens Bangs Stenhus. The cathedral, a small but elegant specimen of sixteenth-century Gothic, is built on the site of an eleventh-century wooden church, only a few tombs from which remain, embedded in the walls close to the altar. Actually, beyond the old tombs, there's little to see inside the cathedral, but plenty to hear when the electronically driven bells ring out each hour – sending a cacophonous racket across the old square of **Gammel Torv**, on which the cathedral stands.

After viewing the cathedral, drop into the **Aalborg Historical Museum**, across the square at Algade 42 (Tues–Sun 10am–5pm; 15kr). The first exhibit here is a dramatic one: the peat-preserved skeleton of a forty-year-old woman who died around 400 AD. In comparison, the rest of the prehistoric section is fairly routine; make instead for the local collections, which provide a good record of Aalborg's early prosperity. The museum also has an impressive, if somewhat incongruous, glassworks collection illustrating the different designs from the various Danish glass-working centres – look out for the armadillo-shaped bottle.

Just off Gammel Torv is another significant feature of old Aalborg, the fifteenth-century **Monastery of the Holy Ghost** (*Helligåndsklostret*), viewable by way of guided tours in summer (check details at the tourist office). These take in the monks' refectory, kept largely unchanged since the last monk left, and the small Friar's room, the only part of the monastery into which nuns (from the adjoining nunnery) were permitted entry. Indeed, this was one of the few monasteries where monks and nuns were allowed any contact at all, a fact which accounts for the reported hauntings of the Friar's room – reputedly by the ghost of a nun who got too friendly with a monk, and as punishment was buried alive in a basement column (the monk was beheaded). Most interesting, however, are the **frescoes** that cover the entire ceiling of the chapel. In more recent times, the corridor outside the chapel was used for shooting practice by the so-called "Churchill Gang", a group of local schoolboys who organized resistance to the Nazis; and much of the monastery now serves as an old folks' home.

The rest of old Aalborg lies to the east across Østerågade, and is a mainly residential area – with just a few exceptions. The sixteenth-century **Aalborghus** (grounds 8am–dusk) is technically a castle but looks much more like a country manor house, and has always had an administrative rather than a military function. Aside from the free theatrical productions staged here in summer, the castle is only worth visiting for the severely gloomy **dungeon** (Mon–Fri 8am–4pm; free), to the right from the gateway, and the underground passageways that run off it. From the castle, Slotsgade leads to the maze of narrow streets around **Vor Frue Kirke**, a dull church but with some meticulously preserved houses surrounding it, many of which have been turned into upmarket craft shops. The best are along the oddly L-shaped Hjelmerstald: notice no. 2, whose ungainly bulge around its midriff has earned it the nickname "the pregnant house".

If you're of Danish descent, or just keenly interested in Danish social history, visit the **Danish Worldwide Archives**, nearby at Arkivgade 1 (Mon–Thurs 9am–4pm, Fri 9am–2pm; free). The story of Danish migration overseas is recorded here through immense stacks of files and books; given enough background facts, details of individual migrants can be traced.

OUTSIDE THE OLD CENTRE

The old centre sets the pleasant tone of the city, but just outside it are a couple of other notable targets. One where you could easily spend an hour or two is the **North Jutland Art Museum** (mid-June to mid-Sept daily 10am–5pm; rest of the year Tues–Sun 10am–5pm; 20kr, free on Tues), on Kong Christians Allé, close to the junction with Vesterbro (bus #14 or a 15-min walk from the centre). Housed in a building designed by the Finnish architect Alvar Aalto, this is one of the country's better modern art collections, strikingly contemporary in both form and content, and featuring – alongside numerous Danish contributions – works by Max Ernst, Andy Warhol, Le Corbusier and, imposingly stationed next to the entrance, Claes Oldenburg's wonderful *Fag-ends in a Colossal Ashtray*. After leaving the museum, you can get a grand, if pricey, view over the city and the Limfjorden by ascending the **Aalborg Tower** (April–Oct daily 10am–5pm; 15kr), on the hill just behind.

From the tower, you may be able to spot what looks like a set of large concrete bunkers on a hill to the southeast of the city. This is, in fact, the **Gug Kirke** (Mon–Fri 9am–4pm), designed by Inger and Johannes Exner and opened in the early 1970s. It's one of the most unusual churches in the country: except for the iron crucifix and the wooden bell tower, the whole thing, including the font, pulpit and altar – decorated by a collage of newspapers – is made of concrete. The idea was to blend the church into the mostly high-rise parish it serves, and for it to function also as a community centre: the perfectly square interior can be turned into a theatre, while the crypt doubles as a café and youth club. It's unique enough to merit a close look; take bus #5 from the city centre.

Eating, drinking and nightlife

In pursuit of **food, drink and nightlife** almost everybody heads for Jomfru Ane Gade, a small street close to the harbour between Bispensgade and Borgergade. Jomfru Ane (literally "young maiden Anne") was a noblewoman and reputedly a witch who, because of her social standing, was beheaded rather than burnt at the stake – though the street nowadays, at least by night, is more synonymous with getting legless than headless. Around midday, the restaurants crammed together here advertise their daily specials with signs: the most reliable are *Fyrtøjet*, at no. 19, and *Regensens*, no. 16, both of which generally have three-course lunches for 75–90kr. Or try *Fellini* at no. 23, serving good-value pizzas and pastas. If it's Saturday, make a beeline for *Fru Jensen* at no. 13, for the inexpensive help-yourself herring buffet.

In the evening, *Fru Jensen* has **live music**, as do several bars along the street; just walk along, listen, and decide which appeals. The better-known Danish rock acts appear at *Skråen*, Strandvejen 19 (☎98/122189), which also holds a café and multi-screen **cinema**. For less mainstream rock music, make for *Café Tusindfryd* at Kattesundet 10. The *Duus* **wine bar**, in the cellar of the Jens Bangs Stenhus (closed Sun), is the place for a quiet evening drink.

Around Aalborg: Lindholm Høje and Rebild Bakker

On the north side of the Limfjorden, **Lindholm Høje** (Tues–Sun 10am–4pm; 20kr) was a major Viking and Iron Age burial ground, and is a captivating place, especially so in the stillness of dawn or dusk. There are a number of very rare Viking "ship monuments" here – burial places with stones arranged in the outline of a ship – as well as more than six hundred cremation graves from the German Iron Age period, probably used by a settlement that was abandoned during the eleventh century. From Aalborg you can get to the site by bus #4 or #11 (running twice an hour for most of the day), or walk there in under an hour: over the Limfjorden bridge, along Vesterbrogade into Thistedvej, right into Viaduktvej, and straight on until Vikingvej appears to the left.

About 30km south of Aalborg is **Rebild Bakker**, a heather-covered hill in close proximity to some scattered beech woods and Rold Skov's dense proliferation of conifers. The area is prime territory for hiking, and has been a **national park** since a group of American expatriate Danes purchased the land and presented it to the Danish government. Nowadays it's the site of the largest American Independence Day celebration outside the USA – a good reason not to be around on July 4 – and is home to the tacky **Lincoln's Log Cabin** (May–Sept daily 10am–5pm; 10kr), a re-creation of Abraham Lincoln's log cabin, filled with mundane articles from 49 American states and facts about Danish migration to them. The Americana doesn't disturb the natural beauty of the area, however, and it can provide a couple of relaxing days. To get there from Aalborg, take a train to Skørping or a bus (#104) to **Rebild**, where there's a **youth hostel** at Rebildvej 23 (☎98/391340), open all year except for a month over Christmas; the adjacent **campsite** (☎98/391110) is also open year-round.

Continue 20km south of Rebild Bakker (or make the hour-long train or bus trip from Aalborg), and you'll reach the town of **Hobro**, worth visiting for the 1000-year-old **Fyrkat**. Fyrkat is a fortress, which is said to have been built by the Viking king, Harald Bluetooth. Fyrkat (April–Oct daily, 10am–5pm; 25kr) is a good place to walk around and get an impression of life during the Viking era. Houses and farms have been reconstructed, and in summer there are demonstrations of trditional Viking activities like bronze casting. Fyrkat is two kilometre's walk from the centre of Hobro.

Frederikshavn

FREDERIKSHAVN is neither pretty nor particularly interesting, and as a major ferry port it's usually full of Swedes and Norwegians taking full advantage of Denmark's liberal drinking laws. But the town is virtually unavoidable if you're heading north, being at the end of the rail route from Aalborg (if you've an international sailing to meet at Hirtshals, change trains at Hjørring). If you're not catching a boat, speed straight on to Skagen (see below); if you are, practical details are liable to be your main concern.

There are just a couple of things worth seeing in Frederikshavn. If you only have half an hour, visit the **Krudttårnet** (April–Oct daily 10am–12.30pm & 1–5pm; 10kr), the squat, white tower near the station, which has maps detailing the harbour's seventeenth-century fortifications (of which the tower was a part) and a collection of weaponry, uniforms and military paraphernalia from the seventeenth to the nineteenth centuries. With more time on your hands, take bus #1 or #2 to the end of the route at

Møllehuset, and walk on through Bangsboparken to the **Bangsbo-Museet** (April–Oct daily 10am–5pm; Nov–March Tues–Sun 10am–5pm; 25kr). Here, comprehensive displays chart the development of Frederikshavn from the 1600s, alongside the slightly grotesque, but very engrossing, Collection of Human Hairwork. The museum's outbuildings store an assortment of maritime articles, distinguished only by the twelfth-century Ellingå Ship, plus a worthwhile exhibition covering the German occupation during World War II and the rise of the Danish Resistance movement.

Practicalities

Buses and **trains** both terminate at the train station; crossing Skippergade and walking along Denmarksgade brings you to the town centre in a few minutes. Arriving **ferries** dock near Havnepladsen, also near the centre, and close to the **tourist office** at Brotorvet 1, on the corner of Rådhus Allé and Havnepladsen (April to mid-June & mid-Aug to Oct Mon–Fri 9am–5pm, Sat 9am–noon; mid-June to mid-Aug Mon–Sat 8.30am–8.30pm, Sun 8.30–11.30am & 4–8.30pm; Nov–March Mon–Fri 9am–5pm; ☎98/423266).

If you're forced to stay, the best-value **hotels** are the *Mariehønen*, Skolegade 2 (☎98/420122; ②), and the *Sømandshjemmet* at Tordenskjoldsgade 15b (☎98/420977; ③). There's also a **youth hostel** at Buhlsvej 6 (☎98/421475; closed Jan), 1500m from the train station (turn right); and a cabin-equipped **campsite**, *Nordstrand*, at Apholmenvej 40 (☎98/429350; April–Sept), 3km north of the town centre, just off Skagensvej.

Skagen

If you have the option, skip Frederikshavn altogether in favour of **SKAGEN**, which perches almost at the very top of Jutland amid a desolate landscape of heather-topped sand dunes, its houses painted a distinctively bright shade of yellow. Forty kilometres north of Frederikshavn, Skagen can be reached by private bus or train (*Eurail* and *InterRail* not valid), both of which leave from Frederikshavn train station roughly once an hour – the bus is the best choice if you're planning to stay at the Skagen youth hostel, as it stops outside.

The Town

Sunlight seems to gain extra brightness as it bounces off the two seas that collide off Skagen's coast, something that attracted the **Skagen artists** in the late nineteenth century. Painters Michael Ancher and Peder Severin (P.S.) Krøyer and writer Holger Drachmann arrived in the small fishing community during 1873 and 1874, and were later joined by Lauritz Tuxen, Carl Locher, Viggo Johansen, Christian Krogh and Oscar Björck. The painters often met in the bar of *Brøndum's Hotel*, off Brøndumsvej, and the owner's stepsister, Anna, herself a skilful painter, married Michael Ancher. The grounds of the hotel now house the **Skagens Museum** (June–Aug daily 10am–6pm; May & Sept daily 10am–5pm; April & Oct daily 11am–3pm; Nov–March Sat & Sun 11am–3pm; 30kr), which comprises the most comprehensive collection of the artists' work. It's an impressive place, not least because so many of the canvases depict local scenes, using the town's strong natural light to capture subtleties of colour; the light, no less powerful today, streams in through the museum's windows. Many of the works, particularly those of Michael Ancher and Krøyer, are outstanding, although the paintings of Anna Ancher, while perhaps the least technically accomplished, often come closest to achieving the naturalism that the artists sought.

A few strides away at Markvej 2, the **Michael & Anna Anchers Hus** (Oct & Jan–April daily 11am–3pm; May to mid-June & mid-Aug to Sept daily 9am–5pm; mid-June to mid-Aug daily 10am–6pm; Nov & Dec Sat & Sun 11am–3pm; 25kr) has been restored with the intention of evoking the atmosphere of their time – through an assortment of squeezed tubes of paint, sketches, paintings, piles of canvases, books and ornaments. Less essential, and a bit overpriced, is **Drachmanns Hus** (June to mid-Sept daily 10am–4pm; 15kr), at Hans Baghsvej 21, on the junction with Skt Laurentii Vej, where Holger Drachmann lived from 1902. Inside the house is a large collection of Drachmann's paintings and sketchbooks, although it was for his lyrical poems, at the forefront of the turn-of-the-century Danish neo-Romantic movement, that he was best known. Such was Drachmann's cultural importance that, on his death, the major Danish newspaper, *Politiken*, devoted most of its front page to him – facsimiles are on display.

The arrival and subsequent success of the artists inadvertently made Skagen fashionable, and the town continues to be a popular holiday destination. But it still bears many marks of its tough past as a fishing community, a history that is excellently documented in **Skagen Fortidsminder** (May–Sept daily 10am–5pm; Oct–April daily 10am–4pm; 25kr), on P.K. Nielsenvej, a fifteen-minute walk south along Skt Laurentii Vej (or the much nicer Vesterbyvej) from the town centre. The museum – built on the tall dune where townswomen would watch for their menfolk to return from the sea during storms – examines local fishing techniques in its main displays, reinforced by photos showing the millions of fish that were strewn along the quay before being auctioned. Among the auxiliary buildings are reconstructions of rich and poor fishermen's houses: the rich fisherman's house includes a macabre guest room kept cool to facilitate the storage of bodies washed ashore from wrecks, while the poor fisherman's dwelling makes plain the contrast in lifestyles – just two rooms to accommodate the parents and their fourteen offspring.

Around Skagen: the buried church and Grenen

Amid the dunes to the south of town, about twenty minutes' walk along Skt Laurentii Vej and Gammel Kirkestræde and onto a signposted footpath, is **Den Tilsandede Kirke**, or "the Buried Church" (June–Aug daily 11am–5pm; 10kr). The name is misleading since all that's here is the tower of a fourteenth-century church, built in what was then a minor agricultural area. The church was assaulted by vicious sandstorms during the eighteenth century: by 1775 the entrance could only be reached with the aid of shovels, and in 1810 the nave and most of the fittings were sold, leaving just the tower as a marker to shipping – while not especially tall, the tower's white walls and red roof are easily visible from the sea. Still under the sands are the original church floor and cemetery. Although part of the tower is open to the public, the great fascination is simply looking at the thing from outside, and comprehending the incredible severity of the storms.

The forces of nature can be further appreciated at **Grenen**, 4km north of Skagen and served by the *Sandormen* tractor-drawn bus, though it's nicer to walk there, down Skt Laurentii Vej and then straight ahead along the beach. This is the actual meeting point of two seas – the Kattegat and Skagerrak – and the spectacle of their clashing waves (the seas flow in opposing directions) is a powerful draw, although only truly dramatic when the winds are strong. On the way back, spare a thought for Holger Drachmann (see above), a man so enchanted by the thrashing seas that he chose to be buried in a dune close to them. His tomb is signposted from the car park.

Practicalities

Skagen's **train station** is on Skt Laurentii Vej, a short walk from the **tourist office** at Skt Laurentii Vej 18 (Mon–Sat 9am–5pm; ☎98/441377). **Staying overnight** in Skagen is infinitely preferable to going back to Frederikshavn any sooner than you have to. For its artistic associations, *Brøndum's Hotel*, Anchervej 3 (☎98/441555; ③), is by far the most atmospheric spot; the fact that few of the rooms have bathrooms and all are far from luxurious keeps the price of doubles down – but book well ahead in summer. A little cheaper is *Skagens Sømandshjem*, Østre Strandvej 2 (☎98/442110; ③). Alternatively, there's the small *Finns Pension*, Østre Strandvej 63 (☎98/450155; ②), and the equally pleasant *Clausens Hotel*, Skt Laurentii Vej 35 (☎98/450160; ②–③). The **youth hostel** is at Rolighedsvej 2 (☎98/442200; closed Dec & Jan), a couple of minutes west of the town centre. Of a number of **campsites**, the most accessible are *Grenen* (April–Sept; ☎98/442546), which has cabins, to the north along Fyrvej, and *Poul Eegs* (April–Sept; ☎98/441470), on Batterivej, left off Frederikshavnvej just before the town centre.

There are plenty of **eating** options in Skagen, though most of them are expensive. For Italian food, try *Italia* or *Alfredo*, both in Havnegade and both serving reasonably priced pizza and pasta dishes. In the same street, *The Kebab House* is excellent and cheap too.

travel details

Trains
Aalborg to: Frederikshavn (20 daily; 1hr 10min).
Århus to: Aalborg (20 daily; 1hr 40min); Copenhagen (5–6 daily; 5hr); Frederikshavn (20 daily; 3hr); Randers (20 daily; 40min); Silkeborg (12–15 daily; 50min); Viborg via Langå (18 daily; 1hr).
Esbjerg to: Århus (16 daily; 3hr 15min); Copenhagen (20 daily; 5hr); Fredericia (27 daily; 1hr 23min); Ribe (14 daily; 36min).
Fredericia to: Århus (25 daily; 1hr 22min); Sønderborg (6 daily; 1hr 55min); Vejle (23 daily; 20min).
Frederikshavn to: Skagen (12 daily; 40min).
Ribe to: Tønder (12 daily; 45min).
Skanderborg to: Århus (25 daily; 15min); Silkeborg (18 daily; 30min).
Sønderborg to: Fredericia(6 daily; 1hr 55min).
Struer to: Holstebro (28 daily; 15min); Thisted (25 daily; 1hr 30min); Vejle (5 daily; 1hr 40min).
Vejle to: Silkeborg (10 daily; 1hr 10min).
Viborg to: Struer (17 daily; 45min).

Buses
Århus to: Copenhagen (2 daily; 4hr).
Frederikshavn to: Skagen (11 daily; 1hr).
Randers to: Ebeltoft (12 daily; 1hr 15min); Grenå (12 daily; 1hr 15min); Viborg (19 daily; 1hr 15min).

Skærbæk to: Havneby (6–8 daily; 25min)
Sønderborg to: Fynshav (7–8 daily; 30min).
Thisted to: Aalborg (14 daily; 2hr 30min); Hanstholm (14 daily; 45min).

Ferries
Århus to: Kalundborg (ferry: 5 daily; 3hr 10min; hydrofoil: 10 daily; 1hr 10min).
Ebeltoft to: Sjællands Odde (ferry; 10 daily, 1hr 40min; hydrofoil; 5 daily; 45min).
Fynshav to: Bøjden (8 daily; 50min).
Grenå to: Anholt (2 daily; 2hr 45min).
Mommark to: Søby (2–4 daily in summer; 1hr).

International Trains
Fredericia to: Flensburg (8 daily; 1hr 45min).

International Ferries
Esbjerg to: Harwich (4–5 weekly in summer; 19hr 45min).
Frederikshavn to: Gothenburg (8 daily; 3hr 15min); Larvik (1 daily; 6hr); Moss (1 daily; 7hr); Oslo (*Stena Line* 1 daily; 10hr).
Grenå to: Halmstad (1–3 daily in summer; 4hr); Varberg (1 daily in summer only; 4hr).
Havneby to: List (June–Oct; 4–8 daily; 55min).
Hirtshals to: Oslo (1 daily in summer; 8–12hr).

PART THREE

NORWAY

Introduction

In many ways **Norway** is still a land of unknowns. Quiet for a thousand years since the Vikings stamped their distinctive mark on Europe, the country nowadays often seems more than just geographically distant. Beyond Oslo and the famous fjords, the rest of the country might as well be blank for all many visitors know – and, in a manner of speaking, large parts of it are. Vast stretches in the north and east are sparsely populated and starkly vegetated, and it is, at times, possible to travel for hours without seeing a soul.

Despite this isolation, Norway has had a pervasive influence. Traditionally its inhabitants were explorers, from the Vikings – the first western European discoverers of Greenland and North America – to more recent figures like Amundsen, Nansen and Heyerdahl. And Norse traditions are common to many other isolated fishing communities, not least northwest Scotland and the Shetlands. At home, too, the Norwegian people have striven to escape the charge of national provincialism, touting the disproportionate number of acclaimed artists, writers and musicians (most notably Munch, Ibsen and Grieg) who have made their mark on the wider European scene. It's also a pleasing discovery that the great outdoors – great though it is – harbours some lively historical towns.

■ Where to go

Beyond **Oslo**, one of the world's most prettily sited capitals, the major cities of interest – in roughly descending order – are medieval **Trondheim**, **Bergen** in the heart of the fjords, hilly, southern **Stavanger** and northern **Tromsø**. All are likeable, walkable cities, worth time for themselves, as well as being on top of startlingly handsome countryside. The perennial draw, though, is the **western fjords** – a must, and every bit as scenically stunning as they're cracked up to be. Dip into the region from Bergen or Åndalsnes, both accessible direct by train from Oslo, or take more time and appreciate the subtleties of the innumerable waterside towns and villages. The **south** of Norway, and in particular the long southern coast, is popular with holidaying Norwegians, with its beaches and whitewashed wooden towns; the central, more remote regions are ideal for hiking and camping.

Far to the north of here Norway grows increasingly barren. The vast lands of **Troms** and

Finnmark were once the home of outlaws and still boast wild and untamed tracts. There are also the Sami tribes and their herds of reindeer, which you'll see on the thin, exposed road up to the North Cape, or **Nordkapp** – the northernmost accessible point of mainland Europe. The Cape is the natural end to the long trek north, although there are still several hundred kilometres further east which could claim that distinction – in fact, right the way to Kirkenes on the Russian border.

■ When to go

Norway is still regarded as a remote, cold country – spectacular enough but climatically inhospitable. **When to go**, however, is not as clear cut a choice as you'd imagine. There are advantages to travelling during the long, dark **winters** with their reduced everything: daylight, opening times and transport services. If you are equipped and hardy enough to reach the far north, seeing the phenomenal **Northern Lights** (*Aurora Borealis*) is a distinct possibility; later, once the days begin to get lighter, **skiing** is excellent; while **Easter** is the time of the great and colourful Sami festivals. But – especially in the north – it is cold, often bitterly so, and this guide has been deliberately weighted towards the **summer** season, when most people travel and when it is possible to camp and hitch to keep costs down. This is the time of the **Midnight Sun**: the further north you go, the longer the day becomes, until at Nordkapp the sun is continually visible from mid-May to the end of July. The box below lists the dates between which the Midnight Sun is visible in different parts of the country.

Something worth noting is that the **summer season** in Norway is relatively short, stretching roughly from the beginning of June to mid-August. Come much later than 16–20 August and

---

THE MIDNIGHT SUN

(whole sun above the horizon)

Alta: May 18–July 27
Bodø: June 4–July 8
Hammerfest: May 16–July 27
Nordkapp: May 13–July 29
Tromsø: May 20–July 20

N.B. These dates may vary by 24 hours either way.

you'll find that tourist offices, museums and other sights cut back their hours, while buses, ferries and trains switch to autumn and winter schedules, too. On the other hand, note that visits during the last two weeks in July (or, on occasion, the last week in July, first in August) coincides with the Norwegian *Felles ferie* – a fortnight when virtually the whole country goes on holiday, filling up campsites, cabins and the roads.

As regards **temperatures**, roughly speaking January and February are the coldest months, July and August the warmest; the Gulf Stream makes the north surprisingly temperate during summer.

Getting There

There's no problem in reaching Norway from the rest of Scandinavia. There are very regular train services from Sweden, year-round ferry connections from Denmark and flights from all the mainland countries. More long-windedly, you can also reach Norway from Iceland, via the Faroes and the Shetland Islands.

■ By train

By **train** you can reach **Oslo** from Stockholm (2–3 daily; 6hr) or from Copenhagen/Gothenburg (3–4 daily; 10hr/5hr); and there are regular services to **Trondheim** (2 daily; 11hr) and **Narvik** (2 daily; 21hr), again from Stockholm. *InterRail/Scanrail* passes are valid – for full details see *Basics*.

■ By ferry

Consider using one of the many ferry services **from Denmark** to Norway. There are connections from **Copenhagen** to Oslo (16hr) with *Scandinavian Seaways*; **Frederikshavn** to Oslo (12hr) and Moss (7hr) with *Stena Line*, and Larvik (6hr) with *Larvik Line*; and **Hirtshals** to Oslo (11hr) and Kristiansand (4hr 30min) with *Color Line*.

Schedules depend on time of year, but on most routes crossings are made once or twice daily during summer and once daily during winter; a few stop altogether in low season. Prices tend to rise sharply in summer but train pass holders get discounts on some routes. All ferries take cars. For fuller details contact the local tourist offices in the relevant Danish towns, or the appropriate ferry companies; and see the Norway and Denmark chapters' "Travel Details" sections.

There's also a year-round ferry service **from Sweden**, linking Strömstad, north of Gothenburg, with Sandefjord, Halden or Fredrikstad. It's operated by *Scandi-Line* (Strömstad ☎0526/150 70; Sandefjord ☎33 46 08 00). The Sandefjord–Strömstad service runs 4–5 times daily all year, taking two and a half hours. Services to Halden and Fredrikstad operate summer only (3–4 daily; 1hr 15min).

From Iceland, the Faroes and Shetlands, there's a service operated by *Smyril Line* (once-weekly June–Aug) which terminates in Bergen. The complete route can take up to three or four days, depending on stopovers.

■ By plane

Norway has international airports at Oslo, Bergen, Stavanger, Kristiansand, Trondheim and Tromsø; most flights from elsewhere in Scandinavia are with *SAS*. A variety of discounts (family/group/student) can make internal Scandinavian flights realistic, though most are only available in summer. Tourist offices will have the latest information, or contact *SAS* or *Braathens Safe*, its competitor, in major Scandinavian cities.

Costs, Money and Banks

Norway has a reputation as one of the most expensive of European holiday destinations. In many ways this is entirely justified as most of what you're likely to purchase – from a cup of coffee to a roll of film and a book – is costly. On the other hand, **accommodation** is reasonably priced in comparison with other north European countries, and Norway's youth hostels are exceptionally good value. **Getting around** is good news too. Most travellers use some kind of train pass and there are numerous discounts available. **Food** is a different matter – it's universally expensive – and the cost of alcohol is enough to make even a heavy drinker contemplate abstinence.

On average, if you're prepared to buy your own picnic lunch, stay in youth hostels, and stick to the less expensive cafés and restaurants, you could get by on around £30/$40 a day, excluding the cost of public transport. Staying in three-star hotels, eating out in medium-range restaurants most nights (but avoiding drinking in bars), you'll get through at least £70/$100 a day. On £130/$180 a day and upwards, you'll be limited only by your energy reserves – though if you're planning to stay in a five-star hotel and to have a big night out, this figure still won't be enough. **Restaurants** don't come cheap, but if you avoid the extras and concentrate on the main courses, around £14/$20 will normally suffice – twice that with a starter and dessert. As always, if you're travelling alone you'll spend much more on accommodation than you would if sharing with at least one other person: most hotels do have single rooms, but they're fixed at 60–80 percent of the price of a double.

■ Money and banks

Norwegian **currency** consists of *kroner*, one of which, a *krone* (crown; abbreviated kr or NOK), is divided into 100 *øre*. Coins in circulation are 50 øre, 1kr, 5kr and 10kr; notes are for 50kr, 100, 500 and 1000kr. You can bring in up to 25,000kr in notes and coins (though there's no limit on travellers cheques). At the time of writing the exchange rate was around 10.4kr to the pound sterling; 6.5kr or so to the US dollar.

All but the tiniest settlements in Norway have a **bank** or **savings bank**, and the vast majority will change foreign currency and travellers cheques. Banks will also handle Eurocheques, and many give cash advances on credit cards. **Banking hours** in Norway are generally Monday–Friday 8.15am–3.30pm, though they close half an hour earlier during the summer (June–Aug) and are open till 5pm on Thursday all year. All major **post offices** change foreign currency and travellers cheques at similar or better rates and they have longer opening hours too, generally Monday to Friday 8am–5pm, Saturday 8am–1pm. You're nearly always charged a commission. If the commission is waived, double check the exchange rate to ensure that it hasn't been lowered to compensate.

Outside banking and post office hours, most major hotels, many travel agents and some hostels and campsites will change money at less generous rates and with variable commissions, as will the **exchange kiosks** to be found in Oslo – see the relevant chapter for addresses and opening hours.

Post and phones

Norway's communication systems are very efficient, and things are made even easier by the fact that nearly all post office and telephone staff speak good English.

Post offices in Norway are plentiful and opening hours are usually Monday–Friday 8am–4pm, Saturday 9am–1pm. Some urban post offices open longer hours, especially the main post office in Oslo (Mon–Fri 8am–8pm, Sat 9am–3pm). At the time of writing, **postage** costs 4.5kr for a postcard or letter under 20g sent within Europe (4kr within Scandinavia), and 5.5kr to countries outside. Mail to the US takes 7–10 days, within Europe 2–3 days.

Norway has a reliable telephone system, run by *Telenor*, and you can make domestic and international **telephone calls** with ease from public phones. Phone booths are plentiful and almost invarably work, but if you can't find one, some bars have pay phones you can use. All the more expensive hotel rooms have phones too, but note that they always attract an exorbitant surcharge for their use.

Public telephones take 1kr, 5kr and 10kr coins, though coin-operated phones are gradually being phased out in favour of those that only take phonecards (*TeleKort*); these can be purchased at newsstands, post offices, major train stations and some supermarkets, in denominations ranging from 35kr to 210kr. An increasing number of public phones also accept major credit cards.

Most phone booths have English instructions displayed inside. To make a reverse charge or collect call, call the operator (they all speak English) on ☎115 (for international calls) or ☎117 (within Norway). Local telephone calls **cost** a minimum of 2kr, while 10kr is enough to start an international call, but not much more. Discount rates on international calls (of around 15 percent) apply from 10pm to 8am. Note that Norwegian telephone numbers have eight digits and there's no area code.

Media

You needn't miss out on TV or newspapers while in Norway, since most British and some American daily **newspapers**, and the odd periodical, are available in most towns from *Narvesen* kiosks, large train stations and at airports. As for the **Norwegian media**, state advertising, loans and subsidized production costs keep a wealth of smaller papers going that would bite the dust elsewhere. Most are closely linked with political parties, although the bigger city-based papers tend to be independent. Highest circulations are claimed in Oslo by the independent *Verdens Gang* and the independent-conservative *Aftenposten*, and in Bergen by the liberal *Bergens Tidende*.

The **television** network has expanded over the last few years, in line with the rest of Europe. Alongside the state channels, NRK and TV2, there are satellite channels like TV Norge, while TV3 is a channel common to Norway, Denmark and Sweden; you can also pick up Swedish TV broadcasts. Many of the programmes are English-language imports, so there is invariably something on that you'll understand – though much of it is pretty unadventurous stuff. Many bars and most hotels are geared up for at least a couple of the big pan-European cable and satellite channels: the *MTV* music station; *CNN*, which provides 24-hour news; Murdoch's *Sky*, with films, news and current affairs; *Superchannel*, a mixture of videos, soaps and movies; and *Eurosport*.

Local tourist **radio** is broadcast during the summer months, giving details of events and festivals; watch for signposts by the roadside and tune in. Otherwise, English radio broadcasts, featuring news from Norway, are repeated several times daily on the FM waveband (93MHz).

Getting Around

Norway's public transport system – a huge mesh of trains, buses, car ferries and passenger express ferries – is comprehensive and reliable. In the winter (especially in the north) services can be cut back severely, but no part of the country is unreachable for long.

All the main air, train, bus and ferry services are detailed in the invaluable (and free) *Rutehefte* (**transport timetables**), an easy-to-use booklet available from either the larger tourist offices in Norway, or in advance from the Norwegian tourist office back home (see p.27). Or check the more hefty *Rutebok for Norge* (195kr, published five times a year) containing every schedule in the country, which some tourist offices and all travel agents hold; ask for photocopies of the relevant pages. Train schedules are included in the free booklet, the *NSB Togruter*, while each separate Norwegian train route has its own little timetable too. All are available at most stations.

■ Trains

Train services are run by *Norges Statsbaner* (*NSB*) – Norwegian State Railways – and operate, apart from a few branch lines, on four main routes, linking Oslo to Stavanger in the south, to Bergen in the west and to Trondheim and on to Bodø in the north. In places, the rail system is extended by a *TogBuss* (literally train-bus) service, with connecting buses continuing on from the train terminal. The nature of the country makes most of the routes engineering feats of some magnitude and worth a trip in their own right – the tiny **Flåm line** and sweeping **Rauma line** to Åndalsnes are exciting examples.

Prices are quite reasonable, the popular Oslo–Bergen run, for example, costing around 470kr one-way for a six-and-a-half-hour journey, and Oslo–Trondheim 550kr for nine hours. Costs can be further reduced by purchasing a **train pass** (see below) or, in some cases, by taking advantage of one of the special **discount fares**. Bookable at least one day in advance, *minipris* tickets can shave about 20 percent off the price of long-distance journeys, the main restrictions being that they are not available at peak periods and on certain trains, stopovers are not permitted; the further you travel, the more economic they become, especially as there's a maximum *minipris* fare of about 430kr. Similarly, the *NSB Kundekort* and *Grønt kort* cost in the region of 450kr, are valid for one year, and entitle holders to 50 percent discounts on many off-peak journeys (*grønne avganger* or so-called "green" departures). For any specific trip, it's always worth checking in advance with the station information desk about special deals and discounts; and here also you can pick up *NSB*'s free leaflets on each of the lines. In terms of **concessionary fares**, there are group and family reductions, while children over 4 and under 16 pay half fare, as do senior citizens.

It's worth noting that inter-city trains and all overnight and international services require an advance **seat reservation** (20kr), whether you have a train pass or not. In high season it's wise to make a reservation on main routes anyway as trains can be packed. **Sleepers** are reasonably priced, certainly in view of the fact that they save you a night's hotel accommodation: a bed in a three-berth cabin costs around 100kr, two-berth 200kr and one-berth at least 420kr – though for a one-berth cabin you'll need a first-class ticket, or rather a **Standard Class** ticket as distinct from **Economy**: NSB don't actually have *first-class* carriages, but do market first-class rail tickets and passes abroad. For further advance information about discounts and tickets, contact the specialist agents listed in the "Getting There" section (p.158).

■ Rail passes

InterRail and *Eurail* passes (see the "Getting There" sections, p.6, p.16) are valid on the Norwegian railway system, as is the *Scanrail* pass, which covers Norway, Sweden, Denmark and Finland (see p.29). There's no longer a pass specific to Norway, though you may be able to buy a *Freedom* (aka *Euro Domino*) pass for Norway before leaving home – again, see the "Getting There" sections on p.6.

■ Buses

Where the train network won't take you, **buses** will – and at no great cost, either: a typical fjord journey, like the Sogndal–Fjaerland trip, costs around 70kr, while the ten-hour bus ride between Ålesund and Bergen is a reasonable 400kr. All tolls and ferry costs are included in the price of a ticket, which can represent a significant saving. You'll need to use buses principally in the western fjords and the far north, though there are also a series of long-distance **express buses** connecting major towns throughout Norway. As a rough guide, most of the longer routes tend to operate once daily, usually early; shorter hauls, although more frequent, often tail off in the late afternoon. **Tickets** are usually bought on board, but travel agents sell advance tickets for the more popular routes. The longest journey, the two-day ride from Bodø/Fauske to Kirkenes, costs around 1470kr. Information on specific routes, and timetables, are available from local tourist offices and bus stations or from *Nor-Way Bussekspress*, Karl Johans gate 2, N–0154 Oslo 1 (☎22 33 01 90; fax 22 42 50 33).

Concessionary fares are generally the same as for the trains (see above), though some bus companies also give discounts for students and train pass holders get a 50 percent reduction on certain bus services. Indeed, for any specific trip, it's always worth checking ahead about special deals and discounts.

Costs can be further reduced by purchasing a **bus pass**. Valid on all express bus routes throughout the country, the *NOR-WAY BusPass* offers a guarantee of a seat without any advance booking (except for groups of more than 8) – the idea being that if one bus gets full, they will lay on another. It is not, however, valid on the vast majority of local bus services. There are 7-day (1375kr) and 14-day (2200kr) passes, and again any toll and ferry costs are almost always covered. Passes for children (aged 4–15) are 75 percent of the adult rate. The pass can be purchased at any of the larger bus stations in Norway, and at the *Nor-Way Bussekspress* office, Karl Johans gate 2, Oslo.

The Nord-Norge Bussen

A long-distance bus service, the **Nord-Norge expressen**, runs between Bodø or Fauske, the northernmost reach of the railway, and Kirkenes, close to the Russian border – a two- or three-day-hour journey usually involving two stopovers. The route is operated by several bus companies who combine to run two buses daily all year as far as Narvik, where you usually have to break your journey before embarking on the next two stages – Narvik to Alta and Alta to Kirkenes – each of which is served by one and sometimes two buses daily. It can be a thrilling ride, though blizzards can play havoc with the schedules between October and May and it has a less-than-thrilling hostess commentary on some of the more spectacular bits. Obviously, if you're embarking on this lengthy trip, a bus pass is your best bet, but you can buy tickets as you go or one all-inclusive ticket in advance: the standard fare is around 1470kr one-way; further details from travel agents and the Bodø or Fauske tourist offices (see also "Travel details" on p.321 and p.343).

■ Ferries

Using a **ferry** in Norway is one of the highlights of any visit – and indeed amongst the western fjords and around the Lofotens they are all but impossible to avoid. The majority are roll-on, roll-off **car ferries**, with prices fixed on a nationwide sliding scale: short journeys (of 10–15min) cost foot passengers 15–20kr, whereas a car and driver pay in the region of 90kr. As a general rule, bus travellers using a ferry will not have to pay any more than the price of their original ticket on buses that cross over on the ferries (the majority), as distinct from those that drop you on one jetty with another waiting on the other side. **Procedures** are straightforward too: foot passengers walk on and pay the conductor, car drivers wait in line with their vehicles on the jetty till the conductor comes to the car window (occasionally there's a drive-by ticket office) to collect the money. One or two of the longer car ferry routes (in particular Bodø–Moskenes) take advance reservations, but the rest operate on a **first-come first-served** basis. In the off season, there's no real need to arrive more than twenty minutes before departure – with the possible exception of the Lofoten Island ferries – but in the summer allow two hours, two and a half to be really safe.

Hurtigbåt passenger express boats

Hurtigbåt **passenger express boats** are hydrofoils that make up for in speed what they lack in enjoyment – unlike the ordinary ferries you're cooped up and can only view the passing landscape through a window. In choppy seas, the ride can be very bumpy too. Nonetheless, they are a very convenient way of saving time: for instance, it takes just four hours for the *Hurtigbåt* service to run from Bergen to Balestrand, the same from Narvik to Svolvaer, and merely two and a half hours to make the trip from Harstad to Tromsø. *Hurtigbåt* services are concentrated on the west coast around Bergen and the neighbouring fjords and the majority operate all year. There's no fixed tariff, so rates vary considerably, though *Hurtigbåt* boats are significantly more expensive than the car ferries: for instance, Bergen to Stavanger, a four-hour trip, costs 450kr, whereas Oslo–Arendal takes almost seven hours and costs 350kr. There are **concessionary fares** on all routes, with children (4–15) and senior citizens getting a 50 percent discount and students often eligible for a 25 percent reduction. In addition, train pass holders may be able to claim a 50 percent discount on various routes, including Bergen–Haugesund–Stavanger, Narvik–Svolvaer, Bergen–Flåm and Flåm–Gudvangen. Ask the local tourist office about further discount deals.

The Hurtigrute

Norway's most celebrated ferry journey is the long and beautiful haul up the coast from Bergen to Kirkenes on the **Hurtigrute** (the word literally means "rapid route") coastal steamer. To many this is the quintessential Norwegian experience and it's certainly the best way to observe the rigours of this extraordinary coastline. Eleven ships combine to provide one daily service in either direction and the boat stops off at over thirty ports on the way. Until fairly recently, the ferry was a vital supply line to the remote towns of northern Norway. The extension of the road system has removed much of its earlier importance, but it continues to act as a delivery service, its survival assured by its popularity with tourists – you may find the lounges full of elderly British and American travellers.

Tickets for the whole round trip, which lasts eleven days and includes all meals, go for anything from 8600kr to 24,000kr depending on whether you're sailing on an old or new vessel, where your cabin is situated, and when you sail – September to March departures are 40 percent cheaper than those in the summer. There are also **concessionary fares** offering 50 percent discounts for senior citizens (over 67), families, groups of ten or more, students, and children (4–15). Note that these discounts are only available for a limited number of cabins in the summertime. If you're over 16 and under 26 and travelling between September and April, another option is a **coastal pass**, which costs 1750kr for 21 days' unlimited travel. Contact a travel agent at home for further details and bookings. Once you're in Norway, either book through a travel agency or with the shippers themselves: *OVDS* (☎76 92 37 00; fax 76 92 37 80) and *TFDS* (☎77 64 82 00; fax 77 64 81 80). Most travel agents and tourist offices have copies of the schedule.

With neither the time, money nor inclination to embark upon an extended voyage with the *Hurtigrute*, a **short jump** along the coast is well worth considering. They are not particularly cheap – especially by comparison with the bus fare – but prices are affordable and last-minute bargains can bring the rates down to amazingly low levels. All the tourist offices in the *Hurtigrute* ports have the latest details and will telephone the captain of the nearest ship to make a reservation on your behalf.

As for **specifics**, although it's a cruise ship you don't need to have a cabin: sleeping in the lounges or on deck is allowed. But plan carefully before buying your ticket, since single tickets allow only one overnight stop. The older ships are the more interesting, and tend to have showers you can use on the lower corridors; newer models have fully self-contained cabins. Car drivers should use the new ships, as the old ones only have room for five or six vehicles, which have to be winched – expensively – on and off. Bikes travel free. A 24-hour cafeteria supplies coffee and snacks, and there's a good restaurant.

■ Planes

Internal flights can prove a surprisingly cheap way of hopping about the country, especially if you're short on time and want to reach, say, the far north. Tromsø to Kirkenes takes the best part of two days by bus; it's an hour by plane.

Domestic air routes are serviced by several **companies** – *Braathens SAFE*, *SAS*, *Coast Air*, *Widerøe Norsk Air* and *Widerøe's Flyveselskap* – and there are good **discounts** available. For instance, *Braathens SAFE* offers a a special youth fare for under-25s which knocks about 50 percent off the full price, though you can't buy the ticket more than seven days in advance and have to pay in full at the time of booking. The same airline also has special *One-way-low-fares* on certain routes and *Billy* tickets, low-price returns bookable at least seven days prior to departure and including a Saturday night away. Otherwise, *Minipris* and *Lavpris* tickets are available on return flights on certain routes and days. In terms of **concessionary fares**, children, families and seniors are all eligible for discounts of up to 50 percent; the details vary year to year, so it's always worth shopping around. But as a baseline, note that the regular standard fare from Oslo to Bergen is around 1000kr one-way, Oslo to Tromsø 2070kr, and Bergen to Trondheim 1300kr.

The two largest carriers offer **air passes** too. *Braathens SAFE* has a *Visit Norway Pass*, which is valid on all the company's routes, the only restriction being that you're not eligible if you are resident in Scandinavia. Under the terms of the pass, short one-way flights within southern or northern Norway cost around 550kr, long one-way flights between south and north are about 1100kr. The dividing line between north and south is drawn through Trondheim, which is counted as belonging to both zones. The pass can be bought either before you get to Norway or when you are there; further details direct from *Braathens SAFE*

(for addresses see p.4) or in Norway, where their main office is at Haakon VII's gate 2, 0161 Oslo (☎67 58 60 00). For the *SAS AirPass*, which can only be purchased before you get to Scandinavia, see "Getting There", p.3.

■ Driving and car rental

Driving in Norway can be a positive adventure. The main roads are excellent, especially when you consider the vagaries of the climate, and, now that most of the more hazardous sections have been ironed out or tunnelled through, driving them is comparatively straightforward. But leave the main roads behind for the narrow byroads that wind across the mountains and you'll be in for some nail-biting experiences – and that's in the summertime. In **winter** the Norwegians close many roads to concentrate their efforts on keeping the main highways open, but obviously blizzards and ice can make driving difficult or dangerous anywhere, even with winter tyres, studs and chains – always seek local advice especially if you're venturing onto minor roads; in the north you can't assume that even the E6 Arctic Highway will be driveable. At any time of the year, the more adventurous the drive, the better equipped you need to be: on remote drives you should pack provisions, take proper hiking gear, check the car thoroughly before departure and carry a spare can of fuel.

Norway's main highways have an "E" prefix – E6, E18 etc; all the country's other significant roads (*riksvei*, or *rv*) are assigned a number and, as a general rule, the lower the number, the busier the road. In our guide, we've used the "E" prefix, but designated the other roads as

---

MAJOR MOUNTAIN PASSES: OPENING DATES

Obviously enough, there's no preordained date for opening mountain roads in the springtime – it depends on the weather with the threat of avalanches often much more of a limitation than actual snow falls. The dates below should therefore be treated with caution and you should seek advice from a local tourist office if in doubt. Should you do head along a mountain road that's closed, sooner or later you're likely to come to a barrier and have to turn round.

E6: Dovrefjell (Oslo–Trondheim). Usually open all year.

E69: Skarsvåg–Nordkapp. Closed late Oct to early May.

Hwy 7: Hardangervidda (Oslo–Bergen). Usually open all year.

Hwy 11: Haukelifjell (Oslo–Bergen/Stavanger). Usually open all year.

Hwy 51: Valdresflya. Closed mid-Nov to late April.

Hwy 55: Sognefjellet. Closed mid-Nov to early May.

Hwy 63: Grotli–Geiranger–Linge (Trollstigen). Closed mid-Oct to late May.

"Highways" (followed by the number). **Tolls** are imposed on certain roads to pay for construction projects, and in theory once the costs are covered the toll is removed. There's a modest toll on entering the country's larger cities (5–15kr) and the older building projects levy a fee of around 20–30kr, but the toll for some of the newer works (like the tunnel near Fjaerland) runs to well over 100kr per vehicle.

Fuel is readily available, even in the north, though here the settlements are so far apart that you'll need to keep your tank full. Current fuel prices are around 8–9kr a litre and there are four main grades – Unleaded (*blyfri*) 95 octane, Unleaded 98 octane, Super 98 octane and Diesel. It's worth remembering that many filling stations don't accept credit cards.

Documentation and rules of the road

Full EU **driving licences** are honoured in Norway, but other nationals will need an **International Driver's Licence** (available at minimum cost from your home motoring organization). If you're bringing your own car, you must have vehicle registration papers, adequate insurance, a first-aid kit, a warning triangle and a green card (available from your insurers or motoring organization). Extra insurance coverage for unforeseen legal costs is also well worth having, as is an appropriate **breakdown policy**. In Britain, the *RAC* and *AA* charge members and non-members about £85 for a month's Europe-wide breakdown cover, with all the appropriate documentation, including green card, provided.

Rules of the road are strict: you drive on the right, with dipped headlights required at all times; there's a speed limit of 30kph in residential areas, 50kph in built-up areas and 80kph on open roads (90kph on motorways and some main roads); seat belts are compulsory for drivers and front-seat passengers (back-seat passengers, too, if fitted). Take note of the speed limits, because if you're stopped for **speeding** there are large spot fines (700kr) payable and rarely any leniency shown to unwitting foreigners. **Drunken driving** is also severely frowned upon. You can be asked to take a breath test on a routine traffic-check; if over the limit, you will have your licence confiscated and may face 28 days in prison.

The *Norges Automobil-Forbund* (*NAF*) patrols all mountain passes between mid-June and mid-August in case of **breakdown**, and there are emergency telephones along some motorways.

NAF's 24-hour Emergency Service number is ☎22 34 16 00. Otherwise, look in telephone directory under "Redningstjeneste".

Car rental

All the major international **car rental** companies are represented in Norway, and addresses are given in the "Listings" sections of larger cities. To rent a car, you'll have to be 21 or over (and have been driving for at least a year), and you'll need a credit card – though the occasional agency will accept a hefty cash deposit. Rental **charges** are fairly high, beginning at around 3600kr per week for unlimited mileage in the smallest vehicle, but include collision damage waiver and vehicle (but not personal) insurance. To cut costs, watch for the special deals offered by the bigger companies (a Friday to Monday weekend rental might, for example, cost you as little as 800kr) or you could go to a smaller, local company (listed in the telephone directory under *Bilutleie*), though you should, in this case, proceed with care. In particular, check the policy for the excess applied to claims and ensure that it includes collision damage waiver (applicable if an accident is your fault), and an adequate level of cover. Bear in mind, too, that it's almost always less expensive to rent your car before you leave home – see p.29.

■ Cycling

Cycling in Norway is not as ludicrous as it sounds, and is a great way of taking in the scenery – just be sure to wrap up warm and dry and not to be over-ambitious in terms of the distances you expect to cover. Cycle tracks as such are few and far between, and mainly confined to the larger towns, but there's precious little traffic on most of the minor roads and cycling along them is a popular pastime. At almost every place you're likely to stay in, you should be able to **rent bikes** – at the tourist office, a sports shop, youth hostel or campsite. Costs are pretty uniform, between 80kr and 100kr a day for a 7-speed bike plus a refundable deposit of around 200kr; mountain bikes are about 30 percent more.

A few tourist offices have maps of recommended cycling routes, but this is a rarity. It is, however, important to check your itinerary thoroughly especially in the more mountainous areas, as cyclists aren't allowed through the longer **tunnels** for their own protection: the fumes can be quite literally life-threatening; discuss your plans with whoever you rent the bike from. You'll also need good lights to ride through the tunnels that aren't prohibited. Bikes nearly always go free on ferries and rural buses, which are usually fitted specially to accommodate them; there's a 25kr fee to take them on trains, and express trains don't take bikes at all.

If you're planning a **cycling holiday**, your first port of call should be the Norwegian tourist office (for addresses see p.27). They provide general cycling advice and issue a map indicating the roads and tunnels that are inaccessible to cyclists. They also have a list of companies offering all-inclusive **cycling tours**. Amongst several, the hiking organization *DNT*, Stortingsgaten 28, Oslo (☎22 83 25 50; fax 22 83 24 78), runs tours of the Hardanger plateau beginning in Finse; *Terra Nova Reisebyrå*, Nygaaten 3, Bergen (☎55 32 23 77; fax 55 32 30 15), offers combined *Hurtigrute* and cycling tours of the west coast; and *Den Rustne Eike*, Vestbaneplassen 2, Oslo (☎22 83 72 31; fax 22 83 63 59), has a varied programme including west coast and Oslo area tours. Obviously enough, tour costs vary enormously, but as a baseline reckon on about 5000kr per week all inclusive.

Accommodation

Inevitably, hotel accommodation is one of the major expenses you will incur on a trip to Norway – indeed, if you're after a degree of comfort, it's going to be the costliest item by far. There are, however, budget alternatives, principally private rooms arranged via the local tourist office, campsites and cabins, and last but not least an abundance of *HI*-affiliated youth hostels.

■ Hotels

Almost universally, Norwegian **hotels** are of a high standard, neat, clean and efficient. Summer prices and more impromptu weekend deals also make many of them, by European standards at least, comparatively economical. Another plus is that the price of a hotel room always includes a buffet breakfast – and especially at the middle to top end of the hotel market, these can be sumptuous banquets. The only negatives are the sizes of the rooms – they tend to be small, especially the singles – and their sameness: Norway abounds in mundane concrete and glass skyrise hotels. In addition to the hotels we've detailed in the guide, all Norwegian hotels, their room rates, summer discounts and facilities, are listed in the free booklet *Overnatting*, available from the Norwegian tourist office.

The summer is also the best time to utilize one of several **hotel discount and pass schemes** in operation throughout Norway. There are seven main ones to choose from and each serves to cut costs, but often at the expense of a flexible, or rather spontaneous, itinerary – advance booking is the norm – and diversity: many people much prefer to mix hotel and hostel accommodation rather than stay in a hotel every night. Most Norwegian hotels are members of one discount/pass scheme or another and you can usually join the scheme at one of the hotels, or at a tourist office; it's also worth checking what's available with your travel agent before leaving home.

■ Pensions and guesthouses

For something a little more informal and less anonymous than the average hotel, **pensions** (*pensjonater* or *hospits*) are your best bet – small, intimate boarding houses usually sited in the larger cities and more touristy towns, which go for about 350–450kr single, 500–700kr double; breakfast is generally extra. A *gjestgiveri* is a **guesthouse** or **inn**, charging the same sort of price. Facilities in all are usually adequate and homely

---

ACCOMMODATION PRICE CODES

All the Norwegian hotels and guest houses listed in the guide have been graded according to the following price bands, based on the cost of the least expensive double room in high season. However, almost every hotel offers seasonal and/or weekend discounts that can reduce the rate by one or even two grades. Many of these bargains are impromptu, but wherever possible we've given two grades, covering both the regular and the discounted rate. Single rooms, where available, are usually between 60 and 80 percent of the cost of a double.

① under 500kr ② 500–700kr ③ 700–900kr ④ 900–1200kr ⑤ 1200–1500kr ⑥ over 1500kr

without being overwhelmingly comfortable; more often than not you'll share a bathroom with others. Some pensions and guesthouses have kitchens available for the use of guests; the local tourist office should know which can offer this facility. The main advantage is that you're more than likely to meet other residents – a real boom (perhaps) if you're travelling alone – and locals.

■ Youth hostels and private rooms

For many budget travellers, as well as hikers, climbers and skiers, the country's **youth hostels** (*Vandrerjhem*) provide the accommodation mainstay: almost one hundred in all, spread right across the country, with handy concentrations in the western fjords, the central hiking and skiing regions and around Oslo. The hostels are invariably excellent and the Norwegian hostelling association, **Norske Vandrerhjem**, Dronningens gate 26, Oslo (☎22 42 14 10; fax 22 42 44 76), puts out a free pamphlet, *Vandrerhjem i Norge*, which details locations, opening dates, prices and telephone numbers. There's just one caveat to the praise: those hostels that occupy schools do tend to be rather drab and institutional.

Prices vary, anything from 90kr to 165kr, although the more expensive ones nearly always include a good breakfast. On average, reckon on paying 110kr a night for a bed, 50kr for breakfast and 80–100kr for a hot meal. Bear in mind also that almost all hostels have a few regular double and family rooms on offer: if you're lucky enough to find one vacant, these are, at around 300kr a double a night, the cheapest rooms you'll find in Norway. Incidentally, non-members can use the hostels, too, for an extra 25kr a night – which can soon mount up, so join the *HI* before you leave home. If you don't have your own sheet sleeping bag, you'll have to rent one for around 40–50kr a time.

It cannot be stressed too strongly that **calling ahead** to reserve a hostel bed in peak season, summer or winter, will save you lots of unnecessary leg work. Many hostels are only open from mid-June to mid-August and most close between 11am and 4pm. There's sometimes an 11pm or midnight curfew, though this is not too much of a drawback in a country where carousing is so expensive. Where breakfast is included, ask for a breakfast packet if you have to leave early to catch transport; otherwise note that hostel **meals** are not always a good buy (exceptions are mentioned in the text). Most, not all, hostels have small

kitchens, but often no pots, pans, cutlery or crockery, so self-caterers should take their own.

Tourist offices in the larger towns and amongst the more touristy settlements of the fjords can often fix you up with a **private room** in someone's house, which may include kitchen facilities. Prices are competitive – from around 150–200kr single, 250–350kr double – though there's usually a booking fee (15–25kr) on top, and the rooms themselves are frequently some way out of the centre. Nonetheless, they're often the best bargain available and, in certain instances, an improvement on the local youth hostel. Where this is the case, we've said so. If you don't have a sleeping bag, check the room comes with bedding – not all of them do; and if you're cooking for yourself, a few basic utensils wouldn't go amiss either.

■ Campsites, cabins and mountain huts

Camping is a popular pastime in Norway and there are literally hundreds of campsites to choose from, anything from a field with a few tent pitches through to extensive complexes with all mod cons. The Norwegian tourist authorities detail around 400 campsites in their free *Camping* brochure, classifying them on a one- to five-star grading depending on the facilities offered. Most sites are situated with the motorist (rather than the cyclist or walker) in mind and a good few occupy key locations beside the main roads. The majority are two- and three-star establishments, where prices are usually per tent, plus a small charge per person; on average expect to pay around 150kr for two people using a tent, with four- and five-star sites on average 20 percent more. During peak season it can be a good idea to **reserve ahead** if you have a car and large tent or trailer; phone numbers are listed in the free camping booklet and throughout the guide.

Camping rough in Norway is more than tolerated; indeed, as in Sweden, it is a tradition enshrined in law. You can camp anywhere in open areas as long as you are at least 150m away from any houses or cabins. As a courtesy, ask farmers for permission to use their land – it is rarely refused. Fires are not permitted in woodland areas or in fields between April 15 and September 15, and camper vans are not allowed (ever) to overnight on lay-bys. A good sleeping bag is essential, since even in summer it can get very cold, and, in the north at least, mosquito repellent and sun-protection cream are vital.

The Norwegian countryside is dotted with thousands of timber **cabins/chalets** (called *hytter*), ranging from simple wooden huts through to comfortable lodges. They are usually two- or four-bedded affairs with full kitchen facilities and sometimes a bathroom, and even TV. Some hostels have them on their grounds, there are nearly always at least a handful of them at every campsite, and in the Lofoten islands they are the most popular form of accommodation, many occupying refurbished fishermen's huts called *rorbuer*. Costs vary enormously, depending on the location, size and amenities of the *hytter*, and there are significant seasonal variations too. However, a one-night stay in a four-bed *hytter* will rarely cost more than 500kr – a more usual average would be about 300kr – and most of the larger versions fall within the 500–700kr price band. If you're travelling in a group, they are easily the cheapest way to see the countryside – and in some comfort. Hundreds of *hytter* are also rented out as holiday cottages by the week. Two main agencies deal with such arrangements nationwide and produce lavish, detailed brochures of the *hytter* on offer. For further details contact *De Norske Hytte Spesialistene*, Norbo Ferie, N-6410 Midsund (☎71 27 82 00; fax 71 27 83 50); or *Den Norske Hytteformidling*, PO Box 3404 Bjølsen, N-0406 Oslo (☎22 35 67 10; fax 22 71 94 13). A third agency, *Fjordhytter Den Norske Hytteformidling Bergen*, Lille Markevei 13, N-5005 Bergen (☎55 23 20 80; fax 55 23 24 04), specializes in western Norway.

One further option for hikers is the chain of **mountain huts** (again called *hytter*) on hiking routes countrywide. Some are privately run, but the majority are operated by **Den Norske Turistforening** (*DNT*), the Norwegian Mountain Hiking Association, and affiliated, regional hiking organizations. Membership of *DNT* costs around 360kr a year and, although you don't have to be a member of *DNT* to use the *hytter*, you soon recoup your outlay as all related costs have one tariff for members, another for non-members. For members staying in staffed huts, a bunk in a dormitory costs 70–100kr, 140kr in a family or double room, with meals starting at 60kr for breakfast, through to 125kr for dinner. At unstaffed huts, where you leave the money for your stay in a box provided, lodging costs about 20 percent less.

Food and Drink

Norwegian food can, at its best, be excellent: fish is plentiful, and carnivores can have a field day trying meats like reindeer steak or elk. But once again all this costs money, and those on a tight budget may have problems varying their diet. Vegetarians, too, won't find much to tempt them. Be prepared to cook for yourself and shop in supermarkets for the consistently cheapest eating. The same can be said of drinking, too: buying from the supermarkets and state off-licences is often the only way you'll afford more than the occasional tipple.

■ Food

Many travellers subsist almost entirely on a mixture of picnic food and hot meals that they rustle up themselves, with the odd snack and café meal thrown in to boost morale. However, there are a number of ways to eat out reasonably inexpensively: a good self-service buffet breakfast, provided by almost every hostel and hotel, goes some way to solving the problem; special lunch deals will get you a hot meal for around 60–70kr; while alongside the regular restaurants – which *are* expensive – there's the usual array of budget pizzerias and cafeterias in most towns.

Breakfast, picnics and snacks

Breakfast (*frokost*) in Norway is a huge self-service affair of bread, crackers, cheese, eggs, preserves, cold meat and fish, washed down by unlimited tea and coffee: it's usually excellent at youth hostels, and memorable in hotels, filling you up for the day for around 50–60kr, when not included in the price of the room.

If you're buying your own **picnic food**, bread, cheese, yoghurt and fruit are all relatively good value, while other staple foodstuffs – rice, pasta, canned fish and vegetables – can cost as much as twice the price you'd pay at home. Anything tinned is particularly pricey, and coffee and tea are also very expensive. Beware of a sandwich spread called *Kaviar* – bright pink, sold in tubes and packed full of additives. Real caviar, on the other hand – from lumpfish rather than sturgeon – is widely available and relatively inexpensive (around 40–45kr for a small jar).

Fast food probably offers the best chance of a hot and filling snack. The indigenous Norwegian stuff, served up from a **gatekjøkken** – a street kiosk or stall – in every town and village, consists mainly of rubbery hot dogs (*varm pølse*), pizza slices and chicken pieces and chips. American-style burger bars are also creeping in. Oslo and

GLOSSARY OF NORWEGIAN FOOD AND DRINK TERMS

Basics and snacks

Appelsin- marmelade	Marmalade	*Kaviar*	Caviar	*Pommes-frites*	Chips
		Kjeks	Biscuits	*Ris*	Rice
Brød	Bread	*Krem*	Whipped cream	*Rundstykker*	Roll
Eddik	Vinegar	*Syltetøy*	Jam	*Salat*	Salad
Egg	Egg	*Melk*	Milk	*Salt*	Salt
Eggerøre	Scrambled eggs	*Mineralvann*	Mineral water	*Sennep*	Mustard
		Nøtter	Nuts	*Smør*	Butter
Flatbrød	Crispbread	*Olje*	Oil	*Smørbrød*	Sandwich
Fløte	Single cream (for coffee)	*Omelett*	Omelette	*Sukker*	Sugar
		Ost	Cheese	*Suppe*	Soup
Grøt	Porridge	*Pannekake*	Pancakes	*Varm pølse*	Hot dog
Iskrem	Ice cream	*Pepper*	Pepper	*Yoghurt*	Yoghurt
Kake	Cake	*Potetchips*	Crisps		

Meat (*Kjøtt*) and game (*Vilt*)

Dyrestek	Venison	*Lever*	Liver	*Spekemat*	Dried meat
Elg	Elk	*Oksekjøtt*	Beef	*Stek*	Steak
Kalkun	Turkey	*Postei*	Paté	*Svinekjøtt*	Pork
Kjøttboller	Meatball	*Pølser*	Sausages	*Varm pølse*	Frankfurter/ Hot dog
Kjøttkaker	Meatcakes	*Reinsdyr*	Reindeer		
Kylling	Chicken	*Ribbe*	Pork rib		
Lammekjøtt	Lamb	*Skinke*	Ham		

Fish (*Fisk*) and shellfish (*Skalldyr*)

Ansjos	Anchovies	*Laks*	Salmon	*Sei*	Coalfish
Blåskjell	Mussels	*Makrell*	Mackerel	*Sild*	Herring
Brisling	Sprats	*Piggvar*	Turbot	*Sjøtunge*	Sole
Hummer	Lobster	*Reker*	Shrimps	*Småfisk*	Whitebait
Hvitting	Whiting	*Rødspette*	Plaice	*Torsk*	Cod
Kaviar	Caviar	*Rokelaks*	Smoked salmon	*Tunfisk*	Tuna
Krabbe	Crab			*Ål*	Eel
Kreps	Crayfish	*Sardiner*	Sardines	*Ørret*	Trout

Vegetables (*Grønsaker*)

Agurk	Cucumber/ gherkin/pickle	*Hvitløk*	Garlic	*Poteter*	Potatoes
		Kål	Cabbage	*Rosenkøl*	Brussel sprouts
Blomkål	Cauliflower	*Linser*	Lentils		
Bønner	Beans	*Løk*	Onion	*Selleri*	Celery
Erter	Peas	*Mais*	Sweetcorn	*Sopp*	Mushrooms
Gulrøtter	Carrots	*Nepe*	Turnip	*Spinat*	Spinach
Hodesalat	Lettuce	*Paprika*	Peppers	*Tomater*	Tomatoes

Fruit (*Frukt*)

Ananas	Pineapple	*Eple*	Apple	*Plommer*	Plums
Appelsin	Orange	*Fersken*	Peach	*Pærer*	Pears
Aprikos	Apricot	*Fruktsalat*	Fruit salad	*Sitron*	Lemon
Banan	Banana	*Grapefrukt*	Grapefruit	*Solbær*	Blackcurrants
Blabær	Blueberries	*Jordbær*	Strawberries	*Tyttbær*	Cranberries
Druer	Grapes	*Multer*	Cloudberries		

Terms

Blodig	Rare, underdone	*Marinert*	Marinated	*Stekt*	Fried
Godt stekt	Well done	*Ovnstekt*	Baked/roasted	*Stuet*	Stewed
Grillet	Grilled	*Røkt*	Smoked	*Sur*	Sour/pickled
Grytestekt	Braised	*Saltet*	Cured	*Syltet*	Pickled
Kokt	Boiled				

Norwegian specialities

Brun saus — Gravy served with most meats, meatcakes, fishcakes and sausages.

Fenalår — Marinaded mutton, smoked, sliced, and served with crispbread, scrambled egg and beer.

Fiskekabaret — Shrimps, fish and vegetables in aspic.

Fiskeboller — Fish balls, served under a white sauce or on open sandwiches.

Fiskesuppe — Fish soup.

Flatbrød — A flat unleavened cracker, half barley, half wheat.

Gammelost — A hard, strong smelling, yellowbrown cheese with veins.

Geitost/Gjetost — Goat's cheese, slightly sweet and fudge-coloured. Similar cheeses have different ratios of goat's milk: cow's milk.

Gravetlaks — Salmon marinaded in salt, sugar, dill and brandy.

Juleskinke — Marinaded boiled ham, served at Christmas.

Kjøttkaker med surkål — Homemade burgers with cabbage and a sweet-and-sour sauce.

Koldtbord — A midday buffet with cold meats, herrings, salads, bread and perhaps soup, eggs or hot meats.

Lapskaus — Pork and vegetable stew, common in the south and east, using salted or fresh meat, or leftovers, in a thick brown gravy.

Lutefisk — Fish (usually cod) preserved in an alkali solution and flavoured; an acquired taste.

Multer — Cloudberries – wild berries, mostly found north of the Arctic Circle and served with cream (*med krem*).

Mysost — Brown whey cheese, made from cow's milk.

Nedlagtsild — Marinaded herring

Pinnekjøtt — Western Norwegian Christmas dish of smoked mutton steamed over shredded birch bark, served with cabbage.

Reinsdyrstek — Reindeer steak, usually served with boiled potatoes and cranberry sauce.

Rekesalat — Shrimp salad in mayonnaise.

Ribbe, julepølse, medisterkake — Eastern Norwegian Christmas dish of pork ribs, sausage and dumplings.

Spekemat — Various types of smoked, dried meats.

Trondhjemsuppe — A kind of milk soup with raisins, rice, cinnamon and sugar.

Bread, cake and deserts

Riskrem — Rice pudding with whipped cream and sugar, served on Christmas Eve.

Trollkrem — Beaten egg whites and sugar mixed with cranberries.

Fløtelapper — Pancakes made from cream, served with sugar and jam.

Knekkebrød — Crispbread.

Havrekjeks — Oatmeal biscuits, eaten with goat's cheese.

Lomper — Potato scones.

Bløtkake — Cream cake with fruit.

Vafle — Waffles.

Kransekake — Cake made from almonds, sugar and eggs, served at celebrations.

Tilslørtbondepiker — Stewed apples and breadcrumbs, served with cream.

Drinks

Appelsin saft	Orange juice	*Mineralvann*	Mineral water	*Brus*	Soft, fizzy drink	*Søt*	Sweet
Fruksaft	Fruit juice					*Tørr*	Dry
Kaffe	Coffee	*Sitronbrus*	Lemonade	*Akevitt*	Aquavit	*Rød*	Red
Te med melk/sitron	Tea with milk/lemon	*Vann*	Water	*Eplesider*	Cider	*Hvit*	White
		Varm sjokolade	Hot chocolate	*Øl*	Beer	*Rosé*	Rosé
Melk	Milk			*Vin*	Wine	*Skål*	Cheers

other cities have branches of *McDonalds* and *Burger King* – hardly health food but at least the standard is consistent and they nearly always have the cheapest coffee in town.

A better choice, and often no more expensive, is simply to get a sandwich, normally a huge open affair called a **smørbrød** (pronounced "smurrbrur"), heaped with a variety of garnishes. You'll see them groaning with meat or shrimps, salad and mayonnaise in the windows of bakeries and cafés, or in the newer, trendier sandwich bars in the larger towns. **Cakes and biscuits** are good, too: watch for doughnuts, Danish pastries (*Wienerbrød*), butter biscuits (*kjeks*) and waffles (*Vafler*).

Good **coffee** is available everywhere, served black or with cream, rich, strong, and, in some places, particularly at breakfast, free after the first cup. **Tea**, too, is ubiquitous, but the local preference is for lemon tea or a variety of flavoured infusions; if you want milk, ask for it. All the familiar **soft drinks** are also available.

Lunch and dinner

For the best deals, you're going to have to eat your main meal of the day at lunchtime (*lunsj*), when **kafeterias** (usually self-service restaurants) lay on the daily special, the **dagens rett**. This is a fish or meat dish served with potatoes and a vegetable or salad, often including a drink, sometimes bread, and occasionally coffee, too; it should go for around 60–70kr. Dipping into the menu is more expensive, but not cripplingly so if you stick to omelettes or cheap cuts of meat. Most department stores and large supermarkets have surprisingly good *kafeterias*; as does every main train station. You'll also find them hidden above shops and offices in larger towns, where they might be called *kaffistovas*; most close at around 6pm. Continental-style **café-bars** have taken off in Oslo, and you'll be able to get similarly priced lunches here – usually more adventurous things like pasta, salads and vegetarian dishes.

Restaurants, serving dinner (*middag*) and real Norwegian food, are out of the range of many budgets, with main courses starting at around 130k, starters and desserts around 50kr. Seafood is good, as are the more obscure meats, but both can be wildly expensive – and the cheapest bottle of wine will set you back at least 150–170kr. Smoked salmon comes highly recommended and, in the north especially, watch out for elk (*elg*) and reindeer steaks (*reinsdyrstek*) – a taste sensation for the curious. Again, the best deals are at lunchtime,

when many restaurants put out a **koldtbord** (the Norwegian *smörgåsbord*), where for a fixed price of around 100–150kr you can get through as much as possible during the three or four hours it's served. Highlights include vast arrays of pickled herring, salmon (*laks*), cold cuts of meat, dried reindeer, a feast of breads and crackers and usually a few hot dishes too – meatballs, soup and scrambled eggs.

In the towns there are a growing number of **ethnic restaurants**, the most affordable of which are the Chinese restaurants and pizza joints, where a huge pizza for two and a couple of small beers will cost around 200kr. Oslo, in fact, has a good array of ethnic restaurants – including Chinese, Japanese, Indian and Moroccan – and altogether the country's widest range of first-class eating places.

Vegetarians

Vegetarians are in for a hard time. Apart from a couple of specialist restaurants in Oslo, there is little you can do except make do with salads, look out for egg dishes in *kafeterias* and supplement your diet from supermarkets. If you are a **vegan** the problem is greater: when the Norwegians are not eating meat and fish, they are attacking a fantastic selection of milks, cheeses and yoghurts. At least you can find out what's in every dish, since everyone speaks English. If you're self-catering, look for **health food shops** (*helse-kost*), found mainly in the larger cities.

■ Drink

When it comes to **drinking**, everything you'll want is available in bars and restaurants, although if it's alcoholic it's taxed up to the eyeballs – a sort of economic rationing, with half a litre of beer costing around 35kr. Outside bars and restaurants, the purchase of alcoholic drinks is controlled and regulated, with state off-licences exercising a monopoly: a symptom of the Norwegians' uneasy relationship with alcohol, which has spawned a strong temperance movement.

What to drink

Although Norwegian alcohol prices are amongst the highest in Europe, it's still worth sampling a couple of local brews. **Beer** is of the lager type and comes in three strengths (class I, II or III), of which the strongest and most expensive is class III. Brands to look for include *Hansa* and *Ringsnes*. **Wine** (all imported) and **spirits** are both way over the top in price, so it's best to take full advantage of your duty-free allowance. One local spirit worth experimenting with at least once is *akevitt*, served ice-cold in little glasses and, at 40 percent proof, real headache material – though more palatable with beer chasers.

Where to drink

Beer is sold in supermarkets and shops all over Norway, though some local communities, particularly in the west, have their own rules and restrictions; it costs about half the price you'd pay in a bar. The strongest beer, along with wines and spirits, can only be purchased from the state-controlled shops, known as **Vinmonopolet**. There's generally one in each small town, though there are more branches in the cities (twenty in Oslo): opening hours are generally Monday–Wednesday 10am–4pm, Thursday 10am–5pm, Friday 9am–4pm, Saturday 9am–1pm, though these times can vary depending on the area; they'll be closed the day before a public holiday. Wine is quite a bargain, from around 55kr a bottle, and there's generally a fair choice of vintages from various South American countries on offer.

Going out for a drink is a different proposition. Wherever you go, a half-litre of beer costs between 35kr and 45kr and a glass of wine at least 30kr. You can get a drink at most **outdoor cafés** and at an increasing number of **bars**, **pubs** and **cocktail bars**. That said, only in the cities is there any kind of "European" bar life and in many places you'll be limited to a drink in the local hotel bar or restaurant. However, in Oslo, Bergen, Stavanger, Trondheim and Tromsø you will be able to keep drinking in bars until at least 1am, until 4am in some places.

As for conventions, despite the obstacles to drinking, the Norwegians take it all very seriously. Like many Scandinavians, they are not social drinkers – asking someone out for a drink during the week labels you an alcoholic – but weekends can be riotous, especially in remoter regions. Incidentally, **buying a round** is virtually unheard of in Norway and people normally pay for their own drinks – something which, considering the prices, is worth remembering.

The country is still littered with people making their own illicit brews in illegal **stills**. If you are invited over "for a drink", be very careful about what you think you are drinking. Swigging something akin to aviation fuel in any sort of quantity can leave you, quite literally, speechless.

Directory

BORDERS There is little formality at the Norway–Sweden border, slightly more between Norway and Finland. However, the northern border with Russia is a different story. There are ornithological reasons why you might want to poke around the area to the east of Kirkenes, but despite the relaxation of tension in the area following the break-up of the Soviet Union, border patrols (from both sides) won't be overjoyed at the prospect. If you have a genuine wish to explore the region, it's best to inform the Norwegian authorities first; or sign on for an organized tour into Russia from Kirkenes.

FISHING Fishing licences are available from hotels, campsites and tourist offices, valid for a day, a week or a season. You'll also need fishing insurance (150kr) if you're fishing for salmon, sea char or freshwater fish, available in any post office. If you take your own fishing tackle, you must have it disinfected before use. More information from the Norwegian Tourist Office.

KIDS There are no real problems with taking children to Norway. They go for half-price on most forms of transport (under-3s or -4s for free), and get the same discount on an extra bed in their parents' hotel room. Family rooms are widely available in youth hostels, while many of the summer activities detailed in this book are geared towards kids anyway. There are also baby compartments (with their own toilet and changing room) for kids under two and their escorts on most trains, and baby-changing rooms at Oslo, Bergen, Trondheim and Bodø train stations. Many restaurants have children's menus; in any case, it's always worth asking if there are cheaper, smaller portions.

LEFT LUGGAGE In most train stations and ferry terminals there are lockers.

PUBLIC HOLIDAYS Everything will be closed on the following days: January 1, Maundy Thursday, Good Friday, Easter Monday, May 1 (May Day), May 17 (Constitution Day), Ascension Day (also in May), Whit Monday, Whit Tuesday, Christmas Day and Boxing Day.

SHOPS Opening hours are Monday–Friday 9am–5pm, Thursday 9am–6/7pm, Saturday 9am–2/3pm. Supermarkets and shopping malls in the main cities have longer opening hours, usually Monday–Friday 8am–8pm, Saturday 8am–4pm. Newspaper kiosks (*Narvesen*) and takeaway food stalls are open in the evenings until 10 or 11pm (weekends, too). And filling stations often sell groceries and stay open until 11pm or so.

SMOKING Since July 1988, smoking has been prohibited in all public buildings, including train stations, and it's forbidden on ferries, all domestic flights and many bus services. Increasingly smoking is confined to a particular area in restaurants and even in bars.

TAX-FREE SHOPPING If you spend more than 300kr at one of 2500 outlets in the tax-free shopping scheme you'll get a cheque for the amount of VAT you paid. On departure at an airport, ferry terminal or frontier crossing, present the goods, the cheque and your passport, and – provided you haven't used the item – you'll get a 10–15 percent refund, depending on the price of the item.

History

Despite its low profile these days, Norway has a fascinating history, its people past explorers and conquerors of northern Europe and its islands, as well as North America. Though at first an independent state, from the fourteenth century onwards Norway came under the sway of first Denmark and then Sweden. Independent again since 1905, it's only recently that Norway has emerged fully onto the international stage, playing a leading part in the increasingly important environmental movement.

■ Early civilizations

The earliest signs of human habitation in Norway date from around 10,000 BC. This, the **Kosma** culture from Finnmark, relied upon seal-fishing for its livelihood. By 8000 BC reindeer-hunters were living in northern Norway, essentially a static people dependent upon flint and bone implements. As the edges of the ice cap retreated from the western coastline (earlier than in Sweden and Finland), these regions began to support a hunting and fishing population. Carvings and **rock drawings** – naturalistic representations of birds, animals and fish – found at Alta in Finnmark have been dated to around 5000 BC.

These Norwegian tribes remained a migratory people for a long time and it took immigrants from the east, most notably the **Boat Axe people** – so-called because of the distinctive shape of their weapons/tools – to bring about real agricultural development.

Around 1700 BC Germanic settlers began to move into Norway from Jutland and southern Sweden. Depictions of **Bronze Age** life (1500–500 BC) are revealed in the rock carvings that became prevalent in southern Norway during this period: pictures of men ploughing with oxen, riding horses, carrying arms and using boats to navigate the coastal water passages. Generally, though, the implements used by ordinary people continued to be of stone. Bronze articles were almost entirely imported, and found mostly in areas settled by the Boat Axe people, who were essentially an aristocratic culture.

Around 500 BC two adverse changes affected Norway. The country suffered with the rest of Scandinavia from a marked deterioration in climate, and the central European advance of the Celts interrupted trade relations with the Mediterranean

world. The poor climate encouraged the development of settled, communal farming in an attempt to improve winter shelter and storage. The early **Iron Age**, though, all but passed Norway by.

The **classical world** knew little of Norway. The Greek geographer, Pytheas of Marseilles, went far enough north to note the short summer nights and probably visited southern Norway, but otherwise what lay beyond was inhospitable and unexplored. Pliny the Elder mentions "Nerigon" as the great island south of the legendary "Ultima Thule", the outermost region of the earth.

Following the collapse of the Roman Empire, Norwegian warriors took full advantage of the **Great Migration period** (fifth to sixth century AD), when whole peoples benefited from the temporary power vacuum. Hoards of appropriated spoils from all over the Mediterranean have been found in Norway. The emphasis on settlement and trade shifted from the west coast to the eastern regions and Trøndelag – areas with easy access to Sweden and its ruling tribe, the *Svear*. Throughout the country, bogs rich in iron ore were exploited and domestic iron-smelting (with its concomitant technical advances) flourished. A farmer class developed, based on a wealth in fields and animals. As all early farms were fundamentally similar, these communities were fairly democratic, although certainly patriarchal. Rural districts evolved with central markets and places of worship.

By the eighth century Norway was a country of **small, independent kingships**, geography preventing any real unity. Only in southeastern Norway, where communication was easier, was there a dynastic grouping whose Swedish connections earned it a place in the **Ynglingatal** – a dynastic list compiled in the late eighth century by the Norwegian *skald* (court poet), Tjodolv. Although the country as a whole remained almost entirely outside the civilized world, advances were being made. There was a specific Merovingian influence on western Norway, which was the only region (apart from northern France) to adopt the short one-edged Saxon sword. And there was an expansion in shipbuilding and seafaring: the iron axe meant that planks could be hewn, and thus it was possible to build vessels fit for the open seas.

■ The Vikings

Overpopulation, internal dissension and the obvious mercantile attractions were all factors in the rapid expansionism that saw Scandinavians suddenly explode upon Europe and the Mediterranean in the ninth century. The patterns of attack and eventual settlement were dictated by the geographical position of the various Scandinavian countries: much as the Swedish Vikings turned eastwards and the Danes south and southwest, so the Norwegians headed west. Norwegian pirates or **Vikings** (from the Norse word *vik*, meaning creek or bay) fell upon the Hebrides, Shetland, Orkney, the Scottish mainland and western Ireland. The Hebrides were quickly overrun, the Pictish population able to offer little resistance, and, with the Isle of Man, formed the basis of a Norse kingdom, providing a base for future attacks upon Scotland and Ireland.

The Norwegians founded Dublin in 836, and from Ireland launched attacks eastwards across the northeast of England. By the end of the century, Norwegian Vikings had also landed and settled in the Faroe Islands and Iceland, while to the south Norwegians were encountering the Muslim power – records indicating attacks by Vikings upon Seville as early as 844.

The raiders soon became settlers, establishing a merchant class at home in Norway. Slave markets in Dublin and elsewhere assisted labour-intensive land clearance schemes; cereal and dairy farming extended into new areas in eastern Norway; and the fishing/hunting economy found new ground in the far north. Othere, a Norwegian chieftain, told Alfred the Great about his home in Finnmark where he kept reindeer and took tribute from the *Sami*.

Pagan culture reached its peak in the Viking period. Western Norway adopted the Germanic *wergild* system of compensation: every free man was entitled to attend the local *Thing* or parliament, while a regional *Lagthing* made laws and settled disputes. Viking craftsmanship is seen at its best in the **ship burials** of Oseberg and Gokstad, which reveal detailed ornamentation and expert carving – both are on display in Oslo's Viking Ship Museum. The Oseberg ship is thought to be the burial ship of Åse, wife of the *Yngling* king Gudrød Storlatnes and mother of Halvan the Black.

It was from this dynastic family that Norway's first king, **Harald Håfrage** (Fair-Haired), king of the tiny Vestfold region, claimed descent. During the ninth century Norway was still a land of petty rulers, much of its southern terrain under Danish influence. Shortly before 900 (the date is unclear) Harald won a decisive victory at Hafrsfjord (near modern Stavanger), which gave him control of the

coastal region as far north as Trøndelag. It sparked an exodus of minor rulers, most of whom left to settle in Iceland. Harald managed to maintain his conquests to the north and, before he died, named his son as his successor.

Erik Bloodaxe held on to his father's throne only briefly before fleeing to Northumbria in 945 (where he had a second short reign in the Viking kingdom of York). His youngest brother, who later became **Håkon the Good** (raised by the English King Athelstan in Wessex), returned to take the throne and, initially, was well received. Confirmed in England, his attempts to introduce Christianity to Norway failed. But he did carry out a number of reforms, establishing a common legal code for the whole of Vestlandet and Trøndelag, as well as introducing the system of *Leidang*, the division of the coastal districts into areas responsible for maintaining and manning a warship. His rule was punctuated by struggles against Erik's heirs, who were backed by Harald Bluetooth (the Danish king). Killed in battle in 960, Håkon was succeeded by Harald Eriksson (one of Bloodaxe's sons), whom Bluetooth killed ten years later in an attempt to halt his growing independence from Denmark. A Danish appointee to the throne, Håkon Sigurdsson, was to be the last genuine heathen to rule Norway. He based his rule at Trøndelag, still staunchly pagan.

In 995 **Olav Tryggvesson**, a Viking chieftain confirmed as a Christian in England, sailed to Norway to challenge Håkon, who was fortuitously murdered by one of his own servants. Claiming descent from Harald Håfrage, Olav founded Nidaros (now Trondheim) as his base in an attempt to force Christianity onto the pagan north. However, his real problem remained the enmity of the Danish-controlled southeastern regions of Norway, and of Bluetooth's son Sweyn, who regarded Norway as his rightful inheritance. In alliance with the Swedish king, Sweyn defeated Olav at the sea battle of Svolder, and Norway was divided up amongst the victors.

Meanwhile, outside Norway, expansionism was underway. Norwegian settlers in **Iceland** established a parliament, the *Althing* in 930, based on Norwegian law. There were further Norwegian Viking discoveries, too. Erik the Red, exiled from Norway and then banished from Iceland for three years for murder, set out in 985 with 25 ships, fourteen of which arrived in **Greenland**, where two communities developed. The **North American** shore had already been sighted by ships blown off course on the way from Norway to Greenland. In 1000 Erik's son, Leif, sailed to Labrador and then south to a region he called Vinland where grapes and corn were found growing wild. Both places, although never settled, marked the now accepted Norwegian "discovery" of North America.

■ The arrival of Christianity

Olav Haraldsson sailed for Norway in 1015, taking advantage of the problems caused by the death of the Danish King Sweyn Forkbeard. Sweyn's son Knud – king (Canute) of England – wasn't able to muster much support from his subordinate Norwegian earls and Olav soon gained recognition as king of Norway. For the first time the king's supporters were powerful inland farmers, a clear indication of how Norwegian society was moving away from its sea-based Viking past. Olav was severe in his attempts to convert Norway into a Christian land and his methods caused bitter opposition, although during his reign the western coast of Norway did adopt a system of church law. However, by 1028 disaffection was at its height and a combined Danish and English fleet led by Knud forced Olav to flee, first to Sweden and then to Russia. Knud's son Sweyn (and his mother, the English Queen Aelfgifu) took the Norwegian crown, only to be faced soon after – in 1030 – by the sensational return of Olav at the head of a scratch army. Olav, however, was defeated by an alliance of local farmers and landowners at **Stiklestad**, the first major Norwegian land battle.

Olav was killed by those who had most to fear from him, those who had already lost influence to a growing royal power. But they were to fare even worse under Sweyn, and reaction against him and Aelfgifu soon grew. In 1035, Olav's young son, Magnus, returned from exile and was made king. People began to look back to Olav as a champion: there was talk of miracles and with the rising Norwegian church looking for a saint to improve its appeal, Olav was canonized. The remains of **St Olav** were reinterred ceremoniously at Nidaros, today's Trondheim, where his memory and alleged miracles hastened the conversion of much of Norway.

On Magnus's death, **Harald Hardråda** (Olav's half-brother) became king and consolidated his grip on the eastern uplands, establishing the boundaries of Norway. Then, turning his attention

southwards, he sailed on England. In 1066, the Norwegian army marched on York but Harald was defeated and killed at Stamford Bridge by the English king Harold Godwinesson. Harald's son, **Olav Kyrre** – the Peaceful – agreed never to attack England again, and went on to reign as king of Norway for the next 25 years. Peace engendered economic prosperity and treaties with Denmark ensured Norwegian independence. Three native bishoprics were established and cathedrals built at Nidaros, Bergen and Oslo. It's from this period, too, that Norway's surviving **stave churches** date: wooden structures resembling an upturned keel, they were lavishly decorated with dragon heads and scenes from Norse mythology, proof that the traditions of the pagan world were slow to disappear.

■ The Age of Greatness

Although Norway was confirmed as an independent power, the twelfth century saw a long period of internal disorder as the descendants of Olav Kyrre struggled to maintain their influence. Civil war ceased only when **Håkon IV** took the throne in 1240. He strengthened the Norwegian hold on the Faroe and Shetland Islands (which now paid tax and accepted a royal governor), and, in 1262, both Iceland and Greenland accepted Norwegian sovereignty. When his claim to the Hebrides was disputed by Alexander III of Scotland, Håkon assembled an intimidatory fleet but died in 1263 in the Orkneys. Three years later the Hebrides and the Isle of Man (always the weakest links in the Norse Empire) were sold to the Scottish crown by Håkon's successor, **Magnus the Lawmender**. Under Magnus, Norway prospered, achieving what was to be its greatest medieval success. The nobility began to assume greater power and were exempted from taxes in the 1270s, but they never became independent feudal lords – scattered farms were difficult to control and castles were rare.

It was in this period that Norwegian **Gothic art** reached its full maturity. Construction of the nave at Nidaros Cathedral began, as did work on Håkon's Hall in Bergen. **Håkon V** was to recover some of the ground lost to the nobility by reducing his Council in numbers and status. New castles were built (especially in Oslo, which became his capital), endowed with royal castellans and garrisons, and all officials were brought under Håkon's immediate control.

Norway, however, was in danger of losing its independence from two quarters. The **Hanseatic League** and its merchants had steadily increased their influence, holding a monopoly on imports and controlling inland trade, too. With strongholds in Bergen and Oslo, the League came to dominate the economy. Secondly, when Håkon died in 1319 he left no male heir and was succeeded by his grandson, the three-year-old son of a Swedish duke. The boy, **Magnus Eriksson**, was elected Swedish king two months later, marking the virtual end of Norway as an independent country until 1905.

Magnus assumed full power over both countries in 1332, but his reign was a difficult one and when the nobility rebelled he agreed that the monarchy should again be split: his three-year-old son, Håkon, would become Norwegian king when he came of age, while the Swedes agreed to elect his eldest son Erik to the Swedish throne. It was then, in 1349, that the **Black Death** struck, spreading quickly along the coast and up the valleys, and killing almost two-thirds of the population.

Håkon VI acceded to the Norwegian throne in 1355 and, despite opposition in Sweden, the idea of union persisted. Håkon married Margaret, daughter of Valdemar (king of Denmark), and when Valdemar died her son Olav took the Danish throne. And on Håkon's death in 1380, Olav inherited the Norwegian throne, too, bringing together the crowns of Denmark and Norway in a union that was to last four hundred years.

■ **The Kalmar Union**

Despite Olav's early death in 1387, Margaret persevered with the union. Proclaimed First Lady by both the Danish and Norwegian nobility, she made a treaty with the Swedish nobles in 1388 that recognized her as regent of Sweden and agreed to accept any king she should nominate. Her chosen heir, **Erik of Pomerania**, was accepted by the Norwegian Council in 1389 as their hereditary sovereign, and in 1397 he was crowned at a diet in Sweden, known as the Kalmar Union.

After Margaret's death in 1412 Norway suffered. All power was concentrated in Denmark, foreigners were preferred in both state and church, and the country became impoverished by paying for Erik's wars against the Counts of Holstein. When Denmark and Sweden formally withdrew their allegiance from Erik in 1439, Norway ceased to take any meaningful part in Scandinavian affairs. Successive monarchs continued to appoint foreigners to important positions, appropriating Norwegian funds for Danish purposes and even mortgaging Orkney and Shetland (1469) to the Scots. Literature languished as the Old Norse language was displaced by the dominant Danish tongue, and only the Norwegian church retained any power.

Briefly, it looked as if Norway might recover some influence. In 1501–2, a Swedish-Norwegian nobleman, **Knut Alvsson**, crossed the border and soon overcame southern Norway as far as Bergen. But he was resisted by the Danish heir to the throne (later Christian II) and treacherously murdered as he sued for peace. Ibsen, for one, later saw this as a terrible blow for Norway, and the country remained neglected and outside the developments that led to the secession of Sweden and the **break-up of the union** in 1523.

■ **Union with Denmark**

Norway had undergone a vigorous "Danicization" during the years of the Kalmar Union, but with the fall of Christian II in 1523, there seemed to be some hope for the country. The nobility rallied under the archbishop of Nidaros, Olav Engelbrektsson, in order to gain terms from the new king, Frederick I. They failed, as they did again on Frederick's death, the ensuing Danish civil war producing victory for Christian III and **the Reformation**. In 1536 Christian, a Protestant, declared that Norway should cease to be a separate country and that the Lutheran faith be established. Norway's national identity was thus further eroded: there was no written Norwegian literature and Danish gradually became the official language; the spoken tongue changed from Old Norse to the bastardized Middle Norwegian; the nobility declined; there was no effective leadership; and even the Church lost power and influence – the only notable church construction was the rebuilding of Nidaros Cathedral.

Lutheranism was slow to take root among the conservative Norwegian peasantry, but it served as a powerful instrument in establishing Danish influence in Norway. The Bible, catechism and hymnal were all in Danish, the bishops were all Danes and, after 1537, so were all the most important provincial Norwegian governors. Also, Frederick II embroiled Norway in the disastrous and inconclusive Northern Seven Years' War (1563–70) with Sweden, after which the tax burden on the country increased again.

During the reign of Frederick's son, **Christian IV**, Norway began to regain some of its former wealth and status. The most active of the Danish kings in Norway, he visited the country often, founding new towns and promulgating the first real national Norwegian Law. The first half of the seventeenth century saw economic advance, too, due to a rapid population growth, marked increases in trade, copper and silver mining, the development of a Norwegian-controlled herring industry and, most importantly, a decline in the power of the Hanseatic League. But the tendency for Danish kings to drag Norway into their wars continued, Norway losing her eastern provinces (Jämtland and Härjedalen) to Sweden in 1645.

Frederick III, already acknowledged as absolute ruler in Denmark, called together the Norwegian Estates in 1661 to acclaim him similarly. The so-called "Twin Kingdoms" (of Denmark–Norway) came into being: Norway was incorporated into the administrative structure of Denmark and granted a *Stattholder* (governor-general) who ruled in Norway through a strict bureaucratic system. There were positive advantages for Norway: the country acquired better defences, simpler taxes, a separate High Court and further doses of Norwegian law.

Despite the full establishment of the Lutheran church in Norway by the end of the seventeenth century, the Reformation brought none of the intellectual stimulus it produced elsewhere. The **Renaissance** followed on late with little to show: the first printing press wasn't established until 1643, and despite the efforts of a small group of Norwegian humanists who completed a set of nostalgic writings about the past, the reading public remained insignificant. The only real expression of the Renaissance spirit was in the towns and buildings put up by Danish king Christian IV (notably Kongsberg, Kristiansand and Christiania – later Oslo): grid-built towns of great elegance.

Under Frederick II's successors, the disputes with Sweden that had beset the century came to a head. The Swedish king, Karl XII, invaded Norway in 1716 only to be repulsed initially by the Norwegian naval hero **Peter Torkenskiold**, who destroyed his fleet. Karl was killed in Norway in 1718 and the **Peace of Frederiksborg** (1720) left Norway in peace for the rest of the eighteenth century.

The **absolute monarchy** of the eighteenth century concerned itself with every aspect of Norwegian life. Missionaries were sent into Finnmark to introduce Christianity to the Sami, and a similar mission was sent to long-neglected Greenland in 1721. Peace favoured the growth of trade and the period saw comparatively little exploitation of the peasantry as tenants – there were still few large estates and no aristocracy on the land. **Culturally** the period saw the emergence of Norway's first modern poet, Peter Dass, whose verses and descriptions of Nordland (in his *Nordland's Trumpet*) were immensely popular; also of Ludwig Holberg, born in Bergen and best known for the 26 comedies he wrote for the Copenhagen Theatre between 1722 and 1727. The Trondheim Scientific Academy was founded in 1760 and a Norwegian Society established in Copenhagen in 1772. With trade monopolies abolished and the number of smallholders increasing, the emergence of a middle class helped shift the mood in Norway towards rejecting the union with Denmark. They wanted the same privileges as the Danes – their own bank, university and treasury.

Despite this, Norway was one of the few countries little affected by the French Revolution. Instead of political action, there was a **religious revival**, with Hans Nielson Hauge emerging as an evangelical leader. His movement, characterized by a marked hostility to officialdom, caused concern and he was imprisoned; yet he provided the nucleus of a fundamentalist layman's movement, still a puritanical force to be reckoned with in parts of west and southwest Norway.

The period leading up to the **Napoleonic Wars** was a boom time for Norway: overseas trade, especially with England, flourished, the demand for Norwegian timber, iron and cargo space heralding a period of unparalleled prosperity. Denmark–Norway had remained neutral throughout the Seven Years' War (1756–63) between England and France, and renewed that neutrality in 1792. However, when Napoleon forced Denmark into his Continental System in 1807, the British fleet bombarded Copenhagen and forced the surrender of the entire Dano-Norwegian fleet. Denmark, in retaliation, declared war on England and Sweden. The move was disastrous for the Norwegian economy, which had suffered bad harvests in 1807 and 1808, and the English blockade of its seaports ruined trade and caused starvation in the country.

Union on an equal footing with Sweden became an increasingly attractive idea to many Norwegians: it offered the best chance to restore lost trade with England. With Crown Prince Bernadotte (formerly one of Napoleon's generals) made heir to the Swedish throne, the idea became a possibility, and following his part in the defeat of Napoleon at Leipzig in 1813, Bernadotte (later Karl Johan XIV) claimed Norway on behalf of Sweden. At the **Peace of Kiel** in 1814 the defeated Danes were forced to cede all rights in Norway to Sweden (although they did keep the dependencies – Iceland, Greenland and the Faroes). Four hundred years of union had ended.

■ Union with Sweden: 1814–1905

Norwegian feeling was that a mere transfer of the union to Sweden did nothing for the country's independence. A Constituent Assembly was summoned to Eidsvoll in April 1814 and produced a **constitution**. Issued on May 17, 1814 (still a national holiday), this declared Norway to be a "free, independent and indivisible realm". However, pressure grew on Norway from the signatories of the Kiel treaty to accept the union and it took a short war with Sweden before the Moss Convention of August 1814 recognized the Norwegian constitution and *Storting* (parliament). Although Bernadotte, as heir and crown prince in Sweden, didn't accede to the throne until 1818, he became regent and virtual ruler of both Sweden and Norway immediately.

The ensuing period was marred by struggles between the *Storting* and the crown over the nature of the union. Although the constitution emphasized Norway's independence, the country remained an inferior partner: the king had a suspensive veto over the *Storting*'s actions; the post of *Stattholder* in Norway could be held by a Swede; while foreign and diplomatic matters concerning Norway remained entirely in Swedish hands. Despite this, **Karl XIV** (as Bernadotte became in 1818) proved a popular king in Norway, and during his reign the country enjoyed a fair amount of independence. From 1836 all the highest offices in Norway were filled exclusively by Norwegians, new penal codes were introduced and democratic local councils established – something that was in part due to the rise of the peasant farmers as a political force.

The layout and buildings of modern Oslo – the Royal Palace, Karl Johans gate, the university – date from the same post-union period, and the gradual increase in prosperity had important **cultural implications**. J.C. Dahl, Norway's great

nature painter, was instrumental in the moves to establish the National Gallery in Oslo in 1836, and Henrik Wergeland, poet, prose writer and propagandist of major talent, remained passionate in his championing of the Norwegian national cause. The influential **temperance movement**, too, gained a foothold in Norway. Acquiring government patronage in 1844, it was instrumental in forcing laws to prohibit the use of small stills – once found on every farm. By the mid-nineteenth century, consumption of spirits had dropped drastically and coffee rivalled beer as the national drink.

Under Oscar I and Karl XV, **pan-Scandinavianism** flourished and then failed, as elsewhere in Scandinavia. This belief in a natural solidarity among Denmark, Norway and Sweden was espoused most loudly by artists and intellectuals, notably Ibsen and Bjørnson. Oscar, a liberal monarch, found himself in some sympathy with the prevailing views, and in 1848 promised aid to Denmark when their troops were forced to withdraw from Schleswig-Holstein in the face of a Prussian advance. Though there was little enthusiasm anywhere for an actual engagement, the gesture was seen as a victory for pan-Scandinavianism. Not so in 1864, though, when Austria and Prussia declared war on Denmark. Karl wanted to help, but Swedish public opinion and the Norwegian *Storting* were unenthusiastic about the prospect, and pan-Scandinavianism died a toothless death. Little more than an academic movement, even in its heyday, the loudest cries of treachery came from **Henrik Ibsen**, whose poetic drama, *Brand*, a spirited indictment of Norwegian authority, had made his name in Norway.

Domestic politics changed, too, with the rise to power in the 1850s of **Johan Sverdrup**. Realizing that independence would only come about if the *Storting* assumed real executive power, his new Reform Society won their first success when a bill was passed to allow annual sessions of parliament. That the *Storting* was increasingly determined to rule emerged in the later struggle over whether the king's ministers should be answerable to parliament. Sverdrup's efforts ensured that a bill was passed to that effect in 1872, and again in 1874 and 1877. Each time, the new king, **Oscar II**, used his suspensive veto until, in 1880, the bill was passed for the third time in an unchanged form. It no longer required royal assent but Oscar claimed an absolute veto in constitutional matters. Sverdrup rallied Norwegian support and the 1882 *Storting* elections returned a formidable *Venstre*

(Left) Party which, in 1884, impeached the supporters of the veto as well as the Prime Minister. Sverdrup headed a new ministry which was to take its authority from the *Storting*, not the crown – in effect a straight transition to full parliamentary government.

Economic growth continued and by 1880 Norway had the world's third largest merchant navy (after the USA and Britain), while whaling expanded with the Norwegian invention of the harpoon. Considerable overpopulation in rural areas at this time was solved to some degree by widespread **emigration** to North America: in 1910 a US census recorded 800,000 of its inhabitants as either first- or second-generation Norwegian.

The *Venstre* Party scored another huge parliamentary majority in 1885. However, the party then split over rows concerning the foreign ministry of the two countries (solely in Swedish hands since 1814) and 1891 saw victory for a Radical Left Party under Johannes Steen, which demanded a separate foreign ministry for Norway. Initial demands were for a separate Norwegian consular service, reasonable enough given the extent of the country's merchant shipping interests. But the king refused to agree and the matter was referred to a Union Committee, which sat inconclusively until Steen assumed power again in 1898 with a new majority government. That year, the Flag Law to remove the Union sign from the Norwegian mercantile marine flag became operational, and further attempts at compromise failed. When the *Storting* finally voted to establish a separate Norwegian consular service in 1905, Oscar again refused to sanction the move. The government resigned, claiming that as the king no longer exercized his constitutional functions the union could be dissolved. A plebiscite in August 1905 returned an overwhelming vote for **dissolution of the union**, which was duly confirmed by the Treaty of Karlstad. A second plebiscite determined that independent Norway should be a monarchy rather than a republic and, in November 1905, Prince Karl of Denmark (Edward VII's son-in-law) was elected to the throne as **Håkon VII**.

Dissolution came at a time of further economic advance, engendered by the introduction of hydroelectric power. Social reforms also saw funds available for unemployment relief, accident insurance schemes and a Factory Act (1909). An extension to the franchise gave the vote to all men over 25 and, in 1913, to women too. The education system was reorganized, and higher sums spent on new arms and defence matters. This prewar period also saw the emergence of a strong Trades Union movement and of a Labour Party committed to revolutionary change.

Culturally, the last years of the nineteenth century were fruitful for Norway. Alexander Kielland, a popular author outside Norway too, wrote most of his works between 1880 and 1891; while Knut Hamsen published his most characteristic novel, *Hunger*, in 1890. Slightly earlier, **Edvard Grieg** (1843–1907), inspired by old Norwegian folk melodies, had composed some of his most famous suites for Ibsen's *Peer Gynt*. Grieg was at the centre of Oslo musical life between 1866 and 1874, his debut concert the first to consist entirely of works by Norwegian composers. The artist **Edvard Munch** was also active during this period, completing many of his major works in the 1880s and 1890s.

■ Between the wars

Since 1814 Norway had had little to do with European affairs and at the outbreak of **World War I** declared itself strictly neutral. Sympathy, though, lay largely with the Western Allies, and the Norwegian economy boomed since its ships and timber were in great demand. By 1916, however, Norway began to feel the pinch, as German submarine action hit both enemy and neutral shipping, and by 1918 Norway had lost half its chartered tonnage and 2000 crew. When the USA entered the war, strict trade agreements were enforced to prevent supplies getting to Germany, and rationing had to be introduced. The price of neutrality was a rise in state expenditure, a soaring cost of living and, at the end of the war, no seat at the conference table. In spite of its losses Norway got no share of the confiscated German shipping, although it was compensated in part by gaining sovereignty of **Spitzbergen** and its coal deposits – the first extension of Norwegian frontiers for five hundred years. In 1920 Norway also entered the new League of Nations.

The decline in world trade, though, led to a decreased demand for Norway's shipping. Bank failure and currency fluctuation were rife, and, as unemployment and industrial strife increased, a developing Norwegian **Labour Party** took advantage. With the franchise extended to all those over 23 and the introduction of larger constituencies, it had a chance, for the first time, to win seats outside the large towns. At the 1927 election the Labour Party, together with the Social Democrats from whom they'd split, were the biggest grouping in the *Storting*. Because they had no overall majority and because many feared their revolutionary rhetoric, they were manoeuvred out of office after only fourteen days. Trade disputes and lockouts continued and troops had to be used to protect scabs.

Prohibition was adopted in 1919 following its wartime introduction but it did little to quell – and even exacerbated – drunkenness. It was abandoned in 1932 and replaced by the government sales monopoly of wines and spirits still in force today. The 1933 election gave the Labour Party more seats than ever. Having shed its revolutionary image, a campaigning reformist Labour Party benefited from the increasing conviction that state control and a centrally planned economy was the only answer to Norway's economic problems. In 1935 the Labour Party, in alliance with the Agrarian Party, took power – an unlikely combination since the Agrarians had boasted **Vidkun Quisling** as their defence spokesperson, a staunch anti-communist and virulent opponent of the Labour Party. In 1933 he'd left to found *Nasjonal Samling* (National Unification), a fascist movement which proposed, among other things, that both Hitler and Mussolini should be nominated for the Nobel Peace Prize. Quisling had good contacts with Nazi Germany but little support in Norway – local elections in 1937 reduced his local representation to a mere seven and party membership fell to 1500.

The Labour government under **Johan Nygaardsvold** presided over an improving economy. By 1938 industrial production was 75 percent higher than it had been in 1914; unemployment had dropped as expenditure on roads, railways and public works increased. Social welfare reforms were implemented and trade union membership increased. When war broke out in 1939, Norway was lacking only one thing – adequate defence. A vigorous member of the League of Nations, the country had pursued disarmament and peace policies since the end of World War I and was determined to remain neutral.

■ World War II

As **World War II** broke – and despite the warning signs from Germany – Norway again emphasized her neutrality. In early 1940, with Hitler preparing an invasion force, the Norwegians were more interested in the Allied mine-laying off the

Norwegian coast – an attempt to prevent Swedish iron ore being shipped from Narvik to Germany. On the same day that they protested to Britain, the **German invasion** of Norway took place: the south and central regions of the country were quickly overrun, the Germans declaring that they were there to protect Norway from the British. King Håkon and the *Storting* left for Elverum, where the government was granted full powers to take whatever decisions were necessary in the interests of Norway – a mandate which later formed the basis of the Norwegian government-in-exile in Britain. The Germans demanded that Quisling be accepted as prime minister but this was rejected outright, and for two months a resistance campaign was fought by the Norwegians. They were no match for the organized German troops and in June both king and government fled to Britain from Tromsø in northern Norway. The country was rapidly brought under Nazi control, Hitler sending **Josef Terboven** to take full charge of Norwegian affairs.

The fascist *NS* was declared the only legal political party in Norway and the media, civil servants and teachers were brought under party control. As **civil resistance** grew, a state of emergency was declared: two trade union leaders were shot, arrests increased and a concentration camp was set up outside Oslo. In February 1942 Quisling was installed as "Minister President" of Norway, but it was soon clear that his government didn't have the support of the Norwegian people. The church refused to cooperate, schoolteachers protested and trade union members and officials resigned *en masse*. In response, deportations increased, death sentences were announced and a compulsory labour scheme was introduced.

Military resistance escalated. A military organization (*MILORG*) was established as a branch of the armed forces under the control of the High Command in London. By May 1941 it had enlisted 20,000 men (32,000 by 1944) in clandestine groups all over the country. Arms and instructors came from Britain, radio stations were set up and a continuous flow of intelligence about Nazi movements sent back. Sabotage operations were legion, the most notable the destruction of the heavy-water plant at **Rjukan**, foiling a German attempt to produce an atomic bomb. Reprisals against the resistance were severe, but active collaboration with the enemy attracted only a comparative handful of Norwegians.

The **government-in-exile** in London continued to represent free Norway to the world, mobilizing support on behalf of the Allies. Most of the Norwegian merchant fleet was abroad when the Nazis invaded and by 1943 the Norwegian navy had seventy ships fighting on the Allied side. In Sweden, Norwegian exiles assembled in "health camps" at the end of 1943 to train as police troops in readiness for liberation.

When the Allies landed in Normandy in June 1944, overt action against the Nazis in Norway by the resistance was discouraged, since the Allies couldn't safeguard against reprisals. By late October, the Russians had crossed the border in the north and forced the Germans to retreat — which they did, burning everything in their path and forcing the local population into hiding. To prevent the Germans reinforcing, the resistance planned a campaign of mass railway sabotage, stopping three-quarters of the troop movements overnight. As their control of Norway crumbled, the Germans finally **surrendered** on May 7, 1945, King Håkon returning to Norway on June 7 — five years to the day since he'd left for exile.

Terboven committed suicide and the *NS* collaborators were rounded up. A caretaker government took office, staffed by resistance leaders, and was replaced in October 1945 by a majority **Labour government**. The Communists won eleven seats, reflecting the efforts of Communist saboteurs in the war and the prestige that the Soviet Union enjoyed in Norway after liberation. Quisling was shot, along with 24 other high-ranking traitors, and thousands of collaborators were punished.

■ Postwar reconstruction

At the end of the war Norway was on its knees: the north had been laid waste, half the mercantile fleet lost, and production was at a standstill. Recovery, though, fostered by a sense of national unity, was quick and it took only three years for GNP to return to its prewar level. Norway's part in the war had increased the country's prestige in the world, a situation acknowledged as Norway became one of the founding members of the **United Nations** in 1945: its first Secretary-General, Tryggve Lie, was the Norwegian Foreign Minister. With the failure of discussions to promote a Scandinavian defence union, the *Storting* also voted to enter **NATO** in 1949.

Domestically, there was general agreement about the form that social reconstruction should take. The laws that introduced the Welfare State in 1948 were passed virtually unanimously by the *Storting*. The 1949 election saw the government returned with a larger majority and Labour governments continued to be returned throughout the following decade, the premiership for most of this time held by **Einar Gerhardsen**. As national prosperity increased, society became ever more egalitarian, levelling up rather than down. Subsidies were paid to the agricultural and fishing industries, wages increased and a comprehensive social security system helped to eradicate poverty. The state ran the important mining industry, was the largest shareholder in the hydroelectric company and built an enormous steel works at Mo-i-Rana to help develop the economy of the devastated northern counties. Rationing ended in 1952 and, as the demand for higher-level education grew, new universities were approved at Bergen, Trondheim and Tromsø.

■ Beyond consensus: modern Norway

The political consensus in favour of Labour began to turn in the early 1960s. Following changes in the constitution concerning the rural constituencies, the centre had realigned itself in the 1950s, the outmoded Agrarian Party becoming the **Centre Party**. Defence squabbles within the Labour Party led to the formation of the **Socialist People's Party** (*SF*), which wanted Norway out of NATO and sought a renunciation of nuclear weapons. The Labour Party's 1961 declaration that no nuclear weapons would be stationed in Norway except under an immediate threat of war did not placate the *SF* who, unexpectedly, took two seats at the election that year. Holding the balance of power, the *SF* voted with the Labour Party until 1963, when it helped bring down the government over the mismanagement of state industries. A replacement coalition collapsed after only one month, but the writing was on the wall. Rising prices, dissatisfaction with high taxation and a continuing housing shortage meant that the 1965 election put a **non-socialist coalition** in power for the first time in twenty years.

Under the leadership of **Per Borten** of the Centre Party, the coalition's programme was unambitious. However, living standards continued to rise and although the 1969 election saw a marked increase in Labour Party support, the coalition hung on to power. Norway had applied twice previously for membership of the

A BRIEF GUIDE TO NORWEGIAN

There are two official Norwegian languages: *Riksmål* or *Bokmål* (book language), a modification of the old Dano-Norwegian tongue left over from the days of Danish dominance; and *Landsmål* or *Nynorsk*, which was developed with the nineteenth-century upsurge of Norwegian nationalism and is based on the Old Norse dialects that came before. You'll see both on your travels but of the two, *Bokmål* is the most common – and is the language we use here.

As elsewhere in Scandinavia, you don't really need to know any Norwegian to get by in Norway. Almost everyone, especially younger people, speaks some English, and in any case many words are not too far removed from their English equivalents; there's also plenty of English (or American) on billboards, the TV and at the cinema. Mastering a hello or a thank you will, however, be greatly appreciated, while if you speak either Danish or Swedish you should have few problems being understood. If you don't, and can't master the Norwegian, a basic knowledge of German is a help too. Of the **phrasebooks**, much the most useful is *Norwegian for Travellers* (Berlitz), though if you intend to visit Denmark and/or Sweden on the same trip, *Traveller's Scandinavia* (Pan) covers all three languages.

PRONUNCIATION

Pronunciation can be tricky. A **vowel** is usually long when it's the final syllable or followed by only one consonant; followed by two it's generally short. Unfamiliar ones are:

ae before an r, as in b**a**d; otherwise as in s**a**y

ø as in f**ur** but without pronouncing the r

å usually as in s**a**w

øy between the ø sound and b**oy**

ei as in s**a**y

Consonants are pronounced as in English except:

c, q, w, z found only in foreign words and pronounced as in the original

g before i, y or ei, as in **y**et; otherwise hard

hv as in **v**iew

j, gj, hj, lj as in **y**et

rs usually as in **sh**ut

k before i, y or j, like the Scottish lo**ch**; otherwise hard

sj, sk before i, y, ø or øy, as in **sh**ut

BASICS

Do you speak English?	*Snakker De engelsk?*	Good morning	*God morgen*
Yes	*Ja*	Good afternoon	*God dag*
No	*Nei*	Good night	*God natt*
Do you understand?	*Forstår De?*	Goodbye	*Adjø*
I don't understand	*Jeg forstår ikke*	Today	*I dag*
I understand	*Jeg forstår*	Tomorrow	*I morgen*
Please	*Vær så god*	Day after tomorrow	*I overmorgen*
Thank you (very much)	*Takk (tusen takk)*	In the morning	*Om morgenen*
You're welcome	*Vær så god*	In the afternoon	*Om ettermiddagen*
Excuse me	*Unnskyld*	In the evening	*Om kvelden*

SOME SIGNS

Entrance	*Inngang*	Police	*Politi*
Exit	*Utgang*	Hospital	*Sykehus*
Gentlemen	*Herrer*	Cycle path	*Sykkelsti*
Ladies	*Damer*	No Smoking	*Røyking forbudt*
Open	*Åpen*	No Camping	*Camping Forbudt*
Closed	*Stengt*	No Trespassing	*Uvedkommende Forbudt*
Arrival	*Ankomst*	No Entry	*Ingen adgang*
Departure	*Avgang*	Pull/push	*Trekk/trykk*

QUESTIONS AND DIRECTIONS

Where? (where is/are?)	*Hvor? (hvor er?)*	Near/far	*i nærheten/langt borte*
When?	*Når?*	Good/bad	*God/dårlig*
What?	*Hva?*	Vacant/occupied	*Ledig/opptatt*
How much/many?	*Hvor mye/hvor mange*	A little/a lot	*Litt/mye*
Why?	*Hvorfor?*	More/less	*Mer/mindre*
Which?	*Hvilket?*	Can we camp here?	*Kan vi campe her?*
What's that called in	*Hva kaller man det på*	Is there a youth hostel	*Er det et vandrerhjini i*
Norwegian?	*norsk?*	near here?	*nærheten ?*
Can you direct me to . . . ?	*Kan De vise meg veien*	How do I get to . . . ?	*Hvordan kommer jeg til . . . ?*
	til . . . ?	How far is it to . . . ?	*Hvor langt er det til . . . ?*
It is/there is (is it/is there?)	*Det er (er det?)*	Ticket	*Billett*
What time is it?	*Hvor mange er klokken?*	Single/return	*en vei/tur-retur*
Big/small	*Stor/liten*	Can you give me a lift	*Kan jeg få sitte på til . . . ?*
Cheap/expensive	*Billig/dyrt*	to . . . ?	
Early/late	*Tidlig/sent*	Left/right	*Venstre/høyre*
Hot/cold	*Varm/kald*	Go straight ahead	*Kjør rett frem*

NUMBERS

0	*null*	9	*ni*	18	*atten*	70	*sytti*
1	*en*	10	*ti*	19	*nitten*	80	*åtti*
2	*to*	11	*elleve*	20	*tjue*	90	*nitti*
3	*tre*	12	*tolv*	21	*tjueen*	100	*hundre*
4	*fire*	13	*tretten*	22	*tjueto*	101	*hundreogen*
5	*fem*	14	*fjorten*	30	*tretti*	200	*to hundre*
6	*seks*	15	*femten*	40	*førti*	1000	*tusen*
7	*sju*	16	*seksten*	50	*femti*		
8	*åtte*	17	*sytten*	60	*seksti*		

DAYS AND MONTHS

Sunday	*søndag*	January	*januar*	July	*juli*
Monday	*mandag*	February	*februar*	August	*august*
Tuesday	*tirsdag*	March	*mars*	September	*september*
Wednesday	*onsdag*	April	*april*	October	*oktober*
Thursday	*torsdag*	May	*mai*	November	*november*
Friday	*fredag*	June	*juni*	December	*desember*
Saturday	*lørdag*				

(Days and months are never capitalised)

GLOSSARY OF NORWEGIAN TERMS AND WORDS

Apotek	Chemist	*Havn*	Harbour	*NRK*	Norwegian State
Bakke	Hill	*Hytte*	Cottage, cabin		TV and Radio
Bokhandel	Bookshop	*Innsjø*	Lake	*Rådhus*	Town hall
Bro/bru	Bridge	*Jernbanestasjon*	Railway station	*Sentrum*	City centre
Dal	Valley	*Kirke/kjerke*	Church	*Sjø*	Sea
Domkirke	Cathedral	*KFUM/KFUK*	Norwegian	*Skog*	Forest
Drosje	Taxi		YMCA/YWCA	*Slott*	Castle, palace
E.Kr	AD	*Klokken/kl.*	o'clock	*Storting*	Parliament
Elv/Bekk	River/Stream	*KNA*	Norwegian equiva-	*Tilbud*	Special offer
Ferje/ferge	Ferry		lent of the RAC	*Torget*	Main town square,
Fjell/berg	Mountain	*MOMS*	Value Added Tax		often home to an
F.Kr	BC	*Museet*	Museum		outdoor market
Foss	Waterfall	*NAF*	Norwegian	*Vann/vatn*	Water or lake
Gate (gt.)	Street		Automobile	*Vei/veg/vn.*	Road
Hav	Ocean		Association	*Å*	River

European Economic Community (EEC) – in 1962 and 1967 – and with de Gaulle's fall in France, 1970 saw a fresh application. There was great concern, though, about the effect of membership on Norwegian agriculture and fisheries, and in 1971 Per Borten was forced to resign following his indiscreet handling of the negotiations. The Labour Party, the majority of its representatives in favour of EEC membership, formed a minority administration. And when the 1972 referendum narrowly voted "No" to joining the EEC, the government resigned.

With the 1973 election producing another minority Labour government, the uncertain pattern of the previous ten years continued. Even the postwar consensus on **Norwegian security policy** broke down on various issues – the question of a northern European nuclear-free zone, the stocking of Allied material in Norway – although there remained strong agreement for continued NATO membership.

In 1983, the Christian Democrats and the Centre Party joined together in a non-socialist coalition, which lasted only two years. It was replaced in 1986 by a minority Labour administration, led by **Dr Gro Harlem Brundtland**, Norway's first woman prime minister. She made sweeping changes to the way the country was run, introducing seven women into her eighteen-member cabinet – a world record. However, her government was beset by problems for the three years of its life: tumbling oil prices led to a recession, unemployment rose (though only to 4 percent) and there was widespread dissatisfaction with Labour's high taxation policies.

At the **general election in September 1989** Labour lost eight seats and was forced out of office – the worst result that the party had suffered since 1930. More surprising was the success of the extremist parties on both political wings – the anti-NATO Left Socialist Party and the right-wing anti-immigrant Progress Party both scored spectacular results, winning almost a quarter of the votes cast, and increasing their representation in the *Storting* many times over. This deprived the Conservative Party (one of whose leaders, bizarrely, was Gro Harlem Brundtland's husband) of a majority it might have expected, the result being yet another shaky minority administration – this time a **centre-right coalition** between the Conservatives, the Centre Party and the Christian Democrats, led by Mr Jan Syse.

The new government immediately faced problems familiar to the last Labour administration. In particular, there was continuing conflict over joining the **European Community**, a policy still supported by many in the Norwegian establishment but flatly rejected by the Centre Party. It was this, in part, that signalled the end of the latest coalition, for after just over a year in office, the Centre Party withdrew from the coalition and forced the downfall of Mr Syse. In his place, Gro Harlem Brundtland was put back in power at the head of a **minority Labour administration** in October 1990, where she remained until her re-election for a fourth period of office in 1993.

■ Present-day politics

The burning issue in the last few years has been **EU membership**. Brundtland and her main political opponents supported an application for membership but, despite the near unanimity of the political parties, the Norwegian people narrowly rejected the EU in a referendum on the terms of membership in the fall of 1994. It was a close call – but in the end an alliance of farmers and fishermen, afraid of the economic repercussions of joining, and women's groups and "green" organizations, who felt that Norway's high standards of social care and environmental controls would suffer, coalesced to swing opinion against the EU.

Quite what Norway will make of this splendid isolation remains to be seen. But with its super-abundance of natural resources, it's hard to imagine that the country will suffer any permanent economic harm.

CHAPTER FOUR

OSLO AND AROUND

O slo is an enterprising city. Something of a poor relation until Norway's break with Sweden at the beginning of the century, it remained dourly provincial until the 1950s, but since then has developed into a go-ahead and cosmopolitan commercial hub of half a million people. The new self-confidence is plain to see in the city centre, a vibrant and urbane place whose relaxed and easy-going air bears favourable comparison with any European capital. Oslo is also the only major metropolis in a country brimming with small towns and villages: its nearest rival, Bergen, is less than half its size. This distinction gives Oslo an unusually powerful – some say overweening – voice in the nation's affairs, whether political, cultural or economic. Inevitably, Norway's big companies are mostly based here, as a rash of concrete and glass tower blocks testify, though these monoliths rarely intercept the stately Neoclassical lines of the late nineteenth-century **town centre**. It's here you should head first, as Oslo's handsome older quarters notch up some excellent museums, are within easy reach of the leafy **Bygdøy peninsula** – home to the world-famous Viking Ship Museum – and field a cosmopolitan street-life and bar scene that surprises many first-time visitors.

The other surprise is Oslo's size. The centre is compact, but the city's vast boundaries (453 square kilometres) encompass huge areas of forest, sand and water. This is no accident. Almost universally, the inhabitants of Oslo have a deep and abiding affinity for the wide open spaces that surround their city – with the waters of the Oslofjord to the south, and the forested hills of the **Nordmarka** inland to the north immensely popular for everything from boating and hiking to skiing. On all but the shortest of stays, there's ample opportunity to join in: the **island beaches** just offshore in the Oslofjord and the open forest and ski jumps at **Holmenkollen** are obvious targets, both within easy reach by ferry or underground train.

Oslo curves round the final shore of the **Oslofjord**, whose tapered waters extend for some 100km from the Skagerrak, the choppy channel separating Norway and Sweden from Denmark. As Norwegian fjords go, Oslofjord is not spectacularly beautiful – its rocky shores are generally low and unprepossessing – but scores of islets diversify the seascape and, amongst a string of workaday industrial settlements, **Fredrikstad** stands out as Norway's only surviving fortified town, its gridiron streets and angular bastions dating from the late sixteenth century. It's best visited as a day trip by train from the capital.

OSLO

The oldest of the Scandinavian capital cities, **OSLO** was founded, according to the Norse chronicler Snorre Sturlason, around 1048 by Harald Hardråde. Harald's son, Olav Kyrre, established a bishopric and built a cathedral here, though the kings of Norway continued to live in Bergen – an oddly inefficient division of church and state, considering the difficulty of communications. At the start of the fourteenth century, Håkon V rectified matters by moving to Oslo, where he built himself the Akershus fortress. The town boomed until 1349 when the bubonic plague wiped out almost half the population, initiating a period of slow decline whose pace accelerated after Norway came under Danish control in 1397. No more than a neglected backwater, Oslo's for-

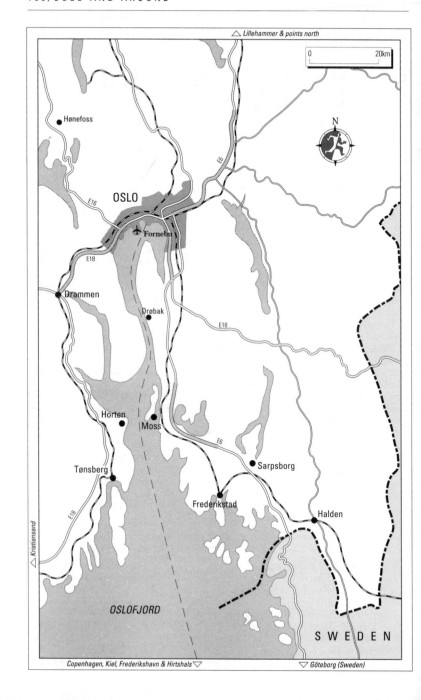

△ *Lillehammer & points north*

0   20km

N

Hønefoss

E6

OSLO

E16

✈ Fornebu

E18

Drammen

Drøbak

E18

Horten

Moss

E6

Sarpsborg

Tønsberg

Frederikstad

E18

Halden

△ *Kristiansand*

S W E D E N

OSLOFJORD

tunes were ultimately revived by the Danish king Christian IV, who moved Oslo lock, stock and barrel, shifting it west to its present site and rejecting its old name (Ås, a Norse word for God, and *Lo*, meaning field) in favour of Christiania in 1624. The new city prospered and by the time of the break with Denmark in 1814, Christiania (indeed Norway as a whole) was clamouring for independence, something it achieved in 1905 – though the city didn't revert to its original name for another twenty years. Today's city centre reflects the late nineteenth and early twentieth century well: wide streets, dignified parks and gardens, solid buildings and long, consciously classical vistas combine to lend it a self-satisfied, respectable air. In Oslo you get the feeling the inhabitants are proud of their wealthy city and of the rapid changes that are under way today – notably an ambitious construction programme and a fast-growing cultural life.

Oslo's biggest draw, though, is its **museums**. The city has a huge variety: Thor Heyerdahl's Kon-Tiki Museum, fabulous Viking ships, the Munch Museum ablaze with a good chunk of the painter's work, the bronze and granite sculptures of Gustav Vigeland, and the moving historical documents of the Resistance Museum – enough to keep even the most battle-weary museum-goer busy for a few days. There's also a decent **outdoor life**, the city sporting a good range of parks, pavement cafés, street entertainers and festivals. Indeed, in summer the whole city virtually lives outdoors, making Oslo a real delight – though in winter, too, the city's prime location amid hills and forests makes it a thriving and affordable ski centre.

Arrival and information

Downtown Oslo is at the heart of a superb public transport system, which makes arriving and departing straightforward and convenient. The principal arrival hub is the area around Oslo S station, at the eastern end of the main thoroughfare, Karl Johans gate. Tourist information is available in Oslo S too.

Train and bus terminals

International and domestic **trains** use the gleaming **Oslo Sentralstasjon**, known as Oslo S (domestic train information ☎22 17 14 00; international information ☎22 36 81 11), sited on the Jernbanetorget at the eastern end of the city centre. There are money exchange facilities here, as well as a post office, a tourist office, and two train information offices, one dealing with enquiries, the other selling tickets and making seat reservations. (The latter are compulsory on many long-distance trains – see p.160.) The station's *InterRail Centre* (mid-June to Sept) has showers and toilets for the use of cardholders.

The central **Bussterminalen** (bus terminal), which is sometimes referred to as Oslo M, is handily placed a short walk to the northeast of Oslo S, under the *Galleriet Oslo* shopping centre. This handles most of the bus services within the city as well as those to and from the airport. Long-distance buses arrive and depart here too, but Express bus travellers (on *Nor-Way Bussekspress* services) and those arriving with *National Express Eurolines* should note that incoming services sometimes terminate on the south side of Oslo S, at the bus stands beside Havnegata. For all bus **enquiries**, consult the Bussterminalen information desk (Mon–Fri 7am–10pm, Sat 8am–5.30pm & Sun 8am–10pm; ☎23 00 24 40).

Airports

In 1998, Oslo's present airport is scheduled to be phased out in favour of a brand new complex that's presently under construction well to the north of the city at Gardermoen. In the meantime, almost all international and domestic flights continue to use **Fornebu**, 7km west of the city. At Fornebu, departures are processed on the upper and arrivals on the lower level, where there are also currency exchange facilities and,

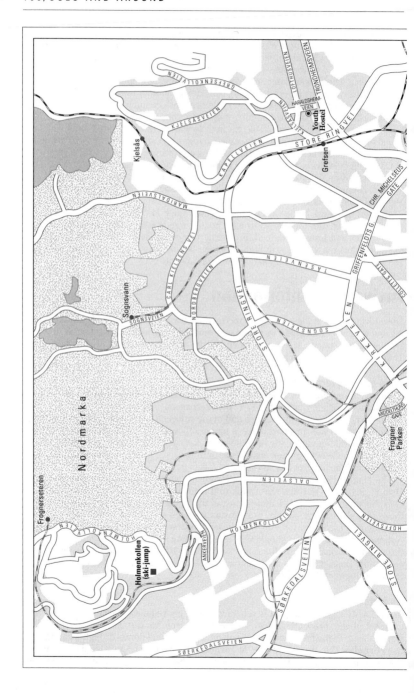

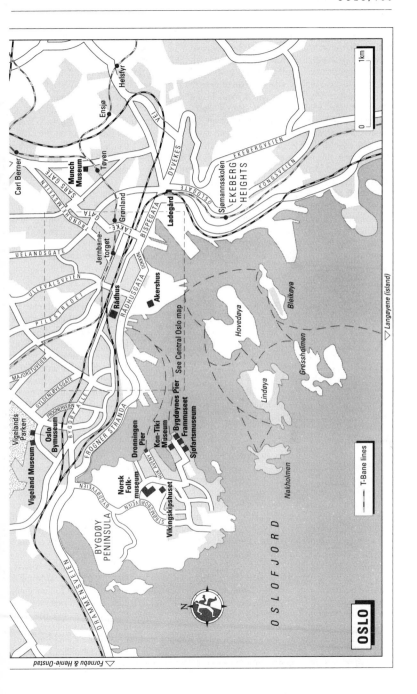

just outside, car rental offices – see "Listings" (p.217) for details. Fornebu is connected with Oslo's main bus terminal by regular *SAS Flybussen* (every 10–15min daily 7.30am–11pm; journey time 25min; 35kr), which leave from the bus stop immediately outside the terminal building; the bus also halts bang in the middle of town at the Nationaltheatret and beside the Stortinget (the parliament building) on Wessels plass. It is, however, cheaper to catch local bus #31 (marked *Tonsenhagen*; every 30min Mon–Sat 6am–midnight, Sun hourly 8am–midnight) to the Nationaltheatret or Jernbanetorget. The #31 bus stop is about 300m from the terminal building: turn right outside the entrance, follow the footpath down to the road and the stop is on the other side; the flat-rate fare is 18kr. **Taxis** into the city centre cost around 120kr. For Fornebu **departures**, the *Flybussen* terminal is inside Oslo's main bus station, though you can also catch the bus from the Nationaltheatret and Stortinget bus stops (every 10–15min Mon–Fri & Sun 6am–9.40pm, Sat 6am–7.40pm).

Enough of **Gardermoen**, Oslo's new airport 50km north of the city, has been completed to allow for its present use by long-haul charter traffic. *SAS Flybussen* (50min; 60kr) link Gardermoen with Oslo's main bus terminal, connecting with incoming and outgoing flights. Obviously, the frequency of the *Flybussen* will be increased as Gardermoen picks up more flights. In the meantime, timetable details are available inside the terminal building at Gardermoen, at the main bus station in Oslo or by calling ☎67 59 62 20.

Ferry terminals

DFDS **ferries** from Copenhagen and *Stena* ferries from Fredrikshavn in Denmarkarrive at the Vippetangen quays, a twenty-minute walk south of Oslo S: take Akershusstranda/Skippergata to Karl Johans gate and turn right, or catch bus #29 marked *Jernbanetorget* (every 15–30min Mon–Fri 6am–midnight, Sat from 7am, Sun from 8am; 5min; 18kr). With *Color Line* from Kiel and Denmark's Hirsthals, you'll arrive at the Hjortneskaia, some 3.5km west of the city centre: from the far side of the quayside car park, bus #56 runs into the centre; this is an infrequent service (every 30min Mon–Fri 6–9.20am & 2.30–5.30pm; 10min; 18kr), but it's mostly linked to ferry arrival times. Failing that, a taxi to Oslo S will cost about 100kr. Ferry ticket office details are given in "Listings", p.218.

Driving into Oslo

Arriving **by car**, you'll have to drive through one of eighteen video-controlled toll points ringed around the city: you pay 12kr to enter. Passholder lanes (blue signs inscribed *Abonnement*) are always located on the left and are for drivers in possession of toll passes; the *Mynt/Coin* (yellow signs) lanes are for exact cash payments only and frequently have a bucket-shaped receptacle where you throw your money; the *Manuell* (grey) lanes are also used for cash payments, but provide change. Oslo's ring roads circle and tunnel under the city; if you follow the signs for "Ring 1" you'll be delivered right into the centre and emerge (eventually) at the *Ibsen P-Hus*, a multistorey car park a short distance from Karl Johans gate.

You won't need your car to sightsee in Oslo, and parking is difficult in any case – you're best off using a **car park**. The *Ibsen P-hus* is at C.J. Hambros Plass 1 (Mon–Fri 6am–12.30am, Sat & Sun 8am–12.30am; ☎22 33 04 80), two blocks from Karl Johans gate, and there are eight other multistorey car parks in the centre, too. Opening times vary, but the majority operate on a similar schedule to the *Ibsen P-hus*, though some, like the *Aker Brygge P-hus*, Sjøgata 4 (☎22 83 80 45), are 24-hour. Costs begin at 5kr for fifteen minutes during the day and evening, mounting up to a maximum charge of 130kr for 24 hours, or 25kr in the evening (6pm–midnight); overnight parking (6pm–9am) costs 80kr. The *Ibsen P-hus* offers a 20 percent discount to Oslo Card-holders (see below).

Alternatively, you can park in pay-and-display car parks and metered spaces around the city (up to 15kr per hour). Identified by blue "P" signs, these on-street, metered spaces are owned and operated by the municipality, remain free of charge from Monday to Friday between 5pm and 8am and over the weekend after 2pm on Saturday. They also provide **free parking** at any time to Oslo Card-holders – but make sure to write your registration number, date and time on the card in the space provided. Note also that Oslo Card-holders still have to observe parking time limits.

Information

The country's main tourist office, the **Norwegian Information Centre** (*Norges Informasjonssenter*, Jan & Dec Mon–Fri 9am–4pm; Feb–May & Sept–Nov Mon–Sat Sat 9am–4pm; June & July daily 9am–6pm; Aug daily 9am–8pm; ☎22 83 00 50), is housed in what used to be the Oslo Vestbane train station at Vestbaneplassen 1, down by the waterfront at the western end of the city centre. Here you'll find some glossy displays and plenty of brochures relating to Norway as a whole, though it specializes on everything to do with Oslo, providing a full range of information, free city maps, guided tours and an accommodation booking service. There's also a tourist office inside **Oslo S** (daily 8am–11pm; ☎22 17 11 24) offering similar services. Both offices sell the Oslo Card and have free copies of various booklets and leaflets, including the *Oslo Official Guide* and *What's On in Oslo* – invaluable listings of events and services in the city.

Specific information for young people is available at **UngInfo**, Møllergata 3 (Mon–Fri 11am–5pm; ☎22 41 51 32).

The Oslo Card

Most visitors succumb to the lure of the **Oslo Card**, a pass that gives free admission to all museums and unlimited free travel on the whole municipal transport system, plus free on-street parking at metered parking places, a 30 percent discount on any *NSB* return train ticket within Norway to or from Oslo, and some useful discounts in shops, hotels and restaurants. Valid for either 24, 48 or 72 hours, it costs 130kr, 200kr and 240kr respectively, with children aged 4 to 15 charged just under half-price. It's available at the tourist offices, most hotels and campsites in Oslo, the *Trafikanten* office (see below) and downtown *Narvesen* newsagents. Note that the card is valid for a set number of hours (rather than days) starting from the moment it is first used, at which time it should either be presented and stamped or (for example, if your first journey is by tram) you should write in the date and time yourself. Bear in mind that in the winter, when opening hours for many sights and museums are reduced, you may have to work hard to make the card pay for itself.

City transport

Compared to other European capitals, Oslo is extremely safe and you're unlikely to be hassled in any shape or form. Naturally, however, the usual cautions apply to walking around on your own late at night, when you should be particularly careful in the vicinity of Oslo S (where the junkies gather) and on the tougher east side of town along and around Storgata. This sense of safety applies in equal measure to the **public transport** system, which is operated by *AS Oslo Sporveier*, whose information office, *Trafikanten*, is on the Jernbanetorget, beneath the high-tech transparent clock tower outside Oslo S (Mon–Fri 7am–8pm, Sat 8am–6pm; ☎22 17 70 30). Apart from selling Oslo Cards and public transport tickets (see below), they give away a useful **transit route map**, the *Sporveins hovedkart,* as well as a **timetable** booklet called *Rutebok for Oslo*, which gives the schedule of every route in the Oslo transport system.

Buses, trams, ferries and the T-bane

Oslo's public transport system consists of buses, trams, a small underground rail system (the *Tunnelbanen*) and local ferries. The Oslo Card is valid on the whole network, but only within the city limits: on services that extend beyond, you pay the fare from the city boundary to your destination. Note also that the *SAS Flybussen* do not accept Oslo Cards and that *NSB* railways, who operate frequent services to some of the outer suburbs, give a 30 percent discount to Card-holders on any return ticket within Norway to or from Oslo.

Almost all city **bus** services originate at the Bussterminalen beside Oslo S. There are around twenty routes operating strictly within the city limits, and other services out of Oslo, too. The vast majority of them pass through Jernbanetorget and another common stop is at the Nationaltheatret, at the west end of the city centre. Most buses stop running at around midnight, though at weekends **night buses** (*nattbuss*) take over on certain routes (flat-rate fare 36kr; Oslo Card and other passes not valid) – full details in the timetable, *Rutebok for Oslo*.

The city's **trams** run on eight routes through the city, crisscrossing the centre from east to west, and sometimes duplicating the bus routes. They are a tad slower than the buses, but a rather more interesting way of getting about. Major stops include Jernbanetorget, Nationaltheatret and Aker Brygge. Most operate regularly throughout the day from 6am to midnight.

The Tunnelbanen – **T-bane** – has eight lines, all of which converge to share a common slice of track that crosses the city centre from Majorstuen in the west to Tøyen in the east, with Jernbanetorget, Stortinget and Nationaltheatret stations in between. From this central section, four lines run westbound (*Vest*) and four eastbound (*Øst*). The system mainly serves commuters from the suburbs, but you'll find it useful for trips out to Holmenkollen and Sognsvann – where the trains travel above ground. The system runs from around 6am until around 12.30am. A series of **local commuter trains**, run by *NSB*, link Oslo with Moss, Drammen and other outlying towns; departures are from Oslo S, with many also making a stop at the Nationaltheatret.

Numerous **ferries** shuttle across the northern reaches of the Oslofjord to connect the city centre with its outlying districts and archipelago. To the Bygdøy peninsula and its museums they leave from the piers behind the Rådhus (late April to Sept), while the all-year services to Hovedøya, Lindøya and the other offshore islets (except Langøyene: June–Aug only) leave from the Vippetangen quay, behind Akershus Castle: to get to the quay, take bus #29 from Jernbanetorget.

Tickets

Flat-fare **tickets** (bought on board the bus, tram or ferry, or at T-bane stations) cost 18kr and allow a free transfer (on to any form of public transport) within one hour; children 4 to 16 years old travel for half price, babies and toddlers free. There are, however, several ways you can cut costs. Best is to buy an **Oslo Card** (see above), though if you're not into museums, then a straight **travel pass** might be a better buy. A 24-hour *Dagskort*, valid for unlimited travel within the city limits, costs 40kr; or there's the *Flexikort* (8 rides; 100kr), as well as passes for longer stays, available from the *Trafikanten* office in Jernbanetorget.

On buses, the driver will check your ticket; on trams you're trusted to have one – and *Flexikort* tickets should be cancelled in the machine. Though the practice might seem widespread, bear in mind that **fare-dodging** is punished by some pretty hefty spot-fines.

Taxis, bicycles and cars

The speed and efficiency of Oslo's public transport system means that you should rarely have to resort to a **taxi**, which is probably just as well as they are expensive. Taxi fares are regulated with the tariff varying according to the hour of the day, but as a sample night-time fare you can expect to pay around 130kr for a ten-minute, five-kilometre ride; during the daytime, it costs about 120kr from Oslo S to Fornebu airport. There are taxi ranks dotted round the city centre and outside all the big hotels. To call a cab ring *Oslo Taxi* on ☎22 38 80 90.

If you want to get about under your own steam, renting a **bicycle** is a pleasant option – the city has a reasonable range of cycle tracks and some roads have cycle lanes. Oslo's main bike rental shop is *Den Rustne Eike*, just along from the tourist office on Vestbaneplassen (May–Oct daily 10am–6.30pm; Nov–April Mon–Fri 10am–6.30pm; ☎22 83 72 31). Their charges begin at 60kr for a 7-speed bike for three hours, 95kr for a mountain bike, rising respectively to 95kr and 170kr for 24 hours. Waterproofs and insurance cost extra, as do helmets (25kr per day), plus there's a refundable deposit of either 750kr or 1000kr. The company also offers bike guided tours and rents machines for children.

Car rental is considerably more pricey – reckon on between 400kr and 500kr a day with CDW and unlimited mileage – though some companies offer a modest discount for Oslo Card-holders. Car rental companies are detailed under "Listings" on p.217. For details of parking in Oslo, see "Arrival and Information", above.

Accommodation

Oslo has the range of hotels you would expect of a capital city, as well as private rooms, a smattering of *pensjonater* (boarding houses) and a trio of youth hostels. To appreciate the full flavour of the city, you're best off staying on or near the western reaches of Karl Johans gate – between the Stortinget and the Nationaltheatret – though the well-heeled area to the north and west of the Royal Palace is enjoyable too. Many of the least expensive lodgings are, however, to be found in the vicinity of Oslo S, and this district – along with the grimy suburbs to the north and east of the station – is ideally avoided. That said, if money is tight and you're here in July and August, your choice of location may well be very limited as the scramble for **budget beds** becomes acute – or at least tight enough to make it well worth calling ahead to check on space. If only for peace of mind, an advance reservation for your first night is recommended. A positive way to cut the hassle is to use the accommodation service provided by the **tourist office**. Both the office inside Oslo S and the Norwegian Information Centre at Vestbaneplassen 1 (see "Information", above), can give you full accommodation lists, or make a reservation on your behalf for a fee of 20kr per person.

Hostels, private rooms and pensjonater

There are two official HI **hostels** in Oslo, both very popular and open to people of any age, though you'll need to be a member to get the lowest rate (non-members pay a modest surcharge of 25kr); the third hostel is rather more basic and geared up for the 16–25 age range. Alternatively, the tourist office can book you into a **private room** for a cost of 170kr for a single, 300kr a double. The supply of private rooms rarely dries up and they're something of a bargain, especially as many also have cooking facilities, but they do tend to be out of the city centre, and there's a minimum two-night stay. Slightly more upmarket than the hostels and private rooms are **pensjonater** (or boarding houses), which start at around 250kr single, 400kr double. There's only a handful of them – and only one near the city centre – and they offer bare but generally adequate accommodation with or without en suite facilities; breakfast is, however, not included and at some places you may need to supply your own sleeping bag.

ACCOMMODATION PRICE CODES

All the Norwegian hotels and guest houses listed in the guide have been graded according to the following price bands, based on the cost of the least expensive double room in high season. However, almost every hotel offers seasonal and/or weekend discounts that can reduce the rate by one or even two grades. Many of these bargains are impromptu, but wherever possible we've given two grades, covering both the regular and the discounted rate. Single rooms, where available, are usually between 60 and 80 percent of the cost of a double.

① under 500kr	② 500–700kr	③ 700–900kr
④ 900–1200kr	⑤ 1200–1500kr	⑥ over 1500kr

City hostels and pensjonater

Cochs Pensjonat, Parkveien 25 (☎22 60 48 36; fax 22 46 54 02). In a handy location behind Slottsparken at the foot of Hegdehaugsveien. No-frills boarding house occupying the third floor of a drab modern block. Some rooms have a kitchen unit. Singles with bath 380kr (300kr without), doubles 510kr (400kr), triples 600kr (480kr) and quadruples 680kr (560kr).

KFUK-KFUM Sleep-In, Møllergata 1 (☎22 20 83 97). The cheapest and most central hostel beds in Oslo, five minutes' walk from Oslo S, near the Domkirke (entrance on Grubbegata). Very basic. No breakfast. Showers and cooking facilities available. July to mid-Aug; reception open 8–11am & 5pm–midnight. 100kr plus an extra 25kr if you need sheets.

Oslo Haraldsheim, Haraldsheimveien 4, Grefsen (☎22 22 29 65; fax 22 22 10 25). Better of the two *HI* youth hostels, 5km northeast of the centre, and open all year except Christmas week. Has 270 beds, most in rooms for four people. The public areas are comfortable and attractively furnished and the rooms are clean and frugal, over half with their own shower and WC. There are self-catering facilities, a restaurant, washing machines and even a solarium. The basic 145kr price includes breakfast (non-members 170kr), while single rooms cost 260kr (330kr with shower), doubles 370kr (450kr). It's a very popular spot, especially with school parties, so advance booking is strongly advised in the summer. Take tram #10 or #11 from the bottom of Storgata, near the Domkirke, to the Sinsenkrysset stop, from where it's a ten-minute walk along the signposted footpath that cuts across the field.

Oslo Holtekilen, Michelets vei 55, 1320 Stabekk (☎67 53 38 53; fax 67 59 12 30). The other *HI* Oslo hostel, but much smaller than Haraldsheim and only open from the end of May to mid-August. It's located 10km west of the city centre and 5km from Fornebu airport. From Oslo M, take bus #151 and the hostel is 100m from the bus stop. There are kitchen facilities, a restaurant and a laundry. Again, the 145kr price includes breakfast; single rooms cost 195kr, doubles 240kr.

Hotels

As far as **hotels** are concerned, a simple en-suite room costs an average 600–700kr, while you hit the comfort zone at about 800kr and luxury from around 900kr. However, almost invariably special offers and seasonal **deals** make the smarter hotels rather more affordable than this. Most of them offer up to 50 percent discounts at weekends (ask for the *weekendpris*), while in July and August – when Norwegians leave town for their holidays – prices everywhere tend to drop radically. Also, nearly every room rate is at least mildly softened by the inclusion of a good self-service buffet breakfast. To check the best deals, head for either of the tourist offices, both of which maintain regularly updated lists of the day's best offers. They'll make the booking for you (for a 20kr fee per person), or try the places on the following list – but always call ahead first.

Ambassadeur, Camilla Colletts vei 15 (☎22 44 18 35; fax 22 44 47 91). One of a long sequence of attractive nineteenth-century town houses graced by wrought-iron balconies. The slightly grimy outward appearance doesn't do justice to the elegantly furnished interior, where each of the bedrooms has a different theme – the "Shanghai" and "Amsterdam", for example. A great location too, just three blocks west of the Slottsparken. Summer and weekend reductions of 50 percent. ③/④

Bondeheimen, Rosenkrantz gate 8 (☎22 42 95 30; fax 22 41 94 37). One of Oslo's most delightful hotels, tastefully decorated with smooth polished pine everywhere you look. It's just two minutes' walk north of Karl Johans gate – and the included buffet breakfast (served in the *Kaffistova*; see "Eating") is excellent. Free coffee, soup and bread in the foyer throughout the evening. The price for a double is 920kr (single 820kr), but look out for weekend and summer discounts of up to 40 percent. ④

City, Skippergata 19 (☎22 41 36 10; fax 22 42 24 29). A popular standby with budget travellers in the seedy side streets around Oslo S. The rooms here are small but reasonably adequate and breakfast is included. ②

Continental, Stortingsgata 24 (☎22 82 40 00; fax 22 42 96 89). Top-notch, long-established hotel bang in the centre of town. Every luxury, plus a sumptuous breakfast. ⑥

Grand, Karl Johans gate 31 (☎22 42 93 90; fax 22 42 12 25). Over a hundred years of tradition, comfort and style in the prime position on Oslo's main street translates into stratospheric room rates. But the food and service here are excellent, and hefty weekend and summer discounts make the comfortable rooms much more affordable. ④/⑥

Imi, Staffeldts gate (☎22 20 53 30; fax 22 11 17 49). Straightforward modern hotel in a quiet part of town to the north of the Slottsparken. Spruce and neat furnishings and fittings. ②/③

Inter Nor Hotel Bristol, Kristian IV's gate 7 (☎22 82 60 00; fax 22 82 60 01). Plush establishment distinguished by its sumptuous public rooms with ornate nineteenth-century embellishments, from chandeliers to columns with fancifully carved arches. ④/⑥

Inter Nor Savoy Hotel, Universitets gate 11 (☎22 20 26 55; fax 22 11 24 80). Attractive choice with pleasant rooms and wood-panelled public areas. In an interesting area too, with bookshops and bars catering primarily for the city's students. At Universitets gate and Kristian Augusts gate, footsteps from Karl Johans gate. ④

Norrøna, Grensen 19 (☎22 42 64 00; fax 22 33 25 65). Unassuming, slightly old-fashioned place occupying part of a nineteenth-century apartment block right in the middle of town, about 400m to the north of the Stortinget. Cheerful and functional but perfectly adequate rooms with modern furnishings. At 850kr per double, it's a bargain that's made even more attractive by summer and weekend discounts of 20 percent. ②/③

Rainbow Hotel Stefan, Rosenkrantz gate 1 (☎22 42 92 50; fax 22 33 70 22). Unremarkable but spick and span modern hotel above the ground-floor shops of a five-storey high-rise. Two hundred rooms. Great location, just a couple of minutes' walk north of Karl Johans gate. Near the top of its price range, it's still one of the city's better deals. ③

Rica Victoria Hotel, Rosenkrantz gate 13 (☎22 42 99 40; fax 22 42 99 43). Large and modern hotel footsteps south of Karl Johans gate. Smart, verging on the luxurious, and popular with visiting business executives. ④/⑤

Camping and cabins

Camping is a fairly easy proposition in a city with plenty of space, the nearest of the sixteen sites dotted within a fifty-kilometre radius being just 3km from the centre. If you're out of luck with rooms in town, some sites also offer **cabins**, or you could telephone the leading cabin and cottage rental agency, *Den Norske Hytteformidling*, Kierschows gate 7 (Mon–Fri 9am–5pm; ☎22 35 67 10), to ask about availability.

Campsites

Bogstad Camping, Ankerveien 117 (☎22 50 76 80; fax 22 50 01 62). Large and well-equipped lakeside campsite, with cabins available for rental (①), 15km northwest of the centre – take bus #32 from Oslo S or Nationaltheatret. It gets crowded, though, so call first. Open all year.

Ekeberg Camping, Ekebergveien 65 (☎22 19 85 68). Medium-sized campground in a rocky, forested parcel of parkland just 3km east of the city centre; bus #24 from Jernbanetorget goes past. Tents only. June–Aug.

Langøyene Camping, Langøyene (☎22 11 53 21). Extremely popular, no-frills campsite on one of the islets just offshore from downtown Oslo. Langøyene has the city's best beaches and an attractive wooded shoreline. To get there, take ferry #94 from the Vippetangen quay, though note that this is a summer-only service (late May to late Aug). Campsite open late May to mid-Aug.

The City Centre

If Oslo is your first taste of Norway, you'll be struck by the light – soft and brilliantly clear in the summer and broodingly gloomy in winter, each season visited by rafts of rain or chilling blizzards. At the time of their construction, the grand late nineteenth- and early twentieth-century buildings that populate **central Oslo** provided the country's emergent bourgeoisie with a sense of security and prosperity, an aura that survives today. Largely as a result, most downtown Oslo remains easy and pleasant to walk around, its airy streets and squares accommodating the appealing remnants of the city's early days as well as a clutch of good museums and dozens of bars, cafés and restaurants.

Despite the mammoth proportions of the Oslo conurbation, the city centre has also stayed surprisingly compact and is easy to navigate by remembering a few simple landmarks. From the train station **Oslo S**, at the eastern end of the centre, the main thoroughfare and city artery **Karl Johans gate** heads directly up the hill, passing the **Domkirke** and cutting a pedestrianized course until it reaches the **Stortinget** (parliament building). From here it sweeps down past the **University** to the **Royal Palace**, which sits in parkland (the **Slottsparken**) at the western end of the centre. South of the palace, on the waterfront, is the brash harbourside development of **Aker Brygge**, across from which is the distinctive twin-towered **Rådhus**. Back towards Oslo S, on the lumpy peninsula overlooking the harbour, is the severe-looking **Akershus Slott**, the city's castle. Between the castle, the Stortinget and Oslo S is a tight, slightly gloomy grid of streets and high buildings that was originally laid out by Christian IV in the seventeenth century. Nowadays the district acts as the city's commercial hub, though its importance is being undermined by Oslo's burgeoning suburbs.

Along Karl Johans gate

Heading west and uphill from Oslo S train station, **Karl Johans gate** begins unpromisingly with a clutter of tacky shops and hang-around junkies, but footsteps away at the corner of Dronningens gate is the curious **Basarhallene**, a circular building of two tiers, whose brick cloisters housed the city's food market in the last century and have since been revived as a tiny shopping complex complete with art shops and cafés. The adjacent **Domkirke** (daily 10am–4pm; free) dates from the late seventeenth century, though its heavyweight tower was remodelled in 1850. Plain and dour from the outside, the cathedral's elegantly restored interior is in delightful contrast, its homely, low-ceilinged nave and transepts awash with maroon, green and gold paintwork, and to either side of the high altar are the stained-glass windows created by Emanuel Vigeland in 1910 (for more on the Vigelands, see p.209). Outside the cathedral, **Stortorvet** was once the main city square, but it's no longer of much account, its nineteenth-century statue of a portly Christian IV merely a forlorn guardian of a second-rate flower market conducted from the backs of delivery vans.

Returning to Karl Johans gate, it's a brief stroll up to the **Stortinget**, the parliament building, an imposing chunk of neo-Romanesque architecture which was completed in 1866. It's open to the public (July to mid-Aug Mon–Sat 11am–2pm; free), but the obligatory guided tour shows little more than can be gleaned from the outside. The narrow piece of park in front, **Eidsvolls plass**, flanks Karl Johans gate, and – along with the gar-

---

It's as well to note again that buying an **Oslo Card** gets you free entrance to all the museums and sights detailed in the following accounts, as well as free transport between them. It's a saving well worth considering, even if you're following a truncated itinerary.

dens further down – is one of the busiest centres of summertime Oslo. It's usually full of jewellery hawkers, ice-cream kiosks and milling people patronizing the nearby pavement cafés, and it gets especially crowded during festivals and live music performances.

On the western side of Eidsvolls plass is the Neoclassical **Nationaltheatret**, built in 1899 and flanked by two stodgy statues of playwrights Henrik Ibsen and Bjørnstjerne Bjørnson. Inside, the red and gold main hall, which seats eight hundred people, has been restored to its turn-of-the-century glory. You can occasionally take a **guided tour** (ask for details at the box office or call ☎22 41 16 40), and this is the best way to see the impressive interior if you can't understand Norwegian, the language of almost every performance. It's also worth noting that the Nationaltheatret is a handy transport terminus. Around the back of the building are two tunnels: the one on the right is for the westbound T-bane, while the one on the left handles local trains and the eastbound T-bane; many city buses and the airport *Flybussen* stop beside the Nationaltheatret too.

Beyond the theatre, standing on the hill at the end of Karl Johans gate, **Det Kongelige Slott**, the Royal Palace, is a monument to Norwegian openness. Built between 1825 and 1848, at a time when other monarchies were nervously counting their friends, it still stands without railings and walls, the Slottsparken grounds freely open to the public. You can't actually go into the palace, but every day at 1.30pm there's quite a snappy changing of the guard. Bang in front of the palace is an equestrian statue of **Karl XIV Johan** himself. Formerly the French General Bernadotte, he abandoned Napoleon and, elected king of Sweden, assumed the Norwegian throne when Norway passed from Denmark to Sweden after the Treaty of Kiel in 1814. Seemingly not content with the terms of his motto (inscribed on the statue), "The people's love is my reward", Karl Johan had this whopping palace built, only to die before its completion.

The University and its museums

Retracing your steps to Karl Johans gate, the nineteenth-century buildings of the **University**, all classical columns and imperial pediments, fit perfectly in this monumental part of the city centre. The **Aula** (July Mon–Fri noon–2pm; free), the main hall between the university's two symmetrical wings, bears huge interior murals by Edvard Munch, the controversial result of a competition held by the university authorities in 1909 (though they weren't actually unveiled, after much heated debate, until 1916). Munch had just emerged (cured) from a winter in a Copenhagen psychiatric clinic when he started on the murals, and the major parts, *The History*, *Sun* and *Alma Mater*, reflect a new mood in his work: confident and in tune with the natural world that he loved. Back outside, during term-time the university steps are usually filled with students; at the beginning of the academic year (around August 20) the pavements are spread with used textbooks which old students sell on to the latest batch of undergraduates.

Around the corner at Frederiks gate 2, the **Historical Museum** (mid-May to mid-Sept Tues–Sun 11am–3pm; rest of the year Tues–Sun noon–3pm; free) comprises the hotchpotch historical and ethnographical collections of the university. The highlight is the Viking and early medieval section, which is displayed on the ground floor. In the rooms to the left of the entrance are several magnificent twelfth- and thirteenth-century stave-church porches and gate posts, alive with dragons and beasts emerging from swirling, intricately carved backgrounds. There are weapons, coins, drinking horns, runic stones, religious bric-a-brac and bits of clothing here too, as well as a superb vaulted room, dating from the late thirteenth century and originating in Ål, near Gol. The rest of the ground floor is taken up by a pretty dire sequence of exhibitions on the Stone, Bronze, Iron and Viking ages. Geared up for school parties, the tiny dioramas are downright silly and detract from the actual exhibits, which (accompanied by long explicatory leaflets) illustrate various aspects of early Norwegian society – from religious beliefs and social structures through to military hardware and trade and craft.

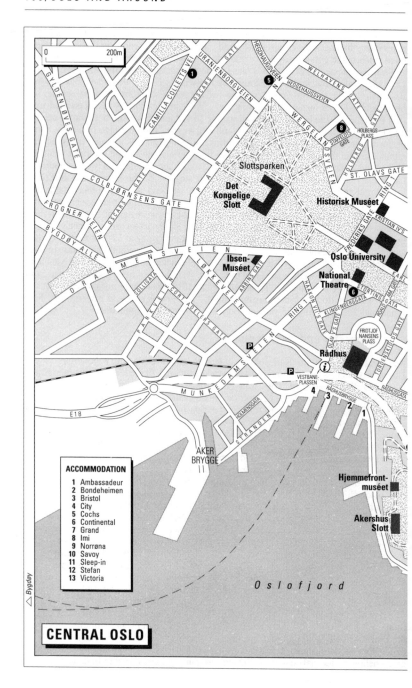

CENTRAL OSLO

ACCOMMODATION

1 Ambassadeur
2 Bondeheimen
3 Bristol
4 City
5 Cochs
6 Continental
7 Grand
8 Imi
9 Norrøna
10 Savoy
11 Sleep-in
12 Stefan
13 Victoria

Slottsparken

Det Kongelige Slott

Historisk Muséet

Oslo University

Ibsen-Muséet

National Theatre

Friodjof Nansens Plass

Rådhus

Vestbane-plassen

Aker Brygge

Hjemmefront-muséet

Akershus Slott

Oslofjord

△ Bygdøy

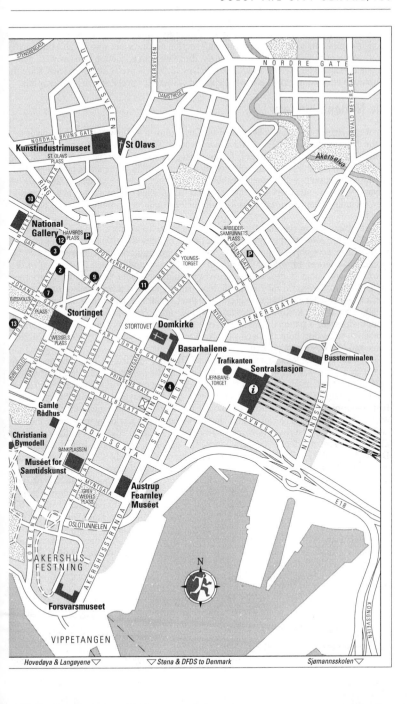

On the second floor, the first part of the **Ethnographical Museum** is devoted to the Arctic peoples and features an illuminating section on the Sami, who inhabit the northern reaches of Scandinavia. Incongruously, there's a coin collection here as well, while it's upstairs again for African and Asiatic art and culture – pretty standard stuff, though temporary exhibitions from around the world sometimes prove worth investigating.

The National Gallery

Norway's largest and best collection of fine art is only a step away from the University in the **Nasjonalgalleriet** (National Gallery; Mon, Wed, Fri & Sat 10am–4pm, Thurs 10am–8pm, Sun 11am–3pm; free), Universitetsgata 13. An approachable collection of works shoehorned into a grand nineteenth-century building, it's short on internationally famous painters – the most notable exception being a fine sample of the work of Edvard Munch – but there's compensation in the oodles of Norwegian artists on display, including examples of the work of all the leading figures up until the end of World War II.

Something of a mishmash, the **first floor** is home to a quirky series of collections, with the large room to the right of the entrance crammed with plaster casts of Italian Renaissance sculptures – including a massive and militaristic equestrian statue by Donatello – and of a horde of Greek and Roman gods and caesars. To the left of the entrance, one room is devoted to Norwegian nineteenth-century sculpture, another holds a set of Novgorod medieval religious paintings and a third a rather timid selection of Old Masters, amongst which the Dutch paintings and those of the German Lucas Cranach – *Reclining Fountain Nymph* and *The Golden Age* – stand out. Nonetheless, for a national gallery there's very little in the way of older works of significance, reflecting both the lack of an earlier royal or aristocratic collection to build upon and Norway's past poverty.

The wide and gracious stairway – where you'll spot a tortured bronze relief of *Helvete* (Hell) by Gustav Vigeland – leads to the kernel of the gallery's collection on the **second floor**, which divides between Norwegian painting on the right-hand side and modern European art to the left. In the latter section is an enjoyable sample of work by the **Impressionists**, assorted bursts of colour from Manet, Monet, Degas and Cézanne, as well as a distant, piercing Van Gogh self-portrait, and later works by the likes of Picasso and Braque. The first room of Norwegian paintings features the work of the country's most important nineteenth-century landscape painters, principally **Johan Christian Dahl** (1788–1857) and his pupil **Thomas Fearnley** (1802–1842). Dahl's giant-sized canvas *Stalheim* is typical of his work, the soft and dappled hues of the mountain landscape with a sleepy village, dotted with tiny figures, whilst his *Hjelle in Valdres* of 1851 adopts the same approach, though here the artifice suffusing the apparent naturalism is easier to detect: the year before, Dahl had completed another painting of Hjelle, but he returned to the subject to widen the valley and heighten the mountains, sprinkling them with snow. Fearnley often lived and worked abroad, but he always returned to Norwegian themes, painting no fewer than five versions of the *Labrofossen ved Kongsberg* (the Labro Waterfall at Kongsberg), a fine moody canvas of dark, louring clouds and frothy water.

From the 1890s, Norwegian landscape painting assumed a mystical and spiritual dimension, with the more literal naturalism of earlier painters abandoned for more symbolic representations, an approach influenced by French painters such as Henri Rousseau. Norwegian artists like **Gerhard Munthe** dipped into lyrical renditions of the Norwegian countryside, cosy, folksy scenes echoed in the paintings of **Erik Werenskiold** and clarified by the somewhat sharper visions of **Harald Sohlberg** (*En blomstereng nordpå* – A Northern Field of Flowers – and the chilly *Vinternatt i Rondane* – Winter Night in the Rondane) and Halfdan Egedius (*Opptrekkende uvaer* – Building up to a Storm). Contemporaneously, **Theodor Kittelsen** (1857–1914) defined the appearance of the country's trolls, sprites and sirens in his illustrations of Asbjørnsen and Moe's *Norwegian Folk Tales*, published in 1883 – and there are examples of his work here in the gallery.

The museum's centrepiece, the **Munch** collection, is however the National Gallery's star turn, gathering together some representative works dating from the 1880s and 1890s up to 1916 in one central room, with several lesser pieces displayed elsewhere. His early work is very much in the Naturalist tradition of his mentor Christian Krohg, though by 1885 Munch is already pushing the boundaries in *The Sick Child*, a heart-wrenching evocation of his sister Sophie's death from tuberculosis. Other works with this same sense of pain include *Mother and Daughter, Moonlight* and one of several versions of *The Scream,* a seminal canvas of 1893 whose swirling lines and rhythmic colours were to inspire the Expressionists. This sample of Munch's work serves as a good introduction to the artist, but for a more detailed appraisal – and a more comprehensive selection of his work – check out the Munch Museum (p.208). Setting aside Munch, who was always an exceptional figure, Norwegian art was reinvigorated in the 1910s by a new band of artists that had trained in Paris under Henri Matisse, whose emancipation of colour from naturalist constraints inspired his Norwegian students. **Henrik Sørensen** (1882–1962), the outstanding figure here, summed up the Frenchman's influence thirty years later: "From Matisse, I learned more in fifteen minutes than from all the other teachers I have listened to" – lessons that inspired Sørensen's surging, earthy landscapes of the lowlands of eastern Norway which he much preferred to the monumental scenery of the west coast. **Axel Revold** (1887–1962) was also trained by Matisse, but he assimilated Cubist influences too – for example his *Sommernatt i Nordland* (Summer Night in Nordland) of 1930 – whilst **Erling Enger** (1899–1990) maintained a gently lyrical approach to the landscape and its seasons. Examples of the work of these and other later artists spreads up from the second to the **third floor**, where there's also a large collection of paintings from the rest of Scandinavia, mostly dating from the first half of the twentieth century.

The Museum of Applied Art

The **Kunstindustrimuseet** (Museum of Applied Art; Tues–Fri 11am–3pm, Sat & Sun noon–4pm; 20kr) occupies an imposing nineteenth-century building some ten minutes' walk from the National Gallery, at St Olavs gate 1: continue to the far end of Universitetsgata, veer to the right and it's at the end of the street. Founded in 1876, this has claim to be one of the earliest applied art museums in Europe, its multifaceted collection particularly strong on period furniture with examples of all major styles – both domestic and imported – from the medieval period down to the present day. The museum spreads out over four floors. The **first floor** accommodates temporary exhibitions (which sometimes raise the cost of admission), while on the **second floor** (to the left of the stairs) is an engaging hotchpotch of Viking tackle from drinking horns, broaches and belts through to religious statuettes and church vestments. The museum's top exhibit is here too, the brightly coloured *Baldishol* tapestry whose intricate twelfth-century design makes it one of the finest early examples of woven tapestry in Europe. Next door, the "Norwegian Gallery" boasts a delightful sample of carved wooden furniture, amongst which the cheerily painted pieces from Gudbrandsdal are outstanding, and alongside is a selection of bedspreads sporting either religious or folkloric motifs. Upstairs, on the **third floor**, a sequence of period interiors illustrates foreign fashions from Renaissance and Baroque through to Chippendale, Louis XVI and Art Nouveau. Moving on again, the **fourth-floor** displays concentrate on ceramics and glassware from the early nineteenth century onwards, with other exhibits on textiles and fashions. The highlight here is the collection of extravagant costumes worn by Norway's royal family at the turn of the twentieth century, fairy-cake affairs especially favoured by Queen Maud, the daughter of England's Edward VII and wife of Haakon VII, not to mention Crown Princess Sonja's consecratory robe from the 1930s.

To the water: the Rådhus and Aker Brygge

Returning to the city centre, the **Rådhus** (May–Sept Mon–Sat 9am–5pm, Sun noon–5pm; Oct–April Mon–Sat 9am–4pm, Sun noon–4pm; guided tours Mon–Fri 10am, noon & 2pm; May–Sept 15kr, Oct–April free), Oslo's modern and controversial City Hall, rears high above the waterfront a couple of minutes' walk south of Karl Johans gate. Constructed of dark brown brick, and opened in 1950 to celebrate Oslo's 900th anniversary after nearly twenty years in the making, initially the building was considered an ugly and strikingly un-Norwegian addition to the city. Nonetheless, its twin towers are a grandiose statement of civic pride, and nowadays rank (in a surprising change of heart) as one of the city's more popular buildings – the obloquy passing to other, more recent additions to the skyline, such as Oslo S. The interior of the Rådhus was equally contentious, much of it a pictorial – and for some, completely over-the-top – record of all things Norwegian. Acres of stylized murals decorate the main hall – the Rådhushallen – with the north wall sporting the massive *From the Fishing Nets in the West to the Forests of the East*, in which the figure of the polar explorer Fridtjof Nansen on the left symbolizes the nation's spirit of adventure, while the dramatist Bjørnstjerne Bjørnson to the right represents intellectual development. On the south wall is a second whopper, the equally vivid *Work, Administration and Celebration,* which took Henrik Sørensen a decade to complete. There's a self-congratulatory nationalism in these murals that's hardly attractive, though this is partly offset by the forceful fresco along the east wall in honour of the Norwegian Resistance of World War II – and taken altogether, the whole is an overwhelming art display that's difficult to beat.

At the back of the Rådhus, beyond the tram lines and shadowed by the bumpy Akershus peninsula, is the central **harbour**, always busy with ferries and boats, with Bygdøy and the little archipelago shimmering in the distance. This is one of downtown Oslo's prettiest spots and handy too for the **Norwegian Information Centre**, located footsteps from the Rådhus in the old, yellow Oslo V train station. Close to the information centre, Oslo's crusty old waterfront warehouses have been turned into the swish **Aker Brygge** shopping-cum-office complex, a gleaming concoction of walkways, circular staircases and glass lifts, all trimmed out with neon and plastic; the bars and restaurants here are some of the most popular in town.

Around Rådhusgata

Running east from the Rådhus, **Rådhusgata** cuts off the spur of land holding Akershus Castle and leads down to the other harbour, where ferries from Denmark dock, the grids of streets on either side a legacy of seventeenth-century Oslo. It's only the layout that has survived, however, as the old timber buildings were almost entirely demolished and replaced by grander stone structures in the nineteenth century, when the district flourished as the commercial heart of the city.

Bankplassen, one block south of Rådhusgata along Kirkegata, has been spruced up and pedestrianized, and its proudest building – the 1907 Art Nouveau structure at no. 4 – has been superbly restored to house the enterprising **National Museum of Contemporary Art** (*Museet for Samtidskunst*; Tues, Wed & Fri 10am–5pm, Thurs 10am–8pm, Sat & Sun 11am–4pm; free). Based on collections originally in the National Gallery, the museum has examples of every major postwar Norwegian artist and there's an extensive sample from the rest of Scandinavia too. The works are displayed in a series of temporary, thematic exhibitions that spread over three floors. Each item is allowed a generous amount of space and so – given that some of the pieces are massive and the museum also hosts prestigious international exhibitions – only a fraction of the permanent collection can be shown at any one time. Nonetheless, Norwegian names to look out for include Bjørn Carlsen, Frans Widerberg, Knut Rose and Bjørn Ransve.

Imaginatively displayed, the exhibits hang from every clean white wall and offset every corner and stairwell, but it's still difficult not to be more impressed by the building itself. The interior – once the head office of the *Norges Bank* – has been stripped of furniture and polished, its echoing halls, offices and rooms resplendent with gilt and marble and ornamental columns and banisters. Visitors get to leave their bags inside one of the bank's old safes, and you can eke out your time in the museum by stopping off in the relaxing *Café Sesam* on the ground floor, which has a decent line in cakes and coffee.

The Astrup Fearnley Modern Art Museum

Opened in 1993, the **Astrup Fearnley Museet for Moderne Kunst** (Modern Art Museum; Tues–Sun noon–4pm, Thurs until 7pm; 30kr), about 200m to the east of the Contemporary Art museum at Dronningens gate 4, occupies a sharp modern building of brick and glass with six-metre high steel entrance doors. It's meant to impress – a suitably posh setting for the display of several private collections and for eminent exhibitions. The exhibits are changed regularly, but the permanent collection does include examples of the work of most major postwar Norwegian artists – for instance Knut Rose and Bjørn Carlsen – as well as a smattering of foreign works from the likes of Francis Bacon and Anselm Kiefer.

Akershus castle and fortress

Though very much part of central Oslo by location, the jutting thumb of land that holds the castle, the **Akershus Slott**, much the most significant memorial to medieval Oslo, is quite separate from the city centre in feel. Built on a rocky knoll overlooking the harbour in around 1300, the original fort was already the battered veteran of several unsuccessful sieges when Christian IV (1596–1648) took matters in hand. The king had a passion for building cities and a keen interest in Norway – during his reign he visited the country about thirty times, more than all the other kings of the Dano-Norwegian union together. So, when Oslo was badly damaged by fire in 1624, he took his opportunity and simply ordered the town to be moved round the bay from its location at the mouth of the river Alna beneath the Ekeberg heights. He had the town rebuilt in its present position, renamed it "Christiania" – a name which stuck until 1925 – and modernized the castle as a Renaissance residence. Around the castle he also constructed a new fortress – the **Akershus Festning** – whose thick earth and stone walls and protruding bastions were designed to combat the threat of artillery bombardment. Refashioned and enlarged on several later occasions – and now bisected by Kongens gate – parts of the fortress have remained in military use to the present day.

There are several entrances to the Akershus complex, but the one to make for is at the west end of Myntgata, from where there's a choice of two marked footpaths. One leads to the **Christiania Bymodell** (June–Aug Tues–Sun 10am–4pm; 20kr), which explains the city's history from 1624 to 1840 by means of an hourly audiovisual performance and a large-scale model of Oslo as it appeared in 1838: drop by to get a better idea of the city's evolution and what the gridded town looked like when it was protected by the fortress. The second footpath leads up to a side gate in the perimeter wall, next to which is a brand new (and crushingly boring) museum-cum-information centre that makes a strange attempt to link the history of the castle with modern environmental concerns. Beyond, there's another choice of signed routes with one path leading to the Defence Museum (see below), the other heading up to the castle and offering some heady views over the harbour on the way. With its twin spires and high gables, the recently renovated **Slott** (May to mid-Sept Mon–Sat 10am–4pm, Sun 12.30–4pm; late April & mid-Sept to Oct Sun only 12.30–4pm; 20k; free guided tour at 11am, 1pm & 3pm, Sun at 1pm) is used mainly for state receptions these days, though the tour takes you through various empty halls and to the chapel. The labyrinthine structure is a tad antiseptic, but exploring the underground passages and dungeons is fun and you get to peek at the Royal Mausoleum. Despite the clinical refurbishment, however, the castle retains a further significance for Norwegians, as it was used as the Nazi HQ during the last war.

The Akershus museums

Housed in a separate building close to the castle entrance, the location of the **Hjemmefrontmuseum** (Resistance Museum; mid-April to Sept Mon–Sat 10am–4pm, Sun 11am–4pm; Oct to mid-April Mon–Sat 10am–3pm, Sun 11am–4pm; 15kr) is particularly apt as captured Resistance fighters were tortured and sometimes executed in the castle by the Gestapo. Labelled in English and Norwegian, the museum's mostly pictorial displays detail the history of the war in Norway from defeat and occupation through resistance to final victory. There are tales of extraordinary heroism here – the determined resistance of hundreds of the country's teachers to Nazi instructions and the story of a certain Petter Moen, who was arrested by the Germans and imprisoned in the Akershus where he kept a diary by picking letters out with a pin on toilet paper: the diary survived, but he didn't. Another section deals with Norway's Jews, of whom there were 1800 in 1939 – the Germans captured 760 and 24 survived – and there's an impressively honest account of Norwegian collaboration, when hundreds of volunteers joined the Wehrmacht, most notoriously the antics of Vidkun Quisling: pressing a button brings up extracts of Quisling's announcement of his assumption of puppet power at the start of the German invasion in April 1940.

Below the castle, a string of ochre-painted barrack blocks fills out the lower portion of the fortress and leads round to the footbridge spanning Kongens gate. On the far side of the bridge, amongst the buildings flanking the parade ground, is the **Forvarsmuseet** or Defence Museum, also known as the Armed Forces Museum (June–Aug Mon–Fri 10am–6pm, Sat & Sun 11am–4pm; Sept–May Mon–Fri 10am–3pm, Sat & Sun 11am–4pm; free). However, this is a poor foil to the quiet heroics of the Resistance collection – a dreary account of the nation's military history illustrated by an assortment of uniforms, rifles and guns, presumably used more for attack than defence. From here, it's a short walk to the main entrance of the Akershus, at the foot of Kirkegata.

Out from the centre

From the jetty behind the Rådhus, ferries shuttle southwest from central Oslo to the **Bygdøy peninsula**, home to the city's showpiece museums, whilst other ferries head south from the Vippetangen quay behind the Akershus to the string of rusticated **islands** that necklace the inner waters of the Oslofjord. The jetty behind the Rådhus is also the departure point for *Hurtigbåt* passenger express boats along the coast to Arendal (late June to mid-Aug 1 daily). Back on the mainland, **east Oslo** is the least prepossessing part of town, a gritty sprawl housing the poorest of the city's inhabitants. You wouldn't come this way were it not for the **Munch Museum**, which boasts a superb collection of the artist's work, though afterwards it's also mildly tempting to pop along the eastern shore of Oslo's principal harbour for the views over the city and to take a gander at the skimpy remains of the medieval town. **Northwest Oslo** is far more prosperous, with big old houses lining the avenues immediately to the west of the Slottsparken. Beyond is the **Frognerparken**, a chunk of parkland with the stunning open-air sculptures of Gustav Vigeland displayed in the **Vigelandsparken**. Further west still, there's more prestigious modern art at the **Henie-Onstad centre**, beyond the city limits in suburban Høvikodden.

The city's enormous reach becomes truly apparent only to the north of the centre in the **Nordmarka**, a massive forested wilderness that stretches inland, patterned by hiking trails and cross-country ski routes. Two T-bane lines provide ready access, clanking their way up into the rocky hills that herald the region. The more westerly grinds on past **Holmenkollen**, a resort whose ski jump forms a crooked finger on Oslo's skyline, before continuing to the **Frognerseteren** terminus, which is still within the municipal boundaries, though the forested hills and lochs around the station feel anything but urban. This feeling of remoteness is duplicated in neighbouring **Sognsvann**, at the end of the other T-bane line.

Southwest: the Bygdøy peninsula

Other than the centre, the place you're likely to spend most time in Oslo is the **Bygdøy peninsula**, across the bay to the southwest of the city, where five separate museums make up an absorbing cultural and historical display; indeed, it's well worth spending a full day – or, less tiring, two half-days – here. The most enjoyable way to reach Bygdøy is by **ferry**. These leave from pier 3 behind the Rådhus (late April & Sept every 40min 9.05am–5.45pm; May–Aug every 40min 9.05am–9.05pm), departing and returning to a similar schedule. They have two ports of call on the peninsula, stopping first at the Dronningen pier, then at the Bygdøynes pier. The two most popular attractions – the Viking Ships and the Norwegian Folk museums – are within easy walking distance of the Dronningen pier; the other three are a stone's throw from Bygdøynes. If you decide to walk between the two groups, allow about fifteen minutes: the route is well signposted but dull. The alternative to the ferry is **bus** #30 (every 30min), which runs all year from Jernbanetorget and the Nationaltheatret to the Folk and Viking Ships, with some services continuing to the other three museums as well.

The Norwegian Folk Museum

About 700m walk uphill from Dronningen pier, at Museumsveien 10, the **Norsk Folkemuseum** (Norwegian Folk Museum; Jan–April & Oct–Dec Mon–Sat 11am–3pm, Sun 11am–4pm; May & Sept daily 10am–5pm; June–Aug daily 9am–6pm; 50kr) combines indoor collections focused on folk art, furniture, dress and customs with an extensive open-air display of reassembled buildings, mostly wooden barns, stables, storehouses and dwellings from the seventeenth to the nineteenth centuries.

At the entrance, pick up a free map and English-language guide (10kr) and begin by visiting the adjacent Norwegian parliament chamber, a cosy nineteenth-century affair complete with ink-wells and quills at the members' seats. The adjoining complex of buildings holds a rather confusing sequence of exhibitions, though at least the signs are in English as well as Norwegian. Some are eminently missable, but the **folk art** section has a delightful sample of quilted bedspreads and painted furniture as well as an intriguing section devoted to **love gifts**, with fancily carved love spoons and mangle boards given by the boys, mittens and gloves by the girls. In rural Norway, it was considered improper for courting couples to be seen together during the day, but acceptable (or at least tolerated) at night – and parents usually moved girls of marrying age into one of the farm's outhouses to assist the process. Look out also for the temporary exhibitions – the museum has a well-deserved reputation for imaginative displays.

By comparison, the open-air collection can't help but seem a little dull. The reconstructed buildings, of which there are over 150, are arranged geographically to emphasize the sense of variety and development, but unless you're really into the nitty-gritty of rural architecture, many of them look remarkably similar. That said, it's worth tracking down the **stave church**, particularly if you don't plan to travel elsewhere in Norway. Dating to the early thirteenth century but clumsily restored in the 1880s when it moved here from Gol, the church is a fairly good example of its type, with steep, shingle-covered roofs, dragon finials and a cramped, wood-scented nave decorated with robust woodcarvings. Elsewhere, the cluster of buildings from **Setesdal** in southern Norway holds some especially well-preserved dwellings and storehouses from the seventeenth century, whilst the **Numedal** section contains one of the museum's oldest buildings, a late thirteenth-century house whose doorposts carry a Romanesque vine decoration. In summer, many of the buildings are open for viewing and costumed guides roam the site to explain the vagaries of Norwegian rural life.

The Viking Ships Museum

A five-minute walk away, south along the main road, is the **Vikingskipshuset** (Viking Ships Museum; daily April & Oct 11am–4pm; May–Aug 9am–6pm; Sept 11am–5pm; Nov–March 11am–3pm; 30kr), a large hall specially constructed to house a trio of ninth-century Viking ships with viewing platforms to enable you to see inside the hulls. The three oak vessels were retrieved from ritual burial mounds in southern Norway towards the end of the last century, each embalmed in a subsoil of clay that accounts for their excellent state of preservation. The size and magnificence of the Viking burial mound denoted the dead person's rank and wealth, whilst the possessions buried with the body were designed to make the afterlife as comfortable as possible. Implicit was the assumption that a chieftain in this world would be a chieftain in the next (slaves were frequently killed and buried with their master or mistress); a belief that was to give Christianity, with its alternative, less fatalistic vision, an immediate appeal to those at the bottom of the Viking pile. That much is clear, but quite how the Vikings saw the transfer to the afterlife taking place is less certain. The evidence is contradictory: sometimes the Vikings stuck the anchor on board the burial ship in preparation for the spiritual journey, but at other times the vessels were moored to large stones before they were buried. Neither was ship burial the only type of Viking funeral – far from it: the Vikings buried their dead in mounds and on level ground, with and without grave goods, in large and small coffins, both with and without boats – and they practised cremation too.

The museum's star exhibit is the **Oseberg** ship, whose ornately carved prow and stern rise high above the hull where thirty oar-holes indicate the size of the crew. Thought to be the burial ship of a Viking chieftain's wife, much of the treasure buried with the boat was retrieved as well – and this is on display at the back of the museum. There are marvellous decorative items, like the fierce-looking animal-head posts and the exuberantly carved ceremonial sleighs, plus a host of smaller, more mundane pieces – buttons, buckets, scissors, combs, a frying pan, cups and needles and suchlike; taken as a whole the grave-goods reveal an attention to detail and a level of domestic sophistication not usually associated with the Vikings.

While the Oseberg ship is 22m long and 5m wide, the sturdier and stronger **Gokstad** boat is a tad longer and wider, its seaworthiness demonstrated in 1893 when a replica was sailed across the Atlantic to the USA. The Gokstad burial chamber was raided by grave robbers long ago, but a handful of items were unearthed and these are exhibited behind the the the third vessel, the **Tune** ship, only fragments of which survive.

The Kon-Tiki, Fram and Maritime museums

A few metres from the Bygdøynes pier, the **Kon-Tiki Museum** (daily April, May & Sept 10.30am–5pm; Oct–March 10.30am–4pm; June–Aug 9.30am–5.45pm; 25kr) is something special. On display inside is the balsawood raft on which, in 1947, **Thor Heyerdahl** made his now legendary journey across the Pacific from Peru to Polynesia. Heyerdahl wanted to prove the trip could be done: he was convinced that the first

Polynesian settlers had sailed from pre-Inca Peru, and rejected prevailing opinions that South American balsa rafts were unseaworthy. Looking at the flimsy raft *Kon-Tiki,* you could be forgiven for agreeing with Heyerdahl's doubters – and for wondering how the crew didn't murder each other after a week in such a confined space. Heyerdahl's later investigations of Easter Island statues and cave graves gave further weight to his ethnological theory, which has now received a degree of acceptance. The whole saga is outlined here in the museum and if you're especially interested, the story is also told in his book *The Kon-Tiki Expedition.* Preoccupied with transoceanic contact between prehistoric peoples, Heyerdahl went on to attempt several other voyages, sailing across the Atlantic in a papyrus boat, *Ra II,* in 1970 to prove that there could have been contact between Egypt and South America; again, the voyage is recorded in a book – *The Ra Expeditions.*

Just over the road, the mammoth triangular display hall is the **Frammuseet** (Jan, Feb & Dec Sat & Sun 11am–3.45pm; March, April, Oct & Nov Mon–Fri 11am–2.45pm, Sat & Sun 11am–3.45pm; early May & Sept daily 10am–4.45pm; late May to Aug daily 9am–5.45pm; 20kr), protecting the beached polar vessel *Fram* – designed by Colin Archer, a Norwegian shipbuilder of Scots ancestry, and launched in 1893. The ship's design was unique, its sides made smooth to prevent the ice from getting a firm grip on the hull, while inside a veritable maze of beams, braces and stanchions held it all together. A veteran of three expeditions, the vessel's finest hour came in 1911 when it carried Roald Amundsen to within striking distance of the South Pole, a feat he achieved a month before Scott of the Antarctic, who died on his way back. Inside the ship, the living quarters will horrify claustrophobics; yet it was in conditions like these that people reached further north and south than ever before.

Next door, the **Norsk Sjøfartsmuseum** (Norwegian Maritime Museum; Jan to mid-May & Oct–Dec Mon, Wed, Fri & Sat 10.30am–4pm, Tues & Thurs 10.30am–7pm, Sun 10.30am–5pm; mid-May to Sept daily 10am–7pm; 30kr) occupies two buildings, the larger of which is a well-designed brick structure with a fairly pedestrian – and surprisingly lightweight – assortment of maritime artefacts. Amongst the assorted models, the only real highlights are a large chunk of a Bergen passenger boat from 1914, complete with daintily decorated cabins, and the canvas and board *Gibraltar boat,* a perilously fragile, homemade craft on which a bunch of Norwegian sailors fled Morocco for British Gibraltar after their ship had been impounded by the Vichy-French authorities. The museum's second building, the **Båthalle** (boat hall), is rather better, holding a diverting selection of wooden boats from all over Norway – inshore sailing and fishing boats mostly dating from the nineteenth century. Afterwards, the museum's reasonably priced terrace café is a handy vantage point for overlooking the bay.

South: the inner Oslofjord

The compact archipelago of low-lying, lightly forested **islands** in the inner Oslofjord is the city's summer playground, and makes going to the beach an unusually viable option for a northern European capital. Jumping on a ferry, attractive enough in the heat of the day, is also one of the more pleasant forms of entertainment during the evenings and, although most of the islets are cluttered with summer homes, the least populated are favourite party venues for the city's preening youth. **Ferries** to the islands (18kr each way, Oslo Card valid) leave from the Vippetangen quay, beside the grain silo at the foot of Akershusstranda – a twenty-minute walk or a five-minute ride on bus #29 south from Jernbanetorget.

Conveniently, **Hovedøya** (ferry #92; mid-March to Sept hourly or every 90min 7.30am–9pm; Oct to mid-March 3 daily; 10min), the nearest island, is also the most interesting, its rolling hills incorporating both farmland and deciduous woods as well as the overgrown ruins of a twelfth-century Cistercian monastery and incidental remains from the days when the island was garrisoned and armed to protect Oslo's harbour. There's a map of the island at the jetty, though on an islet of this size – it's just ten minutes' walk from one end to the other – getting lost is pretty much impossible. There are plenty of footpaths to wander, you can swim from the shingle beaches on the south shore, and there's a seasonal café opposite the monastery ruins. Camping is, however, not permitted as Hovedøya is a protected area – that's why there are no summer homes.

The pick of the other islands is wooded **Langøyene** (ferry #94; June–Aug hourly 10am–6pm; last boat back 7pm; 30min), the most southerly of the archipelago and the one with the best beaches. The H-shaped island has a **campsite**, *Langøyene Camping* (late May to mid-Aug; ☎22 11 53 21), and at night the ferries are full of people armed with sleeping bags and bottles, on their way to join swimming parties.

Northeast: the Munch Museum

Nearly everyone who visits Oslo makes time for the **Munch-museet** and, if you possibly can, it's worth setting aside a half-day for the experience. In his will, Munch donated all the works in his possession to Oslo city council – a mighty bequest of several thousand paintings, prints, drawings, engravings and photographs, which took nearly twenty years to catalogue and organize for display in this purpose-built gallery.

The **museum** is located to the east of the city centre at Tøyengata 53 (June to early Sept daily 10am–6pm; mid-Sept to May Tues, Wed, Fri & Sat 10am–4pm, Thurs & Sun 10am–6pm; 40kr) and is reachable by T-bane – get off at Tøyen and it's a signposted five-minute walk.

Some background

Born in 1863, **Edvard Munch** had a melancholy Christiania childhood, overshadowed by the early deaths of both his mother and a sister from tuberculosis. After some early works, including several self-portraits, he went on to study in Paris – a city he returned to again and again, and where he fell (fleetingly) under the sway of the Impressionists. In 1892 he went to Berlin, where his style developed and he produced some of his best and most famous work, though his first exhibition here was considered so outrageous it was closed after only a week: his painting was, a critic wrote, "an insult to art". Despite the initial criticism, Munch's work was subsequently exhibited in many of the leading galleries of the day, but meanwhile overwork, drink and problematic love affairs were fuelling an instability that culminated in a nervous breakdown in 1908. Munch spent six months in a Copenhagen clinic, after which his health was much improved – and his paintings lost the self-destructive edge characteristic of his earlier work. Generally considered the initiator of the Expressionist movement, for much of the rest of his life Munch wandered Europe, prolifically producing and exhibiting. However, it wasn't until well into his career that he was fully accepted in his own country, where he was based from 1909 until his death in 1944.

The museum

The collection is huge, and only a small part of it can be shown at any one time – an advantage, since you don't feel overwhelmed by what's on display. Also, visiting exhibitions usually limit the Munch paintings to one large gallery, which can appear cluttered, but at least you can reckon on seeing many of the more highly regarded works. There's a basement display on Munch's life and times as well, a methodical trawl providing masses of background information.

In the main gallery, the **early paintings** are typically Munch: deeply and personally pessimistic – *The Sick Child*, one of the first of a series of studies on the same theme, a good example. Even more riveting are the great works of the **1890s**, which form the core of the collection and are considered among Munch's finest achievements. Among many, there's *Dagny Juel*, a portrait of the Berlin socialite Ducha Przybyszewska, with whom both Munch and Strindberg were infatuated; the searing representations of *Despair* and *Anxiety*; the chilling *Virginia Creeper*, a house being consumed by the plant; and, of course, *The Scream* – of which the museum holds several from a total of fifty versions. Consider Munch's words as you view it:

> *I was walking along a road with two friends. The sun set. I felt a tinge of melancholy. Suddenly the sky became blood red. I stopped and leaned against a railing feeling exhausted, and I looked at the flaming clouds that hung like blood and a sword over the blue-black fjord and the city. My friends walked on. I stood there trembling with fright. And I felt a loud unending scream piercing nature.*

Munch's style was never static, however. After recovery from his breakdown and partial withdrawal to the seclusion of the Oslofjord, **later paintings** reflect a renewed interest in nature and physical labour, as in the 1913 *Workers Returning Home*. His technique changed in these later paintings, using streaks of colour to represent points of light, as in the *Death of Marat II*, painted in 1907. Later still, his paintings absorb entirely the landscape, himself and people around him. The light *Village Street, Kragerø* and *Model by the Wicker Chair*, with skin tones of pink, green and blue, reveal at last a happier, if rather idealized, attitude to his surroundings, most evident in works like *Spring Ploughing*, painted in 1919.

The exhibition is punctuated by **self-portraits**, a graphic illustration of Munch's state of mind at various points in his career. There's a palpable sadness in his *Self-portrait with Wine Bottle* of 1906, along with obvious allusions to his heavy drinking, while the telling *In Distress* (1919) indicates that he remained a tormented, troubled man even in his later years. One of his last works, *Self-portrait by the Window* (1940), shows a glum figure on the borderline of life and death, the strong red of his face and green of his clothing contrasted with the ice-white scene visible through the window.

Munch's **lithographs and woodcuts** are shown in a separate section of the gallery: a dark catalogue of swirls and fogs, technically brilliant pieces of work and much more than simple copies of his paintings – indeed, they're often developments of them. In these he pioneered a new medium of expression, experimenting with colour schemes and a huge variety of materials, which enhance the works' rawness: wood blocks show a heavy, distinct grain, while there are colours like rust and blue drawn from the Norwegian landscape. As well as the stark woodcuts on display, there are also sensuous, hand-coloured lithographs, many focusing on the theme of love (in the form of a woman) bringing death.

Northwest: Frogner Park – the Vigeland Sculpture Park and Museum

On the northwest side of the city and reachable on tram #12 from the centre (get off at *Vigelandsparken*), the green expanse of **Frognerparken** (Frogner Park) incorporates one of Oslo's most celebrated and popular cultural targets – the Vigelandsparken, an open-air sculpture park which, along with the Vigeland Museum, commemorates a modern Norwegian sculptor of world renown, **Gustav Vigeland** (1869–1943). Between them, they display a colossal sum of his work, presented to the city in return for favours received in the shape of a studio and apartment, where he lived from 1921 to 1930.

Vigeland began his career as a wood-carver but later, heavily influenced by Rodin, turned to stone and bronze as media. He started work on the **sculpture park** (always open; free) in 1924, and was still working on it when he died in 1943. It's a literally fantastic work, medieval in spirit and complexity. Here he had the chance to let his imagination run riot and, when unveiled, the place wasn't without its critics. From the monumental wrought-iron gates, the central path takes you into a world of frowning, fighting and posing bronze figures, which flank the footbridge over the river. Beyond, the **central fountain**, part of a separate commission begun in 1907, is an enormous bowl representing the burden of life, supported by straining, sinewy bronze Goliaths while, underneath, water tumbles out around clusters of playing and standing figures.

But it's the twenty-metre-high **obelisk** up on the stepped embankment, and the granite sculptures grouped around it, which caused much of the controversy when first erected. It's a humanistic work, a writhing mass of sculpture that depicts the cycle of life as Vigeland saw it: a vision of humanity teaching, playing, fighting, loving, eating and sleeping – and clambering on and over each other to reach the top. The granite children scattered around the steps are perfect: little pot-bellied figures who tumble over muscled adults, and provide an ideal counterpoint to the real Oslo toddlers who splash around oblivious in the fountain.

A five-minute walk from the obelisk, near the river in the southern corner of the park, the **Vigeland-museet** (May–Sept Tues–Sat 10am–6pm, Sun noon–7pm; Oct–April Tues–Sat noon–4pm, Sun noon–6pm; 20kr), on Nobels gate, was the artist's studio during the 1920s. It's still stuffed with all sorts of items related to the sculpture park, including photographs of the workforce, discarded or unused sculptures, woodcuts, preparatory drawings and scores of plaster casts, with the bigger pieces concentrated on the ground floor, the smaller ones up above. Here and there are scraps of biographical information, but Vigeland's last decades were defined by his work: you get the feeling that given half a chance he would have had himself cast and exhibited – as it is, his ashes are stored in the museum's tower.

West: the Henie-Onstad Art Centre

Overlooking the Oslofjord just beyond the city boundary in Høvikodden, the **Henie-Onstad Art Centre** (Mon 11am–5pm, Tues–Fri 9am–9pm, Sat & Sun 11am–5pm & till 7pm June–Aug; usually 50kr but varies with exhibitions; half-price with Oslo Card; ☎67 54 30 50) is one of Norway's most prestigious modern art centres. There's no false modesty here – it's all about art as an artefact of wealth – and the low-slung, modernistic building is a glossy affair on a pretty wooded headland landscaped to accommodate a smattering of sculptures by the likes of Henry Moore and Arnold Haukeland. The centre was founded by the ice skater-cum-movie star Sonja Henie (1910–69) and her shipowner-art collector husband Niels Onstad in the 1960s. Henie won three Olympic gold medals (1928, 1932 and 1936) and went on to appear in a string of lightweight Hollywood musicals. Her accumulated cups and medals are displayed in the centre's basement – prompting a critic to remark "Sonja, you'll never go broke. All you have to do is hock your trophies". Here also are the autographed photos of many of the leading celebrities of the day – though the good wishes of a youthful-looking Richard Milhous Nixon hardly inspire empathy.

The wealthy couple accumulated an extensive collection of twentieth-century painting and sculpture. Matisse, Miró and Picasso, postwar French abstract painters, Expressionists and modern Norwegians all figure highly, but these now fight for gallery space with temporary exhibitions by contemporary artists. It is, therefore, impossible to predict what will be on display at any one time – though you can, of course, telephone ahead to check it out, an especially good idea as the centre also hosts regular concert and theatre performances.

Getting there is straightforward. By car, the centre is close to – and signposted from – the E18, just 12km west of Oslo, beyond the Fornebu airport exit on the way to Drammen. Departing Oslo S – and in most cases from Wessesls plass and the

Nationaltheatret too – buses #151, #153, #161, #162, #251, #252 and #261 all stop on the main road about ten minutes' walk from the centre; make sure to ask the driver to let you off, or you'll find yourself whizzing along the coast to Sandvika.

North: the Nordmarka

Crisscrossed by hiking trails and cross-country ski routes, the forested hills and lochs of the **Nordmarka** occupy a tract of land that extends deep inland from downtown Oslo, but is still within the city limits for some 30km. A network of byroads provides dozens of access points to this wilderness, which is extremely popular with the outdoor-minded citizens of Oslo. *Den Norske Turistforening* (DNT), the Norwegian hiking organization, maintains a handful of staffed and unstaffed huts here, so if you're keen to spend more than a day in the area, head first for DNT's Oslo branch, in the city centre at Stortingsgata 28 (Mon–Fri 8.30am–4pm, Thurs until 6pm; ☎22 83 25 50). They have detailed maps and will arrange a year's DNT membership for around 300kr – a prerequisite if you want to use one of the huts (see p.167 for more on DNT and hiking in general).

For a day trip, one of the easiest and most obvious departure points is **Frognerseteren**, the station at the end of T-bane line #1 just thirty minutes' ride north of the city centre. From the station, there's a choice of signposted trails across the surrounding countryside including the easy one-kilometre stroll to the **Tryvannstårnet** TV Tower (May & Sept daily 10am–5pm; June daily 10am–7pm; July daily 9am–10pm; Aug daily 9am–8pm; Oct–April Mon–Fri 10am–3pm, Sat & Sun 11am–4pm; 30kr), where a lift whisks you up to an observation gallery providing panoramic views on a clear day: even a light mist makes this a pointless excursion. Alternatively, it's just a couple of hundred metres from the Frognerseteren station to the *Frognerseteren Restaurant* (☎22 14 08 90), a splendid wooden lodge offering good food and hillside views. A further twenty-minute tramp downhill from here, either along the road or the adjacent footpath, will bring you to the flashy chalets and hotels of the **Holmenkollen** ski resort, a scene that's dominated by the international **ski jump** (Jan–April & Oct–Dec Mon–Fri 10am–4pm, Sat & Sun 11am–4pm; May & Sept daily 10am–5pm; June daily 10am–8pm; July & Aug daily 9am–10pm; 50kr), an intimidating structure that you can climb for a peek straight down at what is, for most people, a horrifyingly steep descent.

If you're returning to central Oslo, Holmenkollen T-bane station (on line #1) is on the southern edge of the resort, about 1km from the ski jump. To reach it, walk down the main road and watch for the signs just after the *Holmenkollen* restaurant.

Eating

As befits a capital city, Oslo boasts scores of eating places, the sheer variety ensuring there's something to suit almost every budget. Those carefully counting the kroner will find it fairly easy to buy bread, fruit, snacks and sandwiches from stalls, shops and kiosks across the city centre, while fast-food joints offering hamburgers and *pølser* (hot dogs) are legion. Far more interesting are the city's **cafés**. These run the gamut from homely family places to student haunts and ultra-fashionable hang-outs, but nearly all of them serve inexpensive lunches and sometimes bargain evening meals too. Regular **restaurants** are more expensive and frequently rather staid, but even here it's possible to find some excellent deals, especially if you stick to pizzas and pastas in one of the growing band of Italian places. If you've promised yourself a big night out, then you could try one of Oslo's splendid Norwegian restaurants, the most distinctive of which specialize in seafood.

Markets, supermarkets and takeaway snacks

Markets are always good for fruit and vegetables: there are a couple of handy stalls in the Basarhallene beside Karl Johans gate and a small market occupies part of Jernbanetorget, but the main event is on Youngstorget (Mon–Sat 7am–2pm), a brief stroll north of the Domkirke along Torggata. For determined self-caterers, **supermarkets** are thick on the ground. The biggest name is *Rimi*, which has stores dotted across Oslo – central branches are at Rosenkrantz gate 20 and Akersgata 16 (Mon–Fri 9am–5pm, Thurs till 7pm, Sat 9am–2pm).

Takeaway snacks – burgers, *pølser*, pizza slices, kebabs, felafel, chips, etc – are on sale from kiosks and stalls on virtually every street corner. Burger joints, too, have multiplied in the last few years, with *Burger King* now claiming three central branches – at Jernbanetorget 1, Karl Johans gate 8 and Grensen 13. For healthier snacks, numerous bakeries and cake shops sell a reasonable range of sandwiches. The best is *Helios*, Universitetsgata 18 (Mon–Fri 9am–5pm, Sat 9am–3pm), a downtown health and wholefood shop selling sandwiches, pies, quiches and organic breads.

Cafés

For sit-down food, **cafés** represent the best value in town, whether they're traditional *kafeterias* (sometimes self-service), offering solid portions of Norwegian food, or more European-style **café-bars** dishing up salads, pasta and the like in attractive surroundings. Though usually most economical at **lunchtime** (when there's sometimes a dish of the day, the *dagens rett*), the bulk of the places listed below also serve food in the evening until round about 8 or 9pm. Monday is the most common closing day. It's worth noting that quite a few of the establishments detailed below could equally be slotted into our "Drinking" section – the distinction between Oslo's cafés and bars is often very blurred.

Amsterdam, Universitetsgata 11. Done out in the style of a Dutch brown bar, this busy and agreeable café-bar serves up a mixture of Norwegian standbys – meatballs and fishballs – as well as more international dishes, all at moderate prices. Kitchen closes around 8pm. Mon–Sat 11.30am–2.30am, Sun 1pm–midnight.

Bacchus, in the Basarhallene behind the Domkirke. Cosy and cramped café-bar with period decor and a wrought-iron staircase. Attracts a wide-ranging clientele from day-tripping tourists through to art students and the city's eccentrics. Classical music during the day, all sorts at night when the seediness of the surrounding area is more noticeable. Great cakes and pastries plus tasty sandwiches. Mon–Sat 11am–midnight, Sun noon–11pm.

Cappuccino, beside the Basarhallene behind the Domkirke. Outdoor café in one of downtown Oslo's more secluded spots. Pleasant in the daytime, at night the immediate area is rather unsavoury. Serves up inexpensive snacks and light meals. Mon–Sat 11am–11pm, Sun 12.30–11pm.

Celsius, Rådhusgata 19 at Øvre Slotts gate. Hidden through an unlikely looking eighteenth-century gateway, this laid-back café-bar occupies one of Oslo's older buildings and offers delicious Mediterranean-inspired food at around 80kr a dish. It's also a great place for a drink, with plenty of seating and an open courtyard in the summer, log fires in the winter. Tues–Sat 11.30am–1am, Sun 1–10pm.

Ett Glass, Karl Johans gate 33, entrance round the corner near the bottom of Rosenkrantz gate. Trendy, candle-lit café-bar awash with platform shoes and dyed hair. An imaginative menu focusing on light meals and lunches provides some curious delights, though it's a little overpriced. Mon, Tues & Sun noon–1am, Wed–Sat noon–3am, kitchen open till about 9pm.

Falsen, Kongens gate 4. Low-key, functional café favoured by university students. Good Mediterranean-style food with spaghettis at 60kr, moussaka at 65kr. Tues–Fri 11am–5pm, Sat noon–7pm.

Halvorsen's Conditori, Prinsens gate 26. Long-established, traditional café-cum-tea shop across from the Stortinget. Blue rinses abound, but the cakes and pastries are arguably the best in town – at 25–35kr a slice. Mon–Fri 7am–5pm, Sat 9.30am–4pm.

Kaffistova, Rosenkrantz gate 8. Part of the *Hotell Bondeheimen*, this spick and span self-service café serves tasty, traditional Norwegian cooking at very fair prices. There's usually a vegetarian option, too. Mon–Fri 10am–8pm, Sat & Sun 10.30am–5pm.

Kunstnernes Hus, Wergelandsveien 17. The solid-looking art gallery facing the Slottsparken from near the foot of Linstows gate now holds a fashionable café-bar with a good line in lunches and snacks, all reasonably priced. Mon–Thurs 11am–1am, Fri & Sat 11am–3am.

Paleet, Karl Johans gate 37–43. In the basement of this modern shopping mall, fronted by an old facade, is a "Food Street" of a dozen good-value places. What's on offer is superior fast food – order at any of the counters before finding a seat. Two stalls to look out for are *Da Bruno*, with its Italian pastas and pizzas, and *Hellas*, a Greek counter selling dishes for 60kr. Mall open Mon–Fri 10am–8pm, Sat 10am–5pm.

Rorbua, Stranden 71. Near the south end of the Aker Brygge, this cheery café-bar is decked out in all things nautical with poles and nets hanging on the ceiling and thick ropes round the "masts". It's hopelessly over the top, but good fun nonetheless and the seafood is excellent, substantial platefuls costing about 80kr. Daily noon–1am.

Restaurants

Dining out at one of Oslo's **restaurants** can make a sizeable dint in most wallets unless you exercise some restraint. In all but the most expensive of places, a main course will set you back between 150kr and 200kr – not too steep until you add on a couple of beers (at 40kr a throw) or a bottle of wine, which will rush you at least 160kr. On a more positive note, a lousy restaurant meal is unusual as standards are high, though admittedly Norwegian cuisine can lack finesse.

Arcimboldo, Wergelandsveien 17. Fashionable but unpretentious restaurant located inside the Kunstnernes Hus, the old art gallery facing onto the Slottsparken from near the foot of Linstows gate. An imaginative menu featuring both Mediterranean and Norwegian dishes; main courses in the region of 140kr. Mon–Thurs 11am–1am, Fri & Sat 11am–3am.

Engebret Café, Bankplassen 1 (☎22 33 66 94). This smart and intimate restaurant occupies an attractive old building across from the Museum of Contemporary Art. It specializes in Norwegian delicacies such as reindeer and fish, with mouth-watering main courses in the region of 170kr. In summer, there's outdoor seating on the pretty cobbled square in front of the restaurant. Mon–Fri 11am–11pm, Sat noon–11pm. Reservations advised.

Fjordflower, Stranden 30, Aker Brygge (☎22 83 68 97). Boasts one of the widest selections of seafood in the city, with shellfish a particular speciality. Expensive. Mon–Sat 4pm–midnight.

Grand Café, Karl Johans gate 31 (☎22 42 93 90). Eat in style in the café-restaurant where Ibsen once held court – still one of Oslo's most elegant spots. There's a set lunch as well as a full and eclectic menu from which to choose, and while it's not inexpensive, the old-fashioned formality of the place – chandeliers, bow-tied waiters and glistening cutlery – is appealing.

L'Opera, Rosenkrantz gate 13. Smart Italian trattoria with red-checked tablecloths and a menu that covers all the basics – pizza and pasta for around 70kr, meat and fish dishes around twice that. The four-course lunch at 170kr is a good deal. Mon–Fri 4pm–midnight, Sat 2pm–midnight, Sun 2–11pm.

Spaghetteria Santino's, Tordenskiolds gate 8–10. Swish Italian restaurant on a side street off Stortingsgata. Attracts a smart clientele for its first-class pizza and pasta dishes from around 70kr. Mon–Sat 11am–midnight, Sun 2–11pm.

Theatercaféen, in the *Hotel Continental*, Stortingsgata 24–26. Eat in splendid Art Nouveau surroundings and watch the city's movers and shakers doing their thing. A classy, pricey menu of mixed provenance. Mon–Sat 11am–11pm, Sun 11am–10pm.

Vegeta Vertshus, Munkedamsveien 3b, at the junction with Stortingsgata. Near the Nationaltheatret, this unassuming vegetarian restaurant has a help-yourself buffet with fine salads, mixed vegetables, pizza, potatoes and rice. Small platefuls go for around 70kr, while the all-you-can-eat 110kr buffet includes dessert, a drink and coffee; no alcohol is served. Daily 11am–11pm.

Drinking

Downtown Oslo has a vibrant **bar scene**, a noisy, boisterous but generally good-tempered affair, at its most frenetic on summer weekends, when the city is crowded with visitors from all over Norway. The busiest and often flashiest bars are concentrated in the side streets near the Rådhus and down along the Aker Brygge, while other popular but less assertively heterosexual bars are clustered around Universitetsgata and on Rosenkrantz gate. Karl Johans gate weighs in with a string of bars too, some of which are staid and stodgy, others – especially those near Oslo S – a fair bit wilder and less conventional.

Many of Oslo's bars stay open until well after midnight, until 3–4am in some cases, and a number serve snacks and meals as well as drinks, making the distinction between the city's cafés and bars somewhat arbitrary – see under "Eating" for details of café-bars. Remember also that drinks are uniformily expensive, and so, if you're after a big night out, it's a good idea to follow Norwegian custom and start with a few warm-up drinks at home.

Bars and pubs

Barbeint, Drammensveien 20 (close to Parkveien). If you're familiar with Scandinavian bands and cult films then you may recognize a few faces in this jam-packed, fashionable bar. Loud sounds, everything from rap to rock. About ten minutes' walk west of the Nationaltheatret. Daily 8pm–3.30am.

Beer Palace, Holmensgata 3, Aker Brygge. Cramped and crowded bar with old brick walls and a beamed ceiling. Serves over fifty different brands of beer. Daily noon–3.30am.

Børsen – Café Stock Exchange, Nedre Voll gate 19. Occupying part of the old Freemasons' headquarters across from the Stortinget, this combined café, club and restaurant has a cavernous bar (with internet terminals) that's extremely popular at the weekend. Avoid the food. Mon & Tues 4pm–12.30am, Wed & Thurs 4pm–2.30am, Fri & Sat 4pm–4am.

Cruise Café, Stranden 3, Aker Brygge. Standard-issue modern bar done out in shades of brown and cream, with photographs of actors hung on the walls. It's all rather contrived, but the rock – and rock'n'roll – background music is excellent, and there are occasional live, often American, acts here too. Mon, Tues & Sun noon–12.30am, Wed & Thurs noon–2am, Fri & Sat 1pm–2.30am.

The Dubliner Folk Pub, Rådhusgata 28 at Nedre Slotts gate. Stuffed with Irish paraphernalia – from Gaelic road signs to church benches – this medium-sized bar is somewhat self-conscious, but it does offer a mean pint of Guinness and there's often live Irish folk music, Wednesday through Saturday. Open Mon & Tues 11am–1am, Wed–Sat 11am–3am, Sun noon–1am. If you're into Irish bars, the other one to try is **The Seanachie**, a couple of blocks away at Prinsens gate 18 and Kongens gate. It's on the same lines – folksy bygones and regular live folk music (Mon–Sat 11am–2.30am, Sun 2pm–midnight).

Lipp, Olavs gate 2. Part of the *Hotel Continental*, this big and brash bar, all wide windows and wood, is popular with the well-heeled of Oslo – the preening is fun to watch. Mon & Sun 3pm–1.30am, Tues–Sat 3pm–2.30am.

Lorry, Parkveien 12 at the corner of Hegdehaugsveien. A boisterous pub with a piano, frequented mostly by drunk artists and would-be artists and students. There's a wide choice of beers (81 at the last count) and outdoor seating in the summer. A ten-minute walk west of the Nationaltheatret. Daily 9am–2.30am.

Nichol & Son, Olav V's gate 1. Crowded, pint-sized bar whose walls are covered with pictures of Jack Nicholson. They do a good line in daytime snacks and sandwiches. Mon–Wed & Sun 10am–1.30am, Thurs–Sat 10am–3.30am. In the basement below is **Zipper** (Mon–Thurs & Sun 6pm–1.30am, Fri & Sat 5pm–3.30am), an American-style bar with pool table and leather seats.

Palace Grill, Solligata 2. A small American-style bar with Irish beers on draught. Roots, rock and jazz background music, plus occasional live acts. Popular with everyone from yuppies to students. A twenty-minute walk west of the Nationaltheatret: follow Drammensveien, turn left down Cort Adelers gate and it's the first on the right. Mon–Thurs & Sun 3pm–2am, Fri & Sat 3pm–3am.

Savoy Bar, Universitetsgata 11. With its stained-glass windows and wood-panelled walls, this small, intimate bar is an agreeable spot to nurse a beer. Part of the *Savoy Hotel* on the corner of Kristians IV's gate. Daily 5pm–2am.

The Scotsman, Karl Johans gate 17 at Nedre Slotts gate. Many visitors to Oslo seek this bar out – though no one is quite sure why. It's an eccentric kind of place, full of incongruities: the *Angus Steakhouse* restaurant in the basement serves Scottish pizzas and the regular live music acts can be unbelievably bad and/or bizarre, but the place is still packed every night. Outdoor seating on the main drag in summer. Mon–Sat 11am–2.30am, Sun noon–2.30am.

Stravinsky, Rosenkrantz gate 17. Extremely popular bar frequented by twentysomethings, a couple of minutes' walk east of the Rådhus. Mon–Thurs & Sun 8pm–1.30am, Fri & Sat 8pm–2.30am.

Entertainment and nightlife

For all **entertainment listings** it's always worth checking *Natt & Dag*, a monthly Norwegian-language broadsheet available free from cafés, bars and shops. The main alternative is to consult the English-language *What's On in Oslo*, a monthly freebie produced by the tourist office, which contains a day-by-day account of all that is cultural and entertaining, free or otherwise. Summer is the best time to be in Oslo for events of almost every description, although a student presence does keep things active right throughout the year.

Nightclubs

Oslo's liveliest and trendiest **nightclubs** are bang in the middle of town on and around Karl Johans gate. Entry will set you back in the region of 80kr – though, surprisingly, drinks prices are the same as anywhere else. Nothing gets going much before 11pm; closing times are generally around 3–4am.

Barock, Universitetsgata 26. Kitted out in a sort of modern Baroque, with chandeliers, tall mirrors and frescoes, this smart bar-restaurant is attached to one of the more popular dance floors in town, brimming with well-heeled thirtysomethings. Disco begins at 11pm Tues–Sun.

Enka, Karl Johans gate 10. Opposite the Domkirke, an anonymous-looking door leads into what is easily the largest and most popular gay club in Oslo. Spread over several floors, there's a restaurant and a bar, as well as a couple of dance floors. Restaurant and bar open daily from 3pm; disco starts at 10pm Wed–Sun.

Head On, Rosenkrantz gate 11B. A student favourite with the emphasis on funk and rap. Daily 10pm–3.30am.

Kristiania Club, Kristian IV's gate 12. Big, busy but fairly staid nightclub spread over three floors: live salsa and jazz, plus a café and a dance floor. Wed–Sat 8pm–4am.

Snorre, Rosenkrantz gate 11. Extremely popular club incorporating a bar, a restaurant and a large dance floor. Smart, youthful scene – the bouncers impose a dress code aimed against jogging suits and trainers. Student night Thurs. Wed–Sat 9am–3.30am.

Live music: rock, jazz and classical

Tracking down **live music** is straightforward enough, though the domestic rock scene is hardly inspiring – the talent is spread very thin indeed. Otherwise, jazz fans are well served, with several first-rate nightspots dotted round the city centre, whilst classical music enthusiasts can benefit from an ambitious concert programme. For **tickets**, contact the venues direct.

Rock venues

More and more rock bands are including Oslo in their tours, a necessary leavening to what would otherwise be a pretty dull scene. The following venues host regular gigs – at least once a week.

Blue Monk, St Olavs gate 23 (✆22 20 22 90). Crowded, smoky nightspot noted for its live blues, Latin and jazz bands. In the basement is **Sub Pub**, featuring punk, ska and rock music. Daily midnight–3am.

Cruise Café, Stranden 3, Aker Brygge (☎22 83 64 30). This small modern bar showcases live rock, rock'n'roll and blues bands, many from America. Mon, Tues & Sun noon–12.30am, Wed & Thurs noon–2am, Fri & Sat 1pm–2.30am.

Rebekka West, Kristian IV's gate 7 (☎22 41 51 08). Busy and big nightclub with a disco dance floor as well as frequent live acts – anything from punk to Country with contemporary jazz a speciality. Daily 9pm–3.30am.

Rockerfeller Music Hall, Torggata 16 (☎22 20 32 32). Able to accommodate 1500 customers, this is one of Oslo's grandest nightspots – it's even got its own Rock Cinema. Hosts well-known and up-and-coming rock groups with a good sideline in reggae and salsa bands. Torggata runs north from Stortorvet near the east end of Karl Johans gate. Opening times vary according to the gig schedule.

Sentrum Scene, Arbeidersamfunnets plass 2 (☎22 20 60 40). Major venue showcasing big international acts – as well as small-fry local bands. See press for details. Opening times vary with the shows.

Smuget, Rosenkrantz gate 22 (☎22 42 52 02). Large and popular nightclub with bars, a restaurant, a disco and regular live shows by mostly home-grown jazz, rock or blues bands. Daily 8pm–4.30am.

Jazz venues

The Oslo International **Jazz Festival** is held every August, with street parades and concerts at venues throughout the city – details from the tourist office. In October the comparable **Ultima Contemporary Music Festival** gathers together Scandinavian and international talent: ticket and programme information from either the tourist ofice or *Ultima* on ☎22 42 91 20. At other times of the year, try one of the following for regular jazz acts.

Herr Nilsen, C. J. Hambros plass 5 (☎22 33 54 05). Small and intimate bar whose brick walls are decorated with jazz memorabilia. Live jazz – often traditional and bebop – most nights. Air-conditioned. Daily 10am–2.30am.

Original Nilsen, Rosenkrantz gate 11. Popular bar featuring regular live jazz in the evening, with Dixieland a speciality. Daily noon–3.30am.

Rebekka West, Kristian IV's gate 7 (☎22 41 51 08). This large nightclub frequently showcases jazz artists. Daily 9pm–3.30am.

Stortorvets Gjestgiveri, Grensen 1, junction with Grubbegata (☎22 42 88 63). Near the Domkirke, this rabbit warren of a place incorporates a café-bar where there's traditional jazz – particularly Dixieland – every Thurs and Fri night, plus Sat in the early evening.

Classical music and opera

The main venues for **classical music** are the attractively refurbished **Gamle Logen**, the city's old Assembly Rooms at Grev Wedels plass 2 (☎22 33 54 70), and Oslo's **Konserthuset**, Munkedamsveien 14 (Concert Hall; ☎22 83 32 00; box office Mon–Fri noon–8pm, Sat 10am–1pm, ☎22 83 45 10), which is the home of the Oslo Philharmonic Orchestra. The main concert season runs from September to May. In the summertime, **free classical concerts** are given in the courtyard of the Vigeland Museum. Watch out also for good classical programmes at a variety of other venues, including Oslo Domkirke, Akershus Slott, the Munch Museum and the University Aula.

Den Norske Opera is based at Storgata 23 (☎22 42 94 75), and the season runs from September to June. The Oslo Card will get you a 25kr discount on tickets.

Cinema and theatre

Given the popularity of American and English films, **cinemas** are a good source of entertainment for visitors since almost all films are shown in their original language with Norwegian subtitles. They're also surprisingly cheap to get into: tickets average around 50kr and there are reductions of around 20 percent for some matinee and early-evening showings. Also, from May to July, Oslo Card-holders can see any film in any cinema for just 40kr. The main central screens are *Saga*, Stortingsgata 28 at Olav V's gate (☎22 83 42 75); *Klingenberg*, close to the Rådhus at Olav V's gate 4 (☎22 42 59 42); *Sentrum*, Arbeidersamfunnets plass 1 (☎81 54 80 00); and *Eldorado*, Torggata 9 (☎22 42 54 10). Cinema listings – including details of late-night screenings – appear daily in the local press and the tourist office has programme times too.

Nearly all **theatre** productions are in Norwegian, making them of limited interest to tourists. There's a full list of theatres, mainstream and fringe, in the *Oslo Guide*. One of the more interesting venues is **Det Åpne Teater**, Tøyenbekken 34 (☎22 17 39 95), a workshop theatre near Grønland T-bane station, where new plays are performed each week. The **Nationaltheatret**, Stortingsgata 15 (☎22 41 27 10), stages an annual Ibsen Festival, which features productions of Ibsen plays by various international companies – one time you might get to see something in English.

Listings

Airlines *Air France*, Haakon VII's gate 9 (☎22 83 56 30); *Braathens SAFE*, Haakon VII's gate 2 (☎67 59 70 00); *British Airways*, Karl Johans gate 16b (☎22 82 20 00); *Finnair*, Fornebu airport (☎67 53 38 90); *KLM*, Fornebu airport (☎67 58 38 00); *Lufthansa*, Haakon VII's gate 6 (☎22 83 65 70); *SAS*, at *Radisson SAS Scandinavia Hotel*, Holbergs gate 30, and at Fornebu airport (both ☎81 00 33 00).

American Express Travel Service Office, Karl Johans gate 33 (Mon–Fri 9am–6pm, Sat 10am–3pm; ☎22 98 37 20; 24-hr hotline ☎80 01 10 00).

Banks and exchange Banks are open Mon–Fri 8.15am–3.30pm (mid-May to mid-Sept 8.15am–3pm, Thurs till 5pm). Amongst many, *Den Norsk Bank* has downtown branches at Stranden 1, Aker Brygge, and Karl Johans gate 2; *Sparebanken* at Karl Johans gate 3, Storgata 19 and Kirkegata 18. Outside of normal banking hours, the best bet is the exchange office at Oslo S (June–Sept daily 7am–11pm; Oct–May Mon–Fri 8am–7.30pm & Sat 10am–5pm). There are exchange facilities at the two airports: Fornebu (June–Sept Mon–Fri 6.30am–8pm, Sat 7am–5pm, Sun 7am–8pm; Oct–May Mon–Fri 8am–8pm, Sat 8.30am–6pm, Sun 11am–6pm) and Gardermoen (Mon–Fri 6am–9pm, Sat 7am–7pm, Sun 7am–10pm); you can also change money and travellers cheques at the Ekeberg and Bogstad campsites and at larger post offices, where the rates are especially competitive. There are 24-hr ATMs at Oslo S and both airports.

Bookshops There's a wide selection of English-language books and travel guides plus a good sample of Norwegian hiking maps at *Aker Libris*, Fjordalleèn 10, in the Aker Brygge complex. *Tronsmo*, Kristian Augusts gate 19, has long been the city's best-stocked leftist bookshop and many of its titles are in English. *Norlis Antikvariat*, opposite the National Gallery at Universitetsgata 18, sells second-hand and a few new English-language books, as does *J. W. Cappelens Antikvariat*, Universitetsgata 20, which is particularly good on Arctic explorers and their tales. The shop of the Norwegian hiking organization, *Den Norske Turistforening* (DNT), Stortingsgata 28 at Olav V's gate, has a comprehensive collection of Norwegian hiking maps. The Norwegian Cyclists Association, *Syklistenes Landsforening*, Storgata 23 (☎22 41 50 80), has specialist cycling books and maps.

British Council Office and reference library at Fridtjof Nansens Plass 5 (☎22 42 68 48).

Car breakdown For pick-up services, call *Falken Redningskorps* (☎22 95 00 00); *NAF Alarm* (24-hr service; ☎22 34 16 00); or *Viking Redningstjeneste* (24-hr service; ☎22 08 60 00).

Car rental *Avis*, Munkedamsveien 27 (☎22 83 58 00), and at Fornebu airport (☎66 77 10 70); *Bislet Bilutleie*, Pilestredet 70 (☎22 60 00 00); *Budget*, Sonja Henie plass 4 (☎22 17 10 50), and at Fornebu airport (☎67 53 79 24*)*; *Europcar*, Fornebu airport (☎67 53 23 40); *Hertz*, c/o *Radisson SAS Scandinavia Hotel*, Holbergs gate 30 (☎22 20 01 21), and at Fornebu airport (☎67 58 31 00). There are many others – see under "Bilutleie" in the yellow pages.

Credit cards To report lost credit cards, call: *American Express* ☎80 03 32 44; *Diners Club* ☎22 83 06 91; *Mastercard* ☎80 03 02 50; *Visa* ☎22 83 03 90.

Dentist *Oslo Kommunale Tannlegevakt*, Tøyen Senter, Kolstadgata 18 (☎22 67 30 00). Daily 7–10am, plus Sat & Sun 11am–2pm. Otherwise, see under "Tannleger" in the yellow pages.

Embassies *Australia*, information office at Jerbanetorget 2 (☎22 41 44 33), but more serious matters dealt with by UK embassy; *Canada*, Oscars gate 20 (☎22 46 69 55); *Germany,* Oscars gate 45

(☎22 55 20 10); *Ireland*, use UK embassy; *Netherlands,* Oscars gate 29 (☎22 60 21 93); *New Zealand*, use UK embassy; *Poland*, Olav Kyrres plass 1 (☎22 44 86 39); *Spain*, Oscars gate 35 (☎22 55 20 15); *UK*, Thomas Heftyes gate 8 (☎22 55 24 00); *USA*, Drammensveien 18 (☎22 44 85 50). For others, look under "Ambassadeur og Legasjoner" in the yellow pages.

Emergencies Police ☎112; Fire ☎110; Ambulance ☎113. *Oslo Kommunale Legevakt*, Storgata 40 at Hausmanns gate (☎22 11 70 70), has a 24-hour rape and sexual assault counselling service, as well as casualty and outpatient facilities. There's also a 24-hour Crisis Line on ☎22 37 47 00. For a doctor, refer to the yellow pages under "Leger".

Ferry companies *DFDS Scandinavian Seaways* (to Copenhagen), Vippetangen utstikker (pier) #2, beside Akershusstranda (☎22 41 90 90); *Stena* (to Frederikshavn in Denmark), Jernbanetorget 2 (☎22 33 50 00); *Color Line* (to Kiel and Hirtshals, Denmark), Øvre Slotts gate 11 (☎22 94 44 70).

Fishing To fish in the forest lakes of the Nordmarka you need a local licence, a *fiskekort* (165kr), available from sports shops, plus a national licence (90kr), which you can buy from any post office. Common freshwater species include trout, char, pike and perch. For seawater fishing there's no local licence and you only need a national one if you intend to fish for salmon, trout or char. For more information, contact the tourist office, or *Oslomarka Fiskeadministrasjon*, on the outskirts of town at Riflegata 133 (☎22 95 07 98).

Gay Oslo Not much of a scene as such, primarily because Oslo's gays and lesbians are mostly content to share pubs and clubs with heteros. But advice is available and activities and events organized by *LLH* (*Landsforeningen for lesbisk og homofil frigjøring*), St Olavs plass 2 (Mon–Fri 9am–4pm; ☎22 36 19 48). Gay switchboard on ☎22 11 36 60 (Mon–Thurs 8–10pm).

Hiking *Den Norske Turistforening* (*DNT*), Stortingsgata 28 at Olav V's gate (Mon–Sat 10am–4pm, Thurs until 6pm; ☎22 83 25 50), sells hiking maps and gives general advice and information on route planning – an invaluable first call before a walking trip in Norway. Join here to use their nationwide network of mountain huts; the subscription fee of 300kr (concessions 160kr) gives a year's membership.

Laundry *Majorstua Myntvaskeri*, Vibes gate 15 (Mon–Fri 8am–8pm, Sat 8am–5pm); *Mr Clean*, Parkveien 6 at Welhavens gate (daily 7am–11pm). The *Haraldsheim* youth hostel has washing and drying facilities.

Left luggage Lockers and luggage office (daily 6.30am–11pm) at Oslo S.

Library Read foreign newspapers and periodicals at the *Deichmanske Bibliotek*, Henrik Ibsen gate 1 (Mon–Fri 10am–8pm, Sat 9am–3pm).

Lost property Police ☎22 66 98 65; trams, buses & T-bane ☎22 66 49 27; *NSB* railways ☎22 36 80 47.

Newspapers Most English and American newspapers and magazines are widely available in downtown Oslo's convenience stores and *Narvesen* kiosks, with the best selection at Oslo S.

Pharmacy There is a 24-hour service at *Jernbanetorgets Apotek*, Jernbanetorget 4b (☎22 41 24 82). Also, all pharmacies carry a rota in the window advising the nearest open shop.

Police Emergencies ☎112. Otherwise, in case of trouble or lost property (*Hittegods*) go to *Oslo Politikammer*, Grønlandsleiret 44 (Mon–Fri 8.15am–3pm; ☎22 66 90 50).

Post offices Main office: Dronningens gate 15 at Tollbugata (Mon–Fri 8am–6pm, Sat 10am–3pm), with poste restante at counters 37–41. Many other post offices are dotted across Oslo (usual opening hours Mon–Fri 8am–5pm, Sat 9am–1pm), central locations including Karl Johans gate 22, Universitetsgata 2, Sjøgata 1 in the Aker Brygge, and inside Oslo S (Mon–Fri 7am–6pm, Sat 9am–3pm). All post offices exchange currency and cash travellers cheques at very reasonable rates.

Ride share If you want to advertise for shared lifts out of the city, leave your name, address and contact number at the youth information office, *UNGINFO*, Møllergata 3 (Mon–Fri 11am–5pm; ☎22 41 51 32).

Taxis There are taxi ranks dotted all over the city centre, or you can call *Oslo Taxi* on 22 38 80 90.

Telephones International phone calls can be made from any city phone box. The older phone boxes only take coins, the newest version only accepts phone cards – and these are widely available from kiosks and newsagents. Some phone boxes take either cash or a phone card, and a few others accept credit cards. There are phone booths at the main telephone exchange, Kongens gate 21 at Prinsens gate (Mon–Fri 9am–5pm): here, you make the call first and pay later.

Travel agents For discount flights, *BIJ* tickets, *ISIC* cards, etc, try either *Terra Nova*, the travel bureau of the Norwegian youth hostel association at Dronningens gate 26 (☎22 42 14 10); or *KIL-*

ROY travels, Nedre Slotts gate 23 (☎22 42 01 20). *Tourbroker Reisebyrå*, Drammensveien 4 (☎22 83 27 15), specialize in tickets for *National Express Eurolines*. For a full list of Oslo travel agents, see under "Reisebyråer" in the yellow pages.

Vinmonopolet Off-licences at Klingenberggaten 4; Møllergaten 10–12; and at the *Oslo City* shopping complex, Stenersgaten 1.

Winter sports: skating and skiing Skis and equipment can be rented from *Skiservice Tomm Murstad*, Tryvannsveien 2 (☎22 14 41 24), at Voksenkollen T-bane station (line 1). For information on both cross-country and downhill skiing, call into the *Skiforeningen* office at Kongeveien 5 (☎22 92 32 00), in the suburban ski resort of Holmenkollen. Guided ski tours are organized by *Den Rustne Eike*, just along from the tourist office on Vestbaneplassen (May–Oct daily 10am–6.30pm; Nov–April Mon–Fri only; ☎22 83 72 31). In winter there's a floodlit skating rink, *Narvisen*, in front of the Stortinget beside Karl Johans gate; admission is free and skate rental reasonably priced.

Women's movement *Norsk Kvinnesaksforening*, Majorstuveien 39 (☎22 60 42 27), can put you in touch with women's groups in Oslo and the rest of Norway, and provide information on events and activities.

Youth Hostel Association *Norske Vandrerhjem* has its main office and a travel bureau at Dronningens gate 26 (Mon–Fri 8.30am–4pm, June & July till 5pm, Sat 10am–1pm; ☎22 42 14 10). The bureau offers a reliable travel agency service and also provides up-to-date information on hostelling in the rest of the country.

AROUND OSLO

The forested uplands that surround Oslo have little of the splendour of other parts of the country, whether it be far to the north in Norway's finest mountains, or northwest to the fjords. For these delights, you'll have to leave the capital and base yourself elsewhere, but if time is pressing you could get a hint of what all the scenic fuss is about by visiting the narrow straits and chubby basins of the **Oslofjord**, which – around 100km from top to bottom – links the capital with the open sea. This waterway has long been Norway's busiest, an islet-studded channel whose sheltered waters were once crowded with steamers shuttling passengers along the Norwegian coast. Nowadays, the Oslofjord shoreline has been blighted by industry and the only worthwhile destination is **Fredrikstad**, down the eastern side of the fjord on the train route to Sweden, where the old part of town is a riverside fortress whose gridiron streets and earthen bastions have survived in remarkably good condition.

Fredrikstad

Roughly every two hours, trains leave Oslo to thump down the east side of the Oslofjord on their way to **FREDRIKSTAD**, named after the Danish king Frederick II, who had the original fortified town built here at the mouth of the River Glomma in 1567. Norway was ruled by Danish kings from 1387 to 1814 and, with rare exceptions, the country's interests were systematically neglected in favour of Copenhagen. A major consequence was Norway's involvement in the bitter rivalry between the Swedish and Danish monarchies, which prompted a seemingly endless and particularly pointless sequence of wars lasting from the early sixteenth century until 1720. The eastern approaches to Christiania (Oslo), along the Oslofjord, were especially vulnerable to attack from Sweden and the area was ravaged by raiding parties on many occasions. Indeed, Frederick II's fortress only lasted three years before it was burnt to the ground, though it didn't take long for a replacement to be constructed – and for the whole process to be repeated again. Finally, in the middle of the seventeenth century, Fredrikstad's fortifications were considerably strengthened. The central gridiron of cobbled streets was encircled on three sides by zigzag bastions, which allowed the defenders to fire across the flanks and into the front of any attacking force. In turn, these bastions were protected by a moat, concentric earthen banks and outlying redoubts. Armed with 130 cannon, Frederikstad was, by 1685, the strongest fortress in all of Norway – and it has remained in military use ever since, which partly accounts for its excellent state of preservation. The fort was also left unaffected by the development of modern Fredrikstad, an offspring of the timber industry. This new town was built on the west bank of the Glomma while the old fort – now known as the **Gamlebyen** (Old Town) – was on the east.

From Fredrikstad **train** and **bus station**, located in the new part of town, it's a five-minute walk to the River Glomma – head straight down Jernbanegata and take the first left along Ferjestedsveien. From the jetty, the **ferry** (Mon–Fri 5.30am–11pm, Sat 7am–11pm, Sun 9.30am–11pm; 5min; 5kr) shuttles over to the gated back wall of the Gamlebyen. Inside, the low timber and stone houses of the old town, just three blocks deep and six blocks wide, make for a delightful stroll especially as very few tourists venture this way, and on a wet day the streets echo with nothing but the sound of your own footsteps plus the occasional army boot hitting the cobbles as the tiny garrison moves about its duties. There is a **museum** (May–Sept Mon–Sat 11am–5pm, Sun noon–5pm; 20kr), housed in the old *Gamle Slaveri* where prisoners once did hard labour, and the main square holds an unfortunate statue of Frederick II, who appears to have a serious problem with his pantaloons, but it's the general appearance of the place that appeals rather than any specific sight.

Make sure also to take in the most impressive of the town's outlying defences, the **Kongsten Fort**, about ten minutes' walk from the main fortress: go straight ahead from the main gate, take the first right along Heibergs gate and it's signposted on the left. Here, thick stone and earthen walls are moulded round a rocky knoll which offers wide views over the surrounding countryside – an amiably quiet vantage point from where you can spy the layout of the various mounds and trenches that once elaborated the outer lines of defence.

Back on the western side of the Glomma, follow Ferjestedsveien in the opposite direction for the brief walk round to the small park beside the **Domkirke** (late June to mid-Aug, Mon–Sat noon–3pm), a big brown building with stained glass by Emanuel Vigeland. Beyond the church is the centre of modern Fredrikstad, a disinterested kind of place plonked on a bend in the river.

When you've finished with the fortifications, drop by the *Kafé Kongens Torv* (Mon–Sat 10am–4pm, Sun noon–4pm), facing the statue of King Frederick, for a snack, or try the *Balaklavas Gjestgiveri* restaurant, Faergeport gate 78, where the fish dishes average around 120kr. Although it's preferable to treat a visit as a day trip, there is somewhere to **stay** close by – *Fredrikstad Motel & Camping*, Torsnesveien 16 (☎69 32 05 32; fax 69 32 36 66; ①), a rather shoddy establishment about 300m straight ahead from the main gate; it provides tent space as well as inexpensive rooms. Alternatively, there are a couple of hotels on the west side of the river, including the *Victoria*, Turn gate 3 (☎69 31 11 65; fax 69 31 87 55; ④), a perfectly adequate *Best Western* hotel in a modest Art Nouveau building overlooking the park next to the Domkirke.

travel details

Trains

From Oslo to: Bergen (4–5 daily; 6hr 30min); Dombås (3–4 daily; 4hr 20min); Drammen (4–5 daily; 40min); Fredrikstad (8 daily; 1hr 15min); Geilo (4–5 daily; 3hr 20min); Halden (8 daily; 1hr 45min); Hamar (7 daily; 1hr 40min); Hjerkinn (3 daily; 4hr 45min); Kongsberg (4–5 daily; 1hr 20min); Kristiansand (4–5 daily; 5hr); Larvik (2–7 daily; 2hr 15min); Lillehammer (7 daily; 2hr 30min); Moss (8 daily; 50min); Myrdal (4–5 daily; 4hr 30min); Otta (4–5 daily; 4hr 10min); Røros (2–3 daily; 6hr); Stavanger (3 daily; 9hr); Trondheim (3–4 daily; 8hr

15min); Tønsberg (2–7 daily; 1hr 40min); Voss (4–5 daily; 5hr 40min); Åndalsnes (2–3 daily; 6hr 30min).

Buses
From Oslo to: Alta via Sweden (3 weekly; 27hr; reservations obligatory); Arendal (1 daily; 4hr 15min); Balestrand (3 daily; 8hr 15min); Bergen (1 daily; 11hr 40min); Drøbak (hourly; 40min); Fagernes (3 daily; 3hr 20min); Fjaerland (3 daily; 7hr 50min); Grimstad (1 daily; 4hr 40min); Hamar (1 daily; 2hr); Hammerfest via Sweden (3 weekly; 30hr; reservations obligatory); Haugesund (1 daily; 10hr); Kongsberg (1 daily; 2hr); Kristiansand (1 daily; 5hr 40min); Lillehammer (1 daily; 3hr); Lillesand (1 daily; 5hr); Odda (1 daily; 8hr); Otta (2 daily; 5hr); Risør (1 daily; 3hr 30min); Sogndal (3 daily; 7hr); Stavanger (1 daily; 10hr); Stryn (1 daily; 8hr); Voss (1 daily; 10hr 30min).

Ferries
From Oslo to: Dronningen/Bygdøynes (late April & Sept every 40min 9.05am–5.45pm; May–Aug every 40min 9.05am–9.05pm; 10min/15min); Hovedøya (mid-March to Sept hourly or 90min; Oct to mid-March 3 daily; 10min); Langøyene (June–Aug hourly 10am–6pm, last boat back 7pm; 30min).

From Moss to: Horten (hourly 6am–1am; 35min).

Express passenger boats (*Hurtigbåt*)
From Oslo to: Arendal (July to mid-Aug 1 daily; 6hr 45min); Kragerø (July to mid-Aug 1 daily; 4hr 30min); Risør (July to mid-Aug 1 daily; 5hr 10min); Stavern (July to mid-Aug 1 daily; 3hr 15min).

International trains
From Oslo to: Copenhagen via Gothenburg (2 daily); London via Hamburg (2 daily); Paris (1 daily); Rome (1 daily); Stockholm (2–3 daily).

International buses
From Oslo to: Gothenburg (3 daily); Gothenburg/Amsterdam/London (5 weekly); Stockholm (7 weekly; 15hr). Also services to Germany, Italy, Greece, Hungary, Austria and Belgium; information from *Nor-Way Bussekspress* (Bussterminalen, Oslo; ☎23 00 24 40; fax 23 00 24 49).

International ferries
From Moss to: Frederikshavn (1 daily; 7hr).

From Oslo to: Copenhagen (1 daily; 16hr); Frederikshavn (1 daily; 8hr 30min); Hirtshals (6 weekly; 9hr); Kiel (1 daily; 19hr 30min).

CHAPTER FIVE

SOUTH AND CENTRAL NORWAY

P reoccupied by the fjords and the long road to the Nordkapp, few tourists have any inclination to explore **South and Central Norway**. The Norwegians know better. Trapped between Sweden and the fjords, this great chunk of land boasts some of the country's finest scenery, with the forested dales that trail north and west from Oslo heralding the rearing peaks that extend down towards the coast. It's here, within shouting distance of the country's principal train line and the E6 – the main line of communication between Oslo, Trondheim and the north – that you'll find three of Norway's prime **hiking areas**. These are made up of a trio of mountain ranges, each partly contained within a national park – from south to north, Jotunheimen, Rondane and the Dovrefjell. Each park is equipped with well-maintained walking trails and *DNT* huts, and **Otta** and **Kongsvoll**, on both the E6 and the train line, are particularly good starting points for hiking expeditions.

Entirely different, but just as popular with the Norwegians, is the **south coast**, an immediately appealing region whose myriad islets and skerries, beaches and coves

---

STAVE CHURCHES

Of the 29 surviving **stave churches** in Norway, all but a handful are in Southern and Central Norway. Together, they represent the country's most distinctive architectural feature. Their key characteristic is that the timbers are placed vertically into the ground – in contrast to the log bonding technique used by the Norwegians for everything else. Thus, a stave wall consists of vertical planks slotted into sills above and below, with the sills connected to upright posts – or **staves**, hence the name – at each corner. The general design seems to have been worked out in the twelfth century and regular features include external wooden galleries, shingles and finials, but the most fetching churches are those where the central section of the nave has been raised above the aisles to create – from the outside – a distinctive, almost pagoda-like effect. In virtually all the stave churches, the **door frames** (where they survive) are decorated from top to bottom with surging, intricate carvings – fantastic long-limbed dragons, entwined with tendrils of vine – that clearly relate back to Viking design.

The **origins** of stave churches have attracted an inordinate amount of academic debate. Some scholars argue that they were originally pagan temples, converted to Christian use by the addition of a chancel, whilst others are convinced that they were inspired by Russian churches. In the nineteenth century, they also developed a symbolic importance as reminders of the time when Norway was independent. Many had fallen into a dreadful state of repair and were clumsily renovated – or even remodelled – by enthusiastic medievalists with a nationalistic agenda. Undoing this repair work has been a major operation that still continues today. For most visitors, sight of one or two stave churches suffices – and two of the finest are those at Heddal (see p.235) and Borgund (see p.233).

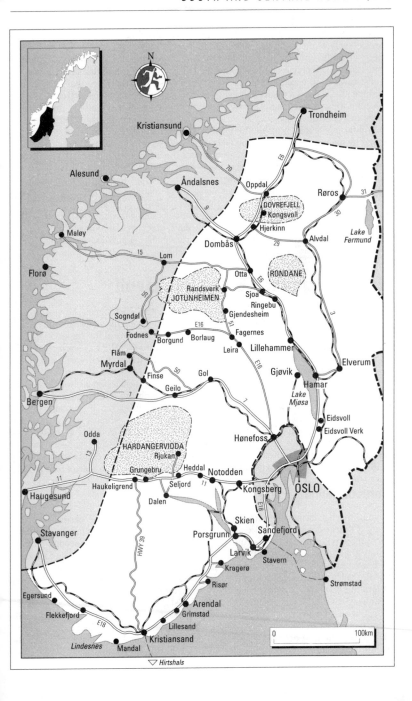

N

Trondheim

Kristiansund

Alesund

Åndalsnes

Oppdal

Røros

31

70

9

DOVREFJELL

Kongsvoll

Hjerkinn

30

29

Lake
Fermund

Maløy

Alvdal

Florø

15

Lom

Dombås

E6

Otta

RONDANE

55

Randsverk

JOTUNHEIMEN

Sjoa

Ringebu

3

Sogndal

Gjendesheim

E16

Fagernes

51

Fodnes

Borgund

Borlaug

Leira

Lillehammer

Flåm

Myrdal

Finse

50

Gol

E16

Gjøvik

Elverum

Bergen

7

Geilo

1

Hamar

Lake
Mjøsa

Odda

HARDANGERVIDDA

Rjukan

Eidsvoll

Eidsvoll Verk

13

Hønefoss

Grungebru

Heddal

Notodden

11

Haukeligrend

Seljord

11

Kongsberg

OSLO

Haugesund

Dalen

E18

Stavanger

Skien

Sandefjord

HWY 39

Porsgrunn

Larvik

Stavern

Kragerø

Strømstad

Risør

Egersund

Arendal

Grimstad

Flekkefjord

E18

Lillesand

0   100km

Lindesnes

Mandal

Kristiansand

▽ Hirtshals

shred a shoreline that extends west from the Oslofjord in the shape of a giant "V". Forested valleys, fells and flatlands back the coast, which is at its prettiest in the east where a handful of old timber ports – **Lillesand**, **Arendal** and **Mandal** – sport bright white, antique clapboard houses along their harbourfronts. **Kristiansand**, easily the largest town on the coast, is different again, a brisk modern place that successfully combines its roles as a resort and major ferry port with connections to Denmark.

Despite these attractions, it's easy to see the whole region as nothing more than a **transport corridor**, especially as a trio of major roads – including the spectacular Hwy 9 to Åndalsnes – branch off the E6 for the fjords, while the south coast is speedily traversed by means of the E18 linking Oslo with Stavanger. In between these, three major roads – the E16 and Hwys 11 and 7 – cut across the interior from the capital to the central fjords and Bergen. But, whichever way you're heading, it would be a great pity if you didn't allow at least a couple of days for the south coast or the national parks in the north.

As you might expect, **bus** services along these main highways are excellent and **trains** are fast and frequent too. Leave the arterial highways, however, and the bus system thins out and travelling becomes a pain without your own vehicle – so much so that it can be worth renting a car locally for a few days. In terms of **accommodation**, roadside campsites are commonplace, there's a reasonable supply of youth hostels and every major town has at least one hotel or guesthouse.

North along the E6 – to Kongsvoll

Hurrying from Oslo to Trondheim and points north, the **E6** remains the most important highway in Norway, and is consequently kept in excellent condition – often with the road works to prove it. Inevitably, the road is used by many of the region's long-distance **buses**, and for much of its length it's also shadowed by Norway's principal **train** line. Heading out of Oslo, both the E6 and the railway thump northwards across the lowlands to clip along the north bank of Lake Mjøsa en route to **Lillehammer**, site of the 1994 Winter Olympic Games and the country's best open-air folk museum. Thereafter, road and rail wriggle on between the **Jotunheim** and **Rondane national parks**, whose magnificent mountains are both within easy reach of the amiable town of **Otta**. Further north still is the beautiful **Dovrefjell** range, which forms a third and equally stunning national park, and one that's best approached from tiny **Kongsvoll**. All three parks are famous for their hiking and an extensive and well-planned system of **hiking trails** networks them. From Kongsvoll, Trondheim (see p.291) is within easy striking distance or you can detour east via either Hwy 29 or 30 to **Røros** (see p.230).

North to Hamar

Beyond the flat farmlands north of Oslo, the E6 curves round the eastern shore of Norway's largest lake, **Lake Mjøsa**, a favourite retreat for Norwegian families, with the surrounding farmland, woods and pastures harbouring numerous second homes. Before the railroad arrived in the 1880s, the lake was a main transport route, crossed by boats during the summer, and in winter by horse and sleigh. It's also halfway country: the quiet settlements around the lake give a taste of small-town southern Norway before the E6 plunges on into wilder regions further north.

Midway round the lake, some 110km from Oslo, lies **HAMAR**, hardly an essential stop, but an amiable, relaxed little place of 15,000 souls whose marinas and waterside cafés make a gallant attempt to sustain a nautical flavour. However insignificant today, Hamar was the seat of an important medieval bishopric and the scant remains of the **Domkirke** – not much more than a chunk of wall with four Gothic arches – are stuck out on the **Domkirkeodden** (cathedral point), a low, grassy headland reached by road or along a pleasant lakeshore footpath that extends the 2km north from the train station. The cathedral is supposed to have been built by the "English Pope" Nicholas Breakspear, who spent a couple of years in Norway as the papal legate before becoming Adrian IV in 1154, but the building, along with the surrounding episcopal complex, was ransacked during the Reformation and local road-builders subsequently helped themselves to the stone. The ruins have now been incorporated into the **Hedmarksmuseet** (daily mid-May to mid-June 10am–4pm; mid-June to mid-Aug 10am–6pm; mid-Aug to mid-Sept 10am–4pm; 30kr), which holds an archeological museum, an open-air folk museum and a medieval herb garden.

Hamar is also as good a place as any to pick up the 130-year-old **paddle steamer**, the *Skibladner*, which shuttles up and down Lake Mjøsa between late May and early September: on Tuesdays, Thursdays and Saturdays the boat makes the round trip across the lake from Hamar to Gjøvik and on up to Lillehammer, whilst on Mondays, Wednesdays and Fridays it chugs down to Eidsvoll and back; there's no Sunday service. Departure details are available at any local tourist office and from the *Skibladner* office, next door to the tourist office in Hamar on Parkgata (Mon–Fri 8.30am–3.30pm; ☎62 52 70 85). Round trips from Hamar to Eidsvoll (2hr 30min) cost 190kr, to Lillehammer (8hr) 240kr – buy tickets on board. One-way fares cost a little over half these rates, but since the lake is not especially scenic a couple of hours on the boat is more than enough for most people.

Practicalities

Hamar **bus** and **train stations** are in the town centre beside the lake. It's here that certain trains from Oslo pause before heading up the loop branch line to Røros (see p.230), a fine four-hour ride over the hills and through huge forests. Some 100m from the train station – turn left out of the terminal building along Stangevegen – is the **tourist office**, at Parkgata 2 (mid-June to mid-Aug Mon–Fri 8am–8pm, Sat & Sun noon–6pm; rest of the year Mon–Fri 8am–3.30pm; ☎62 52 12 17), and next door is the booking office for the *Skibladner* paddle steamer (see above). The jetty for the *Skibladner* ferry is 600m further north.

If you are looking for somewhere to spend the night, there's a fair choice of central **hotel** accommodation, the most attractive option being the lakeshore *Inter Nor Victoria Hotel*, Strandgata 21 (☎62 53 05 00; fax 62 53 32 23; ④), which has a bar and a reasonably good restaurant serving Norwegian favourites. Combined with a **motel** (②), the **youth hostel**, Åkersvikavegen 10 (☎62 52 60 60; fax 62 53 24 60; 120kr, doubles ①), occupies smart modern buildings about 2km south along the lakeshore from the train station – it's in the middle of nowhere, just across from the massive skating arena built for the 1994 Winter Olympics in the shape of an upturned Viking ship.

ACCOMMODATION PRICE CODES

All the Norwegian hotels and guest houses listed in the guide have been graded according to the following price bands, based on the cost of the least expensive double room in high season. However, almost every hotel offers seasonal and/or weekend discounts that can reduce the rate by one or even two grades. Many of these bargains are impromptu, but wherever possible we've given two grades, covering both the regular and the discounted rate. Single rooms, where available, are usually between 60 and 80 percent of the cost of a double.

① under 500kr	② 500–700kr	③ 700–900kr
④ 900–1200kr	⑤ 1200–1500kr	⑥ over 1500kr

Lillehammer

LILLEHAMMER (literally "Little Hammer"), 60km north of Hamar and 170km from Oslo, is Lake Mjøsa's most worthwhile destination. In **winter**, it's *the* Norwegian skiing centre, a young and vibrant place whose rural, lakeshore setting and extensive cross-country ski trails contributed to its selection as host for the 1994 Olympic Winter Games. In preparation for the games, the Norwegian government spent a massive 2 billion kroner on the town's sporting facilities, which are now the best in the country. Spread along the hillsides above and near the town, they include a ski-jumping tower and chair lift, a ski jumping arena with two jumping hills and chair lift, an ice hockey arena and a cross-country skiing stadium that gives access to about 30km of cross-country trails. Several local companies operate all-inclusive winter sports and activity holidays – try *Lillehammer Reiseservice*, Elvegata 19 (☎61 26 36 36; fax 61 26 19 94) – though if this is what you have in mind, you may as well book your holiday with an agent back home (see the "Getting There" sections in *Basics*). Most Norwegians arriving here in winter come fully equipped, but it's possible to rent or purchase equipment when you get here – the tourist office (see below) will advise.

In **summer**, Lillehammer remains a popular holiday spot. Hundreds of Norwegians hunker down in their second homes in the hills, dropping into the town centre for a drink or a meal. Cycling, walking, fishing and canoeing are all popular pastimes and the tourist office can advise on guided tours and equipment rental. But, however appealing the area may be to Norwegians, the countryside round here can't compare with the magnificent wildness of other parts of Norway; that said, Lillehammer is not a bad place to break your journey and there are a couple of handy attractions to keep you busy for a night – but not two.

The art gallery and Maihaugen

Lillehammer's briskly efficient centre, just a few minutes' walk from one end to the other, is tucked into the hillside above the lake and the E6. It has just one notable attraction, its art gallery, the **Kunstmuseum** (mid-June to Aug Mon–Wed 11am–4pm, Thurs–Sun 11am–5pm; rest of the year Tues–Sun 11am–4pm; 30kr; free English guided tours daily in July at 1pm, rest of the year Sat & Sun at noon), which occupies a flashy modern edifice at Stortorget 2. Though specializing in temporary exhibitions of contemporary art (which attract an extra admission charge), the gallery's permanent collection features a small but representative sample of the works of most major Norwegian painters, from Johan Dahl and Christian Krohg to Munch and Erik Werenskiold.

The much-vaunted **Maihaugen open-air museum** (daily May & mid-Aug to Sept 10am–5pm; June to mid-Aug 9am–6pm; 60kr; free 40-min guided tour in English at regular intervals), a twenty-minute walk south from the centre of town along Anders Sandvigs gate (or take hourly bus #7 from the Skysstasjon), is the largest museum of its type in northern Europe. Incredibly, the whole collection represents the lifetime's work of one man, the magpie-ish dentist Anders Sandvig. The Maihaugen holds around 140 relocated buildings, brought here from all over the region, including a charming seventeenth-century presbytery (*prestegårdshagen*), a thirteenth-century stave church (from Garmo), thick log store and smokehouses, summer grazing huts and various workshops. The key exhibits are, however, the two **farms**, complete with their various outhouses and living areas, which date from the late seventeenth century.

The outside area is stocked with farmyard animals, while guides dressed in traditional costume give the low-down on traditional rural life; in summertime there's often the chance to have a go at homely activities, such as spinning, baking, weaving and pottery. You can spend time too in the main museum building, which features temporary exhibitions on folkloric themes. Allow a good half-day for a visit and take advantage of the free guided tour.

Practicalities

The E6 runs along the lakeshore about 500m below the centre of Lillehammer, where the over-large **Skysstasjon**, in Jernbanetorget, at the bottom of Jernbanegata, incorporates the **train station** and the **bus terminal**. There's a **tourist office** here too (late June to mid-Aug Mon–Fri 7.30am–4.30pm, Sat 9.30am–3pm, Sun 11am–4pm; rest of the year Mon–Fri 7.30am–4.30pm, Sat 10am–2pm; ☎61 26 41 99), which is much more helpful than the main tourist office, five minutes' walk away up the hill and off the main street, Storgata, at Elvegata 19. Both offices can help with finding accommodation (though there are no private rooms) and have information on local events and activities.

The popular, modern **youth hostel** (☎61 26 25 66; fax 61 26 25 77; 165kr, rooms ①) occupies part of the Skysstasjon; it's perfect for an overnight visit, but if you're around for longer you may prefer something rather more cosy: a recommended **guesthouse** is *Gjestehuset Ersgaard*, Nordseterveien 201 (☎61 25 06 84; fax 61 25 31 09; ②), a couple of kilometres above town (in the Nordseter direction), which serves excellent breakfasts in its dining room overlooking the town and lake. For **hotel** accommodation in the centre, the *Dølaheimen Breiseth Hotell*, across from the Skysstasjon at Jernbanegata 3 (☎61 26 95 00; fax 61 26 95 05; ④), is a large chain hotel with comfortable rooms.

Lillehammer has a good supply of downtown **restaurants** and **cafés**. The busy *Bøndernes Hus Kafeteria*, at Kirkegata 68 (Mon–Fri 8.30am–7pm, Sat 8.30am–4pm & Sun noon–6pm), is a big, old-fashioned sort of place with cheap and filling self-service meals. Moving up a rung, the *Vertshuset Solveig*, down an alley off the pedestrianized part of Storgata, is cafeteria-style too, but the meals are first-rate with main courses averaging around 100kr; whilst *Thorvald's Spiseri*, Jernbanegata 3, is a more formal restaurant specializing in Italian dishes and seafood. The town has an animated nightlife with **bars** clustered around the western end of Storgata. Places come and go pretty fast, but *Nikkers* and *Pipas*, both a stone's throw from the main tourist office, are the liveliest spots at present.

For getting out into the surrounding countryside, **bikes** can be rented at the youth hostel and the antique *Skibladner* **paddle steamer** shuttles up and down Lake Mjøsa from the jetty about 800m south of the centre – for further details see p.225.

North to Otta and the Jotunheim and Rondane national parks

Heading north from Lillehammer, the E6 and the railway leave the shores of Lake Mjøsa for the **Gudbrandsdal**, the 200-kilometre-long river valley that extends to Dombås and was for centuries the main route between Oslo and Trondheim. Trapped between mountain ranges, the valley has a comparatively dry and mild climate and its soils were good enough to support a string of farming villages, though since the beginning of the century farming has been supplemented by various small-scale industries.

Some 120km north of Lillehammer is **OTTA**, an unassuming little town at the confluence of the rivers Otta and Lågen – and the perfect base for hiking in the nearby Rondane and Jotunheim national parks. Everything you need in Otta is within easy reach: the E6 passes within 100m of the centre, sweeping along the east bank of the Lågen, while the **train station**, **bus terminal** and **tourist office** (mid-June to mid-Aug Mon–Fri 8.30am–7.30pm, Sat & Sun 10am–6pm; rest of the year Mon–Fri 8.30am–4pm; ☎61 23 02 44; fax 61 23 09 60) are all clumped together on the west bank in the Skysstasjon, itself just 100m from the few gridiron streets that pass for the town centre. There are no sights as such, but the stiff hike along the footpath leading up the forested slopes of **Prillarguri** (849m), across the Otta River south of the centre, is a popular outing.

Otta tourist office is exceptionally helpful, providing local bus timetables and offering help on hiking (see below). They also have a small supply of **private rooms** (①) which they will reserve on your behalf for a 20kr fee. Alternatively, the *Grand Gjestegård* (☎61 23 12 00; fax 61 23 04 62; ②), across from the train station, is a pleasant, simple pension, and better than its two rivals along Ola Dahls gate: the *Sagatun Gjestgiveri* (☎61 23 08 14; ①), which with its shared toilets and plain rooms is the nearest thing Otta has to a youth hostel, and the *Otta Hotell* (☎61 23 00 33; fax 61 23 15 24; ②/③), in an unenticing concrete block with a discotheque and swimming pool. The nearest **campsite**, *Otta Camping* (☎61 23 03 09; no fax), occupies a cramped riverside site about 1.5km from town – cross over the bridge on the south side of the centre, turn right and keep going – and has cabins as well as tent pitches. *Øya Camping* (☎61 23 03 31; no fax) is a bigger and better affair with cabins and pitches about 2km north of the town centre on the west bank of the River Lågen. Otta doesn't have much in the way of **restaurants**, but the *Prillarguri Café*, on Storgata, musters a tasty range of Norwegian standbys.

Hiking around Otta

Otta's **tourist office** is the best first stop for information and tips on hiking in the nearby national parks. You can buy maps here detailing routes of varying length and difficulty, and the staff can also advise on the weather and any equipment you might need for longer treks. Getting to the parks using **public transport** is not as easy as you might expect. For **Rondane**, there's a once-daily summertime bus service (mid-June to mid-Aug 1 daily; 1hr) that travels the 20km to the Spranghaugen car park, from where it's an hour's level walk east down the vehicle access road to the staffed *DNT* hut on the lakeshore at **Rondvassbu**; the hut is at the trailhead of several fine Rondane hikes. Note that the bus leaves in the afternoon, which means you'll almost certainly need to overnight here if you're after some hiking. The daily morning service (same summertime period) terminates at Mysuseter, 5km short of Spranghaugen, with a return service heading back to Otta in mid-afternoon. As far as the **Jotunheim** is concerned, there's a weekday, summertime bus from Otta to the staffed *DNT* hut at **Gjendesheim**, set beside the start of several outstanding hikes. The bus leaves early in the morning (late June to mid-Aug Mon–Fri 1 daily; 2hr 30min); from mid-June to mid-September it also runs at the weekend, leaving in the early afternoon. It's 93km from Otta to Gjendesheim, much too far to take a **taxi**, though this a reasonably economic option for the journey from Otta to the Rondane, especially if you can share with other people – enquire at the tourist office, where you can also get information on local **bicycle** and **car** rental.

FROM OTTA TO THE FJORDS

Running west from Otta, **Hwy 15** forms one of the most dramatic approaches to the fjords either straight to Stryn or over the so-called *Ørnevegen* (Eagle's Highway) to Geiranger. You can also branch off Hwy 15 at Lom, taking **Hwy 55** to Sogndal, another extravagantly beautiful road passing through the dales and over mountain passes, with the jagged peaks of the Jotunheim immediately to the east. In terms of public transport, the Oslo–Måløy **bus** (Mon–Fri 1 daily) passes through Otta en route to Stryn; and from mid-June to August, there's a twice-daily service from Otta to Lom and Sogndal. The journey time to Sogndal is just under four hours. For further details see the *Bergen and the Western Fjords* chapter.

Rondane Nasjonalpark

Spreading north and east from Otta towards the Swedish border, the **Rondane**, established in 1962 as Norway's first national park, is now one of the country's most popular hiking areas. Its 580 square kilometres, one-third in the high alpine zone, attract walkers of all ages and abilities. The soil is poor, so vegetation is sparse and lichens, especially reindeer moss, predominate, but then the views across this bare landscape are serenely beautiful and a handful of lakes and rivers along with patches of dwarf birch forest provide some diversity. Most of the mountains, ten of which exceed the 2000-metre mark, are accessible to any reasonably fit and eager walker via a thick network of trails and hiking huts. In the eastern Rondane, the gentle Alvdal Vestfjell is a good target for older walkers or families with small children.

Jotunheimen Nasjonalpark

Norway's most famous walking area, **Jotunheimen Nasjonalpark** ("Home of the Giants") lives up to its name. Here pointed summits and undulating glaciers dominate the skyline, soaring high above river valleys and lake-studded plateaux. Covering only 3900 square kilometres, the park offers an amazing concentration of high peaks, more than two hundred of them rising above 1900m. There are no public roads; all visitors to the area's interior either walk or ski in, usually from either Hwy 55 in the west, or Hwy 51 in the east near Otta. In Jotunheimen, you will find Norway's and northern Europe's two highest peaks, Galdhøpiggen (2469m) and Glittertind (2464m), while the country's highest waterfall, Vettisfossen, with a 275-metre drop, is also located in Jotunheimen, a short walk from the Vetti tourist hut on the west side of the park.

North to Kongsvoll and the Dovrefjell Nasjonalpark

If you avoid the temptation of heading west from Otta along Hwy 15 to the fjords, the E6 and the railway lead the 50km north to **Dombås**, an unappealing crossroads settlement which it's best to ignore – there are other far more pleasant spots for a stopover within a fifty-kilometre radius. Both routes out of Dombås offer tantalizing prospects: Hwy 9 leads the 100km west to Åndalsnes and the Romsdalfjord (see Chapter 6), whilst the E6 plunges north through the mountains towards Trondheim (see Chapter 7); you can make either journey by train as well.

Staying on the E6, it's just 30km to the outpost of **HJERKINN**, stranded on bare and desolate moorland, its train station battened against the wind-blasted ice and snow of winter. There's been a mountain inn here since medieval times, one of the staging posts on the pilgrimage and traders' trail to Trondheim, now just 160km away. The inn's present successor, the *Hjerkinn Fjellstue* (☎61 24 29 27; fax 61 24 29 49; ②), comprises two expansive wooden buildings, with big open fires and simple bedrooms, set on a hill slope overlooking the moors, just over 2km from the train station beside the Hwy 29 to Røros. Coming from the south by road, this is the shortest route to Røros, but Hwy 29 is a real yawn and you're much better off approaching the town via Hwy 30 further north (see below).

Beyond Hjerkinn, the E6 slices across the barren uplands before descending into a narrow ravine, the **Drivdal**. Hidden here, just 13km from Hjerkinn, is **KONGSVOLL**, home of a tiny train station and the charming *Kongsvold Fjeldstue* (mid-Feb to Oct; ☎72 42 09 11; fax 72 42 22 72; ②), a huddle of tastefully restored old timber buildings with reindeer antlers on the outside. It's a lovely spot to break your journey, the bedrooms are simple but perfectly adequate and, as the tiny **information centre** explains, the inn is also slap bang in the middle of the Dovrefjell Nasjonalpark (see below). Incidentally, **train** travellers should note that only some of the Oslo–Trondheim trains stop at Kongsvoll station, 600m down the valley from the inn, and then only by prior arrangement with the conductor. Beyond Drivdal and 105km north of Kongsvoll, the crossroads at Støren, just 50km from Trondheim, is the place to turn off for Røros (see below) – a lovely hundred-kilometre drive along the picturesque Gauldal.

Dovrefjell Nasjonalpark

Bisected by the railroad and the E6, Dovrefjell Nasjonalpark is one of the more accessible of Norway's national parks. A comparative minnow, at just 265 square kilometres, it comprises two distinct zones: the marshes, open moors and rounded peaks that characterize much of eastern Norway spread east from the E6, while to the west the mountains become increasingly steep and serrated as they approach the wild jagged spires of the Romsdal. Beyond the western limits of the park, backing onto the Romsdalsfjord, is the greatest concentration of high peaks outside the Jotunheimen, a favourite destination of European mountaineers, who clamber perpendicular rock faces reckoned to be some of the world's most difficult.

Hiking trails and **huts** lattice the western part of the Dovrefjell and Kongsvoll makes an ideal starting point. It's possible to hike all the way from here to the coast at Åndalsnes, but this takes all of nine or ten days; a more feasible expedition for most visitors is the hike to one of the four snow-tipped peaks of mighty **Snøhetta** (around 2200m) and back again, which can be done in two days. There's accommodation five hours' walk west from Kongsvoll at the unstaffed **Reinheim** hut (mid-Feb to mid-Oct). Further hiking details and maps are available at the park information centre in the *Kongsvold Fjeldstue*.

Røros

Stuck on a treeless mountain plateau, **RØROS** is an airy, blustery place even on a summer's afternoon, when it's full of day-tripping tourists here to survey the old part of town that's little changed since its money-spinning days as a copper mining centre. Until the mining company went bust a decade or so ago, the copper mines had been the basis of life here for over three hundred years. This dirty and dangerous work was supplemented by a little farming and hunting, and life for the average villager can't have been anything but hard. Things have perked up a little since: Røros is now on UNESCO's World Heritage list, and there are firm stylistic controls on its grass-roofed cottages. Film companies regularly use the town as a backdrop for their productions – it has featured as the labour camp in *One Day in the Life of Ivan Denisovich*, a choice that says a lot about the place.

The town and copper mines

In the town centre, **Røros kirke** (early to late June & mid-Aug to mid-Sept Mon–Fri 2–4pm, Sat noon–2pm; late June to mid-Aug Mon–Sat 10am–5pm, Sun 2–4pm; 15kr) is the most obvious target for a stroll, a dominant reminder of the economic power fostered by the mines in the eighteenth century. Built in 1784, and once the only stone building in the town, it's more like a theatre than a religious edifice: a huge structure, capable of seating 1600 people and, like Kongsberg's church (see p.234), designed to overawe rather than inspire. The pulpit is built directly over the altar, a psychological gambit to emphasize the importance of the priest's word. A two-tiered gallery runs around the nave, designed to accommodate occasional labourers on its lower level with undesirables compelled to sit above – they even had to enter via a separate, outside staircase. These byzantine social arrangements are explained in depth on the **guided tour** (late June to mid-Aug 1 daily in English), the cost of which is included in the admission fee.

Immediately below the church, the oldest part of Røros spreads on either side of the river. A huddle of sturdy cross-timbered smelters' cottages, storehouses and workshops squat in the shadow of the humpy **Slegghaugan** (slagheaps) – more tourist attraction than eyesore, and providing fine views over the town and beyond. Here, next to the river, the rambling main works has been tidily restored and faces out onto **Malmplassen** ("Ore Place"), the wide earthen square where the ore drivers arrived from their journey across the mountains to have their cartloads of ore weighed on the

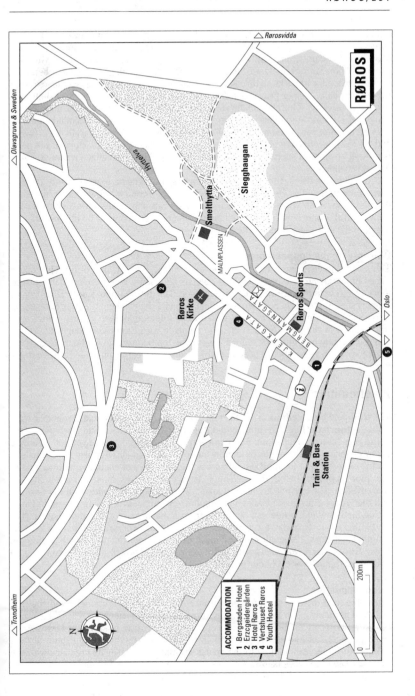

RØROS

△ Rørosvidda

△ Olavsgruva & Sweden

△ Trondheim

▷ Oslo

Hyttelva

Slegghaugan

Smelthytta

MALMPLASSEN

Røros Kirke

Røros Sports

BERGMANNSGATA

KJERKGATA

Train & Bus Station

N

ACCOMMODATION
1 Bergstaden Hotel
2 Erzgeidergården
3 Hotel Røros
4 Vertshuset Røros
5 Youth Hostel

0   200m

outdoor scales. Here too is the smelter's bell, hung in a rickety little tower, which was rung at the start of each shift. The main works, the **Smelthytta** (late June to mid-Aug Mon–Fri 10.30am–6pm, Sat & Sun 10.30am–4pm; rest of the year Mon–Fri 11am–3.30pm, Sat & Sun 11am–2pm; 35kr) – literally "melting hut" – has been converted into a museum, a large three-storey affair whose most diverting section explains the intricacies of copper production from the insides of the cavernous hall that once housed the smelter. There's actually very little to look at – presumably the mining company sold off most of the gear as scrap – and how much you enjoy it depends on your interest in copper production: minuscule dioramas illuminate every part of the process, and there are production charts, examples of the ore and a potted history of the company – all of which is supported by a comprehensive English-language leaflet available free at reception.

Malmplassen is at the top of **Bergmannsgata** which, together with parallel **Kjerkgata**, forms the heart of Røros today. Conspicuously, the smaller artisans' dwellings, some of which have become art and craft shops, are set near the works, away from the rather more commodious dwellings once occupied by the owners and overseers, which cluster round the church.

Olavsgruva: the copper mines

Thirteen kilometres away to the east of town along Hwy 31, one of the old copper mines, the **Olavsgruva**, has been kept open as a museum and there are daily guided tours of the workings throughout the summer (late June to mid-Aug 6 daily; rest of June, rest of Aug & early Sept Mon–Sat 2 daily, Sun 1 daily; rest of the year once weekly, on Sat; 35kr). In July and early August special **buses** make the journey from Røros train station to the mine (60kr return) to coincide with the guided tour, after which you're promptly brought back to town again. The temperature down the mine is a consistent +5°C, so remember to take something warm to wear – you'll need sturdy shoes too.

Practicalities

The **train** and **bus stations** are at the foot of the town centre, a couple of minutes' walk from the **tourist office** (late June to mid-Aug Mon–Sat 9am–8pm, Sun 10am–6pm; rest of the year Mon–Fri 9am–4pm, Sat 10am–4pm; ☎72 41 11 65), where you can pick up a comprehensive booklet on Røros and the surrounding region. They also have details of – and sell maps for – local **hikes** out across the uplands that encircle the town, one of the more popular being the five-hour trek east to the unstaffed *DNT* hut at Marenvollen. The uplands are also popular with **cross-country skiers** in the winter – and the tourist office has a leaflet mapping out several possible skiing routes. For venturing further afield, **bikes** can be rented from *Røros Sports*, on Bergmannsgata (☎72 41 12 18), for 150kr a day for a mountain bike, 100kr for a street bike, plus a 100kr refundable deposit. If you stick around for more than a day, it may be worth buying the 120kr **Røros Card** (*Røroskortet*) from the tourist office, which gives discounts on all manner of things over a 48-hour period.

Accommodation

Either the long drive or the infrequent train service north to Trondheim and south to Oslo will probably mean a night's stay in Røros. Fortunately, there's a reasonable range of central hotel accommodation. The concrete-block **youth hostel** is at Øraveien 25 (☎72 41 10 89; fax 72 41 23 77; all year; 160kr, doubles ①), about 800m south of (and behind) the train station, next to the sports ground, and shares its premises with the *Idrettsparken Hotell* (see below).

Bergstadens, Osloveien 2 (☎72 41 11 11; fax 72 41 01 55). Convenient location at the foot of Bergmannsgata, but a drab, modern hotel with dull double rooms. ③/④

Erzscheidergården, Spell-Olaveien 6 (☎72 41 11 94; fax 72 41 19 00). Easily the best place to stay in town, this guesthouse has charming, unassuming rooms in its wooden main building. Some of the rooms have fine views over town. There's an attractive subterranean breakfast area and a cosy lounge. A real snip at 300–400kr for a double. ①

Idrettsparken Hotell, Øraveien 25 (☎72 41 10 89; fax 72 41 23 77). Connected to the youth hostel (see above), this is not the most appetizing of places to stay. ③

Røros, An-Magritt-veien (☎72 41 10 11; fax 72 41 00 22). One of the *Inter Nor* hotels, this is a big modern place on the northern edge of the centre. ③/④

Vertshuset Røros, Kjerkgata 34 (☎72 41 24 11; no fax). Bang in the centre of town, with cramped doubles; at the bottom of the price category. ②

Eating and drinking

Røros is no gourmet's paradise, but there's just enough choice to get by. The best meals in town are generally served in the *Hotel Røros*, An-Magritt-veien, though it's formal and expensive (closes 10pm). *Papas Pizza*, at the foot of Bergmannsgata in the back of the *Bergstadens Hotel*, is always busy and stays open late. For substantial meals at fairly reasonable prices, the best bet is probably *Otto's Kro Restaurant*, just west of the tourist office at Peder Hiortgata 2, where succulent *entrecôte* goes for 110kr.

From Oslo to the western fjords

Oslo is an easy day's drive, bus or train ride from the fjords of the western coast – which, one could argue, is just as well considering that the forested dales and uplands filling out the interior of southern Norway rarely inspire: in almost any other European country, these elongated valleys would be attractions in their own right, but here in Norway they simply can't compare with the mountains and fjords of the north and west. Almost everywhere, the architecture is routinely modern and most of the old timber buildings that once lined the valleys are long gone – frequently reappearing in the ten-a-penny open-air museums that are a feature of nearly every town.

Of the three major trunk roads crossing the region, the **E16** is the fastest, a quick 350-kilometre haul up from Oslo to the fjord ferry point near Sogndal (see p.275). Its nearest rival, the slower **Hwy 7**, reaches the coast at Eidfjord, near to the Hardangerfjord, a distance of 334km, but in general it's an undistinguished route that's best avoided. For most of its length, Hwy 7 is shadowed by the **Oslo–Bergen railway**, though they part company when the train swings north for its wild and wonderful traverse of the coastal mountains. The third road, **Hwy 11**, which stretches the 418km from Drammen, near Oslo, to Haugesund, but passes near Odda (323km), is a slower route too and has the advantage of passing through **Kongsberg**, an attractive town that makes for a pleasant overnight stay. There are regular long-distance **buses** along all three major roads.

The E16 – to Leira, Borgund and points west

Clipping along the E16 north from Oslo, it's 180km up through a sequence of river valleys to ribbon-like **LEIRA**, where you can break your journey at the **youth hostel** (☎61 36 20 25; fax 61 36 23 05; June to mid-Aug; 85kr, doubles ①), which occupies part of the high school complex beside the road. The next village, unremarkable Fagernes, is where Hwy 51 branches north, running along the edge of the Jotunheim Nasjonalpark, passing near Gjendesheim and finally joining Hwy 15 west of Otta (see p.227).

About 30km further west, the scenery improves as you approach the coast. The road dips and weaves from dale to dale, slipping between the hills until it reaches **LAERDAL** and the stepped roofs and angular gables of the **stave church of Borgund** (daily May & Sept 10am–5pm; June–Aug 8am–7pm; 50kr), set against a forested backdrop. One of the best-preserved stave churches in Norway, Borgund was built beside what was once one of the major pack roads between east and west, though the road fell into disuse when the bubonic plague wiped out most of the local population in the fourteenth century. Much of the church's medieval appearance has been preserved, its tiered exterior decorated by shingles and dragon and Christian cross finials, and culminating in a slender ridge turret. A rickety wooden gallery runs round the outside of the church and the doors sport a swirling intensity of carved animals and foliage. Inside, the dark, pine-scented nave is framed by the upright, wooden posts that define this style of church architecture.

Beyond the church, the valley grows wilder as the E16 travels the 45km down to Fodnes, where the car ferry zips over to Manheller (hourly; 15min; 15kr, car & driver 38kr), some 18km from Sogndal.

Highway 11 – Kongsberg

Forty kilometres west of Drammen (and only an hour or two by train or bus from Oslo), **KONGSBERG** is one of the most interesting towns in the region. The local story has it that the silver responsible for the town's existence was discovered by two goatherds, who stumbled across a vein of the metal laid bare by the scratchings of an ox. True or not, Christian IV, his eye to the main chance, was quick to exploit the find, and his mining centre here marked the beginning of the seventeenth-century silver rush. It turned out that Kongsberg was the only place in the world where silver was to be found in a pure form, and by the following century the town was the largest in Norway – half of its 8000 inhabitants employed in and around the 300-odd mine shafts in the area. The silver-works closed in 1805, when Kongsberg began to make money out of its royal mint, and, a few years later, the armaments factory opened that employs people to this day.

To understand the enormous political power the mines engendered it's necessary to visit **Kongsberg Kirke** (mid-May to Aug Mon–Fri 10am–4pm, Sat 10am–1pm; rest of the year Tues–Fri 10am–noon; 15kr), the largest and arguably most beautiful Baroque church in Norway. It dates from the most prosperous mining period, at the end of the eighteenth century, and sits impressively in a square surrounded on three sides by period wooden buildings. Inside, too, it's a grand affair, with an enormous and showily mock-marbled western wall unusually comprising altar, pulpit and organ: a reverse order that had a political significance – the priest over the altar would exhort the assembled workers to be more industrious in the pursuit of profit. The plush seating arrangements were rigidly, and hierarchically, defined: on the opposite wall is the "King's Box" and boxes for the silver-works managers, while other officials sat in the glass-enclosed "cases". The pews on the ground floor were reserved for their womenfolk, while the sweeping three-tiered balcony was the domain of the Kongsberg petit bourgeoisie, the workers and, squeezing in at the top and the back, the lumpen proletariat.

As for the rest of Kongsberg, it's an agreeable, if quiet, place in summer, with plenty of green spaces. The River Lågen tumbles through the centre, and statues on the old town bridge commemorates various, often foolhardy, attempts to locate new finds of silver (including using divining rods). Enthusiasts will enjoy the mining museum, the **Norsk Bergverksmuseum**, Hyttegata 3 (mid-May to Aug daily 10am–4pm; Sept daily noon–4pm; rest of the year Sun only, noon–4pm; 20kr), housed in the old smelting works at the river's edge along with a pocket-sized ski museum and coin collection. Also, if you haven't already had your fill of open-air museums, the **Lågdalmuseet** (mid-May to Aug daily 11am–5pm; 40kr), on the east side of town off Glitregata, has a ready supply of folksy farm buildings. But merely pottering around Kongsberg is as an enjoyable way as any of spending time here.

The silver mines

The **mines** themselves, the **Sølvgruvene**, are open for tours and make a fine excursion, especially if you have children to amuse. They're hidden in green surroundings 8km out of town in the hamlet of **SAGGRENDA**; drive (or take the local bus from outside the train station) along Hwy 11 in the Notodden direction and look for the sign leading off to the right. The informative eighty-minute **tour** (mid-May to Aug; 50kr) includes a ride on a miniature train through black tunnels to the shafts. There are three or four departures a day; take a sweater as it's cold underground. Back outside, just 350m down the hill, the old ochre-painted, timber workers' compound – the **Sakkerhusene** – has recently been restored and holds some rather half-hearted displays on the history of the mines, as well as a café.

Practicalities

Kongsberg **tourist office** (late June to mid-Aug Mon–Fri 9am–7pm, Sat & Sun 10am–5pm; rest of the year Mon–Fri 9am–4.30pm, Sat 10am–2pm; ☎32 73 50 00) is footsteps from the **train station**, and can help with accommodation – not that there's much of a decision to be made: the **youth hostel** at Vinjesgata 1 (☎32 73 20 24; fax 32 72 05 34; 165kr, double rooms ①) is *the* place to stay, its comfortable, en-suite rooms occupying an attractive timber building close to the town centre. There are two ways to get there – either follow the signs on Hwy 11, or, if you're walking, it's five to ten minutes from the train station to the church and another couple of minutes from there – go round to the back of the church on the right-hand side, then head down the slope and over the footbridge. As for central **hotels**, there are just two options, the mundanely modern *Gyldenløve Hotell*, close to the train station at Hermann Foss gate 1 (☎32 73 17 44; fax 32 72 47 80; ②/③), and the rather more enticing *Grand*, down near the river at Christian Augusts gate 2 (☎32 73 20 29; fax 32 73 41 29; ②/④), where the **restaurant** is first-class. If the weather is good, head for the riverside terrace at the *Gamle Kongsberg Kro* café-restaurant, not far from the church.

West to Heddal, Seljord, Grungebru

A few kilometres outside Kongsberg, Hwy 11 passes into **Telemark**, a county that covers a great forested chunk of southern Norway. Just inside its borders is industrial **NOTODDEN** and 6km beyond that – beside the main road – is the **stave church of Heddal** (mid-May to mid-June & mid-Aug to mid-Sept Mon–Sat 10am–5pm; late June to late Aug Mon–Sat 9am–7pm; Sun all year open at 1pm only; 20kr), whose pretty tumble of shingle-clad roofs was restored to something like their medieval appearance in 1955, rectifying a heavy-handed remodelling in the nineteenth century. Surrounded by a neat cemetery and rolling pastureland, Heddal is actually the largest surviving stave church in Norway. The Christian crosses atop the church's gables alternate with dragon-head gargoyles – a typical mix of symbols in churches of this type. Inside, the twenty masts of the nave are decorated at the top by masks and there's some attractive seventeenth-century wall decoration in light blues, browns and whites, but pride of place goes to the ancient bishop's chair in the chancel. Dating to around 1250, the chair carries a relief retelling the saga of Sigurd the Dragonslayer, a pagan story that Christians soon turned to their advantage, with Jesus taking the place of the Viking, and the dragon becoming the Devil. Across from the church, there's a café and a modest museum illustrating further aspects of Heddal's history.

From Heddal, it's a further 135km west along Hwy 11 to the finely situated **GRUNGEBRU youth hostel** (☎35 07 27 65; fax 35 07 28 16; mid-June to mid-Aug; 90kr, doubles ①), which occupies an isolated huddle of well-kept timber buildings beside the road and overlooking the lake. The lodgings are simple and there are self-catering facilities – note that the hostel provides breakfast but not an evening meal. It's a good spot to overnight: although the scenery bordering Hwy 11 further to the west is wild and dramatic, staying here avoids a night in Odda, the ugly industrial centre that is the nearest significant coastal settlement.

Ninety-five kilometres from Grungebru, the road splits, with Hwy 11 turning southwest to Haugesund (see p.261), a further 102km away. Branching off to the north, Hwy 13 runs the 20km to Odda, passing the waterfalls at **Latefossen**, where two huge torrents empty into the river with a deafening roar.

The South Coast

Arcing out into the Skagerrak, the narrow strait separating Norway and Denmark, Norway's **south coast** may have little of the imposing grandeur of other, wilder parts of the country, but the fretted coastline that extends from the Oslofjord as far as Kristiansand is undeniably lovely. Backed by forests and lakes, it's this part of the coast that attracts Norwegians in their droves, equipped not so much with a bucket and spade, but with a **boat** and navigational aids – for these waters, with their narrow inlets, islands and skerries, make for particularly enjoyable sailing. **Camping** on the offshore islands is easy too, the main restrictions being that you can't stay in one spot for more than 48 hours or light fires on bare rock or amongst vegetation – leaflets detailing all the coastal rules and regulations are available at any local tourist office.

If boats and tents aren't your thing, the coastline has plenty of other attractions, notably the white-painted clapboard and stone houses of tiny towns like **Lillesand**, **Arendal** and, to a lesser degree, **Grimstad**. This portion of the coast is also important for Norway's international trade, since it's just a short hop away from Denmark, and several larger places – like Sandefjord, Larvik and Porsgrunn – have lost all trace of their seventeenth-century roles as timber ports to become industrial centres in their own right. Frankly, these manufacturing towns are best avoided, with the exception of the biggest of them, **Kristiansand**, a lively port and resort with enough sights, restaurants, bars and beaches to while away a night or two. Beyond Kristiandsand lies **Mandal**, an especially attractive holiday spot with a great beach, but thereafter the coast becomes harsher and less absorbing, announcing a sparsely inhabited region where there's precious little to detain you before Stavanger (see the following chapter).

There are regular **trains** from Oslo to Kristiansand and Stavanger, but the rail line runs just inland for most of its journey, only dipping down to the coast at the major resorts – a disappointing ride, the sea views shielded much of the time behind the bony, forested hills. The same applies to the main **road** and **bus** route – the **E18** – for this also stays inland for most of the 300km from Oslo to Kristiansand and again for the 250km on to Stavanger. On the other hand, the E18 makes travelling easy and fast and, once you've settled on a destination, only the tiniest of coastal villages is bothersome to get to – though exploring the surrounding area can be frustrating without your own vehicle. In the summertime, a third option is to take the *Hurtigbåt* **passenger express boat** from Oslo to Arendal. This zips along the coast, nipping in between the islands to call at several coastal villages on its six-hour journey, and serves as a good introduction to the south coast – though at 350kr per person it's expensive.

Along the coast to Risør

Heading south from Oslo, the E18 skirts Tønsberg on the Oslofjord before slipping round the industrial towns of **Sandefjord** and **Larvik** – there's no reason to stop unless you're catching the ferry from Larvik to Frederikshavn (Denmark) or from Sandefjord to Strömstad (Sweden); see "Travel Details" for the possibilities. Beyond, there's a rare view of the sea as you cross the massive bridge spanning the fjord nudging towards **Porsgrunn** and neighbouring **Skien**, the birthplace of Ibsen.

From the Porsgrunn bridge, it's an uneventful 110km along the E10 to Arendal, but the *Hurtigbåt* has a happier time, dropping by the good-looking coastal hamlets of **Stavern** and **Kragerø**, where Edvard Munch spent his summers and produced some of his jollier paintings. The rocky coves and myriad islands along this portion of the coast attract hundreds of Norwegian holiday-makers, who also gather at another of the *Hurtigbåt*'s ports of call, tiny **Risør**.

Arendal

The first place that really merits a stop is **ARENDAL**, 260km from Oslo, and one of the most appealing places on the coast, its sheltered harbour curling right into the town centre, which is pushed up tight against the forested hills. The town's heyday came in the eighteenth century when its shipyards churned out dozens of those sleek wooden sailing ships that then dominated international trade. There's an attractive reminder of the boom times in the grand **Rådhus** (guided tours July & Aug Mon, Tues & Thurs 11am–3pm; 40kr), a four-storey, white timber building from 1812 that faces out over what was once the main city dock. The Rådhus was actually built as a private mansion for a wealthy family of merchants and there are more elegant old buildings immediately behind it in the oldest part of town, known as **Tyholmen**. You can wander these few blocks and then stroll along the boardwalk flanking the **Pollen**, the short and rectangular inner harbour that's bordered by outdoor cafés. For the architectural low-down on the Tyholmen, call in at the tourist office (see below) and sign up for one of their city **walking tours** (July & Aug Mon, Tues & Thurs at 4pm; 1hr 30min; 40kr). Also available at the tourist office are details of all sorts of **boat trips** that leave the Pollen to explore the surrounding coastline, one of the less expensive options being the regular ferry to the offshore islets of Hisøy, Tromøy and tiny **Merdø**, where you can take a peek at the period interior of the **Merdøgaard Museum** (late June to mid-Aug daily noon–4pm; 30kr), an eighteenth-century sea captains' house, and have a swim in the Skagerrak. The sheltered channels round Arendal are ideal for boating and **canoes** can be rented at the town train station; you can buy maps and get advice on routes here too.

Practicalities

Arendal **train station** is an irritating five- to ten-minute walk from the town centre through the smoggy tunnel that leads to the Torvet, the mundane central square located about 150m north of Pollen. **Buses** stop in the larger square, west of Pollen, across from the huge red-brick church with the copper-green steeple. The *Hurtigbåt* **express passenger ferry** (late June to mid-Aug 1 daily) from Oslo arrives at 3.45pm except on Saturdays, when it gets here at a fairly useless 11pm (journey time around 7hr; 350kr). Returning to Oslo, the boat leaves at 4pm, except on Saturday, when it sets off at 9am.

Arendal **tourist office** is in the pedestrianized shopping area just off Torvet at Friholmsgaten 1 (mid-June to mid-Aug Mon–Sat 9am–6pm, Sun noon–5pm; rest of the year Mon–Fri 8.30am–4pm; ☎37 02 21 93). Easily the nicest place **to stay** is the plush *Inter Nor Tyholmen Hotel* (☎37 02 68 00; fax 37 02 68 01; ④/⑤), a smart wooden building on the waterfront at Teaterplassen 2. The more modest *Phønix Hotel*, Friergangen 1 (☎37 02 51 60; fax 37 02 67 07; ②/④), is a straightforward modern hotel footsteps from the west side of Pollen. For **food**, there are a couple of inexpensive cafés on Torvet, but more enjoyable spots include the restaurant of the *Tyholmen Hotel*, and the harbourside *Madam Reiersen* at Nedre Tyholmsvei 3, which serves delicious seafood and fresh pasta dishes. Later on, the café-bars lining the Pollen are lively drinking haunts till the early hours, especially on a warm summer's night.

Grimstad

From Arendal, it's a short 20km south on the E10 by bus or car to **GRIMSTAD**, a brisk huddle of white houses with orange-tiled roofs, stacked up behind the harbour. Nowadays scores of yachts are moored here, but at the beginning of the nineteenth century the town had no fewer than forty shipyards and carried on a lucrative trade with France. It was, therefore, not particularly surprising that when **Henrik Ibsen** left his home in Skien in 1844, at the age of sixteen, he should come to Grimstad, where he worked as an apprentice pharmacist for the next six years. The careless financial dealings of Ibsen's father had impoverished the family and Henrik already had a jaundiced view of Norway's provincial bourgeoisie – opinions confirmed here in tiny Grimstad where Ibsen mocked the worthies of the town in poems like *Resignation* and *The Corpse's Ball*. It was here too that Ibsen picked up first-hand news of the Paris Revolution of 1848, an event that radicalized him and inspired his paean to the insurrectionists of Budapest, *To Hungary*, written in 1849. But Ibsen's connections with the south coast are more usually remembered by the settings of some of his better-known works, particularly *Samfundets Støtter* (Pillars of the Community). The pharmacy where Ibsen lived and worked is now the pocket-sized **Ibsenhuset og Gramstad bymuseum** (Ibsen House and Town Museum; guided tours mid-May to mid-Sept Mon–Sat 11am–5pm, Sun 1–5pm; rest of the year Mon–Fri 10am–3pm; 25kr), which has been returned to something like its appearance in the playwright's day, complete with various Ibsen memorabilia.

The museum is in the centre of town on Henrik Ibsens gate, footsteps from the north side of the harbour. From here, it's a couple of minutes' walk to the pedestrianized part of Storgata, the main drag, and, just off it, the **Reimanngården**, a reconstruction of the first pharmacy where Ibsen worked – the original building was demolished in the 1950s – that now holds an art gallery.

There's nothing much else to see, but the town is an amiable enough place for a brief stroll and everything you need is near at hand: the **bus station** is at the south end of the harbour, a couple of hundred metres from the **tourist office** (June–Aug Mon–Fri 10am–6pm, Sat & Sun 11am–5pm; Sept–May Mon–Fri 8.30am–4pm; ☎37 04 40 41), which has details of the two-hour long **boat cruises** that meander round the skerries just offshore every day throughout the summer. There's also an attractive and central **hotel**, the *Grimstad Hotell*, Kirkegaten 3 (☎37 04 47 44; fax 37 04 47 33; ②/③), which occupies an old, cleverly converted clapboard house in the narrow lanes behind the Ibsen house; the hotel has the best **restaurant** in town. Wine buffs can seek out the locally produced fruit wines of *Fuhr* – with *Fuhr Rhubarb* and *Fuhr Vermouth* representing two daunting challenges for the palate.

Lillesand

Bright and cheerful **LILLESAND**, just 20km south of Grimstad, is one of the more popular holiday spots on the coast, the white-painted clapboard houses of its tiny centre draped prettily round the harbourfront. One or two of the buildings are especially good-looking – notably the sturdy **Rådhus** from 1734 – but it's the general appearance of the place that appeals, best appreciated from the terrace of one of the town's waterfront café-restaurants: choose from either the *Sjøbua brasserie*, midway round the harbour, or the *Beddingen*, near its southern end.

To investigate Lillesand's architectural nooks and crannies, sign up for one of the hour-long **guided walks** (mid-June to Aug daily at 3pm; 30kr), which leave from the tourist office (see below) in the old customs house on the waterfront. They also have information on local **boat trips**, including details of fishing excursions and the timetable of the *badebåten* (bathing boat; July 4 daily; 15min; 20kr), which shuttles over to a bay on the island of Skaurøya, where no one seems to care how chillingly cold the Skagerrak is. Alternatively, a narrow channel, the **Blindleia**, wiggles its way in between the skerries and the mainland south from Lillesand, and this is the route followed by the *M/S Oya*, an old passenger ferry, as it makes the three-hour summertime cruise to Kristiansand (late June to mid-Aug Mon–Sat at 10am; 80kr each way). Other, faster (and slightly more expensive) boats do the trip too – again, details from the tourist office.

Lillesand cannot be reached by train, but there are regular **bus** connections up and down the coast along the E18, which slices through the edge of town. The bus stops footsteps from the south end of the harbour, and the **tourist office** (June–Aug Mon–Fri 10am–6pm, Sat & Sun 11am–5pm; Sept–May Mon–Fri 8.30am–4pm; ☎37 27 23 77) is a five-minute walk away along the harbour to the north. Lillesand has one central **hotel**, the first-rate *Hotel Norge*, Strandgaten 3 (☎37 27 01 44; fax 37 27 30 70; ③/④), a grand old wooden building near the bus stop. The **youth hostel** (☎37 27 07 44; fax 37 27 23 27; mid-June to mid-Aug; 100kr, doubles ①) is located in a dignified timber building too, and even has its own garden, but it's an inconvenient 2km out of town in the middle of nowhere, beside Hwy 402, the road heading inland to Birkeland.

Kristiansand

KRISTIANSAND, some 30km from Lillesand, is Norway's fifth largest town and a major holiday resort – a genial, energetic place which thrives on its ferry connections with Denmark, and its excellent (though often crowded) sandy beaches. In summer, the seafront and adjoining streets are a frenetic bustle of cocktail bars, fast-food joints and flirting holiday-makers, and even in winter Norwegians come here intent on living it up.

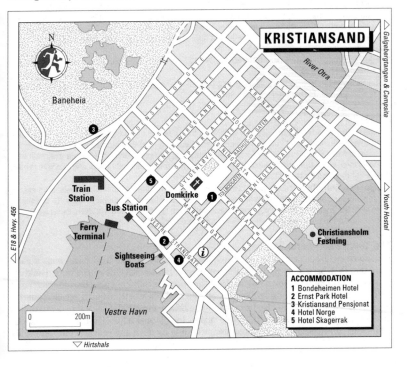

ACCOMMODATION
1 Bondeheimen Hotel
2 Ernst Park Hotel
3 Kristiansand Pensjonat
4 Hotel Norge
5 Hotel Skagerrak

Arrival, information and accommodation

Whether you're coming by **train** (☎38 07 75 00), **bus** (☎38 02 43 80) or *Color Line* **ferry** (☎38 07 88 88), you'll arrive near Vestre Strand gate, on the southwestern edge of the town grid. The **tourist office** is a short walk away, at Dronningens gate 2 (June–Aug Mon–Sat 7am–7.30pm, Sun noon–7.30pm; Sept–May Mon–Fri 8am–4pm; ☎38 02 60 65), and can provide a handy map and information on boat sailing times and island bathing and beaches. Bear in mind that if you **drive** into Kristiansand from the E18, there's a 5kr toll to pay; parking in town is easy. It's pleasant to walk around the centre, but for longer trips, the tourist office offers **bicycle rental** at 50kr a day, plus a 150kr deposit, or for better models, 200kr a day plus 1000kr deposit. Kristiansand has a reasonably good choice of **accommodation** with a fair sprinkling of hotels, a guesthouse or two, a youth hostel and a campsite in or reasonably near the centre – see the list below.

When **moving on**, the obvious route is to push on west along the E18 by train, bus or car. But note also that there are summertime cruises northeast along the coast to Lillesand (July to early Aug 1 daily; 2–3hr; 100kr, 150kr return – see p.238), while Hwy 12 makes the 240-kilometre journey north up **Setesdal** to join Hwy 11; this route into the interior is, however, extremely dull.

HOTELS AND GUEST HOUSES

Bondeheimen, Kirkegata 15 (☎38 02 44 40; fax 38 02 73 21). Located bang in the middle of town, near the Domkirke, the *Bondeheimen* offers modern, comfortable rooms in a grand, converted nineteenth-century mansion. Summer deals bring the price down by about 40kr per double per night, and there's a decent cafeteria as well. ②

Ernst Park, Rådhugaten 2 (☎38 02 14 00; fax 38 02 03 07). A flashily modernized old building with comfortable rooms, but make sure you're not given one that's above the bar-disco. ③/④

Kristiansand Pensjonat, Frobusdalen 2 (☎38 07 05 15; fax 38 07 01 15). Plain and simple rooms in an old and attractive, white-painted timber building on the edge of the city centre, a five- to ten-minute walk from the ferry dock. Something a little different from the run-of-the-mill hotels, and a bargain too. ②

Norge, Dronningens gate 5 (☎38 02 00 00; fax 38 02 35 30). Straightforward modern hotel with plain but adequate rooms. ③

Hotel Skagerrak, Henrik Wergelands gate 4 (☎38 07 04 00; fax 38 07 02 43). Modern building near the ferry terminal. Pleasantly furnished doubles. ③/④

HOSTELS AND CAMPING

Kristiansand Vandrerhjem, Skansen 8 (☎38 02 83 10; fax 38 02 75 05). At 150kr per person per night this is pricey for what you get – cramped rooms in ugly, prefabricated 1960s boxes in the middle of an industrial estate; there's a kitchen and cafeteria, however. About fifteen minutes' walk east of the ferry dock on the tiny peninsula edging the marina; follow Elvegata south and Skansen is near the end of the road on the left. Open all year. Doubles ①.

Roligheden Camping, Framnesveien (☎38 09 67 22). Large and fairly formal campsite 3km east of the town centre behind a dusty gravel car park, which itself edges a yachters' jetty. To get there, drive over the bridge at the end of Dronningens gate, turn right along Marvikveien, then right again at the end, and the site is signposted. Open June to mid-Sept.

The Town and nearby islands

Like so many other Scandinavian towns, Kristiansand was founded by and named after Christian IV, who saw an opportunity to strengthen his coastal defences here. Building started in 1641, and the town has retained the spacious quadrant plan that characterizes all his projects. There are few specific sights, but it's worth a quick stroll around – especially when everyone else has gone to the beach and left the central pedestrianized streets relatively uncluttered. Aside from the **Domkirke** (June–Aug Mon–Sat 9am–2pm) on Kirkegata at Rådhusgaten, which is modern and mock-Gothic and seats nearly two thousand, the only real target is the squat fortress, the **Christiansholm Festning** (mid-May to mid-Sept daily 9am–9pm; free), on Strandpromenaden, whose sturdy circular tower and zigzagging earth and stone ramparts overlook the colourful marina in the east harbour. Built in 1672, the tower's walls are 5m thick, an unnecessary precaution since it has never seen real service, and these days hosts arts and crafts displays.

One of the better moves you can make in Kristiansand is to catch a boat for a **cruise** through the offshore skerries. *M/S Maarten* departs from the quay beside Vestre Strand gate, at the foot of Tollbodgaten, for daily two-hour cruises (mid-June to mid-Aug; 90kr), stopping at several islands that have been designated public (and free) recreation and camping areas, so you can always stay overnight and catch the boat back the next day – but check first with the tourist office (see below) for coastal camping rules and regulations. If you just want a swim without the bother of a boat trip, head for **Galgebergtangen** (Gallows' Point), a pretty rocky cove with a small sandy beach about 1.5km east of the town centre; to get there, go over the bridge at the end of Dronningens gate, take the first major right and follow the signs.

Another possibility is the *M/S Maarten*'s excursion (late June to mid-Aug 3 weekly; 3hr 30min; 140kr) to **Ny Hellesund**, the islet-site of one of the four-hundred coastal defences built by the Germans during the occupation. From the very beginning of World War II, the German admiralty had been trying to persuade Hitler to occupy Norway, partly to avoid their ships being bottled up in the Baltic by the British fleet and partly to open up a wider North Atlantic front against the Allies. It seems, however, that Hitler only took the matter seriously after Vidkun Quisling visited Berlin in late 1939, no doubt encouraged by the Norwegian's virulent anti-Semitism. Subsequently Hitler overestimated both the likelihood of an Allied counter-invasion in the north and Norway's strategic importance, garrisoning the country with nigh on half a million men and building a string of huge coastal artillery batteries.

Eating, drinking and nightlife

Kristiansand's centre is packed with **restaurants** and **cafés**, though beware that standards are very variable – we've given a few of the choicer places below. There's also a fairly active nightlife based around several **bars** which stay open until 2am.

RESTAURANTS AND CAFÉS

Cafeteria Kvikk Lunsj, at the *Bondeheimen Hotel*, Kirkegata 15. Good self-service café with Norwegian favourites at reasonable prices – main courses and daily specials for around 70kr. Open Mon–Sat but closes at 5pm.

Harlekin Restaurant, Vestre Strand gate 32. Opposite the train station, this is a slightly stuffy restaurant but the steaks – from 150kr – are first-rate.

Sjøhuset, Østre Strand gate 12a. An old converted warehouse on the harbour, at the end of Markens gate, decked out in nautical style and serving superb fish courses for 160–180kr underneath wooden beams. Open daily in summer; closed Sun rest of the year.

Sultan, Tollbodgaten 5. Eat Turkish cuisine, mostly meat of various kinds but with some fish dishes, at this pleasant, affordable and very popular restaurant. Main courses in the region of 80–90kr. Daily from around noon till late.

BARS AND NIGHTLIFE

Kick Café Zanzibar, Dronningens gate 8. Arty bar with a terrace at the back, groovy music, and coffee and hot chocolate as well as reasonably cheap beer. Next to the tourist office.

Markens Brød & Sirkus, Tollbodgaten 8 at Markens gate. Café-bar with a vaguely oriental air – large tables and backgammon sets. Upstairs there are discos and live bands nightly, sometimes with fairly well-known faces.

Mandal

MANDAL, just 40km from Kristiansand along the E18, is Norway's southernmost town, an old timber port whose heyday came in the eighteenth century when its pines and oaks were much sought after by the Dutch, who propped many of their canal houses on, and built much of their trading fleet out of timber from around here. Although it's now bordered by a modern mess, Mandal has preserved its quaint old centre, a narrow strip of white clapboard buildings spread along the north bank of the Mandalselva River just before it rolls into the sea. It's an attractive spot, well worth a few minutes' ramble and you can also drop by the municipal **museum** (July to mid-Aug Mon–Fri 11am–5pm & Sun 2–5pm; 20kr), which occupies an antique merchant's house overlooking the river, and exhibits a small but enjoyable collection of nautical paintings – plus a statue by the town's most famous son, Gustav Vigeland (see p.209). It's not these characteristics, however, that make Mandal a popular tourist spot but rather its fine beach, **Sjøsanden**, 1 km from the centre. To get there, walk along the harbour, past the tourist office to the end of the road and turn left; keep on until the car park at the eastern end of the beach. An 800-metre stretch of golden sand that's backed by pine trees and framed by rocky headlands, it's touted as Norway's best beach – and although this isn't saying a whole lot, it's a perfectly enjoyable place to unwind for a few hours.

Mandal isn't served by trains, but there's a fast and frequent bus service here from Kristiansand (hourly; 1hr). Mandal's ugly modern **bus station** is on the north bank of the river and from here it's a brief walk west to the old town centre, just beyond which, facing the river, is the **tourist office**, at Adolf Tidemands gate 2 (Mon–Fri 9am–4pm; ☎38 26 08 20). There are a couple of good places to stay, beginning with the convenient **youth hostel**, the *Kjøbmandsgaarden*, in a cosy, old wooden building across from the bus station at Store Elvegaten 57 (☎38 26 12 76; fax 38 26 33 02; April–Sept; 125kr, doubles ①). They have **boats** and **bikes** to rent – as does the *Inter Nor Solborg Hotel*, Neseveien 1 (☎38 26 66 66; fax 38 26 48 22; ③), an odd-looking but rather attractive modern structure with every mod con; it's on the west side of the town centre, a ten-minute walk from the bus station, below a wooded escarpment. Alternatively, you can **camp** or rent a **cabin** (②) very close to the western end of the beach at the *Sjøsanden Feriesenter* (mid-June to mid-Aug; ☎38 26 10 94), a signposted 2km from the town.

The *Inter Nor Solborg Hotel* has the best **restaurant** in Mandal, but for something less pricey and more informal, head into the centre where you'll find several places including the lively pizzeria-restaurant *Jonas B Gundersen*, and a clutch of **bars** – try *Puben*.

Daily **express buses run** from Mandal along the E18 to Flekkefjord and Stavanger, respectively 90km and 210km away to the west. **Train** travellers have to return to Kristiansand to rejoin the rail network.

Along the coast to Flekkefjord and points west

Heading west from Mandal on the E18, you'll spy precious little of the coast until, after about 70km, you slip round the Fedafjord and scoot down into **FLEKKEFJORD**, a humdrum port that has traditionally depended on its tanneries and lumber. The town straddles a narrow inlet and its tiny centre, on the west side of the bridge, musters a couple of hotels and a **tourist office** (mid-June to mid-Aug Mon–Fri 10am–6pm, Sat 10am–4pm, Sun noon–6pm; rest of the year Mon–Fri 9am–3pm; ☎38 32 12 61), which is located in the old customs house on the Tollbodbrygga pier.

Beyond Flekkefjord, the E18 turns inland, eventually curving round to **EGERSUND**, a desultory port that's the midway point of a daily car ferry connecting Bergen with Hantsholm in Denmark. Egersund also has a **train** station, for it's here the rail line finally returns to the coast after tunnelling across the valleys of the interior – an uninspiring journey as the rail line travels east–west, whilst the region's valleys run north to south.

For the last 80km from Egersund to **Stavanger**, the E18 stays deep inland, but the train has a final coastal flourish, shuttling across long flat plains with the sea on one side and distant hills away to the east – an enjoyable trip until you hit the industrial estates on the peripheries of Stavanger (see the following chapter).

travel details

Trains

From Oslo to: Bergen (4–5 daily; 6hr 30min); Dombås (3–4 daily; 4hr 20min); Drammen (4–5 daily; 40min); Geilo (4–5 daily; 3hr 20min); Hamar (7 daily; 1hr 40min); Hjerkinn (3 daily; 4hr 45min); Kongsberg (4–5 daily; 1hr 20min); Kristiansand (4–5 daily; 5hr); Lillehammer (7 daily; 2hr 30min); Otta (4–5 daily; 4hr 10min); Røros (2–3 daily; 6hr); Stavanger (3 daily; 9hr); Trondheim (3–4 daily; 7hr); Åndalsnes (2–3 daily; 6hr 30min). Trains from Oslo also stop at Sjoa (2 daily; 4hr 30min) and Kongsvoll (3 daily; 4hr 50min) stations on request.

From Kongsberg to: Oslo (5–6 daily; 1hr 30min).

From Kristiansand to: Kongsberg (4–5 daily; 3hr 30min); Stavanger (3–4 daily; 3hr).

From Røros to: Hamar (1–3 daily; 3hr 50min); Oslo (1–3 daily; 6hr); Trondheim (1–2 daily; 2hr 30min).

From Skien to: Larvik (2–7 daily; 45min); Sandefjord (2–7 daily; 1hr); Tønsberg (2–7 daily; 1hr 25min); Oslo (2–7 daily; 3hr).

Buses

From Kongsberg to: Haugesund (1 daily; 8hr 30min); Kristiansand (1–2 daily; 8hr 25min); Oslo (1 daily; 1hr 35min).

From Kristiansand to Flekkefjord (1 daily; 2hr 20min); Kongsberg (1–2 daily; 8hr 25min); Mandal (hourly; 45min); Stavanger (2 daily; 4hr 40min).

From Lillehammer to: Bergen (1 daily; 10hr 25min); Fagernes (1 daily; 2hr 15min).

From Mandal to: Kristiansand (hourly; 45min); Stavanger (1 daily; 4hr).

From Oslo to: Arendal (1 daily; 4hr 15min); Fagernes (3 daily; 3hr 20min); Grimstad (1 daily; 4hr 40min); Kongsberg (1 daily; 2hr); Kristiansand (1 daily; 5hr 40min); Lillesand (1 daily; 5hr); Otta (2 daily; 5hr); Risør (1 daily; 3hr 30min); Sogndal (3 daily; 7hr).

From Otta to: Fagernes (late June to mid-Aug 1 daily; 3hr 30min); Gjendesheim (late June to mid-Aug 1 daily; 2hr); Lom (mid-June to Aug 1 daily; 1hr); Sogndal (mid-June to Aug 1 daily; 4hr 50min).

From Røros to: Trondheim (1–3 daily; 3hr 10min).

From Trondheim to: Bergen (1 daily; 13hr 30min).

Express Passenger Boats (*Hurtigbåt*)

From Oslo to: Stavern (July to mid-Aug 1 daily; 3hr 15min); Kragerø (July to mid-Aug 1 daily; 4hr 30min); Risør (July to mid-Aug 1 daily; 5hr 10min); Arendal (July to mid-Aug 1 daily; 6hr 45min).

International Ferries

From Kristiansand to: Hirtshals (5–6 weekly; 4hr 30min).

From Larvik to: Frederikshavn (5–6 weekly; 6hr 15min).

From Sandefjord: to Strömstad (2 daily; 2hr 30min).

CHAPTER SIX

BERGEN AND THE WESTERN FJORDS

I f there's one familiar – and enticing – image of Norway, it's the fjords: huge clefts in the landscape that occur throughout the country right up to the Russian border, but which are most easily, and impressively, seen on the western coast near Bergen. Wild, rugged and serene, these water-filled wedges of space are visually stunning; indeed, the entire fjord region elicits inordinate amounts of purple prose from the tourist offices, and for once it's rarely overstated. The fjords are undeniably beautiful, especially in the dead of winter, or after the brief Norwegian spring has brought colour to the landscape around early May.

Under the circumstances it seems churlish to complain of the thousands of summer visitors who tramp through on package tours, interrupting the peace and quiet that prevails the other nine months of the year. The rolling mountains are roamed by walkers, the fjords cruised by steady flotillas of white ferries, but if it all smacks too much of package holiday nightmare, don't be put off: there's been little development and what there is is very rarely intrusive. Even in the most popular regions it's easy enough to find spots not yet penetrated by the coach parties.

As for specific destinations, **Bergen**, Norway's second largest city and so-called "Capital of the Fjords", is a welcoming place and boasts some good museums – the best located in an atmospheric old warehouse quarter dating from the city's days as the northernmost port of the Hanseatic trade alliance. As its designation suggests, Bergen is also a handy springboard for the western fjords. Easily reached, to the east, is the **Flåm valley** and its inspiring mountain railway, which trundles down to the **Aurlandsfjord**, a tiny arm of the mighty **Sognefjord**, Norway's longest and deepest. The Sognefjord, lined with pretty village resorts, is the most famous of the country's waterways and is certainly one of the most beguiling, rather more so, in fact, than the **Nordfjord**, lying parallel to the north. Between the two fjords stretches the **Jostedalsbreen** glacier, mainland Europe's largest ice sheet; while north of the Nordfjord there's the tiny S-shaped **Geirangerfjord**, holding perhaps the most spectacular concentration of impressive scenery, though here the tourist hordes can, for once, be off-putting. Further north still, towards the **Romsdalsfjord**, the landscape becomes more extreme, reaching pinnacles of isolation in the splendid **Trollstigen** mountain highway.

Transport in the fjord region

Norway's western fjords comprise perhaps the most confusing region to tour by **public transport**, though this is not due to a poor service. Bus and ferry connections are good, the problem being more one of **access**. By train, you can only reach Bergen in the south and Åndalsnes in the north. For everything in between – the Nordfjord, Jostedalsbreen glacier and Sognefjord – you're confined to buses and ferries, and although they virtually all connect up with each other, it means that there is no set way to approach the fjord region.

We've covered the fjords **south to north** – from the major city Bergen, via Stavanger, the Hardangerfjord, Sognefjord, Nordfjord, Geirangerfjord and Romsdalsfjord, and to Åndalsnes. There are certain obvious connections – from Bergen to Flåm, and from Åndalsnes over the Trollstigen to Geiranger, for example – but routes are really a matter of personal choice; the text details the alternatives. It's a good idea to pick up full **bus and ferry timetables** from local tourist offices whenever you can, and be aware that shorter bus routes are often part of a longer routing on which the buses and ferries link up – meaning that you shouldn't get stranded anywhere.

BERGEN

As it had been raining ever since she arrived in the city, a tourist stops a young boy and asks him if it always rains here. "I don't know" he replies, "I'm only thirteen." The joke isn't brilliant, but it's not too much of an exaggeration either. Of all the things to contend with in the western city of **BERGEN**, the weather is the most persistent and predictable: it rains heavily and relentlessly even in summer, the surroundings often shrouded with mist. But, despite the dampness, Bergen is one of Norway's most enjoyable cities, due not least to its spectacular setting among seven hills, sheltered to the north and west by a series of straggling islands and hairline fjords that fracture the local coastline. There's plenty to see, from Bergen's fine surviving **medieval buildings** through to a whole series of good **museums**, but perhaps more than anything else it's the general flavour of the place that appeals: Bergen is a laid-back, easy-going town with a nautical air, its bustling main harbour, **Vågen**, still very much the main focus. There are other first-rate attractions within easy reach too. Just outside the city limits to the south is **Troldhaugen**, Edvard Grieg's home, and to the north lies the charming open-air museum of **Gamle Bergen** (Old Bergen). If you stay more than a day or two – perhaps using Bergen as a base for seeing the local fjord scenery – you'll soon discover that the city also has the region's best choice of **restaurants** and a decent nightlife to boot.

Arrival, information and city transport

The **train station** (☎55 96 69 00) and **bus station** (*Bystasjonen*; ☎55 32 67 80) are close together on Strømgaten, just a few minutes' walk from Bergen's harbourfront via the pedestrianized shopping street, Marken. If you're heavily laden, a taxi to the harbour will set you back about 50kr. The **airport** is 20km south of the city at Flesland, connected to the centre by the *Flybussen* (every 20–30min Mon–Fri & Sun 6am–9pm, Sat until 7pm; 40kr), which stops at the *Hotel Norge* in Ole Bulls plass, and at the bus station – a half-hour journey. Taxis from the rank outside the arrivals hall charge around 250kr for the same trip.

Ferry and express boat terminals

As well as being a local hub for ferry links with the fjords, Bergen is a busy international port. **International ferries** from Denmark, Iceland, Aberdeen and the Shetland and Faroe islands all arrive at Skoltegrunnskaien, the quay just beyond Bergenhus fortress, as do those from Newcastle, which call at Stavanger and Haugesund on the way here. *Hurtigbåt* **passenger express boats** from Haugesund, Stavanger and the Hardangerfjord, as well as those from Sognefjord and Nordfjord, line up on the opposite side of the harbour at the Strandkaiterminalen; **local ferries** from islands and fjords immediately north of Bergen mostly arrive here too, though short excursions round the Byforden, which adjoins Bergen harbour, leave from beside Torget.

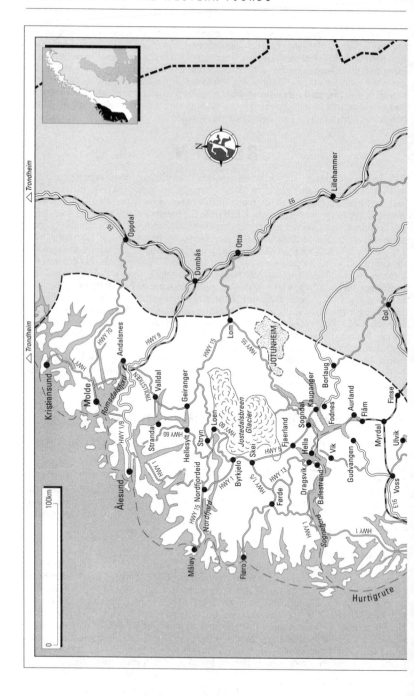

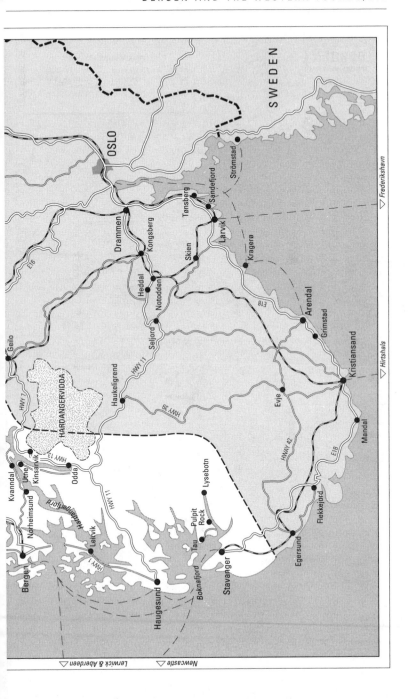

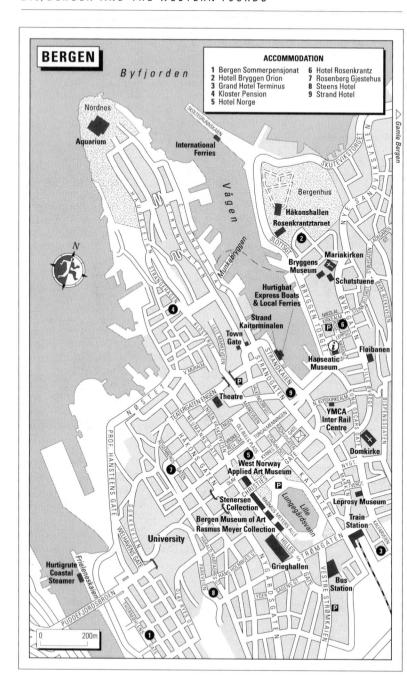

BERGEN

Byfjorden

△ *Gamle Bergen*

ACCOMMODATION

1 Bergen Sommerpensjonat
2 Hotell Bryggen Orion
3 Grand Hotel Terminus
4 Kloster Pension
5 Hotel Norge
6 Hotel Rosenkrantz
7 Rosenberg Gjestehus
8 Steens Hotel
9 Strand Hotel

Nordnes

Aquarium

International
Ferries

Bergenhus

Håkonshallen
Rosenkrantztarnet

Mariakirken

Bryggens
Museum

Schøtstuene

Hurtigbat
Express Boats
& Local Ferries

Strand
Kaiterminalen

Town
Gate

Hanseatic
Museum

Fløibanen

Theatre

YMCA
Inter Rail
Centre

Domkirke

West Norway
Applied Art Museum

Stenersen
Collection

Leprosy Museum

Bergen Museum of Art
Rasmus Meyer Collection

Train
Station

University

Lille
Lungegårdsvann

Hurtigrute
Coastal
Steamer

Grieghallen

Bus
Station

0   200m

Bergen is also a terminal port for the *Hurtigrute* **coastal steamer**, which arrives at the harbour (*Frieleneskaien*) on the southern edge of the city centre, about 1.5km from the train station – beyond the university and close to the Puddefjordsbroen. There are no connecting buses, leaving you with a steep 25-minute walk up through the university and down the other side; far better to take one of the waiting taxis to the city centre (about 50kr).

For **information** on tickets and timetables, see "Listings", p.258.

Driving and parking

If you're **driving** into Bergen, note that a **toll** (5kr) is charged on all vehicles over 50cc entering the city centre from Monday to Friday between 6am and 10pm; pay at the toll-booths. **Parking** is restricted throughout the centre and in an attempt to keep the streets free of traffic, there's an endlessly confusing one-way system in operation. The best advice is to make straight for one of the three central **garages** and leave your car there for the duration of your stay. The largest and most convenient is the *Bygarasjen* (open 24hr), at the *Bystasjonen* bus station, a short walk from the centre. You can only park on the street where there are meters or ticket machines, though this is at least free between 5pm and 8am in most places.

Information and city transport

The **tourist office** is at the beginning of the Bryggen, which runs along the north side of the main harbour, the Vågen (May & Sept Mon–Sat 8.30am–9pm, Sun 10am–7pm; June–Aug daily 8.30am–9pm; Oct–April Mon–Sat 9am–4pm; ☎55 32 14 80). They give away copies of the *Bergen Guide*, an exhaustive consumer's guide to the city, a bus route plan, and endless free brochures. You can also book rooms in private houses here, reserve places on guided tours, buy tickets for fjord sightseeing boats, rent a bike (see below) and exchange money. Similar facilities are available at a seasonal tourist office at the train station (June to late Aug daily 7.15am–11pm). In high season, expect enormous queues at both.

You can walk around most of central Bergen, though if you're intent on seeing the sights and are staying outside of the centre, consider purchasing the **Bergen Card**, a 24-hour (120kr) or 48-hour (190kr) pass which allows free travel on all the city's **buses** and free entrance to – or a substantial discount on – most of the city's sights and many sightseeing trips. It's available at the tourist office, major hotels and the train and bus stations. Otherwise, flat-fare tickets on the bus (14kr) are valid for an hour, though tell the driver if you intend to change. The **Bystasjonen**, on Strømgaten (info on ☎55 32 67 80), is the hub for all buses out into the suburbs and the surrounding area. Another useful link is the tiny orange **ferry** (Mon–Fri 7am–4.15pm; 8kr) across Vågen, from Munkebryggen along Carl Sundsgate to a point near the *SAS Royal Hotel* on the Bryggen.

Bicycle rental is available at the Bryggen tourist office for 50kr per day, plus a refundable deposit of 200kr. Should you need a **taxi**, call *Bergen Taxi* on ☎55 99 70 00, or ☎55 99 70 10 to order one in advance. There's a taxi rank in Ole Bulls plass.

Guided tours and sightseeing

The tourist office offers a plethora of **local tours**: city bus tours, a motorized mini-train ride of the locality and fjord sightseeing trips are just a few examples of what's on offer. They're all detailed in the *Bergen Guide*, which lists prices and departure times. Bear in mind, though, that it's simple and much less expensive to reach most of the destinations under your own steam; exceptions are the guided tours of Bryggen (see "Bryggen and Around", p.252) and the much-vaunted "Norway in a Nutshell" tour to Flåm (1–2 daily; 14hr; from 450kr) – see p.270.

Accommodation

Budget **accommodation** is no great problem in Bergen. There are three youth hostels, a choice of private rooms and guesthouses, and some of the central hotels are surprisingly good value. One of the better bargains are the **rooms** in private houses that you can book through the tourist office, some offering the use of a kitchen. Many are fairly central and the prices are fixed – currently 180kr for a double room (160kr single), 320kr (270kr) for en-suite rooms. They're very popular, so you'll need to get to the tourist office early in summer.

There are several **campsites** on the outskirts of the city, none of them close to the action. Most have four-bunk timber **cabins**, but the cabin specialists for the whole region are *Fjordhytter*, in the city centre at Lille Markveien 13 (☎55 23 20 80).

Hotels

Bryggen Orion, Bradbenken 3 (☎55 31 80 80; fax 55 32 94 14). Deservedly popular mid-range hotel with unassuming but perfectly comfortable modern rooms, just footsteps from the Bergenhus. Breakfasts are magnificent banquets with every type of pickled herring you can think of. ③/④

Grand Hotel Terminus, Zander Kaaes gate (☎55 31 16 55; fax 55 31 85 76). There was a time when the bustles and tweed jackets of Victorian England headed straight for the *Grand* as soon as they arrived in Bergen – and not just because the hotel is next door to the train station. Those days are long gone, but the hotel still has an air of jaded gentility and the rooms are attractive and quiet. ④

Norge, Ole Bulls plass 4 (☎55 21 01 00; fax 55 21 02 99). Bergen's most central top-class hotel, with a full range of facilities from bar to heated swimming pool. ④/⑤

Rosenkrantz, Rosenkrantzgaten 7 (☎55 31 50 00; fax 55 31 14 76). Competent mid-range hotel in an old building just behind the Bryggen. Has everything you'll need and the rooms are neat and trim. ④

Steens, Parkveien 22 (☎55 32 69 93; fax 55 32 61 22). Intimate small hotel in an attractive almost-neo-Gothic terrace near the university. ③

Strand, Strandkaien 2b (☎55 31 08 15; fax 55 31 00 17). Straightforward, pleasant modern hotel overlooking Torget. ④

Guesthouses

Bergen Sommerpensjonat, Thormøhlens gate 18 (☎55 31 13 20). One of the better places offering private rooms, this is a well-furnished set of apartments with fully equipped kitchen and TV room. Located on the far side of the university, about twenty minutes' walk from the centre. Summer only; check with the tourist office. ①

ACCOMMODATION PRICE CODES

All the Norwegian hotels and guest houses listed in the guide have been graded according to the following price bands, based on the cost of the least expensive double room in high season. However, almost every hotel offers seasonal and/or weekend discounts that can reduce the rate by one or even two grades. Many of these bargains are impromptu, but wherever possible we've given two grades, covering both the regular and the discounted rate. Single rooms, where available, are usually between 60 and 80 percent of the cost of a double.

① under 500kr	② 500–700kr	③ 700–900kr
④ 900–1200kr	⑤ 1200–1500kr	⑥ over 1500kr

Kloster Pension, Strangehagen 2 (☎55 90 21 58). One of the best of the budget pensions, with a smashing location amongst old clapboard houses, halfway down the Nordnes peninsula, towards the aquarium (follow Klostergate). Breakfast is included. ①

Rosenberg Gjestehus, Rosenbergsgaten 13 (☎55 90 16 60). Just a short walk from the central streets, close to Johannes Kirke. All rooms have shower and toilet, the price includes breakfast, and there's free coffee for guests all day. Right at the bottom of this price band. ②

Youth hostels

Intermission, Kalfarveien 8 (☎55 31 32 75). Christian-run private hostel close to the train station. Open mid-June to mid-Aug; 100kr.

Bergen YMCA Interrail Centre, Nedre Korskirkealmenning 4 (☎55 31 72 52). Ten minutes' walk from the station, close to Bryggen. Facilities include showers, kitchen, sauna and laundry; there's a supermarket nearby. It has 150 dormitory beds but fills quickly. Open mid-June to Aug. 100kr, including breakfast.

Montana Vandrerhjem, Johan Blyttsveien 30, Landås (☎55 29 29 00; fax 55 29 04 75). An enormous, 200-bed hostel, 5km from the centre – twenty minutes on bus #4 (stop Laegdene) from outside the main post office. A good standby – though it too can fill quickly in summer. 150kr, doubles ①.

Campsites

Bergenshallens Camping, Vilh. Bjerknesvei 24 (☎55 27 01 80). The nearest campsite to the city centre – ten minutes away on bus #3 from the main post office – but conditions are rudimentary. Open mid-June to mid-Aug.

Lone Camping (☎55 24 08 20). Bergen's main campsite, 20km from the centre on Hwy 580. Really only practical for those with their own transport – though it is on the lakeside, with cabins for rent (①), and a café. Open all year.

The City

Founded in 1070 by King Olav Kyrre ("the Peaceful"), **Bergen** was the largest and most important town in medieval Norway, a regular residence of the country's kings and queens, and, from the fourteenth century, a Hanseatic League port, linked to other European and Baltic cities as part of a vigorous trading network. The wealth engendered by this trade meant that Bergen also became a religious centre, supporting thirty churches and monasteries at the height of its influence. However, the League was controlled by German merchants and it was they who ran the self-regulating trading station that grew up on Bergen's main wharf, the Bryggen. In time, this clique came to dominate the region's economy, reducing the locals to a state of dependency until the 1550s. In the post-Hansa period, Bergen's native merchants carried on the monopolistic practices of their predecessors, compelling west coast fishermen to sell their catch through Bergen, an iniquitous system that continued to make Bergen's merchants wealthy right down till the nineteenth century. Fish and fishing still underpin the city's economy today, but Bergen has in recent years also become a major port and minor industrial centre in its own right.

Very little of medieval Bergen has survived, although parts of the fortress – the **Bergenhus** – which commands the entrance to the harbour, date from the thirteenth century. The rest of the city centre divides into several distinct parts, the most interesting being the wharf area, the **Bryggen**, which accommodates an attractive ensemble of eighteenth- and nineteenth-century merchants' trading posts. The Bryggen ends at the head of the central harbour, Vågen, where **Torget** is home to a colourful fish market. From here to the train station stretches one of the older districts, a mainly nineteenth-century area that remains pleasant despite being bashed about by the developers, its narrow lanes leading down to the modern concrete blocks surrounding the central lake, **Lille Lungegårdsvann**. The high-rises here comprise the commercial centre of the city, bounded to the south by a steep hill that's crowned by the **university**.

Torget

Lilian Leland, writing about Bergen in 1890, complained that "Everything is fishy. You eat fish and drink fish and smell fish and breathe fish." Those days are long gone, but now that Bergen is every inch a go-ahead, modern city, tourists flock here seeking out all things piscine. The nearest you'll get to those fishy days now is the **fish market** on **Torget** (Mon–Sat 7am–3pm): vats of ice overspill onto the already slippery square, while at every stall sit huge mounds of prawns and crab-claws, buckets of herring and a thousand other varieties of marine life on slabs, in tanks and under the knife. Fruit, vegetables and flowers also have a place in today's market but it's still the fish that dominate. It's a fine place to pick up the fixings for a picnic lunch, with dressed crabs and smoked-salmon sandwiches on sale at several stalls; load up and idle away time on the quayside, which is a good vantage point for assessing the comings and goings of the local boats and ferries.

Bryggen and around

From Torget, central Bergen spears right and left around the Vågen, with **Bryggen**, on the northerly side of the harbour, the obvious historical and cultural target. The site of the original settlement at Bergen, this is the city's best-preserved quarter, containing, among other things, the distinctive wooden gabled trading posts that front the wharf. The area was once known as **Tyskebryggen**, or "German Quay", after the Hanseatic merchants who operated their trading station here, but the name was unceremoniously dumped at the end of World War II. Hansa influence, based on an ability to trade grain and beer in return for the fish that came down from northern Norway, dates back to the thirteenth century, but only later did the foreign merchants come to dominate local affairs, much to the consternation of local landowners. By the mid-sixteenth century, however, the League was in decline and although the last German merchant hung on till 1764, economic power had long since passed to Norwegians.

The medieval buildings of the Bryggen were destroyed by fire in 1702. Subsequently many were replaced by high-gabled stone warehouses in a style modelled on that of the Hansa period, but a small section of **timber buildings** has survived and now houses shops, restaurants and bars. Although none of these structures was built by the Germans, they carefully follow the original building line: the governing body of the Hansa trading station stipulated the exact depth and width of each merchant's building, and the width of the passage separating them – a regularity that's actually best observed from Øvregaten (see below). The planning regulations didn't end there. Trade had to be carried out in the front section of the building, with storage rooms at the back and the merchant's office, bedroom and dining room on the floor above; the top floor held the living quarters of the employees, arranged by rank. Every activity in this rigidly heirarchical, all-male society was tightly controlled – employees were for-

---

The English-speaking **guided tours of Bryggen** are warmly recommended. They start from the Bryggens Museum daily between June and August at 11am and 1pm, take roughly an hour and a half, and tickets (from the museum) cost 60kr – you can use the same ticket for entry to the Bryggens and Hanseatic museums and the Schøtstuene later in the day.

bidden to fraternize with the locals and stiff fines were imposed for hundreds of "offences", down to swearing, waking up the master and singing at work.

Just along the Bryggen, near the tourist office, the **Hanseatic Museum** (daily June–Aug 9am–5pm; Sept–May 11am–2pm; 35kr) is the best preserved of the early eighteenth-century merchants' dwellings and, kitted out in late Hanseatic style, gives an idea of how things worked. Amongst the assorted bric-à-brac are the possessions and documents of contemporary families, but more than anything else it's the gloomy warren-like layout of the place that impresses, as well as the all-pervading smell of fish. Good though this is, it's the **Bryggens Museum** (May–Aug daily 10am–5pm; Sept–April Mon–Fri 11am–3pm, Sat noon–3pm, Sun noon–4pm; 20kr), next to the *SAS Royal Hotel*, that is Bergen's showpiece, a muddle of things dug up in excavations that started in 1955. The imaginative exhibitions attempt a complete reassembly of medieval life – displaying domestic implements alongside handicrafts, maritime objects and trading items – with the whole lot put into context by the reconstruction of the twelfth-century foundations that were unearthed here.

Behind the museum, the perky twin towers of the **Mariakirken** (late May to mid-Sept Mon–Fri 11am–4pm; rest of the year Tues–Fri noon–1.30pm; 10kr, free in winter) are the most distinguished features of what is Bergen's oldest extant building, a Romanesque-Gothic church dating from the twelfth century. It's still used as a place of worship and was, from 1408 to 1706, the church of the Hanseatic League merchants, who bought it and subsequently installed a fine Baroque pulpit and altar, both of which are well worth a close examination.

Along Øvregaten

Bryggen is – and has been for eight hundred years – bounded by **Øvregaten**, the street that used to mark the extent of the rows of warehouses that reached back from the quayside. Walking along it from the Mariakirken, it's easy to see the old layout of the houses – a warren of tiny passages separating warped and crooked buildings. On the upper levels, the loading bays, staircases and higgledy-piggledy living quarters are still visible; the overhanging eaves of the passageways were designed to shelter trade goods.

Behind the Mariakirken, at Øvregaten 50, is the **Schøtstuene** (June–Aug daily 10am–4pm; May & Sept daily 11am–2pm; Oct–April Sun only, 11am–2pm; 35kr), the old Hanseatic Assembly Rooms, where the merchants would meet to lay down the law or just relax – unlike anywhere else on the trading post, the building was heated in winter. Continue down the street and you'll pass the terminal for the Fløibanen, the funicular railway that runs up to the top of Mount Fløyen (see below), beyond which **Lille Øvregaten** curves round to the **Domkirke** (summer Mon–Fri 11am–2pm) – though this has been restored and rebuilt almost beyond interest. Only the choir and the bottom part of the tower have remained unchanged since the thirteenth century.

Much more promising is the endearingly antiquated collection maintained by the **Lepramuseet** (Leprosy Museum; mid-May to Aug daily 11am–3pm; 15kr), just up from the Domkirke at Kong Oscars gate 59. It's housed in the eighteenth-century buildings of St George's Hospital, ranged around a pretty cobbled courtyard, and tells the tale of the Norwegian fight against leprosy, a serious problem in earlier times. The hospital was the workplace of Norwegian medic Gerhard Henrik Armauer Hansen, who in 1873 was the first person to identify the leprosy bacteria. Small hospital rooms off the central gallery reveal the patients' cramped living quarters, while also on display are medical implements (including cupping glasses for drawing blood) and a few gruesome sketches of sufferers.

Bergenhus

Up the quayside in the other direction, past the warehouses and their narrow passages, lies the **Bergenhus**, a large, roughly star-shaped, mostly earthen fortification dated to the nineteenth century, but including the remnants of earlier strongholds and now used mostly as a park (daily 7am–11pm). Of the two medieval survivors (combined guided tour on the hour every hour; mid-May to mid-Sept daily 10am–4pm; rest of the year Sun noon–3pm; 15kr), one is the **Håkonshallen**, a dull reconstruction of the Gothic ceremonial hall built for King Håkon in the mid-thirteenth century and now standing at the back of a cobbled courtyard flanked by nineteenth-century officers' quarters. Rather better is the adjacent **Rosenkrantztårnet**, a tower whose thirteenth-century winding spiral staircases, medieval rooms and low rough corridors were enlarged in 1565 by the lord of Bergenhus, Erik Rosenkrantz, who used the place as a fortified residence. Incidentally, both buildings were wrecked by the explosion of a German ammunition ship in 1944, and the newness of the rebuilding shows.

The rest of the centre

Having seen Bryggen, you've seen the best of Bergen, though there are almost a dozen other sights and museums scattered around the centre. The liveliest part of town beyond Torget is pedestrianized **Torgalmenningen**, lined with shops and department stores and dotted with benches. Around the corner, **Ole Bulls plass** sports a rock pool and fountain above which stands a rather jaunty statue of local boy Ole Bull himself, the nineteenth-century virtuoso violinist. Ole Bulls plass stretches up to the town **theatre**, *Den Nationale Scene*, at the top of the hill, worth the short walk for a look at the fearsome, saucer-eyed statue of Henrik Ibsen that stands in front. Near here too, just down the hill, at the east end of Strandgaten, stands the only surviving **town gate**, built in 1628 to control access to the city but soon used by the authorities to increase their revenues by imposing a toll.

From Ole Bulls plass, it's an enjoyable fifteen-minute stroll along Klostergaten/Haugeveien, past old clapboard houses with the harbour down below, to the end of the **Nordnes peninsula**. Here, an attractive little park surrounds a marvellous **Akvariet** (Aquarium; daily May–Sept 9am–8pm; Oct–April 10am–6pm; feeding times noon & 4pm; 45kr). It's the best in Norway, with daft-looking penguins, roly-poly seals, and aquatic life from prawns to piranhas. Alternatively, head back into the centre to visit the art museums flanking the lake.

Museums around the lake

Bergen's central lake, **Lille Lungegårdsvann**, is a focus for summertime festivals and events, while ranged along the southern side is a series of art museums, and the **Grieghallen**, Bergen's glass-and-concrete festival hall, built in 1980. This is the main venue for the annual Bergen Festival (see p.257), though it's worth calling in at other times to check out the concert programme.

Of the quartet of art galleries beside the lake, the **Rasmus Meyer collection** (mid-May to mid-Sept Mon–Sat 11am–4pm, Sun noon–3pm; rest of the year Tues–Sun noon–3pm; combined ticket for the Stenersen & Art Museum 35kr), housed in the big building with the pagoda-like roof at Rasmus Meyers Allé 3, is the most diverting. Gifted to the city by one of its old merchant families, the collection contains an extensive collection of Norwegian painting from early landscape painters like Dahl and Fearnley (see p.200), through Christian Krohg and Theodor Kittelsen, to later figures such as Erik Werenskiold. It is, however, for its large sample of the work of Edvard Munch that the museum is usually visited: if you missed out in Oslo (see p.208), this is the place to make amends.

Just along the street are the **Stenersen collection** (same times; combined ticket 35kr), which specializes in temporary exhibitions, and has a modest sample of the work of leading international modern artists like Picasso and Klee; and the **Bergens Kunstforening** (Bergen Museum of Art; same times; combined ticket 35kr), holding Old Masters and yet more Norwegian landscape paintings. Finally, real enthusiasts can head down the street to the **Vestlandske Kunstindustrimuseum** (West Norway Applied Art Museum; mid-May to mid-Sept Tues–Sun 11am–4pm; rest of the year Tues–Sun noon–3pm; 20kr), in the *Permanenten* building at the corner of Christies gate and Nordahl Bruns gate. A lively exhibition programme with the focus on contemporary craft and design brings in the crowds, and some of the displays are very good indeed – which is more than can be said for the permanent collection.

Mount Fløien and Mount Ulriken

When the weather's fine, there's a choice of two mountains to ascend for a bird's-eye view of Bergen and its surroundings. The quaint funicular railway (*Fløibanen*) to the summit of **Mount Fløyen** ("The Vane"), 320m above sea level, runs up the hillside just metres from the Torget, and at the top there's a café-restaurant, a viewing point and footpaths heading off through the woods. It departs every half-hour (Mon–Fri 7.30am–11pm, Sat 8am–11pm, Sun 9am–11pm; May to Sept till midnight) and the return fare is 30kr. Alternatively, the highest of the seven mountains around town, the 642-metre **Mount Ulriken** is reached by the **Ulriksbanen cable car** (daily June–Aug 9am–9pm; Sept–May 10am–5pm; 50kr return); the terminal is behind the Haukeland Sykehus (hospital), which you can reach on city buses #2 or #4, or by taking the shuttle bus from outside the tourist office from (mid-May to mid-Sept daily every 30min 9am–9pm; bus and cable car 70kr return). The views from here are superb, with several footpaths reaching out into the surrounding area.

Around the city

The lochs, fjords and rocky wooded hills surrounding central Bergen have channelled the city's **suburbs** into long ribbons that trail off in every direction. These urban outskirts are not in themselves appealing, but tucked away amongst them are a couple of first-rate attractions, each of which could happily occupy half a day. Edvard Grieg's home, **Troldhaugen**, is south of the city, just beyond **Fantoft stave church**, whereas the open-air **Gamle Bergen** (Old Bergen) is a short way to the north. It's easy to get to all three attractions on public transport, and there are organized excursions of Troldhaugen and Gamle Bergen too, arranged through the tourist office (from about 180kr).

Fantoft stave church and Troldhaugen

Some 5km south of downtown Bergen, just off Hwy 1, **Fantoft Stave Church** (mid-May to mid-Sept daily 10.30am–1.30pm & 2.30–5.30pm; 20kr) was brought here from a tiny village called Fortun in the 1880s. The first owner, a government official, had the structure revamped along the lines of Borgund stave church (see p.233), complete with dragon finials, high-pitched roofs and an outside gallery. In fact, it's unlikely that the original version looked much like Borgund, though this is somewhat irrelevant considering that the church was burnt to the ground in 1992. The present owner is building a replacement, a lengthy process that should be finished in the next year or two.

Back on Hwy 1, it's a further 3km south to the turning that leads to **Troldhaugen** (Hill of the Trolls; Feb & March Mon–Fri 10am–2pm, Sun 10am–4pm; May–Sept daily 9am–5.30pm; Oct & Nov Mon–Sat 10am–2pm, Sun 10am–4pm; 40kr), the lakeside home of **Edvard Grieg** for the last 22 years of his life – though home is something of an exaggeration as he spent several months every year travelling Europe with his music. Norway's only composer of world renown, Grieg has a good share of commemorative monuments in Bergen – a statue in the city park, the *Grieghallen* concert hall – but it's here that you get a sense of the man, an immensely likeable and much loved figure of leftish opinions and disarming modesty: "I make no pretensions of being in the class with Bach, Mozart and Beethoven. Their works are eternal, while I wrote for my day and generation."

A visit begins at the **museum** where Grieg's life and times are exhaustively chronicled and a short film provides yet further insights. From here, it's a brief walk to the **house**, a pleasant and unassuming villa built in 1885, and still pretty much as Grieg left it, with a jumble of photos, manuscripts and period furniture; if you can bear the hagiographical atmosphere, the obligatory conducted tour is quite entertaining – especially for the discovery that Grieg was only five feet tall and bore an uncanny resemblance to Einstein. Grieg didn't, in fact, compose much at home, but preferred to walk round to a tiny **hut** he had built just along the shore. The hut has survived, but today it stands beside a modern concert hall, the **Troldsalen**, where there are **Grieg recitals** from late June through to October (tickets, which include transport, from Bergen tourist office). Finally, Grieg and his wife – the singer, Nina Hagerup – are buried here, in a curious tomb blasted into a rock face overlooking the lake and sealed with twin memorial stones: it's only a couple of minutes' walk down from the main footpath to the graves, but few people venture out to this beautiful, melancholic spot.

Both Fantoft stave church and Grieg's home are reached by regular **bus** (every 20min) from the bus station: take any bus leaving from platforms 19, 20 or 21. For the church, ask to be put off at the Fantoft stop, cross the road, turn right and walk up the hill behind the car park, a ten-minute stretch. For Troldhaugen, get off at the Hopsbroen stop, turn right and about 200m along the road turn left up Troldhaugsveien for an easy twenty-minute stroll to the house.

Gamle Bergen

From Olav Kyrresgate in the city centre, buses #1 and #9 run the 3km north along the fjord shore to Sandviken and the **Gamle Bergen museum** (Old Bergen; mid-May to Aug daily 11am–6pm; hourly guided tours only, on the hour; 30kr). This open-air complex holds a collection of around forty wooden houses, representative of eighteenth- and nineteenth-century Norwegian architecture, their interiors restored to give you an idea of small-town life. Immaculately maintained, with careful cobbled paths and trim gardens, the museum is saved from tweeness by the excellence of the guided tour – an anecdotal affair that can't help but make you grin.

Eating, drinking and entertainment

As you'd expect, there's lots of choice for **eating** in Bergen and you shouldn't have any difficulty finding somewhere decent. Bergen's **nightlife** tends to revolve around the city's students and is at its most active during term-time, but at any time of the year there's a good selection of cafés and **bars** to choose from. **Cultural** events are fairly thick on the ground during the summer, with the largest annual affair, the Bergen Festival, taking place in May.

Eating

For light meals in particular, the **cafés** and **snack bars** that dot the city centre are easily the most enjoyable and often the most economic places to eat, and generally have more character than their nearest rivals, the pizza houses. That said, the fish market on the Torget (Mon–Sat from 7am) remains *the* place for takeaway lunches – dressed crabs, smoked-salmon sandwiches, crab-claws and caviar all being readily available. Bergen also has a clutch of first-rate **restaurants**, most of which specialize in fresh fish and seafood – easily the city's best gastronomic asset.

Cafés and snack bars

Baker Brun, Torget. On the quayside, with a few outdoor seats overlooking the fish market, this bakery sells the city's speciality, the *shillingsboller* – a spiral, sugar-strewn bun – as well as cakes and coffee. Buy French bread here and some seafood from the market and you're away.

Bergen Chinese Restaurant, Lodin Lepps gate 2b. Footsteps from the Bryggen tourist office. Despite the name, this popular spot is as much a café as restaurant, with customers sitting on long benches. Tasty main courses from 70kr.

Café Opera, Engen 24. White wooden building near Ole Bulls plass, its interior busy with a fashionable crew drinking beer and good coffee. Tasty, filling snacks from as little as 35kr.

Kafe Krystall, Kong Oscars gate 16. Swish café-bar near the Domkirke. Delicious seafood, with main courses around 170kr.

Ola's Inn, Vaskerelvsmuget 1. Inexpensive meals served from a wide-ranging menu featuring everything from pizzas to meat balls. Cheerful spot beside Ole Bulls plass. Mon–Fri 10am–9pm, Sat 10am–5pm.

Restaurants

Bryggeloftet & Stuene, Bryggen. This restaurant may be slightly stuffy, but it serves the widest range of seafood in town – mouth-watering meals featuring every North Atlantic fish you've ever heard of, and some you haven't.

La Dolche Vita, Kong Oscars gate 8. Bright, budget-priced pizza and pasta restaurant near the Domkirke – arguably the best of its type in the city.

Enhjørningen, Bryggen. Superbly restored eighteenth-century merchant's house – all low beams and creaking floors – serving excellent Norwegian specialities at fairly high prices. Worth every kroner for an indulgent evening out. The daily buffet lunch (Mon–Sat noon–4pm, Sun 1–4pm) is more affordable, with lashings of salmon, prawns and herring, along with salads, hot dishes, bread, cheese and desserts.

To Kokker, Bryggen. Similar to the *Enhjørningen*, but a tad more formal and without the buffet. First-class seafood. Main courses up to 200kr. Above the *Baklommen* bar. Closed Sun.

Wesselstuen, Engen 14. Old-fashioned Norwegian restaurant – which means lots of burnished wood and brass – with main dishes at 120–140kr, plus a menu of cheaper pasta, omelette and baked potato meals. Off Ole Bulls plass.

Bars and nightclubs

Bryggen Tracteursted, Bryggen. Raucous, earthy bar in one of the old wooden merchants' buildings on the Bryggen. Live music Fri & Sat. Closed Sun.

Dickens, Ole Bulls Plass 8–10. The busiest of the downtown bars, with a young clientele draped across two floors, sitting in side rooms or in the conservatory-style main bar. Food on sale, too, and draught beer. Bit of a meat rack.

Galeien, inside the *Bryggen Orion Hotel*, Bradbenken 3. Fun nightclub with a wide age range, but best enjoyed if you're in a group. A couple of minutes' walk from the Bryggen.

Hulen Stiftelsen, Olav Ryesvei 47. A club in an old air-raid shelter under Nygårdsparken – on the far side of the university from the city centre. Hosts live bands midweek, discos at the weekends. Open Wed & Thurs 8pm–1am, Fri & Sat 9pm–3am.

Sjøboden, Bryggen. Sited inside one of the old timber buildings on the Bryggen, this is a lively spot with frequent live music (of very variable quality).

Festivals and the arts

The **Bergen International Festival** (*Festspillene i Bergen*) is the biggest annual jamboree, usually held over the last twelve days of May and presenting a programme of music, ballet, folklore and drama. Principal venue is the Grieghallen (☎55 21 61 50), where you can pick up tickets and information. Throughout the summer, from May to August, **Sommer Bergen** covers a wide range of activities throughout the city, from fishing competitions to jazz festivals – the tourist office has all the relevant information.

Otherwise, Bergen is pretty big on folk events – singing, dancing and costumed goings-on of all kinds. Catch **folk dancing** at the Bryggens Museum (early June to mid-Aug twice weekly at 9pm; tickets from the tourist office or on the door, 95kr). The other main folk event is *Fana Folklore* (☎55 91 52 40), a staged country festival of Norwegian music, food and dancing on a private estate outside the city. It takes place at 7pm several times a week from June to August and costs 200kr per person, including transport; tickets from hotels and *A/S Kunst*, Torgalmenning 9.

Recitals and concerts
The tourist office has full details of all **musical events** held in and around the city. Specific events to watch out for include concerts by the Bergen Philharmonic (*Bergen Filharmoniske Orkester*), from September to June in the Grieghallen, and summer recitals at Grieg's home, Troldhaugen, from late June to October. For organ recitals, visit Mariakirken by the Bryggen Museum (June–Aug Tues & Thurs at 7.30pm; 50kr). Enthusiasts can catch Bergen's **brass band** playing in the city park beside the Rådhus some summer afternoons.

Listings

Airlines *Braathens SAFE*, Olav Kyrres gate 27 (☎55 23 55 23); *British Airways* enquiries through *Braathens SAFE; Lufthansa*, at the airport (☎55 99 82 30); *SAS*, at the *SAS Hotel* on the Bryggen (☎81 00 33 00).

British consulate Carl Konows gate 34 (☎55 94 47 00).

Car breakdown *Viking Redningstjeneste*, Edvard Griegsvei 3 (24-hr service; ☎55 29 22 22); *NAF*, Marken 12 (24-hr service; ☎55 16 90 20).

Car parking *Parkeringshuset*, Rosenkrantzgaten 4 (Mon–Fri 7am–9pm, Sat 8am–4pm), is central and handy for short stays. For longer stays and/or more flexibility *Bygarasjen*, behind the bus station on Vestre Strømkaien, is open 24hr.

Car rental All the major international car rental companies have offices at the airport, including *Avis* (☎55 22 76 18) and *Hertz* (☎55 22 60 75). In town, there's *Budget*, next to the tourist office at Lodin Lepps gate (☎55 90 26 15), and *Avis* at Lars Hilles gate 20b (☎55 32 01 30).

Cinemas As elsewhere in Norway, cinemas show films in their original language. The thirteen-screen *Konsertpaleet* is in the centre at Neumanns gate 3.

Emergencies Casualty (24hr) and emergency dental care (Mon–Fri 10–11am & 7–9pm, Sat & Sun 3–9pm) at Lars Hilles gate 30 (☎55 32 11 20).

Exchange The main post office has competitive exchange rates for currency and travellers cheques and is open longer hours (see below) than the banks (mid-May to Aug Mon–Fri 8.15am–3pm, Thurs till 5.30pm; rest of the year Mon–Fri 8.15am–3.30pm, Thurs till 6pm). The tourist office and the big hotels offer poor rates.

Ferries *Color Line,* Skuteviksboder 1, Dreggen (☎55 54 86 60) operates car ferries from Bergen's Skoltegrunnskaien to Newcastle; *Fjord Line*, Slottsgaten 1 (☎55 32 37 70), operates car ferries from Skoltegrunnskaien to Egersund and Hanstholm (Denmark); *P&O Scottish Ferries* have car ferries leaving the Skoltegrunnskaien for Aberdeen and Lerwick; and *Smyril Line* car ferries depart from the Skoltegrunnskaien for Iceland and the Faroes (☎55 32 09 70). *Flaggruten* run *Hurtigbåt* passenger express boats from the Strandkai Terminal to Haugesund and Stavanger (☎55 23 87 80); *Fylkesbaatane Reiseservice Hurtigbåt* passenger express boats leave the Strandkai Terminal for Sognefjord and Nordfjord (☎55 32 40 15); and *HSD Hurtigbåt* passenger express boats run from Strandkai Terminal to Norheimsund and Odda (☎55 23 87 80). The *Hurtigrute* coastal steamer sails from the Frieleneskaien. For general information on ferry sailings, contact the tourist office; tickets from local travel agents or the operator.

Gay scene Information on Bergen's low-key gay scene at the main gay café-bar, *Café Finken*, Nygårdsgaten 2a (☎55 31 21 39).

Hiking The *DNT*-affiliated *Bergen Turlag,* Tverrgaten 4–6 (Mon–Fri 10am–4pm; ☎55 32 22 30), will advise on hiking trails in the region, sells hiking maps and arranges guided weekend walks. A year's membership of *DNT* costs 360kr.

Laundry *Jarlens Vaskoteque,* Lille Øvregate 17, near the funicular (Mon–Fri 10am–8pm, Sat 9am–3pm). There's a coffee bar here, too.

Library Strømgaten 6 (Mon–Fri 9am–8pm, Sat 9am–2pm, July & Aug Tues, Wed & Fri till 3pm, Mon & Thurs until 7pm, Sat until 1pm); for foreign newspapers and the Edvard Grieg manuscript collection.

Pharmacy *Apoteket Nordstjernen,* at the bus station (Mon–Sat 7.30am–midnight, Sun 8.30am–midnight; ☎55 31 68 84).

Post office Olav Kyrres gate (Mon–Wed 8am–5pm, Thurs & Fri 8am–6pm, Sat 9am–3pm).

Travel agents The *Norske Vandrerhjem* (Norwegian Youth Hostel Association) travel office is part of *Terra Nova Travel,* Nygaten 3 (Mon–Fri 8.30am–4pm; ☎55 32 23 77), and can advise on all aspects of travel as well as providing literature on the country's hostels. The national student travel organization is *KILROY Travels,* in the Studentsentret – see above (☎55 32 64 00). Otherwise, central travel agents include *Winge Travel Bureau,* Chr. Michelsens gate 1–3, and *Bennett Reisebureau,* Strandgaten 197.

Vinmonopolet Downtown off-licence at Nygårdsgaten 6.

Women's organization *Zonta* is an international women's organization; contact Berit Wollan, St Hanshaugen 56, 5033 Fyllingsdalen (☎55 16 19 92).

THE WESTERN FJORDS

Heading out from Bergen, the **western fjords** beckon. The main coastal highway jerks its way south across the mouths of several fjords on its way to **Stavanger**, the region's lively second town; but far more people choose to head east to the closest of the fjords, **Hardangerfjord**. Northeast from Bergen, there's **Voss**, a winter sports resort of some renown, and **Flåm**, at the end of one of the most exciting trips of them all, the train down the Flamsdal valley to the **Aurlandsfjord** – the most popular fjord trip in Norway, and easily done as a day out from Bergen. Scenic as all this is, it's only beyond here that the fjord region proper begins, north of the Aurlandsfjord, itself an offshoot of one of the most beautiful fjord systems, **Sognefjord**, which cuts inland east from the coast for some 180km. Further north, and running parallel, the **Nordfjord** is smaller at 90km long, but more varied in its scenery, with patches of the **Jostedalsbreen glacier** within sight – and within reach – beyond. The **Geirangerfjord**, further north again, is a marked contrast – tiny, sheer and rugged; while the northernmost **Romsdalsfjord** and its many branches and inlets show signs of splintering into the scattered archipelagos that characterize the northern Norwegian coast. Most importantly, this is a landscape not to be hurried. There's little point in dashing from fjord to fjord – you need to stay put for a while, and go for at least one hike or cycle ride, to really appreciate the fjords in all their magnificent splendour.

At times the sheer size of the fjords is breathtaking – but then the geological movements that shaped them were on the grand scale. During the Ice Age, around three million years ago, Scandinavia was wholly covered in ice, which was extremely thick inland but thinner towards the coast. Under the weight of the ice the river valleys grew deeper, leaving basins when the ice retreated that filled with seawater and became the fjords. Due to the saltwater and the warm Gulf Stream, the fjords remained largely ice-free, and, because the ice had been thinner (ie less heavy) at the coast, were often deeper than the sea itself. The Sognefjord, for example, reaches depths of 1250m, ten times that of most of the North Sea.

FJORD FERRIES

Throughout the text we've detailed the frequency and journey times of **fjord car ferries** and *Hurtigbåt* **passenger express boats**. *Hurtigbåt* services are usually fairly infrequent – three a day at most – whereas many car ferries shuttle back and forth every hour or two from around 7am in the morning until 10pm at night every day of the week; we've given times of operation where they are either different from the norm or particularly useful. **Hurtigbåt fares** are fixed individually with prices starting at around 60kr per hour travelled, but rising to well over 100kr per hour: the four-hour trip from Bergen to Stavanger costs, for example, around 450kr. **Car ferry fares**, on the other hand, are priced according to a sliding scale, with ten-minute crossings running at around 15kr per person (35kr per car and driver), a twenty-minute trip costing 19kr (51kr).

Fjord practicalities

Bergen advertises itself, rather sharply, as "Capital of the Fjords", and the tourist office does organize a barrage of excursions (by bus and ferry) from the city. However, these are an expensive option since most can be done independently. Also, as Bergen is on the western edge of the fjords, the bulk of the day trips involve too much travelling for comfort. A much better option is to use one of the small towns that dot the fjords as a base, especially as once you're actually amidst the fjords, distances are quite modest – at least by Norwegian standards. In the Hardangerfjord system, **Ulvik** is the most appealing base, Sognefjord has **Fjærland** and **Balestrand**, while further north **Loen**, **Åndalsnes** and **Ålesund** all have their advantages.

The convoluted topography of the western fjords has produced a dense and complex **public transport** system that is designed to take you to all the larger villages and towns at least once every weekday, whether by train, bus, car ferry, *Hurtigrute* coastal steamer or *Hurtigbåt* passenger express boat. General transport listings for this chapter are given in "Travel Details" (pp.287–88), and in the text itself we've included local connections where they are especially useful; this information should be used in conjunction with the full **timetables** that are widely available across the region. Bear in mind also, that while there may be transport to your destination, many Norwegian settlements are scattered and you could be in for a long walk once you've arrived – a particularly dispriting experience if it's raining: check the text and, where appropriate, the maps to find out exact locations.

South to Haugesund

The skerries and islets that shred the coastline **south of Bergen** provide a pleasant introduction to the scenic charms of western Norway – and hint at the sterner beauty of the fjords that gash the mainland just a few kilometres to the east. The intricacies of this shoreline, together with the prevailing westerlies, have long made navigation in these parts difficult, while the region's farmers have always struggled to survive on the thin soils that have accumulated on the leeward side of some of the islands.

With great ingenuity, Norway's road-builders have in recent years cobbled together a coastal road, Hwy 1, the **Kystvegen**, which traverses the coast from Bergen to Haugesund and ultimately Stavanger – with three ferry trips breaking up the journey. Travelling this road by **bus** takes a little under six hours, and allows you to see far more than you would on the *Hurtigbåt* **passenger express boat**. The *Kystbussen* leaves Bergen for Haugesund and Stavanger two or three times daily; advance booking is recommended. A one-way ticket to Haugesund costs around 210kr, 340kr to Stavanger, with discounts for students and train pass holders. Car **drivers** should allow six or seven hours for the journey to Stavanger, four or five to Haugesund, which is the best place to stop en route; it's a good idea to pick up car ferry timetables at Bergen tourist office before leaving. The various ferry crossings cost around 220kr per driver and car, 75kr per passenger.

Haugesund

Workaday **HAUGESUND**, two ferry rides and 210km south of Bergen, is a small and lively port that flourished in the nineteenth century from the herring fisheries and is now a major player in the North Sea oil industry. It was here that the first ruler of Norway as one kingdom, Harald Håfagre (Harald the Fair-Haired), was buried, and a granite obelisk, the **Haraldshaugen**, marks his alleged resting place, by the seashore about 2km north of the centre. He gained sovereignty over these coastal districts at a decisive sea battle in 872, an achievement which, according to legend, released him from a ten-year vow not to cut his hair until he became king of all Norway – hence his nickname. Haugesund's other claim to fame is as the town from where a certain baker, in an attempt to improve his fortunes, emigrated to the United States and then changed his name to Monroe. On Haugesund's quayside, there's a **statue** to commemorate the thirtieth anniversary of the death of his daughter, Marilyn.

After you've had a quick look round the brisk, modern gridiron that constitutes the town centre, there's no real reason to tarry, though you could check out any local events with the **tourist office** (June–Aug Mon–Fri 10am–6pm, Sat 10am–3pm; Sept–May Mon–Fri 8am–3.30pm; ☎52 72 50 55), on the harbourfront across from the *Hurtigbåt* ferry terminal. They also supply all the usual information including bus timetables and town plans. From here to the **bus station** is about 600m, straight down Kaigata. For a **place to stay**, the *Rica Saga Hotel*, Skippergata 11 (☎52 71 11 00; fax 52 72 33 36; ②), has pleasant, comfortable doubles, and is just one of several straightforward modern hotels right in the centre of town.

Stavanger and around

STAVANGER is something of a survivor. While other Norwegian coastal towns have fallen foul of the precarious fortunes of fishing, Stavanger has grown and flourished, and now boasts a dynamic economy that has swelled the population to around 100,000. It was the herring fishery that first put money into the town, crowding its nineteenth-century wharves with coopers and smithies, net makers and menders, and when this industry failed the town progressed into shipbuilding and ultimately oil: the port builds the rigs for the offshore oilfields and afterwards refines the oil before dispatch.

None of which sounds terribly enticing, and certainly no one could describe Stavanger as picturesque. But if you have arrived here from abroad by ferry or plane, or find yourself at the end of the south coast's railway line, it's an easy city to adjust to and it's worth sparing at least a little time to see the attractive old town before heading onwards. If you stay longer, you can sally out into the surrounding fjords – among them the outstanding **Lysefjord** – and take advantage of the city's excellent restaurants and lively bars. You'll also hear lots of English spoken: foreign oil workers congregate here and there's even a twice-weekly English-language news section in the local paper, *Stavanger Aftenblad*.

Arrival and information

The **airport** is 14km south of the city at Sola, from where there's a *Flybussen* bus into Stavanger (every 30–40min; 35kr), stopping at the major downtown hotels. The **bus**

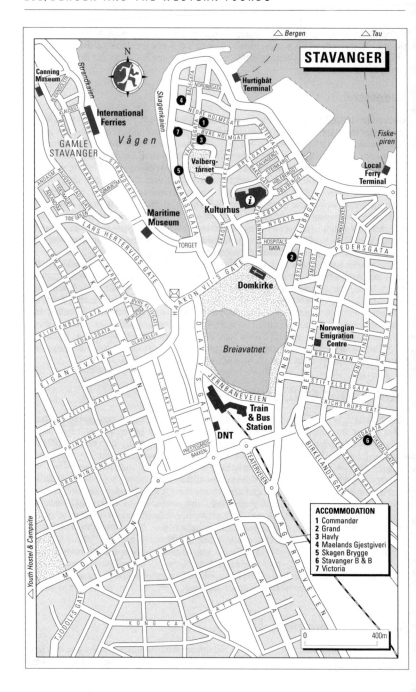

△ Bergen   △ Tau

STAVANGER

Canning Museum

Strandkaien

International Ferries

GAMLE STAVANGER

Skagenkaien

Vågen

Hurtigbåt Terminal

NORDBØGATA

NEDRE HOLMEGATE

ØVRE HOLMGATE

Fiske-piren

Local Ferry Terminal

Valberg-tårnet

Maritime Museum

SKANSEGATA

TORGET

Kulturhus

PEDERSGATA

HOSPITALS GATA

Domkirke

Breiavatnet

Norwegian Emigration Centre

STIFTELSESGATA

Train & Bus Station

ERICHSTRUPS GATE

DNT

PRESTEGÅRDS-BAKKEN

SAUDAGATA

JERNBANEVEIEN

TEATERVEIEN

Youth Hostel & Campsite

MADLAVEIEN

PEDER KLOWS GATE

TJODOLFS GATE

KONG CARLS GATE

LAGÅRDSVEIEN

ACCOMMODATION

1 Commandør
2 Grand
3 Havly
4 Maelands Gjestgiveri
5 Skagen Brygge
6 Stavanger B & B
7 Victoria

0   400m

terminal is on the southern side of the town's central lake, a pint-sized affair that's the most obvious downtown landmark; the **train station** (☎51 56 96 00) is adjacent.

Color Line **ferries** (☎51 52 45 45) from Newcastle and Bergen arrive at the harbour on Strandkaien, a five-minute walk from the main square, Torget. *Hurtigbåt* **passenger express boats** use the terminal at the foot of Kirkegata, which runs south to the central city lake. All the **local express boats and ferries**, for the islands and fjords around Stavanger, arrive at and depart from either the *Hurtigbåt* terminal or the Fiskepiren terminal, just to the east along the harbour (route information on ☎51 52 26 00, Mon–Fri 8am–5pm, Sat 9am–1.30pm).

If you **drive** in, there are several official **parking** places: look for the blue "P" sign. Central car parks include those beside the train station, the post office and on Klubbgata. See "Listings", p.266, for addresses of car rental agencies.

Information and guided tours

The **tourist office** (Mon–Fri 9am–5pm, Sat 9am–2pm; ☎51 89 66 00) is in the central Kulturhus at the top of Sølvberggaten, about 200m north of the lake, and there's a tourist information **kiosk** beside the harbourfront in the summer (July & Aug daily 10am–8pm). They'll give you the free *Stavanger Guide*, a useful listings booklet, and can arrange guided tours (see below). They also sell the **Stavanger Card**, which gives free or discounted rates on sightseeing trips, museum visits and local bus and *Hurtigbåt* journeys; the card costs 110kr for 24 hours, 190kr for 48 hours and 24kr for 72 hours, and is also available from most hotels.

Just about everywhere in Stavanger is walkable, while the town's surroundings are accessible with a variety of local boats and buses that depart from the terminals listed above. For a more formal introduction to the city and surrounding area, consider one of the **guided tours** on offer. There's an enjoyable two-hour walking tour of Stavanger (mid-June to mid-Aug Tues & Thurs at 11am; 80kr), which starts at the harbourside information kiosk and takes in the historic quarter of Gamle Stavanger; the fjords can be seen from sightseeing boats, which depart regularly throughout the summer from Skagenkaien – tickets are available at the quayside from around 200kr.

Accommodation

There's plenty of choice of **accommodation** in Stavanger. Half a dozen hotels cluster Stavanger's compact centre, each offering substantial summer discounts. Alternatively, there are a couple of reasonably convenient, no-frills guesthouses and, further afield, a youth hostel and campsites.

Hotels and guesthouses

Commandør, Valberggata 9 (☎51 89 53 00; fax 51 89 53 01). Handy if slightly down-at-heel central hotel, close to the Valbergtårnet; breakfast included. ②/③

Grand, Klubbgata 3 (☎51 89 58 00; fax 51 89 57 10). Excellent central choice, close to all the bars and restaurants. Smart, modern rooms with cable TV, and the price includes a very good buffet breakfast. ②/③

Havly, Valberggata 1 (☎51 89 67 00; fax 51 89 50 25). Spick and span modern hotel near the Valbergtårnet. ②/③

Maelands Gjestgiveri, Nedre Holme gate 2 (☎51 89 55 85; fax 51 89 55 86). On the east side of the harbour, this utilitarian guesthouse with basic rooms is one of a chain. ①/②

Skagen Brygge, Skagenkaien 28 (☎51 89 41 00; fax 51 89 58 83). Delightful new hotel that's put the squeeze on its competitors. Flashy place with lots of glass and consequently enjoyable views over the waterfront. ③/④

Stavanger Bed & Breakfast, Vikedalsgaten 1a (☎51 52 76 00; fax 51 52 76 05). Straightforward modern hotel in an unexciting residential area a five-minute walk southeast of the central lake. ①

Victoria, Skansegata 1 (☎51 89 60 00; fax 51 89 54 10). Part of the *Inter Nor* chain, a large modern block overlooking the east side of the harbour. The foyer has an oddly Victorian look but the rooms are comfortable and well maintained. ③/⑤

Hostels and camping

Mosvangen Camping, Tjensvollveien 1 (☎51 53 29 71; fax 51 87 20 55). By the lake, next door to the youth hostel. Has cabins and a café as well as tent and caravan pitches. Open late May to early Sept.

Mosvangen Vandrerhjem, Henrik Ibsens gate 21 (☎51 87 29 00; fax 51 87 06 30). *HI* youth hostel with a lakeside setting, a three kilometre walk from the centre: take Madlaveien west from near the station and turn left just beyond the lake onto Tjensvollveien – Henrik Ibsensgate is its continuation. Open all year. Advance reservations advised. Has self-catering and laundry facilities. Breakfasts cost 60kr. 100kr, doubles ①.

The Town

Much of central Stavanger is modern, built with oil money, a flashy and surprisingly likeable ensemble of mini tower-blocks. The only relic of the medieval city is the twelfth-century **Domkirke** (mid-May to mid-Sept Mon–Sat 9am–6pm, Sun 1–6pm; rest of the year Mon–Sat 9am–2pm), up above Torget, whose pointed-hat towers signal a Romanesque church that's suffered from several poorly conceived renovations. The classically simple interior, built by English craftsmen, has fared badly too, spoilt by ornate seventeenth-century additions, including an overly intricate pulpit and five huge memorial tablets adorning the walls of the aisles: all a swirling jumble of richly carved angels, crucifixes, death's heads, animals and apostles. There are organ recitals here every Thursday at 11.15am.

Beside the harbour, on **Torget**, there's a small daily market, with flowers, fruit and veg filling the square, while for fresh fish you should check out the water tanks on the quayside. The streets around **Skagen**, on the jut of land forming the eastern side of the harbour, make up the town's shopping area, a bright mix of mazy lanes and pedestrianized streets that occupies the site of the original Viking settlement. The spiky **Valbergtårnet** (Valberg tower; Mon–Fri 10am–4pm, Sat 10am–2pm; free), atop the highest point here and guarded by three rusty cannons, was a nineteenth-century fire watch; along with some distinctly unthrilling ceramics and textile displays, it offers sweeping views of the city and its industry.

Gamle Stavanger

The town's star turn is **Gamle Stavanger** (Old Stavanger), on the western side of the harbour. Though very different in appearance from the modern structures back in the centre, the buildings here were also the product of a boom when, for much of the nineteenth century, the herring turned up offshore in their millions. Benefiting from this slice of luck, Stavanger flourished and expanded, and the number of merchants and ship owners in the town increased dramatically. Huge profits were made from the exported fish, which were salted and later, with new technology, canned. Today, some of the wooden stores and warehouses flanking the western quayside hint at their nineteenth-century pedigree, but it's the succession of narrow, cobbled lanes behind them that show Gamle Stavanger to best advantage. Formerly the home of local seafarers and cannery workers, the area has been maintained as a residential quarter, mercifully free of tourist tat, and the long rows of white-painted, clapboard houses are immaculately maintained, down to gas lamps, picket fences and tiny terraced gardens. There's little architectural pretension, but here and there flashes of fancy wooden scrolling must once have raised eyebrows amongst the Lutheran population.

The **Hermetikkmuséet** (Canning Museum; early June & late Sept Tues–Fri 11am–3pm, Sun 11am–4pm; late June to mid-Sept daily 11am–4pm; Oct–May Sun 11am–4pm; 30kr), right in the heart of Gamle Stavanger at Øvre Strandgate 88, occupies an old sardine-canning factory and gives a glimpse into the industry that saved Stavanger from collapse at the end of the nineteenth century. The herring largely disappeared from local waters in the 1870s, but the canning factories kept the economy afloat and remained Stavanger's main source of employment until as late as 1960: in the 1920s there were seventy different canneries in the town and the last one closed down in 1983. A visit to an old canning factory may not seem too enticing a prospect, but actually the museum is very good, not least because of its collection of sardine tin labels, called *iddis* in these parts from the local pronunciation of *etikett*, the Norwegian for label. Hundreds have survived, in part because they were avidly collected by the town's children, though this did prompt bouts of adult anxiety – "Labels thefts – an unfortunate collection craze" ran a headline of the *Stavanger Aftenblad* in 1915. The variety of design is quite extraordinary – anything and everything from representations of the Norwegian royal family through to surrealistic labels depicting fish with human qualities. The museum also smokes its own sardines on the first Sunday of every month and every Tuesday and Thursday from mid-June to mid-August, and very tasty they are too.

Eating

Although prices are somewhat inflated by oil business expense accounts, Stavanger is a great place to **eat**, with a series of fine fish and seafood restaurants clustered on the east side of the harbour along Skagenkaien. For something less expensive, you'll have to stick to the more mundane cafés and restaurants in the vicinity of the Kulturhus.

Akropolis, Sølvberggata 14. Footsteps from the Kulturhus, this is a medium-priced Greek restaurant housed in a white wooden building on a cobbled street. Closed Mon.

Dolly Dimple's, Kongsgårdsbakken 1. Basic pizzeria with a few wooden tables and benches. Slices to eat in or take away, and whole pizzas (which will feed two and are excellent) for around 140kr. A few metres up from the Torget.

Konditori Café Tante Molla, Salvågergata 10. Oslo-style coffee house offering tasty, cheap and filling lunches. A short walk from the Kulturhus, down an alley off Østervåg.

Sjøhuset Skagen, Skagenkaien 16. Fine fish and seafood restaurant on the harbour, with monkfish the speciality. Main dishes are around 160–180kr.

Skagen Bageri, Skagen 18. Pleasant coffee house and patisserie on the east side of the harbour.

Drinking and nightlife

Stavanger is lively at night and particularly at the weekend when a rum assortment of oil workers, sailors, fishermen, executives, tourists and office workers gather in the **bars and clubs** on and around the harbourside Skagenkaien to live (or rather drink) it up. Most places stay open until 2am or later, with the rowdier revellers lurching from one bar to the next.

For more subdued evenings, check out the programme at the **Stavanger Konserthus** (☎51 50 88 10) in Bjergsted park, north of the centre beyond Gamle Stavanger, where there are regular concerts by the *Stavanger Symfoniorkester* and visiting artists. There's an eight-screen **cinema**, *Stavanger Kinematografer*, inside the Kulturhus on Sølvberggaten (☎51 50 70 30).

Bars and clubs

Café Garagen, Strandkaien. Busy R&B bar always worth checking to see what's on.

Café Sting, Valberget 3. Right next to the Valbergtårnet, this laid-back wooden café-bar is open to 2am every day. Popular with gays and heteros alike.

Kontoret, Skagen 16. Upmarket bar in old town house, where an older set enjoy civilized drinking in comfortable surroundings.

Newsman, Skagen 14. The best vantage point in town from which to view the weekend mayhem – the bar has an outdoor terrace and gets packed to the gills. Inside, the newspaper theme means papers to read and a trendy clientele. Open until 2am.

New York, Skagenkaien 24. Popular bar-disco, with a gold Statue of Liberty above the door and live bands at the weekend. Open until 4am.

Ovenpaa, Skagenkaien 10. Rowdy rock bar with pool tables and ear-splitting music. Live bands upstairs at weekends.

Taket, Strandkaien. The best club in town, across the harbour from most of the bars. Open Tues & Sun midnight to 4am, Wed–Sat 10pm–4am, though get there at opening time to avoid the queues.

Listings

Airlines *Braathens SAFE*, Strandkaien 2 (☎51 51 10 00); *British Airways*, at the airport (☎51 65 15 33); *SAS*, at the airport (☎51 65 89 00).

Bicycle rental *Sykkelhuset*, Løkkeveien 33 (☎51 53 99 10).

British consulate Prinsens gate 12 (☎51 52 97 13).

Car rental *Avis*, at the airport (☎51 65 19 00); *Budget*, Lagårdsveien 125 (☎51 52 21 33) and at the airport (☎51 65 07 29); *Hertz*, Olav V's gate 13 (☎51 52 00 00) and at the airport (☎51 65 10 96); *Interrent*, Haakon VII's gate 1 (☎51 66 75 20) and at the airport (☎51 65 10 90); *Stavanger Bilutleie*, Kong Karls gate 71 (☎51 52 03 52).

Emergencies Doctor ☎51 53 33 33; dentist: Egil Undem, Kannikbakken 6 (☎51 52 84 52), or see local Saturday newspaper for duty dentist.

Exchange Competitive rates at the main post office (see below).

Ferries International: *Color Line*, Strandkaien (☎51 52 45 45); regional: *Rogaland Traffikselskap* (☎51 89 04 99); *Hurtigbåt* express boats to Bergen: *Flaggruten* (☎51 89 50 90).

Gay scene For nightlife, see *Café Sting*, above. Information from *LLH* gay switchboard (☎51 53 14 46).

Hiking The *DNT*-affiliated *Stavanger Turistforening*, Olav V's gate 18 (Mon–Fri 10am–4pm; ☎51 84 02 00), will advise on local hiking routes and sells a comprehensive range of hiking maps. It maintains around 900km of hiking trails and over thirty cabins in the mountains east of Stavanger – as well as organizing ski schools on winter weekends.

Left luggage In the express boat terminal (Mon–Fri 6.30am–10pm, Sat 6.30am–6pm, Sun 9am–10pm) and the train station (daily 6.30am–11pm, Sat until 4pm).

Laundry *Sentralvaskeriet*, Breibakken 2. Coin-operated launderette.

Petrol 24-hour service, car wash and groceries at *Statoil*, Løkkeveien 115.

Pharmacy *Løveapoteket*, Olav V's gate 11 (☎51 52 06 07). Open daily until 11pm, until 8pm on public holidays.

Post office Haakon VII's gate (Mon–Wed & Fri 8am–5pm, Thurs 8am–6pm, Sat 9am–1pm). Has currency exchange too.

Shopping The main shopping centre is *Arkaden*, Klubbgata 5 (Mon–Fri 10am–8pm, Sat 10am–4pm).

Taxis *Stavanger Taxisentral*, Sjøhagen 10 (☎51 88 41 00).

Travel agents *Winge Reisebureau*, Østervåg 20 (☎51 89 45 00).

Vinmonopolet Off-licence at Olav V's gate 13.

Around Stavanger

Stavanger sits on a narrow promontory just to the south of the wide waters of the **Boknafjord**, which makes a deep indentation in the coast, trailing islets and skerries and linking with the narrower fjords that drill much further inland. The most diverting of these inner fjords is **Lysefjord**, which is famous for its precipitous cliffs and an especially striking rock formation, the **Preikestolen** (Pulpit Rock). There are regular **boat trips** from Stavanger to the Lysefjord, parts of which – including the Preikestolen – are also fairly easy to reach by public transport.

Lysefjord

Framed by mighty cliffs, the pencil-thin **Lysefjord** pierces the mainland, its inky waters stirred by crashing waterfalls and overlooked by the occasional homestead. There are several ways to visit the fjord by **boat** from Stavanger. Departing from the Skagenkaien, *Rødne Clipper Fjord Sightseeing* runs a quick, three-hour circular trip up about half its length (Jan–May, Sept & Oct 5 monthly; June 5 weekly; July & Aug 10 weekly; 190kr), but despite the gushing multilingual commentary, the fjord as seen from the bottom of its cliffs can't help but be disappointingly gloomy – and from this angle Preikestolen hardly makes any impression at all. Rather better is the same company's expedition to **Lysebotn**, at the east end of the fjord, from where a connecting bus tackles the 27 switchbacks up the mountainside to reach the minor road back to Stavanger (May 2 monthly; June–Aug 2 weekly; Sept 1 weekly; 7hr; 275kr). The main advantage of this route are the fabulous views back along the fjord from Lysebotn. You can save money by doing the journey independently: *Rogaland Traffikselskap* runs ferries to Lysebotn from Stavanger's Fiskepiren between three and five times weekly (4hr; 88kr, car & driver 197kr; advance booking required for vehicles). If you're travelling by bus, ask at the tourist office for help in coordinating the ferry trip with the infrequent bus service back from Lysebotn to Stavanger. For more spectacular views, a demanding **hiking trail** leads west from the car park of the *Øygardstøl* café and information centre, just above the last hairpin on the Lysebotn road, to **Kjerag**, a craggy granite plateau about 1000m above the fjord; here too is a much photographed boulder – the **Kjeragbolten** – which is wedged between two rock faces high above the ground. If you tackle the hike, allow between five and six hours for the round trip.

The other celebrated vantage point, **Preikestolen**, is at the mouth of the Lysefjord a good deal closer to Stavanger. It consists of a distinctive 25-metre square table of rock with a sheer 600-metre drop down to the fjord below it on three sides. It's a popular spot and in good weather it can be a little overcrowded, but the views are fabulous all the same. From mid-June to late August, you can get there by public transport: catch the ferry for the forty-minute trip from Stavanger's Fiskepiren to **TAU**, where there's a twice daily connecting bus running the 20km or so on to Preikestolen; the tourist office can tell you which ferries connect with the bus and confirm return times. From the end of the road, it's a three-hour hike to Preikestolen and back along a clearly marked and comparatively easy hiking trail. If you want to hang around, you can stay in the small, pleasant **youth hostel** (June–Aug; ☎94 53 11 11; off season ☎51 84 02 00; fax 51 84 02 14; 105kr, doubles ①) by the car park at the end of the road; reservations are advised.

The Hardangerfjord and around

Only the 120-kilometre-long **Hardangerfjord** is easily and cheaply accessible from Bergen by bus. It's the first of many rattling trips to be made in the fjord region: the road (Hwy 7) twists up the valley past thundering waterfalls and around tight bends before chasing down the other side to **NORHEIMSUND**, sheltered in a bay of the fjord. There is precious little to the town – one main street and a tiny harbour – and the time it takes for the bus to make a stop is all the time you'll need. Like many fjord settlements, it's not the destination but the journey itself that's the real attraction, though you may want to soak up the eminently agreeable surroundings by **staying** overnight at the handsome *Norheimsund Fjord Hotel* (☎56 55 15 22; fax 56 55 15 88; ③).

From Norheimsund, the bus sticks to Hwy 7 as it travels east along the rugged shoreline, a pleasant ride with the Hardangerfjord beginning to split into various subsidiaries in a manner typical of the fjord systems of the whole coast. Every turning seems to bring fresh mountain and fjord views until the bus swings down to **Kvanndal**, where, for drivers at least, there's a choice of routes: you can either press on down the northern shore of the Hardangerfjord towards Ulvik and Voss (see opposite), or stay with the bus route by taking the Kvanndal ferry (hourly; 20min) over to Utne, at the head of the peninsula that divides the Hardangerfjord from the slender Sorfjord.

Little more than a few houses huddled around its harbour, **UTNE** is nevertheless the site of the region's main museum, the **Hardanger Folkemuseum** (May–Aug Mon–Sat 10am–4pm, Sun noon–4pm, July until 6pm; rest of the year Mon–Fri 10am–3pm; hourly guided tours in summer; 25kr), which sports a re-creation of a nineteenth-century farming hamlet as well as putting on regular exhibitions and shows of contemporary art. Few people hang around once they've finished with the museum, but there are several good reasons to spend the night here, not least the comfortable *Utne Hotel* (☎53 66 69 83; fax 53 66 69 83; ③), a cheerful clapboard complex right by the ferry. If you're planning to travel south and then east towards Oslo on Hwy 11 – a route covered on p.233 – Utne is a far better spot to overnight than the next settlement, Odda, a zinc-producing and iron-smelting town, 45km away at the head of the Sorfjord. Utne also makes a good base for hiking in the Hardangervidda Nasjonalpark, across on the east side of the Sorfjord (see below).

Although it's conveniently sited on the foreshore beneath the Hardangervidda park, **KINSARVIK**, linked to Utne by frequent ferries (25min), is a less appealing place to stay if you're intending to spend a few days hiking. Having said that, the **tourist office** here (May, June & late Aug to late Sept Mon–Fri 10am–3.30pm; late June to late Aug daily 10am–7pm; rest of the year Mon–Fri noon–3pm; ☎53 66 31 12) has details of local hiking routes and accommodation, with the big deal in these parts being the *Hotel Ullensvang* (☎53 66 11 00; fax 53 6615 20; ③/④), a massive modern affair plonked on the water's edge 11km to the south in **LOFTHUS**. From Kinsarvik and Lofthus you can also pick up buses heading north to Voss and Bergen.

Hiking trails from the fjord shore in the vicinity of both Lofthus and Kinsarvik climb up to the Hardangervidda plateau, a stiff day's walk leading to the unstaffed *DNT* hut of **Stavali**. From here, paths fan out over the whole of the national park.

The Hardangervidda plateau

Comprising an area of 1000 square kilometres, the **Hardangervidda** is Europe's largest mountain plateau, occupying a great slab of land east of the Hardangerfjord and south of the Bergen–Oslo railway. The plateau is characterized by rolling fells and wide stretches of level ground, its rocky surfaces strewn with lakelets and connecting rivers. The whole plateau is above the tree line, and at times has an almost lunar look to it, an elemental landscape with some variations: there are mountains and a glacier, the **Hardangerjøkulen**, northwest in the vicinity of **Finse**, while the west is wetter – and the flora somewhat richer – than the barer moorland to the east. The lichen that covers the rocks is savoured by herds of reindeer, who leave their winter-grazing lands on the east side of the plateau in the spring, chewing their way west to their breeding grounds before returning east again after the autumn rutting season.

Stone Age hunters followed the reindeer on their migrations and traces of their presence – arrowheads, trapping enclosures – have been discovered over much of the plateau. Later, the Hardangervidda became one of the main crossing points between east and west Norway, with horse traders, cattle drivers and Danish dignitaries cutting across the plateau along cairned trails. These are often still in use as part of a dense network of trails and tourist huts that has been developed by several *DNT*-affiliates in recent decades. Roughly one third of the plateau has been incorporated within the **Hardangervidda Nasjonalpark**, but much of the rest is protected too, so hikers won't notice a great deal of difference between the park and its immediate surroundings. The entire plateau is also popular for winter cross-country hut-to-hut ski touring.

In terms of **access**, there are hiking routes up to the plateau from the east shore of the Sorfjord, notably in the Lofthus-Kinsarik area (see opposite). Alternatively, you can view the Hardangervidda from Hwy 7 between Kinsarvik and Geilo, or from the Oslo–Bergen train line, which tracks across the northern edge of the plateau between Finse (see p.271) and Geilo. Many hikers find the wide skies and lichen-dappled scenery particularly beautiful and walk from one end of the Hardangervidda to the other, a seven- or eight-day expedition.

Ulvik

Tucked away in a snug corner of the Hardangerfjord, the pocket-sized village of **ULVIK** drapes prettily along the shoreline, amidst fruit orchards whose blossom adds a soft pink-white lustre to the green of the hills in springtime. There's nothing particular to see – indeed, the town's main claim to fame is as the place where potatoes were first grown in Norway, in 1765, which just about sums things up. Nonetheless, it's a popular place to unwind, with a cluster of good hotels. **Hiking** trails radiate out from Ulvik into the surrounding countryside, with one of the easiest being the eighteen-kilometre round trip over the adjacent promontory and up along the Osafjord to the smattering of farmsteads that constitute the hamlet of Osa.

Ulvik **tourist office** (mid-May to mid-Sept Mon–Sat 8.30am–5pm, Sun 1–5pm; rest of the year Mon–Fri 8.30am–1.30pm; ☎56 52 63 60) has leaflets covering all the local walks and rents out bikes (100kr per day). You'll find them in the centre beside the bus stop and the jetty – not much public transport comes this way, mainly just summertime *Hurtigbåt* boats from Eidfjord and Norheimsund, and daily buses from Voss. Amongst the **hotels**, the *Ulvik Hotel* (☎56 52 62 00; fax 56 52 66 41; ③/④) is fine, though the plushest place is the *Brakanes Hotel* (☎56 52 61 05; fax 56 52 64 10; ③/⑤); both are beside the fjord, bang in the centre. The *Ulvik Fjord Pensjonat* (☎56 52 61 70; fax 56 52 61 60; May to late Sept; ②), a five-minute walk west from the tourist office along the waterfront, is – if you ignore the stuffed animals in the lounge – another pleasant option, and a good deal cheaper.

Voss, Mjølfjell and Finse

Around 100km east of Bergen, **VOSS** is the first stop for many travellers heading into the fjord region. Impressions are generally favourable, since this is a lakeside town of just 14,000 people, sporting a thirteenth-century church and surrounded by snow-capped hills – however, Voss is essentially a winter sports destination. Although the industrious tourist office does its best to promote the town as a touring centre, it's hard to escape the conclusion that the season is artificially extended to include summer. Consequently, your best bet is to have a quick look round before moving on, unless, that is, you're here either for the skiing or for the much vaunted "Norway in a Nutshell" tour (see below), for which the town is much the most convenient base.

With the lake on one side and the River Vosso on the other, Voss has long been a trading centre on one of the main routes between west and east Norway – though you'd barely guess it from today's modern town. In 1023, King Olav visited to double check the population had all converted to Christianity and stuck a big stone cross here to make his point, and two centuries later another king, Magnus Lagabøte, built a church in Voss to act as the focal point for the whole region. This church, the **Vangskyrkja** (June–Aug daily 9am–5pm; open occasionally in winter; 10kr), still stands, its eccentric octagonal spire rising above stone walls up to 2m thick. The interior is splendid, a surprisingly flamboyant and colourful affair with a Baroque reredos and a folksy rood screen, where a crucified Jesus is attended to by two cherubs. The ceiling is even more unusual, its timbers painted in 1696 with a cotton-wool cloudy sky inhabited by flying angels – and the nearer you get to the high altar, the more of them there are. That's pretty much it as far as specific sights go, though you could take a stroll by the **lake**, Vangsvatnet, or wander the central shops and cafés – if you've come from the hamlets and villages further north shopping might seem something of a treat.

Skiing in Voss

Skiing starts in December and continues until late April, and though there's nothing fancy here, you should be able to get in a few enjoyable days' winter sports. From near the train station, a **cable car** – the *Hangursbanen* – climbs 700m to give access to several short runs, as well as two further ski lifts that take you up another 200m. There's a choice of downhill ski routes of international standard, or you can take longer and gentler downhill routes through the hills above town.

Full **equipment**, for both downhill and cross-country skiing, will set you back around 200–250kr per day; you can rent skis from *Voss Ski & Surf*, at the upper station of the cable car, or from *S. Endeve Sport*, Vangsgata 52 (☎56 51 11 19). Daily lift passes are available, and in January and February some trails are lit for night skiing. Beginners should contact the Ski School, *Skiskule & Skiutleige* (winter daily 9.30am–5pm; ☎56 51 00 32), at the upper station of the cable car. More information on skiing in Voss is available from the tourist office (see below).

Practicalities

Buses stop outside the **train station** at the western end of the town centre; if you're just passing through, there are luggage lockers on the platform. From here, it's a five-minute walk to the **tourist office** (June–Aug Mon–Sat 9am–7pm, Sun 2–7pm; Sept–May Mon–Fri 9am–4pm; ☎56 51 00 51) on the main street, Uttrågata – veer right round the Vangskyrkja and it's on the right. It largely concerns itself with hiking and touring in the surrounding area, but pick up a free *Voss Guide*, which has useful listings, and some timetables. If you plan to go to Flåm via Myrdal (see below), and don't intend stopping over anywhere, consider buying a **"Norway in a Nutshell"** ticket from here (or from the train station), an inclusive train/bus/ferry ticket for the Voss–Myrdal–Flåm–Gudvangen–Voss route. Available from June to mid-September, it costs just over 260kr and is an excellent way of seeing something of the fjords if time is short.

A right turn from the train station and a ten-minute walk along the lake away from the town centre brings you to the excellent **youth hostel** (☎56 51 20 17; fax 56 51 22 05; Jan–Oct; 150kr, doubles ①), overlooking the water; it serves large, cheap evening meals (and good breakfasts) and rents out bikes and canoes. The **campsite**, *Voss Camping* (☎56 51 15 97; all year), is by the lake south of the Vangskyrkja along Prestegardsalléen – turn left from the station and take the right fork at the church. It has a few cabins, laundry facilities, and also offers bikes and boats for rent. As you might expect, there are plenty of cheapish **pensjonater** (① and ②) in Voss, though they're likely to be fully booked in winter; ask at the tourist office about summer deals. Easily the best **hotel** is the nineteenth-century *Fleischer's Hotel* (☎56 51 11 55; fax 56 51 22 89; ④), next door to the train station. Rooms here are plush, the **restaurant** is first rate and there's a terrace bar as well.

Routes on from Voss

From Voss, **express buses** run north along the E16, turning down Hwy 13 to reach the Sognefjord via Vik and the Vangsnes ferry (see p.274). There's also a local bus service (4–6 daily; 1hr 10min) straight along the E16 to Gudvangen, intended to connect with the *Hurtigbåt* express passenger boats from Gudvangen to Flåm, and with ferries to

Kaupanger – but check connections before you set out. Once daily, this service also links with the summertime bus (late June to mid-Sept) from Gudvangen to Flåm and Geilo.

More popular and infinitely more exciting is the **train journey** east from Voss, along the Oslo line as far as either Mjølfjell, Myrdal – where you change for the invigorating ride down to Flåm (see below) – or Finse.

East to Mjølfjell and Finse

The **train route** from Voss **east to Oslo** is one of the most impressive rides in the country, taking in a good number of forests, waterfalls, windswept mountains and wild valleys. Along the way there are a couple of places to break your journey for a day or two's hiking, firstly the thoroughly recommended **youth hostel** at **MJØLFJELL** (☎56 51 81 11; fax 56 51 40 00; April & mid-June to Sept; 90kr, doubles ①), about halfway between Voss and Myrdal. The hostel is actually 6km from Mjølfjell station, but only 300m or so from **ØRNEBERGET** station, just to the east – though far fewer trains stop here. Located in a beautiful, isolated setting, beside a rushing river, the hostel has its own heated pool and is a fine place to rest up for a day or so. You can drive here too: the hostel is at the end of a narrow minor road that begins in Voss; you can't, however drive any further east.

Finse

Beyond Mjølfjell, the higher reaches of the railway line are desolate places even in good weather. All trains stop at **Myrdal**, a remote railway junction in the middle of nowhere, and then proceed to **FINSE**, the railway's highest point, where snow in early August isn't unusual. Finse is nothing more than its station and a few isolated buildings, bunkered down against the howling winds that rip across the plateau in wintertime. Cross-country skiing is particularly energetic here, locals buckling up as soon as they leave the station and zipping off into the distance. You can rent cross-country skiing gear if you want to join in; at other times of the year, you can hike south on the track round the Hardangerjøkulen glacier to reach the trails and huts of the Hardangervidda plateau. Less energetically, pay a visit to the **Rallarmuseet** (summer daily 10am–10pm; 15kr), a museum that records the planning and building of the Oslo–Bergen railway in the late nineteenth century.

There are also **mountain bikes** for rent in Finse, which you can then use to cycle down the old construction road, the gravel- and sometimes asphalt-surfaced *Rallarvegen*, originally laid to provide access for men and materials during the building of the railroad. The most popular stretch of the *Rallarvegen* heads west downhill from Finse to Myrdal station, a distance of 38km, though you may have to dispense with the first 21km (to Hallingskeid) as this is the highest part of the *Rallarvegen* and can be blocked by snow as late as July: check locally for conditions. You'll need to be reasonably fit to make the journey too.

As for **accommodation**, *DNT* operates a fully staffed 150-bed cabin complex, *Finsehytta* (☎56 52 67 32; mid-Feb to mid-May & early July to mid-Sept; ①), and there's also a hotel, *Finse 1222* (☎56 52 67 11; fax 56 52 67 17; Feb–Oct; ②). Heading east from Finse, the train takes forty minutes to reach Geilo, three and half hours more to Oslo.

The train to Flåm and the Aurlandsfjord

Just east of Mjølfjell, the mountain roads finally fizzle out but the railway wriggles on and up to the **Myrdal** junction, at the start of one of Europe's most celebrated branch lines. This is the twenty-kilometre-long, 900-metre plummet down into the **Flåm valley** – a fifty-minute ride not to be missed under any circumstances. The track, which took four years to lay, spirals down the mountainside through hand-dug tunnels, at one point travelling through a reverse tunnel to drop nearly 300m. The gradient of the line is one of the steepest anywhere in the world, and as the train screeches its way down the mountain, past cascading waterfalls, it's good to know that it has five separate sets of brakes, each capable of bringing it to a stop. The tiny train runs all the year round, a local lifeline during the deep winter months.

People have in the past risen to the challenge and **walked from Myrdal** down the old road into the valley, instead of taking the train – an enthralling five-hour hike through changing mountain scenery. The only advice that the tourist office gives about this route is not to walk the other way, *up* to Myrdal, which would take forever, and in any case there's nothing at Myrdal (apart from the train station) if and when you finally get there. If you've come equipped with a decent mountain bike, you could always **cycle** down instead, though the road is too steep to be relaxing.

Flåm

FLÅM village, the train's destination, lies alongside meadows and orchards on the **Aurlandsfjord**, a matchstick-thin branch of the Sognefjord. However, having made the exciting journey, you could be excused for wondering why you bothered. The fjordside complex adjoining the train terminus is crass and commercial – souvenir trolls and the like – and on summer days the tiny village heaves with tourists who pour off the train, eat lunch, and then head out by bus and ferry, having captured the stunning valley on film. But a brief stroll is enough to leave the crowds behind, while out of season, or in the early evening when the day-trippers have moved on, Flåm remains a delight. If you are prepared to risk the weather, early September is probably the best time to visit: the peaks already have snow on them and the vegetation is just turning from green to its autumnal golden brown.

The harbourside complex is ugly, but it does hold everything you'll need, from a supermarket and train ticket office to a **tourist office** (May & Sept Mon–Fri 10.30am–6.30pm; June–Aug daily 8.30am–8.30pm; Oct–April Mon–Fri 8am–4pm; ☎57 63 21 06), where you can buy fjord ferry tickets and pick up local transport information and details on hiking in the area. If you do stay, as well as tent space and cheap cabins (①), there's a small **youth hostel** at *Flåm Camping* (☎57 63 21 21; fax 57 63 23 80; May–Sept; 85kr, doubles ①), a five-minute signposted walk up from the train station. More upmarket rooms are available at either of the small **hotels**: the *Fretheim Hotell* (☎57 63 22 00; fax 57 63 23 03; ④), back from the water behind the old yellow station, and the rather more quiet and attractive *Heimly Pensjonat* (☎57 63 23 00; fax 57 63 23 40; ②), 500m around the fjord towards Aurland.

The *Fretheim* serves breakfast, lunch and dinner. If all you want is a snack and a drink, try the **café** with outdoor seats on the harbour, by the station.

Around Flåm: the Aurlandsfjord and Nærøyfjord

From Flåm there are daily *Hurtigbåt* **passenger express ferries** up the Aurlandsfjord and along the Sognefjord, calling at Aurland, Vangsnes and Balestrand en route to Bergen, five and a half hours away. Another *Hurtigbåt* service (1–3 daily) runs west to the jetty at Gudvangen, a two-hour cruise up the Aurlandsfjord and down to the southern end of the **Nærøyfjord** (the narrowest fjord in Europe), whose high rock faces keep out the sun throughout the winter. It's a superb trip and connecting buses wait at the jetty for onward travel to Voss, a further fine ride up the valley, with the mountains scored by a succession of huge waterfalls.

If you're **driving**, Flåm and Gudvangen are connected by one of the more spirited pieces of tunnelling on display in the fjords – two separate stretches, of 4km and 11km (this section the longest in Norway and the fifth longest in the world), slicing through the mountainside to link the two villages. Local **buses** ply this route, too, beginning in Geilo, then descending the Aurlandals valley to Aurland, before proceeding to Flåm and Gudvangen (late June to mid-Sept 1–2 daily).

The Sognefjord and around

Apart from Flåm, which in any case isn't on the main fjord, the **Sognefjord**'s most appealing spots lie on its north bank, hugged by the highway (variously Hwy 1 and 55) for almost the whole of its length. Roads and transport connections on the south side are, at best, sketchy. To reach Balestrand, the main town on the north side, there are express boats from Bergen or Flåm, or buses from Sogndal to the east.

Balestrand

BALESTRAND is an appealing first stop, a tourist destination since the mid-nineteenth century, when it was discovered by European travellers in search of cool, clear air and picturesque mountain scenery. Kaiser Wilhelm II was a frequent visitor, as were the British, and these days, as the battery of small hotels and restaurants above the quay testifies, the village is used as a touring base for the immediate area. It's very small in scale, though, with farming rather than tourism still the principal occupation round here. If you've an hour or so to spare, take a peek at Balestrand's two attractions, beginning with the **English church of St Olav**, a spiky brown and beige wooden structure built in the general style of a stave church in 1897 at the behest of a British émigré, a certain Margaret Kvikne. In one of those curious hand-me-downs from Britain's imperial past,

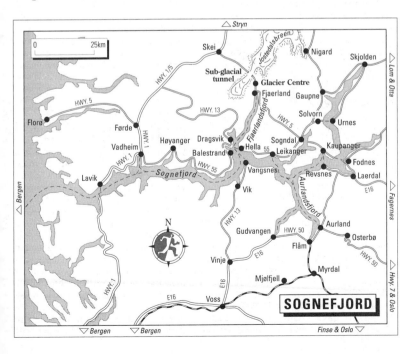

the church remains part of the Diocese of Gibraltar, which arranges English-language services during the summer. The Germans have left their mark, too. About 700m south of the church along the fjord are two marked **Viking burial mounds**, supposedly the tombs of King Bele and his wife, next to which the Kaiser has plonked a statue of the king in a heroic pose – and there's a statue of his son across the fjord in Vangsnes to match (see below).

Practicalities

Buses arrive on the quayside, where you'll also find the **tourist office** (early June & late Aug Mon–Fri 8.30am–4.30pm, Sat 8.30am–2.30pm; mid-June to mid-Aug Mon–Sat 7.30am–9pm, Sun 11am–3pm; rest of the year Mon–Fri 10am–4pm; ☎57 69 12 55), where you can rent bikes (100kr a day) and pick up maps detailing hiking routes in the surrounding mountains. In terms of **accommodation**, the charming *Midtnes Pensjonat* (☎57 69 11 33; fax 57 69 15 84; ②), about 300m from the dock behind the English church, is a pleasantly low-key affair; ask for a room with a fjord view. Another good choice is the **youth hostel** (☎57 69 13 03; fax 57 69 16 70; mid-June to mid-Aug; 145kr, doubles ③), just 150m west of the dock in the comfortable *Kringsjå Hotel*. Both places serve tasty and excellent-value dinners. The grand *Kvikne's Hotel* (☎57 69 11 01; fax 57 69 15 02; May–Sept; ④) dominates much of the waterfront, and it's worth popping into the bar to take a look at the fancy fittings, but don't take a room without having a look first, as some are in a bland modern annexe. The town **campsite**, *Sjøtun Camping* (☎57 69 12 23), occupies a treeless field just beyond the burial mounds, a kilometre or so south of the dock. Most visitors to Balestrand **eat** where they sleep, but you could try the *Kvikne's* restaurant or, more affordably, *Gekkens Café*, upstairs in the pint-sized shopping centre on the quayside.

    Onward connections from Balestrand include daily *Hurtigbåt* passenger express boats to Bergen or Flåm; a daily *Hurtigbåt* service to Fjærland (early June to mid-Sept); and buses to Sogndal, where you change for Fjærland, and to Førde (change for Stryn). There's also a regular summertime passenger ferry (daily 11am–1pm & 3–5pm) that short-cuts the main road by crossing the narrow mouth of the Esefjord to Dragsvik, where **car ferries** operate on a triangular route, south across the fjord to Vangsnes and east to Hella.

North to Fjærland

The most direct route north from Balestrand is by passenger ferry up to the settlement of Fjærland, a lovely trip through the wild **Fjærlandsfjord**. The mountainsides aren't as steep as some, but they're blanketed with a thick covering of trees extending down to the water's edge, while vast vertical clefts in the rock accommodate a succession of tumbling waterfalls. **FJÆRLAND** itself matches its surroundings perfectly – a gentle ribbon of old wooden houses edging the fjord, with the mountains as a backdrop. It's one of the region's most picturesque places, saved from the developers by its isolation: it was one of the last settlements on the Sognefjord to be connected to the road system, with Hwy 5 from Sogndal only completed in 1994. Moreover, it's eschewed the crasser forms of commercialism to become the self-proclaimed "Norwegian Book Town", with a number of old buildings accommodating antiquarian and second-hand bookshops. It also has a splendid **hotel**, the *Hotel Mundal* (☎57 69 31 01; fax 57 69 31 79; May–Sept; ④), whose nineteenth-century turrets, verandas and high-pitched roofs overlook the fjord from the centre of the village. There's a more modest alternative, the *Fjærland Fjordstue Hotell* (☎57 69 32 00; fax 57 69 31 61; ②), a brief walk away along the fjord.

    The *Hotel Mundal* rents out rowing boats and bikes – and it's an easy three-kilometre cycle round the fjord to the **Norsk Bremuseum** (Norwegian Glacier Museum; daily

April, May, Sept & Oct 10am–4pm; June–Aug 9am–7pm; displays 65kr; ☎57 69 32 88), on Hwy 5, which tells you more than you ever wanted to know about glaciers through a hands-on audio-visual display. The museum is one of the Jostedalsbreen Nasjonal-park's three information centres (see p.278). It therefore has the details of all the various **guided glacier walks** on offer, including those on the nearest arm, **Flatbreen** (July to late Aug), though this is a challenging part of the glacier and walks here last between six and eight hours – there are no two-hour or family walks, unlike at Nigardsbreen (see p.279), for example. The starting point is the car park at Øygard, signposted off Hwy 5 near the Bremuseum.

As for **moving on**, Fjærland is on the main Oslo–Sogndal–Førde bus route, with buses stopping beside the Bremuseum. If you're heading north, the road **tunnels** under the Jostedalsbreen glacier to meet Hwy 1 at Skei. The road to Sogndal has a toll of 115kr.

East to Sogndal

From Hella, across the fjord from Dragsvik, the eastbound bus from Balestrand con-tinues for 40km along the water's edge to **SOGNDAL** – bigger and livelier than Balestrand, but not quite as appealing on account of its string of modern concrete build-ings. It sits in a broad valley, surrounded by low, green hills, its appearance consider-ably enlivened by the fruit trees – apples and pears – that grow in abundance in this region. Sogndal is a reasonable place to pause for a night, especially as onward bus ser-vices are good.

Sogndal meanders along the fjord, little more than two long, main streets which meet at a roundabout at the east end of town. The **bus** drops you at the station on the west side of town, in between the two main streets about 500m from the roundabout, where the **tourist office** (June–Aug Mon–Fri 9am–8pm, Sat 10am–1pm, Sun 1–6pm; Sept–May Mon–Fri 11am–4pm; ☎57 67 30 83) occupies part of the Kulturhus. The tourist office has bus and ferry timetables and a small supply of **private rooms** (①). There is more inexpensive accommodation at the **youth hostel** (☎57 67 20 33; fax 57 67 31 45; mid-June to mid-Aug; 90kr, doubles ③), which manages to feel quite homely despite the fact it's housed in a residential folk school (*Folkehøgskule*); it's near the bridge just 400m east of the tourist office. The nicest place to stay, though, is the *Hofslund Fjord Hotel* (☎57 67 10 22; fax 57 67 16 30; ③), a stone's throw from the tourist office; ask for a room with a fjord view.

There's a poor choice of **restaurants** – the best you'll do is either the café and pizza bar of the *Loftesnes Pensjonat*, close to the bus station, or the somewhat stuffy restau-rant of the *Inter Nor Sogndal Hotell* nearby. Self-caterers can stock up in two large **supermarkets** in the centre, including a *Domus*, which has the town's *Vinmonopolet* (liquor store) in its basement.

Onward connections include the express bus northwest to Fjærland and Førde (for Stryn) or east to Oslo via the E16, a route covered on p.233. But much more extraordi-nary is the bus route north along Hwy 55, though note that the road is closed by snow from October to late May or thereabouts. Beyond the turnings to Solvorn and the Nigardsbreen glacier (see below), Hwy 55 squeezes past the western peripheries of the Jotunheimen Nasjonalpark (see p.227) en route to Lom (and Otta). In summer there's a local bus direct to the Nigardsbreen (mid-June to early Sept Mon–Fri 1 daily; 2hr 30min), while another local route links Sogndal with Solvorn (June–Aug 2–3 daily; 25min).

On from Sogndal: Hwy 55 to Solvorn, Urnes and Turtagrø

Some 15km north of Sogndal on Hwy 55, a steep three-kilometres-long turning leaves the main road to snake its way down to **SOLVORN**, an attractive little place clustered on the forested foreshore of the **Lustrafjord**. The village is the site of the *Walaker Hotell* (☎57 68 42 07; fax 57 68 45 44; ③), the most conspicuous part of which is an ugly motel-style block; don't let this put you off lunching here – the main building, an old pastel-painted house with a lovely garden, is just a few strides away.

From the Solvorn jetty, there's a car ferry (mid-June to Aug hourly 8am–5pm; reduced service in winter; 15min) over the fjord to Ornes, from where it's a brief hike up the hill to **Urnes stave church** (June–Aug daily 10.30am–4/5.30pm; 35kr). Apart from the view over the fjord, with the snow-dusted mountains in the background, the church is noted for the fineness of its carvings, the north wall and gables alive with a swirling filigree of strange beasts and delicate vegetation. Actually, in one sense the carvings are bit of a fraud as they were carved for an earlier church that once stood here – about two hundred years before the present structure was erected.

If you're driving, there's a choice of routes from Urnes church. You can can retrace your steps back to Hwy 55 via Solvorn – the route you'll need to take if you're heading to the Nigardsbreen glacier (details on p.279), or you can head north along the minor road that tracks along the east shore of the Lustrafjord to rejoin Hwy 55 at **Skjolden**. It's beyond Skjolden that the most dramatic part of Hwy 55 begins. First the road wriggles up the hillside, twisting and turning until it reaches a mountain plateau which it traverses, providing absolutely stunning views of the jagged, ice-crusted Jotunheimen peaks to the east. This is Norway's highest mountain crossing and if you want to hang around some more, the best of a series of roadside lodges is the attractive **Turtagrø Hotel** (☎57 68 61 16; fax 57 68 61 07; ③), at the west end of the plateau just 17km beyond Skjolden. The hotel is a favourite haunt for mountaineers, but it also provides ready access to the hiking trails that lattice the Jotunheimen Nasjonalpark and there's summer cross-country skiing in the vicinity as well.

Beyond the east end of the plateau, Hwy 55 zips down through forested Leirdal and finally, some 140km from Sogndal, reaches Lom, on Hwy 15.

The Nordfjord and the Jostedalsbreen glacier

Emerge from the Fjærland tunnel (Hwy 5), heading north, and you've just journeyed all the way under the **Jostedalsbreen glacier**. One side of it can be viewed close up at various points along the eastern reaches of the Nordfjord, the next great fjord system to the north – the other, eastern side of the glacier is reachable from the Sognefjord via Hwy 55 (see p.275). Several interconnected stretches of water make up the **Nordfjord**, all differently named but characterized by the same high surrounding mountains and deep green reflective water. However, the Nordfjord does not have quite the lustre of its more famous neighbours, partly because the settlements here, dotted along Hwy 15 on the northern shore, lack any real appeal.

Stryn and around

STRYN, at the eastern end of the Nordfjord system, is the biggest town in the region, but it's an ugly modern sprawl with little to commend it. That said, it's an important transport junction – not least as the starting point for the special summer bus over the Trollstigen to Åndalsnes (mid-June to Aug 1 daily; see p.282) – and, if you're travelling by bus, you may well get stuck in town overnight. **Buses** stop beside the fjord, from where it's a five- to ten-minute walk east to the tatty town centre. The **tourist office** (daily June & Aug 9am–6pm; July 9am–8pm; ☎57 87 23 33) is located in the square just back from the main street (Hwy 15), behind *Johan's Kafeteria*; they take bookings for guided walks on the Jostedalsbreen (see below).

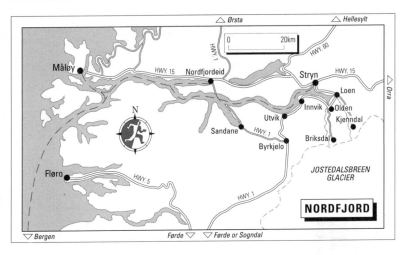

For eminently good-value **rooms**, head for the fjordside *Walhalla Gjestgiveri* (☎57 87 10 72; fax 57 87 18 94; ①), about 200m west of the tourist office along Perhusvegen, which does a good buffet breakfast. The **youth hostel** (☎57 87 13 36; fax 57 87 11 06; late May to mid-Sept; 90kr, doubles ①) is an inconvenient 1500-metre walk up the hill from town – it's not easy to find, so get a map from the tourist office or keep your eyes peeled for the signs on Hwy 15.

The only reasonable **place to eat** in town is *Johan's Kafeteria* on the main street (Mon–Sat 9am–10pm, Sun 11am–10pm), which serves sandwiches, pizzas and the like.

Around Stryn: Loen

Stryn may be unprepossessing, but **LOEN** – just 11km south around the fjord along Hwy 60 – is a good degree better. The hamlet spreads ribbon-like along the low-lying, grassy foreshore within easy striking distance of an arm of the Jostedalsbreen glacier, and is also on the main north–south bus route. Moreover, it's home to one of Norway's more famous hotels, the *Hotel Alexandra* (☎57 87 76 60; fax 57 87 77 70; ③/④), a big and flashy modern block tucked in beneath the hills and fringed by carefully manicured gardens. For lighter bank balances, the motel-style *Hotel Loenfjord* (☎57 87 78 50; fax 57 87 77 70; ②/③), across the road and owned by the same company, offers perfectly adequate rooms.

The *Hotel Alexandra* has all the information you'll need about visiting the nearest glacier nodule, the **Kjenndalsbreen**, to the southeast of Loen. This icy arm is not to be confused with the Briksdalsbreen, which is located south of Olden, a small village just 6km from Loen on Hwy 60; for more on the glacier, see below.

The Jostedalsbreen glacier

You can't help but notice the nearby, lurking presence of the **Jostedalsbreen glacier** at some stage of your wanderings: the 800-square-kilometre ice plateau dominates the whole of the inner Nordfjord region. Lying between the eastern ends of the Nordfjord and Sognefjord, its 24 arms flowing down into the nearby valleys, it is Jostedalsbreen that gives the local rivers and glacial lakes their distinctive blue-green colouring.

GLACIERS DANGERS

- Glaciers are in constant motion and are potentially very dangerous.
- **Never, under any circumstances**, climb a glacier without a guide; never walk underneath a glacier; always heed the instructions at the site.

Catching sight of the ice, nestling between peaks and ridges and licking its way downwards, can be unnerving: the overwhelming feeling is that it shouldn't really be there. As the poet Norman Nicholson wrote of the glacier:

A malevolent, rock-crystal
Precipitate of lava,
Corroded with acid,
Inch by inch erupting
From volcanoes of cold

Which is an evocative and accurate description of a phenomenon that, for centuries, presented an impenetrable north–south barrier, crossed only at certain points by determined farmers and adventurers.

In 1991, the glacier was placed within the **Jostedalsbreen Nasjonalpark** in order to coordinate its conservation. The main benefit of this for tourists has been to provide **guided glacier walks** (*breturar*, June to early Sept only) on its various arms, ranging from two-hour excusions to all-day, fully equipped hikes. Prices start at around 80kr, with a half-day trip weighing in at about 250kr – money well spent if you've never been on a glacier before. There are three national park **information centres**, the most readily accessible one being the Norsk Bremuseum (glacier museum) on the edge of Fjærland (see p.274). The others are the Jostedalsbreen senter (daily April & Oct noon–4pm; May & Sept 10am–4pm; June & Aug 9am–6pm; July 9am–8pm; ☎57 87 72 00; exhibition 50kr) in Oppstryn, 20km east of Stryn on Hwy 15 – easy to get to by car, but a pain by bus – and the isolated Breheimsenteret Jostedal, up a long byroad north of Sogndal, off Hwy 55 on the east side of the glacier (see below). These three centres have displays on all things glacial and issue leaflets outlining all the various guided walks available. Otherwise, local tourist offices and the occasional hotel – like the *Alexandra* in Loen – can advise on visiting the nearest arm of the glacier.

All of these outlets make bookings for guided glacier walks, which are accepted up until about 6pm the evening beforehand, but obviously it's better not to leave it until the last minute. **Equipment** is provided, though you'll need good boots, warm clothes, gloves and hat, sunglasses, and food and drink.

With a vehicle, you can get within easy striking distance of the designated starting points for all the glacier walks. By **bus** it's a little trickier, but it's usually possible with a bit of pre-planning. These starting points are also targets to head for if you just want to get close to the glacier without actually getting on it; we've described three such routes below – though heed the warnings given in the box above, too.

Kjenndalsbreen

With your own transport it's an easy matter to follow the single-track road from Loen for 14km through a beautiful valley skirting the glacial lake to **Kjenndalsbreen**. After 9km, there's a toll post (20kr per car) and then the road gets rougher, eventually petering out at a car park, from where it's a rocky twenty-minute walk to the foot of the glacier. The blue and white folds of ice tumble down the rock face here, split by fissures and undermined by a furious white river fed by plummeting waterfalls.

There are two or three **campsites** along the minor road to the glacier, and a café-souvenir shop at the toll post, good places to stop off if you have to walk here. A much more enticing approach is, however, the **boat** ride along the lake: from **Sande**, just a couple of kilometres up the road from Loen, there are two sailings daily (mid-June to late Aug; 60kr); more information from the *Hotel Alexandra* (see p.277). Note also that guided walks at the end of this valley take in the Bødalsbreen nodule, a little to the north of the Kjenndalsbreen.

Briksdalsbreen

From Stryn a once-daily bus (mid-June to mid-Aug) leaves for the most accessible glacier arm, **Briksdalsbreen**, calling at both Loen and Olden (see above). From Briksdal, 24km south of Olden, it's an easy 45-minute walk to the glacier, passing waterfalls and weaving up the river on the way, and once there it's a simple matter to get close to the ice itself: there's a very flimsy rope barricade and a small warning sign – be careful. If you've lacked photo-opportunities thus far, you can hire a pony and trap at the souvenir/café area by the start of the track, something that will cost you around 130kr – a bit of a swiz when you still have to walk the last bit anyway. Guided glacier walks begin at the café area too.

Nigardsbreen

North of Sogndal, on the east side of the glacier, a byroad branches off Hwy 55 at Gaupne for the 34-kilometre trip up the wild and hostile valley that leads to the **Breheimsenteret Jostedal information centre** (daily May & Sept 10am–5pm; June–Aug 9am–8pm; ☎57 68 32 40; exhibition 60kr). An ultra-modern structure set amid the surrounding peaks, it's appropriately bleak and spare, and as you sip a coffee on the terrace you can admire the glistening glacier dead ahead. From the centre, it's an easy 3-kilometre drive, or walk along the toll road to the shores of an icy green lake where a tiny boat shuttles over to the bare rock slope beside the **Nigardsbreen**, a great rumpled and seamed wall of ice that sweeps between high peaks.

If you're relying on public transport, there's a once-daily **bus** service from Sogndal to the Breheimsenteret (mid-June to early Sept Mon–Fri).

West to Måløy

From Stryn, Hwy 15 travels **west**, cutting inland to skim along the edge of the Hornindalsvatn for the first 50km, before returning to the Nordfjord for the last leg of the journey, the 60km trip down to Måløy. There are panoramic fjord views as you go, but nowhere really warrants a stop, the shoreline villages merely huddles of shops and houses around a landing stage.

Typically, **NORDFJORDEID**, 50km west of Stryn, has one main street of white wooden houses and a **tourist office** (mid-June to mid-Aug Mon–Sat 11am–7pm, Sun noon–7pm; ☎57 86 13 75), which may be able to persuade you of the area's charms – if so, they can book private **rooms** in and around the village. After Nordfjordeid, though, the only real target is the small fishing town of **MÅLØY**, stuck on an island at the fjord's mouth and reached across a "singing bridge": when the wind is in the right direction, the bridge emits an unnervingly high-pitched squeal. Måløy, which is connected to Nordfjordeid, Stryn and Otta by twice-daily bus, is also a *Hurtigrute* **coastal steamer** port, with boats departing south for the leisurely nine-hour cruise to Bergen at 5.30am, north to Ålesund and Kristiansund at 7.30am. There's a *Hurtigbåt* **passenger express boat** service to Bergen as well, and this clips almost five hours off the journey time (1–2 daily; 4hr 20min). Try not to get stuck here overnight, as Måløy is short on **accommodation** – try the *Måløy Hotel* (☎57 85 18 00; fax 57 85 05 89; ③/④).

The Geirangerfjord

The **Geirangerfjord** is one of the region's smallest fjords, but also one of its most breathtaking. A convoluted branch of the Storfjord, it cuts well inland, marked by impressive waterfalls and with a village at either end of the fjord's snake-like profile. You can reach the Geirangerfjord from the north or south. From Stryn and the Nordfjord in **the south**, buses destined for Ålesund run the 40km up Hwy 60 directly to the westernmost village, Hellesylt; if you're approaching **from the north**, Geiranger, the other village, is accessible on a long day trip from Åndalsnes, via the wonderful Trollstigen highway (see p.283). Of the two, Hellesylt makes the better base unless you're keen to join the tourist crowds in Gerainger.

Hellesylt

In Viking times **HELLESYLT** was an important and well-protected port. Traders and warriors would travel the waterways from here as far as England, France and Russia, and many old Viking names survive in the area. Nowadays it's primarily a stop-off on tourist itineraries, most visitors staying just long enough to catch the ferry down the fjord to Geiranger. Consequently, by nightfall Hellesylt is usually quiet and peaceful. For daytime entertainment, there is a tiny **beach** by the ferry quay, the prelude to some very cold swimming. Or you could splash about (as many do) in the waterfall in the centre of the village.

Hellesylt is on the main Bergen/Oslo to Loen, Stryn and Ålesund bus route and **buses** stop beside the jetty. The **tourist office** is on the quayside (June–Aug daily 9am–5.30pm; ☎70 26 50 52), footsteps from the turn-of-the-century, wooden *Grand Hotel* (☎70 26 51 00; fax 70 26 52 22; ②), which has a fine fjordside location, a decent **restaurant** and pleasant rooms. They also sell fishing licences and rent out boats. The hotel's main competitor is the **youth hostel** (☎70 26 51 28; no fax; June-Aug; 100kr, doubles ①), set on the hillside above the village – up the winding road (or take the short-cut path to the right of the waterfall). *Hellesylt Camping* (☎70 26 51 04; summer only) fills out the shadeless field beside the fjord about 300m from the quay.

By ferry along the Geirangerfjord

Fairly regular **car ferries** (May–Sept 4 daily, extra departures June to late Aug; 1hr 10min; 30kr, car & driver 90kr) run between Hellesylt and Geiranger, turning into the Geirangerfjord itself about fifteen minutes after leaving Hellesylt. It's one of the most celebrated trips in the entire fjord region, the S-shaped waters about 300m deep and fed by a series of plunging waterfalls that drop from heights of up to 250m. The falls are all named, and the multilingual commentary aboard the ferry does its best to familiarize you with every stream and rivulet. More interesting are the scattered ruins of abandoned farms, built along the fjord's sixteen-kilometre length by fanatically optimistic settlers over the last couple of centuries. The cliffs backing the fjord are almost uniformly sheer, making farming of any description a short-lived, and back-breaking, occupation – and not much fun for the children either: when they went out to play, they had to be roped to the nearest boulder to stop them dropping into the fjord.

Geiranger

Any approach to **GEIRANGER** is spectacular. Arriving by ferry slowly reveals the little village tucked in a hollow at the eastern end of the fjord, while coming from Eidsdal in the north by road involves thundering along a fearsome set of switchbacks on the

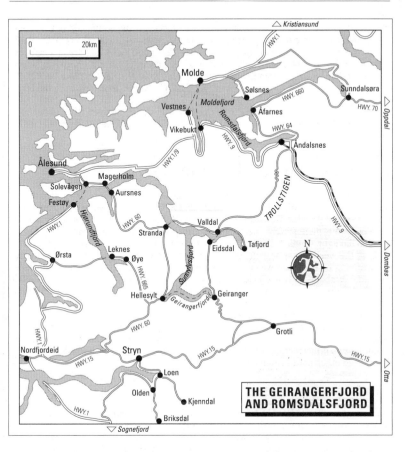

THE GEIRANGERFJORD
AND ROMSDALSFJORD

Ørneveien, the Eagle's Highway, for a first view of the fjord and the village glinting in the distance. Similarly, the road in from Hwy 15 to the south begins innocuously enough, but soon you're squirming round and down the zigzags to arrive in Geiranger from behind.

It's a beautiful setting – one of the most magnificent in all of western Norway – but in the peak season the village itself is chronically overcrowded, with campers and caravanners filling the over-large, fjordside campsite to the gunnels, and, frankly, you'll soon want to leave it behind. If you visit slightly out of season, the true character of the place is more apparent, the fjord hemmed in by sheer rock walls scattered with wisps of hairline waterfalls, the blue waters below bobbed with tiny-looking ferries.

Practicalities

Buses to Geiranger stop by the waterfront, a brief walk from both the **ferry terminal** and the adjacent **tourist office** (June–Aug daily 9am–7pm; ☎70 26 30 99), which pushes expensive boat tours of the fjord, though the car ferry is perfectly adequate. There are several **hotels** to choose from, but be warned that advance reservations are strongly advised in July and August. Both the large and luxurious *Union Hotel* (May–Sept;

☎70 26 30 05; fax 70 26 31 70; ④), high up the hillside on the south side of town, and the ultra-modern timber *Grande Fjord Hotel* (May–Sept; ☎70 26 30 90; fax 70 26 31 77; ②), by the fjord about 1km north of the centre, have good views and are at a safe distance from the crowds. The *Grande Fjord* also has **cabins** (②) and a **campsite**, which is difficult to disentangle from the adjacent *Grande Turist Hytte & Camping* (☎70 26 30 68; fax 70 26 31 17). The **restaurant** of the *Hotel Geiranger*, footsteps from the ferry dock, is first-class.

Summer **buses** from Geiranger to Åndalsnes, over the Trollstigen (see below), currently leave the village daily at 1pm and 6.10pm. Buses to Stryn and Ålesund (1–3 daily) run year-round from Hellesylt, a ferry ride away.

The Romsdalsfjord and around

Travelling up from the south, the crossroads at Dombås is where **Hwy 9** and the **Rauma train line** fork west for the thrilling 100-kilometre rattle down through the alpine mountains of the **Romsdal** valley to the **Romsdalsfjord** – a journey which, to appreciate the increasingly spectacular scenery and engineering, should really be made in daylight. Coming this way, you'll glimpse the tall face of the **Trollveggen** (Troll Wall) to the west as you near the end of the line – at around 1100m, the highest vertical overhanging mountain wall in Europe. As you might expect, this is a haunt of experienced mountaineers (who, incidentally, didn't conquer it until 1965), but since 1980 it has also been attracting BASE-jumping parachutists in search of the ultimate thrill. After a handful of deaths and several serious accidents, jumping off was made illegal in 1986, but it hasn't stopped the fanatical.

Apart from the Hardangerfjord, reached from Bergen, the Romsdalsfjord is the only other Norwegian fjord accessible by train – which explains the number of backpackers wandering its principal town of Åndalsnes. Regular buses and ferries provide easy connections to other fjord settlements nearby.

Åndalsnes

For many travellers **ÅNDALSNES**, connected by fast train with Oslo, is the first – and sometimes only – contact with the fjord country, a distinction it doesn't really warrant. Despite a wonderful setting between lofty peaks and chill waters, the town itself is unexciting: small (with a population of just 3000), modern and industrial, and sleepy at the best of times. You'd do best to get out into the surroundings as soon as possible, either exploring locally or heading onto Tafjord and points south, via the extraordinary Trollstigen, a route that's covered below – as is the other tempting proposition, the journey west to Ålesund. That said, Åndalsnes is a good place to orient yourself at the end of a long journey and can make a useful base, since everything you're likely to need is near at hand.

Practicalities

Buses all stop outside the **train station**, where you'll also find the **tourist office** (mid-June to mid-Aug Mon–Sat 9.30am–6.30pm, Sun 12.30–6.30pm; rest of the year Mon–Fri 8am–3.30pm; ☎71 22 16 22). They provide bus timetables and a wide range of local information that encourages you to use Åndalsnes as a base: the free *Dagsturer* booklet gives details of all sorts of day trips by car, most including a short hike too. They also have details of fishing trips in the fjord (2–3 daily; 4hr; 250kr), local day-long hiking routes, and fixed-rate sightseeing expeditions with *Åndalsnes Taxi* (☎71 22 15 55), who charge 400kr for a brief scoot down the Trollstigen. This is hardly a bargain, though, since local **car rental** firms offer 24-hour deals at around 500kr: *Hertz* (☎71 22

14 24), at the *Hydro* gas station up the hill from the train station on Romsdalsveien, usually has the best offers, but check with the tourist office.

The tourist office also has a small supply of **private rooms** (①), which go for around
300kr per double, but note that most are a good walk from the town centre.
Alternatively, Åndalsnes has a first-rate **youth hostel** (☎71 22 13 82; fax 71 22 68 35;
mid-May to mid-Sept; reception closed 10am–4pm; 100kr, doubles ①), a two-kilometre
hike west out of town: head up the hill out of the centre, turn right at the island at the
major road, go past the Hwy 9 turning to Dombås, but keep on Hwy 9 in the direction
of Ålesund, cross the river and it's on the left-hand side. It's extremely popular, so reservations are pretty much essential. The hostel rents out bikes, and its buffet-style breakfast is one of the best hostellers are likely to get in the whole country – there are facilities for cooking your own evening meals. The other excellent choice, the *Grand Hotel
Bellevue*, Åndalsgata 5 (☎71 22 10 11; fax 71 22 60 38; ③), occupies a big block with
attractive Art Deco touches on a hillock just up from the train station; it's worth paying
extra for a room with a view. Right in the centre, near the station at Vollan 16, *Rauma
Hotell* (☎71 22 12 33; fax 71 22 63 13; ③) is a modern place without much character.
Amongst several local **campsites**, *Åndalsnes Camping og Motell* (☎71 22 16 29; fax 71
22 62 16) has a fine riverside setting about 2km from the town centre – directions are
as for the youth hostel, but turn first left immediately after the river. It's a well-equipped
site with cabins (①) as well as bikes, boats, canoes (170kr per day) and cars available
for rent.

For **food**, the *Buona Sera* pizzeria, a brief walk from the station up the hill out of
town, serves competent Italian food and good steaks, whilst the café of the *Rauma
Hotell* serves inexpensive Norwegian dishes. Local **hiking maps** are sold at *Romsdal
Libris*, opposite the *Rauma Hotell*.

Onward from Åndalsnes

There are special summertime **bus and ferry** services from Åndalsnes over the
Trollstigen to Valldal and Geiranger (mid-June to late Aug 2 daily), with one ferry daily
continuing to Hellesylt, the most pleasant destination of the three; the trip costs 113kr
and rail pass holders get a 50 percent discount. Incidentally, there are buses from
Hellesylt to Ålesund, though it's more straightforward to take a *togBuss* (run by the
train company) straight to Ålesund from Åndalsnes (3 daily; 2hr 20min).

Another option is to take a local **bus** (Mon–Sat 6–8 daily, Sun 4; 1hr 20min) from
Åndalsnes along the northern shore of the Romsadalsfjord to Molde, a workaday industrial town where you can pick up the *Hurtigrute* coastal steamer and the bus making
the short hop north on coastal Hwy 1 to Kristiansund – another *Hurtigrute* port.
Kristiansund has much more to offer than Molde – where you definitely don't want to
get stuck – so check bus connections with Åndalsnes tourist office before you set out.
Note again that rail pass holders get a 50 percent discount on the Hwy 1 buses; also be
careful to distinguish between Kristiansund and the southern coastal town of
Kristiansand: to save confusion, in listings and brochures they are often written as
Kristiansund N and Kristiansand S.

Over the Trollstigen to Valldal

The alarming heights of the **Trollstigen** or "Troll's Ladder", a trans-mountain route
between Åndalsnes and Valldal, are equally compelling in either direction. In summer they are accessible by twice-daily bus (mid-June to Aug), which takes the sweat out
of driving – along with scores of other tourists – round eleven hairpins with a maximum
gradient of 1:12. Drivers (and cyclists) should be particularly careful in wet weather;
and note that the road is generally closed from late September to mid-May – later if the
snows have been particularly heavy.

The Trollstigen starts gently enough, leaving Hwy 9 just 6km southeast of Åndalsnes and running up into a valley surrounded by some of the more famous mountain peaks in Norway: to the right, Kongen and Bispen (the King and the Bishop) are the highest. Soon, though, the sheer audacity of the road becomes apparent, climbing its way across the face of the mountain in huge zigzags, at the halfway point running directly in front of the tumultuous **Stigfossen Falls** – where the bus stops for photographs. On a clear day the views from here are heart-stopping, the water dropping away 180m under the bridge into the valley.

There is nothing at the top except a bare expanse of mountain and a café – the *Trollstigen Fjellstue* – where the bus makes a stop. From here, it's a five-minute walk to the **Utsikten** (viewpoint), where there's a magnificent panorama over the surrounding mountains and valleys. If you're feeling extremely energetic, this is the place to pick up the *Kløvstien*, the original **track** over the mountains – abandoned when the road was built – which has been renovated for walkers. It's well signposted all the way back down towards Åndalsnes, crossing the road in four places, and there's a chain to hang on to on the steeper parts. The walk down the *Kløvstien* takes around four hours, and then there's an easy ninety-minute stroll down the footpath along the Isterdalen valley, which brings you back to Åndalsnes. As usual, come properly equipped, watch for sudden weather changes and be aware of the Trollstigen bus schedules.

Continuing over the mountains, the road travels the Meierdal on its way to **VALL-DAL**, a silent, shadowy village sprawled along the water's edge. If you're marooned, there's a small **youth hostel** (☎70 25 70 31; fax 70 25 75 13; mid-June to Aug; 85kr, doubles ①), 100m from the harbour. However, you'll almost certainly want to press on, heading west along the fjord to either the Linge–Eidsdal ferry (every 30min; 10min), 4km away, or, 12km further on, the Liabygda–Stranda ferry (every 30min; 15min). Most visitors choose the former, the route to Geiranger (see p.280).

Ålesund

At the end of Hwy 9, some 120km west of Åndalsnes, the fishing port of **ÅLESUND** is immediately – and distinctively – different from any other Norwegian town. Neither old clapboard houses nor functional concrete and glass is much in evidence, but instead there's a conglomeration of proud grey and white facades, lavishly decorated and topped with a forest of turrets and pinnacles. There are dragons and human faces, Neoclassical and mock-Gothic facades, decorative flowers and even a pharaoh or two, the whole ensemble seemingly the work of maniacally competitive architects – an observation that contains an element of truth. In 1904, a disastrous fire destroyed the town centre and left 10,000 people homeless. A hectic reconstruction programme saw almost the entire area rebuilt by 1907, in a bizarre Art Nouveau style that borrowed heavily from the German *Jugendstil* movement. Kaiser Wilhelm II, who used to holiday around Ålesund, footed the bill, and the work of the Norwegian architects, most of whom had learnt their craft abroad, is an engaging hybrid of up-to-date foreign influences and folksy local elements.

Walking down pedestrianized **Kongens gate** reveals most of the architectural highlights, but many of the central streets are equally decorative; if you're after exploring every stylistic peccadillo, pick up the free leaflet *On Foot in Ålesund* from the tourist office (see below), where you can also sign up for one of the **guided walking tours** (mid-June to mid-Aug 3 weekly; 1hr 30min; 45kr). The other obvious objective in the town centre is the **park** at the top of Lihauggata. It's a surprise to find monkey puzzle and copper beech trees here, and there's a bust in honour of the town's benefactor, the Kaiser, in which – if you're used to seeing pictures of him as a grizzled older figure in a helmet – he looks disarmingly youthful. The larger statue nearby is of Rollo, a Viking chieftain born and raised in Ålesund, who seized Normandy and became its first duke in 911 – and was an ancestor of William the Conqueror. From the park, several hundred

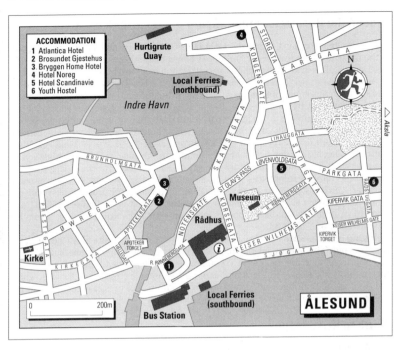

steps lead to the top of the **Aksla**, where the view out along the coast and its islands is fabulous. Otherwise, Ålesund's lively centre, which drapes around its oldest harbour, the **Brosundet**, makes for a pleasant stroll and you can watch the ferries and *Hurtigbåt* coming and going to the islands just offshore.

Practicalities

Ålesund **bus station** is situated on the waterfront across from the **tourist office** in the Rådhus (June–Aug Mon–Fri 8.30am–7pm, Sat 9am–5pm, Sun 11am–5pm; rest of the year Mon–Fri 9am–4pm; ☎70 12 12 02). Southbound local ferries depart from beside the bus station, northbound from the other side of the harbour, beyond which is the quay for the **Hurtigrute coastal steamer**.

One of Ålesund's real pleasures is the quality of its downtown **hotels**. The pick of the bunch is the *Bryggen Home Hotel*, an elegantly converted waterside warehouse at Apotekergata 1 (☎70 12 64 00; fax 70 12 11 80; ④). Next door, in slightly less lavish premises, is the *Brosundet Gjestehus* (☎70 12 10 00; ②), while the *Inter Nor Hotel Scandinavie* occupies a grand old Art Nouveau edifice at Løvenvoldgata 8 (☎70 12 31 31; fax 70 13 23 70; ②/④). The *Hotel Atlantica*, Rasmus Rønneberggata 4 (☎70 12 91 00; fax 70 12 62 52; ②/③), has some balconied rooms overlooking the Brosundet; the rather more mundane *Hotel Noreg*, Kongens gate 27 (☎70 12 29 38; fax 70 12 66 600; ③), is perfectly adequate. If your pocket book doesn't stretch to a hotel, there's a small and central **youth hostel** (☎70 12 04 25; fax 70 12 04 42; May–Aug; 125kr, doubles ①) on Parkgata at the top of Rådstuggata.

For **eating**, the hotels generally boast the best cafés and restaurants, including the popular *Café Brosundet* in the *Hotel Atlantica*, though you could try *Nilles Pizza* at Kirkegata 1. The *Sjøbua Fiskerestaurant*, Brunholmgata 1, serves delicious seafood.

Around the Romsdalsfjord to Molde

Sprawled along the fjord, industrial **MOLDE** is, despite its modern appearance, one of the older towns in the region, but it was blown to smithereens by the Luftwaffe in 1940, an act of destruction watched by King Håkon from the hillside above town, just weeks before he was forced into exile in England. The new town that grew up in its stead is unremarkable, but it does host an **international jazz festival** of some repute, held annually for a week in the middle of July. Tickets are relatively cheap (100–200kr) and there's a smattering of big names among the homegrown talent. Programmes are widely available across the whole region and tickets can be purchased from the ticket office (*Billettkontoret*; ☎71 21 61 00) in Molde Rådhus. Naturally, the big names are sold out months in advance and accommodation is impossible to find during the festival – but the authorities operate a large official campsite a couple of kilometres west of the centre for the duration. At other times of the year, you'll not want to hang around and fortunately the **bus station** and the **ferry terminal** are side by side, minutes from the **tourist office** in the Rådhus (mid-May to Aug Mon–Sat 9am–6pm, Sun 10am–4pm; rest of the year Mon–Fri 8.30am–3pm; ☎71 25 71 33).

Moving on from Molde, Hwy 1 makes the quick 75-kilometre dash north up to Kristiansund. This mostly inland route is followed by the long-distance buses, but if you're driving, take the impressive coastal route, Hwy 64, instead. Eight kilometres of this highway are known as the *Atlanterhavsveien* (Atlantic Highway; 40kr toll), which utilizes a string of bridges and causeways to hop from islet to islet on the edge of the ocean. Occasional local buses use this road too.

North to Kristiansund

From Molde, it takes the express bus just ninety minutes to reach the coastal town of **KRISTIANSUND**, which somehow contrives to look quite dull despite its island-and-sea setting. The town actually straddles three rocky islets, and the enormous natural channel-cum-harbour they create is one of the finest havens on the west coast. The town was founded in the eighteenth century as a fishing port, and there are a handful of old clapboard houses along Fosnagata, just north of the main quay. Up the slope from the quay to the west are the few modern streets that serve as the town centre and nearby too, just south along the the waterfront, is a modern **statue** of a woman carrying a fish, recalling the days when cod was laid out along the seashore to produce the dried cod – the *klippfisk* – that was the main source of income in these parts. Cod fish enthusiasts can get even more clued in by visiting the **Norsk klippfiskmuseum** (mid-June to mid-Aug Mon–Sat noon–5pm, Sun 1–4pm; 25kr), housed in an old warehouse, the Milnbrygga, east across the harbour – small passenger boats, the *Sundbåtene* (Mon–Sat 1 hourly), shuttle between the three islands (two of which are now connected to the mainland by bridge) and levy a flat charge of 10kr per trip. After visiting the *klippfiskmuseum*, you may as well drop by its waterfront neighbours, the **Hjelkrembrygga** (late June to early Aug Sun 1–4pm; 20kr), which displays old sepia photographs of the locality, and the **Woldbrygga** (same times and price), whose old boats and rope-making equipment are lodged in a nineteenth-century barrel factory – though note the restricted opening hours. For something of more general interest, a handful of venerable timber houses makes up the **Gamle Byen** (Old Town), situated on the smallest of the three islands, Innlandet – south across the harbour from the main quay – and here too is the distinctive **Lossiusgården**, a large and handsome eighteenth-century merchant's house, which isn't open to the public.

Practicalities

Buses arriving in Kristiansund – from Molde, Ålesund and Trondheim – all pull up beside the Nordmørskaia quay, where you'll also find the harbourside **tourist office** (July Mon–Fri 9am–8pm, Sat 10am–5pm, Sun 10.30am–6pm; rest of the year Mon–Fri 9am–4pm; ☎71 58 63 80). *Hurtigbåt* **passenger express boats** to Trondheim leave from this quay, as does the boat for Grip. Kristiansund is also a stop for the *Hurtigrute* **coastal steamer**, which docks at Holmakaia, just metres from the Nordmørskaia (daily departures northbound at 11pm, southbound at 5pm). The *Sundbåtene* jetty is a couple of minutes' walk south from the tourist office.

For a **place to stay**, avoid the depressing youth hostel (☎71 67 11 04; fax 71 67 11 58; June–Sept; 100kr, doubles ①), which is anyway a good 1km from the harbourfront, and instead sample the comfortable modernity of the *Inter Nor Grand Hotel*, Bernstorffstrand 1 (☎71 67 30 11; fax 71 67 23 70; ②/④), in the town centre just metres south off Kaibakken, the short main street linking the harbour with the main square, Kongens plass. The plain *City Bed & Breakfast*, down by the harbour at Vågeveien 5 (☎71 67 38 23; ①), is a cheaper choice. In terms of **restaurants**, the *Smia* stands head and shoulders above its competitors, serving superb fish dishes from around 110kr; it's in a converted boat shed close to the harbour at Fosnagata 30. Otherwise, make do with the *China House*, by the harbour at the foot of Kaibakken.

travel details

Trains

From Bergen to: Finse (4–5 daily; 2hr 15min); Geilo (4–5 daily; 3hr); Myrdal (4–5 daily; 1hr 50min); Oslo (4–5 daily; 6hr 30min); Voss (4–5 daily; 1hr 10min).

From Dombås to: Trondheim (3–4 daily; 2hr 30min).

From Myrdal to: Flåm (June to late Sept 11–12 daily; rest of the year 2–4 daily; 50min).

From Åndalsnes to: Dombås (2 daily; 1hr 30min); Oslo (2 daily; 6hr 30min).

Buses

From Balestrand to: Sogndal (2 daily; 1hr 10min); Stryn (Mon–Sat 1 daily; 4hr).

From Bergen to: Aurland (1–2 daily except Sat; 2hr 50min); Dombås (1 daily; 12hr); Flåm (1 daily; 3hr); Gudvangen (1 daily; 2hr 40min); Haugesund (2 daily; 3hr 30min); Hellesylt (Mon–Sat 1 daily; 8hr 15min); Kristiansand (1 daily; 11hr); Stryn (1 daily; 7hr 30min); Nordfjordeid (1–2 daily; 7hr); Norheimsund (3 daily; 2hr); Odda (1 daily; 3hr 30min); Sogndal (3 daily; 4hr 15min); Stryn (Mon–Sat 1 daily; 7hr); Stavanger (2 daily; 5hr 40min);Trondheim (1 daily; 14hr); Utne (1 daily; 2hr 45min); Voss (4 daily; 1hr 45min); Ålesund (1–2 daily; 10hr).

From Flåm to: Aurland (Mon–Fri 2 daily, Sun 1 ; 10min); Gudvangen (Mon–Fri 2 daily, Sun 1 ; 15min).

From Geiranger to: Ålesund (1–3 daily; 3hr 15min); Åndalsnes (June to Aug 2 daily; 3–4hr).

From Molde to: Kristiansund (5 weekly; 2hr); Trondheim (2 daily; 8hr) Ålesund (4–6 daily; 2hr 15min); Åndalsnes (3–8 daily; 1hr 30min).

From Oslo to: Balestrand (3 daily; 8hr 15min); Bergen (1 daily; 11hr); Fagernes (3 daily; 3hr 20min); Fjaerland (3 daily; 7hr 50min); Kaupanger (3 daily; 6hr 45min); Måløy (1 daily; 10hr); Sogndal (3 daily; 7hr); Stryn (1 daily; 8hr).

From Sogndal to: Balestrand (2 daily; 1hr 10min); Bergen (3 daily; 4hr 15min); Kaupanger (2 daily; 20min); Oslo (3 daily; 7hr); Otta (mid-June to Aug 1 daily; 4hr 50min); Solvorn (2 daily; 30min); Stryn (1–2 daily; 4hr 30min); Voss (3 daily; 3hr).

From Stavanger to: Bergen (2 daily; 5hr 40min); Haugesund (2 daily; 2hr 10min); Kristiansand (2 daily; 4hr 40min);

From Stryn to: Bergen (2 daily; 7hr); Hellesylt (1 daily; 1hr); Innvik (1 daily; 40min); Loen (1 daily; 10min); Måløy (1 daily; 1hr); Nordfjordeid (1 daily; 2hr); Olden (1 daily; 20min); Oslo (1 daily; 8hr 30min); Trondheim (1 daily; 8hr); Utvik (1 daily; 50min).

From Voss to: Bergen (3 daily; 4hr); Gudvangen (2 daily; 1hr 20min); Norheimsund (3 daily; 2hr); Odda (1 daily; 2hr 30min); Sogndal (2 daily; 3hr).

From Ålesund to: Bergen (1 daily except Sat; 11hr); Geiranger (1–3 daily; 3hr 15min); Hellesylt (1–2 daily except Sat; 2hr 40min); Kristiansund (5 weekly; 4hr 15min); Molde (4–6 daily; 2hr 15min); Stryn (1–2 daily except Sat; 4hr); Trondheim (1–2 daily; 8hr 10min).

From Åndalsnes to: Geiranger (June to Aug 2 daily; 3–4hr); Kristiansund (2 daily; 3hr); Molde (3–7 daily; 1hr 30min); Valldal (June to Aug 2 daily; 2hr/3–4hr); Ålesund (3–4 daily; 2hr 20min).

Boats

*A plethora of boats shuttles between the settlements dotting the western fjords. There are two main types of service, **car ferries** and **express passenger boats** (**Hurtigbåt**), and these are supplemented by the **Hurtigrute coastal steamer**. Services are frequent and regular, running many times daily up until about 11pm on most routes. Many shorter crossings are detailed in the text; major routes are given below.*

The *Hurtigrute* Coastal Steamer

The daily *Hurtigrute* service departs

Northbound: Bergen at 10.30pm; Florø at 4.45am; Måløy at 7.30am; Ålesund at 3pm; Kristiansund at 11pm; Trondheim at noon.

Southbound: Trondheim at 10am; Kristiansund at 5pm; Ålesund at 12.45am; Måløy at 5.30am; Florø at 8am; arrives Bergen, where the service terminates at 2.30pm.

Journey time from Bergen to Trondheim is 31hr 30min.

Ferries

From Balestrand to: Fjærland (mid-May to Aug 1 daily; 1hr 30min).

From Bruravik to: Brimnes (2 hourly; 25mins).

From Dragsvik to: Vangsnes (hourly; 25min).

From Fodnes (E16) to: Manheller (hourly; 15min).

From Geiranger to Hellesylt (May–Sept 4 daily; Oct-April 2 daily; 1hr 10min).

From Gudvangen to: Kaupanger (2 daily; 2hr).

From Hella to: Dragsvik (every 30min; 10min); Vangsnes (hourly; 15min).

From Kaupanger to: Gudvangen (2 daily; 2hr).

From Stavanger to: Tau (hourly; 45min).

From Utne to: Kinsarvik (2 hourly; 25min).

Express passenger boats (*Hurtigbåt*)

From Aurland to: Balestrand (1 daily; 1hr 20min); Bergen (1–2 daily; 5hr 15min); Flåm (1–3 daily; 20min); Gudvangen (1–3 daily; 1hr 40min).

From Bergen to: Aurland (1–2 daily; 5hr 15min); Balestrand (1–2 daily; 4hr); Flåm (1–2 daily; 5hr 30min); Florø (1–2 daily; 3hr 30min); Måløy (1–2 daily; 4hr 30min); Stavanger (2–5 daily; 3hr 50min).

From Bergen by **bus & Hurtigbåt** to: Kinsarvik (Mon–Sat 2–4 daily; 2hr 20min); Lofthus (Mon–Sat 2–4 daily; 2hr 35min); Odda (Mon–Sat 2–4 daily; 3hr 10min); Utne (Mon–Sat 2–4 daily; 2hr 10min).

From Flåm to Aurland (1–3 daily; 20min); Balestrand (1 daily; 1hr 30min); Bergen (1 daily; 5hr 15min); Gudvangen (1–3 daily; 2hr);

From Gudvangen to: Aurland (1–3 daily; 1hr 40min); Flåm (1–3 daily; 2hr).

From Kristiansund to: Trondheim (1–3 daily; 3hr 30min).

From Stavanger to: Bergen (2–5 daily; 3hr 50min); Haugesund (2–5 daily; 1hr 15min).

From Ålesund to: Molde (Mon–Fri 1 daily; 2hr 15min).

International ferries

From Bergen to: Shetlands/Faroes/Iceland (June to mid-Sept 1 weekly; 11hr/24hr/41hr); Stavanger/Newcastle (2–3 weekly; 4hr/21hr).

From Stavanger to: Newcastle (end of May to mid-Oct 2–3 weekly; 18hr); Hirtshals (2 weekly; 11hr).

CHAPTER SEVEN

CENTRAL NORTHERN NORWAY – TRONDHEIM TO THE LOFOTENS

S tretching up above the western fjords, **Central Northern Norway** comprises the city of Trondheim and the narrow stretch of island-studded coast beyond it – and marks the real transition from rural southern to blustery northern Norway. **Trondheim**, capital of the fertile **Trøndelag** region, is easily accessible from Oslo by train and, with its easy-going air and imposing cathedral, forms a highlight of any itinerary. But travel north of the city, and you begin to feel very far removed from the capital: the express trains that thunder northwards leave the forested south very quickly behind, and travelling becomes more of a slog as the distances between settlements grow ever greater. As Trøndelag gives way to **Nordland** things get increasingly wild, though there is little to stop for between Trondheim and the handsomely sited steel town of **Mo-i-Rana**.

Just north of Mo-i-Rana you cross the **Arctic Circle** – one of the principal targets for many travellers – at a point where the bare and strikingly cruel scenery seems especially appropriate. Beyond here, the mountains of the interior hump down to a fretted, craggy coastline, and even the towns, the largest of which is the port of **Bodø**, have a feral quality about them. Moving on, **Narvik**, in the far north of Nordland, was the scene of some of the fiercest fighting by the Allies and Norwegian Resistance in World War II, but is now a modern port handling vast quantities of iron ore amid some startling rocky surroundings. To the west, reached by road from Narvik or by ferry from Bodø (amongst several ports), lies the offshore archipelago that comprises the **Vesterålen and Lofoten Islands**. This island chain features a comparatively commonplace fjord-indented coastline in the north, between the Vesterålens' **Harstad** and **Andenes**, but to the south the mountain wall that backbones the Lofotens is ravishingly beautiful, and amongst a handful of idyllic fishing villages the pick is **Å**.

Getting around

Transport services are good, which is just as well given the isolated nature of much of the region. The *Hurtigrute* **coastal steamer** stops at all the major settlements on its route up the Norwegian coast from Bergen to Kirkenes, while the islands are accessed by a variety of **ferries** and **express boats**. Known as the "Arctic Highway", the **E6** is the major road route north along the coast from Trondheim, and it's kept in excellent condition – though caravans can make the going very slow. The **train** network reaches as far north as Fauske and nearby Bodø, from either of which **buses** make the link to Narvik, itself the terminal of a separate rail line that runs the few kilometres to the border and then south through Sweden. The only real problem is likely to be **time**. It's a

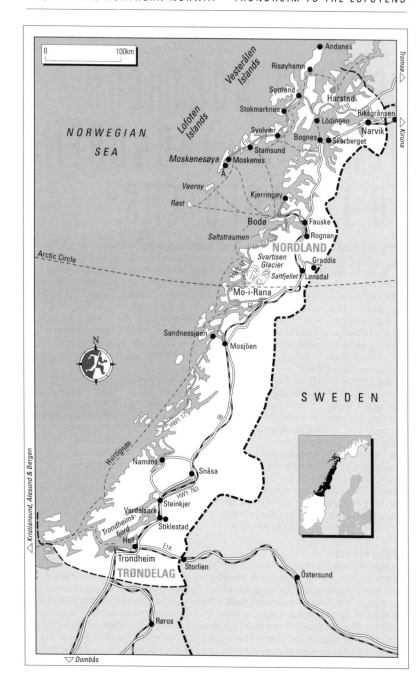

day's journey from Trondheim to Fauske, another day to Narvik, and unless you've days to spare you should think twice before venturing further: the travelling can be arduous and the journey becomes pointless if done at a hectic pace.

Trondheim

Though you might not realize it now, **TRONDHEIM**, an atmospheric city with much of its antique centre still intact, has been a Norwegian power-base for centuries, its age-old importance guaranteed by the excellence of its harbour and its position at the head of a wide and fertile valley. The early Norse parliament, or *Ting*, met here, and the city's grand cathedral was a major pilgrimage centre at the end of a route stretching all the way back to Oslo. Today, it's scarcely credible as Norway's third city, the centre sitting compactly on a small triangle of land, bordered by the River Nid, with the curve of the long and slender Trondheimsfjord beyond. It's a manageable and eminently likeable place, where even the main sights – bar the cathedral – have a low-key quality about them. Despite its university, the pace of the city is slow and provincial, though this is no bad thing, and it's a simple matter to use up a couple of days exploring the central streets and surroundings.

Arrival and city transport

Trondheim is on the E6 highway, 540km – a seven- or eight-hour drive – from Oslo. It's a major stop for the *Hurtigrute* **coastal steamer** (information on ☎73 52 79 60), which docks at the harbour (pier 1: quay 1 for northbound, quay 2 for southbound) behind **Sentralstasjon** (☎72 57 20 20), the gleaming bus and train terminal, from where you simply cross the bridge onto the triangular island that holds central Trondheim. The all-year *Kystekspressen* **express boat** from Kristiansund docks at the Pirterminalen, which is also behind Sentralstasjon. If you're **driving**, a toll of 20kr is levied in either direction on the E6 as you near Trondheim, and there's another municipal toll of 10kr to pay (Mon–Fri 6am–5pm) before you can enter the city itself. **Parking** can be a pain – try the handy *Leuthenhaen P-hus*, in the centre at Erling Skakkesgate 40, or the marginally cheaper (and slightly less convenient) *Bakke P-hus*, east across the bridge from the centre at Nedre Bakklandet 60.

Trondheim **airport** is 35km northeast of the city at Vaernes, and airport buses (45kr) run to Sentralstasjon in the city centre, a 45-minute ride. To get out to the airport, the bus leaves Sentralstasjon 75 minutes before flight departure and calls at the *Royal Garden Hotel* on the way.

The **tourist office** sits right in the centre of town at Munkegaten 18, on the corner of the main square, Torvet (mid-May to late June & mid- to late Aug Mon–Fri 8.30am–8pm, Sat 8.30am–6pm, Sun 10am–6pm; late June to mid-Aug Mon–Fri 8.30am–10pm, Sat 8.30am–8pm, Sun 10am–8pm; Sept to mid-May Mon–Fri 9am–4pm; ☎73 92 94 00). They provide the free and very useful *Trondheim Guide* (also available from information racks at Sentralstasjon), sell hiking maps, and have a limited supply of private rooms (see below), though these are almost entirely out in the suburbs. They will also change money outside banking hours, though at poor rates, and rent out **bicycles** at 80kr per day, plus a refundable deposit of 200kr.

Public transport in town consists of buses and trams (flat-fare tickets 15kr), but in most cases you can just as easily walk. Only if you're heading to one of the outlying museums or the campsite is it worth buying an unlimited 24-hour public transport ticket, the *dagskort* (35kr), from the tourist office.

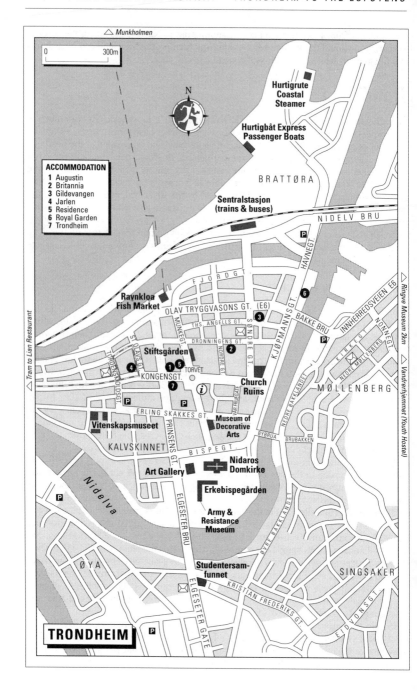

△ *Munkholmen*

0 — 300m

N

Hurtigrute
Coastal
Steamer

Hurtigbåt Express
Passenger Boats

BRATTØRA

ACCOMMODATION
1 Augustin
2 Britannia
3 Gildevangen
4 Jarlen
5 Residence
6 Royal Garden
7 Trondheim

Sentralstasjon
(trains & buses)

NIDELV BRU

HAVNEGT.

△ *Ringve Museum 2km*

△ *Vandrerhjemmet (Youth Hostel)*

INNHERREDSVEIEN E6

NONNEGT.

KIRKEG.

Ravnkloa
Fish Market

FJORDGT.

OLAV TRYGGVASONS GT. (E6)

THS. ANGELLS GT.

DRØNNINGENS GT.

MUNKEGT.

NORDRE GT.

SØNDRE GT.

KJØPMANNSGT.

BAKKE BRU

NEDRE MØLLENBERG

ØVRE MØLLENBERG

△ *Tram to Lian Restaurant*

Stiftsgården

S. OLAVS GT.

TORDENSKJOLDSGT.

KONGENSGT.

TORVET

Church
Ruins

MØLLENBERG

NEDRE BAKKLANDET

i

KONGENSGT.

ERLING SKAKKES GT.

VÅR FRUEGATE

Museum of
Decorative
Arts

BYBRUA

BRUBAKKEN

Vitenskapsmuseet

KALVSKINNET

PRINSENS GT.

BISPEGT.

Art Gallery

Nidaros
Domkirke

Erkebispegården

ELGESETER BRU

Army &
Resistance
Museum

N i d e l v a

ØYA

ØVRE BAKKLANDET

SINGSAKER

Studentersam-
funnet

ELGESETER BRU

ELGESETER GATE

KRISTIAN FREDERIKS GT.

EJLOVONSGT.

TRONDHEIM

ACCOMMODATION PRICE CODES

All the Norwegian hotels and guest houses listed in the guide have been graded according to the following price bands, based on the cost of the least expensive double room in high season. However, almost every hotel offers seasonal and/or weekend discounts that can reduce the rate by one or even two grades. Many of these bargains are impromptu, but wherever possible we've given two grades, covering both the regular and the discounted rate. Single rooms, where available, are usually between 60 and 80 percent of the cost of a double.

| ① under 500kr | ② 500–700kr | ③ 700–900kr |
| ④ 900–1200kr | ⑤ 1200–1500kr | ⑥ over 1500kr |

Accommodation

Beds are plentiful in Trondheim, with a choice of private rooms, two hostels and a selection of reasonably priced hotels and *pensjonater*. The private rooms are particularly good value, though almost all of them are far out from the city centre. Book at the tourist office, where the rate is fixed at 330kr per double per night, plus a 20kr booking fee.

Hotels and guesthouses

Britannia, Dronningensgate 5 (☎73 53 53 53; fax 73 51 29 00). Right in the middle of town, this long-established hotel has a magnificent Art Nouveau breakfast room, complete with Moorish water fountain, Egyptian murals and Corinthian columns. ③/④

Comfort Hotel Augustin, Kongensgate 26 (☎73 52 80 00; fax 73 51 55 01). Routine chain hotel in a big, old brick building, footsteps from Torvet. Functional and perfectly adequate rooms. ②/③

Pensjonat Jarlen, Kongensgate 40 (☎73 51 32 18; fax 73 52 80 80). Basic rooms, bargain prices and handy for the sights. ①

Rainbow Gildevangen, Søndregate 22b (☎73 51 01 00; fax 73 52 38 98). In an imposing old stone building on the north side of Torvet, this chain hotel offers seventy comfortable, modern rooms at economical prices. ②/③

Rainbow Trondheim, Kongensgate 15 (☎73 50 50 50; fax 73 51 60 58). Big and popular chain hotel in an attractive old building right in the centre. Plain, functional doubles. Incidentally, the bar here is one of the few places you can get homemade mead (*mjød*), once – as in medieval England – the most popular brew. ②/③

Residence, Torvet (☎73 52 83 80; fax 73 52 64 60). Package tour favourite on the main square. Overpriced outside summer. ③/④

Royal Garden, Kjøpmannsgate 73 (☎73 52 11 00; fax 73 53 17 66). Stylish modern hotel with sweeping architectural lines and wonderfully comfortable beds. Good summer deals make this one to check out first if you're looking for upmarket lodgings. ③/⑤

Hostels and camping

InterRail Centre, Elgesetergate 1 (☎73 89 95 38). Take bus #41, #42, #48, #49, #52 or #63 along Prinsensgate and ask for the *Studentersamfundet*; or else it's a twenty-minute walk from Torvet. Basic bed and breakfast accommodation run by the university's student society in an unusual round red house with couple of hundred rooms. There's a cheap café, and breakfast is served 7am–noon. Open late June to late Aug, daily 7am–1am ; 90kr.

Sandmoen Motel & Camping (☎72 88 61 35; fax 72 89 03 98). Twelve kilometres south of town, near Heimdal on the E6. Take bus #44 from the bus station, get off at the last stop, walk under the bridge and follow the signs. It has a selection of cabins and rooms – and it's open all year.

Trondheim Vandrerhjem, Weidemannsveien 41 (☎73 53 04 90; fax 73 53 52 88). A twenty-minute hike east from the centre – out over the Bakke bru (bridge), straight uphill along Innherredsveien (the E6), turning right up Nonnegate and it's the third road on the left. Bus #63 from Sentralstasjon and Dronningensgate also runs in that direction – ask the driver to let you off as close as possible. Institutional HI hostel with dorms and rooms. Dorm beds 150kr including breakfast, double rooms 360kr. Open all year except Christmas and New Year.

The City

Central Trondheim, with its animated streets and busy shops, makes for a pleasant stroll. There are a number of sights, including a couple of first-rate museums, but it's the Nidaros Domkirke that is the main focus of a visit.

Nidaros Domkirke

The goal of Trondheim's pilgrims in times past was the colossal cathedral, **Nidaros Domkirke**, Scandinavia's largest medieval building (May to mid-June & late Aug to mid-Sept Mon–Fri 9am–3pm, Sat 9am–2pm, Sun 1–4pm; mid-June to late Aug Mon–Fri 9am–5.30pm, Sat 9am–2pm, Sun 1–4pm; mid-Sept to April Mon–Fri noon–2.30pm, Sat 11.30am–2pm, Sun 1–3pm; 12kr). Gloriously restored following the ravages of the Reformation and several fires, it's still the focal point of any visit to the city and one of the country's architectural highlights. The building, which recalls Trondheim's former name, Nidaros ("mouth of the River Nid"), is dedicated to King – later Saint – Olav.

Born in 995, **Olav Haraldsson** followed the traditional lifestyle of the Viking chieftain from the tender age of twelve, "rousing the steel-storm", as the saga writers put it, from Finland to Ireland. He also served as a mercenary to both the Duke of Normandy and King Ethelred of England, during which time he was converted to Christianity. In 1015, he invaded and conquered Norway to become king. However, Olav's zealous imposition of the new religion alienated many of his followers and he was forced into exile in 1028. Two years later, he was back in Trøndelag, but his army was defeated in the battle of Stiklestad, near Trondheim (see p.298), where Olav lost his life.

Olav may have surrendered his kingdom, but the nationwide church he had founded lost no ground. Needing a local saint to consolidate its position, the church carefully nurtured the myth of Olav and he was subsequently declared a saint. His body was stashed away, and Olav Kyrre, who became King of Norway in 1066, started work on the grand church that was to house the remains in appropriate style. Over the years the church was altered and enlarged to accommodate the growing bands of medieval tourists, achieving cathedral status when the town became an archbishopric in 1152 and becoming the traditional burial place of Norwegian royalty. Since 1814 the cathedral has also been the place where Norwegian monarchs are crowned.

The best time to see the church is in the early morning, when it's comfortably free from tour groups. The magnificent blue-grey soapstone building with its copper-green spire and roof is a true amalgam of styles: the original eleventh-century church was a simple basilica, but subsequent alterations added Romanesque transepts and an early Gothic choir, whose flying buttresses are reminiscent of contemporaneous churches in England. The nave was built in the early thirteenth century, also to an early Gothic design, but it was destroyed by fire in 1719 and the present structure is a painstakingly accurate, late nineteenth-century replica. Inside, the gloomy half-light hides much of the lofty decorative work, but it is possible to examine the striking choir screen whose wooden figures are the work of Gustav Vigeland (see p.209). English-language **guided tours** take place during summer (mid-June to mid-Aug at 11am, 2pm & 4pm; 30min), and you can also take a peek at the assorted baubles of the Norwegian **crown jewels**, kept at the west end of the church (April & May Fri noon–2pm; June to mid-Aug Mon–Fri 9.30am–12.30pm, Sun 1–4pm; mid-Aug to Oct Fri noon–2pm; free). You can climb the cathedral **tower** too, for an extra 5kr (mid-June to mid-Aug same hours).

The churchyard, grounds and nearby river bank are eminently strollable. Behind the Domkirke, to the south, lies the heavily restored archbishop's palace, the

Erkebispegården, where two stone and brick wings are all that survive from the original medieval quadrangle. The archbishops were kicked out during the Reformation and the palace was subsequently used as the city armoury. Many of the old weapons are now displayed in the south wing, which has been turned into the Army and Resistance Museum (**Rustkammeret med Hjemmefrontmuseet**; June–Aug Mon–Fri 9am–3pm, Sat & Sun 11am–3pm; Sept–May Sat & Sun only, 11am–3pm; 5kr). Its most interesting section, on the top floor, recalls the German occupation of World War II, dealing honestly with the sensitive issue of collaboration. The north wing is used for official receptions and, although it's open to visitors (June to mid-Aug Mon–Fri 9am–3pm, Sat 9am–2pm, Sun 12.30–3.30pm), all you'll see is a sequence of empty vaulted halls and some bits and bobs relating to the nineteenth-century reconstruction of the cathedral nave.

Around the Domkirke: museums and galleries

A clutch of museums close to the Domkirke provides some varied entertainment, in particular the delightful Museum of Decorative Arts (**Nordenfjeldske Kunstindustrimueum**; late June to late Aug Mon–Sat 10am–5pm, Sun noon–5pm; rest of the year Mon–Sat 10am–3pm, Thurs till 5pm, Sun noon–4pm; 25kr), a couple of minutes' walk away at Munkegata 5. The museum's extensive collection is shown in rotation, alongside an ambitious programme of temporary exhibitions, with the focus firmly on contemporary arts, craft and design. Begin in the basement, where the historical collection illustrates bourgeois life in Trøndelag from the sixteenth century to 1900 by means of an eclectic combination of furniture, faience, glassware and silver. There are twentieth-century pieces on display here too, notably a fine sample of Art Nouveau, a style that recurs up on the first floor in a room kitted out by the Belgian designer and architect Henri van de Velde. Staying on the first floor, there's an unusual display of **tapestries** illustrating medieval folk-tales, which were produced in Trondheim in the early years of this century. The second floor has modern stuff as well, the highlight being a room devoted to fourteen tapestries by Swedish-born **Hannah Ryggen**, who lived in the Trondheim area from the early 1920s until her death in 1970. The naive style of the tapestries forces home her themes: in the 1930s and 40s railing against Hitler and Fascism, and moving on to more disparate targets – the atom bomb, conformity – in later years. But alongside the protest, there's celebration too: *Yes, We Love This Country* (tapestry 9) is as elegiac an evocation of Norway as you're likely to find.

The city's art gallery, **Trondhjems Kunstforening** (June–Aug daily 10am–4pm; Sept–May Tues–Sun noon–4pm; 20kr), back near the cathedral at Bispegata 7b, is small and less essential, though there's a modest selection of works by Johan Dahl and Thomas Fearnley, the leading figures of nineteenth-century Norwegian landscape painting, as well the first overtly political work by a Norwegian artist: the *Strike* (Streik) was painted in 1877 by the radical Theodor Kittelsen, better known for his illustrations of folk tales, which effectively decided what trolls actually looked like. Also, if you missed the work of Edvard Munch in Oslo (see p.208), there's a modest but diverting selection of his woodcuts, sketches and lithographs here, including several characteristically disturbing works, such as *Lust, Fear* and *Jealous*. Ask for the free inventory at reception.

From here, it's a five- to ten-minute walk northwest across one of the more modern parts of the city centre to the several collections comprising the university's Museum of Natural History and Archeology (**Vitenskapsmuseet**; June–Aug Tues–Fri 10am–6pm, Sat & Sun 11am–6pm; Sept–May Tues–Sat 10am–3pm, Sun 11am–4pm; 25kr), at Erling Skakkesgate 47. At the front, the main building contains an eminently missable assortment of dusty stuffed animals, a second-rate science centre, and a ragbag of largely incomprehensible archeological finds. Ignore these in favour of the smaller building on the left, where there's a small but enjoyable **church art** collection (Oct–April Sun 11am–4pm). Even better is the **historical exhibition** in the old *Suhmhuset* (hay storehouse), a long, low building at the rear, which tracks the development of Trondheim from its foundation in the tenth century to the great fire of 1681. Its excellent range of archeological finds is supported by thoroughly researched, multilingual text investigating everything from sanitary towels to games and attitudes to life and death.

The rest of central Trondheim

Back in the centre, **Torvet** is the main city square, a spacious, open area anchored by a statue of St Olav perched on a tall stone pillar like some medieval Nelson. The broad and pleasant avenues of Trondheim's centre radiate out from here, a gridiron dating back to the late seventeenth century when these thoroughfares doubled as fire breaks. They were originally flanked by long rows of wooden buildings, now replaced for the most part by uninspiring modern structures, although there is one conspicuous survivor in the **Stiftsgården** (early to mid-June Tues–Sat 10am–3pm, Sun noon–5pm; mid-June to mid-Aug Tues–Sat 10am–5pm, Sun noon–5pm; rest of the year open one day a month – details from the tourist office; hourly guided tours on the hour; 30kr), the yellow creation just north of Torvet on Munkegata. Built in 1774–78 as the home of a provincial governor, these days it's an official royal residence. Inside, a long series of period rooms with fanciful Italianate wall paintings reflect the genteel tastes of the early occupants and the anecdotal guided tour manages to bring a smile.

More accessible are the **medieval church ruins** discovered under the library at the far end of Kongensgate, east from Torvet (June–Aug Mon–Fri 9am–4pm, Sat 9am–2pm; Sept–May Mon–Fri 9am–7pm, Sat 10am–3pm; free). The evidence is a bit shaky, but it is believed to have been a chapel dedicated to St Olav, a twelfth-century relic of the days when Trondheim had fifteen or more religious buildings. Excavations uncovered nearly five hundred bodies in the immediate area, which was once the church graveyard, and the group of skeletons on display are neatly preserved under a glass cover.

Following the river south from the library, it's a short walk to the **old town bridge** (*Bybrua*), an elegant wooden reach with splendid views over the early eighteenth-century gabled and timbered warehouses that flank Kjøpmannsgata, most now converted into restaurants and offices. Over the bridge are a few old, brightly painted wooden houses; if these whet your appetite, then you'll enjoy the tangle of narrow alleys and pastel-painted clapboard frontages that fills out the **side streets** north of Kongensgate and west of Prinsensgate. There's nothing special to look at, but it's a pleasant area for a stroll, after which you can wander over to Ravnkloa, the jetty at the north end of Munkegata.

Out from the centre: Munkholmen and Ringve Museum

In summer boats (late May to Aug hourly on the hour 10am–6pm; 28kr return) shuttle out from Ravnkloa to the islet of **Munkholmen**, 2km offshore in the Trondheimsfjord. Originally the city's execution ground, Benedictine monks built an abbey here in the eleventh century and after the Reformation it was converted into a prison-cum-fortress, designed both to hold political prisoners and protect the seaward approaches to the city. There are thirty-minute guided tours of the **fort** (late May to Aug daily 10.30am–5.30pm; 14kr), but most locals use the island as a bathing spot, scrambling round the rocks beneath the walls to the shoreline farthest from the harbour. A half-hour visit to Munkholmen is included in the best of several **boat trips** arranged by the tourist office – "Trondheim from the sea" (late June to mid-Aug Tues–Sun 1 daily; late Aug to early Sept Wed, Fri & Sun 1 daily; 2hr; 80kr).

Eating, drinking and nightlife

Traditionally, Trondheim has never been considered an inspiring place to **eat**, but things are improving and in recent years its smattering of run-of-the-mill Norwegian and ethnic eateries – Chinese, Italian and Indian places make up the bulk – have been supplemented by several first-rate **restaurants**. At the other end of the gastronomic market, the city's mobile **fast-food** stalls are concentrated around Sentralstasjon and along Kongensgate, on either side of Torvet. The town's large student population ensures an active **nightlife**, especially at weekends, when the centre of the action is along Dronningensgate, around the *Britannia Hotel*.

Cafés and restaurants

Benito's Mat og Vinhus, Vår Fruegate 4, off Kongensgate. Short on pasta, long on meat dishes, this is easily the best Italian restaurant in town.

Havfruen, Kjøpmannsgate 7 (☎73 53 26 26). A superb fish restaurant near the cathedral – the best in town with prices to match. Main courses from 170kr. Try to book in advance.

Lian Restaurant, Lianvegen. Up in the forested hills about 10km to the south of the city centre, this restaurant with a terrace bar offers traditional Norwegian food and panoramic views over the Trondheimsfjord. Getting there is enjoyable too – catch the Lian tram from St Olavsgate and keep on it till you reach the terminus, from where it's a couple of minutes' walk up the hill to the restaurant. Unfortunately, at the weekend it's too busy to be much fun. Tues–Sun 10.30am–7pm, later in the summer.

Napoli, Kongensgate 32, at St Olavsgate. Popular spot for tasty Italian food. Pizzas go for around 70kr.

De Ni Muser Café, Bispegata 9. Footsteps from the Art Gallery, this relaxed and fashionable little café serves up tasty snacks and meals based on a variety of European cuisines. Prices are low, and most of the clientele are students. Terrace bar at the back. Tues–Sun 11am–midnight.

O' Martins, Olav Tryggvasonsgate 33 at Jomfrugate. One of the city's better fast-food joints with rock-bottom prices.

Kafé Posepilten, Prinsensgate 32 at Dronningensgate. Laid-back café-bar offering tasty and filling snacks.

Peking House Restaurant, Kjøpmannsgata 63. Competent and reasonably priced Chinese place, specializing in Szechuan dishes.

Bars and clubs

Bobbys Bar, Søndregate 22a. Small, intimate and youthful bar in the town centre.

Breiflabben, Kjøpmannsgate 7. On the floor below the *Havfruen* restaurant, this bar caters for the thirtysomething-plus and often has live jazz Fri & Sat nights.

Carl Johan Møteplass, Olav Tryggvasonsgate 24. Recommended for stylish drinking. Jam-packed at the weekend.

Exit, Dronningensgate. Bar and nightclub that sees most of Trondheim's permed haircuts passing through its doors. Popular – and raucous at the weekend.

Studentersamfundet, Elgesetergate 1. Student centre with cheap drinks, music and dancing during term-time; about twenty minutes' walk south of the city centre along Prinsensgate.

Listings

Airlines *SAS* (☎74 82 35 10); *Braathens SAFE* (☎74 82 32 00); *Widerøe* (☎74 82 49 22).

British consulate Sluppenveien 10 (☎73 96 05 00).

Car rental *Avis*, Kjøpmannsgata 34 (☎73 52 69 15); *Budget,* Elgesetergate 21 (☎73 94 10 25) and at the *Royal Garden Hotel*, Kjøpmannsgata 73 (☎73 52 69 20).

DNT *Trondhjems Turistforening*, at Munkegata 64 (Mon–Fri 9am–4pm; ☎73 52 38 08), is the local branch of the DNT, offering advice on the region's hiking trails and huts. Also organizes guided walks and cross-country skiing trips of various lengths.

Emergencies Fire ☎110; Police ☎112; Ambulance ☎113; Hospital emergency department ☎73 99 88 00; NAF ☎73 96 62 88.

InterRail Centre Rest Point At Sentralstasjon July & Aug, with shavers, toilets and cooking facilities.

Pharmacy *St Olav Vaktapotek*, Kjøpmannsgate 65 (☎73 52 66 66). Mon–Sat 8.30am–midnight, Sun 10am–midnight.

Police Kongensgate 87 (☎73 51 44 11).

Post office Main office at Dronningensgate 10 (Mon–Fri 8am–5pm, Sat 9am–1pm).

Taxis Ranks at Torvet, Sentralstasjon, Søndregata and the *Royal Garden Hotel*; or call ☎73 50 50 73.

Vinmonopolet City centre off-licence at Kjøpmannsgata 32.

North of Trondheim: Stiklestad to Fauske

North of Trondheim, it's a long haul up the coast to the next major places of interest: Bodø, which is the main ferry port for the Lofotens, and the gritty town of Narvik, respectively 740km and 908km away. You can get most of the way there by **train**, a rattling good journey with the scenery becoming wilder and bleaker the further north you go; it takes nine hours to reach **Fauske**, where the railway line reaches its northern limit and turns west for the last 65-kilometre dash across to Bodø. At Fauske, there are **bus** connections north to Narvik, a further five-hour drive away, but many travellers take an overnight break here – though in fact Bodø is a far more pleasant stop.

If you're **driving**, you'll find the E6 – which runs all the way from Trondheim to Narvik and points north – simply too slow-going to cover more than three or four hundred kilometres comfortably in any one day. Fortunately, there are several pleasant places to stop, principally **Steinkjer** and **Snåsa**, in Trøndelag beside the E6, and **Graddis**, a few kilometres off the E6 in the next region up, Nordland. Graddis is sited on the eastern rim of the **Saltfjellet Nasjonalpark**, a wild and windswept mountain plateau that extends from the Swedish border to the **Svartisen glacier** crowning the coastal peaks in the west. The park is a popular destination for experienced hikers, but it's far too fierce an environment for the novice – or the poorly equipped.

Stiklestad

Leaving Trondheim, the E6 tunnels and twists its way round the the fjord to **Hell** – a desperate place with nothing other than its name to recommend it, though in Norwegian *hell* means good fortune – just beyond which the E14 branches off east to Østersund in Sweden. The E6 presses on north, slicing through the valleys and hills of Trøndelag and slipping past the tedious little towns of Levanger and Verdalsøra, where offshore oil platforms are built. From the latter, it's 6km inland off the E6 to **STIKLESTAD**, a straggling village that boasts a museum commemorating Saint Olav's final defeat here, and is the site of one of Norway's biggest St Olav's day celebrations, on July 29.

A descendant of Harald Hafågre (the Fair-Haired), **Olav Haraldsson** (see also p.294) was one of Norway's greatest medieval kings, a Viking warrior turned monarch whose misfortune it was to be the enemy of the powerful and shrewd King Knut of England and Denmark. Knut's bribes that persuaded all but Olav's most loyal allies to change allegiance, and when Olav returned from exile in Sweden in 1030, he was defeated and killed here at the battle of Stiklestad. His role as the founder of the Norwegian church prompted his subsequent canonization and his cult flourished at Trondheim until the Reformation. Olav has long been remembered on the site of his final defeat by the colourful **Olsokspelet** (St Olav's Play), a costume drama performed each year in an open-air amphitheatre in Stiklestad as part of the St Olav Festival. More recently, the government has spent millions building a museum complex fit for a national hero. The amphitheatre now adjoins an **open-air museum** containing some thirty seventeenth- to nineteenth-century buildings imported from the rest of rural Trøndelag. Nearby is a twelfth-century church, original to the site, sitting near to the broad-beamed St **Olav's Kulturhus** (May–Aug daily 9am–8pm; Sept–April Mon–Fri 9am–5pm; ☎74 07 31 00), whose prime exhibit is a melodramatic **museum** (closes 5pm; 30kr) chronicling the events that led to Olav's death by means of shadowy dioramas and a ghoulish soundtrack.

Stiklestad is difficult to reach without your own transport and there's nowhere to stay; a twice-daily train from Trondheim runs to Verdalsøra, from where you have to walk. During the St Olav Festival, however, special trains and buses take visitors to the site; details from the Trondheim tourist office or from the festival office (☎73 52 56 65).

Steinkjer

Back on the E6, it's a further 30km to **STEINKJER**, an unassuming town that sits in the shadow of wooded hills where the river that gave the place its name empties into the fjord. The Germans bombed the town to bits in 1940 as it was the site of an infantry training camp, and the modern replacement is a tidy, rather appealing ensemble that fans out from the long main street, Kongensgate. Here, at no. 37, bang in the centre of town across from the train station, is the *Inter Nor Grand Hotell* (☎74 16 47 00; fax 74 16 62 87; ②/④), which manages to seem quite old-fashioned even though it occupies a modern tower block. The hotel has a reasonable restaurant too, though there are several other options nearby, the pick being the folksy *Trønderstua*, Kongensgate 33, which serves traditional Norwegian fare.

The E6 runs through the town just to the west of Kongensgate, passing the **tourist office** (late June to mid-Aug Mon–Fri 8am–7pm, Sat 10am–5pm, Sun noon–5pm; rest of the year Mon–Fri 8am–4pm; ☎74 16 67 00). There's also a municipal **campsite**, *Guldbergaunet Camping* (☎74 16 20 45; fax 74 16 47 35), in the park on the south bank of the river, about 2km inland from the train station.

Snåsa

On the north side of Steinkjer, there's a choice of routes around the long and slender **Snåsavatnet** lake, with the E6 thumping round the north shore while the more agreeable Hwy 763 meanders through the farmland and wooded hills to the south. At the far end of the lake is **SNÅSA**, a sleepy, sprawling hamlet with a pretty little hilltop church dating from the Middle Ages and very much in the English style. Overlooking the lake on the west side of the village – and 6km from the E6 – is the spick and span **youth hostel** (☎74 15 10 57; fax 74 15 16 15; June–Aug; 110kr, doubles ①), which is part of a larger complex including a comfortably modern if rather spartan **hotel** (all year; ②/③) and a **campsite** (all year) with spaces for tents and caravans as well as huts. There's a restaurant here too, serving mundane but filling Norwegian staples, but note that if you're likely to arrive hungry and late, you should telephone ahead to check it will still be open.

THE COASTAL ROUTE

With time and patience, you can leave the E6 just beyond Steinkjer and strike out along the tortuous **Coastal Route** (the *Kystriksveien*; Hwy 17), which threads its way up the west coast linking many villages that could formerly only be reached by sea. This is an obscure and remote corner of the country: apart from the lovely scenery, there's little of special appeal, and the seven ferry trips that interrupt the 700-kilometre drive north to Bodø (there are no buses) make it very expensive. Alternatively, you can see the highlights in a day by leaving the E6 at **Mo-i-Rana** (see p.300) – pick up a copy of the free booklet on the Coastal Route at the tourist office here – and take Hwy 12 for 35km to join Hwy 17. From the crossroads, it's some 60km to the **Kilboghamn–Jektvik** ferry (Mon–Sat 6 daily, Sun 3; 1hr; car & driver 94kr), a further 30km to the boat from **Ågskardet** to **Forøy** (Mon–Sat 12 daily; 10min; car & driver 35kr), and a final 200km drive into Bodø (see p.302). On the first ferry you cross the Arctic Circle, and after the second you get the chance to see an arm of the Svartisen glacier, viewed across the slender Holandsfjorden.

Into Nordland: Mo-i-Rana and the Svartisen glacier

Beyond Snåsa, the E6 leaves the wooded valleys of the Trøndelag behind for the higher, harsher landscapes of **Nordland**. Rattling past the aluminium plant at Mosjøen, the road wriggles over the mountains along the coast as far as **MO-I-RANA** or "Mo", an unenticing steel town at the end of the Ranafjord. You wouldn't want to stay here, but it is an ideal base for an excursion to the **Svartisen glacier**, one of whose tongues reaches down to a lake 32km from town: proceed north along the E6 for around 13km to Rossvoll, and then follow the signs up the nineteen-kilometre minor road that leads to Svartisvannet lake. Boats run across the lake from late June to August, dropping you a three-kilometre hike away from the glacier, whose name means, graphically, "Black Ice" – strong shoes are essential. Sailings are hourly from mid-July to mid-August (10am–4pm; 20min; 60kr return; information on ☎75 16 23 79); during the rest of the summer, services depend on sufficient customers.

Back in Mo, the **tourist office** (June–Aug Mon–Fri 9am–8pm, Sat 10am–4pm, Sun 1–6pm; Sept–May Mon–Fri 9am–4pm; ☎75 15 04 21), beside the E6, offers free town maps and a range of literature on Nordland, including the free booklet describing the **Coastal Route** (the *Kystriksveien*; Hwy 17), which offers an alternative route north to Bodø (see box on p.299). From Mo tourist office, it's a five-minute stroll north along the fjord (Ole Tobias Olsensgate) to the town centre, where the **bus** and **train stations** are next door to each other. Amongst several modern, downtown **hotels**, both the *Inter Nor Meyergården Hotell*, Ole Tobias Olsensgate 24 (☎75 15 05 55; fax 75 15 40 64; ③), and the *Hotell Ole Tobias*, next door at no. 26 (☎75 15 77 77; fax 75 15 77 78; ③), are perfectly adequate. There's also a no-frills **youth hostel** (☎75 15 09 63; fax 75 15 15 30; May to early Sept; 100kr, double rooms ①), which has a pleasant enough setting on a wooded hillside, a kilometre or so south of town just off (and signposted from) the E6.

The Arctic Circle

Given its appeal as a travellers' totem – and considering the amount of effort it takes to actually get here – crossing the **Arctic Circle**, about 80km north of Mo, is a bit of a disappointment. The landscape, uninhabited for the most part, is undeniably bare and bleak, but the gleaming **Polarsirkelsenteret** (Arctic Circle Centre; daily May & Sept 10am–6pm; June–Aug 9am–10pm) disfigures the scene, a giant lampshade of a building plonked by the roadside and stuffed with every sort of tourist bauble imaginable. You'll whizz by on the bus, the train toots its whistle as it passes by, and drivers can, of course, shoot past too – though the temptation to brave the crowds is strong and even if you resist the Arctic exhibition (40kr), you'll probably get snared by either the "Polarsirkelen" certificate, or the specially stamped postcards. Outside the centre, a couple of simple stone memorials are poignant reminders of crueller times: they pay tribute to the Yugoslav and Soviet POWs who laboured under terrible conditions to build the Nordlandsbanen, the Arctic road to Narvik, for the Germans in World War II.

Saltfjellet Nasjonalpark: Lønsdal and Graddis

The louring mountains in the vicinity of the *Polarsirkelsenteret* are part of the vast **Saltfjellet Nasjonalpark**, a mountain plateau whose spindly pines, stern peaks and rippling moors extend west from the Swedish border as far as the Svartisen glacier. The E6 and the railway cut across this range – in between Mo-i-Rana and Rognan – providing access to its hiking trails, a function that's also served by Hwy 77, which forks east off the E6 to Sweden down the Junkerdal valley. The cairned hiking trails that lattice the mountains are, however, not sufficiently clear to dispense with a compass, weather conditions can be treacherous and, although there's a good network of DNT-affiliated huts, none is staffed and neither are there any provisions: consequently, the region is normally the preserve of experienced hikers. Keys to these huts (most of which are owned by *BOT*, Bodø's hiking association) are available locally.

Among several possible bases for venturing into the Saltfjellet, **LØNSDAL**, around 100km north of Mo and 20km from the Arctic Circle, is the most easily reached, either by train from Trondheim/Mo or Bodø (2–3 daily but check with the conductor; some trains only stop here by request) or on the E6. Not that there's actually much to reach: a one-kilometre long turning off the E6 leads first to the *Polarsirkelen Høyfjellshotell* (☎08 19 41 22; fax 08 19 41 27; ③), a big wooden building buttressed against the elements and with a cosy modern interior, and then to the solitary train station. The hotel is popular, so reservations are advised, and there's not much choice but to have all your meals here – no bad thing.

From Lønsdal, hiking trails head off into the Saltfjellet with one of the more manageable options being the four-hour hike east to **GRADDIS**, where there's a **youth hostel** (☎75 69 43 41; fax 75 69 43 88; mid-June to Aug; 100kr, doubles ③) on the wooded slopes of the Junkedralen, a wild and picturesque ravine between the mountains that is itself a favourite spot to begin exploring the Saltfjellet. The youth hostel is situated off Hwy 77, 18km east of the E6 and close to the Swedish border; there are no buses.

Fauske

Except for a brief stretch of railway line from Narvik into Sweden further north, **FAUSKE** – some 110km north of the Arctic Circle on the E6 – marks the northernmost point of the Norwegian train network and is, consequently, an important transport hub. The town is – along with Bodø – a departure point of the *Nord-Norge ekspressen* (see p.161), the **express bus** service that complements the trains by carrying passengers as far as Kirkenes, close to the Russian border. Get tickets from the bus station in Fauske or buy them on the buses, which leave twice daily from outside the train station. Note that there is a 50 percent discount for *InterRail* pass-holders on the first step of the route, to Narvik (see below), a seven-hour trip that's a gorgeous run past fjords and snowy peaks.

However, most northbound travellers spend the night in Fauske rather than making a quick change onto the connecting bus to Narvik – though in fact Bodø is a better stopover. From Fauske **train station**, it's a five- to ten-minute walk down the hill and left at the T-junction to the **bus station** and adjoining **tourist office** (Mon–Fri 8am–6pm, Sat 10am–2pm; ☎75 64 33 03), which usefully posts the region's ferry time-tables in its windows. Footsteps away, the E6, running parallel to the fjord, forms the main thoroughfare Storgata, accommodating the handful of shops that passes for a town centre. It's here at no. 82 that you'll find the town's only **hotel**, the *Fauske* (☎75 64 38 33; fax 75 64 57 37; ④), a square block whose interior exhibits a surfeit of locally quarried salmon-coloured marble. Nevertheless, the rooms are comfortable and the big breakfast (from 7am; 50kr) is also handy for travellers staying at the spartan **youth hostel** (☎75 64 67 06; June to mid-Aug; 100kr, doubles ①), about 500m west of the hotel and signposted off Storgata. A third option is the *Lundhøgda* **campsite** (☎75 64 39 66; June–Sept), which overlooks the mountains and the fjord about 3km west of the town centre: head out of town along the E80 towards Bodø and watch for the sign which will take you down a country lane flanked by old timber buildings. The campsite takes caravans, has pitches for tents and offers huts for rental (①).

Bodø and around

BODØ, 63km west of Fauske along the E80, can be reached either by bus from Fauske or on the Trondheim train, which terminates here. Founded in 1816, Bodø struggled to survive in its early years, but was saved from insignificance when the herring fishery became exceptionally productive in the 1860s, and the town's harbourfront became crowded with the net menders, coopers, oilskin makers and canneries that kept the fleet going. In the early twentieth century, Bodø accrued several industrial plants and became an important regional centre, but heavy bombing during World War II spared little of the proud nineteenth-century buildings that once flanked the waterfront. Nonetheless, Bodø manages to remain a cheerful modern place within comfortable striking distance of the old trading post of Kjerringøy, one of Nordland's most delightful spots. Bodø is a regular stop on the *Hurtigrute* steamer route and also much the best starting point for a trip to the Lofoten islands (see p.308).

In Bodø itself, the most popular tourist attraction is the Norwegian Aviation Centre (**Norsk Luftfartssenter**; June–Aug Mon–Fri 10am–8pm, Sat 10am–5pm, Sun 10am–8pm; Sept–May Mon–Fri 10am–4pm, Sat & Sun 10am–5pm; 50kr), which tracks through the general history of aviation with the emphasis on domestic civilian and military developments. Rather more interesting than it sounds, the centre's highlights include a flight simulator, an old control tower and a Spitfire, a Tiger Moth and, more unusually, an American U2 spy plane of Gary Powers and Cold War fame. The Aviation Centre is situated on the ring road – Olav V gate – about 2km southeast of the town centre, a dreary walk that you can avoid by catching bus #12 from the bus station – ask the driver to put you off at the City Nord shopping centre, on Gamle Riksvei, from where it's a five- to ten-minute walk west.

If you have your own transport, then consider driving a further 1km south along Gamle Riksvei to the little onion-domed **Bodin kirke** (June–Aug daily 10am–8pm), which sits smugly amongst the surrounding meadows. Dating from the thirteenth century, the church was modified after the Reformation with the addition of a tower and the widening of the windows – at a time when dark, gloomy churches were associated with "Catholic superstition". It is, however, the colourful set of seventeenth-century fixtures that catches the eye, including a lovingly carved Baroque altar board and pulpit.

Practicalities

The *Hurtigrute* **coastal steamer** and the southern **Lofotens ferry** (to Moskenes, Værøy and Røst) leave from the docks respectively 1700m and 700m northeast of the **train station**, which is itself just 300m along Sjøgata from the **tourist office** at Sjøgata 21 (June to late Aug Mon–Fri 9am–9pm, Sat 10am–3pm & 6–8pm, Sun 10am–8pm; rest of the year Mon–Fri 9am–4pm; ☎75 52 60 00; fax 75 52 21 77). The office is good for information on getting to the Lofoten Islands, rents out bikes and also issues an excellent town and district guide. The **bus station** is another 300m along Sjøgata, beside the gigantic *SAS Royal Hotel*. If you're heading further north, note that the same half-price bus deal for rail pass holders travelling from Fauske to Narvik operates from Bodø, too. Close by the bus station, at the west end of Sjøgata, another dock deals with the **hydrofoil** (*Hurtigbåter*) services to the Lofotens, notably to Svolvær and Stokmarknes (see box on p312).

Bodø offers plenty of accommodation choices. The tourist office has a small supply of **private rooms** both in the town and its environs, costing 150kr per person, plus a 15kr booking fee (25kr outside town). Alternatively, the no-frills **youth hostel** is next door to the station at Sjøgata 55 (☎/fax 75 52 11 22; all year; 140kr, doubles ①). Up the accommodation scale, there are several central **hotels**, including the spruce *Norrøna*, close to

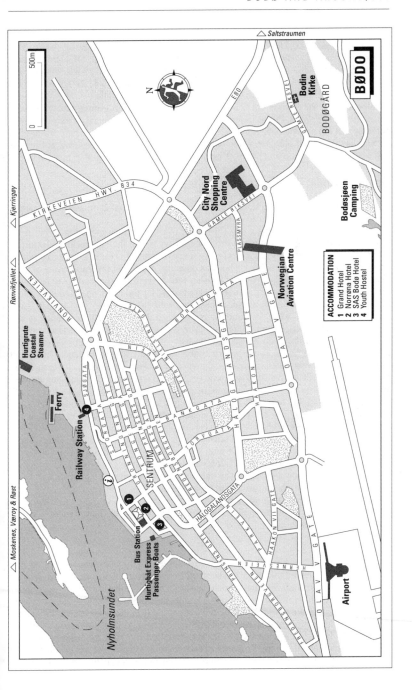

△ Saltstraumen

BØDO

0   500m

N

Kjerringøy △

△ Ranviktfjellet

△ Moskenes, Værøy & Røst

Bodin Kirke

BODØGÅRD

City Nord Shopping Centre

GAMLE RIKSVEI

Bodøsjøen Camping

KIRKEVEIEN   HWY. 834

E80

PLASSMYRA

Norwegian Aviation Centre

RØNVIKVEIEN

Hurtigrute Coastal Steamer

Ferry

Railway Station

BØDINGATA

OLAV V GATE

HAKON VII GATE

HÅLOGALANDSGATA

SJØGATA

BANKGATA

TORVGATA

SENTRUM

ACCOMMODATION
1 Grand Hotel
2 Norrøna Hotel
3 SAS Bodø Hotel
4 Youth Hostel

1

2

3

4

Bus Station

Hurtigbåt Express Passenger Boats

HÅLOGALANDSGATA

PRINSENS GATE

HERNESVEIEN

OLAV V GATE

Airport

Nyholmsundet

i

the bus station at Storgata 4 (☎75 52 55 50; fax 75 52 33 88; ②), and the pleasantly old-fashioned *Grand Hotel*, close by at Storgata 3 (☎75 52 00 00; fax 75 52 27 09; ③/④). The *Radisson SAS Hotel Bodø*, Storgata 2 (☎75 52 41 00; fax 75 52 74 93; ③/⑤), is the swankiest place in town – rooms on the upper floors have great views out to sea. Finally, you can **camp** 3km southeast of the centre at *Bodøsjøen Camping* (☎75 52 29 02), beside the lake not far from the Bodin kirke – take bus #12 from the bus station.

Unfortunately, the town is not so well served when it come to **eating**. Easily the best bet is the *Pizzakjeller'n*, in the basement of the *Radisson SAS*, where an excellent two-person pizza will set you back around 150kr. For **drinking**, the *Peacock Pub*, around the corner, has darts and billiards, while the more fashionable *Paviljongen Bar,* at the east end of the Storgata shopping precinct (the Glasshuset), is a good spot to nurse a beer.

Out from Bodø: Kjerringøy and Saltstraumen

There are two popular excursions from Bodø; while both can be made using public transport, they're much easier to do with your own vehicle.

In summer there's one bus a day (Mon–Sat; 50kr day return including ferry) from Bodø bus station 40km north along the coastal Hwy 834 to the old **trading station** at **KJERRINGØY**, a superbly preserved collection of nineteenth-century timber buildings erected beside a slender channel. This was once the domain of the Zahl family of merchants, who supplied the fishermen of Lofoten with everything from clothes to farmyard foodstuffs. It was not, however, an equal relationship, for the Zahls operated something of a monopoly until the 1910s, allowing them to dictate the price they paid for fish – and many of the islanders were permanently indebted to them. This social division is still very much in evidence at the trading post, where there's a marked distinction between the guest rooms in the main house and the fishermens' bunks in the boat- and cook-houses. Indeed, the family house is remarkably fastidious, with its Italianate busts and embroidered curtains, and a medicine cabinet stocked with formidable Victorian remedies such as a bottle of "Sicilian Hair Renewer." There are enjoyable, hour-long **guided tours** around the place in summer (mid-May to late Aug 3–5 daily, times from Bodø tourist office; 40kr), but to ensure a place and to ask for an English rendition you should call ahead (9–11am; ☎75 51 12 57). Tours loosely coincide with the bus/ferry times, but drivers have much more flexibility as the car ferry (Festvåg–Misten; 15kr; car & driver day return 42kr; 10min) sails at least once an hour – again, schedules from Bodø tourist office. When you've finished with the tour, you can nose around the reconstructed general store, drop by the café and stroll along the fine sandy beach in front of the complex. Should you want to stay overnight, the old parsonage *Kjerringøy prestegård* (☎75 58 34 60 or 75 51 11 43; ①), about 1km north of the trading post along Hwy 834, has simple double rooms in the main building and rather pleasanter ones in the newly renovated cow shed next door. If you're heading back to Bodø to catch a ferry, remember to check the times of the buses.

Saltstraumen

Much less interesting, but far more widely publicized, is the **Saltstraumen**, a narrow channel situated around the bay 33km south of Bodø on Hwy 17, through which billions of gallons of water are forced four times daily, making a headlong rush between inner and outer fjord. The whirling creamy water is at its most turbulent at high tide, and its most violent when the moon is new or full – a timetable is available from Bodø tourist office. Although scores of tourists troop here for every high tide, it has to be said that the scenery is, in Norwegian terms, flat and dull, and the view from the bridge that spans the channel unexciting. Probably the best reason to come here is for the fishing; the fish get trapped between the conflicting currents so you certainly won't leave empty-handed. There's a local **bus** service from Bodø to the Saltstraumen (March to late-Aug Mon–Fri 5 daily, Sat 3, Sun 1), but the times rarely coincide with high tides, though to pass the time you could drop by the **Saltstraumen Opplevelsessenter** (daily May 10am–6pm; June–Aug 10am–10pm; F50), an exhibition near the east end of the bridge, which tells you all you ever wanted to know about tidal currents, and then some.

At enormous expense, the Norwegians have created the **Coastal Route** (the *Kystriksveien*; Hwy 17), which runs south beyond the Saltstraumen, connecting the once-remote villages of the indented shoreline to the road system. Interspersed by no fewer than seven ferry crossings, the highway extends for 700km to Steinkjer – though the shorter detour south to Mo-i-Rana is more economic and much less time-consuming (see box on p.299).

Narvik

Rounding the fjords, twisting and tunnelling through the mountains and rushing over high plateaux dusted with spindly pines, the E6 heads north along the coast from Fauske, reaching, after 170km, the jetty at **Bognes**, where there's a choice of **ferries** – one sails to Lødingen and the E10 on the Lofotens (5–6 daily; 1hr; car & driver 106kr), while the other travels to Skarberget for the E6 and points north (11 daily; 25min; car & driver 55kr).

Eventually, 80km on from Skarberget and five hours from Fauske by bus along the E6, you arrive at **NARVIK**, a relatively modern town established less than a century ago as an ice-free port to handle the iron ore brought by train from northern Sweden. It makes no bones about its main function: the **iron-ore docks** are slap bang in the centre of

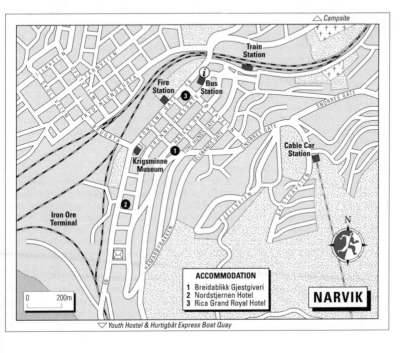

ACCOMMODATION
1 Breidablikk Gjestgiveri
2 Nordstjernen Hotel
3 Rica Grand Royal Hotel

NARVIK

▽ *Youth Hostel & Hurtigbåt Express Boat Quay*

town, with rust-coloured machinery overwhelming the entire waterfront. Yet, for all the mess, the industrial complex is strangely compelling, with its intricate cat's cradle of walkways, conveyor belts, cranes and funnels.

The Town and around

Narvik's first modern settlers were the navvies who built the railway line to the mines in Kiruna, over the border – a Herculean task commemorated every March by a week of singing, dancing and drinking, the locals dressed in nineteenth-century costume. The town grew steadily up to the last war, when it was demolished by fierce fighting for control of the harbour and iron ore supplies. The hulks of German destroyers still lie out in the water, the bodies of hundreds of soldiers and sailors – Nazis and Allied troops – interred in the cemeteries to the north of the town.

Perhaps inevitably, the town centre is rather lacking in appeal, with modern stone replacing the wooden houses and buildings flattened during the war. Nevertheless, try and devote an hour or so to the **Krigsminnemuseum** (War Museum; March to early June & late Aug to Sept daily 11am–3pm; early June to late Aug Mon–Sat 10am–10pm, Sun 11am–5pm; 25kr), in the main square near to the gates of the iron ore terminal. Run by the Red Cross, the museum documents the German saturation bombing of the town, and the bitter and bloody sea and air battles in which hundreds of foreign servicemen died alongside the local population. It's a thoroughly moving account: one display juxtaposes German bullwhips with small toys made by Russian POWs as thanks for food parcels smuggled in by locals, who faced execution if discovered.

If you have a little time to spare, there are summertime **guided tours** of the town (daily at 3pm; 30kr), an easy hour and a quarter's ramble through its older quarters, which includes a visit to the war cemetery. Check with the tourist office about this and the hour-long tour of the dock area (daily at 1pm; 25kr), which leaves from the gates of the *LKAB* complex near the main square: interesting if only for the opportunity to spend an hour amidst the giant, ore-stained contraptions. After its arrival by train, the ore is carried on the various conveyor belts to the quayside where it is shipped out, around thirty million tons of it a year.

Beyond that, it's best to head for the countryside around town. A rather temperamental *fjellheisen* or **cable car** (mid-June to mid-Aug daily 10am–1am; 60kr) – check it's operating at the tourist office before you set out – is located a stiff fifteen-minute walk up above the town behind the bus station, from where it whisks passengers up the first 700m of the mighty **Fagernesfjellet**. From the viewpoint at the top of the cable car, the Lofoten islands are visible on a clear day; it's also a good spot for observing the Midnight Sun (end of May to mid-July).

By train to Sweden: the Ofotbanen

The real highlight of a visit to Narvik is the **train ride** into the mountains behind town that spread east across the Swedish border. Called the *Ofotbanen*, the rail line passes through some wonderful scenery, slipping between hostile peaks before reaching the rocky, barren and lochlet-studded plateau beyond. Completed in 1903, the railroad was a remarkable achievement and it's hard not to be astounded by the hardships the navvies must have endured in the wintertime. There are special day trips from Narvik to the Swedish border, costing 120kr (which includes a video show), but you're better off catching an ordinary train (June to mid-Aug 3 daily; mid-Aug to May 2 daily; 50min; 82kr return) to reach the Swedish border settlement of **RIKSGRÄNSEN**, a hiking and skiing centre on the plateau.

There's a large and surprisingly plush **hotel** here, the *Riksgränsen* (46/980 400 80; fax 46/980 431 25; ②), where you can buy hiking maps and sports gear as well as rent mountain bikes. You can nose around the place for an hour or two before returning by train to Narvik, or alternatively, hike at least a part of the **Rallarvågen**, the old and recently refurbished trail built for the construction workers in the last century, which extends west the 15km to Rombaksbotn on the coast and east to Abisko, deeper in Sweden. A popular option is to walk from Riksgrånsen back towards the coast, joining the return train at one of the Norwegian stations on the way. The area isn't nearly as remote now that the E10 crosses the mountains to the north of the railroad, but the terrain is difficult and weather unpredictable, so hikers will need to be well equipped.

For longer hiking trips, there is a network of **trails and cabins** strung out in the mountains surrounding the railroad. The cabins are maintained by the *Narvik Touring Association* and the keys are kept at the fire station back in town; you'll need to pay a 60kr deposit for their use. Hiking maps are available in Narvik from the *Narvik Libris* bookshop, just up from the museum at Kongensgate 44.

Practicalities

Fifteen minutes' walk from one end to the other, Narvik's sloping centre straggles along the main street, Kongensgate, part of the E6. At the north end of the town centre is the **train station**, from where it's the briefest of strolls to the **bus station** and the neighbouring **tourist office** at Kongensgate 66 (late June to mid-Aug Mon–Sat 9am–7pm, Sun 2–7pm; rest of the year Mon–Fri 9am–4pm; ☎76 94 33 09), which has a full range of bus and ferry timetables. They can also help with ferry reservations. The dock for the passenger-only **express boat** service to Svolvær on the Lofotens (250kr one way; train pass holders half-price) is at the south end of the town centre.

As for **accommodation**, there's a popular, no-frills **youth hostel** (☎76 94 25 98; fax 76 94 29 99; 140kr, double rooms ①) at Havnegata 3, near the express boat harbour. It's open all year except for Christmas and New Year and the price includes breakfast, but note that advance reservations are required from November to February – and are a good idea at other times of the year. If the hostel's full, the cheapest **pensjonat** is the pleasant, unassuming *Breidablikk Gjestgiveri*, Tore Hundsgate 41 (☎76 94 14 18; fax 76 94 57 86; ①) – at the top of Kinobakken, east off Kongensgate just up from the main square. Some of the town's **hotels** have seen better days, but the *Rica Grand Royal Hotel*, just along from the tourist office at Kongensgate 64 (☎76 94 15 00; fax 76 94 55 31; ③/④), retains a little elegance, while the marginally less agreeable *Nordstjernen Hotell*, just south of the square at Kongensgate 26 (☎76 94 41 20; fax 76 94 75 06; ②), boasts a spacious second-floor breakfast room with unsurpassed views of the iron ore terminal. The nearest **campsite**, *Narvik Camping* (☎76 94 58 10; all year), is 2km north of the centre on the E6 and has cabins (①) and boats for rent.

There's only one really recommendable **restaurant** in Narvik, *Bjørns Mat og Vinhus*, just over the bridge from the town square at Brugata 3, which has a comparatively wide-ranging and reasonably priced menu; as a second choice, the *Rallaren* café-bar-cum-grill in the *Rica Grand Royal Hotel* serves filling and inexpensive Norwegian staples.

On from Narvik

There's a choice of several routes on from Narvik. The **rail line** (the *Ofotbanen*), runs east and then south to Abisko, Kiruna and ultimately Stockholm in Sweden, while **bus** travellers can take the *Nord-Norge ekspressen* north to Alta (see p.330) along the E6, one of the most beautiful routes in the country, a succession of switchback roads, lakeside forests, high peaks and lowlands. In summer cut grass lies drying everywhere, stretched over wooden poles that form long lines on the hillsides like so much laundry. Buses also run off the E6 to Tromsø (see the next chapter); and note that rail pass holders get a 50 percent discount on buses south from Narvik to either Fauske or Bodø. There's also an all-year **express boat service** connecting Narvik with Svolvær in the Lofoten Islands, which leaves from the harbour next to the youth hostel.

The Lofoten and Vesterålen islands

A raggle-taggle collection of islands in the Norwegian Sea, the **Lofoten** and **Vesterålen** archipelago is like western Norway in miniature: the terrain is hard and unyielding, and the main – often the only – industry is fishing. The weather is temperate but wet, and the islanders' historic isolation has bred a distinctive culture based, in equal measure, on Protestantism, the extended family and respect for the sea.

The islands were first settled by semi-nomadic hunter-agriculturalists some six thousand years ago and it was they and their Iron Age successors who chopped down the birch and pine forests that once covered the coasts. It was boat-building, however, that brought a brief golden age: by the seventh century, the islanders were able to build oceangoing vessels, a skill that enabled them to join in the Viking bonanza. Local clan leaders became prominent warlords, none more so than the eleventh-century chieftain Tore Hund, one-time liegeman of Olav Haraldsson and one of the men selected to polish the king off at the battle of Stiklestad (see p.298). In the early fourteenth century, the islanders lost their independence and were placed under the control of Bergen: by royal decree, all the fish the islanders caught had to be shipped to Bergen for export. Bergen's merchants were thus able to dictate the prices for both the fish they bought and the goods they sold in return, a system that continued under local merchants until the early years of this century. Since World War II, improvements in fishing techniques and, more recently, the growth in tourism and the extension of the road system, have all combined to transform island life, though this has been offset by the decline of the fishing industry.

Of the two groups, the **Lofoten Islands** are the better known, a string of mountainous, often impossibly beautiful rocky hunks that have everything from seabird colonies in the south to beaches and fjords in the north, the whole mazy coastline freckled by seastacks and skerries. The boat from Bodø, which is the traditional approach, brings you face to face with the islands' most striking feature, the peaks of the **Lofotenveggen** (Lofoten Wall), a 160-kilometre stretch of jagged mountain that appears unbroken due to the islands' proximity to each other.

Understandably, the adjacent **Vesterålen Islands** have been overshadowed as a tourist destination. Here, the mountains are less precipitous and the land more gentle, giving way in the far north to vast tracts of peaty moorland. The villages are less appealing too, formless ribbons straggling along the coast and across any stretch of fertile land that's going, though there are a couple of definite attractions in Harsad and Andenes.

Incidentally, although the archipelago is shared between the counties of Troms and Nordland, the boundary does not coincide with that of the islands: all of Lofotens and the southern half of the Vesterålens are in Nordland, with the remainder in Troms.

Island practicalities: transport and accommodation

Getting to the islands from the mainland by public transport is easy enough (see box on p.312) – indeed, the number of permutations is almost bewildering – but **getting around** them can be more troublesome. **Buses** regularly ply the **E10**, the main island road, which leaves the E6 just north of Narvik to zigzag for almost 400km right down the length of the archipelago. The road crosses from island to island by bridge or tunnel and is only broken once – at the southern tip of the Vesterålens where there's a **car ferry** (every 90min; 25min; 21kr, car & driver 60kr) linking Melbu with Fiskebol in the Lofotens. This is the ferry that carries the Stokmarknes–Svolvær bus. However, the smaller villages dotted along the islands' minor roads can only muster the occasional bus, one of the most useful services running between Sortland and Andenes. To avoid getting stuck, make sure you pick up a bus and ferry **timetable** from any major town beforehand. If you do venture off the beaten track, you'll have to be prepared to **walk** – no bad thing considering the islands do not have a well-developed system of huts and hiking trails, and often the country roads that pattern the islands are far the best way to enjoy the landscape. Another is to go **mountaineering** – Austvågøy has the best climbing and also the best climbing school at Henningsvaer – but the most popular way to get around is by **boat** and there are numerous types of trip on offer.

If you have your own car, it's possible to **drive** from one end of the archipelago to the other, catching the ferry to or from the mainland at Moskenes and Andenes – though this is perhaps too long and tiring an itinerary for many tastes. There are **car rental** outlets at Harstad, Svolvaer and Stamsund, each of them offering special short deals from around 500kr a day, while **bike rental** is available at the Svolvaer tourist office, certain youth hostels and other locations.

As far as **accommodation** goes, the speciality of the Lofotens are its **rorbuer** (fishermen's shacks, literally "row dwellings"), rented out to tourists for overnight stays or longer periods. A certain King Øystein ordered the first of them to be built round the coastline of the island of Austvågøy in the twelfth century, so that visiting fishermen could rest easy instead of sleeping under the upturned hulls of their boats. Traditionally, they were built on the shore, often on poles sticking out of the sea, and usually coloured red, using a paint based on cod-liver oil. At the peak of the fisheries in the 1930s they accommodated around 30,000 men, but since the 1960s, incoming fishermen have preferred to sleep on their boats. Most of the original *rorbuer* disappeared years ago and nowadays they are built by the dozen with the tourist trade in mind. At their best, they are comfortable and cosy seashore cabins, sometimes converted from an original *rorbuer*, with bunk beds and wood-fired stoves; at their worst, they are little better than prefabricated hutches dropped off in the middle of nowhere. Most have space for between four and eight people and cost in the region of 600kr per night, though prices can be anywhere from 400kr to 1000kr. Similar rates are charged in the islands' **sjøhus** (literally "sea houses"), bigger buildings that originated as the quayside halls where the catch was processed and the workers slept. Some of the original *sjøhus* have been cleverly converted into attractive apartments with self-catering facilities, many more into dormitory-style accommodation – though again the quality varies enormously.

A full list of *rorbuer* and *sjøhus* is given in the *Lofoten Info-Guide*, a free booklet that you can pick up at any local tourist office. Otherwise there's a sprinkling of **hotels**, though most of these are modern and bland, as well as a handful of **youth hostels** and **campsites** – many of which dabble in *rorbuer* too.

The Lofoten Islands

Stretched out in a skeletal curve across the Norwegian Sea, the **Lofoten Islands** are the hub of the northern winter fishing industry. At the turn of every year cod migrate from the Arctic Ocean to spawn here, where the waters are tempered by the Gulf Stream. Although January to April are the actual fishing months, fishing impinges on all aspects of the islands' life all year round. At almost every harbour stand massed ranks of wooden racks used for drying the catch (to produce dried cod for export), full and odoriferous in winter, empty in summer like so many abandoned climbing frames.

The Lofotens have their own relaxed pace, with exceptionally mild weather for somewhere so far north: summer days can be spent sunbathing on the rocks or hiking around the superb coastline; and when it rains, as it frequently does, life focuses on the *rorbuer*, cooking freshly caught fish over wood-burning stoves, telling stories and gently wasting time. It sounds rather contrived, and in a sense it is – the way of life here is to some extent preserved like this for tourists. But it's rare to find anyone who isn't less than completely enthralled by it all.

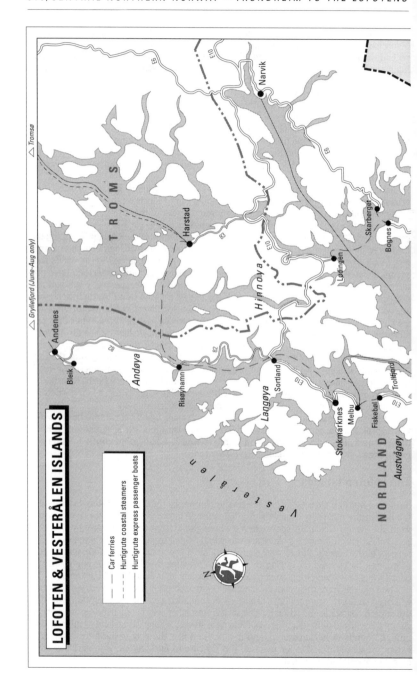

LOFOTEN & VESTERÅLEN ISLANDS

- — — Car ferries
- — · — Hurtigrute coastal steamers
- — — — Hurtigrute express passenger boats

△ Tromsø

△ Gryllefjord (June-Aug only)

Narvik

T R O M S

Harstad

Skarberget

Bognes

Lødingen

Hinnøya

Andenes

Bleik

Andøya

Risøyhamn

Langøya

Sortland

Stokmarknes

Melbu

Fiskebøl

Trollfjord

Vesterålen

N O R D L A N D

Austvågøy

E6

E10

E8

E10

E6

E10

82

83

E10

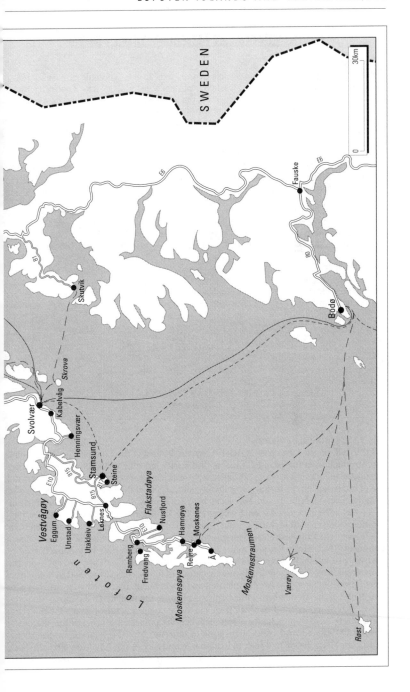

TRANSPORT FROM THE MAINLAND

By coastal steamer

The *Hurtigrute* **coastal steamer** calls at two ports in the **Lofotens**, Stamsund and Svolvær, of which Stamsund is preferable, especially for a short stay. Thereafter the *Hurtigrute* nudges through the Raftsundet, the narrow channel that gives access to the Trollfjord (see p.318) and separates the Lofotens from the **Vesterålens**, where the boat calls at four places: Stokmarknes and Sortland in the south, Risøyhamn in the north and Harstad in the east. Stokmarknes is unremarkable, but it does have the advantage of being near to the Trollfjord; Sortland is downright awful; Risøyhamn is dreary but well on the way to Andenes; and Harstad is a large and busy transport hub.

The *Hurtigrute* leaves Bodø at 3pm daily and foot passenger tickets (available at the quay) cost 245kr to Stamsund, 263kr to Svolvær and 526kr to Harstad, or are free with a Coastal Pass (see p.162). The fare for transporting a car from Bodø to Stamsund is 275kr (Svolvær 290kr; Harstad 350kr), but on the older vessels, where vehicles have to be hoisted on board, there's a 50 percent surcharge. Advance reservations for cars are essential, but can be made just a few hours beforehand by telephoning the captain – ask down at the harbour or at the port's tourist office for assistance. Look out for special deals, which can reduce costs dramatically; they are advertised at local tourist offices.

By car ferry

The principal **car ferry** service from the mainland to the **Lofotens** connects tiny **Skutvik**, midway between Fauske and Narvik, with **Svolvær** (early June to late Aug 7–9 daily; rest of the year 3–4 daily; 2hr; 49kr, car & driver 170kr). Queues are common and you can't book in advance, so drivers need to arrive about two hours before departure to make sure of a place.

A second car ferry service (1–2 daily) links **Bodø** with the southern peripheries of the Lofotens, calling at the small islands of **Røst** and **Værøy** and at the pocket-sized port of **Moskenes**, just a handful of kilometres from the end of the E10. The route varies, but the boat usually sails first to Moskenes (4hr 25min) before visiting one or both of the smaller islands (another 2hr/4hr). The foot passenger fare to Moskenes is 102kr, car and driver 375kr. Queues are usual and drivers need to arrive at least two hours before departure, but advance reservations are possible at a cost of 100kr – ask at Bodø tourist office.

Austvågøy island: Svolvær

SVOLVÆR, on the east coast of **Austvågøy**, the largest of the Lofotens, is a disappointing introduction to the islands: it has all the bustle but little of the charm of the other fishing towns, though it is the administrative and transport centre of the Lofotens and one of the easier places to stay. Despite the poor aspect of the town itself, Svolvær's surroundings are delightful and two local boat trips provide an excellent introduction. Every day several **cruises** leave Svolvær for the **Trollfjord**, an impossibly narrow, two-kilometre long stretch of water up and down which countless excursion boats inch their careful way, eliciting gasps from camera-crazy tourists. The excursion takes three hours and costs 200kr. However, you may well find the ferry ride over to the lovely islet of **Skrova**, just offshore from Svolvær, more to your liking: it's easy to reach on the Svolvær–Skutvik ferry, which calls here a couple of times a day (Mon–Sat) in both directions. The ride takes just twenty minutes and costs about 15kr each way. Svolvær also boasts one of the archipelago's most famous **climbs**, the haul up to the top of the forty-metre-high Svolværgeita ("Svolvær goat"), a stone column perched on a hill behind the town, where lunatic mountaineers leap between the pinnacles (horns) of the summit.

Svolvær's busy **tourist office** (late June to mid-Aug Mon–Fri 9am–10pm, Sat 10am–10pm, Sun 11am–10pm; mid-June to late June & mid-Aug to late Aug Mon–Fri 9am–8pm, Sat 10am–2pm, Sun 4–8pm; rest of the year Mon–Fri 9am–5pm, Sat 10am–2pm; ☎76 07

As far as the **Vesterålens** are concerned, the main car ferry runs from the jetty at **Bognes**, on the E6 between Fauske and Narvik, to **Lødingen** (5–6 daily; 1hr; passengers 33kr, car & driver 106kr), from where it's just 3km to the E10 at a point midway between Harstad and Sortland. A second, seasonal car ferry runs from remote **Gryllefjord**, 110km west of the E6 well to the north of Narvik, to **Andenes** at the northern tip of the Vesterålens (June–Aug; 3 daily; 2hr; car 195kr, passengers 70kr). Note that this is a new service, whose future is uncertain; reservations are strongly advised – telephone, or better still fax *Andøy Reisebyrå* in Andenes (☎76 14 20 22; fax 76 14 20 67).

By express boat

Passenger **express boats** (*Hurtigbåt*) work out slightly cheaper than the coastal steamer and are far faster: one links **Bodø** with Svolvaer and Stokmarknes (Mon–Fri 1 daily; 4hr/5hr 30min; 210kr/250kr); another links **Narvik** with Svolvaer (Mon–Fri & Sun 1 daily; 4hr; 250kr). An express boat also links **Tromsø** with Harstad (1–2 daily; 2hr 30min; around 200kr). In all cases, advance booking through the local tourist office is recommended.

By bus

The main long-distance **bus** services from the mainland to the islands are **Bodø** to Stokmarknes and Svolvær (1–2 daily; 9hr/10hr 30min; 255kr/361kr), and **Fauske** to Harstad (1 daily; 6hr; 272kr). Both of these services use the Bognes-Lødingen ferry. There's also a bus from **Narvik** to Stokmarknes and Svolvær (1 daily; 6hr/8hr; 202kr/308kr).

By plane

You can fly from **Bodø** to the **Lofoten** airports – or rather airstrips – at Svolvær and Leknes (2–3 daily) and Røst (1 daily); beware, though, that the Leknes airport is miles from anywhere you might want to visit, and the onward taxi fare will cost a bomb. To the **Vesterålens**, there are flights from Bodø to Stokmarknes and Andenes (1–3 daily). The carrier is *Widerøe's Flyveselskap* and tickets can be purchased at any travel agent or the *Radisson SAS Hotel Bodø*. Standby, youth and excursion fares make flying to the islands a surprisingly economical option with return fares starting at about 700kr.

---

30 00; fax 76 07 30 01), beside the main square by the harbour, has maps, accommodation lists and details of local public transport. They can reserve you accommodation anywhere in the Lofotens (for a 35kr booking fee), and charge 125kr for making a ferry reservation. Svolvær is a good place to **rent a car**, with both *Avis* and *Budget*, among others, offering some economic short-term deals – from around 500kr per day.

As for **accommodation**, the wooden *Svolvær sjøhuscamping* (☎76 07 03 36; ①), by the seashore at the foot of Parkgata – from the square, turn right up the hill along Vestfjordgata and it's to the right past the library – is a snug fishing house, and the price includes use of the well-equipped kitchen and free showers. Alternatively, the *Hotel Havly* (☎76 07 03 44; fax 76 07 07 95; ③), behind the bus station and near the main square, occupies a plain tower block and has perfectly adequate rooms, while the *Royal Hotel Lofoten* (☎76 07 12 00; fax 76 07 08 50; ③), a few metres up from the main square at the end of Torggata, is a good bit plusher. However, the most popular hotel is the gleaming new *Rica Hotel Svolvær* (☎76 07 22 22; fax 76 07 20 01; ①/③), whose various buildings, in the style of the traditional *sjøhus*, occupy a prime harbourside location.

For **eating**, the café-restaurant of the *Hotel Havly* provides Norwegian standbys at affordable prices, as does the busy café adjoining the *Rimi* superstore, inside the shopping mall just up from the harbour; but for something to savour, head for the *Rica Hotel Svolvær*, which has a first-rate restaurant and a bar.

THE REST OF AUSTVÅGØY: KABELVÅG AND HENNINGSVÆR

From Svolvær, it's just 6km west along the coast to **KABELVÅG**, whose pretty wooden centre, draped around the shore of a narrow and knobbly inlet, is immediately more appealing. Kabelvåg was the most important village on the Lofotens from Viking times until the early years of this century, serving as the centre of the fishery and home to the islands' first *rorbuer* and first inn. The late nineteenth-century **Vågan Kirke**, a big and breezy timber church on the eastern edge of the village beside the E10, is a reminder of these busier times, its hangar-like interior built to accommodate a congregation of over one thousand. The village holds other attractions too, near the cove about 1500m west of the centre in the neighbourhood of Storvågan. Here, the **Lofotmuseet** (Lofoten Island Museum; daily early to mid-June & mid- to late Aug 9am–6pm; mid-June to mid-Aug 9am–9pm; 25kr) tracks through the history of the islands' fisheries and displays the definitive collection of fishing and other cultural paraphernalia. Close by, the **Galleri Espolin** (daily early to mid-June & mid- to late Aug 10am–6pm; mid-June to mid-Aug 10am–9pm) features the paintings and sketches of Kaare Espolin Johnson, a Norwegian artist of local renown.

Buses from Svolvær (Mon–Fri hourly, Sat & Sun 2 daily) drop you near the centre of the village, where there are pleasant **rooms** in the wooden *Kabelvåg Hotel* (☎76 07 88 00; fax 76 07 80 03; ③) near the harbour, not far from the *Præstenbrygga* **restaurant**. Kabelvåg also has a **youth hostel** (☎76 07 81 03; fax 76 07 81 17; mid-June to early Aug; 130kr; doubles ①), in the school building east of the centre across the harbour, 500m from the E10. The nearest *rorbuer* are the modern chalets of the *Nyvågar Rorbuhotell* (☎76 07 89 00; fax 76 07 89 50; ②), by the seashore near the *Galleri Espolin* in Storvågan.

Reachable by bus from Svolvær and Kabelvåg (1–4 daily), **HENNINGSVÆR**, 23km southwest of Svolvær, is a beguiling village, with cramped and twisting lanes of brightly painted wooden houses framing a tiny inlet that cuts the place in half to form a pretty harbour. Almost inevitably, coach parties are wheeled in and out, but it's still well worth an overnight **stay** – advance booking is advisable in summer. The smartest hotel is the modern quayside *Henningsvær Bryggehotel* (☎76 07 47 50; fax 76 07 47 30; Feb–Oct ③), built in traditional style, which makes its older rival, the pastel-painted wooden *Henningsvær Hotell* (☎76 07 49 99; fax 76 07 49 35; ②), look a tad dowdy. The most economical choice is, however, the *sjøhus* of *Den Siste Viking* (☎/fax 76 07 49 11; ①), unadorned accommodation that's right in the centre and doubles as the home of Lofotens' best **mountaineering school**, *Nord Norsk Klatreskole* (same phone number). The school operates a wide range of all-inclusive climbing holidays, catering to various degrees of fitness and experience. Costs vary enormously, but a three-day, one-climb-a-day holiday is in the region of 3000kr. With less time, there are exhilarating **fishing trips** on offer, a morning or afternoon's excursion costing around 250kr, or you could visit the **Karl Erik Harr Gallery** (March & late Aug daily noon–3pm; April & May Wed & Sun noon–3pm; June to mid-Aug daily 10am–9pm; 40kr), which exhibits and sells the work of the artist himself as well as a small selection of early nineteenth-century Lofoten paintings and photographs.

For **food**, the *Bryggehotel* has a first-rate, if pricey restaurant, while there's good seafood at lower prices in the more downbeat *Henningsvær Hotell* restaurant. The commonest of all traditional island dishes – dried and salted cod – can be sampled at the café-bar at *Lars Larsen's Rorbuer.*

Vestvågøy island: Stamsund

It's the next large island to the southwest, **Vestvågøy**, that captivates many travellers to the Lofotens. This is due in no small part to the laid-back charm of **STAMSUND**, whose older buildings string along the rocky, fretted seashore: a jumble of crusty port buildings, wooden houses and *rorbuer*. This is the first port at which the *Hurtigrute* coastal steamer docks on its way north from Bodø, and is much the best place to stay on the island. Getting there by bus from Austvågøy is reasonably easy too, with several buses making the trip daily, though you do have to change at Leknes, the administrative centre of Vestvågøy and the site of the airport, 16km away to the west. If you have your own transport, the quickest way to get to Stamsund is to turn south off the E10 down along Hwy 815 shortly after you cross onto Vestvågøy, a scenic 40km coastal drive.

In Stamsund, the first place to head for is the exceptionally friendly **youth hostel** (☎76 08 91 66; fax 76 08 97 39; closed late Oct & Nov; 75kr, doubles ①), made up of several *rorbuer* and a larger *sjøhus* perched over a pint-sized bay, about 1km down the road from the port and 200m from the Leknes bus stop – ask to be let off. The hostel is officially open from May to mid-August, but it's worth calling at other times to check. Fishing around here is first-class: the hostel rents out rowing boats and lines or you can go on an organized trip for just 150kr; afterwards, you can cook your catch on the hostel's wood-burning stoves. Otherwise, there's just one **hotel**, the glumly modern *Hotel Lofoten* (☎76 08 93 00; fax 76 08 97 26; ③), near the ferry port. More promisingly, you'll find nine comfortable **rorbuer** (☎/fax 76 08 92 83; ④) in the hamlet of Steine, 3km beyond the ferry harbour.

For touring the rest of Vestvågøy, the hostel rents out **bikes** (85kr a day), and is the best source of **information** on everything from fishing to hiking – much better than the village's tourist office, 200m from the ferry dock (mid-June to mid-Aug Mon–Sat 11am–2.30pm & 6–9.30pm, Sun 6–9.30pm; ☎76 08 97 92).

THE REST OF VESTVÅGØY

If you're driving, it's easy to reach the island's windy **west coast**, accessed by a series of turnings off the E10, which slices across Vestvågøy's drab central valley. Beginning in Stamsund, the first part of the journey is the hilly 16km to Leknes, on the E10. From here it's a further 3km to the first signposted byroad, which leads 10km west to **Utakleiv**, a tiny hamlet on the edge of a wide bay and surrounded by austere cliffs. There's more stern scenery at the end of the next turning off the E10, this time at **Unstad**, which is reached along a gravel road that winds up into the hills and tunnels through to the village. There's a marked trail from here along the coast to **EGGUM**, a strenuous 7km **hike** that takes around two hours each way. Eggum, at the end of the third turning off the E10, is itself a lovely spot, arguably the prettiest on the west coast, a huddle of houses dwarfed by the mountains behind and fronted by a vast pebble beach. There's accommodation here, too, at the no-frills *Eggum sjøhus* (☎76 08 19 16; June–Aug; ④).

Without a car these places are difficult to get to: cyclists will face stiff gradients and often strong winds and, although the bus service along the E10 itself is good, there are no regular services off it to the west coast.

South to Moskenes and Å

By any standard the next two islands of the archipelago, **Flakstadøya** and **Moskenesøya**, are extraordinarily beautiful. As the Lofotens taper towards their southerly conclusion, the rearing peaks of the Lofotenveggen crimp a sea-shredded coastline that's studded by a string of fishing villages. Remarkably, the **E10** travels along almost all of this dramatic shoreline, leaving Leknes to tunnel under the sound separating Vestvågøy from Flakstadøya (toll 65kr). About 20km from Leknes, an even more improbable byroad wriggles through the mountains the 6km to **NUSFJORD**, an extravagantly picturesque fishing village in a tight cove. Unlike many fishermen's huts in the Lofotens, which have been erected in response to tourist demand, the ones here are the genuine nineteenth-century article. Inevitably, it's tourism that supports the local economy these days, but it's still a beguiling place and one that holds over thirty comfortably refurbished *rorbuer*, with either one bedroom (sleeping 2–4; ②) or two (sleeping 5; ②). Make reservations in advance with *Nusfjord Rorbuer* (☎76 09 30 20; fax 76 09 33 78).

Back on the E10, it's a further 5km to the **Flakstad kirke**, a distinctive onion-domed, red timber church built of Russian driftwood in 1780. The building announces the beginning of **RAMBERG**, Flakstadøya's administrative centre – if that's what you can call the smattering of services (a garage, a supermarket, etc) that straggles along behind the sandy beach in the shadow of the mountains. Pressing on south, over the first of several narrow bridges, you're soon in **Moskenesøya**, where the road squirms across the mouth of the Kjerkjord, hopping from islet to islet to link the fishing villages of Hamnøya, on the north side of the inlet, and **REINE** to the south. Reine is an odd little place that manages to look a little seedy despite its magnificent surroundings, but it is frequently the departure point for boat trips (see below) and has several *rorbuer* complexes, the neatest of which is *Reine Rorbuer* (☎76 09 22 22; fax 76 09 22 25; ①–②) in the older part of town, at the end of the short promontory just off the E10.

From here, it's about 6km to **MOSKENES**, the midway port between Bodø and the southernmost bird islands of Værøy and Røst – not that there's much here, just a hand-ful of houses dotted round a horseshoe-shaped bay. There is, however, a **tourist office** by the jetty (early June & late Aug Mon–Fri 10am–5pm; mid-June to mid-Aug daily 10am–7pm; ☎76 09 15 99; no fax) and a basic **campsite** (June–Aug) a five-minute walk away up a gravel track.

Six kilometres further south the road ends abruptly at the tersely named **Å**, one of the Lofotens' most delightful villages, its huddle of old buildings rambling over a foreshore that's wedged in tight between the grey-green mountains and the surging sea. Unusually, so much of the old nineteenth-century village has survived that much of Å has been incorporated in the Norwegian Fishing Village (**Norsk Fiskevaersmuseum** Museum; guided tours late June to late Aug daily 11am–6pm; rest of the year Mon–Fri 9am–4pm; 35kr), and you can extend your knowledge of all things fishy by visiting the **Tørrfiskmuseum** (Stockfish Museum; early to mid-June Mon–Fri 11am–4pm; mid-June to late Aug daily 11am–6pm; 35kr) here as well. In addition, you can take advantage of a wide variety of **boat trips**, anything from day-long fishing expeditions beginning in Å (Mon–Sat June–Aug 1 daily; 3hr; 260kr), to Midnight Sun trips (late May to mid-July 1 weekly; 5hr; 190kr) and coastal voyages (June to mid-Aug 1 weekly; 4hr; 290kr), both from Reine. There are also, weather and tides permitting, regular cruises (June to mid-Aug 1 weekly; 4hr; 290kr) from Reine to the **Moskenestraumen** – the terrifying **mael-strom** described by Edgar Allen Poe in his short story "A Descent into the Maelstrom". There are easier places to see one of these in Norway (near Bodø, for instance), but this is the original, of which Poe wrote:

> *Even while I gazed, this current acquired a monstrous velocity. Each moment added to its speed – to its headlong impetuosity. In five minutes the whole sea . . . was lashed into ungovernable fury . . . Here the vast bed of the waters seamed and scarred into a thousand conflicting channels, burst suddenly into frenzied convulsion – heaving, boiling, hissing . . .*

If you want to **stay in Å**, the same family owns the assortment of smart *rorbuer* (①–②) that surround the dock, as well as the adjacent *sjøhus*, which offers very comfortable and equally smart, hotel-standard rooms (②). They also operate the **youth hostel** (all year; 95kr; doubles ①), the bar and the only restaurant, where the seafood is very good. All accommodation reservations can be made on ☎76 09 11 21 (fax 76 09 12 82).

Local **bus #101** runs along the length of the E10 **from Leknes to Å** a couple of times a day from late June to mid-August, less frequently the rest of the year. Buses do not, however, usually coincide with sailings to and from Moskenes. Consequently, if you're heading from the Moskenes ferry port to Å, you'll either have to walk – it's an easy 6km – or take a taxi.

Værøy and Røst

Dangling from the main island chain, **Værøy** and **Røst** are the most southerly of the Lofotens, and the most time-consuming to reach. Indeed, unless you're careful, the irregular ferry schedules can strand you on either for several days – see the box on p.312 for details of services.

It can be well worth making the effort to get here, however, as Værøy and Røst are internationally famous for their **bird colonies**, the crags supporting an incredible number of puffins, the rare sea eagle and eider ducks, as well as cormorants, kittiwakes, guillemots and more recent immigrants like the fulmar and gannet. There are lots of **bird trips** to choose from and for a decent length (say three-hour) excursion you can reckon on paying between 250kr and 350kr. The weather here is uncommonly mild throughout the year, hiking trails ubiquitous, and the occasional beach glorious and deserted.

Of the two islands, **Værøy** is the more visually appealing, comprising a grassy-green, slender coastal strip that ends suddenly in the steep and bare mountains that backbone the island. Just 8km from end to end, Værøy has a few kilometres of road connecting the farmsteads of the plain and squeezing through a narrow pass to wobble along a portion of the coast. The island is, however, best explored on foot, either along the steep and sometimes dangerous footpaths of the mountains, or along the much easier hiking trail that slips down the west coast before crossing a neck of land on its way to Måstad. The inhabitants of this isolated village, which was abandoned in the 1950s, varied their fishy diet by catching puffins from the neighbouring sea cliffs, a difficult task in which they were assisted by specially bred dogs – known locally as puffin dogs.

The **ferry** docks at the southeast tip of the island, about 200m from the **tourist office** (mid-June to mid-Aug Mon–Sat 10am–2pm; ☎76 09 52 10; no fax), which can advise on bike rental, boat tours and accommodation – though you would be foolhardy not to arrange this beforehand: the options are limited to a **guesthouse** at the old vicarage, the *Gamle prestegård* (☎76 09 54 11; fax 76 09 54 84; June–Sept; ②), and a **youth hostel** (☎76 09 53 52; fax 76 09 57 01; mid-May to mid-Sept; 80kr, doubles ①), located in refurbished *rorbuer,* some of which can be rented at any time of the year. Both establishments are some 4km from the jetty. The well-equipped hostel also rents out boats and bikes and runs boat trips to the island's **bird cliffs** at the southwest corner of the island, which are much too steep and slippery to approach on foot.

Even smaller than its neighbour, **Røst** looks very different, its smattering of lonely farmsteads dotted over a pancake-flat landscape interrupted by dozens of tiny lakes. The **airport** is on the edge of the island, a little more than 1km northwest of the main village, itself 2.5km north of the **ferry port**. Again, the **tourist office** (mid-June to mid-Aug Mon–Fri noon–3pm, Sat coincides with the arrival of the boat; ☎76 09 64 11; fax 76 09 62 84) is close to the jetty and the island has a **youth hostel** (☎/fax 76 09 61 09; May–Aug; 95kr, doubles ①), about 1km from the quay. The hostel organizes **boat trips** to the jagged islets that rise high in the ocean to the southwest of Røst, their steep cliffs sheltering hundreds of thousands of seabirds.

The Vesterålen Islands

The spatulate **Vesterålen Islands** lie to the north of the Lofotens, an indistinct grouping that's greener, less stunning and more agricultural than its neighbour. Many travellers simply rush through, demoralized by the sheer mediocrity of the main settlements, Stokmarknes, Sortland and Harstad, and to be frank they don't miss much – providing they take in the trip up the Trollfjord. However, if you have time to spare, a visit to Andenes, tucked away at the far end of the island of Andøya, is just about worth while, and there's a splendid medieval church at Harstad. Bus services between the three main settlements, along the E10 and between Sortland and Andenes are good, and from Harstad there's a useful express passenger ferry up to Tromsø, but otherwise you'll be struggling without your own transport.

The south: the Trollfjord, Stokmarknes and Sortland

The best way **to arrive** is by coastal steamer. A narrow sound – Raftsundet – separates the Lofotens from the Vesterålens, and in summer every ship makes the detour into the two-kilometre-long **Trollfjord**. Slowing to a mere chug, the vessels inch up the narrow gorge, smooth stone towering high above, blocking out the light. At its head the boats effect a nautical three-point turn and then crawl back to rejoin the main waterway. It's very atmospheric, whatever the weather, and free with a Coastal Steamer Pass (see p.162); otherwise a ticket for the three-hour trip from Svolvær to Stokmarknes costs about 180kr.

After the ride, **STOKMARKNES** can't help but feel a bit of a letdown. It's an inconsequential little place trailing along the shoreline in the shadow of the first of the two bridges that cross the straits to Langøya. Drop in to the **tourist office** on the harbourfront (mid-June to late Aug Mon–Fri 10am–6pm, Sat 10am–4pm, Sun 11am–4pm; ☎76 15 29 55), then count on heading out of town – this is a good spot to pick up buses travelling the E10 in either direction. If you do hang around, there's only one passable **place to stay**, the *Kinnarps Turistsenter* (☎76 15 29 99; fax 76 15 29 95; ②/③), a brassy new hotel with *rorbuer* (③) round the back, set on the islet at the end of the first of the two Langøya bridges, about 1km from the town centre. The nearest **youth hostel** (☎76 15 71 06; fax 76 15 83 82; 100kr, doubles ①) is a spartan affair 400m from the car ferry to Fiskebol in the desultory fishing port of **Melbu**, 16km to the south.

Stokmarknes may be inconsequential, but **SORTLAND**, 30km to the north along the E10, is downright ugly. A modern sprawl near the bridge linking Langøya and Hinnøya, the only reason to visit is to change **buses:** the town is something of a transport centre, with certain services – like the bus to Andenes – starting here. The **tourist office** (mid-June to late Aug Mon–Fri 10am–6pm, Sat & Sun 11am–5pm; rest of the year Mon–Fri 10am–5pm; ☎76 12 15 55) is in the centre at Kjøpmannsgata 2, a five-minute walk from the bus station.

North: to Andenes

From Sortland, Hwy 82 begins its hundred-kilometre trek north, snaking along the craggy peripheries of the island of Hinnøya before crossing the bridge over to workaday **Risøyhamn**, the only *Hurtigrute* stop on **Andøya**, the most northerly of the Vesterålen Islands. Beyond Risøyhamn, the scenery is much less dramatic, with the mountains replaced by hills in the west and a vast, peaty moor in the east. Hwy 82 crosses this moorland, an uneventful journey that brings you to the old fishing port of **ANDENES**, whose low-slung buildings trail back from a clutter of wooden warehouses and mini-boat repair yards edging the harbour. "It is the fish, and that alone, that draws people to Andenes. The place itself has no other temptations" said the writer Poul Alm when he visited in 1944, a judgement that today seems a little harsh, though Andenes' appeal remains firmly ocean-based: amongst Scandinavians at least, it is famous for its "**whale safaris**" (late May to mid-Sept daily at 10.30am, often also at 8.30am, 3.30pm & 5.30pm) – a three- to five-hour cruise off the coast with a marine biologist on board to point out sperm, killer and minke whales and dolphins. There's reckoned to be a 90 percent chance of seeing the whales; tickets cost around 600kr for adults (reductions for children), including lunch and a guided tour of the Hvalsenter (Whale Centre – see below) beforehand. Wear warm clothes. Booking at least a day in advance is strongly advised – call the tourist office at the Hvalsenter (see below).

If you're unlucky and can't get on a whale safari, the other recommended **boat trip** (also booked through the tourist office) is the two-hour cruise round the bird island of **Bleiksøya**, a pyramid-shaped hunk of rock populated by thousands of puffins, kitti-wakes, razor bills and, at certain times of year, white-tailed eagles. The boats (June to late Aug daily; 200kr) leave from the jetty at **BLEIK**, an old and remote fishing hamlet around 7km southwest of Andenes; a local bus makes the round trip from Andenes to coincide with sailings.

Back in Andenes, the **Hvalsenter** (Whale Centre; daily late May to mid-June & mid-Aug to mid-Sept 8am–4pm; mid-June to mid-Aug 8am–8pm; 30kr, combined ticket with the *Hisnakul* 50kr), close by the harbour, actually makes for a rather disappointing start to the whale trips. Its lacklustre displays on the life and times of the animal hardly fire the imagination and neither does the massive, deliberately dark and gloomy diorama of a whale munching its way though a herd of squid. Much more diverting is the nearby **Hisnakul** (daily late May to mid-June & mid-Aug to mid-Sept noon–4pm; mid-June to mid-Aug noon–6pm; 40kr), a well-conceived museum-cum-exhibition centre housed in a refurbished timber warehouse, which explores life on Andøya. Short of historical arte-facts, the centre instead offers imaginative displays, like the two hundred facial castings of local people made in 1994 and an assortment of giant imitation bird beaks. There's also a comprehensive explanation of the Northern Lights – Andenes is a particularly good spot for seeing them – illustrated by first-class photographs and a slide show. The third and final museum, the **Polarmuseet** (mid-June to late Sept daily 10am–6pm; 20kr), is beside the harbour too, inside a modest little building with a wooden porch. The interior is mostly dedicated to the Arctic knick-knacks accumulated by a certain Hilmar Nøis, an Andøy man who wintered on Svalbard no fewer than 38 times. The museum also sells tickets for the guided tour of the adjacent **lighthouse** (same hours; 20kr), a forty-metre-high maroon structure built in the 1850s.

PRACTICALITIES

Andenes has one long main street, Storgata, which bisects the town and ends abrupt-ly at the seafront. From the end of the street, the **bus station** is just a few metres away to the east; and the **tourist office** (mid-June to mid-Aug daily 8am–8pm; rest of the year Mon–Fri 8am–4pm; ☎76 14 26 11; fax 76 14 23 77) is located in the Hvalsenter some 300m to the west. Here you can make boat trip reservations and find out about renting bikes (100kr per day) or taking guided walks in the area (from 100kr for 2–4hr). The village has a fair sprinkling of inexpensive accommodation and several households offer **private rooms** – look out for the signs. But considering how isolat-ed a spot this is, you'd be well-advised to call ahead to make a reservation – though, if all else fails, the tourist office will do their best to help you out. One of the nicer places is the *Sjøgata Gjestehus*, Sjøgata 4 (late May to mid-Sept; ☎76 14 19 51; no fax; ③), which offers simple rooms in a pleasant old blue-painted building just 200m from the tourist office. Also on the seafront is the *Lankanholmen* (☎76 14 28 50; fax 76 14 28 55; ③), a modern complex with chalet-style huts, apartments and a small and rather down-at-heel **youth hostel** (mid-May to mid-Sept; same numbers; 140kr, doubles ①). For even more solitude, there are several modern rooms and *rorbuer* at *Hayhusene Bleik* (☎76 14 57 40; fax 76 14 55 51; ①–②), in the lovely hamlet of **Bleik**, 7km down the coast, where the clapboard houses huddle between the craggy hills and the long sandy beach. Andenes has just one **hotel**, the *Norlandia Andrikken*, Storgata 53 (☎76 14 12 22; fax 76 14 19 33; ④; s/p ④), an uninspiring concrete block with rooms to match, less than 1km from the harbour. But the hotel **restaurant** is easily the best place to eat – the Arctic char is superb – while *Jul. Nilsens Bakeri* (Mon–Fri 9am–3pm, Sat 9am–1pm), close to the bus station at Kong Hansgata 1, is good for daytime snacks.

Monday through Saturday, it's easy to reach Andenes by **bus** from Sortland, but when it comes to moving on, your choices are limited: you can, of course, return the way you came, and buses from Andenes meet the *Hurtigrute* in Risøyhamn, or you can take the **ferry** (June–Aug 3 daily; 3hr; 70kr, car & driver 195kr) over to Gryllefjord on the mainland. The **Hvalrutebussen** (June–Aug 1–2 daily), running from Leknes in the Lofotens to Tromsø and Narvik, crosses over on the ferry, but bear in mind that Gryllefjord is a remote spot, a long drive from anywhere. Finally, Andenes has an **airport** with regular flights to Bodø and Tromsø.

Harstad

Readily reached by bus through the mountains from Sortland or round the rugged coastline with the *Hurtigrute* coastal steamer, **HARSTAD**, on the island of Hinnøya, is the region's largest town. It's also home to much of northern Norway's engineering industry, its sprawling docks an unseemly tangle of supply ships, repair yards and cold storage plants spread out along the gentle slopes of the Vågsfjord. Moving on quickly is easy: Harstad is a *Hurtigrute* port, an express passenger boat leaves regularly for Tromsø, and there are frequent buses to the mainland and the Lofotens. But if you're tired of sleepy Norwegian villages, Harstad at least provides a bustling interlude, especially in late June, when the ten-day **Festspillene i Nord-Norge** (North Norway Arts Festival), featuring concerts, theatre and dance, fills the hotels to bursting.

Harstad's only real sight is the **Trondenes kirke** (Sat 9am–noon; summer Mon–Fri 9am–3pm, plus Tues & Thurs 6–8pm, Sun 5–7pm; rest of year Tues–Fri 9am–2pm; free), which occupies a lovely, leafy location beside the fjord 3km north of the town centre, at the end of a slender peninsula. To get there, catch the local "Trondenes" bus (Mon–Sat hourly; 10min) from the station beside the tourist office; by car, follow Hwy 850 north from the centre and watch for the signposted turning on the right; there's also a taxi rank by the bus station.

In medieval times this was the northernmost church in Christendom, the original wooden structure, built at the behest of king Øystein (of *rorbuer* fame – see p.309), dating from the beginning of the twelfth century. The present stone building came a century later, its thick walls and the scant remains of its surrounding ramparts reflecting its dual function as a church and fortress – for these were troubled, violent times. However, the stern outside is in total contrast to the warm and homely interior. Here the dainty arches of the rood screen lead into the choir where each of the three altars is surmounted by a late medieval bas-relief wooden triptych. Of the trio, the central triptych is the finest. Below the main panel – a predictable depiction of the Holy Family – is a curiously cheerful sequence of biblical figures, each of whom wears a turban and sports a big, bushy beard.

Back outside, the walled churchyard holds a Soviet memorial to those eight hundred prisoners of war who died in the area at the hands of the Germans in World War II. There's another reminder of the war in the **Adolf-kanonen** (The Adolf Gun), a massive artillery piece stuck on the north side of the peninsula. It's inside a military zone and the obligatory **guided tour** (mid-June to early Aug daily at 11am, 1pm, 3pm & 5pm; 40kr), which begins at the gate of the compound 1km up the hill from the church, stipulates that you must have your own vehicle to cross from the gate to the gun, a distance of 1km.

PRACTICALITIES

Although Harstad is easy to reach by bus or boat from Sortland, Tromsø and Narvik, it's actually something of a dead end for car drivers, who have to leave the E10 for the final thirty-kilometre drive north into town along Hwy 83. Once you've got there, however, you'll find almost everything you need in the immediate vicinity of the **bus station**. Next door is the **tourist office**, Torvet 8 (mid-June to mid-Aug Mon–Fri 8am–7pm, Sat 9am–7pm, Sun noon–7pm; rest of the year Mon–Fri 8am–4pm; ☎77 06 32 35), which can advise on bike rental. Straight ahead is the jetty for the **Hurtigbåt** express passenger boat, which takes two and a half hours to get to Tromsø; round the back is the dock of the **Hurtigrute** coastal steamer, which takes almost three times as long to make the same trip.

Harstad's comfortable if somewhat institutional **youth hostel** (☎77 06 41 54; fax 77 06 56 33; June to late Aug; 125kr, doubles ①; reception closed 10.30am–6pm) overlooks the fjord from the Trondenes peninsula, about 3km from the town centre, not far from the church; it's easy to reach by local bus from the station. Alternatively, the tourist office arranges **private rooms** for 250kr a double, plus a 25kr booking fee, though most of these are in the suburbs; there are also several central **guesthouses**, the pick being the smart *Sentrum Hospits*, off Havnegata at Magnusgate 5 (☎77 06 29 38; no fax; ①). Among a clutch of bland, modern **hotels**, the *Grand Nordic Hotell*, Strandgata 9 (☎77 06 21 70; fax 77 06 77 30; ②/④), is agreeable enough.

Harstad is no gourmet's paradise, but the *Kaffistova* (Mon–Fri 8am–6pm, Sat 9.30am–2.30pm, Sun 11.30am–4.30pm), across from the *Hurtigbåt* terminal, serves traditional Norwegian standbys at inexpensive rates, and in the evening *tante Augusta*, opposite the *Grand Nordic Hotell*, has a good line in grilled seafood – until around 7pm: arrive later in Harstad and you'll almost certainly have to eat in one of the hotels.

travel details

Trains

From Narvik to: Riksgrånsen (2–3 daily; 50min).

From Trondheim to: Bodø (2–3 daily; 10hr); Dombås (3–4 daily; 2hr 30min); Fauske (2–3 daily; 9hr 20min); Hjerkinn (3 daily; 2hr); 45min); Mo-i-Rana (2–3 daily; 7hr); Oslo (3–4 daily; 7hr); Otta (3 daily; 3hr); Røros (1–2 daily; 2hr 30min); Steinkjer (2–3 daily; 1hr 20min).

Buses

From Bodø to: Fauske (3 daily; 1hr 10min); Harstad (1 daily; 8hr); Narvik (1 daily; 7hr); Svolvær (1 daily; 10hr 20min).

From Fauske to: Bodø (3 daily; 1hr 10min); Harstad (1 daily; 6hr 30min); Honningsvåg (1 daily; 37hr); Narvik (2 daily; 5hr 35min); Nordkapp (1 daily; 38hr); Sortland (1 daily; 5hr 30min); Svolvær (1 daily; 8hr 30min).

From Harstad to: Narvik (1–2 daily; 2hr 40min); Sortland (1–2 daily; 2hr 50min); Svolvær (1–2 daily; 5hr 15min); Å (1–2 daily; 9hr 30min).

From Narvik to: Alta (1 daily; 11hr); Bodø (1 daily; 7hr); Fauske (2 daily; 5hr 35min); Harstad (1–2 daily; 2hr 40min); Sortland (1 daily; 3hr 40min); Svolvær (1 daily; 6hr 30min); Tromsø (2

daily; 4hr 40min); Å (Mon–Fri 1 daily; 9hr 40min).

From Sortland to: Andenes (Mon–Sat 1 daily; 2hr 30min).

From Svolvær to: Leknes (Mon–Sat 1–2 daily; 3hr 10min); Å (Mon–Sat 1–2 daily; 5hr 10min).

From Trondheim to: Bergen (1 daily; 13hr 30min); Dombås (1 daily; 3hr); Kristiansund (1–3 daily; 5hr); Røros (1–3 daily; 3hr 10min); Stryn (1 daily; 7hr 40min); Ålesund (1–2 daily; 8hr).

Nord-Norge Bussen

There are two buses daily from Bodø and Fauske to Nordkjosbotn, one daily continuing to Alta (overnight stops necessary at Narvik and Alta). Two daily continue to Karasjok, the first running on to Kirkenes the same day, the second stopping in Karasjok. See also "Travel Details" in the *Northern Norway* chapter and "Getting Around", p.161.

The *Hurtigrute* Coastal Steamer

The daily *Hurtigrute* service departs at the following times. Journey time from Trondheim to Harstad is 43hr, Tromsø 51hr.

Northbound: Trondheim at noon; Bodø at 3pm; Stamsund at 7.30pm; Svolvær at 10pm; Sortland at 3am; Harstad at 8.15am.

Southbound: Harstad at 8.45am; Sortland at 1.15pm; Svolvær at 7.30pm; Stamsund at 9.30pm; Bodø at 4am; Trondheim at 10am.

Ferries

From Bodø to: Moskenes (1–3 daily; 4hr 15min); Røst (5 weekly; 8hr); Værøy (7 weekly; 7hr).

From Bognes to: Lødingen (5–7 daily; 1hr).

From Fiskebol to: Melbu (11–13 daily; 25min).

From Skarberget to: Bognes (11–14 daily; 25min).

From Svolvær to: Skutvik (early June to late Aug 7–9 daily; rest of the year 3–4 daily; 2hr).

Express passenger boats (*Hurtigbåt*)

From Bodø to: Svolvær (6 weekly; 5hr 30min).

From Harstad to: Tromsø (1 daily; 2hr 30min).

From Narvik to: Svolvær (1 daily except Sat; 3hr 30min).

From Trondheim to: Kristiansund (1–3 daily; 3hr 30min).

International trains

From Narvik to Stockholm (2 daily; 21–24hr).

From Trondheim to: Stockholm (2 daily; 12hr).

CHAPTER EIGHT

NORTH NORWAY

Baedeker, writing one hundred years ago about the remote regions of **North Norway**, comprising Finnmark and the northern reaches of the province of Troms, observed that they possess "attractions for the scientific traveller and the sportsman, but can hardly be recommended for the ordinary tourist." And, to be frank, this is still pretty near the mark today. These are enticing lands, no question, the natural environment they offer stunning in its extremes. But the travelling can be hard, the specific sights well distanced and, when you reach them, subtle in their appeal.

Troms' intricate, fretted coastline has influenced its history since the days when powerful Viking lords operated a trading empire from its islands. Even today, over half the population still lives offshore, inhabiting dozens of tiny fishing villages that are best viewed from the *Hurtigrute* coastal steamer as it pushes along the coast. It is, in fact, the so-called "Capital of the North", **Tromsø**, you should aim for, a lively university town, where King Haakon and his government proclaimed a "Free Norway" in 1940 before fleeing into exile in Britain.

The appeal of **Finnmark** is less obvious, a region covering 48,000 square kilometres yet containing only 2 percent of the Norwegian population. Much of the land was laid waste during World War II, the combined effect of the Russian advance and, more particularly, the retreating German army's scorched-earth policy. It's now possible to drive for hours without coming across a building more than fifty years old. Most travellers head straight for **Nordkapp** (the North Cape), Europe's northernmost point, from where the Midnight Sun is visible between mid-May and the end of July – and some doggedly press on to **Kirkenes**, last town before the Russian border, where you really feel that you are on the edge of Europe. Perhaps surprisingly, few visitors turn inland to the remote Sami towns of **Kautokeino** and **Karasjok**, strange, disconsolate places in the middle of the eerily endless, flat scrub plains of the **Finnmarksvidda**, where winter temperatures plummet to -25°C. Even more adventurously, it's become a little easier these days to reach **Svalbard**, an archipelago 700km north of Norway, frozen solid for most of the year but visitable in July and August, providing you can stump up the substantial wad of money needed to get there – if you do, you'll be rewarded by some extraordinary scenery.

Transport and accommodation

Approaches to the far north are limited but spectacular: trains don't run this far and public transport access is either by coastal steamer (the *Hurtigrute*), bus or plane. The **Hurtigrute** takes the best part of two days to circumnavigate the huge fjords between Tromsø and Kirkenes; **bus** transport is quicker – the Tromsø–Kirkenes trip can be

---

FINNMARK: THE MIDNIGHT SUN AND POLAR NIGHT

On clear nights, the **Midnight Sun** is visible at Alta, Hammerfest and Nordkapp from mid-May until the end of July; the long **Polar Night** runs from the last week in November until the third week in January.

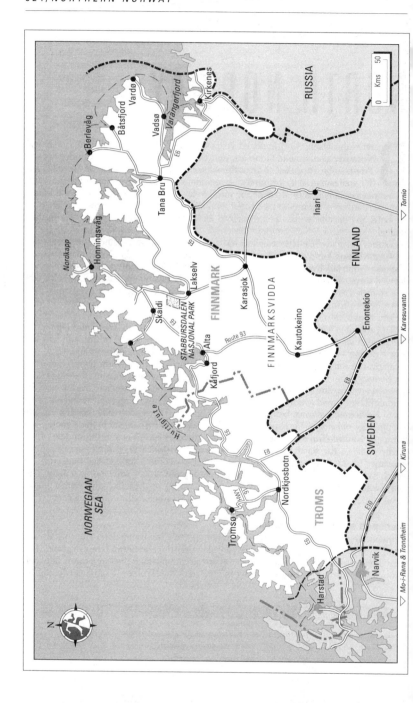

RUSSIA

Kirkenes

Vardø

Båtsfjord

Berlevåg

Vadsø

Varangerfjord

E6

Tana Bru

Inari

Nordkapp

Honningsvåg

E6

Lakselv

FINLAND

Karasjok

FINNMARK

Skaidi

FINNMARKSVIDDA

93

STABBURSDALEN NASJONAL PARK

Alta

Route 93

Kautokeino

Enontekio

Kåfjord

E8

Hurtigrute

E6

SWEDEN

E8

NORWEGIAN SEA

Nordkjosbotn

TROMS

E6

HWY 91

6

Tromsø

Narvik

E10

Harstad

N

0   Kms   50

▷ *Tornio*

▷ *Karesuvanto*

▷ *Kiruna*

▷ *Mo-i-Rana & Trondheim*

done in about a day – and services are efficient and regular throughout the summer (and some of the winter), using the windswept E6 Arctic Highway. Buses also run north off the E6 to Nordkapp and south into the Finnmarksvidda and subsequently Finland. Obviously, these aren't areas you want to get stranded in, so be sure to pick up full **timetables** from any local tourist office. For the longer rides it's a good idea to buy tickets in advance.

The main roads are good – remarkably so considering the winter climate – but **drivers** will find the going slow, even on the main route to Nordkapp. One option, though this has more to do with comfort than speed, is to combine **car and boat** travel – special deals on the *Hurtigrute* can make this surprisingly affordable; local tourist offices will help and advise. If you intend to leave the main roads, you should also be prepared for the worst, since **supplies** of most things are few and far between. Most car rental firms offer deals on **mobile phones** and, especially if you're travelling alone, these can be very reassuring. You'll be able to get **fuel** easily enough at every settlement of any size, but car repairs can take time since workshops are scarce and parts often have to be ordered from the south. If you really want to speed things up, consider **flying** one of the legs of your journey. Summer discounts and special offers make this an economic possibility; ask for details at any *SAS or Braathens* office, and sometimes the tourist office can assist as well.

As for **accommodation**, there's a smattering of youth hostels across the region and a small cache of hotels in all the major towns, as well as a sprinkling of campsites; in any case, if you have a tent and a well-insulated sleeping bag, you can, in theory, bed down more or less where you like, though the hostility of the climate and ferocity of the mosquitoes make most people think (at least) twice. It's also worth remembering that there's a state **off-licence**, a *Vinmonopolet*, in only four towns: Alta, Hammerfest, Vadsø and Kirkenes. Stock up where you can.

Tromsø

TROMSØ has been referred to, rather preposterously, as the "Paris of the North", and though even the tourist office doesn't make any pretence to such grandiose titles now, the city still likes to think of itself as the capital of northern Norway. Which in a way is fair enough, since it's easily the region's most populous town and one with medieval credentials – there's been a church here since the thirteenth century. Tromsø received its municipal charter in 1794, when it was primarily a trading centre, and has since grown into a surprisingly urbane commercial centre with a population of 50,000 people. Not unnaturally, it trades on its geographical position, making much of its university and brewery – the world's northernmost examples of both. But there are other tangible attractions, too, notably two cathedrals, some surprisingly good museums, and an above-average nightlife thanks to the student population.

Arrival and information

At the northern end of the E8, 73km north of Nordkjosbotn on the E6, downtown Tromsø slopes back from the waterfront on the pint-sized island of Tromsøya; the island is connected to the mainland by bridge and tunnel. The *Hurtigrute* **coastal steamer**, on its long journey from Bergen to Kirkenes, docks in the centre of town at the quay at the bottom of Kirkegata. Long-distance **buses** arrive and leave from the adjacent car park. The **airport** is just a few kilometres northwest of the centre at Langnes, and has car rental agencies and a bank; an airport bus (30kr) runs into the city, stopping at the *Radisson SAS Hotel* on Sjøgata and at several other central hotels. The **left-luggage** lockers (15kr per day) in the *Venteromskafé* (☎77 68 20 75) by the *Hurtigrute* dock are acces-

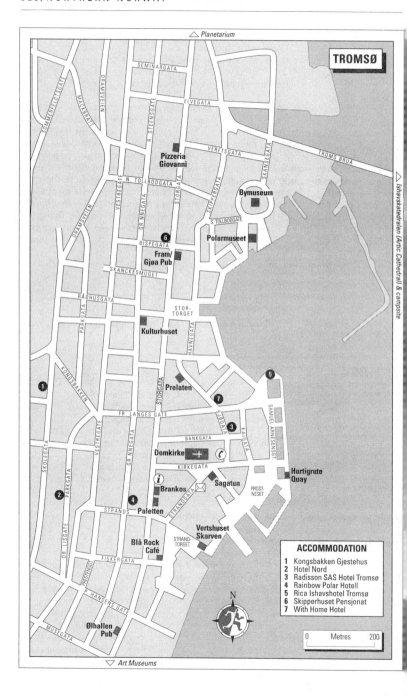

△ *Planetarium*

TROMSØ

SEMINARGATA

ELVEGATA

VERFTSGATA

TROMS BRUA

▷ *Ishavskatedralen (Artic Cathedral) & campsite*

SOMMERFELTSGATE

MACKBRATT

GRAMSVEIEN

OLAVSVEIEN

R. STEENSGATE

N. TOLLBODGATA

VESTREGATE

GRØNNEGATA

STORGATA

SKIPPERGATA

SKANSEGATA

**Pizzeria
Giovanni**

Bymuseum

BISPEGATA

S. TOLLBODGATE

6

Polarmuseet

**Fram/
Gjøa Pub**

SKANCKESMUGET

GRAMSVEIEN

PARKGATA

RÅDHUSGATA

STOR-
TORGET

Kulturhuset

HAVEGATA

KONGSBAKKEN

STORGATA

1

Prelaten

5

7

SAMUEL ARNESENSG

FR. LANGES GATE

VESTREGATE

GRØNNEGATA

SKOLEGATA

PARKGATA

BANKGATA

SJØGATA

KAIGATA

3

Domkirke

KIRKEGATA

**Hurtigrute
Quay**

2

Brankos

Sagatun

PROST-
NESET

STRANDS

4

Paletten

STRANDGATA

**Vertshuset
Skarven**

DR. LISGATE

**Blå Rock
Café**

STRAND-
TORGET

FISKERGATA

PRESTENGT

N

P. HANSENS GATE

**Ølhallen
Pub**

MUSEGATA

ACCOMMODATION

1 Kongsbakken Gjestehus
2 Hotel Nord
3 Radisson SAS Hotel Tromsø
4 Rainbow Polar Hotell
5 Rica Ishavshotel Tromsø
6 Skipperhuset Pensjonat
7 With Home Hotel

0   Metres   200

▽ *Art Museums*

sible Monday through Friday from 6.30am and on Sunday from noon until the boat's midnight arrival; note also that on Saturdays the lockers can be accessed from 10am till midnight only in the height of the season, the rest of the year the café closes at 3pm. The **tourist office** (June to mid-Aug Mon–Fri 8.30am–6pm, Sat & Sun 10am–5pm; rest of the year Mon–Fri 8.30am–4pm, May also Sat 10am–5pm; ☎77 61 00 00) is at Storgata 61, near the Domkirke, and sells a 24-hour **tourist ticket** (50kr) giving unlimited city bus travel, though most places of interest can easily be reached on foot. You can pick up maps and brochures here as well, and book places on various tours and cruises, which start at around 75kr per person for a couple of hours on the surrounding waters.

The town centre is small enough to make **orientation** easy – Stortorget, the main square, is tucked tight against the harbour and the pedestrianized part of Storgata, the main street and north–south axis, bisects it. If you'd like to **rent a bike**, try *Sportshuset*, Storgata 91 (Mon–Fri 9am–5pm, Thurs till 7pm, Sat 10am–3pm), or *Tromsø Sykkelservice ANS*, Kirkegata 1 (April–Oct Mon–Fri 8am–4.30pm, Thurs till 7pm, Sat 10am–2pm; Nov–May Mon–Fri 10am–4pm & Sat 10am–2pm). The central **taxi** office is at Strandveien 30 (☎77 68 80 20), and there are ranks at Strandtorget, by the *Fokus* cinema and the Domkirke.

Accommodation

The tourist office books **private rooms** in town for a 25kr fee: prices are around 100kr for a single, 150–200kr double, so they're well worth considering. Also check with the tourist office about the latest deals at the larger **hotels**, whose weekend and summer discounts can knock up to 40 percent off the regular rate. All the options listed below are centrally situated unless otherwise stated.

Hotels and guesthouses

Hotel Nord, Parkgata 4 (☎77 68 31 59; fax 77 61 35 05). A *pensjonat*, despite the name, with good economical rooms; cheap triples, too. ①

Kongsbakken Gjestehus, Skolegata 24 (☎77 68 22 08; fax 77 68 80 44). Good basic accommodation with impressive views of the city from some rooms. Worth booking ahead in summer. ①

Radisson SAS Hotel Tromsø, Sjøgata 7 (☎77 60 00 00; fax 77 68 54 74). A plush central sky-rise with all the comforts you might expect for the money. Banquet-sized breakfasts. ③/⑤

Rainbow Polar, Grønnegata 45 (☎77 68 64 80; fax 77 68 91 36). Small rooms and few comforts, but summer and weekend prices bring the rates down by around 250kr a room, which is no bad bargain; breakfast included. ②/③

Rica Ishavshotel Tromsø, Fr. Langes gate 2 (☎77 66 64 00; fax 77 66 64 44). A stylish wooden ship-like structure built on the edge of the harbour, this new top-class hotel offers excellent facilities and unsurpassable views of the waterfront. ③/⑤

Skipperhuset Pensjonat, Storgata 112 (☎77 68 16 60). North of Stortorget, by Bispegata, this long-standing favourite with budget travellers has good, cheap rooms. ①
With Home Hotel, Sjøgata 35–37 (☎77 68 70 00; fax 77 68 96 16). Pleasantly situated in the old dock district, a classy hotel with a maritime air. Excellent views along the waterfront. ③/④

Hostels and camping

Tromsdalen Camping (☎77 63 80 37). The nearest campsite to the city, with cabins, is 3km away, over the bridge on the mainland and is open all year; take bus #36 or #30 from outside the *Domus* store on Stortorget.

Tromsø Vandrerhjem, Gitta Jønsons vei 4, Elverhøy (☎77 68 53 19; fax 77 06 63 03). A couple of kilometres from the quay either by bus #24 – from outside the *Sparebanken* on Fr. Langes gate to Elverhøy – or else a steep twenty-minute walk. This large HI hostel is basic and can be noisy; dormitory accommodation plus family and double rooms. A key deposit of 100kr is payable, and there's no curfew. No food is available, but there's a store close by. Open mid-June to mid-Aug; reception closed 11am–5pm 5kr, double rooms ①.

The City

Just off Storgata, bang in the centre of town, the **Domkirke** (Tues–Sun noon–4pm) serves to emphasize how prosperous Tromsø had become by the nineteenth century, the result of its substantial barter trade with Russia. Completed in 1861, it's a handsome structure and one of Norway's largest wooden churches, with an austere beige interior. From here, it's an enjoyable five-minute walk north past summertime buskers to Stortorget, site of a daily fruit and veg **market**; behind this is the waterfront, where fresh fish and prawns are sold direct from inshore fishing boats throughout the summer. Follow the harbour round to the north and you're in the heart of old Tromsø: the raised ground at the water's edge made this area a natural site for fortification as early as the thirteenth century, though a fire in 1969 left few buildings of any interest. One that did survive is the Customs House, built in 1789 and now home to the **Tromsø Bymuseum** (mid-May to mid-Sept daily 11am–6pm; mid-Sept to mid-May Mon–Fri 11am–3pm; 30kr), the town museum, whose mainly nineteenth-century collection takes a stab at summarizing local history and culture. The **Polarmuseet** (daily mid-May to mid-June 11am–6pm; mid-June to Aug 11am–8pm; Sept to mid-May 11am–3pm; 30kr), close by at Søndre Tollbudgata 11, describes hunting in the region throughout the ages by way of good photographs but somewhat stilted reconstructions of the living conditions of fur trappers and seal hunters. It's hard not to be nauseated by the exhibits illustrating the use of barbaric animal traps. The museum has a room devoted to the life of polar explorer Roald Amundsen (1872–1928), who spent thirty years tweeking out some of the secrets of the Arctic and Antarctic, and became the first man to reach the South Pole on December 14, 1911, famously just ahead of his British rival, Captain Scott.

Over the spindly Tromsø bridge, on the other side of the water in the suburb of Tromsdalen, the white and desperately modern Arctic Cathedral (**Ishavskatedralen**; June to mid-Aug Mon–Sat 10am–8pm, Sun 1–8pm; mid-Aug to May daily 3–6pm; 10kr) was completed in 1965. Its striking, glacier-like appearance is created by eleven immense triangular concrete sections, representing the eleven Apostles left after the betrayal, while the entire east wall is made up of a huge stained-glass window, one of the largest in Europe. Another unusual feature is the organ, which is built to represent a ship when viewed from beneath. You can get here on bus #30 or #36 from Havnegata, outside the *Domus* supermarket; or simply walk over the bridge.

From the Ishavskatedralen, it's a five-minute walk – or take bus #28 originating at Havnegata – to the city's **cable car** terminus. From the top (420m), the views of the city and its surroundings are extensive and at the *Fjellstua* restaurant here (☎77 63 86 55) you can treat yourself to a meal with a panoramic backdrop. There are regular daily departures from April to September (10am–5pm), plus an additional evening schedule from June to August (5pm–1am). Note that services are suspended during bouts of bad weather. Tickets cost 50kr.

Back in central Tromsø, on the pocket-sized island of Tromsøya, the eminently successful *Mack* brewery is situated a five-minute walk south of the centre at the corner of Storgata and Musegata. Next door, the best of the city's museums, the **Nordnorsk Kunstmuseum** (Art Museum of Northern Norway; Tues–Sun 11am–5pm; free), is housed in an elegant 1894 building which it shares with the **Tromsø Kunstforening** (Art Society; Tues–Sun 11am–5pm; 10kr). The Art Society uses the ground floor for temporary exhibitions of mainly Norwegian contemporary art, while the two floors up above are the territory of the Art Museum. The emphasis here is on nineteenth- and early twentieth-century Norwegian paintings, mostly loaned from the National Gallery and Museum for Contemporary Art, a competent and regularly rotated sample supplemented by an eclectic assortment of contemporary applied art – predominantly textiles, ceramics and glass. Other temporary exhibitions are often held in the small gardens surrounding the museum building.

Northern Lights Planetarium and Botanical Gardens

A couple of excursions completes the list of things to do in and around Tromsø. About 3km north along the coast from the centre, near the university in the suburb of Breivika, the **Nordlysplanetariet** (Northern Lights Planetarium; June to mid-Aug daily 10am–7pm; 50kr; ☎77 67 60 00) can be reached on bus #37 from outside the *Sparebanken Nord-Norge* on Fr. Langes gate. There are superb film shows here (roughly hourly during the day, but check times in advance if you want the commentary in English) depicting the Northern Lights and Midnight Sun, well worth viewing if the timing of your holiday precludes actually seeing either.

A 250-metre walk east from the Planetarium will take you to the world's most northerly **Botanisk hage** (Botanical Gardens; May–Sept; free), established by the university in 1994, the city's bicentennial year. These four acres of Arctic-Alpine gardens are a pleasant spot for a stroll; thanks to the Gulf Stream, which sweeps up the Norwegian coast, Tromsø's climate is mild enough to allow plants to flourish well beyond their normal northern limits – the city is some 360km above the Arctic Circle.

Eating, drinking and entertainment

Tromsø has an excellent range of places to eat and drink, mostly concentrated in the vicinity of the tourist office and along Storgata. The students' union building, *Studenthuset*, at Skippergata 44 (☎77 68 44 10), has a bar and café, and is good source of **nightlife** information. Cover charges for discos and gigs run to 60kr and upwards.

The **Kulturhuset**, Grønnegata 87 (☎77 68 20 64), is the main venue for cultural events of all kinds – there's a decent bar here as well (see below). There are a couple of **cinemas** in town: the *Fokus*, at Grønnegata 94, and *Verdensteateret*, Storgata 93b. The tourist office has details of screenings. For a less cerebral night out, you can play **pool** at *Tromsø Biljardsenter*, Storgata 46 (open until 11pm).

Cafés and restaurants

Brankos, Storgata 57. Pricey Balkan restaurant with excellent food and arty surroundings. Open evenings only.

Fram Mathus, Storgata 95. Cheap restaurant next to the rowdy *Gjøa Pub*, with whale steak on the menu.

Sagatun, Richard Withs plass 2. Reasonably priced cafeteria meals.

Vertshuset Skarven, Strandtorget 1. Downstairs there's a pub atmosphere and good food; upstairs, the best restaurant in town serves Arctic fish delicacies and reindeer for around 170kr a course.

Bars and nightlife

Blå Rock Café, Strandgata 14. Raucous R&B bar with CD jukebox and weekend discos.

Gjøa Pub, Storgata 95. The cheapest pub in town, teeming with local drunks.

Middagskjelleren, Strandgata 22. Drinks, snacks and live music.

Ølhallen Pub, Storgata 4. Noisy brewery pub, a good place to sample the local beer, *Mack*.

Paletten, Storgata 51. This café-bar maintains an arty reputation by hosting occasional exhibitions.

Teaterkafeen, in the *Kulturhus*, Grønnegata 87. On the corner of Stortorget, this arts centre stays open until 1am most days for trendy (and expensive) drinking and snacks.

Listings

Banks *Sparebanken*, Fr. Langes gate 19; *Kreditkassen*, Grønnegata 78; airport bank open Mon–Fri 10am–6pm.

Car rental *Europcar*, Heiloveien 4, Langnes (☎77 67 56 00; fax 77 67 04 16); *Nord Bilutleie* AS, Fr. Nansensplass 3 (☎77 68 54 11; fax 77 65 78 87); *Avis*, at the airport (☎77 67 53 20; fax 77 67 40 67).

Emergencies Emergency medical care: *Bereitschafts-Arzt* ☎77 68 30 00 (Mon–Fri 4pm–8am, Fri 4pm–Mon 8am). For an ambulance, dial ☎113.

Pharmacy *Svaneapoteket*, Fr. Langes gate 9 (Mon–Fri 8.30am–4pm & 6–9pm, Sat 9am–1.30pm & 6–9pm; ☎77 68 64 24).

Post office Main office at Strandgata 41 (Mon–Fri 8.30am–5pm, Sat 10am–2pm).

Taxi *Tromsø Taxisentral*, Strandveien 30 (24-hr service on ☎77 68 80 20).

Telephone office *Telenor Kundeservice*, Sjøgata 2 (Mon–Fri 8am–4pm).

Travel agents *SAS Luftreisebyrå*, Grønnegata 74 (☎77 61 10 00); *Winge Reisebureau*, Grønnegata 86 (☎77 68 80 00).

Vinmonopolet Off-licence at Storgata 33.

LAPPLAND

The northernmost reaches of Norway, Sweden and Finland, as well as the northwest corner of Russia, are collectively known as **Lappland**. Traditionally, the indigenous population were called "Lapps", though in recent years this name has fallen out of favour and been replaced by the more accurate "Sami", although the changeover is by no means universal.

Into Finnmark: Alta and around

From Tromsø, the E8 and then the E6 follow the coast pretty much all the way to Alta, some 410km – about nine hours – to the north. Drivers can save themselves around 120km (although not necessarily time or money) by cutting across the peninsula south of Tromsø on Hwy 91. This is the route the bus follows, incorporating two ferry crossings, at Breivikeidet–Svensby (7.15am–10pm; 25min; 49k) and Lyngseidet–Olderdalen near Kåfjord (8.15am–9.30pm; 45min; 70kr). Either way, you enter **Finnmark** around 60km short of a second, more northerly **Kåfjord**, a tiny village beside the E6, whose restored nineteenth-century church was built by the English company that operated the area's copper mines until they were abandoned as uneconomic in the 1870s. The Kåfjord itself is an arm of the Altafjord and was used as an Arctic hideaway by the *Tirpitz* and other German battleships during World War II to protect them from the British. From here, it's just 20km further east to Alta.

Alta

Despite the long haul to get here, it's unlikely you'll want to spend more than a night in **ALTA**, whose population of just 16,000 occupies a string of unenticing settlements that straggle along the E6 for several kilometres. It was interesting once; for decades not Norwegian at all but Finnish and Sami, and host to an ancient and much visited Sami fair, until World War II and a series of fires polished off the fair and destroyed all the old buildings except the church – and, to add insult to injury, Alta is now in the grip of a comprehensive new development that has no real centre, and little soul. For all that, it's an important transport junction and hard to avoid: heading to Nordkapp by bus almost certainly means an overnight stop in Alta in order to catch the onward service to Honningsvåg the next day. Buses also head east from here along the E6 to Kirkenes and south down Hwy 93 to Kautokeino. Furthermore, the town does have one remarkable feature that largely compensates for its shortcomings: the **rock carvings at Hjemmeluft** – the most extensive area of prehistoric rock carvings in northern Europe.

The **site** and the attached **museum** (mid-June to Aug daily 8am–11pm; early June & late Aug daily 8am–8pm; Sept daily 9am–6pm; Oct–April Mon–Fri 9am–3pm, Sat & Sun 11am–4pm; 40kr summer, 30kr winter) are on Altaveien, off the E6 as you approach Alta from the west – and about 2km before the shopping complex at Bossekop and the Alta tourist office. There are several hundred carvings, reached through the museum and out along the 5km of wooden walkways you can spot from the E6. They make up an extraordinarily complex tableau of boats, animals and people, recognizable if highly stylized representations whose minor variations – there are four identifiable bands – in subject matter and design indicate successive historical periods. The carvings were executed, it's estimated, between 6000 and 2500 years ago, and although the colours have been retouched by scientists, they are indisputably impressive: clear, stylish, and ultimately rather touching in their simplicity. They provide an insight into a prehistoric culture that was essentially static and largely reliant on the hunting of land animals, with sealing and fishing of lesser importance – the killing done with flint and bone implements. To many experts it seems unlikely that these peoples would have spent so much effort on the carvings unless they had spiritual significance, but this can only be conjecture.

There are guided **tours** of the site in summer and the museum provides a wealth of background information, comparing the carvings, for example, with others found around the world. It also offers a history of the Alta area, particularly the salmon-fishing industry, and documents the conflicts around the development of the nearby hydroelectric power station, which involved flooding land used by the local Sami community.

Practicalities

Buses call at the shopping complex at Bossekop, the original settlement by the water of the Altafjord, and then continue east along the E6 to Alta Sentrum, Elvebakken and Kronstad, the town's other three main foci. At Bossekop you'll find a few facilities – including a café, bank and post office – plus the **tourist office** (June–Aug Mon–Fri 9am–7pm, Sat 9am–4pm, Sun noon–7pm; ☎78 43 77 70), tucked away downstairs in the shopping mall, where you can normally leave your bag while visiting the carvings. They may help with finding **accommodation**, a particularly useful service if you're dependent on public transport – the town's hotels and motels are widely dispersed – and in the height of the season when the town gets crowded with travellers en route to Nordkapp. Also in Bossekop are a couple of modest, motel-style lodgings, the *Alta Gjestestue*, Bekkefaret 3 (☎78 43 55 66; fax 78 43 50 80; ③), and the nearby *Vica Hotell Alta* (☎78 43 47 11; fax 78 43 42 99; ③). Alta Sentrum, some 2km further east, is the newest and least likeable part of town, but it's here you'll find the much more comfortable *North Cape Hotel Alta*, near the main drag at Løkkeveien 61 (☎78 43 50 00; fax 78

43 58 25; ③/④), a brisk, modern place offering substantial summer discounts. Nearby is the **youth hostel**, at Midtbakkveien 52 (☎78 43 44 09; fax 78 43 44 09; mid-June to mid-Aug; 110kr, doubles ①): to get there from Alta Sentrum, head east up the E6 to the next roundabout, where you turn left and then first left again – a ten-minute walk. The hostel has excellent facilities, although food isn't available, and it's pretty much essential to reserve a bed in advance. There are also several **campsites** in the vicinity of Alta, the nearest and best equipped being the four-star *Kronstad Camping* (☎78 43 03 60; fax 78 43 11 55), an all-year site with cabins beside the E6 at the east end of town.

Eating is most cheaply done at the *Alta Gjestestue* (Mon–Fri 7am–10pm, Sat 8am–9pm, Sun 9am–9pm), opposite the filling station in Bossekop, or at the café in the shopping precinct over the road.

The Finnmarksvidda: Kautokeino and Karasjok

Setting aside the slow but steady encroachment of the tourist industry, lifestyles in the remoter parts of the **Finnmarksvidda** have remained much the same for centuries. The main occupations are reindeer-herding, hunting and fishing; and the few thousand semi-nomadic **Sami**, who make up the bulk of the local population, have continued to live in a relatively traditional way, to a pattern dictated by their animals. They remain in the flat plains and shallow valleys of the interior during the winter, migrating towards the coast in early May as the snow begins to melt – though hard to believe, it can get exceptionally hot here in summer. By October, both people and reindeer are journeying back from their temporary summer quarters and preparing for the great **Easter festivals**, when weddings and baptisms are celebrated in Karasjok and Kautokeino. This is without question the best time to be in Finnmark: a celebration of the end of the Polar Night and the arrival of spring, when there are folk music concerts, traditional sports and church services – it's also when the famed reindeer races are run. Summer visits, on the other hand, when most families and their reindeer are at coastal pastures in the north, can be disappointing, with precious little activity.

The best time to **hike** in the Finnmarksvidda is in August and early September – after the peak mosquito season and before the weather turns cold. For the most part the plateau is scrub and open birch forest which makes the going fairly easy, though the many marshes, rivers and lakes can impede progress. There are a handful of clearly demarcated hiking trails and a smattering of appropriately sited huts where you can kip down for the night; for detailed information, ask at the nearest tourist office.

From **Alta**, the only direct route into the vast plain of the Finnmarksvidda is south along Hwy 93 to **Kautokeino**, a distance of 130km. Thereafter, there's a bit more choice, with one road pressing on into Finland, the other, Hwy 92, travelling the 130km east to **Karasjok**, where you can rejoin the E6, well beyond the road to Nordkapp. A few bus services cover these routes but to avoid being stranded you'll need to do some careful studying of the timetables.

Kautokeino

It's a three-hour bus ride from Alta, past a long stretch of scrub, trees, rock and telegraph wires, to **KAUTOKEINO** (*Guovdageaidnu* in Sami), the principal winter camp of the Norwegian Sami and the site of a huge reindeer market in spring and autumn. Nonetheless, it's still a desultory, rather desolate-looking place, though one that has become, strangely enough, something of a tourist draw on account of the pseudo-ethnic jewellers who have moved here – all in search of closer contact with nature. Every summer it's these same jewellers who line the long main street with souvenir booths, attracting Finnish day-trippers like flies. They are not, however, selling tourist tack, and a visit to *Juhl's Silvergallery* (daily summer 8.30am–10pm; winter 9am–8pm), a 3km walk from the centre, following the signs, is a must. In this complex of workshops and showrooms, exquisitely beautiful, high-quality (and high-priced) silver pieces are made and sold, supplemented by a much broader range of quality craftwork.

Back in town, just east of the tourist office, is the small, open-air **Samesk museum** (mid-June to mid-Aug Mon–Fri 9am–7pm, Sat & Sun noon–7pm; rest of the year Mon–Fri 9am–3pm; 20kr), featuring a number of draughty-looking Sami dwellings: you'll see the same little turf huts and skin tents (known as a *lavvu*) all over Finnmark – often housing souvenir stalls.

THE SAMI

Familiarly but erroneously known as "Lapps", there are around 70,000 **Sami** today, stretched across the whole of the northernmost regions of Norway, Sweden and Finland with a couple of thousand on Russia's Kola peninsula too. Among the oldest peoples in Europe, the Same are probably descended from prehistoric clans who migrated here from the east by way of the Baltic. Their language is closely related to Finnish and Estonian, though it's somewhat misleading to speak of a "Sami language" as there are, in fact, three distinct tongues and each of these breaks down into a number of markedly different regional dialects. However, all have many features in common, including a superabundance of ways to express variations in snow and ice conditions.

Originally, the Sami were a semi-nomadic people, living in small communities (*siidas*), each of which had a degree of control over the surrounding hunting grounds. They lived by a combination of hunting, fishing and trapping, but it was the wild reindeer that supplied most of their needs. This changed in the sixteenth century when they switched over to reindeer-herding, with communities following the seasonal movements of the animals. What little contact the early Sami had with other Scandinavians was almost always to their disadvantage – as early as the ninth century a Norse chieftain by the name of Ottar boasted to the English king Alfred the Great of his success in imposing a fur, feather and hide tax on his Sami neighbours.

These early degradations were, however, nothing compared with the dislocation of Sami culture that followed the efforts of Sweden, Russia and Norway to control and colonize their lands. It took the best part of two hundred years for the competing nations to agree on their northern frontiers – the last treaty, between Norway and Russia, was signed in 1826 – and in the meantime hundreds of farmers had settled in "Lappland", to the consternation of its indigenous population.

Things got even worse for the Norwegian Same towards the end of the nineteenth century with new laws that, amongst other things, banned the use of their language in schools and stopped them from buying land unless they could speak Norwegian – an aggressive policy of "Norwegianization" much influenced by the Social Darwinism of the day, and only abandoned in the 1950s.

More recently, the Sami were dealt yet another grievous blow by the **Chernobyl nuclear disaster** of 1986. This contaminated not only the lichen that feeds the reindeer in winter, but also the game, fish, berries and fungi that supplement the Sami diet. Contamination of the reindeer meat meant the collapse of the export market and promises of compensation by the various national governments appeared late in the day, and failed to address the fact that this wasn't just an economic disaster for the Sami – their traditional culture is inseparably tied to reindeer-herding. Partly as a consequence of the necessarily reduced role for reindeer, there has been an expansion in other outlets of Sami **culture**. Traditional arts and crafts have become popular and are widely available in the Finnmarksvidda and in Tromsø; Sami music (*yoik* – rhythmic song-poems) is being given a hearing by World Music and jazz buffs; while in 1987 the first Sami film, "The Pathfinder" (*Veiviseren*), was released to critical acclaim.

Practicalities

Although Kautokeino's main street is all of 1500m long, most of its facilities, including the bus stop, are clustered near the **tourist office** (daily July & Aug 9am–8pm; mid-May to June & Sept 9am–4pm; ☎78 48 65 00), which marks what is effectively the town centre, provides town maps and has a limited supply of **private rooms**, costing from 150kr per person per night. Nearby, there are a small number of similarly modest rooms at *Alfreds Kro og Overnatting* (☎78 48 61 18; ①). The only **hotel** is the run-of-the-mill, modern *Kautokeino Turisthotell* (☎78 48 62 05; fax 78 48 67 01; ③/④), on the north side of town. There are also a couple of **campsites** near the river on the town's southern edge, *Kautokeino Camping* (☎/fax 78 48 54 00) and the adjacent *Haetta's Camping* (☎78 48 62 60). Both have cabins to rent (①). Incidentally, if you want to eat **reindeer**, then this is the place to do it: try *Alfreds Kro* for meals, or, if you have transport and you fancy your Sami food served in a *lavvu*, head for *Madam Bongo* (☎78 48 61 60; at least 3hr advance notice required), 11km west of the town and signposted from the centre.

Karasjok

The only other settlement of any size on the plain, **KARASJOK** (*Kárásjohka*), Norway's Sami capital, is on the main route from Finland to Nordkapp and consequently sees plenty of tourists. Spread across a wooded river valley, it has none of the desolation of Kautokeino, but it still conspires to be fairly dull, despite the siting of the Sami parliament and library here, and the opening of several ethnic jewellery shops and art galleries. The busiest place in town is the *Samelandsenteret* **tourist office** (June to early Aug Mon–Sat 8am–9pm, Sun 10am–8pm; rest of the year Mon–Fri 9am–4pm, Sun 10am–2pm; ☎78 46 73 60; fax 78 46 69 00), which incorporates a Sami souvenir shop, replete with authentic arts and crafts, and a café. During the summer, there are also displays of various traditional Sami skills in the grounds around the centre – the usual sort of stuff with the obligatory reindeer brought along as a backdrop.

A short walk away along the Nordkapp road, past the *North Cape Hotel* and turning right towards the headquarters of the Sami radio station, is **De Sameske Samlinger** (Sami Museum; mid-June to mid-Aug Mon–Sat 9am–6pm, Sun 10am–6pm; April to mid-June & mid-Aug to Oct Mon–Fri 9am–3pm, Sat & Sun 10am–3pm; Nov–March Mon–Fri 9am–3pm, Sat & Sun noon–3pm; 25kr), which attempts an overview of Sami culture and history. The outdoor exhibits comprise an assortment of old dwellings that illustrate, more than anything, the frugality of Sami life, while inside is a large, clearly presented collection of incidental bygones, incorporating a colourful sample of folkloric Sami costumes. You may also want to take a peek at the **Gamle Kirke**, on the opposite side of the river to the main town and the only building left standing at the end of World War II. Of simple design, it dates from 1807, making it easily the oldest surviving church in Finnmark.

A couple of kilometres from the tourist office, off the road to Vadsø and Kirkenes, the tiny Sami Arts Centre (**Samesk Kunstnersenter**; Mon–Fri 10am–3pm, Sat & Sun 11am–3pm; ☎78 46 73 60) showcases the work of contemporary Sami artists, but don't expect folksy paintings – Sami artists are a diverse bunch and as likely to be influenced by post-modernism as reindeer-herding.

However diverting these sights may be, you'll only get a feel for the Finnmarksvidda if you venture out of town. The tourist office has the details of local **guided tours**, with some of the options being dog-sledging, a visit to a Sami camp, a boat trip on the Karasjokka river, cross-country skiing and even gold-panning. The region's most popular long-distance **hike** is the five-day haul across the heart of the Finnmarksvidda from Karasjok to Alta, via a string of stategically located mountain huts – the tourist office can provide full details and advice.

Practicalities

Infrequent bus services may well mean you'll spend the night in Karasjok. From the **bus station**, on Storgata, it's a five- to ten-minute, well-signposted walk west to the tourist office (see above), which has details of a limited number of **private rooms** available for around 200kr per night. Otherwise, the **youth hostel** (mid-June to mid-Aug; 115kr; doubles ③), a short walk from the tourist office on the Alta road, is attached to *Karasjok Camping* (☎78 46 61 35; fax 78 46 66 23), where there are also cabins (①). Alternatively, try along the E6 as it cuts through town, either just east of the centre at the no-frills *Annes Overnatting og Motell* (☎78 46 64 32; ①), where you can also camp, or beside the tourist office at the modern *Karasjok Gjestehus* (☎78 46 74 00; fax 78 46 68 02; ②). Moving upmarket, the *North Cape Hotel* (☎78 46 74 00; fax 78 46 68 02; ②/④), a couple of minutes' walk north of the tourist office along the E6, has reasonably comfortable rooms and runs the unusual *Storgammen* **restaurant**, a wooden turf-covered hut where Sami-style meals can be eaten around an open fire.

Moving on from Karasjok, Hwy 92 heads east into Finland or west the 130km to Kautokeino (several buses weekly). Karasjok is also a stop for the *Nord-Norge Ekspressen*, which continues up the E6 to Kirkenes, or conversely returns to Alta via Lakselv.

Hammerfest

As the tourist office takes great pains to point out, **HAMMERFEST** is the world's northernmost town; it was also, they add, the first town in Europe to have its streets lit by electric light. Hardly fascinating facts, but both give a glimpse of the pride that the locals take in making the most of what is, beyond any doubt, an inhospitable region. And actually it is a wonder the town has survived at all. A hurricane flattened the place in 1856; it was burnt to the ground in 1890; and the retreating Germans mauled it at the end of World War II – yet, instead of being abandoned, Hammerfest was stubbornly rebuilt for a third time. Not the grim industrial town you might expect from the proximity of the offshore oil wells, it is, in fact, a bright and rather elegant port that drapes around a horsehoe-shaped harbour, with an air of prosperity recalling its nineteenth-century heyday as the centre of the *Pomor* (Norwegian–Russian) trade – a trading link it is now keen to revive. But don't get too carried away by expectations: Bill Bryson, in *Neither Here Nor There*, hit the nail on the head with his description of Hammerfest as "an agreeable enough town in a thank-you-God-for-not-making-me-live-here sort of way". Neither is the town's main employer, the *Findus* fish-processing plant, the stuff of Arctic romance.

Running parallel to the harbour, **Strandgata**, the town's main street, is a bustling run of supermarkets, cafés and some rather chic clothes and souvenir shops – inspired by the town's function as a stop-off on the way to Nordkapp. Most action takes place on the main quay, where the **Hurtigrute coastal steamer** docks and the ship's tourists usually spend their hour or so on shore, eating shellfish straight from the stalls along the wharf or buying souvenirs from the small, summertime Sami market.

Beyond that there isn't a great deal to see. Have a quick look inside the **Royal and Ancient Polar Bear Society** (June–Aug Mon–Fri 8am–6pm, Sat & Sun 10am–3pm; free), up from the quay in the basement of the town hall, which is full of stuffed specimens of the majestic animal and sealskin-covered furniture. The society's museum tells the story of Hammerfest as a trapping centre and of its own dubious history as an organization that hunted and trapped polar bears, eagles and arctic foxes. They'll try and cajole you into supporting the organization by becoming a member – honestly, you can live without the certificate. You could also drop by the town's most striking church, the Lutheran **Hammerfest kirke**, west of the centre on Kirkegata, an angular affair, with a large stained-glass window and no altarpiece, which dates from 1961. Another option, if the weather is good, is the short trudge up **Salen** hill for the views out across the bay and over to the nearby islands – and, as a further incentive, there's a restaurant at the top too.

Practicalities

Hammerfest is 60km off the main E6, along Hwy 94, which branches off at Skaidi. It's situated on the island of Kvaløya, which is linked to the mainland by bridge. **Buses** to and from Alta arrive and leave from down by the quay, and there are regular if infrequent connections back to the E6 for Honningsvåg/Nordkapp (change at Skaidi). The **tourist office** (daily mid-May to mid-Aug 9am–7pm; rest of the year 11am–4pm; ☎78 41 21 85) is a short walk from the quay on Strandgata and, if you are going to stay, can provide a map and information sheet. Inexpensive **accommodation** is available at the small and fussy **youth hostel** (late June to late Aug; ☎78 41 36 67; fax 94 78 20 74; 100kr, doubles ①), a twenty-minute walk from the quay at Idrettsveien 52, the road up to the top of Salen hill: from the main drag, Strandgata, turn right up Nybakken and then right again. With more disposable income, try the whopping *Hammerfest Bed and Breakfast*, on the edge of town near the hostel at Skytterveien 24 (☎78 41 15 11; fax 78 41 19 26; ③), or any of the more expensive hotels in the town centre: both the *Hammerfest Hotel*, Strandgata 2 (☎78 41 16 22; fax 78 41 21 27; ④), and more especially the *Rica Hotel Hammerfest*, Sørøygata 15 (☎78 41 13 33; fax 78 41 13 11; ③/④), are perfectly adequate modern hotels with comfortable rooms. There are also a couple of **campsites** with **cabins**: the lakeside *NAF Camping Storvannet* (June to mid-Sept; ☎78 41 10 10; fax 78 41 36 20), a fifteen-minute walk east from the centre out by the sports stadium, has four-bed cabins, while the *Hammerfest Turistsenter* (mid-May to Sept; ☎78 41 11 26), 1500m south of the centre, offers two-bed cabins and rooms (③).

Honningsvåg and Nordkapp

Although **HONNINGSVÅG** is a good bit closer to the North Pole than Hammerfest, it's officially classified as a village, robbing it of the title of the world's northernmost town – hard luck, considering it's barely any smaller nor less hardy in the face of adversity, sitting as it does on the southeast coast of the treeless and windswept island of Magerøya. Yet Honningsvåg has little of the prettiness of its neighbour, being no more than an average fishing village that's only of interest to travellers for its proximity to Nordkapp, 34km away at the northern tip of Magerøya – which, given the hit-and-miss nature of transport in these parts, may mean an overnight stay. This will give you time to drop by the **Nordkapphuset**, next to the bus station, a community and exhibition centre whose staff are exceptionally keen to show you around the small **museum** of local history and culture (mid-June to mid-Aug Mon–Fri 9am–8pm, Sun 1–8pm; rest of the year Mon–Fri 11am–4pm; 20kr). The **tourist office** (same hours; ☎78 47 25 99) is also based here.

Honningsvåg is reached via the E69, which branches off the E6. It's accessible by **bus** from Alta and Hammerfest (change at Skaidi), both around 200km away, as well as Lakselv, with services crossing on the **ferry** from Kåfjord (Jan to mid-May and late Aug to Oct 6 daily; no ferry Oct–Dec; early June to early Aug 16 daily; mid-May to early June and mid-Aug 10 daily; 40min; 34kr, car & driver 107kr). Honningsvåg is also a **coastal steamer** stop, and coming this way you'll arrive at either 5.30pm (northbound) or around 5am (southbound). The journey will be easier and faster when the tunnel linking Magerøya with the mainland is completed – scheduled for 1998.

In terms of **accommodation**, Honningsvåg has a trio of modern, comfortable hotels, including the *Nordkapp Hotel*, footsteps from the bus station at Nordkappgata 4 (☎78 47 23 33; fax 78 47 33 79; ④), and the *Hotel Havly*, about 400m east along the harbour at Storgata 12 (☎78 47 29 66; fax 78 47 30 10; ③). For **food**, there are several sea-sonal takeaway kiosks along Storgata; the *Hotel Havly* has an inexpensive café; and the *Nordkapp Hotel* has a reasonably good restaurant.

Outside of Honningsvåg, there's an unenjoyable **youth hostel/campsite/cabin** com-plex (☎78 47 33 77; fax 78 47 11 77; late May to late Sept; 100kr, doubles ①) 8km away on the road to Nordkapp – and just 50m from the bus stop (see below). Booking is essen-tial for the hostel, which, housed in a wooden chalet, is very basic indeed; camping facil-ities, by contrast, are excellent. Right next door is the *Rica Hotel Nordkapp* (☎78 47 33 88; fax 78 47 32 33; ③/④), with a good if pricey **restaurant**. Three more **campsites** are to be found in a much more attractive setting some 12km further north on the road into the tranquil fishing village of Skarsvåg. Two of them have cabins – *Kirkeporten Camping* (☎78 47 52 33; fax 78 47 52 47) and *Midnattsol Camping/Kro* (☎78 47 52 13; fax 78 47 52 13). If you do stay outside Honningsvåg and are dependent on public transport, note the early departure times of certain **buses** and **ferries**: the southbound coastal steamer leaves Honninsvåg shortly after 6.45am, the first bus to Lakselv at 7am – so you may need to book an early taxi (*Nordkapp Taxisentral;* ☎78 47 22 34).

Nordkapp

Although **Nordkapp** is the real goal, hiking at least some of the winding road out there from Honningsvåg can be rewarding. The road, the last section of the E69, twists its solitary way up from the village and then heads across the tundra of the plateau, with the mountains stretching away on either side. From June to October this is pastureland for herds of reindeer, who graze right up to the road, paying the occasional hiker little heed until they get very close – unlike the traffic which tends to frighten them away. The Sami, who bring them here, combine herding with souvenir selling, setting up camp at the roadside in full costume to peddle clothes, jewellery and antler sets, which many travellers are daft enough to attach to the front of their vehicles.

When visitors finally reach the Nordkapp, many feel desperately disappointed – it is, after all, only a 307-metre-high cliff – but for others there's something about this grey-ish-black hunk of slate, stuck at the end of a bare, wind-battered promontory, that exhil-arates the senses, as it must have done for those prehistoric Sami who established a sacrificial site here. Nordkapp was named (the "North Cape") by the English explorer Richard Chancellor in 1553, as he drifted along the Norwegian coast in an attempt to find the Northeast Passage from the Atlantic to the Pacific. He failed, but managed to reach the White Sea, from where he and his crew travelled overland to Moscow, there-by opening a new, northern trade route to Russia. The account of his exploits, pub-lished by the geographer Richard Hakluyt in his *Navigations*, brought Chancellor's exploits to the attention of seamen across Europe, but it was to be another three hun-dred years before the Northeast Passage was finally negotiated by the Swede Nils Nordenskjøld in 1879. In the meantime, just a trickle of visitors ventured to the North Cape until a couple of royal visitors, the exiled Louis Philippe of Orleans, the king of France, and later, in 1873, the Norwegian Oscar II, opened what was (in nineteenth-cen-tury terms) the tourist floodgates.

Nowdays the modern **North Cape Hall** (summer daily 9am–2am), cut into the rock of the Cape, contains a bank, post office (where you can get your letters specially stamped), exhibitions, souvenir shop and restaurant, and offers – weather permitting – superb views out to sea from a panoramic viewpoint, though you may prefer to absorb the atmosphere by simply walking out along the cliffs.

Getting there

Honningsvåg is the last stop before **Nordkapp** (the North Cape), and there's a variety of ways to travel the final 34km to what is generally, if inaccurately, regarded as

Europe's northernmost point. Something to bear in mind, however you get there, is the **fee** for visiting the Cape, currently a staggering 150kr, whether or not you stop by the North Cape Hall tourist complex (see below). It's hardly much compensation, but the ticket is valid for two days and gives free parking. To dodge the expense and providing you have at least some experience of wilderness hiking, you could instead walk to the actual tip of Europe, the headland of **Knivskjellodden**, which stretches about 1500m further north than its famous neighbour, and is reached along a footpath from the Nordkapp road, a two- to three-hour hike each way.

Nordkapp is, as you might expect, much easier to reach. If you've arrived at Honningsvåg by **coastal steamer**, your best bet is to catch the special coach that gets you there and back within the two-hour stopover. From late May through August, there's also a **bus** connecting Honningsvåg and Nordkapp four times daily (first one to Nordkapp at 11.50am; the last one arriving back in Honningsvåg at 2am); this costs around 100kr return, not including the Nordkapp entrance fee. Other options for getting there include **car rental** – check with the Honningsvåg tourist office for special deals that give four hours' rental for around 600kr – or a **taxi**: these leave from Honningsvåg quayside and charge around 600kr for the return trip, including an hour spent at the Cape. During **winter** access is difficult. The road is closed from November to May or thereabouts, depending on the snow (and the ferry doesn't run to Magerøya from Oct to Dec), but the adventurous are still able to get to Nordkapp by hiring a snowmobile and driver – details from the tourist office. Pick a cloudless "night" if you can, to stand any chance of seeing the Northern Lights.

East to Kirkenes and the Russian border

East of Nordkapp the landscape is more of the same, a bleak and relentless expanse of ocean and barren plateaux. Occasionally the picture is relieved by a determined village commanding sweeping views over the fjords that slice into the mainland, but generally there is little here for the eyes of a tourist. Neither is there anything much to do in what are predominantly fishing and industrial settlements, and there are few tangible attractions beyond the sheer impossibility of the chill wilderness. This in itself can be fascinating, however: it's difficult to feel further estranged from regular western comforts, and after a while the alien scenery becomes strangely compelling.

The most spectacular way to travel is by the **coastal steamer** as far as Kirkenes (from where it then returns to Bergen; see p.162). This also saves you the problem of finding somewhere to stay: **accommodation** is very thin on the ground, being confined to a handful of the larger communities. Campsites are more frequent and most have cabins for rent, but they are geared towards car travellers and are often stuck out in the middle of nowhere. **Buses** run regularly but usually only once a day and not at all overnight, which makes it prudent to plan ahead and book accommodation in advance. Distances are wearyingly long – Hammerfest to Kirkenes is 500km – so it's well worth considering a **standby flight** as a method of getting at least one way quickly: Tromsø to Kirkenes is perhaps the most useful connection, from where you can slowly make your way back west.

The land route east: Lakselv and Tana Bru

The main land route east is via the **E6 Arctic Highway**. This is also the route followed by the *Nord-Norge Ekspressen*, which runs up from Alta, through **Skaidi** (for Hammerfest) and past the turning to the Nordkapp, before continuing south to Lakselv and Karasjok and then turning east for Kirkenes. From Honningsvåg, you can pick the bus up in either Skaidi for points south, or Lakselv for destinations east.

LAKSELV is an unenticing fishing port at the head of the enormous Porsangenfjord, but it does have first-rate fishing on the river (*Lakselv* means salmon river), a small airport from where you can fly to Kirkenes and Tromsø amongst several domestic destinations, and three **hotels** including the standard issue, modern *Lakselv Hotell Best Western*, on Karasjokveien (☎78 46 10 66; fax 78 46 12 99; ③). From Lakselv, the E6 ploughs on south the 75km to Karasjok (see p.334) and then heads 180km east to **TANA BRU**, a Sami settlement (with a couple of campsites and a primitive hotel) around the suspension bridge over the River Tana, one of Europe's best salmon rivers, which sweeps down to the Tanafjord and the Barents Sea. Beyond the village, the E6 follows the southern shore of the **Varangerfjord**, a bleak, weather-beaten run, all colour and vegetation confined to the opposite coastline, with its scattered farms and painted fishing boats. As the road swings inland, it's something of a relief to arrive in Kirkenes (see below).

The sea route east: by coastal steamer

Few people journey beyond Nordkapp to the fishing villages on Norway's far northeast coast and, frankly, unless you are travelling by ship, it's a long ride just to say you have been there. The *Hurtigrute* **coastal steamer**, on the other hand, steers a fine route round the top of the country, nudging its way between tiny islets and bony bluffs, and stopping at the tiny villages of Berlevåg and Båtsfjord, which sit amid a landscape of eerie green and grey rock and cliff, splashes of colour in a land otherwise stripped by the elements. Further on, after pausing at **Vardø**, an interesting place where you might consider an overnight stay, the boat drops by the mundane town of Vadsø before crossing the deep blue waters of the Varangerfjord on the last stage of its journey to Kirkenes (see below). There's snow on the mainland here even in July, which makes for a picturesque chug across the fjord, the odd fishing boat the only thing in sight.

Vardø

With a population of just 3000, **VARDØ** is Norway's most easterly town, built on an island a couple of kilometres from the mainland, to which it's connected by an underwater tunnel. The town's main attraction, located about 1km to the west of the centre and the *Hurtigrute* quay, is the **Vardøhus Festning** (guided tours June–Aug), a star-shaped fortress built in the 1730s at the behest of Christian VI, a singularly unprepossessing monarch who toured Finnmark receiving, according to one of his courtiers, "expressions of abject flattery in atrocious verse". Vardø fortress was constructed to guard the northeastern approaches to the country, but it has never seen active service and its bastions and ramparts have survived pretty much intact. Scrambling around them is good fun, and Vardø's one and only **tree**, a rowan sheltering inside the fortress, is a reminder of what's missing from the flat and barren landscape outside. In fact, Vardø is the only Norwegian town within the Arctic climatic zone, hardly much consolation when you can see your breath on a bright but perishingly cold June afternoon. Within the fortress walls, there is also a small **museum** (mid-June to mid-Aug Mon–Fri 9am–6pm, Sat & Sun 10.30am–6pm; rest of the year Mon–Fri 8.30am–3pm; 20kr), which contains a beam from an earlier medieval stronghold, signed by a later succession of Norwegian kings. Incidentally, these far northern territories were long regarded by the Church as the realm of the Devil, and one of the consequences was that Vardø was the site of Norway's largest late-medieval witch hunt, with over eighty women burned alive, most meeting their deaths at a stake in the fortress grounds.

En route to Kirkenes, the *Hurtigrute* **coastal steamer** reaches Vardø at 5.45am and leaves just thirty minutes later, and heading west it docks here at 5pm and departs at 6pm – not nearly enough time to make it to the fortress and back. You can, however, stay the night. The only central **accommodation** is the no-frills *Gjestegården* pension,

Strandgata 72 (☎78 98 75 29; ① including breakfast), where advance reservations are essential. Otherwise, there's the *Vardo Hotell* (☎78 98 77 61; fax 78 98 83 97; ②) and a **campsite**, *Svartnes Camping* (☎78 98 71 60), on the mainland not far from the tunnel. Incidentally, note that there is no through road west of Vardø, and if travelling **by bus** you will have to return the way you came – along Hwy 98 to Vadsø.

Kirkenes

During World War II the mining town of **KIRKENES** suffered more bomb attacks than any other place in Europe apart from Malta. What was left was torched by the German army retreating in the face of liberating Soviet soldiers, who found 3500 local people hiding in the nearby iron ore mines. The mines are still working and provide the obvious prosperity in what is almost entirely a brand new town, with rows of uniform wooden houses arranged around a central grid behind the harbour.

If it sounds grim, it's not to slight Kirkenes, which has certainly suffered. In fact, it's rather an intriguing town, with some pleasant gardens and residential areas, its surroundings seen to best advantage as you edge in by steamer. It's also one of the few towns in the world which it seems almost churlish to leave quickly, given the effort involved in reaching it. Having arrived, the very least most people do is attempt a short trip across (or to) the nearby border with Russia.

In the town itself, it's worth searching out the **Savio Museum**, housed in the old library in the middle of a residential area at Kongens gate 10b (mid-June to mid-Aug daily 10am–6pm; rest of the year Mon–Fri 10am–4pm; 20kr). This small museum displays the work of the Sami artist John Savio, born in the town in 1902. The artist's particularly tragic life – he was orphaned at the age of three, was ill from childhood, and died in poverty of tuberculosis aged 37– brings a poignancy to the woodcuts he created, which depict Sami life and study loneliness and the power of nature. The museum also hosts contemporary art exhibitions, as does the Norwegian-Russian Art Centre (**Norsk Russisk Kunstsenter**; summer only; ☎78 99 35 80), at Dr. Wessels gate 9.

Practicalities

Kirkenes is the end of the line for both bus and steamer. The **Hurtigrute coastal steamer** spends two hours here every morning preparing for the return journey to Bergen; it docks at a quay just over 1km from the centre. From the **bus station**, down at the central harbour, the *Nord-Norge Ekspressen* leaves daily at 9.15am for Karasjok/Alta. Other buses make the trip to Vadsø and the **airport** (☎78 99 87 08), about 12km west of town. The **tourist office** (June–Aug 8.30am–7pm; Sept-May Mon–Fri 8.30am–4pm; ☎78 99 25 44; fax 78 99 25 25) is in the centre, next to the *Rica Arctic Hotel* at Kongens gate 1, and can provide you with a map and book you a **private room**, though these are rarely convenient for the centre.

The only centrally located budget **accommodation** is the basic *Stenby's Overnatting*, at Riiser Larsens gate 10 (☎78 99 08 20; ①), which has just a few beds available. Or grit your teeth and pay up for the *Rica Arctic Hotel*, Kongens gate 1 (☎78 99 29 29; fax 78 99 11 59; ③/④). You need to book ahead to stay at the **youth hostel** (☎78 99 88 11; mid-June to mid-Aug; 130kr, doubles ①) in Hesseng, some 6km out of town on the E6. There's a **campsite** there too – *Kirkenes Camping* (☎78 99 80 28; fax 78 99 80 28; July–Sept).

The Russian border

The nearest point on the **Russian border** is only 16km southeast of Kirkenes. You can now take photographs of the frontier, provided you don't snap any Russian personnel or military installations – which rather limits the options as there's little else to see. There is a road over into Russia – via the *Storskog grensestasjon* (border station) – but it's not open to casual day-trippers; anyway, the only convenient settlement is the ugly Russian mining town of Nikel, around 60km to the south.

Kirkenes tourist office does, however, have details of more promising **day and weekend tours** into Russia, though most of the more worthwhile trips have to be booked at least ten days in advance. The majority of these trips include the price of a visa – although you'll need to double check this – hence the need for advance booking; reserve a place fewer than ten days ahead and you may be struggling to get it all sorted out, or be charged more for a faster visa service.

Of the companies operating short excursions to **Murmansk**, the best is *Finnmark Fylkesrederi & Ruteselskap (FFR)*, whose head office is in Hammerfest (☎78 41 10 00; fax 78 41 46 55). They run the only *Hurtigbåt* express boat service from Kirkenes to Murmansk (late June to early Aug Mon–Sat 1 daily; 4hr 30min; advance booking essential) and charge 1190kr for the whole day-long trip, including visa, sightseeing and Russian dinner. Try also *Sovjetreiser AS,* Storgata 1, Kirkenes (☎78 99 19 81; fax 78 99 11 42), who offer a one-day Murmansk coach trip for 800kr excluding visa. Otherwise, you'll have to be content with the reflection that if you have made it to Kirkenes and the border, you are further east than Istanbul and as far north as central Greenland.

Svalbard

The **Svalbard archipelago** must be one of the most inhospitable places on earth. Six hundred and forty kilometres north of the Norwegian mainland (and just 1300km from the North Pole), two-thirds of the surface is covered by glaciers, the soil frozen up to a depth of 500m. It was probably discovered in the twelfth century by Icelandic seamen, though it lay ignored until 1596 when the Dutch explorer Willem Barents named the archipelago's main island, **Spitzbergen**, after its "needle-like" mountains. However, apart from a smattering of determined adventurers – from seventeenth-century whalers to eighteenth-century monks – few people had lived here until, in 1899, rich coal deposits were discovered, the geological residue of a lush, tropical forest. The first coal mine opened seven years later and passed from American into Norwegian hands in 1916. Meanwhile, other countries, particularly Russia and Sweden, were getting in on the coal mining act, and when, in 1925, Norway's sovereignty over the archipelago was ratified by international treaty, it was on condition that those other countries who were operating mines could continue to do so. It was also agreed that the islands would be a demilitarized zone, which made them, incidentally, sitting ducks for a German squadron that arrived here to bombard the Norwegian mines in World War II. Today, there are three Norwegian and two Russian settlements, all on the main island – around 4000 people in all.

Despite the hardships, there are convincing reasons to make a trip to this oddly fertile land, which covers around 63,000 square kilometres. Between late April and late August there's continuous daylight; the snow has virtually all melted by July, leaving the valleys covered in flowers; and there's an abundance of wildlife – over a hundred species of migratory birds, arctic foxes, polar bears and reindeer on land, and seals, walrus, even whales offshore. In winter, it's a different story. The Polar Night, when the sun never rises above the horizon, lasts from late October to mid-February; and the record low temperature is a staggering -46°C, which doesn't take into account the wind-chill factor.

Getting there

Needless to say, getting there is an expensive matter. The simplest solution is to **fly**, and *Braathens SAFE* operates services into Svalbard's airport (Longyearbyen) from a variety of Norwegian cities, including Oslo, Bergen, Trondheim and nearest of all Tromsø, on average four times weekly. *SAS* also flies there, but only from Oslo via Tromsø. The

Tromsø–Longyearbyen flight takes an hour and forty minutes and a standard fare with *Braathens SAFE* is about 2290kr return, though special deals can reduce this to around 1700kr.

Adventure "**cruises**" (polar bear spotting and the like) mostly depart from Tromsø: contact the Tromsø tourist office, the Norwegian Tourist Board or *Info-Svalbard*, Postboks 323, N9170 Longyearbyen (☎79 02 23 03; fax 79 02 10 20), for more information. There are many sorts of tour to choose from, so it's difficult to provide guidelines as to price, but in general terms you can expect an all-inclusive, week-long boat trip from Tromsø to cost in the region of 25,000kr, while a four-day flight and accommodation deal from Tromsø to Longyearbyen will be in the region of 4500kr.

It's also possible to organize a tour before you leave home; see the "Getting There" sections in *Basics* for lists of operators.

Longyearbyen and around

Huddled on the narrow coastal plain beside the Isfjorden and below the mountains, **LONGYEARBYEN** lies roughly in the middle of the main island, Spitzbergen, and is the only real Norwegian settlement of any size, with just over 1000 inhabitants. It was founded in 1906, when John M. Longyear, an American mine-owner, established the Arctic Coal Company here, the first to begin production on the archipelago. Longyearbyen now has several shops, five cafés, a cinema, post office, bank, swimming pool, several tour companies, a campsite, youth hostel, guesthouse and three hotels – but note that advance reservations are essential for all accommodation.

The **airport** is 5km from the town; both *Braathens SAFE* (☎79 02 19 22) and *SAS* (☎79 02 16 50) have offices there. The *DNT*-run **campsite** (☎79 02 24 84; late June to early Sept) is next door to the airport, but beware that you'll need to be fully equipped to survive what can be, at any time of the year, a cruel climate. An airport bus runs from the airport into town (30kr), or you can telephone *Maxi-Taxi* (☎79 02 13 05). There's reasonably priced accommodation in the town centre at the unassuming *Svalbard Kro & Hotell* (☎79 02 13 00; fax 79 02 18 06; ③), and nearby is the comparatively swish and newly built *Svalbard Polar Hotel* (☎79 02 35 00; fax 79 02 35 01; ④). Up the hill on the north side of the centre you'll find the functional *Funken Hotel* (☎79 02 24 50; fax 79 02 10 05; ④); beyond here, on the edge of town, are the *Nybyen Gjestehus* (March–Sept; ②), whose simple but adequate rooms occupy refurbished miners' quarters dating from the 1940s, and the **youth hostel** (April–Sept; ①) – both can be booked on the same telephone and fax numbers as the *Funken*. For **eating** you're pretty much limited to the straightforward *Kafé Busen*; the *Longyearbyen Grill og Restaurant* ("*Huset*"), specializing in Arctic dishes, which is across the river on the north side of town, along with a bar and the cinema; or one of the hotel restaurants. The liveliest hang-out is the *Funken Bar*, open till around 11pm, later at weekends.

Trips around Longyearbyen

The real difficulty for the independent traveller is getting around: there's not much point in making the trip only to be stuck in your lodgings. There are four **other settlements** apart from Longyearbyen: **Ny Ålesund** to the northwest and **Sveagruva** to the southeast; and the Russian settlements of **Barentsburg** and **Pyramiden** to the west and north respectively. But there are no road connections, and the only public transport, apart from the airport bus, is a pricey air service to Ny Ålesund. When you also consider that travellers leaving Longyearbyen have to seek permission from, and log their itineraries with, the governor's office, *Sysselmannen på Svalbard*, in Longyearbyen (☎79 02 31 00), and are strongly advised to take a gun (mainly because of the polar bears), you can see the difficulties involved – and understand why the vast majority of visitors opt for a package. It is possible to book onto a **tour** when you arrive, but remember that they are often fully booked months in advance, while prices for individual excursions are prohibitive – primarily because transport is by helicopter, boat or snow-scooter. For advice, contact – preferably by writing, in advance – Longyearbyen's *Info-Svalbard*, Postboks 323, N9170 Longyearbyen (☎79 02 23 03; fax 79 02 10 20), which has details of everything from skiing, hiking and mountaineering tours through to fossil-hunting, boat trips and wildlife "safaris." The largest travel and tour agency in Longyearbyen is *Spitsbergen Travel AS (SpiTra)*, at the *Funken Hotel* (☎79 02 24 50; fax 79 02 10 05).

travel details

Buses

From Alta to: Bodø (1 daily; 15hr); Fauske (1 daily; 14hr); Hammerfest (1 daily; 3hr); Honningsvåg (1 daily; 5hr); Karasjok (1 daily; 5hr); Kautokeino (1 daily; 3hr); Kirkenes (1 daily; 9hr 45min); Lakselv (1 daily; 4hr); Murmansk, Russia (1 daily; 14hr); Narvik (1 daily; 10hr); Oslo (1–2 weekly; 29hr); Skaidi (1daily; 1hr 40min); Tana Bru (1 daily; 8hr 30min); Tromsø (1 daily; 7hr).

From Hammerfest to: Alta (May–Oct 1–2 daily; 3hr); Honningsvåg (Mon–Sat 2 daily, Sun 1; 4hr 20min); Oslo (2 weekly; 29hr); Skaidi (Mon–Sat 2 daily, Sun 1; 1hr 15min).

From Honningsvåg to: Alta (2 daily; 4hr); Bodø (2 daily; 16hr 30min); Fauske (2 daily; 14hr); Lakselv (2 daily; 4hr); Narvik (2 daily; 8hr); Nordkapp (1st week June to 1st week Aug 4 daily; 10 days either side 1–2 daily; 50min).

From Karasjok to: Hammerfest (1 daily; 4hr 30min); Kirkenes (1 daily; 6hr).

From Kautokeino to: Alta (3 weekly; 1hr 40min); Karasjok (Mon, Wed, Fri & Sun 1 daily; 2hr 15min).

From Kirkenes to: Alta (1 daily; 11hr); Karasjok (1 daily; 5hr 30min); Vadsø (1–2 daily; 3hr 30min).

From Lakselv to: Honningsvåg (2 daily; 4hr).

From Nordkojsbotn to: Alta (1 daily; 11hr).

From Tromsø to: Alta (1 daily; 7hr); Kiruna, Sweden (Summer only 1 weekly; 6hr 30min);

Narvik (2-4 daily; 5hr 30min); Nordkjosbotn (3–5 daily; 1hr 30min).

From Vadsø to: Vardø (1 daily; 1hr 30min).

The *Hurtigrute* Coastal Steamer

The daily *Hurtigrute* service departs

Northbound: Tromsø at 3.15pm; Honningsvåg at 5.30pm; Hammerfest at 8pm; Båtsfjord at 3am; Vadsø (Tues, Thurs & Sun only) at 10am; terminates in Kirkenes at either 9.30am or 11.45am.

Southbound: Vadsø (Mon, Wed, Fri & Sat only) at 1.45pm; Båtsfjord at 9.15pm; Honningsvåg 6.45am; Hammerfest 1.15pm; Tromsø at 1.30am.

Journey time from Tromsø to Kirkenes is 43hr.

Ferries

From Kåfjord to: Honningsvåg (June to mid-Aug 11 daily; rest of the year 6 daily; 45min). Two of these ferries daily carry the bus to Nordkapp.

Express passenger boats (*Hurtigbåt*)

From Hammerfest to: Honningsvåg (mid-June to early Aug 2 daily; 2hr 10min).

From Honningsvåg to: Lakselv (late June to early Aug 1 daily; 2hr 30min).

From Kirkenes to: Murmansk (early July to early Aug Mon–Sat 1 daily; 4hr 30min).

From Tromsø to: Harstad (1 daily; 2hr 30min).

PART FOUR

SWEDEN

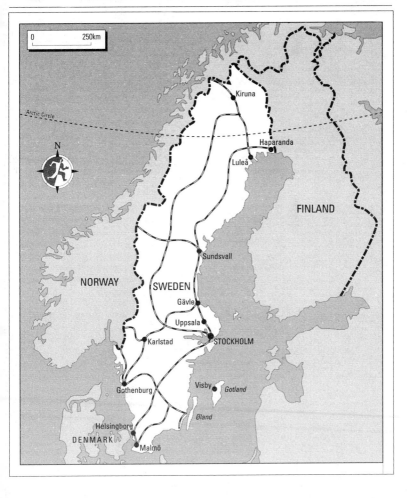

Introduction

Sweden lolls contentedly within an endless natural beauty. Remote, expensive, cold – all of these generalizations may be true, but none is exact. However, Sweden *is* large, clean and efficient and, as it boasts no single concentration of sights (other than in Stockholm), you're as likely to fetch up on a sunny Baltic beach as camp in the forest or hike through national parks.

One aspect of the country most likely to impinge on the cluttered eye of Europeans is the sense of space. Away from the relatively densely populated south, travelling without seeing a soul is not uncommon, and taking in these vast, unpopulated stretches in a limited time can be exhausting – and unrewarding. Better, on a short trip, to delve into one or two regions and experience the atmosphere, to get to know the pervasive nature that shapes the Swedes' attitude to life: once you have broken through the oft-quoted reserve of the people there is a definite emotive feel to the country. And initial contact is easy, as almost everyone speaks functional, often perfect, English.

■ Where to go

The **south and southwest** of the country are flat holiday lands. For so long disputed Danish territory (which the landscape certainly resembles), the provinces now harbour a host of historic ports (including **Gothenburg**, **Helsingborg** and **Malmö**) and less frenetic beach towns – all old and mostly fortified. Off the **southeast** coast, the Baltic islands of **Öland** and **Gotland** are the country's most hyped resorts – and with good reason, supporting a lazy beach life to match that of the best southern European spots, but without the hotel blocks, crowds and tat.

Central and northern Sweden is the country of tourist brochures: great swathes of forest, inexhaustible (around 96,000) lakes and some of the best wilderness hiking in Europe. Two train routes link north with south. The eastern run, close to the **Bothnian coast**, passes old wood-built towns and planned new ones, and ferry ports for connections to Finland. In the centre, the trains of the **Inland Railway** strike off through some remarkably changing landscapes, lakelands to mountains, clearing reindeer off the track as they go. Both routes meet in Sweden's **far north** – home of the Sami, the oldest indigenous Scandinavian people. Here, the Midnight Sun keeps the days long and bright; and in high summer, the sun never sets.

Of the cities, **Stockholm** is supreme. A bundle of islands housing regal and monumental architecture, fine museums and the country's most active culture and nightlife, it is a likely point of arrival and a vital stop-off. Two university towns, **Uppsala** and **Lund**, also demand a visit, while nearly all of the other major cities, chiefly Gävle, Umeå, Gällivare and Kiruna, can make some sort of cultural claim on your attention. Time is rarely wasted in humbler towns either, the immediate beauty of the local surroundings adequately compensating for any lack of specific sights.

■ When to go

Summer in Sweden is short and hectic. From rowdy Midsummer's Night onwards, accommodation is scarce and trains packed as Swedes head out to the country and onto the beaches. Outside the peak month of **July**, things are noticeably quieter. To avoid the rush, September and late May are both usually bright and warm. The **Midnight Sun** extends the days in June and July, and above the Arctic Circle it virtually never gets dark. Elsewhere it stays light until very late, up to midnight and beyond. Thanks to the Gulf Stream, temperatures in Sweden are surprisingly high – see the temperature chart on p.xiii – and on the south coast it can be as hot as any southern European resort.

Winter, on the other hand, can be a miserable experience without the proper clothing. It lasts a long time (November to April solid) and gets very cold indeed: temperatures of -15°C and below are not unusual even in Stockholm. Further north it is positively arctic. The days are short and dark (in the far north the sun barely rises at all) and biting winds cut through the most elaborate of padded coats. On the plus side, the snow stays crisp and white, the air is clean, the water everywhere frozen solid: a paradise for skaters and skiers. Stockholm, too, is particularly beautiful with its winter covering of snow and ice.

Getting There

The cheapest Scandinavian connection with Sweden is from Denmark, by bus and ferry, and regular trains and ferries connect other mainland countries.

■ Trains

There are four possible **train** routes into Sweden **from Norway**. Cheapest are the five-hour run from Oslo to Gothenburg and the slightly longer route from Oslo to Stockholm; the other options are the twelve-hour ride from Trondheim to Stockholm and the day-long (23hr) haul from Narvik.

Trains **from Denmark** (Copenhagen) to Gothenburg or Stockholm use the Helsingør–Helsingborg ferry crossing, with the whole train taken on board – a four-and-a-half- and eight-and-a-half-hour journey respectively.

Anyone under 26 can buy a *BIJ* **ticket** for these routes and all **rail passes** are valid too. Note that a *Scanrail* train pass gives free or discounted travel on various ferry lines between Denmark or Finland and Sweden.

■ Buses

There are several useful **bus** routes into Sweden from other Scandinavian cities, though the frequent services **from Denmark** are the only ones that will get you there quickly. The easiest – and cheapest – connection is on one of the several daily buses **from Copenhagen** to Malmö/Lund, using the Dragør–Limhamn ferry crossing. The *Kystlinjen* service links Kastrup airport and Copenhagen with Helsingborg, using the ferry from Helsingør – this bus then continuing up the southwestern coast of Sweden to Halmstad to connect with trains to Gothenburg.

It's a longer haul **from Norway**, and much more expensive, too: there are several daily buses from Oslo to Gothenburg, the journey taking five or six hours; and one daily bus from Oslo to Stockholm, a nine-hour ride. **From Finland** most routes converge upon Helsinki or Turku and then use the ferry crossings to Stockholm; departures are at least once daily.

■ Ferries and catamarans

Ferry or **catamaran** services to Sweden are plentiful, but can be confusing – not least because several operators run rival services on the same route. To make any sense of the timetables and prices, which change from year to year, check the companies' brochures at any local tourist office. You'll find other details – frequencies and journey times – in the "Travel Details" at the end of each chapter.

In addition, rail passes give **discounts and free travel** on some of the ferry routes. The *Scanrail* pass currently gives free passage on ferries between Helsingør and Helsingborg, and on the Turku–Stockholm and Fredrikshavn–Gothenburg crossings; a 50 percent discount on the routes Helsinki–Stockholm (*Silja Line* only), Vaasa–Umeå and Rønne-Ystad; and a 25 percent discount on the Copenhagen–Malmö route.

From Denmark

Shortest and cheapest ferry crossings are **Helsingør–Helsingborg** (25min) and **Dragør–Limhamn** near Malmö (55min); just walk on board on both ferries. There are also year-round ferry connections to Gothenburg **from Fredrikshavn**, a three-and-a-half-hour journey. And **from Grenå**, *Lion* sails daily to Varberg and Halmstad. Quicker (45min) are the catamaran services to Malmö and Helsingborg **from Copenhagen** – though these crossings are often disrupted by frozen sea between November and March.

The other approach from Denmark is to come via the Danish island of **Bornholm**. Ferries and catamarans from Copenhagen run to Rønne (*Scanrail* gets a 50 percent discount), from where you can cross daily to Ystad, on the southern Swedish coast.

From Finland

Longer ferry journeys link Sweden with Finland, the major crossing being the **Helsinki–Stockholm** route, a fourteen-hour trip with either *Silja* or *Viking*. There are also regular crossings **from Turku** and **from Mariehamn** in the Finnish Åland Islands to Stockholm. If you're aiming for the north of Sweden, then you might be better crossing **from Vaasa**: there are year-round services to Umeå, a journey of four hours.

From Norway

There is one crossing from Norway to Sweden, **from Sandefjord** to Strömstad, north of Gothenburg, which operates all year round (4–5 daily; 2hr 30min).

Costs, Money and Banks

Sweden *is* expensive, but certain bargains make it a better deal than neighbouring Norway and Finland. If you don't already have a rail pass, flying on standby (at least for under-25s) is a fast and affordable option in cutting travel costs. Elsewhere, regional and city discount travel passes ease what could otherwise be a burden. Accommodation, too, can be good value: youth hostels cost an average of 100kr (£10/$16) a night for members (another 35kr for non-members), and are of exceptional quality; campsites are plentiful and cheap. Eating is made bearable by the daily lunch offers found throughout the country – around £5–6/$8–10 for a big, all-inclusive meal plus drink.

Put all this together and you'll find you can exist – camping, self-catering, hitching, no drinking – on around £15/$22 a day, though hardly for any length of time. Stay in hostels, eat lunch, get out and see the sights and this will rise to at least £25/$40. And to these figures add on £3.50/$6 for every drink in a bar, around £2.50/$4 for coffee and cake and £40/$65 minimum a night in a hotel – travelling like this, you're really looking at a figure of more like £60–75/$90–115 a day. Remember, though, that the countryside (and much of your camping) is free, museums usually have low (or no) admission charges and that everything everywhere is clean, bright and works.

Swedish **currency** is the *krona* (plural *kronor*), made up of 100 *öre*. It comes in coins of 50öre, 1kr, 5kr and 10kr; and notes of 10kr, 20kr, 50kr, 100kr, 500kr, 1000kr and 10,000kr. You can change money in **banks** all over Sweden, which are open Mon–Fri 9.30am–3pm, Thurs until 5.30pm, though branches in Stockholm and Gothenburg have longer summer hours (see the various city "Listings" sections). Outside normal banking hours you'll also be able to change money in exchange offices at airports and ferry terminals, and in post offices, as well as at *Forex* exchange offices – again, see the relevant "Listings" sections.

Post and Phones

Communications within Sweden are good, and as most people speak at least some English, you won't go far wrong in the post or telephone office.

Post offices are open Mon–Fri 9am–6pm, Sat 10am–1pm, with some branches closed on Saturday throughout July, Sweden's holiday month. You can buy **stamps** at post offices, most newspaper kiosks, tobacconists and hotels. **Poste restante** is available at all main post offices; take your passport along to claim mail.

For international **telephone calls** either head for the (rare) **telephone office** (*Tele* or *Telebutik*), usually open outside normal shopping hours until around 9pm daily, or dial direct from public **payphones**. This is very easy: the phones take 1kr and 5kr coins (minimum charge 2kr) and the operators all speak English. You can also pay for calls using your credit card – look out for phones marked "CCC". Note that numbers prefixed by ☎020 (often transport information numbers) are all charged at the local rate.

International dialling codes for calling **from Sweden** are given on p.23. For reverse-charge international calls, ring the **overseas operator** on ☎0018. For **directory enquiries**, dial ☎07975 for domestic numbers, ☎07977 for international enquiries.

Media

You'll easily be able to keep in touch with home by tuning into the TV – which relies heavily on English and American programmes – or listening to one of the English-language radio stations. Assuming that you don't read Swedish, you can also keep in touch with world events by buying **foreign newspapers** in the major towns and cities, sometimes on the day of issue, more usually the day after.

Swedish **TV**, as in the rest of Scandinavia, is fairly unchallenging. On top of the two Swedish state channels, *Kanal 1* and *TV2*, there's a commercial station, *TV4*, while the cable station *TV3* is shared with Denmark and Norway. There's also a whole host of satellite and other cable channels – all of which you'll end up glued to if you've blown all your money on a hotel and can't afford to go out. The good news is that imported foreign programmes are in their original language – mostly English.

On the **radio** there's national (Swedish) news in English on *Radio Sweden*: daily in summer at 1.30pm, 2.30pm, 3.30pm, 6pm, 7.30pm, 9.30pm, 10.30pm, 11pm, 11.30pm, 1am and 4.30am (throughout the country on 1179kHz MW; in Greater Stockholm on 89.6FM). Gothenburg local radio also has a daily half-hour programme in English in summer, covering the latest news and giving sightseeing tips. The BBC World Service can be picked up on 6195, 9410, 12095 or 15070 KHz short wave, or in Stockholm on 89.6FM, between 6 and 7am.

Getting Around

Sweden's internal transport system is quick and efficient and runs through all weathers. Services are often reduced in the winter (especially on northern bus routes), but it's unlikely you'll ever get stranded anywhere. In summer, when everyone is on holiday, trains and, to a lesser extent, buses are packed: making seat reservations is a good idea on long journeys.

All train, bus, ferry and plane schedules are contained within the giant **Rikstidtabellen** (timetable), of which every tourist office and travel agent has a copy. It costs 80kr and is not worth buying or carrying around; just ask for photocopies of the relevant pages.

Watch out, too, for city and regional **discount cards**. One payment gets a card valid for anything from a day up to a week, and it usually includes **unlimited local travel** (bus, tram, ferry, sometimes train), museum entry and other discounts and freebies. Often on sale during the summer only (valuable exceptions are those in Stockholm, Gothenburg and Malmö), where useful they are detailed in the text. Otherwise it's worth asking at tourist offices as schemes change frequently.

■ Trains

Swedish State Railways (*SJ* – *Statens Järnvägar*, from abroad ☎08/696 75 40, in Sweden ☎020/75 75 75) has an extensive network, running right from the far south of the country up through northern Sweden, over the Arctic Circle and across the border to Narvik into Norway. Other than flying, it's the quickest way to get around Sweden's vast expanses. The service is excellent, especially on the main routes, and prices not too expensive – a standard-class return from Stockholm to Gothenburg, for example, will cost you 505kr. Sweden is currently introducing a luxurious new high-speed train, the **X2000**, on the main inter-city routes, which can often shave a couple of hours off the normal journey time (see "Travel Details" at the end of each chapter for more information); prices are naturally higher, with a Stockholm–Gothenburg return costing 710kr.

Buying individual **train tickets** is rarely cost-effective, despite the comprehensive system of discounts, which seem to be in continual flux. If you're planning to travel a lot by train, you're gen-

erally better off buying a **train pass**, such as a multi-country *InterRail*, *Eurail* or *Scanrail* pass, which needs to be purchased before you leave home (see *Basics* for details). If you're planning to travel only in Sweden, then it might be worth considering a Sweden-only rail pass; you need to buy this before arriving in Sweden and it currently costs £130 ($210) for seven days' second-class travel, £174 ($280) for fourteen days, with supplements payable on inter-city and express services. The pass should be available from the train ticket agents detailed under "Getting There" in *Basics* – contact the Swedish tourist board (see p.27 for addresses) if you have difficulties.

If you don't have a pass, it's worth checking the latest on any special deals that may be available. Note that one-way train tickets cost half the price of returns, and that you need to make a seat reservation on inter-city services (included in the price). The main discount system is known as the **röd avgång** (red departure), as these services are marked with a red dot in the timetables; on the days they're available, they give a range of discounts depending on the distance travelled. To use the discount you need to have a **reslustkort** (literally, a Wanderlust Card), which costs 150kr and covers two people for a year. On long **overnight** train journeys it's worth paying out for a couchette or a sleeping car. Prices are low, with six-berth couchettes costing only 85k per person, slightly more on international services. Sleepers, where available, start at around 200kr for a two-berth compartment.

One booklet worth picking up is the *SJ Tågtider* **timetable**, which costs 10kr from any train station. Published twice yearly, this is an accurate and comprehensive list of the most useful train services in the country. Otherwise, each train route has its own timetable leaflet, available free from the local station.

The Inlandsbanan

If you're in the country for any length of time at all, then travelling at least a section of the **Inlandsbanan** (Inland Railway) is a must: a single track route, it runs for over 1300km from central Sweden to arctic Gällivare. The line was saved from closure after it was bought by the local authorities along its length, but it now operates from June to August only. *InterRail* and *Scanrail* passes get a 50 percent discount – buy your ticket on the train. No reservations are possible, and timetables vary from year to year: get the latest information by calling ☎063/12 76 95 (fax 10 15 90).

The Pågatågen

In Skåne in southern Sweden, a local private company, **Pågatågen**, operates trains between Helsingborg, Lund and Malmö, and Ystad and Simrishamn. These are fully automated and you buy your tickets from a machine on the platform which accepts coins and notes. Prices on the short hops are low; *InterRail* cards are valid, and the *Scanrail* gets a 50 percent discount.

■ Buses

The main **long-distance bus** companies are *Swebus* (☎020/64 06 40) and *Svenska Buss* (☎020/67 67 67), which operate express routes between large towns, and to and from Stockholm. There are two types of bus: *Expressbussar* run daily, complementing rather than competing with the train system, while the cheaper *Veckoslutsbussar* often only run at weekends (usually Fri & Sun). Fares range from 20kr to 350kr, depending on the distance travelled. In the north there are also many regional bus companies, charging 100–150kr for a one- to two-hour journey. Major routes are listed in the "Travel Details" at the end of each chapter and you can pick up a comprehensive **timetable** at any bus terminal.

Local buses, too, are frequent and regular. Count on using them, as many hostels and campsites are a fair distance from town centres. Flat fares cost 10–15kr, the ticket usually valid for an hour. Most large towns operate some sort of discount system where you can buy cheaper books of tickets – details from the local tourist office and in the text.

Planes

The **plane** network is operated by *SAS* and several smaller companies, such as *Transwede* and *Skyways*, and various deals can make flying a real steal, especially those long slogs north. Average return fares are 1000–1500kr but **under-25s** can fly on standby anywhere in Sweden for 280kr per one-way journey. **Children** under 2 travel free. Most of these fares have to be booked in advance – more details from local travel agents and tourist offices. It's also worth considering an **air pass**, which you'll need to buy in conjunction with your ticket to Scandinavia – *SAS* do one that's valid on all their routes in Sweden, Denmark, Norway and Finland; *Transwede* offer a Nordic air pass, though it's less useful if you're only travelling only in Sweden, where they only fly a handful of routes. See *Basics* for more information.

■ Ferries

Unlike Norway and Finland, domestic **ferry** services in Sweden are few. The various archipelagos on the southeast coast are served by small ferries, the most comprehensive network being within the **Stockholm archipelago**, for which you can buy an island-hopping boat pass – see p.407 for more details. The other major link is between the Baltic island of **Gotland** and the mainland (at Nynäshamn and Oskarshamn), very popular routes in summer for which you should really book ahead. There are discounts for rail pass holders; see p.519 for details on routes. With your own boat it's possible to cross Sweden between Stockholm and Gothenburg on the **Göta Canal** or, alternatively, you can take an expensive cruise along the same route; ticket and journey details are given on p.513. Cheaper day cruises are possible along stretches of the Göta Canal and the Trollhättan Canal; more details are given in the text.

■ Cars, hitching and taxis

Driving presents few problems since roads are good and generally reliable. The only real danger are the reindeer (in the north) and elk (north and further south) that wander onto roads. Watch out in bad light particularly – if you hit one, you'll know about it. As for **documentation**, you need a full licence and the vehicle registration document; an international driving licence and insurance "green card" are not essential. **Speed limits** are 110kph on motorways, 90kph and 70kph on other roads, 50kph in built-up areas. It's compulsory to use **dipped headlights** during daylight hours (on rented cars they will probably come on automatically); and, if you are taking your own car from Britain, remember to get the beam of your headlights adjusted to suit **driving on the right**. If you're motoring into northern Sweden then it's recommended that you fit mud flaps to your wheels and stone guards on the front of caravans. Swedish **drink/driving laws** are among the toughest in Europe and random breath tests the norm. Even the smallest amount of alcohol can lead to lost licences (always), fines (often) and prison sentences (not infrequently).

If you **break down**, call either the police or the *Larmtjänst* (listed in the phone directory), a 24-hour rescue organization run by Swedish insurance companies. You should only use the emergency telephone number (☎112) in the event of an accident.

Car rental and petrol

Car rental is uniformly expensive, though most companies have special weekend tourist rates – from around 500kr, Friday to Monday, for a small car. It's worth checking out local tourist offices in the summer, as they sometimes recommend or operate reasonable weekly deals; otherwise, expect to pay around 3000kr a week, unlimited mileage, for a *VW Golf* or similar-sized car in the summer months. The major international companies are represented in all the large towns and cities – details under the various city "Listings".

Fuel currently costs around 8kr per litre; lead-free fuel is widely available and slightly cheaper. Most filling stations are self-service (*Tanka Själv*) and lots of them have automatic pumps (*Sedel Automat*), where you can fill up at any time using 100kr and 20kr notes.

Hitching and taxis

Despite the amount of holiday traffic and the number of young Swedes with cars, **hitching** is rarely worth the effort, as long-distance lifts are few and far between. Shorter hops are easier to find, especially when travelling along the coasts and in the north, but not having to rely upon hitching as your main means of transport is the best bet. If you do try it, always use a sign and be prepared for long waits.

Taxis are no bargain anywhere. A three-kilometre ride will set you back around 100kr and there's a minimum charge of around 35kr. If you order a taxi by phone, that adds another 30kr to the total – all in all, taxis are worth avoiding in cities where the public transport systems are excellent.

■ Cycling

A much better way to get around independently is to **cycle**. Some parts of the country were made for it, the southern provinces (and Gotland in particular) ideal for a leisurely pedal. Many towns are best explored by bike, and tourist offices, campsites and youth hostels often rent out machines from around 80kr a day, 400kr a week. If you're touring, be prepared for long-distance hauls in the north and for rain in summer. Taking a bike on a train is no simple matter: it will cost you 125kr and you need to hand it in three days in advance of your journey.

The *Svenska Cykelsällskapet* (cycling association; Box 6006, S-164 06 Kista, Stockholm; ☎08/751 6204; fax 751 1935) signposts **cycle routes** in central and southern Sweden; and there's an English-language **guidebook** to cycling in Sweden, available from *Cykelfrämjandet*, Box 6027, S-102 31 Stockholm (☎08/32 16 80). Also, contact the *STF* (see below) for details of cycling package holidays in Sweden, which include youth hostel accommodation, meals and bike rental.

Accommodation

Surprisingly, finding somewhere cheap to sleep is not the hassle that might be expected in an otherwise expensive country – provided you're prepared to do some advance planning. There's an excellent network of youth hostels and campsites, while private rooms and bed and breakfast places are common in the cities. Year-round discounts even make hotels affordable, an option certainly worth considering in the large cities where a city discount card is thrown in as part of the package.

■ Hotels and pensions

Hotels and **pensions** come cheaper than you'd think in Sweden. Although there's little chance of

---

ACCOMMODATION PRICE CODES

All the Swedish pensions and hotels listed in the guide have been graded according to the following price bands, based on the cost of the least expensive double room in high season. However, almost every hotel offers seasonal and weekend discounts that can reduce the rate by one or even two grades. Many of these bargains are impromptu, but wherever possible we've given two grades, covering both the regular and the discounted rate. Single rooms, where available, are usually between 60 and 80 percent of the cost of a double.

① under 500kr   ② 500–700kr   ③ 700–900kr   ④ 900–1200kr   ⑤ over 1200kr

a room under 300kr a night anywhere, you may be lucky during the summer, especially in July, when the Swedes all head south out of the country and hotels drop their prices significantly to attract custom. For the rest of the year, rooms at weekends are much cheaper than midweek, when business travellers push up prices. On average, for a room with TV and bathroom you can expect to pay from 400kr for a single, 600kr a double. Nearly all hotels include a self-service buffet breakfast in the price – which, given its size, can make for a useful saving. It's perhaps worth noting that in summer some of the larger hotels drop their prices even lower than their usual discount rate if you turn up after 6pm without a booking. This is obviously a risky strategy (and breakfast often isn't included in these "late deals"), but it can mean some very cheap rooms.

The best **package deals** are those operated in Malmö, Stockholm and Gothenburg, where 280–300kr (minimum) gets you a hotel bed for one night, breakfast and the relevant city discount card thrown in. These schemes are generally valid from mid-June to mid-August and at weekends throughout the year, but see the accommodation details under the city accounts for more detailed information.

The other option to consider is buying into a **hotel pass** scheme, where you pay in advance for a series of vouchers or cheques which then allow discounts or free accommodation in various hotel chains throughout the country. Further details can be found in the free booklet *Hotels in Sweden*, available from the Swedish Tourist Board, which also lists every hotel in the country.

■ Youth hostels

The biggest choice (indeed, quite often the only choice) lies with the country's huge chain of **youth hostels** (*Vandrarhem*), operated by the *Svenska Turistföreningen* (*STF*, Box 25, S-101 20 Stockholm; ☎08/463 2100, fax 678 1958). There are around 280 hostels in the country (130 open all year), mainly in southern and central Sweden, but also at regular and handy intervals throughout the north. Forget any preconceptions about youth hostelling: in Sweden rooms are family oriented, modern, clean and hotel-like, existing in the unlikeliest places – old castles, schoolrooms, country manors, and even on boats. Virtually all have well-equipped self-catering kitchens and serve a buffet breakfast.

Prices are low (70–125kr plus a 20kr heating supplement in winter; non-members pay an extra 35kr a night) and correspond to one of three grades. It would be impossible to list every hostel in this guide, so consult the *Hostelling International* handbook, or the one published by the *STF* – 60kr from hostels, tourist offices and large bookshops (or available directly from *STF*-address above).

Some tips: hostels are used by Swedish families as cheap hotel-standard accommodation and can fill quickly, so *always* ring ahead in the summer; family rooms are often available for couples; hostels are usually closed between 10am and 5pm, curfews around 11pm/midnight.

Apart from the *STF* hostels, there are a number of **independently run hostels** usually charging similar prices. Many are listed in the booklet of non-affiliated hostels (*SVIF*) and local tourist offices will have more details.

■ Private rooms and B&B

A further option are the **private rooms** in people's houses that most tourist offices can book for you in any reasonable sized town. From around 90–140kr per person (plus a 30–50kr booking fee), they are an affordable and pleasant option: all have access to showers and/or baths, sometimes a kitchen too, and hosts are rarely intrusive. Where rooms are available they are mentioned in the text, or look for the word *Rum* or *Logi* by the roadside.

Farms throughout Sweden offer **B&B** accommodation and self-catering facilities, and lists are available from *Bo på Lantgård*, Skåne Tourist Board, Skiffervägen 38, S-223 78 Lund (☎046/12 43 50, fax 12 23 72), or local tourist offices. It costs roughly 250–300kr a night per person, with discounts for children. If you want to book your B&B accommodation before you leave, the Swedish Tourist Board should be able to point you in the right direction.

■ Campsites

Practically every town or village has at least one **campsite** and these are generally of a high standard, something that is reflected in the price: pitching a tent costs around 100kr a night in July and August (50kr the rest of the year) and there's often a small charge per person, too. Most sites are open June to September, some (around 200, in winter sports areas) throughout the year. The bulk of the sites are approved and classified by the Swedish Tourist Board and a comprehensive listings book, *Camping Sverige*, is available at larger sites and most Swedish bookshops (or, in advance, try one of the map outlets listed in *Basics*). The Swedish Tourist Board also puts out a short free list.

Note that you'll need a **camping card** (49kr from your first stop) at most sites and that **camping gaz** is tricky to get hold of in Sweden – take your own if possible.

Thanks to a tradition known as *Allemansrätt* (Everyman's Right), it's perfectly possible to **camp rough** throughout the country. This gives you the right to camp anywhere for one night without asking permission, provided you stay a reasonable distance (100m) away from other dwellings. In practice (and especially if you're in the north) no one will object to discreet camping for longer periods, although it's as well, and polite, to ask first. The wide open spaces within most town and city borders make free camping a distinct possibility in built-up areas, too.

■ Cabins and mountain huts

Many campsites also boast **cabins**, usually decked out with bunk beds, kitchen and equipment, but not sheets. It's an excellent alternative to camping for a group or couple; cabins go for around 250–350kr for a four-bed affair. Again, it's wise to ring ahead to secure one. Sweden also has a whole series of **chalet villages**, which – on the whole – offer high-standard accommodation at prices to match. If you're interested in a package along these lines, contact the Swedish Tourist Board for more details.

In the more out-of-the-way places, *STF* operates a system of **mountain huts** strung along hiking trails and in national parks. Usually staffed by a warden, and with cooking facilities, the huts cost around 120–200kr a night for members (slightly more in winter). More information and membership details from *STF* (see above).

Food and Drink

"Eating in Sweden is really just a series of heart-breaks."
Bill Bryson, *Neither Here nor There*

There's no escaping the fact that eating and drinking is going to take up a large slice of your daily budget in Sweden – whether you despair quite as much as Bill Bryson depends on what you're prepared to spend. At its best, Swedish food is excellent, largely meat, fish and potato based, but varied for all that, and generally tasty and filling. Unusual foods are the northern Swedish delicacies – reindeer and elk meat, and wild berries – while herring comes in so many different guises, in restaurants and supermarkets, that fish fiends will always be content. Drinking is more uniform, the lager-type beer and imported wine providing no surprises; however, the local spirit, akvavit, is worth trying at least once – it comes in dozens of different flavours.

■ Food

Eating well and cheaply in Sweden are often mutually exclusive aims, at least as far as a sit-down restaurant meal is concerned. Yet it's not impossible to eat good, hot meals cheaply: the best strategy is to fuel up on breakfast and lunch, both of which offer good-value options. There's also a large number of foreign restaurants – principally pizzerias and Chinese restaurants – which are more likely to serve decently priced evening meals.

Breakfast, snacks and self-catering

Breakfast (*frukost*) is almost invariably a help-yourself buffet served in most youth hostels and some restaurants for around 50kr, free in hotels. If you can eat vast amounts between 7am and 10am, it's nearly always good value. Juice, milk, cereals, bread, boiled eggs, jam, salami, tea and coffee appear on even the most limited tables. Swankier venues will also add herring, porridge, yoghurt, paté and fruit. Something to watch out for is the jug of *filmjölk* next to the ordinary milk – it's thicker, sour milk for pouring on cereals. **Coffee** in Sweden is always freshly brewed and very good; often it's free after the first cup, or at least greatly reduced in price – look for the word *Påtår*. **Tea** is less exciting – weak *Liptons* as a rule – but costs around the same, 15kr a cup.

For **snacks** and lighter meals the choice expands, although their availability is inversely related to their health value. A *Gatukök* (street kitchen) or *Korvstånd* (hot-dog stall) will serve a selection of hot dogs, burgers, pizza slices, chicken bits, chips, ice cream, Coke, crisps and ketchup – something and chips will cost around 50kr. These stalls and stands are on every street in every town and village. More upmarket (if that's the word) **burger bars** are spreading like wildfire and a hefty burger and chips meal will set you back a shade over 60kr: the local *Clockburger* is cheaper than *McDonalds*, but both are generally the source of the cheapest coffee in town.

It's often nicer to hit the **konditori**, a coffee shop with succulent pastries and cakes. They're not particularly cheap (coffee and cake cost around 25–30kr) but are generally as good as they look; and the coffee is often free after you've paid for the first cup. This is also where you'll come across *smörgåsar*, open **sandwiches** piled high with an elaborate variety of toppings. Favourites include shrimps, smoked salmon, eggs, cheese, paté and mixed salad – around 40–50kr a time.

For the cheapest eating, it's hard to beat the **supermarkets** and **markets**. Buy the heavier "black" bread rather than the fluffy cheaper white stuff – it's much more filling. A tube of *kaviar*, made from cod roe, is a sort of concentrated Thousand Island spread and good for crispbread (which, itself, is the cheapest thing to buy). Anything tinned is very expensive apart from mackerel and mussels. Yoghurt and milk are good value, and bananas, apples and oranges the cheapest fruits. For those actually **cooking**, pasta, rice, tinned tomatoes, onions, peppers and tinned mushrooms provide filling cheap meals; but tea, coffee and anything frozen or packeted will be at least twice the price it is at home. Stores to watch for are *Åhléns* and *Domus*, national chains with big food halls, weigh-your-own fruit and veg, and "pick and mix" salad bars.

Restaurants: lunch and dinner

Eating in a **restaurant** (*restaurang*) needn't be out of your price range as long as the meal you eat is **lunch**. Most restaurants offer something called the **Dagens Rätt** (daily dish) at around 50–60kr, often the only affordable way to sample real Swedish *Husmanskost* – "home cooking". Served Monday to Friday between 11am and 2pm, this is simply a choice of main meal (usually one meat, one fish dish) which comes with bread/crispbread and salad, sometimes a soft drink or light beer, and usually coffee. Some Swedish dishes, like *pytt i panna* and *köttbullar* (see the food glossary box), are standards. On the whole, though, more likely offerings in the big cities are pizzas, basic Chinese meals and meat or fish salads. Other cheapish places for lunch are **cafeterias**, usually self-service with cheaper snacks and hot meals, which won't be of a

thrilling quality but at least will fill you up: large department stores and train stations are good places to look. If you're travelling **with kids**, look out for the word *Barnmatsedal* (children's menu).

More expensive, but good for a blowout, are restaurants and hotels that put out the **Smörgåsbord** at lunchtime for around 150–200kr. Following the breakfast theme, you help yourself to unlimited portions of herring, hot and cold meats, eggs, fried and boiled potatoes, salad, cheese, desserts and fruit. To follow local custom you should start with akvavit, drink beer throughout and finish with coffee; but this will add to the bill unless it is a fancier and dearer inclusive spread (usually found on Sunday). A variation on the buffet theme is the **Sillbricka**, a specialist buffet where the dishes are all based on cured and marinaded herring – it might simply be called the "herring table" on the menu. This, too, is excellent and runs to about the same price as the *Smörgåsbord*; it's often found in country inns and restaurants.

If you don't eat the set lunch, meals in restaurants, especially at **dinner** (*middag*), can be expensive. Expect to pay at least 400kr for a three-course affair, to which you can add 30–50kr for a small beer, and 150kr for the cheapest bottle of house wine. The food in Swedish restaurants will either be *Husmanskost*, in which case it will generally be marvellous, or French-style nouvelle cuisine – a pricey way to eat carrot shavings and one brussel sprout.

Swedes eat early and lunch in most restaurants is served from around 11am, dinner from around 6pm.

Ethnic restaurants

For years the only **ethnic** choice in Sweden was between the pizzeria and the odd Chinese restaurant and these still offer the best-value dinners. In **pizzerias** you'll get a large, if not strictly authentic, pizza for around 50kr, usually with free coleslaw and bread, and the price generally remains the same whether it's lunch or dinner. As well as the local restaurants, the *Pizza Hut* chain has recently made its mark in Sweden, though it's much more expensive. **Chinese** restaurants nearly always offer a set lunch for around 50kr, and though pricier in the evenings (from around 60–80kr a dish), a group of people can usually put quite a good-value meal together.

In recent years the choice has expanded to include a barrage of **Middle Eastern** kebab take-

GLOSSARY OF SWEDISH FOOD AND DRINK TERMS

Basics and snacks

Bröd	Bread	*Olja*	Oil	*Småkakor*	Biscuits
Frukt Juice	Fruit juice	*Omelett*	Omelette	*Smör*	Butter
Glass	Ice cream	*Ost*	Cheese	*Smörgås*	Sandwich
Grädde	Cream	*Pastej*	Paté	*Socker*	Sugar
Gräddfil	Sour cream	*Peppar*	Pepper	*Soppa*	Soup
Gröt	Porridge	*Pommes*	Chips	*Sylt*	Jam
Kaffe	Coffee	*frites*		*Te*	Tea
Knäckebröd	Crispbread	*Ris*	Rice	*Vinäger*	Vinegar
Mineralvatten	Mineral water	*Salt*	Salt	*Våffla*	Waffle
Mjölk	Milk	*Senap*	Mustard	*Ägg*	Eggs

Meat (*Kött*)

Biff	Beef steak	*Köttbullar*	Meatballs	*Oxstek*	Roast beef
Fläsk	Pork	*Kyckling*	Chicken	*Renstek*	Roast reindeer
Kalvkött	Veal	*Lammkött*	Lamb	*Skinka*	Ham
Korv	Sausage	*Lever*	Liver	*Älg*	Elk
Kotlett	Cutlet/chop				

Fish (*Fisk*)

Ansjovis	Anchovies	*Kräftor*	Freshwater	*Sardiner*	Sardines
Blåmusslor	Mussels		crayfish	*Sik*	Whitefish
Fiskbullar	Fishballs	*Lax*	Salmon	*Sill*	Herring
Forell	Trout	*Makrill*	Mackerel	*Strömming*	Baltic
Hummer	Lobster	*Räkor*	Shrimps/		herring
Kaviar	Caviar		prawns	*Torsk*	Cod
Krabba	Crab	*Rödspätta*	Plaice	*Ål*	Eel

Vegetables (*Grönsaker*)

Blomkål	Cauliflower	*Morötter*	Carrots	*Svamp*	Mushrooms
Brysselkål	Brussel sprouts	*Potatis*	Potatoes	*Tomater*	Tomatoes
Bönor	Beans	*Rödkål*	Red cabbage	*Vitkål*	White cabbage
Gurka	Cucumber	*Sallad*	Salad	*Vitlök*	Garlic
Lök	Onion	*Spenat*	Spinach	*Ärtor*	Peas

Fruit (*Frukt*)

Ananas	Pineapple	*Hallon*	Raspberry	*Persika*	Peach
Apelsin	Orange	*Hjortron*	Cloudberry	*Päron*	Pear
Aprikos	Apricot	*Jordgrubbar*	Strawberries	*Vindruvor*	Grapes
Banan	Banana	*Lingon*	Cranberries	*Äpple*	Apple
Citron	Lemon				

Terms

Blodig	Rare	*Grillat/Halstrad*	Grilled	*Rökt*	Smoked
Filé	Fillet	*Kall*	Cold	*Stekt*	Fried
Friterad	Deep fried	*Kokt*	Boiled	*Ugnstekt*	Roasted/baked
Genomstekt	Well-done	*Lagom*	Medium	*Varm*	Hot
Gravad	Cured	*Pocherad*	Poached	*Ångkokt*	Steamed

Swedish specialities

Björnstek	Roast bear meat; fairly rare but served at Orsa, see p.512.	*Pytt i panna*	Cubes of meat and fried potatoes with a fried egg.
Bruna bönor	Baked, vinegared brown beans, usually served with bacon.	*Potatissallad*	Potato salad.
Fisksoppa	Fish soup.	*Sillbricka*	Various cured and marinaded herring dishes; often appears as a first course at lunchtime in restaurants.
Getost	Goat's cheese.		
Gravad lax	Salmon marinaded in dill, sugar, and seasoning; served with mustard sauce.	*Sjömansbiff*	Beef, onions and potato stewed in beer.
Hjortron	A wild, northern berry, served with fresh cream and/or ice cream	*Ärtsoppa*	Yellow pea soup with pork; a winter dish served traditionally on Thursdays.
Kryddost	Hard cheese with caraway seeds.		
Köttbullar	Meatballs served with a brown sauce and cranberries.	*Ål*	Eel, smoked and served with creamed potatoes or scrambled eggs (*äggröra*).
Lövbiff	Sliced, fried beef with onions.		
Mesost	Brown, sweet cheese; a breakfast favourite.		

Drinks

Apelsin juice	Orange juice	*Mineralvatten*	Mineral water	*Te*	Tea
Choklad	Hot chocolate	*Mjölk*	Milk	*Vatten*	Water
Citron	Lemon	*Öl*	Beer	*Vin*	Wine
Frukt juice	Fruit juice	*Saft*	Squash	*Skål*	Cheers!
Kaffe	Coffee				

aways and cafés, where you'll get something fairly substantial in pitta bread for around 25–30kr. Other ethnic options, however, are exclusive and expensive. **Japanese** and **Indonesian** food (increasingly common) is expense account stuff.

Vegetarians

It's not too tough being **vegetarian** in Sweden, given the preponderance of buffet-type meals available, most of which are heavy with salads, cheeses, eggs and soups. The cities, too, have salad bars and sandwich shops where you'll have no trouble feeding yourself; and if all else fails, the local pizzeria will always deliver the non-meaty goods. At lunchtime you'll find that the *Dagens Rätt* in many places has a vegetarian option; don't be afraid to ask.

■ Drinking

Drinking is notoriously pricey and there is no way of softening the blow – unless you're prepared to forgo bars and buy exclusively in the state liquor shops. Content yourself with the fact that Swedes, too, think it's expensive: you won't find yourself stuck in rounds at the bar that demand a bank loan to pay them off, and it's perfectly

acceptable to nurse your drink as long as you like. It's worth noting, though, that some bars have happy hours, when half a litre of beer goes for around half-price.

What to drink

If you drink anything alcoholic in Sweden, a good choice is **beer**, which – while expensive – at least costs the same almost everywhere, be it café, bar or restaurant: around 40kr for a half-litre of lager-type brew. It's actually very good: unless you specify, it will be *starköl*, the strongest Class III beer – if this is what you want, ask for a *storstark*; cheaper will be *folköl*, Class II and weaker; whilst cheapest (around half the price) is *lättöl*, a Class I concoction notable only for its virtual absence of alcohol. Classes I and II are available in supermarkets, although the real stuff is only on sale in the state-licensed liquor stores – see below – where it's around a third of the price you'll pay in a bar. *Pripps* and *Spendrups* are the two main brands, or watch out for a brew called *50/50*, which is half *Pripps* and half the British *Samuel Smiths*. **Wine** (all imported) is pricey, too, especially in restaurants: a glass of wine in a bar or restaurant costs around 30kr, bottles from 150kr and upwards. And even the Swedish Tourist Board recommend taking in your duty-free quota of **spirits**, though note that if you do buy them in bars, they are all known by their generic English names.

For experimental drinking, **akvavit** is a good bet. Served ice cold in tiny shots, it's washed down with beer – hold onto your hat. There are various different "flavours", too, spices and herbs added to the finished brew to produce some unusual headaches. Or try **glögg**: served at Christmas, it's a mulled red wine with cloves, cinnamon, sugar and more than a dash of akvavit.

Where to drink

You'll find **bars** in all towns and cities and most villages. In Stockholm and the larger cities the move is towards brasserie-type places – smart and flash. Elsewhere, you still come across more down-to-earth drinking dens, often sponsored by the local union or welfare authority, but the drink's no cheaper and the clientele heavily male and drunk. Either way, the bar is not the centre of Swedish social activity – if you really want to meet people, you'd be better off heading for the campsite or the beach.

In the summer, **café-bars** spread out onto the pavement, better for kids and handy for just a coffee. In out of the way places, when you want a drink and can't find a bar, head for a hotel. Wherever you drink you'll find that things close down at 11pm or midnight, though not in Gothenburg and Stockholm where – as long as your wallet is bottomless – you can drink all night.

The Systembolaget

Venturing into a **Systembolaget** (the state off-licence) is a move into a twilight world. Buying alcohol is made as unattractive as possible, everything behind glass and grilles and served by dour, disapproving faces. There is still a real stigma attached to alcohol and its (public) consumption, and punters sneaking out with a brown paper bag full of the hard stuff is not a rare sight. Buying from the *Systembolaget* is, however, the only option for many budget travellers, and apart from strong beer (15kr or so a third-litre), the only

bargain is the wine – from around 50kr a bottle for some surprisingly good European and New World imports. The shops are open Monday to Friday only (9am–6pm); minimum age for being served is 20, and you may need to show ID.

Directory

ANGLING Sweden's 96,000 lakes make for a lot of fishing. It's free along the coast or in the larger lakes, but for anywhere else get a fishing permit from the local tourist office. A leaflet is available from the Swedish National Tourist Board (see *Basics* for addresses).

CUSTOMS Your duty-free limit entering Sweden is one litre of spirits, one litre of wine and two litres of beer (or two litres of wine if no spirits are taken in). Other restrictions, if you're taking in a car/caravan are: no potatoes (seriously!), fresh, smoked or frozen meat and a limit of 5kg of fruit and veg.

EMERGENCIES Dial ☎112 for police (*Polis*), fire brigade (*Brandkår*) or ambulance (*Ambulans*), free of charge from any phone box.

HOLIDAYS Banks, offices and shops are closed on the following days and may shut early on the preceding day: January 1, January 6 (Epiphany), Good Friday, Easter Monday, May 1 (Labour Day), Ascension Day, Whit Monday, Midsummer's Day, All Saint's Day, Christmas Day, Boxing Day.

PHARMACIES *Apotek* in Swedish are generally open shopping hours, although Stockholm has a 24-hour pharmacy. Larger towns operate a rota system of late opening, rota and addresses posted on the doors of each *apotek*.

SHOPS Open Mon–Fri 9am–6pm, Sat 9am–1pm. Some department stores stay open until 8–10pm in cities, and may open on Sunday afternoons as well.

TIPPING Hotels and restaurants include their service charge in the bill, usually ten percent. Where you will frequently have to hand over cash is to cloakroom attendants in bars and discos – around 10kr a time.

History

Sweden has one of Europe's longest documented histories, but for all the upheavals of the Viking times and the warring of the Middle Ages, during modern times the country has seemed to delight in taking a historical back seat. For one brief period, when Prime Minister Olof Palme was shot dead in 1986, Sweden was thrust into the international limelight. Since then, however, it's regained its poise, even though the current situation is fraught. Political infighting and domestic disharmony is threatening the one thing that the Swedes have always been proud of and that other countries aspire to: the politics of consensus, the passing of which, arguably, is of far greater importance than even the assassination of their prime minister.

■ Early civilizations

It was not until around 6000 BC that the **first settlers** roamed north and east into Sweden, living as nomadic reindeer-hunters and herders. By 3000 BC people had settled in the south of the country and were established as farmers; and dating from 2000 BC has discovered indications of a development in burial practices, with **dolmens** and **passage graves** found throughout the southern Swedish provinces. Traces also remain of the **Boat Axe People**, named after their characteristic tool/weapon shaped like a boat. The earliest Scandinavian horse riders, they quickly held sway over the whole of southern Sweden.

During the **Bronze Age** (1500–500 BC) the Boat Axe People traded furs and amber for southern European copper and tin. Large finds of finished ornaments and weapons show a comparatively rich culture. This was emphasized by elaborate burial rites, the dead laid in single graves under mounds of earth and stone.

The deterioration of the Scandinavian climate in the last millennium before Christ coincided with the advance across Europe of the Celts, which halted the flourishing trade of the Swedish settlers. With the new millennium, Sweden made its first mark upon the Classical world. Pliny the Elder (23–79 AD) in the *Historia Naturalis* mentioned the "island of Scatinavia" far to the north. Tacitus was more specific: in 98 AD he referred to a powerful people, the *Suinoes*, who were strong in men, weapons and ships: a reference to the **Svear**, who were to form the nucleus of an emergent Swedish kingdom by the sixth century.

The Svear settled in the rich land around Lake Mälaren, rulers of the whole country except the south. They gave Sweden its modern name: *Sverige* in Swedish or *Svear rike*, the kingdom of the Svear. More importantly, they gave their first dynastic leaders a taste for expansion, trading with Gotland and holding suzerainty over the Åland islands.

■ The Viking period

The Vikings – raiders and warriors who dominated the political and economic life of Europe and beyond from the ninth to the eleventh centuries – came from all parts of southern Scandinavia. But there is evidence that the **Swedish Vikings** were among the first to leave home, the impetus being a rapid population growth, domestic unrest and a desire for new lands. The raiders turned their attention largely eastwards, in line with Sweden's geographical position and knowing that the Svear had already reached the Baltic. By the ninth century the trade routes were well established, Swedes reaching the Black and Caspian seas and making valuable trading contact with the **Byzantine Empire**. Although more commercially inclined than their Danish and Norwegian counterparts, Swedish Vikings were quick to use force if profits were slow to materialize. From 860 onwards Greek and Muslim records relate a series of raids across the Black Sea against Byzantium, and across the Caspian into northeast Iran.

But the Vikings were settlers as well as traders and exploiters, and their long-term influence was marked. Embattled Slavs to the east gave them the name **Rus**, and their creeping colonization gave the area in which the Vikings settled its modern name, Russia. Russian names today – Oleg, Igor, Vladimir – can be derived from the Swedish – Helgi, Ingvar, Valdemar.

Domestically, **paganism** was at its height. Freyr was "God of the World", a physically potent god of fertility through whom dynastic leaders would trace their descent. It was a bloody time. Nine **human sacrifices** were offered at the celebrations held every nine years at Uppsala. Adam of Bremen recorded that the great shrine there was adjoined by a sacred grove where "every tree is believed divine because of the death and putrefaction of the victims hanging there".

Viking **law** was based on the *Thing*, an assembly of free men to which the king's power was subject. Each largely autonomous province had its own assembly and its own leaders: where several provinces united, the approval of each *Thing* was needed for any choice of leader. For centuries in Sweden the new king had to make a formal tour to receive the homage of each province.

■ The arrival of Christianity

Christianity was slow to take root in Sweden. Whereas Denmark and Norway had accepted the faith by the turn of the eleventh century, Swedish contact was still in the east and the people remained largely heathen. Missionaries met with limited success and no Swedish king was converted until 1008, when **Olof Skötonung** was baptized. He was the first known king of both Swedes and Goths (that is, ruler of the two major provinces of Västergötland and Östergötland) and his successors were all Christians. Nevertheless, paganism retained a grip on Swedish affairs, and as late as the 1080s the Svear banished their Christian king, Inge, when he refused to take part in the pagan celebrations at Uppsala. By the end of the eleventh century, though, the temple at Uppsala had gone and a Christian church was built on its site. In the 1130s Uppsala replaced Sigtuna – original centre of the Swedish Christian faith – as the main episcopal seat and, in 1164, Stephen (an English monk) was made the first archbishop.

■ The warring dynasties

The whole of the early Middle Ages in Sweden was characterized by a succession of struggles for control of a growing central power. Principally two families, the Sverkers and the Eriks, waged battle throughout the twelfth century. **King Erik** was the first Sverker king to make his mark: in 1157 he led a crusade to heathen Finland, but was killed in 1160 at Uppsala by a Danish pretender to his throne. Within a hundred years he was to be recognized as patron saint of Sweden, and his remains interred in the new Uppsala Cathedral.

Erik was succeeded by his son **Knut**, whose stable reign lasted until 1196 and was marked by commercial treaties and strengthened defences. Following his death, virtual civil war weakened the royal power with the result that the king's chief ministers, or **Jarls**, assumed much of the executive responsibility for running the country; so much so that when Erik Eriksson (last of the Eriks) was deposed in 1229, his administrator **Birger Jarl** assumed power. With papal support

for his crusading policies he confirmed the Swedish grip on the southwest of Finland. His son, Valdemar, succeeded him but proved a weak ruler and didn't survive the family feuding after Birger Jarl's death. Valdemar's brother Magnus assumed power in 1275.

Magnus Ladulås represented a peak of Swedish royal power not to be repeated for three hundred years. His enemies dissipated, he forbade the nobility to meet without his consent and began to issue his own authoritative decrees. Preventing the nobility from claiming maintenance at the expense of the peasantry as they travelled from estate to estate earned him his nickname Ladulås or "Barn-lock". He also began to reap the benefits of conversion: the clergy became an educated class upon whom the monarch could rely for diplomatic and administrative duties. By the thirteenth century, there were ambitious Swedish clerics in Paris and Bologna, and the first stone churches were appearing in Sweden. The most monumental is the early Gothic **cathedral** built at Uppsala.

Meanwhile the nobility had come to form a military class, exempted from taxation on the understanding that they would defend the crown. In the country the standard of living was still low, although an increasing population stimulated new cultivation. The forests of Norrland were pushed back, more southern heathland turned into pasture, and crop rotation introduced. Noticeable, too, was the increasing **German influence** within Sweden as the Hansa traders spread. Their first merchants settled in Visby and, by the mid-thirteenth century, in Stockholm.

■ The fourteenth century – towards unity

Magnus died in 1290, power shifting to a cabal of magnates led by **Torgil Knutsson**. As Marshal of Sweden, he pursued an energetic foreign policy, conquering western Karelia to gain control of the Gulf of Finland; and building the fortress at Viborg, lost only with the collapse of the Swedish Empire in the eighteenth century.

Magnus's son Birger came of age in 1302 but soon quarrelled with his brothers Erik and Valdemar. They had Torgil Knutsson executed, then rounded on Birger, who was forced to divide up Sweden among the three of them. An unhappy arrangement, it lasted until 1317 when Birger had his brothers arrested and starved to death in prison – an act that prompted a shocked nobility to rise against Birger and force his exile to Denmark. The Swedish nobles restored the principle of elective monarchy by calling on the three-year-old **Magnus** (son of a Swedish duke and already declared Norwegian king) to take the Swedish crown. During his minority a treaty was concluded with Novgorod (1323) to fix the frontiers in eastern and northern Finland. This left virtually the whole of the Scandinavian peninsula (except the Danish provinces in the south) under one ruler.

Yet Sweden was still anything but prosperous. The **Black Death** reached the country in 1350, wiping out whole parishes and killing perhaps a third of the population. Subsequent labour shortages and troubled estates meant that the nobility found it difficult to maintain their positions. German merchants had driven the Swedes from their most lucrative trade routes: even the copper and iron ore **mining** that began around this time in Bergslagen and Dalarna relied on German capital.

Magnus soon ran into trouble, threatened further by the accession of Valdemar Atterdag to the Danish throne in 1340. Squabbles over sovereignty of the Danish provinces of Skåne and Blekinge led to Danish incursions into Sweden and, in 1361, Valdemar landed on Gotland and sacked **Visby**. The Gotlanders were massacred outside the city walls, refused refuge by the Hansa merchants.

Magnus was forced to negotiate and his son **Håkon** – now King of Norway – was married to Valdemar's daughter Margaret. With Magnus later deposed, power fell into the hands of the magnates who shared out the country. Chief of the ruling nobles was the Steward **Bo Jonsson Grip**, who controlled virtually all Finland and central and southeast Sweden. Yet on his death, the nobility turned to Håkon's wife **Margaret**, already regent in Norway (for her son Olof) and in Denmark since the death of her father, Valdemar. In 1388 she was proclaimed "First Lady" of Sweden and, in return, confirmed all the privileges of the Swedish nobility. They were anxious for union, to safeguard those who owned frontier estates and strengthen the crown against any further German influence. Called upon to choose a male king, Margaret nominated her nephew, **Erik of Pomerania**, who was duly elected king of Sweden in 1396. As he had already been elected to the Danish and Norwegian thrones, Scandinavian unity seemed assured.

■ The Kalmar Union

Erik was crowned King of Denmark, Norway and Sweden in 1397 at a ceremony in **Kalmar**. Nominally, the three kingdoms were now in union but, despite Erik, real power remained in the hands of Margaret until her death in 1412.

Erik was at war throughout his reign with the Hanseatic League. Vilified in popular Swedish history as an evil and grasping ruler, the taxes he raised went on a war that was never fought on Swedish soil. He spent his time instead in Denmark, directing operations, leaving his queen Philippa (sister to Henry V of England) behind. Erik was deposed in 1439 and the nobility turned to **Christopher of Bavaria**, whose early death in 1448 led to the first major breach in the union.

No one candidate could fill the three kingships satisfactorily, and separate elections in Denmark and Sweden signalled a renewal of the infighting that had plagued the previous century. Within Sweden, unionists and nationalists skirmished, the powerful unionist **Oxenstierna** family opposing the claims of the nationalist **Sture** family, until 1470 when **Sten Sture** (the Elder) became "Guardian of the Realm". His victory over the unionists at the **Battle of Brunkeberg** (1471) – in the middle of modern Stockholm – was complete, gaining symbolic artistic expression in the **statue of St George and the Dragon** that still adorns the Great Church in Stockholm.

Sten Sture's primacy fostered a new cultural atmosphere. The first **university** in Scandinavia was founded in Uppsala in 1477, the first printing press appearing in Sweden six years later. Artistically, German and Dutch influences were great, traits seen in the decorative art of the great Swedish medieval churches. Only remote **Dalarna** kept alive a native folk art tradition.

Belief in the union still existed though, particularly outside Sweden, and successive kings had to fend off almost constant attacks and blockades emanating from Denmark. With the accession of **Christian II** to the Danish throne in 1513, the unionist movement found a leader capable of turning the tide. Under the guise of a crusade to free Sweden's imprisoned archbishop Gustav Trolle, Christian attacked Sweden and killed Sture. After Christian's coronation, Trolle urged the prosecution of his Swedish adversaries (gathered together under an amnesty) and they were found guilty of heresy. Eighty-two nobles and burghers of Stockholm were executed and their bodies burned in what became known as the

Stockholm Blood Bath. A vicious persecution of Sture's followers throughout Sweden ensued, a move that led to widespread reaction and, ultimately, the downfall of the union.

■ Gustav Vasa and his sons

Opposition to Christian II was vague and unorganized until the appearance of the young **Gustav Vasa**. Initially unable to stir the locals of the Dalecarlia region into open revolt, he left for exile in Norway, but was chased on skis and recalled after the people had had a change of heart. The chase is celebrated still in the **Vasalopet** race, run each year by thousands of Swedish skiers.

Gustav Vasa's army grew rapidly and in 1521 he was elected regent, and subsequently, with the capture of Stockholm in 1523, king. Christian had been deposed in Denmark and the new Danish king, Frederick I, recognized Sweden's *de facto* withdrawal from the union. Short of cash, Gustav found it prudent to support the movement towards religious reform propagated by Swedish Lutherans. More of a political than a religious **Reformation**, the result was a handover of church lands to the crown and the subordination of church to state. It's a relationship that is still largely in force today, the clergy being civil servants paid by the State.

In 1541 the first edition of the Bible in the vernacular appeared. Suppressing revolt at home, Gustav Vasa strengthened his hand with a centralization of trade and government. On his death in 1560 Sweden was united, prosperous and independent.

Gustav Vasa's heir, his eldest son **Erik**, faced a difficult time, not least because the Vasa lands and wealth had been divided among him and his brothers Johan, Magnus and Karl (an atypically imprudent action of Gustav's before his death). The Danes, too, pressed hard, reasserting their claim to the Swedish throne in the inconclusive **Northern Seven Years' War**, which began in 1563. Erik was deposed in 1569 by his brother who became **Johan III**, his first act being to end the war at the **Peace of Stettin**. At home Johan ruled more or less with the goodwill of the nobility, but upset matters with his Catholic sympathies. He introduced the liturgy and Catholic-influenced *Red Book*, and his son and heir Sigismund was the Catholic king of Poland. On Johan's death in 1592, Sigismund agreed to rule Sweden in accordance with Lutheran practice but failed to

do so. When Sigismund returned to Poland the way was clear for Duke Karl (Johan's brother) to assume the regency, a role he filled until declared King **Karl IX** in 1603.

Karl had ambitions eastwards but, routed by the Poles and staved off by the Russians, he suffered a stroke in 1610 and died the year after. The last of Vasa's sons, his heir was the seventeen-year-old Gustav II, better known as Gustavus Adolfus.

The rule of Vasa and his sons made Sweden a nation, culturally as well as politically. The courts were filled and influenced by men of learning; art and sculpture flourished. The **Renaissance** style appeared for the first time in Sweden, with royal castles remodelled – Kalmar being a fine example. Economically, Sweden remained mostly self-sufficient, its few imports luxuries like cloth, wine and spices. With around 8000 inhabitants, Stockholm was its most important city, although **Gothenburg** was founded in 1607 to promote trade to the west.

■ Gustavus Adolfus: the rise of the Swedish Empire

During the reign of **Gustavus II Adolfus** Sweden became a European power. Though still in his youth he was considered able enough to rule, and proved so by concluding peace treaties with Denmark (1613) and Russia (1617), the latter isolating Russia from the Baltic and allowing the Swedes control of the eastern trade routes into Europe.

In 1618 the **Thirty Years' War** broke out in Germany. It was vital for Gustavus that Germany should not become Catholic, given the Polish king's continuing pretensions to the Swedish crown, and the possible threat it could pose to Sweden's growing influence in the Baltic. The Altmark treaty with a defeated Poland in 1629 gave Gustavus control of Livonia and four Prussian sea ports, and the income this generated financed his entry into the war in 1630 on the Protestant side. After several convincing victories Gustavus pushed through Germany, delaying an assault upon undefended Vienna. It cost him his life. At the **Battle of Lützen** in 1632 Gustavus was killed, his body stripped and battered by the enemy's soldiers. The war dragged on until the **Peace of Westphalia** in 1648.

With Gustavus away at war for much of his reign, Sweden ran smoothly under the guidance of his friend and chancellor, **Axel Oxenstierna**. Together they founded a new Supreme Court in Stockholm (and the same, too, in Finland and the conquered Baltic provinces); reorganized the national assembly into four Estates of nobility, clergy, burghers and peasantry (1626); extended the university at Uppsala (and founded one at Åbo – modern Turku); and fostered the mining and other industries that provided much of the country's wealth. Gustavus had many other accomplishments, too: he spoke five languages and designed a new light cannon, which assisted in his routs of the enemy.

■ The Caroleans

The Swedish empire reached its territorial peak under the **Caroleans**. Yet the reign of the last of them was to see Sweden crumble.

Following Gustavus Adolfus' death and the later abdication of his daughter Christina, **Karl X** succeeded to the throne. War against Poland (1655) led to some early successes and, with Denmark espousing the Polish cause, gave Karl the opportunity to march into Jutland (1657). From there his armies marched across the frozen sea to threaten Copenhagen; the subsequent **Treaty of Roskilde** (1658) broke Denmark and gave the Swedish empire its widest territorial extent.

However, the long regency of his son and heir, **Karl XI**, did little to enhance Sweden's vulnerable position, so extensive were its borders. On his assumption of power in 1672 Karl was almost immediately dragged into war: beaten by a smaller Prussian army at Brandenberg in 1675, Sweden was suddenly faced with war against both the Danes and Dutch. Karl rallied, though, to drive out the Danish invaders, the war ending in 1679 with the reconquest of Skåne and the restoration of most of Sweden's German provinces.

In 1682 Karl XI became **absolute monarch** and was given full control over legislation and *reduktion* – the resumption of estates previously alienated by the crown to the nobility. The armed forces were reorganized too and by 1700 the Swedish army had 25,000 soldiers and twelve regiments of cavalry; the naval fleet was expanded to 38 ships and a new base built at **Karlskrona** (nearer than Stockholm to the likely trouble spots).

Culturally, Sweden began to benefit from the innovations of Gustavus Adolfus. *Gymnasia* (grammar schools) continued to expand and a sec-

ond university was established at **Lund** in 1668. A national literature emerged, helped by the efforts of **George Stiernhielm**, "father" of modern Swedish poetry. **Olof Rudbeck** (1630–1702) was a Nordic polymath whose scientific reputation lasted longer than his attempt to identify the ancient Goth settlement at Uppsala as Atlantis. Architecturally, this was the age of **Tessin**, both father and son. Tessin the Elder was responsible for the glorious palace at **Drottningholm**, work on which began in 1662, as well as the cathedral at **Kalmar**. His son, Tessin the Younger, succeeded him as royal architect and was to create the new royal palace at Stockholm.

In 1697 the 15-year-old **Karl XII** succeeded to the throne and under him the empire collapsed. Faced with a defensive alliance of Saxony, Denmark and Russia, there was little the king could have done to avoid eventual defeat. However, he remains a revered figure for his valiant (often suicidal) efforts to prove Europe wrong. Initial victories against Peter the Great and Saxony led him to march on Russia, where he was defeated and the bulk of his army destroyed. Escaping to Turkey, where he remained as guest and then prisoner for four years, Karl watched the empire disintegrate. With Poland reconquered by Augustus of Saxony, and Finland by Peter the Great, he returned to Sweden only to have England declare war on him.

Eventually, splits in the enemy's alliance led Swedish diplomats to attempt peace talks with Russia. Karl, though, was keen to exploit these differences in a more direct fashion. In order to strike at Denmark, but lacking a fleet, he besieged Fredrikshald in Norway in 1718 and was killed by a sniper's bullet. In the power vacuum thus created, Russia became the leading Baltic force, receiving Livonia, Estonia, Ingria and most of Karelia from Sweden.

■ The Age of Freedom

The eighteenth century saw absolutism discredited in Sweden. A new constitution vested power in the Estates, who reduced the new king **Frederick I**'s role to that of nominal head of state. The chancellor wielded the real power and under **Arvid Horn** the country found a period of stability. His party, nicknamed the "Caps", was opposed by the hawkish "Hats", who forced war with Russia in 1741, a disaster in which Sweden lost all of Finland and had its whole east coast burned and bombed. Most of Finland was returned with the agreement to elect **Adolphus Frederick** (a relation of the crown prince of Russia) to the Swedish throne on Frederick I's death, which duly occurred in 1751.

During his reign Adolphus repeatedly tried to reassert royal power, but found that the constitution was only strengthened against him. The Estates' power was such that they issued a stamp with his name when Adolphus refused to sign any bills. The resurrected "Hats" forced entry into the **Seven Years' War** in 1757 on the French side, another disastrous venture as the Prussians repelled every Swedish attack.

The aristocratic parties were in a state of constant flux. Although elections of sorts were held to provide delegates for the *Riksdag* (parliament), foreign sympathies, bribery and bickering were hardly conducive to a democratic administration. Cabals continued to rule Sweden, the economy was stagnant, and reform delayed. It was, however, an age of intellectual and scientific advance, surprising in a country that had lost much of its cultural impetus. **Carl von Linné**, the botanist whose classification of plants is still used, was professor at Uppsala from 1741 to 1778. **Anders Celsius** initiated the use of the centigrade temperature scale; **Carl Scheele** discovered chlorine. A royal decree of 1748 organized Europe's first full-scale census, a five-yearly event by 1775. Other fields flourished, too. **Emmanuel Swedenborg**, the philosopher, died in 1772, his mystical works encouraging new theological sects; and the period encapsulated the life of **Carl Michael Bellman** (1740–95), the celebrated Swedish poet, whose work did much to identify and foster a popular nationalism.

With the accession of **Gustav III** in 1771, the crown began to regain the ascendancy. A new constitution was forced upon a divided *Riksdag* and proved a balance between earlier absolutism and the later aristocratic squabbles. A popular king, Gustav founded hospitals, granted freedom of worship and removed many of the state controls over the economy. His determination to conduct a successful foreign policy led to further conflict with Russia (1788–90) in which, to everyone's surprise, he managed to more than hold his own. But with the French Revolution polarizing opposition throughout Europe, the Swedish nobility began to entertain thoughts of conspiracy against a king whose growing powers they now saw as those of a tyrant. In 1792, at a masked ball in

Stockholm Opera House, the king was shot by an assassin hired by the disaffected aristocracy. Gustav died two weeks later and was succeeded by his son **Gustav IV**, the country led by a regency for the years of his minority.

The wars waged by revolutionary France were at first studiously avoided in Sweden but, pulled into the conflict by the British, Gustav IV entered the **Napoleonic Wars** in 1805. However, Napoleon's victory at Austerlitz two years later broke the coalition and Sweden found itself isolated. Attacked by Russia the following year, Gustav was later arrested and deposed, his uncle elected king.

A constitution of 1809 established a liberal monarchy in Sweden, responsible to the elected *Riksdag*. Under this constitution **Karl XIII** was a mere caretaker, his heir a Danish prince who would bring Norway back to Sweden – some compensation for finally losing Finland and the Åland Islands to Russia (1809) after five hundred years of Swedish rule. On the prince's sudden death, however, Marshal Bernadotte (one of Napoleon's generals) was invited to become heir. Taking the name of **Karl Johan**, he took his chance in 1812 and joined Britain and Russia to fight Napoleon. Following Napoleon's first defeat at the Battle of Leipzig in 1813, Sweden compelled Denmark (France's ally) to exchange Norway for Swedish Pomerania.

By 1814 Sweden and Norway had formed an uneasy union. Norway retained its own government and certain autonomous measures. Sweden decided foreign policy, appointed a viceroy and retained a suspensive (but not absolute) veto over the Norwegian parliament's legislation.

■ The nineteenth century

Union under Karl Johan, or **Karl XIV** as he became in 1818, could have been disastrous. He spoke no Swedish and just a few years previously had never visited either kingdom. However, under Karl and his successor **Oscar I**, prosperity ensued. The **Göta Canal** (1832) helped commercially, and liberal measures by both monarchs helped politically. In 1845 daughters were given an equal right of inheritance. A Poor Law was introduced in 1847, restrictive craft guilds reformed, and an Education Act passed.

The 1848 revolution throughout Europe cooled Oscar's reforming ardour, and his attention turned to reviving **Scandinavianism**. It was still a hope, in certain quarters, that closer cooperation between Denmark and Sweden–Norway could lead to some sort of revived Kalmar Union. Expectations were raised with the **Crimean War** of 1854: Russia could be neutralized as a future threat. But peace was declared too quickly (at least for Sweden) and there was still no real guarantee that Sweden would be sufficiently protected from Russia in the future. With Oscar's death, talk of political union faded.

His son **Karl XV** presided over a reform of the *Riksdag* that put an end to the Swedish system of personal monarchy. The Four Estates were replaced by a representative two-house parliament along European lines. This, together with the end of political Scandinavianism (following the Prussian attack on Denmark in 1864 in which Sweden stood by), marked Sweden's entry into modern Europe.

Industrialization was slow to take root in Sweden. No real industrial revolution occurred and developments – mechanization, introduction of railways, etc – were piecemeal. One result was widespread **emigration** amongst the rural poor, who had been hard hit by famine in 1867 and 1868. Between 1860 and 1910 over one million people left for America (in 1860 the Swedish population was only four million). Given huge farms to settle, the emigrants headed for land similar to that they had left behind – to the Midwest, Kansas and Nebraska.

At home, Swedish **trade unionism** emerged to campaign for better conditions. Dealt with severely, the unions formed a confederation (1898) but largely failed to make headway. Even peaceful picketing carried a two-year prison sentence. Hand in hand with the fight for workers' rights went the **temperance movement**. The level of spirit consumption was alarming and various abstinence programmes attempted to educate the drinkers and, where necessary, eradicate the stills. Some towns made the selling of spirits a municipal monopoly – not a long step from the state monopoly that exists today.

With the accession of **Oscar II** in 1872, Sweden continued on an even, if uneventful, keel. Keeping out of further European conflict (the Austro-Prussian War, Franco-Prussian War and various Balkan crises), the country's only worry was a growing dissatisfaction in Norway with the union. Demanding a separate consular service, and objecting to the Swedish king's veto on constitutional matters, the Norwegians brought

things to a head, and in 1905 declared the union invalid. The Karlstad Convention confirmed the break and Norway became independent for the first time since 1380.

The late nineteenth century was a happier time for Swedish culture. **August Strindberg** enjoyed great critical success and artists like **Anders Zorn** and **Prince Eugene** made their mark abroad. The historian **Artur Hazelius** founded the Nordic and Skansen museums in Stockholm; and the chemist, industrialist and dynamite inventor **Alfred Nobel** left his fortune to finance the Nobel Prizes. An instructive tale, Nobel hoped that the knowledge of his invention would help eradicate war – optimistically believing that mankind would never dare unleash the destructive forces of dynamite.

■ Two World Wars

Sweden declared a strict neutrality on the outbreak of **World War I**, tempered by much sympathy within the country for Germany, sponsored by long-standing language, trade and cultural links. It was a policy agreed with the other Scandinavian monarchs, but a difficult one to pursue. Faced with British demands to enforce a blockade of Germany and the blacklisting and eventual seizure of Swedish goods at sea, the economy suffered grievously; rationing and inflation mushroomed. The **Russian Revolution** in 1917 brought further problems to Sweden. The Finns immediately declared independence, waging civil war against the Bolsheviks, and Swedish volunteers enlisted in the White army. But a conflict of interest arose when the Swedish-speaking Åland Islands wanted a return to Swedish rule rather than stay with the victorious Finns. The League of Nations overturned this claim, granting the islands to Finland.

After the war, a Liberal–Socialist coalition remained in power until 1920, when **Branting** became the first socialist prime minister. By the time of his death in 1924, the franchise had been extended to all men and women over 23 and the state-controlled alcohol system (*Systembolaget*) set up. Following the Depression of the late 1920s and early 1930s, conditions began to improve after a Social Democratic government took office for the fourth time in 1932. A **Welfare State** was rapidly established, meaning unemployment benefit, higher old-age pensions, family allowances and paid holidays. The **Saltsjöbaden**

Agreement of 1938 drew up a contract between trade unions and employers to help eliminate strikes and lockouts. With war again looming, all parties agreed that Sweden should remain neutral in any struggle and rearmament was negligible, despite Hitler's apparent intentions.

World War II was slow to affect Sweden. Unlike 1914, there was little sympathy for Germany, but neutrality was again declared. The Russian invasion of Finland in 1939 (see Finland's History, p.613) brought Sweden into the picture, providing weapons, volunteers and refuge for the Finns. Regular Swedish troops were refused though, fearing intervention from either the Germans (then Russia's ally) or the Allies. Economically, the country remained sound – less dependent on imports than in World War I and with no serious shortages. The position became stickier in 1940 when the Nazis marched into Denmark and Norway, isolating Sweden. Concessions were made – German troop transit allowed, iron ore exports continued – until 1943–44 when Allied threats were more convincing than the failing German war machine. Sweden became the recipient of countless refugees from the rest of Scandinavia and the Baltic. Instrumental, too, by rescuing Hungarian Jews from the SS, was **Raoul Wallenberg**, who persuaded the Swedish government to give him diplomatic status in 1944. Unknown thousands (anything up to 35,000) of Jews in Hungary were sheltered in "neutral houses" (flying the Swedish flag), fed and clothed by Wallenberg. But when Soviet troops liberated Budapest in 1945, Wallenberg was arrested as a suspected spy and disappeared – later reported to have died in prison in Moscow in 1947. However, unconfirmed accounts had him alive in a Soviet prison as late as 1975, and in 1989 some of his surviving relatives flew to Moscow in an attempt to discover the truth about his fate.

The end of the war was to provide the country with a serious crisis of conscience. Physically unscathed, Sweden was now vulnerable to Cold War politics. Proximity to Finland and, ultimately, to the Soviet Union, meant that Sweden refused to follow the other Scandinavian countries into **NATO** in 1949. The country did, however, much to Conservative disquiet, return most of the Baltic and German refugees who had fought against Russia during the war into Stalin's hands – their fate not difficult to guess.

■ Postwar politics

The wartime coalition quickly gave way to a purely **Social Democratic** government committed to welfare provision and increased defence expenditure – non-participation in military alliances didn't mean a throwing down of weapons.

Tax increases and a trade slump lost the Social Democrats seats in the 1948 general election and by 1951 they needed to enter a coalition with the Agrarian (later the Centre) Party to survive. This coalition lasted until 1957, when disputes over the form of a proposed extension to the pension system brought it down. An inconclusive referendum and the withdrawal of the Centre Party from government forced an election which saw no change. Although the Centre gained seats and the Conservatives replaced the Liberals as the main opposition party, the Social Democrats still had a (thin) majority.

Sweden regained much of its international moral respect (lost directly after World War II) through the election of **Dag Hammarskjöld** as Secretary-General of the United Nations in 1953. His strong leadership greatly enhanced the prestige (and effectiveness) of the organization, participating in the solution of the Suez crisis (1956) and the 1958 Lebanon–Jordan affair. He was killed in an air crash in 1961, towards the end of his second five-year term.

Throughout the 1950s and 1960s, domestic reform continued unabated. It was in these years that the country laid the foundations of its much-vaunted social security system, although at the time it didn't always bear close scrutiny. A **National Health Service** gave free hospital treatment, but only allowed for a small refund of doctor's fees, medicines and dental treatment – hardly as far-reaching as the British system introduced immediately after the war.

The Social Democrats stayed in power until 1976, when a **non-Socialist coalition** (Centre–Liberal–Moderate) finally unseated them. In the 44 years since 1932, the Socialists had been an integral part of government in Sweden, tempered only by periods of war and coalition. It was a remarkable record, made more so by the fact that modern politics in Sweden has never been about ideology so much as detail. Socialists and non-Socialists alike share a broad consensus on foreign policy and defence matters, even on the need for the social welfare system. The argument instead has been economic, and a manifestation of this is the **nuclear issue**. A second non-Socialist coalition formed in 1979 presided over a referendum on nuclear power (1980), the pro-nuclear lobby securing victory with the result an immediate expansion of the nuclear programme. However, post-Chernobyl, attitudes have changed, and a more recent referendum has resulted in a commitment to close all Sweden's nuclear power stations by the year 2010, a policy that will cost the government dear in making up the 50 percent shortfall in energy.

■ 1982–89: Olof Palme

The Social Democrats regained power in 1982, subsequently devaluing the krona, introducing a price freeze and cutting back on public expenditure. They lost their majority in 1985, having to rely on Communist support to get their bills through. Presiding over the party since 1969, and prime minister for nearly as long, was **Olof Palme**, probably now the most famous, least-known foreign leader. Assassinated in February 1986, his death threw Sweden into modern European politics like no other event. Proud of their open society (Palme was returning home unguarded from the cinema), the Swedes were shocked by the gunning down of a respected politician, diplomat and pacifist. The country's social system was placed in the limelight, and shock turned to anger and then ridicule as the months passed without his killer being caught. Police bungling was criticized and despite the theories – Kurdish extremists, right-wing terror groups – no one was charged with the murder.

Then the police came up with **Christer Pettersson**, who – despite having no apparent motive – was identified by Palme's wife as the man who had fired the shot that night. Despite pleading his innocence, claiming he was elsewhere at the time of the murder, Pettersson was convicted of Palme's murder and jailed. There was great disquiet about the verdict, however, both at home and abroad: the three legal representatives in the original jury had voted for acquittal at the time; and it was believed that Palme's wife couldn't possibly be sure that the man who fired the shot was Pettersson, since by her own admission she had only seen him once, on the dark night in question and then only very briefly. On appeal, Pettersson was acquitted and released in 1989. The Swedish police appear to believe that they had the right man but not enough evidence to convict, while more recently evidence has pointed to

South African involvement, Palme having been a vocal opponent of Apartheid.

■ 1988–93: Carlsson and Bilot

Ingvar Carlsson was elected the new prime minister after Palme's murder, a position confirmed by the **1988 General Election** when the Social Democrats – for the first time in years – scored more seats than the three non-Socialist parties combined. However, Carlsson's was a minority government, the Social Democrats requiring the support of the Communists to command an overall majority – support that was usually forthcoming but that, with the arrival of the **Green Party** into parliament in 1988, could no longer be taken for granted. The Greens and Communists jockeyed for position as protectors of the Swedish environment, and any Social Democrat measure seen to be anti-environment cost the party Communist support. Perhaps more worryingly for the government, a series of **scandals** swept the country, leading to open speculation about a marked decline in public morality. The Bofors arms company was discovered to be involved in illegal sales to the Middle East, and early in 1990 the Indian police charged the company with paying kickbacks to politicians to secure arms contracts. In addition, there was insider dealing at the stock exchange and the country's Ombudsman resigned over charges of personal corruption.

The real problem for the Social Democrats, though, was the **state of the economy**. With a background of rising inflation and slow economic growth, the government announced an austerity package in January 1990, which included a two-year ban on strike action, and a wage, price and rent freeze – strong measures that astounded most Swedes, used to living in a liberal, consensus-style society. The Greens and Communists would have none of it and the Social Democrat government resigned a month later. Although the Social Democrats were soon back in charge of a minority government, having agreed to drop the most draconian measures of their programme, the problems didn't go away.

The **General Election of 1991** merely confirmed that the model consensus had finally broken down. A four-party centre-right coalition came to power, led by **Carl Bildt**, which promised tax cuts and economic regeneration, but the recession sweeping western Europe didn't pass

Sweden by. Unemployment hit a postwar record and in autumn 1992 – as the British pound and Italian lira collapsed on the international money markets – the krona came under severe pressure. Savage austerity measures did little to help: VAT on food was increased, statutory holiday allowances cut, welfare budgets slashed, and – after a period of intense currency speculation – short-term marginal interest rates raised to a staggering 500 percent. In a final attempt to steady nerves, Prime Minister Bildt and the leader of the Social Democratic opposition, Ingvar Carlsson, made the astonishing announcement that they would ignore party lines and work together for the good of Sweden – and then proceeded with drastic public expenditure cuts.

However, it was too little too late. Sweden was gripped by its worst recession since the 1930s and unemployment reached record levels of 14 percent. Poor economic growth coupled with generous welfare benefits, runaway speculation by Swedish firms on foreign real estate, and the world recession, all contributed to Sweden's economic woes. With the budget deficit growing faster than that of any other western industrialized country, Sweden also decided it was time to tighten up its asylum laws and introduced controversial new visa regulations to prevent a flood of Bosnian refugees.

■ To the present

Nostalgia for the good old days of Social Democracy swept the country in the September of **1994** and Carl Bildt's minority Conservative government was pushed out, allowing a return to power by Sweden's largest party, headed by **Ingvar Carlsson**. Social Democracy was well and truly back, with Carlsson choosing a cabinet composed equally of men and women. New social reforms were implemented, most significantly the 1995 law allowing gay couples to marry, which gives them virtually equal rights with heterosexual couples.

During 1994, negotiations on Sweden's planned membership of the **European Union** were completed and put to a referendum that saw public opinion split right down the middle. While some thought that EU membership would allow Sweden a greater influence within Europe, others were concerned that the country's standards would be forced downwards, affecting the quality of life Swedes had come to expect. However, in

November the vote for membership was won, albeit by the narrowest of margins – just 5 percent – and Sweden joined the Union as of January 1, 1995.

The krona fell to new lows as market fears grew that the minority government wouldn't be able to persuade parliament to approve cuts in state spending. However, the cuts came in the budget – the welfare state was trimmed back further and new taxes announced to try to rein in the spiralling debt: unemployment benefit was cut to 75 percent of previous earnings, sick leave benefits reduced, and lower state pension payments came into force. A new tax was slapped on newspapers but to try to retain some public support, Finance Minister **Göran Persson** reduced taxes on food from a staggering 21 percent to just 12 percent.

Just when everything appeared to be under control, Carlsson announced his resignation in order to spend more time with his family, to be replaced by the domineering Persson. Later, towards the end of 1995, the party was rocked by scandal when it was revealed in the press that Deputy Prime Minister **Mona Sahlin** had been using her government credit card for personal purchases; though she claimed to have paid back every krona, the party lost credibility nonetheless and Sahlin tendered her resignation.

As the cradle-to-the-grave welfare state is abandoned and the gap between rich and poor widens, **racial tension** has become a major social problem. Many Swedes blame their troubles on the rise in the immigrant population – which in Sweden numbers one million out of a total of nearly nine million. Tension began to surface in the early 1990s when refugee housing centres were set on fire and a number of Stockholm immigrants were shot dead. The government has done little to stamp out the violence and neo-Nazi groups are on the rise, with attacks and even murder all too frequent occurrences.

Sweden's economy has recently improved to the point that the country will probably qualify to join the **Single European Currency** in 1999. Opposition to EU membership has continued to grow, however, and recent polls show that a majority of Swedes are in favour of leaving the Union. The government has acknowledged public opinion by declaring that Sweden won't join the single currency – a curious statement given that, unlike Britain, Sweden has failed to negotiate an opt-out clause.

A BRIEF GUIDE TO SWEDISH

Nearly everyone, everywhere in Sweden speaks English, the tourist offices often staffed with what appear to be native Americans (most pick up the accent from films and TV). Still, knowing the essentials of Swedish is useful, and making an effort with the language certainly impresses. If you already speak either Danish or Norwegian you should have few problems being understood; if not, then a basic knowledge of German is a help too. Of the phrasebooks, most useful is *Swedish for Travellers* (Berlitz), or use the section in *Travellers' Scandinavia* (Pan).

PRONUNCIATION

Pronunciation is even more difficult than Danish or Norwegian. A **vowel** sound is usually long when it's the final syllable or followed by only one consonant; followed by two it's generally short. Unfamiliar combinations are:

ej as in m**a**te.

y as in **ewe**.

å when short as in h**o**t; when long as in r**a**w.

ä when before r as in m**a**n; otherwise as in g**e**t.

ö as in f**u**r but without the r sound.

Consonants are pronounced as in English except:

g usually as in **y**et; occasionally as in **sh**ut.

j, dj, gj, lj as in **y**et.

k before i, e y, ä, or ö, like the Scottish lo**ch**; otherwise hard.

qu as **kv**.

sch, skj, stj as in **sh**ut; otherwise hard.

tj like lo**ch**.

z as in **s**o.

BASICS

Hello	*Hej*	Yes	*Ja*	Today	*I dag*
Good morning	*God morgon*	No	*Nej*	Tomorrow	*I morgon*
Good afternoon	*God middag*	I don't understand	*Jag förstår inte*	Day after tomorrow	*I övermorgon*
Good night	*God natt*	Please	*Var så god*		
Goodbye	*Adjö*	Thank you (very much)	*Tack (så mycket)*	In the morning	*På morgonen*
Do you speak English ?	*Talar ni Engelska ?*	You're welcome	*Var så god*	In the afternoon	*På eftermiddagen*
				In the evening	*På kvällen*

SOME SIGNS

Entrance	*Ingång*	Closed	*Stängt*	No smoking	*Rökning förbjuden*
Exit	*Utgång*	Push	*Skjut*	No camping	*Tältning förbjuden*
Men	*Herrar*	Pull	*Drag*	No trespassing	*Tillträde förbjudet*
Women	*Damer*	Arrival	*Ankomst*	No entry	*Ingen ingång*
Open	*Öppen, öppet*	Departure	*Avgång*	Police	*Polis*

QUESTIONS AND DIRECTIONS

Where is . . . ?	*Var är . . . ?*	Good/bad	*Bra/dålig*
When?	*När?*	Left/right	*Vänster/höger*
What?	*Vad?*	Vacant/occupied	*Ledig/upptagen*
Can you direct me to . . .	*Skulle ni kunna visa mig vägen till . . .*	A little/a lot	*Lite/en mängd*
		I'd like	*Jag skulle vilja ha . . .*
It is/There is (Is it/Is there?)	*Det är/det finns (Är det/Finns det?)*	A single room	*ett enkelrum*
		A double room	*ett dubbelrum*
What time is it?	*Hur mycket är klockan?*	How much is it?	*Vad kostar det?*
Big/small	*Stor/liten*	Can we camp here?	*Kan vi tälta här?*
Cheap/expensive	*Billig/dyr*	Campsite	*Campingplats*
Early/late	*Tidig/sen*	Tent	*Tält*
Hot/cold	*Varm/kall*	Is there a youth hostel near here?	*Finns det något van-drarhem i närheten?*
Near/far	*Nära/avlägsen*		

continued overleaf....

continued from previous page

NUMBERS

0	*noll*	9	*nio*	18	*arton*	70	*sjuttio*
1	*ett*	10	*tio*	19	*nitton*	80	*åttio*
2	*två*	11	*elva*	20	*tjugo*	90	*nittio*
3	*tre*	12	*tolv*	21	*tjugoett*	100	*hundra*
4	*fyra*	13	*tretton*	22	*tjugotvå*	101	*hundraett*
5	*fem*	14	*fjorton*	30	*trettio*	200	*tvåhundra*
6	*sex*	15	*femton*	40	*fyrtio*	500	*femhundra*
7	*sju*	16	*sexton*	50	*femtio*	1000	*tusen*
8	*åtta*	17	*sjutton*	60	*sextio*		

DAYS AND MONTHS

Sunday	*söndag*	January	*januari*	July	*juli*
Monday	*måndag*	February	*februari*	August	*augusti*
Tuesday	*tisdag*	March	*mars*	September	*september*
Wednesday	*onsdag*	April	*april*	October	*oktober*
Thursday	*torsdag*	May	*maj*	November	*november*
Friday	*fredag*	June	*juni*	December	*december*
Saturday	*lördag*				

Days and months are never capitalized

GLOSSARY OF SWEDISH TERMS AND WORDS

Berg	Mountain
Bokhandel	Bookshop
Bro	Bridge
Cykelstig	Cycle path
Dal	Valley
Domkyrka	Cathedral
Drottning	Queen (as in *Drottninggatan*, Queen Street)
Färja	Ferry
Gamla	Old (as in Gamla Stan, old town)
Gata (gt)	Street
Hamnen	Harbour
Järnvägsstation	Railway station
Klockan (kl)	O'clock
Kyrka	Church
Lilla	Little (as in Lilla Torget, small square)
Muséet	Museum
Pressbyrå	Newsagent
Rabatt	Rebate/discount
Rea	Sales (and Vrakpriser, bargain)
Riksdagshus	Parliament building
Sjö	Lake
Skog	Forest
Slott	Castle
Spår	Platform (at railway station)
Stadshus	Town hall
Stora	Great/big (as in Storatorget, main square)
Strand	Beach
Stugor	Chalet, cottage
Torg	Central town square, usually the scene of daily/weekly markets
Universitet	University
Väg (v)	Road

CHAPTER NINE

STOCKHOLM AND AROUND

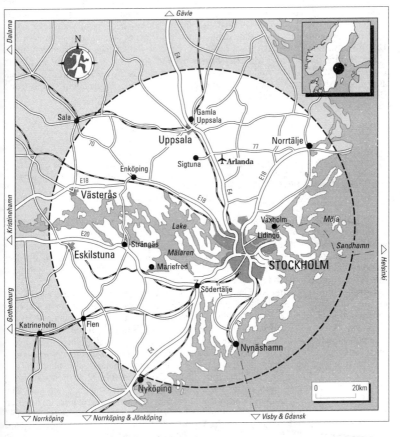

S tockholm is without a shadow of a doubt one of the most beautiful cities in
Europe. Built on no fewer than fourteen islands, where the fresh water of Lake
Mälaren meets the brackish Baltic Sea, fresh air and open space are in plentiful
supply here – one third of the city's total area is made up of water, another third

comprises parks and woodlands. Although the final third is taken over by shops, offices and apartments, it's easy to find a quiet corner to enjoy one of Europe's saner and more civilized capitals. Broad boulevards lined with elegant buildings are reflected in the deep blue water of the Baltic, home to rows of painted wooden houseboats moored alongside the city's cobbled waterfront, while the world's first urban national park offers a unique opportunity to swim and fish virtually in the city centre. Unfortunately, unattractive Sixties-style developments and tangled road junctions mean that some of central Stockholm can be an eyesore, but this is more than compensated for by the wealth of cinemas, bars and restaurants – of which Stockholm has more per capita than most other European capitals.

You can appreciate Stockholm's unique geography by taking one of a number of boat trips around the city. The highlight has to be the **Stockholm archipelago** – a staggering 24,000 islands, rocks and skerries, the Swedish mainland slowly splintering into the Baltic Sea. Easily accessible from the city centre, these islands are a summer paradise for holidaying Stockholmers. A boat trip inland along the serene waters of Lake Mälaren is another easy day trip, with the target of seventeenth-century **Drottningholm**, the Swedish royal residence, right on the lakeside. Alternatively, travelling further along Lake Mälaren brings you to the equally important castle of **Gripsholm** at Mariefred. And still within day trip reach is the ancient Swedish capital and medieval university town of **Uppsala**, easily reached by frequent trains from Central Station, as well as the odd boat.

STOCKHOLM

"It is not a city at all", he said with intensity. "It is ridiculous to think of itself as a city. It is simply a rather large village, set in the middle of some forest and some lakes. You wonder what it thinks it is doing there, looking so important."

Ingmar Bergman interviewed by James Baldwin.

STOCKHOLM often feels like two cities. Its self-important status as Sweden's most forward-looking commercial centre can seem at odds with the almost pastoral feel of its wide open spaces, expanses of open water, and ageing ornate buildings. First impressions can be of a distant and unwelcoming place – provincial Swedes call it the Ice Queen – but stick around for the weekend and you'll see another side to Stockholm, as this is when the population really lets its hair down.

Gamla Stan (pronounced "Gam-la Starn", meaning Old Town) was the site of the original settlement of Stockholm. Today it's an atmospheric mixture of pomp and historical authenticity: ceremonial buildings surrounded on all sides by a latticework of medieval lanes and alleyways. The tiny island of **Skeppsholmen** (pronounced "Shepps-holm-en"), with fantastic views of the curving waterfront, is close by and can be reached by ferry. To the north of Gamla Stan is the modern centre, **Norrmalm**, with its shopping malls, huge department stores and conspicuous wealth, plus the lively Kungsträdgården park and the transport hub of Central Station. Most of Stockholm's eighty or so **museums and galleries** are to be found in Norrmalm, along with the grand residential area of **Östermalm** to the east. Southeast, the green park island of **Djurgården** plays host to two of Stockholm's best-known attractions: the extraordinary preserved seventeenth-century warship, **Vasa**, and **Skansen**, Europe's oldest open-air museum. South of the Old Town lies the island of **Södermalm**, known in English as "the Southside" or as plain "Söder" to its right-on inhabitants. Traditionally Stockholm's working-class area, today it's known for its cool bars and restaurants and lively street-life. To the west of the centre is the island of **Kungsholmen**, which is fast coming to rival its southern neighbour with its trendy eateries and drinking establishments.

Arrival and information

Most planes – international and domestic – arrive at **Arlanda airport**, 45km north of Stockholm. Terminal 2 is used by *Austrian Airlines, Finnair, Maersk, Sabena, Swissair* and *Transwede*; Terminal 5 by all other international airlines; *SAS* domestic flights leave from Terminal 4; other domestic airlines use Terminal 3. Until 1999, when a new high-speed rail link between the airport and city is due to open, the best way to get into Stockholm is to take the the the airport buses, *Flygbussarna* (6.30am–11.30pm; 60kr; ☎08/600 1000), which run at least every ten minutes and call at all terminals en route to the **Cityterminalen** (Stockholm's long-distance bus station), a journey time of about forty minutes; buy your ticket on the bus. **Buses to the airport** leave the Cityterminalen between 4.25am and 10pm; tickets are sold at the booth in the departure area, *not* on the bus. **Taxis** into Stockholm should cost around 350kr – an affordable alternative for a group – choose the ones that have prices displayed in their back windows to avoid being ripped off.

Flights operated by *Malmö Aviation* arrive at the more central **Bromma airport** which is also connected to the Cityterminalen by *flygbussarna* – buses run in connection with flight arrivals and departures, leaving from Gate 23 of the Cityterminalen (40kr; journey time 20min). Buses also link the two airports (7.15am–11.10pm; 60kr; 45min).

By **train**, you'll arrive at and depart from **Central Station**, a cavernous (but heated) structure on Vasagatan in the Norrmalm district of town. Inside there's a *Forex* money exchange office and a very useful room-booking service, *Hotellcentralen* (see "Accommodation" below). All branches of the Tunnelbanan, Stockholm's efficient underground train system, meet at T-Centralen, the metro station directly below the main station. The regional trains that run throughout Greater Stockholm, the Pendeltågen, leave from the main train platforms on the ground level – not from underground platforms.

By **bus**, your arrival point will be the huge glass structure known as the **Cityterminalen**, a hi-tech bus terminal adjacent to Central Station and reached by a series of escalators and walkways from the northern end of the main hall. It handles all bus services: airport and ferry shuttle services, domestic and international buses all leave from here. There's also an exchange office.

There are two main **ferry** companies connecting Stockholm with Helsinki, Turku and Mariehamn in Finland. *Viking Line* ferries dock at Vikingterminalen on the island of Södermalm, where you can catch a bus to Slussen for the frequent T-bana train to T-Centralen. *Silja Line* ferries arrive on the northeastern edge of the city at Siljaterminalen; it's a short walk to either Gärdet or Ropsten T-bana station on the red line, where you can get a train into town. When leaving Stockholm by ferry, note the Swedish names for destinations: Helsinki is *Helsingfors* and Turku, confusingly, is *Åbo*.

Estline sailings from Tallinn in Estonia arrive at Frihamnen at the end of the #41 bus route, which will take you all the way into town. If you're heading for Central Station, get off at the junction of Kungsgatan and Vasagatan and walk the short distance from there; the bus goes directly past the Cityterminalen.

Information

You should be able to pick up a map of the city at most points of arrival, but it's still worth dropping in on one of the city **tourist offices**. Each hands out fistfuls of free information and you'll find a functional (if tiny) **map** in most of the brochures and booklets – though it's probably worth paying 15kr for the better, larger plan of Stockholm

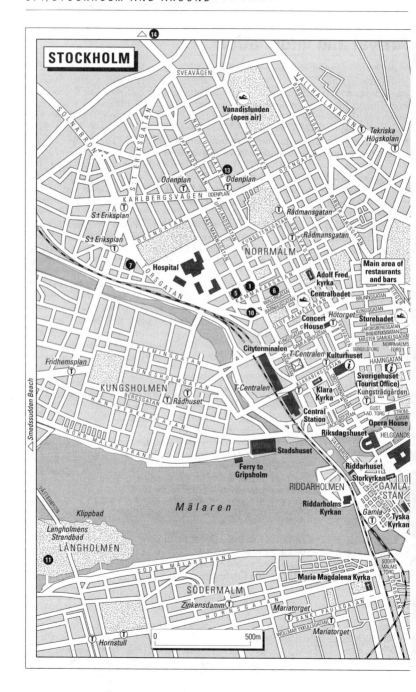

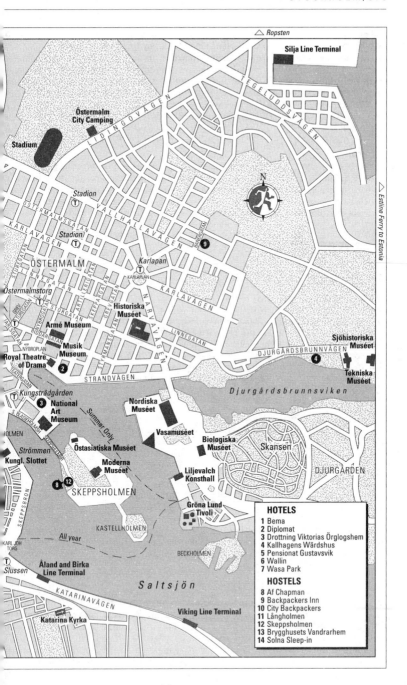

△ Ropsten

Silja Line Terminal

△ Estline Ferry to Estonia

TEGELUDDSVÄGEN

Östermalm City Camping

LIDINGÖVÄGEN

Stadium

N

Stadion Ⓣ

ÖSTERMALMSGATAN

VALLHALLAVÄGEN

Stadion Ⓣ

KARLAVÄGEN

Stadion Ⓣ

STUREGATAN

Karlaplan

KARLAPLAN

ÖSTERMALM

Östermalmstorg Ⓣ

STORGATAN

NYBROGATAN

RIDDARGATAN

ARTILLERIGATAN

SKEPPARGATAN

GREVGATAN

KARLAVÄGEN

NARVAVÄGEN

LINNEGATAN

Historiska Muséet

Sjöhistoriska Muséet

DJURGÅRDSBRUNNVÄGEN

④

Ⓣ NYBROPLAN

Armé Museum

Musik Museum

Royal Theatre of Drama

②

STYRMANSGATAN

STRANDVÄGEN

Tekniska Muséet

Djurgårdsbrunnsviken

Ⓣ **Kungsträdgården**

③ National Art Museum

Nordiska Muséet

S. BLASIEHOLMEN

Summer Only

Strömmen

Kungl. Slottet

Östasiatiska Muséet

Vasamuséet

Biologiska Muséet

Skansen

Moderna Muséet

Liljevalch Konsthall

DJURGÅRDEN

⑧ ⑫

SKEPPSHOLMEN

HOLMEN

KASTELLHOLMEN

Gröna Lund Tivoli

SKEPPSBRON

All year

BECKHOLMEN

KARL JOH TORG

Ⓣ **Slussen**

Åland and Birka Line Terminal

Saltsjön

KATARINAVÄGEN

Katarina Kyrka

Viking Line Terminal

HOTELS

1 Bema
2 Diplomat
3 Drottning Viktorias Örlogshem
4 Kallhagens Wärdshus
5 Pensionat Gustavsvik
6 Wallin
7 Wasa Park

HOSTELS

8 Af Chapman
9 Backpackers Inn
10 City Backpackers
11 Långholmen
12 Skeppsholmen
13 Brygghusets Vandrarhem
14 Solna Sleep-in

and surrounding area produced by the Stockholm Information Service. You can also buy the valuable Stockholm Card (see below) from any tourist office.

The **main office** is on Hamngatan in Norrmalm, on the ground floor of *Sverigehuset* (Sweden House; June–Aug Mon–Fri 8am–6pm, Sat & Sun 9am–5pm; rest of the year Mon–Fri 9am–6pm, Sat & Sun 9am–3pm; ☎08/789 2490, excursion information on ☎08/789 2415; E-mail: info@stoinfo.se; Website : http://www.stoinfo.se). Here you can pick up *Stockholm This Week*, a free listings and entertainments guide, as well as any number of brochures and timetables. Upstairs, the **Swedish Institute** has a good stock of English-language books on Sweden, plus detailed factsheets on all aspects of the country for 1kr each – there's also information to be had on working and studying in the country.

There are **other tourist offices** in the Stadshuset at Hantverkargatan 1 on Kungsholmen (May–Oct daily 9am–3pm; no telephone enquiries) and at the Kaknäs TV tower on Djurgården (daily 9am–10pm; ☎08/789 2435). Lastly, **Kulturhuset**, the monster cultural centre at Sergels Torg 3 in Norrmalm, has a desk on the ground floor offering limited information (Tues–Fri 11am–6pm, Sat & Sun noon–5pm; ☎08/700 0100).

City transport

Stockholm confusingly winds its way across islands, over water and through parkland: the best way to get to grips with it is to equip yourself with a map and walk – it only takes about half an hour to cross central Stockholm on foot. Sooner or later, though, you'll have to use some form of transport and, while routes are easy enough to master, there's a bewildering array of passes and discount cards available. One thing to try to avoid is paying as you go on the city's transport system – a very expensive business. The city is zoned, a trip within one zone costing 13kr with single tickets valid within that zone for one hour; cross a zone and it's another 6.50kr. Most journeys worth making cost 19.50kr. City bus, local train and T-bana **timetables** are easily obtained from the *SL-Center* dotted around the city (see below); timetables for main-line trains operated by Swedish Railways can be found at Central Station.

For public transport **information**, call ☎08/600 1000.

Public transport

Storstockholms Lokaltrafik (*SL*) operates a comprehensive system of buses and trains (underground and regional) that extends well out of the city centre. The main SL information office, the **SL-Center** (Mon–Fri 8am–6pm, Sat 8am–1pm), is at Sergels Torg just by the entrance to T-Centralen (see p.404 for other branches) and has timetables for the city's buses, metro, regional trains and archipelago boats. They also sell a useful **transport map** showing all street names and bus routes (42kr); you should be able to buy this from *Pressbyrå* newsagents too.

The quickest and most useful form of transport is the **tunnelbana** (T-bana), Stockholm's metro system, based on three main lines (red, green and blue) with a smattering of branches. Entrances are marked with a blue letter "T" on a white background. It's the swiftest way to travel between Norrmalm and Södermalm, via Gamla Stan, and it's also handy for a trip out into the suburbs – to the ferry docks and to distant youth hostels and museums. Trains runs from early morning until around midnight – but on Friday and Saturday nights there are services all through the night. The T-bana is something of an artistic venture too: T-Centralen is one

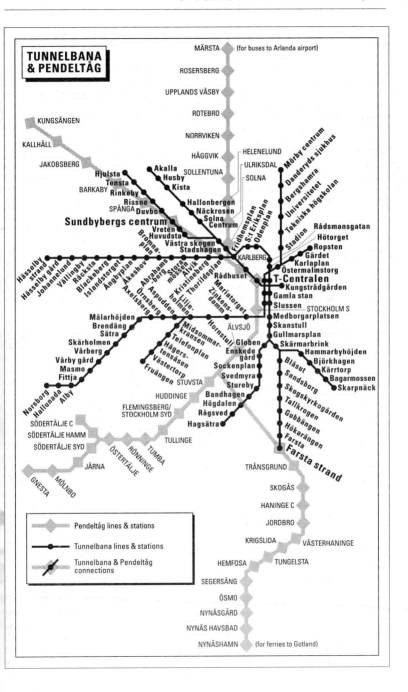

huge papier-mâché cave and Kungsträdgården is littered with statues, spotlights and fountains.

Bus routes can be less direct due to Stockholm's islands and central pedestrianization – for help consult the route map on the back of the *Stockholms innerstad* bus timetable. You should board buses at the front, get off at the back or in the middle and buy tickets from the driver. Night buses replace the T-bana after midnight, except on Friday and Saturday nights.

Ferries provide access to the sprawling archipelago from outside the *Grand Hotel* on Strömkajen (see "Around Stockholm") and also link some of the central islands: Djurgården is connected with Skeppsholmen and Nybroplan in Norrmalm (summer only) and with Skeppsbron in Gamla Stan (all year round). **Cruises** on Lake Mälaren leave from outside the Stadshuset on Stadshusbron and city boat tours leave from outside the *Grand Hotel*, as well as around the corner on Nybroplan.

Travel passes and tickets

The best pass to have, if you're planning to do any sightseeing at all, is the *Stockholmskortet* or **Stockholm Card**, which gives unlimited travel on city buses, ferries, T-bana and regional trains, free museum entry, discounts on boat trips and tours, plus free parking and many other discounts. Cards are sold undated, then are stamped on first use, after which they remain valid for 24 hours. At a cost of 175kr, one card covers an adult and two children under 18. From mid-May to the end of August the card includes an hour's free sightseeing by boat. It isn't valid, though, on ferries to Djurgården or airport buses to Arlanda. You can buy the card from any tourist office in the city (including *Hotellcentralen* in Central Station).

Among the other options, the *Turistkort* or **tourist card** is valid for 24 hours (56kr) or 72 hours (107kr) and gives unlimited travel by bus, T-bana and regional train, plus travel on the trams and ferries to Djurgården. In addition the 72-hour card covers admission to Skansen, the Kaknäs TV tower, Gröna Lund amusement park and the tram museum at Tegelviksgatan 22. Discounts for under-18s or over-65s bring the cost down to 33kr and 70kr respectively. Tourist cards can't be bought in T-bana stations, only from *Pressbyrå* or city tourist offices. Otherwise you can buy a strip of twenty reduced price SL **ticket coupons**, known as *rabattkuponger*, for 85kr – you'll have to stamp at least two for each journey. Buy them at the ticket barriers to any T-bana station.

Finally, if you're staying in Stockholm for a week or a fortnight it's worth considering a **monthly card** or *månadskort*, which allows unlimited travel on virtually everything that moves throughout the whole of Greater Stockholm for a mere 355kr. If you're spending several months in the city at a time it's probably worth buying a **season card**, *säsongskort* – prices vary depending on the time of year. All the above cards need a photograph and can be bought from any SL-Center.

One-way tickets for the **ferries** linking the central islands cost 15kr, rising to 65kr for the longer archipelago trips. Tickets can be bought on board or in advance from the offices of the main ferry company, *Waxholms Ångfartygs AB* (known as *Waxholmsbolaget*), on Strömkajen outside the *Grand Hotel*. If you intend to spend a week or so exploring the islands of the archipelago, it may be worth buying a special pass – see p.407 for details.

Bikes, taxis and parking

Bike rental is centrally available from *Skepp O'Hoj* at Galärvarvsvägen 10 (☎08/660 5757), just over the bridge to Djurgården, or from the nearby *Cykel-och Mopeduthyrningen* at Kajplats 24 along Strandvägen (☎08/660 7959); reckon on paying 180kr per day or 800kr per week for the latest mountain bike, less for a bone shaker. There are other less central places, too, among them *Servicedepån* at Kungsholmsgatan 34 on Kungsholmen (☎08/651 0066), which can rent out tandems.

To get a taxi, you can either attempt to hail one in the street, or more reliably call one of the four main operators: *Taxi Stockholm* (☎08/15 00 00), *Taxi Kurir* (☎08/30 00 00), *Top Cab* (☎08/33 33 33) or *Taxi 020* (☎08/85 04 00). If you do phone for a cab, the meter will show around 25kr before you even get in and will continue to race upwards at an alarming speed – every 10km costs 93kr or thereabouts during the day, 103kr between 7pm and 6am, and 110kr at weekends. A trip across the city centre should add up to around 100–120kr.

If you're driving, be warned that car **parking** in Stockholm is a hazardous business. Firstly, it's forbidden to park within ten metres of a road junction, whether a tiny residential cul-de-sac or a major intersection; nor can you park within the same distance of a pedestrian crossing; and on one particular night of the week (as specified on the rectangular yellow street signs) no parking is allowed, to allow for street cleaning and, in winter, snow clearance. You should never stop in a bus lane or in a loading zone. If your car is towed away (and they are with frightening regularity), go to the compound at Gasverksvägen in Ropsten (Mon–Fri 8am–7pm, Sat 11am–2.30pm; ☎08/651 0000) – a short walk from the T-bana – where surly staff will demand at least 1500kr for its return, an amount that increases on a daily basis. In short, if in doubt, don't park there: look for the words *Gatukontoret* or *Parkeringsbolaget* to indicate valid spaces. For details on **car rental**, see p.404.

Accommodation

Stockholm has plenty of **accommodation** to suit all tastes and budgets, from elegant hotels with waterfront views to some unusually sited youth hostels. However, demand is high, particularly late in the summer, and it's always advisable to book at least your first night's accommodation in advance. You can do this through the *Sverigehuset* tourist office or by calling the hotel or hostel direct.

Alternatively use the services of the excellent **Hotellcentralen**, the room-booking service in the main hall of Central Station (daily May & Sept 8am–7pm; June–Aug 7am–9pm; Oct–April 9am–6pm; ☎08/789 2425), which has comprehensive listings of hotels and hostels plus information on the latest special offers. If you call in to arrange accommodation on the spot you'll be charged a fee of 40kr per room, 15kr for a hostel room, but this is waived if you phone ahead. *Hotellcentralen* also operates the **Stockholm Package** between mid-June and mid-August (and at weekends all year round), an arrangement allowing reduced-price accommodation plus a free Stockholm Card (normally costing 175kr) for each night's stay. At the bottom end of the scale the deal can work out very economical – 300kr per person in a twin room with breakfast, going up to around 500kr in more upmarket hotels, plus *Hotellcentralen*'s regular 40kr booking fee. By calling in advance you can choose a particular hotel – on the day, you get whatever's available.

Hostels and private rooms

Stockholm has wide range of good, well-run **hostel** accommodation, costing from 70kr to 150kr a night per person. There are several official *STF* youth hostels in the city, two of which – *af Chapman* and *Långholmen* – number among the best hostels in Sweden. You'll have to plan ahead if you want to stay at most of the places listed below, particularly in summer. For a **private room**, contact *Hotelltjänst*, Vasagatan 15–17 (☎08/10 44 67), just a few minutes' walk from Central Station. Tell them how much you want to pay, and where in the city you want to stay, and you should land somewhere with a fridge and cooking facilities for around 250kr per person per night.

STF hostels

Af Chapman, Västra Brobänken, Skeppsholmen (☎08/679 5015; fax 611 9875); T-bana Kungsträdgården or bus #65 from Central Station. This square-rigged ship moored at Skeppsholmen has unsurpassed views over Gamla Stan. Without an advance written reservation (preferably two weeks before you arrive), the chances of a space in summer are slim: the drawbacks of a nautical night's accommodation are no kitchen and a lockout between 11am and 3pm. Open all year; reception 7am–noon and 3–10pm, closes every night at 2am; 100kr per bed.

Backpackers Inn, Banérgatan 56 (☎08/660 7515; fax 665 4039); T-bana Karlaplan exit Valhallavägen or bus #41. Fairly central option in a former school; laundry facilities available. Open end of June to mid-Aug; 85kr.

Långholmen, Kronohäktet, Långholmen (☎08/668 0510; fax 720 8575); T-bana Hornstull and follow the signs. Unusual site, inside the old prison on the island of Långholmen, whose cells have been converted into smart hotel and hostel rooms. The hostel is open all year round but between mid-Sept and mid-April there are only 26 beds available; at other times there are over 250. A great location with nearby beaches plus buses to Kungsholmen and the whole of Södermalm on the doorstep; fantastic views of Stockholm and of Lake Mälaren. Open all day; 125kr.

Skeppsholmen, Västra Brobänken, Skeppsholmen (☎08/679 5017; fax 611 7155); T-bana Kungsträdgården or bus #65. A dead central hostel, at the foot of the gangplank to *af Chapman*. Immensely popular, it's little better for speculative arrivals than the ship. No kitchen or laundry facilities. Open all year; lockout noon–3pm; beds cost 70kr or 100kr.

Zinkensdamm, Zinkens väg 20 (☎08/616 8100; fax 616 8120); T-bana Hornstull or Zinkensdamm. Huge hostel with 466 beds available in summer, 202 at other times. Kitchen and laundry facilities. Open all year and all day; beds 100kr or 125kr.

Independent hostels

Brygghusets Vandrarhem, Norrtullsgatan 12N (☎08/31 24 24; fax 31 02 06); T-bana Odenplan. Located close to the top end of Sveavägen around the lively area of Odenplan; 57 beds. Open June–Aug; 110kr.

City BackPackers Vandrarhem, Barnhusgatan 16 (☎08/20 69 20; fax 31 02 06); T-bana T-Centralen. Very central all-year hostel with space for 40 people; 110kr.

Columbus Hotell & Vandrarhem, Tjärhovsgatan 11 (☎08/644 1717; fax 702 0764); T-bana Medborgarplatsen. This friendly hostel has beds at around 120kr, double rooms from 300kr. Open all year.

Gustav af Klint, Stadsgårdskajen 153 (☎08/640 4077; fax 640 6416); T-bana Slussen. Floating hostel/hotel open all year, with cabin beds for around 120kr. Good central location, just a few minutes walk from the Old Town. The hostel accommodation is fine, but if it's full don't be tempted to take one of the hotel rooms – they're not worth the money.

Hotels and pensions

In summer the business trade declines and it's a buyer's market in Stockholm, with double rooms going for as little as 450kr. The cheapest choices on the whole are found to the north of Cityterminalen in the streets to the west of Adolf Fredriks kyrka. But

---

ACCOMMODATION PRICE CODES

All the Swedish pensions and hotels listed in the guide have been graded according to the following price bands, based on the cost of the least expensive double room in high season. However, almost every hotel offers midsummer and weekend discounts, and wherever possible we've given two grades, covering both the regular and the discounted rate. Single rooms, where available, are usually between 60 and 80 percent of the cost of a double.

① under 500kr   ② 500–700kr   ③ 700–900kr   ④ 900–1200kr   ⑤ over 1200kr

don't rule out the more expensive places either: there are some attractive weekend and summer prices that can make a spot of luxury a little more affordable. All the following hotels and pensions include breakfast in the price unless otherwise stated. See p.379 for details of reservation services and the Stockholm Package.

Anno 1647, Mariagränd 3 (☎08/644 0480; fax 643 3700), near Slussen on Södermalm; T-bana Slussen. A seventeenth-century building, all pine floors and period furnishings; handy for the Old Town but not recommended for people with disabilities. ②/③

Bema, Upplandsgatan 13 (☎08/23 26 75; fax 20 53 58); bus #47 and #69 from Central Station. Small pension-style hotel with modern en-suite rooms, ten minutes' walk from the station. A good deal in summer and at weekends. ②

Castle, Riddargatan 14 (☎08/679 5700; fax 611 2022); T-bana Östermalmstorg. Good central hotel popular with jazz and blues musicians (live jazz on summer evenings). All rooms have a bath; good breakfast buffet. ②/⑤

Central, Vasagatan 38 (☎08/22 08 40; fax 24 75 73); T-bana T-Centralen. Modern hotel and the cheapest of all the hotels around the station. ③/④

Columbus, Tjärhovsgatan 11 (☎08/644 1717; fax 702 0764); T-bana Medborgarplatsen. Simple rooms in a building that looks like a school. No en-suite rooms. ②

Diplomat, Strandvägen 7C 5800; fax 783 6634); T-bana Östermalmstorg or buses #47 and #69. Rooms with a view out over Stockholm's grandest boulevard and inner harbour. Suites at the top end of the price range represent much better value than the cheaper rooms at the *Grand*. Summer and weekend deals. ⑤

Drottning Viktorias Örlogshem, Teatergatan 3 (☎08/611 0113; fax 611 3150); T-bana Kungsträdgården. Pension owned by the Swedish Navy, excellent value for such a central location. Older rooms – some en-suite. ③

First Hotel Reisen, Skeppsbron 12–14 (☎08/22 32 60; fax 20 15 59); T-bana Gamla Stan or Slussen. Traditional hotel with heavy wood-panelled interior. All rooms with bathtubs; excellent view over the Stockholm waterfront. ④/⑤

Gamla Stan, Lilla Nygatan 25 (☎08/24 44 50; fax 21 64 83); T-bana Gamla Stan. Elegant rooms in the only halfway affordable Old Town hotel in summer and at weekends, when it drops its rates. ③/④

Grand, Södra Blasieholmshamn 8 (☎08/679 3500; fax 611 8686); T-bana Kungsträdgården. Stockholm's classiest hotel – a late nineteenth-century harbourside building overlooking Gamla Stan – provides the last word in luxury at world-class prices. Only worth considering if you're staying in the best rooms, since suites with a view at the *Diplomat* go for the same price. ⑤

Pensionat Gustavsvik, Västmannagatan 15 (☎08/21 44 50; no fax); buses #47, #53 and #69 from Central Station. Small and cheap pension within ten minutes of the station. ①

Källhagens Wärdshus, Djurgårdsbrunnsvägen 10 (☎08/665 0300; fax 665 0399); bus #69 from Central Station and the centre of town. Highly recommended: twenty rooms painted in different colours in a fantastic spot overlooking the serene water of Djurgårdsbrunnsviken. ③/⑤

King's Lodge, Kungsgatan 37 (☎08/20 88 02; fax 733 5018); T-bana Hötorget. Four former offices now converted into an excellent central hotel, ideal for exploring Sveavägen and cinemaland. Advance booking necessary. No en-suite rooms. ①/②

Mälardrottningen, Riddarholmen (☎08/24 36 00; fax 24 36 76); T-bana Gamla Stan. An elegant white ship moored by the side of the island of Riddarholmen; cabin-style rooms in need of a lick of paint and bit of a polish but still good value for such a central location. ②/③

Queen's Hotel, Drottninggatan 71A (☎08/24 94 60; fax 21 76 20); T-bana Hötorget. En-suite rooms in a good mid-range pension-style hotel. Good breakfast buffet. ②

Scandic Crown Stockholm, Guldgränd 8, Södermalm (☎08/22 96 20; fax 21 62 68); T-bana Slussen. Lots of wooden floors throughout this chain hotel, but it's well worth the price if you get one of the rooms with a fantastic view out over Gamla Stan. ④/⑤

Stockholm, Norrmalmstorg 1 (☎08/678 1320; fax 611 2103); T-bana Östermalmstorg or Kungsträdgården. A penthouse hotel on the top floor of a centrally located office block; good views out over Strandvägen and the harbour. Squeaky wooden floors and faded bathrooms – recommended. ②/⑤

Tre Små Rum, Högbergsgatan 81 (☎08/641 2371; fax 642 8808); T-bana Mariatorget. Six wonderful, bright, clean modern rooms with a Japanese flavour in the heart of Södermalm. Very popular and often full. ①

Wallin, Wallingatan 15 (☎08/20 15 20; fax 791 5050); buses #47 and #69 from Central Station, or a ten minute walk. Decent central hotel with en-suite rooms. ②/④

Zinkensdamm, Zinkens väg 20 (☎08/616 8110; fax 616 8120); T-bana Hornstull or Zinkensdamm. Hotel rooms in a separate wing of the youth hostel (see above). A good choice for the price. ②/③

Camping

With the nearest year-round campsites well out of the city centre, **camping** in Stockholm can prove a bit of a drag. In summer, however, there is a city campsite in Östermalm. The tourist offices provide free booklets detailing facilities at all Stockholm's campsites. In July and August it costs around 100kr for two people to pitch a tent, half that the rest of the year.

Ängby (☎08/37 04 20; fax 37 82 26); T-bana Ängbyplan on the green line towards Välingby. West of the city on the lakeshore. Open all year.

Bredäng (☎08/97 70 71; fax 708 7262); T-bana Bredäng on the red line towards Norsborg. Southwest of the city with views over Lake Mälaren. Open all year.

Östermalms Citycamping (☎08/10 29 03); T-bana Stadion. The most central campsite in town, behind the Stockholm stadium at Fiskartorpsvägen 2. Open late June to mid-Aug.

Solvalla Citycamping, Sundbybergkopplet behind the Solvalla trotting track (☎08/627 0380; fax 627 0370); T-bana Rissne on the blue line towards Hjulsta, then walk 1km. Open all year.

The City

Seeing the sights is a straightforward business in Stockholm: everything is easy to get to, opening hours are long, and the city is a relaxed and spacious place to wander. While the sights and museums may have changed, visitors have been noting Stockholm's aesthetic qualities for 150 years. At one time you would have seen great orchards, grazing cows, even windmills in central Stockholm; the downside then was a lack of pavements (until the 1840s) and no water system (until 1858), open sewers, squalid streets and crowded slums. Later, in the twentieth century, a huge modernization programme was undertaken as part of the Social Democrats' "out with the old and in with the new" policy; the result, unfortunately, can be seen only too clearly around Sergels Torg: five high-rise carbuncles and an ugly rash of soulless concrete blocks that blot the city centre landscape.

But today, the combination of elegant Old Town architecture, wide tree-lined boulevards and great expanses of open water right in the centre all conspire to offer a city panorama unparalleled anywhere in Europe. In addition, Stockholm boasts a bewildering range of museums and galleries, the best of which are described in the account below – for a rundown of the remainder, see p.395.

Old Stockholm: Gamla Stan and Riddarholmen

Three islands make up the **oldest part of Stockholm** – Riddarholmen, Staden and Helgeandsholmen – the whole history-riddled mass a cluster of seventeenth- and eighteenth-century Renaissance buildings backed by narrow medieval alleys. Here, on three adjoining polyps of land, Birger Jarl erected the first fortification in 1255, and for centuries this was the first city of Stockholm. Rumours abound about the derivation of the name Stockholm, but it's generally thought that some sort of wooden drying frames, known as "stocks" were erected on the island that is now home to Gamla Stan thus making it the island, *holm*, of *stocks*. Incidentally, today the word *stock* means log.

Although strictly speaking only the largest island, **Staden**, contains **Gamla Stan**, the Old Town, it's a name that is usually attached to the buildings and streets of all three

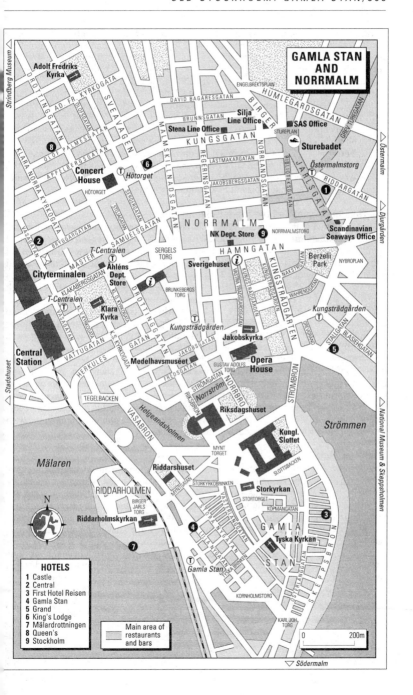

GAMLA STAN
AND
NORRMALM

HOTELS
1 Castle
2 Central
3 First Hotel Reisen
4 Gamla Stan
5 Grand
6 King's Lodge
7 Mälardrottningen
8 Queen's
9 Stockholm

Main area of
restaurants
and bars

0   200m

▽ *Södermalm*

islands. Once Stockholm's working centre, nowadays Gamla Stan is primarily a tourist city, an eminently strollable concentration of royal palace, parliament and cathedral, and one that represents an extraordinary tableau of cultural history. The central spider's web, especially if you approach it over Norrbron or Riksbron, invokes potent images of the past: sprawling monumental buildings and high airy churches form a protective girdle around the narrow streets. The tall dark houses in the centre were mostly those of wealthy merchants, still picked out today by intricate doorways and portals bearing coats of arms. Some of the alleys in between are the skinniest thoroughfares possible, steeply stepped between battered walls; others are covered passageways linking leaning buildings. It's easy to spend hours wandering around here, although the atmosphere these days is not so much medieval as mercenary: there's a dense concentration of antique shops, art showrooms and chi-chi cellar restaurants, though the frontages don't really intrude upon the otherwise light-starved streets. Not surprisingly, this is the most exclusive part of Stockholm in which to live.

The Riksdagshuset and the Medeltidsmuseum

Entering or leaving the Old Town, you're bound to pass the Swedish parliament building, the **Riksdagshuset** (late June to late Aug; guided tours in English at 12.30pm and 2pm; free). Despite the assassination of the former Swedish Prime Minister, Olof Palme, in 1986 (see p.367), Swedish politicians still go freely about their business and you'll often see them nipping in and out of the building or lunching in one of the nearby restaurants. The Riksdagshuset itself was completely restored in the 1970s (though only 70 years old then) and today the grand columned front entrance (seen to best effect from Norrbron) is hardly ever used, the business end being the new glassy bulge at the back – it's here that guided tours perambulate. This being Sweden, the building contains a creche and the seating in the chamber itself is in healthy, non-adversarial rows, with members grouped by constituency rather than party.

In front of the Riksdag (pronounced "Reeks-da"), accessible by a set of steps leading down from Norrbron, the **Medeltidsmuseum** (Tues–Sun 11am–4pm, Wed till 6pm; 30kr) is a museum of medieval Stockholm. Medieval ruins, tunnels and walls were discovered during excavations under the parliament building and have been incorporated into what is a fascinating walk-through underground exhibition. There are reconstructed houses to poke around, models and pictures, boats, skeletons and street scenes, all enhanced by detailed labelling in English.

Kungliga Slottet

Cross over a second section of bridges and up rears the most distinctive monumental building in Stockholm, **Kungliga Slottet**, the Royal Palace – a low, yellowy-brown square building whose two front arms stretch down towards the water. Stockholm's old Tre Kronor (Three Crowns) castle burned down at the beginning of King Karl XII's reign, leaving his architect, Tessin the Younger (see p.406), with a free hand to design a simple and beautiful Renaissance structure. Finished in 1754, the palace is a striking achievement: uniform and sombre from the outside, its magnificent Baroque and Rococo interior is a swirl of state rooms and museums. The sheer size and limited opening hours conspire against seeing everything at once. Outside the hours detailed below, the different sections of the palace have varying and often restricted opening times (the Armoury being the only exception), and some may be closed entirely during state occasions.

The **Apartments** (June–Aug daily 10am–4pm; 45kr) form a relentlessly linear collection of furniture and tapestries. It's all basically Rent-a-Palace stuff, too sumptuous to take in and inspirational only in terms of colossal size. The **Treasury** (same times; 30kr), on the other hand, is certainly worthy of the name, with its ranks of jewel-studded crowns: the oldest is that of Karl X (1650), the most charming are those belonging to princesses Eugëne (1860) and Sofia (1771). Also worth catching is the **Armoury** (daily 11am–4pm; 45kr), less to do with weapons and more to do with ceremony: suits of armour, costumes and horse-drawn carriages from the sixteenth century onwards. It certainly couldn't be accused of skipping over historical detail. King Gustav II Adolf died in the Battle of Lützen in 1632 and the museum displays his horse (stuffed) and the blood- and mud-spattered garments retrieved after the enemy had stripped him down to his boxer shorts on the battlefield. For those with the energy, the **Palace Museum** (June–Aug daily 11am–4pm; 10kr) contains part of the older Tre Kronor castle, whose ruins lie beneath the present building. For real palace junkies, there's also the **Museum of Antiquities** (June–Aug daily 10am–4pm; 40kr) and the **Hall of State** (same times; 10kr). Alongside the palace at Slottsbacken 6, the **Royal Coin Cabinet** (due to reopen at the time of writing; times and price unconfirmed) is home to a stash of coins, banknotes and medals, as well as a number of silver hordes from Viking days.

Into Gamla Stan: Storatorget and around

Beyond the Royal Palace you're into Gamla Stan proper, the streets suddenly narrower and darker. Here, the highest point of old Stockholm is crowned by **Storkyrkan**, the Great Church, consecrated in 1306. Pedantically speaking, Stockholm has no cathedral, but this rectangular brick church fulfils the same role and is the place where the monarchs of Sweden are married and crowned. Storkyrkan gained its present shape at the end of the fifteenth century, with a Baroque remodelling in the the 1730s. Inside, twentieth-century restoration has removed the white plaster from the red-brick columns and although there's no evidence that this was intended in the original, it gives a warm colouring to the rest of the building. Much is made of the fifteenth-century Gothic sculpture of St George and the Dragon, certainly an animated piece but easily overshadowed by the royal pews – more like golden billowing thrones – and the monumental black and silver altarpiece. Organ recitals take place here every Saturday at 1pm.

Stretching south from the church is **Storatorget**, Gamla Stan's handsome and elegantly proportioned main square. Crowded by eighteenth-century buildings whose walls bear wrought-iron lamps, today it's surrounded by narrow shopping streets. In 1520 Christian II used the square as an execution site during the "Stockholm Blood Bath", dispatching his opposition en masse with bloody finality. Now, as then, the streets **Västerlånggatan** and **Österlånggatan**, **Stora Nygatan** and **Lilla Nygatan** run the length of the Old Town on either side of the square, although today their time-worn buildings harbour a succession of art and craft shops and restaurants. Happily though the consumerism is largely unobtrusive and in summer buskers and evening strollers clog the narrow alleyways, making it an entertaining area to wander – and to eat and drink. There are few real targets, though at some stage you'll probably pass the copy of the George and Dragon statue in **Köpmantorget** (off Österlånggatan). Take every opportunity too to scuttle up side streets, where you'll find fading coats of arms, covered alleyways and worn cobbles at every turn.

Just of Västerlånggatan, on Tyska Brinken, is the German Church or **Tyska kyrkan** (Sat & Sun noon–4pm), originally owned by Stockholm's medieval German merchants, when it served as the meeting place of the Guild of St Gertrude. A copper-topped redbrick church atop a rise, it abandoned its secular role in the seventeenth century, when Baroque decorators got hold of it: the result, a richly fashioned interior with the pulpit dominating the nave, is outstanding. Sporting a curious royal gallery in one corner, designed by Tessin the Elder, it came complete with mini palace roof, angels and the three crowns of Swedish kingship.

The Riddarhuset and Riddarholmen

If Stockholm's history has gripped you, it's better to head west from Storatorget towards the handsome Baroque **Riddarhuset** (Mon–Fri 11.30am–12.30pm; 20kr), the seventeenth-century "House of Nobles". It was in the Great Hall here that the Swedish aristocracy met during the Parliament of the Four Estates (1668–1865) and their coats of arms – around 2500 of them – are splattered across the walls. Some six hundred of the noble families survive, the last ennoblement in 1974. Take a look downstairs, too, at the Chancery, which stores heraldic bone china by the shelf load and racks full of fancy signet rings – essential accessories for the eighteenth-century noble-about-town.

Riddarhuset shouldn't really be seen in isolation. It takes only a matter of seconds to cross the bridge onto **Riddarholmen** (Island of the Knights) proper, to visit the **Riddarholmskyrkan** (daily noon–4pm; 20kr). Originally a Franciscan monastery, for over six centuries the church has been the burial place of Swedish royalty. Since Magnus Ladulås was sealed up here in 1290, his successors have rallied round to create a Swedish pantheon and, amongst others, you'll find the tombs of Gustav II Adolf (in the green marble sarcophagus), Karl XII, Gustav III and Karl Johan XIV, plus other innumerable and unmemorable descendants. Walk around the back of the church for stunning views of Stadshuset, the City Hall and Lake Mälaren. Incidentally, the island to the left of Västerbron (the bridge in the distance) is Långholmen; in winter people skate and even take their dogs for walks on the ice along here, as the water freezes solid right up to the bridge and beyond.

Skeppsholmen

Off Gamla Stan's eastern reaches, a ten-minute walk from Storatorget, lies the island of **Skeppsholmen**, home to two of the city's youth hostels. If you're not staying, the main reason to come here is for an eclectic clutch of museums, the most impressive of them just by the Skeppsholmsbron, the bridge onto the island. Other than the museums there's little to detain you on Skeppsholmen or on adjacent microscopic **Kastellholmen**, connected by a bridge to the south. However, both these Baltic islands proved attractive enough to induce the Swedish Navy to settle there in the nineteenth century and some of the old barracks are still visible if you walk around.

The National Art Museum

As you approach the bridge it's impossible to miss the striking waterfront **Nationalmuseum**, Sweden's National Art Museum (Tues 11am–8pm, Wed–Sun 11am–5pm; 40kr), looking right out over the Royal Palace. The impressive collection is contained on three floors: the **ground floor** is taken up by changing exhibitions of prints and drawings, and there's a shop and café here too, as well as lockers for leaving your bags. So much is packed into the museum that it can quickly become confusing and overwhelming – it's worth splashing out on the guidebook.

The **first floor** is devoted to applied art and if it's curios you're after, this museum has the lot – beds slept in by kings, cabinets leaned on by queens, plates eaten off by nobles – mainly from the centuries when Sweden was a great power. There's modern work alongside the ageing tapestries and furniture, including Art Nouveau coffee pots and vases, and examples demonstrating the intelligent simplicity of Swedish chair design.

It's the **second floor**, however, that's most engaging, featuring a plethora of European and Mediterranean sculpture and some mesmerizing sixteenth- and seveteenth-century Russian icons. The paintings are equally wide ranging and of a similarly high quality, including works by El Greco, Canaletto, Gainsborough, Gauguin and Renoir. Something of a coup for the museum is Rembrandt's *Conspiracy of Claudius Civilis*, one of his largest monumental paintings, a bold depiction of well-armed Roman chieftains, displayed in room 33. There are minor works by other later masters (most notably Renoir) and some fine sixteenth- to eighteenth-century works by **Swedish artists**. One, by Carl Gustav Pilo, a late eighteenth-century painting, depicts the coronation of Gustav III in the Storkyrkan in Gamla Stan, the detail interesting since it shows the church with its white plaster columns and not the red brick of today.

Skeppsholmen's museums

Stockholm's museum of modern art, the **Moderna Muséet**, is one of the better modern art collections in Europe, with a comprehensive selection of works by some of the leading artists of the twentieth century. At the time of writing, however, it was closed for renovation and due to reopen in February 1998. In the meantime, the exhibits have been crammed into the premises at Birger Jarlsgatan 57 (Tues–Thurs noon–7pm, Fri–Sun noon–5pm; 50kr). Although the setting isn't perfect, it's still possible to appreciate Dalí's monumental *Enigma of William Tell*, showing the artist at his most conventionally unconventional, and Matisse's striking *Apollo*. Look out, too, for Picasso's *Guitar Player* and a whole host of works by Warhol, Lichtenstein, Man Ray and Francis Bacon. Bus #46 runs from Slussen or Skeppsbron in Gamla Stan to the temporary exhibition space.

A steep climb up the northern tip of the island brings you to **Östasiatiska Muséet** the Museum of Far Eastern Antiquities (Tues noon–8pm, Wed–Sun noon–5pm; 40kr). The reward is an array of objects displaying incredible craftsmanship – fifth-century Chinese tomb figures, delicate jade amulets, an astounding assembly of sixth-century Buddhas, Indian watercolours and gleaming bronze Krishna figures – and that's just one room. Finally, Skeppsholmen's other diversion is the **Arkitektur Muséet** (Tues 11am–8pm, Wed–Sun 11am–5pm; 20kr), on Västra Brobänken, next to the *af Chapman* youth hostel, which stages temporary exhibitions on various aspects of architecture and urban planning within Sweden. Perhaps one for a rainy day.

Norrmalm and Kungsholmen

Modern Stockholm lies immediately to the north and east of Gamla Stan, and is split into two distinct sections. **Norrmalm**, to the north, is the buzzing commercial heart of the city, packed with restaurants, bars, cinemas and shops, while to the east is more sedate Östermalm, a well-to-do area of classy boulevards, covered on p.390. The island of **Kungsholmen**, linked by bridge to the west of Norrmalm, is a mostly residential and administrative district, though with a positive draw in Stockholm's landmark City Hall.

Around Gustav Adolfs Torg

Down on the waterfront, at the foot of Norrbron, is **Gustav Adolfs Torg**, more a traffic island than a square these days, with the nineteenth-century **Operan** (Opera House) its proudest, most notable – and ugliest – building. It was here in an earlier opera house on the same site, at a masked ball in 1792, that King Gustav III was shot by one Captain Ankarström, an admirer of Rousseau and member of the aristocratic opposition. The story is recorded in Verdi's opera *Un ballo in maschera* and you can see Gustav's ball costume, as well as the assassin's pistols and mask, on display in the Palace Armoury in Gamla Stan. The opera's famous restaurant, *Operakällaren*, is hellishly expensive, the trendy café less so.

A statue of King Gustav II Adolf marks the centre of the square, between Operan and the Foreign Office opposite. Look out hereabouts for fishermen pulling salmon out of **Strömmen**, the fast flowing water that winds its way through the centre of the city. Stockholmers have had the right to fish this outlet from Lake Mälaren to the Baltic since the seventeenth century; it's not as difficult as it sounds and there's usually a group of hopefuls on one of the bridges around the square trying their luck.

Just off the square, at Fredsgatan 2 in the heart of Swedish government land is **Medelhavsmuséet**, a sparkling museum devoted to Mediterranean and Near Eastern antiquities (Tues 11am–9pm, Wed–Sun 11am–4pm; 40kr). Its enormous Egyptian section covers just about every aspect of Egyptian life up to the Christian era. As well as several whopping great mummies, the most attractive pieces are the bronze weapons, tools and domestic objects from the time before the Pharaohs. The Cyprus collections are also huge, the largest such gathering outside Cyprus itself, spanning a period of over six thousand years. Additionally the museum contains strong Greek displays and comprehensive collections of Etruscan and Roman art. A couple of rooms examine Islamic culture through pottery, glass and metal work, as well as decorative elements of architecture, Arabian calligraphy and Persian miniature painting.

Walk back towards Operan and continue across the main junction onto Arsenalsgatan to reach **Jakobs kyrka** (daily 11am–5pm), one of the city's many easily overlooked churches. It's the pulpit that draws the attention, a great, golden affair, while the date of the church's consecration – 1642 – is stamped high up on the ceiling in gold figures. There are weekly classical music recitals here, with organ and choir recitals on Saturday at 3pm.

Kungsträdgården

Just beyond the Jacobs kyrka and Operan, Norrmalm's eastern boundary is marked by **Kungsträdgården**, most fashionable and central of the city numerous parks, reaching from the water northwards as far as **Hamngatan**. The mouthful of a name literally means "the king's gardens", though if you're expecting neatly trimmed flower beds and rose gardens you'll be sadly disappointed – it's a great expanse of concrete with a couple of lines of trees. The area may once have been a royal kitchen garden, but nowadays it serves as Stockholm's main meeting place, especially in summer when there's almost always something happening: free evening gigs, theatre and other performances take place on the central open-air stage. Look out too for the park's cafés, in spring packed out with winter-weary Stockholmers soaking up the sun. In winter the park is equally busy, particularly at the Hamngatan end where there's an open-air ice rink, the **Isbanan** (Oct–April daily 9am–6pm; skate rental 30kr). The main tourist office is close by here, in *Sverigehuset*, at the corner of Hamngatan (see p.376).

Hamngatan runs east to **Birger Jarlsgatan**, the main thoroughfare that divides Norrmalm from Östermalm and now a mecca for eating and drinking, but until 1855 the site of two pillories and largely rural (see p.396).

Segels Torg to Hötorget

At the western end of Hamngatan, beyond the enormous *NK* department store, lies **Segels Torg**, the ugliest part of modern Stockholm. It's an unending free show centred on the five seething floors of **Kulturhuset** (Tues–Fri 11am–6pm, Sat & Sun noon–5pm), whose windows look down upon the milling concrete square. Inside this building devoted to contemporary Swedish culture there are temporary art and craft exhibitions together with workshops open to anyone willing to get their hands dirty. The reading room (*Läsesalongen*) on the ground level is stuffed with foreign newspapers, books, records and magazines – a good refuge if it's wet and windy outside. Check the information desk as you come in for details of poetry readings, concerts and theatre performances – admission to Kulturhuset is free but you have to pay to get into any exhibitions or performances. Check out the café on the top floor for delicious apple pie and custard with some of the best views of central Stockholm, though beware that the service often leaves something to be desired.

From the café you'll get a bird's-eye view of the singularly ugly, tall, wire-like column that dominates the massive open space outside and the surrounding spewing fountain (often obscured by soap suds – the local youth think it's a real wheeze to pour packets of washing powder into the fountain). Down the steps, below Sergels Torg, is **Sergels Arkaden**, a set of grotty underground walkways home to buskers, brass bands and demented lottery ticket vendors; look out for the odd demonstration, too, or oddball game – you may spot young Stockholmers running around shivering in their skimpy underwear, having tied the rest of their clothes together in a line to see whose is longest, a singularly Swedish pastime. There are also entrances down here into **T-Centralen**, the central T-bana station, and Stockholm's other main department store, *Åhléns*, not quite as posh as *NK* and easier to find your way around.

A short walk west from Kulturhuset along Klarabergsgatan will bring you to **Central Station** and **Cityterminalen**, hub of virtually all Stockholm's transport. The area around here is given over to unabashed consumerism but as you explore the streets around the main drag, **Drottinggatan**, you'll find little to get excited about – run-of-the-mill clothing shops, twee gift shops punctuated by *McDonalds* and the odd sausage stand. In summer the occasional busker or jewellery stall livens up what is essentially a soulless grid of pedestrianized shopping streets. The only point of culture is the **Klara kyrka** (Mon–Fri 10am–6pm, Sat 10am–7pm, Sun 8.30am–6pm), just to the right off Klarabergsgatan, opposite the station. Another of Stockholm's easily missed churches, hemmed in on all sides with only the spires visible from the surrounding streets, it's a particularly delicate example, with a light and flowery eighteenth-century painted interior and an impressive golden pulpit. Out in the churchyard, a memorial stone commemorates eighteenth-century Swedish poet Carl Michael Bellman, whose popular, lengthy ballads are said to have been composed extempore; his unmarked grave is somewhere in the churchyard.

Three blocks further up Drottinggatan, the cobbled square of **Hötorget** hosts an open-air fruit and veg market on weekdays, as well as the wonderful indoor **Hötorgshallen**, an orgy of Middle Eastern smells and sights and a good place to pick up ethnic snacks. Grab something to eat and plonk yourself on the steps of the **Konserthuset**, one of the venues for the presentation of the Nobel Prizes, and a good place to hear classical music recitals (often free on Sunday afternoons). The tall building opposite is a former department store where Greta Garbo once worked as a sales assistant in the hat department. If this inspires you to go to the movies, you only have to walk across the square to *Filmstaden*, Stockholm's biggest cinema complex; to the east, **Kungsgatan**, which runs down to Stureplan and Birger Jarlsgatan, holds most of the city's other cinemas, interpersed with agreeable little cafés (see p.402).

North to the Strindbergsmuséet

From Hötorget the two main streets of Drottninggatan and Sveavägen run parallel uphill and north as far as Odengatan and the **Stadsbiblioteket** or City Library, in its own little park. Close by, set in secluded gardens between the two roads, sits the eighteenth-century **Adolf Fredriks kyrka**. Although it has a noteworthy past – the French philosopher Descartes was buried here in 1650 before being moved to France – the church would be insignificant today were it not the final resting place for the assassinated Swedish Prime Minister, **Olof Palme**: a simple headstone and flowers mark his grave. A simple plaque now marks the spot on Sveavägen, near the junction with Olof Palmes Gata, where the prime minister was gunned down; the assassin escaped up the nearby flight of steps (see box below).

Continue north along Drottninggatan and you'll come to the "Blue Tower" at no. 85, the last building in which the writer August Strindberg lived and now revived as the **Strindbergsmuséet** (Tues–Sun 11am–4pm; 25kr; T-bana Rådmansgatan). Strindberg lived here between 1908 and 1912 and his house has been preserved to the extent that you must put plastic bags on your feet to protect the floors and furnishings. The study remains as he left it on his death, a dark and gloomy place – he would work with both venetian blinds and heavy curtains closed against the sunlight. Upstairs is his library, a musty room with all the books firmly behind glass, which is a shame because Strindberg wasn't a passive reader: he underlined heavily and made notes in the margins as he read, though these are rather less erudite than you'd expect: "Lies!", "Crap!", "Idiot!" and "Bloody hell!" seem to have been his favourite comments. Good explanatory notes in English are supplied free.

THE ASSASSINATION OF OLAF PALME

The shooting of Prime Minister Olof Palme in February 1986 sent shockwaves through a society unused to political extremism of any kind. Like most Nordic leaders his fame was his security, and his died unprotected, gunned down in front of his wife on their way home from the cinema on Sveavägen. A politically instructive end, it has sadly led to a radical rethink of Sweden's long-established policy of open government. Sweden's biggest ever murder enquiry was launched and as the years went by so the allegations of police cover-ups and bungling grew. When Christer Pettersson was jailed for the murder (see "History", p.367), most Swedes believed that to be the end of the story, but his eventual release only served to reopen the bitter debate. There have been recriminations and resignations within a derided police force and although in the past the most popular suspects were immigrant Kurdish extremists, right-wing terror groups or even a hitman from within the police itself, newer theories have suggested that the corrupt regime in South Africa was behind the killing. Palme was an outspoken critic of Apartheid, leading calls for an economic blockade against Pretoria, and these recent claims are being treated very seriously in Sweden.

Kungsholmen: Stadshuset

Take the T-bana back to the centre, get off at T-Centralen, and it's only a matter of minutes from there, across the Stadshusbron, to the island of **Kungsholmen** and Stockholm's City Hall. Finished in 1923, the **Stadshuset** (guided tours June–Aug 10am, 11am, noon & 2pm; irregularly rest of the year; 30kr) is a landmark of the modern city and one of the first buildings you'll see when approaching Stockholm from the south by train. Its simple, if somewhat drab, exterior brickwork is no preparation for the intricate decor within. If you're a visiting Head of State you'll be escorted from your boat up the elegant waterside steps. For lesser mortals, the only way to view the innards is on one of the guided tours, which reveal the kitschy Viking-style legislative chamber and impressively echoing Golden Hall. The Stadshuset is also the departure point for **boats** to Drottningholm, Mariefred and Uppsala.

Venture further into Kungsholmen and you'll discover a rash of excellent bars and restaurants that has sprung up here – see p.396 – and an excellent **beach** at Smedsudden (buses #54 and #62 to Västerbroplan, then a 5–min walk). Another attraction is the popular **Rålambshovsparken**, where you can take a swim with fantastic views of the City Hall and Old Town.

Östermalm

East of Birger Jarlsgatan the streets become noticeably broader and grander, a uniform grid as far as Karlaplan. **Östermalm** was one of the last areas of central Stockholm to be developed, and with the greenery of Djurgården beginning to make itself felt, the impressive residences hereabouts are as likely to be consulates and embassies as fashionable homes. The first place to head for is the water's edge square, **Nybroplan**, just east along Hamngatan from Sergels Torg, and marked with the white-stone relief-studded **Kungliga Dramatiska Teatern**, Stockholm's showpiece theatre. The curved harbour in front is the departure point for all kinds of archipelago **ferries** and tours (see p.407), and for a summer shuttle service via Skeppsholmen to the Nordiska and Vasa museums over on Djurgården (July & Aug every 15min; 20kr). Look out too for the stone pillars near the water with their snaking lines of multicoloured lights – they're an indication of how clean the city's air and water are at the moment.

Behind the theatre at Sibyllegatan 2 is the innovative **Musikmuséet** (Tues–Sun 11am–4pm; 30kr), containing a range of instruments that visitors are allowed to experiment with. The museum charts the history of music in Sweden using photographs, instruments and sound recordings. Best are the sections that deal with the late nineteenth century, a time when *folkmusik* has been given fresh impetus by the growing labour movement. The concluding parts on "progressive" and "disco" music are brief and uninteresting, with the merest mention of punk and, astonishingly, nothing on ABBA.

The chief feature of this end of the city was once the barracks, a history recalled today by the presence of the **Armémuséet**, opposite the Musikmuséet at Riddargatan 13. Hardly anyone comes to visit its displays of precision killing machines, uniforms, swords and medals, and you're likely to be outnumbered by the alert and omnipresent attendants. At present the museum is closed for renovations – ask at the tourist office to find out when it will reopen.

Just back from the museums, up the hill of Sibyllegatan, **Östermalmstorg** is an absolute find: the square is home to the **Östermalms saluhallen**, an indoor market hall not unlike Norrmalm's Hötorgshallen, but selling more refined delicatessen items – reindeer hearts and the like – and attracting a clientele to match. Wander round at lunchtime and you'll spot any number of fur-coated Stockholmers, sipping Chardonnay and munching shrimp sandwiches.

Historiska Muséet

As you plod your way around Östermalm's rich streets, you're bound to end up at the circular **Karlaplan** sooner or later: a handy T-bana and bus interchange, full of media types coming off shift from the Swedish Radio and Television buildings at the end of Karlavägen. From here it's a short walk (or #44 bus ride) down Narvavägen to the impressive **Historiska Muséet** (Tues–Sun 11am–5pm; 55kr) at nos. 13–17; from Norrmalm, take bus #56 via Stureplan and Linnégatan. The most wide-ranging historical display in Stockholm, it's really two large collections: a museum of National Antiquities and the new underground Gold Room, with its magnificent fifth-century gold collars and other fine jewellery. Ground-floor highlights include a Stone Age ideal home – flaxen-haired youth, stripped pine benches and rows of neatly labelled herbs – and a mass of Viking weapons, coins and boats, much of it labelled in English. Upstairs there's a worthy collection of medieval church art and architecture, with odds and ends turned up from all over the country, evocatively housed in massive vaulted rooms. If you're heading to Gotland, be sure to look out for the reassembled bits of stave churches uncovered on the Baltic island – some of the few examples that survive in Sweden.

Djurgården

When you tire of pounding the streets, there's respite at hand in the form of Stockholm's so-called National City Park, and in particular the section just to the east of the centre, **Djurgården** (pronounced "Yoor-gorn"). Originally royal hunting grounds from the sixteenth to eighteenth centuries, it is actually two distinct park areas separated by the water of **Djurgårdsbrunnsviken** – popular for swimming in summer and skating in winter when the channel freezes over. Also in Djurgården are some of Stockholm's finest **museums**: the massive open-air Skansen, an amazing conglomeration of architecture and folk culture from around the country, and Vasamuséet, the home of a marvellously preserved seventeenth-century warship.

You can walk to Djurgården through the centre out along Strandvägen but it's quite a hike: take bus #44 from Karlaplan or from Norrmalm buses #47 and #69 (only as far at the bridge, Djurgårdsbron, over onto the island) from the centre; or the ferries from Skeppsbron in Gamla Stan (all year) or Nybroplan (July & Aug only).

The Nordiska Muséet, Skansen and Gröa Lunds Tivoli

A full day is just about enough to see everything on Djurgården. Starting with the palatial **Nordiska Muséet**, the Nordic Museum (Tues–Sun 11am–5pm; 50kr, students 30kr), just over Djurgårdsbron from Strandvägen, is the best idea, if only because the same cultural themes pop up repeatedly throughout the rest of the island's exhibitions. The displays are a recent attempt to represent Swedish cultural history (from over the past 500 years) in an accessible fashion, and the Sami section is particularly good. On the ground floor of the cathedral-like interior is Carl Milles's phenomenal statue of Gustav Vasa, the sixteenth-century king who drove out the Danes, and an inspirational figure who wrought the best from the sculptor (for more on Milles, see p.405).

However, it's for **Skansen** (daily 9am–10pm; July & Aug 55kr, rest of the year 45kr) that most people come here: a great open-air museum with 150 reconstructed buildings, ranging from an entire town to windmills and farms laid out on a region by region basis, with each section boasting its own daily activities – traditional handicrafts, games and displays – that anyone can join in. Best of the buildings are the small Sami dwellings, warm and functional, and the craftsmen's workshops in the old town quarter. You can also potter around a small **zoo** and a bizarre **aquarium**, fish cheek by jowl with crocodiles, monkeys and snakes. Partly because of the attention paid to accuracy, partly due to the admirable lack of commercialization (a rarity in Sweden), Skansen manages to avoid the tackiness associated with similar ventures in other countries. Even the snack bars dole out traditional foods and in winter serve up great bowls of warming soup.

Immediately opposite Skansen's main gates (and at the end of the #44 bus route; bus #47 also goes by), **Gröna Lunds Tivoli** (May to mid-Sept daily noon–midnight; shorter hours in winter; 40kr) is not a patch on its more famous namesake in Copenhagen, though decidedly cleaner and less seedy. It's definitely more of a place to stroll through rather than indulging in the rides (none included in the entrance fee), which are frankly tame. At night the emphasis shifts as the park becomes the stomping ground for Stockholm's youth, with raucous music, cafés and some enterprising chat-up lines to be heard.

Vasamuséet

In a brand new building close to the Nordiska Muséet, the **Vasamuséet** (mid-June to mid-Aug daily 9.30am–7pm; rest of the year daily 10am–5pm, Wed till 8pm; 45kr) is without question head and shoulders above anything else that Stockholm has to offer in the way of museums. Built on the orders of King Gustav II Adolf, the *Vasa* warship sank in Stockholm harbour on her maiden voyage in 1628. Preserved in mud for over 300 years, the ship was raised along with 12,000 objects in 1961, and now forms the centrepiece of a startling, purpose-built hall on the water's edge. The museum itself is built over part of the old naval dockyard and was designed to give the impression of a large, soft copper tent, the materials used supposed to relate to navy colours and designs: stone and ochre, tarred black beams mixed in with whites, reds and the green of Djurgården.

Impressive though the building is, nothing prepares you for the sheer size of the **ship** itself: 62m long, the main mast originally 50m over the keel, it sits virtually complete in a cradle of supporting mechanical tackle. Surrounding walkways bring you nose to nose with cannon hatches and restored decorative relief, the gilded wooden sculptures on the soaring prow designed to intimidate the enemy and proclaim Swedish might. Faced with its frightening bulk, it's not difficult to understand the terror that such ships must have generated. Adjacent **exhibition halls** and presentations on several levels take care of all the retrieved bits and bobs. There are reconstructions of life on board, detailed models of the *Vasa*, displays relating to comtemporary social and political life, films and videos of the rescue operation, excellent English explanations and regular English-language **guided tours**.

Thielska Galleriet

At the far eastern end of Djurgården (take bus #69 from Norrmalm), **Thielska Galleriet** (Mon–Sat noon–4pm, Sun 1–4pm; 40kr) is one of Stockholm's major treasures, a fine example of both Swedish architecture and art. The house was built by Fredinand Boberg at the turn of this century for a banker, Ernet Thiel, who then sold it to the state in 1924, when it was turned into an art gallery. Thiel, who knew many contemporary Nordic artists, gathered an impressive collection of paintings over the years, many of which are on display today – there are works by Carl Larsson, Anders Zorn, Edvard Munch, Bruno Liljefors and even August Strindberg. The views, too, are attractive enough to warrant a trip out here.

The TV tower: Kaknästornet

Bus #69 from Norrmalm will take you directly to Stockholm's landmark TV tower, in the northern stretch of parkland known as **Ladugårdsgärdet** (or, more commonly, Gärdet); it's also possible to walk here from Djurgården proper – head northwards across the island on Manillavägen over Djurgårdsbrunnsviken. At 160m, **Kaknäs TV tower** (daily 9am–10pm; 20kr) is the highest building in Scandinavia, allowing fabulous views over the city and archipelago; there's also a restaurant about 120m up should you fancy an airborne cup of coffee. If you come here by bus, you'll pass a gaggle of sundry museums – Dance, Maritime, Technical and Ethnographical – each listed on p.395; while beyond Ladusgårdsgärdet, north of the tower, where windmills used to pierce the skyline, lies first Frihamnen, where the Estonia ferry docks, and just beyond that, Värtahamnen and the *Silja Line* ferry terminal for Finland.

Södermalm

Whatever you do in Stockholm, don't miss the delights of the city's southern island, **Södermalm**, more commonly known simply as Söder, whose craggy cliffs, turrets and towers rise high above the clogged traffic interchange at Slussen. The perched buildings are vaguely forbidding, but venture beyond the main roads skirting the island and a lively and surprisingly green area unfolds: one that's at heart emphatically working-class, though Swedish-style – there are no slums here. To get here, take bus #46 or #48 and get off at Bondegatan, or the #53 to Folkungagatan; alternatively, ride the T-bana to Slussen or, to save an uphill trek, Medborgarplatsen or Mariatorget.

On foot, you reach the island over a double bridge from Gamla Stan into Södermalmstorg – the square around the entrance to the T-bana at Slussen. Just to the south of the square is the rewarding **Stadsmuséet** (Tues–Sun 11am–5pm; 30kr), hidden in a basement courtyard. The Baroque building, designed by Tessin the Elder and finished by his son in 1685, was once the town hall for this part of Stockholm; now it houses a set of collections relating to the city's history as a seaport and industrial centre. Nearby, the Renaissance-style **Katarina kyrka** on Högbergsgatan stands on the site where the victims of the Stockholm Blood Bath – the betrayed nobility of Sweden who'd opposed King Christian II's Danish invasion – were buried in 1520. Their bodies were burned as heretics outside the city walls and it proved a vicious and effective coup, Christian disposing of the opposition in one fell swoop.

That's about as far as specific sights go on Södermalm, although it's worth wandering westwards towards **Mariatorget**, a spacious square where the influence of Art Nouveau is still evident in the architecture. This is one of the most desirable places to live in the city, within easy reach of a glut of stylish bars and restaurants where trendy Stockholmers simply have to be seen. If you're having a bad hair day, you can escape the latest fashions and regress to your childhood at the Museum of Toys, **Hobby-och Leksaksmuseum** at Mariatorget 1C (Tues–Fri 10am–4pm, Sat & Sun noon–4pm; 30kr, children 15kr), which contains everything from tin soliders to space guns, although there's more to interest big kids than little ones, with few toys you can actually play with.

The island is also home to one of Stockholm's most popular **parks**, Tantolunden, located close to the Hornstull T-bana at the end of Lignagatan, complete with open-air theatre in summer. It's also the place to come for **swimming pools** – there are three of them – *Forgrénskabadet* (Medborgarplatsen T-bana), *Erikdalsbadet* (Skanstull T-bana) and the wonderful little *Liljeholmsbadet* (Hornstull T-bana), a pool in a boat-like pontoon contraption that floats in Lake Mälaren: there's single-sex nude swimming here on certain days of the week (see p.404) and the water is never less than 30°C.

You'll probably end up back on Södermalm after dark, since there are some good bars and restaurants in this quarter of town – though it's best to get your bearings during the day, as finding your way around at night can be confusing. The main streets to aim for are **Götgatan**, **Folkungagatan**, **Bondegatan** and **Skånegatan** (see the sections on eating and drinking, starting on p.398).

Långholmen

The name **Långholmen** means "long island" and it's just that, a skinny finger of land off the northwestern tip of Södermalm, crossed by the mighty Västerbron bridge linking Södermalm with Kungsholmen. There's a couple of popular **beaches** here: **Långholmens Strandbad** to the west of the bridge and rocky **Klippbad** to the east; if you don't fancy swimming, take a leisurely stroll through the trees instead for some stunning views over towards the City Hall and Gamla Stan.

You may well find yourself staying here as the island's large prison building has been converted into one of the better hostels in Sweden (see p.380). There's a café here in the summer, and you can sit outside and have a drink in what used to be the prison's exercise yard – narrow, bricked-up runs with iron gates at one end. Alternatively, you could nip back over onto Södermalm and sample the excellent *Lasse i Parken* café (see p.399).

Långholmen is best reached by taking the T-bana to Hornstull and then following the signs to the youth hostel; bus #54 is also handy as it crosses Västerbron on its way between Södermalm, Kungsholmen, Vasastaden and Östermalm – an excellent way of seeing much of the city for very little cost.

Stockholm's parks and gardens

Given Stockholm's sense of space and pleasant aspect, there isn't the same urge as in some cities to head for a park and escape the bustle: even the most built up parts of Norrmalm and Södermalm have a stack of quiet gardens and squares tucked away if you search hard enough. If you're spending only a couple of days in the city, then you'll probably visit **Djurgården** anyway, its excellent range of museums interspersed with rolling parkland, and one of them, Skansen, is open-air itself; see above for more details. Together with Ladugårdsgärdet and **Hagaparken** to the north of town it makes up the country's only National City Park, a vast expanse of urban parkland. Get to Hagaparken by bus #69 towards Frösundavik from the centre of town or prepare yourself for a walk from Odenplan T-bana. Within the park there's a butterfly house, **Fjärilshuset** (Tues–Fri 10am–4pm, Sat & Sun 11am–6pm; 50kr, students 35kr), where you can walk among free-flying butterflies and ogle the tropical birds in a vast bird house; get there on bus #515 from Odenplan. Close by at **Freskati** is the **Bergianska Botaniska Trädgården** (daily 11am–5pm; 10kr), a botanical garden and park whose greenhouse holds the world's largest water lily: take the T-bana to Universitetet (the red line towards Mörby Centrum) and then bus #540.

Closer to the city centre and good for the kids is **Vanadisbadet** (mid-May to mid-Sept daily 10am–6pm; 50kr), a water sports and activity park at the top end of

Sveavägen in Vanadislunden; walk from the T-bana at Odenplan or take bus #52 from the station or Sergels Torg towards Karolinska sjukhuset.

Stockholm's other museums

Stockholm has seventy-odd museums scattered within its limits, and while you'd have to be very keen to want to see the lot, some of the minor collections are worth seeking out: what follows is a brief and biased rundown. Full details can be found in the *Stockholm's Museums* booklet, available from tourist offices. Note that the Stockholm Card gives free entry into most of the following and that the majority are closed on Mondays.

Aquaria

Djurgården, Falkenbergsgatan 2; bus #44 or #47. Tues–Sun 10am–4.30pm; 45kr.

Stockholm's water museum covers every conceivable aspect of the water cycle; part of the admission proceeds is donated to rain forest projects.

Cosmonova, Naturhistoriska Riksmuséet

Frescativägen 40; T-bana Universitetet. Daily 10am–6pm, Thurs till 8pm; 45kr.

Films in the country's only Omnimax theatre show the world of natural history in vivid technicolour; also planetarium shows.

Dansmuséet

Dansens Hus, Barnhusgatan 12–14; T-bana T-Centralen. Tues–Sun noon–4pm; 30kr.

A push-button film archive of world dance, with costume and mark displays – supposedly the only one of its kind in the world.

Junibacken

Galärparken, Djurgården; bus #44 and #47. Tues & Sun 10am–8pm, Wed–Sat 10am–6pm; 75kr, children 55kr.

A family museum based on the stories of the writer Astrid Lindgren.

Liljevachs Konsthall

Djurgårdsvägen 60; bus #44 and #47 or ferry from Skeppsbron (year-round) or Nybroplan (July & Aug). Tues & Thurs 11am–8pm, Wed, Fri, Sat & Sun 11am–5pm; 40kr.

Constantly changing modern art exhibitions with works from Sweden and abroad: everything from photographs of naked men to sculpture displays. Best time to visit is in February and March when the Spring Salon displays the winners of the annual art competition. Consistently good; you may have to queue to get in, but there's an excellent café next door to compensate.

Riksidrottsmuséet

Arenaslingan 5; T-bana Globen. Tues–Sun 11am–4pm; 20kr.

Famous Swedish sportsmen and women go through their paces on newsreel and in exhibition displays.

Sjöhistoriska muséet

Djurgårdsbrunnsvägen 24; bus #69. Daily 10am–5pm; 30kr.

A glance into the Swedish fascination with the sea at this excellent Maritime Museum. There's much detail on early boat-building, a selection of scale models going back to the seventeenth century, and a perfunctory look at the modern Swedish navy, who are evidently proud of their torpedoes.

Vin & Sprithistoriska Muséet

Dalagatan 100; T-bana Odenplan. Tues 10am–7pm, Wed–Fri 10am–4pm, Sat & Sun noon–4pm; 30kr. An unexpectedly fascinating museum devoted to all aspects of wine making and distilling. Worth visiting just for the mechanical sniffing cabinet, whereby you sniff one of the fifty-five spices used to flavour akvavit, guess what it is and press the button for confirmation. This being alcohol-obsessed Sweden, there are no free samples.

Eating

Eating out in Stockholm needn't be outrageously expensive – observe a few rules and accept a few facts and you'll manage quite well. If money is tight, switch your main meal of the day to lunchtime, at least on weekdays, when almost every café and restaurant offers an excellent-value set menu, known as the *Dagens Rätt*, for around 50–60kr. In the evening, look around for the best deals but don't necessarily assume that Italian and Chinese places will be the least expensive; more often than not they're overpriced and the food is tasteless. Having said that, along with the usual Mediterranean and American-style food, there are plenty of other foreign cuisines on offer, particularly Japanese and Thai; plus, of course, a number of traditional Swedish places.

Breakfast, snacks and shopping for food

Stockholmers don't usually go out for **breakfast**, so there are very few places open in the early morning. The only decent option if your hostel or hotel doesn't do breakfast is the restaurant at Central Station, where a large buffet is laid out daily between 6.30am and 10am, costing a good-value 50kr per person. Unless you're desperate, don't bother with **burgers** – you'll pay around 40kr for a large burger and fries at *McDonalds*, only 10kr less than the lunchtime *Dagens Rätt* elsewhere, though coffee is a bargain both here and at *Clock Burger*, the Swedish burger chain. If the nibbles strike it's much more economical to pick up a *korv*, a grilled or fried sausage in bread, for around 10–15kr from a street vendor.

Of the indoor **markets** (both closed Sun), Hötorgshallen in Hötorget is cheaper and more varied than Östermalmshallen in Östermalmstorg. The former is awash with small cafés and ethnic snacks, but be sure to buy your fruit and veg outside where it's less expensive. The latter is posher and downright pricey – while it's pleasant for a wander, you'll find most things cost less in the city's biggest **supermarket** in the basement of the *Åhléns* department store, Sergels Torg. Otherwise, try *Konsum* in Järntorget or *Metro* in the underground arcade at Sergels Torg; neither is particularly cheap. In summer, **fruit and veg** stalls spring up outside many of the T-bana stations, especially those out of the centre.

Cafés and restaurants

The main areas for decent eating, day or night, are the city-centre triangle marked out by Norrmalmstorg, Birger Jarlsgatan and Stureplan; Grev Turegatan in Östermalm; and around Folkungagatan, Skånegatan and Bondegatan on Södermalm. Kungsholmen's restaurants are more spread out, so it's best to have a destination in mind before setting out. Several restaurants in Gamla Stan are also worth checking out, though they tend to be expensive. Vegetarians shouldn't have too much difficulty in finding something to eat. Note that in Sweden as a whole there's a fine distinction between cafés, restaurants and bars, with many places offering music and entertainment in the evening as well as serving food throughout the day (see p.400). Bear in mind that Swedes eat early: lunch is served from 11am and dinner from 6pm.

Norrmalm

Berns, Berzelii Park, Nybroplan. One of the choicest places to eat in town. Made famous by writer August Strindberg, who picked up characters' ideas here for his novel, *The Red Room*. Moderately priced international food under a huge chandelier.

Biblos, Biblioteksgatan 9. A wonderfully trendy spot right in the centre of town – a good place for people-watching. Smoked salmon from 85kr.

Birger Bar, Birger Jarlsgatan 5. If you're a pasta freak this is the place – excellent, cheap pasta until it comes out of your ears. Always busy.

East, Stureplan 13. One of the best eating places in town. Trendy to a T and serving excellent Asian-style dishes plus fish. Lunch 74–106kr, dinner around 150kr.

Enzo & Matilde, Birger Jarlsgatan 9. A wonderful little Italian place tucked away in Birger Jarlspassagen; run by a mad Italian woman who serves up delicious homemade spinach and salmon lasagne and other pasta treats. Lunch 60kr.

Fredsgatan 12, Fredsgatan 12. A delicious mix of Swedish and international cuisine, though on the expensive side. In summer check out the outside bar – it's 5m long.

Hus 1, Sveavägen 57. Popular gay restaurant; unfortunately, the food is rarely up to much and over-priced at that.

Köket och en bar, Sturegallerian 30. Open from 8pm until 6.30am, this is a favourite post-clubbing hangout – but it's pricey.

Lao Wai, Luntmakargtan 74. This was Sweden's first East Asian restaurant and is decidedly good though not especially cheap.

Leonardo, Sveavägen 55. Some of the tastiest pizzas and pasta in Stockholm – always fresh and delicious. Pizzas from the only wood-burning oven in town start at 85kr, pasta dishes from 95kr.

Operakällaren, Operahuset, Gustav Adolfs Torg. A bill at the famous Opera House restaurant will seriously damage your wallet (starters from 150kr) but the daily *smörgåsbord* (Mon–Sat 11.30am–3pm, Sun noon–6pm) is fabulous and just about affordable – around 250kr per person for a spread beyond compare. Otherwise you can get lunch in the *Café Opera* around the back for about 100kr.

Peppar, Torsgatan 34. Attractive Cajun restaurant with decent-sized portions but rather high prices.

Prinsen, Mäster Samuelsgatan 4. Old traditional place frequented by artists, musicians and the like. Fish and meat dishes around 180kr.

Rolfs Kök, Tegnérgatan 41. Popular central restaurant close to Hötorget and specializing in Asian and Cajun stir-fried food. Main dishes around 150kr.

Sawadee, Olofsgatan 6, next to Hötorget T-bana. Attractive Thai restaurant with a wonderful 150kr special dinner and reasonably priced drinks.

Svea Bar & Matsal, Sveavägen 53, just by Rådmansgatan T-bana. Excellent place for a cheap and filling lunch (around 60kr). Set menus in the evenings with dishes around 100kr; cheap beer.

Wayne's, Kungsgatan 14. A popular café for smart city types who pretend to be reading foreign newspapers whilst sipping cappuccinos.

Östermalm

Aubergine, Linnégatan 38. Upmarket and expensive place on one of Östermalm's busiest streets. Lots of wood and glass. Go for the cheaper bar menu, which lists dishes like chicken on a skewer for 85kr.

Grevens Bakficka, Grev Turegatan 7. Affordable and cosy place for lunch, serving pork for 82kr, plaice for 95kr, plus a string of other dishes at around 100kr.

Grodan, Grev Turegatan 16. A favourite with Stockholmers, *Grodan* means "the frog", hence the name *La Grenouille* on the outside. French cuisine at moderate prices.

Gröna Linjen, Mäster Samuelsgatan 10, second floor. A nineteenth-century building housing Scandinavia's oldest vegetarian restaurant. There's good buffet here too.

IKKI, Grev Turegatan 7. A very popular Japanese restaurant, especially at lunchtime. Lots of fish and things grilled on skewers. Affordable.

Il Conte, Grev Turegatan 16. Rumoured to be the best Italian in town. The pasta is excellent and very good value.

Mikael Mat & Dryck, Karlavägen 73. Good tasty Swedish home cooking at excellent prices.

PA & Co, Riddargatan 8. Trend-setting restaurant with international dishes alongside some good old Swedish favourites. Moderate prices.

Saturnus, Erikbergsgatan 6. Good pasta, huge cakes and massive sandwiches – a café that becomes a restaurant in the evening.

Stolen, Sibyllegatan, close to the T-bana exit at Östermalmstorg. The name means "chair" after the dozens of different chairs in the restaurant. Good Italian-style food at reasonable prices – the chicken dishes are especially tasty.

Vassilis Taverna, Valhallavägen 131. Stockholmers say this is the best Greek restaurant in town – try the moussaka, which slips down a treat.

Örtagården, Nybrogatan 31. Top-notch vegetarian restaurant in turn-of-the-century surroundings. Dozens of different salads, warm dishes and soups, served up beneath a huge chandelier.

Gamla Stan

Bistro Ruby, Österlånggatan 14. French bistro in the heart of the old town, tastefully done out in Parisian style. Main dishes cost around 150kr and there's a wide selection of beers.

Eriks, Österlånggatan 17. One of the best places in the old town – good food at reasonable prices – and very popular as a result.

De Fyras Krog, Järntorgsgatan 5. As good a place as any to eat traditional Swedish food – choose between the posh restaurant or the more simple farmhouse-style section.

Den Gyldene Freden, Österlånggatan 51. Stockholm's oldest restaurant, "The Golden Peace" opened in 1772. It certainly isn't cheap – expect to pay around 350kr for just two courses without drinks – but the atmosphere, food and style are unparalleled.

Hermans Hermitage, Stora Nygatan 11. Vegetarian restaurant well worth checking out. Open Mon–Sat to 8pm, Sun to 7pm.

Krokodil, Österlånggatan 7. A good reasonably price place for lunch with a wide and varied menu.

Lilla Karachi, Lilla Nygatan 12. Pakistani restaurant with vegetarian dishes; an interesting change for Stockholm, housed in some of Gamla Stan's old cellar vaults.

Mårten Trotzig, Västerlånggatan 79. Known throughout Sweden for its excellent and stylish food – the splendid setting attracts luvvies and business types from across Stockholm.

Skitiga Duken, Stora Nygatan 35. The name means "dirty tablecloth" but don't let that put you off – a great little Italian place with moderate prices.

Södermalm

Blå Dörren, Södermalmstorg 6. Beer hall and restaurant with pricey but excellent Swedish-style food.

Bonden Mat & Bar, Bondegatan 1C. Small and cosy restaurant with rough brick walls. Dishes cost 100–130kr; try the delicious fillet of chicken with oyster mushrooms in red wine sauce, served with potato gratin.

Bröderna Olssons, Folkungagatan 84. If you like garlic this is the place for you, as every conceivable dish is laced with the stuff.

Creperie Fyra Knop, Svartensgatan 4. A rare treat in Stockholm – excellent crepes at affordable prices, all around 50kr.

Dilan, Nytorget 6. Kurdish restaurant on the south side of the island, where the food comes as spicy as you like it – the *kofteg* and lamb cutlets are particularly recommended.

Dionysos, Bondegatan 56. Over-the-top Greek decor gives this place a friendly feel and the food is excellent: moussaka for 85kr, chicken souvlaki for 70kr.

Ett Rum och Kök II, Blekingegatan 63A. As the name suggests, nothing more than one tiny room and a kitchen serving up French food. Try the salmon with spinach in lime sauce for 129kr or the fillet of goose at 146kr. Closed Sun.

Hannas Krog, Skånegatan 80. A firm favourite and popular haunt of Söder trendies with a mooing cow's head to greet you just inside the entrance. It's crowded and noisy; lunch deals for 58kr, evening dishes around 100–150kr.

Hosteria Tre Santi, Blekingegatan 32. One of Södermalm's better Italian restaurants and excellent value for money – always busy.

Indigo, Götgatan, near the exit from Slussen T–bana. The ideal place to stop off for an afternoon cappuccino. Good pastries too and the carrot cake is a house speciality. Small evening menu.

Indira, Bondegatan 3B. Södermalm's biggest Indian restaurant with a good tandoori-based menu. Prices are reasonable with main dishes in the 70–90kr bracket. Takeaway food too.

Kvarnen, Tjärhovsgatan 4. Small beer hall with simple Swedish food – lunch costs just 40kr. In the evening fish and meat dishes go for 80–90kr.

Lasse i Parken, Högalidsgatan 56. Café housed in an eighteenth-century house with a pleasant garden. Very popular in summer as it's handy for the beaches at Långholmen. Lunch available daily.

Mellis, Skånegatan 83–85. Another popular restaurant on this busy street. Greek, French and Swedish dishes at reasonable prices. A nice place for coffee and cakes too.

Pelikan, Blekingegatan 40. Atmospheric, working-class Swedish beer hall with excellent traditional food; pytt i panna for 58kr, meatballs for 72kr, salmon for 78kr.

Sjögräs, Timmermansgatan 24. A modern approach to Swedish cuisine and very popular – tasty and worth a visit.

Soldaten Svejk, Östgötagatan 15. Lively Czech-run joint popular with students. Large selection of Czech beers including Pilsner Urquell for 39kr. Simple and cheap menu around the 100kr mark.

Spisen, Renstiernas Gata 30. Another trendy hangout in the heart of Söder's restaurant-land, with an emphasis on nouvelle cuisine. Lunch costs 58kr; try the delicious pecan smoked breast of chicken with lemon.

String, Nytorgsgatan 38. If you fancy yourself as a brilliant new writer, or if you just fancy yourself, you'll fit in well in this studenty café. Adopt a ponderous air.

Tre Indier, Möregatan 2. Slightly tucked away but well worth hunting out. A lively Indian restaurant with adjoining bar – the height of fashion.

Kungsholmen

Helmers, Scheelegatan 12. Without a doubt the best restaurant on Kungsholmen. Southern American food with lots of Cajun spices. Very trendy and very busy.

Hong Kong, Kungbrostrand 23. A popular Chinese restaurant and really very good value for money.

La Famiglia, Alströmergatan 45. One of Kungsholmen's better Italian places and a good one for that first date.

Mamas & Tapas, Scheelegatan 3. Delicious Spanish food that draws people from across Stockholm – very popular and deservedly so.

Salt, Hantverkaregatan 34. Located on the island's main road and serving stodgy traditional Swedish fare. Salt is no bad name either – drink a lot of water if you're eating the slabs of pork they serve up.

Vildsvin M Fl, corner of Fleminggatan and Agnegatan. The name means "wild boar and more" – a Basque-run restaurant with a delicious and original menu from that region.

Drinking, nightlife and entertainment

There's plenty to keep you occupied in Stockholm, from pubs, gigs and clubs to the cinema and theatre. There's a particularly good **live music** scene in the bars and pubs, where you'll generally have to pay a cover charge of around 60–80kr. Also, if you don't want to feel very scruffy, wear something other than jeans and trainers – many places won't let you in dressed like that anyway. Be prepared too to cough up around 10kr to leave your coat in the cloakroom, a requirement at many bars as well as at discos and pubs, particularly in winter. As well as the weekend, Wednesday is a busy night in Stockholm with usually plenty going on and queues to get into the more popular places.

Bars, brasseries and pubs

The scourge of Swedish **nightlife** – high alcohol prices – is gradually being neutralized due to increased competition. Over recent years there's been a veritable explosion in the number of bars and pubs in Stockholm. Beer prices have dropped considerably in recent years and on Södermalm especially there are some very good deals, though you'll probably still find yourself paying more than at home. Look on the bright side – you no longer need a bank loan to see you through a night out in Stockholm and Swedish beer is stronger than the stuff you're likely to be used to drinking. **Happy hours** at various places also throw up some bargains – look out for signs outside bars and pubs advertising their particular times.

Despite the increase in bars, however, it's still the case that many Stockholmers do their drinking over a meal, and several of the places listed below are primarily cafés or restaurants. Almost all are open seven days a week.

Norrmalm

Bryggeriet Landbyska Verket, Birger Jarlsgatan 24. The cheap beer prices here attract Stockholm's lads; very busy.

Café Opera, Opera House, Gustav Adolfs Torg. If your Katherine Hamnett gear isn't too crushed and you can stand just one more martini, join the queue outside; open daily till 3am.

Dubliners, Smålandsgatan 8. One of the busiest Irish pubs in town with live music most evenings.

East Bar, Stureplan. Loud music, loud dress and loud mouths. Great fun.

Lydmar, Sturegatan 10. Definitely one of the most popular bars in Stockholm – and very elegant. Dress up a little to get past the beefcake bouncers.

Mushrooms, Nybroplan 6. An ugly low-level building hidden away at Nybroplan but full to bursting with loud, happy beer drinkers.

Sturecompagniet, Sturegatan 4. Three floors of bars – something for everybody and definitely worth a look. Expensive beer.

Svea Bar & Matsal, Sveavägen by the exit to Rådmansgatan T-bana. Cheap beer and a lively atmosphere from early evening onwards.

Tranan, Karlbergsvägen 14. Pricey French restaurant upstairs, but downstairs there's an old workers' beer hall worth a visit.

Trap Bar, Engelbrektsgatan 3. A tiny place which soon gets packed and very claustrophobic.

Gamla Stan

Gråmunken, Västerlånggatan 18. Cosy café-bar, usually busy and sometimes with live music to jolly things along.

Magnus Ladulås, Österlånggatan 26. Rough brick walls and low ceilings make this bar-cum-restuarant an appealing place for a drink or two.

Mårten Trotzig, Västerlånggatan 79. Smart surroundings for an early evening drink before dinner – dress to impress.

Södermalm

Fenix, Götgatan 40. A cheap and nasty American-style bar that's always lively and noisy.

Gröne Jägaren, Medborgarplatsen. Some of the cheapest beer in Stockholm, from 24kr, until 9pm.

Hannas Krog, Skånegatan 80. A good place for a drink before eating in the excellent restaurant.

Kvarnen, Tjärhovsgatan 4. Another busy beer hall – a favourite haunt of southside football fans.

O'Learys, Götgatan 11–13. Södermalm's most popular Irish pub – great fun and handy for stumbling back to the nearby T-bana at Slussen.

Pelikan, Blekingegatan 40. A fantastic old beer hall full of character – and characters.

7:e himlen, Åsögatan/Möregatan. In the same building as the *Tre Indier* Indian restaurant and very popular with southside trendies. The name means "seventh heaven".

Sjögräs, Timmermansgatan 24. A wonderful local little bar that's always busy and lively.

WC, Skånegatan 51. Very busy at weekends with people from across town – handy for the restaurants around Skånegatan and Blekingegatan.

Live music: rock and jazz

Apart from the cafés and bars already listed, there's no shortage of specific venues that put on **live music**; see the list below. Most of these will be local bands, for which you'll pay around 60–70kr entrance, but nearly all the big names make it to Stockholm, playing at a variety of seated halls and stadiums – tickets for these are naturally much more expensive.

The main big venues are the *Stockholm Globe Arena*, Johanneshov (T-bana Gullmarsplan; ☎08/600 3400), which is supposedly the largest spherical building in the world; *Konserthuset* in Hötorget, Norrmalm (☎08/10 21 10); and the *Isstadion* (☎08/600 3400). Check with the tourist office or call the venues direct to find out who's playing.

African Centre, inside Rådhuset T-bana station. Regular African and reggae gigs in this cavernous Algerian-run club; discos until 3am and beyond when there's no band.

Cirkus, Djurgården. Occasional rock and R&B performances.

Cityhallen, Drottninggatan 28, Norrmalm. A big bright bar-restaurant with live Nordic rock and R&B nightly; cheapish food and drink too.

Engelen, Kornhamnstorg 59, Gamla Stan. Live music – jazz, rock and blues – nightly until 3am, but arrive early to get in; the music starts at 8.30pm (Sun 9pm).

Gino, Birger Jarlsgatan 27, Norrmalm. Catch Swedish and international bands performing at one of the city's top nightclubs.

Fasching, Kungsgatan 63, Norrmalm. Local and foreign contemporary jazz. Open Mon–Sat.

Hard Rock Café, Sveavägen 75. R&B bands – often American – several times per week.

Kaos, Stora Nygatan 21, Gamla Stan. Live music from 9pm nightly; rock bands on Fri and Sat in the cellar; and reasonable late-night food.

Melody, Kungsträdgården, Norrmalm. Part of the *Daily News* complex, this central rock venue hosts the most consistent range of live rock music in town – everything from grunge to techno.

Mosebacke Etablissement, Mosebacke Torg 3, Södermalm. Music and cabaret venue, putting on anything from jazz and swing to folk gigs and stand-up comedy.

Stampen, Stora Nygatan 5, Gamla Stan. Long established and rowdy jazz club, both trad and mainstream; occasional foreign names too.

Tre Backar, Tegnérgatan 12–14, Norrmalm; T-bana Rådmansgatan. Good, cheap pub with a live cellar venue. Music every night Mon–Sat until midnight.

Clubs

The **club scene** in Stockholm is limited, with several places doubling as bars or restaurants (where you have to eat). Entrance charges aren't too high at around 40–50kr but beer gets more expensive as the night goes on, reaching as high as 50kr. There is very little crossover with the gay scene; for more gay venues, see below.

Abstrakt, Gamla Brogatan 46, Norrmalm. A hangout for trendy transvestites and other chic people about town. Atmosphere varies from risqué to downright suggestive.

Aladdin, Barnhusgatan 12–14, Norrmalm. One of the city's most popular dance restaurants, close to Central Station, often with performances by live bands. An expensive night out.

Fasching, Kungsgatan 63, Norrmalm. Dancing to live jazz music from midnight onwards.

G-klubben, Skeppsbrokajen, Tullhus 2. Friday night is trendy people night – don't dance too much or your sweat stains will make you unattractive to the other beautiful people.

King Creole, Kungsgatan 18, Norrmalm. Mainstream disco worth checking out for nostalgia value – regular blasts of anything from Big Band to 1960s sounds.

Patricia, Stadsgårdskajen, Södermalm. A former royal yacht for Britain's Queen Mother, today a restaurant-disco-bar with fantastic views of the city out across the harbour and Swedish stand-up comedy nights. Open Wed–Sun; gay on Sun. The food is quite simply fantastic.

Sturecompagniet, Sturegatan 4. Strut to the latest sounds and a fantastic light show – also three floors of bars. Very popular.

Classical music, theatre and cinema

For up-to-date **information** about what's on where, check the special Saturday supplement of the *Dagens Nyheter* newspaper, *På Stan. Stockholm This Week*, free from the tourist office, is also indispensible for **arts listings**, with day-by-day information about a whole range of events – gigs, theatre, festivals, dance – sponsored by the city, many of which are free and based around Stockholm's many parks. Popular venues in summer are Kungsträdgården and Skansen, where there's always something going on. If your Swedish is up to it, there's a free monthly paper, *Nöjesguiden*, that details all manner of entertainment – from the latest films to a club guide. You'll see it in bars and restuarants; pick up a copy and get someone to translate. Or if you're around in summer look out for a similar guide in English, *N&D*.

Classical music and opera

Classical music is always easy to find. Many museums – particularly the Historiska Muséet and Musikmuséet – have regular programmes; there's generally something on at *Konserthuset* in Hötorget, Norrmalm (☎08/10 21 10); *Berwaldhallen*, Strandvägen 69, Östermalm (☎08/784 1800); *Gamla Musikaliska Akademien*, Blasieholmstorg 8 near the National Art Museum (☎08/20 68 18); and *Myntet*, Hantverkargatan 5 (☎08/652 0310). **Operan** (☎08/24 82 40) is Sweden's most famous operatic venue, though for less rarefied presentations of the classics, check the programme at *Folkoperan*, Hornsgatan 72, Södermalm (☎08/658 5300).

If you're after **church music**, you'll find it in Adolf Fredriks kyrka, Norrmalm (lunchtime); St Jakobs kyrka, Norrmalm (Sat at 3pm); Johannes kyrka, Norrmalm; and Storkyrkan, Gamla Stan. For more details, check the listings in *Stockholm This Week*.

Theatre and cinema

There are dozens of **theatres** in Stockholm, but only one has regular performances of **English-language productions**: the *Regina*, Drottninggatan 71 (☎08/20 70 00), which features touring plays; tickets are sold at the theatre box office. If you want tickets for anything else theatrical, it's often worth waiting for reduced-price standby tickets, available from the kiosk in Norrmalmstorg.

Cinema-going is an incredibly popular pastime in Stockholm, with screenings of new releases nearly always full. The largest venue in the city centre is *Filmstaden* in

---

STOCKHOLM WATER FESTIVAL

The **Stockholm Water Festival** is a ten-day annual event in August featuring open-air gigs, street parties, fishing contests, exhibitions, sailing displays and children's events, culminating in a stunning firework display. The tourist office has specific details about each year's events; book accommodation in advance if you're planning your stay to coincide with the festival. Sharpen your elbows and prepare to forge your way through the crowds which briefly transform Stockholm into a bustling city. Luckily the change is brief.

Hötorget, but there's also a good number of cinemas the entire length of Kungsgatan between Sveavägen and Birger Jarlsgatan, always very lively on Saturday night. Tickets cost around 70kr and films are never dubbed into Swedish.

Finally **Kulturhuset** in Sergels Torg has a full range of artistic and cultural events – mostly free – and the information desk on the ground floor gives away programmes.

Gay Stockholm

Given that Stockholm is Sweden's capital city, the **gay scene** is disappointingly small and closeted. Attitudes in general are tolerant but you won't see gay couples walking hand in hand or kissing in the street – just one of the false perceptions of Sweden. Until just a few years ago, when the country freed itself from restrictive tax rules imposed on bars and restaurants, there was only one specifically gay hangout in the whole of the city. Thankfully today things have changed and bars are springing up all over the place. However, a kneejerk reaction by the government in response to the advent of AIDS has forced all gay saunas to close. The four main bars and clubs to be seen at are listed below but beware that all are male-dominated – lesbians have an extremely low profile in Stockholm.

You can get all the latest information from **Hus1** (pronounced "hoos-et", meaning "the house"), the city's main gay centre at Sveavägen 57. The offices above house Sweden's **gay rights group**, the National Association for Sexual Equality – *Riksförbundet för sexuellt likaberättigande* (*RFSL*; ☎08/736 02 12). The centre offers HIV advice (☎08/736 02 11), publishes a free newspaper, and runs a bookstore, a restaurant and radio station. **Gay Pride Week**, which takes place the second week of August, centres on a number of events organized by *Hus1*.

Bars and clubs

Gossip, Sveavägen 36; T-bana Hötorget. A huge club on two floors with lots of dark little corners – great fun. Also an outdoor café in summer. Be there on Thurs, Fri & Sat.

Hus1, Sveavägen 57; T-bana Rådmansgatan. Stockholm's main gay venue – a club, restaurant and bar all rolled into one – and very popular. Friday and Saturday nights are packed. Open daily.

Klubb Häktet, Hornsgatan 82; T-bana Zinkensdamm. A wonderful place with two bars, front and back, as well as a quiet sitting room and a beautiful outdoor courtyard – a real haven in summer. Very popular on Wednesday nights but also open Mon, Tues & Fri–Sun.

Patricia, Stadsgårdskajen; T-bana Slussen. The Queen Mother's former royal yacht attracts queens and more from across Stockholm for fun Sunday evenings. Eat before you groove and there's no entrance fee. A great place for romantic evenings staring out across the harbour. Often hosts drag acts or stand-up comedy.

Listings

Airlines *Aer Lingus*, Dalagatan 3 (☎08/24 93 26); *Aeroflot*, Sveavägen 20 (☎08/21 70 07); *Air France*, Norrmalmstorg 16 (☎08/679 8855); *Air New Zealand*, Kungsbron 1G (☎08/21 91 80); *American Airlines*, at Arlanda airport (☎08/24 61 45); *British Airways*, Hamngatan 11 (☎08/679 7800); *Cathay Pacific*, at Arlanda airport (☎08/797 8580); *Delta AirLines*, Kungsgatan 18 (☎08/796 9600); *Finnair*, Norrmalmstorg 1 (☎08/679 9330); *Icelandair*, Kungstensgatan 38 (☎08/31 02 40); *KLM* and *Northwest*, at Arlanda airport (☎08/593 624 30); *Lufthansa*, Norrmalmstorg 1 (☎08/611 2288); *Malmö Aviation* ☎020/55 00 10; *SAS*, Stureplan 8 (international ☎020/727 555; domestic ☎020/727 000); *Singapore Airlines*, Grev Turegatan 10 (☎08/611 7131); *Transwede*, Vasagatan 36 (☎020/22 52 25); *Qantas*, Kungsgatan 64 (☎08/24 25 02); *United Airlines*, Kungsgatan 3 (☎08/678 1570).

Airports Arlanda ☎08/797 6000; Arlanda flight enquiries *SAS* ☎08/797 3030, other airlines ☎08/797 6100; Bromma ☎08/797 6800.

American Express Birger Jarlsgatan 1 (Mon–Fri 9am–5pm; ☎08/679 5200).

Banks and Exchange Banks are generally open later in central Stockholm than in the rest of the country: Mon–Fri 9.30am–3pm, though some stay open until 5.30pm; the bank at Arlanda is open longer hours and there's also an ATM in the departures hall. *Forex* exchange offices – on the main hall in the Central Station (☎08/411 6734) and downstairs in the T-bana area (☎08/24 46 02), at Cityterminalen (☎08/21 42 80), Vasagatan 14 (☎08/10 49 90), in Sverigehuset (☎08/20 03 89) and at Arlanda airport Terminal 2 (☎08/593 622 71) – offer better value than the banks; also try *Valutaspecialisten* at Kungsgatan 30 (☎08/10 30 00) and at Arlanda Terminal 5 (☎08/797 8557).

Bookshops *Akademibokhandeln*, on the corner of Regeringsgatan and Mäster Samuelsgatan; *Rönnells* (second-hand books), Klarabergsgatan 50; *Aspingtons* (second-hand books), Västerlånggatan 54; *Hedengrens Bokhandel*, Sturegallerian, Stureplan 4; *Sweden Bookshop*, Sverigehuset, Hamngatan 27.

Car breakdown If you need towing call *Larmtjänst*; ☎020/22 00 00.

Car rental *Avis*, Sveavägen 61 (☎08/34 99 10), Vasagatan 16 (☎08/20 20 60), Arlanda airport (☎08/595 115 00), general enquiries ☎08/020/78 82 00; *Budget*, Sveavägen 115 (☎08/33 43 83), Arlanda airport (☎08/797 8470); *Europcar*, Vretenvägen 8, Solna (☎08/627 4800), Arlanda airport (☎08/593 609 40), general enquiries ☎020/78 11 80; *Eurodollar*, Klarabergsgatan 33 (☎08/24 26 55); *Hertz*, Vasagatan 26 (☎08/24 07 20), Arlanda airport (☎08/797 9900), general enquiries ☎020/21 12 11.

Dental problems Emergency dental care at St Eriks sjukhus (hospital), Fleminggatan 22; daily 8am–7pm. After 9pm call the duty dentist on ☎08/644 9200.

Doctor Tourists can get emergency outpatient care at the hospital in the district where they are staying; check with the *Medical Care Information* on ☎08/644 9200.

Embassies and consulates *Australia*, Sergels Torg 12 (☎08/613 2900); *Canada*, Tegelbacken 4 (☎08/453 3000); *Ireland*, Östermalmsgatan 97 (☎08/661 80 05); *New Zealand* – use the Australian Embassy; *UK*, Skarpögatan 6–8 (☎08/671 9000); *USA*, Strandvägen 101 (☎08/783 5300).

Emergencies For police, ambulance or fire service call ☎112.

Ferries Tickets for Finland from *Silja Line*, Stureplan or Värtahamnen (☎08/22 21 40); *Viking Line*, Stadsgårdsterminalen (☎08/452 4255); for Estonia from *Estline*, Frihamnen (☎08/667 0001); for Britain from *Scandinavian Seaways*, Birger Jarlsgatan (☎08/450 4600); for Denmark and other lines in Europe from *Stena Line*, Kungsgatan 12–14 (☎08/14 14 75); for cruises from *Birka Cruises*, Södermalmstorg 2 (☎08/714 5520); for the archipelago from *Waxholms Ångfartygs AB*, Strömkajen (☎08/679 5830)

Laundry Self-service at Sturegatan 4 and St Eriksgatan 97, or try the youth hostels.

Left luggage Lockers at Central Station (from 20kr per day), the Cityterminalen bus station and the *Silja* and *Viking* ferry terminals. Central Station also has a left-luggage office (☎08/762 2549).

Lost property Offices at Central Station (☎08/762 2000); Police, Bergsgatan 39 (☎08/769 3000); *SL*, Rådmansgatan T-bana station, Mon–Fri 10am–5pm (☎08/736 0780).

News in English *Newsday* and *Europe Today* from BBC World Service can be heard on FM 89.6 in Greater Stockholm between 6 and 7am. Radio Sweden also provides news in English, about Sweden only, on the same frequency at several times during the day; info on ☎08/784 7400.

Newspapers At kiosks in Central Station, Cityterminalen or at the *Press Center* with branches in the *Gallerian* shopping centre on Hamngatan and also at Sveavägen 52. Read them for free at *Stadsbiblioteket* (City Library), Sveavägen 73 or at *Kulturhuset* in Sergels Torg.

Pharmacy 24-hour service at *C.W. Scheele*, Klarabergsgatan 64 (☎08/24 82 80).

Police Headquarters at Agnegatan 33–37, Kungsholmen (☎08/401 0000); local police stations at Bryggargatan 19, Tulegatan 4 and Södermangatan 5 in the city centre.

Post office Main office at Vasagatan 28–34, Mon–Fri 8am–6.30pm, Sat 10am–2pm; to collect poste restante take your passport.

SL Travel information Bus, T-bana and regional train (*pendeltåg*) information on ☎08/600 1000; *SL Centers* at Sergels Torg, Mon–Fri 7am–6.30pm, Sat & Sun 10am–5pm; Slussen Mon–Fri 8am–6pm, Sat 8am–1pm; Gullmarsplan (Södermalm) Mon–Thurs 7.30am–6.30pm, Fri 7.30am–5.30pm; Tekniska Högskolan, Mon–Fri 7am–6.30pm, Sat 10am–3pm; Fridhemsplan (Kungsholmen) Mon–Fri 7am–6.30pm.

STF (Svenska Turistföreningen), Drottninggatan 31–33 (☎08/463 2100). Information on Sweden's youth hostels, mountain huts, hiking trails, plus maps and youth hostel membership.

Swimming pools Outdoors at *Vandisbadet*, Vanadislunden, Sveavägen, and at *Eriksdalbadet*, Eriksdalslunden, Södermalm; indoors at *Forsgrénska badet*, Medborgarplatsen 2–4; *Centralbadet*,

Drottninggatan 88; *Sturebadet,* inside Sturegallerian shopping centre, Stureplan (also has masseurs), and at *Liljeholmsbadet,* Bergsunds strand, Liljeholmen – nude male-only swimming sessions on Fri, women only Thurs; non-nude mixed sessions Tues, Wed & Sat.

Toilets Central public toilets in *Gallerian* shopping centre, *Åhléns* and *NK* department stores, T-Centralen and Cityterminalen.

Train information Tickets and information for domestic and international routes with *SJ, Statens Järnvägar* (Swedish State Railways) on ☎020/75 75 75; from abroad call ☎08/696 7540.

Travel agents *KILROY travels,* Kungsgatan 4 (☎08/23 45 15), and out at the University in Freskati at Universitetsvägen 9 (☎08/16 05 15), sell discounted flights and train tickets and *ISIC* cards; *Ticket,* Kungsgatan 60 (☎08/24 00 90), Sturegatan 8 (☎08/611 5020), Sveavägen 42 (☎08/24 92 20); *Transalpino/Wasteels resor,* Birger Jarlsgatan 13 (☎08/679 9870); for cheap flights also check the travel section of the *Dagens Nyheter* newspaper

AROUND STOCKHOM

Such are Stockholm's attractions, it's easy to overlook the city's surroundings; yet after only a few kilometres the countryside becomes noticeably leafier, the islands less congested, the water brighter. As further temptation, some of the country's most fascinating sights are within easy reach, like the spectacular **Millesgården** sculpture museum and **Drottningholm**, Sweden's greatest royal palace. Further out is the little village of **Mariefred**, containing Sweden's other great castle, **Gripsholm** – and like Drottningholm, it's accessible by a fine boat ride on the waters of Lake Mälaren. Other trips in the stunning **archipelago** or to university town of **Uppsala** really merit a longer stay, although if you're pressed for time it's possible to get there and back within a day.

While the Stockholm Card and *turistkort* are valid on bus, T-bana and regional train services within Greater Stockholm, you can't use them on the more enjoyable boat services to Drottningholm or in the archipelago. The quickest way to get to Uppsala is by regional train from Central Station – both cards are valid as far as Märsta, where you'll have to buy a supplementary ticket for the final part of the journey (around 50kr). From mid-June to mid-August there's also a boat service to Uppsala, which leaves Stadshusbron at 10am, arriving at Uppsala at 5.30pm. Boats to Mariefred and Drottningholm also leave from Stadshusbron.

Lidingö and Millesgården

Lidingö is where the well-to-do of Stockholm live, a residential commuter island just northeast of the city centre, which you'll already have glimpsed if you arrived from Finland or Estonia on the *Silja Line* or *Estline* ferries, as they dock immediately opposite. It's worth a second look, though: eagle eyes may have spotted, across the water, the tallest of the statues from the startling **Millesgården** at Carl Milles Väg 2 (daily 10am–5pm; 50kr) – the outdoor sculpture collection of **Carl Milles** (1875–1955), one of Sweden's greatest sculptors and collectors. To **get there**, take the T-bana to Ropsten, then the rickety *Lidingöbanan* over the bridge to Torsvikstorg, from where it's a short walk down Herserudsvägen.

The statues are seated on terraces carved from the island's steep cliffs, many of Milles's animated, classical figures perching precariously on soaring pillars, overlooking the distant harbour: ranked terraces of gods, angels and beasts. A huge *Poseidon* rears over the army of sculptures, the most remarkable of which, *God's Hand,* has a small boy delicately balanced on the outstretched finger of a monumental hand. If you've been elsewhere in Sweden much of the work may seem familiar, copies and casts of the originals adorning countless provincial towns. If this collection inspires, it's worth tracking down three other pieces by Milles in the capital: his statue of *Gustav*

Vasa in the Nordic Museum on Djurgården, the *Orpheus Fountain* in Norrmalm's Hötorget, and at Nacka Strand (reached by bus #404 from Slussen or *Waxholm* boat from Strömkajen) the magnificent *Gud på Himmelsbågen*, a claw-shaped vertical piece of steel topped with the figure of a boy – a stunning marker at the entrance to Stockholm harbour.

The island is also the venue for the world's biggest cross-country running race, the **Lidingöloppet**, held on the first Sunday in October. It's been going since 1965, the thirty kilometre course attracting an international field of around 30,000 runners – quite a sight as they skip or crawl up and down the island's hills. For more information or to find out how to take part, ask at the tourist office in Stockholm.

Drottningholm and Birka

Even if your time in Stockholm is limited, it's worth saving a day for the harmonious royal palace of **Drottningholm** (May–Aug daily 11am–4.30pm; Sept Mon–Fri 1–3.30pm, Sat & Sun noon–3.30pm; 40kr), beautifully located on the shores of leafy Lovön island, 11km west of the city centre. The fifty-minute boat trip there is part of the experience (50kr one-way, 70kr return): it leaves every hour, on the hour, from Stadhusbron to coincide with the opening times. Or take the T-bana to Brommaplan and then buses #301–323 from there – a less thrilling ride, but covered by the *turist-kort* and Stockholm Card.

Drottningholm is perhaps the greatest achievement of the architects **Tessin**, father and son. Work began in 1662 on the orders of King Karl X's widow, Eleonora, Tessin the Elder modelling the new palace in a thoroughly French style – leading to that tired and overused label of a Swedish Versailles. Apart from anything else it's considerably smaller that its French contemporary, utilizing false perspective and trompe l'oeil to boost the elegant, rather narrow interior. On Tessin the Elder's death in 1681, the palace was completed by his son, already at work on Stockholm's Royal Palace. Inside, good English notes are available to help you sort out each room's detail, a riot of Rococo decoration largely dating from the time when Drottningholm was bestowed as a wedding gift on Princess Louisa Ulrika (a sister of Frederick the Great of Prussia). Since 1981 the Swedish royal family has slummed it out at Drottningholm, using the palace as a permanent home, a move that has accelerated efforts to restore parts of the palace to their original appearance – so that the monumental **Grand Staircase** is now exactly as envisaged by Tessin the Elder.

Nearby in the palace grounds is the **Court Theatre** (Slottsteater; May–Aug noon–4.30pm, Sept 1–3.30pm; 40kr), dating from 1766. Its heyday came a decade later when Gustav III imported French plays and acting troupes, making Drottningholm the centre of Swedish artistic life. Take a guided tour and you'll get a flowery though accurate account of the theatre's decoration: money to complete the building ran out in the eighteenth century, meaning that not everything is quite what it seems, with painted papier-mâché frontages masquerading as the real thing. The original backdrops and stage machinery are still in place though, and the tour comes complete with a display of eighteenth-century special effects – wind and thunder machines, trapdoors and simulated lighting. If you're in luck you might catch a **performance** of drama, ballet or opera here (usually June–Aug): the cheapest **tickets** cost 95kr, though decent seats are in the region of 260kr – check the schedule at Drottningholm or ask at the tourist offices in the city. You can also reserve tickets by phone using *BiljettDirekt* (☎077/170 7070) or by calling Drottningholm direct (☎08/660 8225 or 660 8281). With time to spare, the extensive palace grounds also yield the **Chinese Pavilion** (same times as above), a sort of eighteenth-century royal summer house.

Birka

Further into Lake Mälaren lies the island of **Björkö**, known for its rich flora and good swimming beaches. Its real draw, though, is that it holds Sweden's oldest town, **BIRKA**, founded in around 750 AD. A Viking trading centre at its height during the tenth century, a few obvious remains lie scattered about – including the remnants of houses and a vast cemetery. Major excavations were carried out between 1990 and 1995 and a museum, **Birka the Viking Town** (May to mid-Sept daily 10am–5pm; entry with boat ticket) now displays rare artefacts as well as scale models of the harbour and craftsmen's quarters. Get there from Stadshusbron in Stockholm on *Strömma Kanalbolaget* boats (info on ☎08/23 33 75; May to mid-Sept daily at 10am; return from Birka at 3.30pm; 185kr, including entry to Viking Town).

The Archipelago

If you arrived in Stockholm by ferry from Finland or Estonia you'll already have had a tantalizing glimpse of the **Stockholm archipelago**. This array of hundreds upon hundreds of pine-clad islands and islets is the only one of its kind in the world. The archipelago can be split into three distinct sections: inner, centre and outer. In the inner archipelago there's more land than sea, in the centre it's pretty much fifty-fifty, while in the outer archipelago distances between islands are much greater – out here, sea and sky merge into one and the nearest island is often no more than a dot on the horizon. It's worth knowing that if it's cloudy in Stockholm, chances are that the sun will be shining somewhere out on the islands. Even if your trip to the capital is short, don't miss the chance to come out here.

Practicalities

Getting to the islands is easy and cheap, with *Waxholmsbolaget* operating the majority of sailings into the archipelago. Most boats leave from Strömkajen in front of the *Grand Hotel* and the National Museum; others leave from just round the corner at Nybrokajen, next to the Royal Drama Theatre. Buy tickets either on the boats themselves or from the *Waxholmsbolaget* office on Strömkajen, where you can also pick up free timetables to help you plan your route. Timetables are also posted up on every jetty (Swedish: *brygga*). Ticket prices are very reasonable, ranging from 15kr to 65kr depending on the length of the journey. Most boats have a cafeteria or restaurant on board. If you're planning to visit several islands it might be worth buying the **Interskerries Card** (*Båtluffarkort*), which gives sixteen days unlimited travel on all *Waxholmbolaget* lines for 250kr. Or if you've already got an *SL* monthly travel card (see p.378), you can buy a **supplementary Waxholm card** for 215kr, allowing a month's travel anywhere in the archipelago.

Departures to the closest islands are more frequent (often around 4 daily) than those to the outer archipelago; however, if there's no direct service connections can often be made at the island of Vaxholm.

Though there are few hotels in the archipelago, **accommodation** is available in a number of several well-equipped and comfortable **youth hostels**. Opening times vary but all hostels are open in the summer – the most useful are at **Finnhamn** (☎08/542 462 12; all year; 100kr), **Gällnö** (☎08/571 661 17; May–Sept; 100kr) and **Utö** (☎08/501 572 60; all year; 100kr). It's also possible to rent summer **cottages** on the islands – contact the tourist office in Stockholm. You'll need to book way in advance, though, to avoid being pipped to the post by holidaying Swedes. **Campsites** are surprisingly hard to find – you'll be much better off camping rough as a few nights' stay in most places won't cause any problems. Remember, though, that open fires are prohibited all over the archipelago.

Archipelago highlights

Of the vast number of islands in the archipelago, several are firm favourites with Stockholmers, in particular **Vaxholm**; others offer more secluded beaches and plenty of opportunity for lovely walks. The following are a few of the better islands to make for.

Inner and central archipelago

Vaxholm is a popular weekend destination, lying just an hour away from Stockholm. Vaxholm town has an atmospheric wooden harbour with an imposing fortress. This structure superseded the fortifications at Riddarholmen and guarded the waterways into the city, successfully staving off attacks from Danes and Russians in the seventeenth and eighteenth centuries; nowadays, though, it's an unremarkable museum of military bits and pieces. Also within easy reach is **Grinda**, two hours or so away, a thickly wooded island typical of the inner archipelago. Its magnificent sandy beaches have made it a firm favourite with families.

In the central archipelago, low-lying **Gällnö** is covered with thick pine forest. One of the most beautiful islands, it has been designated a nature reserve with deer and eider duck the most likely wildlife you'll spot. Ferries take about two hours to get here from Stockholm.

Svartsö lies in what's considered to be the most beautiful part of the archipelago, near the island of Möja (see below). Known for its fields of grazing sheep, virgin forest and crystal-clear lakes, the good roads make it ideal cycling or walking territory. The sailing from the city again takes around two hours.

Outer archipelago

If you're heading into the outer archipelago from Stockholm, you can sometimes cut the journey time by taking a bus or train to a further point on the mainland and picking the boat up there – where this is the case, we've given details below.

Three hours out of Stockholm, the tiny island of **Finnhamn** lies in the outer archipelago where the islands start to become fewer and where the sea takes over. It's a good place for walking, through forests, meadows and along cliff tops.

Möja (pronounced roughly as "Murr-ya"), three and a half hours from the city, is one of the most popular islands, home to around three hundred people who make their living from fishing and farming. There's a small craft museum in the main town, Berg, and even a cinema, though it's not the place to come if you want to go swimming.

In the southern stretch of the archipelago, **Bullerö** is about as far as you can go before falling into the sea. This beautiful island is home to a nature reserve with walking trails and an exhibition on the archipelago's plentiful flora and fauna. The boat journey takes three hours: get the train from Slussen to Saltsjöbaden, and from there a boat to the island of Nämdö, where you can take the shuttle service to Bullerö.

Sandhamn has been a destination for seafarers since the 1700s and remains so today, its tiny harbour packed full of sailing yachts of all shapes and sizes. The main village is a haven of narrow alleyways, winding streets and overgrown verandas. It takes three and a half hours to get here from Stockholm, but you can save time by taking bus #434 from Slussen to Stavsnäs – the furthest point on the mainland – and picking up a boat there for the hour-long sailing to Sandhamn.

Lying far out in the southern reaches of the archipelago, **Utö** is ideal for cycling, with the sandy beaches at Ålö storsand perfect for a picnic stop. You can also walk over the bathing cliffs at Rävstavik. The journey time from Stockholm is three hours.

Mariefred and Gripsholm

If you've only got time for one boat trip outside Stockholm, make it to **MARIEFRED**, a tiny village to the west of the city whose peaceful attractions are bolstered by one of Sweden's most enjoyable castles. To get there in summer, take the *S/S Mariefred* **steamboat**, which leaves from Klara Mälarstrand near Stadshuset on Kungsholmen (mid-May to mid-June & mid-Aug to mid-Sept Sat & Sun 10am; mid-June to mid-Aug Tues–Sun 10am; 100kr, return 160kr); buy your ticket on board for the three-and-a-half-hour journey. Outside summer, you'll have to travel on an Eskilstuna-bound train as far as **Läggesta**, where connecting buses shuttle passengers to Mariefred, a journey of around an hour.

Mariefred itself – the name derived from an old monastery, Pax Mariae (Mary's Peace) – is as quiet, and quintessentially Swedish, as such villages come. Surrounded by clear water, a couple of minutes up from the quayside and you're strolling through narrow streets whose well-kept wooden houses and little squares haven't changed much in decades. The water and enveloping greenery make for a pleasant stroll: if you call in at the central **Rådhus**, a fine eighteenth-century timber building, you can pick up a map from the **tourist office** inside (June & Aug Mon–Fri 10am–7pm, Sat & Sun 10am–6pm; July daily 10am–6pm; late Aug to mid-Sept Wed–Sun 10am–3pm; ☎0159/297 90). They also arrange **bike rental** (85kr per day; 400kr per week).

Steam train freaks will love the **Railway Museum** (variable hours) in the village – you'll probably have noticed the narrow gauge tracks running all the way to the quayside. There's an exhibition, old rolling stock and workshops, but it's a collection given added interest by the fact that the steam trains still run to and from Mariefred; details below, under "Practicalities".

Gripsholm Castle

Lovely though the village is, touring around it is really only a preface to seeing **Gripsholm** (May, June & Aug daily 10am–4pm; July daily 9am–5pm; April & Sept Tues–Sun 10am–3pm; Oct–March Sat & Sun noon–3pm; 40kr), the imposing red-brick castle built on a round island just to the south: walk up the quayside and you'll spot the path to the castle running across the grass by the water's edge.

In the late fourteenth century, Bo Johnsson Grip, the Swedish High Chancellor, began to build a fortified castle at Mariefred, although the present building owes more to two Gustavs – Gustav Vasa, who started rebuilding in the sixteenth century, and Gustav III, who was responsible for major restructuring a couple of centuries later. Rather than the hybrid that might be expected, the result is rather pleasing – a textbook castle, whose turrets, great halls, corridors and battlements provide an engaging tour. The guide will point out most of the important bits and pieces as you go: there's a vast portrait collection, which includes recently commissioned works of political and cultural figures as well as assorted royalty and nobility; some fine decorative and architectural work; and, as at Drottningholm, a private theatre, built for Gustav III. It's too delicate to use for performances these days, but in summer plays and events take place out in the castle grounds; more information from the tourist office in Mariefred.

Practicalities

Mariefred warrants a night's stay, if not for the sights – which you can exhaust in half a day – then for the pretty, peaceful surroundings. There's only one **hotel**, *Gripsholms Värdshus*, Kyrkogatan 1 (☎0159/130 20; fax 109 74; ③/④), a wonderfully luxurious option overlooking the castle and the water. Otherwise ask at the tourist office about

rooms in the village, which range from 150kr to 420kr per person per night; there are also **cabins** for rent, sleeping six people for 500kr. The nearest **youth hostel** is 15km to the northwest in **Strängnäs** (☎0152/168 61; open all year but advance booking required Sept–May; 100kr), connected by regular bus.

As for **eating**, treat yourself to lunch in *Gripsholms Värdhus*, a beautifully restored inn (the oldest in Sweden). The food is excellent and around 200kr will get you a turn at the herring table, a main course, drink and coffee – all enhanced by the terrific views over to Gripsholm. Alternatively try *Skänken* at the back of the Värdhus, where lunch goes for around 70kr. Or there's the friendly but basic *Jakobs Bistro*, opposite the castle.

When it comes to **leaving Mariefred**, one option is the **narrow-gauge steam train** that leaves roughly hourly between 11am and 5pm (May–Sept: mid-June to mid-Aug daily, otherwise Sat & Sun only; 36kr return, half-price for rail pass holders ☎0159/210 06) for **Läggesta**, a twenty-minute ride away. Here you can pick up the regular *SJ* train back to Stockholm; check connections on the timetable at the tourist office before you leave. Of course it's also possible to get to Mariefred from Stockholm this way.

Eskilstuna and around

Around an hour west of Mariefred on the main train line from Stockholm, **ESKIL-STUNA** is mostly known for the precision tools and instruments manufactured here, but also for its unusually high incidence of violence and murders. Much is made of an impressive industrial heritage in a series of fine museums based in and around the town's oldest houses, which date from the seventeenth century. Of these, the **Radermacher Forges museum** (*Radermachersmedjorna*; April & May daily 10am–4pm: June–Aug Mon–Fri 10am–6pm, Sat & Sun 10am–4pm; Sept–Nov Tues–Sun 10am–4pm; Dec–March Tues–Sat 10am–4pm; ; free) features smiths and wrights working by traditional methods, while on a nearby island, reached by crossing the main Hamngatan and taking a narrow path over the river to Faktoriholmarna, the boring **Faktorimuséet** (Factory Museum; Tues–Sun 11am–4pm; free) has three floors of displays, including several steam engines coaxed into life every Sunday between 1 and 3pm. Next door is the even duller **Vapentekniska Muséet** (Weapons Museum; June–Aug Tues–Sun 11am–4pm; Sept-May Tues, Sat & Sun only; free). To reach these museums from the **train station**, walk for fifteen minutes down Drottninggatan and turn left. The tourist office is also out here by the museums (see below).

More museums can be found in the town centre: the **Konstmuséet** at Kyrkogatan 9 (Tues–Sun noon–4pm, Thurs also 7–9pm; free) is worth a glance for its temporary art exhibitions on the ground floor, while the more interesting **Teatermuséet**, Gillbergavägen 2 (July Tues, Wed & Fri noon–4pm, Thurs noon–8pm; Aug & Sept also Sat & Sun noon–4pm; 30kr), has an odd collection of old photos and newspaper cuttings of old theatre productions.

Practicalities

Eskilstuna's **tourist office** is in Munktellstorget, near the museums (June to late Aug Mon–Fri 9am–6pm, Sat & Sun 10am–4pm; rest of the year Mon–Thurs 9am–5pm, Fri 10am–5pm; ☎016/10 70 00). When it comes to **accommodation**, the cheapest option is the **youth hostel**, located right by a nature reserve at *Vilsta Camping* (☎016/51 30 80; all year; 100kr), a couple of kilometres south of the centre. To get there, turn right out of the station, head along Västermarksgatan to a roundabout, turn right onto Kyrkogatan and keep going along the river until you come to the second bridge – the hostel is on the other side of the river next to an open-air swimming pool. Of the central hotels, the most inexpensive is *Hotell City*, Drottninggatan 15 (☎016/13 74 25; fax

12 42 24; 3; ①). For greater luxury, head for *Hotell Smeden*, Drottninggatan 9 (☎016/13 76 90; fax 12 75 27; ②/④) or the *Stadshotellet Best Western* at Hamngatan 9–11 (☎016/13 72 25; fax 12 75 88; ②/④).

For **eating and drinking**, head for the concentration of places in the central pedestrianized part of town. Best of the bunch is the popular *Brasserie Oscar* at Nybrogatan 5, which offers special student prices. Another brasserie-style restaurant/bar is *Perrongen*, nearby at Nybrogatan 1 – also with student discounts on food. For finer surroundings, check out *Restaurang Tingsgården* at Rådhustorget 2 – the fish is particularly good but nothing comes cheap. Greek food can be had at *Restaurang Akropolis* in Fristadstorget. For a good night's drinking try *Oliver Twist*, a popular pub at Careliigatan 2; other options include *McEwans* at Nybrogatan 5 and *Hamlet Pub Restaurang*, Teatergatan 1.

Around Eskistuna: the Sigurd carving

Twelve kilometres from town in a shady glade near **Sundbyholm**, the **Sigurd carving** is a 1000-year-old runic inscription running for four metres along a slab of stone. The runes are an epitaph for Sigrid, who built a bridge at the site, and are illustrated by scenes from the Icelandic epic poem of Sigrid and the dragon slayer. To get here from Eskilstuna, take the #25 bus (5 daily; 15kr) from the bus station near the church – it passes very close to the stone. There's also excellent **swimming** to be had here in Lake Mälaren.

Uppsala

First impressions as the train pulls into **UPPSALA**, less than an hour from Stockholm, are encouraging. The red-washed castle looms up behind the railway sidings, the cathedral dominant in the foreground. A sort of Swedish Oxford, Uppsala clings to the past through a succession of striking buildings connected with and scattered about its cathedral and university. Regarded as the historical and religious centre of the country, it serves as a tranquil daytime alternative to Stockholm – with an active student-geared nightlife.

Arrival, information and accommodation

Uppsala's **train** and **bus stations** are adjacent to each other, and it's not far to walk down to the **tourist office** at Fyris torg 8 (late June to mid-Aug Mon–Fri 10am–6pm, Sat 10am–3pm, Sun noon–4pm; rest of the year Mon–Fri 10am–6pm, Sat 10am–3pm; ☎018/27 48 00), where you can pick up a handy English guide to the town. This is also the place to rent **bikes** (from 60kr per day). **Boats** to and from Stockholm use the pier south of the centre, at the end of Bävernsgränd. If you're flying in or out of Sweden, you can bypass Stockholm entirely by using the #801 bus link between Uppsala bus station and **Arlanda airport** (every 15–30min, 4.40am–11.40pm; calls at Terminals 5, 4 and 2; journey time 30min).

Accommodation

Though Uppsala is easily within day trip range of Stockholm, you may want to stay around a little longer. As well as a fair range of central hotels, there are two **youth hostels**: an official one at Sunnerstavägen 24 (☎018/32 42 20; May–Aug; 100kr), 6km south of the centre at *STF*'s beautifully sited *Sunnersta Herrgård* (bus #20 from Nybron by Stora Torget); and an independent one in the centre of town at Dragarbrunnsgatan 18 (☎018/10 43 00; all

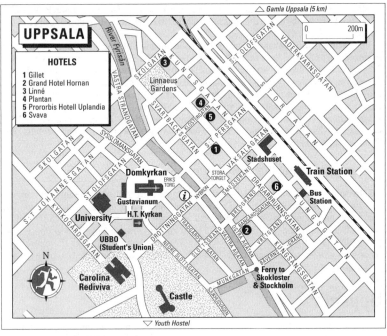

year; 150kr). For **camping**, you can head a few kilometres north to the open spaces of Gamla Uppsala (see below), or use the regular site at *Sunnersta Camping*, by Lake Mälaren in **Graneberg**, 7km from town, near the youth hostel (bus #20).

Grand Hotell Hörnan, Bangårdsgatan 1 (☎018/13 93 80; fax 12 03 11). A wonderfully elegant place with large old-fashioned rooms and restaurant. ③/④

Gillet, Dragarbrunnsgatan 23 (☎018/15 53 60; fax 15 33 80). A stone's throw from the cathedral but with typically average, overpriced, shagpiled rooms. Fans of kitsch should make a point of visiting the restaurant. ③/⑤

Linné, Skolgatan 45 (☎018/10 20 00; fax 13 75 97). Completely overpriced tiny rooms – a last resort when everywhere else is full. ③/⑤

Plantan, Dragarbrunnsgatan 18 (☎/fax 018/10 43 00). Simple, bright and clean rooms with bathroom en-suite and a tiny kitchen. ①

Svava, Bangårdsgatan 24 (☎018/13 00 30; fax 13 22 30; 4/3). A newly built modern hotel with all mod cons including specially designed rooms for people with disabilities and those with allergies. ③/⑤

Provorbis Hotell Uplandia, Dragarbrunnsgatan 32 (☎018/10 21 60; fax 69 61 32). A modern hotel that's gone in for a lot of wood – and small rooms. ③/⑤

The City

Centre of the medieval town and a ten-minute walk from the train station is the great **Domkyrkan** (daily 8am–6pm; free), Scandinavia's largest cathedral. Built as a Gothic brag to the people of Trondehein in Norway that even their mighty church could be overshadowed, it loses out to its competitor by reason of the building material – local brick rather than imported stone – and only the echoing interior remains impressive, particularly the French Gothic ambulatory, sided by tiny chapels and bathed in a golden, decorative glow. One chapel contains a lively set of restored fourteenth-century wall paintings that recount the legend of Saint Erik, Sweden's patron saint: his coronation, crusade to Finland, eventual defeat and execution at the hands of the Danes. The Relics of Erik are zealously guarded in a chapel off the nave: poke around and you'll also find the tombs of Reformation rebel Gustav Vasa and his son Johan III, and that of Linnaeus, the botanist, who lived in Uppsala. Time and fire have led the rest of the the cathedral to be rebuilt, scrubbed and painted to the extent that it resembles a historical museum more than a thirteenth-century spiritual centre; even the characteristic twin spires are late nineteenth-century additions.

The buildings grouped around the Domkyrkan can all claim a cleaner historical pedigree. Opposite the towers, the onion-domed **Gustavianum** (daily July & Aug 11am–3pm; Sept -June noon–3pm; 15kr) was built in 1625 as part of the university and is much touted by the tourist office for its tidily preserved anatomical theatre. The same building houses a couple of small collections of Egyptian, Classical and Nordic antiquities with a small charge for each section (July & Aug daily 11am–3pm).

The current **University** building (Mon–Fri 8am–4pm) is the imposing nineteenth-century Renaissance edifice over the way. Originally a seminary, today it's used for lectures and seminars and hosts the graduation ceremonies each May. The more famous of its alumni include Carl von Linné (Linnaeus) and Anders Celsius, inventor of the temperature scale. No one will mind if you stroll in for a quick look, but to see the locked rooms (including the glorious Augsberg Art Cabinet, an ebony treasure chest presented to Gustav II Adolf) you need to ask in the office inside, to the right of the main entrance (*Vaktmästeriet*); or join a **guided tour** (May–Aug daily 12.30pm & 2pm; 15kr).

A little way beyond the university is the **Carolina Rediviva** (Mon–Fri 9am–5pm, Sat 10am–4pm), the university library. On April 30 each year the students meet here to celebrate the first day of spring (usually in the snow), all wearing the traditional student cap which gives them the appearance of disaffected sailors. This is one of Scandinavia's largest libraries, with around four million books. Adopt a student pose and you can slip in for a wander round and a coffee in the common room. More officially, take a look in the **manuscript room**, where there's a collection of rare letters and other paraphernalia. The beautiful sixth-century Silver Bible is on permanent display, as is, oddly, Mozart's original manuscript for *The Magic Flute*.

After this, the **castle** (no admission) up on the hill is a disappointment. In 1702 a fire that destroyed three-quarters of the city did away with much of the castle, and only one side and two towers remain of what was once an opulent rectangular palace. But the facade still gives a weighty impression of what's missing, like a backless Hollywood set.

Seeing Uppsala, at least the compact older parts, will take up a good half a day. If the weather holds out, use the rest of your time to stroll along the river that runs right through the centre of town. There are several points good for an hour or two's rest in summer and enough greenery to make this stretch more than just pleasant. One beautiful spot is **Linnaeus Gardens** (daily May–Aug 9am–9pm; Sept 9am–7pm; 10kr) over the river on Linnégatan. The university's first botanical gardens, they were relaid by Linnaeus in 1741, some of the species he introduced and classified still surviving.

Gamla Uppsala

Five kilometres to the north of the present city three huge **barrows**, royal burial mounds dating back to the sixth century, mark the original site of Uppsala, **Gamla Uppsala**. This was a pagan settlement – and a place of ancient sacrificial rites. Every ninth year the festival of *Fröblot* demanded the death of nine people, hanged from a nearby tree until their corpses rotted. The pagan temple where this bloody sacrifice took place is now marked by the Christian **Gamla Uppsala kyrka** (Mon–Fri 8.30am–dusk, Sat & Sun 10am–dusk), built over pagan remains when the Swedish kings were first baptized into the new faith. What survives is only a remnant of what was, originally, a cathedral – look inside for the faded wall paintings and the tomb of Celsius, of thermometer fame. Set in the wall outside, there's an eleventh-century rune stone.

There's little else to Gamla Uppsala, and perhaps that's why the site remains so mysterious and atmospheric. There's an **inn** nearby, *Odinsborg*, where – especially if you're with kids – you might want to sample the "Viking lunch": a spread of soup, hunks of meat served on a board, and mead, which comes complete with the horned helmet, an essential item if you're considering pillaging and plundering the afternoon away. And there's an opportunity too, if you're discreet, to **camp** beyond the inn, amid the ghosts.

To get to Gamla Uppsala, take **bus #24** (Mon–Sat every 30min) or **#25** (Sat after 3pm & Sun every 30min) from Dragarbrunnsgatan.

Eating, drinking and nightlife

Eating and entertainment are straightforward in this university town, easier still if you have some form of student ID. For daytime eating there are plenty of **cafés**, particularly in summer, when a glut of open-air places emerges, the most popular on the river. *Café Linné*, just down the street from the Linnaeus gardens, and *Åkanten*, below St Eriks torg, are among the best. Many places stay open until the early hours, an unusual bonus. For snacks and cheap coffee, you could also try the *Alma* café in the basement of the university building. As usual in Sweden, there's a fine distinction between eating and drinking places – though you can eat or drink in many of the following, the "Nightlife" section below pinpoints the liveliest venues for a night out.

Restaurants and bars

Alexander, Östra Ågatan 59. Completely OTT Greek place with busts of famous ancients at every turn. Lunch deal for 50kr.

Café Katalin, Svartbäcksgatan 19. Reasonably priced vegetarian food in a lively setup not dissimilar to *Sten Sture & Co* – and a good second choice if that's full.

Caroline's, Övre Slottsgatan 12. A cheap pizzeria up by the university. Lunch for 45kr.

Domtrappkälaren, St Eriks gränd. One of the most chi-chi places in town – old vaulted roof and great atmosphere. Nothing under 200kr; upstairs, though, you can get an excellent lunch for 60kr.

Elaka Måns, Smedsgränd. A modern bistro-style restaurant with the usual run of fish and mean dishes. Very popular.

Fågelsången, Munkgatan 3. Café that's packed with students at lunchtime; grow a goatee, stare out of the window and ponder the meaning of life.

Güntherska hovkonditori, Östra Ågatan 31. Old-fashioned café serving simple lunch dishes.

Landings, Kungsängsgatan 5. A popular café in the main pedestrian area.

O'Connors, Stora Torget. Irish pub serving food, tucked away on the first floor in the main square; open from 4pm.

Ofvandahls, Sysslomangatan 3–5. A lively café near the old part of town with old wooden tables and sofas – don't leave town without trying the homemade apple, rhubarb or blueberry pie.

Sten Sture & Co, Nedre Slottsgatan 3. An excellent, trendy bar, brasserie and restaurant, serving vegetarian dishes. Outdoor tables in summer.

Svenssons krog/bakficka, Sysslomangatan 15. A wonderful restaurant decked out in wood and glass next to the *bakficka* section which serves pasta dishes.

Svenssons Taverna, Sysslomangatan 14. Diagonally opposite the other Svenssons. A good place for a beer and nibbles. Two of the best places in Uppsala.

Nightlife

At night most of the action is generated by the **students** in houses called "Nations", contained within the grid of streets behind the university, backing onto St Olofsgatan. Not unlike college fraternities, each one organizes dances, gigs and parties of all hues and most importantly all boast very cheap bars. The official line is that if you're not a Swedish student you won't get into most of the things advertised around the town; in practice, being foreign and being nice to the people on the door generally yields entrance, while with an *ISIC* card it's even easier. As many students stay around during the summer, functions are not strictly limited to term-time. A good choice to begin with is *Uplands Nation*, near the river off St Olofsgatan and Sysslomangatan, which has a summer outdoor café open until 3am.

Otherwise, *Sten Sture & Co* puts on **live bands** in the evenings, while *Café Katalin* is open late and has jazz nights. *Club Dacke* is a student frequented summer-only disco on St Olofsgatan, near the Domkyrkan, while one of the liveliest joints is *Rackis*, a music bar out near the student residences on St Johannesgatan (bus #1 to Studentstaden) – there's live music here nearly every night.

Listings

Banks and exchange *Handelsbanken*, Vaksalagatan 8; *Nordbanken*, Stora Torget; *SE-Banken*, Kungsängsgatan 7–9. *Forex* is next to the tourist office at Fyris torg 8.

Bus enquiries *Uppsalabuss* ☎018/27 37 01; city buses leave from Stora Torget; long-distance buses from the bus station adjacent to the train station.

Car rental *Avis*, Spikgatan (☎018/12 55 01); *Budget*, Kungsgatan 80 (☎018/12 42 80); *Europcar*, Kungsgatan 103 (☎018/17 17 30); *Hertz*, Kungsgatan 97 (☎018/12 20 20); *Q8*,Vaksalagatan 95 (☎018/25 26 60); *Statoil*, Gamla Uppsalagatan 48 (☎018/20 91 00);

Cinemas *Filmstaden/Spegeln*, Västra Ågatan 12; *Fyrisbiografen*, St Olofsgatan 10B; *Sandrew*, Smedsgränd 14–20.

Pharmacy at Akademiska sjukhuset, entrance 70 (Mon–Fri 8.30am–9pm, Sat & Sun 9am–9pm; ☎018/66 34 55).

Police ☎018/16 85 00

Post office Dragarbrunnsgatan (☎018/17 96 31).

Systembolaget Off-licences at Svavagallerian (Mon–Thurs 9.30am–6pm, Fri 8am–6pm); Skolgatan 6 (Mon–Fri 9.30am–6pm, Thurs till 7pm).

Taxis *Taxi Direkt* ☎018/12 53 60; *Taxi Uppsala* ☎018/23 90 90.

Telephone office *Telia Butik*, Svartbäcksgatan and Bredgränd

Train enquiries ☎018/65 22 10.

travel details

Trains

From Stockholm to: Boden (2 daily; 14hr); Gothenburg (17 daily; 3hr 15min by X2000, 4hr 30min by intercity); Gällivare (2 daily; 16hr); Gävle (hourly; 2hr); Helsingborg (8 daily; 5hr by X2000, 6hr 30min by intercity); Kiruna (2 daily; 17hr); Luleå (2 daily; 14hr); Läggesta (for Mariefred; 32 daily; 45min by X2000); Malmö (11 daily; 4hr 45min by X2000, 6hr by intercity); Mora (7 daily; 4hr by X2000, 5hr by intercity); Nynäshamn *pendeltåg* for ferries to Gotland (hourly; 1hr); Sundsvall (6 daily; 4hr by X2000, 5hr by intercity); Umeå (1 daily; 11hr); Uppsala (50 daily; 45min); Östersund (4 daily; 6hr).

From Eskilstuna to: Laggesta (for Mariefred; 32 daily; 15min by X2000); Stockholm (32 daily; 1hr by X2000).

From Läggesta to: Stockholm (32 daily; 45min).

From Uppsala to: Gällivare (2 daily; 15hr); Gävle (hourly; 1hr); Kiruna (2 daily; 16hr); Luleå (2 daily; 13hr); Mora (7 daily; 3hr 15min by X2000, 4hr 15min by intercity); Stockholm (50 daily; 45min); Sundsvall (6 daily; 3hr by X2000, 4hr by intercity); Umeå (1 daily; 10hr); Östersund (4 daily; 5hr)

Buses

From Stockholm to: Borlänge (2 on Fri & Sun; 3hr); Falun (2 on Fri & Sun; 3hr 30min); Gävle (3 on Fri, 5 on Sun; 2hr 20min); Gothenburg (Mon–Wed 2 daily, 3 on Thurs, 5 on Fri & Sun, 1 on Sat; 4hr 30min, or 7hr 20min via Kristinehamn or Jönköping); Halmstad (1 on Fri & Sun; 7hr 30min); Haparanda (1 on Fri & Sun; 12hr 45min); Helsingborg (Mon–Thurs 1 daily, 2 on Fri & Sun; 8hr); Jököping (Mon–Thurs 1 daily, 2 on Fri & Sun; 4hr 40min); Kalmar (5 daily; 6hr 30min); Kristianstad (1 on Mon, Thurs, Fri & Sun; 9hr 30min); Kristinehamn (Mon–Thurs 2 daily, Mon–Thurs 2 daily, 3 on Fri & Sun, 2 on Sat; 3hr); Luleå (1 on Fri & Sun; 12hr); Malmö (1 on Fri, 2 on Sun; 10hr 20min); Mora (2 on Fri & Sun; 4hr 40min); Norrköping (Mon–Wed 2 daily, 3 on Thurs, 4 on Fri & Sun, 1 on Sat; 2hr); Rättvik (2 on Fri & Sun; 4hr 10min); Skellefteå (1 on Fri & Sun; 11hr); Umeå (1 on Fri & Sun; 9hr 20min).

International trains

From Stockholm to: Copenhagen (9 daily; 8hr 30min); Narvik (2 daily; 20hr); Oslo (2 daily; 6hr 30min); Trondheim (3 daily; 12hr).

International ferries

From Stockholm to: Helsinki (1 *Viking Line* & 1 *Silja Line* daily; 15hr); Turku (2 *Viking Line* & 2 *Silja Line* daily; 1 daily on each route via the Åland islands); Tallinn (1 every 2nd day); Eckerö on the Åland islands (2–3 daily; 3hr; bus leaves Tekniska Högskolan T-bana 2hr before ferry departure from Grisslehamn).

From Nynäshamn to: Gdansk (3 weekly; 19hr).

Flights

There are fairly regular flights – the most reliable operated by *SAS* – between Stockholm Arlanda and the main northern cities. Timetables are subject to constant change, however, so it's advisable to check with a travel agent.

CHAPTER TEN

GOTHENBURG AND AROUND

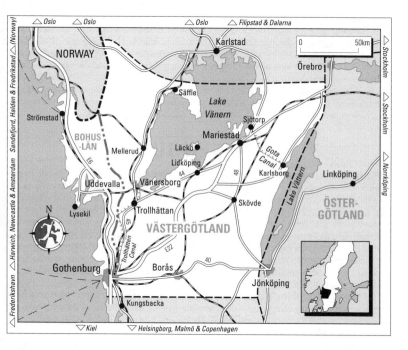

Gothenburg is Sweden's second city and the largest seaport in Scandinavia – facts that have been enough to persuade many travellers arriving here by ferry to move quickly on to the surrounding countryside. But beyond the gargantuan shipyards, Gothenburg's Dutch-designed cityscape of broad avenues, elegant squares, trams and canals is one of the prettiest in Sweden. Moreover, Gothenburg is a surprisingly cultured place, with a new and burgeoning café society, and is worth a lot more time than most visitors give it. The city's image has also suffered from the inevitable comparisons with the capital, and while there is a certain resentment on the west coast that Stockholm wins out in the national glory stakes, many Swedes far prefer Gothenburg's easier-going atmosphere – and its closer proximity to Western Europe. Talk to any Gothenburger and he or she will soon tell you about the more frenetic lives of the "08-ers" – 08 being the telephone code for Stockholm.

The counties to the north and east of the city are prime targets for domestic tourists. To the north, the craggy **Bohuslän coastline**, with its uninhabited islands, tiny fishing villages and clean beaches attracts thousands of holidaymakers all the way to the Norwegian border. The coast is popular with the sailing set, and there are many guest harbours along the way, but the highlight is the glorious fortress island of **Marstrand**, an easy and enjoyable day trip from Gothenburg.

To the northeast of city, the vast and beautiful lakes of **Vänern** and **Vättern** provide the setting for a number of historic towns, fairy-tale castles and some splendid inland scenery, all of which are within an hour's train journey from Gothenburg. The lakes are connected to each other (and to the east and west coasts) by the cross-country **Göta Canal**, and if you're inspired by the possibilities of water transport you could always make the complete four-day trip by boat from Gothenburg to Stockholm. First leg of the journey is up the Trollhättan Canal to **Trollhättan**, a wonderful little town built around the canal and a good place to aim for if you only have time for a short trip out from the city. Beyond here, though, other agreeable lakeside towns vie for your attention, with attractions including the elk safaris on the ancient hills of Halleberg and Hunneberg, near **Vänersborg** on the tip of Lake Vänern, picturesque medieval **Mariestad**, further up the lake's eastern shore, and the huge military fortress at **Karlsborg**, on the western shore of Lake Vättern.

Regular **train** and **bus** services connect most of the region; the only area you may find difficult to explore without a car is the Boshulän coast. **Accommodation** is never a problem, with plenty of hotels, hostels and camping sites in each town.

GOTHENBURG

With its long history as a trading centre, **GOTHENBURG** (Göteborg in Swedish; pronounced "Yur-te-boy") is a truly cosmopolitan city. Founded on its present site in the seventeenth century by Gustav Adolf, Gothenburg was the fifth attempt to create a centre not reliant on Denmark – the Danes had enjoyed control of Sweden's west coast since the Middle Ages, extracting extortionate tolls from all water traffic into Sweden. The medieval centre of trade was sited 40km up the Göta River, but then in order to avoid the tolls it was moved to a location north of the present city; a later incarnation was built on the island of Hisingen, but this fell to the Danes during the battle of Kalmar, and it was another six years before Gustav Adolf founded the city where the main square is today.

Although Gothenburg's reputation as an industrial and trading centre has been severely eroded in recent years – clearly evidenced by the stillness of the cranes in the shipyards by the harbour – the British, Dutch and German traders who settled here during the eighteenth and nineteenth centuries left a rich architectural and cultural inheritance. The city is graced with terraces of grand merchant houses, all carved stone, stucco and painted tiles, while the trade between Sweden and the Far East brought an Oriental influence, still visible in the chinoiserie detail on many buildings. This vital trading route was monopolized for over eighty years by the hugely successful East India Company, whose auction house, selling exotic spices, tea and fine cloth, attracted merchants from all over the world.

Today the city remains a sort of transit camp for business people, though the flashy central hotels that accommodate them say much less about Gothenburg than the restrained opulence of the older buildings, which reflect not only the city's bygone prosperity but also the understatement of its citizens. Gothenburgers may give you the impression they think their surroundings are nothing special, but don't be taken in – they are immensely proud of their elegant city and simply exhibiting a typical Gothenburg modesty.

Arrival and information

From **Landvetter airport**, 25km east of the city, buses run every fifteen minutes via Korsvagan, a junction to the south of the centre, to Central Station in Drottningtorget. The journey takes around 35 minutes (*Flygbuss* daily 5am–11.15pm; 50kr, Gothenburg Card not valid). For airline and airport information numbers, see p.436.

All **trains** arrive at Central Station, on Drottningtorget in the centre of the city. Also here is a *Swebus* office (Mon–Fri 7am–6pm, Sun 10.30am–6pm), where you can buy bus tickets for services to Oslo, which stop outside. Otherwise, **buses** to and from destinations north of Gothenburg use **Nils Ericsonsplatsen** (ticket office Mon–Fri 7.30am–5.45pm, Sat 8am–2pm), just behind the train station. Buses from the south arrive at the **Heden** terminal, at the junction of Parkgatan and Sodra Vagen, from where there are easy tram connections to all parts of the city.

Scandinavian Seaways **ferries** from Britain arrive at Skandiahamn on Hisingen, north of the river (☎031/65 06 00); special buses shuttle to Nils Ericsonsplatsen behind the train station in the city centre (30kr, Gothenburg Card not valid). When leaving, the same bus returns from platform V, ninety minutes before sailings. *Stena Line* ferries from Frederikshavn in Denmark dock at a quay twenty minutes' walk or a regular bus ride from the city centre, while those from Kiel in Germany dock 3km outside Gothenburg – take bus #86 or tram #3 into the centre. Heading back to Germany, *Stena Line* runs a special bus from Ericsonsplatsen at 5.50pm in time for the 7pm crossing.

Information

Gothenburg has two **tourist offices**. Handiest for recent arrivals is the **kiosk** in *Nordstan*, the indoor shopping centre near Central Station (Mon–Fri 9.30am–6pm, Sat 9.30am–3pm). The **main office** is on the canalfront at Kungsportsplatsen 2 (May Mon–Fri 9am–6pm, Sat & Sun 10am–2pm; June & July daily 9am–6pm; Aug daily 9am–8pm; Sept–April Mon–Fri 9am–5pm, Sat 10am–2pm; ☎031/10 07 40). From the train station, it's just five minutes' walk across Drottningtorget and down Stora Nygatan: the tourist office is on the right, opposite the statue of the so-called "Copper Mare" (see p.429). Both offices provide information, free city and tram maps, restaurant and museum listings, and offer a room-booking service, as well as selling the Gothenburg Card. You can also pick up a copy of the fortnightly *Göteborgam*, which contains what's on information in Swedish and English.

The Gothenburg Card

Buying a **Gothenburg Card** (*Göteborgskortet*) is a good way to save money if you intend to do a lot of sightseeing. Available from either of the tourist offices, and from *Pressbyrån* kiosks and hotels, it gives unlimited bus and tram travel within the city, free entry to all the city museums and the Liseberg Amusement Park (not including rides), free car parking (see below), boat excursions, including a day trip to Fredrikshavn in Denmark, plus various other reductions. The card comes in three versions, valid for 24 hours (125kr, children 75kr), 48 hours (225kr, 125kr) or 72 hours (275kr, 150kr).

City transport

Apart from excursions north of the river or to the islands, almost anywhere of interest in Gothenburg is within easy walking distance. The wide streets are pedestrian-friendly and the canals and grid layout of the avenues makes orientation simple. If you're staying further out, however, or approaching from the central transport terminals, some

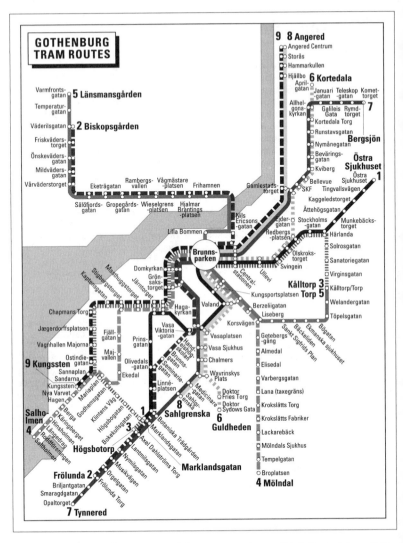

GOTHENBURG TRAM ROUTES

9 **8 Angered**
Angered Centrum
Storås
Hammarkullen
Hjällbo **6 Kortedala**
April-gatan   Januari Teleskop Komet--gatan -gatan torget
Allhel-gona-kyrkan   Galileis Rymd-Gata torget **7**

Varmfronts-gatan **5 Länsmansgården**
Temperatur-gatan
Väderilsgatan **2 Biskopsgården**
Friskväders-torget
Önskeväders-gatan
Mildväders-gatan
Vårväderstorget   Eketrägatan   Rambergs-vallen   Vågmästare-platsen   Frihamnen

Kortedala Torg
Runstavsgatan   **Bergsjön**
Nymånegatan
Beväringsgatan   **Östra Sjukhuset**
Kviberg
Bellevue   Östra Sjukhuset **1**
SKF   Tingvallsvägen
Gamlestads-torget

Sälöfjords-gatan   Gropegårds-gatan   Wieselgrens-platsen   Hjalmar Brantings-platsen
Lilla Bommen
Nils Ericsons-gatan
Redbergs-platsen
Kaggeledstorget
Ättehögsgatan
Eder-gatan   Stockholms-gatan   Munkebäcks-torget
Härlanda
Solrosgatan
Sanatoriegatan
Virginsgatan

Brunns-parken
Domkyrkan
Grön-saks-torget
Järntorget
Central-stationen
Ullevi
Olskroks-torget
Svingein

Chapmans Torg
Jæegerdorffsplatsen   Fjäll-gatan
Vagnhallen Majorna
Ostindie-gatan
Sannaplan
Sandarna
9 Kungssten   Kungssten   Nya Varvet   Hagen
Prins-gatan
Maj-vallen
Olivedals-gatan
Ekedal
Haga-kyrkan
Vasa Viktoria-gatan
Hand-elshög-skolan
Bruns-parks-gatan
Seminarie-gatan
Valand
Kungsportsplatsen   **Kålltorp 3** Kålltorp/Torp
Torp 5
Berzeliigatan   Welandergatan
Liseberg   Töpelsgatan
Korsvägen
Vasaplatsen
Vasa Sjukhus
Chalmers
Wavrinskys Plats
Linné-platsen
Medicinare-gatan
Sahlg-renska
Geteberg-s-gäng   Bäckeliden
Almedal   Ekmanska sjukhuset
Elisedal
Varbergsgatan
Lana (taxegräns)
Krokslätts Torg

Salho-lmen 4
Berga   Härmeberget   Hinsholmen   Långedrag   Roddföreningen   Saltholmen
Mariaplan
Godhemsgatan
Klintens Väg
Högsbogatan
Bokekullsgatan
1
Botaniska Trädgården
8 Sahlgrenska
Axel Dahlströms Torg
Marklandsgatan
6 Guldheden
Doktor Fries Torg
Doktor Sydows Gata
Krokslätts Fabriker
Lackarebäck
Mölndals Sjukhus

Högsbotorp   **3**
Nymilsgatan
Lantmilsgatan
Marklandsgatan
Tempelgatan
Broplatsen
4 Mölndal

Frölunda 2
Briljantgatan
Smaragdgatan
Opaltorget
Musikvägen
Orgelgatan
Frölunda Torg
7 Tynnered

sort of transport may be necessary. A free **transport map** (*Linje Kartan*) is available from either tourist office.

Public transport

The most convenient form of public transport are the **trams**, which clunk around the city and its outskirts on a colour-coded, eight-line system, passing all the central areas every few minutes – you can tell at a glance which line a tram is on as the route colour appears on the front. The main pick-up points are outside Central Station and in

Kungsportsplatsen. During summer, there's the chance to ride on vintage trams from 1902, which trundle through the city centre to Liseberg and Slottsskogen. Gothenburg also has a fairly extensive **bus** network, using much the same routes as the trams, although central pedestrianization can lead to some odd and lengthy detours. You shouldn't need to use them in the city centre; routes are detailed in the text where necessary.

If you have a Gothenburg Card, all public transport within the city is free; if not, **tickets** should be bought from tram and bus drivers. There's no zonal system and adult fares cost a flat-rate 16kr. If you are staying for a couple of days, it's cheaper to buy ticket cards from the *Tidpunkten* offices (travel information centres) at Brunnsparken, Drottningtorget and Nils Ericsonsplatsen, *Pressbyrån* or *Ja* kiosks. A ten-trip ticket card costs 100kr. Stick these in the machines on a tram or bus, and press twice for an adult, once for a child. Trams run from 5am to midnight, after which there is a night service at double the price. **Fare-dodging** carries an instant fine of 600kr – since all the ticket information is posted in English at bus and tram stops, ignorance is no defence.

Finally, a good way to get to grips with the city is to take a **paddan boat tour**, an hour-long trip around the canals and harbour (daily late April to mid-June & early Aug to mid-Sept 10am–5pm; mid-June to early Aug 10am–9pm; mid-Sept to early Oct noon–3pm; 65kr, free with Gothenburg Card after 2pm). Tours leave regularly from moorings on the canal by Kungsportsplatsen.

Cars, taxis and bikes

There is no shortage of **car parks** in the city, with a basic charge of 15kr per hour in the centre. Buying a Gothenburg Card gets you a free parking card, but this is not valid in privately run or multistorey car parks, nor in any car park with attendants. The most useful car parks are the new *Ullevigarage* at Heden, near the bus terminal, the *Lorensbergs* near Avenyn, *Gamla Ullevi* on Alleyn, south of Kungsportsplatsen, and two multistorey car parks at *Nordstan* near Central Station and *Garda-Focus* close to Liseberg. If you don't have a Gothenburg Card, roadside parking areas marked with blue signs are cheaper than parking meters. Some of the larger hotels offer a discount at the multistorey car parks. For information on **car rental** see p.436.

Taxis can be summoned by calling ☎031/65 00 00. There is a 20 percent reduction for women travelling at night, but check with the driver first.

Cycling is a popular and easy way to get around, since Gothenburg boasts a comprehensive series of cycle lanes and plenty of bike racks. The most central place to **rent a bike** is *Sportkälleren* at Bohusgatan 2 (☎031/16 23 46), five minutes from Kungsportsplatsen on the far side of Heden. Outside the centre, try *Cyckelogen* at Bjorcksgatan 45c (☎031/21 11 11), reached by tram #1 or #3 to Härlanda, or *Cykelspecialisten* at Delsjovagen 5B (☎031/40 23 24), tram #5 to St Sigfridsplan. To rent a bike for two days will cost you 250–300kr, a week's rental costs 325–500kr.

Accommodation

Gothenburg has plenty of decent accommodation options, with no shortage of comfortable **youth hostels**, though many are out of the centre, along with **private rooms** and a number of big, central **hotels**. Most of these are clustered together around the train station and offer a high standard of service, if with fairly uniform and uninspiring decor. Summer and weekend reductions mean that even the better hotels can prove surprisingly affordable, and most places also take part in the **Gothenburg Package**, which can cut costs further (see below).

Whenever you turn up, you should have no trouble finding accommodation, though in summer, it's a good idea to book ahead if you are limited to the cheaper hotels, or if you want to stay in the most popular youth hostels (see the listings below).

Youth hostels and private rooms

The cheapest options for accommodation are booking a **private room** (150kr per person in a double room, 200kr for a single) through the tourist office (60kr booking fee; ☎031/10 07 40 for details), or staying in one of the **youth hostels**. All the hostels listed below are run by *STF*, except for *Nordengarden,* and are open all year unless otherwise stated. For stays of a week or more, consider renting out a furnished room with a kitchen; a week's rental costs around 1200kr. For more information, visit *SGS Bostader,* Utlandgatan 24 (Mon–Fri 11am–3pm).

Karralunds Vandrarhem, Olbergsgatan (☎031/84 02 00). Four kilometres from the centre, close to Liseberg Amusement Park – take tram #5 to Welandergatan, direction Torp. Non-smoking rooms available, plus cabins and a campsite (see below). Breakfast can only be ordered by groups. 100kr; book ahead in summer.

Kviberg Vandrarhem, Kvibergsvägen 5 (☎031/ 43 50 55; fax 43 26 50). In Gamlestad (the Old Town before present Gothenburg was founded), ten minutes by tram #6 or #7 from Central Station. Beds in rooms for four cost 110kr; 25kr extra for sheets.

Masthuggsterrassen, Masthuggsterrassen 8 (☎/fax 031/42 48 20). Within a couple of minutes' walk of the *Stena Line* ferry terminal from Denmark; a bed in a room for four costs 125kr.

Nordengarden, Stockholmsgatan 16 (☎031/19 66 31). Private hostel with dorms, a kitchen and free showers. Take tram #1 or #3 to Stockholmsgatan or tram #6 to Redbergplatsen. Booking ahead advisable; 80kr.

Ostkupan, Mejerigatan 2 (☎031/40 10 50; fax 40 10 51). Busy hostel that's only open June–Aug; outside these times, make reservations through *Karralund Vandrarhem* (above). Bus #64 from Brunnsparken to Graddgatan or tram #5 to St Sigfridsplan then bus #62 to Graddgatan (Kalleback direction). 100kr.

Partille, Landvettervagen, Partille (☎/fax 031/44 61 63). Fifteen kilometres east of the city (take bus #503 or #513 from Heden bus terminal; 30min), this hostel has a solarium and day room with TV. 100kr.

M/S Seaside, Packhuskajen (☎031/10 10 35; fax 711 6035). A moored ship at the harbour next to Maritima Centrum, with twenty cabins sleeping one to four. Dorm beds cost 100kr, cabins 175kr; breakfast and sheets extra. Open April–Sept.

Slottskogen, Vegagatan 21 (☎031/42 65 20; fax 14 21 02). Superbly appointed, family-run hostel, just two minutes' walk from Linnegatan and not far from Slottskogen Park Take tram #1 or #2 to Olivedahlsgatan. 100kr; breakfast 40kr.

Torrekulla, Kallered (☎031/795 1495; fax 795 5140). Pleasantly situated hostel, 15km south of the city, with lots of room, a free sauna and a nearby bathing lake. Bus #705 from Heden or a ten-minute train journey from Central Station, then a fifteen-minute walk. 100kr.

Hotels and pensions

The **Gothenburg Package** scheme, coordinated by the tourist office, is a real bargain, as it bundles together accommodation, breakfast and a Gothenburg Card for 360–650kr per person in a twin bedroom, with discounts for children sharing. Around thirty good central hotels take part in the scheme, which operates every Friday to Monday from early June to the end of August, on all major holidays, winter sports holidays and over Christmas. In some hotels it's valid on Thursdays and in others all year round. At the time of writing all the hotels listed below were involved in the Gothenburg Package, and all include breakfast in the price unless otherwise stated. Note that bookings for the Gothenburg Package have to be made through the tourist office; you can't get this offer by contacting the hotels direct.

Alleyn, Parkgatan 10 (☎031/10 14 50; fax 11 91 60). Very central, sensibly priced hotel close to Avenyn and the old town. Price includes room service and parking. ②/③

City, Lorensbergsgatan 6 (☎031/18 00 25; fax 18 81 90). Not to be confused with *City Hotel Ritz* (see below), this is a cheapish and popular place, excellently positioned close to Avenyn. For en-suite rooms you'll pay 300kr more. ①

City Hotel Ritz, Burggrevegatan 25 (☎031/80 00 80; fax 15 77 76). Comfortable hotel close to Central Station; en-suite rooms with cable TV, plus a free sauna. ③

Eggers, Drottningtorget (☎031/80 60 70; fax 15 42 43). The original station hotel, this very characterful establishment has individually furnished bedrooms and a wealth of grand original features. One of the best-value central hotels, with a really low Gothenburg Package price. ③/⑤

Excelsior, Karl Gustavsgatan 9 (☎031/17 54 35; fax 17 54 39). Shabbily stylish 1880 building in a road of classic Gothenburg houses between Avenyn and Haga. It's been a hotel since 1930 and both Greta Garbo and Ingrid Bergman stayed here, as did, more recently, Sheryl Crow. Classic suites with splendid nineteenth-century features cost no more than plain rooms – Garbo's room is no. 535. ②/④

Hotel II, Maskingatan 11 (☎031/779 1111; fax 779 1110). At the harbour, with views across to Hisingen, this is one of the city's most interesting and stylish places to stay, built on the site of an old shipbuilding yard. Take tram #1, #3, #4 or #9 from Järntorget, then the boat, *Älv Snabben* (Mon–Fri 6am–11.30pm every 30min, shorter hours on weekends; 16kr, free with Gothenburg Card), in the direction of Klippan from in front of the *Opera House* at Lilla Bommen – get off at Eriksberg. ③/⑤

Lilton, Föreningsgatan 9 (☎031/82 88 08; fax 82 21 84). One of Gothenburg's least known pensions, close to the Haga district, this is a small, old, ivy-covered place set among trees. ②/③

Maria Erikssons Pensionat, Chalmersgatan 27A (☎031/20 70 30; fax 16 64 63). Just ten rooms, but well positioned on a road running parallel with Avenyn. Breakfast not included. ①

Robinson, Södra Hamngatan 2 (☎031/80 25 21; fax 15 92 91). Facing Brunnspark, this mediocre hotel still boasts its original facade – the building was part of the old Furstenburg Palace (see p.428). Original etched windows on the lift are some of the few features to have survived decades of architectural meddling. All rooms have cable TV; en-suite rooms cost 160kr more. ①/②

Sheraton, Södra Hamngatan 59–65 (☎031/80 60 00; fax 15 98 88). Opposite the train station and exuding all the usual glitz: the atrium foyer is like a shopping mall with glass lifts and fountains; bedrooms are all pastel shades and birch wood. The *Frascati Restaurant* here serves up truffles, duck and salmon. ④/⑤

Cabins and campsites

Two of the following campsites also provide **cabins**, which are worth considering, especially if there are more than two of you. Facilities are invariably squeaky clean and in good working order – there is usually a well-equipped kitchen – but you'll have to pay extra for bedding. Prices for cabins are given below; if you want to **camp**, you'll pay around 100kr for two people in July or August (50kr the rest of the year).

Askims (☎031/28 62 61; fax 68 13 35). Set beside sandy beaches 12km from the centre: take tram #1 or #2 to Linneplatsen, then bus #83, or better still the *Blo Express* (Blue Express; direction Saro)

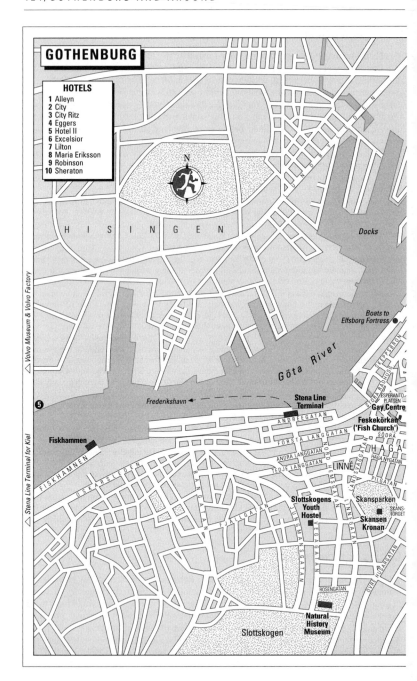

GOTHENBURG

HOTELS
1 Alleyn
2 City
3 City Ritz
4 Eggers
5 Hotel II
6 Excelsior
7 Lilton
8 Maria Eriksson
9 Robinson
10 Sheraton

N

H I S I N G E N

Docks

△ Volvo Museum & Volvo Factory

Boats to
Elfsborg Fortress

Göta River

△ Stena Line Terminal for Kiel

Frederikshavn ←

Stena Line
Terminal

ESPERANTO-
PLATSEN
Gay Centre

Feskekörkan
('Fish Church')

ANDRÉEGATAN

SÖDRA

Fiskhammen

FÖRSTA LÅNGGATAN

ANDRA LÅNGGATAN

TEDJE LÅNGGATAN

H A G A

HAGA NYGATAN

LINNÉ

PILGATAN

FISKHAMNEN

OSKARSLEDEN

BANGATAN

FJÄLLGATAN

LINNÉGATAN

VEGAGATAN

**Slottskogens
Youth
Hostel**

Skansparken

**Skansen
Kronan**

SKANS-
TORGET

LINNÉGATAN

ÖVRE HUSARGATAN

ROSENGATAN

**Natural
History
Museum**

Slottskogen

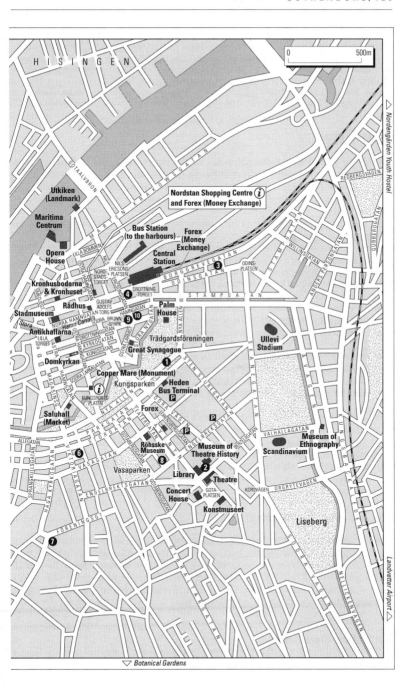

HISINGEN

0   500m

Nordengården Youth Hostel ▷

REDBERGSVÄGEN

GÖTAÄLVBRON

KRÖNHUSGATAN

NILS ERICSONSGATAN

Utkiken
(Landmark)

Nordstan Shopping Centre (i)
and Forex (Money Exchange)

Maritima
Centrum

Bus Station
(to the harbours)   Forex
(Money
Exchange)

LILLA BOMMEN

Opera
House

Central
Station

NILS
ERICSONS
PLATSEN

NORD
STADS
TORGET

BURGGREVEGATAN

ODINS-
PLATSEN

STAMPGATAN

WILLINSGATAN

ANDERS PERSSONSGATAN

GUBBEROGATAN

Kronhusbodarna
& Kronhuset

GUSTAV
ADOLFS
TORG

ODINSGATAN

DROTTNING
TORGET

Rådhus

Stadmuseum

NORRA HAMNGATAN

HAMNGATAN

Palm
House

Stora
Antikhallarna

LILLA
TORGET

Hamn Canal

SÖDRA
BRUNN
SPARK

NYA ALLÉN

Ullevi
Stadium

DROTTNINGGATAN

KYRKOGATAN

KUNGSGATAN

ÖSTRA HAMNGATAN

Trädgårdsföreningen

SKANEGATAN

AVENYN

Domkyrkan

SÖDRA HAMNGATAN

Great Synagogue

STENSGATAN

SÖDRA LARMGATAN

Copper Mare (Monument)

(i)

KUNGSPORTS
PLATEN

Kungsparken

NYA ALLÉN

Heden
Bus Terminal
P

Forex

P

Saluhall
(Market)

VALHALLAGATAN

ALLEGATAN

P

Museum of
Ethnography

SPRÅNGKULLSGATAN

HAGA KYRKOGATAN

PARKGATAN

TEATERGATAN

SÖDRA VÄGEN

ENGELBREKTSGATAN

Röhsske
Museum

Museum of
Theatre History

Scandinavium

KUNGSBACKALEDEN

VASAGATAN

Vasaparken

Library

Theatre

Concert
House

GÖTA-
PLATSEN

Konstmuseet

KORSVÄGEN

ORGRYTEVÄGEN

Liseberg

FÖRENINGSG T

SÖDRA VÄGEN

NELLICKEVÄGEN

Landvetter Airport ▷

▽ Botanical Gardens

from outside Central Station on Drottningtorget. Open May–Aug (office 9am–noon & 3pm–6pm, slightly later Thurs–Sat); four-bed cabins cost 615kr in high season, otherwise 495kr.

Karralunds (see "Private rooms and youth hostels" above for details). Set among forest and lakes, it's open from June 24 to the end of August; four-bed cabins cost 615kr, or 695kr with your own toilet (50kr discount the rest of the year).

Lilleby Havsbad (☎031/56 08 67; fax 56 16 05). Take bus #21 from Nils Ericsonsplatsen and change to the #23 at Kongshallavagen. It takes an hour to reach, but has a splendid seaside location.

The City

Everything of interest in Gothenburg lies south of the **Göta River**, and there's rarely any need to cross the water. This is a fairly compact city, and easy to get around, so you can cover most of the sights in just a day or two, but to get the most from your stay give the city a few more days and slow your pace down to a stroll – which will put you in step with the locals.

At the heart of the city is the historic **old town**, and while Gothenburg's attractions are by no means restricted to this area, its picturesque elegance makes it the best place to start. Tucked between the Göta River to the north and the zigzagging canal to the south, old Gothenburg's tightly gridded streets are lined with impressive facades, and boast an interesting food market and a couple of worthwhile museums – the **Stadsmuseum** and, up by the harbour, the museum of **maritime history**. Just across the canal that skirts the southern edges of the old town is **Trädgårdsforeningen** park, in summer full of picnicking Gothenburgers.

Heading further south into the modern centre, **Avenyn** is Gothenburg's showcase boulevard, alive with showy restaurants and bars. However, it's the roads off Avenyn that hold the area's real interest, with trendy 24-hour café-bars and some of Gothenburg's best museums: in a small area called **Vasaplan** to the southwest, you'll find the **Röhsska Museum** of applied arts and, further south in **Götaplatsen**, the city **Art Museum**. For family entertainment day or night, the famous **Liseberg Amusement Park**, just to the southeast of Avenyn, has been pulling in the crowds since the 1920s.

Vasaplan stretches west to **Haga**, the city's old working-class district now thoroughly gentrified and fashionable. Haga Nygatan, the main thoroughfare, leads on to Linnegatan, the arterial road through the **Linne** district. Fast establishing itself as the most vibrant part of the city, Linne is home to the most interesting evening haunts, with new cafés, bars and restaurants opening up alongside long-established antique emporiums and sex shops. Further out, the rolling **Slottskogen** park holds the **Natural History Museum**, but is perhaps most appealing as a place to relax and enjoy the sun.

The old town and harbour

The **old town** is divided in two by the **Stora Hamn Canal**, to the north of which are most of the main sights and the harbour, where the decaying shipyards make for a dramatic backdrop. The streets south of the Stora Hamn, stretching down to the zigzagging southern canal, are perfect for an afternoon's leisurely stroll, with some quirky cafés, food markets and junk shops to dip into, as well as Sweden's oldest synagogue. Straddling the Stora Hamn is Gothenburg's main square, **Gustav Adolfs Torg**, the best place to start your explorations.

North of the Stora Hamn

At the centre of stately **Gustav Adolfs Torg**, a copper statue of the city's founder, Gustav Adolf, points ostentatiously at the ground where he reputedly declared "Here I will build my city." The statue is a copy, however: the German-made original was kidnapped on its way to Sweden and Gothenburgers commissioned a new one rather than pay the ransom. Although there is little attempt to encourage visitors to enter the buildings surrounding the square, it is worth persisting to discover some exceptional interiors.

To the east of the square, with the canal behind you, stands the **Rådhus** – not the town hall you might expect, but the criminal law courts since 1672. Beyond its rather dull classical colonnaded facade, the interior of its extension was designed by the ground-breaking functionalist architect E.G. Asplund in 1936. Facing the canal, at right angles to the Rådhus, is the white, double-columned 1842 **Borhuset**, the former stock exchange. If you can persuade the attendants to let you in, you'll be rewarded with magnificent banqueting and concert halls, and smaller rooms with a riot of red and blue stucco inspired by the eighteenth-century excavations at Pompeii.

Head north from the square along the filled-in canal of Östra Hamngatan, past the amorphous **Nordstan Shopping Centre**, Sweden's biggest. A dark, depressingly bland complex, its saving graces are a 24-hour pharmacy and the city's second tourist office. If you have time to spare, it's worth taking a short detour along Burggrevegatan to Drottningtorget to see the city's impressive **Central Station**. The oldest in the country, dating from 1856, behind its original facade is a grand and marvellously preserved interior. Look out for the wood beam-ends in the ticket hall, each one carved into the likeness of a city council member of the day.

At its far end, Ostra Hamngatan runs into **Lilla Bommen**. Here Gothenburg's industrial decline comes together with its artistic regeneration to dramatic visual effect: to the west, the cranes of dormant shipyards loom across the sky, a backdrop to industrial-themed sculptures in bronze and pink granite dotted along the waterfront. The new **Opera House** (daily noon–6pm daily; guided tours ☎031/10 80 50; performance info on ☎701 8070) to the left was designed with deliberate industrial styling, the idea being that stage sets should be created within the building as part of a production flow. To the right, **Utkiken** ("Look out"; Jan to mid-May & Sept to mid-Dec Sat & Sun 11am–4pm, May–Aug daily 11am–7pm; 25kr), designed by the Scottish architect Ralph Erskine in the late 1980s, is an 86-metre-high office block taking the form of a half-used red lipstick. Its top storey offers panoramic views of the city and harbour.

Walking west along the quay, it's just a couple of minutes to the **Maritima Centrum** (daily March, April & Sept–Nov 10am–4pm; May–June & Aug 10am–6pm; July 10am–9pm; 45kr, free with Gothenburg Card), which describes itself as "the largest ship museum in the world". Not a dull experience, even for non-enthusiasts, the museum comprises a dozen boats including a 1915 lightship, a submarine and a fire float, each giving a glimpse of how seamen lived and worked on board. The special blue arrow route is designed for those wanting to avoid the ships' steep steps. The original toilets and washrooms on board, for public use, are an experience in themselves. There's also a rather good café and restaurant here too.

From the maritime museum it's a short walk southwest to Gothenburg's oldest secular building, the **Kronhuset** on Kronhusgatan (Tues–Fri 11am–4pm, Sat & Sun 11am–5pm; 30kr). Built by the Dutch in 1642 as an artillery depot for the city's garrison, in 1660 this was where the five-year-old Karl XI was proclaimed king. Set in the eighteenth-century wings of the building is **Kronhusbodarna** (Mon–Fri 11am–4pm, Sat 11am–2pm), a cluster of small, pricey shops specializing in gold, silver and glasswork. You can buy a copy of the city's oldest key from the silversmith here, but your money would be better spent at the atmospheric vaulted café, which serves dunes of meringues as well as sandwich lunches.

A couple of blocks further south, the **Stadsmuseum** or City Museum (April–Sept Mon–Fri noon–6pm, Sat & Sun 11am–4pm; Oct–March closed Mon; 40kr) has emerged, after an extensive reshuffling of the city's collections, as Gothenburg's primary museum. Located at Norra Hamngatan 12, it's housed in Ostindiska Huset, the offices, store and auction house that were constructed in 1750 for the enormously influential **Swedish East India Company**. Granted sole rights to trade with China in 1731, the company monopolized Far East commerce for over eighty years, the only condition being that the spices, silk and porcelain it brought back were to be sold in Gothenburg. The museum itself is well worth a browse, not least for its rich interior, a mix of stone pillars, stained glass and frescoes. Head first to the third floor, where there are exhibitions on the East India Company, allowing a look at the renovated auction hall. Also impressive is the section devoted to industry, a well-designed exhibition relating Gothenburg's twentieth-century history, with displays on shipping and working conditions in the textile factories at the beginning of the century.

South of the Stora Hamn

Across Stora Hamn just to the west of the Stadsmuseum lies **Lilla Torget**, its only draw being a statue of Jonas Alstromer, who introduced the potato to Sweden in the eighteenth century. Walk on to the quayside at **Stenpiren**, the spot where hundreds of emigrants said their last goodbyes before sailing off to create New Sweden in the United States. The original granite **Delaware Monument** was carted off to America in the early part of this century, and it wasn't until 1938 that celebrated sculptor Carl Mille cast a replacement in bronze, which stands here looking out to sea.

Today boats leave Stenpiren for the popular excursion to the island fortress of **Nya Elfsborg** (early May to Aug hourly 9.30am–3pm; 20min; 65kr, free with Gothenburg Card). Built in the seventeenth century to defend the harbour and the city, the surviving buildings have been turned into a **museum** and café. There are guided tours in English (included in the price of the boat trip) around the square tower, chapel and prison cells.

Back at Lilla Torget, walk down Västra Hamngatn, which leads off the southern side of the square, to the city's cathedral; on the way you'll pass **Antik Hallarna** (Mon–Fri 10am–6pm, Sat 10am–2pm), a clutch of pricey antique shops set in a fantastic building with a gilded ceiling and regal marble stairs leading up to a café. A few blocks south of here, to the left off Västra Hamngatan, is the classically styled **Domkyrkan** (Mon–Fri 8am–5pm, Sat 8am–3pm, Sun 10am–3pm). Built in 1827 (the two previous cathedrals were destroyed by fires at a rate of one a century), four giant sandstone columns stand at the portico, and inside there's an opulent gilded altarpiece. The plain white walls concentrate the eye on the unusual post-Resurrection cross, devoid of a Jesus, whose gilded grave clothes are strewn below. Another quirky feature are the twin glassed-in verandas that run down either side, designed for the bishop's "private conversations".

Continuing east past the cathedral and north towards Stora Hamn, the leafy square known as **Brunnspark** soon comes into view, with Gustav Adolfs Torg just across the the canal. The sedate house facing the square is now a snazzy restaurant and nightclub called *The Palace*, but the house was once home to Pontus and Gothilda **Furstenburg**, the city's leading arts patrons in the late nineteenth century. They opened up the top floor as Gothenburg's first art gallery to be lit with electric as well as natural light, and later donated their entire collection – the biggest batch of Nordic paintings in the country – to the city Art Museum. As a tribute to the Furstenburgs, the museum has made over the top floor into an exact replica of the original gallery (see p.430). Staff at *The Palace* know little of its history, but you can still wander upstairs and see the richly ornate plasterwork and gilding much as it was.

Along the southern canal

Following the zigzagging canal that marks the southern perimeter of old Gothenburg – a moat during the days when the city was fortified – makes for a fine twenty-minute stroll, past pretty waterside views and a number of interesting diversions.

Just east of Brunnspark, **Stora Nygatan** wends its way south along the canal's most scenic stretch; on one side are classical buildings all stuccoed in cinnamon and cream, and on the other is the green expanse of Trädgradsföreningen park (see below). Among all the architectural finery sits mainland Sweden's oldest synagogue, the **Great Synagogue** (for tour times call ☎031/17 72 45), which was inaugurated in 1855. This simple domed structure hides one of the most exquisite interiors of any European synagogue: the ceiling and walls are a rich mixture of blues, reds and gold, with Moorish patterns stunningly interwoven with Viking leaf designs. Among its unusual features is a splendid organ, first played at the inauguration ceremony.

Heading south from the synagogue, you'll pass **Kungsportplatsen**, in the centre of which stands a useful landmark, a sculpture known as the "Copper Mare" – though whoever gave it its name obviously didn't see it from below. Also on the square is the main tourist office. A few minutes further on, and a block in from the canal at Kungstorget, is **Saluhallen** (Mon–Fri 9am–6pm, Sat 9am–2pm), a pretty barrel-roofed indoor market built in the 1880s. Busy and full of atmosphere, it's a great place to wander through; outside there's a flower market.

Five minutes from here is another food market, the neo-Gothic **Feskekorka**, or "Fish-church" (Tues–Thurs 9am–5pm, Fri 9am–6pm, Sat 9am–1.30pm). Despite its undeniably ecclesiastical appearance, the nearest the 1874-built Feskekorka comes to religion is the devotion shown by the fish lovers who come to buy and sell here. Inside, every kind of fish lies in gleaming pungent mounds of silver, pink and black flesh, while in a gallery upstairs, there's a very small, very good restaurant (see p.432). Gothenburg's **gay centre** is just behind the Feskekorka at Esperantoplatsen 7 – for more on the city's low-key gay scene, see p.435.

Avenyn and around

Across the canal bridge from Kungportplatsen, the wide cobbled length of Kungportsavenyn runs all the way southeast to Götaplatsen. Known more simply as **Avenyn**, this is the city's grandest and liveliest thoroughfare, lined with nineteenth-century buildings, almost all of their ground floors converted into cafés, bars or restaurants. Gothenburg's young and beautiful strut up and down and sip overpriced drinks at tables that spill onto the street from mid-spring till September. It's enjoyable to sit here and watch life go by, but for all its glamour most of the tourist-oriented shops and brasseries are interchangeable and the grandeur of the city's industrial past is better evoked in the less spoiled mansions along roads like Parkgatan, at right angles to Avenyn over the canal. Here too are a couple of diverting museums.

The Trädgårdsforeningen

Before you cross over into the crowds of Avenyn, take time out to visit the **Trädgårdsforeningen** or Garden Society Park (daily May–Aug 7am–9pm; Sept–April 7am–6pm; May–Aug 10kr, Sept–April free), whose main entrance is just over the canal bridge. For once, this park really does lives up to its blurb – "a green oasis in the heart of the city". Among the trees and lawns are a surprising number of experimental sculptures, designed to blend in with their natural surroundings. Within the park, the **Palm House** (daily June–Aug 10am–6pm; Sept–May 10am–4pm; 20kr, also gives entry to Botanical Garden – see p.431) from 1878 looks like a huge English conservatory and contains a wealth of very unSwedish plant life. Close by is the **Butterfly House** (April, May & Sept Tues–Fri 10am–4pm, Sat & Sun 10am–4pm; June–Aug daily 10am–5pm; Oct–March Tues–Fri 10am–3pm, Sat & Sun 11am–3pm; 35kr), where you can wander among free-flying butterflies from Asia and the Americas. During summer the place goes into overdrive with lunchtime concerts and a special children's theatre.

Vasaplan, Götaplatsen and Liseberg

Once you've had your fill of Avenyn, take one of the roads off to the west and wander into Vasaplan, where the streets are lined with fine nineteenth-century and National Romantic architecture, and the cafés are cheaper and more laid-back. On Vasagatan, the main street through the district, is the excellent **Röhsska Museum**, Sweden's only museum of applied arts (May–Aug Mon–Fri noon–4pm, Sat & Sun noon–5pm; Sept–April Tues noon–9pm, Wed–Fri noon–4pm, Sat & Sun noon–5pm; 35kr). Built in 1916, this is an aesthetic Aladdin's cave, each floor concentrating on different areas of decorative and functional art, from early dynasty Chinese ceramics to European arts and crafts of the sixteenth century. Far more arresting than the gloomy room interiors, however, is the first floor, devoted to twentieth-century decor and featuring all manner of recognizable designs right up to the present – enough to send anyone over the age of 10 on a nostalgia trip.

At the top of Avenyn, **Götaplatsen** is modern Gothenburg's main square, its focal point Carl Milles' **Poseidon**, a giant bronze body-builder nude with a staggeringly ugly face; the size of the figure's penis caused outrage when the sculpture was unveiled in 1930 and it was subsequently dramatically reduced. From the front, Poseidon appears to be squeezing the daylights out of a large fanged fish – symbolic of local trade – but if you climb the steps of the **Concert Hall** to the right, it becomes clear that Milles won the battle over Poseidon's manhood to stupendous effect.

Behind Poseidon looms the impressive **Konstmuseum** (Art Museum; May–Aug Mon–Fri 11am–4pm; Sept–April Tues, Thurs & Fri 11am–4pm, Wed 11am–9pm, Sat & Sun 11am–5pm; 35kr), whose massive, symmetrical facade is reminiscent of 1930s fascist architecture. One of the city's finest museums, it is easy to spend half a day absorbing the diverse and extensive collections. The **Hasselblad Centre** on the ground floor shows excellent changing photographic exhibitions, while upstairs there's postwar and contemporary Scandinavian paintings, a room full of French Impressionists, and a collection of Italian and Spanish paintings from the sixteenth to eighteenth centuries. Best of all, though, are the **Furstenburg Galleries** on the sixth floor, which celebrate the work of some of Scandinavia's most prolific and revered artists from the turn of the century. Well-known paintings by Carl Larsson, Anders Zorn and Carl Wilhelmson reflect a sensitivity to the seasons and landscapes of the Nordic countries and evoke a vivid picture of life in the early years of this century. Look out for Ernst Josephson's sensitive portraits and a couple of Hugo Birger paintings depicting the interior of the Furstenburg Gallery. Also worth a look is an entire room of Larsson's fantastical and bright wall-sized canvases.

Just a few minutes' walk southeast from Götaplatsen lies Sweden's largest amusement park, **Liseberg** (late April to June & late Aug daily 3–11pm; July to mid-Aug daily noon–11pm; Sept Sat 1–11pm, Sun noon–8pm; 40kr, under-7s free; all-day ride pass 195kr, or limited ride tickets for 90kr or 150kr). Dating from 1923, it's a league away from today's more usual neon and plastic versions, with its flowers, trees, fountains and clusters of lights – more Hansel and Gretel than Disneyland. Old and young dance to live bands, and while at night the young and raucous predominate, it is never dangerous. The newest attraction is an ambitious roller coaster called "Hangover". If you're here during the day, it's worth dropping into the surprisingly interesting **Museum of Ethnography** (Mon 11am–9pm, Tues–Fri 11am–4pm, Sat & Sun 11am–5pm; 30kr), just over the highway at Avagen 24. The best exhibits are those on native North and South American culture, including some dramatically lit textiles up to 2000 years old, and rather grislier finds, such as skulls deliberately trephined (squashed) to ward off evil spirits.

Haga and Linne

West of Avenyn, and a ten-minute stroll up Vasagatan (or take tram #1, #3, #4 or #9 towards Linnegatan) lies the city's oldest working-class district, **Haga**, today one of

Gothenburg's most picturesque quarters. Centred on **Haga Nygatan**, Haga is these days the Greenwich Village of Gothenburg, its distinctive stone and wood buildings now the domain of well-off and socially aware twenty- and thirtysomethings, and the cobbled streets lined with alternative and pricey cafés and antique clothes shops. Although there are a couple of good restaurants along Haga Nygatan, this is really somewhere to come during the day, when tables are put out on the street and the atmosphere is friendly and villagey, if a little self-consciously fashionable.

Adjoining Haga to the south, **Skansparken** is hardly a park at all, being little more than the raised mound of land where the **Military Museum** (Tues & Wed noon–2pm, Sat & Sun noon–3pm; 20kr) occupies one of Gothenburg's two surviving seventeenth-century fortress towers, Skansenkronan. The steep climb is worth the effort for good views north towards the harbour; the museum itself consists of a rather feeble collection of wax models in military uniforms throughout the ages.

West of Haga is the more cosmopolitan district of **Linne**, named after the botanist Carl Von Linné, who originated the system of plant classification that's used the world over. Recent years have seen so many new cafés and restaurants spring up along **Linnegatan** – the continuation of Haga Nygatan that runs through the district – that this street of tall, Dutch-style buildings has become a second Avenyn, but without the attitude.

Five minutes' walk south of Linnegatan (or tram #1 or #2 to Linneplatsen) is the huge, tranquil mass of greenery that constitutes the **Slottskogsparken**. Home to farm animals and many varieties of birds, including pink flamingoes in summer, there's plenty here to entertain children. The rather dreary **Natural History Museum** (Tues–Fri 11am–3pm, Sat & Sun 11am–5pm; 30kr) within the grounds prides itself on being the city's oldest, dating from 1833. Its endless cases of stuffed birds both Nordic and foreign seem particularly depressing after the squawking living ones outside, and the only item worth any attention is the world's only stuffed blue whale, which was killed in 1865 and now contains a Victorian café complete with original red velvet sofas – unfortunately, only opened in election years (the Swedish word for a whale also meaning election). On the South side of Slottskogparken are the large, established **Botanical Gardens** (daily 9am–dusk; glasshouses May–Aug daily 8am–6pm, Sept–April Mon–Fri 10am–3pm, Sat, Sun & holidays noon–4pm).

Eating

Gothenburg has a multitude of **eating** places, catering for every taste and budget. The city's status as a trading port has brought with it a huge number of ethnic restaurants, everything from Lebanese to Thai, and the only thing you won't see much of, at least at the lower end of the market, is Swedish food. Naturally, there are some great fish restaurants, and these are among most exclusive around. For less costly eating, there is a growing number of low-priced pasta restaurants to complement the staple pizza parlours and burger bars.

During the past few years, **café life** has really come into its own in Gothenburg, with a profusion of new places throughout the city joining the traditional **konditori** (bakeries with tearoom attached). Nowadays, it's easy to stroll from one café to another at any time of day or night, and tuck into enormous sandwiches and gorgeous cakes. Cafés also offer a wide range of light meals, and are fast becoming about the best places to go for a good food at reasonable prices; the most interesting are concentrated in the fashionable Haga and Linne districts.

Markets and supermarkets

The bustling, historic **Saluhallen** at Kungstorget is a delightful sensory experience, with a huge range of meats, fish, fruits, vegetables and delectable breads; there's also a couple of cheap coffee and snack bars here. A new arrival on the market scene is **Saluhall Briggen**, on the corner of Tredje Långgatan and Nordhamsgatan in the Linne area. More continental and much smaller than Saluhallen, this place specializes in high-quality meats, fish and cheese and mouth-watering deli delights. The **Konsum** supermarket on Avenyn (daily till 11pm) sells a wide range of the usual staples, and has a good deli counter.

Cafés and restaurants

If you want to avoid paying over the odds, then it's generally a good idea to steer clear of Avenyn, where prices are almost double what you'll pay in Haga or Linne, and to eat your main meal at **lunchtime**, when you can fill up on *Dagens Ratt* deals for 40–60kr. Otherwise, you can expect to pay from 80kr to 120kr for a main dish in most restaurants, a lot more in the most exclusive places.

The old town

Ahlstroms Konditori, Korsgatan 2. A classic café/bakery of the old school, the original features have been watered down with modernization, but it's still worth a visit for its good selection of cakes – plus lunches for 52kr.

Broderna Dahlbom, Kungsgatan 12 (☎031/701 7784). Two celebrated brothers run this fine restaurant, serving expensive Swedish and international haute cuisine. Mon–Sat till 11pm.

Feskekorka, in the eponymous fish market (☎031/13 90 51). Excellent fish restaurant but prices seem particularly high when you can see the real cost of the ingredients below. Tues–Thurs 9am–5pm, Fri 9am–6pm, Sat 9am–1.30pm.

Froken Olssons Kafe, Östra Larmgatan 14. Dunes of sandwiches, salads and sumptuous desserts in a rural-style atmosphere. Look out for the mountains of giant meringues on tiered, silver cake trays. Sandwiches 25–50kr.

Mat & Dryck, adjoining Saluhallen market. A pleasant, if basic, place for salad and fresh breads. Daily lunch at 52kr and a choice of twenty beers.

Matilda's, by the side of Salluhallen market. A central, friendly café that's good for a bowl of *café au lait* and a cake.

Avenyn and around

Café Engelen, Engelbreksgatan. Home-baked, excellent-value food at this friendly studenty café. Baked potatoes, lasagne and big sandwiches for 38kr. There's always a vegetarian selection and a good 27kr breakfast. Glorious homemade ice cream and massive range of fruit teas, too. Always open.

GG12, Avenyn 12 (☎031/10 58 26). A well-respected fish restaurant, but extremely expensive.

Gothia Hotel, Massansgatan 24 (☎031/40 93 00). Glitzy hotel with panoramic views from the top-floor piano-bar restaurant. Among other fabulously expensive meals, try the superb king-prawn sandwiches at a whopping 110kr.

Java Café, Vasagatan 23, Vasaplan. Parisian-style studenty coffee house serving a wide range of coffees, and breakfasts for 28kr. Decor includes a collection of thermos flasks dotted among shelves of books. A good Sunday morning hangout.

Junggrens Café, Avenyn 37. The only reasonably priced Avenyn café, with excellent snacks and sandwiches. Atmospheric and convivial, run for decades by a charismatic old Polish woman and her sulky staff. Coffee for only 10kr, sandwiches 12–20kr.

Lai Wa, Storgatan 11, Vasaplan. One of the better Chinese restaurants with a wide variety of dishes at reasonable prices – try the Peking soup. Good lunches.

Le Chablis, Aschebergsgatan 22 (☎031/20 35 45). A somber and elegant fish restaurant set in the candle-lit grandeur of an unusual early twentieth-century stuccoed building with Art Nouveau turrets. All fanned napkins and crisp tablecloths. Extremely expensive.

Restaurant Frågetecken, Södra Vägen 20. Just a minute's walk from Götaplatsen, with a name that translates as "restaurant question mark", this is very popular spot. Eat out in the conservatory, or inside to watch the chefs at work, carefully preparing Balkan-influenced food. They boast of being "famous for breasts": duck at 219kr is the most expensive thing on the menu. Pasta for under 100kr.

Skåne Café, Södra Vägen 59. Big, freshly made sandwiches – smoked salmon for just 20kr – in a very small, basic café, well worth the five-minute walk from Avenyn or Liseberg.

Smaka, Vasaplatsen 3, Vasaplan (☎031/13 22 47). Moderately priced traditional Swedish dishes enjoyed by a lively, young crowd in a striking, modern interior.

Tai Pak, Arkivsgatan, just off Avenyn near Götaplatsen. Decent Chinese restaurant serving a two-course special for 69kr. Individual courses around 65–75kr.

Tintin Café, Engelbrektsgatan 22 (☎031/16 68 12). Very busy, 24-hour café with mounds of food and coffee at low prices (big plate of chicken salad for 40kr) in a laid-back, studenty atmosphere.

28+, Götabergsgatan parallel with Avenyn. Very fine French-style gourmet restaurant, whose name refers to the fat percentage of its renowned cheese, sold in the shop (9am–11pm) near the entrance. Specialities include goose liver terrine. Service is excellent and not snobbish. Lunch Mon–Fri 11.30am–2pm, dinner Mon–Sat 6–11pm.

Wasa Kallare, Vasaplatsen 4, Vasaplan (☎031/13 36 33). Excellent, good-value restaurant serving such delights as pickled raw salmon with stewed potatoes. Snacks like smoked eel sandwich at 55kr.

Haga and Linne

Cedars House, Andra Långgatan 21. Traditional Lebanese food with fifteen-dish mezzes for 225kr (minimum 4 people), also wonderful couscous and lamb dishes. Belly dancing on Fri and Sat nights.

Hemma Hos, Haga Nygatan 12 (☎031/13 40 90). Popular restaurant full of quaint old furniture and serving upmarket and expensive Swedish food – reindeer and fish dishes.

Hos Pelle, Djupedalsgatan 2 (☎031/12 10 31). Sophisticated wine bar off Linnegatan, not cheap but serving snacks as well as full meals, and decorated with wonderful abstract artwork.

Jacob's Café, Haga Nygatan 10. *The* place to sit outside and people-watch; inside the decor is fabulous with some fine Jugrend (Swedish Art Nouveau) lamps.

Johansson's Café & Curiosity Shop, Andre Långgatan 6. Pleasant café, where you can buy the antique ornaments and furniture around you. Sandwiches from 22kr.

Krakow, Karl Gustavsgatan 28 (☎031/20 33 74). Burly staff serving big, basic and very filling Polish food in this large, dark restaurant. Moderate prices.

Le Village, Tredje Långgatan 13 (☎031/24 20 03). Lovely, candle-lit restaurant connected to a big antique shop and serving very well-presented if smallish dishes. The main dining area is expensive – sit in the cheaper bar area where meals start at 65kr.

Linnes Trädgård, Linnegatan 38. This bar and restaurant is a popular, stylish meeting place, with huge windows overlooking the Linnegatan street life. Beautifully presented short menu of fish, meat and pasta (130–170kr). Finish off with the blueberry mousse or the deliciously indulgent honey and pecan parfait. Also a good place for a drink.

Louice Restaurant, Värmlandsgatan 18, off Andra Långgatan. Justifiably popular and unpretentious neighbourhood restaurant, with occasional live music. Standard main courses are expensive but look out for the excellent-value specials at 79kr. There's a full children's menu (35kr) in English.

Sjöbaren, Haga Hygatan 27. A small new fish and shellfish restaurant on the ground floor of a traditional Governor's house building. Moderate prices.

Solrosen, Kaponjargatan 4A (☎031/711 66 97). The oldest vegetarian restaurant in Gothenburg with a wide range of dishes at not outrageous prices.

Solsidan Café, Linnegatan. Lovely café serving delicious cakes; outside seating.

Thai Garden, Andra Långgatan 18 (☎031/12 76 60). Nothing special to look at, but big portions and excellent service at good prices.

Drinking, nightlife and entertainment

There's an excellent choice of places to **drink** in Gothenburg, but aside from a small number of British- and Irish-style pubs, even the hippest bars also serve food and have more of a restaurant atmosphere. Listed below are some of the most popular pubs and bar/restaurants in the city; however, many of the cafés and restaurants listed in the previous section are also good places for a beer, especially those in Avenyn and Linne. Although there are a number of long-established bars in the old town, the atmosphere is generally a bit low-key at night.

There's plenty of other things to do in Gothenburg at night besides drink. The city has a brisk **live music scene** – jazz, rock and classical – as well as the usual cinema and theatre opportunities. The details below should give you some ideas, but it's worth picking up the Friday edition of the *Göteborgs Posten*, which has a weekly listings supplement called "Aveny" – it's in Swedish but not very difficult to decipher. The notice boards in the main hall at the entrance to *Studs*, the student bar in Vasaplan, are also good for gigs, parties and other information on what's going on in the city.

Gothenburg's **gay scene** surprises even Gothenburgers with its half-heartedness, largely put down to the city's high level of tolerance towards lesbians and gays. Most gay activity is run on ultra-organized lines by the state-sponsored national gay association, *RFSL*, based at Esperantoplatsen 7 (see below). The city's few gay clubs are listed below.

Bars and pubs

Although it is not uncommon for Gothenburgers to drink themselves to oblivion, the atmosphere around the bars is generally non-aggressive. Avenyn, late on a Saturday night, is really the only place where you might feel even slightly unsafe.

The old town

Beefeater Inn, Plantagegatan 1. One of a bevy of British-oriented neighbourhood pubs, very in vogue with Gothenburgers. This one really goes overboard, with a stylistic mishmash of red-telephone-box doors and staff in kilts to match the tartan walls.

Dubliners, Östra Hamngatan 50B. Swedes have for a while been overtaken with a nostalgia for all things old and Irish – or at least a Swedish interpretation of what's old and Irish. This is the most popular exponent.

Gamle Port, Östra Larmgatan 18. The city's oldest watering hole with British beer in the downstairs pub and an awful disco upstairs (see "Clubs and live music").

Norrlands Nation, Västra Hamngatan 20. Formerly a university venue, this place is now licensed and is open late. Occasional comedy gigs and music.

The Palace, Brunnsparken. The rather splendid former home of the Furstenburgs and their art galleries (see p.428), this upmarket bar and restaurant is very popular – but pricey.

Avenyn and around

Brasserie Lipp, Avenyn 8. No longer the hippest place on Avenyn, *Lipp* is expensive and so attracts a slightly older crowd – but a crowd it is, especially during summer. Connected to the brasserie is *Bubbles Nightclub* (see "Clubs and live music").

Harley's, Avenyn 10. Very loud young crowd. Not a place for a drink and a chat, unless you stand out on the street.

Niva, Avenyn 9. Bar and restaurant on different levels. Modern interior with a mosaic decor – a stylish bar that's becoming more and more popular.

Scandic Rubinen, Avenyn 24. Glitzy hotel-foyer type of bar. Always packed with tourists and right at the heart of Avenyn.

Studs, Götabergsgatan, off Engelbrecksgatan behind Vasa Church. This is the hub of Gothenburg student life, with a pub, bar and restaurant. The main advantage of the student bar is its prices, with two-for-one beers before 9pm in summer. If you haven't got student ID, friendly bluffing should get you in.

Haga and Linne

Dog & Duck, Viktoriagatan 5. An all-British pub/restaurant, making a valiant attempt at a cosy, nineteenth-century atmosphere. Serves light meals, nachos, burgers and chicken shish kebabs all at around 65kr. Open till 1am, Fri & Sat till 3am.

Indian Palace Pub, Järntorget 4. Just northwest of Haga Nygatan, this place is rather unappealing from outside, with neon arrows coaxing you in. There is a restaurant on the ground floor with a basement pub and pool table.

The Irish Rover, Andra Långgatan 12. Run of the mill Irish/English pub selling *Boddingtons* beer with other lagers, ales and cider on tap, plus a wide range of bottles. Lamb, steaks and trout dishes for 59–95kr.

1252, Linnegatan. The first of the trendy places to be seen in, and the place that put the Linne area on the map. Reasonably priced food considering the location. Outdoor tables in summer.

Clubs and live music

There are no outstanding **clubs** in Gothenburg. The classic nightclub is *Valand*, at Vasagatan 3, just off Avenyn. With three bars, it's where the clubby crowd strut their stuff. *Park Lane*, at Avenyn 36, is a hot, crowded club with three bars, a casino and live entertainment (☎031/20 60 58). *Yaki Da* is attached to *Gamle Port* (see above), and despite having three bars, a stage and a casino, it has a pretty depressing atmosphere; similarly *Bubbles Nightclub* at *Lipp* (see above) is a bit of a disappointment. Sweden's biggest dance floor is said to be at *Rondo*, the dance restaurant at Liseberg Amusement Park – there's always a live band on, and a good atmosphere, with people of all ages dancing.

Gothenburg's **gay clubs** are thin on the ground. *RFSL*, at Esperantoplatsen 7 by the main canal, runs a bar and nightclub called *Touch*, frequented by groups of regulars, who drink here on Wednesday nights and dance on Friday nights. *Bacchus*, at Bellmansgatan 7–9, is the only privately run club. Bigger than *Touch*, it is busiest on Saturday evenings and has a mixed (gay/straight) crowd on Sundays. *Delicious*, in the *NK* department store (weekends only), is a new mixed club.

Live music

Gothenburg's large student community means there are plenty of **local live bands**. The best venue, with the emphasis on alternative and dance music, is *Kompaniet* on Kungsgatan: the top floor is a pub/bar, while downstairs there's dancing to Eurotechno. Drinks are half-price between 8pm and 10pm, the place stays open until 3am daily in summer (winter Wed–Sat only) – and you're likely to be the only foreigner there. Other bars worth checking out are *Klara*, Vallgatan 8, frequented by wannabe poets by day, but with a diverse range of indie and rock bands on Monday nights; and *Dojan*, Vallgatan 3, a small, smoky and crowded rock pub, with live bands every night.

Jazz enthusiasts should head for the trendy *Neffertiti* **jazz club** at Hvitfeldtsplatsen 6 (Mon–Sat from 9pm) – you may have to queue. *Jazzhuset*, Eric Dahlbergsgatan 3 (Wed–Sat 8pm–2am), puts on trad, Dixieland and swing, but is fairly staid and something of an executive pickup joint.

International bands perform at some sizeable stadium-type venues in the city, notably *Scandinavium* (☎031/81 84 00) and the new, colossal arena, *Ullevi Stadium*. Both are off Skånegatan to the east of Avenyn; take tram #1, #3 or #6. Check out the usual listings sources for details of upcoming concerts.

Classical music, cinema and theatre

Classical music concerts are performed regularly in the *Konserthuset*, Götaplatsen, and the *Stora Theatre*, Avenyn. Get hold of programme details from the tourist office.

There are plenty of **cinemas** around the city, screening mostly English-language movies with Swedish subtitles. Most unusual of them is the ten-screen *Bio Palatset*, on Kungstorget, originally a meat market and then a failed shopping mall, its interior is now painted in clashing fruity colours, and its foyer has been excavated to reveal floodlit rocks studded with Viking spears. Another multi-screener is *Filmstaden*, behind the cathedral at Kungsgatan 35.

Theatre in Gothenburg is unlikely to appeal to many visitors. Not only are all productions in Swedish, but the city's council-run theatres also put on plays that make Strindberg look like farce – the lack of audience is not a big concern. Commercial theatres such as the *Lorensberg*, on Lorensbergsgatan near Götaplatsen, go for light comedy shows in Swedish only; like many other theatres in Sweden, it is closed during the summer months.

Listings

Airlines *British Airways*, at the airport (☎020/78 11 44); *Finnair*, Fredsgatan 6 (☎020/78 11 00); *KLM*, at the airport (☎031/94 16 40); *Lufthansa*, Fredsgatan 1 (☎031/80 56 40); *SAS*, at the airport, (☎ 020/91 01 10).

Airport ☎031/94 10 00.

American Express Local agent is *Ticket*, Östra Hamngatan 35 (☎031/13 07 12).

Banks and exchange Most banks are open Mon–Fri 9.30am–3pm, and are found on Östra Hamngatan, Södra Hamngatan and Västra Hamngatan. There are four *Forex* exchange offices, which accept *American Express, Diners Club, Finax* and travellers cheques: Central Station (daily 8am–9pm; ☎031/15 65 16), Avenyn 22 (daily 8am–9pm; ☎031/18 57 60), *Nordstan* shopping centre (9am–7pm; ☎031/15 75 30) and Kungsportsplatsen (daily 9am–7pm; ☎031/13 60 74).

Buses Reservations are obligatory for buses to Stockholm, Helsingborg and Malmo – reserve seats at *Bussresebyra*, Drottninggatan 50 (☎031/80 55 30).

Car rental *Avis*, Central Station (☎031/80 57 80) and at the airport (☎031/94 60 30); *Budget*, Kristinelundsgatan 13 (☎031/20 09 30), at the airport (☎031/94 60 55); *Europcar*, Stampgatan 22 D (☎031/80 53 90), at the airport (☎031/94 71 00); *Hertz*, Stampgatan 16A (☎031/80 37 30), at the airport (☎031/94 60 20).

Doctor *Medical Counselling Service and Information* (☎031/41 55 00); Sahlgrenska Hospital at Per Dubbsgatan (☎031/60 10 00). A private clinic, *City Akuten*, has doctors on duty 8am–6pm at Drottninggatan 45 (☎031/10 10 10).

Emergencies Ambulance, police and fire brigade on ☎90 000.

Ferry companies If you want to book from Gothenburg to Britain or Amsterdam on *Scandinavian Seaways*, use the booking office at Östra Larmgatan 15 (☎031/17 20 50); for general information at Skandiahamn ferry terminal call ☎031/65 06 00. *Stena Line* has no walk-in offices – call ☎031/775 00 00 for information and bookings. *SeaCat* also runs day trips from Gothenburg to Frederikshavn (1hr 45 min; 70kr, Gothenburg Card allows two for the price of one); again there are no walk-in offices – call ☎031/775 08 10.

Left luggage at *Nordstan Service Centre* (see below) or Central Station.

Laundry At *Nordstan Service Centre* (see below).

Newspapers International newspapers from *Press Centre* in *Nordstan* shopping centre or Central Station; or read them for free at the City Library, Götaplatsen.

Nordstan Service Centre In the shopping centre near Central Station (Mon–Fri 10am–6.30pm, Sat 10am–4pm); you can leave luggage (10kr), take a shower here (20kr) and use the laundry service (95kr).

Pharmacy *Apoteket Vasen*, Götagatan 10, in *Nordstan* shopping centre, is open 24 hours every day (☎031/80 44 10).

Police Headquarters at Ernst Fontells Plats (Mon–Fri 9am–2pm; ☎031/61 80 00).

Post offices Main office for poste restante is in Drottningtorget (Mon–Fri 10am–6pm, Sat 10am–noon; ☎031/62 31 62); others on Avenyn (Mon–Fri 10am–6pm, Sat 10am–12.30pm) and at the *Nordstan* shopping centre (Mon–Fri 9am–7pm, Sat 10am–5pm).

Swimming The biggest and best pool is the 1950s *Valhallabadet*, next to the *Scandinavium* sports complex, on Skånegatan.

Telephones Mostly operated by cards, bought at *Pressbyrån* and *Ja* kiosks. In hotels, cafés and older public boxes, you need to insert a minimum of two 1kr coins for a local call.

Trains Central Station ☎020/75 75 75; international train information ☎031/80 77 10.
Travel agents *KILROY travels*, Berzeliigatan 5 (Mon–Fri 9.30am–5pm; ☎031/20 08 60).

AROUND GOTHENBURG

North of Gothenburg, the rugged and picturesque **Bohuslän coast**, which runs all the way to the Norwegian border, attracts countless Scandinavian and German tourists each summer. However, the crowds can't detract from the wealth of natural beauty – rocks, coves, islands and hairline fjords – and the many dinky fishing villages that make this stretch of country well worth a few days' exploration. The most popular destination is the island town of **Marstrand**, with its impressive fortress and richly ornamental ancient buildings, but there are several attractions further up the coast that are also worthwhile targets, not least the centre for Bronze Age **rock carvings** at **Tamunshede**, near Strömstad.

Northeast of the city, the county of **Västergötland** encompasses the southern sections of Sweden's two largest lakes, **Vänern** and **Vättern**. Here the scenery is gentler, and a number of attractive lakeside towns and villages make good bases from which to venture out into the forested coutryside and onto the **Göta Canal**. The waterway connects the lakes to each other (and, in its entirety, the North Sea to the Baltic), and there are a number of ways to experience it, from cross-country cruises to short hops on rented boats. With energy and time to spare, **renting a bike** offers a great alternative for real exploration of Västergötland, using the canal's towpaths, countless cycling trails and empty roads. Nearly all tourist offices, youth hostels and campsites in the region rent out bikes for around 80kr a day or 400kr a week.

The Bohuslän Coast

A chain mail of **islands** linked by a thread of bridges and short ferry crossings make up the county of **Bohuslän** and, despite the summer crowds, it is still easy enough to find a private spot to swim or bathe. Sailing is also a popular pastime among the Swedes, many of whom have summer cottages here, and you'll see yachts gliding through the water all the way along the coast. Another feature of the Bohuslän landscape you can't fail to miss is the large number of **churches** that fill the county – for long stretches these are the only buildings of note. Dating from the 1840s to 1910, they are mostly simple white structures with little variation, usually open between 10am and 3pm, but the clergyman invariably lives next door and will be happy to open up.

Travelling up the coast by **train** is feasible, with services from Gothenburg through industrial Uddevalla and on to **Strömstad**, but trains stop only in the main towns. **Buses** also cover the coast but services are sketchy and infrequent (on some routes there is only one bus a week). If you really want to explore Bohuslän's most dramatic scenery, you need a car. From Gothenburg, the E6 motorway is the quickest route north, with designated scenic routes leading off it every few kilometres.

Kungälv

Just under 20km north of Gothenburg on the E6, the quaint old town of **KUNGÄLV**, overshadowed by the fourteenth-century ruins of Bohus Fortress, is a gem of a place to stop for a few hours. Rebuilt after the Swedes raised it in 1676 to prevent the Danes finding useful shelter, the town now consists of sprawling cobbled streets with pastel-painted wooden houses, all leaning as if on the verge of collapse. The **tourist office** (☎0303/992 00; fax 171 06), in the square below the fortress, will provide you with a useful walking-tour map detailing the history of almost every seventeenth-century property.

The main reason most people visit the town is to see the remains of **Bohus Fortress**. The first defensive wooden fort was built here by the Norwegian king in the fourteenth century, on what was then Norway's southern border. This was replaced by a solid stone building, surrounded by deep natural moats, which managed to withstand six Swedish attacks in the 1560s, and, once it became Swedish, a remarkable fourteen sieges by the Danes in the following century. Where attack failed, Swedish weather has succeeded, however, and today the building is very much a ruin. The fortress is open from May to September, with guided tours, concerts and opera performances in July and August – for full details contact the tourist office.

Once you have seen the fortress and wandered round the village, there is little else to do here, but if you do want to stay, there's a *STF* **youth hostel** a stone's throw from the fortress at Farjevagen 2 (☎0303/189 00; fax 192 95; 100kr).

Marstrand

About 25km west of Kungälv, the island town of **MARSTRAND** buzzes with summer activity, as holiday-makers come here to sail and bathe and take tours around its impressive castle. With ornate wooden buildings lining the bustling harbour, Marstrand is a delightful place and easily visited on a day trip from Gothenburg.

Founded under Norwegian rule in the thirteenth century, the town achieved remarkable prosperity through herring fishing in the following century; rich herring pickings, however, eventually led to greed and corruption, and Marstrand became known as the most immoral town in Scandinavia. The murder of a cleric in 1586 was seen as an omen: soon after the whole town burned to the ground and the herring mysteriously disappeared. The fish – and Marstrand's prosperity – eventually returned in the 1770s, only to disappear again for good forty years later. By the 1820s, the old herring salting houses had been converted into bath houses, and Marstrand had been reborn as a fashionable bathing resort.

From the harbour, it's a lovely walk up the cobbled lane, past the Renaissance-style *Grand Hotel*, to a small square surrounded by exquisite wooden houses, painted in pastel shades. Across the square is the squat, white **St Maria kyrka**; beyond, the streets climb steeply to the castle, **Carlstens Fästning** (June–Sept daily 11am–6pm; 25kr), an imposing sweep of stone walls solidly wedged into the rough rock. You could easily spend half a day clambering around the walls, and down the weather-worn rocks to the sea, where there are always plenty of places to bathe in private. The informal **tours** take an hour and, though none are officially in English, guides are happy to oblige. The most interesting tales are told down in the grim prison cells: Carlstens' most noted prisoner-resident was **Lasse Maja**, a thief who got rich by dressing as a woman and seducing rich farmers. A sort of Swedish Robin Hood, Maja was known for giving his spoils to the poor. Once incarcerated here, Maja ingratiated himself with the officers with his impressive cooking skills, a talent that, after 26 years, won him a pardon from the king.

For 40kr extra, you can take one of the special tours that are run three times a week and lead up through the 1658-built hundred-metre-high towers. The views from the top are stunning, but you have to be fit to get there as the steep, spiral climb is quite exhausting. Once a year, around July 20, the fortress hosts a huge **festival**, with an eigteenth-century-style procession and live theatre. It's a colourful occasion and well worth catching.

Practicalities

Gothenburg Card-holders can get a two-for-one ticket deal on the day trip by boat from Gothenburg; boats leave from Lilla Bommen at 9.30am, arriving in Marstrand at 12.30pm (irregular service in May & June, daily July & Aug). Otherwise, take **bus** #312 from Nils Ericsonsplatsen; buy a 100kr carnet from *Tidpunkten*, next to the bus terminal, which also covers the ferry journey from the mainland.

The **tourist office** at the harbour (June–Aug daily 9am–4pm; rest of the year Mon–Fri 10am–4pm; ☎0303/600 87; fax 600 18) can book **private rooms** for a minimum of two people in either an old barracks (370kr) or in private homes or cottages (450kr). The island's **youth hostel** (open all year; April & May 140kr, June–mid-Aug 200kr, Sept–March 100kr; ☎0303/600 10; fax 606 07) is situated in an atmospheric old bath house overlooking the sea, with a sauna, washing facilities, a swimming pool and a restaurant (see below). Of the several very pleasant **hotels** on the island, finest is the 1892-built *Grand Hotel*, at Paradis Parken (☎0303/603 22; fax 600 53; ④), just 50m from the tourist office and left through the park. *Hotel Alphydden*, Långgatan 6 (☎303/610 30; fax 612 00; ②/③), is a little more basic but perfectly adequate.

About the most interesting place to **eat** on the island is the *American Bar*, close to the harbour, which serves excellent food in huge portions: chicken and cheese salad for 88k, or brie and bacon salad for 67kr – though coffee is a steep 20kr. Decent meals are also served in the restaurant connected to the youth hostel: daily pasta dishes cost 49kr and meat and seafood 90–130kr. At night, the *American Bar*, or neighbouring *Oscars*, which doubles as a nightclub, are good **drinking** haunts.

North to Strömstad

Aside from picturesque scenery and pretty villages, the highlights along this stretch of the coast are the exceptional **marine-life museum** at **Lysekil**, several nature reserves, a wildlife sanctuary and, at **Tanumshede**, an extensive array of Bronze Age **rock carvings**. If you have your own transport, you'll be able to follow the designated **scenic routes**, which lead off the E6; otherwise bus connections from Gothenburg are limited to a few of the main towns. If you have a car, it's easy enough to drive to Strömstad in a day, stopping off at a couple of sights on the way. Athough there are plenty of hotels and hostels along the coast, this is one of the most popular parts of the country for **camping** and caravanning, with loads of sites all the way to Strömstad.

Once off the main E6, you'll soon reach **Tjornbroarna**, a five-kilometre link-up of three graceful bridges connecting the islands of Tjörn and Orust, and affording spectacular views over the fjords. **Orust**, a centre for boat-building since Viking times, is geographically like a miniature Sweden, westerly winds stripping it of trees at the coast, yet with forest running right up to the sea on its eastern shores. The island's *STF* **youth hostel** (☎0304/503 80; all year; 100kr), just outside the village of Stocken, occupies a splendid eighteenth-century wooden manor set in vast grounds.

The largest coastal town in the region is **LYSEKIL**, reached by an express bus from Gothenburg (#840; every 2hr) or, if you're driving, on Route 161 off the E6 at Uddevalla. Not as immediately attractive as other coastal towns, Lysekil does have plenty to recommend it. From the tourist office (☎0523/130 50; fax 125 85) at Sodra Hamngatan 6, it's just five minutes' walk to **Havets Hus** (daily 10am–4pm; 40kr), an exceptional museum of marine life. Chief attraction here is the eight-metre-long glass tunnel, where massive fish swim over and around you; there's also a special touch pool for children to experience the texture of slimy algae and spiky starfish. En route to Havets Hus you'll pass a number of intricately carved villas, a reminder of last century when Lysekil was a popular and genteel bathing resort. Today, nude (segregated) bathing and fishing are popular pastimes and much of the shoreline has been turned into a **nature reserve**, with over 250 varieties of plant life – for guided botanic and marine walks in summer, ask at the tourist office. Walk up any set of steps from the waterfront and you'll reach the town's **church** (daily 11am–3pm), hewn from the surrounding pink granite. If you want to **stay** in Lysekil, try the central *Hotel Lysekil* at Rosikstorg 1 (☎0523/61 18 60; fax 155 20; ②/③).

A possible diversion after visiting Lysekil is to head back along the 162 and turn left for Nordens Ark **wildlife sanctuary** near Åby (about 25km). On the way you'll pass a couple of notable churches, in particular the one at **Brastad**, an 1870s Gothic building with an oddly haphazard appearance – every farm in the neighbourhood donated a lump of its own granite, none of which matched. Don't be put off by the yeti-sized inflatable puffin at the entrance to **Nordens Ark** (open all year; call for times on ☎0523/522 15). This is a unique wildlife sanctuary for endangered animals, where animal welfare is prioritized over human voyeurism. Red pandas, lynx, snow leopards and arctic foxes are among the rare animals being bred and reared at the sanctuary, where the mountainous landscape of dense forest and glades is kept as close as possible to the animals' natural surroundings.

If time allows for only one picture-perfect setting, **FJÄLLBACKA** is an ideal choice. Nestling beneath huge, granite boulders, all the houses are painted in fondant shades, with a wealth of intricate ginger-breading known in Swedish as *snickargladje* ("carpenter's joy"). As you enter Fjallbacka (from Åby you can either go back to the E6 and then take the 163 – around 35km – or follow a more winding route along the coast), it will immediately become apparent that a certain celebrated actress holds sway in the little town. The **tourist office** (June–Aug erratic hours; ☎0525/321 20) is in a tiny, red hut on **Ingrid Bergman's Square**; here a statue of the big-screen idol looks out to the islands, where she had her summer house, and to the sea over which her ashes were scattered. There's not a lot to do here, but if you want to stick around there are plenty of **camping** opportunities and an island **youth hostel** (☎0525/312 34; May–Sept; 100kr).

TANUMSHEDE, a few kilometres further north on the E6, has the greatest concentration of **Bronze Age rock carvings** in Scandinavia, with four major sites in the surrounding countryside. Between 1500 and 500 BC, Bronze Age man scratched images into the ice-smoothed rock, and at Tanumshede you'll see some fine examples of the most frequent motifs: the simple cup mark (which accounts for most), boats, humans and animals. When you reach town, head for the **tourist office** (June to mid-Aug Mon–Sat 10am–6pm; rest of the year Mon–Thurs 9am–4.30pm, Fri 9am–3pm; ☎0525/204 00; fax 298 60), oddly sited in a *Texaco* filling station, which will provide you with explanatory booklets (10kr) in English. There is also a **rock-carving museum** at nearby Vitlyckehallen (May to mid-Sept; 20kr), which explores interpretations of the various images. Tanumshede is reached by five E6 express buses daily from Gothenburg (2hr). There are a smattering of restaurants and nightlife opportunities at the caravan/camping mecca of **Grebbestad**, just a few kilometres southwest of Tanumshede.

Strömstad and the Koster Islands

STRÖMSTAD retains an air of faded grandeur from its days as a fashionable eighteenth-century spa resort. Arriving at the train station, everywhere of interest is easily accessible, and with ferry connections on to Sandefjord, Fredrickstad and Halden in Norway, the town makes a good stopover before heading further north. Though its main attraction is its close proximity to the Koster Islands (see below), Strömstad does have a couple of interesting public buildings. Behind its plain exterior, the town's **church**, a few minutes' walk from the train and bus stations, is an eclectic mix of decorative features, including busy frescoes, model ships hanging from the roof, and gilt chandeliers. More bizarre, however, is the massive, copper-roofed **Stadshus**, the product of a millionaire recluse. Born to a Strömstad jeweller in 1851, Adolf Fritiof Cavalli-Holmgren became a financial whizz kid, moved to Stockholm and was soon one of Sweden's richest men. When he heard that his poor home town needed a town hall, he offered to finance the project, but only if he had complete control over the project, which was to be situated on the spot where his late parents had lived. By the time the mammoth structure was completed in 1917, he was no longer on speaking terms with the city's politicians, and never returned to see the building he had battled to create, which was topped with a panoramic apartment for his private use. Much later, in 1951, it was discovered that he had designed the entire building around the dates of his parents' birthdays and wedding day – January 27, May 14 and March 7, with the dimensions of every room, window or flight of stairs a combination of those numbers. Built entirely from rare local apple granite, the town hall is open to the public, but to view the most interesting areas you have to arrange a free private tour. You can see Adolf's portrait – dated falsely to include his favourite numbers – in the main council chamber.

Practicalities

Strömstad is reached by **train** from Gothenburg (3hr), or the E6 express **bus** between Gothenburg and Oslo (5 daily; 2hr 30min); by car, follow Route 176 off the E6 for the 12km. Both the train and bus stations are on Södra Hammen, opposite the **ferry** terminal for services to Sandefjord in Norway; ferries to Fredrickstad and Halden leave from Norra Hamnen, 100m to the north on the other side of the rocky promontory, Laholmen, as do ferries to the Koster Islands (full details from the tourist office).

The **tourist office** on the quay (June–Aug daily 8am–9pm; Sept–May Mon–Fri 8.30am–5pm; ☎0526/130 25; fax 121 85) can help with **private rooms**, which cost from 125kr per person (50kr booking fee), and **cabins**. The *STF* **youth hostel** is at Norra Kyrkogatan 12 (☎0526/101 93; mid-April to mid-Oct; 100kr), 1km or so from the train station along Uddevallavägen; there's also an independent hostel, *Gastis Roddaren Hostel*, at Fredrikshaldsvagen 24 (☎0526/602 01; all year; 125kr), ten minutes' walk along the road fronting the Stadshus. For a regular, central **hotel** try *Krabban* on Södra Bergsgatan 15 (☎0526/142 00; ②), or the modern, low-built *Hotel Laholmen* (☎0526/12 400; fax 100 36; ②), which enjoys fantastic sea views. The nearest **campsite** is 1km from the train station, along Uddevallavägen.

As befits a resort town, there is no shortage of places to **eat and drink**, most of them around the harbour. The best of the bunch are *Backlund's*, a locals' haunt, with sandwiches at 18kr; *Café Casper*, on Södra Hamngatan, which does lunch specials for 35kr; and *Kaff Doppet,* a more characterful konditori by the station. **Nightlife** in Strömstad boils down to *Skagerack*, a very loud, very young music venue.

The Koster Islands

Sweden's most westerly inhabited islands, the **Koster Islands** enjoy more hours of sunshine than almost anywhere else in the country. **North Koster** is the more rugged, with a grand nature reserve, and takes a couple of hours to walk around. **South Koster** is three times as big, but since no vehicles are allowed on the island, **renting a bike** (ask at the Strömstad tourist office) is the best way to explore its undulating landscape. Both islands are rich in wild flowers, have warm water for swimming, as well as bird- and seal-viewing expeditions during the summer. Outside high season, it's vital to take an early-morning ferry to North Koster (80kr); if you leave later, the only way of making it across onto the south island is to hitch a lift in a local's boat. **Taxi boats** to the islands cost 500kr and can work out economical if there is a group of you; they are the only option if you miss the last ferry back at 9.30pm.

Camping on North Koster is restricted to *Vettnet* (☎0526/204 66), though there are several sites on South Koster, plus a **youth hostel** (☎0526/201 25; May–Sept; 100kr) 1500m from the ferry stop at Ekenäs. You'll also be offered **apartment** rentals for 250–300kr a night, excellent value if there are three or more of you.

The Göta Canal, Trollhättan and Vänersborg

The giant waterway known in its entirety as the **Göta Canal** flows from the mouth of the River Göta to Sweden's largest lake, **Lake Vänern**, via the **Trollhättan Canal**, then cuts across into the formidable **Lake Vättern** and right through southeastern Sweden to the Baltic Sea. If you don't have your own transport then some of the easiest places to see from Gothenburg are the few small towns that lie along the first stretch of the river/canal to Lake Vänern. In particular, **Trollhättan**, where the canal's lock system tames the force of the river to dramatic effect. A few kilometres north of Trollhättan, **Vänersborg**, at the southernmost tip of Lake Vänern, provides a useful base for exploring the natural beauty of nearby hills, the home of Sweden's largest herd of elks. From Gothenburg, regular trains stop at Trollhättan; if you have a car take Route 45.

The Göta Canal

Centuries ago it was realized that lakes Vänern and Vättern, together with the rivers to the east and west, could be used to make inland transport easier. A continuous waterway across the country from Gothenburg to the Baltic would provide a vital trade route, both a means of shipping iron and timber out of central Sweden and of avoiding Danish customs charges levied on traffic though Öresund. It was not until 1810 that Baron Baltzar Von Platten's hugely ambitious plans to carve a route to Stockholm were put into practice by the Göta Canal Company. Sixty thousand soldiers spent seven million working days over 22 years in completing the mammoth task, the canal opening in 1832, shortly after Von Platten's death.

Although the Trollhättan Canal section is still used to transport fuel and timber – the towns on Vänern having their lakeside views blotted by unsightly industrial greyness – this section and the Göta Canal proper, between Vänern and Vättern, are extremely popular tourist destinations, and there's a wide range of canal trips on offer. If cost is not an issue, **Göta Canal Cruises**, Rederiaktiebolaget Göta Kanal, Hotellplatsen 2, Gothenburg (☎031/80 63 15; fax 15 83 11), offer what are dubbed "golden dollar" cruises aboard historic steamers for four-, six- or eight-day jaunts across the country to the Baltic. The emphasis is on glamour and sophistication, with cabins ranging from 13,500kr for four days down to 8200kr. On a smaller budget, **day trips** can be arranged at any tourist office in the region. You can also **rent a boat** or a **bike** to follow the towpaths – ask at the tourist offices for further information.

Trollhättan

Seventy kilometres northeast of Gothenburg, **TROLLHÄTTAN** is the kind of place you might end up staying for a couple of days without really meaning to. A small town, it nevertheless manages to pack in plenty of offbeat entertainment along with some peaceful river surroundings. Built around the fast river that for a couple of hundred years powered its flour mills and sawmills, Trollhättan remained fairly isolated until 1800, when the Göta Canal Company successfully installed the first set of locks to bypass the town's furious local waterfalls. River traffic took off and better and bigger locks were installed over the years. The best time to visit is during the **Fallensdagar** in July (check exact dates with the tourist office), a festival of dancing and music based around the waterfalls. Summer is the only time when the sluices are opened and you can see the falls in all their crashing splendour (May & June Sat & Sun 3pm; July & Aug Wed, Sat & Sun 3pm).

The locks and the steep sides of the falls are the main sights in town, and there are **paths** along the whole system as well as orientation maps. Strolling south along the path towards the Insikten Energy Centre, the network of canal locks is to your left and the beautiful winding river to your right – it's a splendid half-hour's walk, passing a grand, English-style church perched on rocks between the waterways. **Insikten Energy Centre** itself (April, May, Sept & Oct Sat & Sun noon–4pm; mid-June to Aug daily 10am–6pm; free) is considerably more enjoyable than you might imagine, with none-too-scientific explanations of the workings of the nearby **hydroelectic power station** (June–Aug daily guided tours 10am–5pm), a fine 1910 building containing thirteen massive generators.

A little further down at the upper lock, the **Canal Museum** (mid-June to mid-Aug daily 11am–7pm; rest of the year Sat & Sun noon–5pm; 5kr) puts the whole thing in perspective, with a history of the canal and locks, model ships, old tools and fishing gear. Crossing the canal and heading into the town's industrial hinterland, you'll soon reach the **Saab Museum** (June–Aug daily 10am–6pm; Sept–May Tues–Fri 1–4pm; call to arrange a tour on ☎0520/843 44; 10kr), which holds an example of every model built; to demonstrate safety standards, a simulated elk is depicted running into a saloon.

Practicalities

The central **tourist office** (June–Aug Mon–Sat 9am–5pm; Sept–May Mon–Fri 10am–4pm; ☎0520/140 05; fax 872 71), at Gardhemsvagen 9, sells the Trollhättan **Tourist Card** (valid June 10–Aug 18; 20kr), which allows free entrance to most of the town's sites and gives discounts in restaurants, at the swimming pool and on boat trips. The tourist office can also book **private rooms** from 130kr. The former youth hostel overlooking the river is now a **hotel**, *Stromsberg* (☎0520/129 90; fax 133 11; ③/④); the nearest youth hostel is at Hunneberg (see below). There's a **campsite**, close to the centre by the river (June–Aug; ☎0520/306 13), with a heated swimming pool, bike rental, tennis and golf facilities.

Trollhättan's best **cafés** are mostly along Strandgatan by the canal, notably *Bikupan*, a lovely café with a terrace and sandwiches from 20kr, and *Sluss Caféet,* a summer outdoor café overlooking the locks. The cosy *Café Smulan* on Foreningsgatan serves delicious cakes. The most popular **pubs**, also good for evening meals, are *Harry's* at Storgatan 44, and *Cheers* at Kungsgatan 24. Just up the street, *Butler's*, at no. 35, is a traditional late-opening Irish-style pub. Nightlife revolves around the **nightclubs** at *Hotel Swania* (entrance in Strandgatan), and *KK's Bar & Nightclub* at Torggatan 3. Trollhättan's **gay** scene is organized by *RFSL Trestad* (☎0520/41 17 66). From June to August, there are **boats** up the canal to Vänersborg, with the four-hour round trip costing 100kr. Otherwise, **buses** #600 and #605 regularly ply the route.

Vänersborg and around

Dubbed "Little Paris" by the celebrated local poet Birger Sjoberg, **VÄNERSBORG**, on the tip of Lake Vänern 14km north of Trollhättan, doesn't quite live up to the comparison, but is, nonetheless, a charming little resort town. It's main sites are the nearby twin hills of **Hunneberg** and **Halleberg** (see below), both of which are of archeological interest and support a wide variety of wildlife.

Vänersborg's old town is compact and pleasant to stroll around – though the grand buildings are all overlooked by a bleak old prison at the end of Residensgatan. **Skracklan Park**, just a few minutes from the centre, is a pretty place to relax, with its 1930s coffee house and promenade. The bronze statue of Sjoberg's muse, Frida, always has fresh flowers in her hand – even in winter, when the lake is solid ice, locals brave the sub-zero winds to thrust rhododendrons through her fingers.

Although Vänersborg's **museum**, behind the main market square (June–Aug Tues noon–9pm, Wed, Thurs, Sat & Sun noon–4pm; Sept–May Tues noon–7pm, Sat & Sun noon–4pm; 20kr), has more cases of stuffed creatures and lifeless artefacts than most, if you have an hour to spare, the excess makes for fascinating viewing. Its gloomy interior and the collections on display have hardly changed since the doors first opened to the public in 1891. Worth a glance is the caretaker's apartment, preserved in all its 1950s gloom, and a reconstruction of Birger's home, which is darker still.

The **tourist office**'s summer premises have been due to move for several years, but at the time of writing were still at Kungsgatan 15 (June–Aug Mon–Sat 9am–8pm, Sun 10am–6pm; ☎0521/27 14 00). For the rest of the year, the office is on the first floor at Sundsgatan 6b (Mon–Fri 8am–5pm; ☎0521/27 14 02). Apart from the **youth hostel** at Hunneberg (see below), the cheapest place to stay is the friendly and central *Hoglunds* at Kyrkogatan 46 (☎0521/71 15 61; 400kr). **Hotels** include the *Strand* at Hamngatan 7 (☎0521/138 50; fax 159 00; ②). You can **camp** at the lakeside *Ursands Camping* (☎0521/18 666; fax 686 76); get there on **bus** #661, which is really more of a taxi, making six journeys a day and requiring a call an hour beforehand on ☎020/71 97 17. For **eating**, try *Konditori Princess* at Sundsgatan, a pleasant bakery and café full of locals, or make the two-kilometre journey to Värgon's top hotel restaurant (see below). **Nightlife** is pretty limited, the only options being *Club Roccad* on Kungsgatan 23, or *Strommarn*, open till 2pm on Saturday. If you're here with a car, note that two-hour **parking permits** cost 10kr from kiosks and the tourist office.

Halleberg and Hunneberg

The 500-million-year-old twin plateaux of **Halleberg** and **Hunneberg**, just a few kilometres east of Vänersborg, are difficult to get to without your own transport, but well worth the trouble. Crossing the Göta River, you'll first reach **VÄRGON**, home to a renowned, ultra-chic restaurant and hotel, *Ronnums Herrgord* (☎052/ 22 32 70; set lunch 11.30am–2pm, 187kr; ④). Alternatively, you can save your kronor and get a good pizza and salad for 29kr at *Pizzeria Roma* at Nordkroksvagen 1 (☎0521/22 10 70).

Beyond Värgon, the road cuts through the curious, tree-topped hills: early human remains have been found here, as well as the traces of an old Viking fort, but the area is best known as the home of Sweden's biggest herd of elks. **Elk safaris** run in midsummer from Vänersborg's central square (150kr), but disease has reduced the stock to just 120, so don't count on seeing any. Probably the easiest way of spotting the creatures is to drive or walk up the five-kilometre lane around Halleberg at dawn or dusk. Take along some apples: these massive creatures have no qualms about eating from your hand.

Regular **buses** run here from Vänersborg, replaced in summer by a **taxi** service that costs the same; there are just three a day and you need to give one hour's notice (☎020/71 97 17). Also bus #619 runs from Trollhättan straight to Hunneberg, while bus #62 goes to Värgon. The excellent **youth hostel** at Bergagårdsvägen 9 (closed Dec 17–Jan 12, reception daily 8–10am & 5–9pm; ☎0521/22 03 40; fax 684 97; 95kr), at the foot of Hunneberg, dates from 1550 and was used by Danish soldiers to drive the Swedes into the hills. Following their line of retreat up Hunneberg brings you to the **Naturskola Nature Centre** (Mon–Fri 10am–4pm, Sat 10am–2pm, Sun 10am–3pm; ☎0521/22 37 70; free), with a **café** and plenty of information on hand about the wildlife in the hills. A web of nature trails begins here, including special trails for wheelchair users.

Between the lakes: Vastergötland

The county of **Västergötland** makes up much of the region between **lakes Vänern and Vättern** – a wooded landscape that makes up a large part of the train ride between Gothenburg and Stockholm. The most interesting places lie on the southeastern shore of Lake Vänern, notably the pretty town of **Mariestad**, easily reached from Gothenburg, while with more time you can cut south to the western shore of Lake Vättern, and in particular to the colossal fortress at **Karlsborg**. In between the lakes runs the **Göta Canal**, the main regional target for holidaying Swedes in July and August.

Lidköping and around

Although it flanks a grassy banked reach where the River Lidan meets Lake Vänern, **LIDKÖPING**, around 140km northeast of Gothenburg, falls short in charm compared to the rest of the region. On the east bank of the river, the old town square of 1446 faces the new town square, founded by Chancellor Magnus de la Gardie in 1671, on the west; both enjoyed a perfect panorama of Vänern until an unsightly concrete screen of coal-storage cylinders and grain silos was plonked just at the water's edge. The town's claim to fame is the **Rorstrand Porcelain Factory** (Mon–Fri 10am–6pm, Sun noon–4pm; guided tours June & Aug; 15kr); Europe's second oldest, it is situated at the heart of the bleak industrial zone near the lake. The musuem here is pretty uninspiring, but there are some pleasant enough designs on sale at supposedly bargain prices.

Though Lidköping itself has little else to offer, it does make a good base for visiting picturesque **Läckö castle** on the **Kalland peninsula**, a finger of land pointing into Vänern to the west of the town that's brimming with scenic routes and a number of other architectural gems.

Trains arrive at the station by the old square. If you're returning to Gothenburg, change trains at Herrljunga; if you're heading back towards Trollhättan, **bus #5** is quicker, while bus #1 runs directly to Karlsborg (see below) in just under two hours. By **car**, Lidköping is on Route 44, 53km from Vänersborg. The **tourist office** in Nya Stadens Torg (June to mid-Aug Mon–Sat 9am–7pm, Sun 2–7pm; rest of the year Mon–Fri 9am–5pm; ☎0510/835 00; fax 221 99) will help with **private rooms** (from 135kr per person), while the cheapest night's stay is at the **youth hostel**, close by at Nicolaigatan 2 (☎0510/664 30; 100kr). *Park Hotell* (☎0510/243 90; ①/②) at 24 Mellbygatan – which runs south from Nya Stadens Torg – is a pink-painted 1920s villa **hotel**, with huge rooms and original features. Alternatively, try the *Edward Hotell* at Skaragatan 7 (☎0510/22 110; ②), or for more traditional luxury, the *Stadtshotel* (☎0510/220 85; ②/④) on Nya Stadens Torg.

For **snacks** and sandwiches, *Garstroms Konditori* at Mellbygatan 2, just opposite the tourist office, has been serving cakes and coffee since 1857. Full meals can be had at *Gotes Festvaning* across the river at Östra Hamnen (☎0510/217 00), or try the kebabs at *Madonna*, off the main square at Torggatan 6.

Around Lidköping: north to Läckö castle and east to Kinnekulle

Almost everyone heads for Läckö castle, 25km north of Lidköping at the tip of the Kalland peninsula. Officially on its own island, but surrounded by water on just three sides, Läckö is everyone's idea of a fairy-tale castle – all turrets and towers and rendered in creamy white. The castle dates from 1290, but was last modified and restructured by Lidköping's Chancellor, de la Gardie, when he took it over in 1652. Inside there is a wealth of exquisite decoration, which you can see best on a guided tour (daily May–Aug 10am–4pm; Sept 11am–1pm; 30kr). Be warned, however, that Läckö's charms are no secret, and in summer you should be prepared for the crowds. **Bus #132** from Lidköping travels out here hourly in summer (20kr), via the tiny village of Spiken.

Twelve kilometres east of Lidköping by train, **KALLBY** draws visitors for its ancient burial site (turn left at the road junction), where two impressive stones face each other in an Iron Age Cemetery, one carved with a comical, goblin-like figure that's said to be the God Thor. Not far beyond, **Husaby** is a tranquil diversion with great religious and cultural significance. It was here in 1008 that Saint Sigfrid, an English missionary, baptized Olof Skotkonung, the first Swedish king to turn his back on the Viking gods and embrace Christianity. The present three-towered church was built in the twelfth century, just to the west of the well where the baptism is said to have taken place.

Kinnekulle, the "Flowering mountain", is a couple of kilometres on (get off the train at any of the next few stops), an area of woods and lakes interwoven with paths and boasting hundreds of varieties of flowers, trees, birds and other animals. The strange shape of the plateau is due to its top layer of hard volcanic rock, which even four hundred million years of Swedish weather has not managed to wear down, and which makes for something of a botanical and geological treasure trove. There's an *STF* **youth hostel** (100kr; all year; ☎0510/406 53) and **campsite** complex nearby in Hellekis (Råbäck station).

Mariestad and around

Smaller, prettier and more welcoming than Lidköping, lakeside **MARIESTAD**, with its splendid medieval quarter and harbour area, is just an hour's train ride north and an excellent base for a day or two's exploration. What lifts the town beyond postcard status is the extraordinary range of building styles crammed into the centre – Gustavian, Carolean, Classical, Swiss-chalet style and Art Nouveau – like a living museum of architectural design. It's also worth taking a look at the now bishopless **cathedral**, on the edge of the centre, which was built by Duke Karl (who named the town after his wife, Maria of Pfalz) in an attempt to compete with his brother King Johan III's Klara kyrka in Stockholm. To help you explore the town's compact centre, pick up a copy of the walking-tour map from the tourist office, or join one of their free guided **tours** (mid-June to mid-Aug Mon & Thurs).

Mariestad is also an ideal base from which to cruise up Lake Vänern to the start of the Göta Canal's main stretch at **Sjotorp**. There are 21 locks between Sjotorp and Karlsborg (see below), with the most scenic section up to **Lyrestad**, just a few kilometres east of Sjotorp and 20km north of Mariestad on the E20. Lake and canal **cruises** cost 170kr for the day, however long you stay on the boat (contact the tourist office for details).

The **tourist office**, by the harbour on Hamngatan (June–Aug Mon–Fri 8am–7pm, Sat & Sun 9am–6pm; Sept–May Mon–Fri 8am–4pm; ☎0501/100 01; fax 708 19), is opposite the hugely popular *STF* **youth hostel** (☎0501/104 48; book in advance mid-Aug to mid-June; 100kr). Built after the fire of 1693, the hostel is a former tannery with galleried timber outbuildings and an excellent garden café. For a **hotel**, try the olde-worlde 1698-built *Bergs Hotell*, in the old town at Kyrkogatan 18 (☎0501/103 24; ①); *Hotell Viola*, Viktoriagatan 15 (☎0501/195 15; ①); or the imposing *Stadshotellet* on Nya Torget (☎0501/138 00; ②/④), five minutes walk away in the modern centre. The nearest **campsite** is *Ekuddens*, 2km down the river (May–Sept; ☎0501/106 37). Mariestad's trendiest **eating** place is *Café Stroget* on Österlånggatan in the new town area (sandwiches from 20kr). The liveliest **pub/restaurants** are *Buffalo* at Österlånggatan 3 and *Hjorten* at Nygatan 21; the latter also has occasional live music. **Nightlife** options include the disco at *Stadtshotellet* (see above) on Friday and Saturday nights, and year-round live music and dancing at *Ohman's* – also owned by the *Stadshotellet* – at Nygatan 16.

Karlsborg and around

Despite the great plans devised for the fortress at **KARLSBORG**, around 70km southeast of Mariestad on the western shores of Lake Vättern, it has survived the years as one of Sweden's greatest follies. By the early nineteenth century, Sweden had lost Finland – after six hundred years of control – and had became jumpy about its own security. In 1818, with the Russian fleet stationed on the Åland Islands and within easy striking distance of Stockholm, Baltzar Von Platten persuaded parliament to construct an inland fortress at Karlsborg, capable of sustaining an entire town and protecting the royal family and the treasury – the idea being that enemy forces should be lured into Sweden, then destroyed on home territory. With the town pinched between lakes Vättern and Bottensjön, the Göta Canal – also the brainchild of Von Platten and already under construction – was to provide access, but while Von Platten had the canal finished by 1832, the fortress was so ambitious a project that it was never completed. It was strategically obselete long before work was finally abandoned in 1909 and the walls not strong enough to withstand attack from new weaponry innovations. However, parts are still in use today by the army and air force, and uniformed cadets mill around, lending an air of authenticity.

The complex, which is as large as a town, appears austere and forbidding, but you are free to wander through and to enter the **museum** of endless military uniforms; the **guided tour** with special sound and smoke effects is not everyone's idea of a good time. For further information contact the tourist office (see below).

There is no train service to Karlsborg, though there are regular **bus** services from both Lidköping and Mariestad; if you're driving, take Route 202 from Mariestad. The **tourist office**, right by the Göta Canal (June–Aug 9am–5pm; Sept–May Mon–Fri 9am–4pm; ☎0505/173 50; fax 125 91), can book **private rooms** for around 135kr per person. Both the **youth hostel**, 1km to the south (☎0506/449 16; fax 125 91; June–Aug; 100kr), and the **campsite** (☎0505/119 16; June–Sept), 500m to the north of the tourist office, are conveniently located on the banks of Lake Bottensjön.

Forsvik

As far back as the early 1300s, the Karlsborg area maintained an important flour mill, 8km north at **FORSVIK**, run by the monastery that was founded by Sweden's first female saint, Birgitta. Using the height differential between lakes Viken and Bottensjon, first over water wheels and later through power-generating turbines, a sizeable industry emerged, working all manner of metal and wood products. During the Reformation, Forsvik was burnt down, but the creation of the Göta Canal gave the place new life, and it once again became a busy industrial centre. Its paper mill continued to operate until the 1940s, and its foundry until the Swedish shipyard crises in the 1970s. Today the mill is a **museum** (June–Aug noon–6pm; free), which has been restored to its 1940s condition and provides a stimulating picture of Forsvik's industrial past. A bus runs from Karlsborg fairly frequently in summer.

travel details

Trains

From Gothenburg to: Kalmar (2–3 daily; 4hr 20min); Karlskrona (Mon–Fri 1–2 daily; 4hr 40min); Malmö (8–12 daily; 3hr 50min, 3hr by X2000); Stockholm (9–13 daily; 4hr 30min, 3hr 15min by X2000); Strömstad (7–9 daily; 2hr 40 min); Trollhättan (8–15 daily; 40min); Vänersborg (Mon–Fri 10 daily, 4 on Sat & Sun; 1hr 5min).

Buses

From Gothenburg to: Borås (13 daily Mon–Fri, 3 on Sat, 8 on Sun; 55min); Falun/Gävle (1–3 daily; 10hr 30min); Halmstad (3 on Fri & Sun; 2hr); Karlstad (3–5 daily; 4hr); Linköping/Norrköping (3–4 daily, 1 on Sat; 4hr 35min); Mariestad (4–5 daily; 3hr); Oskarshamn (2 on Fri & Sun; 5hr 20min); Oslo (4–5 daily; 4hr 45min); Tanumshede/Strömstad (4–5 daily; 2hr 30min); Trollhättan (2–5 daily; 1hr 5min); Varberg/Falkenberg (2 on Fri & Sun; 50min/1hr 20min).

From Strömstad to: Svinesund (4–5 daily; 20min).

From Mariestad to: Gävle (1 daily Mon–Fri; 7hr 30min); Örebro (1–2 daily; 1hr 30min); Skövde/Jönköping (3–4 daily, 1 on Sat; 1hr 30min/2hr 10min).

From Lidköping to: Vänersborg/Trollhättan (2 on Fri & Sun; 45min/1hr).

International ferries

From Gothenburg to: Harwich (2 weekly; 24hr); Newcastle (June to mid-Aug 1 weekly; 24hr); Frederikshavn (ferries: 4–8 daily, 3hr 15min; catamaran: 3–5 daily, 1hr 45min); Keil (1 daily; 14hr).

From Stömstad to: Sandefjord (mid-June to mid-Aug 2 daily; 2hr 30min); Fredrikstad (mid-June to mid-Aug Mon–Sat 5 daily; 1hr 15min); Halden (mid-June to mid-Aug Mon–Sat 3 daily; 1hr 15min).

CHAPTER ELEVEN

THE SOUTHWEST

There is a real historical interest to the **southwestern** provinces of **Halland**, **Skåne** and **Blekinge**, not least in the towns and cities that line the coast. The flatlands and fishing ports south of Gothenburg were almost constantly traded between Denmark and Sweden, counters won and lost in the fourteenth to seventeenth centuries, and today several fortresses bear witness to the region's medieval buffer status.

Halland, a finger of land facing Denmark, has a coastline of smooth sandy beaches and bare, granite outcrops, punctuated by a number of small, distinct towns. Most charismatic is the old society bathing resort of **Varberg**, dominated by its tremendous thirteenth-century fortress; also notable is the small, beautifully intact medieval core of **Falkenberg**; while for extensive sands with nightlife, too, the regional capital, **Halmstad**, is a popular base.

Further south in the ancient province of **Skåne**, the coastline softens into curving beaches backed by gently undulating fields. This was one of the first parts of the country to be settled, and the scene of some of the bloodiest battles during the medieval conflict with Denmark. Although Skåne was finally ceded to Sweden in the late seventeenth century, the Danish influence died hard, and is still evident today in the thick Skåne accent, often incomprehensible to other Swedes, and in the province's architecture. The latter has also been strongly influenced by Skåne's agricultural economy, the wealth generated by centuries of profitable farming leaving the countryside dotted with **castles** – though the continued income from the land means that most of these palatial homes are still in private hands and not open to the public.

Skåne has a reputation for fertile but mainly flat and uniform countryside; however, it takes only a day or two to appreciate the subtle variety of the landscape, and its vivid beauty – blocks of yellow rape, crimson poppy and lush-green fields contrasting with the region's castles, charming white churches and black windmills. One of the best areas for **walking** and **cycling** is the **Bjäre peninsula**, the thumb of land to the west of the glamorous tennis capital of **Båstad**, where forested hill ranges, spectacular rock formations and dramatic cliffs make for some beautiful scenery. To the south, both **Helsingborg**, with its laid-back, cosmopolitan atmosphere, and Sweden's third city, bustling **Malmö**, are a stone's throw from Denmark, with frequent ferries making the journey in just twenty minutes. Between these two centres, and in contrast to Malmö's industrial heritage, the university town of **Lund** has some classic architecture and a unique atmosphere – an essential target for anyone travelling in the south.

As the countryside sweeps east towards the pretty medieval town of **Ystad**, the southwest corner of Skåne boasts some minor resorts with excellent beaches. Moving east, you enter the splendid countryside of **Österlen**. Unmasked by forest, the pastoral scenery is studded with Viking monuments such as the Swedish Stone Henge at **Ales Stennar**, and, lined with brilliant white beaches backed by several nature reserves, it also offers some of Sweden's most enjoyable cycling. Edging north, the land becomes green and more hilly, the coast featuring a number of interesting little places to stop, such as **Kivik**, with its apple orchards and Bronze Age cairn, and the ancient and picturesque resort of **Åhus**. In the northeast of the county, **Kristianstad** was built as a flagship town by the Danes, and retains its fine, Renaissance structure.

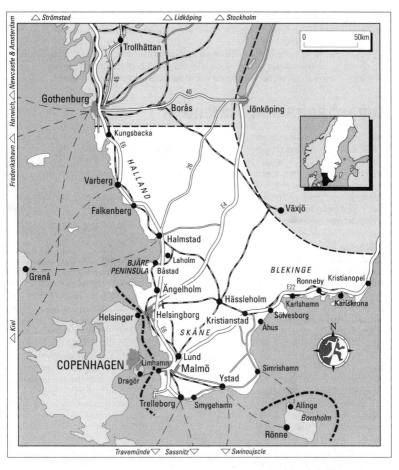

Beyond here to the east, the ledge of land running to the Baltic is **Blekinge**. Among the province's many small, not particularly distinguished resorts, **Karlskrona** stands out. Centred on a number of islands forming a small archipelago, Sweden's second city in the eighteenth century still exudes an air of regal and naval grandeur.

Getting around

The national **train** network follows the coast south from Gothenburg, with frequent trains stopping at all towns as far as Ystad, where the line cuts northeast to Kristianstad. The comfortable, Danish-built *Kustpilen Express* trains run east and west across the country, linking Malmö, Helsingborg and Lund with Kristianstad and Karlskrona. However, some of the most beautiful and less-frequented areas are not covered by the train network, and the **bus** service is skeletal at best, especially along the south coast. There are also certain transport anomalies to look out for: there are trains but no buses between Malmö and Ystad; between Ystad and Kristianstad the train service is very limited, making buses the more efficient option; and, more generally, some train and bus services stop early in the day. It's a good idea to equip yourself with timetables, and the best places to pick them up are the train and bus stations or tourist offices in Gothenburg and Malmö.

With no really steep hills, the southwest is wonderful country for **cycling**, and bike rental outlets are numerous; most tourist offices, youth hostels and campsites also rent out bikes. There are several recognized **walking trails**, mentioned in the text.

Kungsbacka and Tjolöholm

Just beyond the southernmost suburbs of Gothenberg, the small town of **KUNGS-BACKA** is a residential backwater that's of no particular interest to travellers, unless you time your trip to arrive on lively market day (1st Thurs of month). Although Kungsbacka dates from the thirteenth century, when it was just one of a number of prosperous Hanseatic towns along the south coast, the town was razed by fire in 1846, leaving just a couple of houses as testament to its past. It's altogether better to use the town simply as a means of reaching the splendid and unique manor house on the coast at **Tjolöholm**, 15km south.

Tjolöholm

The dream home of Scottish-born merchant and horse-breeder James Dickson, the manor house at **TJOLÖHOLM** (pronounced "chewla-home") was the result of a grand design competition in the 1890s. Enormously wealthy, Dickson wanted a unique house to reflect his British ancestry, the then current Swedish fascination for Romanticism and the latest comfort innovations of the day. The winner of the competition was the 27-year-old Lars Israel Wahlman, who built a stunning Elizabethan-style stately home. Dickson, however, never saw Tjolöholm completed – cutting his finger while opening a champagne bottle, he fatally poisoned himself by wrapping the lead cap around the wound.

In 1901, a village was built around the house, and its little red and white wooden cottages have been immaculately preserved. Along the main driveway, the huge stables and indoor riding track have been converted into an airy café, while the next building contains a **carriage museum** (same times as house – see below), worth a peek to see the bizarre horse-drawn vacuum cleaner. The **interior** of the house (June–Aug daily 11am–4pm; Sept & Oct Sun only 11am–4pm; 45kr) deserves a good hour or so – free pamphlets in English are available (guided tours in English have to be pre-booked). Among the many highlights are the billiard room, where the walls are lined with Belgian marble and punctuated by hot-air vents (part of the avant-garde central heating system), and the sophisticated, regal study, which was oak panelled by Liberty's of London. Sweeping through Blanche Dickson's red boudoir and her four fabulous bathrooms, with sunken baths and showers that sprayed Mrs Dickson from all sides, you're led on to the Charles Rennie Mackintosh-inspired children's nursery, with its simple, white motifs. Once you've had your fill of the mansion, you can while away a pleasant few hours in the grounds, which slope down to a grass-fringed beach.

Practicalities

To get to Tjolöholm, take the **local train** to Kungsbacka from Gothenburg's Central Station (journey time 20min). A special bus runs from here to the house at 11am, returning in the afternoon; if you miss that, bus #732 goes to within 3km of the manor, from where you'll have to walk or hitch. In July and August, there's a special *SJ* **bus** direct to Tjolöholm from Nils Ericsonsplatsen, by Gothenburg station (Sat, Sun & public holidays). By car, turn off the E6 highway just south of Kungsbacka at Fjärås, and follow the signs to Åsa for 2km, from where there are signs for Tjolöholm.

Kungsbacka has a **youth hostel** (☎0300/194 85; mid-June to mid-Aug; 95kr), 2km from the train station on the road to Sarö – turn left from the station then right onto the main road. **Private rooms** at 150kr per person can be booked at the **tourist office** opposite the station (May to late June Mon–Fri 9am–6pm, Sat & Sun 11am–3pm; late June to mid-Aug Mon–Sat 9am–7pm, Sun 11am–3pm; rest of the year Mon–Fri 10am–4pm; ☎0300/345 95; fax 131 34). The only convenient **hotel** is the reasonable *Hotel Halland* at Storgatan 35 (☎0300/775 30; ②/④), almost next to the tourist office. The nearest **campsite** (June–Aug ☎0300/148 29; Sept–May ☎0300/346 48) is 3km away at the *Kungsbacka Sportscenter* – buses run there during school terms (Oct–May).

Varberg

More atmospheric than any other town in Halland, the fashionable little nineteenth-century bathing resort of **VARBERG** boasts surprisingly varied sights – its imposing fortress the most obvious one – plus a laid-back atmosphere, opportunities to swim and plenty of good places to eat.

The Town

All Varberg's sights are concentrated along or near the seafront, with the thirteenth-century moated **fortress** set on a rocky promontory in the sea the most prominent attraction. Home to the Swedish king Magnus Eriksson, important peace treaties with Valdemar of Denmark were signed here in 1343. Standing outside, it's easy to imagine how impenetrable the fortress must have appeared to attackers in the past, as the way in is hardly more obvious today: enter on the sea-facing side by climbing the uneven stone steps to a delightful terrace café, or approach through the great archways towards the central courtyard.

Although tours in English (daily 10am–7pm year-round; tours hourly in July & Aug, children's tours 1.30pm & 2.30pm daily; 20kr, children 10kr) take you into the dungeons and among the impressive cocoa-coloured buildings that make up the inner courtyard, it's the **museum** that deserves most of your attention (mid-June to mid-Aug daily 10am–7pm; rest of the year Mon–Fri 10am–4pm, Sat & Sun noon–4pm; summer 30kr, rest of the year 10kr). The most unnerving exhibit is **Bocksten Man**, a 600-year-old murder victim who was garrotted, drowned, impaled and buried in a local bog until 1936, when a farmer dug him up. His entire outfit preserved by the acid bog, Bocksten Man sports the western world's most complete medieval wardrobe, made up of a cloak, a hood, shoes and stockings. His most shocking feature is the thick, red ringletted hair that cascades around his puny skull, while the three stakes thrust through his body were supposed to ensure that his spirit never escaped to seek out his murderers. Much of the rest of the museum is dispensable, with sections on farming and fishing in

Halland, though the room devoted to the works of the so-called **Varberg School** is worth viewing. A small colony of artists – Richard Bergh, Nils Kreuger and Karl Nordström – who linked up in the last years of the nineteenth century, they developed a national painting style reflecting the moods and atmosphere of Halland, and particularly Varberg. Night scenes of the fortress beneath the stars show a strong Van Gogh influence, but in other paintings, the misty colours create a more melancholy effect.

Overlooking the sea, the custard-and-cream-painted **fortress prison** from 1850 looks incongruously delicate in the shadow of the looming fortress. The first Swedish prison to be built with individual cells, it housed life sentencers, until the last one ended his days here in 1931. Today you can stay in a private youth hostel in the fortress, which has been carefully preserved to retain most of its original features (see below).

A couple of fine remnants from Varberg's time as a spa resort are within a minute of the fortress. Just behind it, facing the town, is the grand **Societeshuset**, set in its own small park. A bridal-like confection of white and pink carved wood, this was where upper-class ladies took their meals after bathing in the splendid **Kallbadhuset** (cold bathhouse), just to the north of the fortress and overlooking the harbour. Somewhat battered by time and the sea winds, but shortly to be renovated, this dainty bathhouse has separate sex naked-bathing areas and is topped at each corner by Moorish cupolas, lending it an imperial air.

Although the Halland coastline is still a little rocky around here, there are several excellent spots for bathing. Head down Strandpromenaden for about five minutes to get to a couple of well-known **nudist beaches**. Alternatively, a few kilometres further north at **Getterön**, a fist of land jutting into the sea, there's a nature centre and extensive bird reserve, as well as a series of secluded coves, reached by regular buses from town.

Practicalities

Varberg is a handy entry point to southern Sweden, linked by a year-round **ferry** service (150kr return; 3hr 45min) to Grenå in **Denmark**. Regular **trains** run down the coast from Gothenburg, and local **buses** cover the 45-kilometre trip south from Kungsbacka (bus #732, changing to #615 at Frillesås). From the **train and bus stations**, turn right down Vallgatan and the town centre is off to the left, the harbour to the right. The **tourist office** in the central square (mid-June to mid-Aug Mon–Sat 9am–7pm, Sun 3–7pm; ☎0340/887 70; fax 111 95) provides free maps of the town. Varberg is easy to walk around, but to explore the nearby coast it might be worth **renting a bike** from *Team Sportia* (75kr a day; ☎0340/124 70), opposite the tourist office.

It's worth booking well in advance for the fortress prison **youth hostel** (☎0340/887 88; all year; 120kr); outside the summer season you have to book through the tourist office (see above). Aside from being spotlessly clean, the prison is much as it was, with original cell doors, complete with spy-holes (each has its own key). If it's full, try the *STF* **hostel** (☎0340/410 43; April–Sept; 100kr) 8km south at **Himle** – bus #652 from the bus station runs within a kilometre. Otherwise, the cheapest **hotel** is the shabby but clean *Hotel Bergklinten*, close to the station at Västra Vallgatan 25 (☎0340/61 15 45; ①); more luxurious are the *Hotel Fregatten* (☎0340/770 00; fax 61 11 21; ②/④), in a former cold-storage warehouse overlooking the harbour, and the more traditional *Stadshotell*, Kungsgatan 24–26 (☎0340/161 00; ②/④). There are a number of **campsites** in the area, the nearest being *Apelvikens Camping* (☎0340/141 78; April–Oct), which is 3km south of the fortress along Strandpromenaden. Alternatively, there are plenty of places to put up a tent for free beyond the nudist beaches.

There are plenty of good places to **eat** in Varberg, mostly along Kungsgatan running north of the main square. The best café in town, great for breakfast, is *Otto's Skafferi*, Kungsgatan 12, serving sumptuous pies and sandwiches. Further down the street, *Harry's Pub & Restaurant* serves a range of pastas all named after English football teams

(75kr) and has a popular happy hour (4–7pm). However, it's worth spending a little extra at the *Societen* in Societets Park, directly behind the fortress, where steaks and fish dishes are served at moderate prices (11.30am–1.30pm). The place comes alive on Thursday and Saturday evenings with foxtrots on the ground floor and a disco in the basement.

Falkenberg

It's a twenty-minute train ride south from Varberg to the well-preserved medieval town of **FALKENBERG**, named after the falcons that were once hunted here. With some lively museums and a long beach, it's a likeable little town but only really comes alive in July and August. Sir Humphrey Davy, inventor of the mining safety lamp, visited in the 1820s to go **fly-fishing** in the River Ätran that runs through town, and as the town's reputation for salmon spread a succession of wealthy English countrymen followed him here, leaving their mark on the town. Today the waters have been so overfished that it costs relatively little to try your hand in the permitted two-kilometre stretch from the splendid 1756-built stone **Tullbron** toll bridge. The tourist office (see below) sell a licence that allows you to catch up to three fish a day (March–Sept; 80kr).

The **old town**, to the west of the curving river, comprises a dense network of low, wooden cottages and cobbled lanes. Nestling among them is the fine twelfth-century **St Laurentii kyrka**, its interior awash with seventeenth- and eighteenth-century wall and ceiling paintings. It is hard to believe that this church functioned at various times as a shooting range, a cinema and a gymnasium, however once the solid neo-Gothic "new" church had been built at the end of the nineteenth century, it was only its secular use that saved it from demolition until reconsecration in the 1920s.

Bypassing the pedestrian County Museum on St Lars Kyrkogatan, head straight for the **new museum** (June–Aug Tues–Fri 10am–4pm, Sat & Sun noon–4pm; Sept–May Tues–Fri & Sun noon–4pm; 20kr) in an old four-storey grain store near the main bridge. While there are the usual archeological collections, the enthusiastic curator has chosen to devote most of the museum to the 1950s, with displays covering Falkenberg's dance bands, along with original interiors of a shoe repair shop and stylized café. The town also boasts a rather unusual **Fotomuseum** (late June to mid-Aug Tues–Thurs 1–8pm; rest of the year Tues–Thurs 5–8pm, Sun 2–6pm): at the time of writing the museum was housed in the owner's home at Karl Salomonssons Vägen 9 (call for directions on ☎0346/803 93) but in July 1997 it's due to move to Sandgatan 13, the home of Falkenberg's oldest purpose-built cinema. Among the thousand or so cameras and other cinematic paraphernalia, there are some superb local peasant portraits, taken in 1898 by Axel Aurelius. Less demanding is a tour of the local **Falken Brewery** (July & Aug Mon–Thurs 10am & 1.15pm; 20kr; book at the tourist office); Sweden's most popular beer, *Falken* has been brewed here since 1896 and is available for sampling at the end of the tour.

Over the river and fifteen minutes' walk south there's a fine, four-kilometre stretch of sandy beach, **Skrea Strand**. At its northern end is the large bathing and tennis complex of **Klitterbadhuset** (Tues & Thurs 6–9am & noon–8pm, Wed noon–8pm, Fri noon–3pm OAPs only & 3–7pm over-16s only, Sat 9am–5pm, Sun 9am–3pm), which offers a fifty-metre saltwater pool and shallow children's pool, a vast sauna, jacuzzi and steam rooms all for 30kr. If you walk all the way down past the wooden holiday shacks at the southern end of the beach, you'll come across some secluded coves; in early summer, the marshy grassland around here is full of wild violets and clover and a great place for **birdwatching**.

Practicalities

Regular **buses** and **trains** drop you close to the centre on Holgersgatan, just a couple of minutes from the **tourist office** in Stortorget (mid-June to Aug Mon–Sat 9am–7pm,

Sun 3–7pm; Sept Mon–Fri 9am–5pm, Sat 10am–2pm; Oct–May Mon–Fri 9am–5pm; ☎0346/174 10; fax 145 26). They can book **private rooms** from 120kr per person, plus 30kr booking fee. The comfortable and well-equipped *STF* **youth hostel** (☎0346/171 11; June to mid-Aug; 100kr) is in the countryside at Näset, 4km south of town – buses #1 and #2 run there until 7pm. It's just a few minutes' walk through the neighbouring **campsite** (☎0346/171 07) to the south end of the beach. The best-located **hotel** for the beach is the sprawling, modern *Nya Hotel Standbaden* (☎0346/580 00; fax 161 11; ③/④ – includes entry to Klitterbadhuset). Rather more interesting is the riverside *Hvitan* (☎0346/820 90; fax 597 96; ②/③), which has a good restaurant and pub, while the cheapest is *Hotel Steria,* a ten-minute walk from the river up Arvidstorpsvägen (☎0346/155 21; fax 101 30; ①).

About the best place for **lunch** is the atmospheric *Falkmanska Caféet*, Storgatan 42, which serves huge baguettes and decadent cakes. The friendly *D.D.* at Hotelgatan 3 (June–Aug daily; Sept–May Wed–Sat), is a smallish restaurant and club serving American food and a 55kr lunch; at night it turns into a dance floor. On the main square, *Harry's Bar* is a busy eating place and pub. The poshest restaurant is *Gustav Bratt*, Brogatan l, near the main square, though its à la carte menu is nothing special. Lunch costs around 150kr.

Halmstad

The principal town in Halland, **HALMSTAD**, was once a grand walled city and important Danish stronghold. Today, although most of the original buildings have disappeared, the town boasts a couple of cultural and artistic points of interest – notably the works of the Halmstad Group, Sweden's first Surrealists – extensive, if rather crowded, beaches within easy reach and a wide range of really good places to eat.

In 1619, the town's **castle** was used by Danish King Christian IV to entertain the Swedish king Gustav Adolf II; records show that there were seven days of solid festivities. The bonhomie didn't last much longer than that, and Christian was soon building great stone and earth fortifications, all surrounded by a moat with four stone gateways into the city. Soon after, a fire all but destroyed the city and the only buildings to survive were the castle and the church. Undeterred, Christian took the opportunity to create a modern Renaissance town with a gridwork of straight streets and the high street, Storgatan, still contains a number of impressive merchants' houses from that time. After the final defeat of the Danes in 1645, Halmstad lost its military significance and the walls were torn down. Today, just one of the great gateways, Norre Port, remains, while Karl XIs Vägen runs directly above the filled-in moat.

The Town

At the centre of the lively market square, **Stora Torg**, is Carl Mille's *Europa and the Bull*, a fountain with mermen twisted around it, all with Mille's characteristically muscular bodies and ugly faces. Flanking one side of the square is the grand fourteenth-century **St Nikolai kyrka** (daily 8.30am–3.30pm), a monumental testament to the town's former importance. Today, the only signs of its medieval origins are the splodges of bare rock beneath the plain brick columns. Leading north from the square, pedestrianized **Storgatan**, which until the 1950s was the old E6 highway, is the main venue for restaurants and nightlife (see below). It's a charming street with some creaking old houses built in the years following the 1619 fire. The great stone arch of **Norre Port** marks the street's end: through here and to the right is the splendid **Norre Katt Park**, a delightful, shady place, with mature beech and horse chestnut trees sloping all the way to the river bank.

By the river at the northernmost edge of the park is a fine **museum** (early June to late Aug daily 10am–7pm, Wed till 9pm; rest of the year 10am–4pm, Wed till 9pm; 20kr, 10kr in winter). While the archeological finds are unlikely to set many pulses racing, upstairs there are some home interiors from the seventeenth, eighteenth and nineteenth centuries, including exquisitely furnished dolls' houses and a room of glorious Gustavian harps and square pianos from the 1780s. The top floor contains a decent sample of the work of the Halmstad Group that's worth a look.

A few kilometres north of the town centre, **Mjållby Arts Centre** is home to the largest collection of works by the **Halmstad Group**, a body of six local artists who championed Cubism and Surrealism in 1920s Sweden. Their work caused considerable controversy in the 1930s and 40s and a quick glance shows how strongly they were influenced by Magritte and Dali. Reputedly the only group of its type to have stayed together in its entirety for fifty years, they sometimes worked together on a single project: you can see a good example at the Halmstad City Library, where an impressive fourteen-metre six-section work adorns the wall above the shelves. To get to the centre, take bus #350 or #351 to the airport, from where it is a one-kilometre walk down the road on the right.

Practicalities

From the **train station**, follow Bredgatan to the Nissan River and just by Österbro (East Bridge) is the **tourist office** (June & Aug Mon–Fri 9am–6pm, Sat 10am–3pm, Sun 1–3pm; July Mon–Sat 9am–7pm, Sun 3–7pm; ☎035/10 93 45; fax 15 81 15), across the bridge from the main square. They can book **private rooms** (from 120kr per person, plus 25kr booking fee in person, 50kr by phone) and sell you a five-day **Halmstad Card** (50kr), which provides free museum entry, free parking and various other discounts. Renting a **bike** is a good way to get out the Mjållby Arts Centre or to the beaches on the coast hereabouts: there's currently one outlet, *Arvid Olsson Cykel*, Norra Vägen ll (Mon–Fri 9.30am–6pm, Sat 9.30am–lpm), which charges a steep 95kr per day for a five-speed bike.

There's a new, central **youth hostel** (☎035/12 05 00; mid-June to mid-Aug; 125–160kr) at Skepparegatan 23, 500m to the west of St Nicolai church, which has showers and toilets in all rooms. Best of the central **hotels** is the very comfortable old *Norre Park Hotel*, Norra Vägen 7 (☎035/21 85 55; fax 10 45 28; ③/④), through the Norre Port Arch north of Storgatan, overlooking the park. The nearest **campsite** is *Hägons Camping*, about 3km from the centre (☎035/12 53 63; fax 12 43 65), which has some **cabins** (3100–4500kr per week).

Eating, drinking and **nightlife** possibilities abound along the cobbled pedestrianized **Storgatan**; prices can be steep in the swisher places. *Daltons* is an alternative bar and restaurant featuring Swedish music and a bar open to the sky in summer. *Gamla Rådhuskällaren*, set in the mellow, candle-lit vaulted cellars of the seventeenth-century law courts, is the place for carnivores, with fine Swedish steaks sold by weight, while Mexican food from 80kr is served at the stylish *Harley's*, also an excellent place for a drink. The best **cafés** are *Konditoria* on Norregatan, next to the *Norre Park Hotel*, which stays open till 10pm, and the old-fashioned *Stånska Hembageriet* at Bankgatan l, just off Storgatan.

Båstad and the Bjäre peninsula

Although linked together geographically, the town of **Båstad** and the attached **Bjäre peninsula** couldn't be more dissimilar. Båstad is a major Swedish sports resort, geared towards the chic pastimes of yachting, golfing and tennis; the peninsula, on the other hand, is a lot less manicured – with both rugged coastlines and lush meadows, it's an area of outstanding natural beauty.

Båstad

The most northerly town in the ancient province of Skåne, **BÅSTAD** has a character markedly distinct from the other towns along the coast. Cradled by the Bjäre peninsula, which bulges westwards into the Kattegat (the water separating Sweden and Jutland), Båstad is Sweden's elite **tennis centre**, hosting the annual Swedish Open at the beginning of July (tickets 100–200kr), plus another sixty tennis courts, five 18-hole golf courses and the well-known *Drivan Sports Centre*. It's all set in very beautiful surroundings, with a horizon of forested hills to the south. Less pleasant, however, is the fact that ever since King Gustav V chose to take part in the 1930 tennis championships, wealthy retired Stockholmers and social climbers from all over Sweden have flocked here to bask in the social glow, something that's reflected in the ostentatiously chic clothes shops and oriental antique specialists that line **Köpmansgatan**, the main thoroughfare.

Practicalities

From the **train station**, it's a half-hour's walk east along Köpmansgatan to the main square, where the **tourist office** (mid-June to mid-Aug daily 10am–6pm; rest of the year Mon–Sat 10am–4pm; ☎0431/750 45; fax 700 55) can book **private rooms** for 140kr per person and rent out **bikes** for 60kr per day. They can also give information on booking tennis courts and renting out sports equipment. To get to the **harbour and beach**, follow Tennisvägen off Köpmansgatan through a luxury residential district until you reach Strandpromenaden; to the west, the old bathhouses have been converted into restaurants and bars.

The *STF* **youth hostel** (☎0431/759 11; fax 717 60; Sept–May; ☎0431/710 30) is next to the *Drivan Sports Centre* on Korrödsvagen, signposted off Köpmangatan. It's open all year, but tends to be reserved for groups in winter, and the number of sporty youngsters here make it one of the noisiest places to stay. The cheaper **hotels** are mostly around the station end of town; beware that prices in Båstad are likely to increase dramatically during the summer due to the tennis. *Hotel Pension Enehall* at Stationsterrasen 10 (☎0431/750 15; fax 724 09; ②) is an unexciting modern hotel just a few metres from the train station. More atmospheric are the *Pensionat Malengården*, Åhusvägen 41 (☎/fax 0431/695 67; from 195kr per person) – take the turning off Köpmansgatan towards the youth hostel – and the *Hotel Pension Furuhem*, close to the train station at Roxmansvägen 13 (☎0431/701 09; fax 701 80; ①); for a harbourside setting, try the *Hotel Skansen* (☎0431/720 50; fax 700 85; ②). **Camping** is not allowed on the dunes; you're best off heading to the Bjäre pensinsula.

Eating and drinking is as much a pastime as tennis in Båstad, and most of the waterside restaurants and hotels both here and on the peninsula offer a 99kr two-course dinner with menus changing weekly. *Pepe's Bodega* at the harbour is a swish pizza place; next door is *Fiskbiten*, a busy fish restaurant, set in a turn-of-the-century bathing house. *Slamficken*, in a neighbouring bathing house, has a popular grill from 6pm, and is also open for breakfast and lunch. Although there are a few **nightclubs**, Båstad is much more geared up for wine sipping in restaurants, only the very young filling the tacky venues along Köpmansgatan.

The Bjäre peninsula

The highlight of the entire region, the **Bjäre peninsula** has a magical quality about it that demands a couple of days' exploration. Its varied scenery ranges from open fields of potatoes and strawberries to cliff formations of splintered red rock and remote, seal-ringed islands thick with birds and dotted with historical ruins. To help you find your way around, buy a large-scale **map** of the area from Båstad tourist office (40kr). The **Skåneleden walking trail** runs round the entire perimeter, which is equally good for cycling (a few gears help, as the terrain can get quite hilly). **Public transport** around the peninsula is adequate: bus #525 leaves Båstad every other hour on weekdays, running through the centre of the peninsula, via Hov and Karup, to Torekov (20min); at weekends you need to call *Båstad taxi* (☎0431/696 66) an hour before you want to leave – be sure to book your return trip (it costs the same as the bus). Bus #524 leaves from Förslov, on the peninsula's southern coast, for Hov, which is useful if you've walked this far. If you don't want to head back to Båstad, bus #523 goes regularly from Torekov south to Ängelholm (50min; see below).

Heading north out of Båstad along the coast road, it's just a couple of kilometres to **Norrvikens Gardens** (May to mid-Sept daily 10am–6pm; 35kr), a paradise for horticulturists. Two to three kilometres further, past *Norrvikens Camping Site* for caravans (April–Oct; ☎0431/691 70), is **KATTVIK**. Once a busy stone-grinding mill village, it is now largely the domain of elderly, wealthy Stockholmers, who snap up the few houses as soon as they appear on the market. Kattvik achieved its moment of fame when Richard Gere chose a cottage here for a summer romance. Otherwise, it contains little more than the friendly *Delfin Bed & Breakfast* (☎0431/731 20; ①), an idyllic base for exploring the region, with vegetarian gourmet cooking and breakfast served under the apple trees.

The sleepy village of **TOREKOV** lies on the peninsula's western coast a few kilometres from Kattvik, and its little harbour is where old fishing boats leave for the nature reserve island of **Hallands Väderö**. Old wooden fishing boats make the fifteen-minute crossing regularly (June–Aug hourly; Sept–May every 2hr; 55kr return), the last one returning at 4.30pm, so it's worth setting off early to give yourself a full day. The island is a glorious mix of trees and sun-warmed bare rocks, with isolated fishing cottages dotted around its edges, while countless birds – gulls, eiders, guillemots and cormorants – fly noisily overhead. If you're lucky, you may be able to make out the seal colony, which lies on the farthest rocks at the southern tip of the island – or ask at Torekov tourist office about organized seal safaris. Check out also the English graveyard, surrounded by mossy drystone walls, which contains the remains of English sailors who were killed in 1809 when stationed here in order to bombard Copenhagen during the Napoleonic Wars.

Ängelholm

The best aspects of peacefully uneventful **ÄNGELHOLM** are its 7km of popular golden beach, and its proximity to elsewhere – Helsingborg is just thirty minutes away by train, the Bjäre peninsula beckons to the north, and the town is also the site of a regional airport. With a range of accommodation and some agreeable restaurants, its not a bad base at all; there is also a surprisingly lively nightlife for a predominantly young crowd. Ängelholm's efforts to sell itself, however, concentrate not on its beaches but on the town mascot, a musical clay cuckoo on sale everywhere – and UFOs. The latter have been big business here since 1946, when a railway worker, Gösta Carlsson, convinced the authorities that he had encountered tiny people from another world. Today Ängelholm hosts international UFO conferences, and the tourist board runs tours to the landing site throughout the summer.

From the train station, it's just a few minutes' walk over the Rönneå River to the main square and tourist office. Not far from here, up Kyrkogatan, is a rather unexciting **handicrafts museum** (May–Aug Tues–Fri 1–5pm, Sat 10am–2pm; 10kr), housed in what used to be the town prison. Should you want to see more of the town, the least strenuous way is a **boat trip** up the river from the harbour (June 8–Aug 11: 4 daily 40-min trips, 45kr; or daily 2-hr return trips, 60kr; ☎0431/203 00). For more freedom of movement, *Skåne Marin*, which runs the tours, also rents out boats and canoes. If none of this appeals, head left from the station 2–3km out to the **beaches**. A free bus runs there from the market square (late June to mid-Aug hourly 10am–4pm).

Practicalities

There are regular **trains** to Ängelholm from Båstad (25min), plus **buses** from Båstad and Torekov. It's a short distance from the train station to the **tourist office** in the main square (June–Aug Mon–Fri 9am–7pm, Sat 9am–4pm, Sun 1–5pm; Sept–May Mon–Fri 9am–4pm; ☎043/821 30; fax 192 07). Ask here about **bike rental**, or go straight to *Hotel Lergöken*, opposite the train station, which charges half the going rate (35kr a day, plus 10kr insurance). The tourist office can also book hotels (20kr fee) or **private rooms** (from 110kr, plus 30kr fee). There's an *STF* **youth hostel** (☎0431/523 64; April–Oct; 95kr) at the beach at Magnarp Strand, 10km north of the train station and reached by local buses. Of several **campsites**, the most convenient for the beach is *Råbocka Camping*, at the end of Råbockavägen (☎0431/105 43; fax 832 45). For a good-value and friendly **hotel**, try *Hotel Lilton* (☎0431/44 25 50; fax 44 25 69; ②/③) at Järnvägsgatan 29, just a few steps from the square and with a great garden café open in summer; failing that, there's the *Hotel Continental* at Storgatan 23 (☎0431/127 00; fax 127 90; ②).

The best place to look for **food** is the harbour. *Hamn Krogen* doesn't look anything special from the outside, but it serves the best fish dishes in Ängelholm – their speciality is Toast Skagen, shrimps and red caviar on toast. A few metres up the beach, in a whitewashed wartime bunker, is the new *Bunken* restaurant and bar, serving fish and chips (35kr) alongside more lavish seafood dishes, and putting on regular live music. The most popular **nightclub** is the cavernous warehouse called *Club Esther*, on Nybrovägen 3, off Industrigatan, the continuation of Järnvägsgatan (Fri & Sat; 40kr). A hundred metres up the road is *Rönneå River*, a busy outdoor club and summer bar.

Helsingborg

It is sometimes joked by locals that the most rewarding sight in **HELSINGBORG** is Helsingør, the Danish town whose castle, Hamlet's celebrated Elsinore, is clearly visible, just 4km over the Öresund. This has less to do with any failings Helsingborg might have, and much more to do with Denmark's cheaper alcohol outlets. Trolley-pulling Swedes converge on Helsingborg from all over the country both to stock up on beer and to spend entire nights on the ferry-laden waters, becoming increasingly drunk for less kronor than they could on land.

Past links between the two towns have been less convivial – in fact, Helsingborg has a particularly bloody and tragic history. After the Danes fortified the town in the eleventh century, the Swedes conquered and lost it again on six violent occasions, finally winning out in 1710 under the leadership of Magnus Stenbock. By this time, the Danes had torn down much of the town and on its final recapture, the Swedes razed its twelfth-century castle, except for the five-metre-thick walled keep (*kärnen*), that still dominates the centre. By the early eighteenth century, war and epidemics had reduced the population to just 700, and only with the onset of industrialization in the 1850s did Helsingborg wake up to a new prosperity. Shipping and the railways turned the town's fortunes around, as evidenced by the formidable late nineteenth-century commercial buildings in the centre and some splendid villas to the north overlooking the Öresund.

Today, a constant through traffic of Danes, Germans and Swedes stay here only long enough to change trains, which is a pity, as there is a youthful, continental feel to this likeable town with its warren of cobbled streets, its cafés and historical sights.

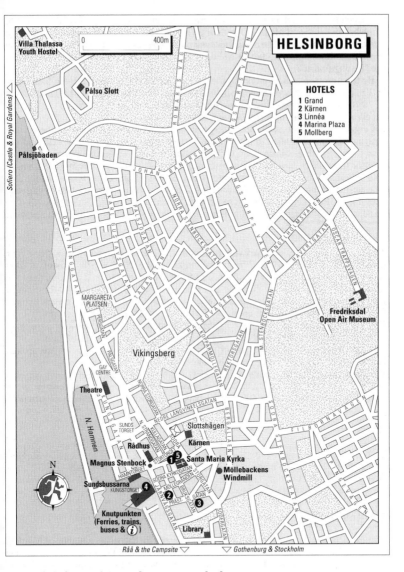

HELSINGBORG

HOTELS
1 Grand
2 Kärnen
3 Linnéa
4 Marina Plaza
5 Mollberg

Arrival, information and accommodation

Unless approaching by car on the E6, chances are you will arrive at the harbourside **Knutpunkten**, the vast, glassy expanses of which incorporate all car, train and passenger **ferry** terminals. On the ground floor behind the main hall is the **bus station**, while the ticket and transport information offices are in front, opposite the tourist office (see below). Below ground level is the combined **train station** for the national *SJ* trains and the lilac-coloured local **Pågatåg** trains, which run south down the coast to Landskrona, Lund and Malmö. One floor up brings you to a *Forex* **currency exchange** office (daily 8am–9pm). The *Sundsbussarna* passenger-only ferry to Helsingør uses the quayside at Hamntorget, 100m away. For ferry ticket details, bus and train information, see "Listings", p.462.

By the entrance to Knutpunkten, the **tourist office** (June–Aug Mon–Fri 9am–8pm, Sat & Sun 9am–5pm; Sept–May Mon–Fri 9am–6pm, Sat 10am–2pm; ☎042/12 03 10; fax 12 78 76) gives out free maps and *Helsingborg This Month*; or for 10kr you can buy the excellent English-language *Helsingborg Guide for Tourists*.

Central Helsingborg is all within easy walking distance, but for the youth hostel and outlying sights you'll need to take a **bus**. Tickets bought on board cost 12kr and are valid for two changes within an hour; if you intend to stay a while, **bus passes** are available for one (25kr), two (35kr), three (50kr) or five (60kr) days. **Cycling** is an enjoyable option but beware that bikes rented from the tourist office don't have handbrakes or gears; other outlets include *Pålsjobaden*, the old bathing house on Drottninggatan, 3km north of the centre, or if you're heading south, *Stadscykeln*, Cindergatan 13. The standard rate is 30kr per day, 120kr per week, with most outlets open only in summer.

Accommodation

The tourist office can book **private rooms** from 125kr per person plus a steep 70kr booking fee (200kr for three or more nights). The *STF* **youth hostel** at Dag Hammarskjöldsväg (☎042/21 03 84; fax 12 87 92; all year; 100kr), 2.5km north of the town centre, is called *Villa Thalassa* and is superbly set around a turn-of-the-century villa – unfortunately the accommodation isn't in the villa itself, but in cabins behind; there are also some holiday cottages (350kr per double). Bus #7 runs north from Knutpunkten (every 20min) to *Pålsjöbaden*, from where it's a one-kilometre walk through forest; after 7pm, bus #44 runs the same route twice an hour till 1am.

There are plenty of central **hotel** options, too: the best-value places are around Knutpunkten and the flashier hotels in the centre.

The Grand, Stortorget 8–12 (☎042/12 01 70; fax 11 88 33). Although new ownership has meant the loss of *The Grand*'s old exclusivity, big summer reductions make its good rooms affordable. ②/⑤

Kärnen, Järnvägsgatan 17 (☎042/12 08 20; fax 14 88 88). Opposite Knutpunkten, this comfortable, recently renovated hotel prides itself on "personal touches", including ominous English-language homilies on each room door; room no. 235 offers: "He who seeks revenge keeps his wounds open". There's a small library, cocktail bar and sauna. ②/④

Linnea, Prästgatan 4 (☎042/21 46 60; fax 14 16 55). Very cheap, central and pleasant. ①/②

Marina Plaza, Kungstorget 6 (☎042/19 21 00; fax 14 96 16). Large, modern and well-equipped hotel right at the harbour, next to Knutpunkten. Popular restaurant and lively pub. ③/④

Mollberg, Stortorget 18 (☎042/12 02 70; fax 14 96 18). Every bit a premier hotel, with a grand nineteenth-century facade, elegant rooms and a brasserie. ②/④

The Town

The most obvious starting point is the waterfront, by the copper statue of Magnus Stenbock on his charger. With your back to the Öresund and Denmark, the **Rådhus** is to your left, a heavy-handed neo-Gothic pile complete with turrets and conical towers. However, the extravagances of provincial nineteenth-century prosperity, and the architect's admiration for medieval Italy make it worth a look inside (July & Aug Mon–Fri, 40-min tours at 10am), especially for the fabulous stained-glass windows that tell the entire history of the town. The original wall and ceiling frescoes – deemed too costly to restore and therefore painted over in 1968 – are currently being uncovered.

The town hall marks the bottom of **Stortorget** – the central "square", so oblong that it's more like a boulevard – which slopes upwards to meet the steps leading to the remains of the medieval castle (there is a lift to the side; June–Aug daily 10am–8pm; Sept–May Mon–Fri & Sun 10am–6pm, Sat 10am–2pm; 5kr, free to children and wheel-chair users). At the top, the massive castellated bulk of **Kärnen** (the keep; daily April, May & Sept 9am–4pm; June–Aug 10am–7pm; Oct–March 10am–2pm; 15kr) is sur-rounded by some fine parkland. Shaped simply as a huge upturned brick, it's worth climbing more for its views than the historical exhibitions. The keep and St Maria kyrka (see below) were the sole survivors of the ravages of war, but the former lost its mili-tary significance once Sweden finally won the day. In the mid-nineteenth century it was destined for demolition and only survived because seafarers found it a valuable land-mark. What cannon fire failed to achieve, neglect and the weather succeeded in bring-ing about, and the keep fell into ruin before restoration began in 1894.

From the parkland at the keep's base, you can wander down a rhododendron-edged path, *Hallbergs Trappor*, to the **St Maria kyrka** (Mon–Sat 8am–4pm, Sun 9am–6pm), which squats in its own square by a very French-looking avenue of beech trees. The square is surrounded by a cluster of quaint places to eat and some excellent shops for picnic food, notably *Maratorgets* on the south side of the square, which sells fruit, and the adjacent *Bengtsons Ost,* a cheese shop. The church itself, begun in 1300 and com-pleted a century later, is Danish Gothic in style and resembles a basilica. Its rather plain facade belies a striking interior, with a clever contrast between the early seventeenth-century Renaissance-style ornamentation of its pulpit and gilded reredos, and jewel-like contemporary stained-glass windows.

Walking back to Stortorget, **Norra** and **Södra Storgatan** (the streets that meet at the foot of the steps to Kärnen) formed Helsingborg's main thoroughfare in medieval times, and are today lined with the town's oldest merchants' houses. Heading south along Södra Storgatan, take the opening to the left of an old sign for the museum (now closed), and after a fairly arduous climb of 92 steps, you'll find a handsome nineteenth-century **windmill**. Around the windmill are a number of exquisite farm cottages with low doorways and eighteenth-century peasant interiors – straw beds, cradles and hand-painted grandmother clocks. A further reward for the climb is to be found at *Möllebackens Väffelbruk* (May–Aug daily noon–8pm), which has been serving home-made waffles using the same recipe since 1912.

Out from the centre: Frederiksdal and Sofiero

Many of the city museum's exhibits have been moved to **Fredriksdal** (May–Sept 10am–6pm; rest of the year reduced hours; 20kr; ☎042/10 59 81), 2km outside the city by bus #2, #3 or #5 from outside the Rådhus. Here a large, open-air museum is set around a fine eighteenth-century manor house; there's plenty to look at, with parks, peasant homes and extensive botanical gardens.

Slightly further afield are the gorgeous **Royal Gardens of Sofiero** (May to mid-Sept 10am–6pm; 30kr), easily reached by bus #252 from Knutpunkten, or by cycling the 4km north along the coast. Built as a summer residence by Oscar II in the 1860s, the house itself looks rather like an elaborate train station, but the real reason to come here is the gardens, given by Oscar to his grandson, Gustav Adolf, when he married Crown Princess Marghareta in 1905. Marghareta created a horticultural paradise, and, as a granddaughter of Queen Victoria, was strongly influenced by English garden design. The rhododendron collection in particular is one of Europe's finest, a stunning array of ten thousand plants, with over five hundred varieties making up a rainbow blanket that stretches down to the Öresund.

Eating, drinking and nightlife

Helsingborg has a good range of excellent **restaurants**, though these can be expen-sive. During the day there are some great **cafés** and konditori, but at night café life is nonexistent; when locals recommend "taking the boat to Helsingør", the entertainment is the boat itself, not landing in Denmark. There are, however, some happening **clubs** for a young crowd.

Cafés and restaurants

Café Annorledes, Södra Storgatan 15. The best home-baked cakes and tarts in town in a friendly 1950s atmosphere.

Fahlmans, Stortorget. A konditori that has been serving elaborate cakes and pastries since 1914.

Grafitti, Knutpunkten, 1st floor. The ideal place if you're hungry, skint and it's past 9pm. Generously filled baked potatoes or baguettes among a young, sometimes rowdy crowd.

Gröna Tallriken, Södra Storgatan 13. A large, bright vegetarian restaurant, also selling health-food products. Californian-style health drinks (15kr), soup (23kr) and meals (48kr).

Ida's, Norra Storgatan. An informal fish and meat restaurant serving the likes of grilled ostrich, kangaroo and great homemade ice cream with hot cloudberry cream. Around 150kr. Closed Mon.

Café Mmmums, Södra Storgatan, behind St Maria kyrka. Hip, stylish café serving huge glass bowls of healthy salads (42kr) and big sandwiches. Also Toronto-style pasta. Daily 9am–7pm.

Pålsjökrog, attached to a lovely old bathhouse 2km north of the centre (☎042/14 97 30). Run by an architect who has designed it to feel like a Swedish country house. It's a special-occasion place serving traditional, well-presented Swedish food (main courses 150kr).

Utposten, Stortorget 17. Very stylish decor – mix of rustic and industrial – at this great, varied Swedish-food restaurant beneath the post office at the steps to Kärnen (2 courses 140kr). Try the delicate and filling seafood and salmon stew at 80kr. Open till 1am.

Bars and clubs

Cardinal, Södra Kyrkogatan 9. Piano bar and nightclub with a steak-oriented restaurant (6pm–1am). The first floor is a popular disco, the second has a quieter piano bar and roulette table (9.30pm–3am). Cover is 60–70kr and you need to be 25 to get in.

Jazz Clubben, Nedre Långvinkelsgatan 22. Sweden's biggest jazz club and well worth a visit on Wed, Fri and Sat evenings for live jazz, Dixieland, blues, Irish folk and blues jam sessions.

Marina, *Hotel Marina* by the harbour. A new club with a crowded, continental atmosphere; minimum age limit is 24. Thurs–Sat 10pm–3am.

Sailor's Inn, *Hotel Marina* at the harbour. This is a pre-disco or post-dinner drinking spot and extremely popular, too. Regular troubadour on Fri night.

Listings

Airport Nearest airport for domestic flights is at Ängelholm, 30km north of town; take the bus from Knutpunkten (1hr before flight departure).

Buses For Stockholm the daily bus leaves from Knutpunkten; reservations essential (☎0625/240 20), but tickets can only be bought on the bus (260kr). For Gothenburg buses leave Fri & Sun only (190kr), no reservations; tickets must be bought from the bus information section at the train booking office.

Car rental Arranged at the tourist office, or direct: *Avis*, Garnisonsgatan 2 (☎042/15 70 80); *Budget*, Gustav Adolfsgatan 47 (☎042/12 50 40); *Europcar*, Muskötgatan 1 (☎042/17 01 15); *Hertz*, Bergavägen 4 (☎042/17 25 40).

Exchange *Forex* in Knutpunkten (lst floor) or Järnvägsgatan 13 (June–Aug 7am–9pm; Sept–May 8am–9pm); maximum 20kr fee.

Ferries to Helsingør Do what the locals do and go back and forth all night: *Scanlines* every 20min (32kr return); Sundbussarna every 20min (30kr return); *Tura* (nonstop ferry; 32kr return). All ferries leave from Knutpunkten; tickets from the first-floor office.

Gay contacts *RFSL*-run café and pub/bar and occasional discos at Pålsgatan 1 (☎042/12 35 32), close to the concert hall, ten minutes' walk from Knutpunkten.

Pharmacy *Björnen*, Drottninggatan 14.

Post office Stortorget 17 (Mon–Fri 9am–6pm, Sat 10am–1pm). You can exchange money here but it costs 35kr per transaction.

Trains The Pågatåg trains from Knutpunkten require a ticket bought from an automatic machine on the platform; international rail passes are valid. It's 50kr one-way to Lund and 60kr one-way to Malmö. Fare dodging invites a 600kr spot fine.

Around Helsingborg: Råå

It's just 7km south from Helsingborg to the pretty fishing village of **RÅÅ**. You can take bus #1A or #1B from the Rådhus, or cycle there along the bike lanes, through the industrial mess of Helsingborg's southern suburbs. Råå's main street, **Råågvagen**, is a subdued place: signs indicate the twelfth-century **Raus kyrka** (left up Lybecksgatan, over the highway and along Rausvägen), but it's nothing special. Råå's main attraction is rather its **harbour**, dense with masts and remarkably untouristy. The **Maritime Museum** here is run by a group of Råå's residents and shows a comprehensive collection of seafaring artefacts. A fascinating, although somewhat stomach-churning sight at the harbour is that of eel sorting: the giant, spaghetti-like creatures are slopped into appropriately coffin-shaped boxes to be separated according to size by fishermen using claw-shaped pincers.

There are a couple of good **eating** places at the harbour. Next door to the museum, the long-established *Råå Wärdshus* serves pricey fish dishes at around 150kr, with lighter snacks and various salads for around 50kr. To the left of the museum, on the pier, *Råå Hamnservering* is the best bet for a cheap meal, with an excellent 58kr lunch buffet. If you want to **stay** your choice is limited to *Råå Camping Site* (☎042/10 76 80; fax 26 10 10), which is advertised as being "waterfront". It is, but the dominant view is of Helsingborg's industrial smog.

Lund

LUND's status as a celebrated university city is well founded. A few kilometres inland and 54km south of Helsingborg, a mass of students' bikes will probably be the first image to greet you, and like in England's Oxford – with which Lund is usually and aptly compared – there is a Bohemian, laid-back eccentricity in the air. With its justly revered twelfth-century Romanesque **cathedral**, its medieval streets, numerous museums and wealth of cafés and restaurants, Lund could well keep you busy for a couple of days. Cultural attractions aside, it is the mix of architectural grandeur and the buzz of student life that lends Lund its unique charm.

Arrival, information and accommodation

Frequent **trains** from Helsingborg (40min) arrive at the **train station** on the western edge of town, also the terminus for **buses** and within easy walking distance of everything of interest. There's also a regular *Intercitybuss* (#999; 65kr) connecting Lund with Copenhagen via Malmö and the Limhamn–Dragør ferry (see p.469). The **tourist office** (June–Aug Mon–Fri 10am–6pm, Sat & Sun 10am–2pm; Sept & May Mon–Fri 10am–5pm, Sat 10am–2pm; Oct–April Mon–Fri 10am–5pm; ☎046/35 50 40; fax 12 59 63), opposite the Domkyrkan at Kyrkogatan 11, hands out free maps and copies of *I Lund*, a monthly diary of events with museum and exhibition listings (the summer edition is in English and Swedish).

Though nowhere is no more than ten minutes' walk away, you might want to consider buying a military **bike** – large, sturdy and khaki green, they are almost indestructible, and if you plan to do a lot of cycling around the region, they're excellent value. Ask at the tourist office or try Harry's *Cykelaffar*, Banvaktsgatan 2 (☎046/211 6946).

There is a decent range of **accommodation** on offer in Lund – nearly all of it in the centre. The tourist office can book **private rooms** for 120–150kr per person, plus a 50kr book-

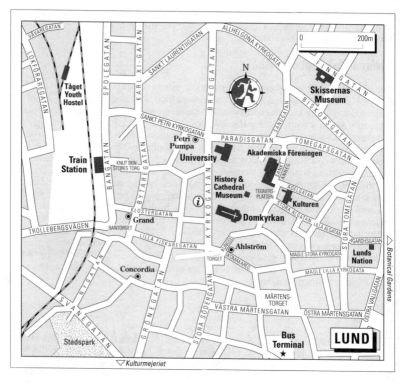

ing fee. Lund's *STF* **youth hostel**, *Tåget*, at Vävaregatan 22, through the tunnel behind the train station (☎046/14 28 20; fax 32 05 68; all year; 100kr), is housed in the carriages of a 1940s train; unfortunately the novelty wears off when you find yourself crammed in three-deep bunks with rope hoists. An alternative is *La Strada*, at Brunnshögsvägen (☎046/32 32 51; fax 521 39; all year; 125kr): take bus #4 from west of Martens Torget 4km to Klosterängsvägen, then follow the bicycle track under the motorway for 1km.

Hotels

Ahlström, Skomakaregatan 3, just south of the Domkyrkan (☎046/211 0174). Average, very central cheapie with the option of en-suite rooms. ①/②

Concordia, Stålbrogatan 1 (☎046/13 50 50; fax 13 74 22). A student hostel until the 1960s, and it still shows. ②/④

The Grand, Bantorget 1 (☎046/211 7010; fax 14 73 01). A grand nineteenth-century hotel, this pink-sandstone edifice straddles an entire side of a small, stately and central square. Unpretentious and comfortable, with a fantastic breakfast buffet. ③/④

Petri Pumpa, St Petri Kyrkogatan 7 (☎046/13 55 19). An exclusive hotel that is best known for its exquisite restaurant (see p.466). ③/⑤

The Town

It's only a short walk east from the train station to the magnificent **Domkyrkan** (Mon, Tues & Fri 8am–6pm, Wed & Thurs 8am–7.15pm, Sat 9.30am–5pm, Sun

9.30am–7.30pm; guided tours 3pm), whose storm-cloud charcoal and white stone give it an unusual monochrome appearance. Before entering, head around the back, past the grotesque animal and bird gargoyles over the side entrances; at the very back is the most beautiful part of the exterior: the three-storey apse above the crypt, crowned with a exquisite gallery.

Beyond the great carved entrance, the majestic interior is surprisingly unadorned, an elegant mass of watery-grey, ribbed stone arches and stone-flagged flooring. One of the world's finest masterpieces of Romanesque architecture, the cathedral was built in the twelfth century when Lund became the first independent archbishopric in Scandinavia, laying the foundation for a period of wealth and eminence that lasted until the advent of Protestantism. There are several interesting features, such as the elaborately carved fourteenth-century choir stalls depicting Old Testament scenes, with grotesque carvings hidden beneath the seats, but most striking is the amazing astronomical clock just to the left of the entrance. Dating from the 1440s, it shows hours, days, weeks and the courses of the sun and moon in the zodiac; if you're here at noon or 3pm, you'll get to see an ecclesiastical Punch and Judy show, as two knights pop out and clash swords as many times as the clock strikes, followed by little mechanical doors opening to trumpet-blowing heralds and the three wise men trundling slowly to the Virgin Mary.

Don't miss the dimly lit and dramatic **crypt**, which has been left almost untouched since the twelfth century. Most of the tombstones are actually memorial slabs, with just one proper tomb containing the remains of Birger Gunnarsson, Lund's last archbishop. A short man from a poor family, Gunnarsson dictated that his stone effigy should be tall and regal. Two pillars are gripped by stone figures – one of a man, another of a woman and child. Legend has it that Finn the Giant built the cathedral for Saint Lawrence; in return, the saint was to guess the giant's name, or failing that, give him the sun, the moon, or his eyes. Preparing to end his days in blindness, Lawrence heard the giant's wife boasting to her baby, "Soon Father Finn will bring some eyes for you to play with". On hearing Lawrence declare his name, the livid giant and his family rushed to the crypt to pull down the columns and were instantly turned to stone.

Just behind the cathedral on Sandgatan, the **History and Cathedral Museum** (Tues–Fri 11am–1pm; free) is for the most part rather dull unless you have a particular interest in the subject, although the statues from Scånian churches in the medieval exhibition do deserve a look, mainly because of the way they are arranged – a mass of Jesuses and Marys bunched together in groups, with the crowd of Jesuses hanging on crosses exuding a Hitchcockian ominousness.

A few minutes' walk north on Tegnerplatsen is the town's best museum, the open-air **Kulturen** (May–Sept daily 11am–5pm, Thurs till 9pm; Oct–April daily noon–4pm, Thurs till 9pm; 40kr). It's easy to spend the best part of a day just wandering around a virtual town of perfectly preserved cottages, farms, merchants' houses, gardens and even churches, brought from seven regions around Sweden and from as many centuries – despite the lack of labelling in English.

Head north from the square along Sandgatan, and then take a right on to Finngatan, in order to reach another rather special museum, **Skissernas Museum** (Museum of Sketches; Tues–Sat noon–4pm, Sun 1–5pm; free). Inside is a fascinating collection of preliminary sketches and original full-scale models of artworks from around the world. One room is full of work by all the major Swedish artists, while in the international room you'll find sketches by Chagall, Matisse, Léger, Mirò and Dufy and sculptural sketches by Picasso and Henry Moore.

As an antidote to museum fatigue, the **Botanical Gardens** (mid-May to mid-Sept 6am–9.30pm; rest of the year 6am–8pm, greenhouses noon–3pm), a few minutes' stroll further southwest down Finngatan (turn left at the end of the street into Pålsjövägen and right into Olshögsvägen), are as much a venue for a picnicking and chilling out as a botanical experience – on hot summer days, clusters of students congregate and stretch out beneath the trees.

Eating, drinking and nightlife

There are plenty of great places to eat and drink in Lund, a great deal of them associated with the university – certain **cafés** are student institutions and a number of the better **restaurants** are attached to student bodies or museums – which serves to keep prices low, especially for beer. However, Lund also boasts a couple of nationally celebrated restaurants that are expensive enough to exclude all except those on business expenses. If you want to buy your own provisions, the market at Mortenstorget, **Saluhallen**, sells a range of fish, cheeses and meats, including Lund's own tasty speciality sausage, *Knake*. Next door to the *Espresso House* (see below) on Sankt Petri Kyrkogata, *Wilderbergs Charkuteri* is a long-established foodie shop brimming with all the ingredients for a picnic.

When it comes to **nightlife**, it's worth knowing that the university is divided into "Nations", or colleges, named after different geographical areas of Sweden and with strong identities. Each nation has its own bar that's active two nights a week, and there are also regular discos. *Lund Nation* is the biggest, based in the red-brick house on Agardhsgatan, while *Småland's Nation* on Kastanjatan, off Mortenstorget, is the trendiest; both are known for hosting **live bands**. Another lively venue is the bright lilac-painted **Mejeriet**, at the end of Stora Södergatan, off the main square. Converted into a music and cultural centre in the 1970s, this 100-year-old dairy now holds a stylish café, concert hall and arts cinema (concert information on ☎046/12 38 11; cinema details on ☎046/14 38 13).

Cafés and restaurants

Café Ariman, Kungsgatan, attached to the Nordic Law Department. A nineteenth-century brick café, this deliberately shabby place is a classic left-wing coffee house – goatees, pony tails and blond dreadlocks predominate. Cheap snacks and coffee.

Café Baguette, Grönegatan. A simple, Mediterranean-style central café, with baguettes from 20kr and fish and meat meals for 70–90kr.

Café Borgen, at the Botanical Gardens. A pleasant café with a basic selection of food, in a castellated building overlooking the water lily pond. June–Aug only.

Espresso House, Sankt Petri Kyrkogata 5, opposite the library. Great atmosphere at this new, stylish coffee and bagel house. A big range of delicious coffees for 12–20kr, with mellow music setting the mood. Daily 8am–11pm.

Fellini, opposite the train station (☎046/13 80 20). Stylish and popular Italian restaurant, decked out in dull chrome and stripped wood. Two-course meals for 135kr. Open late.

Gloria's, Sankt Petri Kyrkogata, near the *Espresso House*. Serving American food, *Gloria's* is very popular with students and tourists. Local bands play Fri & Sat nights, and there's a big, lively garden area at the back. Open till midnight or later.

Kulturen, in front of the museum. Beneath a giant copper beech and facing ancient runestones, this is a busy café, bar and restaurant. A great place to people-watch, with a youngish crowd drinking cheap beer (28kr). Good lunch with vegetarian choice (54kr).

Conditori Lunagård, Kyrkogatan. Classic student konditori, with caricatures of professors adorning the walls. Justly famous for its apple meringue pie.

Petri Pumpa, St Petri Kyrkogatan 7 (☎046/13 55 15). With an extremely expensive, international menu served in cool, elegant surroundings, this restaurant is known as the second best in Sweden.

Stadpark Café, in the park at the end of Nygatan. An old wooden pavilion fronted by a sea of white plastic garden furniture, this place is always busy with families munching on snacks. Big baguettes fill you up for 35–40kr.

Tegners Terass, in the building next to the student union (*Akademiska Föreningen*). Forget any preconceptions about student cafés being tatty, stale sandwich bars. Lunch for 55kr (49kr with student card) is self-service and means as much as you like from a choice of delicious gourmet meals. The main hall is resplendent with gilded Ionic columns; sit inside or on the terrace. Daily 11.30am–2.30pm.

Bars and clubs

Easy, in the Tegners Terass building next to the student union. A new student nightclub (Thurs 7pm–3am; free entry till midnight, then 20kr) with a restaurant (same times) With a student card, 18-year-olds and upwards can get in to the club, otherwise it's strictly over-23s only.

John Bull Pub, Bantorget, adjacent to *Grand Hotel*. English-style, shabby traditional pub.

Lundia, Knutdenstorestorg. Filled with tourists, the atmosphere in this club is rather soulless. Wed–Sat 11pm–3am.

Petri Pumpa Bar, next to *Gloria's*. A glamorous place serving beer from an imported French bar, along with excellent continental lunches for 60–70kr. The sort of bar that has roasted hazelnuts rather than peanuts.

Malmö

Founded in the late thirteenth century, **MALMÖ** became Denmark's most important city after Copenhagen. The high density of herring in the sea off the Malmö coast – it was said that the fish could be scooped straight out with a trowel – brought ambitious German merchants flocking to the city, an influence that can be seen in the striking fourteenth-century St Petri kyrka. Eric of Pomerania gave Malmö its most significant medieval boost, when, in the fifteenth century, he built the castle and mint, and gave the city its own flag – the gold and red griffin of his family crest. It wasn't until the Swedish King Karl X marched his armies across the frozen belt of water to within stiking distance of Copenhagen in 1658 that the Danes were forced into handing back the counties of Skåne, Blekinge and Bohuslän to the Swedes. For Malmö this meant a period of stagnation, cut off from nearby Copenhagan and too far from its own uninterested capital. Not until the full thrust of industrialization, triggered by the tobacco merchant Frans Suell's enlargement of the harbour in 1775, did Malmö begin its dramatic commercial recovery.

Today, the attractive medieval centre, a maze of cobbled and mainly pedestrianized streets, full of busy restaurants and bars, paints a false picture of economic well-being – Malmö, Sweden's third city, is facing commercial crisis. Since its economic heyday between the world wars, a series of miscalculations on top of a country-wide industrial decline have stripped Malmö of its wealth. At Limhamn, where the car ferry from Denmark pulls in, the huge concrete works are now a dormant waste ground and the great limestone quarry just a massive gaping hole: if you arrive here, then your first sight of Malmö is a bizarre blend of industrial decay and the magnificent villas that front the long stretch of sandy beach, which runs all the way to the city centre.

Whatever its problems, Malmö makes for a worthwhile visit, although you won't need more than a day to get a feel for the compact centre; there are also delightful parks, a long and popular beach and some interesting cultural diversions south of the centre. The city's lively nightlife is another inducement to stay a while.

Arrival, information and city transport

All passenger-only **ferries** and **catamarans** from Copenhagen dock at the various terminals along the conveniently central Skeppsbron docks (ticket details are given under "Listings"). Just up from here is the central **train station**. As well as the *SJ* national trains, the Danish-built (and much more comfortable) *Kustpilen* trains run hourly from here to Denmark (change at Hässleholm) and east to Kristianstad, Karlskrona and

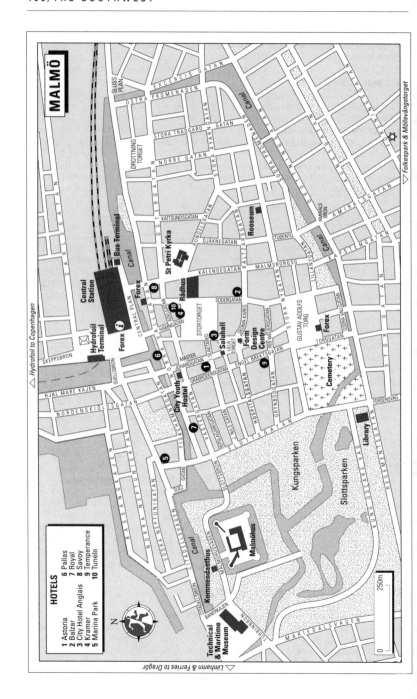

MALMÖ

▷ Hydrofoil to Copenhagen

▷ Limhamn & Ferries to Dragör

▷ Folkespark & Möllevångstorget

SLUSS PLAN

EXERCIS GATAN

ÖSTRA PROMENADEN

STORA TRÄDGÅRD GATAN

DROTTNING TORGET

NORRE GATAN

STORA KYRAN GATAN

SÖDRA PROMENADEN

Canal

Canal

Canal

KATTSUNDSGATAN

Rooseum

RUNDELSGATAN

DJAKNEGATAN

BALTZAR GATAN

AMIRALS BRON

STUDENTG

KALENDEGATAN

MALMSBORGSG

St Petri Kyrka

Bus Terminal

Central Station

Hydrofoil Terminal

Forex

Forex

Rådhus

8

STORTORGET

SÖDERGATAN

2

Saluhall

LILLA TORGET

Form Design Centre

GUSTAV ADOLFS TORG

Forex

TORGGATAN

Cemetery

CARLSGATAN

SKEPPSBRON

HJALMARE KAJEN

NORDENSKIÖLDSGATAN

i

Forex

CENTRAL PLAN

HAMNGATAN

MÄSTER JOHANSGATAN

City Youth Hostel

GRÅBRÖDERSGATAN

3

1

6

4

10

9

5

7

Kungsparken

Slottsparken

Library

Malmöhus

Kommendanthus

Technical & Maritime Museum

Canal

BANERKAJEN

MARIEDALSVÄGEN

FERSENSVÄG

KUNG OSCARS VÄG

REGEMENTSGATAN

SLOTTSGATAN

HOTELS

1 Astoria   6 Pallas
2 Balzar   7 Royal
3 City Hotel Anglais   8 Savoy
4 Kramer   9 Temperance
5 Marina Park   10 Tuneln

N

0   250m

through to Linköping. The frequent local Pågatåg trains to and from Helsingborg/Lund and Ystad use platforms 9–13 at the back. To get to the square outside, Centralplan, site of the main **bus terminal**, either walk through the station or use the exit marked *Lokal stationen*. Frequent buses to and from Lund, Kastrup airport (in Denmark), Kristianstad/Kalmar and Ystad all stop here. Buses from Stockholm, Helsingborg and Gothenburg arrive at **Slussplan**, east of the station, just over Slussbron at the end of Norra Vallgatan. From Sturup **airport**, to the east of Malmö, take an hourly *Flygbuss* into the city centre (Mon–Fri 5.30am–7.30pm, Sat 6.30am–5.30pm; 40min; 60kr). The other possible arrival point is the **Dragør–Limhamn car ferry**, 3km west of the city (see p.475). Bus #82 runs from here up Strandgatan and right up to Central Station. The *Intercitybuss* #999 (Mon–Sat 4 daily 8.30am–5.35pm; 2 on Sun) leaves from Norra Vallgatan via Limhamn and Dragør to Copenhagen's Central Station (50kr).

Information and discount cards

The **tourist office** (June–Aug Mon–Fri 9am–8pm, Sat 9am–5pm, Sun 10am–5pm; Sept–May Mon–Fri 9am–5pm, Sat 9.30am–2pm; ☎040/30 01 50; fax 23 55 20) is inside Central Station. Here you can pick up a wealth of free information, including several good maps and an events and listings brochure, *Malmö This Month*. You can also buy the very useful **Malmö Card** (*Malmökortet*; available for 1, 2 or 3 days; 175kr for a 3-day card), which gives free museum entry, car parking, a guided bus tour and up to eight bus journeys, plus various other discounts on transport, cinemas, concerts and trips around the city. It's also worth considering the two-day **Öresund Runt** (Round the Öresund; 145kr), a ticket that covers any route (or part of it) by ferry, train and hydrofoil to Lund, Helsingborg, Helsingør and across to Copenhagen. There are *Forex* **money exchanges** just opposite the tourist office in Central Station (daily 8am–9pm), on Norra Vägen 60 (7am–9pm) and Gustav Adolfs Torg (9am–7pm).

City transport

Although the city centre is easy to walk around, you'll need to use **buses** to reach some of the sights and some accommodation. Individual tickets cost 12kr and are valid for an hour; a 100kr magnetic card reduces bus fares and can be used by several people at the same time. All tickets are sold on the bus. If you want to use **taxis**, it's worth comparing rates, but for a rough idea of costs: Malmö centre to the airport costs 225kr, Central Station to the soccer stadium 65kr, and to the Limhamm ferry 80kr. A one-hour guided **sightseeing tour** (11am & 1pm; 80kr; free with Malmö Card) leaves from the tourist office, but it's pretty slow-going as it's conducted in Swedish, English and German. Alternatively, you can do your own guided tour on city bus #20, which also leaves from outside the tourist office, where you can buy a brochure pointing out areas of interest for 12kr (several buses an hour; bus ride and brochure free with Malmö Card).

Accommodation

There are some excellent and surprisingly affordable **hotels** in Malmö; the city is eager to attract tourists and competition among hotels can be fierce. Also the tourist office sells a **Malmö Package**, providing visitors with a double room in a central hotel with breakfast and a Malmö Card thrown in. The scheme – along the lines of those in Stockholm and Gothenburg – runs from June to late August, and weekends only for the rest of the year; costs range from 365kr to 650kr per person, depending on the hotel. While it's a good deal, the usual summer reductions at many non-participating hotels may prove even better value. All the hotels listed below participate in the scheme, except for *Hotel Pallas*.

Malmö has two **youth hostels**. The central *City Youth Hostel*, Västergatan 9, is student accommodation let out as a hostel over summer (☎/fax 040/23 56 40; June–Aug; single rooms 125kr, dorms 100kr); it's friendlier and more convenient than the *STF* hostel at Backavägen 18 (☎040/822 20; closed mid-Dec to mid-Jan; 100kr), 5km from the city centre and right by the E6 motorway. To get to the latter, take bus #21A from Centralplan to Vandrarhemmet, cross over the junction past the traffic lights and take first right; the hostel is signposted to the left. The nearest **campsite**, *Camping Sibbarps* at Strandgatan 101 in Limhamn (☎040/34 26 50; all year), is currently in a picturesque spot; however, a controversial new bridge to Copenhagen is being built nearby.

Hotels

Astoria, Gråbrödersgatan 7, a few minutes from the train station across the canal (☎040/786 60; fax 788 70). Recently upgraded, this is a good, plain hotel. ②/③

Balzar, Södergatan 20 (☎040/720 05; fax 23 63 75). Very central hotel between the two main squares. A swanky, traditional place, not remotely Swedish in style. ②/④

City Hotel Anglais, Stortorget 15 (☎040/714 50; fax 611 32 74). A grand, turn-of-the-century hotel in the best central position. Recently renovated and with tasteful rooms. ②/④

Kramer, Stortorget 7 (☎040/20 88 00; fax 12 69 41). Beautiful white-stuccoed, turreted hotel from the 1870s, once Malmö's top hotel. Very luxurious. ③/⑤

Marina Park, Citadellvagen (☎040/23 96 05; fax 30 39 68). Five minutes' walk to the right from the train station, towards Malmöhus. Comfortable, pleasant interior behind a 1950s apartment tower facade. Price includes a good breakfast and free parking. ②

Pallas, Norra Vallgatan 74 (☎040/611 5077; fax 97 99 00). Despite its ornate exterior, this is a rather tatty place. Sami price all year; breakfast 30kr. ①

Royal, Norra Vallgatan 94 (☎040/97 63 03; fax 12 77 12). Small, family-run hotel just up from the train station. Price includes breakfast served in the garden. ②/③

Savoy, Norra Vallgatan 62 (☎040/702 30; fax 97 85 51). No longer prohibitively priced, this is the essence of style, with splendid furnishings and excellent Swedish and international food served in the historical elegance of the *Savoy Dining Rooms*. Attached is the *Bishop's Arms* pub. ③/④

Temperance, Engelbrektsgatan 16 (☎040/710 20; fax 30 44 06). Pleasant central hotel; price includes sauna, solarium and a big buffet breakfast. ②/③

Tuneln, Adelgatan 4 (☎040/10 16 20; fax 10 16 25). The finest small hotel in Malmö and very central. Dating from the Middle Ages, it's beautifully furnished. No summer reduction but discounts at weekends. ③

The City

Standing outside the nineteenth-century train station with its opulent curly-topped pillars and ornate red-brick arches, the **canal** in front of you, dug by Russian prisoners, forms a rough rectangle encompassing the **old town** directly to the south and the moated **castle** to the west, surrounded by a series of lovely and interconnecting parks. First off, though, head down Hamngatan to the main square. On the way you'll pass the striking sculpture of a twisted revolver, a monument to non-violence, that stands outside the grand former Malmö Exchange building from the 1890s.

The old town

Stortorget, the proud main square, necessitated the tearing down of much of Malmö's medieval centre when it was laid out in the mid-sixteenth century. Among the square's elaborate sixteenth- to nineteenth-century buildings, the 1546-built **Rådhus** draws the most attention. A pageant of architectural fiddling and crowded with statuary, restoration programmes last century robbed the building of its original design, leaving the finicky exterior in Dutch Renaissance style. It's impressive, nonetheless, and to add to the pomp, the red and gold Scånian flag, of which Malmö is so proud, hangs from the eaves. There are occasional tours of the interior; check with the tourist office. The cellars, home to *Rådhus Källaven Restaurant* (see "Cafés and restaurants"), have been used as a tavern for more than four hundred years.

On the opposite side of the square, the crumbling, step-gabled red-brick building was once the home of sixteenth-century mayor and Master of the Danish Mint, Jörgen Kocks. Danish coins were struck in Malmö on the site of the present Malmöhus castle (see below), until irate local Swedes stormed the building and destroyed it in 1534. In the cellars here you'll find the *Kockska Krogan* restaurant, the only part accessible to visitors. In the centre of the square, a statue of Karl X, high on his charger, presides over the city he liberated from centuries of Danish rule.

Head a block east, behind the Rådhus, to reach the Gothic **St Petri kyrka** on Göran Olsgatan (Mon–Fri 8am–6pm, Sat 9am–6pm, Sun 10am–6pm), dark and forbidding on the outside but light and airy within. The church has its roots in the fourteenth century, and, although Baltic in inspiration, the final style owes much to German influences, for it was beneath its unusually lofty and elegantly vaulted roof that the German community came to pray – probably for the continuation of the "sea silver", the herrings that brought them to Malmö in the first place. The ecclesiastical vandalism of whitewashing over medieval roof murals started early at St Petri, almost the whole interior turned white in 1553; consequently your eyes are drawn to the two most impressive items: the pulpit and a four-tiered altarpiece, both of striking workmanship and elaborate embellishment. The only part of the church left with its original artwork was a side chapel, the **Krämare Chapel** (from the entrance, turn left and left again). Added to the church in the late fifteenth century as the Lady Chapel, at the Reformation it was considered redundant and sealed off, thus protecting the paintings from the zealous brushes of the reformers. Best preserved are the paintings on the vaulted ceiling, depicting mainly New Testament figures surrounded by decorative foliage, while underfoot the chapel floor is a chessboard of tombs in black, white and red stone.

Södergatan, Malmö's main pedestrianized shopping street, leads south of Stortorget down towards the canal. At the Stortorget end, there's a jaunty troupe of sculptured bronze musicians; further down a collection of lively cafés and restaurants. On the corner of the square, take a peak inside **Apoteket Lejonet**. Gargoyled and balconied on the outside, the pharmacy interior is a busy mix of inlaid woods, carvings and etched glass.

Despite the size of Stortorget, it still proved too small to suffice as the sole main square, so in the sixteenth century **Lilla Torg**, formerly marshland, was sewn on to the southeast corner. Looking like a film set, this little square with its creaky old half-timbered houses, flowerpots and cobbles, is everyone's favourite part of the city. During the day, people congregate here to take a leisurely drink in one of the many bars and wander around the summer jewellery stalls. At night, Lilla Torg explodes in a frenzy of activity, people from all over the city converging on the square.

Walk through an arch on Lilla Torg and you'll reach the **Form Design Centre**, housed in a seventeenth-century grain store. Celebrating Swedish design in textiles, ceramics and furniture, its contents are rather less ambitious than you'd expect. From the turn of the century until the 1960s, the whole of Lilla Torg was a covered market, and the sole vestige of those days, **Saluhallen**, is diagonally opposite the Design Centre. Mostly made up of specialist fine food shops, *Saluhallen* makes for a pleasant, cool retreat on a hot afternoon.

A few streets away but well worth a visit if you're interested in contemporary art is **Rooseum** (Tues–Sun 11am–5pm, guided tours Sat & Sun 2pm; 30kr, free with Malmö Card) on Stora Nygatan. Space is imaginatively used in this elaborate building from 1900, originally constructed to house the Malmö Electricity Company's steam turbines. The main turbine hall forms the central gallery, displaying experimental installations and interesting photographic works. There's also a fine little café here (see p.474).

Malmöhus and around

Take any of the streets running west from Stortorget or Lilla Torg and you soon come up against the edge of **Kungsparken**, within striking distance of the fifteenth-century castle, **Malmöhus** (Tues–Sun June–Aug 10am–4pm; Sept–May noon–4pm; 40kr, free with Malmö Card). For a more head-on approach, walk west (away from the station) up Citadellsvägen; from here the low castle with its grassy ramparts and two circular keeps is straight ahead over the wide moat.

Originally Denmark's mint, the building was destroyed by the Swedes in 1534. Two years later, a new fortress was rebuilt on the site by the Danish King Christian III, only to be of unforeseen benefit to his enemies who, once back in control of Skåne, used it to repel an attacking Danish army in 1677. Serving as a prison for a time (the Earl of Bothwell, Mary Queen of Scots' third husband, its most notable inmate), the castle's importance waned once back in Swedish hands, and it was used for grain storage until opening as a **museum** in 1937. Today, the large, modern complex obliterates views of most of the inner castle walls.

Passing swiftly through the natural history section – a taxidermal Noah's ark with no surprises – the most rewarding part of the museum is upstairs, where an ambitious series of furnished rooms take you from the mid-sixteenth-century Renaissance period through Baroque, Rococco, pastel-pale Gustavian and Neoclassical. A stylish interior from the Jugend (Art Nouveau) period is equally impressive, while other rooms feature Functionalist and post-Functionalist interiors. Just as interesting are the spartan but authentic interiors of the castle itself.

Just beyond the castle to the west along Malmöhusvagen is **Kommendanthuset** (Governor's House), containing a strange combination of military and toy museums. The military section is a fairly lifeless collection of neatly presented medals, rifles and swords, and the usual dummies sporting eighteenth- and nineteenth-century uniforms. The toy museum is more fun, the link between the two museums-in-one being a brigade of toy British soldiers. A little further west running off Malmöhusvagen is a tiny walkway, **Banerkajen**, lined with higgledy-piggledy fishing shacks, selling fresh and smoked fish; just beyond is the **Technical and Maritime Museum** (same times as Malmöhus; 15kr). The technical section has displays on transport, power and local industries (sugar, cement); while upstairs in the science section the main display is a model of Tycho Brahe's observatory on the island of Ven.

Once you've had your fill of museums, the castle **grounds** are good for a stroll, peppered with small lakes and an old windmill. The paths lead all the way down to Regementsgatan and the City Library in the southeastern corner of the park. You can continue walking through the greenery as far as Gustav Adolfs Torg by crossing Gamla Begravnings Platsen, a rather pretty graveyard.

Out from the centre

Tourists rarely head further south of the city than the canal banks that enclose the old town, yet with a few hours to spare, the areas around Amiralsgatan give an interesting insight into Malmö's mix of cultures. A few hundred metres down Amiralsgatan, the splendid copper-domed Moorish building standing out on Föreningsgatan is the restored **Malmö Synagogue**. Designed and built in 1894, the synagogue is decorated with concentric designs in blue and green glazed brick. Strict security measures mean that to see the unrenovated interior you have to telephone the Jewish Comunity offices (ask at the tourist office).

Back on Amiralsgatan, it's a ten-minute walk to **Folkespark**, a quiet garden area at the centre of which stands **Moriskan**, an odd, low building with Russian-style golden minarets topped with sickles. This is Sweden's oldest existing working people's park and was once the prize of the community. Now rather shabby, Folkespark contains a

basic amusement park, and the *Moriskan*, a ballroom. Both, however, are now privately owned, a far cry from the original aims of the park's Social Democratic founders,
carved busts of whom are dotted all over the park.

South of the park, the multicultural character of Malmö becomes apparent. Arabic,
Asian and Balkan *émigré* families predominate and strolling from the park's southern
exit down Möllevången to **Möllevångstorget**, you enter an area populated almost entirely by non-Swedes, with Arabic and Urdu the main languages. The vast Möllevångstorget
is a haven of cafés (see below) and exotic food shops, along with shops selling pure junk.

Along the beach to Limhamn
Separated from the city centre by the delightful **Öresund park**, Malmö's long stretch
of sandy beach reaches all the way to Limhamn, fringed by the Ribersborgs Recreation
Promenade. At the town end of the beach is the **Ribersborgs kallbadhuset** (mid-April
to mid-Sept Mon–Fri, bathhouse 8.30am–7pm, sauna from 11am, Sat & Sun bathhouse
8.30am–4pm, sauna from 9am; mid-Sept to mid-April Mon–Fri, for both noon–7pm, Sat
& Sun 9am–4pm; 28kr, 14kr with Malmö Card), a cold-water bathhouse with a sauna
and café. All the beaches along this stretch, known as the Golden Coast because of the
grand villas overlooking it, boast shallow water.

LIMHAMN (limestone harbour), 3km to the southwest of the city, has an unusual
history and one that will become very apparent if you're staying at the *Sibbarps* campsite or using the Limhamn car ferry to Dragør in Denmark. Once a quiet limestone
quarrying village, Limhamn was taken by storm by a local man with big ambitions
called Fredryk Berg. At the end of the nineteenth century, he had a train line built
between the village and Malmö, and, by winning the support and later affiliation of rival
firms, built up the huge cement works known first as Cementa and later as Euroc.
Heading down Limhamnsvägen (the road running parallel with the beach) to Limhamn
(or take bus #82), the island of **Ön** will come into view. Another of Berg's creations, he
had it built out of waste concrete, and on it constructed apartment houses for factory
workers and a couple of churches. A strongly religious man, he was fond of saying that
the two best things in life were making corporations and attending church, earning him
the nickname "Concrete Jesus".

Eating, drinking and entertainment

Most of Malmö's **eating places** are concentrated in and around its three central
squares (Lilla Torg attracting the biggest crowds). By day, several cafés serve good
lunches and sumptuous cakes; at night, although the range of cuisines isn't that wide,
there are a couple of top places to eat, notably the Italian *Spot Restaurant*. If you want a
change of scene, head south of the centre to Möllenvångstorget, the heart of Malmö's
immigrant community, for cheaper eats and a very un-Swedish atmosphere.
Alternatively, to cut costs, Saluhallen, at the corner of Lilla Torg, is an excellent indoor
market with a few specialist food shops.

Cafés and restaurants
Bageri Café Saluhallen, corner of Lilla Torg. Excellent bagels, baguettes, pies and health foods –
with outside eating, too.

Bro's Jazz Café, Södra Vallgatan 3 (by the canal south of Gustav Adolfs Torg). Good-value, filling
sandwiches named after jazz greats. Patronized by a young, friendly crowd. Open till 1am.

Cyber Space Café, Engelbrektsgatan 13, just east of Stortorget. Stylish, blue-painted internet café,
where you can surf the net while sipping coffee and eating baguettes and pastries. All drinks 10kr.
Half an hour's surfing costs 20kr. Daily 2–10pm.

Café Europa, Södergatan 1. Set in a splendid red-stone building and serving a good à la carte lunch
menu for 55–70kr.

Espresso Rooseum, Gasverksgatan 22. Superb chocolate cake is dished up here in the contemporary art museum. A giant generator takes up most of the room, with seats around the edge. Closed Mon.

Golden Restaurant, corner of Södra Parkgatan and Simrishamnsgatan, to the south of the city. In the main immigrant area, this spartan place serves cheap crêpes, pizza and kebabs.

Gustav Adolfs, Gustav Adolfs Torg. Popular spot, open late at weekends, serving coffee (18kr) in a grand, white-stuccoed building with seating outside. Also a morning coffee and snacks menu.

Conditori Hollandia, Södra Förstadsgatan (south of the canal at Drottninggatan). Traditional, pricey konditori with a window full of melting chocolate fondants.

Johan P. Fish Restaurant, Saluhallen (also accessed from Landbygatan). Understated black and white check decor, with fairly pricey fish dishes on offer.

Kockska Krogan, corner of Stortorget and Suellgatan (☎040/703 20). A very fine old cellar restaurant – but rather overpriced – in the former home of Malmö's sixteenth-century mayor, Jörgen Kock. Closed Sun.

Pelles Café, Tegelgårdsgatan 5. Simple café in a quaint period house, serving huge cheap baguettes and playing jolly, dated music. Outside seating too.

Rådhus Källaven, beneath the town hall on Stortorget. In this gloriously decorative building main dishes cost 200kr, but there's a daily economy meal at 65kr that's well cooked and beautifully served. Outside eating in summer.

Rinaldo's, Saluhallen (also accessed from Landbygatan). Big, fresh rainbow-coloured salads and some wicked desserts.

Spot Restaurant, Stora Nygatan 33 (☎040/12 02 03). Chic Italian restaurant with attached charcuterie. All ingredients imported direct from Italy. During the day, light meals based on ciabatta and panini breads are served. There's an evening menu of fish, cheese and meats. Not too expensive, this is a really great place to eat. Mon 9am–6pm, Tues–Sat 9am–midnight.

Bars

Lilla Torg is the place to go in the evenings. The square buzzes with activity, as the smell of beer wafts between the old, beamed houses, and music and chatter fill the air. It's largely a young crowd, and the atmosphere is like a summer carnival – yellow-jacketed bouncers keep the throng from suffocating. It doesn't make a huge difference which of the six or so bars that you go for – expect to wait for a seat – but as a basic pointer, *Mellow Yellow* is for the 25-plus age group, *Moosehead* is for a younger crowd, and *Victors* even younger and more boisterous, although all are fun. On Möllenvångstorget, south of the centre in the immigrant quarter, *Pub 27* is a popular, laid-back place to drink.

Music and festivals

It used to be that the only entertainment in Malmö was watching rich drunks become poor drunks at the blackjack table in the station bar. Now, if you know where to look, there are some decent **live music** venues and **discos**. The best venues are the very popular *Haket Bistro*, at the *Hotel Temperance*, Engelbrektsgatan, where live music – jazz, salsa or reggae – can be heard from Thursday to Sunday; and *Matssons Musikpub*, Göran Olsgatan 1, behind the Rådhus, which puts on a variety of Scandinavian R&B and rock bands (nightly 9.30pm–2am). Check out *Malmö This Month* for the latest nightclubs and what's on information.

Classical music performances take place at the Concert Hall, Föreningsgatan 35 (☎040/34 35 00; two for the price of one with Malmö Card), home of the Malmö Symphony Orchestra, and at *Musikhögskolan*, Ystadvägen 25 (☎040/19 22 00); check with the tourist office for programme details. Malmö has two annual **festivals** of differing appeal. The **Folkfesten**, held in Kungsparken near Malmöhus in early June, is a sort of mini-Woodstock, devoted to progressive and classic rock. A far more all-encompassing event is the **Malmö Festival** in August, which mainly takes place in Stortorget. Huge tables are set out and cray fish tails are served (free), revellers bringing their own drinks. In Gustav Adolfs Torg, stalls are set up by the immigrant communities, with Pakistani, Sumali and Bosnian goodies and dance shows; meanwhile, rowing competitions take place on the canal.

Listings

Airlines *British Airways*, Sturup airport (☎020/78 11 44); *Finnair*, Baltzarsgatan 31 (☎020/78 11 00); *KLM*, Sturup airport (☎020/50 05 30); *Lufthansa*, Gustav Adolfs Torg 12 (☎040/717 10); *SAS*, Baltzarsgatan 18 (☎040/35 72 00); for airport buses information, see p.469.

Buses From Centralplan to Lund (#130), Kristianstad/Kalmar (#805) and Ystad (#330). From Norra Vallgatan, an *Intercitybuss* (#999; 50kr) runs to Copenhagen via the Limhamn–Dragør ferry.

Car rental *Avis*, Skeppsbron 13 (☎040/778 30); *Budget*, Baltzarsgatan 21 (☎040/775 75); *Europcar*, Mäster Nilsgatan 22 (☎040/38 02 40); *Hertz*, Jorgenkocksgatan 1B (☎040/749 55).

Consulate British Consulate at Gustav Adolfs Torg 8c (☎040/611 55 25).

Doctor On call daily 7am–10pm; ☎040/33 35 00; at other times ☎040/33 10 00.

Exchange Best rates are at *Forex*, Norra Vallgatan 60 (June–Aug daily 8am–7pm), Gustav Adolfs Torg 12 (shorter hours), and at the train station (same hours); or try the Central Station post office (Mon–Fri 8am–6pm, Sat 9.30am–1pm).

Ferries and catamarans *Flygbåtarna*, Skeppsbron (catamaran: 85kr one-way to Copenhagen, 50 percent discount with Malmö Card; ☎040/10 39 30); *SAS*, Skeppsbron (hovercraft to Kastrup airport: 475kr one-way; ☎040/35 71 00); *Scandlines* Limhamn–Dragør ferry crossing (35kr one-way; car plus passengers 350kr one-way; ☎040/16 20 70); *Pilen* catamaran to Copenhagen (29kr one-way; ☎040/23 44 11).

Pharmacy 24-hour service at *Apoteket Gripen*, Bergsgatan 48.

Post office Skeppsbron 1 (Mon–Fri 8am–6pm, Sat 9.30am–1pm).

Soccer Malmö FF is Sweden's only professional soccer club, league champions on several occasions and former finalists in the European Cup. They play at Malmö Stadium, John Erikssons väg; bus #20 from the centre; tickets from around 60kr (info on ☎040/34 26 81).

STF Hiking and youth hostel information from an office inside the post office.

Swimming Adventure pool at *Aq-va-kul*, Regementsgatan 24 (Mon noon–9pm, Tues–Fri 9am–9pm, Sat 9am–6pm, Sun 10am–6pm; 10kr); beaches and pools in Sibbarp near Limhamn (bus #11A; May–Aug Mon–Fri 8am–7pm, Sat & Sun 8am–4pm).

Taxis *City Cabs* ☎040/71 000; *Limhamn taxi* ☎040/13 00 00.

Telephone office *Televerket*, Storgatan 23 (Mon–Fri 8am–9pm, Sat 9.30am–3pm).

Trains Pågatåg information office inside the *Lokalstationen* (Mon–Fri 7am–6pm, Sat 8am–3pm, Sun 9am–3pm).

Southeastern Skåne: the coast to Ystad

The local **Pågatåg train** and the E6 and E14 highways cut directly east towards Ystad, missing out some picturesque, minor resorts and a couple of the region's best beaches, along Sweden's most southwesterly tip. If you have time to explore, and particularly if you have your own transport, this quieter part of the south makes for a delightful few days' exploration. Thirty kilometres south of Malmö (by car or bus #150), you cross an expanse of heathland to which birdwatchers flock every autumn to spot nesting plovers and terns, as well as millions of migratory birds fleeing the Arctic for the Stevns peninsula, south of Copenhagen.

Skanör and Falsterbro

A few kilometres on, at the fan-shaped southwest tip of the country, lie the seaside resorts of Skanör and Falsterbro. Crossing a canal that was dug by Swedes during the last war to provide a transport alternative to occupied Danish coastal waters, you arrive in the early-medieval town of **SKANÖR**, a Hanseatic centre founded to take advantage of the abundance of herring off this stretch of the coast. In the first years of this century, Skanör and its neighbour Falsterbro (see below) became fashionable bathing resorts for rich Malmö families and, although both have since gone in and out of vogue, they are once again desirable destinations for much the same set. There's not much to see in Skanör but its beaches are superb: long ribbons of white sand bordering an extensive bird and nature reserve. From the beach, you can see across the reserve to Skanör's church, half medieval, half High Gothic. Once the herring had moved on to waters new in the sixteenth century, the church never received its intended updates, making it all the more appealing. From the little harbour, it's a pleasant walk to the town square and the lovely old cottages lining Mellangatan. If you want to **stay** – and the beach is worth it – *Hotell Gässlingen* (☎040/47 30 35; fax 47 51 81; Sept–April ④, weekends outside summer ③) at Rådhustorget 6, is a lovely, simple place. If you're **camping**, there are plenty of places to throw down a tent for free, though be careful to avoid the protected bird reserves.

FALSTERBRO, just 2km south, is also very picturesque, attracting Swedish yuppies in force. Along with its castle ruin, eighteenth-century lighthouse and church, it also boasts really fine beaches and is slightly livelier than Skanör. A couple of restaurants worth trying are *Kaptensgården* on Stadsalleyn, an elegant establishment with a garden terrace and occasional live jazz, and, just a few steps up the road, the new *Café Restaurant Allen*, where there's a happy hour noon to 5pm and an afternoon menu of light snacks.

Trelleborg

Following the south coast to the east, the rolling fields are punctuated by World War II concrete bunkers, some now converted into unlikely looking summer houses. Approaching **TRELLEBORG** by bus from Malmö (35min), a curtain of low-level industry blocks the sea – although this won't bother you too much if you're taking one of the ferries over to the German towns of Rostock, Sassnitz or Travemünde. Yet behind the graceless factories, this is a busy little town, its main attractions an inspired reconstruction of a recently discovered Viking fortress and a gallery of works by the sculptor Axel Ebbe.

From the ferry terminals on the seafront, walk up Kontinengatan, past the tourist office (see below), which supplies a good free leaflet, entitled *A Couple of Hours in Trelleborg* in recognition of how long most people stay. A few minutes' further on is the **Axel Ebbe Gallery** in a compact, 1930s Functionalist building that was once the local bank. Ebbe's superb sculptures make for a powerful collection of sensual nudes, all larger than life and in black or white stone. At the turn of the century, Ebbe's gently erotic work was celebrated in Paris, though when his graceful, sprawling *Atlas's Daughter* was unveiled in Copenhagen, it caused an outcry. A few steps into the **Stadsparken**, opposite, is Trelleborg's main square, dominated by Ebbe's *Sea Monster*, a fountain comprising a serpentine fiend intertwined with a characteristically sensual mermaid.

The main shopping promenade, **Algatan**, runs parallel with the seafront, and walking up from the ferry terminal you'll soon come to **St Nicolai's kyrka**, which has some bright ceiling paintings, elaborate sepulchral tablets, and monks' chairs from a Franciscan monastery destroyed during the Reformation. A couple of minutes' stroll from here is Trelleborg's most dramatic new attraction, the **Trelle Fortress** (open all year; free), a much more impressive run-through of local Viking life than the town museum at Östergatan 58. Surrounded by a moat, the original circular fortress, dating from around 980 AD, was built by King Harald Blue Tooth around a seventh-century settlement of pit houses, and is composed entirely of earth and wood. Archeologists have made comparisons with four almost identical forts in Denmark and, using a certain amount of guesswork, have constructed an impressive replica.

Practicalities

The **train station** is close to the ferry terminal; three trains a day run from Malmö to Trelleborg, timed to connect with the Sassnitz ferry, but there are hourly **buses**, stopping at the bus terminal behind the main square. **Ferry** departures to Germany are daily and pretty regular – check "Travel details" at the end of the chapter for schedules.

The **tourist office**, just off Kontinengatan at Hamngatan 4 (mid-June to mid-Aug Mon–Fri 9am–8pm, Sat 9am–6pm, Sun 1–6pm; rest of the year Mon to Fri 9am–5pm; ☎0410/533 22; fax 134 86), is tucked in behind a hot-dog stand, but boasts its own pleasant café, *Garvaregården*. If you do want to **stay**, they can book **private rooms** for 130kr plus a 35kr booking fee. The cheap *Hotel Standard*, Österbrogatan 4 (☎0410/104 38; fax 71 18 66; ①), is central and somewhat shabby, though better than its entrance suggests. At the other end of the spectrum, *Hotel Dannegården*, Standgatan 32 (☎0410/71 11 20; fax 170 76; ③/⑤), is a beautiful 1910 villa surrounded by scented bushes, with just five double rooms in original Art Nouveau style. Even if you don't stay here, it's the finest place for a romantic, though pricey, meal (closed July). Otherwise, there are a couple of reasonable **cafés** on Algatan: *Billings* and *Palmblads*.

Smygehamn and Smygehuk

Around a third of the way from Trelleborg to Ystad along coastal route 9 (bus #183), the hamlet of Smygehamn prides itself on being Sweden's most southerly point. Half a kilometre before you reach this tiny harbour village, neighbouring **SMYGEHUK** has little to it except a particularly cosy **youth hostel** (see below), among a group of old wooden houses clustered around a nineteenth-century **lighthouse**. Walk through the flowers and nettles along the coast and you'll soon reach **SMYGEHAMN**, less than a kilometre away – it's not much more than a tiny harbour surrounded by a few summertime restaurants, a café and a smoked-fish shop. The harbour itself was built out of a limestone quarry, and lime burning was big business here from Smygehamn's heyday in the mid-nineteenth century right up until the 1950s. Lime kilns are still dotted all around, odd, igloo-like structures with cupola roofs. Back from the harbour, Axel Ebbe's *The Embrace* is a good example of his Romantic style – a female nude rises up from the scrubland, embracing the elements.

Smygehuk's **tourist office** occupies a fine, early nineteenth-century corn warehouse by the harbour (June–Aug daily 10am–6pm; ☎0410/240 53), and can book **private rooms** from just 90kr per person, plus 35kr booking fee. The **youth hostel** (see above; ☎0410/245 83; fax 245 09; mid-May to mid-Sept; 100kr) is in the lighthouse keeper's house. The nearest **hotels** are in Trelleborg, 13km away, but *Smygehus Havsbad*, an old bathing house (☎0410/243 90; fax 293 43) just 500m away, has four-bed cabins for 850kr, including breakfast. There's a **restaurant**, sauna and swimming pool here too.

Ystad

An hour by Pågatåg train from Malmö, the medieval market town of **YSTAD** is exquisitely well preserved, with a core of quaint cobbled lanes lined with cross-timbered cottages and a central square oozing rural charm. With the stunningly beautiful coastal region of Österlen stretching northwest from town in the direction of Kristianstad (see p.482) and some excellent walking to the north of town (see p.479), Ystad is a splendid place to base yourself for a day or so. It is also the departure point for **ferries** to the Danish island of Bornholm and to Poland.

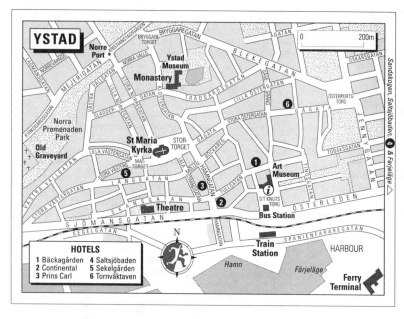

Arrival, information and accommodation

From the **train station**, cross the tracks to St Knuts Torg, where the **tourist office** (mid-June to mid-Aug Mon–Fri 9am–7pm, Sat 11am–7pm, Sun 1–7pm; rest of the year Mon–Fri 9am–5pm; ☎0411/772 79; fax 55 55 85) is next door to the art gallery. St Knuts Torg is also where **buses** from Lund (#X300), Kristianstad (*Skåne Express*) and Simrishamn (#572) will drop you off, and where buses leave for destinations along the coast and into the rest of Skåne. However, there's no bus service from Malmö: either take a Pågatåg train or bus #183 from Trelleborg/Smygehamn to Skateholm and then bus #330 to Ystad; to get to Kristianstad by train, you need to return to Malmö and take the inland train. The **ferry** terminal is behind the train station, signposted "Till Färjorna" – turn left and walk for ten minutes along the quayside. Tickets **to Poland** cost from 220kr one-way (9hr crossing), or you can buy a four-day return for 420kr. One-way tickets and day returns to Bornholm costs 135kr (2hr 30min). **Cycling** is a great way to see the surrounding landscape and bikes can be rented from the tourist office (60kr per day, 300kr per week).

There are several good and reasonably priced **hotels** in town and one at the beach. The **youth hostel** is on the beach at Sandskogen (☎0411/665 66; all year; 95kr), served by buses #572 and #304, but it's only open to groups from September to May. There is a neighbouring **campsite** (mid-April to mid-Sept; ☎0411/192 70) with cabins for rent (from 110kr per person).

Hotels

Bäckagården, Bäckagården 36 (☎0411/198 48; fax 757 15). More a guesthouse than hotel, in a converted home just behind the tourist office. ②

Continental, Hamngatan 13 (☎0411/137 00; fax 332 21). Classic hotel touted as Sweden's oldest, with a grand lobby of marble, Corinthian pillars and crystal chandeliers. Rooms are Italian-style modern, and breakfast is a treat. ③/④

Prins Carl, Hamngatan 8 (☎0411/737 50; fax 665 30). A mid-range place with rooms reserved for non-smokers, others adapted for people with disabilities or allergies. ②/③

Saltsjöbaden, Saltsjöbadsvägen 6 (☎0411/136 30; fax 55 58 30). Renowned for its beach-side position, just east of town, this large, 100-year-old hotel has endless modern corridors tacked on. Sauna and summer-only pool; restaurant in the original saltwater bathing house. ③/④

Sekelgården, Stora Västergatan 9 (☎0411/739 00; fax 189 97). Charming, small family-run hotel in a former merchant's house from 1793. Friendly and informal, with a cobbled courtyard flower garden. En-suite rooms in both the main house and the old tannery at the back. Excellent breakfast. ②/③

Tornväktaven, Stora Östergatan 33 (☎0411/129 54; fax 729 27). Plain and cheap, with breakfast buffet included, this is a reasonable choice if *Sekelgården* is full. No summer reduction. ②

The Town

Turning left from the station and ferry terminals, then right up Hamngatan, brings you to the well-proportioned **Stortorget**, a grand old square encircled by picturesque streets. The **St Maria kyrka** is a handsome centrepiece, with additions from nearly every century since it was begun in the thirteenth century. In the 1880s, changing tastes saw many of the rich decorative features removed, and only the most interesting ones were returned during a restoration programme forty years later. Inside, the early seventeenth-century Baroque pulpit is worth a look for the fearsome face carved beneath it and, opposite, the somewhat chilling medieval crucifix, which was placed here on the orders of Karl XII to remind the preacher of Christ's suffering.

If you stay in Ystad, you'll soon become acquainted with a tradition that harks back to the seventeenth century: from a room in the church's watchtower, a night watchman blows a haunting tune on a bugle every fifteen minutes from 9.15pm to 3am, as a safeguard against the outbreak of fire. The idea was that if one of the thatched cottages went up in flames, the bugle would sound repeatedly for all to go and help extinguish the blaze. The sounding through the night was to assure the town that the watchman was still awake; until the mid-nineteenth century, if he slept on duty he was liable to be executed.

From Stortorget, it's a short stroll up Garvaregränd, past art and craft workshops, and on up Klostergatan to **Ystadbygdens Museum** (Mon–Fri 11am–6pm, Wed till 8pm, Sat & Sun noon–4pm; 30kr). Set in the thirteenth-century Gråbröder (Greyfriars) Monastery, it contains the usual local history collections, given piquancy here by their preserved medieval surroundings. After the monks were driven out during the Reformation, the monastery was at various times a hospital, a poorhouse, a distillery and finally a dump. A decision to demolish it in 1901 was overturned, and today it's definitely worth a visit.

If you want to explore more of the old town, it's still possible to find your way around using a city map from 1753, copies of which are supplied by the tourist office. Not far from the church on the western side of town, **Norra Promenaden**, a strip of mature horse chestnut trees and parkland, is good for a stroll. Here you'll find *Café*

WALKING AROUND YSTAD

The forested lake region 20km north of Ystad provides plenty of hiking possibilities, either along organized trails, or in undeveloped tracts where you can camp rough. Take any bus north in the direction of **Sjöbo** (by car take Route 13), and you'll link with the **Skåneleden** ("Long Trail"), which follows a hundred-kilometre circular route from just outside Ystad. The tourist office (see above) can provide route plans as well as details on where to find places to eat and stay along the way. You can also head north on foot from Ystad to Hedeskoga and then follow trails along a chain of forest-fringed **lakes** – Krageholmsjön, Ellestadssjön and Snogeholmssjön – up to Sövdesjön (a 20-km hike).

Promenaden (also see "Eating, drinking and nightlife"), a white pavilion built in the 1870s to house a genteel café and dance hall.

Eating, drinking and nightlife

There is a fair selection of places to eat in Ystad, including some atmopsheric **cafés** and fine **restaurants**, most of the latter on Stortorget. To start the day, the *Continental* serves a huge **breakfast buffet** (Mon–Fri 7–10am, Sat & Sun 8–10.30am; 60kr), ideal if you've just come off a morning ferry. Aside from the restaurant-bar *Prince Charles Pub* (see below), **nightlife** is pretty minimal – the only trendy club being *Starshine* at Osterportstorg, east from Stortorget (follow Stora Östergatan, on some maps labelled as Gågatan, meaning pedestrianized street). Otherwise, locals tend to take a bus thirty minutes north to **Tingballa**, where there are a couple of dance halls.

Cafés, restaurants and pubs

Café Promenaden, in Norra Promenaden, north of the centre. An excellent café and a good restaurant, specializing in salmon, with 52kr lunches and evening meals for 70–90kr. June–Aug 11am–10pm.

The English Book Café, on Gäsegränd. Down a tiny, cobbled street off Stora Östergatan, inside this precariously leaning wooden house it's all old English china and books to read while you feast on home-baked scones and tea. The gardens are delightful too.

Lotta's, on Stortorget. The most (justifiably) popular restaurant in town, packed each evening in summer. Closed Sat & Sun.

Prince Charles Pub, Hamngatan next door to the *Prins Carl Hotel*. English-style pub and restaurant serving meat and fish dishes in the evenings, with live music on Fri and Sat nights.

Rådhuskälleren, in the cellars of the Rådhus. Rather more sedate than *Lotta's* opposite, with candle-lit lunch (55kr) and dinners (200kr) in a 700-year-old prison; service can be less than convivial. Closed Sun.

Österlen and the coast to Åhus

It's easy to see how the landscape of the southeastern corner of Skåne, known as **Österlen**, has lured writers and artists to its coastline and plains. Here sun-burst yellow fields of rape stand out against a cobalt-blue sky, punctuated only by white cottages, blood-red poppy fields and the odd black windmill. Along with the vivid beauty of the countryside, Österlen has a number of engaging sights, notably the Viking ruin **Ales Stennar**, pretty villages and plenty of sandy beaches. Moving further northeast are the orchards of Sweden's apple region, centred on **Kivik**, while **Åhus**, a low-key resort famous for smoked eels, ends this stretch of the coast.

Unfortunely, **getting around** this part of the country isn't easy, the only major road, Route 9 to Kristianstad via Simrishamn, cutting off the main corner of Österlen. The whole area is poorly served by buses and the only train service is the Pågatåg train from Ystad to Simrishamn: if you haven't got a car, you'll need to do some walking and cycling to make the most of this part of Sweden.

Ales Stennar

Twenty kilometres out of Ystad, near the hamlet of Kåseberga, is the Viking site of **Ales Stennar**. An awe-inspiring Swedish Stone Henge, it is believed to have been a Viking meeting place and consists of 56 stones forming a 67-metre-long boat-shaped edifice, the prow and stern denoted by two appreciably larger monoliths. The site was hidden for centuries beneath shifting sands, which only cleared in 1958. Buried several metres into the sand, it's difficult to imagine how these great stones, not native to the region, were transported here. Ales Stennar stands on a windy, flat-topped hill, and despite the inevitable tourists snapping away at the ancient site (most of whom don't bother to climb up), there's a magestic timelessness at the top that more than rewards your climb.

There are two ways to get to Ales Stennar from Ystad: either take the infrequent **bus** #322 (20min) or rent a **bike** and follow the coastal cycle track through pine forests and past white sandy beaches, following the signs to Kåseberga.

Simrishamn

There's not much to the little fishing town of **SIMRISHAMN**, around 40km from Ystad, although its old quarter of fondant-coloured tiny cottages and its church, orginally built as a twelfth-century fisherman's chapel, are certainly pretty enough. The unexceptional **museum** nearby is full of the usual archeological finds, alongside bits and pieces of farm and fishing equipment. You may want to come here, however, for the summer **catamaran** service to the Danish island of **Bornholm** (see "Travel details"). *Hotell Kockska Garden*, Sturgatan 25 (☎0414/41 17 55; fax 41 19 78; ③), is a comfortable **accommodation** option, housed in a renovated tavern. For **bike rental**, ask at the **tourist office**, Tulhusgatan 2 (mid-June to mid-Aug Mon–Fri 9am–8pm, Sat noon–8pm, Sun 2–8pm; rest of the year Mon–Fri 9am–5pm; ☎0414/41 06 66).

Kivik

Around 20km north from Simrishamn, halfway to Åhus on the coastal road, you'll enter the endless orchards of Sweden's apple-growing region, **Kivik**. The village of **KIVIK** itself has no real centre, but buses stop outside the *Kivik Vardhus* hotel (see below). The uncommercialized harbour is just a few minutes away down Södergatan, and within a couple of kilometres are a number of sights.

Sweden's most notable Bronze Age cairn, **Kungsgraven** (May–Aug daily 10am–6pm; 10kr), is just 500m from the bus stop. A striking 75-metre upturned saucer of rocks, it lay hidden until discovered by a farmer in 1748. At its centre, the burial chamber is entered by a banked entrance passage, and inside are eight floodlit 3000-year-old runic slabs showing pictures of horses, a sleigh and what looks like dancing seals.

Two kilometres from the grave, beyond hilly orchards (follow the signs), is the **Kiviksmusteri** cider factory and the entertaining new **Apple House** (daily 9am–6pm; tours 40kr), an apple museum where each room is infused with a different smell: the room devoted to great apples in history smells of cider, while a room detailing attempts to create an insect-resistant apple summons up apple pie. Other, wackier exhibitions focus on topics such as the symphonic soul of apples. Just 200m beyond the Apple House, **Stenshuvuds National Park** is a perfect place to come back to reality. At almost 100m high, the top of this hill laced with walking trails affords superb views. Self-guided walking tours lead around remnants of an ancient fortress, while there are special wheelchair-accessible paths through the forested hillsides.

Frequent *Skåne Express* **buses** to and from Simrishamn (30min) and Kristianstad (55min) stop outside the *Kivik Vardhus* farmhouse **hotel** (June–Aug; 0414/70074; fax 710 20; ②) and restaurant. For cheaper accommodation, the *STF* **youth hostel** lies in its own attractive gardens on Tittutvägen, north of the harbour, just five minutes' walk from the bus stop (☎711 95; all year; 100kr). For exploring the region further, **bikes** can be rented at the harbourside in midsummer for 75kr a day.

Åhus

Once a major trading port, and in medieval times a city of considerable ecclesiastical importance, **ÅHUS**, 55km north of Simrishamn, today relies on holidaying Swedes for its income. The town is famed for its eels, which appear on menus all over the country, smoked and usually served with scrambled eggs. From the tourist office (see below), it's a short walk up Köpmannagatan to the beautiful old cobbled main square. The twelfth-century **St Maria kyrka**, behind the old Rådhus that houses the town's unexceptional **museum**, is wonderfully preserved, its sheer size attesting to the town's former eminence. However, it's one of the gravestones in the churchyard that really raises the eyebrows: take a look at the headstone of Captain Måns Mauritsson, between the church and the museum. According to the inscription, the captain's wife, Helena Sjöström, was 133 years old when she died, and her daughters were born when she was 82 and 95 respectively. At nearby Västerport (walk to the end of Västergatan from the centre) the **Tobaksmonopolets Lada** (free entry) holds displays of tobacco labels and all the paraphernalia of tobacco processing. For 250 years every garden in Åhus had its own tobacco patch, until the government cancelled its contract with the growers in 1964.

Beyond this, there's little more to do than cut through from the main square down Västra Hamngatan to the waterside, where small pleasure yachts line the harbour, a pretty spot if you avert your eyes from the industrial hinterland to the left. For the **beach**, head out on Järnvägsgatan, behind the tourist office, past a run of old train carriages – there are no trains running now – and left up Ellegatan following signs for **Åhus Strand**.

Practicalities

Unless you're driving, it's easiest to get to Åhus on bus #551 from Kristianstad, 20km to the northwest (see below) – the bus stops outside the **tourist office** at Köpmannagatan 2 (June–Aug Mon–Fri 9am–7pm, Sat 9am–6pm, Sun 2–6pm; Sept–May Mon–Fri 9am–5pm; ☎044/24 01 06; fax 24 38 98). The **youth hostel** (☎044/24 85 35; book through tourist office Sept–May; 100kr) is at Stavgatan 3, just a few metres away. Alternatively, stay on the bus a few minutes longer to get to the beach, where there are plenty of hotels and a **campsite** in the nearby forest (☎044/24 89 69; all year). *Hotel Åhus Strand* (☎044/28 93 00; fax 24 94 80; ②) is a reasonable, if plain choice among the beach hotels. There's a **bike rental** shop on Ellegatan (on the way to the beach) that also rents out double-pedalled buggy bikes at 40kr per hour.

There are some lovely **places to eat** in Åhus. Down by the harbour, the genteel *Gästgivaregård* specializes in Baltic fish dishes at lunchtime, but for the most enjoyable and relaxed dinner, walk 200m along the waterside to *Ostermans* (May–Sept) at Gamla Skeppsbron, a small wooden restaurant at the water's edge, serving just one item – Greenland prawns, bought by weight. Heading back up Västra Hamngatan, *Gallericaféet* (June–Aug) is a small art gallery and garden restaurant, which again specializes in local seafood.

Kristianstad

Twenty kilometres inland, eminently likeable **KRISTIANSTAD** (for its correct pronunciation, try a gutteral "Krwi-chwan-sta") is eastern Skåne's most substantial historic centre – a Renaissance town created in 1614 by Christian IV, Denmark's seventeenth-century "builder-king". A shining example of the king's architectural preoccupations, with beautifully proportioned central squares and broad gridded streets flanking the wide river, it was only to remain in Danish hands for another 44 years.

Arrival, information and accommodation

Local **buses** from Ystad (1hr 30min), Simrishamn (1hr 30min) and Åhus (30min) all stop outside the central bus station on Östra Boulevarden, although the quickest way here is by **train** (1hr 16min from Malmö) on the ultra-comfortable Danish-built *Kustpilen Express* between Malmö and Karlskrona. The **tourist office** (June–Aug

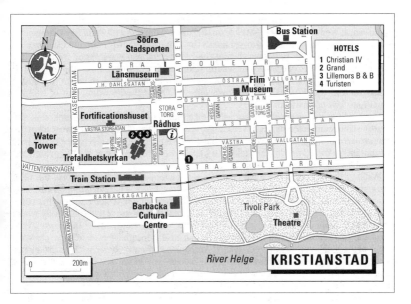

Mon–Fri 9am–8pm, Sat 9am–5pm, Sun 2–6pm; Sept–May Mon–Fri 10am–6pm; ☎044/12 19 88; fax 12 08 98) on Nya Boulevarden displays a list of **private rooms** from 125kr on its door, and can book them for you for a 40kr fee. There is a **campsite** with attached **youth hostel** at *Charlottsborg Camping* (☎044/21 07 67; all year; 100kr), 2km away (bus #22 or #23; Fri & Sat nights bus #17 to Vä from Busstorget, close to Lilla Torget).

All but one of Kristianstad's **hotels** are side by side, just a few steps from the train station. The cheapest is the very comfortable old *Hotel Turisten*, Västra Storgatan 17 (☎044/12 61 50; ①/③), some of whose rooms have bathtubs; alongside at no. 17 is the cosy *Lillemors B&B* (☎044/21 95 25, mobile 070/521 68 00; ②), built in the 1790s. At no. 15 the modern *Grand Hotel* (☎044/10 36 00; fax 12 57 82; ②/⑤) offers friendly service and supremely comfortable beds. The most glamorous place to spend the night, though, is *Hotel Christian IV*, Västra Boulevarden 15 (☎044/12 63 00; fax 12 41 40; ③/⑤). A grand, castle-like confection built at the turn of the century in the old *Sparbank* building, its beautifully renovated features include original fireplaces and parquet floors.

The Town

The most obvious starting point is the **Trefaldighetskyrkan** (Holy Trinity Church; daily 9am–5pm), right opposite the train station, which stands as a symbol of all that was glorious about Christian's Renaissance ideas. The grandiose exterior has seven magnificent spiralled gables, and the high windows allow light to flood the white interior. Diagonally across from the church, the main square, **Storatorg**, hosts the late nineteenth-century **Rådhus**, itself an imitation of Christian's Renaissance design. Inside the entrance, a bronze copy of the king's 1643 bust is something of a revelation, with Christian sporting a goatee beard, one earring and a single dreadlock, his one exposed nipple decorated with a flower motif. Back outside in the square, Palle Pernevi's splintered *Icarus* fountain depicts the unfortunate Greek soul falling from heaven into a scaffolded building site.

North of Storatorg on Östra Boulevarden is the **Länsmuseum** (June–Aug Mon–Fri 10am–5pm, Wed till 8pm; Sept–May Mon–Fri noon–5pm, Wed till 8pm; free), housed in a building that was begun as a royal palace by Christian in 1616, but soon became an arsenal for the Danish partisans during the bloody Scånian wars. Aside from the historical exhibits, there are some interesting textile and art collections on the top floor. If you've time on your hands, it's a pleasant stroll behind the museum to **Södra Stadsporten**, the 1790s southern town gate on Östra Boulevarden, one of the few remaining bits of fortification.

For a panoramic overview of both the town and the local lakes of Hammarsjön and Aradövssjön, connected by the River Helge, walk just a couple of minutes west from the main square to the **water tower** (Mon–Sat 10am–6pm, Sun noon–6pm; free). You take a small lift up the 42 floors (the stairs are kept locked) to the café at the top, which has wall maps to help with orientation.

Walking back through the town centre, a few minutes east of the Storatorg, the **Film Museum**, Östra Storgatan 53 (Tues–Fri & Sun 1–4pm; free), is heralded by a bronze early movie camera outside the door. This was once Sweden's first film studio, where the country's earliest movies were recorded between 1909 and 1911; some of these flickering works are now viewable on videotape inside. From here, wander down any of the roads to the right and you'll reach **Tivoli Park**, where you can stroll beneath avenues of horse chestnut trees; at the park's centre is a green-pained Art Nouveau **theatre**, designed by Kristianstad-born Axel Anderberg, who also created the Stockholm Opera (see p.387). **Sightseeing boats** (*Vattenriket*) splash their way between Kristianstad and Åhus from behind the theatre (June–Aug 3 daily; 65kr, book at the tourist office). At the northern edge of Tivoli Park, there's an art gallery showing temporary exhibitions and housing the **Barbacka Cultural Centre**, which gives information about musical events around the town.

Eating, drinking and entertainment

Kristianstad has a number of really good, stylish and fun places to eat. Of the **cafés**, best are *Fornstuga House*, an elaborately carved Hansel-and-Gretel lodge in the middle of Tivoli Park, and the more central konditori *Du Vanders*, Hesslegatan 6; at *Grafitti Café*, Västra Storgatan 45, you can fill up cheaply on baked potatoes at lunchtime. For fuller meals, *Restaurant Klipper* on Östra Storgatan is an atmospheric cellar restaurant specializing in pricey steaks and the like. Nearby, *Restaurant Roma*, Östra Storgatan 15, is an inexpensive Italian restaurant serving big pizzas at 65kr. The two trendiest eating places, owned by the same people, are the kitsch *Godsfikan,* in the station building (book for Fri or Sat: ☎044/11 05 20), and the more upmarket *Westermanns* on Tivoligatan, serving fine, European-style food.

For a central **drinking** place, check out the 250 or so beers at the *Stänken Pub and Steakhouse*, in the old *Riksbank* on Storatorg, or try the German-owned *Bitte Eine Bit* on Hesslegatan. *Harry's Bar*, Östra Storgatan, is a small and lively place with loud rock music. Kristianstad's hippest **nightclub** is undoubtedly *G Punkten*, upstairs from *Godsfikan* at the train station.

The town hosts two annual festivals: **Kristianstadsdagarna**, a huge seven-day cultural festival in the second week of July (during which the tourist office stays open till 10pm). The annual **Kristianstad and Åhus Jass Festival** runs around the same time, ask for details at the tourist office.

East into Blekinge

The county of **Blekinge** is something of a poor relation to Skåne in terms of tourism. Though tourist offices pump out endless glossy brochures describing the region as "the garden of Sweden", in reality there are some good beaches, plentiful fishing, some fine walking trails and enough cultural diversions to make Blekinge enjoyable for two or three days. The landscape is much the same as in northeastern Skåne: forests and hills with fields fringing the sea. There are, however, a number of islands and a small archipelago south of Karlskrona that are picturesque destinations for short boat trips. If you only have a day or two in the region, it's best to head to the handsome and lively town of **Karlskrona**, the county capital, from where the tiny, fortified hamlet of **Kristianopel** is just 30km away.

Public transport in Blekinge requires some careful timetable studying to avoid being stranded from early evening onwards. Most locals drive, and on weekend evenings there are likely to be no trains or buses between the towns. This fact is keenly observed by taxi drivers, who can charge as much as 250kr to take you between Ronneby and Karlshamn, while hitching is nigh on impossible here. The *Kustpilen Express* train runs from Malmö/Lund to Karlskrona and stops at all the towns detailed below.

Karlshamn

An hour's train ride from either Kristianstad or Karlskrona (see p.487), **KARLSHAMN** is a rewarding goal for a day's exploration. After a disastrous fire in 1763, wealthy merchants continued to build ever more grand houses for themselves as replacements, and some are still standing. The town saw its heyday in the nineteenth century, when it manufactured such goodies as punch, brandy and tobacco. Today, margarine and ice-cream factories flank the harbour, but don't be put off, Karlshamn also has some beautiful little streets of pastel-painted houses, a clutch of museums and, within easy reach, some offshore islands that offer a wooded retreat and clean-water swimming.

From the train station, turn left onto Eric Dahlbergsvägen, and right down Kyrkogatan, which is lined with old, wooden houses painted pale yoghurt shades. **Karl Gustav kyrka**, an unusual late seventeeth-century church, squats at the junction with Drottininggatan. Walking down this street you are retracing the steps of many nineteenth-century emigrants on their way to "New Sweden" in America. The town's **museums** (10kr covers them all) are all close together at the other end of Drottininggatan, at the junction with Vinkelgatan; best of the bunch is **Skottsbergska Gården**, on Drottininggatan (Mon–Fri 10am–5pm; free), an amazingly well-preserved eighteenth-century merchant's house that was inhabited up until the 1940s. On the ground floor, the kitchen is furnished in eighteenth-century style, with an enormous open fireplace, while upstairs there's some splendid Gustavian decoration and wardrobes stuffed with ancient clothes.

On the corner, the **Museum of Local History** (June–Aug Tues–Sun noon–5pm; rest of the year Sat & Sun only) contains usual range of domestic and marine exhibits; more interesting are the various buildings out through the old courtyard, where among the authentic interiors there's a tobacco-processing works. Finally, if you've time on your hands, choose the **Punch Museum** (June–Aug Tues–Sun noon–5pm) over the gallery in the same warehouse at Vinkelgatan 9. It's an intriguing place, displaying the workings of Karlshamn Flaggpunch, the factory that blended this potent mixture of sugar, arrak and brandy, until it was forced to close down in 1917.

Practicalities

A short walk from the station, the harbourside **tourist office** is on the corner of Ågatan and Ronnebygatan (mid-June to mid-Aug Mon–Fri 9am–8pm, Sat 10am–2pm & 5–8pm, Sun noon–7pm; rest of the year Mon–Fri 9am–5pm; ☎0454/165 95; fax 842 45) and will book **private rooms** (100kr per person plus 40kr booking fee) and **cottages** (850kr per week for 2) anywhere in the region. The squeaky new *STF* **youth hostel** sits next to the train station at Surbrunnsvägen 1c (☎0454/140 10; May–Sept; 100kr). The nearest campsite (May–Sept; ☎0454/812 10) is by the sea at **Kollevik**, 3km out of town; take bus #312 from the train station or Stortorget. Of the central **hotels**, the cheapest is the *Bode Hotel,* Södra Fogdelyckegatan (☎0454/315 00; ①); the *Hotel Carlshamn,* Varvsgatan 1 (☎0454/890 00; fax 891 50; ②/④), by the harbour, is the luxury option.

Karlshamn has an extraordinarily good **vegetarian restaurant**, *Gourmet Grön* at Drottninggatan 61 (Mon–Fri 11.30am–3pm & 6–1am, Sat noon–3pm), serving a gourmet buffet with as much as you can eat for a remarkable 50kr during the day, 100kr in the evening. There's an Italian menu, too, and superb homemade desserts. Alternatively, you can sit outside at the *Terrassen Restaurant,* Ronnebygatan 12, to eat a wide range of fish and meat dishes.

The laid-back but dated annual **rock festival**, staged on the west bank of the river at Bellvue Park, occurs in mid-June, when the streets become littered with inebriated revellers. In the third week of July, the **Baltic Festival** is far bigger, an impressive, all-consuming town celebration with plenty of drinking and merriment.

Ronneby

Much of **RONNEBY** has been destroyed by development and, arriving by train, even the summer sun can't improve the view of banal buildings ahead. There is, however, a tiny **old town**, a few minutes' walk up the hill to the left, testament to the fact that in the thirteenth century this was Blekinge's biggest town, trading with the Hanseatic League. Only when the county became Swedish four centuries later did Ronneby fall behind neighbouring Karlskrona. Today, the main attraction is the beautifully preserved collection of spa houses, a couple of kilometres over the river at **Ronneby Brunnspark** (see below).

In the town itself, walk up hill to the left of the train station, and turn left again onto the main street, Kungsgatan. There is nothing much of interest here until you reach **Helga Korskyrkan** (Church of the Holy Cross). With its whitewashed walls, blocked-in arched windows and red-tiled roof, the church looks like a Greek chapel presiding over the surrounding modern apartment buildings. Dating originally from the twelfth century, this Romanesque church took quite a bashing during the Seven Years' War (1563–70) against the Danes. On the night of what is known as the **Ronneby Blood Bath** in September 1564, all those who had taken refuge in the church were slaughtered – you can still see the gashes in the heavy oak door in the north wall that were made during the violence.

In 1775 the waters here were found to be exploitably rich in iron, and Ronneby soon became one of Sweden's principal spa towns, centred on **Ronneby Brunnspark**. Just fifteen minutes' walk from the train station up the hill and over the river (or take bus #211), the park's houses stand proudly amid blazing rhododendrons and azalias. One such property is now a fine *STF* youth hostel (see below), with the wonderful café-bar **Wiener Café** next door. There are pleasant **walks** through the beautifully kept park, past a duck pond, and into the wooded hills behind, picking up part of the **Blekingeleden** walking trail. Also through the trees are some unexpected gardens. On summer Sunday mornings the park is the site of a giant **flea market**, selling genuine Swedish antiques alongside general tat.

Practicalities

From Karlshamn, there are frequent **train** and **bus** services to Ronneby. The **tourist office** (June–Aug Mon–Fri 9am–7pm, Sat 10am–4pm, Sun noon–4pm; Sept–May Mon, Wed & Fri 9am–5pm, Tues & Thurs 9am–7pm; ☎0457/176 50; fax 174 44) is in the Kulturcentrum, close to the church in the tiny old town. Without a doubt the best place to stay is at the *STF* **youth hostel** (☎/fax 0457/263 00; closed Dec to early Jan; 100kr) in Ronneby Brunnspark, whose owners also run the inaptly named *Grand Hotel* (☎0457/268 80; fax 268 84; ②) in a modern apartment building opposite the train station at Järnvägsgatan 11. Less central is *Strandgården*, Nedre Brunnsvägen 25 (①), a small, family-run pension near the youth hostel.

For **eating and drinking** in town, try *Nya Wienerbageriet* on Västra Torgatan, off the main square, for filling lunches, including a daily pasta dish for 50kr. At the back is a stylish new **bar** (Thurs–Sat 7pm till late) with occasional live music. Just off Stortorget is the best konditori, the *Continenta*. There are also a few places near the station: *Restaurant & Pub Piaff,* on Karlskronagatan, is an established pizza restaurant, with outside tables; a few steps away is an intimate, traditional pub, *Jojjes Pub Bar*; though *Wiener Café* in Ronneby Brunnspark is the most popular place to drink.

Karlskrona

Blekinge's most appealing destination, **KARLSKRONA** is the regal county capital, located on the largest link in a chain of breezy islands. Founded by Karl XI in 1680, who picked it as an ice-free southern harbour for his Baltic fleet, everything about the town today revolves around its maritime heritage. The wide avenues and stately squares were built to accommodate the king's naval parades, and cadets in uniform still career around streets named after Swedish admirals and battleships. However, even if you're not a naval fan, Karlskrona has plenty to offer, particularly the picturesque old quarter

around the once-busy fishing port at Fisktorget and some short cruises around the islands in the archipelago; however, due to military restrictions no bathing is allowed on them (there's good swimming off the nearby island of **Dragsö** or at the fine bath-house in town).

Arriving by **train** or **bus**, you'll pass the island of **Hästö**, once home to Karlskrona's wealthiest residents, before arriving a few minutes later in the town centre on **Trossö**, connected to the mainland by the Österleden main road. Climb uphill past Hoglands Park to the main square, **Stortorget**, at the highest point and geographical centre of the island. It's a vast and beautiful square, dominated by two complementary **churches**, both designed by Tessin the Younger and stuccoed in burnt orange with dove-grey stone colonnades. **Fredrikskyrkan** (Mon–Fri 11am–3pm, Sat 9.30am–2pm) is elegant enough, but the interior of the circular domed **Trefaldighetskyrkan** (Mon–Fri 11am–3pm, Sat 9.30am–2pm; guided tours on request) holds more interest. Built for the town's German merchant community in 1709, the domed ceiling is its most remarkable feature, painted with hundreds of rosettes and brilliantly shaded to look three-dimensional. The altar is also distinctive, golden angelic faces peering out of a gilded meringue of clouds.

Head between the churches, down the wide, cobbled Södra Kungsgatan, which is divided down the centre by the walls of a tunnel that once carried trains between the station and the harbour. The leafy square ahead is **Amiralitets Torget** and perched at its centre is the huge, peeling wooden bell tower of the **Admiralty Church.** To get to the church itself, head down Vallgatan on the left of the square and the beautifully proportioned wooden church is up on your right. Built in 1685, it's the oldest entirely wooden church in Sweden. Outside the entrance, take a look at one of the city's best-known landmarks: the wooden statue of **Rosenbom**, a local beggar who one night forgot to raise his hat to thank the wealthy German figurehead carver, Fritz Kolbe. When admonished for this, Rosenbom retorted, "If you want thanks for your crumbs to the poor, you can take my hat off yourself!". Enraged, Kolbe struck him between the eyes and sent him away, but the beggar froze stiff and died in a snow drift by the church. Next morning, Kolbe found the beggar's body and, filled with remorse, carved a figure of Rosenbom to stand at the spot where he died, designing it so that you have to raise his hat yourself to give some money.

Follow Vallgatan down to the waterside and you'll come to the Aspö ferry terminal, where boats leave for the **Maritime Museum** on Stumholm Island, next to a new art gallery (check opening times and price at the tourist office). Among its vast and graphic collections, the most striking include ship figureheads and a few intriguing items in a display on naval punishment.

For more of a feel of old Karlskrona, wander west past the military hardware towards the **Björkholmen** area. Here a couple of tiny wooden early eighteenth-century houses in little gardens survive, homes that the first craftsmen at the then new naval yard built for themselves. Nearby **Fisktorget**, originally the site of a fish market, is pleasant for a stroll, though nowadays the boats around here are likely to be pleasure yachts; this is the terminal for boat and river trips. The dull **Blekinge Museum** on Fisktorget (Mon–Fri 10am–4pm, Sat & Sun 11am–4pm; free) is worth a visit for the pleasant summertime café rather than the exhibits on shipbuilding and the like.

Practicalities

Karlskrona's **tourist office** (June & Aug Mon–Fri 10am–6pm, Sat 10am–2pm; July Mon–Fri 10am–7pm, Sat 10am–4pm, Sun noon–6pm; Sept–May Mon–Fri 10am–5pm; ☎0455/834 90; fax 822 55) is in the library just off Stortorget. You can book **private rooms** here for around 125kr per person and rent cheap, green military **bikes** for 25kr a day. As usual, the cheapest bed is to be had in the *STF* **youth hostel**, centrally located at Bredgatan 16 (☎0455/834 81; mid-June to mid-Aug; 100kr). The nearest **camping** is out on Dragsö island (☎0455/153 54), around 2.5km away: take bus #7 from the bus station to Saltö, from where it's a ten-minute walk. Most appealing of the modern **hotels** is the *Hotel Carlskrona*, on Skeppsbrokajen at Fisktorget (☎0455/196 30; fax 259 90; ②/④); or there's the traditional 1890-built *Statt Hotel* (☎0455/192 50; fax 169 09; ②/④) on the main street at Ronnebygatan 37–39. If those are out of your range, *Hotel Conrad* on Västra Köpmangatan (☎0455/823 35; ①/②), halfway up the hill towards Stortorget, is plain and reasonable, while the *Hotel Aston*, Landbrogatan 1 (☎0455/194 70; ①/②), is more central.

Most of the town's **konditori** are indistinguishable, two exceptions being the pleasant *Café Tre G* on Landbrogatan, opposite Hoglands Park, which serves baked potatoes, cakes and sandwiches, and *Systrarna Lindkvists Café*, Borgmästaregatan 3, across from the tourist office. The majority of Karlskrona's **restaurants** are along central Ronnebygatan. Best of the bunch is the Italian-style *Ristorante Il Divino* at no. 29; a few metres up, *Red Light* serves kebabs and light meals. A more unusual setting for a meal is the *Old Water Works*, between the big churches on Stortorget, which does Greek food. The most popular summer **pub** is *Jolen*, Norra Kungsgatan 1, with outside terrace drinking; the rest of the year, locals go to the *Kings Crown* on Stortorget.

Ferries to Gdynia in Poland depart from the ferry terminal once daily (10hr 30min); daytime tickets cost 320kr return and 180kr one-way, night-time 410kr and 230kr.

Kristianopel

Arriving by road at **KRISTIANOPEL**, 30km northeast of Karlskrona, there is not the slightest hint that this idyllic village of just 38 inhabitants was once a strategic fortification with a bloody history; if you're here outside July, you'd also be amazed to know that the place bursts with up to two thousand holidaymakers at that time, contributing to a sense of revelry seldom found in the rest of Sweden.

It's only when you've walked past the minute, untouched cottages in their tumbling gardens and all the way to the tiny harbour that you spot the two kilometres of three-metre-thick **fortification walls** that surround the settlement. A 1970s reconstruction, they were built over the original fortifications erected in 1600 by Danish King Christian IV to protect against Swedish aggression. The walls were finally raised by the Swedes after the little town had spent 77 years changing hands with alarming regularity. There is little in the way of specific sights in Kristianopel, the only building worth a brief look being the **church**, near the village shop; inside is an eye-catching altar, decorated with vividly drawn trees. It's a replacement for a medieval church that burnt to the ground in 1605, killing all the village women, children and elderly, who were huddled inside for protection. Today, it's just a grassy mound near the campsite.

Practicalities

Getting to Kristianopel is tricky by public transport. **Bus** #120 from Karlskrona (to Kalmar) only runs along the main E22, stopping at Fågelmara, 6km from the village; from September, bus #122 from Karlskrona goes all the way to the village. Alternatively **bikes** rented in Karlskrona can be taken on the #120 bus at no extra cost, and **hitching** is easier here than in most places.

For accommodation in the village you are limited to the **youth hostel/campsite** (☎/fax 0455/661 30; all year; tents & caravans only; hostel 85kr), tucked inside the low walls overlooking the sea, or the one **hotel**, a simple eighteenth-century farmhouse called *Gästgiferi* (☎/fax 0455/660 30; April–Sept; ①), to the left of the main road into the village. At the campsite you can rent a **rowing boat** (10kr per hour, 50kr per day).

There are three **restaurants** in the village, at the hotel and hostel/campsite. Just by the campsite, the basic and wooden *Värdshuset Pålsgården* serves basic food and opens late every night in July as a pub. A few minutes away, *Restaurant Sjöstugan* is a slightly more upmarket pizza restaurant, with glorious views over to the nearest islands. If you want to cook for yourself there are a couple of shops on the campsite, and another near the church (Mon–Fri 9am–6pm, Sat & Sun 9.30am–noon).

Every July, the two campsite restaurants are the focus for a wide range of **music** and **night-time entertainment**, ranging from Country and Western to Eurovision Song Contest favourites, blues, jazz and rock'n'roll.

travel details

Express trains

Daily express trains operate throughout the region, in particular **Oslo–Copenhagan** (via Gothenburg, Varberg, Halmstad and Helsingborg) and **Stockholm–Copenhagen** (via Helsingborg). Both routes have a branch service through to Malmö. Despite complicated timetabling, the service is frequent and regular north or south between Gothenburg and Helsingborg/Malmö.

Trains

From Helsingborg to: Gothenburg (11 daily; 2hr 40min); Lund/Malmö (10–12 daily; 40–50min).

From Karlskrona to: Emmaboda for connections to Växjö, Stockholm & Kalmar (1–2 hourly; 40min).

From Kristianstad to: Karlshamn (hourly; 50min); Karlskrona (hourly; 1hr 50min); Ronneby (hourly; 1hr 20min).

From Malmö to: Gothenburg (8–10 daily; 3hr 45min); Hässleholm/Kristianstad (4 daily; 47min); Karlskrona (hourly; 3hr 15min); Lund (3 hourly; 13min); Ystad (Mon–Fri hourly, 5 on Sat & Sun; 50min).

Buses

From Ängelholm to: Torekov (3–5 daily; 45min).

From Båstad to: Torekov (5 daily; 30min).

From Helsingborg to: Båstad (4 daily; 55min); Halmstad (6 daily; 1hr 50min).

From Karlskrona to: Stockholm (Fri & Sun; 7hr 30min).

From Kristianstad to: Kalmar (1 daily; 3hr); Lund/Malmö (1 daily; 2hr 30min/2hr 45min).

From Malmö to: Gothenburg (Mon–Thurs 1 daily, 3 on Fri & Sun; 4hr 25min); Halmstad/Falkenberg/ Varberg (2 on Fri & Sun; 2hr 25min/2hr 55min/3hr 20min); Helsingborg (Mon–Thurs 1 daily, 6 on Fri & Sun; 1hr 5min); Jönköping (Mon–Thurs 1 daily, 3 on Fri & Sun; 4hr 30min); Kristianstad/Kalmar (1 daily; 2–5hr 30min); Lund (hourly; 20min); Mellbystrand (1 on Fri & Sun; 2hr); Stockholm (Mon–Thurs 1 daily, 3 on Fri & Sun; 9hr); Trelleborg (hourly; 35min).

From Ystad to: Kristianstad (Mon–Fri 5–6 daily, 3 on Sat & Sun; 1hr 55min); Lund (Mon–Fri 3 daily; 1hr 15min); Malmö (3 daily; 1hr); Simrishamn (Mon–Fri 3 daily, 1 on Sat & Sun; 50min); Smygehamn (Mon–Fri 5 daily, 2 on Sat & Sun; 30min).

International ferries, hydrofoils and catamarans

From Halmstad to: Grenå (2 daily; 4hr).

From Helsingborg to: Helsingør (3 hourly; 25min).

From Karlskrona to: Gdynia, Poland (1 daily; 10hr 30min).

From Limhamn (Malmö) to: Dragör (14–18 daily; 55min).

From Malmö to: Copenhagen (*Flygbåtarna* and *Pilen* hydrofoils hourly, 45min; *Shopping Linjen* hydrofoil 5 daily, 45min).

From Simrishamn to: Allinge on Bornholm (summer only catamaran 3–4 daily).

From Trelleborg to: Rostock (3 daily; 6hr); Sassnitz (5 daily; 3hr 45min); Travämunde (2 daily; 7–9hr).

From Varberg to: Grenå (2 daily; 4hr).

From Ystad to: Rönne on Bornholm (3–5 daily; 2hr 30min); Swinoujscie, Poland (2 daily; 7–9hr).

CHAPTER TWELVE

THE SOUTHEAST

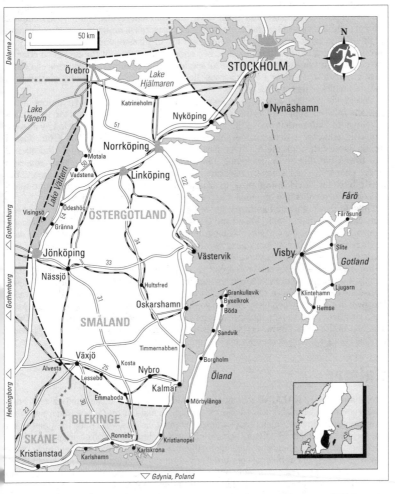

A lthough a less obvious target than the coastal cities and resorts of the southwest, Sweden's **southeast** certainly repays a visit. Impressive castles, ancient lakeside sites and numerous glass-making factories hidden amongst forests are some of the mainland attractions, while off the east coast, Sweden's largest

Baltic islands offer beautifully preserved medieval towns and fairy-tale landscapes. Train transport, especially between Stockholm and the towns close to the eastern shore of Lake Vättern, is good; speedy, regular services mean that you can even visit some places as day trips from Stockholm.

Småland county in the south encompasses a varied geography and some stridently different towns. The glorious historic fortress town of **Kalmar** is a worthwhile stop; it deserves more time than it it's usually given, being a jumping-off point for the island of Öland. Further inland, great swathes of dense forest are rescued from monotony by the many **glass factories** that continue the county's tradition of glass production, famous the world over for design and quality. By the mid-nineteenth century, agricultural reforms and a series of bad harvests in Småland saw mass emigration to America and in **Växjö**, the largest town in the south, the art of glass-making and the history of Swedish emigration are the subject of two superb museums. At the northern edge of the county, **Jönköping** is a great base for exploring the beautiful eastern shore of **Lake Vättern**; it's also worth venturing across the water to visit the island of **Visingsö**, rich with remnants of its royal history.

The idyllic pastoral landscape of **Östergotland** borders the eastern shores of the lake and reaches as far east as the Baltic. Popular with domestic tourists, the small lakeside town of **Vadstena** is one of the highlights, its medieval streets dwarfed by austere monastic edifices, a Renaissance palace and an imposing abbey. The **Göta Canal** wends its way through the northern part of the county to the Baltic and a number of fine towns line the route, including **Linköping**, with its unusual open-air museum where people live and work in a re-created nineteenth-century environment. Just to the north, bustling **Norrköping** grew up around the textile industry, a background that's preserved in a collection of handsome red-brick and stuccoed factories.

Outside the fragmented archipelagos of the east and west coasts, Sweden's only two true islands are in the Baltic: Öland and Gotland, adjacent slithers of land with unusually temperate climates. Though they've long been targets for domestic tourists, these days an increasing number of foreigners are discovering their charms – sun, beaches and some impressive historic (and prehistoric) sights. **Öland** – the smaller island and closer to the mainland – is less celebrated, but its mix of dark forest and flowering meadows makes it a tranquil spot for a few days' exploration. **Gotland** is known for its medieval Hanseatic capital, **Visby**, a stunning backdrop to the carnival atmosphere that pervades the town in summer, when ferry-loads of young Swedes come here to sunbathe and party – it's also one of the most popular places for Swedes to celebrate **Midsummer's Night**. The rest of the island, however, is little visited by tourists, and all the more worth while for that. Both islands are ideal for cycling, and it's easy to rent **bikes**.

Kalmar

Bright and breezy **KALMAR**, set among a huddle of islands at the southeastern edge of the county of Småland, has treasures enough to make it one of southern Sweden's most delightful towns – a fact that's missed by most visitors, who have their sights set on the Baltic island of Öland, separated from Kalmar by a six-kilometre bridge. Surrounded by fragments of ancient fortified walls, the seventeenth-century "**New Town**" is a mass of cobbled streets and lively squares, lined with some lovely old buildings, and within two minutes' walk of the train station is an exquisite fourteenth-century **castle**, scene of the Kalmar Union, which united Sweden, Norway and Denmark as a single kingdom in 1397, and now one of Scandinavia's finest preserved Renaissance palaces. Just a short walk in the other direction, there's a fascinating exhibition on the **Kronan**, one of the world's biggest warships, which sunk off Öland over three hundred years ago. Even now, new finds are being discovered, helping to piece together the world's most complete picture of seventeenth-century maritime life.

Arrival, information and accommodation

Kalmar's **tourist office** at Larmgatan 6, at the junction with Ölandsgatan (early June &
late Aug daily 9am–7pm; mid-June to mid-Aug daily 9am–9pm; Sept–May Mon–Fri
9am–5pm; ☎0480/153 50; fax 174 53), is within spitting distance of the **train station**
(several trains daily from Gothenburg and Stockholm) and **bus terminal**. Here you
can get a decent map of Kalmar; information on Öland is dealt with on the island itself.
Kalmar can be explored easily on foot, but if you want to strike out into the surrounding countryside, you can rent a **bike** from *Team Sportia*, Södravägen 2, or at the campsite, *Stensö Camping* (see below).

The tourist office arranges **private rooms** from 175kr per person, 250kr for a double, plus a 50kr booking fee. Other budget accommodation options include the **youth
hostel**, ten minutes' walk away at Rappegatan 1c (☎0480/129 28; fax 882 93; all year;
100kr), on the next island to the north, **Ängö**. Next door, *Hotel Svarnen* (①) is run by
the same staff. The nearest **camping** is on Stensö island, 3km from the centre, where
you can rent cheap cabins. Local buses head out this way – check details with the
tourist office. Kalmar boasts several attractive central **hotels**, such as the 1906-built
Stadshotel, Stortorget 14 (☎0480/151 80; fax 158 47; ②/⑤), and the castle-like
Frimurarehotellet on Larmtorget (☎0480/152 30; fax 858 87; ②/③).

Kalmar Slott

Beautifully set on its own island, a short way from the train and bus stations, the first stones of **Kalmar Slott** (May–Sept Mon–Sat 10am–5pm; rest of the year shorter hours; 30kr) were probably laid in the twelfth century. A century later, it became the most inpenetrable castle in Sweden under King Magnus Ladulås. The biggest event to take place within its walls was in 1397, when Danish Queen Margareta instigated the Union of Kalmar, which gave her sovereignty over all of Scandinavia. Subsequently the castle passed repeatedly between Sweden and Denmark, but despite eleven sieges, it remained almost unscathed. By the time Gustav Vasa became King of Sweden in 1523, Kalmar Slott was beginning to show signs of stress and strain, and the king set about rebuilding it, while his sons Eric XIV and Johan III took care of decorating the interior. Preserved in fantastic detail as a fine Renaissance palace, it well illustrates the Vasa family's concern to maintain Sweden's prestige in the eyes of foreign powers.

Today, if the castle doesn't appear to be defending anything in particular, this is due to a devastating fire in the 1640s, after which the town was moved to its present site on the island of Kvarnholmen – though the Old Town (Gamla Stan) beyond the castle still retains some winding old streets that are worth a look. Unlike many other southern Swedish castles, this one is storybook accurate: turrets, ramparts, a moat, drawbridge and a dungeon, with a fully furnished interior that's fascinating to wander through. Among the many highlights is King Johan's bedroom, known as the **Grey Hall**. His bed, which was stolen from Denmark, is decorated with carved faces on the posts, but all their noses have been chopped off – the guilty Johan believed that the nose contained the soul and didn't want the avenging souls of the rightful owners coming to haunt him. The **King's Chamber** (King Eric's bedroom) is the most intriguing room, with its wall frieze a riot of vividedly painted animals and a secret door allowing escape onto the roof should Eric be attacked by his younger brother Johan, who he believed wanted to kill him. This isn't as paranoid as it sounds, since Eric's death in 1569 is widely believed to have been caused by arsenic poisoning.

The rest of the town

Opposite the castle, Kalmar's **Konstmuseum** (June–Aug Mon–Fri 10am–5pm, Sat & Sun noon–5pm; Sept–May Mon–Fri 10am–5pm & 7–9pm, Sat & Sun noon–5pm; 30kr) displays changing exhibitions of contemporary art, with an emphasis on late 1940s and 50s Expressionism, and a first-floor exhibition devoted to chair design throughout the ages. The top floor contains one largish gallery of nineteenth- and twentieth-century Swedish nude and landscape paintings.

It's far better to head back into the elegantly gridded Renaissance New Town, which is laid out around the grand **Domkyrkan** (daily 9am–6pm) in Stortorget. Designed in

1660 by Nicodemus Tessin the Elder (as was the nearby Rådhus), after a visit to Rome, this vast and airy church in Italian Renassiance style is today a complete misnomer: Kalmar has no bishop and the church has no dome. Inside, the altar, designed by Tessin the Younger, shimmers with gold, as do the *Faith* and *Mercy* sculptures around it.

The Kronan Exhibition

Housed in a refurbished steam mill on Skeppsbrongatan, a few minutes' walk from the Domkyrkan, the awe-inspring **Kronan Exhibition** is the main attraction of the **Länsmuseum**, Kalmar's county museum (daily mid-June to mid-Aug 10am–6pm; rest of the year 10am–4pm; 40kr). The royal ship *Kronan*, built by the British Francis Sheldon, was one of the world's three largest ships, twice the size of the *Vasa*, which sank off Stockholm in 1628 (see p.392). Fully manned, the *Kronan* went down in 1676, blown apart by an explosion in its gunpowder magazine, and the lives of 800 of its 842 crew were lost, their bodies preserved for more than three hundred years on the Baltic sea bed.

It wasn't until 1980 that super-sensitive scanning equipment detected the where-abouts of the ship, 26m down off the coast of Öland. A salvage operation was led by a descendant of the ship's captain, Admiral Lorentz Creutz, and the amazing finds are displayed in an imaginative walk-through reconstruction of the gun decks and admiral's cabin, accompanied by sound effects of cannon fire and screeching gulls. While the ship's treasure trove of gold coins is displayed at the end of the exhibition, it's the incredibly well-preserved clothing – hats, jackets, buckled leather shoes and even silk bows and cuff links – that brings this exceptional show to life. Other rooms detail the political nature of the wars between the Swedes, Danes and Dutch at the time of the sinking.

Eating and drinking

There's a generous number of good places to **eat** in Kalmar. The liveliest night-time area is **Lärmtorget**, where restaurants, cafés and pubs serve Swedish, Indonesian, Chinese, Greek, Italian and English food. For daytime snacks try *Kullzenska caféet*, Kaggensgatan 26, a charming eighteenth-century **konditori**.

Restaurants and bars

Ernesto Spaghetti & Cocktail Bar, opposite *Krögers* on Lärmtorget. Serves a huge range of piz-zas (50–60kr) and pastas (55–75kr), as well as traditional Italian salads, antipasto and meat courses (120kr) in upmarket surroundings.

Ernesto Steakhouse, at the harbour. A glassy building similar in style to its Italian sister restau-rant, this one serves more substantial and expensive meat and fish meals. Daily lunch is reasonable, though, at 55kr.

Krögers on Lärmtorget. The most popular pub/restaurant, where a relaxed crowd eat light Swedish meals like *Kottbullesmörgäs* (meatball sandwiches; 40kr) or rather less Swedish fish and chips (66kr), plus meat dishes and pastas. There's live music every Sunday from September to April.

Lodbroks Café & Pub, entered from Norra Långgatan 20. The romantic dining room is sophisti-catedly rustic, with a short but unusual menu: try the speciality, fried anchovies and parsley with sour cream (32kr). A good-value breakfast is served 7am – 1pm (20kr).

Ming Palace, Fiskeragatan 7. The best Chinese restaurant in town, with a lunch special at 50–60kr. To find it, head towards the base of the castellated old water tower.

O'Keefe's, part of the *Stadshotel*. A pub with a good atmosphere.

Oscar Bar & Brasserie, on Lärmtorget. A pleasant Greek-inspired place serving a three-course meal for 99kr and pan pizzas for 60kr; there's also a well-stocked bar.

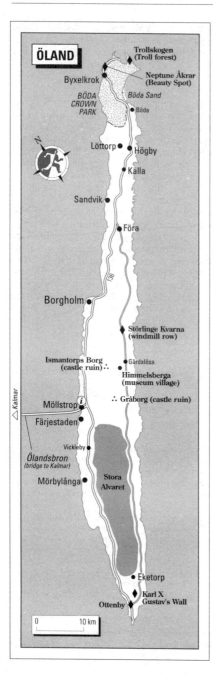

Öland

Linked to mainland Sweden by a six-kilometre bridge, the island of **Öland** is the kind of place a Swedish Famous Five would come on holiday: mysterious forests and flat, pretty meadows to cycle through, miles of mostly unspoilt beaches, wooden cottages with candy-striped canopies, windmills, and ice-cream parlours. Swedes have been coming here in droves for over a century, but since becoming popular with non-domestic tourists, it's now visited by 55,000 people every July and August. Despite this onslaught, which clogs the road from the bridge north to the main town, **Borgholm**, this long, splinter-shaped island retains a very likeable old-fashioned holiday atmosphere, with a labyrinth of **walking trails** and **bicycle routes** and some of the best bathing opportunities in Sweden.

A royal hunting ground from the mid-sixteenth century until 1801, Öland was ruled with scant regard for its native population. Peasants were forbidden from chopping wood or owning dogs or weapons, while Kalmar's tradesmen exploited the trade restrictions to force low prices for the islanders' produce. Danish attacks on Öland saw seven hundred farms destroyed, and following a succession of disastrous harvests in the mid-nineteenth century, a quarter of the population packed their bags for a new life in America. This century, Öland's young are just as likely to migrate to the Swedish mainland.

Today, Öland's attractions include numerous ruined castles and Bronze and Iron Age burial cairns, runic stones and forts, all set amid rich and varied fauna and flora and striking geography. To the south is a massive limestone plain known as the **Alvaret**, whose thin covering of soil is pierced by tiny flowers in summer. In central Öland, the Ice Age left the limestone more hidden and the area is blanketed with forest, while to the north, the coastline is craggy and irregular with dramatic-looking *rauker* – stone pillars, weathered by the waves into jagged shapes.

Getting to the island

If you're **driving**, take the Ängö link road to Svinö (clearly signposted), just outside Kalmar, which takes you over the bridge to Möllstorp on Öland. **Cycling** over the bridge is forbidden, but there's a free bus from Svinö especially for bikes, which drops you off outside the island's main tourist office in Möllstorp. If you're **hitching**, you can try your luck with the free bus, too, as the bridge has no footpath. **Bus** timetables change with the seasons, but buses #101 and #106 are safe bets, running almost hourly from Kalmar bus station to Borgholm (50min), less regularly in the evenings. Buses also run to Färjestaden, hub of the island's bus network, a couple of kilometres south of Möllstorp.

There are two **ferry** services to Öland. The more popular car ferry takes you from **Oskarshamn**, 80km north of Kalmar, to Byxelkrok (in north Öland) twice a day at 1.30am and 5.30pm (2hr; 120kr one-way, 160kr return; car & driver 190kr, car & passengers 490kr; bikes 40kr). A passenger-only ferry also runs frequently from **Timmerrabben**, 40km north of Kalmar, to Borgholm (70kr one-way; bikes 30kr).

Information and getting around

Öland's main **tourist office** is in a large pink building in **Möllstorp**, next to the end of the bridge (April & May Mon–Fri 9am–6pm, Sat 10am–5pm, Sun 10am–4pm; June, Aug & Sept Mon–Fri 9am–7pm, Sat 10am–6pm, Sun 10am–4pm; July Mon–Sat 9am–7pm, Sun 10am–6pm; Oct–March Mon–Fri 9am–5pm; ☎0485/39 90 20; fax 390 10). Pick up a bus timetable and the *Ölands Karten* (49kr), an excellent if costly map. While you're at the tourist office, pop into the nature centre, *Naturum*, where a twenty-metre model of the island lights up to show all the areas of interest.

It's worth noting the shape and size of Öland before forming ambitious plans to cover it all by bike; although the island is geared for cycling, with endless cycle tracks along the flat roads, if you want to explore it from north to south, you're looking at 130km. **Bike rental** is available in Kalmar, Borgholm and at most of the campsites, hostels and the odd farm, for around 40kr per day, 200kr per week. If you have a **car**, orientation could not be simpler: there is just one main road, Route 136, which runs from the lighthouse at the island's northernmost tip to the lighthouse in the far south, mostly parallel with the west coast; a smaller road runs off the 136 down the east of the island, south from Föra. Though an efficient **bus** network connects most places in Öland, the service is infrequent and you should be prepared for a lot of waiting around, particularly in the south – you need to time trips carefully to avoid being stranded, though **hitching** is not impossible in the far south.

Borgholm

Walking the simple square grid of streets that makes up **BORGHOLM**, Öland's "capital", it's clear that tourism is the lifeblood of this villagey town. Although swamped well beyond its capacity each July by tens of thousands of visitors, cramming its pizzerias and bars and injecting a riotous carnival atmosphere, Borgholm is in no way the tacky resort it could be. Encircled by the flaking, turreted villas that were the pride of the town during its first period as a holiday resort in the nineteenth century, most of the centre is a friendly, if bland, network of shops and restaurants leading to a very pleasant harbour.

The only real attraction here is **Borgholms Slotts ruin** (May–Aug daily 10am–6pm; free), just to the southwest of the centre. A colossal stone fortification with rows of huge arches and corridors open to the skies, it is reached either through a nature reserve, signposted from the town centre, or from the first exit south off Route 136.

When the town was founded in 1816, with just 33 inhabitants, the twelfth-century castle, rebuilt throughout subsequent centuries, was already a ruin.

A few hundred metres south of the castle is the present royal family's summer residence, **Solliden Park**, an Italian-style villa built to a design specified by Swedish Queen Victoria (the present king's great grandmother) in 1903. A huge, austere red-granite bust of Victoria rises out of the trees at the entrance car park. The villa itself is closed to the public but the gardens (mid-May to mid-Sept daily 1–6pm; 35kr) make for a pleasant stroll, or you could just head for the delightful thatch-roofed café, *Kaffetorpet* (same times as the garden), by the car park.

Just to the north of the town centre, **Blå Rör** is Öland's largest Bronze Age cairn, a huge mound of stones excavated when a coffin was discovered in 1849. In the 1920s, burnt bones indicating a cremation grave were also discovered, along with bronze swords and tweezers – common items in such tombs. However, there's nothing much to see there now and you're better off visiting **Forngard**, Köpmangatan 23 (mid-May to Aug Mon–Sat noon–6pm; 20kr), a museum of Öland life whose most interesting exhibits come from the historical sites around the island. The ground-floor displays includes bits of ancient skulls, some Viking glass, Bronze Age jewellery and grave finds.

Practicalities

Set in quiet, park-like gardens, the large and stately *STF* **youth hostel** at Rosenfors (☎0485/107 56; May to mid-Aug; 100kr) is 1km from the town centre – ask the bus driver to stop at the *Q8* filling station just before Borgholm proper, 100m from the hostel. The tourist office will book **private rooms** in person only, from 120kr per person, booking fee 25kr (50kr for stays of 2–5 days). The local **campsite**, *Kapelludden's Camping* (☎0485/101 78; fax 129 44), is on a small peninsula five minutes' walk from the centre; there are no cabins. However, here, as on the rest of the island, there's no shortage of beautiful spots for camping rough.

Of the **hotels** in the centre of town, *Hotel Borgholm*, Trådgårdsgatan 15 (☎0485/770 60; fax 124 66; ③), has smart rooms, while facilities at the vast *Strand Hotel*, Villagatan 4 (☎0485/888 88; fax 124 27; ③), include a shopping mall, disco and nightclub, pool and sauna. Eight kilometres south of Borgholm on Route 136 lies one of the few really fine hotels on the island, *Halltorps Gästgiveri* (☎0485/850 00; fax 850 01; ④), set in a beautiful eighteenth-century manor house.

There is a pronounced summer holiday feel to the town's **restaurants** and bars. Pizza places abound around Stortorget and down to the harbour, all much the same and not cheap at 65–85kr for a pizza. *Mama Rosa*, right at the harbour on Södra Långgatan, is smarter than most and has a more varied menu. On the far side of the harbour, *Skeppet* is a jolly little Italian restaurant open in summer, hidden behind 1940s industrial silos. For the finest food with matching prices, head for *Backfickan* at *Hotel Borgholm*, whose chef is something of a celebrity in Sweden. More fun (and less costly) is the restaurant-bar *Båtan* (mid-June to Aug), a 1915-built pleasure boat, moored at the harbour, with live music daily. For **drinking**, *Pubben*, Storgatan 18, is a cosy pub with 46 varieties of whisky. The only **nightclub** worth checking out, *Rooky Bar* (daily 6pm–2am), is on Södralanggatan, 500m from the harbour.

North Öland

It's the north of the island that has the most varied landscape, with some unexpected cultural and social diversions to boot. Heading up Route 136, there's no shortage of idyllic villages, dark woods and flowery fields. At **FÖRA**, about 20km north of Borgholm, there's a good example of a typical Öland church, which doubled as a fortress in times of war. Proud, forlorn **Källa kyrka**, about 7km north, has been empty since 1888 and sits in splendid isolation, 2km outside **KÄLLA** – take care not to confuse it with the present church by the road sign. Surrounded by brightly flowering meadows, this dull-white medieval church is bounded by drystone walls, and its grounds littered with ancient, weathered tombs. Inside, the lofty interior has seen plenty of action: built of limestone in 1130 to replace an earlier stave church, it was regularly attacked by heathens from over the Baltic seas. Modernized in the fourteenth century, when Källa was a relatively important harbour and trading centre, and stripped of its furnishings in the nineteenth century, a row of six models of the church in various incarnations are the only interior features.

HÖGBY, a few kilometres on, has the only remaining tied church houses on the island, relics of the medieval Högby kyrka nearby, but there's not a great deal to stop for. At nearby **LÖTTORP** you can engage in an unusual if expensive dining experience: follow the signs east for 4km down country lanes to the *Lammet & Grisen* restaurant, housed in a Spanish hacienda (daily 5.30pm–midnight). The only dishes on the menu are salmon and spit-roasted lamb and pork (hence the restaurant's name), with baked potatoes, flavoured butters and sauces – all you can eat for 210kr.

Continue north and west off the 136 across the island to witness the striking sight of the **Byrums Rauker**: solitary limestone pillars formed by the sea at the edge of a sandy beach. From here, the north of Öland is shaped like a bird's head, the beak facing east and with a large bite out of its crown. The best **beaches** are along the east coast; starting at Böda Sand, the most popular stretch is a couple of kilometres north at **Kyckesand**; and there's a nudist beach just to the north, marked by a large boulder in the sea.

There are some gorgeous areas of natural beauty in the far north. The nature reserve of **Trollskogen** (Trolls Forest), to the east – so-called because it is exactly the kind of place you would imagine trolls to inhabit, with twisted, gnarled trunks of ancient oaks all shrouded in ivy – offers some excellent walking. Around the western edge of the north coast, the waters are of the purest blue, lapping against rocky beaches; on a tiny island at the tip stands Långe Eric Lighthouse, a handsome 1845-built obelisk and a good goal for a walk or cycle ride. **Neptune Åkrar**, 3km south along the western coast is covered with lupin-like flowers forming a sheet of brilliant blue to rival the sea beyond. The name, given by Carl Von Linné, means Neptune's Ploughland, since the ridged land formation looks like ploughed fields. The only town in this region is **BYXELKROK**, a quiet place with an attractive harbour where ferries dock from mainland Oskarshamn.

Practicalities

There's not much in the way of proper hotels north of Borgholm (see above), but high-standard **campsites** abound, mostly beside a beach and marked every couple of kilometres off the 136. The most extensive site is *Krono Camping* at Böda Sand (☎0485/222 00; fax 223 76), 50km north of Borgholm and 2km off the main road at the southern end of the beach. Cabins range from 3000kr per week for four people, up to 4700kr with a water supply. Facilities are extensive, with shops, restaurants and a bakery at the site. The *STF* **youth hostel**, *Vandrarhem Böda* at Mellböda (☎0485/220 38; fax 221 98; all year; 100kr), just south of Böda's campsite, is big and well equipped. An unusual alternative is to stay at the nearby *Bödabaden Öland Square Dance Centre* (☎0485/220 12 or 220 85; fax 220 07; all year; ①), Europe's only square-dancing theme park, with tournaments and courses every day. The en-suite cabins are fairly upmarket, more like basic hotel rooms. Just 6km northwest at **Byxelkrok**, *Solö Värdhus* (☎0485/283 70; all year; ②) is a pleasant enough **hotel**; here you'll find the only likely **nightlife** venue in the north of Öland, at the restaurant, pub and disco *Sjöstugan* (April noon–5pm, May noon–8pm, June–Aug noon–2am), right by the shore.

Central Öland

Cutting eastwards from Borgholm (take bus #102), following signs to Räpplinge, brings you to **Störlinge Kvarna**, a row of seven windmills by the roadside. A sign tells you this is the island's longest line of post-mill type windmills, but as you'll probably have already seen several windmills by now, there's no real inducement to stop. A couple of kilometres south, **GÄRDSLÖSA** has the island's best preserved medieval church. Its exterior has been maintained so well that it's almost too pristine, but inside is worth a look for its 1666-made pulpit and thirteenth-century ceiling paintings; these were whitewashed over in 1781, but uncovered in 1950.

The preserved village of **Himmelsberga**, a few kilometres further south, is an **open-air museum** (May to mid-Sept daily 10am–6pm; 30kr) in a gorgeous setting. Since the decline of farming in the middle of this century, most of Öland's thatched farmhouses have been rather brutally modernized; Himmelsberga, however, escaped and two of its original farms opened as museums in the 1950s. Subsequently, buildings were brought from all over the island, and it is now an extensive collection of crofters farms, a smithy and a windmill.

East from Himmelsberga, the ancient castle ruin of **Ismantorps Borg** (dating from around 450 AD) only warrants a visit if you fancy a walk along a lovely wooded path. A huge, circular base of stones, you can see the foundations of 88 rooms inside – if you try. **Gråborg**, passed by bus #102, another 10km south of here, is Öland's largest ancient castle ruin, with 640-metre-long walls. Built around 500 AD and occupied through the Middle Ages, when the Gothic entrance arch was built, today the walls encircle little more than a handful of hardy sheep.

South Öland

Dominated by **Stora Alvaret**, the giant limestone plain on which no trees can grow, the south of the island is sparsely populated, with its main town the rather dull **Mörbylånga**. You won't see any bare rock, however, only a meadow landscape sprouting rare alpine plant life that has stoically clung on since the Ice Age. **Buses** run so infrequently here that you'll need to carefully check times at Färjestaden, just south of the bridge, which is where the few southbound services begin. However, the lack of regular transport means that **hitching** is a feasible option here. Facilities as a whole are fewer than in the north, so it's worth stocking up before you head off. Despite the difficulties of travelling in southern Öland, its great advantage is that summer crowds thin out here, allowing you to explore the most untouched parts of the island in peace.

The prettiest village south along the 136 is **VICKLEBY**, equidistant between Färjestaden to the north and Mörbylånga to the south, and the site of a remarkable art and design school, **Capella Gården**, the brainchild of furniture designer Carl Malmsten. An idealist, Malmsten's dream was to create a school that stimulated mind, body and soul – an idea that shocked Stockholm society at the time. In 1959, he bought a range of picturesque farmhouses at Vickleby, and opened an art and design school for adults that still runs today. The students' work, including some lovely ceramic and wood pieces, is on sale in a big annual exhibition. If you do visit, it's best to call the studios beforehand (☎0485/361 32).

Of all the forts on Öland, the one most worth a visit is at the village of **EKETORP**, reachable by bus from Mörbylånga. The site (May to mid-June & late Aug daily 9am–5pm; guided tours in English 1pm; 45kr) includes an archeological museum containing the finds of a major excavation in the 1970s. Three settlements were discovered, including a marketplace from the fourth century and an agricultural community dating from 1000AD. The result is a wonderful achievement in popular archeology, actual physical evidence being thin on the ground. The best of the finds, such as jewellery and weapons, are on show in the museum, and there's a workshop, where, if you feel inclined, you can have a go at leather work or "authentic" ancient cookery. If you head south from here, you'll come to a stone wall that cuts straight across the island. Called **Karl X Gustav's Wall**, it was built in 1650 to fence off deer and so improve hunting. A strain of 150 fallow deer still roams about today at **Ottenby**, in the far south of the island. Öland's largest estate, built in 1804, this is now a birdwatcher's paradise, with a huge nature reserve and Ottenby **bird station**, which has been the national centre for migrating birds since 1946. With two protected bird observation towers, and a bird museum, you have to be keen for the area to hold much appeal – there's absolutely nothing else here.

Practicalities

The main **tourist office** at Möllstorp (see p.497) will book **private rooms** from 150kr per person per night, with a 25kr booking fee, more for longer stays. *Mörby Youth Hostel* (☎/fax 0485/493 93; all year; 100kr), 15km south of the bridge, is a **hostel and hotel** combined, the only difference being that the price of hotel rooms (①) includes sheets and breakfast; bus #105 stops right outside. *Top 12* is a kind of hotel, with a **campsite**, 10km south of the bridge at Haga Park; the beach here offers good windsurfing. For a **regular hotel**, try *Hotel Kajutan* (☎0485/408 10; ③), a pleasant old place at the harbour behind the bus station in **Mörbylånga**. At Vickleby there's the popular *Hotel Bo Pensionat* (☎0485/360 01; ②), in a traditional row of village houses; book ahead in high season.

Småland

Thickly forested and studded with lakes, **Småland County** makes up the southeastern wedge of Sweden, and although appealing at first, the uniformity of the scenery means it's easy to become oblivious to the natural beauty. Småland is frequently somewhere people travel through – from Stockholm to the southwest, or from Gothenburg to the Baltic coast – yet beneath the canopy of greenery, there are a few vital spots of interest, alongside opportunities for hiking, trekking, fishing and cycling.

Historically, Småland has had it tough. The simple, rustic charm of the pretty painted cottages belies the intense misery endured by generations of local peasants; in the nineteenth century, this lead to a massive surge of emigration to America. Subsistence farming had failed, and the people were starving, consequently a fifth of Sweden's population left the country – most of them from Småland. Their plight is vividly retold at the **House of Emigrants** exhibition in **Vaxjö**, a town that makes an excellent base for exploring the region, but the county's main tourist attraction remains the many **glass factories** hidden away in the forest.

Växjö

Founded by Saint Sigfrid in the eleventh century, **VÄXJÖ** (pronounced "veh-quer") is by far the handiest place to base yourself if you are interested in touring the region's glassworks. Deep in the heart of Småland county (110km from Kalmar), the town itself boasts two superb museums: the newly renovated and extensive **Smålands Museum**, notable for being home to the **Swedish Glass Museum**; and the **House of Emigrants**, which explores the mass emigration from Sweden in the nineteenth and early twentieth centuries. While the town centre doesn't hold much else of appeal, the romantic castle ruin of **Kronoberg** is within easy reach, just 4km to the north of town.

The Town

The newly renovated **Smålands Museum**, behind the train station (June–Aug Mon–Fri 11am–6pm, Sat & Sun 11am–4pm; Sept–May Tues, Wed & Fri 11am–6pm, Thurs 11am–8pm, Sat & Sun 11am–4pm; 30kr), contains two permanent exhibitions: an intelligently displayed history of Smålands manufacturing industries and the rather more appealing "four hundred years of Swedish glass". The latter's exhibits range from sixteenth-century place settings to eighteenth- and nineteenth-century etched and simple coloured glass, along with stylish Art Nouveau-inspired pieces; most appealing, though, are the wide-ranging displays of contemporary glass in the extension building, which are all mounted on white wood plinths. If you're intending to visit any of the glassworks (see below), it's a good idea to come here first and gauge the different styles.

The plain building directly in front of the museum contains the inspired **House of Emigrants** (June–Aug Mon–Fri 9am–6pm, Sat 11am–3pm, Sun 1–5pm; Sept–May Mon–Fri 9am–5pm, Sat 11am–3pm, Sun 1–5pm; 25kr), with its moving "Dream of America" exhibition. The museum presents a living picture of the intense hardship faced by the Småland peasant population from the mid-nineteenth century. Due to agricultural reforms and a series of bad harvests, between 1860 and 1930 a million Swedes – a sixth of the population – emigrated to America, most of them from Småland. Creative techniques, including English-language telephone narratives, succeed in tracing individual lives and recounting the story of the industry that grew up around emigration fever. Most boats left from Gothenberg and, until 1915, sailed to Hull in Britain, where passengers crossed to Liverpool by train to board the transatlantic ships. Conditions on board were usually dire: the steamer *Hero* left Gothenburg in 1866 with 500 emigrants, nearly 400 oxen and 900 pigs, calves and sheep sharing the accommodation.

The attached **Research Centre** (Mon–Fri 9am–4pm; ☎0470/201 24) charges 100kr per day to help interested parties trace their family roots, using passenger lists from ten harbours, microfilmed church records from every Swedish parish, and records of such bodies as the Swedish New York Society, Swedes in Australia and the Swedish Congo Veterans Association. It's worth booking ahead during the peak season of May to mid-August.

There's not much else to see in the centre, but take a quick look at the very distinctive **Domkyrkan** (daily 8am–8pm; June–Aug guided tours 9am–5pm), with its unusual twin green towers and apricot-coloured facade. Regular restorations, the most recent in 1995, together with a catalogue of sixteenth-century fires and a lightning strike in 1775 have left nothing of note except a unique 1775 organ. There are, however, some brilliant new glass ornaments by Göran Wärff, one of the best known of the contemporary Glass Kingdom designers. The cathedral is set in the **Linné Park**, named after the Carl Von Linné, who was educated at the handsome adjacent school (closed to the public).

Kronoberg Castle

Set on a tiny island in Lake Helgasjön, the ruins of **Kronoberg Castle** lie 4km north of the town centre in a beautiful and unspoilt setting – follow the signs for Evedal, or take hourly bus #1B from the bus station. The Bishops of Växjö erected a wooden fortress here in the eleventh century, but it was Gustav Vasa who built the present stone version in 1540. Entered over an old wooden bridge set at a narrow spot in the lake, it's a perfect ruin, leaning precariously and complete with rounded tower and deep-set lookouts. Some new brick archways and a couple of reinforced roofs, added in the 1970s, stop the whole thing collapsing. Between the ruin and the grass-roofed centuries-old café *Ryttmästargården* (see below), the old paddle steamer *Thor* makes regular excursions around Lake Helgasjön and up to Lake Asassjön, the perfect way to appreciate the lakeland scenery.

Practicalities

Hourly **trains** from Kalmar pull into the station, alongside the **bus station** in the middle of town, from where it is a short walk to the **tourist office** at Kronobergsgatan 8 (mid-June to mid-Aug Mon–Fri 9am–6pm, Sat 10am–2pm, Sun 11am–3pm; Sept to mid-June Mon–Thurs 9.30am–4.30pm, Fri 9.30am–3pm; ☎0470/414 11; fax 478 14). Here you can book **private rooms** from 110kr, 25kr extra for sheets, plus a 50kr booking fee. The splendid *STF* **youth hostel** (☎0470/630 70; fax 632 16; all year; 100kr) at **Evedal**, 5km north of the centre, occupies an eighteenth-century house set in parkland on tranquil

Lake Helgasjön (with its own beach); to get there, take Linnegatan north, following signs for Evedal, or take bus #1C from the bus terminal to the end of the route (last bus is at 4.15pm, 3.15pm on Sat), or bus #1A, which leaves you with a 1500-metre walk, but runs daily till 8.15pm. Next to the hostel is a **campsite**, *Evedal Camping* (☎0470/630 34; fax 631 22), with new four-person cabins for 450kr. Of the hotels, the most striking is the *Teater Park*, in the central Concert Hall building (☎0470/399 00; fax 475 77; ②/④). Otherwise, try the no-frills *Esplanad*, Norra Esplanaden 21A (☎0470/225 80; fax 262 26; ①/②), or the good-value *Värend*, Kungsgatan 27 (☎0470/104 85; fax 362 61; ①/③).

One of the pleasures of Växjö and its surrounds is the wealth of really good **eating** experiences, though few of them come cheap. A couple of **cafés** with strong gourmet leanings are run by the same people: the recently opened *Café Momento* in Smålands Museum (open museum hours) serves tasty Italian snacks, plus salads and soups, while the same food is available in summer in *Café Ryttmästargården*, an eighteenth-century cottage overlooking the Kronoberg castle (to get there in the evening you'll need your own transport). The best **restaurant** food – fresh lake fish is the speciality – is served at the lakeside *Evedal Vardhus*, next door to the youth hostel on Lake Helga.

The Glass Kingdom

Within the landscape of dense birch and pine forests, threaded by lakes, that stretches between Kalmar and Växjö, lie the bulk of Småland's celebrated **glassworks**. The area is dubbed **Glasriket**, or the "Glass Kingdom", with each glassworks signposted clearly from the spidery main roads. This seemingly odd and very picturesque setting for the industry is no coincidence. King Gustav Vasa pioneered glass-making in Sweden when he returned from Italy in the mid-sixteenth century and decided to set up a glassworks in Stockholm. However, it was only Småland's forests that could provide the vast amounts of fuel needed to feed the furnaces, and so a glass factory was set up in 1742, named *Kosta* after its founders, Koskull and Stael von Hostein. Today, *Kosta* is the largest glassworks in Småland.

GLASS-MAKING AND BUYING GLASS

Demonstrations of the **glass-making process**, held in a dozen or so of the glassworks, can be mesmerizing to watch. The process involves a glass plug being fished out of a shimmering, molten lake (at 1200°C) and then turned and blown into a graphite or steel mould. In the case of wineglasses, a foot is then added, before the piece is annealed (heated and then slowly cooled) for several hours. It all looks deceptively simple and mistakes are rare, but it nevertheless takes years to become a servitor (glass-maker's assistant), working up through the ranks of stem-maker and bowl-gatherer. In smaller works, all these processes are carried out by the same person, but in many of Småland's glassworks, you'll see the bowl-gatherer fetching the glowing gob for the master blower, who then skilfully rolls and shapes the syrupy substance. When the blower is attaching stems to wineglasses, the would-be handle will slide off or sink right through if the glass is too hot; if too cold, it won't stick – and the right temperature lasts a matter of seconds.

If you want to **buy glassware**, which is marketed with a vengence, don't feel compelled to snap up the first things you see. The same batch of designs appear at most of the glassworks, a testament to the fact that *Kosta Boda* and *Orrefors* are the main players nowadays; many of the smaller works have been swallowed up, even though they retain their own names. This makes price comparison easier, but don't expect many bargains; the best pieces go for thousands of kronor. You may find it useful to see the glassware exhibition in Väjxö's Småland's Museum first to get an idea of the various styles and where you can find them (see p.501).

Visiting the glassworks

Of the twenty or so glassworks still in operation in Småland, thirteen have captivating glass-blowing **demonstrations** on weekdays, several have permanent **exhibitions** of contemporary work or pieces from the firm's history and, without exception, all have a **shop**, usually open slightly longer hours. **Bus** services to the glassworks, or at least within easy walking distance, are extremely limited, and without your own transport it is almost impossible to see more than a couple in a day – however, you'll probably find this is enough.

While each works has individual design characteristics, the *Kosta Boda* and *Orrefors*, its main rival, give the best picture of what is available. **Orrefors** is easiest reached from Kalmar: take Route 25 to Nybro, then Route 31 or a train from Växjö to Nybro, then bus #138, #139 or #140 to the factory (June to mid-Aug; glass-blowing Mon–Fri 8am–3.30pm, Sat 10am–3pm, Sun 11am–3pm; exhibition Mon–Fri 9am–3pm, Sat 9am–4pm, Sun 11am–4pm).

The **Kosta Boda** and **Åfors** glassworks are operated by the same team, with the biggest collection at *Kosta* (June to mid-Aug; glass-blowing Mon–Fri 10am–3pm, Sat 9am–3pm, Sun 11am–4pm). The historical exhibition here (Mon–Fri 9am–6pm, Sat 9am–4pm, Sun 11am–4pm) contains some delicate turn-of-the-century glassware designed by Karl Lindeberg, while if you're looking for simple modern works, Anna Ehrener's bowls and vases are the most elegant pieces. These can be bought in the adjacent shop, alongside current designs that tend towards colourful high-kitsch. To get to *Kosta* from Växjö, take Route 23 in the direction of Oskarshamn, then Route 31 southeast and onto Route 28. By public transport, bus #218 makes the hour-long trip direct from Växjö bus station.

Strömbergshyttan glassworks, near Hormantorp, is the best bet for a short trip from Växjö. With both *Kosta* and *Orrefors* displays (June to mid-Aug; shop only Mon–Fri 9am–6pm, Sat 9am–4pm, Sun 11am–4pm), it's more comprehensive than nearby *Sandvik*, an *Orrefors* company. To get there, head south down Route 30 from Växjö, or take bus #218 (the *Kosta* bus; 40min). If you're driving, continue on to the small, traditional **Bergdala** works, 6km north of Hovmantorp, which produces Sweden's distinctive blue-rimmed glassware (mid-June to mid-Aug; glass-blowing Mon–Fri 9am–2.30pm, Sat 10am–3pm, Sun noon–4pm).

To the north, **Rosdala** produces glass for lampshades (mid-June to mid-Aug; glass-blowing Mon–Fri 8am–3pm, though closed most of July), with some of the ugliest 1970s designs on display in its museum (Mon–Fri 9am–6pm, Sat 10am–4pm, Sun 11am–4pm). There's no public transport here: from Växjö, take Route 23 to Norrhult-Klavreström, then Route 31 north. Smaller **Johansfors**, set on the lakeside to the south of the region, specializes in stem-ware (exhibition and shop Mon–Fri 9am–6pm, Sat 10am–4pm, Sun noon–4pm) – take Route 28 from *Kosta*. Nearby **Skruf** has the most basic, jam-jar style collection, which is also about the cheapest, but is one of the few to charge (5kr) for museum entry.

Jönköping

Perched at the southernmost tip of Lake Vättern, **JÖNKÖPING** (pronounced "Yun-shurp-ing") is one of the oldest medieval trading centres in the country, having won its town charter in 1284. Today it is famous for being the home of the matchstick, the nineteenth-century manufacture and worldwide distribution of which made the town a wealthy place. Matches are no longer made here: in 1932 the town's match magnate, Ivar Kruger, shot himself rather than face bankruptcy, bringing a swift end to the industry. Despite the town's bland centre, its location and ample accommodation and eating possibilities make it a viable base for touring the lake. Jönköping's renovated historical core, focused on the match museum, is the most interesting part to explore.

The biggest of the match factories, built in 1844, now houses **Tändsticksmuséet**, the match museum (May–Aug Mon–Fri 10am–5pm, Sat & Sun 11am–3pm; Sept–April Tues–Thurs noon–4pm, Sat & Sun 11am–3pm; 25kr) at Västra Storgatan 18. Inside, however, it isn't too thrilling, just a collection of matchbox labels and match-making machines and not much else. Opposite, the **Radio Museum** displays every type of radio from early crystal sets to Walkmans. A couple of metres away and set in another old match factory is **Kulturhuset**, a trendy centre with rooms for band rehearsals and antiquarian and alternative bookshops (Mon–Fri 5–7pm). During summer (June–Aug), the centre is converted into a private youth hostel (see below). There's also a good cheap café here and next door is *Bio,* a stylish art-house cinema. From September to May, there's also a bustling early-morning Saturday market on the street outside the centre.

The only other museum to bother with is the **Länsmuseum** (daily 11am–5pm, Wed till 8pm; 20kr), on Dag Hammarskjölds Plats, across the canal between lakes Vättern and Munksjön. A mishmash of oddities, with exhibits on garden chairs throughout the ages, bonnets, samovars and doll's houses, it is like wandering around a well-stocked junk shop – and there's no English labelling. The best part is the well-lit collection of paintings and drawings by **John Bauer**, a local artist who enthralled generations of Swedes with his Tolkienesque representations of gnomes and trolls in the *Bland Tomtar och Troll* books.

Practicalities

The **train** and **bus stations** are next to each other on the lake's edge. Just over the bridge, the **tourist office** is located in the *Djurläkartoget* shopping centre (mid-June to mid-Aug Mon–Fri 8am–6pm, Sat 10am–1pm; rest of the year Mon–Fri 8am–4.30pm; ☎036/10 50 50; fax 12 83 00). Here you can arrange a **private room** at 150kr per person; the town's **youth hostel** (☎036/19 05 85; mid-June to mid-Aug; 110kr) is just a few steps west of the train station. The *Rosenlund* **campsite** (☎036/12 28 63; all year) is right on the lakeside, 3km from the town centre on the route of several buses. Most prestigious of the town's **hotels** is the imposing *Stora Hotel,* Hotellplan (☎036/10 00 00; fax 71 93 20; ②/④); or try the less luxurious *Grand Hotel,* Hovrättstorget (☎036/71 96 00; fax 71 96 05; ①/②), or *Prize Hotel City,* just three minutes from the station at Västra Storgatan 25 (☎036/71 92 80; fax 71 88 48; ①/②).

Jönköping has plenty of good and lively places to **eat** and **drink**. However, some close for the summer, when many of the townsfolk head off to the coast, while others are closed on Fridays and Sundays. *Anna-Gretas Matsal & Café,* Västra Torget, is the oldest and friendliest **café** in town, opening at 7am or earlier for the market traders, while the in-crowd frequent *Café Bla Bla,* a laid-back café-bar on Smedjegatan. For more substantial eating, try the decent Indian food at *Taj Mahal,* Kapellgatan 15, which also does takeaways, or the American-diner-style *Trottoaren Restaurant,* connected to the grand *Stora Hotell* at Hotellplan, where full meals (from 159kr) are served at incongruously linen-laid tables.

Many of the town's bars also serve food: most popular are *G och Company,* Smedjegatan 36, which features loud music and a summer beer garden, and the new *Karlsonns Salonger,* Västra Storgatan 9. The trendiest **club** is the stylish *Gruvan* (50kr), housed in a former match factory by the match museum.

Along the shore of Lake Vättern

The road heading north along the eastern shores of **Lake Vättern** offers the most spectacular scenery and delightful historical towns in the region. Jönköping can be used as a base for excursions, but there are plenty of places to eat and stay along the way to historic Vadstena (see below). It's perfect for **trekking**, too, with several walking paths, the most established being Södra Vätternleden, John Bauerleden and Holavedsleden.

Six kilometres east of Jönköping on the E4 – initially called Östra Storgatan – is **HUSKVARNA**, originally named *Husqvarna* after the arms factory that was based here, now a sewing machine and motorbike manufacturer. Buses make the trip in around ten minutes. On the way, you'll pass *Rosenlundsbadet*, the best bathhouse and sauna in Jönköping (Mon noon–8pm, Tues & Thurs 6.30am–8pm, Wed & Fri 8am–8pm, Sat & Sun 10am–5pm), next door to *Elmia*, a huge, featureless exhibition hall that hosts ice-hockey matches and classical concerts.

However, it's altogether more rewarding to take a northward route, on either the E4, or the more picturesque *Grännavagen* (the old E4). There are no trains here, but buses #120 and #121 make the trip to Gränna in around an hour and there's a quicker express bus twice a day too.

Gränna and Visingö

An excellent target for a day trip, **GRÄNNA**, 40km north of Jönköping, is for Swedes irrevocably associated with pears, striped candy and hot-air ballooning (see below). It's easy to while away a whole afternoon in the cafés here, while there are several lovely places to stay should you want to linger. Approaching from the south, the Gränna Valley sweeps down to your left, with the hills to the right, most notably the crest of Grännaberget, which provides a majestic foil to some superb views over Lake Vättern and its island, **Visingsö**.

Per Brahe, one of Sweden's first counts (see below), built the town, using the symmetry, regularity and spaciousness in planning that he had learnt while governor of Finland. If you arrive in late spring, the hills around Gränna are a confetti of pear blossom, Per Brahe having encouraged the planting of pear orchards – the Gränna pear is still one of the best-known varieties today. The main roads were all designed so Brahe could look straight down them as he stood at the windows of his now-ruined castle, **Brahehus**. The gardens along the main street, **Brahegatan**, remain mostly intact, and until the 1920s there were no additions to the original designs.

Next to the tourist office on Brahegatan is the fascinating **S A Andree museum** (daily mid-May to mid-June 10am–5pm; July & Aug 10am–6pm; rest of the year 10am–4pm; 20kr), dedicated to Salomon August Andree, the Gränna-born balloonist, who led a doomed attempt to reach the North Pole by balloon in 1897. Born at Brahegatan 37, Andree was fired by the European obsession of the day to explore and conquer unknown places, and also by the nationalist fervour sweeping through the country, which gained him funding from Alfred Nobel, King Oscar and Baron Oscar Dickson. However, after a flight lasting only three days, the balloon made a forced landing on ice just 470km from its departure point, and after six weeks trekking the men died either from the cold, starvation or poisoning from trichinosis, after eating the raw meat of a polar bear they had managed to spear. It was 33 years before their frozen, preserved bodies and their equipment were discovered by a Norwegian sailing ship. Highlights of the poignant displays are the diary of 25-year-old crew member Nils Strindberg, and some film taken by the team, including sequences of them dragging their sledges across the sheets of ice.

Visingsö

From Gränna a twenty-minute ferry crossing (June-Aug every 30 min; otherwise hourly; 16kr, 150kr return with a car) drops you on the island of **Visingsö**, which is just 12km by 3km wide. A lagoon at the harbour makes swimming here less chilly than the deep waters of Vättern usually allow. During the twelfth and thirteenth centuries, Swedish kings often lived on the island, and five medieval monarchs died here, including Magnus Ladulås in 1290. It was in the mid-sixteenth century that Eric XIV decided that Sweden should follow the example of continental monarchies, and bestow titles and privileges on deserving noblemen. He created the title of Count of Visingsborg, whose lands included Visingsö, and awarded it to Per Brahe the Elder, who enjoyed a spate of castle building here. However, after Brahe the Younger's death in 1680, the Crown took back much of the land, including the island.

Arriving at the dock, you're likely to be met by a horse and trap called a *remmalag*, a tempting way to cover the three-kilometre trip (42kr return) to **Kumlaby** church, the oldest relic on the island, dating back to the twelfth century. With beautifully painted ceiling and walls, the church's truncated tower was designed for the astronomy classes organized by Brahe the Younger, whose school was the first in the region to accept women. Between June and August, you can climb the steps of the tower for a fine view of the island (daily 9am–8pm). **Bikes** can be rented from near the dock to see the remains of **Näs castle**, at the southern tip of the island. This was once a major power centre in Sweden, though there's little sign of its erstwhile glory. **Visingsborg Slott**, near the ferry terminal, is also an empty shell, its roof burned off by Russian prisoners celebrating the death of Karl XII in 1718.

Practicalities

Gränna's **tourist office** is on Brahegatan, right beside the S A Andree Museum (June–Aug Mon–Fri 9–6pm, Sat 10am–2pm; rest of the year Mon–Fri 10am–4pm; ☎0390/410 10; fax 102 75). Two **youth hostels** serve the town: the first is close to the tourist office, where you can make bookings (mid-June to early Aug; 100–110kr), the second right on the beach near the ferry (☎0390/107 06; May–Sept; 120kr). You can also arrange **private rooms** through the tourist office (from 100kr plus 30kr fee).

Grand Hotel Ribbagården, just off Brahegatan, is a really charming **hotel**, packed full of antiques (☎/fax 0390/108 21; ②/③); it's been a hotel since 1922, and for 970kr you can stay in the room Greta Garbo used. Gränna's other famous hotel is the castle-like *Hotel Gyllene Uttern*, or "Golden Otter" (☎0390/108 00; fax 418 80; ③/④, annexe rooms ②/③), 3km south of town close to the main road.

There are several excellent **cafés** in Gränna, all on Brahegatan, except for *Café Stugan* (May 10am–9pm; June–Aug 10am–10pm), a steep climb from the market square, which specializes in shrimp sandwiches and Swedish cheesecake. Back in town, *Café Amalia* sells superb lingonberry ice cream, which you can enjoy on a terrace overlooking the rooftops and lake. There's only one drinking place of note, *Gränna Pub* at *Café Hjorten*, also on Brahegatan, a very pleasant restaurant and bar, with a beer garden and a pizza parlour downstairs.

Vadstena and Motala

With its beautiful lakeside setting, 60km north of Gränna, **VADSTENA** is the most evocative town in Östergotland and a fine place for a day or two's stay. At one time a royal seat and an important monastic centre, the town's main attraction nowadays is a gorgeous moated **castle**, planned in the sixteenth century by Gustav Vasa as part of his defensive ring to protect the Swedish heartland around Stockholm. The cobbled, twisting streets, lined with cottages covered in climbing roses, also hold an impressive **abbey**, whose existence is the result of the passionate work of fourteenth-century Saint Birgitta, Sweden's first female saint.

The castle and abbey

Vadstena boasts a number of ancient sites and buildings, notably the Rådhus, Sweden's oldest courthouse, but the town's top attraction is its castle, **Vadstena Slott** (daily June & Aug 10am–1pm; July 10am–4pm; 35kr). With four seven-metre-thick round towers and a grand moat, it was originally built as a fortification to defend against Danish attacks in 1545, but was then prettified into a palace to house Gustav Vasa's mentally ill third son, Magnus. His elder brother, Johan III, was responsible for its lavish decorations, but fire destroyed it all just before completion, and to save on costs, the post-fire decor was merely painted on the walls – down to the swagged curtains that can still be seen today.

From the end of the seventeenth century, the building fell into decay and was used as a grain store; the original hand-painted wooden ceilings were chopped up to make into grain boxes. As a result, there wasn't much to see inside, but a recent drive to buy up period furniture from all over Europe has re-created more of an atmosphere. Portraits of the Vasa family have also been crammed in, displaying some very unhappy and ugly faces that make for entertaining viewing. It's worth joining the regular English-language tours to hear more of the Vasa family saga, but if you're short on time, the most interesting area to aim for are the dark, vaulted towers.

A few minutes' walk away, at the water's edge, stands Vadstena's **abbey church** (daily May 9am–5pm; June & Aug 9am–7pm; July 9am–8pm), the architectural legacy of Saint Birgitta. Birgitta came to Vadstena as a lady-in-waiting to King Magnus Eriksson and his wife, Blanche of Namur, who lived at Bjälbo Palace. Married at 13, and after giving birth to eight children, she began to experience visions and convinced her royal employers to give up their home in order to set up a convent and monastery. Unfortunately, she died abroad before her plans could be completed, and the work was continued by her daughter Katarina, with the church finally consecrated in 1430. Birgitta's specification that the church should be "of plain construction, humble and strong" is fulfilled from the outside, but within the sombre, grey exterior hides a celebrated collection of medieval artwork. More memorable than the crypts of various royals is the statue, now devoid of hands, of Birgitta "in a state of ecstasy". To the right, the rather sad "Door of Grace and Honour" was where each Birgittine nun entered the abbey after being professed – the next time she passed through the doorway would be in a coffin on her funeral day. Birgitta's bones are encased in a red velvet box, decorated with silver and gilt medallions, in a glass case down stone steps in the Monk's choir stalls. Although now housing a restaurant and a hotel, the **monastery** and palace-turned-**nunnery** on either side of the abbey are open for tours, though they won't occupy you for long.

Practicalities

Express **bus** #840 runs to Vadstena from Gränna (50min) and Jönköping (90min) twice daily on weekdays, once on Sundays. By car, it's a straight run along the E4 and Route 50 north from Gränna or southwest on Route 50 from Motala (see below). Vadstena itself is easily walkable, but for striking out into the Östergotland countryside, **bikes** can be rented (90kr per day or 300kr per week) from the quaint old **tourist office** at Rådhustorget (May Mon–Fri 9am–5pm, Sat 10am–noon; June & Aug Mon–Fri 10am–6pm, Sat 10am–1pm, Sun 4–7pm; July Mon–Fri 10am–7pm, Sat 10am–1pm & 5pm–7pm, Sun 4pm–7pm; ☎0143/151 25; fax 151 29). You can also buy a **Vadstena Card** here for 60kr, covering a sightseeing tour and entry to the castle and Vadstena's minor museums; it's only worth it if you intend to see the lot.

A list of **private rooms** is supplied by the tourist office, while Vadstena's *STF* **youth hostel** is close to the lake at Skänningegatan 20 (☎0143/103 02; fax 104 04; all year but book ahead outside midsummer; 100kr). Mostly housed in converted historic buildings, the main **hotels** are fairly expensive. The *Vadstena Kloster Hotel*, in the 1369-built nunnery next to the abbey (☎0143/315 30; fax 136 48; ③/④) is still very atmospheric, especially the original Kings Hall where breakfast is served; non-residents can also breakfast here for 50kr (Mon–Fri 7.15am–9am, Sat & Sun 8.30am–10am). Run by the same company is the grand and comfortable *Vadstena Slottshotel*, opposite the castle on Ayslen (☎014/103 25; ③/④).

Eating in Vadstena is equally costly. The pick of the **cafés** is the extremely busy *Gamla Konditori* on Storgatan just up from the tourist office, while the best **restaurant** in town is *Vadstena Valven*, Storgatan 18, which does a lunch special at 55kr and fish specialities in the evening (closed Sun outside summer). *Restaurant Rådhus Källeren,* in the cosy cellars of the sixteenth-century courthouse on Rådhustorget, doubles as a **pub**, where Vadstena locals hang out on Thursday and Saturday evenings. For decent pizzas, try *Pizza Firenze* at Storgatan 13.

Motala

At **MOTALA**, 16km north of Vadstena and reached by regular #16 buses, the Göta Canal tumbles into Lake Vättern through a flight of five locks. It's one of the most popular spots on the canal, the town designed by the waterway's progenitor, Baltzar Von Platen: where lake and canal meet, a promenade cuts a smooth arc around the bay, while Motala fans out behind. You'll pass Von Platen's grave, beside his statue, on the canalside walk. Pleasant though strolling around the lake is, it's worth taking the opportunity to cruise down a stretch of the canal, something that's easiest during the peak summer season (mid-June to mid-Aug), though not impossible at other times of the year. In summer, **boats** run along the canal to Borensburg, 20km east, leaving Motala at 10.30am and taking around five hours for the round trip (150kr, lunch on board 80kr). Alternatively, you could cover the same journey by **bike**; the tourist office can advise about boat tickets and bike rental places.

The town itself is, for the most part, rather bland. However, the new **Motor Museum** (May–Sept daily 10am–8pm; 40kr) at the harbour edge is much more entertaining than it sounds. Far from the usual showrooms of shiny vehicles, this is really a museum of style, and great fun even if you've not much interest in cars. Each of the unusual motors is displayed in context, with music appropriate to the era blaring from radio sets. On the hill behind the town, there is a small **Radio Museum** (June–Aug daily 11am–4pm; 10kr), recalling the days when "Motala Calling" was as redolent to Swedes as "This is London" is to avid BBC World Service listeners. Just up from the Motor Museum is the **Canal and Navigation Museum** (May Mon–Fri 9am–4pm; June & Aug Mon–Fri 8am–6pm; July daily 8am–8pm; 20kr), which details the canal's construction and demonstrates the operation of a lock.

An ambitious new project intended (perhaps optimistically) to generate tourism for Motala is **Locomotiv 2000** (July–Sept Mon & Fri–Sun 10am–6pm, Tues & Thurs 10am–8pm; 25kr). Set in the old workshop buildings at Motala Verkstad, on the narrow strip of land to the east of the centre, between the waterways of Göta Canal and Motala Ström, its regularly changing exhibitions are aimed at creating a "smithy for ideas", a sort of museum of environmental history with an emphasis on future technological breakthroughs. Not exactly a recipe for relaxation, but it can be teamed up with a pleasant water trip. To get to the centre, you can take a boat up Motala Ström or bus #322; bus #301 stops a kilometre short.

Just 3km west of the centre, **Varamon Beach**, with its kilometre of golden sand, claims to be Scandinavia's largest inland bathing beach. While that is not strictly true, it does have the warmest waters in Lake Vättern, and on hot summer days the beach is thick with bronzing bodies. It's also a popular windsurfing site.

Practicalities

Trains pull in parallel with the canal about a kilometre from the centre. For the **tourist office** (June–Aug daily 10am–6pm; Sept-May daily 10am–5pm; ☎0141/22 52 54; fax 521 03) at Fokes Hus, turn left along Östermalmsgatan, right along Vadstenavägen and left into Repslagaregatan. This brings you past the central Stora Torget and the **bus station**; the tourist office is on the right, close to the harbour. There's a second, summertime tourist office at the harbour itself (June to mid-Aug daily 8am–8pm), which rents out **bikes** (60kr per day, 250kr per week).

Private rooms for around 180kr can be booked through the main tourist office; while the *STF* **youth hostel** at Varamon (☎/fax 0141/57436 or mobile 0103/871 28; 95kr) is right on the beach – take bus #301 from Stora Torget. There's a popular summer café here, too. There's also a well-equipped **campsite** on the beach called *Z-Parkens Camping* (☎0141/21 11 42), alongside *Varamon Chalet Colony,* some pretty wooden cabins overlooking the lake (book through the tourist office). The main town-centre **hotels** are entirely business-oriented, but the only option if you value en-suite bathrooms. *Stadshotellet* on Storatorget (☎0141/21 64 00; fax 21 46 05; ②/④) has large, shabby rooms, and *Palace Hotel,* Kungsgatan 1, just off Storatorget (☎ 0141/21 66 60; fax 57 221; ③/④), is much the same. A better choice if you're a non-smoker and don't mind sharing a bathroom is the cosy new *Hotel Urban Hjarne* at Bispmotalagatan 11 (☎0141/ 23 52 00; fax 21 75 45; ①), run by the Salvation Army.

Most of Motala's **restaurants**, grouped around Storatorget, are nondescript and offer daily lunches for around 50kr. *Teatercaféet*, next to the tourist office, is a pleasant option for sandwiches, cake and coffee. Most of the **pubs** cater for a very young crowd, but a good alternative for food and drink all day is *Hallen*, housed in an old market hall just off Storatorget near the *Stadshottelet*.

Örebro

Beyond Motala, Lake Vättern runs out of decent-sized towns and it isn't until **ÖREBRO** – 60km north of the lake – that you reach a signficant settlement. Strategically located on the main route from southwest Sweden to Stockholm, its light industrial hinterland promises

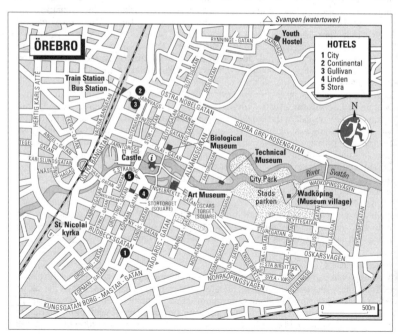

little, and even Örebo's proudest boasts are anti-climatic: it's Sweden's sixth most populous city, lying on the shores of Hjälmaren, the country's fourth largest lake. Yet the heart of Örebro comes as a pleasant surprise, the much fortified thirteenth-century **castle** forming a magnificent backdrop for the cultivated contours of the water-lily-studded **River Svatån**. Aside from the town's attractions, **Lake Tysslingen**, a few kilometres west, makes for a good afternoon excursion by bike. In spring, several thousand whooper swans settle here on their way to Finland and make spectacular viewing from observation towers.

Arrival, information and accommodation

Örebrö is just three hours from Stockholm on the main east–west **train** line. From the train and bus stations it's a short walk along Östra Bangatan and then to the right to reach the helpful **tourist office** in the castle (June–Aug Mon–Fri 9am–7pm, Sat & Sun 10am–5pm; rest of the year Mon–Fri 9am–5pm, May also Sat noon–4pm; ☎019/21 21 21; fax 10 60 70). The town centre is easy to see on foot, but if you want to get out into the countryside, you can rent a **bike** from the Technical Museum on Hamnplan, or at any *Pressbyrån* (40kr per 24 hours, 180kr per week). Another option is take a **boat trip** around nearby **Lake Hjälmaren** on *M/S Linnea* or *M/S Gustav Lagerbjelke* (2hr, 60kr; 3hr, 200kr).

    Private rooms can be booked at the tourist office for 130kr per person, plus a 25kr fee. The *STF* **youth hostel** has recently moved to new premises at Fanjunkarevägen 5 (☎019/31 02 40; fax 31 02 56; 100kr), an old army barracks just to the north; take bus #31 to Rynninge and get off one stop before the end of the line. If you're **camping**, the nearest site is 2km south of town at **Gustavsvik** (☎019/19 69 50; fax 19 69 90; mid-May to Aug). Of Örebrö's rather uninspiring **hotels**, the oldest and most luxurious is the central *Stora Hotellet*, Drottninggatan l (☎019/12 43 60; fax 611 78 90; ②/④), supposedly haunted by the ghost of a young woman and her mother. *City Hotel,* Kungsgatan 24 (☎019/10 02 00; fax 13 74 46; ②/③), and *Hotel Continental,* opposite the train station at Järnvägsgatan 2 (☎019/11 95 60; fax 11 73 10;43; ①/④), are similiar mid-range hotels; while *Hotel Gullvivan*, Järnvägsgatan 20 (☎019/611 90 35; fax 18 94 50; ①/③), is a cheaper option. Finally, there's the basic but perfectly adequate *Hotel Linden*, Köpmangatan 5 (①).

The Town

A fort has defended the town ever since a band of German merchants settled here in the thirteenth century, attracted by the presence of iron ore in the area. Enlarged by King Magnus Eriksson, the structure was further fortified by Gustav Vasa, whose son Karl IX did what Vasa's sons invariably did and turned it into a splendid Renaissance castle, raising the walls to the height of the medieval towers and plastering them in cream stucco. After the town lost its importance, **Örebro Castle** fell into disuse and was saved by becoming a storehouse and a prison.

    The fairy-tale exterior you see today is the result of renovation in the 1890s, when the castle was carefully restored to reflect both its medieval and Renaissance grandeur. The same cannot be said for the interior: valiant **tour guides** (May–Sept 5 daily; English tour at 2pm; 50kr) face a real challenge as there is no original furniture, and today many of the rooms are used by the county governor or for conferences. If you do join a tour, the few features of interest are some finely inlaid doors and floors dating from the 1920s, depicting historical events at Örebrö, and a large portrait of Karl XII and his family, all their faces painted to look the same – all have popping eyes, the result of using arsenic to whiten their faces. On the top floor there are a few local exhibits moved here from the old county museum.

    Nearby, at the top of the very oblong Stortorget, **St Nicolai kyrka** originates from 1260, but following extensive restoration in the 1860s there's little of its medieval character left. Recent renovations have tried to undo the damage, but today it's the contemporary art exhibitions on show here that catch the eye. Historically, however, the church is significant, as it was here in 1810 that the unknown figure of Napoleon's marshal, Jean Baptiste Bernadotte, was elected successor to the Swedish throne. The present royal family are descendants of the new King Karl Johan, who never spoke a word of Swedish.

Following the river eastwards brings you to the **Art Museum** (June–Aug Mon 11am–4pm, Tues–Sun 11am–6pm; Sept–May Tues–Sun noon–4pm; 25kr), a surprisingly spacious series of galleries housed in what was the Länsmuseum (see p.505). Much of the work on show is mediocre, the best room showing a collection by the late nineteenth-century local artist, Axel Borg. A little further up the river, past the appealing Stadspark, stands **Wadköping** (daily May–Aug 11am–5pm; Sept–April 11am–4pm; shops and exhibitions closed Mon). This is an entire village of centuries-old wooden cottages and shops brought to the site to form a living open-air museum. It's all extremely pretty but very staged. Some of the cottages have been reoccupied, and the twee little shops sell pastel-coloured wooden knick-knacks.

Eating and drinking

There are plenty of atmospheric places in Örebro for enjoying a wide range of good **food**. If you're here in July, though, be prepared for some of the smaller restaurants to be locked for the holidays. In the daytime, delicious organic home-baked goodies are served at *Café Stadsträdgården*, in the greenhouses at the entrance to Stadpark (Mon–Fri 11am–6pm, Sat & Sun 11am–5pm). For sheer fun, the *Medeltidspuben*, *Drottning Blanka* (Queen Blanka's Medieval Pub) serves medieval-style meals, such as wild boar, in the windowless, candle-lit depths of the castle's torture chamber and prison – a main course and drink costs around 80kr. Excellent meals can be had in the trendy *Ett Rum Och Kök* at Ringgatan 30, about ten minutes' walk from the castle. There's a bar there called *Garage* made out of half a red Volvo Amazon, the classic 1950s sports saloon. The best pizzas in town, along with meat dishes and pasta, are served at the upmarket *Wärdshuset Gyllen Oxen,* Ringgatan 19. For **drinking**, head for *Björnstugan*, on Kungsgatan, which is always busy.

Linköping

Sixty kilometres east of Lake Vättern in the county of Östergötland, **LINKÖPING**'s range of appealing buildings stand as testament to its 900-year-old history. The architectural highlights are the remarkable Domkyrkan and an entire village caught in a late nineteenth-century time warp – **Gamla Linköping**, a few kilometres to the west. Linköping's best-kept secret, however, missed by all but a handful of visitors, is a unique art exhibition that reveals more about eighteenth-century Swedish society than any number of old houses could hope to do.

The Town and around

With its soaring, 107-metre-high spire, the elegant **Domkyrkan** (June & July Mon–Sat 9am–7pm, Sun 9am–6pm; rest of the year Mon–Sat 9am–6pm, Sun 10am–6pm), set in a swathe of greenery, dates from 1232 – though the bulk of the present, sober building was completed around 1520 – and is built entirely of local hand-carved limestone. Stonemasons from all over Europe worked on the building and, with a belfry and the west facade added as late as 1885, you can make out a number of styles from Romanesque to Gothic. The venerable old buildings around the Domkyrkan include the much rebuilt thirteenth-century castle which, like so many others, was fortified by Gustav Vasa and beautified by his son Johan III.

Five minutes' wander down Ågatan in the direction of the Stångån River, the town's most unexpected cultural diversion is in the unlikely setting of the **Labourers' Educational Association** (ABF) at Snickaregatan 22. On the fourth floor is a priceless collection of 85 brilliantly executed pictures by the celebrated artist **Peter Dahl**, illustrating all the *Epistles of Bellman*. Carl Michael Bellman was an eighteenth-century poet/songwriter who sought to expose the hypocrisies of contemporary Swedish society, telling of life in pubs, of prostitutes and of the wild and drunken sexual meanderings of high-society men and women, all set against fear of the Church and final damnation. Officially, the ABF closes for July, but if you walk round the corner onto Storgatan and to the left of the *Spar Bank*, a set of elevators leads to a second entrance, where someone should let you in.

Just one block back on St Larsgatan, **St Lars kyrka** (Mon–Thurs 11am–4pm, Fri 11am–3pm, Sat 11am–1pm) is frequently bypassed, standing as it does within a few metres of the great Domkyrkan. Consecrated by Bishop Kol in 1170, the present interior has had too many face lifts to show many signs of its age. However, it was a plan to reinforce the floor that brought the discovery of a number of twelfth-century engraved stone and wood coffins. There are no signs to direct you, but beneath the church, in candle-lit half light, complete twelfth-century skeletons reside in new glass coffins, alongside some remarkably preserved wood coffins and the exposed remains of the original church, rebuilt in the 1730s. To see it all, just ask whoever is selling postcards to unlock the door leading to the basement.

Gamla Linköping

Just 3km west of Linköping proper, **Gamla Linköping** (Mon–Fri 10am–5.30pm, Sat & Sun noon–4pm; free) is a remarkable open-air museum, essentially different from the others you may have seen in that it is a true living environment. An entire town of houses, shops and businesses has been brought here from Linköping, along with streetlighting, fences, signs and even trees, to re-create the town as an identical copy of its nineteenth-century incarnation – even the street plan is exactly the same. Fifty people live here, and there's a massive waiting list for eager new tenants, despite the drawbacks of not being allowed to alter the properties and the fact that tourists trundle through year-round. Craftsmen work at nineteenth-century trades, and most shops are open every day, including a small chocolate factory, gold- and silversmiths, a woodwind workshop and linen shops; there's a cafeteria and an open-air theatre, with performances throughout the summer. Buses #203 and #205 run here from Resecentrum (Sept–May every 20min).

Canal trips

Linköping is riddled with waterways and a number of trips offer to chance to explore them. The **Göta Canal** is the most obvious target, wending its way from Motala through Borensberg to the seven-sluice Carl Johan Lock at Berg, just north of Linköping, where it meets Lake Roxen. South of the city, the less well-known **Kinda Canal** has a manually operated triple lock at Tannefors, and you can head south for 35km through a mix of canal and river to Rimforsa.

There are endless combinations of canal and river trips, with mystifying cost options, from a basic Göta Canal trip for two adults for 210kr, to a more glamorous spree on the *M/S Nya Skärgården* to Söderköping (35km east) and back in a steamer from 1915 (bookings on ☎070/637 17 00). For a less ambitious trip, boats also head down the Kinda Canal/Stångån River to a pleasant outdoor café at Tannefors. For the least expensive canal experience, you can rent canoes or bikes along the old towpath at *Hotel Östergyllen* (see below).

Practicalities

All **trains** and **buses** arrive at and leave from **Resecentrum** (travel centre) in the north of the town centre. Linköping is easy to walk around, with the reference point of the Domkyrkan spire rarely out of sight. The main **tourist office** (Mon–Fri 9am–6pm; June–Aug also Sat & Sun 9am–3pm; ☎013/20 68 35 or 31 46 00; fax 14 21 55) is just a few minutes' walk west from Resecentrum, in the airy Concert and Congress Hall – cross Järnvägsgatan, head down Järnvägsavenyn and it's on the left. A helpful smaller **evening office** is based at the *Ekoxen Hotel*, Kostergatan 68 (Mon–Fri 6–10pm; June–Aug also Sat & Sun 3–10pm) – from Järnvägsavenyn turn right down Klostergatan, and it's at the far end on the right.

The tourist office will book **private rooms** from 150kr per person (no booking fee). Every room in Linköping's *STF* **youth hostel**, Klostergatan 52A (☎013/14 90 90; fax 14 83 00; 100kr), has its own mini-kitchen and en-suite shower and toilet. *Glyttinge Camping*, a modern **campsite** with four-bed cabins, is 3km east of town at Berggårdsvägen (☎013/17 49 28; mid-April to Sept); take bus #201. Linköping is not a popular holiday destination with Swedes, and several of the smaller **hotels** close for July – the plus side is that some of those that stay open drop their prices dramatically. Best value is the comfortable family-run *Hotellet Östergyllen,* Hamngatan 2 (☎013/10 20 75; fax 12 59 02; ①), which also operates **cycling and canoeing packages**. For a little more luxury, try the *Ekoxen,* Klostergatan 68 (☎013/14 60 70; fax 12 19 03; ②/⑤), which has every facility, including a pool.

Linköping is a likeable spot to spend an evening, and the liveliest and most appealing places to **eat and drink** after dark are all on Ågatan, running up to the Domkyrkan. Some of them are open during the day, too. A couple of **café-konditori** around Storatorget serve the best cakes and sandwiches: *Lind's*, on the edge of the square is better than its neighbouring rivals. For bigger meals, try *B.K.* on Ågatan, a fun place with a huge cocktail bar and an elegant restaurant serving unusual dishes like crocodile, kangaroo and frogs' legs (90–139kr), or *Gula Huset*, also on Ågatan, which serves an extensive vegetarian buffet for 55kr at lunchtime and big portions of Swedish meat and fish dishes or pizzas (74kr) later on – it's also the cheapest place to drink. The national organization *RFSL* runs a **gay** bar, *Joy Café* at Nygatan 58, open afternoons in summer; for entry to the popular Friday-night pub, however, you need to be a member.

Norrköping and around

It is with good reason that the dynamic, youth-oriented town of **NORRKÖPING** calls itself Sweden's Manchester. Like its British counterpart, Norrköping's wealth came from its textile industry, which thrived in the eighteenth and nineteenth centuries (the Swedish word for corduroy is *manchester*). The legacy from this period is the town's most appealing feature: it is one of Europe's best-preserved industrial urban landscapes, with handsome red-brick and stuccoed mills reflecting in the waters of Motala Ström.

It was this small, rushing river that attracted the Dutch industrialist Louis De Geer to the town in the late seventeenth century, and his paper mill, still in operation today, became the biggest factory, to be followed by numerous wool, silk and linen factories. Today, many buildings are painted a strong, tortilla-chip yellow, as are the trams – De Geer's favourite colour has become symbolic of the town. Textiles kept Norrköping booming until the 1950s, when foreign competition began to sap the market, and the last big textile mill closed its doors in 1992. Like Manchester, Norrköping has also become a nucleus for music-inspired youth culture, popularized by Ulf Lundell, one of Sweden's most famous singer-songwriters, and home to the country's best-known working-class rock band, Eldkvarn.

Norrköping has one of the highest immigrant populations in Sweden. The first to come here were the Jews in the mid-eighteenth century. Today's immigrant communities are mostly from Asian and Arabic countries, though in the past few years there's been a considerable influx from the former Yugoslavia.

Arrival, information and accommodation

The helpful **tourist office** at Drottninggatan 11 (June–Aug Mon–Fri 9am–7pm, Sat & Sun 9am–3pm; rest of the year Mon–Fri 9am–5pm; ☎011/15 15 00; fax 16 08 78) is five minutes' walk from the **train** and **bus** terminals. They sell a range of good-value cards and packages: the **Norrköping Runabout Card** (295kr) is valid for three days and gives free admission to Kålmorden Djurpark and Löfstad Manor, free museum entry, plus various other freebies like boat trips and tours; the more ambitious **Östergötland County Card** (325kr) covers more trips and throws in a Vadstena Card; while a **Runabout Package** (mid-June to mid-Aug) gives discounts on accommodation along with a Runabout Card. Ask at the tourist office, too, about the 1902 **vintage tram**, which loops around on a sightseeing tour during summer. Regular yellow trams run around the centre on two lines, costing a flat 15kr, valid for an hour.

The tourist office will book **private rooms** from 130kr per person, plus a 60kr booking fee, or can just provide a list for you. There are two *STF* **youth hostels**. *Turistgården* (☎011/10 11 60; fax 18 68 63; all year; 90kr), Ingelstadsgatan 31, is just a few hundred metres behind the train station, or there's the more picturesque one at Abborreberg, 5km east of town. The closest **campsite** is by the rock carvings at Himmelstalund, *City Camp* on Utställningsvägen (☎011/17 11 90; fax 17 09 82) – walk west along the river, or take bus #118 from the bus station. The cheapest central **hotel**, *Hotel Centric*, Gamla Rådstugugatan 18–20 (☎011/12 90 30; fax 18 07 28; ①/②), close to the train station and parallel with Drottninggatan, is reasonable enough, but for a more upmarket experience, try for a room at the turn-of-the-century *Grand Hotel*, bang in the centre at Tyska Torget 2 (☎011/19 71 00; fax 18 11 83; ②/⑤). The *President Hotel*, next to the theatre at Vattengränden 11 (☎011/12 95 20; fax 10 07 10; ③/⑤), is pleasant too.

The Town

From the train station to the north of the town, Drottninggatan runs as a straight north–south central artery, crossing Motala Ström. Just a few steps down from the station, the small but pretty **Carl Johans Park** boasts the unusual feature of 25,000 cacti, all formally arranged in thematic patterns. Over the river and following the tram lines up cobbled Drottninggatan, a right turn into Repslagaregatan leads into **Gamla Torget**, overlooked by a charismatic sculpture of Louis De Geer by Carl Milles. From here, the steely modern riverside **Concert Hall** is fronted by trees, providing a lovely setting for the *Kråkholmen Louis De Geer* café (see below). It's worth stepping inside the Concert Hall for a moment, as its surface modernity belies the fact that this was once one of De Geer's paper factories. You can also pick up information on the symphony orchestra's weekly concerts.

Through the impressive, eighteenth-century paper mill gates to the left, and across a wooden bridge behind the hall is the **Arbets (Work) Museum** (daily 11am–5pm; free), housed in a triangular, yellow-stuccoed factory from 1917. Known as "The Iron" – though its shape and colour are more reminiscent of a wedge of cheese – the building was considered by Carl Milles to be Europe's most beautiful factory. It's a splendid place, with seven floors of exhibitions on living conditions, workers' rights and daily life in the mills. Take the stairs down, rather than the lift, to see a touching exhibition in the stairwell about the life of Alva, a woman who spent 35 years as a factory worker here. Next door, over another little bridge, is the excellent **Stadsmuseum** (Tues–Fri

10am–4pm, Thurs till 8pm, Sat & Sun 11am–5pm; free). Set in an interconnecting (and confusing) network of old industrial properties, the most engaging of the permanent exhibitions is a trade street featuring the workplaces of a milliner, confectioner, chimney sweep and, in a backyard, a carriage maker.

Back across the river, follow the bank west for ten minutes into the countryside, to reach the **Färgargården**, an open-air dyeworks museum (May–Aug Tues–Sun noon–4pm, free), ranged in a huddle of wooden nineteenth-century houses. A better reason to come here than the exhibitions or the garden of plants used to make dyes, is the oudoor café, open whenever the weather is good during summer.

Any interest you have in Swedish art can be satisfied at Norrköping's **Konstmuseum**, at the southernmost tip of Drottninggatan (Tues–Sun noon–4pm, Wed till 8pm; 30kr), as it's full of some of the country's best-known modernist works. Founded by a local snuff manufacturer at the turn of the century, the galleries offer a fine, well-balanced progression from seventeeth-century Baroque through to up-to-the-minute twentieth-century paintings. Coming out of the art museum, the bunker-like, concrete building to the right is the town **library**, more interesting and user-friendly than most, with a big range of international newspapers and free use of the Internet.

Eating and drinking

There is a fair selection of eating places in Norrköping, most of them doubling up as bars. However, it's the Norrköping custom to have a drink at home before heading out to the pubs, so the city only starts coming alive from 10pm or so. If you want to carry on after the bars close, the most popular **nightclub** and restaurant is *Tellus* (Wed, Fri & Sat 9pm–3am), beneath *Pub Vasa* at Kungsgatan 38; the food here is basic and cheap.

Far and away the friendliest and most stylish **restaurant** and **bar** is *Guskelov*, Dalsgatan 13, at the opening to the industrial area and next door to the concert hall, which specializes in fish. *Pub Wasa*, on the riverside at Kungsgatan 38, is a popular drinking spot, effectively decked out as a ship interior. Across the road, *Cromwell House* is a little more upmarket, serving light meals like omelettes or chicken wings for around 85kr. If your budget is up to it, *Restaurant La Mansion*, Södra Promenaden 116, offers venison, salmon and the like in the setting of a former home of a textile mill manager. Two-course lunches are a steep 135kr.

Around Norrköping: Löfstad Manor and Kålmorden Djurpark

The following are all easy trips from Norrköping; within even closer reach are the rock carvings at **Himmelstalund**, a couple of kilometres west of the centre. These carvings date from around 1500 BC and show with unusual clarity ships, weapons, animals and men; while burial mounds, though nothing much to look at, attest to Iron Age and Viking settlements in the area. To get there take bus #118 from Norrköping.

Löfstad Manor

Just 10km southwest of town, **Löfstad Manor** (May Sat & Sun only; June to mid-Aug daily; tours hourly on the hour noon–4pm; 30kr) is a fine country home dating from the 1650s, but rebuilt a hundred years later after a fire ravaged all but its shell. The same family owned Löfstad until the last, unmarried daughter, Emily Piper, died in 1926. She willed the house, its contents and the whole estate to the Museum of Östergotland, which has kept it untouched since her death. Generations of ancestors before Emily all made their mark, and there's a splendid collection of eighteenth- and nineteenth-century Baroque and Roccoco furniture and pictures. Emily's most notable ancestor was Axel Fersen, who, during the French Revolution, tried in vain to save King Louis XVI and Queen Marie-Antoinette. His motives may not have been entirely political – rumoured to have been the queen's lover, it's thought that the portrait of Marie Antoinette's daughter in the drawing room is a portrait of his daughter, too. The areas with the most authentic lived-in feel are the kitchen and servants quarters, while in the servant's quarters you can see Miss Piper's bathroom, with her ancient bathrobe still hanging from the door. The tour guide whisks you round pretty quickly and it's a good idea to ask for English translations before the tour gets underway.

Bus #481 runs from Norrköping bus terminal to Löfstad (just ask for Löfstad Slott). Getting back can be a problem, especially on weekend afternoons, but you may be able to get a ride from another visitor. There's a pleasant **restaurant** in one wing of the house, serving traditional Swedish food, plus a cheaper café in the stables.

Kolmården Djurpark

In the other direction, 28km northeast of Norrköping, **Komården Djurpark** is one of the country's biggest tourist attractions. A combined zoo, safari park and dolphinarium, it's understandably popular with children, who have their own zoo as well as access to a gaggle of other diversions and enclosures. If your views on zoos are negative, it's just about possible to be convinced that this one is different; there are no cages, but instead sunken enclosures, rock barriers and moats to prevent the animals from feasting on their captors. There's certainly no shortage of things to do either: there's a cable-car ride over the safari park, a tropical house, working farm and dolphin shows.

If you're interested in just one or two specific attractions in the park, it might be as well to call first (☎01/24 90 00), as the safari park can be closed in bad weather. Generally, though, most things are open daily (from 10am until around 4–6pm). Entrance charges vary according to what you want to see, but a combined ticket for everything runs from 160kr to 200kr, depending on the season. If you don't have your own transport, take bus #432 from Norrköping bus terminal (hourly; 50min). Should you want to stay, there's a **hotel**, the *Vidmarkshotellet* (☎011/15 71 00; ②/④), at the park, or you can **camp** at *Kolmården Camping* (☎011/39 82 50), close by at the water's edge.

Nyköping and around

The county of Södermanland – known as Sörmland – cuts diagonally to the northeast of Norrköping above Bråviken bay. Its capital, the very small historic town of **NYKÖPING**, has seen a lively past, but today is used by most visitors simply as a springboard for the picturesque coastal islands to the east. This is a pity, as its under-rated charms include an excellent museum, in and around the ruins of its thirteenth-century castle, and a harbour that bustles with life in summer.

A late twelth-century defensive tower, built to protect the trading port at the estuary of the Nyköping River, was converted into a fortress by King Magnus Ladulås, and it was here in 1317 that the infamous **Nyköping Banquet** took place. One of Magnus's three sons, Birger, invited his brothers Erik and Valdemar to celebrate Christmas at Nyköping and provided a grand banquet. Once the meal was complete, and the visiting brothers had retired to bed, Birger had them thrown in the castle's dungeon, threw the key into the river and left them to starve to death. It wasn't until the nineteenth century that the key was found by a boy fishing in the river, though whether the rusting key on display is the genuine item, no one knows. Gustav Vasa fortified the castle with gun towers in the sixteenth century, and his son Karl, Duke of Södermanland, later had it converted it into a regal Renaissance Palace. The following century all but the King's Tower was devastated by fire, and never rebuilt.

Today, the riverside tower and connected early eighteenth-century house built for the county governor form a **museum complex** (July daily noon–4pm; rest of the year closed

Mon; 20kr). Wandering through the original gatehouse beneath Karl's heraldic shield, you reach the extensively restored **King's Tower**. Climbing up to the first floor you'll pass carefully stacked bits and pieces excavated from Karl's palace – most notably some spectacular Ionic column tops. On the first floor, a model of the fortress fronted by a dashboard of buttons allows you to follow the events of the Nyköping Banquet – complete with gory details. The top floor has some evocative exhibits, including a bizarre 3-D cameo depicting the dead King Gustavus Adolfus lying in state, with his widow and six-year-old Queen Kristina looking on. It's the old **Governor's Residence**, however, that has the most exquisite collections. Here you can climb the stairs, lined with menacing portraits, to an exceptional run of magnificently decorated rooms from each stylistic period. Among the highlights is the Jugend room – probably the finest example you'll see in Sweden.

Once you've seen the castle and museum, Nyköping offers a pleasant walk along the river bank, lined with people fishing, to the popular harbour and marina, a regular goal for the Stockholm yachting set – the capital being just 100km away by road or train; the flat water inside the 1500-metre-long breakwater is also an important venue for canoe racing.

Practicalities

The **train station**, where buses also stop, is at the opposite end of town from the harbour, though the distance is easily walkable. The cental **tourist office**, on Rådhus Storatorget (June to mid-Aug Mon–Fri 8am–5pm, Sat & Sun 10am–5pm; rest of the year Mon–Fri 8am–5pm; ☎0155/24 82 00; fax 24 88 00), will book **private rooms** from 125kr (no booking fee). The delightful *STF* **youth hostel** is set in the castle grounds at Brunnsgatan 2 (May to mid-Sept; rest of the year groups only; ☎0155/21 18 10; 70–100kr). The nearest **camping site**, which has cheap cabins, is *Oppeby Camping* (May–Sept; ☎0155/21 13 02), 2km northwest of the centre near the E4. Among the **hotels**, *Kompaniett*, on Folkungavägen by the harbour (☎0155/28 80 20; fax 28 16 73; ②/⑤), is stylish – and good value, since breakfast, afternoon tea and a buffet dinner are included in the price. Otherwise, try the cheap but adequate *Hotel Wictoria*, Fruängsgatan 21 (☎0155/21 75 80; fax 21 44 47; ①/②).

Most of the **eating and drinking** is, unsurprisingly, done at the harbour, but for the best daytime **café**, head for *Café Hellmans* on Västra Trädgårdgatan 24 (Mon–Fri 7.30am–6pm, Sat 9am–4pm, Sun 10am–4pm), just off Stora Torget, where you can sit outside in the courtyard in summer. *Tova Stugen*, behind the castle grounds close to the harbour, serves light lunches in low, grass-roofed fifteenth-century cottages brought here from around Södermanland. Nyköping's lively **restaurant** and **bar** scene is based around the old wooden storage buildings along the harbourside. Try the popular *Restaurant Hamn Magasinet*, where two-course meals (including a vegetarian option) cost 166kr. Serving similar food, *Lotsen* is more laid-back and cheaper.

If you're driving from Nyköping to Stockholm, it's a straight run on the E4; it's also a quick **train** journey (1hr 15min). The **bus** route is convoluted, involving one of five buses to either Trosa or Vagnhärad, then bus #782 to Liljeholmen, followed by a subway trip to the city centre.

Around Nyköping

Hundreds of **islands** are accessible from Nyköping, served by regular boat trips from town. The most popular excursion is to the nature reserve on **Stendörren**, from where boats continue to the idyllic little coastal town of Trosa. Around 30km west of town, Stendörren offers some fine walking between the islands, which are connected by footbridges. **Trosa** – also reachable by road, 40km along the E4 – is ideal for tranquil riverside walks, with some forested trails and picture-perfect, red wooden cottages around the old centre.

M/S Labrador leaves the dock at Nyköping for Stendörren and Trosa at 9am (mid-June to mid-Aug Thurs & Fri). It costs 80kr to get to Stendörren, 120kr for Trosa; the return boat leaves at 3.20pm. Alternatively you can stay on Trosa in the *STF* **youth hostel** (☎015/65 32 28; June to mid-Aug; 85kr). If you don't want to return to Nyköping, take bus #702 from Trosa bus terminal to Liljeholmen (1hr), where you can connect with public transport to Stockholm. **Camping** near Trosa is possible at *Nynäs Camping* (mid-April to mid-Oct; ☎015/64 10 09). There's only one cabin, so it's worth booking well in advance.

Gotland

Rumours about good times on **Gotland** are rife. Wherever you are in Sweden, one mention of this ancient Baltic island will elicit a typically Swedish sigh followed by an anecdote about what a great place it is. You'll hear that the short summer season is an exciting time to visit; that it's hot, fun and lively. Largely, this is all true: the island was a distinctly youthful feel as young, mobile Stockholmers desert the capital for a boisterous summer spent on its beaches. The flower power era also makes its presence felt with a smattering of elderly VW camper vans lurching off the ferries, but shiny Saabs outnumber them fifty to one. During summer, bars, restaurants and campsites are packed, the streets swarm with revellers, and the sands are awash with bodies. It's not everyone's cup of tea: to avoid the hectic summer altogether, come in late May or September when, depending on your bravado, you can still swim.

Gotland itself, and in particular its capital, **Visby**, has always seen frenetic activity of some kind. A temperate climate and fortuitous geographical position attracted the Vikings as early as the sixth century and the lucrative trade routes they opened, through to Byzantium and western Asia, guaranteed the island its prosperity. With the ending of Viking domination, a "Golden Age" followed, Gotland's inhabitants sending embassies, maintaining trading posts and signing treaties with European and Asian leaders. However, by the late twelfth century the island's autonomy had been undermined by the growing power of the Hanseatic League, under whose influence Visby became one of the great cities of medieval Europe, famed for its wealth and strategic power. A contemporary ballad had it that "The Gotlanders weigh their gold with twenty pound weights. The pigs eat out of silver troughs and the women spin with golden distaffs."

This romantic notion of the island's prosperity persisted right into this century, when Gotlanders began relying on tourism to prop up the traditional industries of farming, forestry and fishing. Twentieth-century hype makes great play of the sun, and it's true that the flowers that give Gotland its "Island of Roses" tag have been known to bloom at Christmas. It's not all just tourist brochure fodder, however: nowhere else in Scandinavia is there such a concentration of unspoilt medieval country churches, 93 of them still in use and providing the most permanent reminder of Gotland's ancient wealth.

Getting there: ferries and planes

Ferries to Gotland are numerous and, in summer, packed, so try and plan well ahead. *Gotlandslinjen*, the ferry line, has booking centres in both Nynäshamn and Oskarshamn. Or, in Stockholm, call into *Gotland City* (☎08/23 61 70; fax 411 79 65), Kungsgatan 57, which can provide information and sell advance tickets. One-way fares cost around 135kr during high season (June to mid-Aug), 175kr on Friday, Saturday and Sunday; and there are student discounts (30 percent) on all crossings. Night sailings in summer are packed out so it may be worth while booking an en-suite cabin (1016kr return for 2 people). Taking a bicycle costs 35kr. See "Travel Details" for a full run-through of ferry schedules and frequencies. The nearest port to Stockholm is **NYNÄSHAMN**, where there's a **youth hostel** (☎08/520 208 34; all year, advance book-

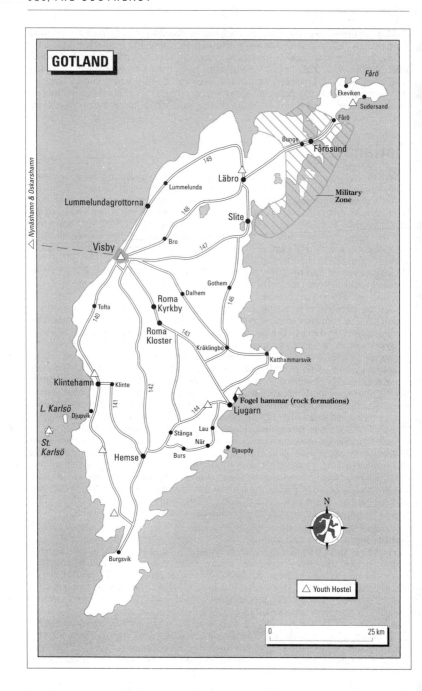

GOTLAND

Fårö

Ekeviken

Sudersand

Fårö

Bunge

Fårösund

149

Läbro

Lummelunda

Military Zone

Lummelundagrottorna

148

Slite

Bro

147

Nynäshamn & Oskarshamn

Visby

Gothem

Dalhem

146

Roma Kyrkby

Tofta

140

Roma Kloster

143

Kräklingbo

Katthammarsvik

Klintehamn

Klinte

142

L. Karlsö

Djupvik

141

144

◆ **Fogel hammar (rock formations)**

Ljugarn

St. Karlsö

Stånga

Lau

När

Hemse

Burs

Djaupdy

Burgsvik

N

△ Youth Hostel

0   25 km

ing essential Sept–May) not far from the train station at Nickstabadsvägen 17. From Gothenburg or the southwest of the country, **OSKARSHAMN** may well be the easier port, a little over six hours by train from Gothenburg. Be warned that the limited food on board the ferries is expensive, so it's worth stocking up before you leave.

Recent competition between the two airlines servicing the island has made **flying** an economical option – at least for under-24s. One-way fares from Stockholm can be as little as 296kr standby. Local tourist offices can provide up-to-date prices.

Visby

Undoubtedly the finest approach to **VISBY** is by ship, when you can see the old trading centre as it should be seen – from the sea. If you sail on one of the busy summer night-time crossings, it's good to get out on deck for the early sunrise. By 5am the sun is above the city, silhouetting the towers of the cathedral and the old wall turrets.

Arrival and information

Visby **airport** is 3km from town, a five-minute ride on the airport bus (30kr). A **taxi** into the centre will cost around 65kr. All the huge **ferries** serving Visby dock at the same terminal, just outside the city walls (and off our map). Just turn left and keep walking for the centre. Alternatively, a short way to the right along the harbourfront will bring you to *Gotlandsresor* at Färjeleden 3, which has a room-booking service (see "Accommodation", below).

The main **tourist office** is within the city walls in Donnersplats (mid-April to May Mon–Fri 8am–5pm, Sat & Sun 10am–4pm; June to mid-Aug Mon–Fri 7am–7pm, Sat & Sun 10am–7pm; rest of the year Mon–Fri 9am–4pm; ☎0498/20 17 00; fax 27 89 40). Here you can buy the excellent *Turistkarta Gotland* (25kr), a map with descriptions of all the points of interest. There's also a selection of **tours** available, some of which are worth considering if time is short: a walking tour of Visby (May–Aug daily at 11.30am; 70kr) and separate day-long tours of the south and north of the island by bus (May–Aug 1–2 weekly; 300kr), though beware that they only run when enough people are interested.

Getting around

Visby itself is best explored on foot. Despite its warren-like first appearance, it's a simple matter to find your way around the narrow, cobbled streets. The main square, **Storatorget**, is signposted from almost everywhere, and early arrivals will be rewarded by the smell of freshly baked bread from the square's bakery. Modern Visby has spread beyond the limits defined by its old city walls, and today the new town gently sprawls from beyond **Österport** (East Gate), a few minutes' walk up the hill from Storatorget. From here, in **Östercentrum**, the **bus terminal** serves the rest of the island; the tourist office has free timetables.

For getting around the island, it's hard to resist the temptation to rent a **bike**. Most ferry arrivals at Visby are plagued by people hustling bikes, and if you don't have one you might as well succumb here. Bike rental is also on offer on Korsgatan or, as a last resort, at Österport, though this is the least helpful outlet. Most places charge around 50kr a day, and if you want to try a tandem, it's best to arrive early as they are unusually popular. If you intend striking out into the countryside beyond Visby – undiscovered by most of the young summer crowd – it's worth knowing that bikes can easily be rented, and more cheaply, at various towns to the south of Visby, though Gotland's bike outlets like to appear vague about this possibility. For trips further afield, bear in mind that bikes can be taken on the island's buses for a flat fee of 20kr. Ask at the tourist office for a free map of the **cycle route** that circumnavigates almost the entire island, signposted out of Visby.

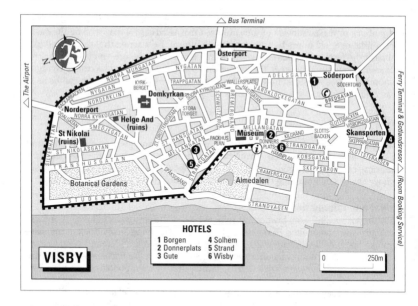

Accommodation

Finding **accommodation** in Visby should seldom be a problem; the abandoned-looking souls wrapped in sleeping bags and collapsed in the parks are only there through alcoholic excesses the night before, not homelessness. There are plenty of hotels (though few are particularly cheap), several campsites and cabins, and a youth hostel. The *Gotlandsresor* office, at Färjeleden 3 (☎0498/20 10 20; fax 20 12 70), and the tourist office (see above) can help with **private rooms** from 120kr per person, as well as **cottages**. More information and advice is available at *Gotlands Turist Service* at Österport (Mon–Fri 9am–6pm; ☎0498/20 60 00; fax 24 90 59), which has better access to accommodation information than the tourist office.

The well-equipped **youth hostel**, *Gotlands Ice Hockey Federation Youth Hostel* (☎0498/24 82 02; fax 24 82 70; all year; 150kr), is set in the forest 3km from Visby centre, behind the city's ice hockey hall (ask the bus driver to drop you at *Isall*). If you don't have your own transport, hitching is easy from the main road, but a taxi back will cost around 80–90kr. Chiefly, though, Gotland is a place for **camping**. After the success of Ulf Lundell's youth-culture novel *Jack*, which extolled the simple pleasure of getting wasted on a beach, Gotland became the place to go for wild summer parties: at many campsites, the most exercise you'll get is cycling to and from the Systembolaget. The closest campsite, *Nordenstrands* (May–Sept; ☎0498/21 21 57), is 1km outside the city walls – follow the cycle path that runs through the Botanical Gardens along the seafront.

HOTELS

Borgen, Adelsgatan 11 (☎0498/27 99 00; fax 24 93 00). Attractive family hotel in the middle of the action, yet with lovely, peaceful gardens. En-suite rooms, sauna and solarium. ③/④

Donnersplats, Donnersplats 6 (☎0498/21 49 45; fax 21 49 44). A popular, central hotel also offering two- to three-bed apartments for 950kr. Booking essential in July and Aug. ③/④

Gute, Mellangatan 29 (☎0498/24 80 80; fax 24 80 89). Very central and reasonably comfortable; reductions may be possible if you appear at the last minute. ③/④

Hamn, Färjeleden 3 (☎0498/20 12 50; fax 20 12 70). Opposite the harbour, this is the most convenient hotel for early-morning ferries back to the mainland. All rooms have TV, shower and toilet and breakfast (included) is served from 5am. Open May–Sept. ②

Solhem, Solhemsgatan 3 (☎0498/27 90 70; fax 21 95 23). Just outside the city walls at Skansporten, this large hotel is considerably shabbier than its price suggests. Only an option if all other central hotels are full. ④

Strand, Strandgatan 34 (☎0498/21 26 00; fax 27 81 11). A rather glamorous place in the heart of town, with a sauna, steam bath, indoor pool and a stylish atmosphere. ④/⑤

Wisby, Strandgatan 6 (☎0498/20 40 00; fax 21 13 20). Splendid, central hotel in a building dating back to the Middle Ages; it was a grain store until 1850. Fine breakfasts (open to non-residents for 65kr). However, in May, June and Aug the price goes up to 1410kr. ⑤

The City

Visby is much older than its medieval remnants suggest. The name derives from its status as a Stone Age sacrificial site – "the settlement", *by*, at "the sacred place", *vi* – but it's the medieval trappings that give the city its distincly Mediterranean air. The magnificent **defensive wall** that encircles Visby is the most obvious manifestation of its previous importance. It was hardly a new idea to fortify trading centres against outside attack, although this land wall, built around the end of the thirteenth century, was actually aimed at isolating the city's foreign traders from the island's own locals. Annoyed at seeing all their old trade monopolized, the Gotlanders saw something sinister in the wall's erection and didn't have to wait long to be vindicated. In 1361, during the power struggle between Denmark and Sweden, the Danish king, Valdemar III, took Gotland by force and advanced on Visby. The burghers and traders, well aware of the wealth of their city, shut the gates and sat through the slaughter outside. Excavations this century revealed the remains of two thousand bodies, more than half of them women, children and invalids. **Valdemar's Cross**, a few hundred metres east of Söderport (South Gate), marks their mass grave. Erected by the survivors of the carnage, it reads: "In 1361 on the third day after St James, the Goths fell into the hands of the Danes. Here they lie. Pray for them."

Back inside the city walls, the merchants surrendered, and a section of the wall near Söderport was broken down to allow Valdemar to ride through as conqueror. Valdemar's Breach is recognizable by its thirteen crenellations representing, so the story goes, the thirteen knights who rode through with the Danish king. Valdemar soon left clutching booty and trade agreements, and Visby continued to prosper while the island's countryside around it stagnated, its people and wealth destroyed.

The old **Hanseatic harbour** at Almedalen is now a public park and nothing is much more than a few minutes' walk from here. Pretty **Packhusplan**, the oldest square in the city, is bisected by curving Strandgatan, which runs southwards to the fragmentary ruins of **Visborg Castle**, overlooking the harbour. Built in the fifteenth century by Erik of Pomerania, the castle was blown up by the Danes in the seventeenth century. In the opposite direction, Strandgatan runs northwest towards the sea and the lush **Botanical Gardens**, just beyond which is the **Jungfrutornet** (Maiden's Tower), where a local goldsmith's daughter was walled up alive – reputedly for betraying the city to the Danes.

Strandgatan itself is the best place to view the impressive merchants' houses looming over the narrow streets, with storerooms above the living quarters and cellars below, notably **Burmeisterska house** (June–Aug daily 11am–6pm; free). One of the most picturesque buildings is the old pharmacy, **Gamla Apoteket** (June–Aug Mon–Fri 2–6pm, Sat 10am–1pm; 10kr), a lofty place with gloriously higgledy-piggledy windows. Strandgatan's small Natural History Museum (June–Aug daily 11am–5pm; free) is largely missable, unlike the fine **Gotlands Fornsal Museum**, next door at Strandgatan 14 (mid-May to Aug daily 11am–6pm; Sept to mid-May Tues–Sun noon–4pm; 30k). Housed in a mid-eighteenth-century distillery, there are five storeys of exhibition halls covering eight thousand years of history, plus a good café and bookstore. Among the most impressive sections is the **Hall of Picture Stones** in Room 1, a collection of richly carved key-hole shaped stones dating mostly from the fifth to seventh centuries. The **Hall of Prehistoric Graves** is equally fascinating, its glass cases displaying skeletons dating back six thousand years. Rooms 9 to 13 trace the history of **medieval Visby**, with exhibits including a trading booth, where the burghers of Visby and foreign merchants dealt in commodities – furs, lime, wax, honey and tar – brought from all over Northern Europe. A series of tableaux bring the exhibition up to 1900, starting with Eric of Pomerania, the first resident of Visborg Castle, and leading on through the years of Danish rule, up to the island's industrial boom. There's a wax model of Anna Margareta Donner, a member of the eighteenth-century trading dynasty whose name you'll spot all over town.

Strolling around the twisting streets and atmospheric walls is not something that palls quickly, but if you need a focus, aim for **Norra Murgatan**, above the cathedral, once one of Visby's poorest areas. At the end nearest Norderport you'll be treated to the best view of the walls and city rooftops, along with a rare opportunity to climb onto the ramparts. **Kruttornet**, the dark, atmospheric tower on Strandgatan (June–Aug daily 10am–6pm), affords more grand views; while the roof of the **Helge And** church ruin (May–Sept daily 10am–6pm), which has been reinforced to allow access to the second floor, provides another central vantage point. Or head for **Studentallén** on the water's edge, from where the sunsets are magnificent.

VISBY'S CHURCHES

At the height of its power, Visby maintained sixteen **churches** and while only one, the Cathedral of St Mary, is still in use, the ruins of eleven others – very often only their towers or foundations – can be seen. The **Domkyrkan** (Mon–Fri & Sun 8am–9pm, Sat 8am–6.30pm) was built between 1190 and 1225 and as such dates from just before the great age of Gothic church-building on the island. Used as both warehouse and treasury in the past, it's been heavily restored, and about the only original fixture left is the thirteenth-century sandstone font. Most striking are its towers, one square at the western front and two slimmer eastern ones; originally each had spires, but since an eighteenth-century fire, they've been crowned with fancy Baroque cupolas, giving them the appearance of inverted ice cream cones. Inside, have a look beneath the pulpit, decorated with a fringe of unusually hideous angels' faces.

Seventeenth- and eighteenth-century builders and decorators found the smaller churches in the city to be an excellent source of free limestone, tiles and fittings – which accounts for the fact that most are today in ruins. Best of what's left is the great **St Nicolai** ruin, just down the road from the Domkyrkan, once the largest church in Visby. Destroyed in 1525, its part-Gothic, part-Romanesque shell hosts a week-long **chamber music festival**, starting at the end of July; tickets range from 100kr to 300kr and are available from the tourist office – which also sells a rather disappointing guide, *The Key to all of Gotland's Churches*.

Eating, drinking and nightlife

Visby's centre is small enough to wander around and size up the lunchtime eating options. More specifically, **Adelsgatan** is lined with cafés and snack bars, Wallersplats and Hästgatan are busy at lunchtime, while **Strandgatan** is the focus of Visby's evening parade. For good, cheap food all day, try Saluhallen, the market opposite the harbour: here you can buy fresh baked bread, fish and fruit and eat it at tables overlooking the water. Visby's restaurants and bars see plenty of life during the day, but at night they positively heave with young bodies – many of them drunk. **Donnersplats**, opposite the tourist office, is also lively at night, with lots of takeaway food stalls. Alternatively, head down to the **harbour**, where forests of masts make a pretty backdrop to the loud, happy beat of music and revellers grooving away on the dance floors. Note that many of Visby's discos and clubs open in the late afternoon, from around 4pm onwards, for "After Beach" sessions of relatively cheap beer.

Gotlanders also enjoys a unique licence from the state to brew their own **beer**, the recipe differing from household to household. It's never on sale, but summer parties are awash with the murky stuff – be warned, it is extremely strong. There are central off-licences in Storatorget and at Östervägen 3, with the island's other Systembolaget at Hemse, Slite, Klintehamn, Färösunds and Burgsvik.

DAYTIME CAFÉS

Café Björkstugan, Späksgränd. In a fabulous, lush garden on the prettiest central cobbled street, this little café serves pies and coffee.

Madame Donners Café, Donnersplats. A splendidly picturesque café with a garden; the tables inside once belonged to the venerable Mrs Donner. Main courses include cod with almonds at 50kr, and open sandwiches for 20kr.

Café Ryska Gården, Stortorget. A rustic place specializing in *saffranspanskakka*, a saffron-yellow rice pie, rather stronger in colour than taste; along with Gotland's own salmberry jam and cream.

Skafferiet, Adelsgatan. A lovely eighteenth-century house turned into a cosy café boasting a lush garden at the back. Baked potatoes and great cakes.

RESTAURANTS AND BARS

Bakfickan, corner of St Katarinegatan and Stortorget. A quiet, relaxed little restaurant, with a tiled interior. Also a good place for a drink.

Barbeque Garden, Strandgatan 15. On the site of Visby's medieval town hall, this is a huge garden pizza restaurant, with indoor and outdoor seating. Lots of cocktails, and a bright if not exactly trendy atmosphere.

Café Boheme, Hästgatan 9. A mellow but lively candle-lit place, serving inexpensive salads, sandwiches and pizzas and lots of cakes, including a rather good *kladdkaka* (gooey chocolate pie). Closed Sun & Mon outside summer.

Burmeister, Strandgatan. Busy place serving a full à la carte menu with starters around 80kr, pasta 90kr and main courses at 160kr. Expect long queues.

Friheten, Donnersplats. A lively pub attached to *Wisby Hotel*. Loud, live bands reverberate Fri & Sat evenings.

Gutekällaren, Lilla Torggränd, just a couple of steps up from *Henry's Bar*. Quiet fish and meat restaurant with an uncharacteristically sober atmosphere; à la carte and grill menu and cheaper bar food for around 50kr.

Henry's Bar, corner of St Hansgatan and Lilla Torggränd. One of the busiest joints, with a big, traditional pub, dancing and a steady queue to get in. Burgers, ribs, chicken and salads are served with the beers, for around 60–90kr.

Munk Källeren, Lilla Torggränd, opposite *Gutekällaren*. Massively fashionable and subsequently crowded. There's an extensive à la carte menu, entirely in English.

MEDIEVAL WEEK

During the first week of August, Visby becomes the backdrop for a boisterous re-enactment of the conquest of the island by the Danes in 1361. **Medieval Week** sees music in the streets, medieval food on sale in the restaurants (no potatoes – they hadn't yet been brought to Europe) and on the first Sunday a procession recreating Valdemar's triumphant entry through Söderport to Stortorget. Here, modern-day burghers are stripped of their wealth and then the procession moves onto the Maiden's Tower – all good touristy fun with a genuine carnival atmosphere to boot.

The rest of the island

There is a real charm to the rest of Gotland – rolling green countryside, forest-lined roads, fine beaches and small fishing villages, and everywhere the rural skyline is dominated by churches, the remnants of medieval settlements destroyed in the Danish invasion. Yet perhaps because of the magnetic pull of Visby, very few people bother to go and explore. The **south** of the island, in particular, boasts numerous wonderful and untouched villages and beaches; while the **north**, though pretty, can be adequately seen on a day trip from the capital.

Cycling around the island is immensely enjoyable, since the main roads are free of traffic and any minor roads positively deserted. Gotland's **buses**, though regular, are very few indeed. Outside Visby, they tend to run only twice daily – morning and evening. **Hitching**, however, is an accepted means of transport, and unless you have a specific destination in mind, it's often just as well to go wherever the driver is heading. As you go, keep an eye out for the waymarkers erected in the 1780s to indicate the distance to *Wisby* (the old spelling). They are calculated in Swedish miles (ie 10 km) and appear every quarter-mile, though the mile markers are the most ornate.

The Southeast

The so-called "capital" of the south, **HEMSE**, around 50km from Visby (buses ply the route), is little more than a main street, but there are a couple of banks and a good local café, *Bageri & Conditori Johansson* on Storgatan – if you're camping or without your own transport, this is the place to stock up with food. You can rent **bikes** from two places on Ronevägen, off Storgatan: *Hemse Krog* is a general rental shop with bikes, while next door, *Ondrell's* (☎0498/48 03 33) is incredibly cheap (40kr per day, 20kr each day after or 160kr per week); it also rents trailers. There's not a lot else to Hemse, except a **swimming pool** (June–Aug Mon–Thurs 2–8pm, Fri 5–8pm; 35kr), signposted "simhall", off Storgatan at the north end of the town. Hemse **bus station**, parallel with Storgatan (head down Ronevägen for one block and turn left), is oddly sited in a boarded-up and vandalized house.

Along Route 144 west towards Burs, the countryside is a glorious mix of meadows, ancient farms and dark, mysterious forest. **BURS** itself has a gorgeous thirteenth-century saddle church, so called because of its low nave and high tower and chancel. There's a fabulously decorated ceiling, medieval stained-glass windows and ornately painted pews. Nearby, *Burs Café* is a friendly locals' joint serving cheap, filling meals. Turning right out of Burs, the scenery is a paradise of wild, flowering meadows and medieval farmholdings, all untouched by the centuries, with ancient windows and carved wooden portals. The next place you come to is the tranquil and pretty hamlet of **NÄR**, notable for its church, set in an immaculate churchyard. The tower originally served as a fortification in the thirteenth century, but more arresting are the bizarre portraits painted on the pew ends right the way up the left side of the church. All depict women with demented expressions and bare, oddly placed breasts. A couple of kilometres north and just beyond the village of **LAU**, *Garde* **youth hostel** (☎0498/49 11 81; fax 49 11 81; open all year, pre-book outside summer; 95kr) provides some of Sweden's strangest accommodation: the cluster of buildings is situated right by the local football pitch, and the clean bathroom facilities are shared with anyone doing football practice. There's a food shop around the corner from the hostel reception and a café-bar in the village.

For beaches, and the nearest thing Gotland has to a resort, the lively and charming town of **LJUGARN** makes a good base. The **tourist office** (daily May & mid-Aug to mid-Sept 11am–4pm; June 9am–6pm; July to mid-Aug 8am–7pm) is just off the main road as you approach town and has plenty of information about the southeast of the island. Though full of touristy restaurants, the village manages to retain an authentic feel and is famous for its *rauker* – tall limestone pillars rising up from the sea. A delightful cycle or stroll down Strandvägen follows the coastline through woods and clearings carpeted in *blåeld*, the electric blue flowers for which the area is known. The *rauker* stand like ancient hunched men, their feet lapped by the waves. This is one place where it's easy to find a range of eating places to suit most tastes, and accommodation, unlike most of the island, is not restricted to camping or hostels. "*Rums*" are advertised in appealing-looking cottages all over the little town – the tourist office can also make bookings from 100kr (plus 30kr fee) – and there's a **youth hostel** (☎0498/49 31 84; all year; 95kr) on Strandridaregården. Gotland's oldest **B&B**, *Badpensionatet*, is here too (☎0498/49 32 05; ②); it opened its doors in 1921. All rooms are en-suite and there's also a restaurant, the only one in town that's open all year. Some of the best cakes in Sweden are to be found in Ljugarn, at *Café Espegards* on Storvägen, where there's a permanent queue. Finally, *Brunna Dorren* is a pleasant old stuccoed house now home to a pizza restaurant, with a big garden where beer is served overlooking the sea.

Heading back west from Ljugarn, Route 144 passes through **LYE**, a charming if sleepy hamlet with an antique shop and café. **STÅNGA** is just a few kilometres on, and worth stopping at for its fourteenth-century church with unusual wall tablets running down the facade. These have been attributed to Egypticus, a sculptor named for his influences since his identity has never been discovered. By the golf course outside is *Gumbalda Golf* (☎0498/48 28 80; fax 48 28 84; ①), a stylish **place to stay** at a very reasonable price; special golf packages are on offer, and the green fee for the eighteen-hole course is 200kr per day.

Stora and Lilla Karlsö

The two **islands** of Stora Karlsö and Lilla Karlsö, lying over 6km off the southwest coast, have been declared **nature reserves**, and both have bird sancturaries where razorbills, guillemots, falcons and eider duck breed relatively undisturbed. **Lilla Karlsö** is reached from Djupvik, 7km south of Klintehamn (no buses); return tickets, from the harbour office there, cost 120kr. There is a restaurant on the island, serving lunch and dinner – you need to book all meals, including breakfast if you're staying overnight in the hostel-style accommodation (☎0498/24 10 19; 100kr).

Stora Karlsö is reached from Klintehamn: tickets are available from the harbour office for sailings at 9am and 11am (150kr return; 45min). The only accommodation is in the tiny, very basic fishermen's huts that comprise the *STF* **youth hostel** (☎0498/24 500; fax 24 52 60; 100–200kr per hut for 4). No camping is allowed on the islands.

The north: Visby to Slite

Thirteen kilometres north of Visby are the **Lummelundagrottarna** (daily May–Aug 9am–6pm; Sept 9am–4pm; 40kr), limestone caves, stalagmites and stalactites that form a disappointingly dull and damp stop. There's a more interesting natural phenomenon 10km to the north, where you'll see the highest of Gotland's coastal **limestone stacks**. These are the remnants of reefs formed over four hundred million years ago: the fact that they're well above the tide line is proof of earlier, higher sea levels. This stack, 11.5 metres high and known as **Jungfruklint**, is said to look like the Virgin and Child – something you'll need a fair bit of imagination to deduce.

Instead of taking the coastal road from Visby, you could head inland instead towards **BRO**, which has one of the island's most beautiful churches. Several different building stages are evident from the Romanesque and Gothic windows in the tower, but the most unusual aspect is the south wall with its flat-relief picture stones, carved mostly with animals, that were incorporated from a previous church on the site.

On the whole, it's far better to press on north, where many of the secluded cottages serve as summer holiday homes for urban Swedes. Much of the peninsula north of **Lärbro** is prohibited to foreign tourists due to the army's presence, just the main road corridor to Fårösund being open to allow access the lovely **Fårö island** beyond (see below). You can go as far as **BUNGE** without special permission, and it's worth making the journey to visit its bright fourteenth-century fortified church and open-air museum (mid-May to mid-Aug daily 10am-6pm; 30kr). **SLITE**, just to the south of Lärbro and open to everyone, is the island's only really ugly place – day-trip buses pass right through its cement factories, quarries and monumentally dull architecture. Beyond this, though, Slite has a sandy beach and good swimming. If you don't mind paying for your camping, then the campsite (☎0498/22 08 30; May–Sept) isn't a bad choice, right on the beach.

Fårö

If you're worried about straying into forbidden territory, check with the tourist office in Visby, which arranges special day-long **bus trips** (June–Aug Tues & Thurs; 300kr) to **Fårö** (Sheep Island). However, it is possible for foreigners to get there independently: take the bus to **Fårosund**, then the half-hourly free ferry crossing (year-round; 15min) from the quay ten minutes' walk to the south, on the main road. There's a down-at-heel but surprisingly good working-men's café in town, *Färösund Grill*, which serves excellent sandwiches (25kr) and almond tart (10kr), with good, cheap coffee. Just opposite is *Bungehallen*, a very well-stocked supermarket (open daily till 10pm).

Most of Fårö island itself is flat limestone heath, with shallow lakes and stunted pines much in evidence. In winter (and sometimes in summer, too) the wind whips off the Baltic, justifying the existence of the local windmills – and of the sheep shelters, with their steeply pitched reed roofs, modelled on traditional Fårö houses. Examples of both line the road as you leave the ferry. The best place to head for (and the target of most of the Swedish holiday-makers) is the five-kilometre white sand arc at **Sundersandsviken**; much of the rest of the swimming is done at **Ekeviken**, on the other side of the isthmus. The remainder of the coastline is rocky, spectacularly so at **Lauterhorn** and, particularly, **Langhammars**, where limestone stacks are grouped together on the beach. At Lauterhorn you can follow the signs for Digerhuvud, a long line of stacks leading to the tiny fishing hamlet of **Helgumannen**, which has no more than a dozen shacks on the beach, now used as holiday homes. Continuing along the same rough track brings you to a junction; right runs back to the township of Fårö; left, a two-kilometre dead-end road leads to Langhammars.

The only place to stay is the *STF* **hostel** at Fårö, *Fårögården* (☎0498/22 36 39; mid-May to Aug; 100kr), which has its own small restaurant.

travel details

Trains

From Hallsberg to: Gothenburg (hourly; 2hr 40min); Stockholm (hourly; 1hr 30min).

From Jönköping to: Falköping (for Stockholm & Gothenburg; hourly; 45min); Nässjo (for Stockholm & Malmö; hourly; 35min).

From Kalmar to: Emmaboda (16 daily; 35min); Gothenburg (5 daily; 4hr 15min), plus more frequent local trains from Emmaboda and Växjo; Malmö (8 daily; 3hr 40min); Stockholm (5 daily; 6hr 30min); Växjo (10 daily; 1hr 15min).

From Motala to: Hallsberg (for Örebro, Stockholm & Gothenburg; 6 daily; 45min); Mjölby (for Malmö & Stockholm; 2 daily; 1hr 15min).

From Norrköping to: Linköping (1–2 hourly; 25min); Malmö (11 daily; 3hr 15min); Nyköping (5 daily; 40min); Stockholm (hourly; 1hr 40min).

From Örebro to: Gävle (6 daily, some changing at Falun; 3–4hr); Hallsberg (for Stockholm & Gothenburg; 1–2 hourly; 20min); Motala (6 daily; 1hr 30min); Stockholm (7 daily; 3hr 10min).

From Oskarshamn to: Gothenburg (3 daily; 5hr 30min); Nässjo (3 daily; 2hr 25min); Jönköping (3 daily; 3hr 20min).

From Växjo to: Kalmar (6 daily; 1hr 40min); Karlskrona (2 daily; 1hr 30min); Gothenburg (8 daily; 3hr 20min).

Buses

From Jönköping to: Gothenburg (Mon–Fri 2 daily, 3 on Sun; 2hr 15min); Gränna/Vadstena/Motala/Örebro (up to 2 daily; 30min/ 1hr 20min/1hr 40min/3hr 5min); Växjo (1 on Fri & Sun; 1hr 20min).

From Kalmar to: Gothenburg (1 daily; 6hr); Lund/Malmö (1 daily; 5hr 30min/5hr 45min); Oskarshamn/Västervik/Stockholm (3 daily; 1hr 25min/2hr 35min/6hr 50min).

From Motala to: Norrköping/Stockholm (2 on Fri & Sun; 1hr 35min/3hr 25min).

From Norrköping to: Löfstad Manor (every 2hr; 20min); Kolården Djurpark (5 daily; 1hr); Linköping/Jönköping/Gothenburg (6 daily; 30min/2hr 40min/4hr 55min); Kalmar (5 daily; 4hr 15min); Stockholm (5 daily; 2hr 10min).

From Växjo to: Jönköping/Linköping/Norrköping/Stockholm/Uppsala (1 on Fri & Sun; 1hr 20min/3hr 30min/4hr/6hr 30min/7hr 30min).

Ferries

From Nynäshamn to: Byxelkrok (mid-June to mid-Aug 3 daily); Visby (mid-June to mid-Aug 2–3 daily; rest of the year night sailings only; 5–6hr).

From Oskarshamn to: Visby (mid-June to mid-Aug 2 daily; rest of the year night sailings only; 3hr day, 6hr night).

From Timmernabben to: Borgholm (mid-June to mid-Aug 3 daily).

CHAPTER THIRTEEN

THE BOTHNIAN COAST: GÄVLE TO HAPARANDA

S weden's east coast forms one edge of the **Gulf of Bothnia** (*Bottenhavet*), a corridor of land that with its jumble of erstwhile fishing towns and squeaky-clean contemporary urban planning is quite unlike the rest of the north of the country. The coast is dominated by towns and cities: the endless forest so dominant in other parts of the north has been felled here to make room for settlements. Almost the entire coastline is dotted with towns that reveal a faded history. Some, like **Gävle** and **Hudiksvall**, still have their share of old wooden houses, promoting evocative images of the past, though much was lost during the Russian incursions of the eighteenth century. Cities like **Sundsvall**, **Umeå** and **Luleå** are more typical – modern, bright and airy, they rank as some of Sweden's liveliest and most likeable destinations. Throughout the north you'll also find traces of the religious fervour that swept the region in centuries past: **Skellefteå**, **Piteå** and **Luleå** all boast excellently preserved *kyrkstäder* or parish villages, clusters of gnarled old wooden cottages dating from the 1700s, where villagers from outlying districts would spend the night after making the lengthy journey to church in the nearest town.

However, the highlight of the Bothnian Coast is undoubtedly the stretch known as the **Höga Kusten**, or High Coast, between Härnösand and Örnsköldsvik – for peace and quiet, this is easily the most idyllic part of central Sweden. Its indented coastline is best seen from the sea, with its shimmering fjords reaching deep inland, tall cliffs and a string of pine-clad islands that make it possible to island-hop up the coast. There's also good hiking to be had here in the **Skuleskogen national park**. The weather may not be as reliable as further south but you're guaranteed clean beaches – often all to yourself – crystal-clear waters and some fine walking.

Getting around

The **train** line hugs the coast until just beyond Härnösand, where intercity services terminate. From here a branch line swings inland, joining up in Långsele with the main line north to Kiruna and on to the Norwegian port of Narvik. There are regular services between Stockholm and Sundsvall, stopping at Gävle, Söderhamn and Hudiksvall; from Sundsvall a handful of trains continues on to Härnösand, sometimes with a direct connection from Stockholm. There's also a handy train and bus connection to Sundsvall from the inland town of Östersund (see "Travel details" at the end of the chapter). Beyond Härnösand things get more tricky and it's easier to continue north by **bus** from Härnösand up the High Coast towards Örnsköldsvik and on to connect with the main train line at Boden or Luleå. Island-hopping by **ferry** along the High Coast is a wonderful way to make your way north and to take in one of northern Sweden's most beautiful regions. There are frequent bus services north from Örnsköldsvik via Umeå, Skellefteå and Piteå to Luleå and Boden.

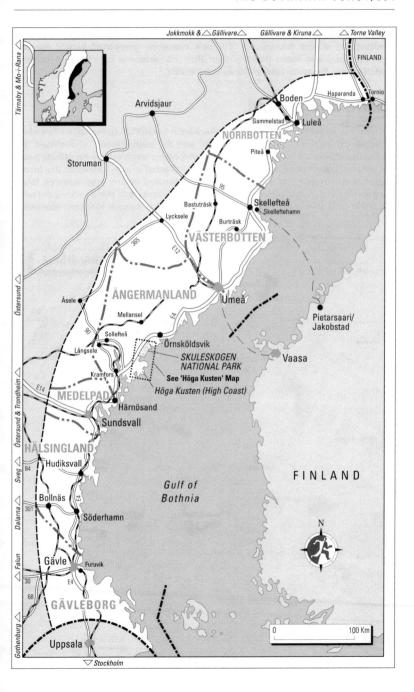

Over recent years the number of ferry services between the Bothnian coast and **Finland** has shrunk dramatically. The only remaining year-round service operates between Umeå and Vaasa (journey time 4hr). The future of the crossings between Skellefteå and Pietarsaari and Kokkola is uncertain.

Gävle and around

It's only two hours north by train from Stockholm to **GÄVLE** (pronounced "Yerv-le"), principal city of the county of Gästrikland and the southernmost in Norrland, the region that makes up two-thirds of Sweden and covers more or less everything north of Uppsala. Gävle is an old city – its town charter granted in 1446 – although this knowledge doesn't prepare you for the modern, sophisticated centre: large squares, broad avenues and proud monumental buildings. Almost completely rebuilt after a devastating fire in 1869, the layout of the city reflects its industrial success in the late nineteenth

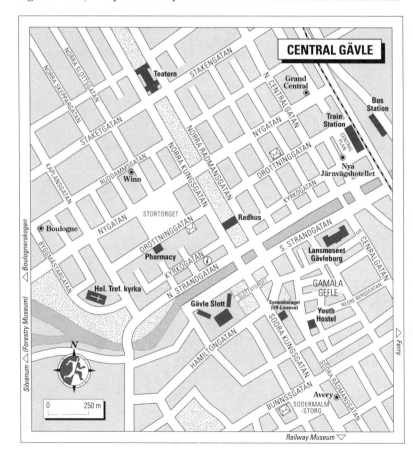

CENTRAL GÄVLE

century, when Gävle was the export centre for the iron and timber produced locally. Today, though, the city is more famous as the home of *Gevalia* coffee, which you're certain to taste during your time in Sweden.

Arrival, information and accommodation

The city centre is concentrated in the grid of streets that spreads southwest from the **train station** on Stora Esplanadgatan. You'll find left-luggage lockers (15kr) on the main platform. The bus station, for both local and long-distance services, is on the other side of the train station: use the subway that runs under the train tracks. The **tourist office** (June–Aug Mon–Sun 9am–6pm; Sept–May Mon–Fri 9am–4pm; ☎026/14 74 30) is located in Berggrenska Gården at Norra Kyrkogatan 14, where there's also a summertime open-air café serving the best homemade bread in town.

The tourist office can arrange private **apartments** from 170kr per person per night (reductions for longer stays); you don't need to book in advance. Gävle has two **youth hostels** – one is superbly located in the old quarter at Södra Rådmansgatan 1 (☎026/62 17 45; fax 61 59 90; all year; 100kr); the other is out on the coast, at Bönavägen 118 in Engeltofta, 6km northeast of the city and reached by bus #5 from Rådhuset (☎026/961 60; fax 960 55; May–Aug; 100kr). The nearest **campsite** is at the Furuvik Amusement Park (☎026/980 28 or 19 90 00; see p.536); buses #821, #838 and #832 run there roughly every half-hour.

ACCOMMODATION PRICE CODES

All the Swedish pensions and hotels listed in the guide have been graded according to the following price bands, based on the cost of the least expensive double room in high season. However, almost every hotel offers seasonal and weekend discounts that can reduce the rate by one or even two grades. Many of these bargains are impromptu, but wherever possible we've given two grades, covering both the regular and the discounted rate. Single rooms, where available, are usually between 60 and 80 percent of the cost of a double.

① under 500kr   ② 500–700kr   ③ 700–900kr   ④ 900–1200kr   ⑤ over 1200kr

---

Hotels

Aveny, Södra Kungsgatan 31 (☎026/61 55 90; fax 65 15 55). A small family-run hotel south of the river. ①/③

Boulogne, Byggmästargatan 1 (☎/fax 026/12 63 52). Small, basic hotel serving breakfast on a tray. Close to Boulognerskogen park. ①/②

Grand Central, Nygatan 45 (☎026/12 90 60; fax 12 44 99). One of the smartest hotels in town with old-fashioned rooms. ③/④

Nya Järnvägshotellet, Centralplan 3 (☎026/12 09 90; fax 10 62 42). The cheapest hotel in Gävle with toilet and shower in the corridor but perfectly adequate. ①/②

Winn, Norra Slottsgatan 9 (☎026/17 70 00; fax 10 59 60). Another smart hotel with its own pool, sauna and sunbeds. ③/④

The City

Central Gävle is easy to navigate, with the broad, dead straight streets of the modern city bisected by a stretch of park that runs roughly north–south. To the south, cut off by the river, lies Gamla Gefle, the small part of the city that survived the fire and the first place to head for.

Gamla Gefle

The part of the city known as **Gamla Gefle** passes itself off today as the old town, though unfortunately there's not much left of it. If you stay in the youth hostel you'll be right on the edge of the few remaining narrow cobbled streets – notably Övre Bergsgatan, Bergsgränd and Nedre Bergsgränd – with their pastel-coloured wooden cottages complete with window boxes bursting with summer flowers. For a glimpse of social conditions a century ago, visit the **Joe Hill-Gården** (June–Aug daily 10am–3pm; free; other times by arrangement on ☎026/61 34 25) at Nedre Bergsgatan 28. Joe Hill, born in the house as Johan Emanuel Hägglund in 1879, emigrated to the United States in 1902, where with a new name he went on to become a working-class hero – his songs and speeches served as rallying cries to comrades in the International Workers of the World; then, framed for murder in Salt Lake City, he was executed in 1915. The syndicalist organization to which he belonged runs the museum, a collection of standard memorabilia – pictures and belongings – given piquancy by the telegram announcing his execution and his last testament.

On the other side of Gamla Gefle, on the canalside at Södra Strandgatan 20, is the county museum, **Länsmuséet Gävleborg** (Tues 10am–4pm, Wed–Fri till 9pm, Sat & Sun 1–5pm; 25kr). Its extensive displays of artwork by most of the great Swedish artists from the 1600s to the present day, including Nils Kreuger and Carl Larsson, make this a rarity among provincial museums and attract visitors from across the country. Also on show are displays on the ironworks and fisheries in the area, as well as work by local artist Johan-Erik Olsson (popularly known as Lim-Johan), whose vivid imagination and naive technique produced some strangely childlike paintings.

The rest of the city

The modern city lies over the river, its broad streets and tree-lined avenues designed to prevent fires from spreading. From the sculpture-spiked **Rådhus** up to the beautiful nineteenth-century theatre, a central slice of parks, trees and fountains neatly splits the city. All the main banks, shops and stores are in the grid of streets on either side of the central avenue, while the roomy **Storatorget**, sporting a phallic monolith, has the usual open-air market (Mon–Sat from 9am), selling good-quality fruit and veg.

Gävle's other main sights – none of them major – are out of the centre but close enough to reach on foot. Back at the river by the main double bridge, **Gävle Slottet**, the seventeenth-century residence of the country governor, lost its ramparts and towers years ago and now lurks behind a row of trees like some minor country house. You can't go inside for a poke around, although you can arrange a visit to the **Fängelsemuséet** (Prison Museum) on the premises by contacting the tourist office. From Gävle Slottet a short walk along the river leads to a wooden bridge, across which is Kaplansgatan and the **Heliga Trefaldighets Kyrka**, the Church of the Holy Trinity, a seventeenth-century masterpiece of wood-carved decoration. Check out the pulpit, towering altarpiece and screen – each the superb work of a German craftsman, Ewardt Friis. Cross back over the river and take a stroll down Kungsbäcksvägen, a narrow street lined with old wooden houses painted yellow, green and orange, with tulips and wild roses growing outside their front doors. Keep going alongside the riverside path from here and in about fifteen minutes you'll come to **Silvanum** (Tues–Fri 10am–4pm, Wed till 9pm, Sat & Sun 1–5pm; free) at Kungsbäcksvägen 32, northern Europe's largest forestry museum – interesting only if you're desperate to learn more about the unforgiving forest that you'll become well acquainted with as you travel further north. Continue and you'll come to the rambling **Boulognerskogen**, which opened in the mid-nineteenth century and still provides an oasis of trees, water and flowers just outside the city centre – a good place for a picnic and a spot of sunbathing on a sunny day.

On a rainy day you may find yourself contemplating the **Sveriges Järnvägsmuséet**, the national railway museum at Rälsgatan 1 (Tues–Sun 10am–4pm; 30kr, free with

InterRail pass). Now housed in the old engine shed, the fifty or so locomotives, some of them over 100 years old, are of limited appeal to non-enthusiasts. If you walk here from the train station along Muréngatan, you'll pass the old dockside **warehouses** off Norra Skeppsbron, a reminder of the days when ships unloaded coffee and spices in the centre of Gävle. Today, strolling past the red wooden fronts with fading company names, it feels as though you're wandering around an old Hollywood movie set rather than the backstreets of a northern Swedish city.

Eating, drinking and entertainment

There's a fair choice of **eating places** in Gävle, but for the best options stick to the central grid of streets around Storatorget and spots up and down the central esplanade between Rådhuset and the theatre. Nearly all cafés and restaurants double up as bars, and some also mutate into nightclubs too.

Cafés, bars and restaurants

Arken, boat moored alongside Norra Skeppsbron. Great for atmosphere on a summer evening; two courses of fish or seafood for 125kr, three courses 150kr.

Brända Bocken, Storatorget. Young and trendy with outdoor seating in summer. Beef and pork dishes, hamburgers and salmon for around 80kr; beer 39kr.

Café Artist, Norra Slottsgatan 9. Trendy, relaxed hangout with cosy sofas and wooden panelling. Fish and meat dishes for around 140kr, smaller dishes like *pytt i panna* for 60–70kr.

Kungshallen, Norra Kungsgatan 17. Next to the theatre. Mammoth pizzas cost 44–60kr, while beer goes for 29kr – in short, a steal.

O'Leary's, Södra Kungsgatan 31. Incredibly busy place to do your boozing and boogying. Attracts a young crowd.

Skeppet, in the *Grand Central Hotel*, Nygatan 45. Fine fish and seafood in a maritime atmosphere, with prices to match. Lunchtime pasta menu for 75kr.

Tennstoppet, Nygatan 38. Cheap and cheerful hamburger restaurant with sausage and chips 40kr, egg and bacon 49kr, mixed grill 50kr.

Österns Pärla, Ruddammsgatan 23. No surprises in this Chinese restaurant, serving regular dishes for 80–90kr.

Heartbreak Hotel, Norra Strandgatan 15. Pub, bistro-style bars and nightclub. Much improved since it's started to attract a post-teen crowd.

38°, Norra Kungsgatan 7A. Once the trendiest place to drink, now less popular but still worth checking out.

Listings

Bank *Nordbanken*, Norra Kungsgatan 3–5.

Bus information Local buses operated by *Länstrafiken* ☎020/91 01 09; long-distance operated by *Swebus* ☎026/14 40 00.

Car rental *Avis* ☎026/51 57 50; *Budget* ☎026/51 48 20; *Hertz* ☎026/51 18 19; *Statoil* ☎026/12 01 12.

Cinema *Filmstaden* and *Sandrew*, Norra Slottsgatan.

Gay contacts Fjärde Tvärgatan 55 (☎026/18 09 67). Switchboard Sun 7–9pm; café Wed 6.30–9pm; parties second Sat in the month 9.30pm–2.30am.

Pharmacy Nygatan 31 (☎026/10 02 46).

Post office Drottninggatan 16 (☎026/12 13 90).

Systembolaget Off-licence at Södra Kungsgatan, near Gävle Slottet.

Taxi *Gävle Taxi* ☎026/12 90 00 or 10 70 00.

Around Gävle: beaches, Limön and the Furuvik Amusement Park

If the sun's shining you'll find locals catching the rays at the sandy beach of **Rullsand**, which stretches for about 3km. Bus #838 should go there in the morning and return in the evening but check with the tourist office for the latest details. More accessible nearby beaches are **Engeltofta** (near the youth hostel) and **Engesberg**, both reached by bus #5 from Rådhuset. Other good beaches plus some walking paths can be found on the island of **Limön**, reached by summer ferry from Skeppsbron (3 daily; 30kr) – one service a day stops at Engeltofta on the way.

In the other direction is the **Furuvik Amusement Park** (May to late June Mon–Fri 10am–4pm, Sat & Sun 10am–5pm; July daily 10am–6pm; early Aug daily 10am–5pm; 95kr, children 55kr), with a zoo, fairground, parks and playgrounds. Ride coupons cost 12–24kr a time, or you can buy a pass (*Åkband*) for 95kr. Buses #821, #838 and #832 leave for Furuvik roughly every half-hour from the bus station.

Söderhamn and Hudiksvall

On the first leg of the coastal journey further into Norrland the railway sticks close to the coast. If you are in no great rush to reach the bigger towns and tourist centres further north, **Söderhamn** and **Hudiksvall** both suit a leisurely stop, though Hudiksvall's distinctive wood-panel architecture gives it the edge over Söderhamn.

Söderhamn

It's easy to see that **SÖDERHAMN** was once much more important than it looks nowadays. Founded in 1620 at the head of a ten-kilometre-long fjord, its glory days came several decades later and the seventeenth-century **Ulrika Eleonora kyrka** that towers over the Rådhus gives hints of the wealth the city once had, which was earned primarily from fishing. Relics from an earlier church on the same site are kept in **Söderhamns Museum** (July to early Aug daily noon–5pm; 10kr), halfway up Oxtorgsgatan from the main square, Rådhustorget. The museum is housed in a former rifle-manufacturing workshop, from the days when Söderhamn supplied the weapons that helped Sweden to dominate northern Europe.

A number of fires have taken their toll on Söderhamn, the most devastating, in 1876, destroying virtually everything in its path. As a result the modern town is built on the familiar grid pattern, with space for central parks and green spaces. For a better appreciation of the layout of the town, climb up the white 23-metre-high **Oskarsborg tower** (June–Aug daily 9am–9pm): follow the path signposted from down by the railway tracks. From up here the surrounding forests that enclose the town stretch away as far as the eye can see. To explore further, you can leave town on a series of **walking paths** striking out from near the hospital; go up Kyrkogatan from under the railway bridge near Rådhustorget and continue up the hill onto the footpath, turn left into Krongatan and head for the hospital, past the helipad and turn right into the forest.

Söderhamn's main tourist attraction, however, is the **Fjärilshuset** (Butterfly House; daily May–Sept 9am–5pm; Oct–April 10am–3pm), where you can watch myriad different species of butterfly fluttering around in a tropical rain forest environment. The Butterfly House is in the village of Ina and the bus to the youth hostel (see below) passes close by – it's only a ten-minute ride.

If you've time to spare, it's easy to take a **boat trip** out into Söderhamn's archipelago, which is made up of about five hundred islands; the largest, Storjungfrun (literally The Great Virgin), has given its name to the stretch of coast around Söderhamn and Hudiksvall, *Jungfrukusten* or The Virgin Coast. Boats (info on ☎026/12 77 66) leave from the opposite end of town to Rådhustorget – walk down the main street and along the canal for about fifteen minutes to reach the jetty.

Practicalities

Söderhamn's **train station** is in the centre, while the **tourist office** is out of town on the way to the Butterfly House (June to early Aug Mon–Fri 9am–7pm, Sat & Sun noon–5pm; rest of the year Mon–Fri 9am–4pm; ☎0270/753 53) and can provide information on boat trips and hiking routes in the area. If you're planning on **staying** overnight you won't be overwhelmed with choices: the central *First Hotel Statt*, Oxtorgsgatan 17 (☎0270/414 10; fax 135 24; ②/④), is the luxury option, though summer sees its prices drop considerably. If money is tight, you'll be better off at the **youth hostel** (☎0270/452 33; fax 453 26; June–Aug; 100kr) 13km west of town in **Mohed**. The hostel and a year-round **campsite** are beautifully located beside a lake in deep pine forest; to get here take hourly bus #64 or #100; the #100 continues to **Bollnäs**, about thirty minutes' ride away and handy for main-line trains north to Boden, Luleå, Gällivare and Kiruna.

A fair number of decent bars and restaurants have opened in Söderhamn in recent years. **Eating** places are mostly to be found along the main pedestrian street, Köpmangatan. Try the Indian food at *Restaurang Tandoori*, at the Rådhus end of the street; next door at *Mosquet Restaurant* you'll find pizzas and pasta for 40–55kr, fish dishes for double that. For a more upmarket culinary experience, at prices to match, try *Restaurang Faxe* on Kungsgatan or the *Stadsrestaurang* inside the *First Hotel Statt* on Oxtorgsgatan. The Chinese restaurant *Mandarin Palace*, in Köpmantorget next to the bus station, has *Dagens Rätt* for 53kr. For coffee and cakes, *TeWe's Konditori* on Köpmangatan can't be beaten. **Drinking** is best done at *Dino* on Oxtorgsgatan 17, *Bryggeriet* at Dammgatan 3, or at the Irish pub *Tigern* at Västra Storgatan 20 (under the railway bridge from Rådhustorget and turn left).

Hudiksvall

The oldest town in Sweden north of Gävle, **HUDIKSVALL** has had its fair share of excitement over the years. Originally founded in 1582, around the Lillfjärden bay at the mouth of the River Hornån, at the beginning of the seventeenth century the sea had receded so far that Hudiksvall was forced to move – the bay is now several hundred metres away from the water's edge. An important commercial and shipping centre, it bore the brunt of the Russian attacks on the northeast Swedish coast in 1721 and to this day its church is pockmarked with cannon holes; every other building was razed to the ground. The oldest part of the city is split into two main sections. Turn right out of the train station and cross the narrow canal, Strömmingssundet (Herring Sound), and you'll soon see the small old **harbour** on the right; this area is known as **Möljen**. Here the wharfside is flanked by a line of red wooden fishermen's cottages and storehouses, all leaning into the water; it's a popular place for locals to while away a couple of hours in the summer sunshine. The back of the warehouses hide a run of bike and boat repair shops, handicraft studios and the like.

More impressive and much larger than Möljen, **Fiskarstan** (Fishermen's Town), down Storgatan beyond the *First Hotel Statt*, contains neat examples of the so-called "Imperial" wood-panel architecture of the late eighteenth and nineteenth centuries. It was in these tightly knit blocks of streets with their fenced-in plots of land that the fishermen used to live during the winter. Take a peek inside some of the little courtyards – all window boxes and cobblestones. The history of these buildings is put into perspective in the excellent **Hälsinglands Museum** (Tues–Fri 9am–4pm, Wed till 8pm, Sat & Sun 11am–3pm; 20kr, free on Sat) on Storgatan, which traces the development of Hudiksvall as a harbour town. Have a look at the paintings by **John Sten** upstairs: born near Hudiksvall, his work veered strangely from Cubism to a more decorative fanciful style.

The best time to visit Hudiksvall is July 5–21, when the town hosts the **Musik vid Dellen**, a multifarious cultural festival including folk music and other traditional events; information and tickets from the tourist office.

Practicalities

Hudiksvall's **train** and **bus stations** are conveniently opposite each other and it's just two minutes' walk along the main road to the town centre. The **tourist office** (mid-June to mid-Aug Mon–Fri 9am–7pm, Sat 10am–6pm, Sun noon–6pm; rest of the year Mon–Fri 9am–4pm; ☎0650/191 00) is behind the old warehouses near the wharf. As for **accommodation**, the *First Hotel Statt* at Storgatan 36 (☎0650/150 60; fax 960 95; ②/④) is the priciest hotel in town, though good value in midsummer, or there's the cheaper *Hotell Temperance* near the station at Håstagatan 5 (☎/fax 0650/311 07; ①/②). The nearest **youth hostel** (☎0650/132 60; all year; 100kr) is located out at the Malnbaden **campsite**, 3km from town – bus #5 runs there hourly (10am–6pm) in summer, otherwise you'll need to take a taxi from the bus station (80kr each way). Sited on the bay, it has a large sandy beach and offers bike rental.

Oddly enough, Hudiksvall has fewer **eating and drinking** opportunities than smaller Söderhamn. The one and only **bar** in town is the *Tre Bockar* at Bankgränd, opposite the fishermen's warehouses at Möljen; at lunchtime the *Dagens Rätt* and a beer goes for 69kr. A popular eating place is *Bolaget* at Storgatan 49, where main dishes cost around 85kr, pizzas 45kr. Alternatively, try the smarter *Le Bistro* on Hamngatan, which has a 3–11pm happy hour for food and drink, or the town's top restaurant, *Bar o Kök*, attached to *First Hotel Statt* on Storgatan.

Sundsvall

The capital of the tiny province of Medelpad, **SUNDSVALL**, known as "Stone City", is immediately and obviously different. Once home to a rapidly expanding nineteenth-century sawmill industry, the whole city burned to the ground in June 1888, and nine thousand people lost their homes. Rebuilding began at once and within ten years a new centre constructed entirely of stone had emerged. The result is a living document of turn-of-the-century urban architecture, designed and crafted by architects who were involved in rebuilding Stockholm's residential areas at the same time. Wide streets and esplanades that were intended to serve as fire breaks formed the backbone of their work. However, the reconstruction was achieved at a price: the workers who had laboured on the new stone buildings were shifted from their homes in the centre and moved south to a poorly serviced suburb, highlighting the glaring difference between the wealth of the new centre and the poverty of the surrounding districts.

Arrival, information and accommodation

From the **train station** it's a five-minute walk to the city centre: turn left and go under the road bridge. The helpful **tourist office** (mid-June to mid-Aug Mon–Fri 9am–8pm, Sat & Sun 10am–8pm; rest of the year Mon–Fri 11am–5pm, Thurs till 6pm; ☎060/61 42 35) is in the main square, Storatorget. The **bus station** is at the bottom of Esplanaden, though if you want information or advance tickets for the express bus south to Stockholm or north to Örnsköldsvik or Sollefteå (also inland to Östersund),

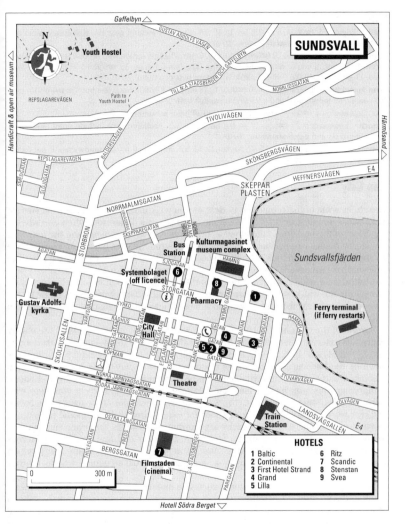

Gaffelbyn

SUNDSVALL

N

Youth Hostel

GUSTAV ADOLFS VÄGEN

TILL GAFFELBYN

NORRLIDSGATAN

Handicraft & open air museum

REPSLAGAREVÄGEN

Path to
Youth Hostel

TILL N:A STADSBERGET

TIVOLIVÄGEN

Härnösand

REPSLAGAREVÄGEN

BALDERSVÄGEN

SKÖNSBERGSVÄGEN

HEFFNERSVÄGEN

E4

SKEPPAR
PLASTEN

SMEDGATAN

SJUKGATAN

NORRMALMSGATAN

STORBRON

SKEPPAREGATAN

NOBELSVÄGEN

Bus
Station

**Kulturmagasinet
museum complex**

HAMNG

Sundsvallsfjärden

ÅGATAN

SJÖGATAN

**Systembolaget
(off licence)**

6

8

STORGATAN

i

Pharmacy

STRANDGATAN

1

**Ferry terminal
(if ferry restarts)**

HAMNGATAN

**Gustav Adolfs
kyrka**

VÄNGRAND

KYRKOGATAN

NYBROGATAN

HAMNPLAN

RÅDHUSGATAN

TRÄDGÅRDSGATAN

**City
Hall**

ESPLANADEN

ESPLANADEN

BANKGATAN

4

GATAN

SKOLHUSALLÉN

KÖPMANGATAN

5 2 9

3

GATAN

NORRA JÄRNVÄGSGATAN

SÖDRA JÄRNVÄGSGATAN

Theatre

GATAN

STUVARVÄGEN

THULEGATAN

ÖSTRA LÅNGGATAN

LANDSVÄGSALLÉN

KÖLVÄGEN

E4

FREDS

**Train
Station**

BERGSGATAN

7

**Filmstaden
(cinema)**

TILL S:A STADSBERGET

PARKGATAN

0   300 m

HOTELS			
1	Baltic	6	Ritz
2	Continental	7	Scandic
3	First Hotel Strand	8	Stenstan
4	Grand	9	Svea
5	Lilla		

Hotell Södra Berget

visit *Y-Bussen* at Trädgårdsgatan 13 (☎060/17 19 60). For other bus information contact the tourist office. The airport is 20km north of town, linked by an airport bus to connect with flights to and from Stockholm.

The tourist office has a limited supply of **private rooms** for between 125kr and 150kr per person, plus a 60kr booking fee. Other budget options include the slightly grotty **youth hostel** (☎060/61 21 19; fax 61 78 01; all year; 100kr) outside town at Norra Berget, the mountain overlooking the city (take bus #72 or #73). However, there's no shortage of reasonably priced hotels. The nearest **campsite**, *Fläsians Camping* (☎060/554475; May to mid-Sept), also has cabins for 200–400kr per day; it's outside town – ask at the tourist office for directions.

Hotels

Baltic, Sjögatan 5 (☎060/15 59 35; fax 12 45 60). Centrally located near the Kulturmagasinet and the harbour; perfectly adequate rooms. ②/④

Continental, Rådhusgatan 13 (☎060/61 26 07). Central budget option with around ten basic rooms; serves breakfast. If you've no luck here, try the *Lilla Hotellet* at no. 15 (☎060/61 35 87), or the *Svea* at no. 11 (☎060/61 16 05) – there's little to choose between them. ①/②

First Hotel Strand, Strandgatan 10 (☎060/12 18 00; fax 61 92 02). Smartest hotel in town with over 200 rooms, an indoor pool and a wicked breakfast buffet. ②/⑤

Ritz, Esplanaden 4 (☎060/15 08 60). The cheapest hotel in Sundsvall. ①

Scandic, Esplanaden 29 (☎060/17 16 00; fax 12 20 32). Facilities here include eight cinemas, a sauna, sunbeds and a golf simulator. ③/⑤

Stenstan, Sjögatan 11 (☎060/15 07 20; fax 12 34 56). Renowned for its sandwiches if not for its rooms or Finnish-speaking staff. ②/③

The City

The sheer scale of the rebuilding is clear as you walk into town from the train station. The style is simple, uncluttered limestone and brick, the dimensions often overwhelming. Most of the buildings functioned as offices as well as residences, and the four- and five-storey houses are palatial structures. As you stroll the streets you can't help but be amazed by the tremendous amount of space right in the heart of the city – it's hard to believe that Sundsvall is the most densely populated city in northern Sweden. **Esplanaden**, a wide central avenue, cuts the grid of streets in two, itself crossed by **Storgatan**, the widest street. **Storatorget**, the central square of the city, is home to various impromptu exhibitions as well as a fresh fruit and veg market (Mon–Sat from 9.30am).

Several of the buildings in the centre are worth a second look, not least the sturdy bourgeois exterior of **Sundsvalls Museum** (Mon–Thurs 10am–7pm, Fri 10am–6pm, Sat & Sun 11am–4pm; free), housed within four nineteenth-century warehouses down by the harbour. The buildings stood empty for twenty years before a decision was taken to turn them into what's now the **Kulturmagasinet** (Culture Warehouse), comprising museum, library and café. Magasinsgatan, an old street complete with railway tracks, still runs between the warehouses, a reminder of the days when coffee and rice were transported to the harbour for export. Inside, the regional museum is worth a quick look, as is the nearby art exhibition. Towards the other end of town, follow the main pedestrian street, Storgatan, to its far end and you'll come across **Gustav Adolfs kyrka** (daily June–Aug 10am–4pm; Sept–May 11am–2pm), which marks one end of the new town, a soaring red-brick structure whose interior resembles a large Lego set.

Beyond the city's design, the most attractive diversion is the tiring three-kilometre climb to the heights of **Gaffelbyn**, the hill that overlooks the city to the north; walk up Storgatan, cross over the main bridge and follow the sign to the youth hostel. If you'd prefer to spare your legs, buses #4, #72 and #73 go much of the way. The view on a clear day is fantastic, giving a fresh perspective on the city's planned structure and the restrictive nature of its location, hemmed in on three sides by hills and the sea. From here you can see straight across to Södra Berget, the southern hill, with its winter ski slopes. **Norra Bergets Hantverks och Friluftsmuseum** (summer Mon–Fri 9am–6pm, Sat noon–4pm, Sun 11am–4pm; winter Mon–Fri 9am–4pm; free) is an open-air handicrafts museum with the usual selection of twee wooden huts and assorted activities, though you can try your hand at baking some *tunnbröd*, the thin bread that's typical of northern Sweden. The bake-your-own offer is included in the Activity Card, which you can buy from the museum or its bakery for 40kr.

Eating, drinking and entertainment

For **eating**, Storgatan has a handful of pizza places and restaurants, most offering daily lunch offers. Over the last couple of years restaurants have mushroomed and you'll find a good choice – something you may want to make the most of if you're heading further north. Sundsvall's **bars** generally have a good atmosphere, though nightclubs are rather thin on the ground.

Cafés and restaurants

Athena restaurang och pizzeria, Köpmangatan 7. All the Greek favourites from tzatziki to souvlaki, as well as pizzas; around 100kr.

Café Charm, corner of Storgatan 32 and Köpmangatan (near the post office). A good choice for coffee and cakes with free refills and calorific cream concoctions; closes at 6pm.

China Restaurant, Esplanaden, near the bus station. Chicken dishes for 72kr, meat 76kr and duck 93kr – also takeaway.

Fem rum och kök, Östra Långgatan 23. Tastefully designed five-room restaurant offering northern Swedish delicacies such as reindeer and elk; around 150kr for a main dish.

Restaurang Seaport, in the *First Hotel Strand*, Strandgatan 10. A chi-chi international brasserie with gourmet dishes and accompanying clientele. Reckon on at least 200kr for dinner.

Saigon Palace, Trädgårdsgatan 5. Vietnamese restaurant with good prices – chicken in peanut sauce for 87kr.

Skeppsbrokällaren, next to *Hotell Baltic* on Sjögatan. Reindeer in cinnamon sauce is a speciality (185kr), though there are also cheaper dishes on offer.

Skippers, Storgatan 40. A lively place for lunch (57kr) – choose from pork, lasagne, burgers or salad.

Bars and nightlife

Dublin, Nybrogatan 16. Irish pub with a broad selection of different beers, Irish music and darts.

Hoagy's, in the *First Hotel Strand*, Strandgatan 10. A tasteful piano bar where tired and emotional locals can be found rounding off an evening's boozing – open till 3am with beers for 25kr during the 8–11pm happy hour.

Jop's, Trädgårdsgatan 35. The most popular pub in town with beers for 39kr; also has darts and local bands at weekends – *the* place to drink.

Macken, Sjögatan 25. Done out as a 1950s-style filling station with beer on tap from petrol pumps – during happy hour (5–9pm) beers start at 28kr.

Mercat Cross, Esplanaden 27. Scottish pub with staff in kilts. Expensive.

O'Bar, Bankgatan 11. A good lively bar nearly the ugly fish fountain, with beers from 36kr – if your pocket can take the pace, it's a good place for cocktails.

Skippers, Storgatan 40. Known for its huge selection of beers and buzzing atmosphere. Happy hour Mon–Thurs & Sat 5–8pm, Fri 4–8pm.

Listings

Airport Information and reservations: ☎060/18 80 00 or 19 75 20.

Banks *Handelsbanken*, Storgatan 23; *Nordbanken*, Kyrkogatan 15; *SE-Banken*, Storgatan 19.

Bus station Sjögatan (☎060/15 31 00).

Car rental *Bilbolaget*, Bultgatan 1 (☎060/18 08 90); *Budget*, at the airport (☎060/57 80 06); *Shell*, Bergsgatan 114 (☎060/61 6 051).

Cinema *Filmstaden*, far end of Esplanaden over the railway lines.

Gay contacts Basement on the corner of Skolhusallén amd Östra Långgatan (☎060/171 30). Café Wed & Sun 7–10pm; disco 2nd and last Sat of month 10pm–2.30am; pub Fri 10pm–2.30am; switchboard Thurs 8–10pm (☎060/15 77 78).

Hospital Lasarettsvägen 19 (☎060/18 10 00).

Pharmacy Storgatan 18 (Mon–Fri 9am–6pm, Sat 10am–3pm; ☎060/18 11 17); also at the hospital (☎060/18 11 17).
Police Storgatan 37 (☎060/18 00 00).
Post office Köpmangatan 19 (☎060/19 60 00).
Systembolaget Off-licence at Torggatan 1 (Mon–Wed & Fri 9.30am–6pm, Thurs 9.30am–7pm).
Taxi *Taxi Sundsvall* ☎060/19 90 00; *City Taxi* ☎060/12 00 00.
Train enquiries Parkgatan ☎060/18 30 00.

Härnösand

From Sundsvall it's an hour's train trip north along the coast to **HÄRNÖSAND**, a pleasant little place at the mouth of the River Ångerman. Founded in 1585, the town has had its fair share of disasters: two great fires in 1710 and 1714, only to be followed by a thorough ransacking by invading Russians in 1721. Yet despite this, the town is stuffed full of architectural delights and is definitely worth a stop on the way north. Härnösand marks the beginning of the stunningly beautiful county of Ångermanland – one of the few areas in Sweden where the countryside resembles that of neighbouring Norway, with its low mountains, craggy coastlines and long fjords reaching far inland. The town is also a good base from which to explore the nearby High Coast (see p.545), or alternatively you can head inland to connect up with the main train line north at Långsele.

The Town and around

For such a small provincial place, Härnösand reeks of grandeur and self-importance – each of its proud civic buildings a marker of the confidence it exudes. The town centre is on the island of **Härnön**, and its main square, **Stora Torget**, was once chosen by local worthies as the most beautiful in Sweden. From the square, take a stroll up Västra Kyrkogatan to the heights of of the Neoclassical **Domkyrkan** (daily 10am–4pm), which dates from the 1840s though it incorporates bits and pieces from earlier churches on the site: the Baroque altar is eighteenth-century, as are the VIP boxes in the nave. The cathedral holds two records: as well as being the smallest in Sweden, it's also the only white cathedral in the country. From the cathedral turn right and follow the road round and back down the hill until you come to the narrow old street of Östanbäcksgatan, with its painted wooden houses that date back to the 1700s. For a taste of the town's architectural splendour, take a walk up the main street, Nybrogatan, where the grand building that houses the Länsstyrelsen (County Administration) and *Mitt Sverige Turism* (a good source of information on the High Coast; see below) is particularly beautiful, with a pastel orange facade. From the top of the hill here some good views can be had back over the town and the water.

Beaches and the Murberget open-air museum

The long, sandy **beaches** in nearby **Smitingen**, fifteen minutes away by bus #14 (4 daily from the bus station, over the bridge from the train station), are generally regarded as some of the best in Norrland. Closer to town, there are pebble beaches near the Sälsten campsite. Continue round the coast from here and you'll eventually reach the **open-air museum** (June–Aug daily 11am–5pm; 40kr) at **Murberget**, which is the second biggest in Sweden after Skansen (see p.392). Buses #2 and #52 run there hourly from the bus station. Around eighty buildings have been transplanted here, including traditional Ångermanland farmhouses and the old Murberg church which is popular for local weddings. In the nearby **Länsmuseet** (County Museum; daily 11am–5pm; 25kr) worthy exhibitions demonstrate how people settled the area two thosand years ago, alongside desperately dull displays of birds' feet, silver goblets and spectacles from more modern times; if you're into armoury, then you're in for a treat – the museum also has a collection of hunting weapons, peasants' weapons and army weapons from the seventeenth to the nineteenth centuries.

Practicalities

Härnösand's **tourist office** (June–Aug daily 9am–8pm; Sept–May Mon–Fri 10am–4pm; ☎0611/881 40) is near the train station at Järnvägsgatan 2, inside the building marked Spiran; if you're travelling further afield in Ångermanland, and in particular up to the High Coast, you're better off visiting the *Mitt Sverige Turism* tourist office (same times; ☎0611/290 30) at Nybrogatan 15, where the helpful staff can advise on transport and accommodation in the area.

Härnösand's **youth hostel** (☎0611/104 46; mid-June to early Aug; 100kr), where you're likely to get your own self-contained apartment, is a fifteen-minute walk from the centre up Nybrogatan and then left. The nearby **Sälstens Camping** (☎0611/181 50) is around 2km from the centre, next to a string of pebble beaches; it also has a small selection of four-bed cabins for 250kr per night and rents out bikes to guests. Of the town's three **hotels**, *Hotell Royal*, near the station at Strandgatan 12 (☎0611/204 55; ①/②), and *Hotell City*, Storgatan 28 (☎277 00; ①/③), are the cheapest options, with little to choose between them. The *Scandic Hotell* at Skeppsbron 9 (☎0611/105 10; ③/④) is not as good value.

The most popular **pub-restaurant** is *Kajutan* on the pedestrianized Storgatan, linking Stora Torget and Nybrogatan: reckon on 80kr for burgers and the like, with beer from 42kr. If you feel like splashing out on some northern Swedish delicacies, *Restaurang Apothequet*, located in an old pharmacy at Nybrogatan 3, is the place: reindeer costs around 180kr, cloudberries 70kr, or there are two-course set meals for 149kr. Other eateries include the neighbouring *Nybrokällaren*, which serves lunch from 11am to 2pm; the popular pizzeria *Matverkstaden* at Storgatan 5; and the *Rutiga Dukan* café, near the cathedral at Västra Kyrkogatan 1, which does good-value lunches and delicious home-baked pastries and pies.

North to Örnsköldsvik: the Höga Kusten

The term **Höga Kusten**, meaning High Coast, refers to the beautiful stretch of the Bothnian coast between Härnösand and Örnsköldsvik, characterized by rolling mountains and verdant valleys that plunge precipitously into the Gulf. The rugged shoreline is composed of sheer cliffs and craggy outcrops of rock, along with some peaceful sandy coves. Offshore are dozens of islands, some no more than a few metres in size, others much larger and covered with dense pine forest; it was on these islands that the tradition of preparing the foul-smelling *surströmming* (fermented Baltic herring) is thought to have first started. The coastline is best seen from the sea and a trip out to one of the islands gives a perfect impression of the scale of things; however, it's also possible to walk virtually the entire length of the coast on the *Höga Kusten leden*, a long-distance hiking path that extends 130km from the new bridge just north of Härnösand to Varvsberget in Örnsköldsvik.

There are two options for seeing the coast **from Härnösand**: either take one of the *E4-Expressen* buses from the bus station for Örnsköldsvik – these pass through the tiny villages of Ullånger and Docksta (jumping-off points for the island of Ulvön) and skirt round the Skuleskogen National Park – and you'll get a flavour of the High Coast from the road; or take the *E4-Expressen* part of the way up the coast; it leaves Härnösand at 11.55am for Bönhamn (change at Lunde and Nordingrå; check the latest details with *Mitt Sverige Turism*), from where a small boat leaves for the island of Högbonden.

The islands

A trip out to the islands off Höga Kusten has to rank as the highlight of any trip up the Bothnian coast. Using a combination of buses and boats you can make your way to three of the most beautiful islands in the chain: **Högbonden**, **Ulvön** and **Trysunda**. Högbonden only has connections to the mainland, which means doubling back on yourself a little to take the bus up the coast to reach the boat which sails out to Ulvön from Ullånger and Docksta.

Högbonden

After just ten minutes' boat ride from the mainland, the steep sides of the tiny round island of **Högbonden** rise up in front of you. There are no shops (bring all provisions with you), no hotels, no flush-toilets – in fact the only building on Högbonden is a light-house situated at the highest point on a rocky plateau where the pine and spruce trees have been unable to get a foothold. The lighthouse has now been converted into a **youth hostel** (π0613/230 05; mid-May to Sept; groups only except mid-June to mid-Aug; 100kr) with just 27 beds and stunning views. To make the most of it you need to stay a couple of nights, exploring the island's gorge and thick forest by day, and in the evenings relaxing in the traditional wood-burning **sauna** down by the sea.

To **get there**, take the 11.55am Luleå-bound bus from Härnösand, get off at Lunde and get the bus to Nordingrå, then change again to get to Bönhamn, from where the *M/F Högbonden* (mid-June to mid-August every 2hr 10am–6pm; book ahead at other times on π0614/179 54, π0613/23118 or mobile 010/254 9050; 60kr return) makes the ten-minute trip out to the island. Tell the bus driver you're taking the boat over to Högbonden and he'll ring the skipper to ask him to wait for the bus; the same applies on the trip back to the mainland.

Ulvön

The largest island in the chain, **Ulvön** is really two islands, Norra Ulvön and, across a narrow channel, the uninhabited Södra Ulvön. Before the last war Ulvön boasted the biggest fishing community along the High Coast but many islanders have since moved to the mainland, leaving around forty permanent residents.

All boats to the island dock at the main village, **Ulvöhamn**, a picturesque one-street affair with red and white cottages and tiny boathouses on stilts. The island's only **hotel**, *Ulvö Skärgårdshotell* (π0660/340 09; fax 340 78; ③), is at one end of the street, just to the right of where the *M/S Kusttrafik* from Ullånger and Docksta puts in. Walk a short distance to the left of the quay and you'll come to a tiny wooden hut that functions as a summer **tourist office** (π0660/340 93) – you can also rent bikes here for 60kr per day. Continue and you'll soon reach the seventeenth-century fisherman's chapel, decorated with flamboyant murals; the road leading uphill to the right just beyond here will take you to the **youth hostel** (π0660/34068; June–Aug; 95kr). Another 4km on is the old fishing village of **Sandviken**, now a minuscule holiday village renowned for its long sandy beach (*M/S Otilia II* to Örnsköldsvik sometimes puts in here). Back in Ulvöhamn, at the other end of the main street is the village shop; *M/F Ulvön* to Trysunda and Köpmanholmen leaves from the quay just in front, while *M/S Otilia II*, for Örnsköldsvik, docks just on the other side of the jetty. The shop also looks after the keys for the pine **cabins** on the island (π0660/310 13 or 340 14; fax 305 17 or 341 59).

To **get here**, make your way to **Docksta** on the E4-Expressen bus, from where *M/S Kusttrafik*, operated by *Höga Kusten Båtarna* (π0613/105 50 or 130 00; 75kr), leaves daily at 10.15am (June–Aug), arriving in Ulvöhamn at 11.30am, and returning at 3pm. To get to Docksta from Högbonden, take the bus from Bönhamn via Nordingrå back to Lunde, where you can connect with the frequent E-4 buses that stop there on their way between Sundsvall and Umeå (bus information: ☎060/15 31 00, 21 12 00 or 71 14 00). There are frequent bus services to Docksta **from Härnösand**. It's also possible to reach Ulvön from Örnsköldsvik on the *M/S Otilia II* (☎0660/125 37 or 880 15; late June to early Aug 1 daily at 9.30am, returning 3pm; 70kr one-way).

Trysunda

Boats from Ulvön, just an hour away, dock in **Trysunda**'s narrow U-shaped harbour, around which curves the island's tiny village. This is the best preserved fishing village in Ångermanland and it really is a charming little spot with its forty or so red and white houses right on the waterfront and a seventeenth-century chapel with wonderful murals. The island's gently shelving rocks make it ideal for bathing and there's no shortage of secluded spots. Trysunda is also crisscrossed with walking paths leading through the gnarled and twisted dwarf pines. You can stay on the island in the tiny **youth hostel** (☎0660/430 38; early June to Aug; 95kr).

Getting here is simple from Ulvöhamn, since the *M/F Ulvön* (☎010/254 2108; 30kr one-way) makes the trip at least once a day all year round, before continuing on to **Köpmanholmen** back on the mainland (25kr; 45min), where there's a youth hostel (☎0660/33496; mid-May to Aug; 100kr) plus regular buses to Örnsköldsvik.

The High Coast Trail and Skuleskogen

The High Coast Trail (*Höga Kusten Leden*) stretches 130km from Veda, near Härnösand, to Varvsberget, virtually in the centre of Örnsköldsvik, and is divided up into thirteen stages (each 7–12km long) with free overnight cabins. It takes in the magnificent **Skuleskogen national park**, noted for its dense forests, coastal panoramas and sharp-edged ravines. The park is home to the unusual long-beard lichen *(Usnea longissima)*, which grows on spruce trees, as well as many varieties of bird, such as woodpecker (including the rare whitebacked woodpecker), capercaillie, hazel and black grouse, wren, coal tit and crested tit; other residents include elk, roe deer, lynx, fox, badger, ermine, marten, mink, mountain hare and squirrel. A number of well-marked paths lead through the park in addition to the trail.

It's also possible to do some **climbing** in the park. Trails of varying difficulty lead up **Skuleberget** (285m) near Docksta, and anyone in normal shape can make it safely to the summit for some magnificent views. If you're out to do some serious climbing, you can rent equipment at Skule Naturum, on the route of buses between Härnösand and Örnsköldsvik.

For more **information**, contact *Mitt Sverige Turism* in Härnösand (☎0611/290 30), which sells a small map book for the High Coast for 40kr, or the tourist office in Örnsköldsvik (see below).

Örnsköldsvik

About 120km north of Härnösand beyond the High Coast lies the port of **Örnsköldsvik** (usually shortened to **Ö-vik**), an ugly modern city stacked behind a superbly sheltered harbour. The town's only saving grace is its **museum** at Läroverksgatan 1 (Tues–Fri 10am–4pm, Wed till 8pm, Sat & Sun 11am–4pm; 10kr). From the long-distance bus station, walk up the steps on the other side of Strandgatan, which will bring you out on Storgatan, then continue east along either Läroverksgatan or Hamnagatan to get to the museum. Ignore the typical collections of prehistoric finds and dreadful nineteenth-century furniture and ask to be let into the adjacent workshop, which conceals a sparkling documentation of the work of locally born artist, **Bror Marklund**. Most of his art was commissioned by public bodies and goes unnoticed by travellers who brush against it all the time: his *Thalia*, the goddess of the theatre, rests outside the City Theatre in Malmö; and his figures adorn the facade of the Historical Museum in Stockholm. Inside the workshop, look for the brilliantly executed jester plaster casts, one of Markland's most easily identifiable motifs. The only other vaguely interesting thing to do in town is to take a stroll along the harbourside past the old warehouses and the impressive culture and business centre known as *Arken*.

Practicalities

If you've opted to come to Ö-vik by **train** you'll have to alight at Mellansel on the main line from Stockholm to Kiruna, about 30km to the northwest; to get into town take one of the frequent buses. This is also the arrival and departure point for the **E4-buses** that run the entire length of the coast from Sundsvall and Luleå as well as services from Östersund (information on ☎0660/21 12 00). Boats to and from Ulvön dock at the *Arken* quay in front of the bus station along Strandgatan.

The **tourist office** (June to late Aug Mon–Fri 9am–7pm, Sat 10am–2pm, Sun 10am–3pm; rest of the year Mon–Fri 10am–5pm; ☎0660/125 37; fax 880 15) is at Nygatan 18 and can provide information on the Höga Kusten islands. There's only one budget **hotel**, the *Strand City Hotell*, right in the centre at Nygatan 2 (☎0660/106 10; fax 21 13 05; ①/③), a cheerful hostel-like establishment. Rather more agreeable rooms can be found both at the swanky *First Hotell Statt* (☎0660/101 10; fax 837 91; ②/④) at Lasarettsgatan 2, and the more functional *Hotell Focus* up the hill at no. 9 (☎0660/821 00; fax 838 67; ②/④). The **youth hostel** (☎0660/702 44; all year; 100kr) is 7km southwest of town in **Överhörnäs** – take the bus marked Köpmanholmen (18kr) and ask the driver to stop and let you off.

For **eating**, head for the lively harbourside, where many restaurants have outside tables overlooking the waters of the Örnsköldsviksfjärden: try the brasserie-style *Arkenrestaurangen*, next to the harbour, where main dishes go for around 120kr; next door, the *Arken* pub is a good place for a beer. More upmarket are *StrandKaj 4*, serving up local delicacies such as whitefish for 145kr, and the nearby *Fina Fisken*, with fish dishes from 110kr. Of the pizzerias, the best are *Il Padrino* on Läroverksgatan, just off Stora Torget, and *Restaurangen Mamma Mia* on Storgatan. Off Storatorget, between Hemköp and the Sparbanken, is the *China Tower restaurangen*, which doubles as a pub. However, the place to do your **drinking** is in one of the two bars at the *First Hotell Statt* at Lasarettsgatan 2. On the corner of Viktoriaesplanaden and Strandgatan there's *Hamncompaniet*, a bar and disco popular with 18- to 25-year-olds.

Umeå

UMEÅ is the biggest city in northern Sweden, with a population of around 100,000, whose average age is an incredible 35. Strolling around the centre, you'll notice that those who aren't in pushchairs are pushing them, while the cafés and city parks are full of teenagers. Demographically it's probably Sweden's most youthful city, no doubt influenced by the presence of Norrland University and its 20,000 students. With its fast-flowing river and wide, stylish boulevards, Umeå is a distinctly likeable city and it's no bad idea to spend a couple of days here sampling some of the bars and restaurants – the variety of which you won't find anywhere else in Norrland.

Arrival, information and accommodation

It's a ten-minute walk from either the **train station** or **long-distance bus station** to the centre, down on one of the many parallel streets that lead in the general direction of the river. The bus station will also be your point of arrival if you come to Umeå by ferry from Vaasa; *Silja Line* dock at nearby Holmsund, from where connecting buses run inland to Umeå. A good first stop is the **tourist office** (mid-June to mid-Aug Mon–Fri 8am–8pm, Sat 10am–5pm, Sun 11am–5pm; rest of the year Mon–Fri 9am–6pm, Sat 11am–2pm; ☎090/16 16 16) in Renmarkstorget, an ugly concrete square. The staff here are very helpful and dish out among other things a free newspaper with detailed listings; they also have a supply of **private rooms** from 150kr per night (booking fee 25kr). Otherwise, the nearest **campsite** is the lakeside *Umeå camping stugby* (☎090/16 16 60; fax 12 57 20; all year), 5km out of town on the E4 at Nydala; it also has **cabins** for four to six people for 560kr, individual double rooms in other cabins for 225kr and *trätält* (tiny two-bed huts) for 160kr per night; facilities include washing machines and bike rental. Buses #6 and #7 together provide a frequent service on weekdays, and the #69 runs every half-hour at weekends; get off at Nydala and the campsite is about a five-minute walk towards Nydalabadet. Umeå's bright and newly renovated **youth hostel** (☎090/77 16 50; fax 77 16 95; all year; 100kr) is in the centre at Västra Esplanaden 10.

Hotels

First Hotel Grand, Storgatan 46 (☎090/77 88 70; fax 13 30 55). Newly renovated and rather chic, in a good central location. ②/④

Pilen, Pilgatan 5 (☎090/14 14 60). One of the cheaper smaller hotels with weekend and summer deals. ①/②

Strand, Västra Strandgatan 11 (☎090/12 90 20; fax 12 18 40). A perfectly adequate budget hotel. ②/③

Tegs, Verkstadsgatan 5 (☎090/12 27 00; fax 13 49 90). The cheapest hotel in town with basic but decent rooms. ①/②

Wasa, Vasagatan 12 (☎090/77 85 40; fax 77 85 49). Another good hotel in a lively central location. ②/③

Winn, Skolgatan 64 (☎090/12 20 20; fax 12 54 28). Close to the bus station and good for nearby restaurants and bars. ②/④

Umeå Plaza, Storgatan 40 (☎090/17 70 00; fax 17 70 50). Umeå's smartest hotel: the bathrooms have loudspeakers and marble washbasins, and there are superb views from the fifteenth-floor sauna suite. ②/⑤

The City

Umeå is known as the "City of Birch Trees", for the trees that were planted along every street following a devastating fire in 1888. Most of the city was wiped out in the blaze but rebuilding began apace and two wide esplanades were constructed to act as fire breaks should a similar disaster occur again. You'll be hard pushed to find any of the original wooden buildings, but around the little park in front of the **Rådhus**, lingering bits of turn-of-the-century timber architecture still look out over the river responsible for the town's name: *uma* means "roar" and refers to the sound of the rapids along the River Ume, now converted into hydroelectric power further upstream.

As well as its ambience, Umeå offers one terrific museum complex, **Gammlia**, which merits a good half-day's attention. The original attraction around which everything else developed is the **Friluftsmuseum** (mid-June to mid-Aug daily 10am–5pm; free), an open-air group of twenty regional buildings, the oldest the seventeenth-century gatehouse on the way in. As usual, the complex is brought to life by people dressed in period costume – in the bakery you can watch them preparing traditional unleavened *tunnbröd* – while cows, pigs, goats, sheep and geese are kept in the yards and farm buildings. The main collection is housed in the indoor **Västerbottens Museum** (mid-June to mid-Aug Mon–Fri 10am–5pm, Sat & Sun noon–5pm; rest of the year Tues–Fri 9am–4pm, Sat noon–4pm, Sun noon–5pm; free): three exhibitions that canter through the county's history from prehistory (including the oldest ski in the world dated at 5200 years old) to the Industrial Revolution. It's all good stuff, well laid out and complemented by an array of videos and recordings, with a useful English guidebook available. Linked to Västerbottens Museum is the **Bildmuseum** (mid-June to mid-Aug daily noon–5pm; rest of the year Tues–Sat noon–4pm, Sun noon–5pm; free), which houses the university art collection, featuring contemporary Swedish work by artists such as Carl Larsson and Anders Zorn and a cobbled-together set of old masters. Back outside, county history continues in the separate **Fiske och Sjöfartsmuseum** (mid-June to mid-Aug daily noon–5pm; rest of the year Tues–Sat noon–4pm, Sun noon–5pm; free), an attempted maritime museum but really no more than a small hall clogged with fishing boats.

If you've a bike (see "Listings" for rental details), it's a gentle day's cycle along the riverside cycle track (*Umeleden*) to Norrfors and its 5000-year-old rock carvings in the dried-up river bed. Back down the southern side of the river, the path leads past the massive hydroelectric station and **Bölesholmarna**, two islands that can also be reached easily on foot from the city centre in about fifteen minutes, an ideal spot for picnics and barbecues, as well as a quick dip in the small lake in the middle of the islands. The route is detailed on a free map available from the tourist office.

Eating, drinking and entertainment

Eating and drinking possibilities are enhanced in Umeå by the number of students around: most of the restaurants can be found around the central pedestrianized Kungsgatan or Rådhusesplanaden. For a quick bite, the best **café** in town is *Konditori Mekka*, close to the train station at Rådhusesplanaden 17, serving heavenly pastries and free coffee refills. Otherwise, try the café in the library, *Stadsbiblioteket*, patronized by an intellectual-looking crowd sporting goatees and spectacles. Another good spot for coffee and cake is on board the *Vita Björn*, the white boat moored down from the Rådhus.

Restaurants and bars

Brasseriet Skytten, Rådhusesplanaden 17. *The* drinking place to be seen and to do the seeing – always packed out.

China Hall, Kungsgatan 60. Reasonably priced Chinese and Japanese food with the option to fry your own at your table.

Lottas Krog, Nygatan 22. Eighty different beers – everything from McEwans to Marstons bitter – of which a dozen are on tap, including Guinness. Pub menu with a 65kr special of entrecôte and potatoes.

Mucky Duck, Vasaplan. Bar frequented by an older crowd; 47 types of beer.

Rådhuskällaren, under the *Grand Hotell* at Västra Rådhusgatan 1. Top-notch food under a vaulted ceiling – bring a full wallet.

Restaurang Charlotta, corner of Nygatan and Rådhusesplanaden. Probably the most expensive place in town: reindeer, sole, lamb, lobster, salmon – reckon on 400kr per head – in a sophisticated wooden interior.

Scruffy Murphy, Norrlandsgatan 5. A popular Irish pub with traditional fittings and atmosphere. Also has a cheap and good buffet.

Skytten, near the train station at Järnvägstorget. Two restaurants in one, a brasserie and a more upmarket place. Wide menu at reasonable prices.

Teater Caféet, Vasaplan. Outdoor seating in summer. Grill specialities and lighter dishes. Three courses for 139kr or very good gravadlax for 109kr. Service not always great. Happy hour daily 3–6pm.

V&R, inside the *Plaza Hotell* at Storgatan 40. Very smart and chi-chi; everything from vegetarian lasagne for 69kr to fillet of lamb for 159kr.

Listings

Banks *Föreningsbanken*, Renmarkstorget 9; *Handelsbanken*, Storgatan 48; *Nordbanken*, Rådhusesplanaden 3; *SE-Banken*, with ATM, Kungsgatan 52; *Sparbanken Norrland*, Rådhustorget.

Bike rental *Cykel & Mopedhandlar'n*, Kungsgatan 101 (Mon–Fri 9.30am–5.30pm, Sat 10am–1pm; ☎090/14 01 70); *Oves Cykelservice*, Storgatan 87 (Mon–Fri 8am–5pm; ☎090/12 61 91); count on around 50kr per day, with discounts for longer periods.

Buses Long-distance bus station, Järnvägstorget 2 (☎090/13 20 70); city buses at Vasaplan (☎090/16 22 40).

Cinemas *Filmstaden*, Östra Rådhusgatan 2D; *Saga*, Kungsgatan 46; *Sandrew*, Skolgatan 68; *Spegeln*, Storgatan 50.

Ferry tickets *Silja Line* in Renmarkstorget (Mon–Fri 9am–5pm; ☎090/14 21 00).

Gay contacts *RFSL* (Swedish Gay Rights Association) at Box 38, S-901 02, Umeå; *Club Feliz*, Östra Esplanaden 5, first floor, café Wed 7–10pm; 1st & 3rd Sat in the month disco 9pm–1am; switchboard Wed 7–10pm (☎090/77 47 10).

Pharmacy Renmarkstorget 6, or at the hospital, Norrlands Universitetssjukhus.

DAY TRIPS TO FINLAND

Silja Line operate a year-round service between Umeå and **Vaasa in Finland** with a crossing time of around 4hr. Out of season a day return goes for as little as 95kr; in summer (mid-June to mid-Aug) for 195kr. On a day trip it's usually possible to leave Umeå at 8am, returning on the 10pm sailing from Vaasa, but beware that times vary depending on the time of year. Normal one-way fares are 150–210kr, double that for a standard return. Boats sail from the port of **Holmsund**, southeast of Umeå; buses leave the long-distance bus station an hour before the boat departure. Tickets and information from *Silja Line* in Renmarkstorget (☎090/14 21 00).

Police Götgatan 1 (☎090/15 20 00).
Post office Vasaplan (Mon–Fri 8am–6pm, Sat 10am–2pm; ☎090/15 05 00).
Swimming pools Indoor at *Umeå simhall* at Rothoffsvägen 12 (☎090/16 16 40); outdoor at Nydalabadet, by the campsite.
Systembolaget Off-licence at Kungsgatan 50A (Mon–Thurs 9.30am–6pm, Fri 8am–6pm) and at Vasagatan 11 (Mon–Fri 9.30am–6pm, Thurs till 7pm).
Taxi *City Taxi* ☎090/14 14 14; *Taxi Umeorten* ☎090/13 20 00; *Umeå Taxi* ☎090/14 10 00; *Lillebil* ☎090/441 44.
Train station Järnvägsallén 7 (☎090/15 58 00).

Skellefteå and around

"In the centre of the plain was Skellefteå church, the largest and most beautiful building in the entire north of Sweden, rising like a Palmyra's temple out of the desert", enthused the nineteenth-century traveller Leopold von Buch, for there used to be a real religious fervour about **SKELLEFTEÅ**. In 1324 an edict in the name of King Magnus Eriksson invited "all those who believed in Jesus Christ or wanted to turn to Him" to settle between the Skellefte and Ume rivers. Many heeded the call and parishes mushroomed on the banks of the Skellefte. By the end of the eighteenth century a devout township was centred on the monumental church, which stood out in stark contrast to the surrounding plains and wide river. Nowadays more material occupations support the town and the tourist office makes the most of modern Skellefteå's gold and silver refineries, while admitting that the town centre doesn't have much to offer: concentrate instead on the church and its nearby *kyrkstad* or parish village.

PARISH VILLAGES

Parish villages are common throughout the provinces of Västerbotten and Norrbotten. The **kyrkstad** consists of rows of simple wooden houses grouped tightly around the church. After the break with the Catholic Church in 1527, the Swedish clergy were determined to teach their parishioners the Lutheran fundamentals. Church services became compulsory: in 1681 it was decreed that those living within 10km of the church should attend every Sunday, those between 10km and 20km every fortnight and those between 20km and 30km every three weeks. Within a decade parish villages had appeared throughout the region to provide the travelling faithful with somewhere to spend the night after attending church. The biggest and most impressive is at Gammelstad near Luleå (see p.554), and another good example can be seen in Öjebyn near Piteå (p.552). Today they're no longer used in their traditional way but many people still live in the old houses, especially in summer, and sometimes even rent them out to tourists.

Skellefteå's church and parish village, **Bonnstan**, are within easy striking distance of the centre: head west along Nygatan and keep going for about fifteen minutes. On the way you'll pass the **Nordanå Kulturcentrum**, a large and baffling assortment of buildings that's home to a theatre, a twee period grocer's shop (*Lanthandel*) and a dire **museum** (Mon noon–7pm, Tues–Thurs 10am–7pm, Fri–Sun noon–4pm; free) containing three floors of mind-numbing exhibitions on everything from the region's first settlers to swords. Tucked away to the side of the Lanthandel is *Nordanå Gårdens Värdshus*, a pleasant restaurant serving lunches for 60kr.

The first part of Bonnstan you come to is the **kyrkstad** – five long rows of weatherbeaten log houses with battered wooden shutters (the houses are protected by law and any modernization is forbidden, including the installation of electricity). Take a peek inside, but bear in mind that they're privately owned by local people who use them as summer cottages. To the right of the parish village you'll find the **kyrka** (daily Sept to mid-June 10am–4pm; mid-June to Aug 10am–6pm), a proud white Neoclassical building with four mighty pillars supporting the domed roof. Inside there's an outstanding series of medieval sculptures; look out too for the 800-year-old Virgin of Skellefteå, a walnut carving near the altar and one of the few remaining Romanesque images of the Virgin.

Practicalities

Skellefteå's small centre is based around a modern paved square flanked by Kanalgatan and Nygatan; at the top of the square is the **bus station** and the summer **tourist office** (late June to early Aug Mon–Fri 10am–7pm, Sat & Sun 10am–3pm; ☎0910/73 60 20), which deals with all enquiries including accommodation; at other times of the year, visit the main office at Kanalgatan 56 (Aug–May Mon–Thurs 8am–5pm, Fri 8am–4pm; ☎0910/73 60 20). Check at the tourist office about the current situation regarding **ferry** sailings from nearby Skelleftehamn (connecting bus from the bus station) to Pietarsaari (in Swedish, Jakobstad) in Finland; or contact *Båtiken,* Kanalgatan 65 (Mon–Fri 9am–5pm; ☎0910/141 60).

There are four central **hotels** to choose from: cheapest is the *Hotell Viktoria* at Trädgårdsgatan 8 (☎0910/174 70; ①/②), a family-run establishment on the top floor of a block on the south side of the main square; virtually next door at Torget 2, *Hotell Malmia* (☎0910/77 73 00; fax 77 88 16; ②/④) has perfectly adequate rooms and is the centre of Skellefteå's nightlife (see below); nearby at Stationsgatan 8 is the dark and dingy *Skellefteå Stadshotell* (☎0910/141 40; fax 126 28; ②/④); the smartest hotel is the *Scandic* (☎0910/383 00; ③/④) at Kanalgatan 75, across Viktoriagatan. The **youth hostel** (☎0910/372 83; mid-June to mid-Aug; 100kr) is well worth seeking out at Elevhemsgatan 13: a newly renovated yellow building by the southern bank of the River Skellefte, half an hour's walk from the centre. Head east on either Storgatan or Nygatan, turn right onto Viktoriagatan, cross the river over Viktoriabron and take the first left, Tubölegatan, to its end, then keep to the gravel path rather than the main road and the hostel is on the left. For **campers**, *Skellefteå campingplats* (☎0910/188 55) is 1500m north of the centre on Mossgatan, just off the E4; it also has **cabins** for 250kr per night.

Skellefteå's **restaurants** aren't exactly impressive, though *Kulturkrogen*, by the bus station on Södra Järnvägsgatan, has tasty beef and salmon for around 150kr. The restaurant on the veranda at the *Scandic Hotel* offers northern Swedish specialities for around 150kr. Among the usual cluster of pizzerias, the best are *Pizzeria Pompeii* at Kanalgatan 43, where pizzas cost 60kr, and *Pizzeria Dallas* at Köpmangatan 9, which serves fourteen different varieties at 35kr. The best spot for **lunch**, if you can catch it when it's open, is *Urkraft* at the corner of Nygatan and Tjärhovsgatan. Good cakes can be had at *Café Carl Viktor*, Nygatan 40, or the twee *Lilla Mari* at Köpmangatan 13. **Drinking** is best done at *MB* (Malmiabaren) in *Hotell Malmia* on the main square; in summer there's outdoor seating and a great atmosphere.

North from Skellefteå: Piteå

With no train station – the nearest are at Bastuträsk (Mon–Fri 2 buses daily) and Jörn (Mon–Sat 2 buses daily, 1 on Sun) – the easiest way to continue north from Skellefteå is by using one of the frequent **E4-buses**, which stop in the small town of **PITEÅ** before terminating in Luleå (see p.559).

Located in Sweden's most northerly county, Norrbotten, Piteå's history goes back to the beginning of the fourteenth century, when it was situated at what is today the near-by village of **Öjebyn**. When granted its town charter in 1621, the town was still situated 20km west of its current location but an extensive fire razed much of the town and the decision was taken to up sticks and move to the coast. Modern Piteå is an anodyne mix of squares and pedestrianized shopping streets and squares, as well as being home to one of Sweden's biggest paper producers, and the sole reason to stop here is to visit the parish village, **Öjebyns kyrkstad**, 6km out of town (bus #1 runs there hourly until 4.15pm from the bus station at the end of pedestrianized Prästgårdsgatan). The village's small wooden cottages, grouped around a fifteenth-century stone church on Kyrkovägen, are privately owned and most of them still have no electricity. Debate continues as to whether this parish village is the oldest in Sweden – a title that's also claimed by nearby Luleå's parish village.

Practicalities

If you want to stay, the tourist office at Noliagatan 1 (summer daily 8am–8pm; winter Mon–Fri 8am–5pm; ☎0911/933 90) can fix up **private rooms** for 200–600kr per person per night. Other than that you're looking at the town's two **hotels**, the comfortable, olde-worlde *Stadshotellet* at Olof Palmes gata 1 (☎0911/197 00; fax 122 92; ③/④), and the less characterful *Time Hotell*, off the main square at Uddmansgatan 5 (☎0911/910 00; fax 194 00; ②/③). The nearest **youth hostel** is located in a former agricultural college at Öjebyn (☎0911/963 85; mid-June to mid-Aug; 95kr).

For **eating**, your best bet is *Pentryt* at Sundsgatan 29 (closed Fri), which has lunch deals for around 50kr – it serves food until 8pm then mutates into a bar and disco. Another reasonable choice is *Pigalle*, across the road at Sundsgatan 36. The best pizzeria is *Ängeln* at Källbogatan 2, while *Golden Dragon* serves up bland Chinese meals as well as pizzas. For cafés try *Röda Lyktan* inside the Småstaden shopping centre on the main street, or the 1960s time warp *Ekbergs Konditori* at Storgatan 50. **Drinking** dens can be found downstairs at the *Stadshotellet* in the *Cockney Pub*, and in the cheaper bar of the *Time Hotell*, especially busy on Friday nights.

Luleå

Last stop on the E4-bus line, **LULEÅ** lies at one end of the *Malmbanan*, the iron-ore railway that connects the ice-locked Gulf of Bothnia with the ice-free Norwegian port of Narvik in the Norwegian Sea. The town's wide streets and lively atmosphere have an immediate appeal, making this a much better stop-off than nearby Boden (see p.556), 25 minutes down the train line. If you're heading north for the wilds of the Torne valley, Gällivare and Kiruna, or indeed to the sparsely populated regions inland, it's a good idea to spend a day or so here enjoying the sights and the impressive range of bars and restaurants: Luleå is the last oasis in a frighteningly vast area of forest and wilderness spreading north and west.

Luleå was founded in 1621, centred on the medieval church and parish village of nearby Gammelstad (meaning Old Town; see p.554). Even in those days trade with Stockholm was important, but as the industry expanded Gammelstad's tiny harbour proved inadequate to the task and in 1649, by royal command, the city was moved lock,

stock and barrel to its present site – only the church and parish village remained, today one of the city's main attractions. Shipping is still an important part of the local economy but over recent years Lulea has become the hi-tech centre of northern Sweden, specializing in metallurgy, research and education.

Arrival, information and accommodation

The **train** and **bus** stations are at one end of the string of parallel streets that make up the centre, and it takes about five minutes to walk between the two. Luleå's **tourist office** is a good ten minutes away in the Kulturcentrum Ebeneser at Storgatan 43B (mid-June to mid-Aug Mon–Fri 9am–7pm, Sat & Sun 10am–4pm; rest of the year Mon–Fri 10am–7pm, Sat 10am–4pm; ☎0920/29 35 00 or 29 35 05). Ask here about the town's free bike service: a number of ex-army bikes, painted red, white and blue, are available for use – take one and leave it wherever you choose. The tourist office is also the place to ask about boat trips to some of the hundreds of mostly uninhabited islands in the archipelago off the coast here.

The tourist office has a small number of **private rooms** for about 200kr per person, though they can't be booked by phone. Unfortunately the nearest **youth hostel** (☎0920/523 25; fax 524 19; all year; 100kr), fifteen minutes out at **Gäddvik** (Pike Bay), is too close to the main E4 for a quiet night's sleep; to get there, take hourly bus #6 from outside the train station and tell the bus driver to let you off at the hostel. The nearest **campsite** (☎0920/500 60), also reached on bus #6, is another five minutes on from the hostel.

Hotels

Amber, Stationsgatan 67 (☎0920/102 00). A cosy family-run place with good summer prices. ②/④
Arctic, Sandviksgatan 80 (☎0920/109 80). A smart little hotel that's very handy for the train station. ③/⑤
Aveny, Hermelinsgatan 10 (☎0920/22 18 20). One of the smaller hotels with reasonable summer prices. ②/④
Luleå Stads, Storgatan 15 (☎0920/670 00). The oldest and smartest of the city's hotels, with tasteful retro rooms, right in the centre of town. Discounts at weekends only. ④/⑤
Park, Kungsgatan 10 (☎0920/211 49). The cheapest of Luleå's hotels; basic but perfectly fine, with a shower and toilet in the corridor. ①

The City

There's only really one main street, the long **Storgatan**, south of which, past the main square, Rådhustorget, is the **Domkyrkan**. The medieval original disappeared centuries ago and the latest model to stand on the site, built in 1893, contains a modern barrage of copper chandeliers hanging like Christmas decorations. Walking west up Köpmangatan from the cathedral you'll find the **Norrbottens Museum** (June to mid-Aug Mon–Fri 10am–7pm, Sat & Sun noon–7pm; rest of the year Mon 1–5pm, Tues–Fri 9am–4pm, Sat & Sun noon–4pm; free) at Storgatan 2. Among the usual dull resumé of county history are some good displays on the Sami culture that begins to predominate northwest of Luleå (see the following chapter). Just south of the Domkyrkan, **Konstens Hus** at Smedjegatan 2 (Tues–Fri 11am–6pm, Wed 11am–8pm, Sat & Sun noon–4pm; free) is worth a look for some interesting works by local and not-so-local artists and sculptors.

If the weather's good, the next stop should be the **Gültzauudden** – a wooden promontory with a sandy beach; its odd name derives from the German shipbuilder, Christian Gültzau, who helped to make Luleå a shipbuilding centre. For more room to stretch out, you're better off taking the *M/S Stella Marina* out to the island of **Klubbviken**, the prettiest of the score of tiny islets that lie in the archipelago offshore. Here you'll find an enormous sandy beach and enough privacy to satisfy even the most solipsistic of souls. Boats leave from the southern harbour (Södra Hamnen) from the end of June to early August (June & Aug 2 daily, July 5 daily).

Gammelstad

The original settlement of Luleå, **GAMMELSTAD**, is 10km northwest of the city centre. When the town moved to the coast a handful of the more religious stayed behind to tend the church and the attached **parish village** remained in use. One of the most important places of historical interest north of Uppsala, the site is set to become the latest addition to the UNESCO World Heritage List. The church itself (daily June & Aug 10am–6pm; July 10am–8pm) is one of the largest of its kind in Norrland, completed at the end of the fifteenth century and adorned with the work of church artists from far and wide: both the decorated choir stalls and the ornate triptych are medieval originals, while the sumptuous pulpit is a splendid example of Bothnian Baroque, its intricacies trimmed with gilt cherubs and red and gold bunches of grapes. Look out for the opening above the south door, through which boiling oil was generously poured over unwelcome visitors.

Around 450 cottages are gathered around the church, making this the biggest parish village in Sweden, though nowadays they're unoccupied except during important religious festivals. Guided walks can be arranged with Gammelstad's **tourist office** (mid-June to mid-Aug daily 9am–6pm; ☎0920/543 10), located in one of the cottages. Down the hill from the tourist office is the **Friluftsmuséet Hägnan** (June to early Aug daily 11am–5pm; rest of Aug & early Sept Sat & Sun noon–4pm; free), an open-air heritage park whose main exhibits are two old farmstead buildings from the eighteeenth century. During the summer there are demonstrations of rural skills such as sheep-rearing, the crafting of traditional wooden roof slates and the baking of *tunnbröd*, northern Sweden's unleavened bread.

Getting to Gammelstad from Luleå is straightforward. **Buses** #8 and #9 make the thirty-minute trip from Hermelinsparken, at the west end of Skeppsbrogatan, every half-hour on weekdays, replaced by the #32 at weekends and in the evenings; the last bus back is at 10pm.

Eating and drinking

While the restaurants on Storgatan may be a little pricier than those in the side streets, you'll probably find that the extra kronor are worth it for a lively atmosphere. As usual, you can happily do an evening's drinking in the restaurants listed below.

Ankaret, Köpmangatan 16, near the Domkyrkan. Good fish dishes for around 100kr.

Bryggan, inside *Stads Hotell* at Storgatan 15. Expensive reindeer and other northern Swedish specialities – nothing under 150kr.

Cook's Krog, inside *SAS Luleå* hotel at Storgatan 17. The place to come if you want steak. Around 150kr.

Restaurang Corsica, Nygatan. Traditional Corsican dishes make this a welcome change. Entrecôte for 89kr, beer 35kr.

Fiskekyrkan, in Södra Hamnen. One of the cheaper restaurants in town with pasta and other simple dishes for less than 100kr. Its outdoor tables on the harbourside make it a popular drinking place in summer.

Pimpinella, Storgatan 40. Liveliest and trendiest drinking spot in town with tables out in the street during summer.

Tallkotten, inside *Stads Hotell* at Storgatan 15. Trendy place decked out in blue and yellow serving everything you could imagine, including ostrich, but with the emphasis on northern Swedish dishes. Count on spending 100–150kr; 60kr for lunch.

WillGott, Storgatan 11. Smart restaurant with a lunch buffet or pasta for 70kr; meat and fish dishes for 120kr.

Ängeln, corner of Nygatan and Storgatan. Simple place serving pizza and pasta. Under 100kr.

Listings

Banks *Handelsbanken*, Storgatan, between *Stads Hotell* and the tourist office; *Nordbanken*, Köpmangatan, near the pharmacy.

Bus station Kvarteret Loet (☎0920/890 85).

Car rental *Avis* ☎0920/22 83 55; *Biluthyrning i Luleå*, Varvsgatan 35 (☎0920/121 87); *Budget*, Robertviksgatan 3 (☎0920/131 11); *Dahlgrens Biluthyrning*, Sandviksgatan 72B (☎0920/21 10 30); *Hertz*, Gammelstadsvägen 23 (☎0920/22 56 00 or 22 56 10); *Europcar* ☎0920/10 165.

Gay contacts Information by post from Box 95, 971 04 Luleå (☎0920/22 61 66). Switchboard Sun 7–10pm (☎0920/170 55).

Pharmacy Köpmangatan 36c (Mon–Fri 9am–6pm, Sat 9am–2pm, Sun 1–4pm; ☎0920/22 03 95).

Police Skeppsbrogatan 37 (☎0920/29 50 00).

Post office Storgatan 53 (☎0920/840 00).

Systembolaget Off-licence on Köpmangatan (Mon–Fri 9.30am–6pm, Thurs till 7pm).

Taxi *Taxi Luleå* ☎0920/100 00; *6:ans Taxi* ☎0920/666 66.

Boden

Twenty-five minutes by train from Luleå, **BODEN** is a major transport junction for the entire north of the country; from here trains run northwest to Gällivare and Kiruna and eventually onto Narvik in Norway, and south to Stockholm and Gothenburg. There also used to be a branch line to Haparanda (see below) and on to Finland, but this has now closed and the route served only by buses. Its strategic location means that in summer Boden's tiny train station can be filled with backpackers; if you've got time, it's well worth stepping out into the town.

Boden's position, roughly halfway along the coast of Norrbotten at the narrowest bridging point along the Lule River, was no doubt one of the reasons that the **Överluleå kyrka** (mid-June to end June & early Aug Mon–Fri & Sun 1–5pm; July Mon–Fri & Sun 1–7pm) and its **parish village** were founded here in 1826. The church is a twenty-minute walk from the train station, down the modest main street, **Kungsgatan**, over the bridge and right along Strandplan; the church impresses most by its location, perched on a hillock overlooking the water, surrounded by whispering birch trees. The surrounding cottages of the parish village once spread down the hill to the lake, Bodträsket, complete with their stables and narrow little alleyways. Nowadays they're rented out as superior **hostel accommodation** during the summer (see below).

Today Boden is Sweden's largest military town and everywhere you look you'll see spotty-faced young men kitted out in camouflage gear and black boots strutting purposefully (if somewhat ridiculously) up and down the streets; there are infantry, tank, artillery and air corps here. The first garrison was established in 1901 and a fortress completed in 1907. Atop a hill about 3km southeast of the centre – a forty-minute walk from the train station – is **Svedjefortet** (summer daily 11am–7pm; 10kr), offering good views of the town. Blasted out of the hill there's an underground fortress where you can see old cannons from 1894 and 1917, as well a selection of military uniforms. On the southwest edge of town lies the **Garnisonsmuséet** (Garrison Museum; summer daily 11am–4pm; 10kr), proudly displaying the largest collection of military uniforms north of Stockholm.

Practicalities

Ask at the summer **tourist office** at the train station (daily June & Aug 9am–6pm; July 9am–9pm; ☎0921/624 10) or at the main office at Färgaregatan 5 (rest of the year Mon–Fri 8am–5pm; ☎0921/623 14) about the possibility of staying in one of the parish **cottages** – rates vary from 265kr (in June) to 345kr (July) for two people, but they're often booked up way in advance. Boden's **campsite** (☎0921/62407) is a few minutes' walk from the church, following the path along the lakeside; here you can rent canoes (30kr an hour, 150kr a day) and bikes (50kr a day). Of the **hotels**, the cheerful *Hotell Standard*, outside the station at Stationsgatan 5 (☎0921/160 55; fax 175 58; ①), also provides hostel accommodation for 15- to 35-year-olds (90kr), or there's the more upmarket *Hotell Bodensia* in the centre at Kungsgatan 47 (☎0921/177 10; fax 192 82; ②/④).

Eating in Boden, you won't be overwhelmed by choice. For a solid meal, try *Panelen* at the station end of Kungsgatan, while for pizza or pasta you're best off at *San Marino*, Garnisonsgatan 41, or *Restaurang Romeo* in the pedestrianized centre, both with pizzas from 50kr, pasta from 70kr. *Café Ollé* at Drottninggatan 4 does a 50kr lunch deal and tasty open sandwiches. Boden's best drinking spot is *Olivers Inn*, on Kungsgatan just before the bridge.

Haparanda and around

Hard by the Finnish border and at the very north of the Gulf of Bothnia, **HAPARAN-DA** is hard to like. Trains no longer run to the town (the nearest stations are Boden in Sweden and Kemi in Finland) but the defunct train station sets the tone of the place – a grand-looking building reflecting Haparanda's aspirations to be a major trading centre after World War I. That never happened and walking up and down the streets around Torget can be a pretty depressing experience; the signpost near the bus station doesn't help matters either, reinforcing the feeling that you're a very long way from anywhere: Stockholm 1100km, the North Cape 800km and Timbuktu 8386km.

To fully understand why Haparanda is so grim, you need to know a little history: the key is the neighbouring Finnish town of **Tornio** (Torneå in Swedish). From 1105 until 1809 Finland was part of Sweden and Tornio was an important trading centre, serving markets across northern Scandinavia. But things began to unravel when Russia attacked and occupied Finland in 1807; the Treaty of Hamina then forced Sweden to cede Finland to Russia in 1809 – thereby losing Tornio. It was decided that Tornio had to be replaced and so in 1821 the trading centre of Haparanda was founded, on the Swedish side of the new border along the River Torne. However, it proved to be little more than an upstart compared to its neighbour across the water. Nearly two hundred years on, with Sweden and Finland now members of the European Union, Haparanda and Tornio have declared themselves a "Eurocity" – one city made up of two towns from different countries.

There are only a couple of sights in town: the train station building from 1918 and the peculiar **Haparanda kyrka**, a monstrous modern construction that looks like a cross between an aircraft hangar and a block of flats topped off in dark coloured copper. When the church was finished in 1963 it caused a public scandal and it has even been awarded a prize for being the ugliest church in Sweden.

Practicalities

There are no border formalities and you can simply walk over the bridge to Finland and wander back whenever you like; it's worth remembering that Finland is an hour ahead of Sweden.

Haparanda's **tourist office** (June–Aug Mon–Fri 9am–8pm, Sat & Sun 10am–2pm; Sept–May Mon–Fri 9.30am–5pm; ☎0922/615 85) is in the bus station off Norra Esplanaden, near the bridge to Finland. The smart **youth hostel** (☎0922/611 71; all year; 100kr) nearby at Strandgatan 26 has the cheapest beds in town, with good views across to Finland. To reach the **campsite**, *Sundholmens Camping* (☎0922/618 01 or 100 03), at Järnvägsgatan 1, right at the other end of town, walk along the river down Strandgatan, take a right onto Storgatan, cross the railway lines and follow the signs; the campsite also has some four-bed cabins for 270kr. Alternatively, try the cheap and cheerful pension *Resandehem*, in the centre of town at Storgatan 65B (☎0922/120 68; ①), or if you've a bit more money to spend, the town's sole hotel, *Haparanda Stadshotel* at Torget 7 (☎0922/614 90; fax 102 23; ②/④).

Tornio (see p.696) has many more **bars** and **restaurants** than its Swedish neighbour, so you may want to do what the locals do and nip over into Finland for a bit of high life, especially at the weekend. Otherwise, the best meal to be had in Haparanda is the lunch served at the *Stadshotel* in the main square – a help-yourself deal for 59kr. Pizzas from 38kr and beer from 25kr are served up at *El Paso Pizzeria* on Storgatan, close to Torget, and at the Chinese pizza parlour *Lei-Lane* at Köpmangatan 15. *Nya Konditoriet* on Storgatan is the best place for coffee and cakes. When it comes to **drinking**, head for the pub *Ponderosa* at Storgatan 82 or the *Gulasch Baronen* pub attached to the *Stadshotel*.

Around Haparanda: Kukkolaforsen

If you're stuck in Haparanda for a day or two, it's worth making the trip 15km north to **KUKKOLAFORSEN**. On the last weekend in July the impressive rapids here are the scene of the *Sikfesten* or Whitefish Festival. This local delicacy is caught in nets at the end of long poles, fishermen dredging the fast, white water and scooping the whitefish out onto the bank, then grilling them on large open fires. Originally a centuries-old fisherman's harvest festival, it's now largely an excuse to get plastered, with a beer tent, evening gigs and dancing the order of the day. It costs 100kr to get in on the Saturday, 60kr on the Sunday, although if you're staying in the adjacent campsite (☎0922/310 00; fax 310 30), which also has cabins (270kr), you should be able to sneak in for free.

River rafting down the rapids can also be arranged here, either through the campsite or at the tourist office in Haparanda – 180kr gets you the gear, helmet and life jacket, and pays for a short trip down-river plus a certificate at the end. Trips go at 1pm and 6pm. Finally, the **sauna** at Kukkolaforsen has been declared the best in the country by the Swedish Sauna Academy; after boiling yourself up in temperatures over 100°C, step out onto the veranda with a cool beer, breathe the crisp air heavy with the scent of pine, and listen to the roar of the rapids. And don't forget to wave to Finland across the river.

Moving on from Haparanda: bus routes

Swedish buses head north on the Swedish side of the border through the beautiful Torne valley to Pajala (Mon–Fri 3 daily, 1 on Sun), from where connections can be made to either Gällivare or Kiruna, or with a change at Vittangi to Karesuando. Alternatively, if you are heading on into Finland, Finnish buses connect Haparanda with Tornio and Kemi roughly every hour. Times are posted up at the bus station in Haparanda. There's also a once-daily direct afternoon bus from Haparanda to Rovaniemi (journey time 3hr).

travel details

Trains

From Boden to: Gothenburg (1 daily; 17hr 30min); Gällivare (3 daily; 2hr); Gävle (2 daily; 12hr 30min); Kiruna (3 daily; 3hr); Luleå (5 daily; 25min); Narvik (2 daily; 6hr 30min); Stockholm (2 daily; 14hr); Uppsala (2 daily; 13hr).

From Gävle to: Boden (2 daily; 12hr 30min); Falun (5 daily; 1hr); Gällivare (2 daily; 14hr); Hudiksvall (8 daily; 1hr 30min); Härnösand (3 daily; 3hr 30min); Kiruna (2 daily; 15hr 30min); Luleå (2 daily; 12hr); Stockholm (hourly; 2hr); Sundsvall (8 daily; 2hr 30min); Söderhamn (8 daily; 50min); Umeå (1 daily; 9hr); Uppsala (hourly; 1hr); Örebro (6 daily; 3hr); Östersund (4 daily; 4hr).

From Hudiksvall to: Gävle (8 daily; 1hr 30min); Härnösand (3 daily; 2hr); Sundsvall (9 daily; 1hr);

Stockholm (8 daily; 3hr 20min); Uppsala (8 daily; 2hr 40min).

From Härnösand to: Långsele (4 daily; 2hr); Sollefteå (5 daily; 1hr 40min); Stockholm (3 daily; 6hr); Sundsvall (8 daily; 1hr).

From Luleå to: Boden (5 daily; 25min); Gothenburg (1 daily; 18hr); Gällivare (3 daily; 3hr); Kiruna (3 daily; 4hr); Narvik (2 daily; 7hr); Stockholm (2 daily; 14hr 30min); Uppsala (2 daily; 13hr 30min).

From Sundsvall to: Gävle (8 daily; 2hr 30min); Hudiksvall (9 daily; 1hr); Härnösand (8 daily; 1hr); Långsele (3 daily; 2hr); Stockholm (7 daily; 5hr); Söderhamn (9 daily; 1hr 45min); Östersund (6 daily; 4hr 15min).

From Söderhamn to: Gävle (8 daily; 50min); Hudiksvall (9 daily; 40min); Härnösand (3 daily; 2hr

45min); Stockholm (8 daily; 2hr 40min); Sundsvall (9 daily; 1hr 45min); Uppsala (8 daily; 2hr).

From Umeå to: Boden (1 daily; 5hr); Gothenburg (1 daily; 14hr); Gällivare (1 daily; 8hr); Gävle (1 daily; 9hr); Kiruna (1 daily; 9hr); Luleå (1 daily; 5hr 40min); Stockholm (1 daily; 11hr); Uppsala (1 daily; 10hr).

Buses

The E-4 express buses

Following the withdrawal of branch line rail services to the coastal towns north of Sundsvall (except Umeå), the *E-4 bussarna* run four times daily between Sundsvall and Luleå, generally connecting with trains to and from Sundsvall. The buses are reliable and all have toilet facilities on board. Buy your tickets from the bus driver before boarding. From Sundsvall the buses call at Härnösand (45min); Lunde (for connections to the High Coast; 1hr 35min); Ullånger (1hr 55min); Örnsköldsvik (2hr 40min); Skellefteå (6hr 30min); Piteå (7hr 45min) and Luleå (8hr 45min).

Other important routes: services run from the coast into central northern Sweden, often linking up with the Inlandsbanan. There's also one service from Umeå to Mo-i-Rana in Norway. For buses from Härnösand and Örnsköldsvik to the High Coast see p.543.

From Boden to: Haparanda (6 daily; 2hr 15min), Luleå (6 daily; 30min).

From Haparanda to: Boden (6 daily; 2hr 20min); Luleå (9 daily; 2hr 30min); Pajala (4 daily; 3hr 30min).

From Luleå to: Boden (6 daily; 30min); Gällivare (2 daily; 3hr 30min); Haparanda (9 daily; 2hr 30min); Jokkmokk (3 daily; 3hr); Kiruna (2 daily; 5hr); Pajala (2 daily; 3hr 30min).

From Skellefteå to: Arvidsjaur (2 daily; 2hr); Bastuträsk (for main-line train connections; 5 daily; 1hr); Jörn (for main-line train connections; 2 daily; 1 hr).

From Piteå to: Älvsbyn (for main-line train connections; 6 daily; 1hr).

From Umeå to: Dorotea (2 daily; 3hr 15min); Mo-i-Rana (Norway; 1 daily; 8hr); Storuman (3 daily; 3hr 40min); Strömsund (2 daily; 4hr 30min); Tärnaby (3 daily; 5hr 30min); Vännäs (for mainline train connections; 22 daily; 30min).

From Örnsköldsvik to: Mellansel (for main-line train connections; 11 daily; 40min); Åsele (for connections to Dorotea and Vilhelmina 1 daily; 3hr).

Services to and from Stockholm

The only long-distance service up the Bothnian Coast is #887, operated by *Swebus Express*, though it only runs as far as Bollnäs and Edsbyn, calling at Gävle and Uppsala en route. For information call *Swebus* on ☎020/640 640 or from abroad on ☎08/655 00 90.

International ferries

From Skellefteå to: Pietarsaari (Jakobstad in Swedish). Future of sailings uncertain. Check with *Silja Line* on ☎090/14 21 00.

From Umeå to: Vaasa (mid-June to mid-Aug 3–4 daily; rest of the year 1–2 daily; 3hr 30min).

Flights

There are fairly regular flights – the most reliable operated by *SAS* – between Stockholm Arlanda and the main northern cities. Timetables are subject to constant change, however, so it's advisable to check with a travel agent.

CHAPTER FOURTEEN

CENTRAL AND NORTHERN SWEDEN

In many ways the long wedge of land that comprises **central and northern Sweden** – from the shores of **Lake Vänern** up to the Finnish border north of Arctic Circle – encompasses all that is most typical of the country. This vast area of land is really one great forest broken only by the odd village or town. Rural and underpopulated, it fulfils the image most people have of Sweden: lakes, pine forests, wooden cabins and reindeer. Swedes across the country lived like this until just one or two generations ago, taking their cue from the people of these central lands and forest who were the first to rise against the Danes in the sixteenth century. They shared their land, uneasily, with the Sami and their reindeer, earliest settlers of the wild lands in the far north of the country.

Folklorish **Dalarna** county is the most intensely picturesque region. Even a quick tour around one or two of the more accessible places gives an impression of the whole: red cottages with white doors and window frames, sweeping green countryside, summer festivals and water bluer than blue. Dalarna's inhabitants maintain a cultural heritage (echoed in contemporary handicrafts and traditions) that goes back to the Middle Ages. And the county is *the* place to spend Midsummer, particularly Midsummer's Eve, when the whole region erupts in a frenzy of celebration.

The privately owned **Inlandsbanan**, the great Inland Railway, cuts right through central and northern Sweden and links virtually all the towns and villages covered in this chapter. Running from **Mora** to **Gällivare**, above the Arctic Circle, it ranks with the best European train journeys, an enthralling 1100km travelled over two days. Certainly it's a much livelier approach to the north than the east coast run up from Stockholm. Buses connect the rail line with the **mountain villages** that snuggle alongside the Norwegian border – the Swedish *fjäll*, or fells, not only offer some of the most spectacular scenery in the country but also some of the best, and least spoilt, hiking in Europe. North of Mora, **Östersund** is the only town of any size, situated by the side of the Great Lake reputed to be home to Sweden's very own Loch Ness monster. From here trains head in all directions: west to Norway through the country's premier ski resort, **Åre**, south to Dalarna and Stockholm, east to Sundsvall on the Bothnian coast and north to Lappland.

The wild lands of the **Sami** make for the most fascinating trip in northern Sweden. Omnipresent reindeer are a constant reminder of how far north you are, but the enduring Sami culture, which once defined much of this land, is now under threat. The problems posed by tourism are escalating, principally the erosion of grazing land under the pounding feet of hikers, making the Sami increasingly economically dependent on selling souvenirs and handicrafts. The Chernobyl nuclear accident in 1986 led to a fundamental change in living patterns, the result of the fallout affected grazing lands and even today reindeer in certain parts of the north are unfit for human consumption.

Further north, around industrial **Gällivare** and **Kiruna**, and as far as the Norwegian border at **Riksgränsen**, the rugged (potentially dangerous) **national parks** offer a

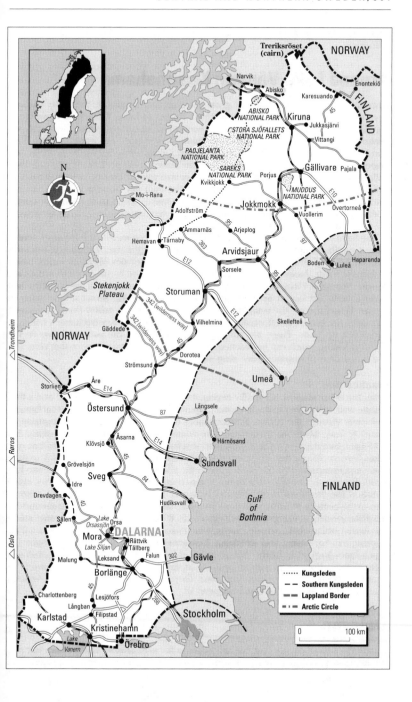

Treriksröset (cairn)
NORWAY
Narvik
Abisko
Enontekiö
Karesuando
FINLAND
ABISKO NATIONAL PARK
Kiruna
STORA SJÖFALLETS NATIONAL PARK
Jukkasjärvi
Vittangi
PADJELANTA NATIONAL PARK
SAREKS NATIONAL PARK
Porjus
Gällivare
Pajala
N
Mo-i-Rana
Kvikkjokk
Jokkmokk
MUDDUS NATIONAL PARK
Övertorneå
Adolfström
Vuollerim
Ammarnäs
Arjeplog
Hemavan
Tärnaby
363
Arvidsjaur
E12
Sorsele
Boden
Luleå
Haparanda
Stekenjokk Plateau
Storuman
342 (wilderness way)
Skellefteå
342 (wilderness way)
Vilhelmina
E12
Gäddede
45
NORWAY
Strömsund
Dorotea
Umeå
△ Trondheim
Åre
E14
Storlien
Långsele
Östersund
87
△ Røros
Klövsjö
Åsarna
E14
Härnösand
Grövelsjön
Sveg
84
Sundsvall
Idre
Drevdagen
45
Hudiksvall
Sälen
Lake Orsasjön
Orsa
Gulf of Bothnia
FINLAND
△ Oslo
DALARNA
Mora
Rättvik
Lake Siljan
Tällberg
Malung
Leksand
Falun
302
Gävle
Borlänge
Charlottenberg
Lesjöfors
Karlstad
Långban
Filipstad
786
Stockholm
Kristinehamn
Lake Vänern
Örebro

.... **Kungsleden**
— — **Southern Kungsleden**
═══ **Lappland Border**
—··— **Arctic Circle**

0   100 km

chance to hike and commune with nature like nowhere else; this is the last wilderness in Europe.

Around Lake Vänern: Kristinehamn

Once the southern terminus of the great Inlandsbanan train route, the pretty harbour town of **KRISTINEHAMN**, on the northern fringes of **Lake Vänern**, is nowadays a popular target for holidaying Swedes. It's been an important port since the fourteenth century, when iron from the Bergslagen mines was shipped out from the town. Five hundred years later one of the country's earliest railways speeded up the process: cars loaded with iron ore coasted downhill from the mines to the port, the empty cars then pulled back to mines across the whole of the central mining area of Sweden, known as Bergslagen, by horses and oxen. In summer the train line became a popular tourist route, thereby subsidizing a line that could never make a profit from its regular traffic. Today, however, the Inlandsbanan starts in Mora (see opposite) and large sections of the track north of Kristinehamn have been ripped up.

The town is proud, and rightly so, of its towering fifteen-metre-high **Picasso sculpture**, a sandblasted concrete pillar standing guard over the river entrance to the town at Rönneberg. The striking piece is one of the Les Dames des Mougins series, based on Picasso's wife, Jacqueline, and was raised and decorated by the Swedish artist **Carl Nesjar**. Seeing as Picasso only provided a photograph of a model of the sculpture and never actually set foot in Sweden, the "Picasso sculpture" tag seems a little unfair to Nesjar. To get there – the sculpture is 6km from the centre – follow Presterudsvägen out along the cycle track/footpath that skirts the river, past Kristinehamn's flotilla of garish private boats. There are some good beaches along the path, and also on the island of **Vålön**, which can be reached from the statue by a boat service that runs several times a day in summer (June–Aug daily 10am–6pm).

Practicalities

From the **train station**, served by regular trains from Stockholm, turn left and a five-minute walk brings you to the large main square, Södra Torget, and a river that branches its way through the centre. Kristinehamn's **tourist office** is at Västerlånggatan 22 (June & Aug Mon–Sat 9am–6pm, Sun noon–6pm; July Mon–Fri 9am–8pm, Sat 9am–6pm, Sun noon–6pm; Sept–May Mon–Fri 9am–4pm; ☎0550/881 87); you can rent bikes here for 75kr a day. The nearest **youth hostel** (☎0550/147 71; mid-May to Aug; 85kr) and **campsite** (☎0550/881 95) are in the village of Kvarndammen (take the E18 in the direction of Örebro) – the campsite also rents out bikes (100kr a day). Pick of the **hotels** is the *Stadshotellet* (☎0550/150 30; fax 41 12 35; ⑤) on Södra Torget, a lovely turn-of-the-century building with modern rooms and a restaurant. More economical is the *Hotel Fröding* at Kungsgatan 44 (☎0550/151 80; fax 101 30; ③), or you could ask at the tourist office about private rooms, which can be rented from 100kr, plus a 25kr booking fee. For **eating and drinking**, *Restaurant Sjöjungfrun* at Vålösundsvägen 117 (open June–Aug), right by the Picasso statue at Rönneberg, serves top-quality fish and meat dishes. For lunch, you're best off at *Roma Restaurant*, a busy pizzeria at Skaraborgsvägen 13, with pizzas from 50kr. The most popular place to drink is *Arklow's* Irish pub and restaurant, at Hamnbrogatan 18.

Dalarna

Dalarna is a large county that not only takes in the area around **Lake Siljan** but also the ski resorts of **Sälen** and **Idre**, close to the Norwegian border. It holds a special misty-eyed place in the Swedish heart, and should be on your list of destinations, though not to the exclusion of places further north. Verdant cow pastures, gentle rolling meadows sweet with the smell of summer flowers, and tiny rural villages make up most of the county, although the land to the northwest of Lake Siljan (created millions of years ago when a metorite crashed into the earth) slowly rises to meet the chain of mountains that forms the border with Norway. One small lakeside town can look pretty much like another, so restrict yourself to one or two before moving on further north: Leksand and Mora are the best options, and Rättvik may also be worth a visit if you've time (see below). If you're here for more than a couple of days, the nearby industrial towns of **Falun** and **Borlänge** can be a relief after the folksiness of the lakeside and the tourist hordes that dominate the area in summer. North of Mora the county becomes more mountainous and less populous and the only place of any note is **Orsa** with its fascinating **bear park**.

Trains operated by the national rail company, *SJ*, call at all the towns around the lake and terminate in Mora; Falun can be reached by changing at Borlänge. From Mora the private **Inlandsbanan** railway takes over – though Orsa, Sälen and Idre can all be reached by bus from Mora. Another good way to get about, especially around Lake Siljan, is to rent a **bike** from one of the tourist offices – this region is a popular Swedish holiday destination so there's no shortage of accommodation.

Around Lake Siljan

Things have changed since Baedeker, writing in 1889, observed that "Lake Siljan owes much of its interest to the inhabitants of its banks, who have preserved many of their primitive characteristics . . . In their idea of cleanliness they are somewhat behind the age". Today it's not the people who captivate but the scenery: **Lake Siljan** is what many people come to Sweden for, its gentle surroundings, traditions and local handicrafts weaving a subtle spell. There's a lush feel to much of the region, the vegetation enriched by the lake, which adds a pleasing dimension to what are essentially small, low-profile towns and villages. Only Mora stands out as being bigger and busier, with the hustle and bustle of holiday-makers and countless caravans in summer.

Mora

If you've only got time to see part of the lake, then **MORA**, the largest of the settlements, is the place to head for, especially if you're travelling further north, as it's the starting point of the Inlandsbanan (see p.564). Mora's main draw is the work of Sweden's best-known artist, **Anders Zorn** (1860–1920), who moved here in 1896 and whose paintings are exhibited in the excellent **Zorn Museum** at Vasagatan 36 (Mon–Sat 9am–5pm, Sun 11am–5pm; 25kr) – look out for the self-portrait and the especially pleasing *Midnatt* (Midnight) from 1891, which depicts a woman rowing on Lake Siljan, her hands blue from the cold night air. You might also want to wander across the lawn and take in his home, **Zorngården** (Mon–Sat 10am–4pm, Sun 11am–4pm; 30kr), where he lived with his wife, Emma. The other museum in town worth considering is the **Vasaloppsmuséet** (mid-Feb to Sept daily; 30kr), also on Vasagatan but on the other side of the church. Here you'll find an exhibition on the history of the *Vasaloppet* (see p.569) – a ski race that started 500 years ago with the attempts of two Mora men to catch up with King Gustav Vasa, who was fleeing from the Danes. Once you've covered the town's sights, you might want to take a **cruise** on the lake aboard the lovely old steamship *M/S Gustaf Wasa* (timetables vary; info on ☎010/252 3292 or 204 7724); count on 120kr for a round trip to Leksand and back or 80kr for a two-hour lunch cruise.

Mora's **tourist office** (mid-June to mid-Aug Mon–Fri 9am–8pm, Sat 10am–8pm, Sun 11am–8pm; rest of the year Mon–Fri 9am–5pm, Sat 10am–1pm; ☎0250/265 50) is located at Ångbåtskajen, down on the quayside near Mora Strand train station, which is

ACCOMMODATION PRICE CODES

All the Swedish pensions and hotels listed in the guide have been graded according to the following price bands, based on the cost of the least expensive double room in high season. However, almost every hotel offers seasonal and weekend discounts that can reduce the rate by one or even two grades. Many of these bargains are impromptu, but wherever possible we've given two grades, covering both the regular and the discounted rate. Single rooms, where available, are usually between 60 and 80 percent of the cost of a double.

① under 500kr   ② 500–700kr   ③ 700–900kr   ④ 900–1200kr   ⑤ over 1200kr

nothing more than a platform. The main station, Mora, is the place to go for information on *SJ* and Inlandsbanan trains, but it's further from the centre, so unless you're staying at the youth hostel get off at the next stop, Mora Strand.

The cheapest place to stay is the **youth hostel** (☎0250/381 96; all year; 100kr) at Fredsgatan 6; get off the train at Mora station, turn left, and keep walking for about five minutes along the main street, Vasagatan. Mora's **campsite**, *Mora Camping* (☎0250/15352), is a ten-minute walk from the centre along Hantverkaregatan, which begins near the bus station: there's a good beach nearby, as well as a lake for swimming. Among the **hotels**, biggest and best is the *Mora Hotell* at Strandgatan 12 (☎0250/717 50; fax 189 81; ②/③), opposite Mora Strand train station, with a choice of modern and old-fashioned rooms. *Hotell St Mikael* (☎0250/159 00; fax 380 70; ②), Fridhemsgatan 15, is small with tasteful rooms, while *Hotell Kung Gösta* is handy for the main train station (☎0250/150 70; fax 170 78; ②/③).

As for **eating and drinking**, all the hotels serve up a decent *dagens rätt* for around 55kr with little to choose between them. *Wasastugan*, a huge log building at Tingnäsvägen between the main train station and the tourist office, also does 55kr lunches, but it's particularly lively in the evenings, with meat and fish dishes from 80kr. Alternatively, head for the highly regarded *Strandrestaurangen*, next to the tourist office on Strandgatan, which serves any pizza you could imagine for 59kr. In summer coffee and cakes can be enjoyed outside at *Helmers Konditori* and at *Mora Kaffestugan*, virtually next door to each other on Kyrkogatan. Despite its name, *Café Gabbis*, inside

INLANDSBANAN PRACTICALITIES

The **Inlandsbanan**, the great inland railway that links Dalarna with Lappland, is today a mere shadow of its former self. Spiralling costs and low passenger numbers forced Swedish Railways to sell the line in 1992, at which point services on the southern section between Mora and Kristinehamn had already been abandoned. The railway was bought by the fifteen municipalities the route passes through, and the private company, *Inlandsbanan AB*, was launched. It now operates only as a tourist venture in summer – generally from mid-June to the end of August. InterRail and ScanRail passes give a 50 percent **discount** – buy your ticket on board; it's not possible to reserve seats in advance. Timetables are approximate and the train is likely to stop whenever the driver feels like it; maybe for a spot of wild strawberry picking or to watch a beaver damming a stream. It's certainly a fascinating way to reach the far north of the country but not to be recommended if you're in a rush. Taken in one go the whole journey lasts two days, with an overnight stop in Östersund. Take it easy and make a couple of stops along the route and you'll get much more out of it. Special guides available on board contain commentaries and information about places along the route. For **timetables** and other **information** contact *Inlandståget AB*, Kyrkgatan 56, S-831 34 Östersund (☎063/12 76 95 or 10 15 90; fax 51 99 80).

the *Mora Hotell* on Strandgatan, is in fact a pub and one of the liveliest places in the evening besides *Wasastugan*.

Rättvik

Situated at the eastern bulge of the lake, 37km from Mora, **RÄTTVIK** is altogether much smaller and quieter: one tiny shopping street, a jetty out into the lake and an outdoor swimming pool and that's about the sum of it. While there's not much in the way of sights, what Rättvik does have is access to plenty of gorgeous countryside. Get out of the village as soon as you can and head up for the viewing point at **Vidablick** – about an hour's walk and a stiff climb but the view is worth it – you can see virtually all of Lake Siljan, and the surrounding hillsides, covered in forests broken only by the odd farm. You can get to the viewing point by walking on marked trails through the forests above Rättvik: pick up a free map of town from the tourist office (see below) and ask for advice on how to get there. In the forest itself there are a couple of information boards showing the different trails – Vidablick has a small café and a shop to reward your efforts. The quickest way back down to Rättvik is to take one of the steep roads down the hill (ask the staff in the shop to point out the correct one), go left at the end onto Wallenkampfvägen and then right along Mårsåkervägen towards Lerdal, and you'll see some of the most beautifully located residential houses in Dalarna – all wood logs and flowers and with a view out over the lake.

Rättvik's **tourist office** is handily situated in the train station (mid-June to mid-Aug Mon–Fri 9am–8pm, Sat 10am–8pm, Sun 11am–8pm; rest of the year Mon–Fri 9am–5pm, Sat noon–4pm; ☎0248/702 00). The best and cheapest place to stay is the **youth hostel** (☎0248/105 66; all year; 100kr) on Centralgatan, built in traditional Dalarna style out of large pine logs and surrounded by trees; get there by following Domarbacksvägen, just 1km from the train station. There are two **campsites** in town, one across the road from the youth hostel (☎0248/561 10), the other right on the lakeside behind the railway tracks (☎0248/516 91). When it comes to **hotels** there's not much choice: the best in town is the average *Hotell Lerdalshöjden* (☎0248/511 50; fax 511 77; ③) on Bockgatan, or there are some comfortable pine cabins at *Hotell Hantverksbyn* (☎0248/302 50; fax 306 60; ②), about 3km out of Rättvik.

There's a dearth of good places to **eat and drink** in Rättvik and most people head off to Leksand or Mora for a night out. A decent bet is *Restaurant Anna* on Vasagatan – a cosy restaurant with lunch for 55kr and local specialities in the evening for 100kr and upward; otherwise you're looking at *Tre Krögare* on pedestrianized Storgatan, which serves burgers for 40kr and meat dishes for 80kr, and has a happy hour (Wed–Sun 3–8pm); or *Bella Pizza* at Ågatan 11, where pizzas go for around 50kr.

Leksand

LEKSAND is perhaps the most popular and traditional of the Dalarna villages and is certainly worth making the effort to reach at Midsummer, when festivals recall age-old dances performed around the Maypole. Incidentally, Sweden's Maypoles aren't erected until June: spring comes late here, and in May there are few leaves on the trees and often some lingering snow. Celebrations culminate in the **church boat races**, an aquatic procession of sleek wooden longboats that the locals once rowed to church every Sunday. The race starts on Midsummer's Day in nearby Siljansnäs and continues for ten days around the lake, reaching Leksand on the first Saturday in July. Between twenty and twenty-five teams take part in the races, all cheered on by villagers at the water's edge. Check the latest details at the tourist office (see below). Another event worth coming here for is **Musik vid Siljan** – Music by Lake Siljan – nine days of nonstop classical, jazz and dance band music performed in churches, on the lakeside and at various locations out in the surrounding forest. The festival takes place in the first week of July, but check with the tourist office for the latest details.

At other times there's little to do in Leksand other than to rest up and take it easy for a while. Stroll along the riverside down to **Leksands kyrka**, which enjoys a magnificent setting, its peaceful churchyard lined with whispering spruce trees and overlooking the river and the lake. One of the biggest town churches in the country, Leksand's church has existed in its present form since 1715, although the oldest parts date back to the thirteenth century.

All trains between Mora and Börlange stop in Leksand; from the **train station** it's a five-minute walk to the **tourist office** on Norsgatan (☎0247/803 00; mid-June to mid-Aug Mon–Fri 9am–8pm, Sat 10am–8pm, Sun 11am–8pm; rest of the year Mon–Fri 9am–5pm, Sat 10am–1pm) – head up Villagatan then turn left onto Sarbanksgatan. Leksand's comfortable **youth hostel**, one of the oldest in Sweden, is over the river, around 2.5km from the train station in Parkgården (☎0247/152 50; all year; 100kr). Otherwise, there are two hotels to choose between: *Hotell Moskogen* at Insjövägen 50 (☎0247/146 00; 144 30; ③), which offers discounts for longer stays, and the unextraordinary *Hotell Korstäppen* at Hjortnäsvägen 33 (☎0247/123 10; fax 141 78; ③). The tourist office can also book four-bed **cabins** in the area from 450kr per night. If you're camping, the nearest **campsite**, *Leksands Camping*, is a twenty-minute walk from the tourist office along Tällbergsvägen (☎0247/803 13 or 803 12). The best place to eat **lunch** is at *Café Kulturhuset*, just up from the tourist office on Norsgatan – in summer there are tables in the garden at the back. Alternatively try *Bosporen*, a basic pizzeria in the tiny pedestrianized centre of town, which does lunch for 60kr. For a **drink** head for the pub and disco *Restaurant City*, which also does pizzas, kebabs and pasta to eat in or take away.

Borlänge

In comparison with nearby Falun (see below), **BORLÄNGE** is ugly and dull. As the biggest town in Dalarna, it developed as a steel and paper mill centre, industries that still dominate the town today. If it's a rainy day, you might want to investigate the three museums. Best of these is the **Jussi Björling Muséet** at Borganäsvägen 25 (Jan to mid-May & mid-Sept to Dec Tues–Fri noon–5pm; mid-May to mid-Sept Mon–Fri 11am–6pm, Sat 10am–2pm, Sun noon–5pm; 20kr), which commemorates Borlänge's most famous son and world famous tenor. It's a toss up as to which of the other two is more dull: the **Geologiska muséet** at Floragatan 6 (Mon–Fri 11am–2pm, Sat 11am–5pm; 10kr) has mind-numbing displays of rocks, minerals and fossils, whereas the **Framtidsmuséet** at Jussi Björlingsvägen 25 (Mon 1–5pm, Tues–Fri 10am–5pm, Sat & Sun noon–5pm; 25kr) is a museum of the future with a planetarium. Much better is to pass the museums over in favour of a stroll round the river; start at the open-air **craft village**, *Gammelgården*, with its small collection of old wooden houses on Stenhålsgatan.

From the central train station, walk past the green Liljekvistska parken to get to the **tourist office** (mid-June to mid-Aug daily 9am–7pm; rest of the year Mon–Fri 10am–6pm; ☎0243/665 66) on Borganäsvägen. Should you need to stay, the **youth hostel** (☎0243/22 76 15; all year; 100kr) is within easy walking distance of the centre at Kornstigen 23 A, while the **campsite**, *Mellsta Camping*, is more of a trek out, beautifully located by the river on Mellstavägen. There are a number of identikit **hotels** in the centre of town, all with pleasant modern rooms, though only *Hotel Gustaf Wasa* (☎0243/810 00; fax 806 00; ②/④) has bath tubs. Otherwise, try *Hotel Brage* (☎0243/22 41 59; fax 871 00; ②/④) at Stationsgatan 1, or the smaller and cheaper *Hotell Saga* (☎0243/21 18 40; ①) at Borganäsvägen 28.

When it comes to **eating**, you can't fail to notice Borlänge's proliferation of pizzerias: best of the bunch is *La Pizza* on Tunagatan. Greek specialities are served up at *En Liten Röd* on Vattugatan, Chinese food at *Le Mandarin* in Svea Torget, and Mexican and

Cajun delights at *Broken Dreams* inside *Hotel Gustaf Wasa*. The best food in town, though, is served up at the smart restaurant in the *Hotel Brage,* while traditional Swedish dishes can also be sampled at the intimate *Balders Krog* on Målaregatan. The most popular **pubs** in town are the *Flying Scotsman* in the Framtidsmuséet building on Jussi Björlingsvägen, and the *Hotel Brage*'s bar. Pick of the **cafés** is *Café 18.96*, set in a wonderful old pink wooden house on Sveagatan.

Falun

Twenty minutes by train from Börlange, **FALUN** is another essentially industrial town, though a pleasant one at that, founded on the business of **copper mining**. At their peak in the seventeenth and eighteenth centuries, the mines here produced two-thirds of the world's copper ore and the town acquired buildings and a layout commensurate with its status as Sweden's second largest town. In 1761, however, two devastating fires wiped out virtually all of central Falun and the replacements were built mostly of brick. The few old wooden houses to survive can be found in the areas of Elsborg (southwest of the centre), Gamla Herrgården and Östanfors (north of the centre), which are worth seeking out for an idea of the cramped conditions the mine-workers had to live in.

The **mines** themselves, out of town at the end of Gruvgatan, were said by the botanist Carl von Linnaeus to be as dreadful as hell itself and conditions were indeed appalling. An unnerving element of eighteenth-century mining was the omnipresence of copper vitriol gases, a strong preservative. A recorded case exists of a young man known as Fat Mats, whose body was found in the mines in 1719. He'd died 49 years previously in an accident but the corpse was so well preserved that his erstwhile finacée, by then an old woman, recognized him immediately. Hour-long **guided tours** can be arranged (March, April & Sept to mid-Nov Sat & Sun only 12.30–4.30pm; May–Aug daily 10am–4.30pm ☎023/158 25 or 711 4 75; 55kr), beginning with a lift ride that takes you down 55m to a network of old mine roads and drifts – be warned that the temperature drops to around 6–7°C. Make sure you also peer into the Great Pit, *Stora Stöten*, which appeared on Midsummer Day in 1687 – the result of a huge underground collapse caused by extensive mining and the unplanned driving of galleries and shafts.

Apart from the mines, Falun's attractions boil down to **Dalarnas Museum** at Stigaregatan 2–4 (May–Aug Mon–Thurs 10am–5pm, Fri–Sun noon–5pm; Sept–April Mon, Tues & Thurs 10am–5pm, Wed 10am–9pm; 20kr), which includes sections on the county's folk art, and on the hill overlooking town, Sweden's **National Ski Stadium** (*Riksskidsstadion*; ask for directions from the tourist office), where you can take a lift up to the top of the ninety-metre ski jump for a terrifying peer down.

Practicalities

From the **train** and **bus stations**, east of the centre, take the pass under the main road and head towards the shops in the distance to reach Stora Torget and Falun's **tourist office** (mid-June to mid-Aug Mon–Sat 9am–7pm, Sun 11am–5pm; rest of the year Mon–Fri 9am–5pm, Sat 9am–1pm; ☎023/836 37). The nearest **youth hostel** (☎023/105 60; all year; 100kr), a modern affair, is about 3km from the train station at Hälsinggårdsvägen 7 in Haraldsbo – take bus #701 or #704 from the centre; the **campsite** (☎023/835 63) is up at Lungnet by the National Ski Stadium, about fifteen minutes' walk from town. Central **hotels** include the swanky *First Hotel Grand* at Trotzgatan 9–11 (☎023/187 00; ②/④), and the more homely *Hotell Bergmästaren*, near the train station at Bergskolegränd 7 (☎023/636 00; ②/④).

In terms of **eating and drinking** places, Falun far outstrips the towns around Lake Siljan – in quality as well as choice. Most popular is the trendy *Banken Bar & Brasserie* at Åsgatan 41, housed in an old bank building decorated with bank notes and serving burgers, baked potatoes, fish and the like from around 80kr. Next door is the posh but cosy *Två rum och kök*, where meat and fish dishes start at 135kr. Another popular spot is *Rådhuskällaren*, a cellar under the town hall in Stora Torget serving delicious if somewhat pricey food – reckon on 120kr upwards and at least 165kr for a bottle of wine. *De Niro*, opposite Dalarnas Museum, is an inordinately popular pizzeria-cum-nightclub with bouncers on the door and regular cheap meal deals.

Drinking establishments, other than the above restaurants, include the excellent *Pub Engelbrekt* at Stigaregatan 1, and the average English-themed *King's Arms* at Falugatan 3. For entertainment value, though, the best time to be in Falun is in mid-July, when musicians from all over the world take over the town for a four-day **International Folk Music Festival** (check latest dates with the tourist office).

Sälen and Idre

The major ski resort of **SÄLEN** in effect also encompasses the surrounding slopes and mountains of Lindvallen, Högfjället, Tandådalen, Hundfjället, Rörbäcksnäs and Stöten. Each site has its own slope but looks to the village of Sälen for shops and services – not least the Systembolaget. **Buses** call at each resort in turn, terminating in Stöten. In summer there's just one bus a day from Mora (#95; 1hr 40min), plus a direct daily service (#801) from Gothenburg.

There are no sights as such: like neighbouring Idre (see below), Sälen is a base for outdoor activities during the summer and skiing in winter. In **summer** fishing, canoeing and beaver safaris are all available through the tourist office, plus there's some fantastic **hiking** to be had in the immediate vicinity (see below). In **winter** snow is guaranteed from November to May, making Sälen the biggest ski centre in the Nordic area, with over a hundred pistes. However, unless you've booked a package in advance (see *Basics*), prices are high and hotels may be full up.

Your first port of call should be the **tourist office** (late June to early Aug & Dec–April daily 9am–6pm; rest of the year Mon–Fri 9am–6pm; ☎0280/202 50) on the one straggly main street that runs through the village. Best bet for summer **accommodation** is the wonderfully situated *Högfjällshotellet* (☎0280/870 00; fax 211 61; ②/④) at Högfjället – just on the tree line with good views of the surrounding hills – a bus runs there twice a day. If you really want to be out in the wilds and get away from it all, head for the **youth hostel** (☎0280/820 40; all year; 100kr) at Gräsheden, near Stöten. The hostel staff will pick you up from the bus stop in Stöten if you call ahead.

Idre

The twice-daily bus from Mora follows the densely forested valley of the Österdalälven on its near three-hour journey to another of Sweden's main ski resorts, **IDRE**, before continuing up the mountain to the ski slopes at Idrefjäll. In winter the place is buzzing – not just with people but also with reindeer who wander down the main street at will; they're drawn here by the salt on the roads which they lick for minerals.

Idre is a tiny one-street affair, with a bank, supermarket and post office, definitely the place to stay if you're here in summer. The **tourist office** (mid-June to mid-Aug Mon–Fri 8am–7pm, Sat 8.30am–7pm, Sun 9am–7pm; rest of the year Mon–Fri 9am–5pm, Sat & Sun 10am–2pm; ☎0253/207 10) is at the far end of the main street when approaching from Mora. It can help arrange all sorts of activities, from fishing to horse-riding, and has plenty of information on hiking in the area.

For **accommodation** try the small and comfortable *Hotell Idregården* (☎0253/200 10; fax 206 76; ①/③) on the main road in from Mora – its **bar** is a popular spot at weekends. When it comes to **eating** there's precious little choice – either *Idregården* which is famous for its ostrich and wild game, or *Kopparleden*, complete with plastic flowers, which does simple fry-ups. In the ski resort of **Idrefjäll** there's just one **hotel**, *Idre Fjäll* (☎0253/410 00; fax 401 58; ②/⑤), which offers numerous activities as well as skiing, but for all practical matters you'll need to go down to the village, which is known as **Idrebua**. It's essential to book ahead.

Hiking around Sälen and Idre

The best **hiking route** is the little-known southern stretch of the **Kungsleden**, which starts at the *Högfjällshotellet* above Sälen and runs, with a break in the middle, to Storlien. It's an easy path to walk, with overnight cabins along its length, the majority operated by *Svenska Turistföreningen*, plus three fell stations at the Storlien end. From Idre you can join the path near the border at **Grövelsjön**, renowned for its stark and beautiful mountain scenery (twice-daily bus from both the village and Idrefjäll), where there's also an STF **fell station** (☎0253/230 90; Feb–April, mid-June to Sept, Christmas & New Year; 195–380kr, 50kr discount for IH members). Latest information from the tourist office in Idre or from the fell station in Grövelsjön. See p.585 for more on the Kungsleden.

An alternative is to follow the ninety-kilometre **Vasaloppsleden** (90km) to Mora. This footpath traces the route taken by skiers on the first Sunday in March during the annual *Vasaloppet* race (see p.563). A detailed map of the route, which starts just outside Sälen in **Berga**, is available from the tourist offices in Sälen and Mora.

The Inlandsbanan: Orsa to Östersund

First stop for the Inlandsbanan on its long way north is the tiny town of **ORSA**, 21km from Mora. If you get off the train here you're entering bear country: it's reckoned that there are a good few hundred **brown bears** roaming the dense forests around town, though few sightings are made, except by the hunters who cull the steadily increasing numbers. Your best bet of seeing one is to visit the **Orsa Grönklitt björnpark** (daily mid-May to early June & late Aug to mid-Sept 10am–3pm; early June to late Aug 10am–5pm; 55kr), the biggest bear park in Europe, 13km outside town (reached by once-daily bus #118 from Mora, which you can pick up at Orsa train station). The bears here are not tamed or caged, but wander around the 900 square kilometres of the forested park at will. It's the humans who are restricted, having to clamber up viewing towers and along covered-in walkways. Funny, gentle and vegetarian for the most part, occasionally the bears are fed the odd dead reindeer or elk that's been killed on the roads. Out of season they hibernate in specially constructed lairs that are monitored by closed circuit television cameras.

From the train station ion Järnvägsgatan it's a short walk to the **tourist office** on Centralplan (mid-June to mid-Aug Mon–Fri 9am–8pm, Sat 10am–8pm, Sun 11am–8pm; rest of the year Mon–Fri 9am–5pm, Sat 9am–1pm; ☎0250/521 63). If you need to stay over, the best bet is the **youth hostel** (☎0250/421 70; closed late April to mid-May & Nov; 100kr), beautifully located on Moravägen by the side of Lake Orsa, just 1km east of the centre. There's also a well-equipped **youth hostel** at the park (☎0250/462 00; all year; 100kr).

Härjedalen county: Sveg and Klövsjö

A sparsely populated fell region stretching north and west to the Norwegian border, **Härjedalen** is excellent terrain for walking. Until 1645 the county belonged to Norway, something that has left its mark in the local dialect. Some of Sweden's most magnificent scenery can be seen here – more than thirty mountains exceed the 1000-metre mark, the highest peak being **Helags** (1797m), whose icy slopes support Sweden's southermost glacier. Härjedalen is also home to the largest single population of bears in the country, as well as a handful of shaggy musk oxen, ferocious creatures that have wandered over the border from Norway.

Härjedalen's main town – and the first major stop on the Inlandsbanan after Orsa – is **SVEG** (pronounced "Svay-gg"), site of a 1273 parliament called to hammer out a border treaty Sweden and Norway. Since then things have quietened down considerably and even on a Friday night in midsummer you're likely to find yourself alone in the wide streets lined with grand old wooden houses. A graceful river runs right through the centre of town and there are some delightful meadows and swimming spots just a few minutes' walk from the centre.

Sveg's **tourist office** (☎0680/107 75 or 130 25) is on an unnamed road and can be tricky to find; your best bet is to follow the green tourist information signs. If you're keen to **stay overnight**, try the ramshackle **youth hostel**, a fifteen-minute walk from the station at Vallervägen 11 (☎0680/103 38; advance booking required Oct–May; 100kr). In the same building is the rather shabby *Hotell Härjedalen* (same phone; ①); more upmarket is the *Hotell Mysoxen* (☎0680/71 12 60; fax 100 62; ②/③), the other side of Torget on the corner of Fjällvägen and Dalagatan. The **campsite** (☎0680/107 75) is open all year and is a stone's throw from the tourist office by the riverside. Your best chances of not **eating** alone are at the cramped *Kornan* pub, pizzeria and café, near the corner of Kyrkogatan and Dalagatan, or at the *Knuten* pizzeria in the main square, Torget.

Klövsjö

A thoroughly charming place with its log cabins set in rolling verdant pastures, **KLÖVSJÖ** has gained the reputation of being Sweden's most beautiful village. There's some justification to this – the distant lake and the forested hills that enclose the village on all sides create the feeling that's it's in a world of its own. Ten farms continue to work the land much as in days gone by – ancient grazing rights still in force mean that horses and cows are free to roam through the village at will. Flowering meadows, trickling streams, wooden barns and the smell of freshly mown hay drying on frames in the afternoon sun cast a wonderful spell. Once you've taken a look at **Tomtangården** (daily July to mid-Aug), a preserved seventeenth-century farm estate, there's not much else to do except breathe the bitingly clean air and admire the beauty – you won't find anywhere as picturesque as this. Unfortunately you can't stay here because there are no rooms to let, but the **tourist office** on the main road (mid-June to mid-Aug Mon–Sat 9am–7pm, Sun noon–7pm; rest of the year Mon–Fri 9am–5pm; ☎0682/212 50) has cabins to rent in the vicinity (375–500kr per day, 2000–2500kr per week).

To **reach Klövsjö**, get off the train at **Åsarna**, a centre for skiing, from where buses make the twenty-minute trip to the village four times a day. In summer at least, it's fairly easy to find accommodation in Åsarna, at the well-equipped **campsite** (☎0687/302 30; fax 0687/303 60) or **youth hostel** (☎0687/302 30; all year; 100kr). Opposite the train station, the *Åsarna Hotell* (☎0687/300 04) is smarter, with a restaurant and bar. The skiing centre itself is on the one and only main road, a few minutes from the train station, and there's a **tourist office** in the same complex (daily June–Aug 8am–9pm; Sept–May 8am–7pm; ☎0687/301 93).

Östersund

Having reached **ÖSTERSUND**, it's worth stopping at what is the only large town until Gällivare, inside the Arctic Circle. If you're heading north this really is your last chance to indulge in a bit of high life – the small towns and villages beyond have few of the entertainment or culinary possibilities available here. What's more, Östersund is also a major transport hub, the E14 running through town on its way to the Norwegian border, while as well as the summer Inlandsbanan service, there are trains west to Åre and Storlien (the latter with connections to Trondheim in Norway), east to Sundsvall and

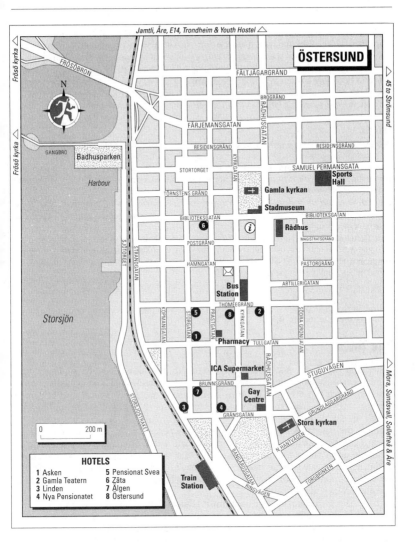

south to Stockholm and Gothenburg, plus express buses north to Gallivåre, which run all year and are a better option than the Inlandsbanan if you're in a hurry.

Arrival, information and accommodation

From the **train station** on Strandgatan, its' a five-minute walk north to the town centre; the **bus station** is more central, on Gustav III's Torg. A couple of blocks to the north, the helpful **tourist office** (June and early to mid-Aug Mon–Sat 9am–7pm, Sun 10am–7pm; July Mon–Sat 9am–9pm, Sun 10am–7pm; rest of the year Mon–Fri 9am–5pm; ☎063/14 40 01) is opposite the minaret-topped Rådhus at Rådhusgatan 44.

For accommodation, the modern STF **youth hostel** (☎063/13 91 00; mid-June to early Aug; 100kr) is ten minutes' walk from the train station at Södra Gröngatan 34. More atmospheric, though, is a night spent inside *Jamtli*, a wonderful independent **hostel** amid the old buildings in open-air museum grounds; phone direct (☎063/10 59 84) or ask the tourist office to book you a room for a 40kr fee. **Campers** can stay either at *Östersunds Camping* (☎063/14 46 15; all year), a couple of kilometres south down Rådhusgatan; or over on Frösön at *Frösö Camping* (☎063/14 46 15; June–Aug) – take bus #3 or #4 from the centre.

Hotels

Asken, Storgatan 53. Only eight rooms – all en-suite but rather plain and simple; one is reserved for people with allergies. ①/③

Gamla Teatern, Thoméegränd 20 (☎063/51 16 00; fax 13 14 99). Without doubt the finest in town, situated in an atmospheric turn-of-the-century theatre with sweeping wooden staircases. The main stage is now a restaurant. ②/③

Linden, Storgatan 64 (☎063/51 73 35). Cramped and basic rooms all with facilities en suite. ①/③

Östersund, Kyrkgatan 70 (☎063/12 45 00; fax 10 63 86). A massive modern hotel with 126 rooms – high on quality but low on charm. ②/④

Nya Pensionatet, Prästgatan 65 (☎063/51 24 98). Tastefully decorated turn-of-the-century hotel with just seven rooms and toilet and shower in the corridor; 100m from the train station. ①

Pensionat Svea, Storgatan 49 (☎063/51 29 01). Seven twee rooms with toilet and shower in the corridor. Discounted rates for longer stays. ①

Zäta, Prästgatan 32 (☎063/51 78 60). Simple and plain but comfortable, with cable TV and a sauna. ①/③

Älgen, Storgatan 61 (☎063/51 75 25). Small and central with plain yet comfortable en-suite rooms; handy for the train station. ①/③

The Town

Östersund sits on the eastern shore of the mighty **Storsjön** (Great Lake), lending the town a seaside holiday atmosphere, unusual this far inland, and it's an instantly likeable place in which to fetch up. The town itself is made up of the familiar grid of parallel streets lined with modern quadruple-glazed apartment blocks designed to keep the winter freeze at bay (temperatures regularly plummet as low as -20°C). Strolling through the pedestrianized centre is a relaxed experience; take time out and sip a coffee around the wide open space of Stortorget and watch Swedish provincial life go by, or amble down one of the many side streets that slope in an intoxicated fashion down to the still deep waters of the lake. Here you may be lucky enough to spot Sweden's own Loch Ness monster, **Storsjöodjuret**, a vast dog-headed creature, of which sightings are numerous if unsubstantiated.

The main attraction in town is **Jamtli Historieland** (late June to mid-Aug daily 11am–5pm; 60kr), an impressive open-air museum, a quarter of an hour's walk north of the centre along Rådhusgatan. For the first few minutes it's a bit bewildering, full of people milling around in traditional country costume, farming and milking much as their ancestors did. They live here throughout the summer and everyone is encouraged to join in – baking, tree-felling, grass-cutting. While kids naturally love it, you'd have to be pretty cynical not to enjoy the enthusiastic atmosphere. Some intensive work has been done on getting the settings right: the restored and working interiors are gloomy and dirty, with no hint of the usual pristine historical travesty. In the woodman's cottage, presided over by a bearded lumberjack who makes pancakes for the visitors, shoeless and scruffy children snooze contentedly in the wooden cots. Outside, even the planted crops and roaming cattle are accurate to the period, while an old-fashioned local store, *Lanthandel*, has been set up among the wooden buildings around the square near the entrance. The **Länsmuséet** on the same site (late June to mid-Aug 11am–5pm; rest of the year Tues

11am–8pm, Wed–Sun 11am–5pm; 40kr) shows off the county collections: a rambling houseful of local exhibits that includes monster-catching gear devised by lakeside worthies last century. The museum's prize exhibits are the awe-inspiring Viking Överhögdal tapestries, which date from the ninth or tenth centuries – discovered in an outhouse in 1910, the tapestries are crowded with brightly coloured animals and buildings.

Back in the centre, apart from the **Stadsmuseum** (Mon–Fri noon–4pm, Sat & Sun 1–4pm; free) – a crowded two hundred years of history in a building the size of a shoebox – next to the old church on Rådhusgatan, and the **Gamla Kyrkan** (Mon–Fri 1–3pm) itself, there's not a vast amount in the way of sights. The **harbour** is a better bet, a fleet of tiny boats and a couple of light aircraft bobbing about on the clean water. Immediately to the right of the harbour is the tiny **Badhusparken** – an inordinately popular spot in summer for catching a few rays.

Finally, it's possible to go monster-spotting on a **lake cruise** on board *S/S Thomée* – a creaking old wooden steamship built in 1875. Routes and timetables vary but always include a two-hour trip around the lake (55kr), amongst other destinations; for more information contact the tourist office (see below).

Frösön

Take the foot- or road bridge across the lake from Badhusparken and you'll come to the island of **Frösön**. People have lived here since prehistoric times and Frösön's name derives from the Viking settlement on the island and its association with the pagan god of fertility, Frö. There's plenty of good walking here, as well as a couple of historical stops. Just over the bridge in front of a red-brick office block, look out for the eleventh-century **rune stone** that tells of a man called Östmadur (East Man), son of Gudfast, who brought Christianity to the people of Jämtland – presumably from some point to the east. From here you can clamber up the nearby hill of Öneberget, where you'll find the fourth-century settlement of Mjälleborgen – the most extensive in Norrland.

Follow the main road west and up the main hill for about 5km to the beautiful **Frösö kyrka** (or take bus #3 from the centre), an eleventh-century church with a detached bell tower. In 1984 archeologists digging under the church's altar came across a bit of birch stump surrounded by the bones of bears, pigs, deer and squirrels – evidence of the cult of ancient gods, the *Aesir*, and indication that the site has been a place of worship for almost two thousand years. Today the church is one of the most popular in Sweden for marriages – especially at Midsummer, for which you have to book years in advance.

Eating, drinking and nightlife

Gastronomically there's more choice in Östersund than for a very long way north. Most of the city's eating places, many doubling up as bars, are located south of Stortorget. For **breakfast**, the train station café is good value and always busy. For **coffee** and cakes try *Wedemarks Konditori*, Prästgatan 27, where you can also make up your own sandwiches.

Restaurants and bars

Brunkullans Krog, Postgränd 5. Undoubtedly the best eating experience in Östersund, with traditional Swedish and international dishes served in an old-fashioned wooden interior. Prices start at around 130kr. In summer you can sit out at tables in the garden, where a cheaper menu is served.

Captain Cook, Hamngatan 9. A selection of delicious Australian-style grilled delights in the 100–120kr range; extremely popular, for drinking as much as eating.

Restaurang G III/O'Keefes, *Hotell Östersund*, Kyrkgatan 70. One of the town's most popular drinking holes and a less exciting restaurant.

Kashmir/Ljungen, Tegelbruksvägen 11. A fair trek on foot from the centre but if you're longing for curry this is the place – it's the only Indian restaurant in Norrland.

Kvarterskrogen, Storgatan 54. Smart linen tablecloths and prices to match – lamb, entrecôte, beef and sole, none of it under 150kr.

Lokalen, Rådhusgatan 64, entrance round the corner in Gränsgatan. Norrland's only gay café, this place is open Monday to Friday from noon to 6pm. It also holds regular parties too. See "Listings" for more information.

Ming Palace, Storgatan 15. The best Chinese in town with the usual array of dishes hovering around 90kr.

Skafferiet, Stortorget 8. A delicious fish restaurant in the Saluhallen – watch out for the hanging fishing nets. Good lunches for 65kr.

Restaurang Volos, Prästgatan 38. Cheap pizzas and some good authentic Greek food. Look out for special offers on beer.

Listings

Airlines *SAS* ☎063/15 10 10; *Nordic East* ☎063/430 10.

Airport 1km from the centre on the island of Frösön. Buses leave Kyrkgatan in time for departures.

Bike rental *Cykelogen* (Mon–Sat only; ☎063/12 20 80) at Kyrkogatan 45, where mountain bikes cost about 100kr per day; *Cykelprojektet* (☎063/14 15 77), by the bus station, with bikes from 30kr.

Buses *Swebus* operates all local buses; information on ☎063/16 82 61. The daily *Inlansexpressen* buses between Gallivare and Mora stop at the bus station.

Car rental *Avis* at the airport (☎063/448 70) or at Bangårdsgatan 9 (☎063/10 12 50); *Budget*, Köpmangatan 25 (☎063/10 44 10); *Europcar*, Hofvallsgränd 1 (☎063/51 72 40); *Hertz*, Köpmangatan 25 (☎063/10 21 12); *Statoil*, Frösövägen (☎063/51 11 44).

Gay contacts *Lokalen* café at Rådhusgatan 64 (☎063/13 19 00), entrance round the corner in Gränsgatan, weekdays noon–6pm; parties first Sat in the month. Switchboard Mon–Fri 10am–6pm (☎063/10 06 68). Information from Box 516, 831 26 Östersund, or on switchboard number.

Pharmacy Prästgatan 51 (Mon–Fri 9am–6pm, Sat 9am–4pm,Sun 11am–4pm).

Police ☎063/15 25 00.

Systembolaget Off-licence at Prästgatan 18 (Mon–Fri 9.30am–6pm) and Kyrkgatan 82 (Mon–Fri 9.30am–6pm, Thurs till 7pm).

Taxi *Taxi Östersund* ☎063/51 72 00.

West from Östersund

The E14 and the train line follow the route trudged by medieval pilgrims on their way to Nidaros (now Trondheim) over the border in Norway, a twisting route that threads its way through sharp-edged mountains rising high above a bevy of fast-flowing streams and deep, cold lakes. Time and again the eastern Vikings assembled their armies beside the holy Storsjön lake to begin the long march west, most famously in 1030 when King Olaf of Norway collected his mercenaries for the campaign that led to his death at the Battle of Stiklestad. The Vikings always crossed the mountains as quickly as possible and so today – although the scenery is splendid – there's nothing much to stop for en route, other than the winter-skiing and summer-walking centres of Åre and Storlien.

Åre

ÅRE (pronounced "Or-re"), two hours by train from Östersund, is Sweden's most prestigious ski resort with 44 lifts and snow guaranteed between December and May. During the snowbound season rooms are like gold dust and prices sky-high: if you do come to ski, book accommodation well in advance through the tourist office or better still come on a package tour (see *Basics*). Equipment rental isn't too expensive: downhill and cross-country gear costs 100–150kr per day, around 500kr per week – contact the tourist office.

In summer the Alpine village is a quiet haven for ramblers, sandwiched as it is between the river and a range of craggy hills overshadowed by the mighty 1420-metre-high Åreskutan mountain. A network of **walking tracks** crisscrosses the hills, or for a more energetic scramble, take the **Kabinbanan**, Sweden's only cable car (75kr return), up to a viewing platform from where it's a thirty-minute clamber to the summit. The view is stunning – on a clear day you can see over to the border with Norway and a good way back to Östersund. Beware that even the shortest walk back takes two hours and requires some stamina.

The **tourist office** (July,Aug & mid-Dec to March daily 9am–6pm; rest of the year Mon–Fri 9am–3pm; ☎0647/177 20) is in the square, 100m up the steps opposite the train station. It has detailed mountain maps and endless information on hiking in the nearby mountains and further afield – ask for the excellent *Hiking in Årefjällen* booklet. They can also help with mountain biking in the area.

If you're tempted to stay, the tourist office can help fix up a **private room** from around 125kr in summer, almost all of them with kitchen, shower and TV. Otherwise, the cheapest option is the unofficial **youth hostel** known as *Åre Backpackers Inn* (☎0647/177 31; 150kr), in the park below the square; the **campsite** (☎0647/525 20; closed Sept–Nov) is five minutes' walk from the station – head to the right.

For **food** Åre's not up to much, but there are several cheap places around the square: try the cheerful *Café Bubblan*, which does reasonable lunches of pies and sandwiches for 54kr, or the more substantial dishes served at *Labands Krog Grill & Pizzeria*. At the cable car terminus, *Bykrogen* serves decent main meals from 100kr but note that it closes at 7pm.

Storlien

Just 6km from the Norwegian border and a favourite feasting spot for the region's mosquitoes, **STORLIEN** is the place to stop if you plan to do some hiking, which is good and rugged around here. Incidentally, the countryside hereabouts is also prime berry-picking territory, the rare cloudberry grows here, and mushrooms, in particular canterelles, can be found in great number. There's not much here though: a **tourist office** in an old train carriage at the station (June–Aug daily 10am–5pm; rest of the year open telephone enquiries on ☎0647/701 70), a couple of hotels, a supermarket and mile upon mile of open countryside. Storlien's **youth hostel** (☎0647/700 50; closed mid-June to mid-July; 100kr) is a four-kilometre walk across the railway tracks to the E14 and then left down the main road towards Storvallen. If you're merely after a bed for the night, then **Ånn**, halfway between Åre and Storlien, is the best bet: all trains between Östersund and Åre and Storlien stop there and the youth hostel (☎0647/710 70; all year; 100kr) is right opposite the station. Of Storlien's **hotels**, *Hotell Storlien* (☎0647/701 51; fax 0647/705 22; ③), right by the train station, has mega-cheap rooms in summer – from 95kr per person in a double room. **Eating and drinking** is not easy, with just two options, the better of which is the *Le Ski* restaurant, nightclub and bar at the train station; otherwise, coffee, waffles and sandwiches are available at *Café Storliengården* (Tues–Sun 9am–5pm), a two-minute walk from the station.

Moving on from Storlien, trains operated by Norwegian Railways leave daily for Trondheim in Norway. In the opposite direction there are services to Stockholm and Gothenburg via Östersund, while the afternoon train from Trondheim to Storlien connects with sleeper services to both these destinations.

North to Gällivare

After Östersund the **Inlandsbanan** slowly snakes its way across the remote Swedish hinterland, a vast and scarcely populated region where the train often has to stop for elk and reindeer – and occasionally bears – to be cleared from the tracks. On the other occasions that the train comes to a halt with no station in sight, it's usually for a reason – a spot of berry-picking, perhaps – while at the Arctic Circle everyone jumps off for photos.

Route 45, the **Inlandsvägen**, sticks close to the train line on its way north to Gällivare – if you're not bound to the train this should be your preferred road north. It's easy to drive and well surfaced for the most part, though watch out for suicidal reindeer – once they spot a car hurtling towards them they'll do their utmost to throw themselves underneath it. **Bus** travellers on the daily *Inlandsexpressen* from Östersund to Gällivare will also take this route.

Vilhelmina and Storuman

Three and a half hours up the Inlandsbanan from Östersund, **VILHELMINA** is a pretty little town that once was an important forestry centre. However, the timber business has since moved out of town and the main source of employment today is a telephone-booking centre for Swedish Railways. Its name – from Fredrika Dorotea Vilhelmina, the wife of King Gustav IV Adolf – may suggest great things but Vilhelmina remains a quiet little place with just one main street. Principal attraction is the **parish village**, nestling between Storgatan and Ljusminnesgatan, whose thirty-odd wooden cottages date back to 1792 when the first church was consecrated. It's since been restored and today the cottages can be rented out via the **tourist office** (mid-June to mid-Aug Mon–Fri 8am–8pm, Sat & Sun noon–6pm; rest of the year Mon–Fri 8am–5pm; ☎0940/152 70) on the main Volgsjövägen, a five-minute walk up Postgatan from the **train station**, which also serves as the **bus** station.

Vilhemina's **youth hostel** (☎0940/141 65; mid-June to early Aug; 95kr) is centrally located in a school boarding house at Tallåsvägen 34; contact the tourist office to make bookings out of season. It's only about ten minutes' walk to the campsite, *Rasten Saiva Camping* (☎0940/107 60; May–Oct), which has four-berth cabins for rent for 200–450kr, as well as a great sandy **beach**; head down Volgsjövägen from the centre and take the first left after the youth hostel. There are two central **hotels** in town: the ostentatious *Hotell Wilhelmina* (☎0940/554 20; fax 101 56; ②/④) at Volgsjövägen 16 and the friendly *Lilla Hotellet* (☎0940/150 59; ②) at Granvägen 1.

Eating and drinking doesn't exactly throw up a multitude of options: try the à la carte restaurant at *Hotell Wilhelmina* for traditional northern Swedish dishes and 60kr lunches, or the plain *Pizzeria Quinto,* Volgsjövägen 27. For coffee and sandwiches head for *Dagnys Café* next to the parish village, which also has a lunch menu for 55kr. In the evenings locals gravitate towards *Sven Dufvas Krog* in the main square for a drink or two.

Storuman

STORUMAN, about an hour and a half up the line from Vilhelmina, is a transport hub for this part of southern Lappland. **Buses** run northwest up the E12, skirting the Tärnafjällen mountains, to Tärnaby and Hemavan before wiggling through to Mo-i-Rana in Norway and in the opposite direction down to Umeå via Lycksele, where there are connections on to Vindeln and Vännäs on the main coastal rail line. A direct bus, *Lapplandspilen,* also links Storuman with Stockholm.

There's not much to Storuman itself – the centre consists of one tiny street that supports a couple of shops and banks. The **tourist office** (late June to mid-Aug 8am–8pm; rest of the year Mon–Fri 9am–5pm; ☎0951/333 70 or 105 00) is located in the train station and gives out a handy map of town. While it's possible to stay here – the **youth hostel** (☎0951/104 28; mid-June to mid-Aug; 100kr) is just 400m left of the station and the luxurious *Hotell Toppen* (☎0951/117 00; fax 121 57; ②/④) only a ten-minute walk up the hill at Blå Vägen 238 – it's much better to head off into the mountains for some good **hiking** and **fishing**.

If you do stay, try the **restaurant** at *Hotell Toppen*, which has a lunch buffet for 60kr, or alternatively there's the basic, reasonably priced *Bel Ami Pizzeria* in the main square. Better is *Bettys Krog*, opposite the train station, which also does decent pizzas and lunch deals.

Tärnaby and Hemavan

Four **buses** daily make the two-hour drive northwest from Storuman to the tiny mountain village of **TÄRNABY**, birthplace of Ingmar Stenmark, double Olympic gold medallist and Sweden's greatest skier. It's a pretty place: yellow flower-decked meadows run to the edge of the mountain forests here, the trees felled to leave great swathes that accommodate World Cup ski slopes. At the eastern edge of the village as you approach from Storuman, the **Samigården** (late June to mid-Aug daily 10am–4pm; 10kr) is a pleasant introduction to Sami history, culture and customs. The museum recalls older times when, after a kill in a bear hunt, the gall bladder was cut open and the fluid drunk by the hunters. The **tourist office** (mid-June to mid-Aug daily 9am–8pm; rest of the year Mon–Fri 8.30am–5pm; ☎0954/104 50) on the main street can provide information on fishing and hiking in the area. One popular walk is across the nearby Laxfjället mountain, with its fantastic views down over the village – it can be reached by chair lift from either of the two hotels mentioned below. If it's sunny, head for the **beach** at Lake Laisan, where the water is often warm enough to swim – take the footpath which branches off right from Sandviksvägen past the **campsite**. If the round trip is too much for one day there are several inexpensive places **to stay** – try the *Tärnaby Fjällhotell*, Östra Strandvägen 16 (☎0954/104 20; fax 106 27; ①/②), which also has four-bed apartments (395kr), or *Fjällvindens Hus* (☎0954/104 25; fax 106 80; ①/②) on Skyttevägen, which also rents out two- to six-bed cabins (410kr).

Buses continue on to **HEMAVAN**, which marks the beginning and the end of the 500-kilometre *Kungsleden* trail – see p.585. If you need to stay, head for the **youth hostel** (☎0954/305 10; mid-June to Sept; 100kr) on Blå Vägen, the main road into the village from Tärnaby – it's known as *FBU-Gården*. If you have your own transport, continue along the E12 towards Norway to the gay-friendly *Sånninggårdens Restaurant & Pensionat* (☎0954/330 38; fax 330 06; ①), dramatically located next to a range of craggy mountains and renowned for its excellent food – try the mountain char with cream and chive sauce (117kr). Incidentally, the pension is the last stop for the *Lapplandspilen* bus to and from Stockholm.

Sorsele

SORSELE (pronounced "Sosh-aye-le") is the next major stop on the Inlandsbanan, although major is perhaps a misleading word to use for this pint-sized dreary town. On the Vindel River, Sorsele became a cause célèbre among conservationists in Sweden forcing the government to abandon its plans to regulate the flow here by building a hydroelectric power station. The river remains in its natural state today – seething with rapids – and is one of only four in the entire country that haven't been tampered with in some form or other. During the last week in July the river makes its presence felt with the **Vindelälvsloppet**, a long-distance race held over four days (Wed–Sat) that sees hundreds of competitors flog themselves over the 350km from nearby Ammarnäs down to Vännäsby near Umeå. It's quite a spectacle – needless to say, accommodation at this time is booked up months in advance. The other big event is the **Vindelälvsdraget**, a dog sleigh race held over the same course in the second week of March (Thurs–Sun). The town is also an ideal base for **fly-fishing** – the Laisälven and Vindelälven are teeming with grayling and brown trout and a number of local lakes are stocked with char; more details from the **tourist office** (July & Aug Mon–Fri

9am–8pm, Sat & Sun 10am–6pm; rest of the year Mon–Fri 9am–3pm; ☎0952/109 00) at the train station on Stationsgatan. In the same building there's a small **museum** (same times; 20kr) detailing the life and times of the Inlandsbanan – worth a look if you're using the train at any time, though unfortunately all labelling is in Swedish.

Accommodation in Sorsele boils down to a rather drab hotel, *Hotell Gästis* (☎0952/107 20; fax 551 41; ②/④) at Hotellgatan 2; a riverside **campsite** (☎0952/101 24) with **cabins** (from 2850kr per week); and a small **youth hostel** (☎0952/100 48; mid-June to early Aug; 95kr), just 500m from the train station at Torggatan 1–2. **Eating** options are similarly scant: at lunchtime head for the hotel, which has simple dishes for around 50kr, or the dreary pizzeria *La Spezia* on Vindelvägen. Other than that you're left with *Grillhörnan* near the train station, with its greasy burgers and pizzas (40–60kr); the bakery in the same building is the place to buy fresh bread. There are no **bars** in Sorsele, like many of the villages in this part of Sweden, but you can find expensive beer at all the restaurants mentioned above.

Arvidsjaur and the Arctic Circle

An hour and a quarter north of Sorsele on the Inlandsbanan, **ARVIDSJAUR** is by far the largest town you'll have passed since Östersund – though that's not saying much. Drab housing areas spread out either side of a nondescript and indeterminate main street, Storgatan. For centuries this was where the region's Sami gathered to trade and debate, their agenda hijacked by the Protestant missionaries who established their first church here in 1606. The success of the Swedish settlement was secured when silver was discovered in the nearby mountains and the town flourished as a staging point and supply depot. Despite these developments, the Sami continued to assemble here on market days and during religious festivals, building their own **parish village** of simple wooden huts at the end of the eighteenth century. About eighty have survived and are clumped unceremoniously towards the north end of town next to a modern yellow apartment block; the **Lappstaden** (June–Aug daily 11am–5pm; 20kr; other times you can walk in for free) is still used today for the *Storstämningshelgen* festival over the last weekend in August, as well as for auctions and other events throughout the year. There are still around twenty Sami families in Arvisdjaur, making their living from reindeer husbandry.

There's no real reason to tarry, but if you want to stay, head for the **tourist office** (mid-June to mid-Aug daily 8.45am–7pm; rest of the year Mon–Fri 9am–5pm; ☎0960/175 00) at Garvaregatan 4, just off Storgatan and five minutes' walk from the station up Lundavägen. They'll fix you up with a **private room** for around 110kr, plus a booking fee of 25kr. There's also a cosy private **youth hostel**, *Lappugglans Turistviste*, conveniently situated at Västra Skolgatan 9 (☎0960/124 13; 100kr); or you could try *Camp Gielas* (☎0960/134 20), which also has **cabins**, set beside Tvätttjärn, one of the town's dozen or so lakes, a few minutes walk along Strandvägen and Järnvägsgatan from the tourist office. There are two **hotels** in town: *Hotell Laponia* at Storgatan 45 (☎0960/555 00; ②/④), with comfortable, modern en-suite rooms and a swimming pool, and the more basic *Centralhotellet*, handy for the train station at Järnvägsgatan 63 (☎0960/100 98; ①/②). Be warned that in winter much of the hotel accommodation will be full of test drivers from Europe's leading car companies, who come to the area to experience driving on the frozen lakes – book well in advance to secure a room.

For snacks and coffee try *Kaffestugan* at Storgatan 21, which also does sandwiches and salads for 40–50kr. There's a small choice of **restaurants** – for pizzas and Italian food try *Athena* at Storgatan 10, which has a 60kr lunch deal. Next door at Storgatan 8, *Cazba* serves up pizzas for the same price but has less atmosphere. For finer food, head for the restaurant at *Hotell Laponia*, where delicious à la carte meals, including local reindeer, go for 100–150kr. The **bar** here is the place to be seen of an evening but be prepared to shell out 45kr for a beer. Another popular spot, though no cheaper, is *Pegs Pub* at Skogsgatan 5.

The Arctic Circle

A couple of hours north of Arvidsjaur the Inlandsbanan finally crosses the **Arctic Circle** just south of Jokkmokk (see below). This is occasion enough for a bout of whistle-blowing as the train pulls up to allow everyone to take photos of the hoardings announcing the crossing: due to the earth's uneven orbit the line is creeping northwards at a rate of up to 15m a year and the circle is now around 1km north, but for argument's sake this spot is as good as any. Painted white rocks curve away over the hilly ground, a crude but popular representation of the Circle: one foot on each side is the standard photographic pose. If you find the godforsaken place appealing there's a **campsite** (contact the tourist office in Jokkmokk for erratic opening times); a taxi into Jokkmokk will cost around 100kr for the seven-kilometre ride.

Jokkmokk

During his journey in Lappland, the botanist Carl von Linné said, "If not for the mosquitoes, this would be earth's paradise"; his comments were made after journeying along the river valley of the Lilla Luleälven during the short summer weeks when the mosquitoes are at their most active. The town's Sami name comes from one particular bend (*mokk*) in the river (*jokk*), which runs through a densely forested municipality the size of Wales with a minuscule population of just 6500; needless to say, **JOKKMOKK** is a welcome oasis, though not an immediately appealing one. Once wintertime Sami quarters, a market and church heralded a permanent settlement by the beginning of the seventeenth century. Today, as well as being a well-known handicrafts centre, the town functions as the Sami capital and is home to the *Samiras Folkhögskola*, the only further education college teaching handicrafts, reindeer husbandry and ecology in the Sami language.

Jokkmokk's fantastic **Ájtte museum** (*ájtte* means storage hut in Sami), a brief walk east of the centre on Kyrkogatan, off the main Storgatan (mid-June to Aug Mon–Fri 9am–6pm, Wed till 8pm, Sat & Sun 11am–6pm; rest of the year Mon–Fri 9am–4pm, Sat & Sun noon–4pm; 40kr), is the place to really mug up on the Sami. Displays and exhibitions recount the tough existence of the original settlers of northern Scandinavia and show how things have slowly improved over time – today's Sami are more dependent on snow scooters and helicopters to herd their reindeer than on the age-old methods employed by their ancestors. There are some imaginative temporary exhibitions on Sami culture and local flora and fauna, and the museum staff can also arrange day trips into the surrounding marshes for a spot of mushroom-picking (and mosquito-swatting). Close to the museum on Lappstavägen, the **alpine garden** (mid-June to mid-Aug daily noon–7pm; other times by arrangement; ☎0971/101 00 or out of season 170 70; 25kr) is home to moor-king, mountain avens, glacier crowfoot and other vegetation to be found on the fells around Jokkmokk.

Have a look, too, at the **Lapp kyrka**, off Stortorget, a recent copy of the eighteenth-century church that stood on this site. The octagonal design and curiously shaped tower betray the Sami influence, but the surrounding graveyard wall is all improvisation: the space in between the coarsely hewn timbers was used to store coffins during winter, waiting for the thaw in May when the Sami could go out and dig graves again – temperatures in this part of Sweden regularly plunge to -30°C and below in winter.

The great **winter market**, known simply in Swedish as *Jokkmokks marknad* (market), still survives, now nearly 400 years old, held in the first week of February (Thurs–Sun), when 30,000 force their way into town, increasing the population almost tenfold. It's the best and coldest time of the year to be in Jokkmokk – there's a Wild West feeling in the air – with lots of drunken stall holders trying to flog reindeer hides and other unwanted knick-knacks to even more drunken passers-by – and all in positively Arctic temperatures. The **reindeer races** can be a real spectacle: held on the frozen Talvatissjön lake behind *Hotell Jokkmokk*, man and beast battle it out on a specially marked out track on the ice; however, the reindeer often have other ideas and veer off with great alacrity into the crowd every now and then, sending spectators fleeing for cover. Staying in town at this time of year means booking accommodation a good year in advance (some private rooms become available in the autumn before the market). A smaller and less traditional autumn fair is held at the end of August (around the 25th) – an easier though poorer option.

During summer, Talvatissjön is the preferred spot for catching Arctic char and rainbow trout, though to **fish** here you need a fishing permit (*fiskekort*), available from the tourist office. There's a cleaning table and fireplace laid on, should you catch anything. It's also possible to go **whitewater rafting** around Jokkmokk on the Pärlälven just to the west of town – there are two different routes, one for beginners and a more turbulent stretch of water for those who live life in the fast lane – safety equipment is included in the price (350kr); for more information contact *Äventyrarna* on ☎0971/126 96.

Practicalities

Coming by train from Stockholm, get off at Murjek, from where buses run west to Jokkmokk four times a day. Jokkmokk's **tourist office** (daily mid-June to mid-Aug daily 9am–7pm; Winter Market 8am–6pm; rest of the year 8.30am–4pm; ☎0971/121 40), at Stortorget 4, is a five-minute walk from the train station along Stationsgatan. They've got all sorts of printed information, useful if you're considering hiking in the region, and can arrange **private rooms** for around 100kr, plus a 10kr booking fee. The **youth hostel** (☎0971/559 77; all year; 100kr) is located in a wonderful old house with a garden at Åsgatan 20. To get to the **campsite**, *Jokkmokks Turistcenter* (☎0971/123 70), 3km southeast of town on the Lule River, off the main E97 to Luleå and Boden, you're best off renting a bike from the tourist office (50kr per day). Of the town's two **hotels**, *Hotell Jokkmokk* has a convenient and attractive lakeside setting at Solgatan 45 (☎0971/553 20; fax 556 25; ②/④), though its en-suite rooms are very ordinary and the restaurant a 1970s throwback; *Hotell Gästis* at Herrevägen 1 (☎0971/100 12; ①/②) is nothing to write home about: simple en-suite rooms with modern decor.

Jokkmokk has a limited number of **eating** and **drinking** possibilities. The cheap and cheerful *Restaurang Milano* at Berggatan has lunch for 50kr and pizzas for around 60kr at other times. Pizzas are also on the menu at the rather nicer *Restaurang Opera* at Storgatan 36, along with the usual range of meat and fish dishes. If you're gagging for a steak, head for *GJ's Stekhuset* on Föreningsgatan, where a slab goes for 50kr at lunchtime. For traditional Sami dishes, such as reindeer, head for the restaurant at the Ájtte museum, where lunch costs 50kr – the cloudberry and ice cream here is simply divine. Your first choice for drinking should be *Restaurang Opera* (see above); failing that, try *Restaurang Milano* and, in the evenings, the *Bakfickan* bar inside *Hotell Jokkmokk* – if you've drunk your way round Jokkmokk this far you won't mind the late-night drunken company here.

Southeast of Jokkmokk: Vuollerim

Forty-five kilometres southeast of Jokkmokk on Route 97 to Boden and Luleå lies **VUOLLERIM**, site of a 6000-year-old winter settlement from the Stone Age. Archeological digs have uncovered evidence of habitation in the area – well-preserved remains of houses, storage pits, tool and weapon shards, fires, rubbish dumps and drainage works. A small and excellent **museum** (June–Aug Mon–Fri 9am–6pm; Sept–May Mon–Fri 9am–4pm; 50kr) covers the development of the various sites and finds and a slide show takes you on a local journey through time, reconstructing the probable life of the inhabitants. The whole thing really comes alive when a minibus carts you off to the digs themselves with archeologists providing a guided tour in

English – without them the whole thing would be nothing more than a mudbath to the untrained eye. The museum is on the edge of tiny Vuollerim at Murjeksvägen 31. To **get here** from Jokkmokk, take the Boden/Luleå bus and get off at the Statoil filling station, then walk 1km up the road towards the village; the bus to Murjek goes right to the museum. Incidentally, the site is on a narrow, wooded promontory that juts out into the lake – a great place for a picnic.

Gällivare

Last stop on the Inlandsbanan and by far the biggest town since Östersund, **GÄLLIVARE** is far more pleasant than you'd imagine from the surrounding industry. Strolling around its open centre, heavily glazed and insulated against the biting cold of winter, is a great antidote to the small inland villages along the train route. There's a gritty ugliness to Gällivare that gives the place a certain charm: a steely grey mesh of modern streets that has all the hallmarks of a city, although on a scale that's far too

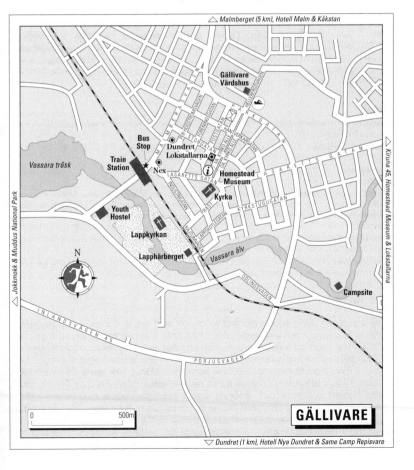

modest for the title to be applied with any justification. It's also an excellent base for hiking in the nearby national parks (see p.583).

Arrival, information and accommodation

Arriving in Gällivare's **train station** on Lasarettsgatan, you're only five minutes' walk from the **tourist office** (June to mid-Aug daily 9am–8pm; rest of the year Mon–Fri 9am–4pm; ☎0970/166 60) at Storgatan 16, which provides good free maps and hiking information; downstairs in the same building there's a café and upstairs a simple **museum** dealing with Sami history and forestry. The tourist office can fix you up with a **private room** for around 125kr per person, plus a booking fee of 20kr, or you could sample the town's **youth hostel** (☎0970/143 80; reservations required in Oct; 100kr or 70kr for a dorm bed) behind the train station – cross the tracks by the metal bridge; because of the town's position on routes north to Kiruna and Narvik (and south to Stockholm and Gothenburg), booking ahead in summer is advised. This is a wonderful place to stay in winter when the Vassara träsk lake is frozen – snow scooters whizz up and down its length under the eerie Northern Lights, clearly visible in Gällivare. If the hostel's full, try the small and rather less friendly **private hostel**, *Lapphärberget* (☎0970/125 34; 100kr), near the Lappkyrkan. There's also a **campsite** (mid-May to mid-Sept; ☎0970/186 79) by the river and off the main E45 between Porjusvägen and Jokkmokk. If you've your own transport, undoubtedly the best place to stay is in the simple wooden huts at the reconstructed shantytown, **Kåkstan**, up at Malmberget (☎0970/183 96 or mobile ☎070/537 6977; or book through the tourist office).

Hotels

Dundret, Per Högströmsgatan 1 (☎0970/145 60). Small pension with just seven rooms; shower and toilet in the corridor. ①/②

Gällivare Värdshus, Klockljungsvägen 2 (☎0970/162 00). Grotty on the outside but fine on the inside – German-run and central, with small hostel-style rooms. ②/③

Lokstallarna, at the Homstead Museum, Storgatan 16 (☎0970/153 75). Hostel-style en-suite accommodation. Open March–Aug. ①

Malm, Torget 18, Malmberget (☎0970/244 50). Basic rooms without bathrooms, but very cheap at 150kr in summer. The hotel rents out 21-gear **city bikes** for 100kr per day – if you book one day in advance they'll bring them down to the tourist office for collection; otherwise take bus #1 up to Malmberget. ①

Nex, Lasarettsgatan 1 (☎0970/110 20; fax 154 75). Smart, tastefully decorated rooms; unfortunately it's closed at weekends. ②/④

Nya Dundret (☎0970/145 60; fax 148 27). The best hotel in Gällivare, but it's at the top of the Dundret mountain, so you'll need your own transport to get here. ③/⑤

The Town

Gällivare is one of the most important sources of **iron ore** in Europe, and if you've any interest in seeing a working mine, don't wait until Kiruna's tame "tourist tour" (see p.585). The modern mines and works are distant, dark blots, tucked away at Malmberget up on the hill overlooking Gällivare. There are two separate tours, both running from June to August: one of the underground **iron ore mine** (Mon–Fri 10am & 2pm; 160kr), the other to the open cast **copper mine** (Mon–Fri 2pm; 140kr), which is the biggest in Europe and incidentally also Sweden's biggest gold mine – gold is recovered from the slag produced during the extraction of the copper. The ear-splitting noise produced from the mammoth-sized trucks in the mine (they're five times the height of a man) can be quite disconcerting in the confined darkness. This tour also takes in **Kåkstan**, the shantytown where the miners lived over a hundred years ago –

rows of reconstructed wooden huts either side of an unmade street (it's also possible to stay here – see above).

Gällivare occupies the site of a Sami village and one theory has it that the town's name comes from the Sami language – Djellivare: a crack or gorge (*djelli*) in the mountain (*vare*). Down by the river near the train station, you'll come across the Sami church, **Lappkyrkan** (mid-June to Aug daily 10am–2pm), a mid-eighteenth-century construction. It's known as the *Ettöreskyrkan* (one öre church) after the one öre subscription drive throughout Sweden that paid for it.

Walks in the area

There's precious little else to see or do in Gällivare and you'd be wise to use your time exploring the marshes and forests of one of the nearby **national parks**: Padeljanta, Stora Sjöfallet or **Muddus**, which lies south of town, hemmed in by the Inlandsbanan on one side and the train line from Boden to Gällivare on the other. The park is easy to reach with your own car but public transport will only take you within 12km – take the bus to Ligga and then walk to Skaite and the beginning of the network of trails (see p.584).

Train travellers unfortunately barely catch a glimpse of the park which is shrouded by dense forest, and will have to be satisfied with the **Dundret** mountain, overshadowing the town, which is the target of Midnight Sun spotters. You can walk up to the *Björnfällan* restaurant (the name means "bear trap"), about a four-kilometre hike on a well-marked path, and the views are magnificient, but this isn't the very top. Buses head up the winding road especially for the Midnight Sun, leaving daily at 11pm from the train station (mid-June to mid-July), returning at 1am; tickets, available from the tourist office, cost 140kr return and include the ubiquitous Swedish waffle covered with cloudberries and cream.

Eating and drinking

If you're arriving from one of the tiny villages on the Inlandsbanan, the wealth of **eating and drinking** possibilities in Gällivare will make you quite dizzy; if you're coming from Luleå, grit your teeth and bear it. A good place for lunch is *Restaurang Peking* at Storgatan 21B, which has reasonable Chinese food for 57kr but is closed on Mondays – there are also pizzas on offer. The best pizzeria in town is *Pizzeria Dylan* in the Arkaden shopping centre, which also does takeaways but is closed in the evening. The restaurant in the *Nex Hotell* on Lasarettsgatan does good lunches for 50–60kr and although it's pretentious and expensive it does serve excellent local delicacies such as Arctic char and reindeer – reckon on 100–150kr. At lunchtime you could also try *Café Forell* at Hantverkaregatan 7, which specializes in fish dishes and has a good salad bar. Coffee and cakes can be consumed at *Åhults Bageri & Café* at Lasarettsgatan 19 or in *Hembyggdskaféet* under the tourist office. As for **drinking** the place to be seen is the rustic *Kai's Pub* at Storgatan 15, with a happy hour from 3pm to 8pm; the bar in the *Nex Hotell* is also popular.

Hiking in the National Parks

It's not a good idea to go **hiking in the national parks** of northern Sweden on a whim. Even for experienced walkers, the going can be tough and uncomfortable in parts, downright treacherous in others. Mosquitoes are a real problem: it's difficult to imagine the utter misery of being covered in a blanket of insects, your eyes, ears and nose full of the creatures. Yet this is one of the last wilderness areas left in Europe: the map of this part of the country is little more than vast areas of forest and mountains; roads and human habitation are the exception rather than the norm. Reindeer are a common

sight since the parks are breeding grounds and summer pasture, and Sami settlements are dotted throughout the region – at Ritsem and Vaisaluokta, for example. Although there are some good short trails in the national parks, suitable for beginners, the goal for more ambitious hikers is the northern section of the **Kungsleden** trail, which crosses through several of the parks.

National parks

Muddus is the place recommended for beginnners, a pine forest and marshland park between Jokkmokk and Gällivare, home to bears, lynx, martens, weasels, hares, elk and in summer also reindeer; the whooper swan is one of the most commonly sighted birds. The park's western edges are skirted by Route 45 and the easiest approach is to leave the highway at Liggadammen (buses from Gällivare) and then follow the small road to Skaite. You can also reach the park from the southeast via Nattavaara and Messaure. An easy hiking trail of 50km starts at Skaite, with cabins along the route and a campsite by the Muddus falls.

Beginning about 120km northwest of Gällivare, the tract of wilderness edging Norway contains no fewer than three national parks, with the low fells, large lakes and moors of Padjelanta and Stora Sjöfallet parks acting as the eyebrows to the sheer face of the mountainous and inhospitable Sarek park. **Padjelanta** is the largest national park in Sweden; the name come from the Sami language and means "the higher country", an apt description for a high tableland almost exclusively above the treeline and home to thousands of reindeer. A 150-kilometre trail, the Padjelanta Trail, runs from Kvikkjokk (reached by bus from Jokkmokk) north through Stora Sjöfallet to Vaisaluokta (across the lake from Ritsem) and is good for inexperienced walkers – allow at least a week. From Vaisaluokta there are buses back to Gällivare.

The real baddie is **Sarek**, the terrain officially classed as "extremely difficult". There are no tourist facilities, trails, cabins or bridges; the rivers are dangerous and the weather rotten – and definitely not for anyone without Chris Bonington-type experience.

Kungsleden: Abisko to Hemavan

Kungsleden is the most famous and popular of Sweden's hiking trails, a 500-kilometre route from **Abisko** in the north to **Hemavan**, near Tärnaby (see p.577), in the south. It's a well-marked trail, passing through various sections of the national parks, which is traditionally split into five sections. From Abisko to Kvikkjokk, north of the Arctic Circle, and in the south between Ammarnäs and Hemavan there are STF cabins and fell stations. Huts are placed at 15–20-kilometre intervals, a distance that can be covered in one day, while shelter from the wind is provided at various places along the route. The Kungsleden is an easy trail to walk: the streams are all crossed by bridges and patches of marshy ground overlaid with wooden planks; there are also boat services or rowing boats for crossing the several large lakes on the route.

If you're looking for total isolation this is not the trail for you – it's the busiest in the country. A handy tip is to go against the flow: most people start from Abisko, but if you walk the route in reverse you'll find it easier going – or avoid July.

Kiruna and around

KIRUNA was the hub of the battle for the control of the iron ore supply during World War II. From here ore was transported north by train to the great harbour at Narvik over the border in Norway. Much German fire power was expended in an attempt to interrupt the supply to the Allies and wrest control for the Axis. In the process, Narvik suffered greviously, whilst Kiruna – benefiting from supposed Swedish neutrality – made a packet selling to both sides.

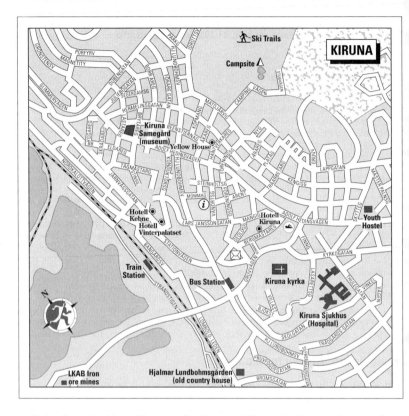

Today the train ride to Kiruna rattles through sidings, slag heaps and ore works, a bitter contrast to the surrounding wilderness. Brooding reminders of Kiruna's prosperity, the **mines** still dominate the town and much more depressingly than in neighbouring Gällivare, two hours back down the train line: despite the new central buildings and open parks, the town retains a gritty industrial air. **Guided tours** of the mines are arranged by the tourist office (July & Aug 4 daily; 90kr; minimum age 10; out of season group bookings only). A coach takes visitors through the underground road network and then stops off at a "tourist mine", a closed off section of a leviathan structure containing service stations, restaurants, computer centres, trains and crushing mills. During the dark winter months it's possible to visit the mines on a Japanese mushroom tour – in search of shiitakes (Mon–Fri at 4pm, returning 10pm, Sat & Sun at 8am, returning 8pm; 125kr; mushrooms picked cost 25kr per 100g; book through the tourist office or direct on ☎0980/124 16).

All the other sights in town are firmly wedded to the all-important metal in one way or another. The tower of the **Rådhus** (June–Aug daily 9am–6pm; Sept–May Mon–Fri 9am–5pm) is obvious even from the train station, a strident metal pillar harbouring an intricate latticework, clock face and sundry bells that chime raucously at noon. It was designed by Bror Marklund and the whole hall unbelievably won the 1964 award for the most beautiful Swedish public building. Inside there's a tolerable art collection and Sami handicraft displays in summer.

Only a few minutes up the road, **Kiruna kyrka** (daily 11am–5pm; July until 10pm) causes a few raised eyebrows. Built in the style of a Sami hut, it's a massive origami creation of oak beams and rafters the size of a small aircraft hangar. *LKAB*, the iron ore company that to all intents and purposes *is* Kiruna and which paid for its construction, was also responsible for the nearby **Hjalmar Lundbohmsgården** (June–Aug daily 10am–8pm; Sept–May Mon–Fri 10am–4pm; free), a country house once used by the managing director of the company and "founder" of Kiruna. Displays inside mostly consist of turn-of-the-century photographs featuring the man himself and assorted Sami in their winter gear. Visit before going down the mine and everything will take on an added perspective – without the mine, Kiruna would be a one-reindeer town instead of the thriving place it is today.

The **Kiruna Samigård** (mid-June to Sept daily 8am–6pm; rest of the year Mon–Fri 8am–4pm; 20kr) at Brytaregatan 14 is the most rewarding exhibition of Sami culture in town. The handicrafts may be familiar but what won't be is the small display of Sami art, really very good. There's a café and souvenir shop where you can buy a piece of antler bone or reindeer skin to take home.

Practicalities

Arriving by **train**, it's a brisk ten-minute walk from the station up the steep hill to the **tourist office** (mid-June to Aug Mon–Fri 9am–8pm, Sat & Sun 9am–6pm; rest of the year Mon–Fri 9am–4pm; ☎0980/188 80) in Folkets Hus, in the central square off Mommagatan. Kiruna's **youth hostel** (☎0980/171 95; mid-June to mid-Aug; 100kr) is 2km from the train station at Skyttegatan 16, up in the centre of town; turn right out of the train station and follow the signs. It fills quickly in summer, as does the **campsite** (☎0980/131 00), a twenty-minute walk north on Campingvägen, in the Högalid part of town; cabins (②) are available here too. Kiruna also has a number of central **hotels** – try *Hotell Vinterpalatset* at Järnvägsgatan 18 (☎0980/831 70; fax 130 50; ②/⑤), which has a superb sauna and jacuzzi suite on the top floor. Round the corner at Konduktörsgatan 7, *Hotell Kebne* (☎0980/123 80; ②/⑤) is also handy for the train station and has good-quality rooms. There are also a couple of other low-priced options: *Yellow House* at Hantverkaregatan 25 has hostel-style rooms with shared bathrooms for 100kr per person, while the rooms at *Hotell Kiruna,* Bergmästaregatan 7 (①/②), are basic but slightly more comfortable (reservations for both on ☎0980/137 50).

Kiruna's hardly a centre of haute cuisine, but **eating** at the inordinately popular *Mats & Mums,* Bergmästaregatan 10, is the best bet – the window through into the adjacent swimming pool makes an unusual setting for a meal of burgers or Arctic specialities (100–150kr). Good food is also served at *Restaurang Lapplandia*, in the same building as *Hotell Kiruna* at Bergmästaregatan 7 – don't be put off by the ugly brown facade. Coffee and cakes are served up at *Brända Tomten* on Meschplan. Kiruna's most popular **bar** is the Western-style *Mommas* in the main square, alongside the tourist office. The grotty drinking den that is *Restaurang Arran*, across the square at Föreningsgatan 9, often serves staggeringly cheap beer before 11pm and attracts a corresponding clientele – go in with a friend.

Around Kiruna: Jukkasjärvi

The tiny village of **JUKKASJÄRVI** is a mecca for any tourist travelling in Lappland in winter: the **ice hotel** that is built here late every October is also the world's biggest igloo and stands proudly by the side of the Torneälven river until it melts in May. One thousand tons of ice and two thousand tons of snow are used to make the igloo, whose exact shape and design changes from year to year. There is usually a bar in the entrance hall, several bedrooms with compacted snow beds covered with reindeer hides, an exhibition hall, cinema and chapel where local couples can marry. Winter temperatures are generally around -20 to -30°C which means that inside the igloo it's normally around -5°C. Guests who choose to stay are provided with specially made sleeping bags as used by the Swedish army, who do their Arctic survival training here – don't wear pyjamas or you'll sweat. If you chicken out, there are also cabins for rent on the site; all bookings are handled by *Jukkas AB* at Marknadsvägen 63 (☎0980/211 90; fax 214 06; rooms and cabins both ③). You can **eat** across the road at *Jukkasjärvi Wärdhus*, where lunch goes for around 60kr.

In **summer** Jukkasjärvi is a good place to commune with nature: river-rafting, canoeing and hiking are possible – details on the above number.

From Kiruna to the Norwegian border

Since 1984 there's been a choice of ways to continue your journey towards Norway: by train on the last leg of the long run from Stockholm or Luleå, and also by road. The **Nordkalottvägen** runs parallel to the railway on the Swedish side of the border, threading its way across barren plateaux (the lakes up here are still frozen in mid-June) before slicing though the mighty Norwegian mountains. It's an exhilarating run that passes the start of the **Kungsleden** trail at Abisko: get off the train at Abisko Turiststation (not Abisko Ö, which is the village) and the adjoining fell station offers all sorts of useful advice for hikes from half a day upwards. See p.585 for further details. Both train line and road continue on to Riksgränsen, the last settlement in Sweden, where it's possible to ski right up to late June. There's a **hotel** here, *Hotell Riksgränsen* (☎0980/400 80; fax 431 25; ③/⑤), opposite the train station – but nothing more.

The Torne Valley

The gently sloping sides of the lush **Tornedalen** (Torne Valley) are one of the most welcoming sights in northern Sweden. Stretching over 500km from the mouth of the Gulf of Bothnia to Sweden's remote northern tip, the three rivers, Torne, Muonio and Könkämä mark out the long border between Sweden and Finland in the far north of Scandinavia. The valley is refreshingly different from the coast; the villages here are small and rural, often no more than a couple of wooden cottages surrounded by open flower meadows running down to the river's edge; and different too from the heavily wooded inland regions of the country, the open plains here providing much needed grazing land for the farmers' livestock. **Buses** run from Haparanda up the valley and you can break the journey whenever you feel like it to take in one of the many lakes swirling in mist.

Pajala

The valley's main village is pretty **PAJALA** (pronounced "pie-allah") – a place which has earned itself something of a reputation in Sweden. To celebrate the village's recent 400th anniversary, the local council placed ads in Swedish newspapers inviting women from the south of the country up to Lappland to take part in the birthday festivities; the predominance of heavy-labouring jobs in the north of Sweden has produced a population imbalance, around three men to every woman, and explains the ridiculously macho behaviour that prevails in these parts. Journalists outside Sweden soon heard about the ads and before long busloads of women from across Europe were heading north to take part in a drunken, debauched bash. The plan worked, however, with dozens of east European women losing their hearts to gruff Swedish lumberjacks and beginning new lives north of the Arctic Circle. However, it remains to be seen whether the effects of several winters of 24-hour darkness, coupled with temperatures of -25°C, will tip the balance back.

Undoubtedly the third week of September, the **Römpäviiko** – the "romp week" – as this ongoing cultural festival is called, is the liveliest time to be in the village. At any other time Pajala is a great place to rest up in for a day or so; take a walk along the riverside or head off in search of the great grey owl (*strix nebulosa*) that sweeps through the nearby forests; the huge wooden model in the bus station will give you an idea of what the bird looks like: lichen grey with long slender tail feathers and a white crescent between its black and yellow eyes.

Pajala's **tourist office** (mid-June to Sept Mon–Fri 9am–6pm, Sat & Sun 9am–1pm; rest of the year Mon–Fri 9am–5pm; ☎0978/714 41) is located in the bus station and can provide information on the surrounding area. Close by at Soukolovägen 2, *Pajala Wärdhus* (☎0978/101 00 or 712 00; fax 714 64; ②/④) has cosy little **rooms** and all meals are included in the price, or there's the similar *Hotell Smedjan* at Fridhemsvägen 1 (☎0978/108 15; fax 717 75; ②/④). But the best place to stay is right at the other end of the village: *Pajala Camping* (☎0978/718 80 or 719 32; May–Sept) offers stunning views over the lazy Torne river, plus some simple **cabins** with cold water.

For **eating and drinking**, head for the *Pajala Wärdhus* at lunchtime for the cheapest meals – *dagens rätt* goes for 52kr, for traditional northern Swedish delicacies count on at least 100kr; beer comes cheap here at weekends when there's also a popular disco in the basement. *Bykrogen*, just round the corner, is a cheap and cheerful pizzeria with pizzas from 40kr.

Heading north: Karesuando and Treriksröset

A bus leaves Pajala once daily for Sweden's northernmost village, **KARESUANDO** (currently at 1.25pm; change in Vittangi to arrive at 5.25pm), a singularly ugly place where the land is in the grip of permafrost all year round and life is pretty tough. Karesuando is 250km north of the Arctic Circle and deep in Sami country – here national borders carry little significance, people cross them without as much as a bat of an eyelid as they go about their everyday business.

If you're heading for **Treriksröset** – a cairn where Sweden, Norway and Finland meet – you'll be forced to stay the night here because the bus to Karesuando doesn't connect with services on the other side of the border in Finland (see below); stock up on tourist brochures from the **tourist office** (mid-June to mid-Aug daily 9am–6pm; ☎0981/202 05) or bring a good book. The basic *Hotell Grape* (☎0981/200 22; fax 202 65; ②/④) or *Karesuando Camping* (☎0981/201 39) are your two choices for **accommodation**. Alternatively there's a **youth hostel** across the river in Finnish Kaaresuvanto (from Sweden call ☎009 358/167 7771).

To continue to Treriksröset, cross the River Könkämä to **Kaaresuvanto** (remember Finnish time is an hour ahead), from where buses leave in summer for Kilpisjärvi – there's no road on the Swedish side of the border. From here there are two choices: an eleven-kilometre hike down a track to the cairn or a twenty-minute **boat** ride across the lake (July to mid-Aug 10am, 1pm & 5pm Finnish time; 85kr return; minimum 4 passengers; information on Swedish mobile ☎010/666 8715), which shortens the hike to just 3km.

travel details

Trains

From Borlänge to: Gävle (5 daily; 1hr 30min); Falun (8 daily; 15min); Malung (5 daily; 2hr); Mora (7 daily; 1hr 20min); Stockholm (10 daily; 2hr 40min); Uppsala (10 daily; 2hr); Örebro (4 daily; 2hr).

From Falun to: Borlänge (8 daily; 15min); Gävle (5 daily; 1hr); Stockholm (8 daily; 3hr); Uppsala (8 daily; 2hr 45min); Örebro (4 daily; 1hr 45min).

From Gällivare to: Boden (3 daily; 2hr); Gothenburg (1 daily; 19hr 30min); Gävle (2 daily; 14hr); Kiruna (3 daily; 1hr); Luleå (3 daily; 2hr

20min); Stockholm (2 daily; 16hr 30min); Umeå (1 daily; 7hr); Uppsala (2 daily; 15hr 30min).

From Kiruna to: Abisko (3 daily; 1hr 20min); Boden (3 daily; 3hr); Gothenburg (1 daily; 20hr 30min); Luleå (3 daily; 3hr 20min); Narvik (3 daily; 3hr); Riksgränsen (3 daily; 2hr); Stockholm (2 daily; 17hr 30min); Uppsala (2 daily; 16hr 30min).

From Kristinehamn to: Stockholm (10 daily; 2hr 45min); Oslo (2 daily; 4hr)

From Mora to: Borlänge (7 daily; 1hr 20min); Leksand (7 daily; 45min); Rättvik (7 daily; 30min); Stockholm (7 daily; 4hr by X2000, 5hr by InterCity); Tällberg (7 daily; 35min); Uppsala (7 daily; 3hr 15min by X2000, 4hr 15min by InterCity)

From Östersund to: Gothenburg (1 daily; 11hr); Stockholm (4 daily; 6hr), Storlien (4 daily; 3hr); Sundsvall (6 daily; 4hr 15min); Trondheim (3 daily; 5hr 30min); Uppsala (4 daily; 5hr 15min); Åre (4 daily; 1hr 45min).

The Inlandsbanan

Timetables are liable to change from year to year but following is a rough idea of services and times. Currently the service runs from mid-June to the end of August. Latest information on ☎020/53 53 53.

From Arvidsjaur to: Jokkmokk and Gällivare (4 weekly); Storuman, Vilhelmina and Östersund (6 weekly).

From Gällivare to: Jokkmokk and Arvidsjaur (4 weekly); Storuman, Vilhelmina and Östersund (4 weekly).

From Mora to: Orsa, Sveg, Klövsjö and Östersund (4 weekly).

From Östersund to: Klövsjö, Sveg and Mora (4 weekly); Jokkmokk and Gällivare (4 weekly); Vilhelmina, Storuman, Arvidsjaur (1 daily).

Buses

From Arvidsjaur to: Gällivare (1 daily; 2hr); Östersund (2 daily; 7hr).

From Gällivare to: Arvidsjaur (1 daily; 2hr); Jokkmokk (4 daily; 1hr 30min); Kiruna (4 daily; 2hr 10min); Luleå (2 daily; 3hr 15min); Pajala (3 daily; 2hr 20min); Ritsem (1 daily; 3hr 30min); Östersund (1 daily; 11hr).

From Jokkmokk to: Gällivare (4 daily; 1hr 30min); Kvikkjokk (1 daily; 1hr 50min); Murjek (4 daily; 50min).

From Kiruna to: Gällivare (4 daily; 2hr 10min); Jukkasjärvi (6 daily; 40min); Karesuando (1 daily; 3hr 30min); Luleå (2 daily; 4hr 45min); Pajala (3 daily; 3hr 30min); Nikkaluokta (2 daily; 1hr 10min).

From Kvikkjokk to: Jokkmokk (2 daily; 1hr 50min).

From Mora to: Grönklitt bear peak (1 daily; 1hr); Idre (2 daily; 3hr); Malung (2 daily; 2hr); Orsa (12 daily; 20min); Sälen (1 daily; 1hr 40min); Särna (4 daily; 1hr 50min); Östersund (2 daily; 5hr).

From Murjek to: Jokkmokk (4 daily; 50min).

From Storuman to: Tärnaby (5 daily; 2hr); Hemavan (4 daily; 2hr 20min).

From Åsarna to: Klövsjö (4 daily; 15min); Östersund (7 daily; 1hr 20min).

From Östersund to: Arvidsjaur (2 daily; 7hr); Gällivare (1 daily; 11hr); Mora (2 daily; 5hr); Umeå (2 daily; 6hr).

International trains

From Kristinehamn to: Oslo (2 daily; 4hr).

Flights

There are fairly regular flights – the most reliable operated by *SAS* – between Stockholm Arlanda and the main northern cities. Timetables are subject to constant change, however, so it's advisable to check with a travel agent.

PART FIVE

FINLAND

Introduction

Mainland Scandinavia's most culturally isolated and least understood country, Finland has been independent only since 1917, having been ruled for hundreds of years by imperial powers: first the Swedes and then the Tsarist Russians. Much of its history involves a struggle simply for recognition and survival.

During the Swedish period, the Finnish language (one of the world's strangest and most difficult) was regarded as fit only for peasants – which the majority of Finns were – and attempts were later made to forcibly impose Russian. All publications were in Swedish until the *Kalevala* appeared in the early nineteenth century. A written collection of previously orally transmitted folk tales telling of a people close to nature and living by hunting and fishing, the *Kalevala* instantly became regarded as a truly Finnish history, and formed the basis of the **National Romantic** movement in the arts that flourished from the mid-nineteenth century, stimulating political initiatives towards Finnish nationalism.

It's not surprising therefore that modern-day Finns have a well-developed sense of their own culture, and the legacy of the past is strongly felt – in the still widely popular Golden Age paintings of Gallen-Kallela, Edelfelt and others, the music of Sibelius, the National Romantic architecture (paving the way for modern greats like Alvar Aalto); or in the fact that the scars of the 1918 Civil War, which split the nation following independence, have yet to heal fully. Equally in evidence, even among city dwellers, are the deeply ingrained down-to-earth values of rural life, along with a sense of spirituality epitomized by the sauna, which for Finns is a meaningful ritual rather than an exercise in health. A small but significant proportion of Finns actually come from **Karelia** – a large tract of land now scythed in two by the Finnish–Russian border and sparsely inhabited, but historically a homeland distinct from Finland *and* Russia, and one whose traditional peasant culture is highly revered.

Some elderly rural dwellers are prone to suspicion of anything foreign, but in general the Finnish population is much less staid than its Nordic neighbours. Nonetheless, the years of optimism encouraged by the success of the country's subtle politics – following the Scandinavian consensus model domestically but pioneering a unique foreign policy based on the need to live peacefully next door to a superpower – seem to have come to an end. The world recession has bitten deep into the Finnish economy, while the disintegration of the Soviet Union has left an extremely volatile situation brewing on Finland's doorstep.

■ Where to go

The country is mainly flat and filled by huge forests and lakes, and you'll need to travel around a lot to appreciate Finland's wide regional variations. The **South** contains the least dramatic scenery, but the capital, **Helsinki**, more than compensates, with its brilliant architecture and superb collections of national history and art. Stretching from the Russian border in the east to the industrial city of **Tampere**, the vast waters of the **Lake Region** provide a natural means of transport for the timber industry – indeed, water here is a more common sight than land. Towns lie on narrow ridges between lakes, giving even major manufacturing centres green and easily accessible surroundings.

Ostrobothnia, the upper portion of the west coast, is characterized by near-featureless farmlands and long sandy beaches, which are – to Finns at least – the region's main draw. Here too you'll also find the clearest Swedish influence: in parts up to a third of the population are Swedish-speaking – known as Finland-Swedes – and there's a rich heritage from the days of Swedish trading supremacy. **Kainuu** is the thickly forested heart of the country, much of its small population spread among scattered villages. The land begins to rise as you head north from here, folding into a series of fells and gorges that are ripe for spectacular hiking. **Lappland**, completely devoid of large towns, contains the most alluring terrain of all, its stark and haunting landscapes able to absorb any number of visitors on numerous hiking routes. A distinctive element of the area are the **Sami** people, semi-nomadic reindeer herders whose traditional way of life remains relatively untainted by modern culture.

■ When to go

The official Finnish holiday season is early July to mid-August, and during these weeks there's an exodus from the towns to the country regions. The best time to visit the rural regions is either side of these dates, when things will be less crowded and less hectic – though no cheaper.

In **summer**, regarded as being from June to early September, Helsinki and the South and the Lake Region enjoy mild and sunny weather. Temperatures are usually 18–24°C (65–75°F), sometimes reaching 32°C (90°F) in the daytime, but they drop swiftly in the evening, when you'll need a light jacket. The north is always a few degrees cooler and often quite cold at night, so carry at least a thick jumper. The **Midnight Sun** can be seen from Rovaniemi northwards for two months over midsummer; the rest of the country experiences a night-long twilight from mid-June to mid-July.

Winter, roughly from late October to early April in the south, plus a few weeks more on either side in the north, is painfully cold. Helsinki generally fluctuates between 0°C and -20°C (32°F and -4°F), the harshest months being January and February; in the north it's even colder, with just a few hours of daylight; and in the extreme north the sun doesn't rise at all. The snow cover generally lasts from November to March in the south, a few weeks longer in the north. On the plus side, Finland copes easily with low temperatures and transport is rarely disrupted.

The best time for **hiking** is from May to September in the south and from June to September in the north. You'll need a good-quality tent, a warm sleeping bag, rainwear, spare warm clothing, thick-soled waterproof boots, a compass and detailed maps. Maps and other equipment can be bought in tourist centres close to the hiking routes. See p.35 for more on hiking.

Getting There

How hard it is to get to Finland obviously depends on which part of Scandinavia you're coming from. From the east coast of Sweden it's easy, with regular ferry crossings from a number of points and usually good onward links once you've arrived. Further north, Sweden and Norway both have land borders with Finland and these are no fuss to cross by bus – or in one place a train – although in a few spots you may have to wait several days between connections. From Denmark, it's impossible to get to Finland without passing through Sweden unless you fly, although there is a direct bus service and fairly frequent trains.

■ From Denmark

The **bus** link from Copenhagen to Finland runs four times a week to Helsinki, via Stockholm and Turku.

Naturally, it's a fairly exhausting journey, taking 25 hours. Especially if you've got an *InterRail*, *BIJ* or *Nordturist* pass, it's a much better idea to take the **train**: there are one or two daily from Copenhagen to Turku (21hr) and Helsinki (25hr).

■ From Sweden

The most frequent **ferries** from Sweden to Finland run between Stockholm and **Helsinki** and are operated by the *Silja* and *Viking* lines. Each company has a year-round overnight service, leaving at 6pm and arriving at 9am. Both lines also run a twice-daily service from Stockholm to **Turku**, which takes ten or eleven hours. Quicker still (6–10hr) are the daily services between Stockholm and **Mariehamn**, run by *Silja*, *Viking* and *Birka Line*.

For current details and the latest news on the numerous discounts availabe – ranging from 50 percent reductions to free passage for holders of *InterRail* or *Eurail* cards, plus reductions for children and senior citizens – check with a travel agent or the relevant ferry office. Taking the train from Stockholm to Helsinki is a further option – see "Travel details" for more details.

Lastly, it's quite possible to **drive** to Finland from Sweden – a beautiful journey in the summer or early autumn. The efficient main E4 highway follows the Gulf of Bothnia through Sweden, giving the opportunity to experience Swedish and Finnish Lappland. The border crossing is around 1020km north of Stockholm at Haparanda/Tornio.

■ From Norway

In the Arctic North, buses connect the Norwegian–Finnish border towns of Karasjok–Karisganiemi and Skipbotn–Kilpisjärvi, and the Finnish border villages of Polmak and Nuorgam; fares and schedules, beyond what we've included under "Travel Details" at the end of the relevant chapters, can be checked at any tourist office or bus station.

■ By plane

Finnair have non-stop **flights to Helsinki** from Copenhagen (3 daily), from Stockholm (8 daily) and from Oslo (11 daily). There are also eleven flights a week **to Tampere** from Stockholm and twelve a week from Oslo. To get to Tampere from Copenhagen you need to connect in Helsinki. **Turku** is served by daily flights from Stockholm –

from elsewhere you need to connect via Helsinki. Check with a travel agent for occasional bargain fares between Scandinavian cities.

Costs, Money and Banks

If you're arriving from Norway or Sweden, Finland's prices will come as little surprise. Though the cost of a meal or the bill for an evening's drinks can come as a shock, for the most part prices in Finland are comparable with those in most European capitals, and there is no shortage of places catering for those on tighter budgets. Bargain lunchtime "specials" are common and travelling costs, in particular, can come as a pleasant surprise.

There are ways to cut **costs**, and we've detailed them where relevant, but as a general rule you'll need £20–30/\$30–45 a day to even live fairly modestly – staying mostly at youth hostels or campsites, eating out every other day and supplementing your diet with food from supermarkets, visiting only a few selected museums and socializing fairly rarely. To live well, and see more, you'll be spending closer to £50/\$75.

Finnish **currency** is the *markka* (plural *markkaa*), which divides into 100 *penniä*. Notes come as 1000mk, 500mk, 100mk, 50mk and 10mk; coins are 5mk, 1mk, 50p, 20p, 10p and 5p. The **exchange rate** at the time of writing was 7.10mk to £1 (10.65mk to US\$1).

As usual, one of the best ways to carry money is as travellers cheques. These can be changed at most **banks** (Mon–Fri 9.15am–4.15pm), the charge for which is usually 15mk (though several people changing money together need only pay the commission once). You can also change money at hotels, though normally at a much worse rate than at the banks. In a country where every markka counts, it's worth looking around for a better deal: in rural areas some banks and hotels are known not to charge any commission at all. Some banks have currency exchange desks at transport terminals which open to meet international arrivals, and these are the best places to head outside normal banking hours.

Major **credit and charge cards** – *Amex, MasterCard, Visa, Diner's Club* – are usually accepted by hotels, car rental offices, department stores, restaurants and sometimes even by taxis. However, it's still advisable to check beforehand.

There are no restrictions on the amount of money you can take in or out of Finland.

Post and Phones

In general, communications in Finland are dependable and quick, although in the far north, and in some sections of the east, minor delays arise due simply to geographical remoteness.

Unless you're on a hiking trek through the back of beyond, you can rest assured your letter or postcard will arrive at its destination fairly speedily. The cost of mailing anything weighing under 20g to other parts of Europe is 3.20mk priority class, 2.60mk for economy; to the rest of the world prices are 3.40mk or 2.40mk respectively. You can buy **stamps** from a **post office** (Mon–Fri 9am–5pm; longer hours at the main post office in Helsinki), from street stands or *R-kioski*, and at some hotels. **Post restante** is available at the main post office in every large town.

An out-of-order **public phone** is virtually unheard of in Finland, although many of them only take phonecards, which you can buy in a number of denominations from kiosks and tobacconists. The minimum cost of a **local call** is 2mk. Phones that accept money take 1mk and 5mk coins, and a few older ones also accept two 50p coins, which run out rapidly so have a supply of small change to hand. **International calls** are cheapest between 10pm and 8am. The bill for using a **hotel phone** is often dramatically more expensive.

The Media

The biggest-selling **Finnish newspaper**, and the only one to be distributed all over the country, is the daily *Helsingin Sanomat* (10mk). Most of the others are locally based and sponsored by a political party, except for the second most popular daily rag, *Uusi Suomi* (10mk), which is an independent paper that publishes an English-language resumé of the day's news. All newspapers carry entertainment listings; only the cinema listings – where the film titles are translated into Finnish – present problems for non-Finnish speakers. A better source of what's on information, if you're in Helsinki, Tampere or Turku, is the free *City* (appearing fortnightly in Helsinki, monthly in Turku and Tampere), which carries news, features and entertainment details on the surrounding area in Finnish and English. For **rock music** listings, the fortnightly *Rumba* (15mk) has a rundown of forthcoming gigs and festivals throughout the country.

Overseas newspapers, including most British and some US titles, can be found, often on the day of issue, at the *Academic Bookstore*, Pohjoisesplanadi 39, in Helsinki. Elsewhere, foreign papers are harder to find and less up-to-date, though they often turn up at the bigger newsagents and train stations in Turku, Tampere and, to a lesser extent, Oulu.

Finnish **television**, despite its three channels (one of which is called *MTV*, but is unrelated to the round-the-clock music station), isn't exactly inspiring and certainly won't keep you off the streets for long. Moderately more interesting is the fact that, depending on where you are, you might be able to watch Swedish, Estonian and Russian programes. A few youth hostels have TV rooms, and most hotel room TVs have the regular channels plus a feast of cable and satellite alternatives. As with films shown in the cinema, all Finnish TV programmes are broadcast in their original language with subtitles.

Getting Around

Save for the fact that traffic tends to follow a north–south pattern, you'll have few headaches getting around the more populated parts of Finland. The chief form of public transport is the train, backed up, particularly on east–west journeys, by long-distance coaches. For the most part trains and buses integrate well, and you'll only need to plan with care when travelling through sparsely inhabited areas such as the far north and east. Feasible and often affordable variations come in the form of boats, planes, bikes, and even hitching – though car rental is strictly for the wealthy.

The complete **timetable** (*Suomen Kulku-neuvot*) for train, bus, ferry and air travel within the country is published every two months and costs 95mk from stations and kiosks. This is essential for plotting complex routes; for simplified details of the major train services, pick up the *Taskuaikataulu* booklet (7mk) from any tourist office or train station.

■ Trains

The swiftest land link between Finland's major cities is invariably the reliable **train service**, operated by the national company, *VR*. Large, comfortable express trains (and a growing number of "ICs", super-smooth state-of-the-art Inter-City trains) serve the principal **north–south** routes several times a day, reaching as far north as Kemijärvi and Kolari in southern Finnish Lappland. Elsewhere, especially on

east–west hauls through sparsely populated regions, rail services tend to be skeletal and trains are often tiny one- or two-carriage affairs. The Arctic North is not served by trains at all.

InterRail, *BIJ* and *Scanrail* passes are valid on all trains; if you don't have one of these and are planning a lot of travelling, get a **Finnrail Pass** *before* arriving in Finland from a travel agent or Finnish Tourist Office (for addresses, see p.27). This costs £74/$119 for three days' unlimited travel within a month, £100/$169 for five days, or £136/$229 for ten days.

Otherwise train **fares** are surprisingly reasonable. As a guide, a one-way, second-class ticket from Helsinki to Turku, a trip of around 200km, costs around 94mk; Helsinki to Kuopio (465km) costs around 196mk, and Helsinki to Rovaniemi (900km) around 304mk. If you've brought a car with you, car sleeper services are a convenient way of covering long distances. A one-way trip from Helsinki to Rovaniemi for a car and up to three passengers costs around 950mk, including sleeping berths.

Tickets are valid for a month, and you can break your journey once, provided the ticket is stamped at the station where you stop – and as long as the total distance covered is 80km or more. You should **buy tickets** from station ticket offices (*lippumyymälä*), although you can also pay the inspector on the train. If there are three or more of you travelling together, **group tickets**, available from a train station or travel agent, can cut the regular fares on journeys over 80km by at least 20 percent. **Senior citizens** with *Rail Europ* cards are entitled to a 30 percent discount on regular tickets, or 50 percent if they are over 65 and buy a Finnish Senior Citizens railcard (50mk). **Seat reservations**, costing 20mk (20–80mk supplement on ICs), can be a good idea if you're travelling over a holiday period or on a Friday or Sunday evening.

■ Buses

Buses – run by local private companies but with a common ticket system – cover the whole country, and are often quicker and more frequent than trains over the shorter east–west hops, and essential for getting around the remoter regions. In the Arctic North there are no railways, so all public transport is by road.

Fares are fixed according to distance travelled: Helsinki to Lahti (100km) costs around 84mk,

Helsinki to Kuopio (400km) around 216mk. Express buses charge a supplement of 12–15mk. All types of ticket can be purchased at a bus station or at most travel agents; only ordinary one-way tickets can be bought on board the bus, though on journeys of 80km or less there's no saving in buying a return anyway. On return trips of over 80km, expect a reduction of 10 percent. To cut costs, there is a slightly bewildering array of **discounted tickets** available: three or more people travelling 80km or more qualify for a **group reduction** of 20 percent; holders of *YIEE/FIYTO* cards (but not *ISIC* cards) can get a 30 percent reduction on trips of similar length. **Students** can also buy a bus travel discount card for 50mk, which gives 35–50 percent reductions on journeys of 80km or more; these are available from bus stations on presentation of a photo and proof of full-time education. Similar reductions can be claimed by those **over 65**. If you're going to travel a lot by bus, the cheapest way of working things is to get a **Coach Holiday Ticket**, which gives 1000km of bus travel over any two-week period for 350mk; buy it from any long-distance bus station, though exactly how much money it saves will obviously depend on your itinerary. For information, the free bus **timetable**, *Suomen Pikavuorot*, which lists all the routes in the country, can be picked up at most long-distance bus stations.

■ Planes

With their range of discounts, domestic **flights** can be comparatively cheap as well as time-saving if you want to cover long distances, such as from Helsinki to the Arctic North. That said, travelling by air means you'll miss many interesting parts of the country; another point to bear in mind is that flights from smaller towns to the bigger centres – Helsinki, Tampere and Oulu – tend to depart at around 6am. The **Finnair Holiday Ticket**, which costs the equivalent of $500, covers ten domestic flights in a thirty-day period. Holiday tickets are restricted to foreigners but can be bought inside or outside Finland, from *Finnair* offices or travel agents. There's also a variety of off-peak summer reductions which can be checked at travel agents and airline or tourist offices in Finland.

■ Ferries

Lake travel is aimed more at holidaying families than the budget-conscious traveller. **Prices** are high considering the distances, and progress is slow as the vessels chug along the great lake chains. If you have the time, money and inclination, though, it can be worth taking one of the shorter trips simply for the experience. There are numerous routings and details can be checked at any tourist office in the country and at Finnish Tourist Offices abroad.

■ Cycling

Cycling can be an enjoyable way to see the country at close quarters since the only appreciable hills are in the far north and extreme east. Villages and towns may be separated by several hours' pedalling, however, and the scenery can get monotonous. Finnish **roads** are of high quality in the south and around the large towns, but are much rougher in the north and in isolated areas; beware the springtime thaw when the winter snows melt and sometimes cover roads with water and mud. All major towns have bike shops selling spares – and Finland is one of the few places in the world where you can buy bicycle snow tyres with tungsten steel studs. Most youth hostels, campsites and some hotels and tourist offices offer **bike rental** from 70mk per day, 200mk per week; there may also be a deposit to pay of 150–200mk.

■ Driving and hitching

With such a good public transport network, **renting a car** is only worth considering if you're travelling as a group of four or five as it's extremely expensive (as is petrol). The big international companies such as *Avis*, *Budget*, *EuropCar* and *Hertz*, and the similarly priced Finnish company, *Oy Polarpoint*, have offices in most Finnish towns and at international arrival points. They all accept major credit cards; if paying by cash, you'll need to leave a substantial deposit. You'll also need a valid driving licence, at least a year's driving experience, and to be a minimum of 19–23 years old, depending on the company you rent from.

Rates for a medium-sized car are 200–400mk per day, with reductions for longer periods, down to around 2400mk for a fortnight's use. On top of this, there's a surcharge of up to 5mk per km (which may be waived on long-term loans) and a drop-off fee of around 350mk if you leave the car somewhere other than the place from which it was rented. For more details on car rental before arriving in Finland, visit an office of one of the international companies mentioned above, or ask at a Finnish Tourist Board office.

If you **bring your own car** to Finland, it's advisable (though not compulsory) to have a Green Card as proof of insurance. If you have one and are involved in an **accident**, report it at once to the Finnish Motor Insurer's Bureau, Bulevardi 28, 00120 Helsinki (☎09/19251).

Once underway, you'll find the next financial drain is **fuel**, which costs 5.35mk a litre (unleaded). **Service stations** are plentiful (except in the far north, where they are few and far between) and usually open from 7am to 9pm from Monday to Saturday, often closed on Sunday – although in summer many stay open round the clock in busy holiday areas. Though **roads** are generally in good condition there can be problems with melting snows, usually during April and May in the south and June in the far north. Finnish **road signs** are similar to those throughout Europe, but be aware of bilingual place names (see p.605); one useful sign to watch for is *Keskusta*, which means "town centre". **Speed limits** vary between 40–60kph in built-up areas to 100kph – if it's not signposted, the basic limit is always 80kph. On motorways the maximum speed is 120kph in summer, 100kph in winter.

Other **rules** of the road include: using **headlights** when driving outside built-up areas, as well as in fog and in poor light; and the compulsory wearing of **seatbelts** by drivers and all passengers. As elsewhere in Scandinavia, penalties for **drunk driving** are severe – the police may stop and breathalyse you if they think you've been driving erratically. In some areas in the north of the country, **reindeer and elk** are liable to take a stroll across a road, especially around dusk. Although these are sizeable creatures, damage (to the car) is unlikely to be serious; still, all such collisions should be reported at the nearest police station.

Hitching is generally easy, and sometimes the quickest means of transport between two spots. Finland's large student population has helped accustom drivers to the practice, and you shouldn't have to wait too long for a ride on the busy main roads between large towns. Make sure you have a decent road map and emergency provisions/shelter if you're passing through isolated regions. While many Finns speak English, it's still handy to memorize the Finnish equivalent of "let me out here" – *jään pois tässä*.

■ City transport

It's only in and around very small towns and villages that you may struggle to get about by means other than foot. In cities and larger towns, **public transport** takes the form of a comprehensive bus network (together with trams in Helsinki) with fares of 8–15mk for a single journey. After midnight, **taxis** (*taksi*) may be your only option. These can be hailed in the street, found at taxi ranks or phoned for (look under *Taksiasemat* in the phone book). Taxis are cheaper in the north than the south, and most expensive of all in Helsinki. Basic charges are normally around 14mk plus 6–7mk per kilometre, with additional charges at night and at weekends. With several people sharing, taxis can be an affordable way to travel between isolated towns when public transport is scarce.

Accommodation

Whether you're at the end of a long-distance hiking trail or in the centre of a city, you'll find at least some kind of accommodation in Finland to suit your needs. You will, however, have to pay dearly for it: prices are high and only by being aware of special offers and the cheap times in which to travel will you be able to sleep well on a budget.

■ Hotels

Finnish **hotels** (*hotelli*) are rarely other than polished and pampering: TV, phone and private bathroom are standard fixtures, breakfast is invariably included in the price, and there's often free use of the sauna and swimming pool too. Costs can be formidable – frequently in excess of 500mk for a

---

ACCOMMODATION PRICE CODES

The Finnish hotels listed throughout the guide have been graded according to the following price bands, based on the rate for a double room in summer. However, many hotels offer summer and/or weekend discounts, and in these instances we've given two grades, covering both the regular and the discounted rate.

① Under 275mk ② 275–350mk ③ 350–450mk ④ 450–550mk ⑤ 550–750mk ⑥ 750mk and over

double – but planning ahead and taking advantage of various discount schemes and seasonal reductions can cut prices, often to as little as 300mk.

In **major cities**, particularly Helsinki, there can be bargains in business-oriented hotels during July and August, and on Fridays, Saturdays and Sundays throughout the year. Exact details of these change frequently, but it's worth checking the current situation at a local tourist office. Reductions are also available to holders of Helsinki Cards and the similar card issued for Tampere. Otherwise, between July and August you're unlikely to find anything under 350mk by turning up on spec. Hotels in **country areas** are no less comfortable than those in cities, and often a touch less costly, typically 250–300mk. However, space is again limited during summer.

Expense can be trimmed a little under the *Finncheque* system: you can buy an unlimited number of 200mk **vouchers**, each valid for a night's accommodation for one person in any of the 200 participating hotels from mid-May to September. There are three price categories: Group III are double rooms with breakfast included, Group II carries a supplement of 40mk per person, and Group I a supplement of 80mk. You can only buy the *Finncheque* outside Finland at a Finnish Tourist Board office or a specialist travel agent, who will also supply addresses of the hotels involved. Don't worry about buying more vouchers than you might need – they are refundable at the place of purchase. Another discount is that offered by the downmarket *Scanhotel* chain, whose "Scandic Holiday Cheque" can be more useful to the budget-conscious. Valid at all *Arctia* hotels in Finland throughout the year, prices range from 450mk per room including breakfast, though beware that some hotels add on a "quality surcharge". The Cheques are widely available from travel agents outside Finland.

In many towns you'll also find **tourist hotels** (*matkustajakoti*), a more basic type of hotel, broadly akin to British-style bed and breakfast (without the breakfast). They charge 200–300mk per double room, but may well be full throughout the summer. The facilities of **summer hotels** (*kesähotelli*), too, are more basic than regular hotels, since the accommodation is in student blocks which are vacated from June to the end of August: there are universities in all the major cities and in an impressive number of the larger towns. Reservable with any Finnish travel agent, summer hotel prices are around 225mk per person. Bear in mind that identical accommodation –

minus the bed linen and breakfast – comes a lot cheaper in the guise of a youth hostel.

■ Youth hostels

Often the easiest and cheapest place to rest your head is a **youth hostel** (*retkeilymaja*). These exist throughout the country, in major cities (which will have at least one) and isolated country areas. It's always a good idea to phone ahead and reserve a place, which many hostel wardens will do for you. If you're arriving on a late bus or train, say so when phoning and your bed will be kept for you; otherwise bookings are only held until 6pm. Things are quieter after mid-August, although a large number of hostels close soon after this date – check that the one you're aiming for doesn't. Similarly, many hostels don't open until June.

Overnight **charges** vary between 60mk and 150mk, depending on the type of accommodation, with hostels ranging from the basic dormitory type to those with two- and four-bedded rooms and at least one bathroom for every three rooms. Bed linen, if not already included, can be rented for an extra 20–30mk. With a Hostelling International Card (not obligatory) you can get a 15mk reduction per person per night. The Finnish hostel association's office in Helsinki sells International Guest Cards (90mk) that do the same job. Their guide, *Suomen Retkeilymajat*, available directly from them at *Suomen Retkeilymajajärjestö* at Yrjönkatu 38B, 00100 Helsinki (☎09/694 0377), lists all Finnish hostels, and the very helpful staff here can also provide a free Finland map showing all hostels marked blue or red, the former being open all year, the latter open in summer only.

All youth hostels have wardens to provide general assistance and arrange **meals**: most hostels offer breakfast, usually for 22–28mk, and some serve dinner as well (around 45mk). Hostel breakfasts, especially those in busy city hostels, can be rationed affairs and – hunger permitting – you'll generally be better off waiting until you can find a cheapish lunch somewhere else (see "Food and Drink" below). The only hostel breakfasts really worth taking advantage of are those offered at summer hotels, where hostellers can mingle with the hotel guests and, for 25–30mk, partake of the help-yourself spread.

■ Campsites and camping cottages

There are some 200 official **campsites** (*leirintäalue*) in Finland, and around 150 more operating on a less formal basis. Most open from May to September, although around seventy stay open all year. The approved sites, marked with a blue and white tent sign in a letter C, are classified by a star system: one-star sites are in rural areas and usually pretty basic, while on a five-star site you can expect excellent cooking and laundry facilities and sometimes a well-stocked shop. The cost for two people sharing is 30–90mk, depending on the site's star rating. Campsites outside major towns are frequently very big (a 2000-tent capacity isn't uncommon), and they're very busy at weekends during July and August. Smaller and more remote sites (except those serving popular hiking routes) are, as you'd imagine, much less crowded.

Holiday villages have been sprouting up throughout Finland in the last few years and there are now around 200 of them. Standards vary considerably, with accommodation ranging from basic cabins to luxurious bungalows. All provide fuel, cooking facilities, bed linen and often a sauna – but you'll need to bring your own towels. Costs range from 700mk to 3000mk per week, though for a luxury bungalow you be might paying up to 6000mk. Camping cottage cheques, available from travel agents for 70mk per cabin per night, can be used at some ninety campsites and holiday villages throughout the country from May 15 to September 15 – an economical option if there are enough of you.

Without an *International Camping Card* (see *Basics*) you'll need a *National Camping Card*, available at every site for 20mk and valid for a year. If you're considering **camping rough**, remember it's illegal without the landowner's permission – though in practice, provided you're out of sight of local communities, there shouldn't be any problems.

■ Hiking accommodation

Hiking routes invariably start and finish close to a campsite or a youth hostel. Along the way there are several types of basic accommodation. Of these, a *päivätupa* is a cabin with cooking facilities which is opened during the day for free use; an *autiotupa* is an unlocked hut which can be used by hikers to sleep in for one night only – there's no fee but often no space either during the busiest months. A *varaustupa* is a locked hut for which you can obtain a key at the Tourist Centre at the start of the hike – there's a smallish fee and

you'll almost certainly be sharing. Some routes have a few *kämppä* – cabins originally erected for forest workers but now used mainly by hikers; check their exact location with the nearest tourist centre. On most hikes there are also marked spots for pitching your own tent and building fires. For fuller hiking details see the *Ostrobothnia, Kainuu and Lappland* chapter.

Food and Drink

Finnish food is full of surprises and demands investigation. It's pricey but you can keep a grip on the expense by indulging most often at markets and at the many down-to-earth dining places, saving restaurant blowouts for special occasions. Though tempered by many regulations, alcohol is more widely available here than in much of Scandinavia: there are many places to drink but also many people drinking, most of them indulging moderately but some doing it to excess on a regular basis, regarding themselves as the last true Finns.

■ Food

Though it may at first seem a stodgy, rather unsophisticated cuisine, **Finnish food** is an interesting mix of western and eastern influences. Many dishes resemble those you might find elsewhere in Scandinavia – an enticing array of delicately prepared fish (herring, whitefish, salmon and crayfish), together with some exotic meats like reindeer and elk – while others bear the stamp of Russian cooking: solid pastries and casseroles, strong on cabbage, pork and mutton.

All Finnish restaurants will leave a severe dent in your budget, as will the foreign places, notably the innumerable pizzerias, that you'll come across all over the country. The golden money-saving rule is to treat **lunch** (*lounas*, usually served 11am–2pm) rather than the much dearer **dinner** (*päivällinen*, usually from 6pm) as your main meal. Also, eke out your funds with stand-up snacks and by selective buying in supermarkets. If you're staying in a hotel, don't forget to load up on the inclusive **breakfast** (*aamiainen*) – often an open-table laden with herring, eggs, cereals, porridge, cheese, salami and bread.

Snacks, fast food and self-catering

Economical **snacks** can be found in market halls (*kauppahalli*), where you can find basic foodstuffs

GLOSSARY OF FINNISH FOOD AND DRINK TERMS

Basics

Juusto	Cheese	Maito	Milk	Piirakka	Pie
Kakku	Cake	Makeiset	Sweets	Riisi	Rice
Keitto	Soup	Perunat	Potatoes	Voi	Butter
Keksit	Biscuits	Piimä	Buttermilk	Voileipä	Sandwich
Leipä	Bread				

Meat (*Lihaa*)

Häränfilee	Fillet of beef	Kinkku	Ham	Sianliha	Pork
Hirvenliha	Elk	Lihapyörykat	Meatballs	Poro	Reindeer
Jauheliha	Minced beef	Nauta	Beef	Vasikanliha	Veal
Kana	Chicken	Paisti	Steak		

Seafood (*Äyriäisiä*) and Fish (*Kala*)

Ankerias	Eel	Rapu	Crayfish	Silakat	Baltic herring
Graavilohi	Salted salmon	Sardiini	Sardine	Silli	Herring
Hauki	Pike	Savustettu lohi	Smoked salmon	Suolattu	Pickled herring
Hummeri	Lobster				
Katkaravut	Shrimps	Savustettu silakat	Smoked Baltic herring	Taimen or forelli	Trout
Lohi	Salmon	Siika	Large, slightly oily, white fish	Tonnikala	Tuna
Makrilli	Mackerel			Turska	Cod
Muikku	Small whitefish				

Egg dishes (*Munaruoat*)

Hillomunakas	Jam omelette	Kinkkumunakas	Ham omelette	Pekonimunakas	Bacon omelette
Hyydytetty muna	Poached egg	Munakas	Omelette	Perunamunakas	Potato omelette
Juustomunakas	Cheese omelette	Munakokkeli	Scrambled eggs	Sienimunakas	Mushroom omelette
Keitetty muna	Boiled eggs	Paistettu muna	Fried egg		

Vegetables (*Vihannekset*)

Herneet	Peas	Paprika	Green pepper	Sieni	Mushroom
Kaali	Cabbage	Pavut	Beans	Sipuli	Onion
Kurkku	Cucumber	Peruna	Potato	Tilli	Dill
Maissintähkät	Corn on the cob	Pinaatti	Spinach	Tomaatti	Tomato
		Porkkana	Carrot		

Fruit (*Hedelmä*)

Appelsiini	Orange	Luumu	Plums	Pähkinä	Nut
Aprikoosi	Apricot	Mansikka	Strawberry	Persikka	Peach
Banaani	Banana	Meloni	Melon	Raparperi	Rhubarb
Greippi	Grapefruit	Omena	Apple	Sitruuna	Lemon
Kirsikka	Cherry	Päärynä	Pear	Viinirypäle	Grape

Sandwiches (*Voileipä*)

Kappelivoileipä	Fried French bread with bacon and topped by a fried egg	Oopperavoileipä	Fried French bread with hamburger and egg
Muna-anjovisleipä	Dark bread with slices of hard-boiled egg, anchovy fillets and tomato	Sillivoileipä	Herring on dark bread, usually with egg and tomato

continued overleaf...

continued from previous page

Finnish Specialities

Kaalikääryleet	Cabbage rolls: cabbage leaves stuffed with minced meat and rice	Piparjuuriliha	Boiled beef with horseradish sauce
Kaalipiirakka	Cabbage and mincemeat pie	Porkkanalaatikko	Carrot casserole; mashed carrots and rice
Karjalanpaisti	Karelian stew: beef and pork with onions	Poronkäristys	Sautéed reindeer stew
Kurpitsasalaatti	Pickled pumpkin served with meat dishes	Sianlihakastike	Gravy with slivers of pork
		Silakkalaatikko	Casserole with alternating layers of potato, onion and Baltic herring, with an egg and milk sauce
Lammaskaali	Mutton and cabbage stew or soup		
Lasimestarin silli	Pickled herring with spices, vinegar, carrot and onion		
Lihakeitto	Soup made from meat, potatoes, carrots and onions	Stroganoff	Beef with gherkins and onions, browned in a casserole, braised in stock with tomato juice and sour cream
Lindströmin pihvi	Beefburger made with beetroot and served with a cream sauce		
		Suutarinlohi	Marinated Baltic herring with onion and peppers
Lohilaatikko	Potato and salmon casserole		
Lohipiirakka	Salmon pie	Tilliliha	Boiled veal flavoured with dill sauce
Makaroonilaatikko	Macaroni casserole with milk and egg sauce		
		Venäläinen silli	Herring fillets with mayonnaise, mustard, vinegar, beetroot, gherkins and onion
Maksalaatikko	Baked liver purée with rice and raisins		
Merimiespihvi	Casserole of potato slices and meat patties or minced meat	Wieninleike	Fried veal cutlet

Drinks

Appelsiinimehu	Orange juice	Konjakki	Cognac	Tonic vesi	Tonic water
Gini	Gin	Limonaati	Lemonade	Vesi	Water
Kahvi	Coffee	Olut	Beer	Viiniä	Wine
Kalja	Dark ale	Tee	Tea	Viski	Whisky
Kivennäisvesi	Mineral water				

along with local and national specialities. Adjoining these halls are cafeterias, where you will be charged by the weight of food on your plate. Look out for *karjalan piirakka* – oval-shaped Karelian pastries containing rice and mashed potato, served hot with a mixture of finely chopped hard-boiled egg and butter for 5–10mk. Also worth trying is *kalakukko*, a chunk of bread with pork and whitefish baked inside it – legendary around Kuopio but available almost everywhere. Expect to spend around 15mk for a chunk big enough for two. Slightly cheaper but just as filling, *lihapiirakka* are envelopes of pastry filled with rice and meat – ask for them with mustard (*sinappi*) and/or ketchup. Most train stations and the larger bus stations and supermarkets also have cafeterias proffering a selection of the above and other greasier nibbles.

Less exotically, the big **burger** franchises are widely found, as are the *Grilli* and *Nakkikioski* roadside fast-food stands turning out burgers, frankfurters and hot dogs for 14–20mk; they're always busiest when the pubs shut.

Finnish **supermarkets** – *Sokos*, *K-Kaupat*, *Pukeva* and *Centrum* are widespread names – are fairly standard affairs. In general, a substantial oval of dark ryebread (*ruisleipä*) costs about 7–10mk, ten *karjalan piirakkas* 14mk, a litre of milk 7mk, and a packet of biscuits around 12–14mk. Unusually, Finnish tinned **soup** (*keitto*) can be an excellent investment for self-catering, a usually flavoursome option containing hunks of meat and vegetables.

Coffee (*Kahvi*) is widely drunk and costs 7–12mk per cup; in a *baari* or *kahvila* it's sometimes consumed with a *pulla* – a kind of doughy bun. Coffee is normally drunk black, although milk is always there if you want it; you'll also commonly find espresso and cappuccino, although these are more expensive. **Tea** (*tee*) costs 5–10mk, depending on where you are and whether you want to indulge in some exotic brew. In rural areas, though, drinking it is considered a bit effete. When ordering tea, it's a good idea to insist that the water is boiling before the teabag is added – and that the bag is left in for more than two seconds.

Mensas, restaurants and pizzerias

If you're in a university town, the campus cafeteria or **student mensa** is the cheapest place to get a hot dish. Theoretically you have to be a student but you are unlikely to be asked for ID. There's a choice of three meals: *Kevytlounas* (*KL*), the "light menu", which usually comprises soup and bread; *Lounas* (*L*), the "ordinary menu", which consists of a smallish fish or meat dish with dessert; and *Herkkulounas* (*HL*), the "delicious menu" – a substantial and usually meat-based plateful. All three come with bread and coffee, and each one costs 15–22mk. Prices can be cut by half if you borrow a Finnish student ID card from a friendly diner. The busiest period is lunchtime (11.30am–12.30pm); later in the day (usually 4–6pm) many mensas offer price reductions. Most universities also have cafeterias where a small cup of coffee can cost as little as 3mk.

If funds stretch to it, you should sample at least once a *ravintola*, or **restaurant**, offering a lunchtime buffet table (*voileipäpöytä* or *seisova pöytä*), which will be stacked with tasty traditional goodies that you can feast on to your heart's content for a set price of around 75mk. Less costly Finnish food can be found in a *baari*: designed for working people and generally closing at 5pm or 6pm, a *baari* serves a range of Finnish dishes and snacks (and often the weaker beers; see "Drink", below). A good day for traditional Finnish food is Thursday, when every *baari* in the country dishes up *hernekeitto ja pannukakut*, thick pea soup with black rye bread, followed by oven-baked pancakes with strawberry jam, with buttermilk to wash it down – all for around 35mk. You'll get much the same fare from a *kahvila*, though a few of these, especially in the big cities, fancy themselves as being fashionable and may charge a few markkaa extra.

Although *ravintola* and *baaris* are plentiful, they're often outnumbered by **pizzerias**, as varied in quality here as they are in any other country but especially worth while for their lunch specials, when a set price of 35–55mk buys a pizza, coffee and everything you can carry from

the bread and salad bar. Many of the bigger pizza chains offer discounts for super-indulgence – such as a second pizza for half-price and a third for free if you can polish off the first two. **Vegetarians** are likely to become well acquainted with pizzerias – specific vegetarian restaurants are thin on the ground, even in major cities.

■ Drink

Finland's **alcohol laws** are as bizarre and almost as repressive as those of Norway and Sweden, but unlike in those countries, boozing is tackled enthusiastically, even regarded by some as an integral part of the national character. Some Finns, men in particular, often drink with the sole intention of getting paralytic; younger Finns are more inclined to regard the practice simply as an enjoyable social activity.

What to drink

Finnish spirits are much the same as you'd find in any country. **Beer** (*olut*), on the other hand, falls into three categories: "light beer" (I-Olut) – more like a soft drink; "medium-strength beer" (*Keskiolut*, III-Olut) – more perceptibly alcoholic and sold in many food shops and cafés; and "strong beer" (A-Olut or IV-Olut), which is on a par with the stronger international beers, and can only be bought at the *ALKO* shops and fully licensed (Grade A) restaurants and nightclubs.

The main – and cheapest – outlet for alcohol of any kind is the **ALKO** shop (Mon–Thurs 10am–5pm, Fri 10am–6pm, Sat 9am–2pm). Even the smallest town will have one of these, and prices don't vary. In an ALKO shop, strong beers like *Lapin Kulta Export* – an Arctic-originated mind blower – and the equally potent *Karjala*, *Lahden A*, *Olvi Export*, and *Koff* porter, cost 7.90–8.40mk for a 300ml bottle. Imported beers such as *Heineken*, *Carlsberg* and *Becks* go for 9.90–10.20mk a bottle. As for **spirits**, *Finlandia* vodka and *Jameson's* Irish Whiskey are 150mk and 190mk respectively per litre. There's also a very popular rough form of vodka called *Koskenkorva*, ideal for assessing the strength of your stomach lining, which costs 140mk. The best bargain in **wine** is reputedly the Hungarian variety, which changes hands for around 35mk per bottle, though you can buy bottles in ALKO for under 30mk. French wines range from 42mk to 285mk a bottle.

Where to drink

Most **restaurants** have a full licence, and some are actually frequented more for drinking than eating; it's these that we've listed under "Drinking" throughout the text. They're often also called bars or pubs by Finns simply for convenience. Just to add to the confusion, some so-called "Pubs" are not licensed; neither are *Baari*, mentioned above.

Along with ordinary restaurants, there are also **dance restaurants** (*tanssiravintola*). As the name suggests, these are places to dance rather than dine, although most do serve food as well as drink. They're popular with the over-forties, and before the advent of discos were the main places for people of opposite sex to meet. Even if you're under 40, dropping into one during the (usually early) evening sessions can be quite an eye-opener. Expect to pay a 14–35mk admission charge.

Once you've found somewhere to drink, there's a fairly rigid set of **customs** to contend with. Sometimes you have to queue outside the most popular bars since entry is permitted only if a seat is free – there's no standing. Only one drink per person is allowed on the table at any one time except in the case of *porter* – a stout which most Finns mix with regular beer. There's always either a doorman (*portsari*) – whom you must tip (5–7mk) on leaving – or a cloakroom into which you must check your coat on arrival (again 5–7mk). Bars are usually open until midnight or 1am and service stops half an hour before the place shuts. This is announced by a winking of the lights – the *valomerkki*.

Some bars and clubs have **waitress/waiter service**, whereby you order, and pay when your drinks are brought to you. A common order is *iso tuoppi* – a half-litre glass of draught beer, which costs 15–25mk (up to 35mk in some nightclubs). This might come slightly cheaper in **self-service** bars, where you select your tipple and queue up to pay at the till.

Wherever you buy alcohol, you'll have to be of **legal age**: at least 18 to buy beer and wine, and 20 or over to have a go at the spirits. ID will be checked if you look too young – or if the doorman's in a bad mood.

Directory

CANOEING With many lakes and rivers, Finland offers challenges to every type of canoe enthusiast, expert or beginner. There's plenty of easygoing paddling on the long lake systems, innumerable thrashing rapids to be shot, and abundant sea canoeing around the archipelagos of the south and southwest coast. Canoe rental (available wherever there are suitable waters) costs around 20mk per hour, 50–165mk per day, or 400mk per week, with prices dependent on the type of canoe. Many tourist offices have plans of local canoeing routes, and you can get general information from the Finnish Canoe Association, Radiokatu 2, 00240 Helsinki (☎09/158 2363).

CUSTOMS There are few, if any, border fomalities when entering Finland from another Scandinavian country by land (although the crossing from Norway at Näätämö is – at least in theory – closed to non-Scandinavians from 10pm to 7am). The same applies when crossing by sea; only by air do you usually need to show your passport.

DENTIST Seeing a dentist can be very expensive: expect to spend a minimum of 100mk. Look under "Hammaslääkäri" in the phone book, or ask at a tourist office.

DOCTOR Provided you're insured, you'll save time by seeing a doctor at a private health centre (*Lääkäriasema*) rather than queuing at a national health centre (*Terveyskeskus*). You are required to present a doctor's referral and a written statement confirming that you will pay the bill in order to stay in hospital.

EMERGENCIES ☎112.

FISHING Non-Scandinavians need a General Fishing Licence if they intend to fish in Finland's waterways; this costs 80mk (20mk for a 7-day period) from post offices and is valid for one year. In certain parts of the Arctic North you'll need an additional licence costing 30mk and obtainable locally. Throughout the country you'll also need the permission of the owner of the particular stretch of water, usually obtained by buying a permit on the spot. The nearest campsite or tourist office will have details of this, and advise on the regional variations on national fishing laws.

MARKETS In larger towns, these usually take place every day except Sunday from 7am to 2pm. There'll also be a market hall (*kauppahalli*) open weekdays 8am–5pm. Smaller places have a market once or twice a week, usually including Saturday.

NUDE BATHING Sections of some Finnish beaches are designated nude bathing areas, sometimes sex-segregated and occasionally with an admission charge of around 10mk. The local tourist office, or campsite, will have the facts.

PHARMACIES *Kemikaalikauppa* sell only cosmetics; for medicines you need to go to an *apteekki*, generally open daily 9am–6pm.

PUBLIC HOLIDAYS Shops and banks close on these days and most public transport will operate a Sunday schedule; museum opening hours may also be affected. January 1, May 1, December 6, December 24, 25 and 26. Variable dates: Epiphany (between January 6 and 12), Good Friday and Easter Weekend, the Saturday before Whit Sunday, Midsummer's Eve, All Saint's Day (the Saturday between October 31 and November 6).

SAUNAS These are cheapest at a public swimming pool, where you'll pay 10–20mk for a session. Hotel saunas, which are sometimes better equipped than public ones, are more expensive (30–40mk) but free to guests. Many Finnish people have saunas built into their homes and it's common for visitors to be invited to share one.

SHOPS Supermarkets are usually open Mon–Fri 9am–8pm, Sat 9am–6pm. Some in cities keep longer hours, for example 8am–10pm. In Helsinki the shops in Tunneli are open until 10pm. In the weeks leading up to Christmas some stores and markets are open on Sunday too.

FINNISH AND SWEDISH PLACE NAMES

On most maps and many transport timetables cities and towns are given their Finnish names followed by their Swedish names in parentheses. Both Swedes and Finnish-Swedes will frequently use the Swedish rather than the Finnish names. The main places in question are listed below, with the Finnish name first.

Helsinki (Helsingfors)
Porvoo (Borgå)
Turku (Åbo)
Pori (Björneborg)

Tampere (Tammerfors)
Mikkeli (St Michel)
Savonlinna (Nyslott)

Vaasa (Vasa)
Kokkola (Gamlakarleby)
Oulu (Uleåborg)

History

Finland's history, inextricably bound with the medieval superpowers, Sweden and Russia, and later with the Soviet Union, is a stirring tale of a small people's survival – and eventual triumph – over what have often seemed impossible odds. It's also a story that's been full of powerful contemporary resonances, as the other Baltic nations have succesfully striven to regain their own independence.

■ First settlements

As the ice sheets of the last Ice Age retreated, parts of the Finnish Arctic coast became inhabited by tribes from eastern Europe. They hunted bear and reindeer, and fished the well-stocked rivers and lakes: relics of their existence have been found and dated at around 8000 BC. Pottery skills from outside were introduced around 3000 BC, and trade with Russia and the east flourished. At the same time, other races from the east were arriving and merging with the established population: the **Boat Axe** culture (1800–1600 BC), which originated in central Europe, spread as Indo-Europeans migrated and the seafaring knowledge they possessed enabled them to begin trading with Sweden from the Finnish west coast. This is indicated by **Bronze Age** findings (around 1300 BC) concentrated in a narrow strip along the coast. The previous settlers withdrew eastwards and the advent of severe weather brought this period of occupation to an end.

■ The arrival of the Finns

The antecedents of the Finns were a primordial race based in central Russia who moved outward in two directions. One tribe went south, eventually to Hungary, and the other westward to the Baltic where it mixed with Latgals, Lithuanians and Germans. The latter, the "Baltic Finns", were migrants who crossed the Baltic around 400 AD to form an independent society in Finland. In 100 AD the Roman historian Tacitus had already described a wild and primitive people called "the Fenni". This is thought to have been a reference to the earliest **Sami**, who occupied Finland before this. With their more advanced culture, the Baltic Finns absorbed this indigenous population, although some of their pre-existing customs were maintained. The new Finns worked the land, utilized the vast forests and made lengthy fishing expeditions on the lakes.

■ The pagan era

The main Finnish settlements were along the west coast facing Sweden, with whom trade was established. The cessation of this trading, caused by the Swedish Vikings' opening up of routes to the east, in turn forced these western communities into decline. Meanwhile the Finnish south coast was exposed to seaborne raiding parties and most Finns moved inland and eastwards, a large number settling around the huge Lake Ladoga in **Karelia**. Eventually the people of Karelia were able to enjoy trade in two directions – with the Varangians to the east and the Swedes to the west. Groups from Karelia and the more northern territory of Kainuu regularly ventured into Lappland to fish and hunt. At the end of the pagan era Finland was split into three regions: Varsinais-Suomi ("Finland proper") in the southwest, Häme in the western part of the lake region, and Karelia in the east. Although they often helped one another, there was no formal cooperation between the inhabitants of these areas.

■ The Swedish era (1155–1809)

At the start of the tenth century, pagan Finland was neighboured by two opposing religions: Catholicism in Sweden on one side and the Orthodox Church of Russia on the other. The Russians wielded great influence in Karelia, but the west of Finland began to gravitate towards Catholicism on account of its high level of contact with Sweden. In 1155, King Erik of Sweden launched a crusade into Finland, and although its real purpose was to strengthen trade routes, it swept through the southwest leaving the English **Bishop Henry** at **Turku** to establish a parish. Henry was killed by a Finnish yeoman, but became the patron saint of the Turku diocese and the region became the administrative base of the whole country. Western Finland generally acquiesced to the Swedes, but Karelia didn't, becoming a territory much sought after by both the Swedes and the Russians. In 1323, under the **Treaty of Pähkinäsaari**, an official border was drawn up, giving the western part of Karelia to Sweden while the Russian principality of Novgorod retained the eastern section around Lake Ladoga. To emphasize their claim, the Russians founded the Orthodox **Valamo Monastery** on an island in the lake.

Under the Swedish crown, Finns still worked and controlled their own land, often living side by side with Swedes, who came to the west coast to safeguard sea trade. Finnish provincial leaders were given places among the nobility and in 1362 King Håkon gave Finland the right to vote in Swedish royal elections. When the Swedish throne was given to the German Albrecht of Mecklenburg, in 1364, there was little support for the new monarch in Finland, and much violent opposition to his forces who arrived to occupy the Swedish-built castles. Once established, the Mecklenburgians imposed forced labour and the Finnish standard of living swiftly declined. There was even a proposal that the country should be sold to the Teutonic Order of Knights.

In a campaign to wrest control of the Swedish realm, a Swedish noble, **Grip**, acquired control of one Finnish province after another and by 1374 was in charge of the whole country. In doing this he was obliged to consider the welfare of the Finns and consequently living conditions improved. Another effect of Grip's actions was to underline Finland's position as an individual country – under the Swedish sovereign but distanced from Sweden's political offices.

A testament by Grip was intended to ensure that Finnish affairs would be managed by the Swedish nobility irrespective of the wishes of the monarch. The nobility, however, found themselves forced to look for assistance to Margrethe, Queen of Denmark and Norway. She agreed to come to the Swedes' aid provided they recognized her as sovereign over all the Swedish realm including Finland. This resulted in the **Kalmar Union** of 1397.

While the Finns were barely affected by the constitution of the Union, there was a hope that it would guarantee their safety against the Russians, whose expansionist policies were an increasing threat. Throughout the fifteenth century there were repeated skirmishes between Russians and Finns in the border lands and around the important Finnish Baltic trading centre of Viipuri (now Russian Vyborg).

The election of King Charles VIII in 1438 caused a rift in the Union and serious strife between Sweden and Denmark. He was forced to abdicate in 1458 but his support in Finland was strong, and his successor, Christian I, sent an armed column to subdue Finnish unrest. While Turku Castle was under siege, the Danish noble **Erik Axelsson Tott**, already known and respected in the country, called a meeting of representatives from every Finnish estate where it was agreed that Christian I would be acknowledged as king of the Union.

Tott went on to take command of Viipuri Castle and was able to function almost independently of central government. Although he planned to make Viipuri the major centre for east–west trade, resources had to be diverted to strengthening the eastern defences. During the 1460s Novgorod was forced into Moscow's sphere of influence and finally absorbed altogether. This left Finland's eastern edge more exposed than ever before. Novgorod had long held claims on large sections of Karelia, and the border situation was further confused by the Finnish peasants who had drifted eastwards and settled in the disputed territories. Part of Tott's response to the dangers was to erect the fortress of **Olavinlinna** (in the present town of Savonlinna) in 1475, actually inside the land claimed by Russia.

Tott died in 1481 and **Sten Sture**, a Swedish regent, forced the remaining Axelssons to relinquish their familial domination of Finland. By 1487 Sture had control of the whole country, and appointed bailiffs of humble birth – instead of established aristocrats – to the Finnish castles in return for their surplus revenue. These monies were used to finance Sture's ascent through the Swedish nobility. As a result nothing was spent on maintaining the eastern defences.

Strengthened by an alliance with Denmark signed in 1493, Russia attacked Viipuri on November 30, 1495. The troops were repulsed by the technically inferior Finns, an achievement perceived as a miracle. After further battles it was agreed that the borders of the Treaty of Pähkinäsaari would remain. However, the Swedes drew up a bogus version of the treaty in which the border retained its fifteenth-century position, and it was this forgery which they used in negotiations with the Russians over the next hundred years.

Within Finland a largely Swedish-born nobility became established. Church services were conducted in Finnish although Swedish remained the language of commerce and officialdom. Because the bulk of the population was illiterate, any important deed had to be read to them. In the thirteenth and fourteenth centuries, any Finns who felt oppressed simply moved into the wild lands of the interior – out of earshot of church bells. Partly because the peasants still placed their faith in their ancient creeds, the **Reformation** was able to pass through Finland without bloodshed.

By the time **Gustav Vasa** took the Swedish throne in 1523, many villages were established in the disputed border regions. Almost every inhabitant spoke Finnish. but there was a roughly equal division between those communities who paid taxes to the Swedish king and those who paid them to the Russian tsar. In the winter of 1555, a Russian advance into Karelia was quashed at Joutselkä by Finns using skis to travel speedily over the icy roads, a victory that made the Finnish nobility confident of success in a full-scale war. While hesitant, Vasa finally agreed to their wishes: 12,000 troops from Sweden were dispatched to eastern Finland, and an offensive launched in the autumn of 1556. It failed, with the Russians reaching the gates of Viipuri, and Vasa retreating to the Åland Islands, asking for peace.

In 1556 Gustav Vasa made Finland a Swedish Grand Duchy and gave his son, Johan, the title Duke of Finland. It was rumoured that **Duke Johan** not only spoke Finnish but was an advocate of Finnish nationalism. These claims were exaggerated, but the duke was certainly pro-Finnish, surrounding himself with Finnish nobles and founding a chancery and an exchequer. He moved into Turku Castle and furnished it in splendour. However, the powers of his office, as defined by the Articles of Arboga, were breached by a subsequent invasion of Livonia and he was sentenced to death by the Swedish Diet in 1563, although the king's power of pardon was acknowledged. Finland was divided between loyalty towards the friendly duke and the need to keep on good terms with the Swedish crown, now held by Erik XIV. The Swedish forces sent to collect Johan laid siege to Turku castle for three weeks, executing thirty nobles before capturing the duke and imprisoning him.

The war between Sweden and Denmark over control of the Baltic took its toll on Erik. He became mentally unbalanced, slaying several prisoners who were being held for trial, and, in a moment of complete madness, released Johan from detention. The Swedish nobles were incensed by Erik's actions and rebelled against him – with the result that Johan became king in 1568.

In 1570 Swedish resources were stretched when hostilities again erupted with Russia, now ruled by the aggressive Tsar Ivan ("the Terrible") IV. The conflict was to last 25 years, a period known in Finland as **"The Long Wrath"**. It saw the introduction of a form of conscription instead of the reliance on mercenary soldiers, which had been the norm in other Swedish wars. Able-bodied men aged between 15 and 50 were rounded up by the local bailiff and about one in ten selected for military service. Russia occupied almost all of Estonia and made deep thrusts into southern Finland. Finally the Swedish-Finnish troops regained Estonia and made significant advances through Karelia, capturing an important eastern European trading route. The war was formally concluded in 1595 by the **Treaty of Täyssinä**. Under its terms, Russia recognized the lands gained by Sweden and the eastern border was altered to reach up to the Arctic coast, enabling Finns to settle in the far north.

Sweden was established as the dominant force in the Baltic, but under Gustav II, who became king in 1611, Finland began to lose the special status it had previously enjoyed. Its administration was streamlined and centralized, causing many Finnish nobles to move to Stockholm. Civic orders had to be written rather than passed on orally, and many ambitious Finns gave themselves Swedish surnames. Finnish manpower supported Swedish efforts overseas – the soldiers gaining a reputation as wild and fearless fighters – but brought no direct benefit to Finland itself. Furthermore, the peasants were increasingly burdened by the taxes needed to support the Swedish wars with Poland, Prussia and Germany.

Conditions continued to decline until 1637, when **Per Brahe** was appointed governor-general. Against the prevailing mood of the time, he insisted that all officers should study Finnish, founded Turku University – the country's first – and instigated a successful programme to spread literacy among the Finnish people. After concluding his second term of office in 1654 he parted with the terse but accurate summary: "I was highly satisfied with this country and the country highly satisfied with me."

A terrible harvest in 1696 caused a **famine** that killed a third of the Finnish population. The fact that no aid came from Sweden intensified feelings of neglect and stirred up a minor bout of Finnish nationalism led by **Daniel Juslenius**. His book, *Aboa Vetus Et Nova*, published in 1700, claimed Finnish to be a founding language of the world and Finns to be descendants of the tribes of Israel.

In 1711 Viipuri fell to the Russians. Under their new tsar, Peter ("the Great"), the Russians quickly spread across the country, causing the nobility to flee to Stockholm and Swedish commanders to be more concerned with salvaging their army than saving Finland. In 1714, eight years of Russian occupation – **"The Great Wrath"** – began. Descriptions of the horrors of these times have been exaggerated, but nonetheless the events confirmed the Finns' long-time dread of their eastern neighbour. The Russians saw Finland simply as a springboard to attack Sweden, and laid waste to anything in it which the Swedes might attempt to regain.

Under the **Treaty of Uusikaupunki**, in 1721, the tsar gave back much of Finland but retained Viipuri, east Karelia, Estonia and Latvia, and thus control of the Baltic. Finland now had a new eastern border that was totally unprotected. Russian occupation was inevitable but would be less disastrous if entered into voluntarily. The Finnish peasants, with Swedish soldiers forcibly billeted on them, remained loyal to the king but with little faith in what he could do to protect them.

The aggressive policies of the Hats in the Swedish Diet led to the 1741 declaration of war on Russia. With barely an arm raised against them, Russian troops again occupied Finland – the start of **"The Lesser Wrath"** – until the **Treaty of Turku** in 1743. Under this, the Russians withdrew, ceded a section of Finland back to Sweden but moved their border west.

■ The Russian era (1809–1917)

In an attempt to force Sweden to join Napoleon's economic blockade, Russia, under Tsar Alexander I, attacked and occupied Finland in 1807. The **Treaty of Hamina**, signed in September of that year, legally ceded all of the country to Russia. The tsar had needed a friendly country close to Napoleon's territory as a reliable ally in case of future hostilities between the two leaders. To gain Finnish favour, he had guaranteed beneficial terms at the Diet (based in Porvoo) in 1809 and subsequently Finland became an **autonomous Russian Grand Duchy**. There was no conscription and taxation was frozen at its current level, making it virtually nothing for years to come, while realignment of the northern section of the Finnish–Russian border gave additional land to Finland. Finns could freely occupy positions in the Russian empire, although Russians were denied equal opportunities within Finland. The long period of peace that ensued saw a great improvement in Finnish wealth and well-being.

After returning Viipuri to Finland, the tsar declared Helsinki the **capital** in 1812, regarding Turku as too close to Sweden for safety. The "Guards of Finland" helped crush the Polish rebellion and fought in the Russo-Turkish conflict. This, along with the French and English attacks on Finnish harbours during the Crimean War, accentuated the bond between the two countries. Many Finns came to regard the tsar as their own monarch.

There was, however, an increasingly active **Finnish-language movement**. A student leader, the future statesman **Johan Vilhelm Snellman,** had met the tsar and demanded that Finnish replace Swedish as the country's official language. Snellman's slogan "Swedes we are no longer, Russians we cannot become, we must be Finns" became the rallying cry of the **Fennomen**. The Swedish-speaking ruling class, feeling threatened, had Snellman removed from his university post and he retreated to Kuopio to publish newspapers espousing his beliefs. His opponents cited Finnish as the language of peasants, unfit for cultured use – a claim undermined by the efforts of a playwright, **Aleksis Kivi**, whose works marked the beginning of Finnish-language theatre. In 1835, the collection of Karelian folk tales published in Finnish by **Elias Lönnrot** as the *Kalevala* was the first written record of Finnish folklore, and became a literary focal point for Finnish nationalism.

The liberal tsar Alexander II appointed Snellman to Turku University, from where he went on to become minister of finance. In 1858 Finnish was declared the official language of local government in areas where the majority of the population were Finnish speaking. And the Diet, convened in 1863 for the first time since the Russian takeover, finally gave native-tongued Finns equal status with Swedish speakers. The only opposition was from the so-called **Svecomen**, who sought not only the maintenance of the Swedish language but unification with Finland's westerly neighbour.

The increasingly powerful Pan-Slavist contingent in Russia was horrified by the growth of the Finnish timber industry and the rise of trade with the west. They were also unhappy with the special status of the Grand Duchy, considering the Finns an alien race who would contaminate the eastern empire by their links with the west. Tsar Alexander III was not swayed by these opinions but, after his assassination in 1894, Nicholas I came to power and instigated a **Russification process**. Russian was declared the official language, Finnish money was abolished and plans were laid to merge the Finnish army into the Russian army. To pass these measures the tsar drew up the unconstitutional **February Manifesto**.

Opposition came in varying forms. In 1899, a young composer called **Jean Sibelius** wrote *Finlandia*. The Russians banned all performances of it "under any name that indicates its patriotic character", causing Sibelius to publish it as *Opus 26 No. 7*. The painter **Akseli Gallen-Kallela** ignored international art trends and depicted scenes from the *Kalevala* with his brush, as did the poet **Eino Leino** with his pen. Students skied to farms all over the country and collected half a million signatures against the Manifesto. Over a thousand of Europe's foremost intellectuals signed a document called *Pro-Finlandia*.

But these had no effect, and in 1901 the **Conscription Law** was introduced. This forced Finns to serve directly under the tsar in the Russian army. A programme of civil disobedience began, the leaders of which were soon obliged to go underground, where they titled themselves the *Kagel* – borrowing a name used by persecuted Russian Jews. The Finnish population became divided between the "compliants" (acquiescent to the Manifesto) and the "constitutionalists" (against the Manifesto), splitting families and even causing the rival sides to do their shopping in different stores.

The stand against conscription was enough to make the Russians drop the scheme, but their grip was tightened in other ways. A peaceful demonstration in Helsinki was broken up by cossacks on horseback, and in April 1903 the tsar installed the tough **Bobrikov** as governor-general, giving him new and sweeping powers. The culmination of sporadic acts of violence came on June 16, 1904, when the Finnish civil servant **Eugen Schauman** climbed the Senate staircase and shot Bobrikov three times before turning the gun on himself. After staggering to his usual Senate seat, Bobrikov collapsed and died – and his assassin became a national hero.

In 1905, the Russians suffered defeat in their war with Japan and the general strike that broke out in their country spread to Finland, the Finnish labour movement being represented by the Social Democratic Party. The revolutionary spirit that was moving through Russia encouraged the conservative Finnish Senate to reach a compromise with the demands of the Social Democrats, and the result was a gigantic upheaval in the Finnish parliamentary system. In 1906, the country adopted a single-chamber parliament (the *Eduskunta*) elected by national suffrage – Finnish women being the first in Europe to get the vote. In the first election under the new system the Social Democrats won eighty seats out of the total of two hundred, making it the most left-wing legislature seen so far in Europe.

Any laws passed in Finland, however, still needed the ratification of the tsar, who now viewed Finland as a dangerous forum for leftist debate (the exiled Lenin met Stalin for the first time in Tampere). In 1910, Nicholas II removed the new parliament's powers and reinstated the Russification programme. Two years later the **Parity Act** gave Russians in Finland status equal to Finns, enabling them to hold seats in the Senate and posts in the civil service. The outspoken anti-tsarist parliamentary speaker **P.E. Svinhufvud** was exiled to Siberia for a second time.

As World War I commenced, Finland was obviously allied with Russia and endured a commercial blockade, food shortages and restrictions on civil liberties, but did not actually fight on the tsar's behalf. Germany promised Finland total autonomy in the event of victory for the kaiser and provided clandestine military training to about two thousand Finnish students – the *jäger* movement who reached Germany through Sweden and later fought against the Russians as a light infantry battalion on the Baltic front.

■ Towards independence

When the tsar was overthrown in 1917, the Russian provisional government under Kerensky declared the measures taken against Finland null and void and restored the previous level of autonomy. Within Finland there was uncertainty over the country's constitutional bonds with Russia. The conservative view was that prerogative powers should be passed from the deposed ruler to the provisional government, while socialists held that the provisional government had no right to exercise power in Finland and that supreme authority should be passed to the *Eduskunta*.

Under the **Power Act**, the *Eduskunta* vested in itself supreme authority within Finland, leaving only control of foreign and military matters residing with the Russians. Kerensky refused to recognize the Power Act and dissolved the Finnish parliament, forcing a fresh election. This time a bigger poll returned a conservative majority.

The loss of their parliamentary majority and the bitterness felt towards the bourgeois-dominated Senate, who happily complied with Kerensky's demands, made the Social Democrats adopt a more militant line. Around the country there had been widespread labour disputes and violent confrontations between strikers and strike-breaking mobs hired by landowners. The Social Democrats sanctioned the formation of an armed workers' guard, soon to be called the **Red Guard**, in response to the growing **White Guard** – a right-wing private army operating in the virtual absence of a regular police force. A general strike was called on November 13, which forced the *Eduskunta* into reforms after just a few days. The strike was called off but a group of dissident Red Guards threatened to break from the Social Democrats and continue the action.

After the Bolsheviks took power in Russia, the conservative Finnish government became fearful of Soviet involvement in Finnish affairs and a *de facto* **statement of independence** was made. The socialists, by now totally excluded from government, declared their support for independence but insisted that it should be reached through negotiation with the Soviet Union. Instead, on December 6, a draft of an independent constitution drawn up by **K.J. Ståhlberg** was approved by the *Eduskunta*. After a delay of three weeks it was formally recognized by the Soviet leader, Lenin.

■ The Civil War

In asserting its new authority, the government repeatedly clashed with the labour movement. The Red Guard, who had reached an uneasy truce with the Social Democratic leadership, were involved in gunrunning between Viipuri and Petrograd, and efforts by the White Guard to halt it led to full-scale fighting. A vote passed by the *Eduskunta* on January 12, 1918, empowered the government to create a police force to restore law and order. On January 25, the White Guard was legitimized as the Civil Guard.

In Helsinki, a special committee of the Social Democrats took the decision to resist the Civil Guard and seize power, effectively pledging themselves to **civil war**. On January 27 and 28, a series of occupations enabled leftist committees to take control of the capital and the major towns of the south. Three government ministers who evaded capture fled to Vaasa and formed a rump administration. Meanwhile, a Finnish-born aristocrat, **C.G.E. Mannerheim**, who had served as a cavalry officer in the Russian army, arrived at the request of the government in Ostrobothnia, a region dominated by right-wing farmers, to train a force to fight the Reds.

Mannerheim, who had secured a 15 million markkaa loan from a Helsinki bank to finance his army, drew on the German-trained *jäger* for officers, while the Ostrobothnian farmers – seeking to protect their landowning privileges – along with a small number of Swedish volunteers, made up the troops. Their initial task was to "mop up" the Russian battalions remaining in western Finland, which had been posted there by the tsar to prevent German advancement in the world war, and which by now were politicized into Soviets. Mannerheim had achieved this by the beginning of February, and his attention then turned to the Reds.

The Whites were in control of Ostrobothnia, northern Finland and parts of Karelia, and were connected by a railway from Vaasa to Käkisalmi on Lake Ladoga. Although the Reds were numerically superior they were poorly equipped and poorly trained, and failed to break the enemy's line of communication. Tampere fell to the Whites in March. At the same time, a German force landed on the south coast, their assistance requested by White Finns in Berlin (although Mannerheim opposed their involvement). Surrounded, the leftists' resistance collapsed in April.

Throughout the conflict, the Social Democratic Party maintained a high level of unity. While containing revolutionary elements, it was led mainly by socialists seeking to retain parliamentary democracy and believing their fight was against a bourgeois force seeking to impose right-wing values on the newly independent state. Their arms, however, were supplied by the Soviet Union, causing the White taunt that the Reds were "aided by foreign bayonets". Many of the revolutionary socialists within the party fled to Russia after the civil war, where they formed the Finnish Communist Party. The harsh treatment of the Reds who were captured – 8000 were executed and 80,000 were imprisoned in camps where more than 9000 died from hunger or disease – fired a resentment that would last for generations. The Whites regarded the war as one of liberation, ridding the country of Russians and the Bolshevik influence, and setting the course for an anti-Russian Finnish nationalism.

Mannerheim and the strongly pro-German *jäger* contingent were keen to continue east, to gain the whole of Karelia from the Russians, but the possibility of direct Finnish assistance to the Russian White Army, seeking to overthrow the Bolshevik government, came to nothing through the Russian Whites' refusal to guarantee recognition of Finland's independent status. Later that year, a provisional government of independent Karelia was set up in Uhtua. Its formation was masterminded by Red Finns, who ensured that its claims to make Karelia a totally independent region did not accord with the desires of the Finnish government. The provisional government's congress, held the following year, further confirmed a wish for separation from the Soviet Union and requested the removal of the Soviet troops who now held positions vacated by the Allies. This was agreed with a proviso that Soviet troops retained a right to be based in eastern Karelia. The collapse of the talks caused the provisional government and its supporters to flee to Finland as a Finnish battalion of the Soviet Red Army moved in and occupied the area. Subsequently the Karelian Workers' Commune, motivated by the Finnish Communists and backed by Soviet decree, was formed.

A few days later, the state of war which existed between Finland and Russia was formally ended by the **Treaty of Tartu**. The existence of the Karelian Workers' Commune gave the Soviet negotiators a pretext for refusing Finnish demands for Karelian self-determination, claiming the new set-up to be an expression of the Karelian people's wishes. The treaty was signed in an air of animosity. A bald settlement of border issues, it gave Finland the Petsamo area, a shoulder of land extending to the Arctic coast.

■ The Republic

The White success in the civil war led to a right-wing government with a pro-German majority, which wanted to establish Finland as a monarchy rather than the republic allowed for under the 1917 declaration of independence. Although twice defeated in the *Eduskunta*, Prime Minister **J.K. Paasikivi** evoked a clause in the Swedish Form of Government from 1772, making legal the election of a king. As a result, the Finnish crown was offered to a German, Friedrich Karl, Prince of Hessen. Immediately prior to German defeat in the world war, the prince declined the invitation. The victorious Allies insisted on a new Finnish government and a fresh general election if they were to recognize the nation's independent status. Since the country was now compelled to look to the Allies for future assistance, the request was complied with, sealing Finland's future as a republic. The first president was the liberal **Ståhlberg**.

The termination of the monarchists' aims upset the unity of the right and paved the way for a succession of centrist governments. These were dominated by two parties, the **National Progressives** and the **Agrarians**. Through a period of rapidly increasing prosperity, numerous reforms were enacted. Farmers who rented land were given the opportunity to buy it with state aid, compulsory schooling was introduced, laws regarding religious freedom were passed and the provision of social services strengthened. As more farmers became independent producers, the Agrarians, claiming to represent the rural interests, drew away much of the Social Democrats' traditional support.

Finnish economic development halted abruptly following the world slump of the late 1920s. A series of strikes culminated in a dock workers' dispute which began in May 1928 and continued for almost a year. It was settled by the intervention of the Minister for Social Affairs on terms perceived as a defeat for the strikers. The dispute was seen by the right as a communist-inspired attempt to ruin the Finnish export trade at a time when the Soviet Union had re-entered the world timber trade. It was also a symbolic ideological clash – a pointer to future events.

Moves to outlaw communist activity had been deemed an infringement of civil rights, but in 1929 the *Suomen Lukko* was formed to legally combat communism. It was swiftly succeeded by the more extreme and violent **Lapua Movement** (the name coming from the Ostrobothnian town, where a parade of communist youth had been brought to a bloody end by "White" farmers). The Lapuans rounded up suspected communists and communist sympathizers, and drove them to the Russian border, insisting that they walk across. Even the former president, Ståhlberg, was kidnapped and dumped at the eastern town of Joensuu. The Lapuans' actions were only half-heartedly condemned by the non-socialist parties, and in private they were supported. But when the Lapuans began advocating a complete overthrow of the political system, much of this tacit approval dried up.

The government obtained a two-thirds majority in the elections of October 1930 and amended the constitution to make communist activity illegal. This was expected to placate the Lapuans but instead they issued even more extreme demands, including the abolition of the Social Democrats. In 1932, a coup d'état was attempted by a Lapuan group who prevented a socialist member of parliament from addressing a meeting in Mäntsälä, 50km north of Helsinki. They refused to disperse, despite shots being fired by police, and sent for assistance from Lapuan bases around the country. The Lapuan leadership took up the cause and broadcast demands for a new government. They were unsuccessful because of the loyalty of the troops who surrounded the town on the orders of the then prime minister, Svinhufvud. Following this, the Lapuans were outlawed, although their leaders received only minor punishments for their deeds. Several of them regrouped as the Nazi-style Patriotic People's Movement. But unlike the parallel movements in Europe, there was little in Finland on which Nazism could focus mass hatred, and, despite winning a few parliamentary seats, it quickly declined into insignificance.

The Finnish **economy** recovered swiftly, and much international goodwill was generated when the country became the only nation to fully pay its war reparations to the USA after World War I. Finland joined the League of Nations hoping for a guarantee of its eastern border, but by 1935 the League's weakness was apparent and the Finns looked to traditionally neutral **Scandinavia** for protection as Europe moved towards war.

■ World War II

The Nazi–Soviet Non-Aggression Pact of August 1939 put Finland firmly into the Soviet sphere. Stalin had compelled Estonia, Latvia and Lithuania to allow Russian bases on their land, and in October was demanding a chunk of the Karelian isthmus from Finland to protect Leningrad, as well as a leasing of the Hanko peninsula on the Finnish Baltic coast. Russian troops were heading towards the Finnish border from Murmansk, and on November 30 the Karelian isthmus was attacked – an act that triggered the **Winter War**.

Stalin had had the tsarist military commanders executed, and his troops were led by young communists well versed in ideology but ignorant of war strategy. Informed that the Finnish people would welcome them as liberators, the Soviet soldiers anticipated little resistance to their invasion. They expected to reach the Finnish west coast within ten days and therefore carried no overcoats, had little food, and camped each night in open fields. The Finns, although vastly outnumbered, were defending their homes and farms as well as their hard-won independence. Familiarity with the terrain enabled them to conceal themselves in the forests and attack through stealth – and they were prepared for the winter temperatures, which plunged to -30°C (-18°F). The Russians were slowly picked off and their camps frequently surrounded and destroyed.

While Finland gained the world's admiration, no practical help was forthcoming and it became simply a matter of time before Stalin launched a better-supplied, unstoppable advance. It came during February 1940 and the Finnish government was forced to ask for peace. This was granted under the **Treaty of Moscow**, signed in March by President **Kyösti Kallio**, who cursed "let the hand wither that signs such a paper" as his hand put pen to paper. The treaty ceded 11 percent of Finnish territory to the Soviet Union. There was a mass exodus from these areas, with nearly half a million people travelling west to the new boundaries of Finland. Kyösti Kallio was later paralyzed on his right side.

The period immediately following the Winter War left Finland in a difficult position. Before the war, Finland had produced all its own food but was dependent on imported fertilizers. Supplies of grain, which had been coming from Russia, were halted as part of Soviet pressure for increased transit rights and access to the important nickel-producing mines in Petsamo. Finland became reliant on grain from Germany and British shipments to the Petsamo coast, which were interrupted when Germany invaded Norway. In return for providing arms, Germany was given transit rights through Finland. Legally, this required the troops to be constantly moving, but a permanent force became stationed at Rovaniemi.

The Finnish leadership knew that Germany was secretly preparing to attack the Soviet Union, and a broadcast from Berlin had spoken of a "united front" from Norway to Poland at a time when Finland was officially outside the Nazi sphere. Within Finland there was little support for the Nazis, but there was a fear of Soviet occupation. While Finland clung to its neutrality, refusing to fight unless attacked, it was drawn closer and closer to Germany. Soviet air raids on several Finnish towns in June 1941 finally led Finland into the war on the side of the Nazis. The ensuing conflict with the Russians, fought with the primary purpose of regaining territory lost in the Winter War, became known as **the Continuation War**. The bulk of the land ceded under the Treaty of Moscow was recovered by the end of August. After this, Mannerheim, who commanded the Finnish troops, ignored Nazi encouragement to assist in their attack on Leningrad. A request from the British prime minister, Winston Churchill, that the Finns cease their advance, was also refused, although Mannerheim didn't cut the Murmansk railway which was moving Allied supplies. Even so, Britain was forced to acknowledge the predicament of its ally, the Soviet Union, and declared war on Finland in December 1941.

In 1943, the German defeat at Stalingrad, which made Allied victory almost inevitable, had a profound impact in Finland. Mannerheim called a meeting of inner-cabinet ministers and decided to seek a truce with the Soviet Union. The USA stepped forward as mediators but announced that the peace terms set by Moscow were too severe to be worthy of negotiation. Germany meanwhile had learned of the Finnish initiative and demanded an undertaking that Finland would not seek peace with Russia, threatening to withdraw supplies if it was not given. (The Germans were also unhappy with Finnish sympathy for Jews. Several hundred who had escaped from central Europe were saved from the concentration camps by being granted Finnish citizenship.) Simultaneously, a Russian advance into Karelia made Finland dependent on German arms to launch a counterattack. An agreement with the Germans was signed by President **Risto Ryti** in June 1944 without the consent of the *Eduskunta*, thereby making the deed invalid when he ceased to be president.

Ryti resigned the presidency at the beginning of August and Mannerheim informed Germany that the agreement was no longer binding. A peace with the Soviet Union was signed in Moscow two weeks later. Under its terms, Finland was forced to give up the Pestamo region and the border was restored to its 1940 position. The Hanko peninsula was returned but instead the Porkkala peninsula, nearer to Helsinki, was to be leased to the Soviet Union for fifty years. There were stinging reparations. The Finns also had to drive the remaining Germans out of the country within two weeks. This was easily done in the south, but the bitter fighting that took place in Lappland caused the total destruction of many towns. It was further agreed that organizations disseminating anti-Soviet views within Finland would be dissolved and that Finland would accept an Allied Control Commission to oversee war trials.

■ The postwar period

After the war, the Communist Party was legalized and, along with militant socialists expelled from the Social Democratic Party, formed a broad leftist umbrella organization – the **Finnish People's Democratic League**. Their efforts to absorb the Social Democrats were resisted by that party's moderate leadership, who regarded communism as "poison to the Finnish people". In the first peace-time poll, the Democratic League went to the electorate with a populist rather than revolutionary manifesto – something that was to characterize future Finnish communism. Both they and the Social Democrats attained approximately a quarter of the vote. Bolstered by two Social Democratic defections, the Democratic League narrowly became the largest party in the *Eduskunta*. The two of them, along with the Agrarian Party, formed an alliance ("The Big Three Agreement") that held the balance of power in a coalition government under the premiership of Paasikivi.

Strikes instigated by communist-controlled trade unions allowed the Social Democrats to accuse the Democratic League of seeking to undermine the production of machinery and other goods destined for the Soviet Union under the terms of the war reparation agreement, thereby creating a scenario for Soviet invasion. Charges of communist vote-rigging in trade union ballots helped the Social Democrats to gain control of the unions. The Democratic League won only 38 seats in the general election of 1948, and rejected the token offer of four posts in the new government, opting instead to stay in opposition. Their electoral campaign wasn't helped by the rumour – almost certainly groundless – that they were planning a Soviet-backed coup.

To ensure that the terms of the peace agreement were adhered to, the Soviet-dominated Allied Control Commission stayed in Finland until 1947. Its presence engendered a tense atmosphere both on the streets of Helsinki – there were several incidents of violence against Soviet officers – and in the numerous clashes with the Finnish government over the war trials. Unlike the eastern European countries under full Soviet occupation, Finland was able to conduct its own trials, but had to satisfy the Commission that they were conducted properly. Delicate manoeuvring by the Chief of Justice, **Urho Kekkonen**, resulted in comparatively short prison sentences for the accused, the longest being ten years for Risto Ryti.

The uncertain relationship between Finland and the Soviet Union was resolved, to some extent, by the signing of the **Treaty of Friendship, Cooperation and Mutual Assistance** (FCMA) in 1948. It confirmed Finnish responsibility for its own defence and pledged the country not to join any alliance hostile to the Soviet Union. In the suspicious atmosphere of the Cold War, the treaty was perceived by the western powers to place Finland firmly under Soviet influence. The Soviet insistence that the treaty was a guarantee of neutrality was viewed as hypocritical while they were still leasing the Porkkala peninsula. When it became clear that Finland was not becoming a Soviet satellite and had full control over its internal affairs, the USA reinstated credit facilities – carefully structured to avoid financing anything that would be of help to the Soviets – and Finland was admitted to western financial institutions such as the IMF and World Bank.

The postwar **economy** was dominated by the reparations demand. Much of the bill was paid off in ships and machinery, which established engineering as a major industry. The escalating world demand for timber products boosted exports, but inflation soared and led to frequent wage disputes. In 1949 an attempt to enforce a piece-work rate in a pulp factory in Kemi culminated in two workers being shot by police, a state of emergency being declared in the town, and the arrest of communist leaders. Economic conflicts reached a climax in 1956 after right-wingers in the *Eduskunta* had blocked an annual extension of government controls on wages and prices. This caused a sharp rise in the cost of living and the trade unions demanded appropriate pay increases. A general strike followed, lasting for three weeks until the strikers' demands were met. Any benefit, however, was quickly cancelled out by further price rises.

In 1957, a split occurred in the Social Democrats between urban and rural factions, the former seeking increased industrialization and the streamlining of unprofitable farms, the latter pursuing high agricultural subsidies. At the annual party conference, **Väinö Tanner** was elected chairman. His hopes for restoring unity were dashed by the pro-urban secretary Leskinen, who filled the party with his supporters. By 1959 the breakaway ruralists had set up the Small Farmers' Social Democratic Union and formed a new trade union organization, causing a rift within the country's internal politics that was to have important repercussions in Finland's dealings with the Soviet Union. Although the government had no intention of changing its foreign policy, Tanner had a well-known antipathy to the Soviet Union. Coupled with a growing number of anti-Soviet newspaper editorials, this precipitated the **"night frost"** of 1958. The Soviet leader, Khruschev, suspended imports and deliveries of machinery, causing a rise in Finnish unemployment. **Kekkonen**, elected president in 1956, personally intervened in the crisis by meeting with Khruschev, angering the Social Democrats, who accused Kekkonen of behaving undemocratically; meanwhile the Agrarians were lambasted for failing to stand up to Soviet pressure.

In 1960, Tanner was re-elected as chairman and the Social Democrats continued to attack Kekkonen. The Agrarians refused to enter government with the Social Democrats unless they changed their policies. As global relations worsened during 1961, the Soviet Union sent a note to Kekkonen requesting a meeting to discuss the section of the 1948 treaty dealing with defence of the Finnish–Soviet border. This was the precursor to the **"note crisis"**. The original note went unanswered, but the Finnish foreign secretary went to Moscow for exploratory talks with his opposite number. Assurances of Soviet confidence in Finnish foreign policy were given, but fears were expressed about the anti-Kekkonen alliance of conservatives and Social Democrats formed to contest the 1962 presidential election. Kekkonen again tried to defuse the crisis himself: using his constitutional powers he dissolved parliament early, forcing the election forward by several months and in so doing weakened the alliance. Kekkonen was re-elected and foreign policy remained unchanged. This was widely regarded as a personal victory for Kekkonen and a major turning point in relations with the Soviet Union. Through all subsequent administrations, the maintenance of the **Paasikivi-Kekkonen line** on foreign policy became a symbol of national unity.

Following Tanner's retirement from politics in 1963, the Social Democrats ended their stand against the established form of foreign policy, making possible their re-entry to government.

Throughout the early 1960s there was mounting dissatisfaction within the People's Democratic League towards the old pro-Moscow leadership. In 1965, a moderate non-communist was elected as the League's general secretary, and two years later he became chairman; a similar change took place in the communist leadership of the trade unions. The new-look communists pledged their desire for a share in government. The election of May 1966 resulted in a "popular front" government dominated by the Social Democrats and the People's Democratic League, under the prime ministership of **Rafael Paasio**.

This brought to an end a twenty-year spell of centre-right governments in which the crucial pivot had been the Agrarian Party. In 1965, the Agrarians changed their name to the Centre Party, aiming to modernize their image and become more attractive to the urban electorate. A challenge to this new direction was mounted by the **Finnish Rural Party**, founded by a breakaway group of Agrarians in the late 1950s, who mounted an increasingly influential campaign on behalf of "the forgotten people" – farmers and smallholders in declining rural areas. In the election of 1970 they gained 10 percent of the vote, but in subsequent years lost support through internal divisions.

The communists retained governmental posts until 1971, when they too were split – between the young "reformists" who advocated continued participation in government, and the older, hardline "purists" who were frustrated by the failure to implement socialist economic policies, and preferred to stay in opposition.

■ Modern Finland

Throughout the postwar years Finland promoted itself vigorously as a **neutral country**. It joined the United Nations in 1955 and Finnish soldiers became an integral part of the UN Peace-Keeping Force. In 1969 preparations were started for the European Security Conference in Helsinki, and in 1972 the city was the venue for the **Strategic Arms Limitation Talks (SALT)**, underlining a Finnish role in mediation between the superpowers. But an attempt to have a clause stating Finland's neutrality inserted into the 1970 extension-signing of the FCMA Treaty was opposed by the Soviet Union, whose foreign secretary, Andrei Gromyko, had a year earlier defined Finland not as neutral but as a "peace-loving neighbour of the Soviet Union".

In 1971 the revelations of a Czech defector, General Sejna, suggesting that the Soviet army was equipped to take over Finland within 24 hours should Soviet defences be compromised, brought a fresh wave of uncertainty to relations with its eastern neighbour; as did the sudden withdrawal of the Soviet ambassador, allegedly for illicit scheming with the People's Democratic League.

The stature of Kekkonen as a world leader guaranteed continued support for his presidency. But his commitment to the Paasikivi-Kekkonen line ensured that nothing potentially upsetting to the Soviet Union was allowed to surface in Finnish politics, giving – as some thought – the Soviet Union a covert influence on Finland's internal affairs. Opposition to Kekkonen was simply perceived as an attempt to undermine the Paasikivi-Kekkonen line. Equally, the unchallengeable nature of Kekkonen's presidency was considered to be beyond his proper constitutional powers. A move in 1974 by an alliance of right-wingers and Social Democrats within the *Eduskunta* to transfer some of the presidential powers to parliament received a very hostile reaction, emphasizing the almost inviolate position that Kekkonen enjoyed. Kekkonen was re-elected in 1978, although forced to stand down through illness in 1981. In 1982 the former Social Democrat prime minister **Mauno Koivisto** became president.

Because Finland is heavily dependent on foreign trade, its well-being has closely mirrored world trends. The international financial boom of the 1960s enabled a string of social legislation to be passed and created a comparatively high standard of living for most Finns – albeit not on the same scale as the rest of Scandinavia. The global **recession** of the 1970s and early 1980s was most dramatically felt when a fall in the world market for pulp coincided with a steep increase in the price of oil. This brought about an economic crisis that forced Kekkonen to appoint an emergency centre-left government to deal with the immediate problems. Inflation was brought down, but the recession has only recently begun to lift. Industry is heavily concentrated in the south, causing rural areas further north to experience high rates of unemployment and few prospects for economic growth – save through the rising levels of tourism.

The election of 1987 saw a break with the pattern of recent decades. Non-socialist parties made large gains, mainly at the expense of the Rural Party and Communists, while the Social Democrats lost just one seat – far fewer than anticipated. Initially it was hoped by the left that the slimness of the conservative majority in the new government would allow the Social Democratic prime minister Kalevi Sorsa to remain in office: in the event the National Coalition leader **Harri Holkeri** formed a cabinet.

Frequently, though, the Holkeri government appeared inept. The lowering of the full-pension retirement age from 65 to 55 placed a financial burden on the state that it was ill equipped to deal with, while official reaction to events in the Soviet Union fell well short of public expectation – the government's hesitancy and apparent deference to Moscow perhaps being a case of old habits dying hard.

Public disillusionment with the Holkeri coalition resulted in large gains for the Centre Party in the election of March 1991. The Centre Party chairman, 47-year-old **Eske Aho**, subsequently became prime minister, leading a new coalition with many of its members reflecting the comparative youth and fresh ideas of its leader.

In 1992, celebrations to mark 75 years of Finnish independence were muted by the realization that the country was entering a highly critical period facing more problems (few of its own making) than it had for many decades. The end of the Cold War had diminished the value of Finland's hard-won neutrality, the economic and ethnic difficulties in the former Soviet Union are still being watched with trepidation, while the global **recession** hit Finland just as the nation lost its major trading partner of the last fifty years (the Soviet Union). Such events have forced Finland to pin its hopes for the future on closer links with western Europe.

Throughout the early 1990s Finland's economic depression was among the worst in the industrial west, with its banking system in crisis and unemployment figures almost the highest in Europe. On January 1, 1995, Finland became a full member of the European Union, a generally welcome development, and the same year the Social Democratic Party's **Martti Ahtisaari** was elected as president, with the general election resulting in a coalition win for the Social Democrats, their Chairman Paavo Lipponen forming a majority government that includes Conservatives, Socialists, the Swedish Folk Pary and the Green Party. The government declared its main tasks to be cutting unemployment by half and reducing national spending to decrease the national debt. While the economic situation has been slowly improving

A BRIEF GUIDE TO FINNISH

Finnish has nothing in common with the other Scandinavian languages. It belongs to the Finno-Ugrian group, and its grammatical structure is complex: with fifteen cases alone to grapple with, it's initally a tricky language to learn, although once a basic vocabulary is attained things become less impenetrable. Usefully, compared to other languages, there are very few actual words in Finnish – the majority of terms being compounded. English is widely spoken, particularly by young people and around the main towns. Swedish is a common second language and the first of the Finland-Swedes, found mainly in the western parts of the country.

Of the few available phrasebooks, *Finnish For Travellers* (Berlitz) is the most useful for practical purposes; the best Finnish-English dictionary is *The Standard Finnish Dictionary* (Holt, Rinehart and Winston).

PRONUNCIATION

In Finnish, words are pronounced exactly as they are written, with the stress always on the first syllable: in a compound word the stress is on the first syllable of each part of the word. Each letter is pronounced individually, and doubling a letter lengthens the sound: double "kk"s are pronounced with two "k"-sounds and the double "aa" pronounced as long as the English "a" in "car". The letters b, c, f, q, w, x, z and å are only found in words derived from foreign languages, and are pronounced as in the language of origin.

a as in f**a**ther but shorter

d as in ri**d**ing but sometimes soft as to be barely heard

e between the e in p**e**n and the i in p**i**n.

g (only after 'n') as in si**n**ger

h as in **h**ot

i as in p**i**n

j like the y in **y**ellow

np like the m in **m**other

o like the aw in l**a**w

r is rolled

s as in **s**aid but with the tongue a little further back from the teeth

u as in b**u**ll

y like the French u in "s**u**r"

ä like the a in h**a**t

ö like the ur in F**ur** but without any "r"-sound.

BASICS

Do you speak English?	*Puhutteko englantia ?*	Good day	*hyvää päivä* (usually shortened to *päivä*)
Yes	*kyllä/joo*		
No	*ei*	Goodnight	*hyvää yötä*
I don't understand	*En ymmärrä*	Goodbye	*hyvästi*
I understand	*Ymmärrän*	Yesterday	*eilen*
Please	*olkaa hyvä*	Today	*tänään*
Thank you	*kiitos*	Tomorrow	*huomenna*
Excuse me	*anteeksi*	Day after tomorrow	*ylihuomemnna*
Good morning	*hyvää huomenta*	In the morning	*aamulla/aamupäivällä*
Good afternoon	*hyvää päivää*	In the afternoon	*iltapäivällä*
Good evening	*hyvää iltaa*	In the evening	*illalla*

SOME SIGNS

Entrance	*Sisään*	Open	*Avoinna*	Police	*Poliisi*
Exit	*Ulos*	Closed	*Suljettu*	Hospital	*Sairaala*
Gentlemen	*Miehille/Miehet/Herrat*	Push	*Työnnä*	No Smoking	*Tupakointi kielletty*
Ladies	*Naisille/Naiset/Rouvat*	Pull	*Vedä*	No Entry	*Pääsy kielletty*
Hot	*Kuuma*	Arrival	*Saapuvat*	No Trespassing	*Läpikulku kielletty*
Cold	*Kylmä*	Departure	*Lähtevät*	No Camping	*Leiriytyminen kielletty*

QUESTIONS AND DIRECTIONS

Where's...?	*Missä on...?*	How much ?	*Kuinka paljon ?*
When ?	*Koska/million ?*	How much is that ?	*Paljonko se maksaa ?*
What ?	*Mikä/mitä ?*	I'd like	*Haluaisin*
Why ?	*Miksi ?*	Cheap	*Halpa*
How far is it to...?	*Kuinka pitkä matka on ...n ?*	Expensive	*Kallis*
Where can I get a	*Mistä lähtee saada juna ...n ?*	Good	*Hyvä*
train to...?		Bad	*Paha/Huono*
Train/bus/boat/ship	*Juna/bussi (or) linja-*	Here	*Täällä*
	auto/vene/laiva	There	*Siellä*
Where is the youth	*Missä on retkeilymaja ?*	Left	*Vasen*
hostel ?		Right	*Oikea*
Can we camp here ?	*Voimmeko leiriytyä tähän ?*	Go straight ahead	*Ajakaa suoraan eteenpäin*
Do you have	*Onko teillä mitään*	Is it near/far ?	*Onko se lähellä/kaukana ?*
anything better/	*parempaa/isompaa/halvem*	Ticket/ticket office	*Lippu/matkalippu*
bigger/cheaper ?	*paa ?*	Train/bus station/	*Rautatieasema/linja-*
It's too expensive	*Se on liian kallis*	bus stop	*autoasema/bussipysäkki*

NUMBERS

0	*nolla*	9	*yhdeksän*	18	*kahdeksantoista*	80	*kahdeksankymmentä*
1	*yksi*	10	*kymmenen*	19	*yhdeksäntoista*	90	*yhdeksänkymmentä*
2	*kaksi*	11	*yksitoista*	20	*kaksikymmentä*	100	*sata*
3	*kolme*	12	*kaksitoista*	21	*kaksikymmentäyksi*	101	*satayksi*
4	*neljä*	13	*kolmetoista*	30	*kolmekymmentä*	151	*sataviisikymmentäyksi*
5	*viisi*	14	*neljätoista*	40	*neljäkymmentä*	200	*kaksisataa*
6	*kuusi*	15	*viisitoista*	50	*viisikymmentä*	1000	*tuhat*
7	*seitsemän*	16	*kuusitoista*	60	*kuusikymmentä*		
8	*kahdeksan*	17	*seitsemäntoista*	70	*seitsmänkymmentä*		

DAYS AND MONTHS

Monday	*maanantai*	January	*tammikuu*	July	*heinäkuu*
Tuesday	*tiistai*	February	*helmikuu*	August	*elokuu*
Wednesday	*keskiviikko*	March	*maalisku*	September	*syyskuu*
Thursday	*torstai*	April	*huhtikuu*	October	*lokakuu*
Friday	*perjantai*	May	*toukokuu*	November	*marraskuu*
Saturday	*lauantai*	June	*kesäkuu*	December	*joulukuu*
Sunday	*sunnuntai*				

Days and months are never capitalised

GLOSSARY OF FINNISH TERMS AND WORDS

Joki	River	*Museo*	Museum
Järvi	Lake	*Pankki*	Bank
Kauppahalli	Market hall	*Posti*	Post office
Kauppatori	Market square	*Puisto*	Park
Kaupungintalo	Town hall	*Rautatieasema*	Train station
Katu	Street	*Sairaala*	Hospital
Keskusta	Town centre	*Taidemuseo*	Art museum
Kirkko	Church	*Tie*	Road
Kylä	Village	*Tori*	Square
Linna	Castle	*Torni*	Tower
Linja-autoasema	Bus station	*Tuomiokirkko*	Cathedral
Lipputoimisto	Ticket office	*Yliopisto*	University
Matkailutoimisto	Tourist office		

over the last few years, unemployment remains high and the future of the welfare state is uncertain. In 1996 Finland joined the European Monetary Union and in early 1997 the issues being considered by Finland's government are whether the country should become a member of NATO and the ERM, proposals for which there is currently considerable opposition. As for Finland's relationship with its eastern neighbour, the sense of threat induced by the former Soviet Union has weakened dramatically. This is partly due to the growing economic and touristic links between Finland and the newly independent states of the former USSR, but also because Finland has had to turn inward and concentrate on solving its own domestic problems.

CHAPTER FIFTEEN

HELSINKI AND THE SOUTH

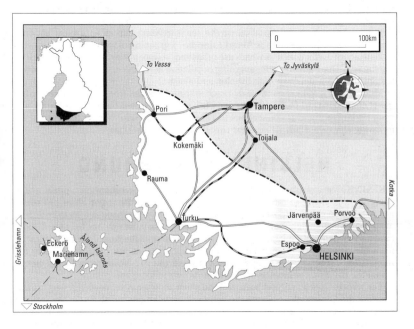

The southern coast of Finland makes up the most populated, industrialized and richest part of the country, with the densest concentration – not surprisingly – around the capital, **Helsinki**. A city of half a million people with the friendliness of a peasant village on market day, Helsinki's innovative architecture and batch of fine museums and galleries collectively expose the roots of the national character – while at night the pubs and clubs strip it bare. It may seem the perfect prelude to exploring the rest of Finland, and in the practical sense it is, being the hub of the country's road, rail and air traffic routes. However, if you can, you should try to arrive in Helsinki *after* seeing the rest of the country. Only with some prior knowledge of Finland does the significance of the city as a symbol of Finnish self-determination become clear.

A couple of towns **around Helsinki** evince the change from ruralism to modernism even further. **Porvoo** sits placidly locked in the nineteenth century, while the suburbs of **Espoo** form a showpiece of twentieth-century urban design. Further away, in the country's southeastern extremity, the only community of significant size and importance between Helsinki and the Russian border is the shipping port of **Kotka** – not wildly appealing in itself but at the heart of a coastal region typified by historically intriguing small towns and villages, and a fair number of geological oddities.

Helsinki only became the capital in 1812, after Finland had been made a Russian Grand Duchy and Tsar Alexander I had deemed the existing capital, **Turku**, too close to Sweden for comfort. Today Turku, facing Stockholm across the Gulf of Bothnia, handles its demotion well. Both historically and visually, it's one of Finland's most enticing cities; indeed, the snootier elements of its Swedish-speaking contingent consider Åbo (the Swedish name for Turku) the real capital and Helsinki just an uncouth upstart.

Between Helsinki and Turku, along the entire southern coast, only small villages and a few slightly larger towns break the continuity of forests. Around Turku, though, things are more interesting, with the two most southerly of the Finland-Swedish communities: **Rauma**, with its unique dialect and well-preserved town centre; and the likeably downbeat **Pori**, a town that's gained notoriety from its annual jazz festival.

Where this corner of Finland meets the sea it splinters into an enormous archipelago, which includes the curious **Åland Islands** – a grouping of thousands of fragments of land, about half a dozen of which are inhabited, connected by small roadways skirting the sea. There's a tiny self-governing population here, Swedish-speaking but with a history that's distinct from both Sweden and Finland.

Much of the region is most easily reached from Helsinki, from where there are frequent connections to Turku. Rauma and Pori are best reached by bus from Turku, and from Pori there are easy connections to Tampere and the Lake Region (covered in the following chapter). Daily ferries also connect Turku to the Åland Islands.

HELSINKI AND AROUND

HELSINKI has a character quite different from the other Scandinavian capitals, and in many ways is closer in mood (and certainly in looks) to the major cities of eastern Europe. For years an outpost of the Russian empire, its very shape and form is derived from its powerful neighbour. Yet throughout this century the city has become a showcase for independent Finland, much of its impressive **architecture** drawing inspiration from the dawning of Finnish nationalism and the rise of the republic. Equally the **museums**, especially the National Museum and the Art Museum of the Ateneum, reveal the country's gradual assimilation of its own folklore and culture.

The streets have a youthful buzz, and the short summer is acknowledged by crowds strolling the boulevards, cruising the shopping arcades and socializing in the outdoor cafés and restaurants; everywhere there's prolific **street entertainment**. At night the pace picks up, with a great selection of pubs and clubs, free rock concerts in the numerous parks, and an impressive quota of fringe events. It's a pleasure just to be around, merging with the multitude and witnessing the activity.

Much of central Helsinki is a succession of compact granite blocks, interspersed with more characterful buildings, alongside waterways, green spaces and the glass-fronted office blocks and shopping centres you'll find in any European capital. The city is hemmed in on three sides by water, and all the things you might want to see are within walking distance of one another – and certainly no more than a few minutes apart by tram or bus.

Arrival, information and city transport

However you arrive you'll be deposited somewhere close to the heart of town. Helsinki's **airport**, Vantaa, is 20km to the north and served by frequent airport buses (30-min journey; 24mk). These stop at the new suburb of Pasila, at the *Finnair* terminal behind the *Inter-Continental Hotel*, halfway between the city centre and the Olympic Stadium, before continuing to the train station. A cheaper, if slightly slower, airport connection is city bus #615; this costs 15mk and runs from the airport to the bus terminal beside the train station. City bus #614 runs from the airport to the other bus station, Simonkatu, but only a few times a day.

The **ferry** lines *Viking* and *Silja* have their terminals on opposite sides of the South Harbour (docks known respectively as Katajanokka and Olympic) and disembarking passengers from either have a walk of less than 1km to the centre. The **train station**, equipped with luggage lockers, is right in the heart of the city centre, next door to one of the two city bus terminals. All trams stop immediately outside or around the corner in Mannerheimintie. Just across Mannerheimintie and a short way up Simonkatu is the second city bus terminal and the **long-distance bus station**.

Information

The **City Tourist Office**, at Pohjoisesplanadi 19 (May–Sept Mon–Fri 9am–7pm, Sat & Sun 9am–3pm; Oct–April Mon–Fri 9am–5pm, Sat 9am–3pm; ☎09/169 3757; fax 169 3839), supplies free street and transport maps, along with the useful free tourist magazine *Helsinki This Week* and the stylish *Helsinki Happens* guide. While here, try and get hold of the excellent *Helsinki On Foot* brochure, useful although it tends to mix Finnish and Swedish street names on its maps. If you're staying for a while and plan to see as much of the city and its museums as possible, consider purchasing a **Helsinki Card** (available from the tourist office), which gives unlimited travel on public transport and free entry to over forty museums. The three-day card (165mk) is the best value, although there are also two-day (135mk) and one-day (105mk) versions.

For information on the rest of the country, visit the **Finnish Tourist Board** at Eteläesplanadi 4 (June–Aug Mon–Fri 8.30am–5pm, Sat 10am–2pm; Sept–May Mon–Fri 8.30am–4pm), on the other side of Esplanadi from the City Tourist Office. Next door to the tourist board office is *Edita*, the best place for **maps** of Finland, the Baltic and Scandinavia generally; there's a second branch at Annankatu 44 (both open Mon–Fri).

City transport

The central area and its immediate surrounds are covered by an integrated transport network of buses, trams and a small metro system. A single journey costs 9mk and unlimited transfers are allowed within one hour. A **multi-trip** ticket gives ten rides for 75mk. You can also buy a **tourist ticket** covering the city and surrounding areas such as Espoo and Vantaa for one (45mk), three (90mk) or five days (135mk), which permits travel on buses and trams displaying double arrows (effectively all of them); obviously, this is only a cost-cutter if used frequently. If you don't intend to leave the city proper, you're better off with a **Helsinki only tourist ticket**, again available in one- (25mk), three- (50mk) or five-day (75mk) versions. Single tickets can be bought on board, others from the bus station, R-kioski stands or tourist office. On **buses** you enter at the front and must either buy or show your ticket. On **trams**, get on at the front or back, and stamp your ticket in the machine. It's unlikely that you'll be asked to show your ticket except on some of the old vehicles on the #1 tram route, which have a seated conductor instead of a machine. **Metro** tickets can be bought from the machines in the stations. As for routes, tram #3T follows a figure-of-eight route around the city and if you're pushed for sightseeing time will take you past the most obvious attractions. If you're tempted to fare-dodge, it's worth knowing that there's a 250mk spot fine on buses and trams, though it's rare for inspectors to appear. **Taxis** have a basic charge of 12mk, with a further 7mk per km, plus a 7mk evening surcharge after 6pm, and a 13mk surcharge from 10pm Saturday until 6am Sunday.

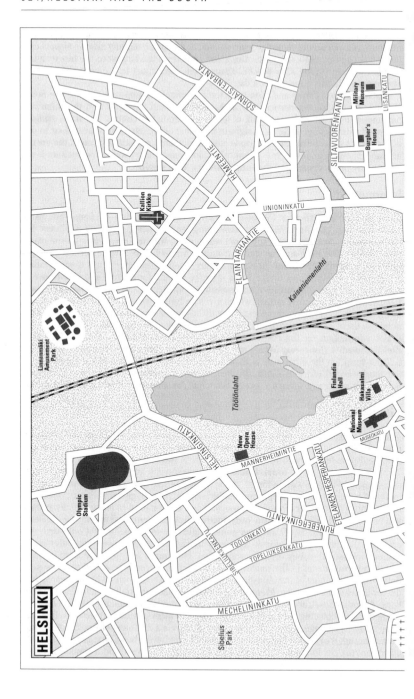

HELSINKI

Military Museum

LIISANKATU

SILTAVUORENRANTA

Burgher's House

SÖRNÄISTENRANTA

HÄMEENTIE

UNIONINKATU

Kallion Kirkko

ELÄINTARHANTIE

Kaisaniemenlahti

Linnanmäki Amusement Park

Töölönlahti

Finlandia Hall

Hakasalmi Villa

New Opera House

National Museum

MUSEOKATU

HELSINGINKATU

MANNERHEIMINTIE

ETELÄINEN HESPERIANKATU

Olympic Stadium

RUNEBERGINKATU

SIBELIUKSENKATU

TÖÖLÖNKATU

TOPELIUKSENKATU

MECHELININKATU

Sibelius Park

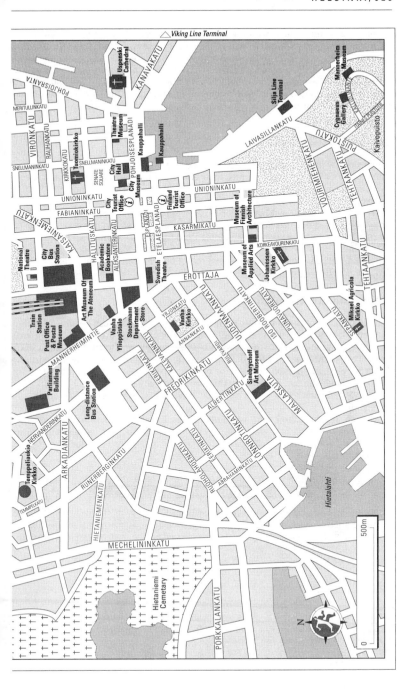

Viking Line Terminal

Uspenski Cathedral

KANAVAKATU

POHJOISRANTA

MERITULLINKATU

VIRONKATU

RAUHANKATU

Theatre Museum

Silja Line Terminal

Mannerheim Museum

LAIVASILLANKATU

Cygnaeus Gallery

PUISTOKATU

HANNE TESTER

Kaivopuisto

KIRKKOKATU

Tuomiokirkko

SNELLMANINKATU

Kauppahalli

Kauppahalli

SNELLMANINKATU

Senate Square

City Hall

City Museum

POHJOISESPLANADI

UNIONINKATU

UNIONINKATU

UNIONINKATU

FABIANINKATU

City Tourist Office

Finland Tourist Office

Museum of Finnish Architecture

TEHTAANKATU

VOURIMIEHENKATU

KAISANIEMENKATU

HALLITUSKATU

KASARMIKATU

ETELÄESPLANADI

KORKEAVUORENKATU

Museum of Applied Arts

Johannessen Kirkko

National Theatre

City Bus Station

Academic Bookstore

ALEKSANTERINKATU

Swedish Theatre

EROTTAJA

Art Museum Of The Ateneum

Vanha Ylioppistalo

Stockmann Department Store

YRJÖNKATU

Vanha Kirkko

ANNANKATU

UDENMAANKATU

ISO ROOBERTINKATU

PUNAVUORENKATU

Mikael Agricola Kirkko

SEPÄNKATU

Train Station

Post Office & Postal Museum

MANNERHEIMINTIE

KEKUSKATU

FREDRIKINKATU

BULEVARDI

Sinebrychoff Art Museum

ALBERTINKATU

MALLASKUJA

Parliament Building

Long-distance Bus Station

NERVANDERINKATU

ARKADIANKATU

RUNEBERGINKATU

LÖNNROTINKATU

ERIKINKATU

RUOHOLAHDENKATU

ABRAHAMINKATU

Temppeliaukio Kirkko

TEMPPELIKATU

HIETANIEMENKATU

Hietalahti

MECHELININKATU

Hietaniemi Cemetary

500m

PORKKALANKATU

N

0

Join one of the guided **walking tours** run by the Helsinki Tourist Association, Lönrotinkatu 7B (☎09/603 417), and you'll finish up knowing more about the city than most of its residents do. The two-hour walks cost 30mk. For details, phone the above number or ask at the city tourist office. There are also numerous **boat sightseeing tours** from the harbour costing around 40mk for an hour or 60mk for two hours. These run from around 11am to 7pm, and brochures are available at the tourist office, or from touts at the harbour itself.

Accommodation

There's plenty of **accommodation** in Helsinki, but by far the bulk of it is in mid-range hotels. Various discounts can reduce their cost but if they're still beyond your means there are a couple of cheaper summer hotels, several tourist hotels and a few hostels. Wherever you stay, you should book as far ahead as possible: the various cut-price hotel deals get snapped up quickly, and hostel space is tight in summer. If you want a hotel or hostel bed but don't have anything planned before arrival, you can book a room for a 12mk fee through the very helpful **Hotel Booking Centre** in the train station, to the left of the platforms near the left luggage office (mid-May to mid-Sept Mon–Fri 9am–9pm, Sat 9am–7pm, Sun 10am–6pm; rest of the year Mon–Fri 9am–6pm; ☎09/171 133; fax 175 524).

Hotels and tourist hotels

Although the cost of a room in one of Helsinki's top-flight **hotels** can be unusually high, the better hotels aren't necessarily out of reach: many of them drop their rates dramatically in the summer tourist season, while nearly everywhere offers reductions at weekends. To take advantage of any bargains, it's essential to book as early as possible – either by phoning the hotel directly or making a reservation through a travel agent. However much you pay, it's unlikely that you'll leave any Helsinki hotel feeling ripped off: service and amenities – such as the inclusive help-yourself breakfast – are usually excellent.

Though they lack the luxury of regular hotels, the city's **tourist hotels**, providing basic accommodation in private rooms without bathrooms, and usually inexpensive meals, can be a good-value alternative to a regular hotel, especially for three or four people sharing.

ACCOMMODATION PRICE CODES

The Finnish hotels listed throughout the guide have been graded according to the following price bands, based on the rate for a double room in summer. However, many hotels offer summer and/or weekend discounts, and in these instances we've given two grades, covering both the regular and the discounted rate.

① Under 275mk	② 275–350mk	③ 350–450mk
④ 450–550mk	⑤ 550–750mk	⑥ 750mk and over

Hotels

Academica, Hietaniemenkatu 14 (☎09/402 0206; fax 441 201). A well-placed summer hotel with morning sauna and pool; see also "Hostels" below. ②

Anna, Annankatu 1 (☎09/648 011; fax 602 664). Small and central, with a cosy atmosphere despite its past as a Christian mission. ③/⑤

Anton, Paasivuorenkatu 1 (☎09/750 311; fax 701 4527). A bit out of the way, just north of the centre close to Hakaneimentori, but well priced at weekends. ③/④

Arctia Hotel Marski, Mannerheimintie 10 (☎09/68061; fax 642 377). Opposite the Stockmann department store and named after Marski (Marshal) Mannerheim, this is one of the best hotels in the city, though less atmospheric than the *Palace*, below. ⑤/⑥

Arthur, Vuorikatu 19 (☎09/173 441; fax 626 880). You can save money in this good-quality hotel by getting a room without a bathroom – but do it early. ③

Cumulus Kaisaniemi, Kaisaniemenkatu 7 (☎09/171 146). Ageing but clean rooms that can be good value at weekends. ③/⑥

Cumulus Seurahuone, Kaivokatu 12 ☎09/69141; fax 6914010). A stylish, classic hotel opposite the train station, with the historic *Cafe Socis* attached. Big, splendid rooms with original features. ③/⑤

Finn, Kalevankatu 3b (☎09/640 904). A modern, compact and peaceful place, virtually in the city centre. ③

Grand Marina, Katajanokanlaituri 7 (☎09/16661; fax 664 764). The vast former harbour customs house from the 1930s, now transformed into an elegant, very Scandinavian-looking hotel just a few strides from the arrival point of *Viking Line* boats from Sweden. ④/⑥

Helka, Pohjoinen Rautatiekatu 23 (☎09/613 580; fax 441 087). Rather plain-looking exterior but very welcoming on the inside; and within easy reach of everything. Some weekend reductions. ③/④

Inter-Continental, Mannerheiminie 46 (☎09/40551; fax 405 5255). Next door to the *Sokos Hesperia* and slightly less expensive, though the service is equally excellent. ⑥

Lord Hotel, Lönnrotinkatu 29 (☎09/680 1680; fax 680 1315). Designed as a mock-castle but not really of the standard its image suggests. ③/⑤

Marttahotelli, Uudenmaankatu 24 (☎09/646 211; fax 680 1266). A clean and cosy hotel, though the rooms are on the small side. No alcohol served. ③/④

Palace Hotel, Eteläranta 10 (☎09/134 561; fax 654 786). Luxurious and overlooking the Olympic Harbour; there are no reductions for rooms with a sea view unless you're really pushy, but a quiet day in summer can bring substantial reductions. ⑤/⑥

Radisson SAS, Runeberginkatu 2 (☎09/69580; fax 6958 7100). Five-star, white-tiled and glamorous, resembling buildings like the Opera House and Finlandia Hall, this is not surprisingly expensive; visit in summer, when rates are cut by half. ⑤/⑥

Satakuntalo, Lapinrinne 1 (☎09/695 851; fax 694 2226). Another handily located summer hotel which doubles as student accommodation in winter. Shared bathrooms. ①

Sokos Helsinki, Yliopistonkatu 12 (☎09/131 401; fax 176 014). The best aspect of this place is its location, a stone's throw from Senate Square in one of the prime central streets. ③/④

Sokos Hesperia, Mannerheimintie 50 (☎09/43101; fax 431 0995). Swish and business-oriented, this is one of the major hotels just past the parliament building; weekend reductions. ④/⑥

Sokos Klaus Kurki, Bulevardi 2–4 (☎09/618 911; fax 608 538). Recently renovated and perfectly situated for exploring the city. Usually offers weekend rates. ④/⑤

Sokos Torni, Yrjönkatu 26 (☎09/131 131; fax 131 1361). Next door to the classic sauna and pools on Yrjönkatu. On a clear day, the thirteenth-floor bar gives views all the way to Estonia, but the drinks are pricey, as are the rooms – though weekend rates can drop dramatically. ④/⑤

Sokos Vaakuna, Asema-Aukio 2 (☎09/131 181; fax 1311 8234). In the heart of the city facing the train station, built to coincide with the 1952 Olympic Games, this smartly refurbished hotel still contains many of its original, quintessentially Finnish architectural features. ④/⑤

Tourist hotels

Erottajanpuisto, Uudenmaakatu 9 (☎09/642 169; fax 680 2757). Usefully positioned, and especially good value for several people sharing. ①

Lönnrot, Lönnrotinkatu 16 (☎09/693 2590; fax 693 2482). Close to the Old Church and everything central. Basic but quite endurable. ①

Matkakoti Margarita, Itäinen Teatterikuja 3 (☎09/669 707 or 656 695). Fairly basic place with a Russian atmosphere, set in a quiet street close to the train and bus stations, and quite adequate for a night's rest. It also rents rooms cheaply by the day for those arriving in the city early and leaving later the same day. ②

Omapohja Gasthaus, Teatterikuja 3 (☎09/666 211). Downstairs from *Matkakoti Margarita*, this one has four rooms with showers and toilets en suite and rooms are complete with colour TVs and a microwave oven for use of guests. ②

Hostels

Though the staple accommodation option of budget travellers, Helsinki's **hostels** are not without drawbacks: curfews are common in dormitories, and there is sometimes a limit imposed on the length of stay during the peak summer period.

Academica, Hietaniemenkatu 14 (☎09/402 0206; fax 441 201). Hostel-type accommodation is available in this summer hotel (see "Hotels" above) on production of an *IYHF* or student card. June–Aug only. 90–115mk.

Euro Hostel, Linnankatu 9 (☎09/622 0470 fax 655 044). Comfortable place in a clean modern building with free morning sauna and twin beds (not bunks) in the up-and-coming but quiet Katajanokka area, close to the *Viking Line* arrival point; take tram #4. Open all year; 115–175mk per person.

Kallion retkeilymaja, Porthaninkatu 2 (☎09/7099 2590). The hostel of the Helsinki Youth Office. One large dormitory for men and three smaller rooms for women; 50mk per person. Open mid-May to Aug; closed 10.30am–3pm. Two kilometres from the centre, close to Hakaniemi metro station. Trams #1, #2, #3B and #7 stop nearby.

Stadionin retkeilymaja, in the Olympic Stadium (☎09/496 071; fax 496 466). A three-kilometre hike from the city centre up Mannerheimintie; the hostel entrance is on the far side of the stadium complex. With its own *Cafe Pinja*, this is a great venue for a youth hostel, though breakfast (25mk) is not served in very sporting quantities and the place is often crowded.Trams #3T, #4, #7A and #10 stop outside. Open all year; 60–135mk.

Campsites

Of Helsinki's two **campsites**, only one makes a reasonable base if you're planning to spend time in the city. This is *Rastila* (☎09/316 551; fax 344 1578), 13km to the east in Itäkeskus, on the metro line and also served by buses #90, #90A, #965 and #98. It's open all year and there's always plenty of space. The other site is *Oittaa* (☎09/862 585), about 30km to the west, which is open from June to mid-August; take a train to Espoo and then a bus.

The City

Following a devastating fire, and the city's appointment as Finland's capital in 1812, Helsinki was totally rebuilt in a style commensurate with its rank: a grid of wide streets and Neoclassical, Empire-style brick buildings, modelled on the then Russian capital, St Petersburg. This forms the basis of the modern city, which divides into four fairly distinct portions. It's a tribute to the vision of planner Johan Ehrenström and architect Carl Engel that in and around **Senate Square** the grandeur has endured, often quite dramatically. The square itself, overlooked by the gleaming Lutheran Cathedral, is still the city's single most eye-catching feature; and, just a few blocks away, past the South Harbour and the waterside market, **Esplanadi** remains a handsome tree-lined avenue. Meeting one end of Esplanadi, the great artery of **Mannerheimintie**, the main route into the centre from the suburbs, carries traffic and trams past Finlandia Hall and the Olympic Stadium on one side, and the National Museum and the streets leading to Sibelius Park and the vast Hietaniemi Cemetery on the other. The bulge of land that extends **south of Esplanadi** has long been one of the most affluent sections of town. Dotted by palatial embassies and wealthy dwellings, it rises into the rocky **Kaivopuisto park**, where the peace is disturbed only by the rumble of the trams and the summer rock concerts.

Along the seafront are old Mediterranean-style villas, which continue into the narrow streets of the exclusive Eira quarter. Divided by the waters of Kaisaniemenlahti, the districts of **Kruununhaka** and **Hakaniemi** contain what little is left of pre-seventeenth-century Helsinki – in the small area up the hill behind the cathedral, compressed between the botanical gardens and the bay; over the bridge is a large marketplace and the hill leading past the formidable **Kallio kirkko** towards the modern housing districts further north. Helsinki also has innumerable offshore islands, the biggest of which are **Suomenlinna** and **Seurasaari**. Both of these, despite their location just minutes away from the city centre, offer untrammelled nature and a rewarding crop of museums.

Senate Square and Esplanadi

The heart of Helsinki lies in and around **Senate Square**, a compact area of broad bustling streets, grand buildings, famous (to Finns) shops and the most popular promenading spot in the entire country.

Around Senate Square

Most of the streets leading into Senate Square are fairly narrow and unremarkable, a fact that simply serves to increase the impact as the square comes into view and you're struck by the sudden burst of space, by the graceful symmetry of the buildings and most of all the exquisite form of the **Tuomiokirkko** or Lutheran Cathedral (May–Sept Mon–Fri 9am–5pm, Sat & Sun 9am–6pm; Oct–April Mon–Fri 10am–4pm, Sat 10am–6pm, Sun noon–6pm), raised on granite steps that support it like a pedestal. Designed, like most of the other buildings on the square, by Engel, and overseen by him until his death in 1840, it was finally completed, with a few variations, in 1852. Among the post-Engel additions are the statues of the Twelve Apostles that line the roof, which may seem familiar if you've visited Copenhagen: they're copies of Thorvaldsen's sculptures for Vor Frue Kirke. After the Neoclassical extravagances of the exterior, the spartan Lutheran interior comes as a disappointment; better is the gloomily atmospheric **crypt** (June–Aug daily 10am–4pm; entrance on Kirkkokatu), now often used for exhibitions – when there's likely to be an admission charge.

The buildings around the square contribute to the pervading sense of harmony, and although none is open to the public, some are of great historical significance. The **Government Palace** (*Valtioneuvosto*), known as the Senate House until independence and seating the Senate from 1822, consumes the entire eastern side. It was here that an angry Finnish civil servant became a national hero by assassinating a much-hated Russian governor-general in 1904; shortly afterwards he killed himself. Opposite are the Ionic columns of **Helsinki University** (*Helsingin Yliopisto*), next door to which is the **University Library** (*Yliopiston kirjasto*), considered by many to be Engel's finest single building (only students and bona-fide researchers are allowed in).

Between Kirkkokatu and Rauhankatu, just north of the square, is **The House of Scientific Estates** (*Säätytalo*), the seat of the Diet that governed the country until 1906, when it was abolished in favour of a single-chamber parliament elected by universal suffrage (at the time, Europe's most radical parliamentary reform). In the small park behind the Government Palace is the **House of Nobility** (*Ritarihuone*), where the upper crust of Helsinki society rubbed shoulders a hundred years ago. One place anyone can enter, although it's only worthwhile if you're keen on Finnish drama, is the **Theatre Museum**, just off the square at Aleksanterinkatu 12 (June–Aug Sat & Sun noon–5pm; groups only at other times; 10mk), which has some small displays on two of the National Theatre's leading figures – Aleksis Kivi and Kaarlo Bergbom (see p.638 for details on Helsinki's other theatre museum).

Directly opposite the cathedral at Alexanderinkatu 18 is Helsinki's oldest stone building, **Sederholm House** (June–Aug daily 11am–5pm, Sept–May Wed–Sun

11am–5pm; 15mk), dating from 1757. It was recently restored to house a small museum concentrating on aspects of eighteenth-century life in the city with particular relevance to industrialist Johan Sederholm. There are exhibitions on trade, education and construction, but what makes it perhaps most enjoyable is the eighteenth-century music collection – you can ask to hear a range of classical CDs while you wander around. A more high-tech record of Helsinki life can be found one block south from Sederholm at the new **City Museum**, Sofiankatu 4 (Mon–Fri 9am–5pm, Sat & Sun 11am–5pm; 15mk). Here, a permanent exhibition entitled "Time" gives glimpses of Helsinki from its roots as a country village right up to today's national capital. It's an impressive show, beautifully lit with fibre optics and halogen lamps, though the chronology jumps around disconcertingly.

The square at the eastern end of Aleksanterinkatu is overlooked by the red and green onion-shaped domes of the Russian Orthodox **Uspenski Cathedral** (May–Sept Tues–Fri 9.30am–4pm, Sat 9am–noon, Sun noon–3pm; Oct–April Tues & Thurs 9am–2pm, Wed noon–6pm & Fri noon–4pm; tram 4) on Katajanokka, a wedge of land extending out to sea between the North and South Harbours and currently the scene of a dockland development programme, converting the area's old warehouses into pricey new restaurants and apartments for Helsinki's yuppies. In contrast to its Lutheran counterpart, the cathedral is drab outside but on the inside has a rich display of icons and other mesmerizing adornments, incense mingling with the sound of Slavonic choirs.

Esplanadi and around

Walking from the cathedral towards the South Harbour takes you past the **President's Palace**, noticeable only for its conspicuous uniformed guard, and the equally bland **City Hall**, used solely for administrative purposes. There's more colour and liveliness among the stalls of the **kauppatori** or market square (Mon–Thurs 8am–5.30pm, Fri 8am–6pm, Sat 8am–3pm) along the waterfront, laden with fresh fruit and vegetables; around the edge of the harbour you can buy fresh fish directly from the boats moored there. If your principles allow it, the market is also the best place to buy fur – mink and fox hats and coats are cheaper here than in the city's many fur salons. The **kauppahalli** (market hall) with its interior of original carved mahogany and carved pediments (Mon–Fri 8am–5pm, Sat 8am–2pm), a bit further along, is a good place for snacks and watching tourists contemplating the reindeer kebabs and Russian caviar.

Across a mishmash of tram lines from the South Harbour lies **Esplanadi**. At the height of the Swedish/Finnish language conflict that divided the nation during the mid-nineteenth century, this neat boulevard was where opposing factions demonstrated their allegiance – the Finns walking on the south side and the Swedes on the north. Nowadays it's dominated at lunchtime by office workers, later in the afternoon by buskers, and at night by couples strolling hand-in-hand along the central pathway, seemingly oblivious to the whistles and leers of the young bucks occupying the seats. Musical accompaniment is provided free on summer evenings from the hut in the middle of the walk – expect anything from a Salvation Army band to rock groups. Entertainment of a more costly type lies at the far end of Esplanadi in the dreary off-white horseshoe of the **Swedish Theatre** building, its main entrance on Mannerheimintie.

West to Mannerheimintie

If you think Esplanadi is crowded, wait until you step inside the brick Constructivist exterior of the **Stockmann Department Store**, at the junction of Mannerheimintie and Aleksanterinkatu, Europe's largest department store, selling everything from bubble gum to Persian rugs. On the fifth floor is the **Stockmann Museum** (Mon–Thurs noon–1pm; free), a small and surprisingly interesting exhibition on the history of the century-old enterprise. What you won't see in the museum is any reference to the popularity of the massive *Forum* shopping mall, directly across Mannerheimintie, which has been cutting into the *Stockmann* profits in recent years. The **Academic Bookstore** is part of *Stockmann*'s, though it has its own entrance on Aleksanterinkatu. There's an extensive collection of books here (more titles allegedly than in any other bookstore in Europe), including many English-language paperbacks and a sizeable stock of foreign newspapers and magazines.

Opposite *Stockmann*'s main entrance is a statue by Felix Nylund, the *Three Smiths*, which commemorates the workers of Finland who raised money to erect a building for the country's students. This building is the **Vanha Ylioppistalo** – the old Students' House – its main doors facing the statue. The Finnish Students' Union is based here, now owning some of the most expensive square metres of land in Finland and renting them out at considerable profit. In the Vanha, as it's usually known, is the **Vanhan Galleria** (during exhibitions usually 10am–6pm; free), a small gallery with frequent modern art events. It's worth becoming acquainted with the building's layout during the day, as it contains a couple of lively bars that are well worth an evening visit. Taking a few strides further along Mannerheimintie brings you to the *Bio* cinema and, beside it, steps lead down into a little modern courtyard framed by burger joints and pizzerias, off which runs the entrance to **Tunneli**, an underground complex containing shops, the central metro station and a pedestrian subway to one of the city's most enjoyable structures – the train station.

The train station and National Theatre

Erected in 1914, **Helsinki train station** ranks among architect Eliel Saarinen's greatest achievements. In response to criticism of his initial design, Saarinen jettisoned the original National Romantic features and opted for a style more akin to late Art Nouveau. Standing in front of the huge doors (so sturdy they always give the impression of being locked), it's hard to deny the sense of strength and solidity the building exudes. Yet this power is tempered by gentleness, a feeling symbolized by four muscular figures on the facade, each clasping a spherical glass lamp above the heads of passers-by. The interior details can be admired at leisure from either one of the station's two restaurants. Later, Saarinen was to emigrate to America; his son in turn became one of the best-known postwar American architects, whose most famous creation is the *TWA* terminal building in New York.

Beside the station is the imposing granite form of the **National Theatre**, home of Finnish drama since 1872. "Finnish culture" was considered a contradiction in terms by the governing Swedish-speaking elite right up to the mid-nineteenth century, and it was later felt (quite rightly) to pose an anti-Russian, pro-nationalist threat to Finland's Tsarist masters. Finnish theatre was so politically hot during the Russification process that it had to be staged away from the capital, in the southwest coastal town of Pori. At the forefront of Finnish drama during its early years was Aleksis Kivi, who died insane and impoverished before being acknowledged as Finland's greatest playwright. He's remembered here by Wäinö Aaltonen's bronze sculpture. Interestingly, nobody knows for sure what Kivi actually looked like, and this imagined likeness, finished in 1939, came to be regarded as the true one.

Just across from the train station is the surprisingly enjoyable **Posti Museo** (Postal Museum; Mon–Fri 10am–7pm, Sat & Sun 11am–4pm; free), inside the city's main post office. What could have been the country's dullest museum is in fact remarkably innovative, displaying the unlikely-looking implements connected with more than 350 years of Finnish postal history, along with interactive computer games, multivision screens and a special crayoning area for toddlers. There's also a pleasant café. An additional incentive to visit are the free postcards with which you can stuff your pockets upon leaving.

The Art Museum of the Ateneum

Directly opposite the open square of the bus station is the **Art Museum of the Ateneum** (Tues & Fri 9am–6pm, Wed & Thurs 9am–8pm, Sat & Sun 11am–5pm; 10mk, 45mk for special exhibitions). Chief among the museum's large collection of Finnish paintings is the stirring selection of Golden Age works from the late nineteenth century – a time when the spirit of nationalism was surging through the country and the movement towards independence gaining strength; indeed, the art of the period was a contributing factor in the growing awareness of Finnish culture, both inside and outside the country. Among the prime names of this era were **Akseli Gallen-Kallela** and **Albert Edelfelt**, particularly the former, who translated onto canvas many of the mythic scenes of the *Kalevala*; however, all but one of Gallen-Kallela's works, the unrepresentative *Kallervo Goes To War*, have been moved to Turku (see p.654). Slightly later came **Juho Rissanen** with his moody and evocative studies of peasant life, and **Hugo Simberg**, responsible for the eerie *Death and the Peasant* and the powerful triptych *Boy Carrying a Garland*. Cast an eye, too, over the works of **Helene Schjerfbeck**, for a long time one of the country's most underrated artists but now enjoying an upsurge in popularity – and collectability. Among the best examples of pure Finnish landscape are the works of **Pekka Halonen**: *Pioneers in Karelia* is typical, with soft curves expressively denoting natural scenes.

This cream of Finnish art is assembled on the first floor, appropriately placed directly off the main landing of the grand staircase that leads up from the entrance. Continue to the second floor and you'll find the provocative expressionism of **Tyko Sallinen** and the November Group, most active around 1917, some token **foreign** masters – a couple of large Munchs, a Van Gogh, a Chagall and a few Cézannes – and several much more recent installations by innovative contemporary Finnish artists. Before you leave, check out the excellent art bookshop on the ground floor.

North along Mannerheimintie

Mannerheimintie is the logical route for exploring north of the city centre. The wide thoroughfare is named after the military commander and statesman C.G.E. Mannerheim, who wielded considerable influence on Finnish affairs in the first half of the twentieth century. He's commemorated by a statue near the busy junction with Arkadiankatu, a structure on which the city's bird population has left its mark. Directly behind this is the site of the large National Contemporary Art Museum, being built at the time of writing, which is due to open some time in 1998.

The Parliament Building and National Museum

The section of Mannerheimintie from *Stockmann*'s northwards passes a number of outstanding buildings, the first of which is the **Parliament Building**, on the left (guided tours July & Aug Mon–Fri 2pm, Sat 11am & noon, Sun noon & 1pm; Sept–June Sat & Sun only; when in session, access is to the public galleries only; free). With its pompous columns and choking air of solemnity, the porridge-coloured building was the work of J.S. Sirén, and completed in 1931. Intended to celebrate the new republic, its style was drawn from the revolutionary Neoclassicism that dominated public buildings from Fascist Italy to Nazi Germany, and its authoritarian features can appear wildly out of place, though it's worth a look nonetheless.

From here onwards things improve, with the **National Museum** (June–Aug Tues 11am–8pm, Wed–Sun 11am–5pm; Sept–May Tues 11am–8pm, Wed–Sun 11am–4pm; 15mk), whose design was the result of a turn-of-the-century competition won by the three Young Turks of Finnish architecture – Armas Lindgren, Herman Gesellius and Eliel Saarinen. With National Romanticism at its zenith, they steeped their plan in Finnish history, drawing on the country's legacy of medieval churches and granite castles (even though many of these were built under Swedish domination), culminating in a weighty but slender tower that gives the place a cathedral-like profile. The entrance is guarded by Emil Wikström's sculptured bear and the interior ceilings are decorated by Gallen-Kallela with scenes from the *Kalevala*.

The museum may seem the obvious place to discover what Finland is all about but, especially if you've spent hours exploring the copiously stocked national museums of Denmark and Sweden, you might well find the collections disappointing. Being dominated by other nations for many centuries, Finland had little more than the prerequisites of peasant life to call its own up until the mid-1800s (when moves towards Finnish nationalism got off the ground), and the rows of farming and hunting tools alongside endless displays of bowls and spoons from the early times do little to fire the imagination. The most interesting sections of the museum are those relating to the rise of Finnish self-determination and the early years of the republic. Large photographs show the enormous crowds that massed in Helsinki's streets to sing the Finnish anthem in defiance of their (then) Russian rulers, and cabinets packed with small but intriguing objects outline the left–right struggles that marked the early decades of independence and the immediate postwar years – periods when Finland's political future teetered precariously in the balance, a long way from the stability and prosperity enjoyed in more recent times.

Finlandia Hall to the Olympic Stadium

Stylistically a far cry from the National Museum building but equally affecting, **Finlandia Hall** (guided tours when not in use, usually at noon and/or 2pm; ☎09/40241; fax 446 259; or check at the city tourist office for the latest details) stands directly across Mannerheimintie, partially hidden by the roadside foliage. Designed by the country's premier architect, **Alvar Aalto**, a few years before his death in 1976, Finlandia was conceived as part of a grand plan to rearrange the entire centre of Helsinki. Previously, Eliel Saarinen had planned a traffic route from the northern suburbs into a new square in the city centre, to be called Vapaudenkatu (Freedom Street) in celebration of Finnish independence. Aalto plotted a continuation of this scheme, envisaging the removal of the rail-freight yards, which would enable arrivals to be greeted with a fan-like terrace of new buildings reflected in the waters of Töölönlahti. Finlandia was to be the first of these, and only by looking across from the other side of Töölönlahti do you perceive the building's soft sensuality and the potential beauty of the greater concept. The design, however, has obvious faults, the most apparent being that the vast marble panels are curling away from the walls. Inside the hall, Aalto's characteristic wave pattern (the architect's surname, as it happens, means "wave") and asymmetry are in evidence. From the walls and ceilings through to the lamps and vases, the place has a quiet and graceful air. But the view from the foyer is still of the rail-freight yards, and the great plan for a future Helsinki is still under discussion.

Next door is **Hakasalmi Villa** (Wed–Sun 11am–5pm; 15mk), one of four satellite museums belonging to the new City Museum (see below). An Italian-style Neoclassical villa built in the 1840s by a councillor and patron of the arts whose collection inspired the founding of the museum, it houses long-term temporary exhibitions, often strikingly designed and worth a peek – recent topics have included the growth of the city, music and design. Finland's new **Opera House** (Mon–Fri 9am–6pm, Sat 3–6pm, Sun open 2hr before performances) a little way beyond Finlandia, is, like so many contemporary Finnish buildings, a Lego-like expanse of white-tiled facade. Its light-flooded interior is enlivened by displays of colourful costumes, though, and its grounds and entrance spiked with minimalist black granite sculptures.

From this point on, the decisive outline of the **Olympic Stadium** becomes visible. Originally intended for the 1940 Olympic Games, the stadium eventually staged the first postwar games, in 1952. From the **Stadium Tower** (Mon–Fri 9am–8pm, Sat & Sun 9am–6pm; 5mk) there's an unsurpassed view over the city and a chunk of the southern coast. If you're a stopwatch and spikes freak, ask at the tower's ticket office for directions to the **Sport Museum** (Mon–Fri 11am–5pm, Sat & Sun noon–4pm; 10mk), whose mind-numbing collection of track officials' shoes and swimming caps overshadows a worthy attempt to present sport as an integral part of Finnish culture. The nation's heroes, among them Keke Rosberg and Lasse Virén, are lauded to the skies. Outside, Wäinö Aaltonen's sculpture of Paavo Nurmi captures the champion runner of the 1920s in full stride, and full nudity – something that caused a stir when the sculpture was unveiled in 1952.

West of Mannerheimintie

As there's little of note north of the stadium, you should cross Mannerheimintie and follow the streets off it, which lead to **Sibelius Park** and Eila Hiltunen's monument to the composer made from 24 tons of steel tubes, like a big silver surrealist organ. Next to this, the unfortunate side work is an irrefutably horrid sculpture of Sibelius' dismembered head. The shady and pleasant park is rudely cut by a main road called Mechelininkatu. Following this back towards the city centre brings you first to the small Islamic and Jewish cemeteries, and then to the expanse of tombs comprising **Hietaniemi Cemetery** (usually open until 10pm). A prowl among these is like a stroll through a "Who was Who" of Finland's last 150 years: Mannerheim, Engel and a host of former presidents are buried here; just inside the main entrance lies Alvar Aalto, his witty little tombstone consisting partly of a chopped Neoclassical column; behind it is the larger marker of Gallen-Kallela, his initials woven around a painter's palette. It's to the cemetery that local school kids head when skipping lessons during warm weather, not for a smoke behind the gravestones but to reach the **beaches** that line the bay just beyond its western walls. From these you can enjoy the best sunset in the city.

On the way back towards Mannerheimintie, at Lutherinkatu 3, just off Runeberginkatu, is **Temppeliaukio kirkko** (Mon, Tues, Thurs & Fri 10am–8pm, Wed 10am–7pm, Sat 10am–6pm; in winter closed Tues 12.45pm–2.15pm; tram 3B). Brilliantly conceived by Timo and Tuomo Suomalainen and finished in 1969, the church is built inside a large lump of natural granite in the middle of an otherwise ordinary residential square. Try and see it from above if you can (even if you have to shin up a drainpipe), when the copper dome that pokes through the rock makes the thing look like a ditched flying saucer. The odd combination of man-made and natural materials has made it a fixture on the tourist circuit, but even when crowded it's a thrill to be inside. Classical concerts frequently take place here, the raw rock walls making for excellent acoustics – check the noticeboard at the entrance for details.

South of Esplanadi: Kaivopuisto and Eira

From the South Harbour it's a straightforward walk past the *Silja* terminal to Kaivopuisto, but it's more interesting to leave Esplanadi along Kasarmikatu, for some small, offbeat museums. First of these is the **Museum of Finnish Architecture** (Tues–Sun 10am–4pm, Wed until 7pm; free) at no. 24, which is aimed at the serious fan: architectural tours of less accessible buildings both in Helsinki and around the country can be arranged here. Combined with an extensive archive, it's a useful resource for a nation with an important architectural heritage.

A block from Kasarmikatu is Korkeavuorenkatu, with the excellent **Museum of Applied Arts** at no. 23 (June–Aug daily 11am–5pm; Sept–May Tues–Sun 11am–5pm, Wed until 8pm; 20mk), which traces the relationship between art and industry in Finnish history. There are full explanatory texts and period exhibits, from Karelianism – the representations of nature and peasant life from the Karelia region in eastern Finland that dominated Finnish art and design in the years just before and after independence – to the modern movements, along with the postwar shift towards the more familiar, and less interesting, pan-Scandinavian styles.

Kaivopuisto park

Kasarmikatu ends close to the base of a hill, from where footpaths lead up to the Engel-designed **Astronomical Observatory**. Down on the other side and a few streets on is the large and rocky **Kaivopuisto** park. In the 1830s this was developed as a health resort, with a spa house that drew Russian nobility from St Petersburg to sample its waters. The building, another of Engel's works although greatly modified, can be found in the middle of the park's central avenue, today pulling the crowds as a restaurant.

Off a smaller avenue, Itäinen Puistotie, runs the circular Kallionlinnantie, which contains the house where Gustaf Mannerheim spent the later years of his life, now maintained as the **Mannerheim Museum** (Fri–Sun 11am–4pm, other times by appointment; 30mk; ☎09/635 443). A Finnish-born Russian-trained military commander, Mannerheim was pro-Finnish but had a middle-class suspicion of the working classes: he led the right-wing Whites during the Civil War of 1918, and two decades later the Finnish campaigns in the Winter and Continuation wars (for more on which, see the "Military Museum", below). His influence in the political sphere was also considerable, and included a brief spell as president. While acknowledging his importance, the regard that Finns have for him these days, naturally enough, depends on their own political viewpoint.

Ideology aside, the house is intriguing. The interior is left much as it was when the man died in 1951, and the clutter is astounding. During his travels Mannerheim raided flea markets at every opportunity, collecting a remarkable array of plunder – assorted furniture and antiques, ornaments and books from all over the globe. Upstairs is the camp-bed which Mannerheim found too comfortable ever to change, and in the wall is the vent inserted to keep the bedroom as airy as a field-tent.

If he had lived a few decades earlier, one of Mannerheim's Kallionlinnantie neighbours would have been Frederik Cygnaeus, art patron and Professor of Aesthetics at Helsinki University. In 1860 Cygnaeus built a summer house at no. 8, a lovely yellow-turreted affair, and filled it with an outstanding collection of art. Later he donated the lot to the nation and today it's displayed as the **Cygnaeus Gallery** (Wed 11am–7pm, Thurs–Sun 11am–4pm; 10mk). Everything is beautifully laid out in the tiny rooms of the house, whole walls of work by the most influential of his contemporaries. The von Wright brothers (Ferdinand, Magnus and Wilhelm) are responsible for the most touching pieces – the characteristic bird and nature studies. Look out, too, for a strange portrait of Cygnaeus by Ekman, showing the man sprouting sinister wings from under his chin.

The edge of Kaivopuisto looks out across a sprinkling of little islands and the Suomenlinna fortress. You can follow one of the pathways down into **Merikatu**, along which lie several of the Art Nouveau villas lived in by the big cheeses of Finnish industry during the early part of the century. Easily the most extreme of these is no. 25, the Enso-Gutzeit villa, now portioned off into offices and with a lingering air of decay hanging over its decorative facade, making the squat little statues strewn around the garden seem quite indecent.

Eira

Inland from Merikatu, the curving alleys and tall elegant buildings of the **Eira** district are landmarked by the needle-like spire rising from the roof of **Mikael Agricola kirkko**, named after the translator of the first Finnish Bible but making no demands on your time. A few streets away, the twin-towered **Johannes kirkko** is again not worth a call in itself but functions as a handy navigation aid, being close to the junction of Merimenhenkatu and Yjrönkatu. Following the latter takes you past the partly pedestrianized Iso Robertinkatu, before reaching Bulevardi and the square containing **Vanha kirkko** or Old Church. A humble wooden structure, and another example of Engel's work, this was the first Lutheran church to be erected after Helsinki became the Finnish capital, predating that in Senate Square by some years but occupying a far less glamorous plot – a plague victim's burial ground dating from 1710.

Heading left along Bulevardi brings you to the wide Hietalahdentori, a concrete square that perks up with a daily morning flea market and, in summer, an evening market between 3.30 and 8pm. Across the road is the Sinebrychoff brewery, which besides bestowing a distinctive aroma of hops to the locality, finances the **Sinebrychoff Art Museum** at no. 40 (Mon, Thurs & Fri 9am–5pm, Wed 9am–9pm, Sat & Sun 11am–5pm; 10mk, 30mk for special exhibitions). This rather precious museum houses mostly seventeenth-century Flemish and Dutch paintings, along with some excellent miniatures, delicately illustrated porcelain and refined period furniture.

Kruununhaka and Hakaniemi

North of Senate Square is the little district of **Kruununhaka**. Away from the general city hubbub, its closely built blocks shield the narrow streets from the sunlight, evoking a forlorn and forgotten mood. At Kristianinkatu 12, the single-storey wooden **Burgher's House** (Mon & Wed 10am–4pm, Tues noon–8pm, Sat & Sun 11am–4pm; 10mk) stands in vivid contrast to the tall granite dwellings around it – and gives an indication of how Helsinki looked when wood was still the predominant building material. The interior has been kitted out with mid-nineteenth-century furnishings, the period when the city burgher did indeed reside here.

Kristianinkatu meets at right-angles with Maurinkatu, a short way along which is the **Military Museum** (Mon–Fri & Sun 11am–4pm; 10mk), a rather formless selection of weapons, medals and glorifications of armed-forces life, but with some excellent documentary photos of the Winter and Continuation wars of 1939–44. Finland was drawn into World War II through necessity rather than choice. When Soviet troops invaded eastern Finnish territories in November 1939, under the guise of protecting Leningrad, they were repelled by technically inferior but far more committed Finns. The legends of the "heroes in white" were born then, alluding to the Finnish soldiers and the camouflage used in the winter snows. Soon after, however, faced with possible starvation and a fresh Soviet advance, Finland joined the war on the Nazi side, mainly in order to continue resisting the threat from the east. For this reason, it's rare to find World War II spoken of as such in Finland: much more commonly it's divided into these separate conflicts.

Hakaniemi

The western edge of Kruunanhaka is defined by the busy Unionkatu (if it's a sunny day, take a stroll around the neat **botanical gardens**, just off Unionkatu), which continues northwards across a slender body of water into **Hakaniemi**, a district chiefly visited for its **kauppahalli** (Mon–Fri 8am–5pm, Sat 8am–2pm).

Although Hakaniementori is surrounded by drab storefronts and office blocks, the indoor market is about the liveliest in the city – mainly due to its position near a major junction for city buses and trams, as well as a metro station. From the square you can see right up the hill to the impressive Art Deco brickwork of the **Kallio kirkko**, beyond which is the busy Sturenkatu and the open green area partly consumed by **Linnanmäki amusement park** – the scene of several killings several years back when its roundabouts and dodgems provided the backdrop for a bout of teenage gang warfare. Since then, the park has reverted to providing innocent amusements and you should have no qualms about walking past it, after crossing Sturenkatu, on the way to the **Museum of Workers' Housing** at Kirstinjuka 4 (May–Sept Mon noon–8pm, Tues & Wed 10am–4pm, Sat & Sun 11am–6pm; 15mk), for some fascinating social history. The series of wooden buildings that now hold the museum were built during the early 1900s to provide housing for the impoverished country folk who moved to the growing, increasingly industrialized city to work as street cleaners and refuse collectors. Six of the one-room homes where the new arrivals settled have been re-created with period furnishings, and a biography on the door describes each flat's occupants – woeful tales of overcrowding, overwork, and sons who left for America and never returned.

Suomenlinna

Built by the Swedes in 1748 to protect Helsinki from seaborne attack, the fortress of **Suomenlinna** stands on five interconnected islands, reached by half-hourly ferry from the South Harbour, which make a rewarding break from the city centre – even if you only want to laze around on the dunes. (These were created by the Russians with sand shipped in from Estonia to strengthen the new capital's defences after they'd wrested control of Finland.) If you're feeling inquisitive, there are hour-long summer **guided walking tours** (June–Aug daily 11.30am & 1.30pm – check with tourist office for English-language tours; 20mk), beginning close to the ferry-landing stage. Suomenlinna has a few museums, none particularly riveting, although the **Nordic Arts Centre** (Tues–Sun 11am–5.45pm; closed Aug; free), with its small displays of contemporary arts from the Nordic countries, is worth a browse. Of the others, the **Ehrensvärd Museum** (early May–Aug daily 10am–5pm; Sept daily 10am–4.30pm; Oct & March to early May Sat & Sun 11am–4.30pm; 10mk) occupies the residence used by the first commander of the fortress, Augustin Ehrensvärd. He oversaw the building of Suomenlinna and now lies in the elaborate tomb in the grounds; his personal effects remain inside the house alongside displays on the fort's construction. The **Armfelt Museum** (mid-May to Aug daily 11am–5.30pm; Sept Sat & Sun 11am–5.30pm; 6mk) contains the eighteenth- and nineteenth-century family heirlooms of the Armfelt clan, who lived in the Joensuu Manor at Halikko. Finally, the **Coastal Artillery Museum** (mid-May to Aug daily 11am–5pm; Sept daily 11am–3pm; Oct to mid-May Sat & Sun 11am–3pm; 5mk) records Suomenlinna's defensive actions and – for an extra 10mk – visitors can clamber around the darkly claustrophobic World War I submarine *Vesikko*.

Seurasaari and around

A fifteen-minute tram (#4) or bus (#24) ride from the city centre (get off one stop after the big hospital on the left, from where it's a one-kilometre walk) lies **Seurasaari**, a small wooded island delightfully set in a sheltered bay. The three contrasting museums on or close by the island make for a well-spent day. Access to the island proper is by a bridge at the southern end of Tamminiementie, conveniently close to the **Helsinki City Art Museum** (Wed–Sun 11am–6.30pm; 20mk). Though one of the best collections of modern Finnish art, with some eerily striking work, the museum is hardly a triumph of layout, with great clumps of stuff of differing styles thrown at the walls. But the good pieces shine through. Be warned, though, that during temporary exhibitions the permanent stock is locked away.

A few minutes' walk from the art museum, towards the Seurasaari bridge, is the long driveway leading to the **Urho Kekkonen Museum** (July & Aug daily 11am–5pm, Thurs until 7pm; Sept–June Tues–Sun 11am–5pm; 15mk), the villa where the esteemed former president lived from his retirement until his death is 1980, and which has been the official home of all Finnish presidents since 1940. Whether they love him or loathe him, few Finns would deny the vital role Kekkonen played in Finnish history, most significantly by continuing the work of his predecessor, Paasikivi, in the establishment of Finnish neutrality and what became known as the "Paasikivi-Kekkonen line". He accomplished this largely through delicate negotiations with Soviet leaders – whose favour he would gain, so legend has it, by taking them to a sauna – narrowly averting major crises and seeing off the threat of a Soviet invasion on two separate occasions. Kekkonen often conducted official business here rather than at the Presidential Palace in the city. Yet the feel of the place is far from institutional, with a light and very Finnish character, filled with birchwood furniture, its large windows giving peaceful views of surrounding trees, water and wildlife.

Close by, in another calm setting across the bridge on Seurasaari itself, is the **Open-Air Museum** (June–Aug daily 11am–5pm, Wed until 7pm; first half of Sept Mon–Fri 9am–3pm, Sat & Sun 11am–5pm; second half of Sept Sat & Sun 11am–5pm; second half of May Mon–Fri 9am–3pm, Sat & Sun 11am–5pm; 15mk), a collection of vernacular buildings assembled from all over Finland, connected up by the various pathways that extend all around the island. There are better examples of traditional Finnish life elsewhere in the country, but if you're only visiting Helsinki this will give a good insight into how the country folk lived until surprisingly recently. The old-style church is a popular spot for city couples' weddings.

Aside from the museums and the scenery, people also come to Seurasaari to strip off. Sex-segregated **nudist beaches** (10mk) line part of the western edge – also a popular offshore stop for the city's weekend yachtsmen, armed with binoculars.

Outlying museums

Helsinki has a few other **museums** outside the centre that don't fit into to any walking tour. All are within fairly easy reach with public transport, and sometimes a little legwork.

Gallen-Kallela Museum

At Gallen-Kallelantie 27 on the little Tarvaspää peninsula. Mid-May to Aug Tues–Thurs 10am–8pm, Fri–Sun 10am–5pm; Sept to mid-May Tues–Sat 10am–4pm, Sun 10am–5pm; 35mk. Take tram #4 from the city centre to the end of its route (on Saunalahdentie), then walk 2km along Munkkiniemi on the bay's edge, to a footbridge which leads over the water and towards the poorly signposted museum. Alternatively, bus #33 runs from the tram stop to the footbridge about every twenty minutes.

This museum is housed inside the Art Nouveau studio home of Gallen-Kallela, where the influential painter lived and worked from 1913, though it's a bit of an anticlimax, with neither atmosphere nor a decent display of the artist's work. There are a few old paints and brushes under dirty glass coverings in the studio, while in an upstairs room are the pickled remains of reptiles and frog-like animals collected by Gallen-Kallela's family. Inscribed into the floor is a declaration by Gallen-Kallela: "I Shall Return". Unless you're a huge fan, it's probably not worth the bother.

The Cable Factory museums (Kaapelitehdas)

A clutch of museums now occupies what was formerly a cable factory to the west of the city centre at Tallberginkatu 1F, accessible on tram #8. All are open Tues–Fri noon–6pm, Wed until 8pm, Sat & Sun noon–5pm; 10mk.

Although the **Hotel and Restaurant Museum** is specifically designed for aficionados of the catering trade, the photos on the walls of its two rooms reveal a fascinating social history of Helsinki, showing hotel and restaurant life from both sides of the table, alongside a staggering selection of matchboxes, beer mats emblazoned with the emblems of their establishments, and menus signed by the rich and infamous.

Despite its grand title, the **Photographic Museum of Finland** comprises a shabby herd of old cameras that suggest Finnish photography never really progressed beyond the watch-the-birdie stage. Amends are made by the innovative temporary collections of photos that regularly adorn the walls. The third museum in the complex is the city's main **Theatre Museum** (see also p.629), displaying a permanent collection of costumes, stage sets and lights. Frequent temporary exhibitions focus on different aspects behind the scenes in Finnish theatre.

Eating and drinking

Eating in Helsinki, as in the rest of the country, isn't cheap, but there is plenty of choice, and with careful planning plenty of ways to stretch out funds. Other than all-you-can-eat **breakfast** tables in hotels (hostel breakfasts in the city tend to be rationed), it's best to hold out until **lunch**, when many restaurants offer a reduced fixed-price menu or a help-yourself table, and in almost every pizzeria you'll get a pizza, coffee, and all you can manage from the bread and salad bar for under 40mk. **Picnic food**, too, is a viable option. Use the markets and market halls at the South Harbour or Hakaniementori for fresh vegetables, meat and fish. Several supermarkets in Tunneli, by the train station, stay open until 10pm. The popular **Forum** shopping centre, a somewhat downtrodden version of the *Stockmann* looming up directly opposite, has a number of popular, inexpensive eateries on two floors, while the **precinct** opposite the train station contains a range of mid-standard, filling eateries open till late.

Throughout the day, up until 5pm or 6pm, you can also get a coffee and pastry, or a fuller snack, for 10–25mk at one of the numerous **cafés**. The best cafés are stylish, atmospheric affairs dating from the turn of the century. Alternatives include myriad multinational hamburger joints and the slightly more unusual *Grilli* roadside stands, which sell hot dogs, sausages and the like; if you're tempted, experts claim the *Jaskan Grilli*, in Töölönkatu behind the National Museum, to be the best of its kind. If you're hungry and impoverished (and are, in theory at least, a student), you can get a full meal for 12–15mk from one of the **student mensas**, two of which are centrally located in the main university building at Aleksanterinkatu 5, and at Hallituskatu 11–13. One or the other will be open during the summer; both are open during term time. The mensas can be cheaper still in the late afternoon, from 4pm to 6pm, and are also usually open on Saturdays from 9am to 1pm. As for **evening eating**, there are plenty of restaurants serving reasonably priced ethnic foods, as well as a number of Finnish haute cuisine places.

Cafés

Aalto, in the Academic Bookstore, Pohjoisesplanadi 39. Designed by the world-famous Finnish architect, the interior of this cafeteria makes it worth sitting down to appreciate after a morning's book browsing. Good salads for 40mk and great cakes (20mk).

Avec, *Stockmann Department Store*. Serves cakes, stylish sandwiches and drinks in pleasant surroundings.

Caramelle, by Villa Hakasalmi, Karamzininkatu 2. A small, intimate café serving gorgeous gooey cakes. Open summer Mon–Fri 11am–5pm, Sat & Sun 11am–4pm; shorter hours in winter.

Ekberg, Bulevardi 9. Nineteenth-century fixtures and a deliberately *fin-de-siècle* atmosphere, with starched waitresses bringing the most delicate of open sandwiches and pastries to green marble tables.

Eliel, on the ground floor of the train station. An airy, vaulted Art Nouveau interior with a good-value self-service breakfast (Mon–Sat 7–10am, Sun 8–10am; 29mk) – and a roulette table.

Engel, Aleksanterinkatu 26. Named after the Berlin-born designer of all the buildings you can see from its window, a haven of fine coffee, pastries, cakes and intellectual chit-chat, just across from Senate Square. Try the smoked-fish salad (39mk).

Esplanad, Pohjoisesplanadi. The best place for cheaper food. Filled baguettes (20mk), a choice of fresh soups daily and always a queue.

Fazer, Kluuvikatu 3. Helsinki's best-known bakery, justly celebrated for its lighter-than-air pastries. Another branch is in the *Forum* Shopping Centre opposite *Stockmann*. At either, try the speciality

Bebe, a praline cream-filled pie for 8mk. Café Mon–Fri 7.45am–11pm, Sat 8.30am–11pm, Sun noon–10pm; shop Mon–Fri 7.45am–6pm, Sat 9am–3pm.

Kappeli, in Esplanadi Park. An elegant glasshouse with massive wrought-iron decorated windows overlooking Esplanadi and the harbour, with lots of live entertainment outside and in during the summer. The cellar is also a great spot for an evening drink – see *Kappelin Olutkellari*, under "Drinking". Daily June–Aug 8am–4am; Sept–May 9am–4am.

Mini Succes, Korkeavourenkatu 2. Freshly baked bread, doughnuts and pastries every day.

Monetario/Bubbling Under, Kaivakatu 8, opposite the train station. A combination of 1960s-style bar and futuristic bubbling glass columns, serving cheap coffee (5mk) at high stools. Daily 9am–2am.

Socis, Kaivokatu 12. Big, cosmopolitan and very beautiful – though also very expensive. Mon–Sat 10am–midnight, Sun noon–10pm.

Strindberg, corner of Mikonkatu and Pohjoisesplandi. Stylish outdoors coffee sipping – though it's expensive if you want to eat, with a menu listing such items as smoked reindeer with lapland cheese followed by glow fried grayling and arctic cloudberry for 115mk. Mon–Thurs 7.30am–midnight, Fri 7.30am–1am, Sat 9am–1am, Sun 10am–midnight.

Tamminiementie, Tamminiementie 8. A good stop-off when visiting the City Art Museum or Seurasaari Island, for high-quality tea (or coffee) served in elegant surroundings, with Chopin playing in the background.

Tomtebon Kahvila, opposite the Kekkonen Museum at Seurassari. Coffee served with homemade cookies and cakes in a lovely old wooden villa set in a lush garden. June–Aug daily 11am–5pm; Sept–May Sat & Sun 11am–4pm.

Ursula (1), Kaivopuisto. On the beach at the edge of the Kaivopuisto park, with a wonderful sea view from the outdoor terrace.

Ursula (2), Pohjoisesplanade 21. Elegant place for good cakes and tarts. There's courtyard eating at the back, near the entrance to a beautiful interior design shop. Daily 9am–10pm.

Victor, 32 Bulevardi. Enticing selection of reasonably priced lunch dishes that attract a regular local clientele; large windows for watching the world go by.

Restaurants

Foreign restaurants are reasonably plentiful in Helsinki, and in a typical **pizzeria** you can expect to pay 50–60mk per person for dinner, provided you don't drink anything stronger than mineral water. There are also a few **vegetarian** restaurants, which charge about the same. **Finnish** restaurants, on the other hand, and those serving **Russian** specialities, can be terrifyingly expensive; expect to spend around 150mk each for a night of upmarket overindulgence. Restaurants are usually open daily until around 1am, though the kitchens close at about 11pm. It's best to check first if you want to eat late, especially at the more expensive places, which tend to close a little earlier.

Finnish and Russian

Alexander Nevski, Pohjoisesplanadi 17 (☎09/639 610). A very fine, classic Russian restaurant with live music. June–Aug Mon–Sat noon–1am, Sun 6pm–midnight; Sept–May Mon–Fri 11am–midnight, Sat noon–midnight, Sun 6pm–midnight.

Bellevue, Rahapajankatu 3, behind the Uspenski Cathedral (☎09/179 560). A superb Russian restaurant ironically opened in 1917, the year Finland won independence from Russia. Expensive but gourmet Russian food. Try Marshal Mannerheim's favourite of minced lamb flavoured with herring. Mon–Fri 11am–midnight, Sat & Sun 5pm–midnight.

Havis Amanda, Unioninkatu 23. An excellent fish restaurant, though pricey and somewhat staid.

Holvari, Yrjönkatu 15. Specializes in mushrooms, personally picked by the owner and providing the basis of tasty soups and stews.

Houne ja Keittiö, Huvilakatu 28. The name means literally "a room and a kitchen", and this tiny place is just that, producing fine home-cooked dishes from a small selection starting at a bargain 40mk. Closed at weekends.

Hullu Kukko, Simonkatu 8. Nothing special to look at, but great fish soup and excellent pizzas (52mk).

Iso-Ankkuri, Pursimiehenkatu 16. Fairly downbeat and used mostly by local people, but with a filling, unextravagant menu.

Kannu, Punavuorenkatu 12. Much of the original interior, designed by Alvar Aalto, remains in this locals' haunt, where the staff dish up stodgy, down-to-earth Finnish food.

Kasakka, Meritullinkatu 13. Over the top spirit-of-the-Tsars atmosphere and great food in this old-style Russian restaurant.

Katajanokan Kasino, Laivastokat 1. A gourmet and theme restaurant, in which you can feast on à la carte elk or reindeer in anything from a mock wartime bunker to the "Cabinet Room", decorated with markers to Finnish independence. A great place if someone else is paying.

Katarina, Aleksanterinkatu 22–24. An inspired if immensely costly mating of Finnish and French cuisines.

Kynsilaukka Ravintola Garlic, Fredrikinkatu 22. Pricey, but the ultimate if you like garlic.

Kuu, Töölönkatu 27. Unpretentious place to consume equally unpretentious inexpensive Finnish food.

Ravintola Lappi, Annankatu 22. A fine, though not cheap Finnish restaurant specializing in real Finnish foods like pea soup and oven pancakes, as well as Lappish specialities of smoked reindeer and warm cloudberries.

Saslik, Neitsytpolku 12 (☎09/348 9700). Highly rated for its Russian food, served amid lush, Tsarist-period furnishings and accompanied by live music. Mon–Sat 11am–midnight, Sun 1pm–midnight.

Sea Horse, Kapteeninkatu 11. Serves a range of fairly inexpensive Finnish dishes, and is renowned for its Baltic sprats.

Sipoli, Kanavaranta 3. A tastebud-thrilling, formal and glamorous – though financially ruinous – choice of six gourmet dishes, several based on traditional Sami fare.

Terrace Bar, Stockmann Department Store, sixth floor. Situated on the top floor and with bright, relaxed Lloyd loom style seating. A small salad and soup costs 42mk, or go for dishes from the grill (11am–7pm), such as potato and anchovy bake (42mk) or grilled chicken (47mk).

Ethnic and vegetarian

Ani, Telakkakatu 2. Turkish food at its best from the 38mk open table laid out at lunchtime.

Aurinkotuuli, Lapinlahdenkatu 25a. A good range of vegetarian dishes at prices to suit all but the tightest of budgets.

Green Way, Erottajankatu 11. Wholefood place with a well-stocked fruitshake and juice bar.

Kairinmaru, Korkeavuorenkatu 4 (☎09/639 180). A good Japanese place with sushi and a takeaway service. If eating in, it's best to book ahead.

Kasvis, Korkeavuorenkatu 3. Literally a "vegetable restaurant", and one of the oldest and best (though not the cheapest) in the country. Good vegetarian shop attached.

Namaskar, Mannerheimintie 100. The pick of a slowly growing band of Indian restaurants struggling to make an impression on Helsinki eating habits. Currently the most expensive Asian restaurant in the city.

Sukhothai, Runeberginkatu 32. The least expensive and quite possibly the best of the city's crop of new Thai restaurants.

Wienerwald, Kaivakatu, opposite the train station. A sort of Austrian-style Pizza Hut with good-value Austrian fish and meat dishes and wide range of Austrian sausages. Try half a roasted chicken and potato salad for 37mk.

Zucchini, Fabianinkatu 4. A friendly and stylish vegetarian restaurant.

American

Cantina West, Kasarmikatu 23. Fiery Tex-Mex food in a lively, western-themed restaurant spread over several floors. Gets loud late at night.

Chico's, Mannerheimintie 68. Very friendly, inexpensive all-American eatery with pizzas and burgers starting at around 50mk, alongside speciality dishes from the Deep South and Mexico. Mon–Fri 11am–midnight, Sat noon–midnight, Sun 1pm–midnight.

La Havanna, Uudenmenkatu 9–11. Pioneering Cuban eaterie doing great things with seafood, but make sure you come at lunchtime – at night it's packed with boozers. See "Drinking".

Planet Hollywood, Mikonkatu 9. Much hyped American diner opened by the likes of Finnish film director Renny Harlin, Bruce Willis, Demi Moore and Geena Davis, and crammed with movie memorabilia.

Italian and pizzas

Mama Rosa, Runeberginkatu 55. A classic pizzeria also serving fish, steaks and pasta. One of the best mid-priced restaurants in the city that's not surprisingly always full. Daily 11am–midnight.

Pasta Factory, Mastokatu 6. Intimate and discreetly stylish Italian place. Quite affordable.

Pizza No.1, Mannerheimintie 18, second floor of the *Forum* shopping centre. Standard pizzas, but good deals at lunchtime and an entertaining selection of English cricket memorabilia on the walls.

Drinking

Although never cheap, alcohol is not a dirty word in Finland, and **drinking**, especially beer, can be enjoyed in the city's many café-like pubs, which are where most Helsinki folk go to socialize. You'll find one on virtually every corner, but the pick of the bunch are listed below. Only the really swanky places have a dress code, and they are usually too elitist – and expensive – to be worth bothering with anyway. Sundays to Thursdays are normally quiet; on Fridays and Saturdays on the other hand, it's best to arrive as early as possible to get a seat without having to queue. Most drinking dives also serve food, although the grub is seldom at its best in the evening (where it's good earlier in the day, we've included it under "Restaurants"). If you want a drink but are feeling anti-social, or just very hard-up, the cheapest method, as ever, is to buy from the appropriately named *ALKO* shop: there are self-service ones at Fabiankatu 7 and Vuorikatu 7.

Pubs and bars

Angleterre, Fredrikinkatu 47. Utterly Finnish despite the flock wallpaper and Dickensian fixtures – good for a laugh and cultural disorientation.

Aseman Yläravintola, second floor of the train station. Socially much more interesting than the *Eliel* downstairs (see "Cafés"), this is a lively and diverse place for a drink, surrounded by architect Saarinen's fabulous features. Don't risk it if you've a train to catch.

Ateljeebaari, *Hotel Torni*, Yrjönkatu 26. On the thirteenth floor of a plush hotel: great views, great posing – but be warned that the women's toilet has bizarre ceiling-to-floor windows. Drinks are pricey.

Black Door, Iso Robertinkatu 1. Excellent selection of beers and fair prices, with seats oustide on a small terrace.

Bulevardia, Bulevardi 34. Many customers are technicians or singers from the neighbouring Opera House who swoop in after a concert. Join them for the Art Deco decor – matt-black furniture designed by 1930s architect Pauli Blomstedt, and burr-birch walls.

Elite, Etläinen Hesperiankatu 22. Once the haunt of the city's artists, many of whom would settle the bill not with money but with paintings – a selection of which lines the walls. Especially good in summer, when you can drink on the terrace.

Happy Days, Pohjoisesplanadi 2. Spend a few hours in this sometimes rowdy summer-only bar and you'll encounter a cross-section of Helsinki characters – some coming, some going, others falling over.

La Havanna, Uudenmenkatu 9–11. A Cuban restaurant, though there's much more boozing than dining in the evenings, and not much space to move as Latin American music fills the smoky air. A must. See also "Restaurants".

Juttutupa, Säästöpankinranta 6. The building was once HQ of the Social Democrats; they built it with a tower to allow their red flag to fly above the neighbouring church spires. The decision to take up arms, which culminated in the 1918 civil war, was made here and photos commemorate the fact. Apolitical entertainment is provided on Wed, Fri and Sat by an accordian and/or violin player, encouraging enjoyable singalongs.

Kaarle XII, Kasarmikatu 40. Fine Art Nouveau features hewn into the red granite walls make this the most traditional-looking of the city's bars; not that the customers allow the surroundings to inhibit their merrymaking.

Kannus, Eerikinkatu 43. The fights and drunken sailors that made this a Helsinki legend for fifty years have given way to new management and an attempt to re-create a 1960s Americana look, complete with pool table and movie-poster tablecloths (and rarely any fights).

Kappelin Kellari, in Esplanadi Park. The entrance is to the side of this distinctive multipurpose building of glass and fancy ironwork (see also "Cafés" above). A garrulous and gloriously eclectic clientele.

Kosmos, Kalevankatu 3. This is where the big media cats – TV producers, PR people, the glitzier authors – hang out and engage in loud arguments as the night wears on. The wonderful interior is unchanged since the 1920s, but you'll only see it if you get past the extremely officious doorman.

Kultainen Härkä, Uudenmenkatu 16–20. Load your plate from the inexpensive salad bar by day; drink, and heckle the singer tinkling the piano, by night.

Ma Baker's, Mannerheimintie 12. A good place to initiate yourself into drinking Helsinki-style; open until 3am, it has a reputation as a last-chance pick-up spot.

Meri Makasiini, Hietalahdenranta 4. Slightly out-of-the-way but worth sampling on a Fri or Sat night when the customers spill onto the terrace to drink and gaze at the cranes of the city's cargo harbour.

Mulligans, Mannerheimintie 10. Live Irish music every night at this likeable pub.

No Name, Töölönkatu 2. Looks like an American cocktail bar and pulls an intriguing cross-section of Finns on the razzle.

Richard's Pub Rikhardinkatu 4. Close to the editorial offices of the major Helsinki newspapers. Usually contains a few hacks crying over lost scoops.

Salve, Hietaladenranta 11. Filled with nautical paraphernalia but no longer the seedy sailors' haunt that it was. Worth a call, to eat or drink, although the recently hiked-up prices suggest the place has ideas above its station.

St Urho's Pub, Museokatu 10. One of the most popular student pubs – which accounts for the lengthy queue that forms from about 9pm on Fri and Sat.

Vanhan Kahvila, Mannerheimintie 3. A self-service and hence comparatively cheap bar. It fills quickly, so try to arrive early for a seat on the balcony overlooking the bustle of the streets below.

Vanhan Kellari, Mannerheimintie 3. Downstairs from the *Vanhan Kahvila*, its underground setting and bench-style seating help promote a cosy and smoky atmosphere. Rumour has it that this is where the Helsinki beat poets of the early 1960s drank, and where they now bring their children.

Vastarannan Kisski, Salomonkatu 15, A crowded pub with a wide selection of beers both on tap and bottled.

William K, Mannerheimintie. A cosy, locals' pub with old Indian carpets for tablecloths and every beer you could want, though the imported ones are expensive.

Zetor, Kaivopiha, near the train station. A loud, country-themed bar designed by the people who run the Leningrad Cowboys rock group.

Nightlife and entertainment

Helsinki probably has a greater and more diverse number of ways to spend the evening than any other Scandinavian city; there is, for example, a steady diet of **live music**. Finnish rock bands, not helped by the awkward metre of their native language, often sound absurd on first hearing, but at least seeing them is relatively cheap at 20–35mk – around half the price of seeing a British or American band – and sometimes even free. The best gigs tend to be during term-time, but in summer there are dozens of free events in the city parks, the biggest of which take place almost every Sunday in Kaivopuisto. Many bands also play on selected nights in one of the growing number of surprisingly hip **clubs and discos**, in which you can gyrate, pose or just drink into the small hours – admission is usually 20–30mk.

For up-to-the-minute details of **what's on,** read the entertainments page of *Helsingin Sanomat*, or the free fortnightly paper *City* (found in record shops, bookshops and department stores), which has listings covering rock and classical music, clubs, cinema, theatre and opera. You could also drop into **Kompassi,** Simonkatu 1 (☎09/612 1863), a youth service centre with information on festivals, concerts and events, or else simply watch out for posters on the streets. **Tickets** for most events can be bought at the venue or, for a small commission, at a couple of agencies: *Lippupalvelu*, Mannerheimintie 5 (Mon–Fri 9.30am–4.30pm, Sat 10am–2pm; ☎09/179 568 or 9700 4700), and *Tiketti*, Yrjönkatu 29c (Mon–Fri 9am–5pm; ☎09/693 2255). Both of these are open slightly longer hours in winter.

Clubs and music venues

Bar Fat Mama, Kaisaniemenkatu 6. Very eclectic, marginal music performed live. Daily from 10.30pm.

Bar 52, Fabiankatu 29. Live 1950s music in a cool, laid-back atmosphere.

Café Barock, Fredrikinkatu 42. Huge restored old church with eating, drinking and dancing in an offbeat atmosphere.

Berlin, Töölönkatu 3 (☎09/499 002). Depending on the night, you'll find the latest acid and hip-hop sounds, heavy rock, or black-music specials.

Botta, Museokatu 10 (☎09/446 940), joined to *St Urho's Pub* (see "Drinking", above). Vibrant dance music of various hues most nights.

Helmi, Eerikinkatu 14. The only non-gay venue on this street – very crowded and loud, with a good bar selection.

Kaivo, Kaivopuisto Park. One of the city's longest established late-night party spots, come here to dance, drink and join the very long taxi queues for home.

KY-Exit, Pohjoinen Rautatiekatu 21 (☎09/407 238). Sometimes has visiting foreign bands, more often lively disco nights for clubbers in their early twenties.

Manala, Dagmarinkatu 2. Two floors and long queues for anything from ballroom dancing to grinding to MTV's latest offerings.

Nylon, Kaivokatu 12. Somewhat pretentious but certainly hip small club run by the city's Live Music Association. Popular late at night.

Olutkellari, *Merihotelli*, John Stenberginranta 6 (☎09/708 711). Acoustic blues on Mon & Tues.

Orfeus, Eerikinkatu 3 (☎09/640378). Free live jazz and blues on Thurs, Fri & Sat.

Storyville, Museokatu 8. Buzzing jazz joint, with live dixieland, swing or be-bop on stage every night. Open till the small hours.

Super Bad Soul Club, at *Victor's*, Eteläranta 16 (☎09/661 112). As the name suggests, a celebration of the sounds (and the clothes) of American soul and funk of the early 1970s. Thurs only.

Tavastia, Urho Kekkosenkatu 4–6 (☎09/694 3401). A major showcase for Finnish and Swedish bands. Downstairs has the stage and self-service bar; the balcony is waitress service.

Teatro, Yrönkatu 31. A young crowd at this popular venue built in an old cinema; it's more mainstream than *Fat Mama*, with a cover charge of 50–60mk.

Vanha Maestro, Fredrikinkatu 51–53 (☎09/644 303). The place to go if you fancy some traditional Finnish dancing, and a legend among the country's enthusiasts of *humpa* – a truly Finnish dance, distantly related to the waltz and tango. Afternoon and evening sessions most days (entry 10–30mk).

Vanha Ylioppilastalo, Mannerheimintie 3 (☎09/176 616). The main venue for leading indie bands from around the world; see also the *Vanha* bars under "Drinking".

Gay Helsinki

The **gay scene** in Helsinki, though it's still small, has really blossomed during the past couple of years, gaining a much higher profile and wider acceptance, at least among the city's younger and more cosmopolitan population. Most of the gay **cafés/bars** are within a couple of minutes' walk of each other around **Eerikinkatu**, the most hip being *H2o* at no. 14, a dark, stylish and continental-style café-bar. On the other side of the road, *Stonewall* (Tues–Thurs & Sun 5pm–2am, Fri 5pm–3am, Sat 2pm–3am) is a more traditional basement bar serving good food in a slightly less welcoming atmosphere – go before 9pm for happy hour, when beers are 15mk. A street away is the popular night club *Don't Tell Mama*, Annankatu 32, and next door to that is *Café Escale*, a gay boozer's hangout with little charm. Newest on the scene is *Lost & Found*, Annankatu 6 (Mon–Fri 2pm–4am, Sat & Sun 1pm–4am), a very stylish gay drinking and eating place with a sweeping bar – try the fine salmon and herb soup (36mk). Back on Eerinkatu is Finland's one and only gay **bookstore**, the well-stocked *Baffin Books* (Mon–Fri noon–7pm, Sat 10am–3pm). For information and advice, contact the national gay and lesbian organization **SETA**, Oikokatu 3 (☎09/135 8303), during office hours.

Cinema

Both the latest blockbusters and a good selection of fringe **films** are normally showing somewhere in Helsinki. A seat is usually 25–30mk, although some places offer a 15mk matinee show on Mondays; this isn't loudly advertised but discreetly indicated by hand-written notices outside the venue. Check the listings in *City* or pick up a copy of *Elokuva-Viikko*, a free weekly leaflet that lists the cinemas and their programmes. English-language films are shown with Finnish subtitles – there's no overdubbing. If you're at a loose end, the three-screened *Nordia*, Yrjönkatu 36 (☎09/1311 9250), commonly has an excellent programe of new art-house films and cult classics – at cheap prices.

Listings

Airlines *British Airways*, Keskuskatu 7 (☎09/650 677); *Finnair*, Mannerheimintie 102 (☎09/81881); *SAS*, Phojoisesplanadi 23 (☎09/177 433).

Airport Enquiries ☎09/8292451; *Finnair* terminal for airport buses (☎09/410411).

Books The *Academic Bookstore* at Pohjoisesplanadi 39 has several floors containing thousands of books in various languages on all subjects, including a large stock of English paperbacks.

Car rental *Avis*, Fredrikinkatu 67 (☎09/441 114); *Budget*, Toinen linja 29 (☎09/735 964); *Europcar*, Mannerheimintie 50 (☎09/408 443).

Doctor ☎008.

Embassies *UK*, Itäinen Puistotie 17 (☎09/661 293); *USA*, Itäinen Puistotie 14 (☎09/171 931); *Canada*, Pohjoisesplanadi 25B (☎09/171 141). Citizens of Australia and New Zealand should contact the Australian Embassy in Stockholm, and Irish citizens the relevant authority in Amsterdam.

Emergencies Ambulance and Fire ☎112; Police ☎10022.

Exchange Outside banking hours at the airport 6.30am–11pm; and slightly more cheaply at Katajanokka harbour (where *Viking* and *Finnjet* dock) daily 9–11.30am & 3.45–6pm. Also *Forex* in the central train station (daily 8am–9pm), though it doesn't accept *Visa*; and *Postipankki*, opposite the station (Mon–Fri 8am–8pm, Sat 10am–6pm), which handles cash advances on all major cards.

Ferries Reservations & information: *Silja Line* ☎0990/330 000, fax 01255/240 268 (daily 8am–8pm); *Tallink* ☎09/2282 1211, fax 649 808 (Mon–Sat 8.30am–7pm); *Viking Line* ☎09/12351 (daily 7am–9.30pm).

Hitching *Radio City* on 96.2MHz has a phone-in lift service each Thursday (☎09/694 1366) – and they speak English.

Hospital Töölö Hospital, Töölönkatu 40 (☎09/4711), has a first-aid unit; Helsinki University Central Hospital, Haartmaninkatu 4, has an emergency department (same phone number).

Late shops The shops in Tunneli, the underground complex by the train station, are open Mon–Sat 10am–10pm, Sun noon–10pm.

Laundry Self-service at Punavuorenkatu 3 (Mon–Fri 7am–9pm, Sat & Sun 9am–9pm) and Mannerheimintie 93 (Mon–Thurs 9am–5pm, Fri 8am–1pm); they're not cheap – 20–58mk for a load.

Left luggage For 10mk at the long-distance bus station (Mon–Thurs & Sat 9am–6pm, Fri 8am–6pm), or in the train station (Mon–Fri 7am–10pm).

Libraries In Finnish, *kirjasto*; central branches at Topeliuksenkatu 6 in Töölö, at Rikhardinkatu 3 near Esplanadi, and at Viides linja 11, close to Kallio kirkko (all Mon–Fri 9.30am–8pm, Sat 9.30am–3pm).

Lost-property office (*Löytötavaratoimisto*) Sixth floor, Päivänteentie 12A (June–Aug Mon–Fri 8am–3.15pm; Sept–May Mon–Fri 8am–4.15pm; ☎09/189 3180, fax 189 2829).

Media There's a tourist-oriented "News in English" on ☎09/040. See also "What's On".

Pharmacy *Yliopiston Apteeki*, Mannerheimintie 96 (☎09/415 778), is open 24 hours; its branch at Mannerheimintie 5 is open daily 7am–midnight.

Police Olavinkatu 1 (☎09/694 0633).

Post office The main office is at Mannerheimintie 11 (Mon–Fri 9am–5pm); poste restante at the rear door (Mon–Fri 8am–9pm, Sat 9am–6pm, Sun 11am–9pm). Stamps from post offices or the yellow machines in shops, which take 1mk and 5mk coins.

Transport information In Finnish only; planes ☎09/821 122 or 818 500; long-distance buses ☎9600 4000 (expensive recorded message); train timetables ☎09/010 0121; city transport ☎09/765 966. For ferry information, see above.

Travel agents *KILROY travels*, Kaivokatu 10D (☎09/680 7811), is the Scandinavian youth travel agent, specializing in discounted tickets for students and young people. *Suomen Matkutoimisto* (*SMT*), the Finland Travel Bureau, Alexanderinkatu 17, organizes trips to Russia and the necessary visas.

What's on Listings in *Helsinki This Week* (monthly), and the *Helsinki Guide* (issued each summer), from the city tourist office, hotels and hostels.

Women's movement Although it's closed throughout July, the place to make contact is the Finnish feminists' union: *Naisasialiitto Unioni*, at Bulevardi 11A (☎09/642 277), where there's also *Naistenhuone*, a women's bookshop-café (Mon–Fri 4–9pm, Sat noon–6pm, Sun 2–6pm).

Around Helsinki

To be honest, there's little in Helsinki's outlying area that's worth venturing out for. But three places, all an easy day trip from the city, merit a visit: the visionary suburbs of

FINLAND'S LINKS WITH ESTONIA

Following Estonia's regaining of its independence, a growing number of passenger vessels are plying the 85-kilometre route across the Baltic between Helsinki and the Estonian capital, Tallinn. Unless you go on the day trip offered by *Estonian New Line* (see below), you'll need an Estonian **visa** to make the journey. These cost 40mk from the Estonian Consulate, Second Floor, Eteläranta 2A (☎09/79719), and usually take three to four days to be issued, though you can get one immediately by paying 100mk.

Estonia and Finland have similar languages, a common ancestry, and histories which had largely run parallel up until the Soviet Union's annexation of Estonia in 1940. Despite the decades of Soviet occupation, **Tallinn**, within its medieval walls, is a beautifully maintained Hanseatic city with many museums and some fine old churches just a few minutes' walk from the harbour. If you have time, take a look, too, at the enormous Song Festival Grounds just outside the old centre, scene of the much-publicized pro-independence rallies of the late 1980s.

While independence has brought Estonians many new freedoms, it hasn't brought them any money. The introduction of the kroon (rhymes with "prawn", not "prune"), a new version of the pre-Soviet currency, did little to ease the uphill struggle faced by the country's economy.

Crossings are offered by *Tallink Finland OY* (tickets from South Harbour booking office; ☎09/2282 1211, fax 649 808), *Eestin Linjat* (Keskuskatu 1; ☎09/228 8544, fax 2288 5222), *Silja Line* (☎09/18041; fax 180 4276) and *Viking Line* (Mannerheimintie 14; ☎09/12351; fax 647 075). You should expect to pay between 80mk and 130mk for a one-way ticket; cars cost 140–200mk.

Espoo; the home of the composer Sibelius, at **Järvenpää**; and the evocative old town of **Porvoo**, which also serves as an obvious access route to the underrated southeastern corner of the country.

The Espoo area

Lying west of Helsinki, the suburban area of **Espoo** comprises several separate districts. The nearest, directly across the bay, is the "garden city" of **TAPIOLA**. In the 1950s Finnish urban planners attempted to blend new housing schemes with the surrounding forests and hills, frequently only to be left with a compromise that turned ugly as expansion occurred. Tapiola was the exception to this rule, built as a self-contained living area rather than a dormitory town, with alternating high and low buildings, abundant open areas, parks, fountains and swimming pools. Much praised on its completion by the architectural world, it's still refreshing to wander through and admire the idea and its execution. The **tourist office** on the thirteenth floor at Keskustorni 13 (May–Aug Mon–Fri 8am–5pm, Sat 10am–2pm; Sept–April Mon–Fri 8am–5pm; ☎09/460 311; fax 466 378) handles enquiries about the whole Espoo area.

Walking about 3km north of Tapiola, past the traffic-bearing Hagalundintie, brings you to the little peninsula of **Otaniemi** and a couple more notable architectural sites. One of these is the Alvar Aalto-designed campus of Helsinki University's technology faculty; the other – far more dramatic – is the *Dipoli* student union building on the same campus. Ever keen to harmonize the artificial with the natural, architects Reimi and Raili Pietilä here created a building which seems fused with the rocky crags above Laajalahti, the front of the structure daringly edging forward from the cliff face.

Though the town of Espoo itself has little to delay you, just beyond lies the hugely absorbing **Hvitträsk** (June–Aug Mon–Fri 10am–7pm, Sat & Sun 10am–6pm; April, May, Sept & Oct Mon–Fri 11am–6pm, Sat & Sun 11am–5pm; 15mk), the studio home built and shared by Eliel Saarinen, Armas Lindgren and Herman Gesellius until 1904, when their partnership dissolved amid the acrimony caused by Saarinen's independent (and winning) design for Helsinki's train station. Externally, this is an extended and romanticized version of the traditional Finnish log cabin, the leafy branches that creep around making the structure look like a mutant growth emerging from the forest. Inside are frescoes by Gallen-Kallela and changing exhibitions of Finnish art and handicrafts. Both Eliel Saarinen and his wife are buried in the grounds.

Buses run throughout the day from Helsinki **to Tapiola** but you usually need specifically to request them to stop there; check the details and times at the bus station or the city tourist office. To get from central Helsinki **to Hvitträsk**, take the local (line L) train to Louma (10 daily; 37min) and follow the signs for 3km, or take bus #166 from Helsinki (3 daily; 55min). Guided tours of Hvitträsk plus Sibelius's home (see below) starting from next to the *Sokos Hotel Vaakuna* on Station Square, cost 195mk (40mk with Helsinki Card) and last four hours (call ☎09/601 966 for reservations).

Järvenpää: Ainola

Thirty-eight kilometres north of Helsinki in **JÄRVENPÄÄ**, easily reached by either bus or train, is **Ainola** (May & Sept Wed–Sun 11am–5pm; June–Aug Tues–Sun 11am–5pm; for guided tours combined with Hvitträsk, see above) – the house where Jean Sibelius lived from 1904 with his wife, Aino (sister of the artist Eero Järnefelt), after whom the place is named.

Though now regarded as one of the world's greatest composers, **Jean Sibelius**, born in Hämeenlinna in 1865, had no musical background whatsoever, and by the age of nineteen was enrolled on a law course at Helsinki University. He had, however, developed a youthful passion for the violin and took a class at the capital's Institute of Music. Law was soon forgotten as Sibelius's real talents were recognized, and his musical studies took him to the cultural hotbeds of the day, Berlin and Vienna. Returning to Finland to teach at the Institute, Sibelius soon gained a government grant, which enabled him to begin composing full time, the first concert of his works taking place in 1892. His early pieces were inspired by the Finnish folk epic, the *Kalevala*, and by the nationalist sentiments of the times. Sibelius even incurred the wrath of the country's Russian rulers: in 1899 they banned performances of his rousing *Finlandia* under any name that suggested its patriotic sentiment; to circumvent this, the piece was published as "Opus 26 No. 7".

While the overtly nationalistic elements in Sibelius's work mellowed in later years, he continued composing with what's regarded as a very Finnish obsession with nature: "Other composers offer their public a cocktail," he said, "I offer mine pure spring water". He is still highly revered in his own land, although he was also notorious for his bouts of heavy drinking, and a destructive quest for perfection which fuelled suspicion that he had completed, and destroyed, two symphonies during his final thirty years. This was an angst-ridden period when no new work appeared, which became known as "the silence from Järvenpää". Sibelius died in 1957, his best-known symphonies setting a standard almost impossible for younger Finnish composers to live up to.

The house is just the kind of home you'd expect for a man who would include representations of flapping swans' wings in his music if one happened to fly by while he was at work: a tranquil place, close to lakes and forests. Indeed, the wood-filled grounds are as atmospheric as the building, which is a place of pilgrimage for devotees: books, furnishings and a few paintings are all there is to see. His grave is in the grounds, marked by a marble stone inscribed simply with his name. For more tangible Sibelius memories, and more of his music, visit the Sibelius Museum in Turku (see p.655).

While in Järvenpää, it would be a pity to miss out on a visit to the **Halosenniemi Museum** (Jan–April & Sept–Dec Tues–Sun 11am–4pm; late April to Aug Tues–Sun 11am–6pm; 25mk). On the Tuusula Lakeside road, just a few minutes' walk from Ainola, this is the rustic home of Pekka Halonen, one of Finland's most renowned artists. A lovely serene place, its National Romantic decor has been painstakingly restored to house some of his pictures and painting materials in their original setting.

Porvoo

One of the oldest towns on the south coast, **PORVOO**, 50km east of Helsinki, with its narrow cobbled streets lined by small wooden buildings, gives a sense of the Finnish life that predated the capital's bold squares and Neoclassical geometry. This, coupled with its elegant riverside setting and unhurried mood, means you're unlikely to be alone. Word of Porvoo's peaceful time-locked qualities has spread.

First stop should be the **tourist office** at Rauhankatu 20 (Mon–Fri 8am–4pm, Sat 10am–2pm; ☎019/580 145; fax 582 721), over the road from the bus station, for a free map of the town. The immediate area is comparatively recent, but look in at the preserved **Johan Ludwig Runeberg House**, at Aleksanterinkatu 3 (May–Aug Mon–Sat 10am–4pm, Sun 11am–5pm; Sept–April Wed–Sat 10am–4pm, Sun 11am–5pm; 10mk), where the man regarded as Finland's national poet lived from 1852 while a teacher at the town school. Despite writing in Swedish, Runeberg greatly aided the nation's sense of self-esteem, especially with *Tales of Vänrikki Ståhl*, which told of the people's struggles with Russia in the 1808–09 conflict. The first poem in his collection *Our Land* later provided the lyrics for the national anthem. Across the road, the **Walter Runeberg Gallery** (May–Aug Mon–Sat 9.30am–4pm, Sun 10.30am–5pm; Sept–April Tues–Sat 11am–4pm, Sun 11am–5pm; 15mk) displays a collection of sculpture by Runeberg's third son, one of Finland's more celebrated sculptors. Among many acclaimed works, he's responsible for the statue of his father that stands in the centre of Helsinki's Esplanadi.

The old town (follow the signs for "Vanha Porvoo") is built around the hill on the other side of Mannerheimkatu. Near the top, its outline partially obscured by vegetation, is the fifteenth-century **Tuomiokirkko** (May–Sept Mon–Fri 10am–6pm, Sat 10am–2pm, Sun 2–5pm; Oct–April Tues–Sat 10am–2pm, Sun & hols 2–4pm). It was here in 1809 that Alexander I proclaimed Finland a Russian Grand Duchy, himself Grand Duke, and convened the first Finnish Diet. This, and other aspects of the town's past, can be explored in the **Porvoo Museum** (May–Aug daily 10am–4pm; Sept–April Wed–Sun noon–4pm; 15mk) at the foot of the hill in the old town's main square. There are no singularly outstanding exhibits here, just a diverting selection of furnishings, musical instruments and general oddities, largely dating from the years of Russian rule.

Practicalities

Buses run all day from Helsinki to Porvoo, and a one-way trip costs around 40mk. Idling around the town is especially pleasant late in the day as the evening stillness descends, and the last bus back to the city conveniently departs around midnight. There's also a **boat**, the *J.L. Runeberg*, which sails from Helsinki's South Harbour in summer (Tues, Wed & Fri–Sun at 10am, arriving 1.15pm; returns to Helsinki at 3.15pm; 95mk one-way).

If you've exhausted Helsinki, **spending a night** in Porvoo leaves you well placed to continue into Finland's southeastern corner (see below). If possible, try to arrange accommodation while in Helsinki, particularly if you're after hotel bargains – rates in Porvoo are steep. There is, however, a **youth hostel**, open all year, at Linnankoskenkatu 1 (☎019/523 0012), and a **campsite** (☎019/581 967), open from June to mid-August, 2km from the town centre.

THE SOUTHEAST

As it's some way from the major centres, foreign tourists tend to neglect the extreme **southeastern corner** of Finland; Finns, however, rate it highly, flocking here to make boat trips around the small islands and to explore the many small communities, which enticingly combine a genuine rustic flavour with sufficient places of minor interest to keep boredom at bay. For Finns, the region also stirs memories: its position on the Soviet border means it saw many battles during the Winter and Continuation wars, and throughout medieval times it was variously under the control of Sweden and Russia. It's an intriguing if not exactly vital area, worth two or three days of travel – most of it by bus, since rail lines are almost nonexistent.

East to Kotka

If Porvoo seems too tourist-infested, make the 40km journey east to **LOVISSA**, an eighteenth-century fishing village pleasantly free from Helsinki day-trippers. The village, whose 8000-strong population divides into equal numbers of Finnish- and Swedish-speakers, is overlooked by the two old **fortresses** of Rosen and Ungern, both worth exploring. The **tourist office** (June–Aug Mon–Fri 9am–6pm, Sat 9am–4pm; Sept–May Mon–Fri 9am–4pm, Sat 9am–2pm; ☎019/555 234; fax 532 322), on the market square, can supply details of how to get to them; off the square, a row of prettily preserved houses points the way to the **district museum** (Tues–Sun noon–4pm; 10mk), containing, besides the usual local hotchpotch, a fine stock of turn-of-the-century romantic postcards. Later on, if you have the cash, spend it on a slap-up meal at *Degerby Gille*, Sepänkuja 4, a restaurant set in a seventeenth-century house that's one of the town's most important historical sights; if you don't, poke your head around the restaurant's door anyway to marvel at the wonderfully maintained interior.

In the bay off Lovissa there's a less welcome modern sight – one of the country's two **nuclear power stations**. Finland's Cold War balancing act between East and West led to the country buying its nuclear hardware from both power blocs; this one has spent the past thirty years producing plutonium for (allegedly) Soviet nuclear weapons. The other, Western-backed, at Olkiluoti (near Rauma), is newer and still the subject of much argument. The Finnish public is divided over the merits of nuclear power in general: the country takes about 40 percent of its energy from nuclear sources, but the growing anti-nuclear movement is calling for a switch to hydroelectric power. Whatever the outcome of the debate, mindful of the design flaws in Soviet-built reactors, the view is an unnerving one.

If you have the time, a couple of smaller settlements on the way to Kotka can comfortably consume half a day. In 1809, the Swedish–Russian border was drawn up in this area, splitting the region of Pyhtää in two. Some 20km from Lovissa is **RUOTSINPYHTÄÄ** (or Swedish Pyhtää), whose local **tourist office** (☎019/618 474; fax 618 475) is heroically positioned on the bridge over the inlet that once divided the two feuding empires. Historical quirks aside, the main attraction here, unappetizing though it may at first sound, is the seventeenth-century **iron works** – now turned into craft studios, with demonstrations of carpet-weaving, jewellery-making and painting. It's all quite enjoyable to stroll around on a sunny day. You should also visit the oddly octagonal-shaped **wooden church** (June–Sept daily noon–3pm; Oct–May Sun noon–4pm – book with the tourist office) to admire Helene Schjerfbeck's beautiful altarpiece. It was here, incidentally, that a Finnish TV company filmed a very popular soap opera, *Vihreän Kullanmaa* ("the Land of the Green Gold"), making good use of the contrast between the spacious mill-owners' houses and the cramped workers' cottages.

The village of **PYHTÄÄ**, whose position on the Russian side of the border meant it retained its Finnish name, is a twenty-minute bus ride further east. There's a **stone church** here (June–Sept daily noon–3pm; Oct–May Sun only), one of the oldest in the country, dated at around 1301. Its interior frescoes are primitive and strangely moving, and were discovered only recently when the Reformation-era whitewash was removed. From the quay on the other side of the village's sole street, there's a ferry service to the nearby islands, including Kaunissaari ("Beautiful Island"), where you can connect with an evening motorboat straight on to Kotka.

The land route to Kotka takes you through **SILTAKYLÄ**, a small town significant only for the hills around it and its **tourist information** counter at the town hall, beside the main road, which has information on walks in the district. The hills afford great views over a dramatic legacy of the Ice Age: spooky Tolkienesque forests and many miles of a red-granite stone known as *rapakivi* that's unique to southeast Finland, covered by a white moss. A number of marked hiking trails lead through the landscape, strewn with giant boulders, some as big as four-storey buildings and supporting their own little ecosystem of plant and tree life. After a day's trek, you can reward your efforts with food and drink – or even a swim – at the not too pricey *Pyhtään Motelli* (☎05/343 1661), which despite its name is situated on the edge of Siltakylä.

Kotka

After the scattering of little communities east of Porvoo, **KOTKA**, a few kilometres on from Siltakylä, is immense by comparison, the only large town between Helsinki and the Russian border. Built on an island on the Gulf of Finland, Kotka's past reflects its closeness to the sea. Numerous battles have been fought off its shores, among them the Sweden–Russia confrontation of 1790, which was the largest battle ever seen in

Nordic waters: almost 10,000 people lost their lives. Sixty-odd years later, the British fleet virtually reduced Kotka to rubble during the Crimean war. In modern times the sea has been the basis of the town's prosperity: sitting at the end of the Kymi river with a deep-water harbour, the town makes a perfect cargo transit point – causing most locals to live in fear of a major accident occuring in the industrial section, or in the freight yards. Only two roads link Kotka to the mainland and a speedy evacuation of its inhabitants would be almost impossible.

The town itself has little to delay you; it's more a place to eat and sleep than anything else. Only the eighteenth-century Orthodox **St Nicolai Kirkko** (Tues–Sun noon–2pm) survived the British bombardment, and even that is not particularly interesting, although you should make a point of visiting the **Langinkoski Imperial Fishing Lodge** (May–Aug daily 10am–7pm; Sept & Oct Sat & Sun only), off the main island, about 5km north of the town centre (take bus #20). It was here that Tsar Alexander III would relax in transit between Helsinki and St Petersburg; the wooden building, a gift to him from the Finnish government, is most striking for its un-Tsar-like simplicity and the attractive setting in the woods near the fast-flowing Kymi river.

Practicalities

Rail and road connections bring you right into the compact centre, where the **tourist office** at Keskuskatu 7 (June–Aug Mon–Fri 9am–4pm, Sat 10am–2pm; Sept–May Mon–Fri 9am–4pm; ☎05/227 4424; fax 15676) will fill you in on local bus details – essential for continuing around the southeast.

As for practical needs in Kotka, grumbling stomachs can be quietened in *Kairo*, Satamakatu 7, an authentic seamen's **restaurant**, popular with eastern European sailors. *Cap Horn*, Kotkankatu 9, also serves food, though it's mainly a drinking place; otherwise, there's gourmet *Kesäravintola Meriniemi* at Kaivokatu 16. A good-value **hotel** to try is the pleasant *Hotelli-Gasthau Merikotka*, Satamakatu 9C (☎05/15222; fax 15414; ②), or there's the more upmarket *Seurahoune*, Keskuskatu 21 (☎05/186090; fax 186881; ④). The nearest **youth hostel**, *Kärkisaariis*, is 6km north of Kotka in Mussalo (bus #20), overlooking a spectacular bay (☎05/604215; mid-May to mid-Sept; contact the Kotka tourist office if booking outside these times). There's also a **campsite** in Mussalo (☎05/605 055; April–Sept) and, next door, the *Hotel Santalahti* (same phone number; ②), where anybody can drop in to use the cheapish **cafeteria**.

TRIPS TO RUSSIA

Overland from Helsinki

Two **trains** – a Russian and a Finnish one – leave Helsinki every day for the seven- to eight-hour trip to **St Petersburg**; there's also a Russian overnight service. All border formalities are carried out on the train, but you must have a Russian visa before you leave – the tourist office has a list of travel agencies that can arrange visas, though be warned that they take a week to process. A one-way second-class ticket costs 265mk, including seat reservation, first-class tickets are 429mk, or 487mk for a sleeping compartment.

Day cruises

If sailing to St Petersburg for a short visit sounds more attractive, you could book a place on one of the four cruises a year operated by *Kristina Cruises*: there's one in June, one in July and two in August. All leave Helsinki at 5pm, arrive in St Petersburg 9am the following morning and return at 11pm the next day. You don't need a visa for one of these excursions, but you do need to fill in a questionnaire for the tour operator at least a week before departure. For more information, contact *Kristina Cruises*, Korkeavuorenkatu 2, Kotka (☎05/218 1011; fax 214 624).

Hamina and east to the Russian border

Twenty-six kilometres east of Kotka is **HAMINA**, founded in 1653 and sporting a magnificently bizarre town plan, the main streets forming concentric circles around the centre. It was built this way to allow the incumbent Swedish forces to withstand attack – the town being the site of many Swedish–Russian battles. Besides the layout, however, there's not an awful lot to amuse in the town, although you can pick up suggestions and local information from the **tourist office** at Rautatienkatu 8 (Mon–Fri 8am–4pm; ☎05/749 525; fax 749 5381).

The tourist office can give you the latest schedule of the bus that runs to Virolahti, 31km east, and within a few kilometres of the **Salpalinjan Bunkkerit** or Salpa Line Bunkers – fortifications that stretched from here to Lappland and were intended to protect Finland from Soviet attack during the run-up to the Winter War of 1939. Massive hunks of granite blocked the way of advancing tanks. These days Finnish war veterans are eager to show off the bunker's details and lead visitors to the seats (and controls) of ageing anti-tank guns. Buses to Viipuri, the formerly Finnish town now on the wrong side of the border (see p.676), also pass through Hamina; again, details are best checked at the tourist office.

The only other place to aim for in the vicinity (to reach it you'll need your own transport – no buses cover the route) is **YLÄMAA**, 27km north of Vaalima on the road to Lappeenranta (see p.675). Here you'll come upon one of the world's two **spectrolite** mines. Spectrolite is a kind of feldspar, first discovered in Canada (where the only other mine is), although Finnish spectrolite is considered far superior. This can be appreciated in the mine shop's display of dazzlingly beautiful jewellery and watches made from the mineral, which vary in colour according to the angle of the light striking them. It's remarkable stuff, though unfortunately it doesn't come cheap.

THE SOUTHWEST

The area between Helsinki and Finland's **southwestern** extremity is probably the blandest section of the whole country. By road or rail the view is much the same, endless forests interrupted only by modest-sized patches of water and virtually identical villages and small towns. Once at the southwestern corner, however, things change considerably, with islands and inlets around a jagged shoreline, and the distinctive Finland-Swedish coastal communities.

Turku

There is very little in Åbo which has entertained me in the survey, or can amuse you by the description. It is a wretched capital of a barbarous province. The houses are almost all of wood; and the archiepiscopal palace, which has not even a single storey, but may be called a sort of barrack, is composed of no better materials, except that it is painted red. I inquired if there was not any object in the university, meriting attention; but they assured me that it would be regarded as a piece of ridicule, to visit it on such an errand, there being nothing within its walls except a very small library, and a few philosophical instruments.

A Tour Round The Baltic, Sir N.W. Wraxall, 1775.

TURKU (or **Åbo** as it's known in Swedish) was the principal town in Finland when the country was a province of Sweden, losing its status in 1812, along with most of its buildings in a ferocious fire soon after – occurrences that clearly improved the place, if the

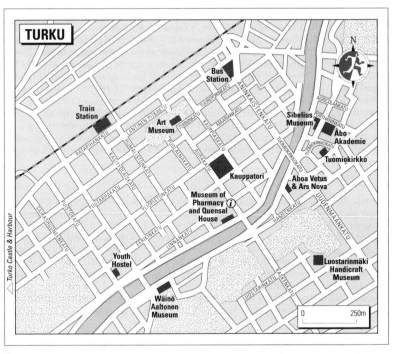

above quotation is to be believed. These days Turku is small and highly sociable –
thanks to the boom years under Swedish rule, and a high ration of students from its two
universities – bristling with history and culture, and with a sparkling nightlife to boot.

Arrival, information and accommodation

The river Aura splits the city, its tree-lined banks forming a natural promenade as well
as a useful landmark for finding your way around. The interesting older features, the
cathedral and castle, are at opposite ends of the river, while the main museums are
along its edge. There are gleaming department stores, banks and offices on the northern side of the river in Turku's central grid, where you'll also find the **tourist office** at
Aurakatu 4 (June to mid-Sept Mon–Fri 8.30am–7.30pm, Sat & Sun 10am–5pm; mid-Sept
to May Mon–Fri 8.30am–6pm, Sat & Sun 10am–7pm; ☎02/233 6366; fax 233 6488).
Close by is the **kauppatori** and the effervescent **kauppahalli** (Mon–Fri 8am–5pm, Sat
8am–2pm). Outside banking hours, you can **change money** at Eerinkatu 12 (Mon–Fri
8am–6pm, Sat 10am–2pm; June–Aug also Sun). Both the **train station** and **bus station**
are within easy walking distance of the river, just north of the centre.

Accommodation

If you turn up at the weekend having made an early reservation, there can be some
good deals in Turku's mid-range **hotels**: *Hotel Julia*, Eerikenkatu 4 (☎02/336311; fax
251 1750; ③/⑤), *Cumulus*, Eerikenkatu 28 (☎02/338 211; fax 338 2299; ③/⑤), or
Seurahuone, Eerikinkatu 23 (☎02/337 301; fax 251 8051; ③/④). Note, however, that
their prices rise substantially during the week, in which case you'll be better off trying

the less luxurious **tourist hotels**: *Astro Hotel,* Humalistonkatu 18 (☎02/251 7838; fax 251 5516; ①), *Good Morning Hotel Turku,* Yliopistonkatu 29A (☎02/232 0921; fax 251 8870; ①/②) or *Nukkumatti Hotel,* Satakunnant 177 (☎02/211 0112; fax 211 0113; ②).

At the budget end of the market, Turku has an excellent official **youth hostel**, *Turku City Hostel,* beautifully situated by the river in the city centre at Linnankatu 39 (☎02/231 6578; fax 231 1708; open all year) – take bus #30 from the train station. There is also a friendly **bed and breakfast** place at Vanha Littoistentie 27 (☎02/237 3902 or 9400 905556), with single rooms for 100mk, doubles for 150mk and triples for 200mk. The nearest **campsite** (☎02/262 3260) is on the small island of Ruissalo, overlooking Turku harbour. It's open from June to mid-August and takes about fifteen minutes to reach on bus #8. Ruissalo is a good place to visit anyway, for its two sandy beaches, a botanical garden sporting a host of rare and spectacular plants, and fine views to the archipelago.

The City

Arriving in Turku by train, you'll quickly make the pleasing discovery that the town's major places of interest unintentionally arrange themselves into a very logical pattern. By beginning at the Art Museum, a few strides from the station, and from there moving south through the town centre and heading westwards along the river's edge, you'll be able to see everything worth seeing in a day – although allowing two days might be more sensible if you want to have energy left for the Turku nightlife. During the 1970s and 80s parts of Turku were subjected to some thoughtless redevelopment, resulting in a number of really hideous buildings and a new national byword, the "Turku Disease". However, streets of intricately carved wooden houses still survive around the Port Arthur area, a lovely part of town for simply strolling around.

The Art Museum

Though it's not much of a taster for the actual city, **Turku Art Museum** (Tues, Fri & Sat 10am–4pm, Wed & Thurs 10am–7pm, Sun 11am–6pm; 20–40mk, depending on the exhibition), housed in a purpose-built Art Nouveau granite structure close to the train station, is one of the better collections of Finnish art, with works by all the great names of the country's Golden Age – Gallen-Kallela, Edelfelt, Pekka Halonen, Simberg and others – plus a commendable stock of moderns. Not least among these are the wood sculptures of Kain Tapper and Mauno Hartman, which stirred up heated debate on the merits of carefully shaped bits of wood being presented as art when they were first shown during the 1970s.

The Cathedral and around

To get to grips with Turku itself, and its pivotal place in Finnish history, cut through the centre to the river, and the tree-framed space that, before the great fire of 1879, was the bustling heart of the community, and which is still overlooked by the **Tuomiokirkko** (June–Aug Mon–Fri 9am–8pm, Sat 9am–3pm, Sun noon–4.30pm; Sept–May Mon–Fri 10am–4pm, Sat 10am–3pm, Sun noon–4.30pm; free guided tours in English at 2pm, 3pm & 4pm). The cathedral, erected in the thirteenth century on the "Knoll of Sheep", a pre-Christian place of worship, was at the centre of the Christianization process inflicted by the crusading Swedes on the pagan Finns, and grew larger over the centuries as the new religion became stronger and Swedish involvement in Finland escalated. The building, still the base of the Finnish church, has been repeatedly ravaged by fire, although the thickness of the walls enabled many of its medieval features to survive. Of these, it's the tombs that catch the eye: Torsten Stålhandske, commander of the Finnish cavalry during the seventeenth-century Thirty Years' War, in which Sweden sought to protect its domination of the Baltic and the Finns confirmed their reputatation as wild and fearless fighters, lies in a deliriously ornate coffin (to the right as you enter) opposite Samuel Cockburn and Patrick Ogilvie, a couple of Scots who fought alongside him. On the left-hand side, Catharine Månsdotter, the commoner wife of the Swedish king Erik XIV, with whom, in the mid-sixteenth century, she was imprisoned in Turku Castle, is as popular in death as she reputedly was in life, judging by the numbers who file past her simple black marble sarcophagus. The window behind it carries her stained-glass image – and if you crane your neck to the left, you can see a wall plaque bearing the only known true likeness of her. For 10mk you can visit the **cathedral museum** upstairs (same times as cathedral), which gives a stronger insight into the cathedral's past. There's an assortment of ancient jugs, goblets, plates and spoons, though more absorbing are the collections of church textiles – funeral flags and the like – at the far end.

Immediately outside the cathedral is a statue to **Per Brahe**, governor-general of Finland from 1637 and the first Swedish officer to devote much attention to the welfare of the Finns, encouraging a literacy programme and founding the country's first university. The site of this is within the nearby yellow Empire-style buildings, although the actual seat of learning was moved to Helsinki during the era of Russian rule. Next to these are the oldest portions of the **Åbo Akademi** – Finland's only remaining Swedish-language university – while the modern, Finnish-language **Turku University** is at the other end of Henrikinkatu: these days both are more notable as places for eating rather than sightseeing.

Turku's newest and most splendid museum is the combined **Aboa Vetus** and **Ars Nova** (May–Aug daily 10am–7pm; Oct–April Tues–Sun 11am–7pm; 35mk, or 50mk for both) on the bank of the Aurajoki River just a few steps from the university. Translating as "Old Turku, New Art", the place was intended to be simply a modern art gallery, but when the building's foundations were dug a warren of medieval lanes and cellars came to light, an unmissable opportunity to present the history and archeology of the city. Glass flooring allows a near-perfect view of the remains. The New Art part comprises a collection of 350 striking works, alongside frequent temporary exhibitions. There's a great café here, and the *Aboa Vetus* magazine (in English), though pricey at 40mk, is informative and helpful, especially as the guided tours are only in Finnish.

Back past the cathedral and across Piispankatu is the sleek low form of the **Sibelius Museum** (Tues–Sun 11am–3pm, Wed also 6–8pm; 15mk). Although Sibelius had no direct connection with Turku, this museum is a fitting tribute to him and his contribution to the emergence of an independent Finland. Chances are that the recorded strains of *Finlandia* will greet you as you enter: when not the venue for live concerts (which usually take place during the winter), the small but acoustically perfect concert area pumps out recorded requests from the great man's oeuvre; take your place beside dewy-eyed Finns for a lunch hour of Scandinavia's finest composer. Elsewhere, the Sibelius collection gathers family photo albums and original manuscripts, along with the great man's hat, walking stick and even a final half-smoked cigar. Other exhibits cover the musical history of the country, from intricate musical boxes and the frail wooden *kantele* – the instrument strummed by peasants in the *Kalevala* – to the weighty keyboard instruments downstairs.

The Observatory and Maritime Museum

On the other side of the cathedral from the Sibelius museum, you'll see a small hill topped by the wooden dome of the **Observatory and Maritime Museum** (mid-April to mid-Sept daily 10am–6pm; 10mk). Not worthy of too much time, this was designed – rather poorly – by Carl Engel, who had arrived in Turku seeking work in the days before his great plan for Helsinki made him famous. Originally the building was intended to serve the first Turku University as an observatory, but disputes between Engel and his assistants and a misunderstanding of scientific requirements eventually rendered the place useless for its intended purpose. To make things worse, the university moved to Helsinki, and the building was then turned into a navigational school. Despite various nautical and astronomical odds and ends, the chief attraction is the great view over Turku and out to the archipelago from the top-floor windows. The old water tower outside the observatory regularly hosts minor art exhibitions in summer.

The Luostarinmäki, Aaltonen and pharmacy museums

From the water tower, head directly down the side of the hill to the far more engrossing **Luostarinmäki Handicrafts Museum** (daily May–Sept 10am–6pm; Oct–April 10am–3pm; 15mk), one of the best – and certainly the most authentic – open-air museums in Finland. Following a severe fire in 1775, rigorous restrictions were imposed on the town's new buildings, but due to a legal technicality they didn't apply in this district. The wooden houses here were built by local working people in traditional style and evolved naturally into a museum as descendants of the original owners died and bequeathed their inherited homes to the municipality. The unpaved streets run between tiny wooden houses, which once had goats tethered to their chimneys to contain the turfed roofs. The chief inhabitants now are the museum volunteers who dress up in period attire and demonstrate the old handicrafts.

A short walk from the handicrafts museum, on the southern bank of the river, is another worthwhile indoor collection: the **Wäinö Aaltonen Museum** (Tues–Sun 11am–7pm; 13mk, more during special exhibitions). Unquestionably the best-known modern Finnish sculptor, Aaltonen, born in 1894, grew up close to Turku and studied for a time at the local art school. His first public show, in 1916, marked a turning point in the development of Finnish sculpture, introducing a freer, more individual style to a genre struggling to break from the restraints of the Neoclassical tradition and French realism. Aaltonen went on to dominate his field totally throughout the 1920s and 30s and his influence is still felt today; the man's work turns up in every major town throughout the country, and even the parliament building in Helsinki was designed with special niches to hold some of his pieces. Much of his output celebrates the individuals who contributed to the growth of the Finnish republic, typically remembering them with enormous heads, or as immense statues that resemble haulking chunks of socialist realism. But Aaltonen, who died in 1966, really was an original, imaginative and sensitive sculptor, as the exhibits here demonstrate. There's also a roomful of his paintings, some of which show perhaps why he concentrated on sculpture.

Across the river from the Aaltonen museum, there's a sign in the grass which spells out TURKU:ÅBO. Not far away from this is a wooden staircase running up to the front door of the **Museum of Pharmacy and Quensel House** (May–Sept daily 10am–6pm; Oct–April daily 10am–3pm; 10mk). Quensel was a court judge who moved to the house in 1694, and it later became the home of Professor Josef Gustaf Pipping – the "father of Finnish medicine" – in 1785. Period furnishings remain, proving just how wealthy and stylish the life of the eighteenth-century bourgeoisie actually was. Many chemists' implements from around the country are on show, among them some memorable devices for drawing blood.

Turku Castle

The town's museums, and its cathedral and universities, are all symbols of Turku's elevated position in Finnish life, though by far the major marker to its many years of importance stands at the western end of Linnankatu. Follow the signs for *Turun Linna*, or take bus #1 from the harbour, and you'll eventually see, oddly set among the present-day ferry terminals, the relatively featureless and unappetizing exterior of **Turku Castle** (May–Sept daily 10am–6pm; Oct–April Tues–Sun 10am–3pm; 20mk). Fight any dismay though, since the compact cobbled courtyards, maze-like corridors and darkened staircases of the interior make the castle a good place to wander – and to dwell on the fact that this was the seat of the government of the country for centuries; and that much of Finland's (and a significant portion of Sweden's) medieval history took shape within these walls. Unless you're an expert on the period, you'll get a migraine trying to figure out the importance of everything that's here, and it's a sensible idea to buy one of the guide leaflets on sale at the entrance. The castle probably went up sometime around 1280, when the first bishop arrived from Sweden; gradual expansion through the following years accounts for the patchwork effect of its architecture – and the bewildering array of finds, rooms and displays. The majority of the fortification took place during the turbulent sixteenth century, instigated by Swedish ruler Gustavus Vasa for the protection of his son, whom he made Duke Johan, the first Duke of Finland. Johan pursued a lavish court life but exceeded his powers in attacking Livonia and was sentenced to death by the Stockholm Diet. Swedish efforts to seize Johan were successful only after a three-week siege, and he was removed to Stockholm. The subsequent decision by the unbalanced Erik XIV to release Johan resulted not only in Johan becoming king himself, but also in poor Erik being imprisoned here – albeit with a full quota of servants and the best food and wine. The bare cell he occupied for a few weeks contrasts strongly with the splendour from Johan's time, offering a cool reminder of shifting fortunes. There's a gloom-laden nineteenth-century painting here, by Erik Johan Löfgren, of Erik with his head on the lap of his queen (Catharine Månsdotter), while the lady's eyes look askance to heaven.

Eating, drinking and entertainment

You'd need to be very fussy not to find somewhere to **eat** in Turku that's to your liking. Walking around checking the lunchtime offers can turn up many bargains, plus there's the usual selection of economical pizzerias.

Cafés and restaurants

Foija, Aurakatu 10. Good pizzas for under 50mk.

Gadolinia, Henrikenkatu. This student mensa is part of Åbo Akademi – look for the sign saying "Rouka" – and, as usual, the cheapest option in town

Herman, Läntinen Rantakatu 37 (☎02/230 3333; fax 230 3334). On the riverside, set in a bright and airy storehouse dating from 1849. Since Turku hosted the Tall Ships Race in 1996, the whole area has been renovated – ask to reserve the single table for two overlooking the river. Fantastic food that comes at a price, with main courses running from 48mk to 100mk.

Italia, Linnankatu 3. Sizeable pizzas at very affordable prices

Pinella, Porhaninpuisto. Café in an antique wooden pavilion, serving decadent chocolate brownies and ice cream (15mk), as well as main dishes such as cold smoked reindeer pancakes (60mk).

Pizzeria Dennis, Linnankatu 17. Decent, well-priced pizzeria.

Café Qwensel, in a courtyard behind the Pharmacy Museum. Fabulous cakes in atmospheric eighteenth-century surroundings.

Turun Hotelli Ravintola Oppilaitos, in the Data Centre close to Turku Hospital and Sports Hall – take the train one stop to Kupittaa. Run by the catering college, the service here is almost too efficient and the food usually excellent.

Bars and entertainment

The riverside restaurant *Samppalinna*, on Itäinen Rantakatu, is a good night-time **drinking** venue. Other popular bars are *Olavinkrouvi*, Hämeenkatu 30, which draws numerous students; *Pub Peltimies*, part of the *Rantasipi Hotel* at Pispalantie 7 (see also below); and *Erik XIV*, Eerikinkatu 6, which also serves decent food. Consider also the "English-style" pub: *Hunter's Inn*, part of *Hotel Julia* but with its own entrance at Brahenkatu 3. Floating restaurants are popular among tourists, if not with too many locals, and the boats change each summer, though the names Papa Joe, Svarte Rudolf and Lulu reappear year after year: all have decent enough restaurants, beer and often put on live music.

For something more energetic than boozing to fill the nights, there are several **discos**, most of them within the bigger hotels. *Börs Night Club*, in the *Hotel Hamburger Börs*, Kauppiask 6, is one of the best known. *Submarina*, in the *Marina Palace* hotel at

Linnankatu 32, is the trendiest spot on a Saturday night for the latest hip-hop and house sounds; not far behind are *Rendez-Vous*, in the *Rantasipi Hotel* at Pispalantie 7, and *Time Out*, Puutarhakatu 8. More sedate, and with a slightly older clientele, are *Kilta*, Humalistonkatu 8, and *Casanova*, Eerikinkatu 12.

During August, the **Turku Music Festival** packs thousands into a number of venues for performances in a wide range of musical genres (information on ☎02/251 1162). If your tastes are for classical music, try and get a ticket for the **Turku Philharmonic Orchestra**, based in the Concert Hall at Aninkaistenkatu 9 (ticket office Mon–Fri 11am–2pm; ☎ 02/232 2816). One of the oldest orchestras in Europe, dating from 1790, today it performs symphony and chamber music concerts, sometimes in the afternoon. Alternatively, check with the tourist office for a rundown of the week's films: Turku has five **cinemas**, the largest, with five screens, being the *Julia*, Eerikinkatu 4. There are usually two screenings a night, at 6.30pm and 8.30pm.

Travelling on from Turku

Continuing from Turku **north along the coast**, there are direct bus services to the nearest main towns, Rauma and Pori. The train to Pori takes virtually a whole day and involves going via Tampere and changing at least once, possibly three times. From **Turku harbour** ferries sail through the vast archipelago to the Åland Islands, and on to Sweden. The harbour is 3km from the city centre and bus #1 covers the route frequently. There's also a daily sailing to the Åland Islands from **Naantali**, 16km from Turku; a direct bus links Turku to the Naantali docking stage. While pleasant enough, with its wooden buildings and slight passageways, Naantali isn't worth hanging around for more than a few hours, and with regular buses there's no need to stay, though there's a tourist office should you need further information (☎02/850 850).

Rauma and Pori

Small and largely unsung **RAUMA**, 90km north of Turku, is one of the oldest towns in the country, its eighteenth- and nineteenth-century buildings evoking a strong historic flavour. Strangely for the west coast, it's a mainly Finnish-speaking community, although with a studied and archaic dialect that many ordinary Finns find hard to understand. Such insularity perhaps goes back to the mid-sixteenth century, when the inhabitants were forced to move their seafaring skills to the newly founded Helsinki – making Rauma a ghost town for some time. This past is documented in the **History Museum** in the eighteenth-century town hall at Kauppakatu 13 (Tues–Fri 10am–4pm, Tues also 6–8pm, Sat 10am–2pm, Sun 11am–5pm; free), with further evidence on show at **Marela**, Kauppakatu 24 (summer daily 10am–5pm; rest of the year closed Mon; 10mk), a house preserved in the style of a rich shipowner's home from the turn of the century.

There's a **tourist office** at Valtakatu 2 (June–Aug daily 8am–3pm; Sept–May Mon–Fri 9am–4pm; ☎02/834 4551; fax 822 4555) for practical information. If you need to stay, it's just 1km from the town centre to *Poroholma*, the combined **youth hostel** and **campsite** (☎02/822 4666; mid-May to Aug); otherwise, the *Cumulus, Aittakarinkatu* 9 (☎02/37821; ③), boasts two saunas, a pool and summer terrace. For a filling lunch, try the *Villa Tallbo*, Petäjäksentie 178 (☎02/8220733; fax 8239 733), occupying the restored *fin-de-siècle* summer villa of a shipowner.

Pori

Due to its yearly jazz festival – increasingly rock- and pop-oriented in recent years – **PORI** has become one of the best-known towns in Finland. For two weeks each July, its streets are full of music and the 100,000 people who come to hear it. Throughout the rest of the year Pori reverts to being a small, quiet industrial town with a worthy region-al museum and a handful of architectural and historical oddities. The central section, despite its spacious grid-style streets, can be crossed on foot in about fifteen minutes.

In the centre of Pori at Hallituskatu 14, just across the road from the tourist office (see below), stands the **Pori Theatre**, the temporary home of Finnish-language theatre during the period of Russification, when Finnish drama was considered too provocative to take place in a larger centre like Turku or Helsinki. Built in 1884, it has a striking Renaissance facade, and the tiny interior – seating just 300 – is heavy with the opulence induced by its frescoes and sculptured chandeliers. To see inside, ask at the tourist office. Also within a few steps, at Hallituskatu 11, is another good stop – the **Satakunta Museum** (Tues–Sat 11am–5pm; 10mk), its three well-stocked floors tracing the roots of both Pori and the sur-rounding Satakunta region. The town's life is chronicled here through medieval findings, late nineteenth-century photos and shop signs, and typical house interiors, alongside inter-esting memorabilia from the powerful labour movement of the 1930s.

Pori's strangest sight, however, is in the big Käppärä cemetery, a twenty-minute walk along Maantiekatu. In the cemetery's centre is the Gothic-arched **Juselius Mausoleum** (May–Aug daily noon–3pm; Sept–April Sun noon–2pm; free), erected in 1898 by a local businessman, F.A. Juselius, as a memorial to his daughter, Sigrid, who died aged 11. The leading Finnish church architect of the time, Josef Steinbäck, was called on to design the thing, while Gallen-Kallela decorated the interior with some of his best large-scale paintings. The artwork was adversely affected by both fire and the local sea air, but has been restored by Gallen-Kallela's son from the original sketches, enabling the structure to fulfil its purpose as powerfully, and as solemnly, as ever.

Practicalities

It's a short walk from either the **bus station** – into Isolinnankatu and straight on – or the **train station** – follow Rautatienpuistokatu – into the centre of town, where the **tourist office** is opposite the theatre on Hallituskatu (June to mid-Aug Mon–Fri 8am–6pm, Sat 9am–1pm; mid-Aug to May Mon–Fri 8am–4pm; ☎ 02/621 1273; fax 621 1275). The nearest **youth hostel** is about 5km from the centre, at Tekniikantie 4 (☎02/637 8400; fax 637 8125; May–Aug) – buses #30, #31, #32, #40, #41 and #42 stop nearby. The city's **campsite**, *Isomäki* (☎ 641 0620), is a little closer, just 2km from the centre in the Isomäki Sports Centre, next to the outdoor swimming pool, but it's only open during the jazz festival; buses #7 and #8 run from the centre to the hospital (*sairaala*) close by. At other times of year, you'll need to head 20km out to the *Yyteri* site (☎02/638 3778), though it does have a shop, café, sauna and many cabins; ask at the tourist office for directions. Among the **hotels**, you could try the *Cumulus*, Itsenäisyydenkatu 37 (☎02/623 8000; fax 623 8449; ②/③), one of the larger places and with its own restaurant. A smarter hotel is the *Vaakuna*, Gallen-Kallelankatu 7 (☎02/528 100; fax 528 182; ③/④), a business-oriented hotel with good weekend dis-counts.

In the **evening** most people gravitate to the town centre and watch a procession of highly polished cars heading aimlessly up and down the main streets. Cafés and bars fall in and out of favour quite rapidly, although one of the most consistently popular is *Anton's* on Antinkatu, where a 7mk cup of coffee comes with a cloudberry liqueur chocolate. Otherwise, for eating there are numerous fast-food outlets – particularly *gril-lis*. Check out also the all-year spin-off from the jazz festival, the *Jazz-Café*, at Eteläranta 6 on the banks of the Kokemäenjoki.

If you're planning to come here for the **jazz festival**, it's best to have accommodation fixed up in advance, since hotels, the hostel and the campsite become very crowded – the tourist office endeavours to house as much of the overspill as possible in private homes or in local schools. As for **tickets**, advance booking forms can be obtained from

Finnish tourist offices outside the country. Also, during the course of the festival there's a Festival Centre at Eteläranta 6, which sells tickets (30–190mk) and hands out programmes and information. Obviously the big names sell out well in advance.

The Åland Islands

The **Åland Islands**, all 6000-plus of them, lie scattered between Finland's southwest coast and Sweden. Politically Finnish but culturally Swedish, the Ålands cling to a weird form of independence, with their own parliament and flag (a red and yellow cross on a blue background). The currency is Finnish but the language is Swedish – which explains why the main and only sizeable town is more commonly known by its Swedish name of **MARIEHAMN** than by the Finnish **Maarianhamina**.

The Ålands (**Ahvenanmaa** in Finnish) were in Swedish hands through the Middle Ages, but, coveted by the Russians on account of their strategic location on the Baltic, they became part of the Russian Grand Duchy of Finland in 1807. When Finland gained independence, the future of the Ålands was referred to the League of Nations (though not before several Åland leaders had been imprisoned in Helsinki on a charge of high treason). As a result, Finnish sovereignty was established, in return for autonomy and complete demilitarization: the Ålanders now regard themselves as a shining example of Nordic cooperation, and living proof that a small state can run its own affairs while being part of a larger one.

The Ålands' ancient history is as interesting as the modern: many Roman coins have been found, there are scores of Viking burial mounds, and the remains of some of the oldest Finnish churches. The excellent **Åland Museum** (May–Aug daily 10am–4pm, Tues until 8pm; Sept–April Tues–Sun 11am–4pm, Tues also 6–8pm; 15mk) in Mariehamn's Stadshusparken tells the full story, and is complemented by the ship-shaped **Åland Maritime Museum** on Hamngatan (June–Aug daily 10am–5pm; Sept–May daily 10am–4pm; 20mk), 1km away at the other end of Storagatan, which celebrates the fact that, despite their insignificant size, the Ålands once had the world's largest fleet of wooden sailing ships.

Smaller local history museums in Åland's other communities reflect the surprisingly strong regional differences among the islands; it seems the only thing that's shared are the ubiquitous Åland maypoles – which stand most of the year round – and the fact that specific sights generally take a back seat to the various forms of nature. There are, however, several things worth making for. To the northeast of Mariehamn, in Tosarby Sund, are the remains of **Kastelholm**, a fourteenth-century fortress built to consolidate Swedish domination of the Baltic. Strutted through by numerous Swedish monarchs, it was mostly destroyed by fire in the mid-nineteenth century and is now being restored. In summer guided tours run several times a day (20mk) from the gate to the nearby open-air **Jan Karlsgärden Museum**. The Russians also set about building a fortress, **Bomarsund**, but before it could be completed the Crimean War broke out and an Anglo-French force stormed the infant castle, reducing it to rubble; just the scattered ramparts remain. Both would-be castles are on the same bus route from Mariehamn.

Elsewhere, you can trace the route of the old **post road**, the only mail link from Stockholm to what was then Tsarist St Petersburg. To their long-lasting chagrin, the Åland people were charged with seeing the safe passage of the mail, including taking it across the frozen winter sea – and quite a few died in the process. The major remnant of these times is the nineteenth-century Carl Engel-designed **Post House** in **ECKERÖ**, at the islands' western extremity. Standing on the coast facing Sweden, the building was intended to instil fresh arrivals with awe at their first sight of the mighty Russian empire. Despite retaining its grandeur, it now looks highly incongruous amid the tiny local community.

Having waded through the history, all that's left to say is that the Ålands have sea, sun and beckoning terrain in unlimited quantities – which is precisely their appeal. Nowadays the Ålands' primary source of income is summer tourists, especially Swedes on day trips to Mariehamn. Elsewhere the flat and thickly forested islands contain plenty of secluded spots to search out and enjoy.

Practicalities

Ferries from Finland and Sweden (see "Travel Details") stop in Mariehamn's West Harbour and there's a **tourist office** a few minutes away at Storagatan 11 (June–Aug daily 9am–6pm; Sept–May Mon–Sat 10am–4pm; ☎018/ 27300), which can provide the latest details regarding travel and accommodation. You're going to have a hard time finding **somewhere to stay** if you turn up in summer on spec and without a tent: there are no official youth hostels on the islands and, although there are a number of cheapish guesthouses, some of which offer hostel-type facilities, these fill quickly. If you're at a loose end in Mariehamn, try *Kronan* at Neptunigatan 52 (☎018/12617; ②), or *Kvarnberget*, Parkgatan 28 (also ☎018/12617; ②). The wise option, though, is to camp: there are plentiful **campsites** (in isolated areas you should be able to camp rough with no problems) and a fairly thorough **bus service** covering the main islands. **Cycling** is a sound alternative to the buses, offering not only more freedom but also rental rates slightly cheaper than on the mainland. Most of the islands not linked by road bridge can be reached by small and often free local ferries. If you're feeling lazy, or don't have much time, get a feel of the place by taking one of the **guided bus tours** that leave Mariehamn most weekdays from June to August. They cost 50mk, and last a few hours – check schedules with the tourist office.

travel details

Trains

Helsinki to: Espoo (30 daily; 30min); Järvenpää (38 daily; 30min); Jyväskylä (9 daily; 4hr); Kajaani (4 daily; 7hr 30min); Kuopio (7 daily; 5hr 30min); Lahti (13 daily; 1hr 30min); Luoma (30 daily; 37min); Mikkeli (7 daily; 3hr 30min); Oulu (7 daily; 6hr 30min); Rovaniemi (4 daily; 9hr 30min); Tampere (19 daily; 2hr); Turku (12 daily; 2hr).

Pori to: Tampere (7 daily; 1hr 40min).

Turku to: Tampere (8 daily; 1hr 50min).

Buses

Hamina to: Virolahti (2–3 daily; 35–55min).

Helsinki to: Joensuu (4 daily; 8hr 55min); Jyväskylä (8 daily; 5hr); Kotka (7–9 daily; 1hr 30min–2hr 10min); Lahti (26 daily; 1hr 30min); Mikkeli (8 daily; 4hr); Porvoo (18 daily; 1hr); Tampere (16 daily; 3hr); Tapiola (4 daily; 35min); Turku (21 daily; 2hr 30min).

Kotka to: Hamina (3 daily; 35min).

Mariehamn to: Bomarsund (5 daily; 30min); Eckerö (5 daily; 45min); Kastelholm (5 daily; 30min).

Porvoo to: Kotka (8–10 daily; 40min); Lovisa 8–10 daily; 1hr); Phytää (8–10 daily; 1hr 40min).

Rauma to: Pori (4 daily; 45min).

Turku to: Pori (7 daily; 2hr); Rauma (10 daily; 1hr 30min).

Ferries

Naantali to: Mariehamn (1 daily; 7hr 30min).

Turku to: Mariehamn (2 daily; 5hr 20min).

International Trains

Helsinki to: Moscow (1 daily; 16hr 30min); St Petersburg (2 daily; 10hr).

International Buses

Hamina to: St Petersburg (1 daily; 5hr 30min); Viipuri (1 daily; 2hr 30min).

International Ferries

Helsinki to: Stockholm (2 daily; 15hr); Tallinn (3–4 daily; 3–5hr).

Mariehamn to: Kappellskär (3 daily; 7hr); Stockholm (Mon–Thurs 3 daily, Fri–Sun 2 daily; 6hr).

Turku to: Stockholm (2 daily; 12hr).

CHAPTER SIXTEEN

THE LAKE REGION

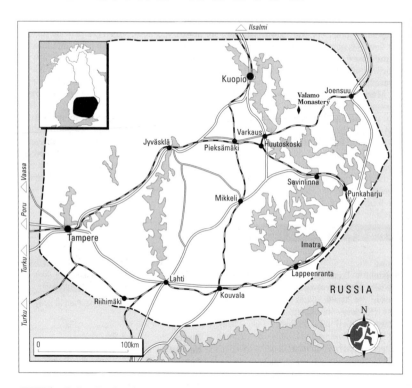

The **Lake Region** is unique in Finland, if not in Scandinavia. Extensive lake chains, chiefly the Päijänne and Saimaa systems, consume a third of the country, particularly the chunk that bulges towards Russia. Each chain features countless bays, inlets and islands, while the dense surrounding forests are interspersed by streaky ridges. The settlements that flourished here grew up around the paper mills, which used natural waterways and purpose-built canals to transport the timber to pulping factories powered by gushing rapids.

Wherever you go, water is never far away, further pacifying an already tranquil, verdant landscape. Even **Tampere**, Finland's major industrial city, is likeable for its lakeside setting as much as for its cultural delights. It's also the most accessible of the region's cities, being on the railway line between Helsinki and the north. Also reachable from Helsinki, **Lahti** only fulfils its promise as a winter sports resort; during summer the town is comparatively dull and lifeless. Diminutive **Mikkeli** has more character, and makes a good stopover en route to the atmospheric eastern part of the Lake

Region, where slender ridges furred with conifers link the few sizeable landmasses. Its regional centre, **Savonlinna**, stretches delectably across several islands, and boasts a superbly preserved medieval castle. To get a sense of Karelian culture visit **Joensuu**, **Lappeenranta** or the city of **Kuopio**, three towns where many displaced Karelians settled after World War II. In the heart of the region lies **Jyväskylä**, whose wealth of buildings by Alvar Aalto draws modern architecture buffs to what is otherwise a typically sleepy town. Down-to-earth **Iisalmi** is effectively a bridge between the Lake Region and the rougher, less watery terrain further north.

Unless you want total solitude (which is easily attained), it's advisable to spend a few days in the larger towns and make shorter forays to the smaller ones, leaving time to spare for exploring the more thinly populated areas. Although the western Lake Region is mostly well served by **trains**, connections to – and within – the eastern part are awkward and infrequent. With daily services between the main towns and less frequent ones to the villages, **buses** are handier for getting around. To really explore the countryside, it's necessary to rent a car or bicycle. Slow, expensive ferries also link the main lakeside towns, while practically every community runs short pleasure cruises.

Tampere and around

"Here it was as natural to approve of the factories as in Mecca one would the mosques", wrote John Sykes of **TAMPERE** in the 1960s and you soon see what he meant. Although Tampere is Finland's biggest manufacturing centre and Scandinavia's largest inland city, it's a highly scenic place, with leafy avenues, sculpture-filled parks and two sizeable lakes. The factories that line the Tammerkoski rapids in the heart of the city actually accentuate its appeal, their chimneys standing as bold monuments to Tampere's past – it's no coincidence that the town is known colloquially as Finland's Manchester. Its rapid growth began just over a century ago, when Tsar Alexander I abolished taxes on local trade, encouraging the Scotsman James Finlayson to open a textile factory here, drawing labour from rural areas where traditional crafts were in decline. Metalwork and shoe factories soon followed, their owners paternally supplying culture to the workforce by promoting a vigorous local arts scene. Free outdoor rock and jazz concerts, lavish theatrical productions and one of the best modern art collections in Finland maintain such traditions to this day.

Arrival, information and accommodation

Almost everything of consequence is within the central section of the city, bordered on two sides by the lakes Näsijärvi and Pyhäjärvi. The main streets run off either side of Hämeenkatu, which leads directly from the **train station** across Hämeensilta – the bridge over Tammerkoski, famous for its weighty bronze sculptures by Wäino Aaltonen, representing four characters from local folklore. Although there's little call to

---

ACCOMMODATION PRICE CODES

The Finnish hotels listed throughout the guide have been graded according to the following price bands, based on the rate for a double room in summer. However, many hotels offer summer and/or weekend discounts, and in these instances we've given two grades, covering both the regular and the discounted rate.

① Under 275mk   ② 275–350mk   ③ 350–450mk
④ 450–550mk   ⑤ 550–750mk   ⑥ 750mk and over

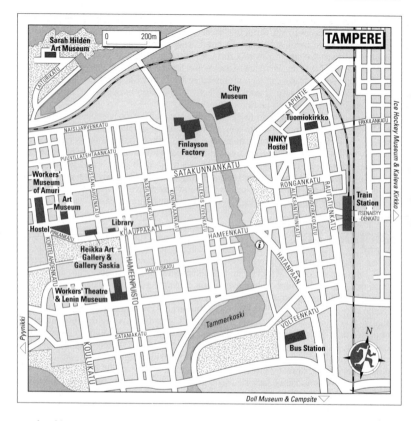

use local **buses**, most routes begin from the terminal on Hämeenkatu. At Hämeenkatu 1 there's a useful late-opening **exchange** office (June–Aug daily 9am–6pm; Sept–May closed Sun). Tampere's **tourist office**, Verkatehtaankatu 2 (June–Aug Mon–Fri 8.30am–8pm, Sat 8.30am–6pm, Sun 11am–6pm; Sept–May Mon–Fri 8.30am–5pm; ☎03/212 6652 or 6775; fax 219 6463), hands out copies of the excellent, free *Tampere Today* guide. In summer they also organize two-hour sightseeing tours (daily 2pm; 40mk).

Accommodation

Budget travellers are catered for best during the summer, when both the main **youth hostels** are open. *NNKY* (the Finnish YWCA, open to both sexes) stands opposite the cathedral at Tuomiokirkonkatu 12A (June to late Aug; ☎03/222 5446); the second official hostel is the bigger, much more impersonal summer hotel *Domus*, at Pellervonkatu 9 (☎03/255 0000; fax 255 0009), behind the Kaleva kirkko. *Uimahallinmaja*, centrally located at Pirkankatu 10–12 (☎03 222 9460; fax 222 9940), 1km from the train station, is a superb cheap hotel-style hostel open all year, with rooms sleeping one to four people (105–170mk per person), plus dorm beds (95mk). Of Tampere's regular **hotels**, the *Victoria*, Itsenäisyydenkatu 1 (☎03/242 5111; fax 242 5100; ③), and *SokosHotel Villa*, Sumeliaksenkatu 14 (☎03/262 6267; fax 262 6268; ③), are both handily placed and well priced, or an early booking might get you some luxury beside the lake at the *Rosendahl*, Pyynikinti 13 (☎03/244 1111; fax 223 3375; ④), a couple of kilometres from the city centre. As usual, however, the least expensive lakeside option is a **campsite** – *Härmälä* (☎03/265 1355; mid-May to late Aug; bookings at other times of year on ☎90/6138 3210), 5km to the south and accessible by bus #1. Tents can be pitched for 70mk, while cabins for three people cost 120mk, those sleeping five 300mk.

The City

Short, broad streets make central Tampere very easy to explore. From the train station, Hämeenkatu runs across the Tammer River into the heart of the city and almost everything of interest lies within a few minutes' walk of this busy thoroughfare. You'll need to cross back over the river (most easily done by following Satakunnankatu), however, to reach Tampere's historic cathedral – and to see the Finlayson factory, on which the city's fortunes were founded.

Hämeenkatu and north

Walking the length of Hämeenkatu from the train station leaves you in front of the upwardly thrusting neo-Gothic **Aleksanterin kirkko** (daily May–Aug 10am–6pm; Sept–April 11am–3pm). With its riot of knobbly ceiling decorations, the effect inside is something like an ecclesiastical train station, with an unusually unpleasant artexed alter. To the left, following the line of greenery up the slender Hämeenpuisto, is the Tampere Workers' Theatre and, in the same building but with a separate entrance on Hallituskatu, the **Lenin Museum** (Mon–Fri 9am–5pm, Sat & Sun 11am–4pm; 15mk). After the abortive 1905 revolution in Russia, Lenin lived in Finland and attended the Tampere conferences, held in what is now the museum. It was here that he first encountered Stalin, although this is barely mentioned in either exhibition: one concentrates on Lenin himself, the other on his relationship with Finland. For a detailed explanation, borrow the English-language brochure from reception.

Several blocks north of Hämeenkatu, the Amuri district was built during the 1880s to house Finlayson's workers. Some thirty homes have been preserved as the **Workers' Museum of Amuri** (early May to mid-Sept Tues–Fri 9am–5pm, Sat & Sun 11am–6pm; rest of the year Tues–Sat 9am–5pm, Sun 11am–5pm; 15mk) at Makasiininkatu 12, a simple but affecting place that records the family life of working people over a hundred-year period. In each home is a description of the inhabitants and their jobs, and authentic articles from the relevant periods – from beds and tables to family photos, newspapers and biscuit packets.

Just around the corner at Puutarhakatu 34 is the **Art Museum of Tampere** (Tues–Sun 10am–6pm; 15mk, up to 40mk during special exhibitions; guided tours by arrangement ☎03/219 6577), whose first floor holds powerful if staid temporary exhibitions on such subjects as the treasures of Indonesia and, from August 1997, ancient Mexican art; the large basement galleries are filled with contemporary local work. If you're looking for older Finnish art, head instead for the far superior **Hiekka Art Museum**, a few minutes' walk away at Pirkankatu 6 (Wed, Thurs & Sun noon–3pm; other times by arrangement ☎03/212 3975 or 212 3973; 15mk). Kustaa Heikka was a gold- and silversmith whose professional skills and business acumen made him a local big shot around the turn of the century. The art collection he bequeathed to Tampere reflects his interest in traditional lifestyles; borrow a catalogue from reception, since most pieces are identified only by numbers. Amongst the most notable work (including sketches by Gallen-Kallela and Helene Schjerfbeck) are two of Heikka's own creations: a delicately wrought brooch marking the completion of his apprenticeship, and a finely detailed bracelet with which he celebrated becoming a master craftsman. Well worth the diversion, and free too, is the next-door **Gallery Saskia** (daily noon–6pm), show-ing intriguing new work that you won't catch elsewhere.

Nearby stands the **Tampere Library**, Pirkankatu 2 (June–Aug Mon–Sat 9.30am–7pm; Sept–May Mon–Fri 9.30am–8pm, Sat 9.30am–3pm), an astounding feat of user-friendly modern architecture. The work of Reimi and Raili Pietilä (who also designed the epic Kalevala kirkko – see below), and finished in 1986, the library's curving walls give it a warm, cosy feel; believe it or not, the building's shape was inspired by a certain type of grouse (a stuffed specimen of which sits in the reception area). Strolling around is the best way to take in the many small, intriguing features, and will eventually lead you up to the top-floor café, which gives a good view of the cupola, deliberately set eleven degrees off the vertical – to match the off-centre pivot of the earth. In the basement of the library, with its own entrance at Hämeenpuisto 20, **Moomin Valley** (May–Aug Mon–Fri 9am–5pm, Sat & Sun 10am–6pm; Sept–April Wed–Fri 9am–5pm, Sat & Sun 10am–6pm; 15mk) re-creates with dolls and 3D dis-plays scenes from the incredibly popular Moomin children's books of Finnish author Tove Jansson.

The Näsijärvi lakeside

Just north of Tampere's central grid-plan streets, the tremendous **Sara Hildén Art Museum** (daily 11am–6pm; 15mk), built on the shores of Näsijärvi, displays Tampere's premier modern art collection by means of changing exhibitions. The museum is on the other side of Paasikiventie from Amuri (take a #16, or the summer-only #4 bus from the town centre or train station).

Occupying the same waterside strip as the Hildén collection is **Särkänniemi**, a tourist complex incorporating a dolphinarium, aquarium, planetarium and observation tower. Seen from the tower – an unmistakable element of Tampere's skyline – the city seems insignificant compared to the trees and lakes that stretch to the horizon. The rapids that cut through them can be identified from afar by the factory chimneys along-side. The tower is open from 10am to 8pm during summer, and there's a 12mk admis-sion charge, waived if you're using the tower restaurant; the other diversions cost 20–30mk apiece and are rarely uncrowded with families. To make a day of it, buy the 70mk Särkänniemi Passport (50mk in winter), valid for all parts of the complex. There's a café here too, serving uninspired pizza and quiche.

The Cathedral and around

Cross to the eastern side of the Tammer River along Satakunnankatu and you'll not only see – foaming below the bridge – the rapids that powered the **Finlayson factory**, but also the factory itself, still standing to the north and nowadays holding several crafts workshops.

Immediately ahead, the **Tuomiokirkko** stands in a grassy square, a picturesque cathedral in the National Romantic style, designed by Lars Sonck and finished in 1907 (daily May–Aug 10am–6pm; Sept–April 11am–3pm; guided tours 11am & 5pm). It's most remarkable for the gorily symbolic frescoes by Hugo Simberg – particularly the *Garden of Death*, where skeletons happily water plants, and *The Wounded Angel*, show-ing two boys carrying a bleeding angel through a Tampere landscape – which caused an ecclesiastical outcry when unveiled. So did the viper (a totem of evil) which he placed amongst the angel wings on the ceiling; Simberg retorted that evil could lurk anywhere – including a church.

After viewing the cathedral, you've more or less completed a circular trek around the city and seen all that the central part has to offer, except for the glittering *Koskikeskus* shopping mall near the station.

Out from the centre

To learn about Tampere's origins, take a pleasant walk along the shores of Pyhäjärvi to the **City Museum** (Tues–Sun 11am–5pm; 10mk), housed in a converted factory just across the river from the great Finlayson factory. Its most interesting section deals with the early twentieth century – a turbulent time for both Tampere and Finland. As an industrial town with militant workers, Tampere instigated a general strike against the Russification of Finland, filling the streets with demonstrators and painting over the Cyrillic names on trilingual street signs. After independence the city became a Social Democratic stronghold, and one ruthlessly dealt with by the right-wing government following the civil war of 1918 – yet the municipal administration remains amongst the most left-leaning in Finland.

On a totally different note, Itsenäisyydenkatu runs uphill behind the train station to meet the vast concrete folds of the **Kaleva kirkko** (daily May–Aug 10am–6pm; Sept–April 11am–3pm; guided tours at 11am & 5pm). Built in 1966, it was a belated addition to the neighbouring **Kaleva estate**, which was heralded as an outstanding example of high-density housing in the 1950s. Though initially stunning, the church's interior lacks the subtlety of the city library, despite being designed by the same team – perhaps because Reimi and Raili Pietilä based their plan on a fish this time.

Continuing past the church, follow the signs for *Jäähalli* (Ice Hall) to the ice hockey stadium just off Kekkosentie (or take bus #18, #19, #25 or #27 from the centre). The **Ice Hockey Museum** here (open during matches or by special request; ☎03/212 4200; 10mk) accords due honour to the local teams Ilves and Tappora, which have won more national championships than all of Finland's other teams combined. Other exhibits include a vast collection of hockey sticks from around the world, and a white puck used during the immediate postwar period, when artificial ice was unavailable and matches were played on the blue ice of frozen lakes.

Eating, drinking and entertainment

Tampere boasts an eclectic range of restaurants and cafés to suit most pockets. Several places in the *Koskikeskus* shopping mall, Hatanpään valtatie 1, offer cheap lunchtime specials, but, as usual, the cheapest **places to eat** are the student mensas – in the university at the end of Yliopistonkatu, just over the railway line from the city centre – where full meals can cost as little as 10mk with a student card, 16mk without. There are all the usual pizza places: *Rosso*, on the second floor of the *Hostel Uimahallin Maja*, Pirkankatu 10–12, is open till 11.45pm nightly, while *Martina*, Hämeenkatu 5A, does an unusual Mexican pizza (43mk). For quiet posing, *Café Strindberg* (daily 7am–2am), next to the theatre at Hämeenpuisto 1, serves fine cakes, pies and excellent filled baguettes (32mk), as well as breakfasts and more substantial lunches; there's another branch at the train station. For carnivores, *Tiiliholvi,* Kauppakatu 10 (Mon–Fri 11am–3pm & 5pm–midnight) is known for its good but pricey steaks, while *Henricks*, Satamakatu 7 (Mon–Sat 11am–midnight, Sun 11am–6pm), serves up French cuisine in a more intimate atmosphere. If you want to try a Tampere speciality, head for the Laukontori open-air market, by the rapids, where the local black sausage, *mustamakkara*, is sold.

There are numerous **supermarkets** for buying your own provisions. Try the big *Sokos* store at Hämeenkatu 21; *Anttila*, Puuthakatu 10; or *Forum*, Kuninkaankatu 21 – all of which are central. Slightly further out, and cheaper, are *City Market*, Sotilaankatu 11, and *Sokos Market* at Sammonkatu 73. There's also a large **kauppahalli** at Hämeenkatu 19 (Mon–Fri 8am–5pm, Sat 8am–2pm), and open-air markets at Laukontori (Mon–Fri 6am–2pm, Sat 6am–1pm), Keskustori (first Mon of month 6am–6pm) and Tammelantori (Mon–Fri 6am–2pm, Sat 6am–1pm).

Bars and entertainment

Tampere at night is very much alive and buzzing, with numerous late-night bars, cafés and clubs. One of the most popular **pubs** is the Irish *Dublinin Ovet* ("Doors of Dublin") at Kauppakatu 16, though the best place for Guinness is *Pikilinna* on Pinninkatu, to the east of the city centre, a small football fans' pub with an ambience all its own. Another summertime favourite is *Falls*, down by the rapids. Live **jazz** bands perform at the laid-back *Tullikamari*, a nightclub set in an old customs house behind the train station on Itsenäisyydenkatu (Independence Street), and named after the 1918 Civil War between the white and red armies. Almost opposite the tourist office is *Paapankapakka*, a swing-style jazz club with up and coming bands. *Café Europa* on Aleksanterinkatu is more of a meeting place than an all-night hangout, though it does have live music, while on the same street, the extremely popular rock disco *Doris* in the basement of *Restaurant Katupoika* is the place where locals go to drink beer and dance till morning. On warm nights the locals head out to the Pyynikki area, a natural ridge on the edge of Tampere, beside Pyhäjärvi. Tickets for the **Pyynikki Summer Theatre** cost around 70mk, but it's worth trekking out just to look at the revolving auditorium which slowly rotates the audience around during performances, blending the surrounding woods, rocks and water into the show's scenery.

There are a couple of good **gay bars**, the friendliest and most laid-back in the country being *Mixei* on Otavalankatu 3 (Tues–Sun 10am–3am; disco Fri & Sat 10pm–3am). Entrance is just 10mk and – rarely for Finland – there's no compulsory cloakroom charge. Also unique is Finland's only **lesbian bar**, *Nice Place,* Hämeenpuisto 29 (Fri & Sat 3pm–2am) – though open to anyone, the customers are usually women relaxing over coffee.

Around Tampere – and moving on

Half an hour from Tampere on the busy rail line to Helsinki, **HÄMEENLINNA** is revered as the birthplace of Sibelius and Finland's oldest inland town. Though somewhat self-important, it's nonetheless worth a visit if you have time. The major attraction is **Hämeenlinna** (daily May–Aug 10am–6pm; Sept–April 10am–4pm; 14mk), the sturdy thirteenth-century castle from which the town takes its name. Next comes the **Sibelius Childhood Home** (daily May–Aug 10am–4pm; Sept–April noon–4pm; 2mk) at Hallituskatu 11, where the great composer was born, now reverentially restored to how it was during the first years of his life. A few blocks away at Viipurintie 2, the **Art Museum** (Tues–Sun noon–6pm, Thurs until 8pm; 3mk) musters a mundane collection of minor works by major Finnish names, among them Järnefelt, Gallen-Kalella and Halonen.

Seeing all this won't take long, and any spare hours are better spent in the outlying area of **Hattula**, roughly 5km from Hämeenlinna's centre. The local **Hattulan kirkko** (daily May to mid-Aug 11am–5pm; mid-Aug to April noon–4pm; 15mk) is probably the finest medieval church in Finland – outwardly plain, with an interior totally covered by 180 sixteenth-century frescoes of biblical scenes. En route to the church, a combined **youth hostel** (May to mid-Aug) and **campsite** (June–Aug; both ☎03/682 8560) face Hämeenlinna across the river, 4km from the town centre. Camping costs 70mk at night, beds in chalets from 200mk.

Moving on from Tampere

Tampere has excellent **train and bus links** to the rest of Finland. To reach the rest of the Lake Region, however, there are two main choices. Aiming for Jyväskylä (simplest by train) also puts you within comparatively easy reach of Varkaus, Joensuu and Kuopio. Alternatively, heading for Lahti (to which there are direct buses; by train change at Hyvinkää) makes more sense if you want to press on to Mikkeli, or see more of the eastern Lake Region, such as Lappeenranta and Savonlinna.

Jyväskylä

JYVÄSKYLÄ is the most low-key and provincial of the main Lake Region towns, despite the industrial section that takes up one end and a big university which consumes the other – though the latter does provide something of a youthful feel. Jyväskylä also has more than its fair share of buildings by **Alvar Aalto**. The legendary architect grew up here and opened his first office in the town in 1923, and his handiwork – a collection of buildings spanning his entire career – litters the place.

After some minor projects, Aalto left Jyväskylä in 1927 for fame, fortune and Helsinki, but returned in the 1950s to work on the teacher-training college. By the 1970s this had grown into the **Jyväskylä University**, whose large campus halts traffic where the main road gives way to a series of public footpaths, leading to a park and sports ground. Although Aalto died before his ambitious plan for an Administration and Cultural Centre was complete, the scheme is still under construction along Vapaudenkatu. Across the road from the (perhaps intentionally) uninspiring police station – unveiled in 1970 – stands a **city theatre** resembling a scaled-down version of Helsinki's Finlandia (free guided tours start from the tourist office at 2pm daily in summer).

The town's museums are clustered together on the hill running down from the university towards the edge of the lake, Jyväsjärvi. At the request of the town authorities rather than through vanity, Aalto built the **Alvar Aalto Museum** at Alvar Aallon Katu 7 (Tues–Sun 11am–6pm; 10mk, free on Fri). The architect's best works are obviously out on the streets, making this collection of plans, photos and models seem rather superfluous. But the Aalto-designed furniture makes partial amends. The first floor hosts temporary art exhibitions and the ground floor has a pleasant if unexciting café. Aalto also contributed to the exterior of the nearby **Keski-Suomen Museo** (Museum of Central Finland; Tues–Sun 11am–6pm; 10mk, free on Fri), with two separate exhibitions: one devoted to Middle Finland – well designed but with no English translations – and the other representing each decade of the twentieth century through the car number plates, music and kitchen gadgetry of the day. The collection of room interiors is worth the visit alone. Walking back towards the town centre along

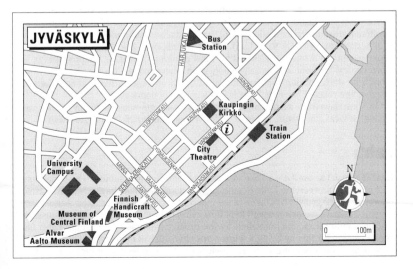

Keskussairaalantie brings you to the **Finnish Handicraft Museum**, beside the main road at Seminaarinkatu 32 (Tues–Sun 11am–6pm; 10mk, free on Fri). Preserved in its 1910 style, the building is a centre for research into the origins and development of all kinds of crafts, and the displays range from bell-making to spectrolite jewellery – all far more stylish than you might expect. Another place to see is the nineteenth-century **Kaupungin-kirkko** (June–Aug daily 10am–5pm; ask at the tourist office about the free guided tours), opposite the tourist office. The church was the centrepiece of Jyväskylä life a century ago, but declined in importance as the town gained new suburbs and other churches. Despite recent restoration – when the interior was repainted in its original pale yellow and green – the church looks authentically dingy.

Practicalities

From the train and bus stations, right in the centre, it's a short walk to the **tourist office**, in a beautiful wooden building at Asemakatu 6 (June–Aug Mon–Fri 8am–6pm, Sat & Sun 10am–6pm; Sept–May Mon–Fri 8am–5pm; ☎014/624 903; fax 624 904), which can supply a useful free leaflet on the local buildings designed by Aalto. For **accommodation**, the family-run and central *Hotel Milton*, Hannikaisenkatu 29 (☎014/213 411; fax 631 927; ②), is a good choice, right by the train station. The local **youth hostel** (☎/fax 014/253 355; open year-round) is a state-of-the-art affair, 4km from the centre, off Laajavuorentie – take bus #2 from Vapaudenkatu. The nearest **campsite** (☎014/624 895; June–Aug) is 2km north off the E4 – take Puistokatu and then continue along Taulumäentie, or take bus #8.

Eating options veer from the pizza establishments along the main streets to the more upscale *Kissanviikset* ("the Cat's Whiskers") at Puistokatu 3, which serves some sizeable and just about affordable fish dishes at lunchtime. The most lurid of the pizzerias is the turquoise, pink and yellow *Sohwi* at Vaasankatu 21, which doubles as a bar. Among the cafés, *Kahvila Ruustinna* at Kauppakatu 11 serves deliciously calorific cakes, while *Book Café Beckers* at Seminaarikatu 28 (Mon–Sat noon–5pm, Sun noon–3pm), just beyond the craft museum, occupies a maze of old wooden carved buildings that holds art galleries and a bookshop.

The university hosts events in and out of term-time, so it's always worth checking the student **mensas** for posters. The neighbourhood around the university is also a focus for the town's **nightlife**, such as it is. Two notable haunts are *Ilokivi*, Keskussairaalantie 2, often featuring art exhibitions and live bands; and the smoky *Ruthin ravintola*, Seminaarinkatu 19 (daily 9am–1am), where members of the philosophy and politics departments get down to chess and/or hard drinking. *Alvari*, at Kauppakatu 30, is a more central hangout whose easy-going atmosphere makes it a popular **gay** venue, though its dark interior contains the usual quota of those drinking themselves into oblivion; the relaxed bar *Free Time* is just a couple of doors away.

On Thursdays there's a **gay night** at *Becker's Book Café* (see above); for further information on local gay events, call in at SETA, Yliopistonkatu 26 (☎014/310 0660).

Lahti

LAHTI doesn't know if it's a Lake Region town or a Helsinki suburb. The major transport junction between the Lake Region and the south, Lahti lacks any lake area atmosphere; its entire growth has taken place this century (mostly since Alvar Aalto opened several furniture factories, which kept him going between architectural commissions) and local cultural life is diminished by the relative proximity of Helsinki. Lahti finds compensation for this by being a **winter sports** centre of international renown: three enormous ski jumps hang over the town, and there's a feeling of biding time when summer grass rather than winter snow covers their slopes. Unless you're here to ski, Lahti isn't a place you'll need or want to linger in – the town can easily be covered in a day. Head first for the **observation platform** on the highest ski jump (May–Sept 11am–6pm, Sat & Sun 10am–5pm; 20mk), whose location is unmistakeable. From such a dizzying altitude the lakes and forests around Lahti stretch dreamily into the distance, and the large swimming pool below resembles a puddle (when frozen in winter it's used as a landing zone).

The only structures matching the ski jumps for height are the twin radio masts atop Radiomäki hill, between the train station (a 15-min walk away) and the town centre. Steep pathways wind uphill towards the **Radio Ja TV Museo** (Radio and Television Museum; call ☎03/818 4512 for opening times; 15mk), inside the original transmitting station at the base of one of the masts. Here, two big rooms are packed with bulky Marconi valves, crystal sets, antiquated sound-effect discs, room-sized amplifiers and intriguing curios. Look out for the *Pikku Hitler* – the German-made "little Hitler", a wartime portable radio that forms an uncanny facsimile of the dictator's face.

At Radiomäki's foot, the distinctive red brickwork of Eliel Saarinen's **town hall** injects some style into the concrete blocks that make central Lahti so dull and uniform. Built in 1912, many of its Art Nouveau features were considered immensely daring at the time, and although most of the originals were destroyed in the war, careful refurbishment has re-created much of Saarinen's design. Viewable during office hours, the interior is definitely worth seeing. Lahti's other notable building is at the far end of Mariankatu, which cuts through the town centre from the town hall: the **Ristinkirkko** (daily 10am–3pm), whose white roof slopes down from the bell tower in imaginative imitation of the local ski jumps. Interestingly, this was the last church to be designed by Alvar Aalto: he died during its construction and the final work was overseen by his wife. Outside, Wäinö Aaltonen produced one of his most discreetly emotive sculptures to mark the war graves in the cemetery.

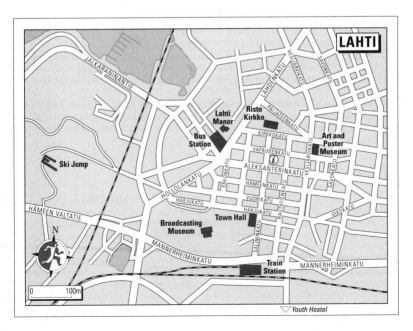

By now you've more or less exhausted Lahti, although Hämeenkatu, running parallel to the far more hectic Aleksanterinkatu, contains a number of little art galleries owned by local artists, and a few second-hand bookshops. The **Art Museum** (daily 11am–4pm; 20mk), just around the corner at Vesijärvenkatu 11, exhibits nineteenth- and twentieth-century works, most notably by Gallen-Kallela and Edelfelt; the adjacent **Poster Museum** (separate entrance at Vapaudenkatu 22; daily 11am–7pm; 15mk) mounts temporary displays and a biannual international poster festival.

Finally, near the hazardous web-like junction by the bus station is the wooden nineteenth-century Lahti Manor, hidden behind a line of trees. Now a **Historical Museum** (Mon–Fri 10am–5pm, Sat & Sun 11am–5pm; 20mk), it contains regional paraphernalia, numerous Finnish medals and coins, plus an unexpected hoard of French and Italian paintings and furniture.

Practicalities

The **tourist office** is at Torikatu 3B (June–Aug Mon–Fri 8am–5pm, Sat & Sun 10am–2pm; Sept–May Mon–Fri 8am–4pm; ☎03/818 4566 or 4568; fax 818 4564). Though the official **youth hostel** at Kivikatu 1 (☎03/782 6324; fax 818 4564) is open all year, it's a monotonous thirty-minute walk from the centre: go under the train station tunnel, along Launeenkatu, right into Tapparakatu and through a housing estate. Buses #9 and #51 run between the hostel and the town centre although only the latter goes to the train station. With this in mind, it's worth trying the slightly pricier **private hostel**, *Patria*, at Vesijärvenkatu 3 (☎03/782 3783), near the train station, which also has double rooms (①). For a more luxurious night's stay, the best choice is the *Seurahuone*, Aleksanterinkatu 14, which boasts a sauna and pool, and TV and VCR in all rooms (☎03/85111; ④). About 4km to the north of Lahti at **Mukkula** is a lakeside **campsite** with cottages (☎03/306 554; June–Aug; 200mk, camping 35mk per person), reached directly by bus #30 from the bus station at the end of Aleksanterinkatu.

Low-priced **eating** options include *Grilli Serdika* at Hämeenkatu 21, which claims to be the cheapest steakhouse in Lahti, while the best place for cakes and pastries is the central *Café Sinuhe*, Mariankatu 21. You'll find the larger **supermarkets** clustered along Savonkatu. Though hardly remarkable for its nightlife, Lahti holds its own compared to smaller towns in the Lake Region. For an evening **drink**, try the lively *Marco Polo* in the *Seurahuone Hotel* (see above), or *Jokeri*, slightly further along the street. The terrace-style café on Mariankatu offers more refined forms of social intercourse.

Train and bus connections onwards from Lahti are fairly good. Mikkeli, to the north, is the sensible target if you're ultimately making for Kuopio, but Lappeenranta is a better destination if you're keen to discover the small towns and glorious scenery of the eastern Lake Region.

Mikkeli

In 1986 a Helsinki bank robber chose the market square in **MIKKELI** as the place to blow up himself, his car and his hostage. This, the most violent event seen in Finland for decades, was perhaps an echo of Mikkeli's blood-spattered past. In prehistoric times the surrounding plains were battlegrounds for feuding tribes from east and west, the Finnish Infantry has a long association with the town, and it was from Mikkeli that General Mannerheim conducted the campaign against the Soviet Union in the Winter War.

Military matters are a strong local feature, but you don't need to be a bloodthirsty warmonger to find interest in the town's military collections – the insights they provide into Finland's recent history can be fascinating. More generally, Mikkeli lacks the heavy industry you'll find in some Lake Region communities, functioning instead as a district

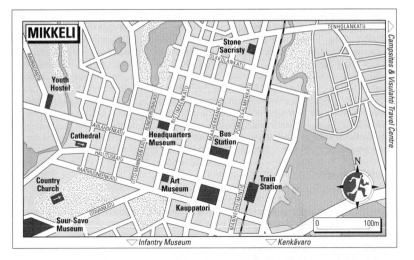

market town (the daily crowds and activity within its kauppatori seem out of all proportion to its size), while sporting a handsome cathedral and a noteworthy art collection.

The military museums

Older Finns visiting Mikkeli tend to make a beeline for the office used by Mannerheim, preserved as the **Headquarters Museum**, Päämajankatu 1–3 (mid-May to Aug daily 10am–5pm; 5mk). It's not so much the exhibits – centrepiece is Mannerheim's desk, holding his spectacles and favourite cigars – but the fact that the Winter War, which effectively prevented a Soviet invasion of Finland in 1939 (see p.613), was waged and won from this very room that gives the museum its special importance. An adjoining room has photo displays and a short slide show about Mannerheim's days in Mikkeli.

Mannerheim spent some of those days in the **Mikkeli Club**, a cross between a speakeasy and a masonic lodge, which still exists, occupying what is now part of the *Sokos* department store on Hallitutskatu, facing the kauppatori. The club's walls are lined with photos of Mannerheim and his staff, although less prominence is given to the snaps of the Marshal riding with Hitler during the Führer's birthday visit (these are in an unmarked folder usually lying on a side table). The club is not strictly open to the public but the tourist office (see below) can arrange for interested individuals to be shown around.

A few minutes' walk from the town centre is the **Infantry Museum**, Jääkärinkatu 6–8 (mid-May to mid-June & mid-Aug to mid-Sept Tues–Sun 10am–5pm; mid-June to mid-Aug daily 10am–5pm; mid-Sept to mid-May Wed, Sat & Sun noon–5pm; 10mk), which records the key armed struggles that marked Finland's formative years as an independent nation. Assorted rifles, artillery pieces and maps of troops' movements provide the factual context, but it's the scores of front-line photos and display cases of troops' letters and lucky charms that reveal the human story. A second, substantially less interesting, section of the museum concentrates chiefly on the Finnish role in the United Nations Peace-Keeping Force.

The rest of the town

Raised in 1897, Mikkeli's Gothic Revival **Cathedral** (daily 10–11am only) sits primly on a small hill at the western end of Hallituskatu. Inside, Pekka Halonen's 1899 altarpiece draws the eye, a radiant Christ against a dark, brooding background. Take a close look, too, at Antii Salmenlinna's stained-glass paintings and you'll spot depictions of three Finnish towns (Viipuri, Sortavala and Käkisalmi) ceded to Russia after World War II.

Down the road from the cathedral, the excellent **Art Museum**, at Ristimäenkatu 5A (Tues–Fri & Sun noon–6pm, Sat noon–3pm; 10mk), stages some stimulating temporary exhibitions of the latest Finnish art and has two permanent displays of artworks bequeathed to the town. The Martti Airio Collection is a forceful selection of early twentieth-century Finnish impressionism and expressionism – Tyko Saalinen's *Young American Woman* and *On the Visit* are particularly striking. The museum's other benefactor was the Mikkeli-born sculptor Johannes Haapasalo, who left nearly three hundred finished works and over a thousand sketches to the museum. One of Haapasalo's better works can be seen beside the cathedral: called *Despair*, it marks the graves of Mikkeli's Civil War dead.

If you've ever wondered how vergers in eighteenth-century Finland kept their church congregations awake, the answer (a big stick) can be seen at the tiny **Stone Sacristy**, to the north at Porrassalmenkatu 47 (June–Aug daily 11am–5pm; free); the church which the sacristy served was demolished in 1776. Several other historic items from the Mikkeli diocese sit in the room, a wooden pulpit, a "shame bench" (for women deemed unvirtuous) and a wood-framed bible among them. While here, spare a thought for the twelfth-century graveyard on which the sacristy stands, and the 22 twentieth-century corpses entombed beneath its concrete floor.

A fifteen-minute walk from the town centre along Otavankatu (easily combined with a visit to the Infantry Museum) leads to the **Country Church** (June to mid-Aug Mon–Thurs 11am–5pm, Sun noon–5pm), believably claimed to be one of the largest wooden churches in Finland. Size aside, the church is a modest sight, but is a more satisfying time-filler than the small stone building in its grounds which houses the **Suur-Savo Museum** (April–Sept Tues–Sun 11am–3pm, Wed also 4–6pm; free), a hotchpotch of broken clocks, cracked crockery, and even a bent-wheeled penny-farthing bicycle, purporting to be a record of regional life.

Kenkävaro and Visulahti

Should the urge to weave, sew or create something in clay suddenly strike, **Kenkävaro**, Pursialenkatu 6 (mid-June to mid-Aug Mon–Fri & Sun 10am–6pm, Sat 10am–2pm; 25mk), run by the local handicrafts association, has several workshops that can provide the necessary tools and instruction. Even if artistic urges don't stimulate a call, Kenkävaro's historical associations might: the workshops occupy the buildings of Finland's oldest vicarage, most of it dating from 1869 – and the main building holds a very nice café (see below).

Kenkävaro is a good place to occupy young minds and hands and another is the less traditional **Visulahti Travel Centre**, 5km from Mikkeli (bus #1) on the road to Kuopio (mid-May to mid-Aug daily; 25–40mk for each section, 60mk for a combined day ticket). It includes a waxworks, motor museum and dinosaur theme park with a host of displays and rides.

Practicalities

The **train and bus stations** are both within a few minutes' walk of Mikkeli's centre, where the **tourist office** faces the kauppatori at Hallituskatu 3a (June to mid-Aug Mon–Fri 9am–5.30am, Sat 9am–2pm; mid-Aug to May Mon 9am–5pm, Tues–Fri 9am–4.30pm; ☎015/151 444; fax 151 625).

Of Mikkeli's **hotels**, the top-notch *Sokos Hotel Vaakuna*, Porrassalmenkatu 9 (☎015/20201; fax 202 0421; ③/⑤), is a good bet, or if that's too pricey, try *Gasthaus Mikkeli*, Nuijamiestenkatu 63 (☎015/150 225; ②). The nearest official **youth hostel**, one of the most beautiful in the country, is *Löydön kartano* (☎015/664 101; fax 664 109; open all year), 20km to the south at Kartanontie 71 in **Risteena** (some Kouvola-bound buses stop there). The family-run hostel occupies a large, atmospheric pink-painted wooden house, for two hundred years home to an aristocratic Russian general and his descendants, who bought it in 1752. Beds are 60mk and a generous breakfast costs 30mk. Mikkeli also has a couple of **campsites** within striking distance on local bus routes: *Visulahti* (☎015/18281; mid-May to Aug), 5km away beside the Visulahti Travel Centre (see above); and *Mäntyniemi*, Ihastjärventie 40B (☎ 015 174220), 7km from the centre.

When it comes to **eating**, a tasty range of paellas, pizzas and lasagne dishes are served up by the mid-priced *Sevilla*, Maaherrankatu 12, and *Café Aurinkoisia* on Porrassalmenkatu, opposite the market square, serves filling, cheap lunches. You'll sacrifice atmosphere but save a few markkaa by eating at *Rosso*, Maaherrankatu 13 (open daily until 10 or 11pm), which provides the town's cheapest pizzas (30mk). The main square hosts a particularly good daily market selling fresh breads, fish, fruit and snacks.

Lappeenranta

Likeable **LAPPEENRANTA** provides an excellent first taste of the eastern Lake Region, conveniently sited on the main rail line between Helsinki and Joensuu and along all the eastern bus routes. It's a small, slow-paced town where summer evenings find most of the population strolling around the linden-tree-lined harbour. Once holding a key position on the Russian border, Lappeenranta boasts historical features that its neighbouring towns don't share and provides an eye-opening introduction to political conflicts that not only affected medieval Finland but also had an impact on recent generations.

The Town and fortress

After calling in at the **tourist office** (late June & July Mon–Fri 8am–8pm, Sat 9am–3pm, Sun 10am–3pm; rest of June & Aug Mon–Fri 8am–6pm, Sat 9am–3pm; Sept–May Mon–Fri 9am–3pm; ☎05/415 6860; fax 415 6140), which faces the **bus station**, a ten-minute walk along Kauppakatu from the **train station**, let gravity pull you down the hill into the town centre and towards the harbour. Strolling and snacking from the numerous stands selling the local specialities – spicy meat pastries called *vetyjä* and *atomeja* – are the primary harbourside pursuits.

If you're feeling more energetic, climb the steep path on the harbour's western side, which brings you to the top of the town's old earthen ramparts and into the Russian-built Fortress area, where Lappeenranta's past soon becomes apparent. Its **origins** as a trading centre reach back to the mid-1600s, but it was with the westward shift of the Russian border in 1721 that the town found itself in the front line of Russian–Swedish conflicts. After the Peace of Turku in 1743, the border again moved, this time leaving Lappeenranta inside Russian territory. Subsequently, a garrison of the Tsar's army arrived and, by 1775, had erected most of the stone buildings of the **fortress** on the short headland that forms the western wall of the harbour.

Several of these structures still line the cobblestoned Kristiinankatu, which leads across the headland before descending to the shores of the lake, three of them housing museums. Unless you've a particular interest in the military role of horses and the uniforms worn by their riders, however, the collections of the **Cavalry Museum** (June–Aug Mon–Fri 10am–6pm, Sat & Sun 11am–5pm; Sept–May Sun 11am–5pm; 20mk) can safely be ignored. A better quick stop is the **Orthodox Church** (June to mid-Aug Tues–Sun noon–4.30pm; rest of the year shorter hours), just opposite, where the glow of beeswax candles helps illuminate the icons of what is Finland's oldest Orthodox church, founded in 1785.

Step back across Kristiinankatu and you're outside the **South Karelian Art Museum** (June–Aug Mon–Fri 10am–6pm, Sat & Sun 11am–5pm; Sept–May Tues–Sun 11am–5pm, Thurs until 8pm; 20mk), which rotates its permanent stock of paintings with south Karelian connections – mostly a mundane bunch of landscapes and portraits, although some important Finnish artists are represented – and stages exhibitions of emergent regional artists in an adjoining building.

The most rewarding of the three museums is at the end of Kristiinankatu: the **South Karelian Museum** (June–Aug Mon–Fri 10am–6pm, Sat & Sun 11am–5pm; Sept–May Tues–Sun 11am–5pm, Thurs until 8pm; 20mk). Surprisingly though, it isn't collections from Lappeenranta that form the main displays here but ceramics, souvenirs and sporting trophies from Viipuri, a major Finnish town 60km from Lappeenranta that was ceded to the Soviet Union after World War II (see the box below). Many who left Viipuri to stay on the Finnish side of the border began their new lives in Lappeenranta, and it's mostly they who shed a tear when looking at these reminders (including a large-scale model) of their home town. Elsewhere in the museum are numerous Karelian costumes, subtle differences in which revealed the wearer's religion and (for women) marital status, and worthy displays on hunting, farming and traditional handicrafts.

Practicalities

Reward yourself after a tour of the Fortress area with coffee and a home-baked pie or cake at *Café Majurska*, close to the Orthodox church on Kristiinankatu. Sour rye bread and the softer *rieska* bread are easily found in Lappeenranta's marketplace or by the harbour, where you'll also find stuffed waffles and *atomi* and *vety* pastries, local favourites. For more substantial **eating**, try the fair-priced pizzas at *Pifferia*, Raatimiehenkatu 13, or the tasty fish dishes at *Majakka*, Satamatie 4, facing the harbour. A good choice for affordable and swiftly served pizzas, meat, fish and vegetarian dishes is *Huvi Retki* at Valtakatu 31. Should you be in Lappeenranta on a Sunday, the traditional Finnish lunches served at *Pitotalo Miekkala*, Partalantie 136, are enough to satisfy a huge appetite, though it's advisable to book first (☎05/458 1882). In fact, as traditional South Karelian cookery relies on lengthy oven baking and roasting, if you want to try local specialities, it's often necessary to reserve a table and order your food in advance.

VIPURI

Before it was ceded to the Soviet Union in 1944, **VIIPURI** was one of Finland's most prosperous and cosmopolitan towns: being the Saimaa waterway's main link to the Baltic Sea, it was a major port, its population a mixture of Finns, Swedes, Russians and Germans. The town also acquired several architecturally acclaimed buildings, most notably its Alvar Aalto-designed library, before it came under Moscow's control.

With many of its 1930s buildings still standing, Viipuri today has a strange time-locked quality. Lack of Soviet investment (Viipuri was never allowed to challenge Leningrad's place as the USSR's major western seaport) resulted in a dearth of new construction, but also allowed many of the town's once elegant structures to reach advanced states of dilapidation. With post-Soviet Russian entrepreneurs appearing on the scene with a host of speculative building projects (none of which includes plans for conservation) it seems old Viipuri – and the picture of prewar Finland that it gives – could well be razed to the ground.

From Lappeenranta, there's a **daily bus to Viipuri** (100mk return), which twice a week continues to St Petersburg (360mk return). Russian visas, which can take up to ten days to acquire, are necessary for the journey. An alternative is a **visa-free day trip by boat** from Lappeenranta (150–200mk); there are several daily during the summer – check details with the tourist office.

Lappeenranta is easily covered in a day, though you may well need to stay overnight between transport links. The pick of several high-standard **hotels** are *Lappee*, Brahenkatu 1 (☎05/67861; ③), and *Hotel Cumulus*, Valtakatu 31 (☎05/677 811; ③/⑤), which contains the *Huvi Retki* restaurant (see above). There are also some cheaper **guesthouses**, such as *Matkahovi*, Kauppakatu 52 (☎05/415 6705; ①). The town's two **youth hostels** are 2km west of the centre: *Karelia Park*, Korpraalinkuja 1 (☎05/675 211; fax 452 8454), and *Huhtiniemi*, Kuusimäenkatu 18 (☎05/ 451 5555; fax 451 5558), which is also where you'll find the local **campsite** (same phone number).

Savonlinna and around

Leisurely draped across a series of tightly connected islands, **SAVONLINNA** is one of the most relaxed towns in Finland. The significance of Savonlinna's woodworking industries and its commercial importance as a major junction on the Saimaa route pales beside the income from tourism and the cultural kudos of its annual international opera festival. The town is packed throughout July (when the opera festival takes place) and early August, but on either side of the peak season its streets and numerous small beaches are uncluttered. The easygoing mood, enhanced by the slow glide of pleasure craft in and out of its harbour, makes Savonlinna a superb base for a two- or three-day stay. This gives ample time to soak up the mellow atmosphere, discover the local sights, and to explore the curiosities – such as a remarkable modern art centre and a huge nineteenth-century church – that lie within the town's idyllic surrounds.

The Town

Savonlinna's centrally placed passenger harbour and kauppatori are pleasant spots to mingle with the crowds and enjoy a snack from one of the numerous food stalls. Within a few strides, you might poke your head inside the **Savonlinna Art Gallery**, Olavinkatu 40 (July daily 10am–8pm; rest of the year Tues–Sun 11am–5pm; 15mk), which provides a spacious home for temporary shows usually mounted in tandem with those at the Regional Museum (see below), or the smartly restored **Pikkukirkko**

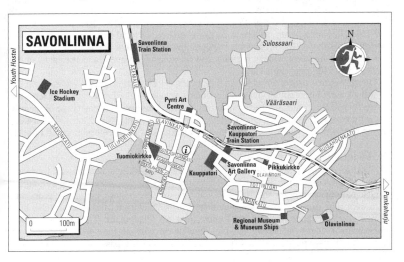

(June to mid-Aug daily 10am–6pm), a Lutheran Church which began life serving the
Greek Orthodox faithful. Fine as these places may be, however, none of them holds a
candle to Savonlinna's greatest possession: the engrossing Olavinlinna Castle, a fifteen-
minute walk from the harbour, at the end of Linnankatu.

Perched on a small island and looking like some great, grey sea monster surfacing
from the deep, Savonlinna's **Olavinlinna Castle** (daily June to mid-Aug 10am–5pm;
mid-Aug to May 10am–3pm; 20mk) was founded in 1475 to guard this important lake-
transport junction at the eastern extremity of what was then the Swedish empire – a
region being eyed by an expansionistic Russia. The Swedes built walls 5m thick to
resist attack on the eastern side, but the castle was to switch hands fairly frequently in
later years; the last change saw the Russians moving in after the westward shift of the
border that followed the 1743 Peace of Turku. They added the incongruous Adjutant's
Apartment which, with its bright yellow walls and curved windows, resembles a large
piece of Emmenthal cheese. With military importance lost when Finland became a
Russian Grand Duchy in 1809, the castle ended its pre-Restoration days rather igno-
miniously as the town jail.

The castle can only be visited on guided **tours**, included in the admission fee, which
begin on the hour from the entrance. The guides' commentary is a vital aid to comprehending the complex historical twists and turns that the castle endured, and for pointing out the numerous oddities, such as the sole original indoor toilet, in the maiden's
chamber, through which there's a sheer drop to the lake below.

Occupying an 1852 granary a stone's throw from the castle, the **Savonlinna
Regional Museum** (July daily 10am–8pm; rest of the year Tues–Sun 11am–5pm; 10mk
June–Aug, 5mk rest of the year; ticket also covers the art gallery – see above) is among
the Lake Region's better accounts of the evolution of local life, beginning with an
intriguing display on the prehistoric rock paintings found near Savonlinna. The bulk of
the museum, however, charts hunting and farming techniques, and the birth of the
area's tar and logging industries.

The museum's **upper level** holds temporary art exhibitions, often culled from the
country's most interesting private collections. Outside, docked at the end of a jetty, are
three turn-of-the-century steamers known as the **Museum Ships** (June–Aug only,
same times as regional museum; admission with same ticket), which earned their keep
plying the Saimaa waterways, sometimes travelling as far as St Petersburg and Lübeck.

Practicalities

While there are very few trains into Savonlinna from Parikkala, 59km away, there is a
choice of **train stations**: Savonlinna-Kauppatori is by far the most central, although if
you're making straight for the *Malakias* youth hostel (see below), get off at Savonlinna,
1km west. The **bus station**, served by three buses a day from Mikkeli and Helsinki, is
also a short distance west of the centre, just off Olavinkatu. The **tourist office**,
Puistokatu 1 (daily late June & July 8am–10pm; rest of June & Aug 8am–6pm;
Sept–May 9am–4pm; ☎015/273 492; fax 514 449), faces the passenger harbour. They

rent out bikes for 35mk a day and can supply useful route maps for cycling in the area.

Savonlinna has several budget-priced **accommodation** possibilities and some good hotels. However, don't expect the big discounts you might find elsewhere, as the hotels have no shortage of summer business. If you're not deterred, the stylish *Hotel Tott*, Satamakatu 1 (☎015/575 6390; fax 514 504; ⑥), is a sound choice, with apartments on offer (680mk) as well as rooms. Two of Savonlinna's **summer hotels** also have **dormitory** accommodation: *Malakias*, Pihlajavedenkatu 6 (☎015/739 5430; fax 272 524; ②), 2km west of the centre, and the handier *Vuorilinna* (same phone number; ②) on Vääräsaari, the island linked by a short bridge to the kauppatori – though the hostel section here is closed in July. *Hotel Hospits*, Linnankatu 20 (☎015 515661; fax 515120; ③ in July, ② rest of the year), also has good-value rooms, but you'll need to book ahead as it's very popular. There's a marked absence of **campsites** in Savonlinna. The nearest is *Vuohimäki* (☎015/537 353; fax 272524; June to late Aug), 7km west of the centre and served by local buses.

When it comes to **eating**, the usual pizza joints line Olavinkatu – *Pizza Capero*, at no. 51, is as good as any of them. For **Finnish food**, sample the 35mk lunches at *Snellman*, Olavinkatu 31, or try the better but pricier (54mk) *Majakka*, Satamakatu 11. With a bit more to spend, go for the Chinese restaurant at Olavinkatu 33, where main courses are 60–70mk, although the most adventurous place to dine is *Paviljonki*, Rajalahendenkatu 4 (Mon–Fri 11am–9pm, Sat & Sun 10am–6pm), where Finland's top trainee chefs serve up their latest creations. The service is excellent, the food imaginative and well prepared. Lunch here costs 45mk, 55mk on Sundays.

North of Savonlinna: Villa Rauhalinna

Completed in 1900 in the village of Lehtiniemi, 16km north of Savonlinna, **Villa Rauhalinna** was built by a high-ranking officer in the Russian army as a silver-wedding present to his wife. The villa is a phenomenal example of intricate and ornate carpentry, and is decorated throughout with many of its original fixtures and fittings. It's not a museum, however, and while visitors are free to explore most of the villa, and the tree-filled grounds that extend to the lakeside, most people make the day trip from Savonlinna to partake of the slap-up Russian lunch buffet (July, daily 135mk; June & Aug Sun only, 85mk) served in the dining room.

If eating in the villa is beyond your means, bring a picnic to consume beside the lake and take the opportunity to discover something of the privileged lifestyles of well-heeled Russians in turn-of-the-century Finland. Regular **buses** run to Lehtiniemi from Savonlinna, but it's more in keeping with the spirit of the place to arrive by **boat** (at 30mk return, only slightly pricier than the bus) from the passenger harbour. If you can't face leaving the villa, a few double rooms are available (☎/fax 015/523 119; ③).

East of Savonlinna: Punkaharju Ridge and beyond

According to local belief, the **Punkaharju Ridge** is the healthiest place to breathe in the world, thanks to an abundance of conifers that super-oxygenate the air. This narrow seven-kilometre strip of land between lakes Puruvesi and Pihlalavesi begins 24km to the east of Savonlinna, and three roads and a railway line are squeezed onto this slender thread of land. With the water never more than a few metres away on either side, this is the Lake Region at its most beautiful, and easily reached on any train heading this way from Savonlinna.

Along the ridge, at the centre of things, you'll find **Lusto**, a recently built national forest museum (daily 10am–6pm; 35mk). Designed, predictably, from wood, its permanent exhibits examine how forests function and survive; there's also a shop stocked with wooden items, though perhaps the best part is the restaurant-café, where you can fill up on sauteed reindeer, fillet of elk and *kuusenkerkkä*, a gloriously rich cake of smetana, pine kernels and Lappish berries. For exploring the area further, you can rent bikes here for 35mk a day.

The most atmospheric **place to stay** is *Punkaharjun Valtionhotelli*, Punkaharju 2 (☎015/739 611; fax 441 784; summer ⑤, winter ④), an ornate wooden house on the ridge that still summons up the Tsarist era, despite an insipid restoration. Cheaper but decidedly ugly is *Gasthaus Punkaharju*, Palomäentie 18 (☎015/441 371 or 473 123; fax 441 771; ③).

Retretti Arts Centre

The ridge runs into the village of Punkaharju, but first passes by the incredible **Retretti Arts Centre** (daily May–Aug 10am–8pm; Sept to late June 10am–7pm; 65mk, students 55mk), a place devoted to the visual and performing arts. The unique element is the setting – man-made caves gouged into three-billion-year-old rock. Outside, in the large sculpture park, fibreglass human figures by Finnish artist Olavi Lanu entwine cunningly with the forms of nature; tree branches suddenly become human limbs and plain-looking boulders slowly mutate under your gaze into a pile of male and female torsos. Inside the caves, the main exhibitions are changed every year and are selected, believe it or not, to complement the raw rock walls. Besides more strange pieces by Lanu, the interior also features underground streams, whose gushings and bubblings underpin the music piped into the air. After this, the collection of Finnish painting upstairs in the regular gallery can only seem ordinary.

The few daily **trains** between Savonlinna and Parikkala (a spur of the Helsinki–Joensuu line) call at Retretti train station; their timings can be very inconvenient, however, and **buses** provide a more reliable alternative. Another option, though an expensive one (130mk return), is to travel by **boat** from Savonlinna's passenger harbour. All these transport details should be checked at the tourist office as the details fluctuate frequently. One way to enjoy the art without keeping an eye on your watch is to stay virtually next door at *Punkharjun Lomakeskus* (☎015/739 611; fax 441 784), an extensive camping area with simple huts (from 200mk) and fully equipped cottages (from 600mk) as well.

Kerimäki Church

Though, like Retretti, it lies to the east of Savonlinna (23km distant), without independent transport the village of Kerimäki is near-impossible to reach without first returning to Savonlinna, from where there are several daily buses and a summer boat service (check the latest details at the tourist office). The reason to come to this otherwise unremarkable village on the shores of Lake Puruvesi is to see the **Kerimäki kirkko** (daily June to late Aug Mon–Fri 9am–8pm, Sat 9am–6pm, Sun 9am–8pm; last week of Aug 10am–6pm; at other times call ☎015/541 177 to arrange a visit), an immense wooden church, built in 1848 to hold 5000 people and claimed to be the largest wooden church in the world. Complete with double-tiered balconies, and a yellow- and white-painted exterior beaming through the surrounding greenery, it truly is an astonishing sight – but you won't find much else in Kerimäki to occupy your day.

Varkaus, Valamo Monastery and Joensuu

Due to the preponderance of water in the vicinity, **train connections** around Savonlinna are extremely limited, only running east to Parikkala to link with Helsinki-bound express trains, which stop there on their way north. The express train from Helsinki also calls at Parikkala on the way north to **Joensuu** (a major town of the eastern lake region) but if arriving from Savonlinna, you're left with a wait of several hours for the northbound connection. Unless you want to spend half a day drinking coffee at tiny Parikkala's train station, a sensible alternative is to travel by bus to the industrial town of **Varkaus**, from there picking up a train on the Turku–Joensuu line. In all cases, the latest timetables should be carefully checked before making firm plans.

Valamo Monastery, which lies between Varkaus and Joensuu, makes for an intriguing stop, but one fraught with difficulties unless you have your own transport.

Varkaus

The sawmills and engineering factories that dominate diminutive but commercially important **VARKAUS** sit amid gentle hills and dense forests. On a good day, the billowing chimneys and steel pipes are artily mirrored in the placid waters of the town's lakes; on a bad day, unwelcome smells fill the air and there can be few Finnish towns where nature seems so obviously to be losing the battle against heavy industry. Even if you hate Varkaus on arrival, stick around long enough to see the Canal and Mechanical Music museums: in their very different ways, both are unique in Finland.

The Town

In such a place, it seems appropriate that **Varkaus kirkko**, on Savontie (June–Aug Mon–Fri 9am–6pm, Sat & Sun noon–6pm; Sept–May closed Sat & Sun), should be designed in a severe functional style. Inside, the church is notable less for its architecture than an immense altar fresco, measuring almost 300 square metres, painted – with the aid of several helpers and a large amount of scaffolding – by revered Finnish artist Lennart Stegerstråle.

A short walk from the church, a group of yellow wooden buildings from 1916 holds the **Museum of Workers' Housing**, Savontie 7 (Wed 3–7pm, Thurs–Sun 11am–3pm; 15mk), comprising a briefly interesting succession of single rooms furnished to show typical living conditions from the 1920s (when Varkaus factory labourers kept pigs and cows to remind them of their country origins) to the 1960s. The **Museum of Esa Pakarinen**, also in the workers' housing complex (same times as above; same ticket valid) remembers a tremendously popular Finnish comic actor of the postwar years who was a Varkaus resident. Pakarinen's forte was playing the fool (he rejoiced in the on-screen nickname "wood head") and singing with his false teeth removed. Besides assorted mementoes of his glittering career, a TV runs videos of Pakarinen's finest films – though the subtleties are well and truly lost on non-Finnish speakers.

A fifteen-minute walk from Savontie along factory-dominated Ahlströminkatu brings you to the **Varkaus Museum**, Wredenkatu 5A (Wed 11am–7pm, Thurs 9am–4pm, Fri & Sat 9am–3pm, Sun 10am–6pm; free), which provides some proof – with displays on the beginnings of local settlements and early agricultural life – that Varkaus did exist before the discovery of iron ore in local river beds set the town on course to becoming an engineering base. Much of the museum, however, charts the rise and rise of the local firm founded in 1909 by Walter Ahlström (after whom most things in the town appear to be named); by the 1950s, the company was – and continues to be – among the world's leading innovators in industrial machinery.

The canal and mechanical music museums

Leaving the town centre on Taipaleentie takes you over the rapids that made lake transport around Varkaus difficult until 1835, when a rough canal was built a kilometre east of the ferocious waters (look for the tower above the locks of the modern-day Taipale Canal). Following successive poor harvests, emergency labour was used to built a second, wider canal in 1867. Before this task was completed, 227 labourers had died from hunger or disease and been buried in mass graves; their final resting places can still be seen at the end of a rough track on Varkausmäki hill, some 7km from Varkaus. Rather than make the long and morbid trek to the grave sites, however, a visit to the **National Central Canal Museum**, inside a former warehouse beside the modern canal (opening times uncertain at the time of writing; check at the tourist office), provides all the background you'll need on the building of the Varkaus canals and the growth of canals generally in Finland. It's less drab than you might expect: the early canals not only opened up important new transport routes in the pre-motorized days, but had a major strategic importance in the border disputes between Finland and Russia.

Close to the canal museum, the bizarre and superb **Museum of Mechanical Music**, Pelimanninkatu 8 (July daily 10am–6pm; rest of the year Tues–Sat 11am–6pm, Sun 11am–5pm; 40mk) is really more of a personal show than a museum, with the eccentric German curator and his family singing along with his extraordinary collection of music-making devices – from an ancient pianola to a prototype stereo gramophone – gathered from all over Europe and restored to working order.

Practicalities

From the **bus and train terminals** on Relanderinkatu, it's a walk of just a few minutes to Kauppakatu, Varkaus's main street. To reach the **tourist office** at Kauppatori 6 (June to mid-Aug Mon–Fri 9am–6pm, Sat 9am–2pm; rest of the year Mon–Fri 9am–4.30pm; ☎017/552 7311), however, you'll need to walk for a further ten minutes along Taipaleentie.

There's little incentive to spend longer than you have to in Varkaus but if you do need to **stay overnight**, try the adequate but old-fashioned *Keskus-Hotelli*, Ahlströminkatu 18 (②); around the corner stands the more modern *Oscar*, Kauppatori 4 (☎017/579 011; ④/⑤). A more basic alternative is *Joutsenkulma*, Käämeniementie 20 (☎017/556 4688; ②). The only truly budget accommodation in town is the *Taipale* **campsite** (☎017/552 6644; June–Aug), on Leiritie.

Varkaus isn't the nation's culinary hot spot, and **eating** cheaply is limited to the café in the *Joutsenkulma* (see above), which has a simple menu, or the local branch of *Rosso*, Ahlströminkatu 21, plying the usual pizzas.

Valamo Monastery

The original **Valamo Monastery**, on an island in Lake Ladoga, was the spiritual headquarters of Orthodox Karelia from the thirteenth century onwards. In 1940, however, with Soviet attack imminent, the place was abandoned and rebuilt well inside the Finnish border, roughly halfway between Varkaus and Joensuu.

Volunteer workers arrive each summer to assist the monks in their daily tasks, and shorter-term visitors are welcome to imbibe the spiritual atmosphere and enjoy the tranquillity of the setting, though the somewhat austere regime won't suit everyone. Without transport of your own, **getting to the monastery** is not easy. The only bus that stops at the gates, 4km from the main road, is a once-daily service from Joensuu; the two daily buses from Helsinki stop nearby. Although the monks insist this is not a hostel, it is possible **to stay** cheaply overnight (☎017/570 1506; fax 570 1510)

Joensuu

Whether you arrive by bus or train (the terminals are adjacent to one another), the kilometre-long walk into the centre of **JOENSUU** – the capital of what was left of Finnish Karelia after the eastern half was ceded to the Soviet Union in 1944 – is one of the most enjoyable introductions to any Lake Region town: the route crosses the broad Pielisjoki River and then the narrow Joensuu Canal before reaching Eliel Saarinen's epic Art Nouveau town hall and the wide kauppatori.

Pleasing first impressions apart, compact and modestly sized Joensuu doesn't have too much beyond the usual round of local museums and churches to fill your time – a day will cover it with ease.

The Town

Considering the devastation caused by the war, Joensuu has a surprising number of nineteenth-century buildings intact. These include the wood-framed structure housing the **tourist office** at Koskikatu 1 (mid-June to mid-Aug Mon–Fri 8am–6pm, Sat 9am–2pm, July also Sun 10am–2pm; rest of the year Mon–Fri 9am–4pm; ☎013/267 5300; fax 123 933), and the red-brick former schoolhouse which now holds the **Art Museum**, at Kirkkokatu 23 (Tues & Thurs–Sun 11am–4pm, Wed 11am–8pm; 15mk, free on Wed). The museum's minor pieces and an unexpected crop of Far Eastern and Greek antiquities fails to divert attention from Edelfelt's finely realized portrait, *The Parisienne* – worth the admission fee alone. Some of Finland's more radical new artists get a showing just across from the museum's entrance at the **Gymnasium Gallery** (hours vary; usually free).

Leaving the art museum and glancing either way along the aptly named Kirkkokatu (Church Street), you'll spot Joensuu's major churches standing at opposite ends. To the right, the neo-Gothic **Lutheran Church** (June to mid-Aug Mon 11am–7pm; other times by arrangement ☎013/2021) can seat a thousand worshippers but, aside from Antti Salmenlinna's impressive stained-glass windows, doesn't differ wildly from its counterparts in other towns. A few years older, the icon-rich **Greek Orthodox Church** (mid-June to mid-Aug Mon–Fri noon–6pm; other times by arrangement ☎013/122 564) is more deserving of a swift peek inside.

Retrace your steps by crossing back over the river and you'll find yourself on the small island of Ilosaari, where the **Northern Karelia Museum** (Tues, Thurs & Fri noon–4pm, Wed noon–8pm, Sun 10am–6pm; 10mk) assembles a large collection of traditional costumes in its efforts to chronicle Karelian life and culture. Despite the over-abundance of cloth, the museum is a good place to get a grasp of the history and the trials and tribulations of rural life in this part of Finland.

More modern concerns become evident if you take a Friday evening stroll along the birch-tree-lined banks on the town side of the river. You'll find scores of locals flogging unwanted household goods and clothes, and others operating impromptu fast-food stands – all in an effort to earn a few extra markkaa and lessen the effects of economic recession.

If butterflies don't appeal and you find yourself with a day to spare but no desire to move beyond the town's environs, take a trip through the cactus-filled greenhouses of Joensuu University's **Botanical Gardens**, Heinäpurontie 70 (early May to Aug daily except Tues 10am–6pm; rest of the year Mon & Wed 10am–3pm, Thurs 10am–8pm, Sun noon–2pm; 20mk). Afterwards, you could explore the gardens themselves, which are claimed to hold a specimen of every plant native to northern Karelia – there are many more of these than you might expect.

A tradition shared among the Baltic countries is song festivals. If you're in any doubt as to the sheer scale of these events, take a look at the huge **Song Bowl** which sits beside the Pyhäselkä lake, just southwest of Joensuu's centre. Or, better still, be around during the **Joensuu Song Festival** in June, when up to 11,000 singers can be found harmonizing together. While the song festival may have deep roots, tropical butterflies and Joensuu are a more recent combination. Strange as it may seem, a bunch of Malaya's finest are flown in every week (butterflies have a very short lifespan) to keep up the colourful stocks of the **Tropical Butterfly Garden** (times vary: call ☎013/129 380 to check; 30mk), bizarrely situated on an industrial estate, 2km west of the town centre.

Practicalities

Besides the tasty morsels which can be picked up for a few markkaa inside the kauppahalli (beside the kauppatori), Joensuu's bargain **eating** options include the usual pizza joints – *Rosso*, Siltakatu 8, is the most dependable. For something more extravagant, try the French and Finnish cuisine and subdued atmosphere provided by an old-fashioned live orchestra at the *Hotel Kimmel* restaurant, Itäranta 1. For good Hungarian food, head for *Astoria*, overlooking the river at Rantakatu 32, where you can eat outside in warm weather.

For an overnight stop, you'll find some very good summer rates at the central and comfortable *Hotel Vaakuna*, Torikatu 20 (☎013/277 511; fax 277 3210; ③). Elsewhere, there are **dorm beds** as well as regular double rooms at the central summer hotel *Elli*, Länsikatu 18 (☎013/225 927; fax 225 763; ①). The *Partiotalo*, a **youth hostel** run by the Scouts organization (☎013/123 381; June–Aug), is located 1km north of the town centre, at Vanamokatu 25; the town **campsite** is beside the Pyhäselka lake in Linnunlahti (☎013/126 272, winter reservations ☎013/225 733; fax ☎013/123 933; June–Aug).

CROSSING THE RUSSIAN BORDER: SORTAVALA

If you've visited Joensuu's art museum, you'll have seen a scale model of **Sortavala**, one of the many Finnish towns to come under Soviet control following the postwar realignment of the border. Since the collapse of the Soviet Union, it's been possible for Finns (and indeed any other westerners equipped with Russian visas) to visit the town with comparative ease. Despite occupying a scenic position on the shores of Lake Ladoga, Sortavala itself has no intrinsic appeal whatsoever. The **journey from Joensuu to Sortavala** takes nearly four hours and there's a daily bus throughout most of the summer; get the latest details from the Joensuu tourist office.

North from Joensuu: Nurmes

Should Joensuu be as rural as you want to get, swing inland (you'll have to do this by bus) to the more metropolitan Kuopio (see below). Otherwise, continue north from Joensuu into some of the eastern Lake Region's least populated but scenically most spectacular sections, where there are hilltop views out above the tips of fir trees across watery expanses that stretch far into Russia. With its daily train link from Joensuu, the small town of **NURMES** makes the obvious base for exploration but you'll need private transport – or a lot of careful juggling with local timetables and costly sightseeing trips – to find the best of the landscape. There's a small **tourist information desk** (mid-June to mid-Aug daily 9.30am–9pm) at Nurmes train station, and a larger **tourist office** on Lomatie (daily June to mid-Aug 8am–10pm; rest of the year 8am–4pm; ☎013/481 770; fax 481 775). Budget **accommodation** in Nurmes can be found at two hostels, *Pompannappi*, Koulukatu 16, and *Hyvärilä*, on Lomatie, which is also the location of the town's campsite. All three share the same phone and fax numbers. There's also an exceedingly ordinary, central **hotel**, *Nurmeshovi*, Kirkkokatu 21 (☎013/480 750; ②/③).

Kuopio

Sited on a major inland north–south rail route and the hub of local long-distance bus services, **KUOPIO** has the feel – and, by day, much of the hustle and bustle – of a large city but is in fact only marginally bigger than most of the other Lake Region communities. Nonetheless, it's an important Finnish town and, especially if you're speeding

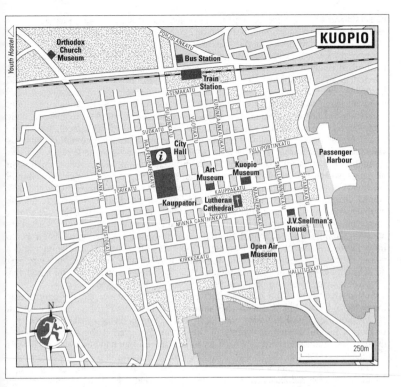

north to spend the bulk of your time in Lappland, provides both a break in the journey and an enjoyable taste of the region.

The Town

Kuopio's broad kauppatori, overlooked by the nineteenth-century city hall, is very much the heart of the town, with live jazz and rock music issuing from its large stage in summer. Walk the kilometre eastwards from here along Kauppakatu, towards the busy passenger harbour on the Kallavesi lake, and you'll pass most things worth seeing in town – with the exception of the extraordinary Orthodox Church Museum (see below).

At Kauppakatu 35, the **Kuopio Art Museum** (Mon–Sat 9am–4.30pm, Wed until 8pm, Sun 11am–6pm; 10mk; for guided tours call ☎017/182 642) fills a sturdy granite building with an enterprising assortment of contemporary exhibitions, and, on the upper floor, keeps a less stimulating stock of twentieth-century Finnish painting with local connections. Further along the same street at no. 23, the **Kuopio Museum** (May–Aug Mon–Sat 9am–4pm, Wed until 8pm, Sun 11am–6pm; Sept–April closed Sat; 15mk) charts the evolution of local settlements, from motley Stone Age findings to the thousand-and-one uses that tree bark was put to in pre-industrial Finland. The switch from rural to urban life caused great changes in Finnish society, but one thing that remained constant was a dependency on coffee: using the original fittings, the museum re-creates a Kuopio institution – Alli Karvonen's coffee shop, which dispensed the caffeine-laden nectar from 1933 to 1969 in cups etched with Finnish landscapes. Unless stuffed reindeer munching plastic lichen and a bleak collection of painted wooden insects set your pulse racing, the rest of the museum can be ignored, but keep an eye out for Juho Rissanen's study of naked Nordic men building a wall, on the staircase – a fresco that turns many heads.

Leave the museum and you only need to cross the road to look inside the **Lutheran Cathedral** (daily June–Aug 10am–5pm; Sept–May 10am–3pm), a handsome creation erected in 1815 using local stone. Although spacious, the cathedral's interior could hardly be described as opulent, but years ago it did contrast dramatically with the cramped living quarters of most Kuopio folk. Walk south along Kuninkaankatu until you reach Kirkkokatu and the **Kuopio Open-Air Museum** (mid-May to mid-Sept daily 10am–5pm, Wed until 7pm; rest of the year Tues–Sun 10am–3pm; free), where the stock of mostly wooden dwellings reveals the up-against-it domestic conditions that prevailed, at least for Kuopio's poorer inhabitants, from the 1840s to the 1930s.

Another old house, interesting for a quite different reason, stands at Snellmaninkatu 19, preserved as **J.V. Snellman's Home** (mid-May to Sept daily 10am–5pm, Wed until 7pm; rest of the year by appointment – call ☎017/182 624, in winter ☎017/182 625; 10mk). From 1844, when the 39-year-old Snellman married his 17-year-old bride, the couple spent several years in this large but far from grand home. At the time, Snellman was earning a living as head of Kuopio's elementary school after the country's Swedish-speaking ruling class had booted him out of his university post, angry at his efforts to have Finnish made an official language. Aided by a few original furnishings and a colour scheme devised by Snellman, the house may be fairly authentic, but there isn't actually a lot to see – though that shouldn't deter anyone with an interest in Finnish history from paying their respects (for more on Snellman, see p.609).

Set on the brow of the hill marking Kuopio's northwest corner, the enormously impressive **Orthodox Church Museum**, Karjalankatu 1 (May–Aug Tues–Sun 10am–4pm; Sept–April Mon–Fri noon–3pm, Sat & Sun noon–5pm; 20mk), draws the Orthodox faithful from many parts of the world. Yet even if the workings of the Orthodox religion are a complete mystery to you, there's much to be enjoyed: elaborate Russian-made icons, gold-embossed bibles, gowns and prayer books, and lots more.

The placing of the museum in Kuopio is no accident. This part of Finland has a large Orthodox congregation, many of them (or their parents) from the parts of eastern Finland that became Soviet territory after World War II. Many objects from the original Valamo Monastery (see p.682), likewise caught on the wrong side of the border, are also on display here.

Practicalities

Adjacent to one another at the northern end of Puijonkatu, Kuopio's **train and long-distance bus stations** are an easy walk from the the town centre. There are good bus and train connections north from Kuopio to Iisalmi (see below) and on to Kajaani and Oulu (see the following chapter), as well as with Helsinki and all the main southern towns. The **tourist office** faces the kauppatori at Haapaniemenkatu 17 (June to mid-Aug Mon–Fri 9am–8pm, Sat 9am–4pm; rest of the year Mon–Fri 9am–5pm; ☎017/182 584; fax 261 3538).

The rock-bottom budget **accommmodation** options are both some distance from the centre of town: the **youth hostel** *Hostelli Rauhalahti* is a four-kilometre trek to the south at Katiskaniementie 8 (☎017/473 111; fax 473 470), while the **campsite** (☎017/312 244; May–Aug) is 6km to the south. Local buses frequently change their route numbers, so check the latest details at the tourist office.

Staying centrally costs more, although there are no-frills double rooms (and a few dorm beds) at *Puijohovi*, Vuorikatu 35 (☎017/261 4943; ①). More luxurious accommodation, with lake views and private saunas, can be found at *Puijonsarvi*, Minna Canthinkatu 16 (☎017/170 111; ③/④). Otherwise, try *Cumulus*, Puijonkatu 32

(☎017/154 111; fax 154 299; ③/④), or the glitzier *Arctia Hotel Kuopio*, Satamakatu 1 (☎ 017/195 111; fax 195 170; ⑤).

Eating, drinking and nightlife

The **evening market**, held nightly during summer at the passenger harbour, is a good place to sample *kalakukko* – a kind of bread pie, baked with fish and pork inside it. While it's to be found all around the country, Kuopio is *kalakukko*'s traditional home and at least one stall here will be selling it, warm and wrapped in silver foil; a fist-sized piece costs about 15mk.

Away from the harbourside market, it's the usual pizza joints that provide most nourishment at the most reasonable price: *Rosso*, Haapaniemenkatu 24–26, or *Pizza Marito* on Tulliportinkatu, are just two of many. The town's finest restaurant is undoubtedly the *Musta Lammas*, down in the cellar vaults at Satamakatu 4 (Mon–Sat 5pm–midnight; ☎017/ 262 3494), which has been in business since 1862. Several of the pubs mentioned below also offer good-value **lunches**; for something more exotic, try the Mexican food at *Amarillo*, Kirjastokatu 10, where lunches cost around 35mk.

Kuopio has a reputation for being the stamping ground of some of Finland's best rock musicians, and the town has a number of **pubs** where you can hear live muic. *Henry's Pub*, Kauppakatu 18, sees jam sessions and some live bands; *Freetime* (part of *Amarillo*; see above) at Kirjastokatu 10, and *Emigrant's*, Kauppakatu 16, are less music-oriented but are usually enjoyable drinking spots. For a more mellow evening out, try the upmarket *Sampo*, Kauppakatu 13, noted for its fine fish restaurant. Out of central Kuopio (but close to the campsite; see above), the *1001 Yöta* bar at *Hotel Rauhalahti* stages some wild bashes on Friday nights, and often lays on free transport from the town centre. Find out what's happening there by asking at the tourist office, or try phoning the bar itself (☎017/473 111).

Iisalmi

The farmland around **IISALMI**, an hour by bus from Kuopio, makes a welcome break from pine forests and marks the centre of northern Savolax, a district that, in public opinion polls, is regularly voted the least desirable place in which to live. The reason for this is slightly mysterious – the modestly sized town looks nice enough – but might be due to the locals' reputation for geniality mixed with low cunning. Whether this is innate, or a defensive reaction by country folk who've been pitchforked into urban life, is debatable.

Whatever the truth, two museums give a very good insight into local life. The **District Museum** (daily noon–8pm; free), at Kivirannantie 5 on the shores of the Palosvirta river – cross the river from the centre of town and turn left – reveals the down-at-heel life of the peasantry; while the **Juhani Aho Museum** (May–Aug 10am–6pm; other times by arrangement ☎017/150 1388; free) in Mansikkaniemi, 5km along the Kajaani road by local bus, shows how the other half lived. Aho was a major influence on Finnish literature as it emerged around the turn of the century, and the simple buildings filled with the author's possessions manage to convey the commitment of the artists who came together in the last years of Russian rule.

Aside from a few hotels, such as *Artos* on Kyllikinkatu (☎017/812 244; fax 814 941; ②/③) and the tiny *Hotel Restentti,* Puistotie 21 (☎017/862 660; fax 862 535; ②), accommodation in the town is limited. However, the **tourist office** at Kauppakatu 22 (June–Aug Mon–Fri 8am–6pm, Sat 10am–2pm; Sept–May Mon–Fri 8am–3.30pm; ☎017/822 346; fax 826 760), on the corner with the main street, Pohjolankatu, can point you towards summertime budget options on the outskirts, and to **campsites** with cabins, such as *Koljonvirta Camping,* Ylemmäisentie (☎017/825 252, winter bookings ☎501 391; mid-May to mid-Aug).

travel details

Buses

Joensuu to: Kuopio (5 daily; 2hr 30min); Valamo monastery (1 daily; 1hr 10min).

Kuopio to: Jyväskylä (3 daily; 2hr 15min).

Lahti to: Mikkeli (6 daily; 2hr 15min); Savonlinna (2 daily; 3hr 45min).

Lappeenranta to: Imatra (hourly; 37min).

Mikkeli to: Savonlinna (4 daily; 1hr 45min).

Savonlinna to: Kuopio (4 daily; 3hr 40min); Parikalla (2 daily; 1hr 20min); Punkaharju (2 daily; 50min); Varkaus (4 daily; 2hr 20min).

Tampere to: Helsinki (5 daily; 2hr); Pori (5 daily; 1hr 45min); Turku (5 daily; 2hr 30min).

Varkaus to: Joensuu (2 daily; 2hr); Kuopio (8 daily; 1hr 15min).

International Buses

Joensuu to: Sortavala (1 daily in summer; 3hr 45min).

Lappeenranta to: St Petersburg (2 weekly; 4hr); Viipuri (1 daily; 1hr 30min).

Trains

Iisalmi to: Kajaani (4 daily; 1hr); Oulu (3 daily; 3hr 30min).

Jyväskylä to: Tampere (9 daily; 2hr).

Kuopio to: Iisalmi (5 daily; 1hr); Jyväskylä (5 daily; 1hr 50min); Kajaani (4 daily; 2hr 15min); Mikkeli (6 daily; 1hr 45min).

Lahti to: Mikkeli (5 daily; 1hr 45min).

Lappeenranta to: Helsinki (8 daily; 2hr 40min); Järvenpää (1 daily; 2hr 20min); Lahti (8 daily; 1hr 15min).

Mikkeli to: Kuopio (5 daily; 1hr 30min).

Savonlinna to: Parikkala (1 daily; 48min).

Tampere to: Hämeenlinna (21 daily; 53min); Helsinki (12 daily; 2hr 15min); Jyväskylä (9 daily; 2hr); Oulu (7 daily; 5hr); Pori (6 daily; 1hr 45min); Savonlinna (2 daily; 4hr); Turku (7 daily; 2hr 15min).

Varkaus to: Joensuu (3 daily; 1hr 30min).

CHAPTER SEVENTEEN

OSTROBOTHNIA, KAINUU AND LAPPLAND

etween them, these three regions take up nearly two-thirds of Finland, but unlike the populous south or the more industrialized sections of the Lake Region, they're predominantly rural, with small communities separated by long distances. Despite this, or perhaps because of it, each region has a very individual flavour and equally distinct people.

Living along the coast of **Ostrobothnia** are most of the country's Swedish-speaking Finland-Swedes, a modestly sized section of the national population whose culture differs from that of either Swedes or Finns. Distance from wartime ravages has enabled the towns in this area to retain some of their old wooded form (and usually their Swedish name is used as often as the Finnish), while much of the region's affluence stems from the adjacent flat and fertile farmlands. The main reason you're likely to be here are the numerous ferry connections from Sweden: **Vaasa** and **Kokkola** are the chief entry points, although there are lesser ones to the north and south. Overall, though, given the lack of exciting scenery – save for a few fishing settlements scattered along the jagged shoreline – and the social insularity of the place, you'd be generous to devote more than a couple of days to it. Even busy and expanding **Oulu**, the region's major city, has an off-putting anodyne quality, causing its best aspect to be the ease of transport in and out – although you could always join the Swedes drinking their way into oblivion slightly further north at the border town of **Tornio**.

Kainuu is the thickly forested, thinly populated heart of Finland and – something perhaps felt more strongly here than anywhere else in the country – is traditionally peasant land. Over recent decades Kainuu has suffered a severe economic decline as wealth has become concentrated in the south. There's a surprising level of poverty in some parts, but this is being alleviated by the marketing of the area's strong natural appeal: woods, rivers, hills and wide stretches of barely inhabited country. The only sizeable town, **Kajaani**, still retains many wooden buildings. It's a good base for wider explorations by foot, bike or canoe, and, since no railways serve the territory beyond, it's the hub of a bus network which connects the region's far-flung settlements. **Kuhmo**, east of Kajaani, is notable for the web of nature trails and hiking routes around it, while heading north through the twin villages of **Suomussalmi** and **Ämmänsaari** and on past **Kuusamo**, the landscapes become wilder: great gorges, river rapids and fells, visited by reindeer as often as people. Hikers here are well catered for by a number of marked tracks, in addition to totally uninhabited regions traversable only with map, compass and self-confidence. The villages have little to offer beyond accommodation and transport to and from the end-points of the hikes, so stay away if you're not the hiking type.

Much the same applies to **Lappland**, probably the most thrilling place to hike in the world. **Rovaniemi**, the main stopover en route, can provide little except factual information on the area beyond, and trains to Kemijärvi (there are no services to points north), but it is the junction for the two major road routes into the **Arctic North**. Here

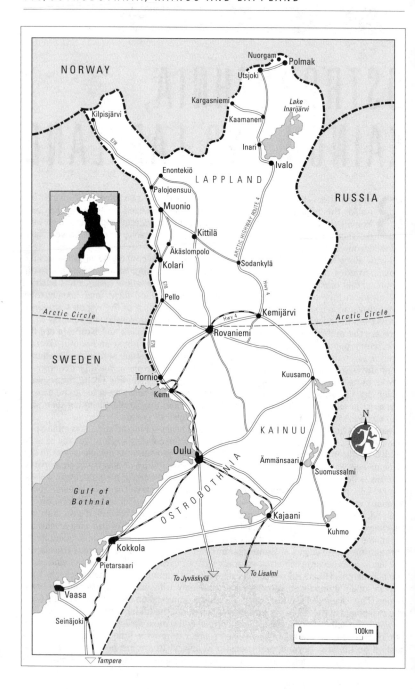

you'll find wide open spaces that are great for guided treks through gold-panning country and along the edges of the mountain chains, which continue far into Sweden and Norway. Elsewhere you can be totally isolated, gazing from barren fell-tops into Russia. But while the Arctic settlements are small, and few and far between, the whole region is home to several thousand Sami, who've lived in harmony with this special, often harsh environment for millennia. Discovering their culture and way of life can be as exciting as experiencing the Arctic North itself.

Vaasa

The lifeblood of **VAASA** is its harbour, through which the produce of southern Ostrobothnia's wheat fields is exported and the lucrative tourist traffic from Sweden arrives. Years of steady income have given the town a staid, commercial countenance, and its wide avenues (the old centre was obliterated by fire a century ago) are lined by shipping offices, consulates and a plethora of boozing venues aimed at Swedes from Sundsvall or Umeå, who come here to get smashed – yet another reason to get the first bus or ferry out.

Seventy-odd years ago Vaasa was briefly the seat of the provisional government after the Reds (an alliance of Communists and Social Democrats who took up arms against Finland's repressive Civil Guard) had taken control of Helsinki and much of the south at the start of the Civil War in 1918: it was among Ostrobothnia's right-wing farmers that the bourgeois-dominated government drew most of its support. This barely endearing fact is recalled by the reliefs of the then president Svinhufvud, and Mannerheim, who commanded the Civil Guard, on the front of the town hall and by the monument outside it.

Since then, it seems, little besides drunkenness has broken the peace. The apex of local cultural activity is the **Ostrobothnia Museum** (Mon–Fri noon–8pm, Sat & Sun 1–6pm; 10mk) at Museokatu 3, which recounts the history of the town and boasts an enjoyable collection of sixteenth- and seventeenth-century Dutch, Italian and Flemish art. Another way to pass the hours is to take the local bus that skirts across a ring of islands off the coast to reach the windswept little fishing village of **Björköby**.

Practicalities

Buses from Pori and **trains** from Seinäjoki, the nearest connection points to Vaasa, both pull in at the northern end of the town centre, within walking distance of the **tourist office** at Raastuvankatu 30 (June–Aug Mon–Fri 8am–7pm, Sat & Sun 10am–7pm; Sept–May Mon–Fri 8am–4pm; ☎06 /325 1145; fax 325 3620). If you have to stay overnight before moving on, **hostels** are your best bet. The official one is part of the summer hotel *Tekla* at Palosaarentie 58 (☎06/327 6411; fax 321 3989), which is open all year round and lies about 3km from the centre by bus; slightly nearer and prici-

---

ACCOMMODATION PRICE CODES

The Finnish hotels listed throughout the guide have been graded according to the following price bands, based on the rate for a double room in summer. However, many hotels offer summer and/or weekend discounts, and in these instances we've given two grades, covering both the regular and the discounted rate.

① Under 275mk	② 275–350mk	③ 350–450mk
④ 450–550mk	⑤ 550–750mk	⑥ 750mk and over

er are the hostels *Olo*, Asemakatu 12 (☎06/317 4558), and *Evankelinen Kansanopisto*, Rantakatu 21–22 (☎06/317 4913; fax 312 4072). In the summer months, there's the further option of the **campsite**, *Wasa Camping* (☎06/317 3852, winter bookings ☎06/312 5888; fax 312 5989), which is 2km from the town centre but close to the ferry harbour. The most pleasant central **hotel** is the small *Astor*, Asemakatu 4 (☎06/317 6200; fax 317 6484; ③/⑤), where for 100mk extra you can get a room with its own sauna; the newest is the *Silveria*, Ruutikellarintie 4 (☎06/326 7511; fax 326 7510; ③/④), with morning sauna, swimming and breakfast included in the room price.

Travel connections

Some **trains** from Vaasa (whose station is at the end of Hovioikeudenpuisto-kirkko) go directly to Tampere, but it's quicker to get there by changing at Seinäjoki (which all trains from Vaasa pass through), on the main line between Helsinki and Oulu.

There are numerous buses (but no trains) **south from Vaasa** to Pori and Turku (covered in the *Helsinki and the South* chapter). On the way, some 70km south of Vaasa, is Kaskö (in Swedish, Kaskinen), a small port receiving sailings from Gävle, and the neighbouring Kristiinankaupunki (Kristinestad), notable only for its surviving seventeenth-century layout; both settlements have direct rail links to Seinäjoki.

Travelling **north from Vaasa** by bus to the major coastal city of Oulu involves a mildly scenic journey passing fishing hamlets along the archipelago, and the small and still largely wooden towns of Uusikaarlepyy (Nykarleby) and Pietarsaari (Jakobstad). Aside from the **ferry from Skellefteå** in Sweden, which docks at Pietarsaari, there's no special reason to come here; if you arrive by boat, you'll need to take the bus to Kokkola to venture further into Finland.

Kokkola

Deep offshore waters have allowed **KOKKOLA** to industrialize its harbour, so that passengers steaming in from Skellefteå are greeted by views of a massive oil refinery. There's nothing quite so dramatic about arriving in Kokkola proper, which is 5km from the harbour and linked by a bus service that usually meets the ferry.

The ferry schedules make it difficult to avoid spending a night here, and the cheapest option is the *Tankkari* **youth hostel** at the *Suntinsuu* **campsite** (☎06/831 4006; fax 831 0306; hostel open June–Aug, campsite mid-May to Sept), just across the town bypass from the centre. There's also a tourist hotel, the *Touristi*, Isokatu 22 (☎06/831 8968; ③). With a little more money to spend, try *Sokos Hotel Vaakuna*, Rantakatu 16 (☎06/827 7000; fax 822 5185; ③/④), or the optimistically named *Grand*, Pitkänsillankatu 20B (☎/fax 06/831 3411), with doubles at 250mk including breakfast. For what it's worth, the **tourist office** on Mannerheiminaukio (June–Aug Mon–Fri 9am–5pm, Sat 9am–1pm; Sept–May Mon–Fri 8am–4pm; ☎06/831 1902; fax 831 0306) can point you towards the only remotely interesting local sight: the **English Park**, at one end of Isokatu, which contains a boat captured when the British fleet tried to land here in 1854, during the Crimean campaign. A much more welcome sight, though, is the **train station** at Isokatu's other end. **Travelling on** from Kokkola is straightforward since the town is on the main rail line between Oulu and Helsinki.

Oulu

Despite **OULU**'s role as national leader in the computing and microchip industries, the city still has sufficient remnants from the past to remind visitors of its nineteenth-century status as a world centre for tar. The black stuff was brought by river from the

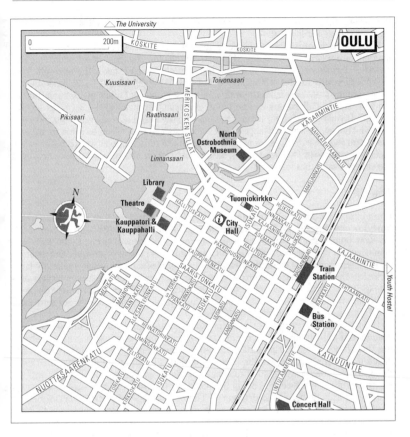

forests of Kainuu, and the international demand for its use in ship- and road-building helped line the pockets of Oulu's merchants. Their affluence and quest for cultural refinement made the town a vibrant centre, not only for business but also for education and the arts. Today, a handsome series of islands, a couple of highly conspicuous old buildings, and the nightlife fuelled by the roaming fun-hungry students from the university, bring colour into Oulu's otherwise pallid tones. Though it has its share of faceless office blocks, there's an ancient feel to the place, too, as seen in tumbledown wooden shacks around the intricately carved Kauppahalli.

Arrival and accommodation

Despite its size, Oulu is little more than a stopover on the way to somewhere else, being handy for **trains** in various directions, most usefully the direct services to and from Helsinki, Kajaani in the east (see p.697) and Rovaniemi in the north (see p.701). Arriving here, you'll find the platforms of the **train station** feed conveniently into an underground walkway with two exits: one runs to the nearby **bus station** (with regular services to and from Kuusamo), while the other leads directly into the compact city centre, just a few minutes' walk from the **tourist office** (July Mon–Sat 9am–6pm, Sun

10am–4pm; rest of the year Mon–Fri 9am–4pm; ☎08/314 1295; fax 314 1310), close to the City Hall at Torikatu 10.

Low-cost **accommodation** is, unfortunately, limited. The very central *Turisti*, Ratateinkatu 9 (☎08/375 233; fax 311 0701; ②), has the cheapest **hotel** beds, and also provides dorm-style accommodation in the summer, when it takes the overspill from the official **youth hostel** at Kajaanintie 36 (☎08/311 8060; fax 311 6573; June–Aug), a fifteen-minute walk east from the train and bus stations. Of Oulu's mainstream hotels, the best summer discounts can be found at *Apollo*, Asemakatu 31–33 (☎/fax 08/374 344; ②). If you're looking for luxury, the *Eden* on the island of Nallikari (☎08/550 4100; fax 554 4103 ④/⑤) won't disappoint – it's got a superb pool and offers spa treatments and steam rooms, as well as a fine restaurant. Bus #5 runs there, as well as to the cabin-equipped **campsite** (☎08/554 1541), 4km from town on Mustassaari Island; nearby is the sliver of sand that locals call a beach.

The City

From either the bus or train station, it's just a few minutes' walk straight ahead to the **harbour** and the neighbouring **kauppatori** and **kauppahalli** (Mon–Thurs 8am–4pm, Fri 8am–5pm, Sat 8am–3pm), an appealing, ornate place and a good spot for some cheap eating. There's a local joke about Oulu putting its buildings on water and its boats on land, which derives from the former steamship *Hailuoto*, sitting permanently land-locked in the marketplace, where – at least for the time being – it serves traders as a café (6.30am–2.30pm), overlooked by the sleekly modern **library** and **theatre** rising on stilts from the waters of Rommakonselkä. The library frequently stages **art and craft exhibitions**, which are usually worth a look.

The **City Hall**, a few minutes' away on Kirkkokatu, retains some of the Renaissance grandeur of the late nineteenth century, when it was built as a luxury hotel, symbolizing the affluence and cosmopolitan make-up of the tar-rich town. A local newspaper called it "a model for the whole world. A Russian is building the floor, an Austrian is doing the painting, a German is making the bricks, an Englishman is preparing the electric lighting, the Swede is doing the masonry, the Norwegian is carving the relief and the Finn is doing all the drudgery." The present-day drudgery is performed by local government officials who've become accustomed to visitors stepping in to gawp at the wall-paintings and enclosed gardens that remain from the old days. While inside, venture up to the second floor, where the Great Hall still has its intricate Viennese ceiling-paintings and voluminous chandeliers.

Further along Kirkkokatu, the copper-domed, yellow-stuccoed **Tuomiokirkko** (summer daily 10am–7pm; reduced hours rest of the year) was built in the 1770s following a great fire that more or less destroyed the city, but underwent a full and successful restoration in 1996. Stowed away inside the cathedral, but available for perusal on request, is a portrait of Johannes Messinius, the Swedish historian, supposedly painted by **Cornelius Arenditz** in 1612; restored and slightly faded, it's believed to be the oldest surviving oil painting in Finland, despite the efforts of the Russian cossacks who lacerated the canvas with their sabres in 1714. The small park outside the cathedral is a former cemetery, and bits of clothing and bone found beneath the floor of the seventeenth-century cellar of the pleasant *Franzen Café*, on the corner of Kirkkokatu and Linnankatu, have been reburied beneath the cafe's tiled floor – the barman can point out the spot. Cross the small canal just north of the cathedral to reach Ainola Park, and continue along the footpath to find the **North Ostrobothnia Museum** (June–Aug Mon–Thurs 10am–6pm, Sat 10am–4pm, Sun 11am–5pm; Sept–May Mon–Thurs & Sat 10am–4pm, Sun 11am–5pm; 10mk). It's packed with tar-stained remnants from Oulu's past, a large regional collection, and an interesting Sami section. There's no English labelling, but the displays are mostly self-explanatory.

If the future does more to excite your imagination than the past, skip the museum in favour of **Tietomaa**, or Computer Land, a few minutes' walk away at Nahkatehtaankatu 6 (May to mid-Aug daily 10am–6pm; reduced hours rest of the year; 50mk), several floors of powerful computer games and simulations – and a chance to experience the wonders of Virtual Reality.

Koskikeskus, the university and botanical gardens

A more Finnish-like way to explore Oulu is by packing a picnic lunch and setting off for the four small islands across the mouth of Rommakonselkä, collectively known as **Koskikeskus**. The first island, Linnansaari, has the inconsequential remains of Oulu's sixteenth-century castle; next comes Raatinsaari, followed by Toivonsaari, and the rapids that drive a power station designed by Alvar Aalto, with twelve fountains added by the architect to prettify the plant. Pikisaari, the fourth island, is much the best to visit, reached by a short road bridge from Raatinsaari. A number of tiny seventeenth-century wooden houses here have survived Oulu's many fires, and Pikisaari has become the stamping ground of local artists and trendies, with several **art galleries** and **craft shops**, and the *Kuusrock* **rock festival** in the third week of July.

The islands can also be glimpsed through the windows of buses #27, #32 and #33, all of which pass through Koskikeskus on the twenty-minute ride to the **university**. It's not a bad destination if you're at a loose end, if only for the opportunity to gorge in the student mensa. To work up an appetite, try finding the **Geological Museum** (June–Aug Tues–Sun 11am–3pm; Sept–May Tues, Thurs & Sun 11am–3pm; free) or the **Zoological Museum** (Mon–Fri 8.30am–3pm, Sun 11am–3pm; free), both secreted within the university's miles of corridors. The former is much as you'd expect, with a large collection of rare gems; the latter's best feature are the painstakingly hand-painted habitats created for each of the numerous specimens of stuffed Finnish wildlife.

Once you've ventured onto the campus you may as well take a look at the tropical and Mediterranean flora inside the two glass pyramidal structures that comprise the **Botanical Gardens** (June–Aug Tues–Fri 8am–5pm, Sat & Sun 10am–5pm; open-air gardens June–Aug daily 7am–5pm; Sept–May Tues–Fri 8am–3pm, Sat & Sun noon–3pm; 10mk).

Eating, drinking and nightlife

Oulu boasts some delightful **cafés** for lunch and the odd snack, the best including *Sokeri Jussi*, set in an old salt warehouse on Pikisaari and, just over the bridge from the mainland, the *Café Pilvikirsikka*, in an old greenhouse in Hupisaari park; *Café Koivuranta* is also popular, a wooden-built café on the riverside. *Café Saara* is a peaceful place to stop off for a coffee, right in the centre at Kirkkokatu 2. For **cakes**, the finest outlet in Oulu is *Katri Antell* on Rotuaari, with the more basic *Bisketti* just opposite. If you're stuck for somewhere to go on a Sunday, *NUKU*, the Youth Cultural Centre, has a laid-back café in an atrium courtyard at Hallituskatu 7. Finally, for a little more class, venture into the Concert Hall on Lintulammentie, a short walk south of the bus station. A coffee in the hall's café isn't cheap, but it does allow you to admire the gleaming Italian marble interior, with the bonus of live classical music during summer (Mon–Sat 12.30–1pm).

For a waterside **meal**, try the central *Neptunus*, which serves good fish and meat dishes in a boat moored behind the rusting Hailuoto by the market square. Another place to fill up with good food is the *Franzen Café*, in a charismatic old building opposite the cathedral at Kirkkokatu 2 (Mon–Fri 11am–2pm & 4pm–midnight, Sat 4pm–midnight; ☎08/311 3224) – as well as the ultra-swish street-level restaurant, there's a cellar bar serving German beers and sausages. Otherwise, load up in any of Oulu's pizzerias – the most popular is *IMadison* at Isokatu 18. *Oskarin Kellari,* at Rautatienkatu 9 near the train station, is a good choice for a reasonably priced meal, despite its grim outward appearance.

Nightlife and entertainment

Oulu's **nightlife** revolves around numerous **cafés** and **pubs**, the best of the bunch being the friendly *Rauhala*, in the Ainola Park at Mannenkatu 1: it's open daily from 2pm until 2am, with live music on Wednesday, Friday and Saturday from 10pm. One of the trendiest bars, with occasional live music, is *V.P.K.* in the old fire station on Uusikatu – you need to be aged 20 or over to get in. Otherwise, head for *Hilpeä Huikka* or the nightclub *Yöhuikka* in the *Apollo Hotel* building on Mäkeliininkatu (which also hosts karaoke nights). The most popular Irish pub is *Leskinen*, near Akateeminen Kirjakauppa, while *Never Grow Old* at Hallituskatu 13 is a long-standing reggae pub. For bigger band sounds, try *Café Rumba,* Pakkahuonenkatu 19. *Kujasen Baari*, Pakkahuonenkatu 30, is a lesbian-friendly pub but open to all. In addition, there are a couple of rather uninspiring nightclubs: *Dorian*, Asemakatu 26, whose decor consists of shards of shattered mirror, and *Donna*, at the *Hotel Cumulus*, Kajaaninkatu 17.

On to Tornio: Kemi

If you want to cross overland into Sweden, the place to make for is Tornio, 130km northwest of Oulu – reached by a once-daily train or more frequent buses from **Kemi**, a small town on the Oulu–Rovaniemi train route around 110km northwest of Oulu. Although otherwise undistinguished, in Kemi you can join a four-hour "cruise" on a genuine **arctic ice-breaker** between January and April, which costs 720mk. Details from the tourist office at Kauppakatu 22 (☎016/199 465; fax 199 468), or from *Sampo Tours*, at Ajos Harbour, 15km from Kemi.

Tornio

Situated on the extreme northern tip of the Gulf of Bothnia, **TORNIO** makes a living by selling booze to fugitives from Sweden's harsh alcohol laws, and catering to Finns who are here to enjoy the beach, to fish, or shoot the Tornionjoki Rapids. After the Swedish–Russian conflict of 1808–09, the border between Sweden and Finland was drawn around **Suensaari**, an oval piece of land jutting from the Swedish side into the river, on which central Tornio now sits. With no formalities at the customs post on the bridge linking the two countries, the traffic in liver-damaged Swedes from nearby Haaparanta (in Swedish, Haparanda) is substantial. If you're **arriving by bus** the journey will terminate in Suensaari. From the **train station**, walk across the bridge immediately opposite to get onto the island.

The dominant features of the town are its bars and restaurants, so numerous that it is pointless to list them. Simply stroll around Hallituskatu and Kauppakatu and drop into the ones with the most promising noises. Always lively are *Pub Tullin*, Hallituskatu 5, and *Aarninholvi*, Aarnintie 1, while everyone who sets foot in Tornio seems to visit *Pizzeria Dar Menga*, Kauppakatu 12–14, one of the cheapest spots for solid nourishment. For coffee and fresh bread and cakes, it's hard to beat *Karkiaisen Leipomo*, Länsiranta 9. Alternatively, you can buy a bag of salted and smoked whitefish along the banks of the rapids (roughly 12mk for a meal's worth).

If you're not into drinking and feel uneasy with the boozy atmosphere, try visiting the seventeenth-century **Tornionkirkko** (summer Mon–Fri 9am–5pm) on the edge of the town park, or climbing the **observation tower** (June–Aug daily 9am–10pm). Otherwise there's only the **Tornio River Valley Historical Museum** (summer Tues–Fri noon–7pm, Sat & Sun noon–5pm; free), near the corner of Torikatu and

Keskikatu, or the possibility of some diversion suggested by the **tourist office**, in the Green Line Centre at the Swedish border (June to mid-Aug Mon–Fri 8am–8pm, Sat & Sun 10am–8pm; rest of the year Mon–Fri 8am–4pm; ☎016/432 733; fax 480 048).

It might be slightly cheaper to join the drunken legions staggering back across the border to sleep in Haaparanta (see p.557), but should you choose to stay in Tornio, there's a **youth hostel**, *Suensaari*, centrally placed at Kirkkokatu 1 (☎016/481682; fax 480 048; June to mid-Aug), plus a **campsite** on Matkailijantie (☎016/445 945; fax 480 048), with cottages going for around 200mk a night. Among the hotels, *Kaupunginhotelli,* Itäranta 4 (☎016/43311; fax 482 920; ③), boasts a trio of restaurants and five saunas.

Kajaani and around

KAJAANI, 178km southeast of Oulu by bus, could hardly be more of a contrast to the communities of the Bothnian coast. Though small and pastoral, the town is by far the biggest settlement in this very rural part of Finland, where trains and buses are rare and the pleasures of nature take precedence over anything else. Obviously there's little daily bustle or nightlife, but the place offers some insight into Finnish life in one of the less prosperous regions. Fittingly, it was in Kajaani that Elias Lönnrot wrote the final parts of the *Kalevala*, the nineteenth-century collection of Finnish folk tales that extolled to the hilt the virtues of traditional peasant life.

From the gloriously Art Nouveau **train station**, Kauppakatu leads directly into Kajaani's minuscule centre, but turn left into Asemakatu and you'll spot the decorative exterior of the **Kainuu Museum** at no. 4 (Mon–Fri noon–3pm, Wed until 8pm, Sun noon–5pm; 5mk, ticket covers the art museum too). Inside, an engrossingly ramshackle collection of local art and history actually says a lot about the down-to-earth

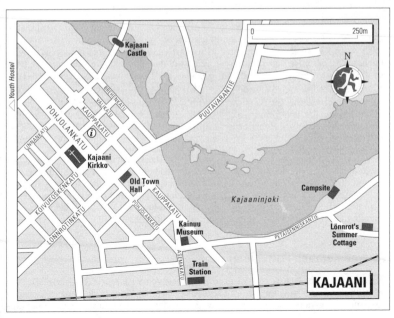

qualities of the area. Bypassing this and heading straight for the centre, you'll find the **Old Town Hall** (whose designer, Carl Engel, is famous for Helsinki's Senate Square) at the junction of Kauppakatu and Lönnrotinkatu. Slightly further on stands the dramatic **Kajaani kirkko** (summer daily 10am–8pm), whose wooden frame, weird turrets and angular arches were heralded as the epitome of neo-Gothic style when the church was completed in 1896. Resembling a leftover from a *Munsters* set, its spectral qualities are most intense by moonlight.

More historically significant, perhaps, but far less thrilling, is the ruined **Kajaani Castle**. Built in the seventeenth century to forestall a Russian attack, it later served as a prison where, among others, Johannes Messenius, the troublesome Swede, was incarcerated. Although there's constant talk of schemes to rebuild it, the castle was ruined so long ago that nobody's sure what it actually looked like, and the present heap of stones is only worth seeing if you're already idling along the riverside beside it.

Given the lack of other evening activities, idling is what you're likely to be doing if you stay here overnight. The problem of complete boredom is no less severe for the local youth, who've taken to lining the pavements of Kauppakatu in their hundreds, waiting for something to happen. About the only other way to pass the sunset hours is to take a quiet walk along the riverside footpath, from the corner of Ammakoskenkatu and Brahenkatu. The route passes the **open-air theatre**, and provides a chance to gaze at logs sliding blissfully towards destruction at the pulp mill up ahead. Following the river in the other direction leads to **Lönnrot's summer cottage**. Built by Elias for his wife, the small wooden structure now stands totally empty, insignificant and isolated; the only acknowledgement of its existence seems to be the name of the neighbouring *Elias Restaurant*: an odd outcome for a man whose life's work was so influential – and so revered.

Practicalities

Once you've arrived in Kajaani, you may well find yourself staying for the night. The official **youth hostel**, at Pohjolankatu 4 (✆/fax 08/622 254) is open all year, while the summer-only **campsite**, *Onnela Camping* (✆08/622703, ✆08/615 0200 in winter; fax 629 005; June –Aug) is by the river, not far from the Lönnrot Cottage. If you're prepared to trek, *Hotel Kajnuunportti*, 3km south of town on Route 5 at Kajnuunportti (✆08/613 3000; fax 613 3010; ②) offers rooms for five, with a kitchen, as well as regular singles and doubles. For up-to-date information on accommodation and onward transport, head for the **tourist office** at Pohjolankatu 16 (June–Aug Mon–Fri 9am–6pm, Sat 9am–1pm; rest of the year Mon–Fri 9am–5pm; ✆08/615 5555; fax 615 5664).

There's not a huge number of decent places to **eat** in Kajaani, the two most reliable options being as much pizza as you can eat for 40mk at *Casa Blanca*, Kolvukoskenkatu 17, or the odd blend of Finnish and Spanish food at *Restaurant Sevillia*, upstairs at the *Sokos Hotel Valjus*, Kauppakatu 20.

Buses provide the easiest way of **moving on** from Kajaani. The only rail links are west to Oulu (4 daily via Kontiomäki), or the twice-daily service south to Joensuu and the eastern Lake Region, plus the four daily connections for Iisalmi, Kuopio and beyond. The best direction to head for more rural delights is east towards Kuhmo, where the scenery gets increasingly spectacular, especially around Sotkamo (39km from Kajaani) and the acclaimed beauty spot of **Vuokatti** – a high pine-clad ridge commanding views all the way to Russia. The rolling hills make this Finland's premier ski-training area.

Around Kajaani: Paltaniemi

There's an hourly bus from Kajaani to the preserved village of **PALTANIEMI**, 9km away on the shores of Oulujärvi – an attractive place but, since the closure of its campsite, one without anywhere to stay. In contrast to down-at-heel Kajaani, eighteenth-century Paltaniemi was home to Swedish-speaking aesthetes who were lured here by the importance of Kajaani Castle during the halcyon days of the Swedish empire. Their transformation of Paltaniemi into something of a cultural hotbed seems incredible given the tiny size and placid setting of the place, but evidence of a refined pedigree isn't hard to find. Most obviously there's the **Paltaniemi kirkko** (summer only, daily 10am–6pm), built in 1726, a large church whose interior is deliberately chilled in order to preserve **frescoes** painted by Emmanuel Granberg between 1778 and 1781, which include a steamy vision of hell in the gruesome *Last Judgement*.

It's also fun to ferret around behind the pews, trying to decipher centuries-old graffiti. Even Tsar Alexander I paid a visit to Paltaniemi after Finland had become a Russian Grand Duchy, and his impromptu meal in a stable is reverentially commemorated in the **Tsar's Stable**, by the church. **Hövelö**, the old cottage across the road, was the birthplace of **Eino Leino**, whose poems captured the increasingly assertive mood of Finland at the turn of the century: his life and the history of Kajaani Castle form the subject of a rather dull exhibition.

Kuhmo

With belts of forests, hills and lakes, and numerous nature walks and hikes within easy reach, **KUHMO** makes a fine base for exploring the countryside. The terrain is in some ways less dramatic than further north, but then again it's far less crowded.

You can get more details of hiking routes, maps and other practical information from the **tourist office** (June–Aug Mon–Fri 8am–6pm, Sat 9am–4pm; Sept–May Mon–Fri 8am–5pm; ☎08/655 6382; fax 655 6384) in the town hall, on the corner of Kainuuntie and Koulukatu. The tourist office can also explain how best to reach the **Kalevala Village**, on the outskirts of the town. This large-scale re-creation of a completely wooded Karelian village provides an illuminating and valuable account of traditional building methods, plus it's a good excuse for pricey souvenirs – and some interesting handicrafts – to be sold to the many genuine Karelians who visit. It's also the only thing close to Kuhmo of appeal to non-hikers.

Low-budget accommodation options in Kuhmo include the **youth hostel** *Piilolan Koulu* (☎08/655 6245; fax 655 6139), which has rooms as well as dorms, though it's only open in late June and July. *Hotel Kalevela*, 3km from the centre (☎08/655 4100; fax 655 4200; ⑤), is a fair bet for a clean, modern room and can also rent out **canoes** and **bikes**. The town **campsite** (☎08/655 6388; fax 655 6384; June–Aug) is just under 2km from the centre along Koulukatu.

HIKING ROUTES AROUND KUHMO

The local section of the several hundred kilometres of track that make up the **UKK hiking route**, an enormous trek forking off in two directions, starts from the Kuhmo sports centre and winds 70km through forests and the Hiidenportti canyon. Several other hikes begin further out from Kuhmo and can be reached by buses from the town. **Elimyssalo**, to the east, is a 15km track through a conservation area, and also to the east is **Kilpelän-kankaan**, where a cycle path runs 3.5km across heathland, passing a number of Winter War memorials. To the north, **Sininenpolku** is a 12km hike over a ridge, past small lakes and rivers. In the northwest, **Iso-Palosenpolku** has two paths through a thickly forested area, where there are overnight shelters. Additionally, several **canoeing routes** trace the course of the old tar-shipping routes between Kuhmo and Oulu.

Continuing northwards from Kuhmo leads only to more hiking lands, and if you need urbanity, nightlife and easy living, now's the time to own up and duck out. If not, and your feet are itching to be tested over richly vegetated hills, gorges, river rapids, and hundreds of kilometres of untamed land, simply clamber on the bus for Suomussalmi.

Around Ämmänsaari and Suomussalmi

Although separated by a lake, Kiantajärvi, **ÄMMÄNSAARI** and **SUOMUSSALMI** are really twin settlements. Ämmänsaari is on the main road, Route 5, about 100km from Kajaani, while the smaller Route 41 covers the similar distance from Kuhmo to Suomussalmi. The villages themselves are connected by a more or less hourly bus service. Ämmänsaari, the administrative centre for northern Kainuu, is a good place to gather details of hiking and accommodation in the wilds: contact the **tourist office**, Jalloniemi, by Route 5 (summer Mon–Fri 8am–8pm, Sat noon–4pm, Sun noon–6pm; winter Mon–Fri 8am–4pm; ☎08/719 1243; fax 711 189). You can stay overnight there at the **campsite** (☎08/711 209 or 050/566 4252; June–Aug) or the tourist hotel *Kianta-Baari*, Ämmankatu 4 (☎08/711173; ①); in Suomussalmi the budget option is the tourist hotel *Wanhan Kalevan Majatalo*, Kainuuntie 24 (☎08/715018; ①). Buses from Ämmänsaari and Suomussalmi run to the main hiking areas in the province, usually on a daily basis.

To the east, something of the old Karelian culture can still be felt in the tiny villages of Kuivajärvi and Hietajärvi, close to the Russian border. Near Kuivajärvi is the **Saarisuo Nature Reserve**, where an eight kilometre hiking trail traverses a protected forest and marshy areas that are home to a wide variety of bird life. Adjacent is a youth hostel (☎08/723 179; fax 711 189; April–Sept) which serves breakfasts for 30mk.

Close to **HOSSA**, an old Sami village on the road to Kuusamo, are eight hiking paths, ranging from just 1km to 25km and graded according to difficulty, which pass through pine forests and over ridges between limpid lakes. Dotted about are old tar pits, lumber camps and a few traditional *laavu* shelters – crude slope-roofed huts open to the elements on one side, used by early lumber workers and based on the design of peasant hunters. All the hikes begin 8km from the village, which has a **campsite** (☎/fax 08/732 310) that's open all year, and a **holiday village** (☎08/732 322; fax 732 307), both with affordable cabins. In Hossa village itself, make time to visit the new *Hossa Guiding Centre*, which has one room given over to a huge floor map and another full of useful information. Just south of Hossa, in the Ruhtinansalmi area, is the **Martinselkonen Nature Reserve**, known locally as the "last wilderness". Rarely visited by tourists, the reserve has no marked paths or facilities, just a few disused barns remaining from the tree felling which ended in this area fifty years ago. Take local advice before venturing into it.

Kuusamo and around

KUUSAMO, 120km north of the twin villages and reached by daily express buses from Oulu, plus regular services from Rovaniemi, is a dull town organized around those who prefer to experience nature from the warm side of a hotel window. But it's also the starting point for the **Kuusamo Bear Circuit** (*Karhunkierros*), one of the most popular hiking routes in Finland: a seventy-kilometre trek weaving over the summit of Rukatunturi, dipping into canyons and across slender log suspension bridges over thrashing rapids. Herds of hikers are a far more common sight than bears, but the hike is still a good one – on and off the main track there are several interesting shorter routes. From Kuusamo, take the bus to **Ristikallion** for the start of the hike. Along the route, wilderness huts are placed roughly at ten-kilometre intervals, though during peak months these are certain to be full.

Fortunately there's no shortage of places to pitch your own tent, and about halfway along the route are three **campsites**, *Juuma* (☎08/863 212), *Jyrävä* (☎08/863 236) and *Retkietappi* (☎08/863 218), all open from June to August. For full details of local hiking and accommodation, and the many summer events that bring some life to the town, call in at the **Karhuntassu Tourist Centre** at Torangintaival 2 (☎08/850 2910; fax 850 2901). As for accommodation in Kuusamo itself, as well as the **youth hostel** across the street from the bus station at Kitkantie 35 (☎08/852 2132; fax 852 1134; June–Aug), there's the good-value *Viikinki Hotelli* on Juhanpie (☎08/852 3619; ②), with saunas and breakfast included.

The tougher **Six Fells Hiking Route** starts south of **Salla**, about 115km from Kuusamo. A bus runs there from both towns, three times a day Monday to Friday, pulling up at the Salla Tourist Centre (☎016/839 651; fax 839 657), which marks the beginning of the trail. Should you need to stay, there's a **hotel** here, *Hotel Revontuli* (☎016 879 711; fax 837 760; ③), plus some nearby **cabins** (with showers) costing 245mk a night (☎016/831 931; fax 837 765). The 35-kilometre hike includes some stiff climbs up the sides of spruce-covered fells. From the bare summits you can enjoy spectacular views. **Niemelä**, close to the road between Kuusamo and Salla, marks the other end of the trail. From Salla you can continue by bus directly to Ivalo in the Arctic North (see p.707), or to Kemijärvi to meet the train for Rovaniemi (see below).

Rovaniemi and around

Relatively easy to reach by train or bus from Ostrobothnia, Kainuu or Helsinki, **ROVANIEMI** is touted as the capital of Lappland. An administrative centre just south of the Arctic Circle it may be, but tourists who arrive on day trips from Helsinki expecting sleighs and tents will be disappointed by a place that looks as Lappish as a palm tree. The wooden huts of old Rovaniemi were razed to the ground by departing Germans at the close of World War II, and the town was completely rebuilt during the late 1940s. It's now really quite dismal, with its uniform greyish-white buildings and an unnerving newness to everything – even the smattering of antique shops contains nothing older than 1970s junk. Alvar Aalto's bold but impractical design has the roads forming the shape of reindeer antlers – which is fine if you're travelling by helicopter, but makes journeys on foot take far longer than they need to. All in all, Rovaniemi is a mess, and most visitors only use it as a short-term stopover, or as a base for studies in Lapp culture.

The Town

An essential stop if you have any interest in Lappish culture is **Arktikum**, in the northern part of town at Pohjoisranta 4 (May–Aug daily 10am–6pm; Sept–April Tues–Sun 10am–6pm; 50mk) and by far the most fascinating museum in Rovaniemi. Its great arched atrium emerges from the ground like a U-boat, with almost all the exhibition areas submerged beneath banks of stone. The centre contains both the **Provincial Museum of Lappland** and the **Arctic Centre**, together providing a varied insight into the history and present-day lives of the peoples of the Arctic North. Displays range from raincoats made of seal intestine, arctic fox and caribou hide and polar bear trousers, to superb photographic displays on reindeer husbandry today – modern technology has made its mark, with cellular phones, snowmobiles and four-wheel drive buggies now the norm. There are also pictures of the horrific devastation the German soldiers left, burning every building in site when they were forced to retreat in 1944. Taking an intelligent, non-sentimental approach, the museum superbly evokes the remarkable Sami culture and is well worth a couple of hours before you head north.

Back in the centre, **Lappia**, an Aalto-designed building a short way down Ratakatu from the bus and train stations at Hallituskatu 11, contains a theatre and concert hall,

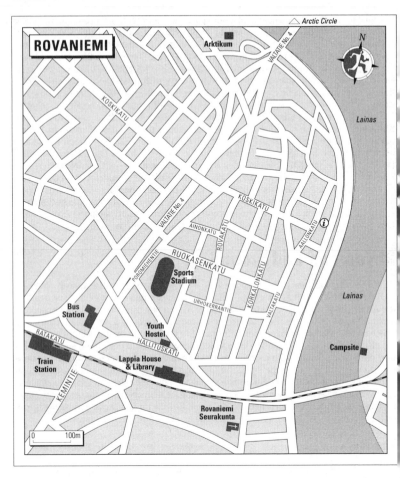

and a **library** (June to mid-Aug Mon–Fri 11am–7pm, Sat 10am–3pm; rest of the year Mon–Fri 11am–8pm, Sat 10am–4pm) that has a **Lappland Department**. Situated at the bottom of the stairwell from the main lending section, the section consists of a staggering hoard of books in many languages covering every Sami-related subject, plus relevant magazine and newspaper articles. This constantly growing collection is already the largest of its kind, and probably the best place in the world for undertaking research into the subject.

Other points of interest in Rovaniemi are few. At Kirkkotie 1, **Rovaniemi Seurakunta** (daily mid-May to early Aug 9am–9pm; Sept 9am–7pm; other times by arrangement), the parish church, repays a peek on account of its jumbo-sized altar fresco, *Fountain of Life* by Lennart Segerstråle, an odd work that pitches the struggle between good and evil into a Lappland setting. About the only other thing meriting a look is the **J. Martiinni Knife Factory** (Mon–Fri 8am–4pm) at Marttinintie 6 in the industrial area, reached either on foot or by bus #4. In the kingdom of the sharp edge the Martiinni name reigns supreme, and if you're looking for a knife the prices in the factory shop are cheaper than anywhere else – plus you can have your name inscribed on the blade. Prices range from a few markkaa to 300mk for the latest model.

If you have more time to kill and the weather isn't too cold (Rovaniemi's prone to chilly snaps even in summer), visit one of the two outdoor museums that lie near each other just outside town, accessible by buses #3 or #6. The **Ethnographical Museum Pöykkölä** (June–Aug Tues–Sun 1–4pm; 5mk) is a collection of farm buildings that belonged to the Pöykkölä family between 1640 and 1910, and forms part of a potpourri of things pertaining to reindeer husbandry, salmon-fishing and rural life in general. About 500m up the road is the **Lappish Forestry Museum** (June to mid-Sept Tues–Sun noon–6pm; 10mk) where the reality of unglamorous forestry life is remembered by a reconstructed lumber camp.

The Arctic Circle

Some people are lured to Rovaniemi solely for the dubious thrill of crossing the **Arctic Circle**. While the "circle" itself doesn't remain constant, its man-made markers do – 8km north of town along Route 4. Bus #4 goes to the circle from the bus station, as does #8, which also calls at the stops in town with "Arctic Circle" emblazoned on them. Both buses depart roughly hourly. Near the circle and served by the same buses is the **Santa Claus Village** (June–Aug daily 8am–8pm; Sept–May Mon–Fri 11am–7pm, Sat 10am–4pm; free). In the early 1960s, plans were mooted to create a monstrous Father Christmas village to capitalize on Lappland's seasonal association once and for all. Mercifully the scheme was abandoned and a compromise reached. Considering its tourist pitch, the place – inside a very large log cabin – is quite within the bounds of decency: you can meet Father Christmas all year round, contemplate the reindeer grazing in the adjoining farm and leave your name for a Christmas card from Santa himself (I've been waiting nine years for mine).

Practicalities

Both bus and train stations are close to each other, just a couple of minutes' walk from the city centre. The **tourist office** (June to mid-Aug Mon–Fri 8am–6pm, Sat & Sun 11.30am–4pm; Sept–May Mon–Fri 8am–4pm; ☎016/346 270; fax 322 2767) is to the northeast at Koskikatu 1, just a few minutes' walk from the basic but friendly all-year **youth hostel** at Hallituskatu 16 (☎/fax 016/344 644). It's always crowded in summer, so try to book in advance. Budget alternatives are the guesthouse *Outa*, at Ukkoherrantie 16 (☎016/312 474; ①), or the more costly summer hotels *Ammatioppilaitoksen*, at Kairatie 75 (☎016/392652; ②), and *Domus Arctica*, Ratakatu 6 (☎016/23535; ②). With a little more money to spend, try the *Oppipoika*, Korkalonkatu 33 (☎016/20321; fax 16969; ③/④), in the same building as the hotel and restaurant school (see below) and boasting a pool and two saunas, as well as good food. Rovaniemi's **campsite** (☎016/345 304) is at Jäämerentie 1, on the far bank of Ounasjoki, and equipped with a café and sauna.

There are a few pleasant **cafés** in town, best being the small *Antinkaapo*, just a few buildings up from *Valentina Conditoria*, another good spot for sticky buns. For filling food at very reasonable prices, *Cafe Kisälli,* Korkalonkatu 35 (Mon–Fri 8.30am–5pm), and the neighbouring *Oppipoika Restaurant* (daily 11am–11pm) are both run by the local hotel and catering school. At the café you can fill up on delicious schnitzels or pike perch with potatoes and vegetables for 30mk. The restaurant at the *Hotel Polar* is also good, specializing in reindeer-derived dishes (try the 30mk reindeer soup).

In the **evening** the few students of the Lappland University can usually be found socializing in *Lapinpaula* (often known by its nickname *Tupsu*) at Hallituskatu 24, or *Tivoli*, Valtakatu 19. *Sampo*, Korkalonkatu 32, plays host to serious drinkers – a more relaxed atmosphere prevails at *Roy*, Maakuntakatu 24. Drinking is really one of the few things to do here other than watching logs float downriver. The hotels tend to host any **nightlife** there is: *Hotel Lapponia*, Koskikatu 23, is popular, while *Doris*, at the *Hotel Vaakuna*, Koskikatu 4, attracts an older crowd. The town wakes up a bit when ROPS, the Rovaniemi **football team**, are playing at home. You'll hear the cheering all over town and be able to see the game for free through gaps in the fencing – the stadium is on Pohiolankatu and the season runs through the summer. Despite what you might assume from the modest facilities, ROPS is one of the country's best teams.

The Arctic North

Bottled inland by the northern tip of Norway, Finland's **Arctic North** mixes forests, lakes and rivers with tracts of desolate upland that rise high above the tree line. In these uncompromising latitudes, some of the indigenous Sami population still herd their reindeer and maintain their traditions despite serious threats from a number of sources – most dramatically in recent years, Chernobyl fallout. The Sami tend to remain far from the prying eyes of the tourist, though their angular tipis, wreathed in reindeer antlers and skins, smoked salmon and all sorts of Arctic trinkets, are to be found along the region's main roads during the summer, in what can seem a rather crass, commercially inspired conformity. This racial stereotyping is intended to appeal to the wallets of the thousands of motorists who use the **Arctic Highway**, the E75/4, the fastest approach to the Nordkapp (see p.336). But don't let this put you off: the Arctic wilderness is a ready escape, its stark and often haunting landscapes easily accessible.

Two main roads lead north from Rovaniemi: the Arctic Highway, which services the **northeast**, linking the communities of Sodankylä, Ivalo, Inari and Karigasniemi; and Route 79/E78, which crosses the **northwest**, connecting Muonio and Kilpisjärvi. Inari and Sodankylä are the only settlements worth a second look, but what lies around the Arctic North's minuscule communities will hold your gaze for much longer – provided you take the trouble to do at least some **hiking**. If you're planning to travel north from Rovaniemi on one route then back on the other, be warned that there are no roads in between, only rough tracks – with no facilities – traversing some desolate landscape. For safety, you need to either retrace your steps to Rovaniemi before taking the other route, or travel in an arc into Norway and over the other side, a journey by car of around four hours.

The Northeast: Sodankylä and the Arctic Highway

North of Rovaniemi, it's an uneventful 130-kilometre drive along the Arctic Highway to **SODANKYLÄ**, a modest, comfortable town, whose modern appearance belies its ancient foundation. From the late seventeenth century, Finnish settlers and Christian Sami gathered here on high days and holidays to trade and to celebrate religious festivals. Unusually, their wooden **church** of 1689 has survived intact (summer daily 10am–6pm), its rough-hewn timbers crowding in upon the narrowest of naves with the pulpit pressing intrusively into the pews. The old church nestles beside the Kitinen River in the shadow of its uninspiring nineteenth-century replacement and a stone's throw from the **Alariesto Art Gallery** (June–Aug Mon–Sat 10am–5pm, Sun noon–6pm; Sept–May Mon–Fri 10am–5pm, Sat 10am–4pm, Sun noon–4pm; 10mk). The gallery features the work of Andreas Alariesto, a twentieth-century Sami artist of some renown. Each canvas is an invigorating representation of traditional native life and custom, notably a crystalline *View from the Arctic Ocean* embellished with chaotic boulders, predatory fish jaws and busy Sami. A useful catalogue available at reception explains the background to all the exhibits.

THE ARCTIC NORTH: HIKING AND PUBLIC TRANSPORT

The best way to experience the Arctic North is to get off the bus – the only form of public transport – and explore slowly, which means on foot. The rewards for making the physical effort are manifold. There's a tremendous feeling of space here and the wild and inhospitable terrain acquires a near-magical quality when illuminated by the constant daylight of the summer months (the only time of year when hiking is feasible).

Many graded **hiking routes** cover the more interesting areas, with most of the more exhilarating of them distributed among the region's four national parks: **Pyhätunturi**, southeast of Sodankylä; **Urho Kekkonen** and **Lemmenjoki**, further north off the Arctic Highway; and **Pallas-Ounastunturi**, near Muonio in the northwest. There are challenges aplenty for experienced hikers, though mere novices need have nothing to fear, provided basic common sense is employed. The more popular hikes can become very busy and many people find this an intrusion into their contemplation of the natural spectacle – others enjoy the camaraderie. If you are seeking solitude you'll find it, but you'll need at least the company of a reliable compass, a good-quality tent – and emergency supplies.

We've assembled a broad introduction to the major hikes and described the type of terrain that you'll find on them. Bear in mind that these aren't definitive accounts as conditions and details often change at short notice; always gather the latest information from the nearest tourist centre or park information office.

Hiking rules and tips

Obviously you should observe the **basic rules** of hiking, and be aware of the delicate ecology of the region: don't go starting fires in any old place (most hikes have marked spots for this) and don't pitch your tent out of specified areas on marked routes. You should always check that you have maps and spare supplies before setting out, and never aim to cover more ground than is comfortable. Bathe your feet daily to prevent blisters, and carry some form of mosquito repellent – the pesky creatures infest the region.

Hiking accommodation

To be on the safe side, you shouldn't go anywhere without a good-quality **tent**, although the majority of marked hikes have some form of basic shelter (see p.600), and most have a **youth hostel** and **campsite** (plus comfy hotels for those who can afford them) at some point on the trail. These fill quickly, however, and few things are worse than having nowhere to relax after a long day's trek – so make an advance reservation whenever possible.

Public transport

Buses run far less frequently in the Arctic North than elsewhere in Finland, but services along the Arctic Highway are quite good and all the larger settlements are reached by bus at least once a day. Other buses run to schedules designed to deliver and collect hikers from either end of the busier trails. Be sure to check timetables carefully and plan several days ahead: get the special northern bus timetable from the tourist office in Rovaniemi if possible, or refer to the more general nationwide timetable, *Pikavuoro Aikataulut*, available at the bigger bus stations. Forward planning applies equally to accommodation (see above). On your way northwards, you'll almost certainly meet people returning from hikes, whose advice can be very useful.

Sodankylä is little more than an elongated main street, Jäämerentie, and all the main facilities – the **bus station**, post office and petrol stations – are within a few metres of each other. At the time of writing the **tourist office** was planning to move from its old home in the Alariesto Gallery; ask at the gallery for its new location.

Sodankylä has a handful of **hotels**, the most convenient of which are the *Hotelli Kultaisen Karhun Majatalo* (☎016/613 801; fax 613 810: ③), a five-minute walk from the bus station at Sodankyläntie 10, and the nearby *Hotel Sodankylä*, Unarintie 15 (☎016/617 121; fax 613 545; ③). There's also a **campsite** (☎016/612 181; fax 611 503; early June to mid-Aug) and a **youth hostel** (☎016/611 960; fax 611 503; same dates), a ten- to fifteen-minute walk from the centre: cross the bridge, veer left along Savukoskentie and follow the signs. As for **meals**, the pizzas served up at *Poronsarvi*, Jäämerentie 52, are the best in town, or for a wider choice of meat and fish dishes, try *Ravintola Revontuli* on the same street. *Matkanuisto Kahvio*, Sompiontie 4, is a reasonable café though stuffed with tacky souvenirs.

Around Sodankylä: Pyhätunturi National Park

Off the Arctic Highway some 65km southeast of Sodankylä lies **Pyhätunturi National Park**, and the steep slopes and deep ravines of the most southerly of Finland's fells. Here, the 45-kilometre **Pyhätunturi and Luostotunturi hiking route** rises from marshlands and pine woods and rounds five fell summits. Five kilometres from the start is the impressive waterfall of the Uhrikuru gorge, after which the track circles back for a short stretch, eventually continuing to Karhunjuomalampi (The Bear's Pool). There's a *päivätupa* here, but the only other hut on the route is by the pool at Pyhälampi.

Near the hike's starting point are an **information centre** (☎016 813 777; fax 812 032), a **campsite** (☎016/852 103; fax 852 140; late June to mid-Aug), and two reasonably priced hotels, *Pyhätunturi* (☎016/856 111; fax 882 740; ②) and *Pyhän Asteli* (☎016/852 141; fax 852 149; ②). The hike ends at Luostotunturi, where accommodation includes the *Luosto Hotel* (☎016/624 400; fax 624 410; ③), and the more basic *Luostonhovi* (☎016 624421; fax 624 297; ①). The daily **bus** between Sodankylä and Kemijärvi (on the rail line from Rovaniemi) stops close to both ends of the trail.

Continuing north: Urho Kekkonen National Park

Travel north by car from Sodankylä on the Arctic Highway for 110km and you'll arrive at *Koilliskaira Visitor Centre* (June–Sept daily 10am–7pm; Oct–May Mon–Fri 10am–4pm; ☎016/626 251; fax 626 113) – it's impossible to reach by public transport. Here you can reserve cabin beds, get information on dozens of hikes – and watch film about the terrain. Just 100m from the centre lurks a gaggle of tourist establishments: the **Gold Museum and Panning Centre** (55mk), the *Gold Prospector* restaurant serving Lappish specialities for 45–100mk, reindeer omelette being the cheapest dish, and a **guesthouse** (②) with **cabins** (200mk). Twenty kilometres further north (130km from Sodankylä) is the turning for *Tunturikeskus Kiilopää*, a popular and well-equipped fell-walking centre on the edge of the **Urho Kekkonen National Park**. The park is one of the country's largest, incorporating the uninhabited wilderness that extends to the Russian border – pine moors and innumerable fells lacerated by gleaming streams and rivers.

With regular bus connections to north and south, the fell centre is easily the most convenient base for exploring the park. It's at the head of several walking trails, from the simplest of excursions to exhausting expeditions using the park's chain of wilderness cabins. The centre's **reception desk** (daily 8am–11pm; ☎016/667 101; fax 667 121) sells detailed trail maps for 40–65mk, rents out mountain bikes (110mk per day;

500mk per week), organizes guided walks, and arranges accommodation in the adjoining, year-round **youth hostel** (same phone number). There's also a good restaurant and, that Finnish prerequisite, a sauna (25mk).

Ivalo and Inari

Try not to get stuck in **IVALO**, on the Arctic Highway 40km north of the fell centre, a town of singular ugliness. If you do have to stay, however, the riverside *Hotel Kultahippu*, Petsamontie 1 (☎016/661 825; fax 662 510; ③), and the cheaper *IMotel Petsamo*, Petsamontie 14 (☎016 661 106; fax 661 628 ①), are the most palatable overnight options, both including breakfast and sauna in the price. There is no longer an official **tourist office** here, the nearest being in Inari (see below), though in summer there's a small information area in the shop called *Porotuote* on the main road through the village

The road heading north to Inari winds around numerous lakes dotted with islands – it's a spectacular route if you can time your trip with the glorious Lappish **Ruska**, a season that takes in late summer and autumn, when the trees take on brilliant citrus colours that reflect in the still waters. **INARI** itself, 35km away, is slightly more amenable than Ivalo, straggling along the bony banks of the Juutuanjoki River as it tumbles into the freezing cold, islet-studded waters of Lake Inarijärvi. There's nothing remarkable about the village itself, but it's a pretty little place with several appealing diversions. The bus stops outside the **tourist office** in Inari House (June–Aug daily 9am–8pm; Sept–May Mon–Fri 9am–3pm; ☎016/676 363; fax 676 364). As well as accommodation information, you can get a fishing licence (39mk) here, and visit the building's permanent Sami handicrafts exhibition (free), whose exhibits show a marked contrast in quality with the tourist souvenirs that pop up everywhere here. Close by, the open-air **Sami Museum** (daily June to mid-Aug 8am–10pm; mid-Aug to early Sept 8am–8pm; 20mk) is shortly to be replaced with a roofed-in centre designed to rival Arktikum (see the Rovaniemi section, above). It currently features a re-sited nineteenth-century village, a cluster of old, relocated tipis and various reconstructions illustrating aspects of Sami life – principally handicrafts and hunting and fishing techniques. Beginning about 2km from the museum, the five-kilometre **Pielppajärvi Wilderness Church hiking trail** leads to the isolated remains of a 1752 church.

From the river bridge, *Arktinen Inari* operates daily two-hour **lake cruises** in summer (June & Aug at 2pm; July at 10am, 2pm & 6pm; Sept by arrangement; ☎016/6975 1352 in June & Aug, ☎016/6034 81701 in July; 50mk), as well as similarly priced fishing trips; or, if you're travelling in a group, you can rent a twelve-seat boat and a guide for two and a half hours for three to eleven people (150mk flat fee). Whole-day fishing trips can be arranged through the tourist office for 950mk for three people, including equipment and food.

Many travellers pass through Inari during the summer, so make a point of booking accommodation ahead of arrival. There's a **campsite**, *Uruniemi Camping*, (☎016/671 331; March, April & June to late Sept), on the southern outskirts of the village, with cottages to rent; the *Inarin Kultahovi* **hotel** (☎016/671 221; fax 671 250; ③) offers comfortable rooms with river views, plus an excellent, reasonably priced **restaurant**. If money's tight, stick to the popular *Terassikavla Café*, beside the bus stop.

Around Inari: Lemmenjoki National Park

A vast tract of birch and pinewood forest interrupted by austere, craggy fells, marshland and a fistful of bubbling rivers, **Lemmenjoki National Park**, about 40km southwest of Inari, witnessed a short-lived gold rush in the 1940s. A few panners still remain, eking out a meagre living.

The park's most breathtaking scenery is to be found on its southeastern side along the Lemmenjoki river valley. To get there, take the **daily bus from Inari** to **Njurgalahti**, a tiny settlement on the edge of the park about 12km off Route 955 (the district's main road), which is where the 55-kilometre-long, two-day hike down the river valley begins; taking the twice-daily boat (June–Aug) from Njurgalahti to Kultasatama cuts 20km off the hike's full distance.

At **Härkäkoski**, hikers cross the river by a small boat, pulled by rope from bank to bank; the track then ascends through a pine forest to **Morgamoja Kultala**, the old gold-panning centre, where there's a big unlocked hut for the use of hikers. There are a couple of other huts set aside for hikers on the trail, but the nearest **campsite** (June–Aug; ☎/fax 016/673 001), with cottages, is back on the main road at **Menesjärvi**. The holiday village (☎/fax 016/673 435) in the hamlet of **Lemmenjoki** is far closer, with four-berth **cabins** from around 150mk per day. At present there's no information centre in the park and further enquiries should be directed to the Ylä-Lappi district forestry office on ☎016/687 701 (fax 662 648).

North from Inari: crossing into Norway

Travelling north from Inari is rather pointless unless you're aiming for Norway. The Finnish section of the Arctic Highway continues to dreary **KAAMANEN**, though on the way, just past a sign for *Jokitörmä Hostel*, is a bold, stark and deeply evocative memorial in rusty red metal to the war in Finland, September 15, 1944. In simple words, it states "the battles of the light infantrymen in the wilds of Lappland were brought to an end in Kaamaren, Inari at the end of October 1944. 774 killed, 262 missing, 2904 wounded". In Kaamanen there's a **campsite** with cottages that's open all year (☎016/672 713). The route then swings westwards on its way to the Nordkapp, exiting Finland at **KARIGASNIEMI**, an unprepossessing hamlet that has a restaurant (*Soarve Stohpu*) with pleasant rooms in the adjoining *Kalastajan Majatalo* (☎/fax 016/676 171; ①), though its bar is permanently full of drunken locals. There are also two **campsites**: *Lomakylä* (☎016/676 160 or 676 136), which is open all year, and the *Tenorinne* (early June to mid-Sept; ☎016/676 113).

From Kaamanen, a minor road branches due north to **UTSJOKI**, a small border village beside the Tenojoki River. The nearest **campsite** (mid-June to mid-Aug; ☎016/678 803) is a few kilometres away, by the river's edge in Vetsikko. The road on from Utsjoki runs parallel to the Norwegian border, then crosses it just beyond the hamlet of **Nuorgam**, where there's a guesthouse, the *Matkakoti Suomenrinne* (☎016/678 620), open from mid-June to mid-August, and a year-round **campsite** (☎016/678 312). Once across the border, it's a 160-kilometre journey to Kirkenes in Norway (see p.338).

The Northwest

Heading northwest from Rovaniemi, Route 79 sticks close to the banks of the Ounasjoki River before it reaches the straggling settlement of **KITTILÄ**, a distance of 150km. There's little to detain you here – the departing German army burnt the place to the ground in 1944 and the rebuilding has been uninspired – though both the **youth hostel**, Valtatie 5 (mid-June to early Aug; ☎016/648 508), and neighbouring **campsite** are conveniently located beside the main road.

It's a further 20km to the dishevelled ski resort of **SIRKKA**, whose surrounding hills boast seven hiking (or, in winter, cross-country skiing) routes, including the enjoyable river and fell walking of the eighteen-kilometre Levi Fell trail. All seven tracks begin in or near the centre of Sirkka, where there's a good range of **places to stay**. *Sirkantähti* (☎016/641 491; ④) is one of the better hotels, or try the cheaper *Hullu Poro*, just off the main road (☎016/641 506; ②).

Muonio and Pallas-Ounastunturi National Park

Modest **MUONIO** lies 60km west of Sirkka beside the murky river that separates Finland from Sweden. What passes for the town centre falls beside the junction of the

E78, the main north–south highway, and Route 79. Despite a rash of green tourist information signs, outside the high season you'll be lucky to find any form of information office. Muonio's summertime **tourist office** (summer Mon–Fri 11am–7pm; ☎016/532 605) is attached to a small snack bar. You're better off asking about the surrounding area at the year-round **youth hostel** *Lomamaja Pekonen*(☎/fax 016/532 237) close by; the nearest **campsite** (☎016/532 491) is 3km back along the road to Sirkka.

There's no need to stay long in Muonio, however. You will need to change here for buses to Kilpsijärvi (see below), but otherwise should continue on the once-daily bus from Rovaniemi to Enontekiö/Hetta – which passes through **Pallas-Ounastunturi National Park**, a rectangular slab of mountain plateau whose bare peaks and coniferous forests begin about 30km northeast of Muonio. One bus a day leaves Muonio at 9.30am Monday to Friday for the National Park, stopping outside the park's **information office** (summer Mon–Fri 11am–6pm, Sat & Sun 9am–4pm; ☎016/532 452; fax 532 929). The best places to camp around here are south of Munio on Route 21 – ask for details at the information office or in Muonio.

Pallastunturi marks the start of the **Pallas-Hetta hiking route**, an arduous 56-kilometre trail that crosses a line of fell summits with several *autiotupa*, *varastupa* and camping areas en route, as well as a sauna about halfway along in the hut at **Hannukurun**. The highest point is the summit of Taivaskero, near the start. The track ends at Lake Ounasjärvi, which you'll need to cross by boat. There's no **ferry service** at all between 11pm and 7am, but at other times, if the boat isn't there, you should raise the flag to indicate that you want to cross.

On the other side, you'll find a **National Guiding Office** (late Feb to early May & June to late Sept Mon–Fri 9am–6pm, Sat & Sun 9am–5pm; rest of the year Mon–Fri 8am–4pm, July & early Aug till 10pm), where you can buy maps and make reservations for a host of cottages in the twin villages of **ENONTEKIÖ/HETTA**, where there's also a **youth hostel** (☎016/521 361; fax 521 049; mid-Feb to April & June to mid-Sept; rooms ①) and a trio of **campsites**: *Hetan Lomakylä* (☎016/521 521; all year;), *Kotatieva* (☎016/521 062; June to mid-Aug) and *Ounasloma* (all year, but call ahead ☎016/521 055). Three hundred metres from the Guiding Office, the *Hetta Hotel* (☎016/521 361; ③) offers a plush alternative, with several rooms overlooking the lake. The hotel sells trail maps and rents out canoes and a full range of walking and camping equipment. It's also the best place to **eat** for miles around. For excellent free information on hiking, **Lapland Guiding** (☎016 521 230; fax 521 403), next door to the youth hostel, is a sensible first stop.

OTHER HIKES IN THE PARK: THE PALLAS-OLOS-YLLÄS TRAIL

The Hetta-Pallas trail is the park's most impressive walk and also the one with the best transport links. There are several other options, though, notably the 87-kilometre **Pallas-Olos-Ylläs hiking trail**, which also begins from Pallastunturi. With several unlocked huts on its route, this track twists south past fells and lakes until it leaves the park and reaches the Muonio–Sirkka road close to the swanky *Olostunturi Hotel* (☎016/536 111; fax 536 444; ④/⑤). The hotel serves primarily for winter skiing, but the hills that surround it are crisscrossed by a number of shorter walking trails. The reception desk has all the details plus the times of the Rovaniemi–Muonio bus: on the slower services, the bus stops here after it's been to Pallastunturi.

The Pallas-Olos-Ylläs trail continues south, soon reaching the dam on the Särkijoki river before proceeding down to Lake Äkäkasjärvi, where there's a café in a former grain mill. From here, the track heads onto the eastern slopes of Äkäkero, passing the remarkably good-value *Äkäskero Hotel* (☎016/533 077; fax 533 078; ② including sauna and 5-course meal) and continuing for 4km to the tiny settlement of **ÄKÄSLOMPOLO**, on the upper slopes of Yllästunturi, where there's an all-year **hostel** (☎016/569 255; fax 569 351).

BUSES INTO NORWAY AND SWEDEN

Once daily, the Rovaniemi/Muonio to Kilpisjärvi bus continues to Skibotn in **Norway**. From Skibotn, there's a daily service along the coastal highway – north to Alta and south to Tromsø. Unfortunately, the bus schedules rarely connect, so you'll almost certainly have to hitch to avoid a night in Skibotn. Similarly, the Finnish bus to Karesuvanto usually arrives too late for passengers to cross the bridge to **Sweden**'s Karesuando and catch the early-morning bus to Kiruna.

The **bus service** on from Äkäslompolo is dreadful: there's a once-weekly summer service to Kolari, eventually reaching Tornio on the E78, but to reach Muonio, 76km north of Kolari, you'll have to hitch.

Continuing north from Muonio: Kilpisjärvi and around

The thumb-shaped chunk of Finland that sticks out above the northern edge of Sweden is almost entirely uninhabited, a hostile Arctic wilderness whose tiny settlements are strung along the only road, the E78. For the most part this seems a gloomy route of desolate landscapes and untidy villages, comparing poorly with the splendour of the parallel road to the south that connects Sweden's Kiruna and Norway's Narvik. However, the E78 does have its moments as it approaches the Norwegian frontier, with the bumpy uplands left behind for dramatic snow-covered peaks.

From the E78, you might cross into Sweden via **KARESUVANTO**, a dreary village 95km north of Muonio, to reach the Kiruna–Narvik road. Otherwise there's little reason to cross the border here or stay longer than you need to in Karesuvanto – if you do, use the all-year **campsite** (☎016/522 079), which has some smart, green-painted cabins (150mk for a twin-bed cabin). Otherwise, try the *Ratkin Hotel* (☎016/522 101; fax 522 104; ③), which has a good restaurant.

There's more to be said for continuing for 110km on the E78 to the hamlet of **KILPISJÄRVI** on the Norwegian frontier. Just 25km south of Kilpisjärvi itself on the one ribbon of road is the welcoming *Peeran Retkeilykeskus* **youth hostel** (☎/fax 016/532 659), serving good food. At Kilpisjärvi itself, perched beside the coldest of lakes in the shadow of a string of stark tundra summits, the *Kilpisjärvi Tourist Hotel* (☎016/537 761; fax 537 767; ②) has a gorgeous location that means it gets booked up months ahead for the March to mid-June period; however, 5km further down the road, the tourist hotel *Kilpisjärvi Tourist Centre* (☎016/537 771; fax 537 702; ①) offers rooms and cottages in just as fine a setting. Both places sell maps covering a number of **local hikes**, the most popular of which are the brace of ten-kilometre trails running to the top of the neighbouring Saanatunturi, 1029m high. The main way up (and down) is the track on the steep north side, although another route runs behind the fell to the northern shore of Saanijärvi, where there's a *päivätupa*.

Another option is the 24-kilometre loop trail, beginning and ending at Kilpisjärvi, that runs north through the **Malla Nature Reserve** to the **Three Countries Frontier** where Finland, Norway and Sweden meet. The track crosses by footbridge the rapids of Siilajärvi, after which a secondary track ascends to the summit of Pikku Malla. The main route continues to Iso Malla. There's a steep and stony section immediately before the waterfalls of Kihtsekordsi, and then a reindeer fence marking the way down to an *autiotupa* beside the Kuokimajärvi lake. From the tourist office, a stone path leads to the cairn marking the three national borders. There's a **campsite** at the tourist centre (mid-March to mid-May & mid-June to mid-Sept) and, nearby, a private **hostel**, *Saananmaja* (☎016/537 746).

travel details

Trains

Kokkola to: Helsinki (9 daily; 5hr); Oulu (8 daily; 2hr 30min); Tampere (9 daily; 3hr 45min).

Oulu to: Kajaani (3 daily; 2hr 20min); Kemi (9 daily; 1hr 10min); Rovaniemi (7 daily; 2hr 30min).

Rovaniemi to: Kemijärvi (1 daily; 1hr 15min).

Vaasa to: Helsinki (4 daily via Seinäjöki; 4hr 30min); Kokkola (3 daily; 2hr 30min); Oulu (3 daily; 5hr 30min); Tampere (4 daily; 2hr 30min).

Buses

Inari to: Kaamanen (6 daily; 1hr 45min); Karigasneimi (2 daily; 1hr 45min); Utsjoki (2 daily; 3hr 45min).

Kajaani to: Ämmänsaari (1 daily; 2hr 30min direct, longer by slower indirect routes); Kuusamo (1 daily; 4hr 10min direct, also slower indirect routes).

Kemi to: Tornio (4 daily; 30min).

Kolari to: Äkäslompolo (1 weekly; 55min).

Kuusamo to: Ristikallion (1 daily; 1hr 15min); Rukatunturi (2 daily; 50min); Salla (2 daily; 3hr).

Luosto to: Sodankylä (1 daily; 40min).

Muonio to: Kilpisjärvi (1 daily; 3hr 45min).

Oulu to: Kuusamo (6 daily; 4hr).

Pallastunturi to: Enontekiö (1 daily; 2hr 30min); Muonio (1 daily; 40min).

Pietarsaari to: Kokkola (6 daily; 40min).

Rovaniemi to: Enontekiö/Hetta (2 daily; 5hr 15min); Inari (2 daily; 6hr); Ivalo (3 daily; 5hr); Kiilopää (1 daily; 4hr); Kilpisjärvi (2 daily; 7hr 45min); Kittilä (4 daily; 2hr 30min–2hr 50min); Muonio (2 daily; 4hr); Pallastunturi (1 daily; 4hr 45min); Sodankylä (4 daily; 1hr 40min).

Sodankylä to: Kemijäarvi (5 daily; 2hr).

Suomussalmi and Ämmänsaari to: Kuusamo (3 daily; 2hr 45min).

Tornio to: Äkäslompolo (1 weekly; 3hr 45min).

Utsjoki to: Nuorgam (2 daily; 55min).

Vaasa to: Pori (5 daily; 2hr 45min); Turku (6 daily; 5hr).

International Ferries

Kokkola to: Skellefteå (1 daily in summer; 4hr 30min).

Pietarsaari to: Skellefteå (1 daily; 4hr 30min).

Vaasa to: Sundsvall (late April to May 3 daily; 8hr 30min); Umeå (4 daily in summer; 4hr).

INDEX

Note that the letters Å, Ä, Æ, Ø and Ö come at the end of the alphabet.

A

Aalborg (D) 146
Abisko (S) 585
Accommodation 30
  in Denmark 50
  in Finland 598–600
  in Norway 165
  in Sweden 352
Addresses in Scandinavia 42
Airlines
  in Australasia 19
  in Britain 4
  in Ireland 11
  in North America 14
Ales Stennar (S) 480
Alta (N) 331
Andenes (N) 318
Andersen, Hans Christian 113
Arctic Circle 42, 300, 579, 703
Arctic North, The 704–710
Arendal (N) 237
Arvidsjaur (S) 578
Aurlandsfjord (N) 272

B

Balestrand (N) 273
Banks 22
Banks
  in Denmark 47
  in Finland 595
  in Norway 158
  in Sweden 348
BERGEN (N) 245–259
  Accommodation 250
  Arrival 245
  Bars and clubs 257
  Bergenhus 253
  Bryggen 252
  Cafés and snack bars 257
  City transport 249
  Fantoft Stave Church 255
  Festivals 257
  Gamle Bergen Museum 256
  Information 249
  Listings 258
  Mount Fløien 255
  Mount Ulriken 255
  Museums 254
  Restaurants 257
  Torget 252
  Troldhaugen 255

Øvregaten 253
Bering, Vitus 132
Birka (S) 407
Bjäre Peninsula (S) 456
Bleik (N) 319
Blixen, Karen 94
Boden (S) 556
Bodø (N) 302
Bohuslän Coast, The (S) 437
Boknafjord (N) 266
Books 37–41
Borgholm (S) 497
Borlänge (S) 566
Bornholm (D) 106
Borre 105
Bothnia, The Gulf of (S) 530
Briksdalsbreen (N) 279
Bro (S) 527
Bullerö (S) 408
Bunge (S) 528
Burs (S) 526
Byxelkrok (S) 499
Båstad (S) 456

C

Camping 31
Car rental in Scandinavia 29
Charlottenlund (D) 87
Christiansø (D) 107
Consulates 21
COPENHAGEN (D) 69–93
  Accommodation 74
  Arrival 71
  Bars 90
  Cafés 88
  Christiania 84
  Christiansborg 82
  Christianshavn 83
  City transport 74
  Clubs 91
  Gay Copenhagen 91
  Indre By 77
  Information 71
  Listings 92
  Little Mermaid 81
  Live music 90
  Pizzerias 88
  Tivoli Gardens 84
Costs
  in Denmark 47
  in Finland 595
  in Norway 158
  in Sweden 348
Credit cards 22
Crime 32

D

Dalarna (S) 562
Danish language, The 67

Daugbjerg (D) 145
Disabled travellers 34
Dovrefjell Nasjonalpark (N) 229
Dragør (D) 87
Drink
  in Denmark 54
  in Finland 603
  in Norway 170
  in Sweden 357
Driving to Scandinavia from Britain 8
Drottningholm (S) 406
Dueodde (D) 106

E

Ebeltoft (D) 142
Eckerö (F) 660
Egersund (N) 242
Eggum (N) 315
Eketorp (S) 500
Elk safaris (S) 444
Elmelunde (D) 105
Embassies 21
Enontekiö (F) 709
Esbjerg (D) 123–125
Eskiltuna (S) 410
Espoo (F) 647
Estonia, travelling to 646
European Union 66, 184, 368
Eurostar 7
Exchange 22

F

Falkenberg (S) 453
Falster (D) 104
Falsterbro (S) 476
Falun (S) 567
Fanefjord (D) 105
Fanø (D) 125
Fauske (N) 301
Ferries to Scandinavia from Britain 8, 9
Ferry companies in Ireland 11
Finnhamn (S) 408
Finnish language, The 618
Finnmark (N) 330, 332
Finse (N) 271
Fishing
  in Denmark 55
  in Finland 604
  in Norway 171
  in Sweden 358
Fjällbacka (S) 440
Fjærland (N) 274
Flakstadøya (N) 315
Flekkefjord (N) 242

Flights to Scandinavia
  from Australasia 18
  from Britain 3–6
  from Ireland 11
  from North America 12–17
Flights within Scandinavia 29
Flåm (N) 272
Food in Denmark 51
  in Finland 600
  in Norway 167
  in Sweden 354
Forsvik (S) 447
Fredensborg Slot (D) 98
Fredericia (D) 129
Frederiksborg Slot (D) 98
Frederikshavn (D) 150
Frederiksø 107
Fredrikstad (N) 219
Fåborg (D) 118
Fårö (S) 528
Föra (S) 498

G

Gallen-Kallela, Akseli 610
Gamla Uppsala 413
Gammelstad (S) 554
Gay Scandinavia 33
Geiranger (N) 280
Geirangerfjord (N) 280
Gilleleje (D) 97
Gjendesheim (N) 228
Glaciers 42
Glass Kingdom, The (S) 503
Glass-making 503
GOTHENBURG (S) 417–437
  Haga 430
  Information 419
  Linne 431
  Liseberg 430
  Listings 436
  Live music 435
  Markets and supermarkets 431
  Old Town, The 426
  Restaurants 432
  Theatre 436
Gotland (S) 519–528
Graddis (N) 301
Grieg, Edvard 179, 255
Grimstad (N) 238
Grinda (S) 408
Gripsholm (S) 409
Grungebru (N) 235
Gränna (S) 506
Gudhjem (D) 106
Gällivare (S) 581–583
Gällnö (S) 408
Gärdslösa (S) 500
Gävle (S) 532–535
Göta Canal (S) 442

H

Hald Ege (D) 144
Halleberg (S) 444
Halmstad (S) 454
Hamar (N) 224
Hamina (F) 652
Hammarskjöld, Dag 366
Hammerfest (N) 335
Hanstholm (D) 146
Haparanda (S) 557
Hardangerfjord (N) 267
Hardangervidda Nasjonalpark
  (N) 268
Harstad (N) 320
Hattula (F) 668
Haugesund (N) 261
Havneby (D) 127
Health 24
Helge Steamer, The (D) 118
Hellebæk (D) 97
Hellesylt (N) 280
Helsingborg (S) 458–463
Helsingør (D) 95–97
HELSINKI (F) 622–646
  Accommodation 626–628
  Arrival 622
  Art Museum of the Ateneum
    632
  Bars and pubs 642
  Cafés 639
  Cinema 645
  City transport 623
  Clubs 644
  Eira 635
  Esplanadi 630
  Gay Helsinki 644
  Hakaniemi 636
  Information 623
  Kaivopuisto 635
  Kruununhaka 636
  Listings 645
  Live music 644
  Mannerheimintie 632
  Museums 638
  National Museum, The 632
  National Theatre 631
  Olympic Stadium, The 633
  Restaurants 640
  Senate Square 629
  Seurasaari 637
  Suomenlinna 637
Hemavan (S) 577
Hemse (S) 526
Henningsvær (N) 314
Hetta 709
Heyerdahl, Thor 206
Hiking in Scandinavia 35
Hillerød (D) 98
Hindsholm Peninsula (D) 117

History
  of Denmark 56–66
  of Finland 606–620
  of Norway 173–184
  of Sweden 359–368
Hjerkinn (N) 229
Hjerl Hede 145
Holsterbro (D) 146
Honningsvåg (N) 336
Hornbæk (D) 97
Horsens (D) 132
Hotels in Scandinavia 30
Hudiksvall (S) 537
Humlebæk (D) 94
Hunneberg (S) 444
Huskvarna (S) 506
Hämeenlinna (F) 668
Härjedalen (S) 569
Härnösand (S) 542
Höga Kusten (S) 543
Högbonden (S) 544
Högby (S) 499

I

Ibsen, Henrik 178, 238
Idre (S) 568
Iisalmi (F) 687
Inari (F) 707
Inlandsbanan, The (S) 350, 564,
  569
Insurance 25
InterRail passes 6
Ivalo (F) 707

J

Jelling (D) 131
Joensuu (F) 682–684
Jokkmokk (S) 579
Jostedalsbreen glacier (N) 277
Jotunheim (N) 228
Jotunheimen Nasjonalpark (N)
  229
Jukkasjärvi (S) 587
Jyväskylä (F) 669
Järvenpää (F) 647
Jægerspris (D) 102
Jönköping (S) 504

K

Kaamanen 708
Kabelvåg (N) 314
Kajaani (F) 697
Kallby (S) 445
Kalmar (S) 492–495
Kalundborg (D) 101
Karasjok (N) 334
Karesuando (S) 589

Karesuvanto (F) 710
Karigasniemi (F) 708
Karlsborg (S) 446
Karlshamn (S) 485
Karlskrona (S) 487
Kattvik (S) 457
Kautokeino (N) 332
Kerimäki Church (F) 680
Kerteminde (D) 116
Kierkegaard, Søren 85, 97
Kilpisjärvi (F) 710
Kinnekulle (S) 445
Kinsarvik (N) 268
Kirkenes (N) 340
Kiruna (S) 585–587
Kittilä (F) 708
Kivik (S) 481
Kjenndalsbreen (N) 278
Kjerringøy (N) 304
Klövsjö (S) 570
Kokkola (F) 692
Kolding (D) 128
Kolmården Djurpark 517
Kongeshus Mindepark (D) 145
Kongsberg (N) 234
Kongsvoll (N) 229
Korsør (D) 102
Koster Islands (S) 441
Kotka (F) 650
Kragerø (N) 237
Kristianopel (S) 489
Kristiansand (N) 239
Kristianstad (S) 482
Kristiansund (N) 286
Kristinehamn (S) 562
Kuhmo (F) 699
Kukkolaforsen (S) 558
Kungälv (S) 437
Kungsbacka (S) 450
Kungsleden (S) 585
Kuopio (F) 684–687
Kuusamo (F) 700
Källa (S) 498
Køge (D) 102

L

Ladby Boat (D) 117
Laerdal (N) 233
Lahti (F) 670
Lakselv (N) 339
Langeland (D) 119
Lappeenranta (F) 675–677
Lappland 330
Lapps *see* Sami
Larvik (N) 236
Lau (S) 526
Legoland (D) 132
Leira (N) 233

Lejre Historical-Archeological
  Centre (D) 101
Leksand (S) 565
Lemmenjoki National Park (F) 707
Lidingö (S) 405
Lidköping (S) 445
Lilla Karlsö 527
Lillehammer (N) 226
Lillesand (N) 238
Limfjordslandet (D) 146
Limhamn (S) 473
Lindholm Høje (D) 150
Linköping (S) 512
Ljugarn (S) 526
Loen (N) 277
Lofoten Islands (N) 308–317
Lofthus (N) 268
Lolland (D) 105
Longyearbyen (N) 342
Louisiana (D) 94
Lovissa (F) 649
Luleå (S) 552
Lund (S) 463–467
Lye (S) 527
Lyngby (D) 87
Lysefjord (N) 267
Lysekil (S) 439
Lysgård (N) 145
Läckö (S) 445
Lønsdal (N) 301
Löfstad Manor 516
Lönnrot, Elias 609
Löttorp (S) 499

M

Malla Nature Reserve (F) 710
MALMÖ (S) 467–475
  Accommodation 469
  Arrival 467
  Bars 474
  Cafés 473
  City centre 470–473
  City transport 469
  Festivals 474
  Information 469
  Limhamn 473
  Listings 475
  Music 474
  Restaurants 473
Mandal (N) 242
Mannerheim, C.G.E. 611
Maps 27
Maribo (D) 105
Mariefred (S) 409
Mariehamn (F) 660
Marielyst (D) 104
Mariestad (S) 446
Marstal (D) 120
Marstrand (S) 438

Media
  in Denmark 47
  in Finland 595
  in Norway 159
  in Sweden 349
Midnight Sun, the 157, 323
Mikkeli (F) 672–675
Milles, Carl 405
Millesgården (S) 405
Mjølfjell (N) 271
Mo-i-Rana (N) 300
Molde (N) 286
Money 22
  in Denmark 47
  in Finland 595
  in Norway 158
  in Sweden 348
Monroe, Marilyn 261
Mora (S) 563
Moskenes (N) 316
Moskenesøya (N) 315
Motala (S) 509
Muddus National Park (S) 584
Munch, Edvard 179, 201, 208
Muonio (F) 708
Murmansk (N) 341
Måløy (N) 279
Møn (D) 105
Mønsted (D) 145
Möja (S) 408

N

Narvik (N) 306
Nielsen, Carl 114
Nigardsbreen 279
Nobel, Alfred 365
Nordfjord (N) 276
Nordfjordeid (N) 279
Nordkapp (N) 337
Norheimsund (N) 267
Norrköping (S) 514
North Cape *see* Nordkapp
Northern Lights, The 42
Norwegian language, The 182
Notodden (N) 235
Nurmes (F) 684
Nusfjord (N) 316
Nyborg (D) 109–111
Nykøbing (D) 104
Nyköping (S) 517–519
Nynäshamn (S) 519
När (S) 526
Nærøyfjord (N) 272
Næstved (D) 104

O

Odense (D) 111–116
Olav, Saint 298
Orsa (S) 569

Oskarshamn (S) 521
OSLO (N) 185–219
  Accommodation 193
  Akershus Castle 203
  Arrival 187–191
  Astrup Fearnley Modern Art
    Museum 203
  Bars and pubs 214
  Bygdøy Peninsula 205
  Cafés 212
  Cinema and theatre 216
  Clubs 215
  Defence Museum 204
  Frogner Park 209
  Henie-Onstad Art Centre 210
  Historical Museum 197
  Holmenkollen 211
  Hovedøya 207
  Information 191
  Karl Johans Gate 196
  Kon-Tiki Museum 206
  Langøyene 208
  Listings 217
  Live music 215
  Markets and supermarkets 212
  Munch Museum 208
  Museum of Applied Art 201
  National Gallery 200
  National Museum of Contemporary
    Art 202
  National Theatre 197
  Nordmarka 211
  Norwegian Folk Museum 205
  Rådhus 202
  Resistance Museum 204
  Restaurants 213
  Royal Palace 197
  University 197
  Vigeland Sculpture Park 209
  Viking Ships Museum 206
Otta (N) 227
Oulu (F) 692–696

P

Package tours
  from Australasia 20
  from Britain 9
  from Ireland 12
  from North America 17
Padjelanta National Park (S) 585
Pajala (S) 588
Pallas-Ounastunturi National Park
  (F) 709
Palme, Olof 367, 390
Paltaniemi (F) 698
Parish villages (S) 550
Piteå (S) 552
Polar Night, The 323
Police 32
Pori (F) 658
Porsgrunn (N) 237
Porvoo (F) 648

Post
  in Denmark 47
  in Finland 595
  in Norway 159
  n Sweden 349
Post offices 23
Public holidays
  in Denmark 55
  in Finland 605
  in Norway 171
  in Sweden 358
Pulpit Rock (N) 267
Punkaharju Ridge (F) 679
Pyhää (F) 650
Pyhätunturi National Park (F) 706

R

Rail passes 6, 16, 20, 29
Ramberg (N) 316
Randers (D) 141
Rauma (F) 658
Rebild Bakker (D) 150
Reine (N) 316
Retretti Arts Centre (F) 680
Ribe (D) 125
Ribe, Nightwatchman of 126
Riksgrånsen (N) 306
Ringsted (D) 103
Risør (N) 237
Romsdalsfjord (N) 282
Rondane (N) 228
Rondane Nasjonalpark (N) 228
Rondvassbu (N) 228
Ronneby (S) 486
Roskilde (D) 99–101
Rovaniemi (F) 701–704
Rudkøbing (D) 119
Ruotsinpyhtää (F) 650
Russia, travelling to 340, 651, 684
Råå (S) 463
Rättvik (S) 565
Rømø (D) 127
Rønne (D) 106
Røros (N) 230
Røst (N) 317

S

Saggrenda (N) 235
Saltfjellet Nasjonalpark (N) 300
Saltstraumen (N) 304
Sami, The 333, 561, 579, 701
Sandefjord (N) 236
Sandhamn (S) 408
Sandvig (D) 107
Santa Claus 703
Sarek National Park (S) 585
Savonlinna (F) 677–679
Sexual harassment 32
Sibelius, Jean 610, 647, 655, 668

Siljan, Lake (S) 563
Silkeborg (D) 133
Siltakylä (F) 650
Simrishamn (S) 481
Sirkka (F) 708
Skagen (D) 151
Skaidi (N) 338
Skandeborg (D) 132
Skanör (S) 476
Skellefteå (S) 550
Skien (N) 237
Skuleskogen National Park (S)
  545
Slite (S) 528
Småland (S) 501–505
Smygehamn (S) 477
Smygehuk (S) 477
Snåsa (N) 299
Sodankylä (F) 704
Sogndal (N) 275
Sognefjord (N) 273
Solvorn (N) 275
Sorsele (S) 577
Sortland (N) 318
Spitzbergen (N) 341
Stamsund (N) 315
Stavanger (N) 261–266
Stave churches 222
Stavern (N) 237
Stege (D) 105
Steinkjer (N) 299
Stiklestad (N) 298
STOCKHOLM (S) 371–405
  Accommodation 379–382
  Arrival 373
  Bars and pubs 400
  Breakfast 396
  Cafés 397–399
  Cinema 402
  City transport 376–379
  Clubs 401
  Djurgården 391
  Gamla Stan 382
  Gay Stockholm 403
  Information 373
  Kulturhuset 388
  Kungliga Slottet 384
  Kungsholmen 390
  Listings 403
  Live music 401, 402
  Medeltidsmuseum 384
  National Art Museum 386
  Normalm 387
  Parks and gardens 394
  Restaurants 397–399
  Riksdagshuset 384
  Skeppsholmen 386
  Storatorget 385
  Södermalm 393
  Theatre 402
  Östermalm 390

Stockholm Archipelago, The (S) 407
Stokmarknes (N) 318
Stora (S) 527
Store Heddinge (D) 103
Storebælt Exhibition Centre (D) 111
Storlien (S) 575
Storuman (S) 576
Strindberg, August 389
Stryn (N) 276
Strömstad (S) 440
Stånga 527
Sundsvall (S) 538–542
Suomussalmi (F) 700
Svalbard (N) 341
Svaneke (D) 106
Svartsö (S) 408
Sveg (S) 570
Svendborg (D) 117
Svolvær (N) 312
Swedish language, The 369
Sälen (S) 568
Söderhamn (S) 536
Sønderborg (D) 128

T
Tampere (F) 663–668
Tana Bru (N) 339
Tanumshede (S) 440
Tapiola (F) 647
Tau (N) 267
Telemark (N) 235
Telephones 23
  in Denmark 47
  in Finland 595
  in Norway 159
  in Sweden 349
Thisted (D) 146
Three Countries Frontier 710
Tisvildeleje (D) 97
Tjolöholm (S) 450
Torekov (S) 457
Torne Valley, The (S) 588
Tornio (F) 696
Tour operators
  in Australasia 20
  in Britain 10
  in Ireland 11
  in North America 17
Tourist offices 26
Trains to Scandinavia
  from Britain 6
  from Ireland 12
Transport
  in Scandinavia 29
  in Denmark 48–50
  in Finland 596

in Norway 160
in Sweden 350
Travel agents
  in Australasia 18
  in Britain 4
  in Ireland 11
  in North America 13
Travellers' cheques 22
Trelleborg (S) 476
Trollfjord (N) 318
Trollhättan (S) 442
Trollstigen (N) 283
TROMSØ (N) 325–330
TRONDHEIM (N) 291–298
Trysunda (S) 545
TURKU (F) 652–658
Tärnaby (S) 577
Tønder (D) 127

U
Ulvik (N) 269
Ulvön (S) 544
Umeå (S) 546–550
UPPSALA (S) 411–415
Urho Kekkonen National Park (F) 706
Utne (N) 268
Utsjoki 708
Utö (S) 408

V
Vaasa (F) 691
Vadstena (S) 507
Valamo Monastery (F) 682
Valdemar's Slot (D) 118
Valldal (N) 284
Varberg (S) 451
Vardø (N) 339
Varkaus (F) 681
Vaxholm (S) 408
Vejle (D) 130
Vesterålen Islands (N) 318–321
Vestvågøy (N) 315
Viborg (D) 142
Vickleby (S) 500
Vigeland, Gustav 209
Viipuri, Russia 676
Vikings 56, 173, 359
Vilhelmina (S) 576
Villa Rauhalinna (F) 679
Visas 21
Visby (S) 521–525
Visingsö (S) 506
Voss (N) 269
Vuollerim (S) 580
Vänern, Lake (S) 442, 562

Vänersborg (S) 443
Värgon (S) 444
Västergötland (S) 444
Vättern, Lake (S) 442, 505–507
Växjö (S) 501
Værøy (N) 317

W
Wallenberg, Raoul 366
Winter sports 36
Women in Scandinavia 32
Working in Scandinavia 36
World Service 42

Y
Ylämaa (F) 652
Youth hostels 31
Ystad (S) 477–480

Å
Å (N) 316
Åhus (S) 481
Åland Islands (F) 660
Ålesund (N) 284
Åndalsnes (N) 282
Åre (S) 574
ÅRHUS (D) 133–141
  Accommodation 135
  Arrival 134
  City transport 134
  Domkirke 135
  Eating 138
  Listings 132
  Live music 139
  Modern Århus 136
  Nightlife 139
  Old Århus 135
  Rådhus 136

Ä
Äkäslompolo (F) 709
Ämmänsaari (F) 700
Ängelholm (S) 457

Æ
Ærø (D) 119
Ærøskøbing (D) 119

Ø
Ørneberget (N) 271
Østerlars (D) 107
Öland (S) 496–501

Ö
Örebro (S) 510–512
Örnsköldsvik (S) 545
Östersund (S) 570–574

Stay in touch with us!

ROUGH*NEWS* is Rough Guides' free newsletter.
In three issues a year we give you news, travel
issues, music reviews, readers' letters and the
latest dispatches from authors on the road.

I would like to receive ROUGH*NEWS*: please put me on your free mailing list.

NAME ....

ADDRESS ....

Please clip or photocopy and send to: Rough Guides, 1 Mercer Street, London WC2H 9QJ, England
or Rough Guides, 375 Hudson Street, New York, NY 10014, USA.

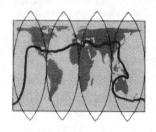

THE LOWEST PRICE CAR RENTAL AROUND THE

AND THAT'S A PROMISE†

For convenient, low-price car rental – all around the world – choose Holiday Autos. With a network of over 4,000 locations in 42 countries, when you're off globetrotting you won't have to go out of your way to find us.

What's more, with our lowest price promise, you won't be flying round and round in circles to be sure you're getting the best price.

With Holiday Autos you can be sure of the friendly, efficient service you'd expect from the UK's leading leisure car rental company. After all, we've won the Travel Trade Gazette 'Best Leisure Car Rental Company' award and the Independent Travel Agents' 'Top Leisure Car Rental Company' award time and time again. So, we've quite a reputation to maintain.

With Holiday Autos you simply don't need to search the globe for down-to-earth low prices.

For further information see your local Travel Agent or call us direct on **0990 300 400**

Holiday Autos
WE KNOW YOU HAVE A CHOICE